SHAKESPEARE SURVEY

69

Shakespeare and Rome

EDITED BY

PETER HOLLAND

CO-EDITOR FOR THEMED ARTICLES
EMMA SMITH

CAMBRIDGE
UNIVERSITY PRESS

CAMBRIDGE
UNIVERSITY PRESS

University Printing House, Cambridge CB2 8BS, United Kingdom

Cambridge University Press is part of the University of Cambridge.

It furthers the University's mission by disseminating knowledge in the pursuit of
education, learning and research at the highest international levels of excellence.

www.cambridge.org
Information on this title: www.cambridge.org/9781107159068

First published 2016

Printed in the United Kingdom by TJ International Ltd. Padstow Cornwall

A catalogue record for this publication is available from the British Library

ISBN 978-1-107-15906-8 Hardback
ISSN 0080-9152

EDITOR'S NOTE

Volume 70, on 'Creating and Recreating Shakespeare', the theme of the World Shakespeare Congress in 2016, will be at press when this volume appears. The theme of volume 71 will be 'Shakespeare and London'.

Submissions should be addressed to the Editor to arrive at the latest by 1 September 2017 for volume 71. Pressures on space are heavy and priority is given to articles related to the theme of a particular volume. Submissions may be made either as hard copy sent to the Editor at The Shakespeare Institute, Church Street, Stratford-upon-Avon CV37 6HP, or as an e-attachment to pholland@nd.edu. All articles submitted are read by the Editor and at least one member of the Advisory Board, whose indispensable assistance the Editor gratefully acknowledges. Unless otherwise indicated, Shakespeare quotations and references are keyed to *The Complete Works*, ed. Stanley Wells, Gary Taylor, John Jowett and William Montgomery, 2nd edition (Oxford, 2005).

Philip Edwards, a former member of the Advisory Board, died in the last year. Philip served from volume 26 (1973) to volume 33 (1981). He was a fine scholar who contributed greatly to Shakespeare studies. Here I wish to mention only his generous and perceptive assistance to successive Editors of *Shakespeare Survey* over those years and long thereafter.

I would also like to thank Emma Smith who co-edited the themed section in this volume with such enthusiasm and discrimination. Working with her has been enormous fun and I'm very grateful for her assistance.

CONTRIBUTORS

CHRISTIAN M. BILLING, *University of Hull*
MARIACRISTINA CAVECCHI, *Università degli Studi di Milano*
KATHARINE A. CRAIK, *Oxford Brookes University*
DAVID CURRELL, *American University of Beirut*
DOMINIQUE GOY-BLANQUET, *University of Amiens*
PATRICK GRAY, *Durham University*
BARBARA HODGDON, *University of Michigan*
BRADLEY J. IRISH, *Arizona State University*
RUSSELL JACKSON, *University of Birmingham*
HEATHER JAMES, *University of Southern California*
MICHAEL P. JENSEN, *Ashland, Oregon*
ROS KING, *University of Southampton*
JANE KINGSLEY-SMITH, *University of Roehampton*
PETER KIRWAN, *University of Nottingham*
MATS MALM, *University of Gothenburg*
GEORGE MANDEL, *Oxford Centre for Hebrew and Jewish Studies*
ROBERT S. MIOLA, *Loyola University, Maryland*
INEKE MURAKAMI, *University at Albany, SUNY*
VERENA OLEJNICZAK LOBSIEN, *Humboldt-Universität, Berlin*
REIKO OYA, *Keio University, Tokyo*
STEPHEN PURCELL, *University of Warwick*
TOM REEDY, *Denton, Texas*
THOMAS RIST, *University of Aberdeen*
KATE RUMBOLD, *University of Birmingham*
ESTHER B. SCHUPAK, *Bar-Ilan University*
CHARLOTTE SCOTT, *Goldsmiths College, University of London*
JAMES SHAW, *University of Oxford*
MICHAEL SILK, *King's College London*
CERI SULLIVAN, *Cardiff University*
DENISE A. WALEN, *Vassar College*
ROBERT N. WATSON, *University of California, Los Angeles*
PETER WOMACK, *University of East Anglia*
JOHN WYVER, *University of Westminster*

CONTENTS

CONTENTS

ILLUSTRATIONS

LIST OF ILLUSTRATIONS

LIST OF ILLUSTRATIONS

PAST THE SIZE OF DREAMING?
SHAKESPEARE'S ROME

ROBERT S. MIOLA

Ethereal Rumours
Revive for a moment a broken Coriolanus
(T. S. Eliot)

Confronting modernity, the speaker in 'The Wasteland' recalled the ancient hero and Shakespeare's play (his 'most assured artistic success', Eliot wrote elsewhere) as fragments of past grandeur momentarily shored against his present ruins. Contrarily, Ralph Fiennes revived *Coriolanus* in his 2011 film because he thought it a modern political thriller:

For me it has an immediacy: I know that politician getting out of that car. I know that combat guy. I've seen him every day on the news and in the newspaper – that man in that camouflage uniform running down the street, through the smoke and the dust. I've seen the people protesting on the streets, in their hoodies and jeans. You know, that's our world.[1]

Critics of Shakespeare's Rome have always occupied a place along the spectrum marked by these extremes, some thinking it depicts a world elsewhere and long ago, others that it reflects contemporary times, either those of the playwright or of his audiences.

Shakespeare first encountered Rome as ancient world through his grammar-school education, specifically his study of Latin authors such as Ovid, Vergil, Horace, Cicero, Caesar, Seneca, Plautus, Terence, Livy, Suetonius, Tacitus and others; this education made Rome more significant and accessible than Athens, Jerusalem, or cities in Asia and the East. Allusions and representations throughout the canon evoke the ancient city and its famous citizens, its customs, laws and code of honour, its enemies, wars, histories and myths. But Shakespeare knew Rome as a modern city of Italy as well, land of love, lust, revenge, intrigue and art, setting or partial setting for eight plays. Portia disguises herself as Balthazar, a 'young doctor of Rome' (*Merchant*, 4.1.152); Hermione's statue is said to be the creation of 'that rare Italian master, Giulio Romano' (*The Winter's Tale*, 5.2.96). And Shakespeare knew both ancient and modern Rome as the centre of Roman Catholicism, home of the papacy, locus of forbidden devotion and prohibited practice, city of saints, heretics, martyrs and miracles. The name 'Romeo', appropriately, identifies a pilgrim to Rome. Margaret wishes the college of Cardinals would choose her bead-praying husband Pope 'and carry him to Rome' (*2 Henry VI*, 1.3.65), whence Cardinal Pandolf in *King John* and Cardinal Campeius in *Henry VIII*. Despite such presence, criticism has been slow to recognize the connections between Shakespeare's ancient and modern cities. For most commentators today, Shakespeare's Rome is the classical *urbs* he depicted in one narrative poem, *The Rape of Lucrece*, and five plays, *Titus Andronicus*, *Julius Caesar*, *Antony and Cleopatra*, *Coriolanus* and, to a lesser extent, *Cymbeline*, which has only four

---

[1] Ralph Fiennes in Christopher Wallenberg, 'Stage to Screens: Ralph Fiennes Talks to Playbill.com About Wrestling *Coriolanus* Onto the Big Screen', *Playbill*, 20 November 2011, p. 2, www.playbill.com/news/article/stage-to-screens-ralph-fiennes-talks-to-playbill.com-about-wrestling-coriol-184750

scenes in Rome, the rest in Britain and Wales. (Some have argued also for *Hamlet*, wherein Horatio claims to be 'more an antique Roman than a Dane', 5.2.293.)

It was not ever thus. The most influential book yet written on the subject, M. W. MacCallum's *Shakespeare's Roman Plays and their Background*,[2] considered only *Julius Caesar*, *Antony and Cleopatra* and *Coriolanus* as the Roman plays and, though noting French Senecan drama, only North's Plutarch as the background. MacCallum exhaustively analyzed character, all the while methodically comparing passages from Plutarch's *Lives* to Shakespeare's text. So doing, he advanced well beyond the insight of the first editor, Nicholas Rowe (1709), who praised the 'virtue and philosophical temper' of Shakespeare's Brutus, his Antony's 'irregular greatness of mind', these figures portrayed 'exactly as they are described by Plutarch, from whom certainly Shakespeare copied 'em'.[3] Charting additions, omissions and contradictions, MacCallum defined the subject and the principal approach for most of the following century, culminating in the word-by-word semiotic analyses of Alessandro Serpieri;[4] but he excluded *Titus Andronicus* as Shakespeare's juvenilia, relegating it to the 'vestibule and forecourt of his art'.[5] Introducing the 1967 reprint of MacCallum's book, T. J. B. Spencer justly noted its importance and some deficiencies – this exclusion, the relentless emphasis on character, and the lack of any stage sense. A decade earlier Spencer's own article 'Shakespeare and the Elizabethan Romans' had begun correction by considering *Titus Andronicus* as authentically Roman, Shakespeare's attempt 'not to get it all right, but to get it all in',[6] and by stating (overstating, actually) that Elizabethan Romans, despite literary admiration for Cicero, were 'Suetonian and Tacitan rather than Plutarchan',[7] that is, imperial rather than republican. Spencer's fellow contributor to the same *Shakespeare Survey* volume, J. C. Maxwell, included *Titus* in his review of Shakespeare's Roman plays, though he thought, prophetically, some of it by George Peele.[8] After exhaustive review of the scholarship and the application of some

twenty-one tests, Vickers, of course, has now conclusively demonstrated Peele's hand in the play, even if some contest the details.[9]

John W. Velz's magisterial 1978 review in *Shakespeare Survey* expanded Shakespeare's Rome to include *Lucrece*, *Titus Andronicus* and *Cymbeline*.[10] (After its appearance, Michael Platt felt obliged to revise his *Rome and Romans according to Shakespeare* to take into account the missing plays.)[11] Velz's subtitle, moreover, 'authenticity or anachronism?', pithily identified a central question for commentators on Shakespeare's ancient world. Nahum Tate, along with such luminaries as Dryden, Pope and Johnson, saw historical verisimilitude in Shakespeare's representations. In 1662 Margaret Cavendish actually went further, declaring them improvements on the originals: 'certainly Julius Caesar, Augustus Caesar and Antonius did never really act their parts better, if so well, as he hath described them'.[12] On the other side, Ben Jonson thought 'ridiculous' Shakespeare's description of Caesar as never doing wrong but with 'just cause',[13] a phrase that

---

[2] M. W. MacCallum, *Shakespeare's Roman Plays and their Background* (London, 1910; rpt. with an introduction by T. J. B. Spencer, New York, 1967).

[3] Brian Vickers, ed., *William Shakespeare: The Critical Heritage*, 6 vols. (London, 1974-81), vol. 2, p. 200.

[4] Alessandro Serpieri, et al., eds., *Nel laboratorio di Shakespeare: Dalle fonti ai drammi*, vol. 4, *I Drammi Romani* (Parma, 1988); Alessandro Serpieri, 'Shakespeare and Plutarch: intertextuality in action', in *Shakespeare, Italy, and Intertextuality*, ed. Michele Marrapodi (Manchester, 2004), pp. 45–58.

[5] MacCallum, *Roman Plays*, p. 177.

[6] T. J. B. Spencer, 'Shakespeare and the Elizabethan Romans', in *Shakespeare Survey 10* (Cambridge, 1957), pp. 27–38; p. 32.

[7] Spencer, 'Elizabethan Romans', p. 31.

[8] J. C. Maxwell, 'Shakespeare's Roman Plays: 1900–1956', in *Shakespeare Survey 10* (Cambridge, 1957), pp. 1–11.

[9] Brian Vickers, *Shakespeare, Co-Author: A Historical Study of Five Collaborative Plays* (Oxford, 2002).

[10] John W. Velz, 'The Ancient World in Shakespeare: Authenticity Or Anachronism? A Retrospect', in *Shakespeare Survey 31* (Cambridge, 1978), pp. 1–12.

[11] Michael Platt, *Rome and Romans according to Shakespeare* (Salzburg, 1976; rev. 2nd edn, Lanham, MD, 1983).

[12] Vickers, ed., *Critical Heritage*, vol. 1, p. 43.

[13] Vickers, ed., *Critical Heritage*, vol. 1, p. 26.

does not appear in the Folio as we have it. Thomas Rymer (1693) mocked Shakespeare for putting Caesar and Brutus in 'fools' coats' and making them 'Jack Puddings in the Shakespeare dress'.[14] And, Velz observed, 'from the time of John Dennis's *Essay on the Genius and Writings of Shakespear* (1712) it has been a scholarly parlour game to enumerate Shakespeare's blunders in the Roman plays'[15] – the clock striking in Rome, the night clothes of Brutus and Portia, other anachronisms and anatopisms. Velz argued that critics in the mid to late twentieth century reformulated the perennial question by asking not whether Shakespeare's Rome and Romans were authentic, but whether the playwright and his audience thought them so; most, he thought, now answered in the affirmative. He also declared that Shakespeare presented Rome as a 'world apart', a place with its own politics, national character and institutions and called attention to its symbolic topography (walls, gates, Capitol, forum, battle-fields), rhetoric and sources, especially Vergil.

Not only has Shakespeare's Rome grown larger for readers today, so has its 'background'. Again, Spencer began the process by reviewing Elizabethan historians of Rome, for example William Fulbecke and Richard Reynoldes, who, like Shakespeare in *Titus Andronicus*, portrayed the city as a place of 'garboyles' or tumults.[16] Glossing *Julius Caesar* and *Antony and Cleopatra*, Leeds Barroll comprehensively reviewed classical, medieval and renaissance accounts of Roman history since the time of Augustus.[17] From this plenitude Anne Barton argued that Livy's *Ab urbe condita* (along with Machiavelli's *Discorsi*) contributed to *Coriolanus* its unusual regard for the citizens (hers a distinctly minority view of the plebeians, by the way) and its critical view of Coriolanus, who makes the patrician error of identifying himself as the Republic.[18] *L'etat ce n'est pas moi*, he learns too late. Vergil has now become a well-recognized source of image and action, even as Shakespeare writes against him, transforming Aeneas and Dido, for example, into Antony and Cleopatra.[19] Ovid, Jonathan Bates demonstrated,[20] inspires in the Roman plays a luminous and significant network

of mythic allusion to Tereus, Procne, Philomel, Astraea, Mars, Venus and Hercules. Others have suggested Lucan's *Pharsalia* as a deep source for the imagery of parricidal *saevitia*,[21] Machiavelli for the disillusioned politics of *Julius Caesar*,[22] and Cicero and anti-Ciceronian oratory for the rhetoric of *Coriolanus*.[23]

By the late twentieth century the model implicit in traditional *Quellenforschung*, wherein an author reads a book and tags borrowings by verbal iteration, has yielded to more spacious, accommodating models of intertextuality. 'Background' can now include subtexts beneath texts, contexts alongside, which may or may not have been read by the author, intertexts betwixt and between the author, original audience and modern reader. The master of sources traditionally defined, Geoffrey Bullough, actually served as unacknowledged harbinger of these changes with his endlessly capacious category of 'analogue'; Bullough contributed

---

[14] Vickers, ed., *Critical Heritage*, vol. 2, p. 55.

[15] Velz, 'Authenticity or Anachronism?', p. 1.

[16] Spencer, 'Elizabethan Romans', pp. 29–32.

[17] J. Leeds Barroll, 'Shakespeare and Roman History', *Modern Language Review*, 53 (1958), 327–43.

[18] Anne Barton, 'Livy, Machiavelli, and Shakespeare's Coriolanus', in *Shakespeare Survey 38* (Cambridge, 1985), pp. 115–29.

[19] See John W. Velz, '"Cracking strong curbs asunder": Roman Destiny and the Roman Hero in Coriolanus', *English Literary Renaissance*, 13 (1983), 58–69; Robert S. Miola, *Shakespeare's Rome* (Cambridge, 1983); Barbara J. Bono, *Literary Transvaluation: From Vergilian Epic to Shakespearean Tragicomedy* (Berkeley, CA, 1984); Heather James, *Shakespeare's Troy: Drama, Politics, and the Translation of Empire* (Cambridge, 1997).

[20] Jonathan Bate, *Shakespeare and Ovid* (Oxford, 1993).

[21] Clifford Ronan, *'Antike Roman': Power Symbology and the Roman Play in Early Modern England, 1585–1635* (Athens, GA, 1995).

[22] Robin Headlam Wells, '*Julius Caesar*, Machiavelli, and the uses of History', in *Shakespeare Survey 55* (Cambridge, 2002), pp. 209–18.

[23] Michael West and Myron Siberstein, 'The Controversial Eloquence of Shakespeare's Coriolanus – an Anti-Ciceronian Orator?', *Modern Philology*, 102 (2005), 307–31; John Kerrigan, 'Coriolanus Fidiussed', *Essays in Criticism*, 62 (2012), 319–53.

wide-ranging and searching essays on classical and early modern representations of Brutus, Caesar, Antony, Cleopatra and Coriolanus.[24] Another forerunner, Emrys Jones, introduced Euripides's *Hecuba*, intermediated somehow, as a model for the structural movement from suffering to revenge in *Titus Andronicus*; he also presented the dispute between Agamemnon and Menelaus in *Iphigeneia in Aulis* as prototype for the quarrel scene (4.2) in *Julius Caesar*.[25] Jones did not need to claim that Shakespeare read Euripides in Greek, or to compile verbal echoes, or to trace precise filiations in order to note structural and tonal similarities. Anne Barton similarly compared the 'divided catastrophe' in three plays of Sophocles, imitated by later playwrights, to that in *Antony and Cleopatra*; in all cases the second event forces a reappraisal and radical change of view.[26] Naomi Conn Liebler has argued for Herodian's *History* as 'con-text' for *Titus Andronicus*, insisting on the hyphen to indicate a text that is not mere background but that must be *read with*.[27] Jane Grogan has made a persuasive case for Herodotus's depiction of the dying Persian empire as 'intertext' for *Titus Andronicus*.[28] Now, more than ever, 'Tutte le strade portano a Roma', 'all roads lead to Rome'.

The movement to intertextuality, along with various other critical changes that decentred the author, placed Shakespeare and his Roman plays among various competing cultural and literary discourses. Consequently, critics began to attend to other dramatic representations of Rome. In an Italian monograph, Vanna Gentili surveyed the field, focusing on Lodge's *The Wounds of Civil War* and Edmund Spenser.[29] Warren Chernaik called attention to other playwrights and to variant traditions in the reception of Tacitus, though he disappointingly provided a series of discrete discussions rather than integrated analysis.[30] Most perceptively, Clifford Ronan analyzed the forty-three extant English Roman plays between 1585 and 1635, demonstrating that early modern stage Romans are distinctive and extraordinary in seven areas: 'military and governmental achievements, humanistic patronage of the arts, an ostensibly king- or godlike clemency, and the powers of

self-control and self-denying *constantia*'. These four virtues come with three vices: a pride that could become 'factiousness and a sensitivity to insult', a 'fondness for rituals of superiority' and 'downright savage cruelty'.[31] Taking Shakespeare as her central point, Julia Griffin has usefully surveyed Caesar plays from 1545 to 1762 under three headings, those dramatizing Catiline's conspiracy, the civil war with Pompey, or the assassination.[32]

Among other playwrights, Ben Jonson has begun to command deserved attention, his *Sejanus* and *Catiline* now not simply dismissed as pedantic foils to Shakespeare's more successful representations. This demeaning trend started with Leonard Digges (1640), who contrasted the 'ravished' spectators of Brutus and Cassius at 'half-sword parley' with those who could not 'brook a line / Of tedious though well-laboured *Catiline; / Sejanus* too was irksome'.[33] (The trend continues in Martindale and Martindale.)[34] But Ian Donaldson has described *Sejanus* (in which Shakespeare acted) as a deliberate and critical response to the

---

[24] Geoffrey Bullough, ed., *Narrative and Dramatic Sources of Shakespeare*, vol. 5, *The Roman Plays* (London, 1964).

[25] Emrys Jones, *The Origins of Shakespeare* (Oxford, 1977).

[26] Anne Barton, '"Nature's piece 'gainst fancy": The Divided Catastrophe in *Antony and Cleopatra*' (1974), *Essays, Mainly Shakespearean* (Cambridge, 1994), pp. 113–35.

[27] Naomi Conn Liebler, 'Getting it all right: *Titus Andronicus* and Roman History', *Shakespeare Quarterly*, 45 (1994), 263–78.

[28] Jane Grogan, '"Headless Rome" and Hungry Goths: Herodotus and *Titus Andronicus*', *English Literary Renaissance*, 43 (2013), 30–61.

[29] Vanna Gentili, *La Roma Antica degli Elisabettiani* (Bologna, 1991).

[30] Warren Chernaik, *The Myth of Rome in Shakespeare and his Contemporaries* (Cambridge, 2011).

[31] Ronan, *'Antike Roman'*, p. 65.

[32] Julia Griffin, 'Shakespeare's *Julius Caesar* and the Dramatic Tradition', in *A Companion to Julius Caesar*, ed. Miriam Griffin (Malden, MA, 2009), pp. 371–98. See also her witty study of the two poets in *Julius Caesar* and elsewhere: 'Cinnas of Memory', in *Shakespeare Survey 67* (Cambridge, 2014), pp. 299–309.

[33] Vickers, *Critical Heritage*, vol. 1, p. 28.

[34] Charles Martindale and Michelle Martindale, *Shakespeare and the Uses of Antiquity: An Introductory Essay* (London, 1990).

ambivalences of *Julius Caesar*.[35] Chernaik included the Horatian *Poetaster* as well in the mix, explained the republicanism of *Sejanus* as a warning against tyranny, and explored Jonson's changes from Sallust in *Catiline*.[36] Tom Cain reviewed the circumstances and probable causes of the Privy Council's concern about 'popery and treason' in *Sejanus*, Jonson's ancient world providing a disturbing mirror to his own.[37] Inga-Stina Ewbank examined *Catiline* in the contexts of both Roman plays and Stuart politics.[38] Not coincidentally Donaldson, Cain and Ewbank all served as editors in the grand publication of the Cambridge Ben Jonson (print and electronic editions), a vast repository of scholarship – replete with texts, records and search capacities – that enables and invites further study of Jonson's Rome. We await also the Oxford Thomas Heywood and other editions that will inspire more informed accounts of Rome in contemporary representations.

Seen together, Shakespeare's Roman works depict momentous political changes over almost a millennium of Roman history. *Lucrece* dramatizes the expulsion of the Tarquin tyrants in 509 BC and the start of the Republic, the problems of which are on full display in *Coriolanus* – the battles, uprisings, elections and betrayals that occurred between 491 and 488 BC. *Julius Caesar* portrays the events immediately before and after Caesar's assassination, 15 March 44 BC. The march of history toward Empire continues in *Antony and Cleopatra* with Antony's defeat in the battle of Actium in 31 BC and the prophecy of the Pax Augusta beginning in 27 BC, 'the time of universal peace' (4.6.4). *Cymbeline* provides perspective on that Roman Empire from the outside, from the court of the British king who died in AD 41. *Titus Andronicus* depicts the decay of empire and the invasions of the Goths, *c.* AD 300–400.

Consequently, notice of political themes has been a constant preoccupation in the critical history. Paul A. Cantor (1976) believed that *Coriolanus*, *Julius Caesar* and *Antony and Cleopatra* 'form a kind of historical trilogy, dramatizing the rise and fall of the Roman Republic, in a sense the tragedy of Rome itself, in which the Republic is corrupted and eventually destroyed by its very success in conquering the world'.[39] He identified *thumos* (defined as 'public spiritedness') as characteristic of the republic and *eros* as characteristic of the empire. But this study, Gary Miles pointed out, makes some unhistorical assumptions; the essential virtue in a Roman aristocrat's life in both republic and empire was *dignitas*, or public standing, as evident in *elogia*, portraiture and official deifications.[40] Shakespeare adds a post-classical emphasis on integrity, on interior life.[41] Andrew Hadfield takes up other political themes, viewing *Lucrece* and *Titus* as warnings against tyranny and *Julius Caesar* as exhibiting the decay of republican institutions, though he strains to accommodate this play to his reading of Shakespeare as republican sympathizer.[42] Virtually no one has assented to Barbara L. Parker's claim that Plato's *Republic* constitutes a direct source for the politics of Shakespeare's Rome; her monograph cites commonplace ideas a few verbal echoes, and then succumbs to the fallacy of misplaced specification.[43] And few have found many engaging ideas in the largely derivative monographs of Vivian

[35] Ian Donaldson, '"Misconstruing everything": *Julius Caesar* and Sejanus', in *Shakespeare Performed: Essays in Honor of R. A. Foakes*, ed. Grace Ioppolo (Newark, DE, 2000), pp. 88–107.

[36] Chernaik, *Myth of Rome*.

[37] Tom Cain, ed., *Sejanus*, volume 2 of *The Cambridge Edition of the Works of Ben Jonson*, ed. David Bevington, Martin Butler and Ian Donaldson, 6 vols. (Cambridge, 2012), quoted from p. 201.

[38] Inga-Stina Ewbank, ed., *Catiline*, in *Cambridge Edition of the Works of Ben Jonson*, ed. Bevington, Butler and Donaldson, vol. 4, pp. 6–18

[39] Paul A. Cantor, *Shakespeare's Rome: Republic and Empire* (Ithaca, NY, 1976), quoted at p. 16.

[40] Gary B. Miles, 'How Roman are Shakespeare's "Romans"?', *Shakespeare Quarterly*, 40 (1989), 257–83.

[41] As also noted by Cynthia Marshall in 'Shakespeare, Crossing the Rubicon', in *Shakespeare Survey 53* (Cambridge, 2000), pp. 73–88.

[42] Andrew Hadfield, *Shakespeare and Renaissance Politics* (London, 2004) and *Shakespeare and Republicanism* (Cambridge, 2005).

[43] Barbara L. Parker, *Plato's Republic and Shakespeare's Rome: A Political Study of the Roman Works* (Newark, DE, 2004).

Thomas and Charles Wells.[44] More specifically and helpfully, Peltonen examines the connections between the arts of rhetoric and citizenship in *Coriolanus*, topics of perennial interest.[45]

It has become standard practice to discern in the Roman works topical political parallels: many compare Lucrece's concern for her chastity and Elizabeth's cult of virginity, for example, the Imperial Rome of *Antony and Cleopatra* and the court of James I, the civic unrest in *Coriolanus* and the Midlands revolts, the dreams of monarchy and nationhood in *Cymbeline* and those of Stuart ideology. In a sensitive and detailed reading of *Julius Caesar* in 1599, James Shapiro discusses many Elizabethan concerns in Shakespeare's ancient Rome: worry over assassination and succession, controversy over the calendar and the suppression of ceremonies and debate about 'the uses of the classical past, republicanism, tyranny, holiday, popularity, censorship, political spin and the silencing of opposing voices'.[46] Two challenging essays have sought wider political application. John Drakakis examines *Julius Caesar* as a case history in the mechanisms of power, as relevant today as it was in the Globe: the theatrical imagery exposes 'the discursive mechanisms, at the moment that it seeks to reinforce, the historical and material determinants, of political power'. The play is 'not so much as a celebration of theatre as an unmasking of the politics of representation per se'.[47] Martha Nussbaum reads *Julius Caesar* as profoundly anti-republican in that its Roman citizens, contrary to those in the sources, are too fickle and self-centred to govern themselves, incapable of rising to the necessary love of principles and institutions that guarantee freedom and equality for all. Shakespeare's play and his Brutus, she argues, get rewritten in the passionate republicanism of the American (1776) and Indian (1947) revolutions.[48]

Along with politics, religion has always fascinated visitors to Shakespeare's Rome, particularly its pagan ethos of honour, shame and fame. In a seminal essay, D. J. Gordon observed in *Coriolanus* Shakespeare's critical treatment of this ethos as self-destructive.[49] Glory, the principal form of immortality open to these Romans,

appears here as the stinking breath of the multitude or, as Falstaff put it, 'What is that "honour"? Air' (*1 Henry IV*, 5.1.135). The role of Stoicism has also been much in conversation. Shakespeare's reading of Cicero, Seneca and Plutarch, Geoffrey Miles argued, furnished the vision of *constantia* as steadfastness and invariability that underlies three Roman plays.[50] According to Aristotelian ethical theory, Shakespeare explores the defect of constancy in Antony, its balanced presence in Brutus, and its excess in Coriolanus – a consistent reading if a bit too schematic. Gordon Braden has sharply focused attention on the most immutably alien and pagan element in Shakespeare's Roman world, namely suicide. Lucrece, Portia, Brutus, Cassius, Antony and Cleopatra all kill themselves as climactic gestures of self-control and self-assertion (though Cleopatra, of course, is a special case). Despite Augustine's and Dante's admonitions, as well as Chapman's and Fletcher's examples in their plays, Shakespeare's self-slaughtering Romans do not consider life after death. In the case of Brutus, 'Shakespeare has cleanly excised the look to the afterlife that would have seemed authoritative in North and been nearly instinctive

[44] Vivian Thomas, *Shakespeare's Roman Worlds* (London, 1989); Charles Wells, *The Wide Arch: Roman Values in Shakespeare* (New York, 1993).

[45] Markku Peltonen, 'Political rhetoric and citizenship in *Coriolanus*', in *Shakespeare and Early Modern Political Thought*, ed. David Armitage, Conal Condren and Andrew Fitzmaurice (Cambridge, 2009), pp. 234–52.

[46] James Shapiro, *1599: A Year in the Life of William Shakespeare* (London, 2005), p. 189.

[47] John Drakakis, '"Fashion it thus": *Julius Caesar* and the Politics of Theatrical Representation', in *Shakespeare Survey* 44 (Cambridge, 1992), pp. 65–73; pp. 71 and 72.

[48] Martha C. Nussbaum, '"Romans, countrymen, and lovers": Political Love and the Rule of Law in *Julius Caesar*', in *Shakespeare and the Law: A Conversation among Disciplines and Professions*, ed. Bradin Cormack, Martha C. Nussbaum, and Richard Strier (Chicago, 2013), pp. 256–81.

[49] D. J. Gordon, 'Name and Fame: Shakespeare's *Coriolanus*', in *Papers, Mainly Shakespearean*, ed. G. I. Duthie (Edinburgh, 1964), pp. 40–57.

[50] Geoffrey Miles, *Shakespeare and the Constant Romans* (Oxford, 1996).

in a Christian writer, and replaced it with a foursquare bleakness: the only thing lasting forever is farewell'.[51]

Shakespeare's Romans, then, differ distinctly from Puccini's Roman Tosca, who cries 'O Scarpia, avanti a Dio' ('O Scarpia, onward to God') as she jumps to her death from Castel' Sant'Angelo, the pagan gesture of suicide thus located in explicitly Christian contexts, physical and metaphysical. Yet critics have detected elsewhere and in other ways significant Christian presences and absences in Shakespeare's Rome. J. L. Simmons thought 'the antedating of Christian Revelation' 'the most significant historical factor' in *Julius Caesar, Antony and Cleopatra* and *Coriolanus*.[52] Trapped in Augustine's Earthly City, Shakespeare's Romans are doomed to tragic failure. This study explains credibly the bleak sense of constriction in Shakespeare's Roman world but is itself too narrow and single-minded. Noting in *Julius Caesar* plentiful reference to contemporary religious issues, David Kaula well discussed Caesar's holy blood in Calphurnia's dream, source of 'tinctures, stains, relics, and cognizance' (2.2.89); the 'sacrifice' of Caesar and subsequent bathing in this blood strongly evoke Christian rituals.[53] In a much admired essay, Stanley Cavell went further, seeing Coriolanus as competing with Christ, the 'lamb' the wolf loves or, in his view, who loves the wolf.[54] Among other parallels, he compared Coriolanus's refusal to show his wounds with Christ's showing of his wounds to Thomas, and the appearance of three women to Coriolanus to the appearance of three women at the Crucifixion 'whose names begin with the same letter of the alphabet (I mean begin with M's not with V's)'.[55] We have all learned to appreciate the mysterious operations of Shakespeare's religious memory but this seems like free association in service of over-determined Christological resonance.

In his edition of *Titus Andronicus*, Jonathan Bate suggestively interpreted the Goths who join Lucius's army against the corrupt city as harbingers of constitutional reform and as pre-figurations of the Protestants who effected another *translatio*

imperii in the sixteenth century.[56] Attempting an overview, Robert S. Miola explored the clash between classical *anima* and Christian soul in *Lucrece*, the sacrament of violence in *Titus Andronicus*, and pagan oracle as Holy Scripture in *Cymbeline*. 'The drifted humanist imagination apprehends the other as other and as itself.'[57] Also discussing *Cymbeline*, Sarah Beckwith argued that the final reconciliation scene 'links the languages of confession, acknowledgment, and recognition to create the unprecedented peace that is the "mark of wonder" in this play, the play that harmonizes Britain with ancient and contemporary Rome'.[58] Her persuasive analysis of religious language and imagery in the last scene shows the creation of a restored community and nation.

Whether classical or Christian, Shakespeare's Rome presents to most readers and audiences a world of values coded as masculine – honour, constancy, self-control, courage, *virtus* – a world, in other words, especially suited to the interrogation of feminist and gender criticism. Janet Adelman powerfully argued that Coriolanus's masculinity 'is constructed in response to maternal power, and in the absence of a father; . . . the hero attempts

---

[51] Gordon Braden, 'Fame, eternity, and Shakespeare's Romans', in *Shakespeare and Renaissance Ethics*, ed. Patrick Gray and John D. Cox (Cambridge, 2014), pp. 37–55; p. 46.

[52] J. L. Simmons, *Shakespeare's Pagan World: The Roman Tragedies* (Charlottesville, VA, 1973), quoted at p. 7.

[53] David Kaula, '"Let us be sacrificers": Religious Motifs in *Julius Caesar*', *Shakespeare Studies*, 14 (1981), 197–214; see also Jack Heller, '"Your statue spouting blood": *Julius Caesar*, the Sacraments, and the Fountain of Life', in *Word and Rite: The Bible and Ceremony in Selected Shakespearean Works*, ed. Beatrice Batson (Newcastle upon Tyne, 2010), pp. 77–93.

[54] Stanley Cavell, '"Who does the wolf love?" Reading *Coriolanus*', *Representations*, 3 (1983), 1–20; quoted at p. 8.

[55] Cavell, '"Who does the wolf love?"', p. 12.

[56] Jonathan Bate, ed., *Titus Andronicus* (London, 1995).

[57] Robert S. Miola, '"An alien people clutching their gods?" Shakespeare's Ancient Religions', in *Shakespeare Survey 54* (Cambridge, 2001), pp. 31–45; p. 32.

[58] Sarah Beckwith, *Shakespeare and the Grammar of Forgiveness* (Ithaca, NY, 2011), p. 105.

to recreate himself through his bloody heroics, in fantasy severing the connection with his mother even as he enacts the ruthless masculinity that is her bidding'.[59] Coriolanus ultimately fails to construct an identity apart from his mother and dies 'helpless and unarmed, his multiply-penetrated body the sign of his mother's presence in him'.[60] Adelman writes mesmerising prose, extremely sensitive to the language of the play, but this anti-heroic reading ultimately construes Volumnia as both male and female when it suits (is she ever portrayed as multiply penetrated?); it reduces Roman *virtus* to compensatory phallic aggression (displaced from oral fixation), and turns Coriolanus into a helpless 'child', pathetic rather than tragic.[61] Pondering the Egyptian Queen's revulsion at 'some squeaking Cleopatra' boying her 'greatness' (5.2.216), as well as the theatrical history of the play, Juliet Dusinberre argued that productions should assert 'women's control', not weakness; the play exposes 'the performative nature of gender categories, offering us a world we can recognize'.[62] Gail Kern Paster boldly described blood as a trope of gender in *Julius Caesar* and argued that the assassination 'discloses the shameful secret of Caesar's bodiliness: by stabbing and displaying his body, the conspirators cause the fallen patriarch to reveal a womanly inability to stop bleeding'.[63] From a different angle, Coppélia Kahn continued this investigation, discovering a larger pattern of wounding that includes Lavinia's mutilation, Portia's stab of her thigh, Antony's attempted suicide, and Coriolanus's gashes and scars; in this copiously bleeding world she discussed the place of the women – the oppositional Cleopatra, the chaste, sacralized Lucrece and Lavinia, and the frighteningly Roman Volumnia.[64] Despite their differences these studies have all reckoned the costs and contradictions of Roman *machismo* and forcefully located women centrally within and without Roman walls.

Such developments in feminist and gender studies have led to new studies of early modern sexuality, the body and homosexuality that further illuminate Shakespeare's Rome. Cynthia Marshall analyzed *Titus Andronicus* as pornography,

particularly its display of a raped, mutilated woman that pushes 'the erotics of pain, suffering, and dominance to new limits'.[65] Gail Kern Paster revised her essay on Caesar for *The Body Embarrassed* (1993), which explores early modern constructions of the humoral body and the disciplines of shame, and has sparked new interest in early modern blood, physiology and corporeality. Discovering a discourse of phlebotomy in Shakespeare's Rome, Belling discusses contaminated blood and bloodletting as both purge and revenge in *Lucrece*, *Titus Andronicus*, and *Coriolanus*.[66] Balizet examines the bleeding child, son and daughter, in *Titus Andronicus* and the relation of blood to domestic identity and to 'home'.[67] Hoffman argues that Coriolanus's blush acts against Galenic humoral determinism and 'motivates a process of moral consciousness and complexional reform through which his soul is purified'.[68] (This is a bit much since Coriolanus never actually

[59] Janet Adelman, *Suffocating Mothers: Fantasies of Maternal Origin in Shakespeare's Plays, 'Hamlet' to 'The Tempest'* (London and New York, 1992), p. 146. (This work contains a revised version of 'Anger's My Meat: Feeding, Dependency, and Aggression in *Coriolanus*', 1980).

[60] Adelman, *Suffocating Mothers*, p. 162.

[61] Adelman, *Suffocating Mothers*, p. 161.

[62] Juliet Dusinberre, 'Squeaking Cleopatras: Gender and Performance in *Antony and Cleopatra*', in *Shakespeare, Theory, and Performance*, ed. James C. Bulman (London, 1996), pp. 46–67; p. 64.

[63] Gail Kern Paster, '"In the spirit of men there is no blood": Blood as Trope of Gender in *Julius Caesar*', *Shakespeare Quarterly*, 40 (1989), 284–98; p. 285.

[64] Coppélia Kahn, *Roman Shakespeare: Warriors, Wounds, and Women* (London, 1997).

[65] Cynthia Marshall, 'The Pornographic Economy of *Titus Andronicus*', in *The Shattering of the Self: Violence, Subjectivity, and Early Modern Texts* (Baltimore, 2002), pp. 106–37; p. 11.

[66] Catherine Belling, 'Infectious Rape, Therapeutic Revenge: Bloodletting and the Health of Rome's Body', in *Disease, Diagnosis and Cure on the Early Modern Stage*, ed. Stephanie Moss and Kaara L. Peterson (Aldershot, 2004), pp. 113–32.

[67] Ariane M. Balizet, *Blood and Home in Early Modern Drama: Domestic Identity on the Renaissance Stage* (New York, 2014), pp. 89–120.

[68] Tiffany Hoffman, 'Coriolanus' Blush', in *Embodied Cognition and Shakespeare's Theatre: The Early Modern Body-Mind*, ed.

blushes but only mentions the possibility twice, 1.10.69, 2.2.146). In 2010 Maria del Sapia Garbero and others published twenty-one essays in *Questioning Bodies in Shakespeare's Rome*, a wide-ranging study of what John Dee called 'anthropo-graphie' or 'the description of man', 'both a transdiscipline and a field of enquiry imagined on the model of the new cartography'.[69] The collection moves beyond the reinterrogated human body to wider scientific and philosophical applications.

Queer theory has much to address in Shakespeare's Roman works, the most baroque examples of male military eroticism, of course, appearing in *Coriolanus*, where Martius wants to embrace Cominius, 'In arms as sound as when I wooed, in heart / As merry as when our nuptial day was done, / And tapers burnt to bed-ward!' (1.7.30–2). Aufidius greets his former enemy as a newlywed anticipating the wedding night: 'more dances my rapt heart / Than when I first my wedded mistress saw / Bestride my threshold' (4.5.117–19). He embraces Coriolanus on stage and remembers dreaming often of him, 'Unbuckling helms, fisting each other's throat' (126). In a comprehensive study of homosexual desire in the Renaissance, Bruce Smith explained that these Roman warriors assert their masculinity by bonding and competing, yet by keeping at a distance in a kind of 'communal narcissism'.[70] Jonathan Goldberg wrote that Aufidius and Volumnia are 'versions of each other, lovers and enemies', that *Coriolanus* equates 'hetero and homo desire *and its betrayal*'. 'Coriolanus's career of attempted self-authorship', however, finally 'represents a desire to become a machine, to "live" in some realm that is not biological'.[71] The sensationally titled essay, 'The Anus in *Coriolanus*', thus dwindles to a tamely conventional conclusion. The contributors to *Shakesqueer* (2011) might have provided further insight into the strange concentricity of military and amorous impulses and into the undercurrents of homoerotic desire in Shakespeare's Rome had they spent more energy on the textual, critical and performance histories of the works and less on confession and self-congratulation.[72] Much more remains to be said.

Recent race and ethnic studies have also opened our eyes to the many non-Romans in and outside of Shakespeare's city and, more importantly, to the extent that city constructs its identity by demonizing and expelling outsiders. Ania Loomba noted that the dominant patriarchy of Rome casts Tamora and Aaron as 'embodiments of pure evil; the supposedly uncontrollable sexuality of women and blacks motivates their liaison'.[73] Exploring stage stereotypes of blackness, Arthur Little called Aaron additionally 'the sexually potent mastermind behind Lavinia's rape'.[74] But these and many other critics note that Rome proves to be child-devouring whereas Aaron barters his own life for his infant's. Elsewhere Loomba cites Antony Sher and Gregory Doran recalling black South African audiences identifying with Aaron, who delights in his 'coal-black' hue (4.2.98), and their boisterous approval of his defiance.[75] A Moor and a villain, Aaron complicates race distinction in Shakespeare's Rome and helps to dismantle the oppositions between civilized Roman and barbarous Goth.

Laurie Johnson, John Sutton and Evelyn Tribble (New York, 2014), pp. 173–89; pp. 173–4.

[69] Maria Del Sapio Garbero, Nancy Isenberg and Maddalena Pennacchia, eds., *Questioning Bodies in Shakespeare's Rome* (Göttingen, 2010), p. 14.

[70] Bruce R. Smith, *Homosexual Desire in Shakespeare's England: A Cultural Poetics* (Chicago, 1991), p. 59.

[71] Jonathan Goldberg, 'The Anus in *Coriolanus*', in *Shakespeare's Hand* (Minneapolis, 2003), pp. 176–86; pp. 183 and 185 respectively.

[72] Madhavi Menon, ed., *Shakesqueer: A Queer Companion to the Complete Works of Shakespeare* (Durham, 2011).

[73] Ania Loomba, *Gender, Race, Renaissance Drama* (Oxford, 1989), p. 47.

[74] Arthur L. Little, Jr, *Shakespeare Jungle Fever: National-Imperial Re-Visions of Race, Rape, and Sacrifice* (Stanford, CA, 2000), p. 63.

[75] Ania Loomba, *Shakespeare, Race, and Colonialism* (Oxford, 2002), p. 75. On their 1995 production, see Natasha Distiller, *Shakespeare and the Coconuts: On Post-Apartheid South African Culture* (Johannesburg, 2012), pp. 71–96.

The category of 'race' itself has been shown to be problematically indeterminate. To early moderns, race did not simply mean 'skin color', Margo Hendricks has demonstrated, but referred also to 'difference born of a class-based concept of geneal-ogy, a psychologized (and essentialized) nature, or group typology'.[76] Thus Little can treat Antony as white male who transgresses the boundaries that demarcate race: 'in going primitive, Antony goes Egyptian, in effect African'; he ends up as a 'kind of white African'.[77] The archetypal anti-Roman out-sider, Cleopatra, 'with Phoebus' amorous pinches black' (1.5.28), deeply interrogates the play's con-structions of racial difference, colonial conflict, gen-der and national oppositions, as Kim Hall has noted.[78] The colour of the historical Cleopatra's skin has occasioned much recent dispute since Martin Bernal's *Black Athena*[79] and Mary Lefkowitz's bristling response, *Not out of Africa*.[80] Joyce Green MacDonald devotes a chapter to this controversy before dismissing it for Shakespeare, concluding that *Antony and Cleopatra* 'is finally so convinced of the cosmic import of Cleopatra's racial difference from the Romans that it cannot be both-ered to be consistent about her skin color'.[81] Perhaps, but directors and actors have usually chosen to cast an actress of one colour or another in the role and this decision has consequences. Celia R. Daileader surveys the various impersonations of blackness in the history of modern stage Cleopatras.[82] Of course, whiteness studies now hold that whiteness is a raced position and not simply the invisible and normative default. From this point of view, Francesca T. Royster explores the constructions of racial identity for Tamora, also depicted as anti-Roman other, and for Cleopatra.[83] Aebischer examines the relation of 'whiteness' to beauty in Renaissance Cleopatras from Jodelle to Shakespeare.[84] Whatever the merits of her 1963 per-formance, Elizabeth Taylor's pale, voluptuous Cleopatra, masked in blue eye-shadow and mascara, adorned in sixty-five costumes, including one of 24-carat gold cloth, had a long dramatic history.

As racially other, however defined, Shakespeare's Cleopatra has struck many as paradoxically Roman, particularly in her refusal to be led in triumph and in her suicide. As such she recalls Horace's famous Cleopatra (*Carmina*, 1.37), the hated foreign queen ('fatale monstrum', 'doom-bringing portent'), who nevertheless faces death with serene countenance ('voltu sereno') and manly ('nec muliebriter') Roman fortitude. Shakespeare again addresses the paradoxes of racial alterity in his last portrayal of an anti-type to Rome, the Britons. Critics have var-iously discussed the shifting perplexities of *Cymbeline*, which mixes conflicting historical and mythical accounts to feature the English and Welsh, ancient Romans and modern Italians, a chauvinistic defiance of Rome, and finally an agreement to pay it tribute. Jodi Mikalachki notes that dramas set in Roman Britain tend to conclude with a masculine embrace that exorcizes resistant female savagery and promises peaceful union with the Empire.[85] Griffiths disagrees, arguing that inclu-sion of Renaissance Italians in the play, idlers, phi-landerers and worse, undermines the final fraternal

---

[76] Margo Hendricks, 'Surveying "Race" in Shakespeare', in *Shakespeare and Race*, ed. Catherine M. S. Alexander and Stanley Wells (Cambridge, 2000), pp. 1–22; p. 20.

[77] Little, *Jungle Fever*, p. 104.

[78] Kim F. Hall, *Things of Darkness: Economies of Race and Gender in Early Modern England* (Ithaca, NY, 1995).

[79] 2 vols. (New Brunswick, NJ, 1987 and 1991).

[80] New York, 1996.

[81] Joyce Green MacDonald, *Women and Race in Early Modern Texts* (Cambridge, 2002), p. 60.

[82] Celia R. Daileader, 'The Cleopatra Complex: White Actresses on the Interracial "Classic" Stage', in *Colorblind Shakespeare: New Perspectives on Race and Performance*, ed. Ayanna Thompson (New York, 2006), pp. 205–20.

[83] Francesca T. Royster, 'Cleopatra as Diva: African-American Women and Shakespearean Tactics', in *Transforming Shakespeare: Contemporary Women's Re-visions in Literature and Performance*, ed. Marianne Novy (New York, 1999), pp. 103–25; 'White-limed Walls: Whiteness and Gothic Extremism in Shakespeare's *Titus Andronicus*', *Shakespeare Quarterly*, 51 (2000), 432–55; *Becoming Cleopatra: The Shifting Image of an Icon* (New York, 2003).

[84] Pascale Aebischer, 'The Properties of Whiteness: Renaissance Cleopatras from Jodelle to Shakespeare', in *Shakespeare Survey 65* (Cambridge, 2013), pp. 221–38.

[85] Jodi Mikalachki, 'The Masculine Romance of Roman Britain: *Cymbeline* and Early Modern English Nationalism', *Shakespeare Quarterly*, 46 (1995), 301–22.

hug and reveals that Rome itself, like Britain, is an unstable, discursive construct.[86] Martin Butler convincingly and comprehensively reviews the competing myths of nationhood in the period and explains the dual view of the Romans as predatory and beneficent: 'The split identity of the Romans stages an Oedipal scenario' that expresses the 'trauma of inheritance'. Britain must repudiate the Rome that is evil father and restore relations with the Rome that is good father, bestower of the imperial patrimony. Paying tribute does not imply base submission but rejection of isolation and a claiming of place in the changing world order. 'Victory puts relations with Rome on a new footing, making Britain more a competitor than a colony'. Philharmonus's final prophecy of the eagle flying west into sunlight foretells 'a westering of empire to British dynasties as yet unborn'.[87]

Performance criticism also now illuminates Shakespeare's Rome and the particular staging challenges of the plays – the grisly horrors of *Titus Andronicus*, the mid-play climax of *Julius Caesar*, the dizzying locale shifts of *Antony and Cleopatra*, the crabbed diction and unlikeable hero of *Coriolanus*, the mixing of genres in *Cymbeline*. The study of performance receives increasing attention in the introductions and annotations of multivolume editions (New Arden 3, New Cambridge, Oxford, Norton Critical) and in separate studies and series. Cambridge University Press publishes the *Players of Shakespeare* volumes, consisting of essays on Shakespearian roles by RSC actors, and a *Shakespeare in Production* series, wherein specific references to productions gloss the text of the play. Richard Madelaine's *Antony and Cleopatra*, for example, notes the many different ways productions have lifted the dying Antony to Cleopatra in the monument – machinery, linen strips, stairs, stage illusion – as well as the many different moods of Cleopatras with the asp – coquettish (Harriet Faucit), rapturous (Isabella Glyn), childish (Vivien Leigh), queenly (Peggy Ashcroft), reluctant (Lindy Davis), affectionate (Vanessa Redgrave) and joyful (Judi Dench).[88] Sarah Hatchuel and Nathalie Vienne-Guerrin have edited a volume of essays, *Shakespeare on Screen:*

The Roman Plays,[89] wherein Russell Jackson examines film depictions of the plebeians, and Samuel Crowl, Dominique Goy-Blanquet and Lois Potter each explore *Julius Caesar*, the last noting the difficulty of turning Stoic imperturbability into effective drama. Mariangela Tempera amusingly catalogues references to the Roman plays in films ranging from Alfred Hitchcock's *Spellbound* (1955) to Mark Waters's *Mean Girls* (2004): 'What's so great about Caesar? Brutus is just as cute. People totally like Brutus as much as Caesar . . . We should totally just stab Caesar!' (p. 310). Among other contributions, José Ramón Diaz-Fernández provides a remarkably comprehensive bibliography that lists film and television adaptations, filmed stage performances, animated versions, derivatives and citations, and educational videos.

The Shakespeare in Performance series of Manchester University Press has also contributed substantially by focusing on the material conditions of significant productions as well as on their actors, scenic design, medium of adaptation and contexts – historical, political and social. Discussing *Titus Andronicus*, Alan Dessen praises Deborah Warner's production (1987) for trusting the script, that is, for restoring material cut by Peter Brook, John Barton and Trevor Nunn, and for its brilliant use of dark comedy. The reviser, Michael Friedman, notes the adoption of this dark comedy in productions from 1989 to 2009, as well as three other interpretive lines: stylized, following Peter Brook (1955); realistic, following Jane Howell (1985); and political, following Douglas Seale (1967).[90] Andrew James Hartley adroitly surveys the production history of *Julius Caesar*, noting its lack of a unifying central figure,

---

[86] Huw Griffiths, 'The Geographies of Shakespeare's Cymbeline', *English Literary Renaissance*, 34 (2004), 339–58.

[87] Martin Butler, ed., *Cymbeline* (Cambridge, 2005), pp. 51 and 50 respectively.

[88] Richard Madelaine, *Shakespeare in Production: 'Antony and Cleopatra'* (Cambridge, 1998), pp. 288–91, 320.

[89] Rouen, 2009.

[90] Michael D. Friedman, *Shakespeare in Performance: 'Titus Andronicus'* (Manchester, 2013) (incorporates Alan Dessen's 1989 edition).

the opacity of Brutus, the early placement of the assassination, the disunity of the last two acts, the absence of romance, strong female characters and humour.[91] Hartley shows how Orson Welles's landmark 1937 production reshaped the play through staging, costuming, lighting and cutting to reflect the rising threat of European fascism and the ineffectuality of conscientious liberalism. Subtitled *The Death of a Dictator*, Welles portrayed Caesar as Mussolini, Hitler, or any charismatic tyrant, and the people as the lawless, violent mob that tears apart Cinna the poet in a scene restored after two hundred and fifty years of absence from the stage (p. 43). Those who manipulate the mob, not the mob itself, threaten the Republic and civilization in Joseph Mankiewicz's film *Julius Caesar* (1953), which highlights the sinister Brando as Antony in the Proscription scene. Hartley convincingly explores the scene and play in the context of McCarthyist extremism and Mankiewicz's own troubles with anti-Communist hysteria. Focusing on Deborah Warner's 2005 *Caesar*, its core uncertainty, its revelation of media misconstruction, Hartley declares that 'the word which ghosts twenty-first-century productions most clearly is "spin"' (p. 5). In this series, Robert Ormsby astutely discusses *Coriolanus*, illuminating the metamorphoses of Bertolt Brecht's mid-twentieth century Marxist production, with its focus on social and political forces over individuals, its presentation of the plebeians as 'wronged, aware, and finally brave and united'.[92] Rejecting Brecht's cautious optimism about politico-social change, Gabor Székely's production (Budapest, 1985) showed that 'the futility of participating in a degraded public sphere has a profoundly corrosive effect on anyone who attempts to do so' (p. 158). Ormsby argues that Ralph Fiennes's film employs Hollywood conventions, especially 'narrative clarity, frenetic editing techniques and an abundance of explosive violence' (p. 223) to depict Coriolanus as 'failed action hero'.

Like Titus Andronicus and Coriolanus, we return inevitably to Rome, where we began, or more precisely to the principal place Shakespeare's Rome began, Plutarch's *Lives*. Recent changes in classical scholarship under the rubric of 'Reception'

studies have radically transformed understanding of ancient texts and the subsequent processes of reading and revivication. Early theorists such as Hans Robert Jauss and Wolfgang Iser have inspired Charles Martindale, Lorna Hartwick and a new generation of classical scholars to move beyond the metaphors of classical 'tradition' and 'legacy' to recognize more flexible and dynamic relationships between authors, texts and readers. A Greek or Latin text is no longer an unchanging and eternal deposit, 'quod semper, quod ubique, quod omnibus creditum est' ('what always, everywhere, and by everyone is believed'), passed on to later generations, but a work whose meaning is realized by the very acts of reading, translating, interpreting, revising and adapting that constitute its history. Thus readers of Shakespeare's Rome today begin by noting how Plutarch himself refashions sources, including Greek epic, drama and history. Indeed, North's Plutarch is one largely unexplored source for Shakespeare's mediated contact with Homer and Greek tragedy.[93] Plutarch writes as a Greek ethnographer for whom Rome is to some degree an alien civilization and as a biographer with a keen eye for dramatic scenes. Moderns reading Shakespeare reading Plutarch thus participate in a series of complicated interactions.

The rise of this new *Rezeptionsästhetik* enforces the realization that Shakespeare never read Plutarch at all: he read North's English translation (probably the 1595 edition) of Amyot's French translation (1559) of Plutarch's *Lives*. As in so many ways, MacCallum was ahead of his time here, printing in his Appendix B Greek, Latin, French and English versions of Volumnia's speech to Coriolanus, a close and sustained Shakespearian borrowing

---

[91] Andrew James Hartley, *Shakespeare in Performance: 'Julius Caesar'* (Manchester, 2014).

[92] Robert Ormsby, *Shakespeare in Performance: 'Coriolanus'* (Manchester, 2014), p. 51.

[93] On the latter, see the suggestive discussion of Christopher Pelling, 'Seeing a Roman Tragedy through Greek Eyes: Shakespeare's *Julius Caesar*', in *Sophocles and the Greek Tragic Tradition*, ed. Simon Goldhill and Edith Hall (Cambridge, 2009), pp. 264–88.

though intermediations. Also printing parallel passages in Greek, French and English in a spirited plea for attention to translation, John Denton notes North's imposition of an alien, moralizing (Puritan) viewpoint at times, such that the tribunes become flattering and busy prattlers and the common people more fickle and objectionable.[94] Plutarch, moreover, simply remarks that candidates for office wore no tunic under the toga in order to demonstrate humility whereas North invents a separate 'gown';[95] all these changes Shakespeare magnifies in *Coriolanus*. Another astute commentator, Christopher Pelling notes contradictions of Plutarch but also continuations: Shakespeare finishes what Plutarch started, particularly in his characterization of Volumnia and emphasis on Coriolanus's anger.[96] As editor and translator of Plutarch's *Caesar* (Oxford, 2011), Pelling observes further that Plutarch and Shakespeare make the same kind of changes to their source: alteration in sequence, conflation, chronological compression, transfer of action from one character to another, creation of a context and imaginative elaboration. Moreover, Shakespeare sometimes seems to 'sense the real Plutarch even when his translators stray' (p. 65): he elaborates on the idea of sacrifice (*katarkhesthai*) in the killing of Caesar (whether grand intention or self-delusion on the conspirators' part), though Amyot and North miss it entirely. And he conveys some of the ambivalence of the untranslatable *daimon* that ranges through Plutarch's account, first as Caesar's spirit, then as Brutus's; Pompey's spirit haunts the first half of the play but Caesar's 'spirit' finally destroys Brutus. Poutiainen focuses on Shakespeare's encounters with the untranslatable Greek terms *daimon* and *psuché* – gesturing to a wide and fertile field for future study.[97]

Gordon Braden notes that Shakespeare, at other times, follows North in his mistakes, reproducing the erroneous 'Lydia' for 'Libya' (*Antony*, 3.6.10), for example, and substituting 'womb' for the 'corpse' Volumnia warns Coriolanus about treading upon (5.3.125).[98] The playwright felicitously transforms North's confusing account of Brutus on suicide (simultaneously opposing and endorsing self-slaughter) by showing him changing his

mind in response to the suggestion of public dishonour, of being 'led in triumph / Thorough the streets of Rome' (5.1.108–9). Colin Burrow, furthermore, gives a fresh and searching account of Plutarch's conceptual contributions to Shakespeare's Rome – 'the balanced ethical judgements of the *Lives*, their perplexing blend of anti-Stoicism and their apparent valorization of passion, their conjunction of political analysis and gossip, their constant and self-conscious attempts to reconcile a whole range of conflicting historical sources'.[99] Burrow points to the two visions of ancient Rome present in *Julius Caesar*, the city of moral order, marmoreal values, of honour and fame, and that of 'ghosts, spirits, blood, pollution, sacrifices, portents, and murder' (p. 224). He observes also passages important to Shakespeare that he chose not to dramatize in *Coriolanus*.

Others have looked at classical receptions beyond Plutarch. Niall Rudd has deftly explored Shakespeare's 'creative reminiscence' of many classical texts in *Titus Andronicus*.[100] Pramit Chaudhuri has reviewed Peele's and Shakespeare's Latin quotations from Horace, Ovid and Seneca in this play,

---

[94] John Denton, 'Plutarch, Shakespeare, Roman Politics and Renaissance Translation', in *Shakespeare's Plutarch, Poetica*, ed. Mary Ann McGrail (Tokyo, 1997), 187–209.

[95] John Denton, '"Wearing a gown in the market-place or a toga in the Forum": Coriolanus from Plutarch to Shakespeare via Renaissance Translation', in *Shakespeare e la sua Eredità*, ed. Grazia Caliumi (Parma, 1993), pp. 97–109.

[96] Christopher Pelling, 'The Shaping of Coriolanus: Dionysius, Plutarch, and Shakespeare', in *Shakespeare's Plutarch, Poetica*, ed. McGrail, 3–32.

[97] Hannu Poutiainen, 'Autoapotropaics: *Daimon* and *Psuché* between Plutarch and Shakespeare', *Oxford Literary Review*, 34 (2012), 51–70.

[98] Gordon Braden, 'Plutarch, Shakespeare, and the alpha males', in *Shakespeare and the Classics*, ed. Charles Martindale and A. B. Taylor (Cambridge, 2004), pp. 188–205.

[99] Colin Burrow, *Shakespeare and Classical Antiquity* (Oxford, 2012), p. 214.

[100] Niall Rudd, '*Titus Andronicus*: The Classical Presence', in *Shakespeare Survey 55* (Cambridge, 2002), pp. 199–208; p. 208.

carefully comparing original contexts, exploring errors and conflations, precisely calibrating the dramatic ironies.[101] In the age of Classical Reception studies investigation of sources is no longer the elephants' graveyard of literary criticism but its symphony hall, where one can hear complex polyphonies composed of enchanting harmonies and more enchanting dissonances.

The burgeoning study of early modern print publication and the history of the book has also furnished exciting perspectives. Colin Burrow observes that the 1594 *Lucrece* quarto features a similar ornament to *Venus and Adonis* Q2 (1594), thus making 'an attractive pair of books to buy at Harrison's shop at the sign of the White Greyhound'.[102] Typography identifies twenty-three lines as sententiae for readers to copy and memorize. These strategies did not succeed, however, according to Katherine Duncan-Jones, who speculates that *Lucrece*'s initial unpopularity caused the publisher Roger Jackson to print an edition in 1616 that features twelve numbered headings, summaries, heavy use of italics, minor verbal substitutions and the misleading advertisement, 'Newly revised'.[103] One need not agree that the 1594 version was a 'Purple Cow' (p. 522) to appreciate the new marketing plan. Burrow also notes that *Lucrece* Q9 (1655) contains Quarles's *Tarquin Banished, or the Reward of Lust*, thus shifting the focus from politics to 'individual crime and punishment'.[104] Extending these insights, Sasha Roberts comprehensively examines the early modern transmission of *Lucrece* in printed quartos, in manuscript marginalia and in subsequent quotation in commonplace books, anthologies and other texts.[105] She wonderfully demonstrates the 'provisionality and instability of poetic meaning ... in the hands of the dissenting reader, the innovative stationer, and the commonplacer' (p. 142). Sonia Massai discerns in the Fourth Folio (1685) text of *Coriolanus* the sophisticated corrections and ingenious alterations that signal the presence of an editor rather than a printing-house proofreader; she proposes, plausibly, Nahum Tate.[106] And finally, Nadia Bishai observes that all three quartos of *Titus Andronicus* (1594–1611) appeared for sale at a single bookshop, the Sign of the Gun, by one stationer, Edward White, who specialized in crime literature.[107] She thus situates *Titus Andronicus* in the London book trade and proposes contemporary crime literature as a new material and literary context.

Burrow's admirable edition of Shakespeare's *Sonnets and Poems* reveals other significant shifts in the critical winds of the twenty-first century, especially renewed attention to the history of reading, to early modern quotation and appropriation of Shakespeare's Roman works. Searching manuscript miscellanies, Burrow notes one revision that confuses the pronouns so that Lucrece's hand lies under Tarquin's cheek rather than her own, thus suggesting 'post-coital fulfilment rather than imminent rape' (p. 44). In print sources he adduces Sir John Suckling's 1646 rewriting of some verses in the six-line stanzas of *Venus and Adonis* instead of the original rhyme royal, and W. B.'s quotation of a few lines about Tarquin in *The Philosopher's Banquet* (1633) under the rubric 'Of Princes' (pp. 44, 51–2). Peter Holland's brilliant edition of *Coriolanus* expands this reading of readings into a central hermeneutic principle, showing how the play 'fires writers and crowds, politicians and theatre workers to explore its possibilities'[108] across a wide range of cultural expressions: Poel's 1931

---

[101] Pramit Chaudhuri, 'Classical Quotation in Titus Andronicus', *ELH*, 81 (2014), 787–810.

[102] Burrow, ed., *Complete Sonnets and Poems* (Oxford, 2002) p. 42.

[103] Katherine Duncan-Jones, 'Ravished and Revised: The 1616 Lucrece', *Review of English Studies*, 52 (2001), 516–23.

[104] Burrow, ed., *Complete Sonnets and Poems*, p. 44.

[105] Sasha Roberts, 'The Malleable Poetic Text: Narrative, Authorship, and the Transmission of Lucrece', in *Reading Shakespeare's Poems in Early Modern England* (Basingstoke, 2003), pp. 102–42.

[106] Sonia Massai, *Shakespeare and the Rise of the Editor* (Cambridge, 2007), pp. 180–9.

[107] Nadia Bishai, '"At the signe of the gunne": Titus Andronicus, the London Book Trade, and the Literature of Crime, 1590–1615', in *Titus out of Joint: Reading the Fragmented 'Titus Andronicus'*, ed. Liberty Stanavage and Paxton Hehmeyer (Newcastle upon Tyne, 2012), pp. 7–48.

[108] Peter Holland, ed., *Coriolanus* (London, 2013), p. 8.

production examining militarism, T. S. Eliot's fragmentary encounters, Delmore Schwartz's epic, the politically explosive revival of the Comédie-Française, the later adaptations of Brecht, Grass and Osborne, up through the most recent productions and films. Holland fluently includes performances as critical responses and as readings arising from their individual cultural moments. He extends his purview backwards in time as well, to the early modern translations of Livy, Vergil, Plutarch and to Dionysius of Halicarnassus, noting linguistic losses and additions in Amyot and North, transpositions, and transformations. And he also looks around to the wide context of contemporary reference, including three marginal drawings probably by Nicholas Udall in a 1549 edition of Livy, notices in a William Herbert poem (1604), in John Bodenham's poetic anthology *Bel-vedere* (1600), and in various political works to various purposes.[109]

Holland acknowledges the utility of searchable databases in this survey but warns about their potential to mislead. That said, the databases and digital resources now available certainly have the potential to transform future studies of Shakespeare's Rome. Most Shakespeare scholars know British Literary Manuscripts Online, Early English Books Online (and the Text Creation Partnership), The Union First-Line Index of English Verse, Literary Manuscripts Online, Scriptorium, the Folger and British Library databases and links, and many digital bibliographies, editions and reference materials. But they will also find treasures in classical databases (L'Année Philologique, Thesaurus Linguae Graecae, Thesaurus Linguae Latinae, The Perseus Project, The Loeb Classical Library's Digital Edition); many universities, including Cambridge, offer a full list of online classical resources that provide access to texts, vases, images, papyri, dictionaries, commentaries and early Christian writers. There is also Gallica, the digital library of the Bibliothèque Nationale de France, and the astonishing collection of the Bavarian State Library, MDZ (Münchener DigitalisierungsZentrum Digitale Bibliothek).

At a few keystrokes one can trace lexical patterns in classical and early modern texts, search images and translations, read *editiones principes*, rare early modern translations, including Latin ones, commentaries on ancient texts by Camerarius, Melanchthon, Winshemius and Stiblinus, medieval and early modern European poetry, drama and prose. Shakespeare's Rome can now appear in wider and deeper literary and cultural contexts, as part of the larger humanist project of classical exchange that begins with Petrarch and includes French Senecan playwrights, La Pléiade (especially du Bellay's *Les Antiquités de Rome*), Renaissance epics, Italian genre experiments, the Spanish Siglo de Oro, Protestant German adaptations, visual art, sculpture and architecture.

Think you there was or might be such a Rome as this? The critical and theatrical histories indicate no end to the possibilities, no limit to the ethereal rumours that can revive for a moment a broken Coriolanus. Recent scholarship reveals a Rome entirely unimagined by previous generations, as do recent productions on stage and screen. Julie Taymor's gripping *Titus Andronicus* (1999) featured in the publicity shots and opening scenes Romans in blue war paint, thus mimicking their historical enemies as Caesar famously described them ('Omnes vero se Britanni vitro inficiunt, quod caeruleum efficit colorem, atque hoc horridiores sunt in pugna aspectu' (*De Bello Gallico*, 5.14.2), 'The Britons in truth dye themselves with woad, which makes a blue colour, and thereby have a more terrifying appearance in battle'). Lucrece has moved from page to stage: Jane Lapotaire dissolved 'the neat stanzas of the poem ... into a twenty-minute aria of pain' in Gregory Doran's reading at the Swan;[110] Callie Kimball's dramatization (2007), replete with additional female characters – Augusta and Maia (her maids), Sabina (representing the raped Sabine women), and

---

[109] Holland, ed. *Coriolanus*, pp. 102–4.

[110] George Simmers, 'The Rape of Lucrece: Staging the Unstageable', *OhmyNews International Podcasts* (2006), http://english.ohmynews.com/articleview/article_view .asp?menu=c10400&no=316563&rel_no=1

Sylvia (Rhea Sylvia, raped and murdered mother of Romulus and Remus) – gave voice to Lucrece's anguish while depicting her in context of larger cultural histories.[111] Paolo and Vittorio Taviani's prize-winning *Cesare Deve Morire* (2012) films prisoners in Rebibbia rehearsing and performing *Julius Caesar*, in the close and tense confines of the jail the inmates play their parts with riveting menace, machismo and barely controlled violence but also with surprising humour and emotion, as the translated poetry resounds in guttural and lyrical Italian dialects, shouted, spoken, whispered. The film testifies finally to the humanity of the prisoners and the liberating power of theatre. At the Globe also in 2012 Italian audiences and reviewers applauded Baracco's Italian *Giulio Cesare* as 'a sort of guiding light showing them the way out of the dark ages of Berlusconismo'.[112] Recently (and inanely), Michael Almereyda (2014) refashioned the national struggle of *Cymbeline* into an American urban war between the 'Briton' motorcycle gang and the corrupt police of a city called 'Rome', whose leader is a black Officer Lucius. In the spring of 2016, Rosy Colombo, general editor of the journal *Memoria di Shakespeare*, and others held an international Shakespeare conference in Rome titled 'Memoria di Roma'. Nothing is past the size of dreaming. A place of the imagination, Shakespeare's Rome 'will on / The way it takes, cracking ten thousand curbs / Of more strong link asunder than can ever / Appear in your impediment' (*Coriolanus*, 1.1.67–70).

---

[111] Krystyna Kujawinska Courtney, 'Callie Kimball's The Rape of Lucrece (2007): A Woman's Creative Response to Shakespeare's Poem', *Borrowers and Lenders: The Journal of Shakespeare and Appropriation*, 7 (2012/13), www.borrowers.uga.edu/380/show

[112] Sonia Massai, 'Art of Darkness: Staging *Giulio Cesare* at the Globe Theatre', in *Shakespeare Beyond English: A Global Experiment*, ed. Susan Bennett and Christie Carson (Cambridge, 2013), pp. 92–100; pp. 98–9.

PUNS AND PROSE: REFLECTIONS ON SHAKESPEARE'S USAGE

MICHAEL SILK

'Puns and prose' and 'Shakespeare's usage': under this heading, I shall be offering reflections on two aspects of Elizabethan/Jacobean literary usage in general, of non-comic ('serious') Shakespearian usage in particular,[1] and, representatively, of the usage in that most familiar of Shakespeare's serious verse dramas, and dramatic hybrids, *Hamlet*. I shall be doing this from a comparative perspective:[2] a perspective that helps to bring to prominence the distinctive, and not merely the discussible. Points of reference will range from Sanskrit drama to the history of the English language, from postmodern theory to the insights of Coleridge and Jean Paul, and from Renaissance Italy and Reformation Germany to ancient Greece and, especially, Rome – though it will soon become apparent that, contrary to received opinion, not all roads actually lead to Rome.

Among much that arrests the reader or hearer of the serious verse drama of the Elizabethan/Jacobean age[3] are pervasive punning and the extensive use of prose. Both have been widely discussed, but discussions focus largely on local efficacy: what is the rationale or effect of *these* switches from verse to prose, or *those* bits of wordplay? What interests me in the first instance are the two phenomena and their larger, literary-historical and comparative-literary, significance – though, inevitably and properly, rationales and effects will figure in my discussion too.

In England, punning, and wordplay in general,[4] is famously characteristic of Shakespeare and his age, across the genres, in contrast to the age or ages preceding: the later Middle Ages and the early sixteenth century.[5] Shakespeare is only one of many to practise punning in his age, but punning

is profusely and particularly exploited by Shakespeare, from the sonnets to the tragedies, and very notably in *Hamlet*, where (as Molly Mahood put it) we have more 'quibbles' than in any other Shakespearian tragedy, many of them from the lips of Hamlet himself.[6] Our hero's first words (as everyone points out) are punning: 'A little more than kin and less than kind' (words

My thanks to audiences at the London Shakespeare Seminar and the University of Exeter for helpful comments on oral versions of this chapter, and especially to Margreta de Grazia, for subsequent comments and advice.

[1] 'Serious' by conventional or classicizing norms (subsuming, in this case, the histories and the tragedies), irrespective of the fact that comedy can be serious, in a serious sense of the word: M. S. Silk, *Aristophanes and the Definition of Comedy* (Oxford, 2000), pp. 301–49.

[2] With particular points of reference in poetics and in the classical tradition (broadly understood, as in Michael Silk, Ingo Gildenhard and Rosemary Barrow, *The Classical Tradition: Art, Literature, Thought* (Chichester, 2014)).

[3] Hereinafter, sometimes referred to as 'Elizabethan', for the sake of brevity.

[4] Wordplay is wider than punning, of course. I am broadly concerned with wordplay in general, but with punning in particular; and when I appeal to 'wordplay' in what follows, this will often be no more than *variatio* for punning, as the context should make clear.

[5] 'Punning is as rarely found in [English] medieval drama as in the poems and prose works of late Middle English writers like Chaucer and Gower': N. F. Blake, *The Language of Shakespeare* (Basingstoke, 1989), p. 19. The claim is overstated (cf. e.g. R. A. Shoaf, 'The Play of Puns in Late Middle English Poetry', *On Puns: The Foundation of Letters*, ed. Jonathan Culler (Oxford, 1988), pp. 44–61), but the right way round.

[6] M. M. Mahood, *Shakespeare's Wordplay* (London, 1957), p. 112.

addressed to, or at, the king, 1.2.65). His last words (as not everyone seems to acknowledge) are punning, too: 'The rest is silence' (5.2.310), with 'rest' as remainder ('All the rest is mute'),[7] but with activated connotations of 'rest' as repose (the 'everlasting rest' of death, the 'rest' that 'flights of angels sing thee to'),[8] while an additional reference is suggested to Hamlet's own words a few lines earlier: 'this fell sergeant Death / Is strict in his *arrest*'.[9] Death is indeed, for Hamlet, not only an end to speech, but a subjection, on one or other level, to the law; and his active presence in the play is – literally – defined by puns.

Commenting on Shakespeare's puns, half a century ago, Mahood suggested:

To Elizabethan ways of thinking, there was plenty of authority for [punning]. It was to be found in Scripture (*Tu es Petrus* . . .) and in the whole line of rhetoricians, from Aristotle and Quintilian, through the neo-classical textbooks that Shakespeare read perforce at school, to the English writers such as Puttenham whom he read later for his own advantage as a poet.[10]

Scripture, I shall come back to – but this talk of authority from 'rhetoricians' and 'textbooks', and 'Puttenham' too, I find puzzling. Mahood's remarks are prefigured, or followed, by a bevy of scholars from Sister Miriam Joseph to, more recently, Jane Donawerth and, most recently, Sophie Read,[11] who is more nuanced with regard to the rhetoricians and the textbooks, but still seems to assume a significant relationship. I am puzzled, not because I doubt the large impact of formal rhetoric on the literature of this period, but because of what we find when we look, specifically, at how those classical or classical-derived authorities actually respond to puns.

In the handbooks of Shakespeare's time, we find, in the first place, a set of four pun-related 'figures': paronomasia, antanaclasis, syllepsis, asteismus. In Elizabethan usage these often problematic labels can generally be said to refer respectively to wordplay based on the addition, change, or loss of a 'letter'; to repetition of a word in different senses; to a kind of zeugma; and to a witty riposte that may (but need not) involve 'a word having two significations'.[12] In these terms, Hamlet's opening

'kin'/'kind' wordplay is an example of paronomasia, whereas his closing 'rest', involving a mode of secondary connotation play acknowledged by sensitive readers of poetry from the late-nineteenth century onwards,[13] fails to correspond to any of the four types: contemporary theory (as often) is not coextensive with creative practice.[14] Then again, the handbooks frequently assume (and their labels are frequently illustrated by) tame examples.[15] 'Blame not other men . . . nor mislike

---

[7] *All's Well*, 2.3.78. 'Last words': not counting 'O, O, O, O!'

[8] *Romeo*, 5.3.110; *Hamlet*, 5.2.313.

[9] *Hamlet*, 5.2.288–9 (my italics).

[10] Mahood, *Wordplay*, p. 9.

[11] Miriam Joseph, *Shakespeare's Use of the Arts of Language* (New York, 1947), e.g. p. 165; Jane Donawerth, *Shakespeare and the Sixteenth-Century Study of Language* (Urbana, IL, 1984), e.g. p. 118; Sophie Read, 'Puns: Serious Wordplay', in *Renaissance Figures of Speech*, ed. Sylvia Adamson, Gavin Alexander and Katrin Ettenhuber (Cambridge, 2007), pp. 80–94.

[12] Paronomasia and antanaclasis: see e.g. Henry Peacham, *The Garden of Eloquence* (rev. edn, 1593), p. 56. Syllepsis: e.g. Angel Day, *The English Secretory* (1592), p. 87 (here and elsewhere, I cite premodern orthography in modernized form, where possible). Asteismus: Peacham, *Garden*, pp. 33–4. Asteismus is clearly marginal to punning, and, though put on a par with the other types by (e.g.) Joseph, *Arts of Language*, p. 165, is understandably ignored by (e.g.) Read, 'Puns', p. 80; in antiquity, in any case, it is a subspecies of *irony* (see Heinrich Lausberg, *Handbuch der literarischen Rhetorik*, vol. 1 (Munich, 1960), p. 303). Meanwhile, Renaissance readings of these figures are themselves inconsistent. For instance, John Hoskins, *Directions for Speech and Style* (1599?), ed. H. H. Hudson (Princeton, NJ, 1935), thinks that paronomasia can subsume alliteration ('a pleasant touch of the same letter . . . with a different meaning', p. 15) and antanaclasis simple repetition (p. 44).

[13] Cf. e.g. Nietzsche on Horace's *Odes* in 1888: 'This mosaic of words, in which every word, as sound, as *locus*, as concept, pours out its powers left and right and over the whole' (*Twilight of the Idols* [*Götzendämmerung*], 'What I Owe to the Ancients', section 1). Earlier anticipations of the principle include Walter Whiter's observations on semantic overlap in *A Specimen of a Commentary on Shakespeare* (1794).

[14] Cf. Margreta de Grazia, 'Homonyms Before and After Lexical Standardization', *Deutsche Shakespeare-Gesellschaft West, Jahrbuch*, 127 (1990), 143–56; p. 154.

[15] Recent scholarship, conversely, likes to attach Renaissance labels to more striking examples: so e.g. Read, 'Puns', pp. 82–3, 261, on syllepsis.

at all their want of *pity*, that have no mean to *pity* yourself': Angel Day, exemplifying antanaclasis in 1592.[16] Such instances, frankly, have little relevance to the range and inventiveness of Elizabethan wordplay, Shakespearian or other.

But in case we are still in any danger of supposing that the handbooks somehow do provide significant authorization for Elizabethan practice, we need to acknowledge the fact that, apart from a general commendation of 'figures' among the arts of language,[17] what we find there is a common restriction of punning – under whatever label – to comedy and other non-serious usage. So Peacham, in 1593, says paronomasia should be 'sparingly used, and especially in grave and weighty causes',[18] while Puttenham, in 1589, associates its use with 'the comical poet and the epigrammatist',[19] and Scaliger, in 1581, is explicit that any such figures do not belong 'in serious poetry', but only in 'epigrams, satire and comedy'.[20] And in the ancient sources for these treatises, we find the same. Representatively, the *Ad Herennium* indicates that figures like paronomasia ('adnominatio', in Latin) are 'more suitable for entertainment' ('delectatio') than for serious discourse,[21] while Quintilian actually declares that uses of 'antanaclasis' tend to be 'insipid, *even* in jokes' ('*etiam* in iocis frigidum').[22] And when Puttenham, in 1589, translates 'asteismus' as 'the merry scoff', the restriction to (and tone of) comic usage is symptomatically built into the label.[23] Renaissance theorists do sometimes praise conceits – clever combinations or elaborations of thought, especially in images – and conceits may involve wordplay, but the official line is in any case to associate conceits themselves with light usage. So William Scott, in 1599, associates 'pleasant and well-disposed conceits' with the epigram, and commends 'witty conceits' as 'merry, graceful and savoury jests',[24] a proposition anticipated by Aristotle's *Rhetoric* (on which more later).[25] Meanwhile, philosophically minded students of language tend to deplore any kind of verbal slipperiness – from Aristotle in logician's mode ('avoid equivocations') to Francis Bacon in 1605 (cautioning, sternly, against 'the great sophism of all sophisms')[26] – while some wordplay is condemned

outright by the figure-brokers, even, notably 'cacemphaton' (coarse innuendo, as in Hamlet's 'country matters'), which Puttenham, for instance, includes among the 'vices or deformities in speech and writing'.[27]

In fact, the nearest thing to theoretical enthusiasm for serious-poetic wordplay in the whole premodern era is in seventeenth-century Spain: Gracián's treatise on the conceit (1642/9), which enthuses over paronomasia as one of the mechanisms of wit, though in satire and the epigram more than serious poetry.[28] In the sixteenth century, one might also point to a discussion in Castiglione's *Courtier* (1528), where one of the characters in the dialogue approves a good-natured use of witty

---

[16] Day, *Secretory*, p. 57 (my italics).

[17] It is 'an imperfection in man's utterance to have none use of figure at all': George Puttenham, *The Art of English Poesy* (1589), 3.2.

[18] Peacham, *Garden*, p. 56.

[19] Puttenham, *Poesy*, 3.19 (with 'prosonomasia', mistakenly, for 'par-').

[20] Julius Caesar Scaliger, *Poetices libri septem*, 4.33: 'conveniunt epigrammati, satyro et comoediae' (on 'Allusio, Inversio, Paronomasia').

[21] *Rhetorica Ad Herennium*, 4.32.

[22] Quintilian, *Institutio Oratoria*, 9.3.69 (my italics). Cf. Cicero and Castiglione, n. 29 below.

[23] Puttenham, *Poesy*, 3.18. Read ('Puns', p. 84) and others misrepresent this association of punning and laughter as a marginal, or else later, development. Outside etymological play (pp. 24–5 below), the association is fairly constant from antiquity to the end of the eighteenth century.

[24] William Scott, *The Model of Poesy*, ed. Gavin Alexander (Cambridge, 2013), pp. 29, 40.

[25] Below, pp. 22–3 .

[26] Aristotle, *Rhetoric*, 3.5.4 (*mē amphibolois legein*); Bacon, *The Advancement of Learning*, 2.14.7.

[27] *Hamlet*, 3.2.111; Puttenham, *Poesy*, 3.21–2 (albeit for him 'cacemphaton' is not the most 'intolerable' of 'vices'). Cf., in antiquity, Quintilian, *Institutio*, 8.3.44–7.

[28] But without subservience to rhetoric: 'Gracián's originality consists precisely in the fact that he . . . declares the system of antique rhetoric to be insufficient': Ernst Robert Curtius, *European Literature and the Latin Middle Ages*, trans. W. R. Trask (London, 1953), p. 297. Baltasar Gracián, *Agudeza y Arte de Ingenio* (title of the 1649 revised edition of the work first published in 1642 as *Arte de Ingenio, tratado de la Agudeza*), *Discreto* 32.

wordplay in courtly discourse, echoing a comparable discussion in Cicero – but neither in Castiglione nor in his Ciceronian source is there unqualified commendation for such wordplay, nor any sense, again, that it properly belongs in serious poetic contexts.[29]

The assumption that Renaissance rhetoric necessarily underpins Elizabethan practice in any case seems surprising, given that in some particulars that practice (and not least Shakespeare's) is strikingly independent of rhetorical principles. Take obscurity – condemned by every rhetorician, old or new (as also by Sidney and Ben Jonson, among others)[30] – but not exactly unexampled in poetic practice, especially (though not only) in later Shakespeare.[31]

But a more interesting case (and the one that concerns me) is another familiar phenomenon across the Elizabethan/Jacobean dramatic spectrum – the use of prose in verse drama, including (what most concerns me) serious verse drama, and not least *Hamlet*, where large parts of the play are in prose, much of it spoken by Hamlet himself:

HAMLET. . . . what make you at Elsinore?
ROSENCRANTZ.   To visit you, my lord, no other occasion.
HAMLET. . . . Were you not sent for? Is it your own inclining? . . .
GUILDENSTERN. My lord, we were sent for.
HAMLET. I will tell you why . . . I have of late – but wherefore I know not – lost all my mirth, forgone all custom of exercise; and indeed it goes so heavily with my disposition that this goodly frame, the earth, seems to me a sterile promontory. This most excellent canopy the air, look you, this brave o'erhanging, this majestical roof fretted with golden fire – why, it appears no other thing to me than a foul and pestilent congregation of vapours. What a piece of work is a man! How noble in reason, how infinite in faculty . . . And yet to me what is this quintessence of dust?   (2.2.272–310)

If, like punning, prose has a pervasive presence in the serious verse drama of the Elizabethan/Jacobean age, it is even more obvious than is the case with punning that this presence has no authority from the rhetorical tradition. This is not because Renaissance

or ancient rhetoricians avoid confronting the issue of specific usage in different genres, though Renaissance rhetoricians certainly do so less than the likes of Quintilian in antiquity. It is simply because there are no relevant precedents for prose in serious drama before English drama in this age, not anywhere.

In classical antiquity, all consequential drama was in verse:[32] in some of Aristophanes' comedies (all in verse) we find a few lines of prose (for ceremonial formulae or the like);[33] in ancient tragedy, Greek or Roman, there is no parallel at all.

29 *Il libro del cortegiano*, 2.57–61, based on Cicero, *De Oratore*, 2.248–54, where Cicero's speaker discusses the verbal sources of 'laughter' ('risus'), especially those involving wit ('facetiae'). Wit (we learn) may involve 'equivocations' ('ex ambiguo dicta', 2.250), but the outcome, though certainly 'clever' ('acuta'), tends to 'startle rather than amuse' ('admirationem magis quam risum movet', 2.254). Instances of such wordplay do make the speaker sound 'educated' ('ut belle et litterate dicta laudantur', 2.253) – but this, in context, is less than a ringing endorsement. Though offering up-to-date examples (of aristocratic banter), Castiglione follows Cicero closely, Italianizing two key phrases: 'laudate per ingeniose che per ridicule' and 'più presto movano maraviglia che riso' (2.58). Both writers, of course, assume the association of puns with the comic, which witty 'equivocations', paradoxically, are liable to contravene. These qualifications and alignments are glossed over by Donawerth, *Language*, p. 122, in a discussion of the Castiglione passage.
30 Representative swipes at obscurity: Quintilian, *Institutio*, 8.3.82; Horace, *Ars Poetica*, 26; Puttenham, *Poesy*, 3.21 ('extreme darkness'); Sir Philip Sidney, *An Apology for Poetry* (c. 1580), ed. G. Shepherd, rev. R. W. Maslen (Manchester, 2002), p. 95 ('obscure definitions'); Ben Jonson, *The Poetaster* (1601), 5.3.569 ('dark and dangerous'); Roger Ascham, *The Schoolmaster* (1570), 2.5 ('the sense is hard and dark . . . which fault. . .') (in G. Gregory Smith, ed., *Elizabethan Critical Essays*, vol. 1 (Oxford, 1904), p. 42).
31 Cf. e.g. Frank Kermode, *Shakespeare's Language* (London, 2000), pp. 4–16. With classical precedent in mind, one might compare the flagrant obscurity of the parodos of Aeschylus' *Agamemnon*, along with the negative comments on Aeschylean style by 'Euripides' in Aristophanes' *Frogs*, 924–30.
32 The Sicilian Sophron's long-lost prose mimes (fifth century BC) are hardly, for present purposes, consequential.
33 Along with a couple of instances in 'Old Comedy' elsewhere: full listing in Aristophanes, *Thesmophoriazusae*, ed. Colin Austin and S. Douglas Olson (Oxford, 2004), pp. 150–1 (on *Thesmo.* 295–311).

In some medieval French and English mystery or miracle plays of the fourteenth and fifteenth centuries, there are possible, or apparent, incidental occurrences of prose[34] – but identification of prose in such cases is often complicated by the vagaries of later copyists and by the elusiveness of verse norms (notorious in late medieval and very early modern England) – while in Henry Medwall's morality play *Nature* (written *c.* 1490?), we find one short passage in prose, ostensibly prefiguring Elizabethan usage.[35] In Italian drama, conversely, no parallels are apparent. Indeed, in world literature, before the Elizabethan age, there seems to be only the single, obviously unrelated, precedent of Sanskrit drama of the mid first millennium AD.[36]

Meanwhile, though, in other genres, compositions mixing verse and prose are attested across the ages.[37] In Western traditions, mixed forms are familiar, albeit never exactly a norm. In antiquity, we have the so-called Menippean satire, whose diverse manifestations, from Varro to Petronius to Martianus Capella, are not only not fully 'serious', in the conventional sense, but occupy a section of the generic spectrum remote from drama of any kind.[38] Satire apart, mixed forms make an intermittent appearance in Western literatures, from Boethius's *Consolation*, in late antiquity, to Lewis Carroll's *Alice*, via Dante's *Vita Nuova* and Sannazzaro's pastoral *Arcadia* of 1485. Looking back explicitly to Boethius and Sannazzaro, Sidney, in his *Apology*, duly alludes to such 'mingled prose and verse',[39] which he himself uses in the *Old Arcadia*, while, at the end of the Elizabethan age, William Scott alludes, in turn, to Sidney's usage, and then to the now established use of prose in English verse comedy – though (perhaps revealingly) he makes no acknowledgement of its use in the serious drama of his time.[40]

At all events, in serious, 'high' drama before Elizabethan England, there is effectively no such use. In Renaissance Italy, all such drama is, on the classical model, entirely in verse, though in the sixteenth century prose comedy becomes a new norm, as in Machiavelli's *Mandragola* (1518) and Ariosto's *I Suppositi* (1509), which George Gascoigne translates, as *The Supposes*, in 1566: the

earliest English prose play. But in serious drama, we find no prose – and no mixture. The use of prose in verse drama is effectively the invention of Elizabethan England, first in comedy (where practice is established by at least the early 1580s), and then, remarkably, in serious drama, like *Hamlet*.

If one consults Vickers or, before Vickers, Crane,[41] one finds a lucid account of the conventions established by the playwrights for the use of prose in serious drama: for low or prosaic speakers (like Rosencrantz and Guildenstern in *Hamlet*); for letters and proclamations (like Hamlet's letter to Horatio: 4.6.12–30); for comic matter (like the banter of the gravedigger clowns in *Hamlet*, 5.1); and for madness, first attested in high drama in Kyd's *Spanish Tragedy* (1589?).[42] In *Hamlet*, the hero's 'antic' mode (1.5.173) famously finds expression in prose – though not much of his prose is visibly 'antic' (disturbed, distorted, deranged), nor is his non-antic prose always comic or prosaic or low: 'What a piece of work is a man! How noble in reason, how infinite in faculty . . . And yet to me what is this quintessence

---

[34] Summary in Traudi Eichhorn, 'Prosa und Vers im vorshakespeareschen Drama', *Shakespeare-Jahrbuch*, 84–6 (1948–50), 140–98; pp.141–8.

[35] *Nature*, 1.836–41, a 'whispered "aside"', often cited as 'the earliest known prose in English drama': A. H. Nelson, *The Plays of Henry Medwall* (Woodbridge, 1980), p. 204. The status of such an isolated instance, however, surely remains unclear, as does the possibility of any significant connection between this passage (or any apparent earlier passages) and Elizabethan usage.

[36] Summary overview: H. W. Wells, *The Classical Drama of India* (London, 1963), pp. 115–30.

[37] See J. Harris and K. Reichl, eds., *Prosimetrum: Crosscultural Perspectives on Narrative in Prose and Verse* (Cambridge, 1997).

[38] Overview: Joel C. Relihan, *Ancient Menippean Satire* (Baltimore, MD, 1993).

[39] Sidney, *Apology*, p. 97.   [40] Scott, *Poesy*, pp. 19, 78–9.

[41] Brian Vickers, *The Artistry of Shakespeare's Prose* (London, 1968), pp. 5–6 (and cf. 17–18, 331); Milton Crane, *Shakespeare's Prose* (Chicago, 1951), pp. 2–3, 30.

[42] In all drama, the earliest attested use of prose to indicate 'insanity or temporary distraction' is in *The Rare Triumphs of Love and Fortune* (1582?): J. F. Macdonald, 'The Use of Prose in English Drama before Shakespeare', *University of Toronto Quarterly*, 2 (1933), 465–81; p. 470.

of dust?' But the elaborate set of conventions is a reality – clearly marked in earlier Shakespeare, as in other dramatists, and still a factor in *Hamlet* – and astonishingly it is established in Elizabethan England within a few years of audacious experiment. The apparent stages of this development were set out by Macdonald in 1933.[43] The first attested use of prose in verse tragedy, or other serious drama, is seemingly in Marlowe's *Tamburlaine* (1587?), and within a dozen or so years, by the time of *Hamlet* (1600?), the usage is pervasive, a once comic practice has been established across the board, and all the conventions are there. Such a rapid development of artistic norms has few parallels in Western art. One thinks perhaps of certain phases of cinema, or of jazz, in the twentieth century. The rapid development is remarkable in any event.

And no less remarkable: just as this development with prose is seemingly a purely English phenomenon, so too (though matters here are certainly less cut and dried) is the *scale* and the *proliferation* of wordplay in the Elizabethan/Jacobean age, across the genres (*tout court*), and in serious drama not least. I find no close parallel anywhere, and, in particular, no close parallel in any of the serious verse traditions in the creative heartland of classicizing Europe: in Renaissance Italy or France. In fourteenth-century Italy, there is prominent wordplay in Petrarch,[44] as there is in sixteenth-century France, in Maurice Scève's Petrarchan *Délie* (1544) and the Pléiade poetry of Joachim Du Bellay, but hardly on the Elizabethan scale, and during these centuries there is nothing in French or Italian literature to match the proliferation in England. In fifteenth-century French farces and so-called Fools' Plays ('soties'), and pre-eminently in Rabelais, in the second quarter of the sixteenth century, wordplay abounds – but all this is comic usage, as is, in Germany, Fischart's Lutheran-Rabelaisian *Geschichtklitterung* ('Hotchpotch History', 1582). Luther himself, along with others of his era, has his quota of polemical wordplay in his theological writings,[45] though no such exuberance extends to his hymns. In medieval Latin and the neo-Latin of the Renaissance, wordplay characterizes a range of texts, from the tenth-century heroic poem *Waltharius* to the *Cenodoxus*, a miracle play by the Jesuit Jakob Bidermann (1602), but here as elsewhere we find nothing like the Elizabethan proliferation, across the genres and in virtually every form of serious discourse. Only in Elizabethan England do we seem to find this (and, inter alia, the supposed authorizing of wordplay by the rhetoricians evidently made little impression on classicizing circles on the Continent).

It which point, one might again ponder the phenomenon of the conceit. A fashion for conceits becomes a pan-European phenomenon in the earlier part of the seventeenth century: metaphysical conceits in England, Italian *concettismo*, *préciosité* in France – and *conceptismo* in Spain, associated especially with satire and the satirical essay, as in Gracián's *Agudeza*. But, irrespective of the fact that these movements, broadly, reach their peak after the Jacobean age, and that Gracián, in particular, is not primarily focused on high-serious usage, we should bear in mind, once again, that the conceit is not in itself, or not necessarily, a matter of wordplay at all. In the French tradition, for instance, *préciosité* subsumes the use of so-called 'pointes' (in effect, often, punning conceits), but also much else besides.[46] And the same is true of the ancient equivalent, or near equivalent, of the conceit, Aristotle's 'witticisms' (*ta*

---

[43] Macdonald, 'Prose'. More recent commentators fail to spell out the facts.

[44] Cf. p. 25 below.

[45] Representative example: Luther's 1511 publication of what he called *Die Lügend von S. Johanne Chrysostomo* (in effect, 'the Lie-gend of St John Chrysostom') – 'wordplay . . . typical of the rhetoric of the polemical writings of the Reformation period' (M. E. Kalinke, *The Book of Reykjahólar* (Toronto, 1996), p. 3). Exemplifying the common disjunction between theory and practice, Luther himself purports to espouse a doctrine of 'one word, one meaning' and 'dissociation of language from . . . figures': Richard Waswo, *Language and Meaning in the Renaissance* (Princeton, NJ, 1987), pp. 245, 248.

[46] Cf. Florence Vuilleumier, 'Les Conceptismes', in *Histoire de la rhétorique dans l'Europe moderne, 1450–1950*, ed. Marc Fumaroli (Paris, 1999), pp. 517–37; and, summarily, Curtius, *European Literature*, pp. 292–4.

asteia) in *Rhetoric*, 3.11. Aristotle's interesting, if untidy, discussion is mostly about metaphor and simile (prefiguring one main tendency of seventeenth-century conceits).[47] He does also refer to, and exemplify, wordplay, under the heading of 'homonymy' (*homōnumia*) and 'changes of a letter' (*ta para gramma*), but much more briefly and (as he makes explicit) largely 'in jokes' (*en tois geloiois*).[48]

The distinctiveness of the situation is apparent. Puns and prose break through the barriers – in England: a remarkable pair of developments, or experiments, in one country, one culture, without much reference to classical or classicizing theory, or to current or recent practice in other prestige European traditions.

In England, the prose experiment is short-lived. In the drama of the later seventeenth century, a classicizing decorum is restored. The verse tragedies that the likes of Dryden compose are more orderly and, when Shakespeare is adapted (as he repeatedly is, by Dryden and others), the prose is liable to be attenuated, especially in the mouths of heroic characters. The same period, of course, likewise takes sharp exception to punning. There are copious criticisms of wordplay, often with explicit reference to the earlier period. 'Shakespeare played with words to please a quibbling age': so writes Robert Gould in 1685. In 1709 Nicholas Rowe echoes the verdict: 'As for his jingling sometimes, and playing upon words, it was the common vice of the age he lived in.' In 1672, Dryden had been more specific, levelling the criticism at Jonson ('not free from the lowest and most grovelling kind of wit, which we call clenches') and Sidney ('perpetually playing with his words'), after already denouncing Shakespeare himself ('his comic wit degenerating into clenches') in 1668.[49]

By the early eighteenth century, it is a critical topos that punning characterized the whole Elizabethan/Jacobean age, from Shakespearian verse to (even) solemn prose. After castigating Shakespeare's 'vice', Rowe adds: 'we find it in the pulpit, made use of as an ornament to the sermons of some of the greatest divines of those times'. Addison, in 1711, is more explicit: 'The age in which the pun chiefly flourished was the reign of

King James the First ... The greatest authors in their most serious works made frequent use of puns. The sermons of Bishop Andrewes and the tragedies of Shakespeare are full of them.'[50] By way of qualification to Addison's periodizing (and my own, too), one should acknowledge that punning does not come to a sudden halt after the death of James I in 1625. Wordplay is still on display in the Caroline age, as it still is (more or less) in Milton.[51] But the Elizabethan/Jacobean age is unquestionably the peak; and it is hardly a coincidence that the word 'pun' only surfaces after the Jacobean period, and is, from the first, pejorative. The word is first attested, as Read points out, in a royalist pamphlet by John Taylor in 1643, in a list of 'frivolous forms' of language.[52] 'Pun' (along with synonyms like the now obsolete 'clench', or 'clinch') was pejorative, and it remained pejorative until Coleridge's 'defence of Shakespeare's puns and plays on

---

47 'Most witticisms are derived from metaphor or surprise': Aristotle, *Rhetoric*, 3.11.6.

48 Aristotle, *Rhetoric*, 3.11.8 and 3.11.6.

49 Robert Gould, 'The Play-House', in the version of the poem printed in Gould's *Works*, vol. 2 (1709), p. 245; Nicholas Rowe, 'Some Account of the Life etc. of Mr. William Shakespeare', prefixed to his 1709 Shakespeare edition; John Dryden, 'Defence of the Epilogue' (*sc.* to the second part of *The Conquest of Granada*), in John Dryden, *Of Dramatic Poesy and Other Critical Essays,* vol. 1, ed. George Watson (London, 1962), pp. 178–9; Dryden, *Of Dramatic Poesy*, in Watson, ed., *Essays*, vol. 1, p. 67.

50 In *The Spectator*, 61 (10 May 1711). The Shakespeare/Andrewes version of the topos is still influential: it helps to shape Sophie Read's argument (Read, 'Puns') in 2007.

51 In his polemical prose, but also some of his elevated verse: see e.g. John Leonard, 'Self-Contradicting Puns in *Paradise Lost*', in *A Companion to Milton*, ed. Thomas Corns (Chichester, 2008), pp. 393–410. At least some of the punning in *Paradise Lost* is 'comic', however – notably at 6.609–27, where Satan and Belial 'in pleasant vein / Stood scoffing' (628–9), prompting Landor's *bon mot* (*Imaginary Conversations*, 'Southey and Landor': 1846): 'It appears then on record that the first overt crime of the refractory angels was punning: they fell rapidly after that.'

52 Read, 'Puns', pp. 82, 261; Taylor, *Mercurius Aquaticus*. The *OED* classes 'pun' with other pejorative 'clipped words' of that era, like 'mob'.

words', in the wake of the brilliant *aperçus* of the German theorist, Jean Paul, in 1804.[53]

As the seventeenth century leaves Jacobean vices behind, and especially from the Restoration onwards, there is (everyone agrees) a discernible change of attitudes to wordplay. But this change is widely represented as a shift from official approval (as supposedly in the rhetoricians) to official disapproval. It is, rather, a shift from less than enthusiastic acknowledgement, or suspicion, to outright condemnation – and if we need more evidence of the suspicion, we find it in Shakespeare himself. Notwithstanding the pervasive use of wordplay throughout and across his drama, his characters are repeatedly made to respond to punning dismissively, which surely represents conventional attitudes and expectations. In *Richard II*, Gaunt plays on 'gaunt', and Richard responds: 'Can sick men play so nicely with their names?' (2.1.84). In *The Merchant of Venice*, Lancelot plays on 'Moor' and 'more', and Lorenzo comments: 'How every fool can play upon the word' (3.5.41). In *Cymbeline*, Guiderius warns his brother: 'And do not play in wench-like words with that / Which is so serious' (4.2.231–2). And even Hamlet, wordplayer supreme, responds in similar vein to the gravedigger: 'We must speak by the card, or equivocation will undo us' (*Hamlet*, 5.1.133–4). Elizabethan/Jacobean practice is one thing; conventional attitudes are seen to be another.

But if this conventional suspicion is the norm, there is indeed one significant exception, one arena in which wordplay and the challenges it presents are authorized and accepted. In the time-honoured practice of (so-called) etymology,[54] familiar to Shakespeare's age in, above all, the world of biblical exposition, a special version of wordplay has a special authority. As Mahood's example serves to remind us,[55] biblical etymology centres on proper names (though the range is certainly wider): '*Tu es Petrus* . . .', or in the King James Bible, and the original Greek, 'Thou art Peter [*Petros*], and upon this rock [*petra*] I will build my church' (Matthew 16: 18).

The etymological tradition is complex and extensive; many currents are involved, from philosophy to grammar – but (significantly) rhetoric hardly at all. In ancient rhetorical theory, etymology has a marginal presence under 'invention' ('inventio');[56] under style ('elocutio'), where puns and other figures belong, it is never discussed. Like rhetoric, though, etymology has a significant presence in the ancient world. There are notable, if isolated, examples in early and classical Greek literature, from Homer to tragedy to the apophthegms of the philosopher Heraclitus;[57] Euripides's play on 'Pentheus' as 'a name fit for *calamity* [sc. *penthos*]' is representative.[58] The long life of etymology as a theoretical category effectively begins with Plato's *Cratylus*, an influential text in the Renaissance, especially via Ficino's commentary.[59] In the first century BC, etymology was intensively discussed, and applied, by Varro (Roman grammarian and, coincidentally, prolific author of Menippean satire); and Varro's theorizations significantly impinge on Roman poets, especially Ovid,[60] but also, and above all, on the Christian traditions of theological and biblical exegesis, from Augustine all the way to Lancelot Andrewes.[61]

---

[53] Jean Paul, *Vorschule der Ästhetik*, 2.52 ('Das Wortspiel'). 'Defence . . . words' is one of the subheadings in Coleridge's notes on *Richard II*, for a lecture given in 1813: Coleridge, *Shakespearean Criticism*, vol. 1, ed. T. M. Raysor (London, 1960), p. 137.

[54] 'So-called', because etymology in modern usage refers to origins, diachronically, whereas the premodern concept concerns immanent meaning, in effect syn- (or pan-) chronically.

[55] Above, p. 18.

[56] As 'notatio': see esp. Cicero's *Topics* (essentially a treatise on 'invention': *Topics*, 2.6–8), 8.35–7.

[57] Summary in Robert Maltby, 'Etymology', in *The Oxford Classical Dictionary*, ed. S. Hornblower et al., 4th edn (Oxford, 2012), pp. 542–3.

[58] Euripides, *Bacchae*, 508 (my italics).

[59] Published in 1484, as *Argumentum in Cratylum vel de recta nominum ratione*.

[60] Varro, *De Lingua Latina*, esp. books 2–4. Ovid: see F. Ahl, *Metaformations: Soundplay and Wordplay in Ovid and Other Classical Poets* (Ithaca, NY, 1985).

[61] On the earlier period, see Mark Amsler, *Etymology and Grammatical Discourse in Late Antiquity and the Early Middle Ages* (Amsterdam, 1989), pp. 15–56.

In the Western Middle Ages, dominated by Christianity, etymology is formative. It is enshrined in the seventh-century text that did more than any other to transmit classical learning to the Latin West, Bishop Isidore's encyclopedia, called, precisely, *Etymologies* (*Etymologiae*), where Isidore declares: 'Once the etymology is known, scrutiny of each thing is more straightforward.'[62] For medieval, and then Renaissance, minds, etymology (in the words of Ernst Robert Curtius) is a substantive 'category of thought'.[63] And via Augustine, in particular, it becomes a preoccupation of Reformation biblical interpretation, as it is in Bishop Andrewes: the Andrewes that Addison and others bracket with Shakespeare (as fellow offender), the Andrewes whose 'sacramental' wordplay Sophie Read, plausibly, contrasts with Shakespeare's. Andrewes, for instance, lights and lingers on the phrase 'verbum infans', the incarnation of the divine *word* in the *baby* Jesus, where the word 'without speech' – *in-fans* – is itself an *in-fant*; and, as Read puts it, 'Andrewes accepts the pun as a mark of divine grace'.[64]

Read, plausibly, *contrasts* such usages with Shakespeare's – but might they be connected at source, through one or other etymological current? Without particular reference to Shakespeare, Hannah Crawforth's recent study probes some of the implications and applications of the etymology tradition in English poetry, and poets' thinking, from Spenser to Milton.[65] Neither she nor anyone seems to have suggested that in the Elizabethan/Jacobean age the *explosion* of wordplay as such is directly prompted by the etymology tradition – and, if nothing else, the special, and longstanding, connection of etymology with proper names[66] might seem to tell against any such definitive linkage. However, Screech has argued that Rabelais's wordplay is both stimulated and shaped by this tradition;[67] and of course cases like Gaunt's play on his name in *Richard II* might be said to reflect it directly, as might the well-known play on 'will' in the sonnets – and indeed the long line of poetic name-plays that reaches an earlier peak in Petrarch's obsessive wordplay with his 'Laura' in the *Canzoniere*.[68]

In Petrarch, Ovid is a huge presence, as he is, subsequently, in the Renaissance; and in the *Metamorphoses* – the most influential of all Ovidian texts for the Renaissance – Ovid offers significant etymological play himself, even using that mode in the very first line to enact the 'changed forms' that constitute his subject: the *Metamorphoses* is a poem about '*muta-tas ... formas*'.[69] Might Ovidian-Petrarchan precedent be a significant factor for Elizabethan/Jacobean practice? Possibly – but if so (or *even* if so), I come back to the question: why – as with prose in verse drama – specifically in England?

Offering external historical explanations for stylistic developments like these may well be thought a mug's game, but – if only (though, I hope, not only) – to encourage debate, I suggest three big factors.[70] The first, and presumably least, is, indeed,

---

[62] Isidore, *Etymologiae*, 1.29.1.

[63] Curtius, *European Literature*, pp. 495–500.

[64] Read, 'Puns', pp. 89–90 (citing Andrewes's sermons of 1611 and 1618), where 'sacramental' is Peter McCullough's characterization, endorsed by Read herself.

[65] Hannah Crawforth, *Etymology and the Invention of English in Early Modern Literature* (Cambridge, 2013).

[66] See e.g. J. J. O'Hara, *True Names: Vergil and the Alexandrian Tradition of Etymological Wordplay* (Ann Arbor, MI, 1996), p. 9; Amsler, *Etymology*, pp. 82–100; Curtius, *European Literature*, pp. 496–500.

[67] M. A. Screech, *Rabelais* (London, 1979), pp. 377–97 (esp. p. 393).

[68] Where the beloved's name is linked variously with 'lauro' (laurel tree and laurel crown), as well as quite different entities like 'l'aura' ('the breeze'), 'l'auro' ('gold').

[69] Ahl, *Metaformations*, p. 51. Ovid, *Metamorphoses*, 1.1–2: 'In nova fert animus *mutatas* dicere *formas* / corpora' ('My soul moves me to tell of *forms changed* into new bodies': my italics).

[70] I exclude the commonly repeated claim that the proliferation of punning is a 'reaction to the poverty' of English vocabulary (Blake, *Language of Shakespeare*, p. 20). Not only does the 'explanation' fail to explain *why* England (other nations felt the same 'poverty'); as a causal explanation (rather than a comment on effect), it is quaintly utilitarian – as if Elizabethan writers punned out of patriotic duty. More thought-provoking is de Grazia's suggestion ('Homonyms', pp. 150–1) that punning is less exceptionable, or even identifiable, in an age without 'fixed pronunciation and spelling', before 'dictionaries codified vocabulary and prescribed

the impact of the Reformation and its etymological preoccupations, which (if nothing else) must have helped to intensify awareness of the possibilities of language. But the impact of Reformation practices is in no sense peculiar to England (nor indeed is etymology in this age peculiar to Protestantism: Ficino? Rabelais?). We need something more.

My suggestion for a second, bigger factor, then, is the distinctive bent of Elizabethan writing, especially dramatic writing, towards literary hybridization. The use of prose in serious verse drama ignores classicizing Renaissance norms, as does the proliferation of 'comic' wordplay (beyond the sphere of etymology) in 'serious' verse.[71] And both of these predilections share a brisk unconcern with generic purity or decorum, as bequeathed by antiquity and as reinstated by Renaissance humanism – in line with the well-known hybridity of so much English drama in this age. As Samuel Johnson insisted, in the mid eighteenth century, Shakespearian tragedy in particular, ignoring 'strict', classicizing norms, tends towards the mixed mode of tragicomedy: a 'bastard kind', as William Scott calls it.[72] Yet Shakespearian tragedy is far from being the only 'bastard kind' in its time. In this connection, John Lyly is an interesting witness. His *Midas* (1589?) is a prose comedy that combines elements from pastoral allegory and elsewhere, and in the preface to the play Lyly suggests that 'If we present a mingle-mangle, our fault is to be excused, because the whole world is become an hodge-podge.' The whole world, hardly – but England, arguably, yes. The punning and the prose, in England, reflect a spirit of non-classical or even anti-classical (anti-classical-generic) experiment.

And yes: though it is, these days, apparently unfashionable to say so, England, compared with Italy (in earlier centuries) or France (in the Elizabethan century) is only half in the classicizing Renaissance (Germany, by comparison, is hardly in the Renaissance at all),[73] while – not irrelevantly – the English experiments come at a time when Italy (well past *its* Renaissance) is itself a culture of experiment, not least in new dramatic hybrids, of which opera is one and pastoral tragicomedy (like

Battista Guarini's *Il pastor fido*) another. And quite apart from the direct influence on English drama of Guarini's new hybrid, in particular,[74] the very phenomenon of such experiments is itself likely to have been a further stimulus to English experimentation in general.

In itself, the English development of prose in serious verse drama might be said to belong to a larger, and earlier, set of formal innovations, the most momentous of which is the displacement of long-verse rhyming lines by blank-verse iambics – pioneered in Henry Howard's translation of Virgil, *Aeneid* 4, around 1540, which itself reflects the innovation of blank verse in Italy (by Gian Giorgio Trissino in his tragedy, *Sofonisba*, in 1515). Unlike prose in verse drama, however, that development, at least, is hardly anti-classical; it might indeed be said to restore a non-rhyming equivalent to the ancient world's 'stichic' verse norms, rather.[75]

---

usage' – but the suggestion invites the riposte: why is punning not then equally pervasive in English usage (or Italian usage etc.) in *earlier* centuries? Why *now*?

71 It might be added that Hamlet's 'antic' punning is, at least in part, relatable to the characteristic idiom of 'the stock figure of the Antic-Vice', 'the dominant stage figure through the middle of the sixteenth century' and a figure relatable in turn to the comic clown: Margreta de Grazia, *'Hamlet' without Hamlet* (Cambridge, 2007), pp. 180, 183, following Robert Weimann, *Shakespeare and the Popular Tradition in the Theater*, ed. R. Schwartz (Baltimore, MD, 1978).

72 Johnson, *Preface to Shakespeare* (1765), in Samuel Johnson, *The Major Works*, ed. Donald Greene (Oxford, 1984), pp. 423–4; Scott, *Poesy*, p. 24. What Patricia Parker calls 'the often arbitrary boundaries of genre' (*Shakespeare from the Margins* (Chicago, 1996), p. 1) are anything but arbitrary in the 'strictly' classical tradition that looks back to (e.g.) Horace, *Ars Poetica*, 86–7, or Aristotle, *Rhetoric*, 3.7, on *to prepon* ('decorum').

73 England, like *Spain*? Cf. n. 78 below.

74 *Il pastor fido* was first published in 1589; the first attested opera, *Dafne*, by Jacopo Peri and Ottavio Rinuccini, belongs to the same year. The text of Guarini's play was printed in England in 1591.

75 As Milton argues ('ancient liberty recovered') in his headnote to the 1674 edition of *Paradise Lost*. More relevant is Lois Potter's suggestion that rhythmic contrasts between stanzaic verse and 'sing-song fourteeners' in earlier sixteenth-century English plays prefigure 'the verse-prose distinction as

But England, in the Elizabethan age, is only half in a classicizing mindset anyway. This is an age when English architecture is still, mostly, Gothic;[76] an age when the headmaster of one of the new humanist schools (Richard Mulcaster, first head of Merchant Taylors', founded in 1561) can say, 'I honour the Latin, but I worship the English';[77] and an age when even the learned Christopher Marlowe (Cambridge scholar, and translator of Lucan and Ovid) can put prose into his serious verse dramas (from *Tamburlaine* to *Doctor Faustus*), apparently unconstrained by classical norms altogether. As everyone used to say – but seemingly less often, these days – England for a time gets the best of both worlds: access to the riches of classical antiquity, without being overpowered by them (and Shakespeare, least of all).[78]

So: alongside the Reformation penchant for etymology, we have the impetus to experiment with literary hybrids, within a nominally classicizing Renaissance culture; and we have a third big factor, peculiar to England, and more to do with punning than prose: the distinctive hybridity of the English *language*, relative to German on one side, and Italian and French on the other, a configuration precisely parallel to the relationship (or non-relationship) of the four cultures in question to the Renaissance itself.[79]

Thanks to the huge influence of Norman French after the Conquest, and further borrowings from French in the centuries that follow, English emerges from the Middle Ages as a distinctive de facto linguistic hybrid, with a mass of Latin-derived vocabulary on a Germanic base: 'a surprisingly intimate alliance of . . . the Germanic and Romance' (as the German philologist, Jacob Grimm, put it in 1851).[80] And the new hybrid is not just any kind of hybrid. Thanks to the coincident phenomenon of Middle English elimination of inflectional endings, and the reduction of inherited polysyllables more generally, English (now also the beneficiary of many new Latinate loan words) presents a remarkable pattern of syllabic contrasts. Short, often monosyllabic, 'native' words (where 'native' actually subsumes many of the earlier French borrowings) jostle with long Latinate loan words and

neologisms, as in Shakespeare's textbook example: 'this my hand will rather / The *multitudinous* seas *incarnadine*, / Making the green one red'.[81] English 'particles', observes William Scott in 1599, are 'mostly . . . monosyllables' – 'as are all almost of our Saxon appellatives'.[82]

Over the course of the second millennium AD, virtually all European cultures debate their own 'language questions', beginning with Italy, in the fourteenth century. In England, such a 'question' surfaces in the fourteenth century too, when Higden's *Polychronicon* deplores the fact that, thanks to population mixtures, 'the language of the country has been corrupted'.[83] In Shakespeare's age, the English 'language question' is hotly debated, and a new linguistic consciousness focuses in large part on the history of the language, including its mixed inheritance.[84] That mixture (it is clear) can now be seen, not as a cause for shame, but as a strength.

---

it is usually understood in later Elizabethan drama': 'Elizabethan Experiments', in *The Revels History of Drama in English, vol. 2, 1500–1576*, ed. T. W. Craik et al. (London, 1980), pp. 233–57; pp. 237–8.

[76] Cf. the sketch by Colin Burrow, *Shakespeare and Classical Antiquity* (Oxford, 2013), pp. 15–19. Shakespeare is himself compared to Gothic architecture by later readers as different as Alexander Pope (in the preface to his Shakespeare edition of 1725) and August Wilhelm Schlegel (in the opening pages of his *Vorlesungen über dramatische Kunst und Literatur*, 1816).

[77] Mulcaster, *The First Part of the Elementary* (1582), p. 254.

[78] 'Fortunately in England, as also in Spain, the strength of native taste was sufficiently powerful to counteract the great prestige of neo-classic form': M. C. Bradbrook, *The Growth and Structure of Elizabethan Comedy*, 2nd edn (Cambridge, 1973), p. 5.

[79] So Silk, Gildenhard and Barrow, *Classical Tradition*, p. 121.

[80] In a speech, 'Über den Ursprung der Sprache'.

[81] *Macbeth*, 2.2.59–61 (my italics, for Latinate polysyllables); on the passage, and the wider issues here, see Silk, Gildenhard and Barrow, *Classical Tradition*, pp. 141–7.

[82] Scott, *Poesy*, p. 60.

[83] *Polychronicon* (c. 1327), translated (from Latin to English) by Trevisa in the 1380s: Silk, Gildenhard and Barrow, *Classical Tradition*, p. 144.

[84] There is a new 'interest in the history of the English language arising in Early Modern England as a result of early attempts to study Anglo-Saxon, the antiquarian movement, biblical humanist practices and the growth of lexicography': Crawforth, *Etymology*, p. 7.

As Scott observes, 'we can by easy change draw the words of any language to have the very habit of English'.[85] And (it is no less clear) the mixture is perceived as a strength, not least because of the syllabic contrasts. Thus, in the mid 1590s, Richard Carew pinpoints the aesthetic advantages of the new syllabic range: 'the long words that we borrow, being intermingled with the short of our own store, make up a perfect harmony'.[86]

Among much else, the large number of monosyllables in the language creates a range of homophones and homonyms that simply make puns more readily available. Mahood provides a list of Shakespeare's favourite wordplay words. At the top of the list, in descending order of frequency, are: 'dear', 'grace', 'will', 'light', 'lie', 'crown', 'heart'/'hart' and 'son'/'sun'.[87] But more profoundly, learned Elizabethan discussions of the language – the mixture, the history, the syllabicity too – surely play a special part in stimulating the kind of consciousness that expresses itself in wordplay. English semi-independence from Renaissance classicizing is (I propose) the determining factor that emboldens even learned writers both to develop the use of prose in serious verse drama and to seize the opportunities for wordplay, there as elsewhere – while the conditions for this latter exploitation are peculiarly operative in the new age of general language awareness. In all of which, classicizing rhetoric plays only a very minor part. Puns and prose in serious drama achieve their impressive outcomes, largely in spite of the classicizing of the age, almost in defiance of that classicizing.

And what else, if anything, do puns and prose have in common? The logic of prose usage in Elizabethan verse drama, as summed up by Vickers and Crane, and as still represented in earlier Shakespeare, is what elsewhere I have called 'differential stability'. As in Greek tragedy (with its differentiations between high-style spoken dialogue and even higher-style sung lyrics), or as in most of the Western world's novels (differentiated between more formal narrative and less formal direct speech), there are shifts and switches within a single work, but the shifts and switches operate according to a specifiable formula.[88] But in, for instance, *Hamlet*, without abandoning the principle, Shakespeare far exceeds it: he *de*stabilizes. When the inanities of 'Full thirty times hath Phoebus' cart' are in verse, and the powerful message of 'What a piece of work is a man' is in prose, one can fairly say that the time, indeed, is 'out of joint':[89] the very structures of literature, and experience, have become unpredictable.

The logic of punning in serious poetry is – or *may* be – comparable. Generalizing about the rationale or effect of puns is tricky, and in some ways the modern abandonment of the problematic apparatus of the rhetoricians in favour of the single category of 'the pun' has merely substituted one set of problems for another. 'The rest is silence' has little in common with (say) 'Time flies like an arrow; fruit flies like a banana' (Groucho Marx).[90] Theorists of punning in recent years like to relate it, in neo-Saussurian fashion, to 'the arbitrariness of the sign'.[91] This is seriously misleading. Hamlet's relentless punning is not about 'the sign', but about truth and appearance,[92] illusion and disillusion, the excruciating disparity between what should be and what is.[93] More specifically, Groucho's wordplay might be said to be about the sign, self-referentially; 'The rest is silence' plainly isn't. As far as 'serious' punning is

---

[85] Scott, *Poesy*, p. 49.

[86] Carew, *The Excellency of the English Tongue*, attached to the 1614 edition of William Camden's *Remains Concerning Britain*: Silk, Gildenhard and Barrow, *Classical Tradition*, p. 145.

[87] Mahood, *Wordplay*, p. 51.

[88] Silk, *Aristophanes*, pp. 102–11 (where stability, 'differential' and other, is contrasted with stylistic 'mobility'; examples from *Hamlet* on pp. 109–10).

[89] *Hamlet*, 3.2.148, 2.2.305, 1.5.189.

[90] Widely attributed to Groucho, though seemingly first cited in print by Anthony Oettinger, 'The Uses of Computers in Science', *Scientific American*, 215.3 (1966), 161–72; p. 168.

[91] So e.g. Jonathan Culler, 'The Call of the Phoneme', in Culler, *On Puns*, pp. 1–16; pp. 11–13.

[92] Cf. Mahood, *Wordplay*, p. 54. Crane, *Prose*, pp. 146, 155, reads Hamlet's prose in a similar spirit.

[93] Cf. Coleridge on 'the death-bed feeling in which all things appear as puns and equivocations': *Shakespearean Criticism*, vol. I, p. 135.

concerned, Jean Paul's is a superior insight: puns celebrate coincidence – in life.[94] The world, not the language, is at stake.

Prose in verse drama threatens to undermine an assumed one-to-one relationship between genre and language, but then the newly-established conventions (prose for comic matter, and so on) restore at least a differential stability, until experiments like Shakespeare's, in *Hamlet* and elsewhere, now subvert that stability too. But if prose in verse drama threatens the assumed relationship between genre and language, so punning tends to undermine an assumed one-to-one relationship between – yes – language and object, but *thereby* to undermine the stability *of that object itself*, of life and experience itself. Dr Johnson's notorious distaste for Shakespeare's punning is revealing here. Johnson has no problem with Shakespeare's tragicomic tendencies, because 'mingling' tragedy and comedy 'approaches nearer than either to the appearance of *life*'.[95] Conversely (and even more than Dryden or Rowe), he is appalled by Shakespeare's wordplay: 'a quibble was to him the fatal Cleopatra for which he lost the world, and was content to lose it'.[96] For Johnson, writing in 1765, punning threatens 'the world' indeed. Let us call to mind the seemingly defensive insistence with which (in an era of growing intellectual instability) Johnson affirms, precisely, the stabilities of human existence. 'The province of poetry,' he declares, a few years earlier, 'is to describe nature and passion, *which are always the same*'.[97] Hamlet's punning (like his prose) makes 'nature', and 'passion' too, feel random and variable, instead.

But if punning creates, or even celebrates, coincidence, etymology ('sacramental' or otherwise) finds *links*: it creates, or (as Heidegger might say) discloses, relationships.[98] In this sense, one can only agree with Read in contrasting, not relating, Shakespeare and Andrewes. Shakespeare's punning and, so too, his experiments with prose, beyond the newly established stability, are not mechanisms of disclosure so much as open-ended modes of exploration,[99] in this most exploratory of ages.

---

[94] Jean Paul, *Vorschule der Ästhetik*, 2.52. Read, 'Puns', p. 84, acknowledges 'the fortuitousness of the connections [punning] insists on', without pursuing the implications.

[95] Johnson, *Preface to Shakespeare*, p. 424 (my italics).

[96] Johnson, *Preface to Shakespeare*, p. 429.

[97] Johnson, *Rasselas* (1759), ch. 10 (my italics).

[98] *Pace* the loose thinking that leads Culler to call etymology 'the diachronic version of punning' (for good measure, conflating etymology as understood in modern historical linguistics with the very different premodern and early modern concept: n. 54 above) ('The Call of the Phoneme', p. 2).

[99] As far as wordplay is concerned, a different, and prospectively more plausible, kind of 'disclosure' is suggested by Parker's argument that in Shakespearian drama *systems of thematic* puns (my terms, not hers) create 'linkages' that 'expose ... the orthodoxies and ideologies of the texts they evoke' (*Shakespeare from the Margins*, p. 13). The unstated premise is that – in, or especially in, thematic usage – 'puns often link together unrelated imagery': Kenneth Muir, 'The Uncomic Pun', *Cambridge Journal*, 3 (1950), 472–85; p. 483. But this hardly points to the logic of 'uncomic' punning as such, which is better suggested by Muir's observation that Shakespeare's puns can also 'seem to shoot out roots in all directions' (p. 483).

'AWAY WITH HIM! HE SPEAKS LATIN': *2 HENRY VI* AND THE USES OF ROMAN ANTIQUITY

DAVID CURRELL

Shakespeare's English history plays, and particularly the early histories, have rarely attracted notice for their engagement with the literature and culture of classical antiquity. The wealth and complexity of allusion and adaptation evinced in other works has, understandably, absorbed most commentators and anchored most overviews and theorizations of Shakespeare's practices.[1] But though they had smallest Latin and least Greek, the early histories engage in a significant way with the texts, mythologies, ideologies and rhetoric of classical antiquity, and especially of the Latin texts underpinning the grammar school curriculum of the late sixteenth century. The network of allusions to Rome and the sprinkling of spoken Latin in *2 Henry VI* comprise a purposive and patterned stratum of poetic design clustering around and characterizing the two contending houses.[2] Allusions to books 1 and 2 of the *Aeneid* bind Queen Margaret and the Duke of Suffolk as would-be Virgilian sufferers operating in a Lucanian polity. Meanwhile, the Duke of York puts his greater skills in the Latin tongue and capacity to outwit humanist statecraft in the service of stratagems that include inciting Jack Cade, whose status within the play as an uneasy parody of York is deepened by his systematic attack on learning and education.

An important exception to the critical generalization drawn above is Andrew Hadfield's study of the engagement across the three *Henry VI* plays and *Richard III* with the political and military crises of the civil war at the end of the Roman Republic. Hadfield identifies so dominant an influence from

[1] Robert Kilburn Root, *Classical Mythology in Shakespeare* (1903; repr. New York, 1965) and J. A. K. Thomson, *Shakespeare and the Classics* (London, 1952) are in essence compendia of Shakespearian references to classical myths and texts and enumerate several in the *Henry VI* plays. The principal works that have contributed to contemporary critical understandings of Shakespeare's classical intertextuality include passing or no reference to these plays: Robert S. Miola, *Shakespeare's Rome* (Cambridge, 1983); Charles Martindale and Michelle Martindale, *Shakespeare and the Uses of Antiquity: An Introductory Essay* (London, 1990); Jonathan Bate, *Shakespeare and Ovid* (Oxford, 1993); Heather James, *Shakespeare's Troy: Drama, Politics, and the Translation of Empire* (Cambridge, 1997); Miola, 'Reading the Classics', in *A Companion to Shakespeare*, ed. David Scott Kastan (Oxford, 1999), pp. 172–85; *Shakespeare and the Classics*, ed. Charles Martindale and A. B. Taylor (Cambridge, 2004); Warren Cherniak, *The Myth of Rome in Shakespeare and his Contemporaries* (Cambridge, 2011); Colin Burrow, *Shakespeare and Classical Antiquity* (Oxford, 2013). On classical intertextuality in later history plays, see Judith Mossman, 'Henry V and Plutarch's Alexander', *Shakespeare Quarterly*, 45 (1994), 57–73; and 'Plutarch and Shakespeare's Henry IV parts 1 and 2', *Poetica*, 48 (1997), 99–117.

[2] For an account of the critical history concerning the relationship between the 1594 quarto, *The First part of the Contention betwixt the two famous Houses of Yorke and Lancaster* (hereafter Q) and *The second Part of Henry the Sixt* in F, see Ronald Knowles, ed., *King Henry VI, Part Two*, The Arden Shakespeare (Walton-on-Thames, 1999), pp. 111–41. Lawrence Manley cites Madeleine Doran's suggestion, made in 'Henry VI, Parts II and III': Their Relation to the 'Contention' and the 'True Tragedy' (Iowa City, 1928), p. 65, that the omission of almost all of the Latin present in F from Q may be attributable to a want of proficiency in that language on the part of the reporter or the country audiences for whom the Q text was prepared as an abridgement for a touring

Lucan and Roman historians that he labels the plays collectively 'Shakespeare's *Pharsalia*'.[3] He instructively discusses selected passages across all four plays, especially allusions to Julius Caesar, and adduces some of Lucan's grotesqueries as possible influences, but in general argues less on the basis of the plays' verbal texture than on the overall picture of dysfunctional governance and the resultant mutually destructive assertions of sovereignty. The period 1593–4 saw the publication of the quarto *The First part of the Contention* together with the quarto *The Most Lamentable Romaine Tragedie of Titus Andronicus*, *Venus and Adonis* and *Lucrece*, and warrants the excavation of links with contemporary interest in republicanism and the Roman literature that informed it.[4] In advancing the maximal version of a provocative thesis, however, Hadfield is selective, and, but for the notable instance of Edward's 'Et tu Brute, wilt thou stab *Cesar* too?' in the octavo *True Tragedie of Richard Duke of Yorke*, omits interpretation of the actual Latin present in these texts.[5] I aim to show that literary and linguistic engagements with Roman antiquity in *2 Henry VI* are substantial and various, and that while Lucan may be even more crucial than Hadfield posits, Virgil's *Aeneid* is just as important.

My investigations are energized by Colin Burrow's capacious conception of classical antiquity and its functions in Shakespeare's culture, and his insights into the strategies by which Shakespeare harnessed its semiotic potentials at specific moments of his poetic career. Notably, 'Shakespeare knew very well that reading something in a grammar long ago does not necessarily mean that one understands it, nor that one grasps the force of a quotation when it is used in a new context', and that knowledge, paired with insight into the dramatic potential of *representing* misunderstanding, misquotation and forgetfulness, made for a treatment of classical antiquity in *2 Henry VI* (one of the small minority of plays to which Burrow does not make explicit reference) of greater subtlety, continuity and power than initially appears.[6] The ways in which *2 Henry VI* handles classical linguistic material, mythological reference and the

sociology of Latinity illuminate key characters and actions, and underscore how deeply and from how early a date these elements, and the dramatic strategies for drawing poetic resonance from them, penetrate the Shakespearian canon. As in better-known instances, grammar books and the schoolroom scene of instruction form a key part of Shakespeare's representation.[7] Beyond – and at the same time arising from – the differential classical 'typing' of Queen Margaret, Suffolk, Gloucester and York, *2 Henry VI* represents a social revolt that is also a revolt against literacy. Jack Cade is killed (after ordering the killing of a clerk and a humanist lord), yet his dominance over Act 4 of *2 Henry VI* conveys Shakespeare's

---

company, and adds a third possibility: 'that no one in Pembroke's Men . . . could speak Latin': 'From Strange's Men to Pembroke's Men: *2 Henry VI* and *The First part of the Contention*', *Shakespeare Quarterly*, 54 (2003), 253–87; p. 270. There may be further warrant for Manley's hypothesis in the Q version of the confrontation of Jack Cade and Lord Saye. In F, Cade says, 'Away with him, away with him! He speaks Latin' (4.7.53); Q has a comical sequence of guesses as to what language Saye has used (TLN 1811–14). While this near total absence of Latin text and the diminishment of classical allusions in Q versus F is relevant to theories of revision or reconstruction, I am here not principally concerned with chronology or attribution, and do not find prior attempts to illuminate the latter on the basis of classical references dispositive. J. W. Binns discusses three instances of Latin quotation in *2 Henry VI* in his overview of editorial issues surrounding Latin in Shakespearian texts, 'Shakespeare's Latin Citations: The Editorial Problem', in *Shakespeare Survey 35*, ed. Stanley Wells (Cambridge, 1982), pp. 119–28; pp. 122–3.

3 Andrew Hadfield, *Shakespeare and Republicanism* (Cambridge, 2005), p. 103.

4 Hadfield, *Republicanism*, pp. 99–102. On republican discourses and their presence in the theatre of the early 1590s, see also Patrick Cheney, *Marlowe's Republican Authorship: Lucan, Liberty, and the Sublime* (New York, 2009).

5 Hadfield, *Republicanism*, pp. 118–19. The line occurs on sig. E2r in the facsimile of the *True Tragedie* reproduced in John D. Cox and Eric Rasmussen, eds., *King Henry VI, Part 3*, The Arden Shakespeare (London, 2001), p. 403.

6 Burrow, *Classical Antiquity*, p. 25.

7 On the pedagogy and curricula of the early modern English grammar school see T. W. Baldwin, *Shakespeare's Small Latine and Lesse Greeke*, 2 vols. (Urbana, 1944); Jeff Dolven, *Scenes of Instruction in Renaissance Romance* (Chicago, 2007), pp. 15–64; and Burrow, *Classical Antiquity*, pp. 22–50.

ambivalences regarding the conduct and consequences of humanist education that informs but
also sets a limit point to its sceptical politics.

'DIDO WOULD UNFOLD': QUEEN MARGARET AND VIRGIL

At a moment of crisis at the Lancastrian court in the
wake of the assassination of the protector, 'good
Duke Humphrey' of Gloucester, King Henry turns
to Queen Margaret's favourite, the Duke of
Suffolk, and lambasts the conspirator for offering
hypocritical comfort.[8] Her political and marital
ascendency suddenly in question, Queen
Margaret attempts to meet rhetorical fire with
fire, aiming to overwhelm the King's anger and
incipient independence by articulating the pangs of
disprized love:

> QUEEN.　How often have I tempted Suffolk's
> 　　tongue –
> 　The agent of thy foul inconstancy –
> 　To sit and witch me, as Ascanius did
> 　When he to madding Dido would unfold
> 　His father's acts, commenced in burning Troy!
> 　Am I not witched like her? Or thou not false like him?
> 　　　　　　　　　(2 Henry VI, 3.2.114–19)

Queen Margaret calls Henry 'agent of ... foul
inconstancy' for his tears over Gloucester and
wrath at Suffolk (murderer of Gloucester but
minion of the Queen). She is as victimized as
Dido, and he as faithless as Aeneas. But in
making the boy Ascanius the seductive teller
of Troy tales at Dido's court is she not herself
foully inconstant to Roman literary history?
In Virgil's *Aeneid*, Venus has substituted her
son Cupid for Ascanius to influence Dido's
disposition while Aeneas narrates his own
exploits. Can one encounter this passage and
not concur with Paul Vincent that the author
is betraying 'gross ignorance of the most
famous book of the most famous work of
poetry in Latin', exposing 'fundamental gaps
in his knowledge of the classics'? If so, does
not the authorship disintegrate? After all, there
are some dozen '*bona fide* classical allusions', so

'we must conclude that the classical allusions
in *2 Henry VI* do not all trace back to the
same source, and that Shakespeare's sole
authorship of the play is more problematic
than most scholars today are prepared to
accept'.[9] This conclusion is precipitant, whatever models of co-authorship one is inclined to
entertain.[10]

As a first step towards explicating this passage,
it is crucial to realize that Dido 'viewed awry'
constitutes something like a Shakespearian
signature:

> LORENZO.　In such a night
> 　Stood Dido with a willow in her hand
> 　Upon the wild sea banks, and waft her love
> 　To come again to Carthage.　(*Merchant*, 5.1.9–12)

> ANTONY.　Where souls do couch on flowers we'll
> 　　hand in hand,
> 　And with our sprightly port make the ghosts gaze.
> 　Dido and her Aeneas shall want troops
> 　And all the haunt be ours.　(*Antony*, 4.15.51–4)

> ADRIAN.　Tunis was never graced before with such
> 　　a paragon to their queen.
> GONZALO.　Not since widow Dido's time.
> ANTONIO. *(to Sebastian)*　Widow? A pox o'that!
> 　How came that 'widow' in? Widow Dido!
> SEBASTIAN.　What if he had said 'widower Aeneas'
> 　too? Good lord, how you take it!

---

[8] I cite *2 Henry VI* from Knowles's Arden edition (see n. 2)
unless otherwise specified. I cite Q from the facsimile in
Knowles (pp. 376–407) and use his through-line numbering.
For 'good Duke Humphrey' see 1.1.156, 159, 190; 2.2.74;
3.2.123, 248; 4.1.76; cf. 3.2.183–4.

[9] Paul Vincent, 'Unsolved Mysteries in *Henry the
Sixth, Part Two*', *Notes & Queries*, 48 (2001), 270–4; pp.
273–4.

[10] Vincent prepares for his analysis of allusion with more
conventional stylometrics (working with the rate and
distribution of 'O'/'Oh' and 'you'/'ye' spellings, and
of compound words of varying inventiveness, see
pp. 272–3), but the extended reliance on Queen
Margaret's speech to clinch a distinction between 'university' and 'non-university' authorship, I will argue, vitiates
the ultimate claim.

ADRIAN. *(to Gonzalo)* 'Widow Dido' said you? You
make me study of that: she was of Carthage, not of
Tunis.

GONZALO.   This Tunis, sir, was Carthage.

ADRIAN.   Carthage?

GONZALO.   I assure you, Carthage.

(*Tempest*, 2.1.79–90)

Lorenzo contaminates his Dido with a willow
borrowed from Ovid's Ariadne, Antony effects
a second and posthumous divorce from Sychaeus
that he may overgo a literary avatar of Augustus,
and Gonzalo garbles geography. Even Tamora's
lascivious evocation of the famous lovers, 'curtained with a counsel-keeping cave' (*Titus*,
2.2.24), appears, if not awry, then wry: the
epithet 'counsel-keeping' is hardly consistent
with the encounter's availability as an exemplum,
bruited through time and space by Virgilian
Fama.

Vincent alleges a second and similarly telltale
solecism a few lines earlier, when Queen
Margaret recalls her stormy voyage to England
and refers to Aeolus, divine keeper of the winds,
as 'he that loosed them forth their brazen caves'
(*2 Henry VI*, 3.2.89). He follows Thomson, who
pointed to the alleged oddity of the epithet
'brazen' ('an absurd name for a cave'), while
unhelpfully noting that while *Aeneid* 1.52ff. is
one classical locus for Aeolus, there are several
other possibilities. A 'confused recollection' of
the bronze wall surrounding Aeolus's island,
mentioned at *Odyssey* 10.3ff., is the classicist
Thomson's improbable suggestion.[11] A likelier
source for the epithet are the 'brazen doors' of
Aeolus's realm and the fetters of 'Vulcan's sturdy
brass' with which Jupiter promises to restrain the
winds in Marlowe and Nashe's *Dido, Queen of
Carthage*.[12] In any event, on the basis of these
two 'errors' Vincent states 'there is more than
one detail here at odds with the venerated original
of these lines', and infers that 'university men' like
Peele or Marlowe 'could not have written these
lines'.[13]

Rather than find this speech Shakespearian on
the basis of its unconsciousness of error, I find it
Shakespearian on the basis of its consciousness of

misprision; moreover, Queen Margaret's swerve
from the *Aeneid* is of a piece with the splicing,
twisting and knotting of Latin texts evident
throughout the play.[14] Burrow's account of
another alleged howler offers a useful starting
point: 'But when he uses the name of Aristotle
here [*Troilus*, 2.2.165] ... he makes what would
now be called an obvious anachronism as well as
an error ... A Richard Farmer would say that
this "mistake" shows that Shakespeare did not
"know" Aristotle. But Shakespeare's references
to classical authorities are theatrically motivated
performances rather than scholarly citations.'[15]
The purposive error, as Burrow proceeds skilfully to elucidate, is a Shakespearian technique –
and I mean 'error' less in the sense it would
take in the schoolroom than in its etymological
sense of wandering: a literary deviation that
calls attention to itself and in its dramatic
context illuminates a character's desire or
affect.[16]

---

[11] Thomson, *Classics*, pp. 88–9.

[12] Christopher Marlowe, *The Complete Plays*, ed.
Frank Romany and Robert Lindsey (London, 2003), 1.1.62
and 118.

[13] Vincent, 'Unsolved Mysteries', p. 273.

[14] Robert S. Miola, 'Vergil in Shakespeare: From Allusion to
Imitation', in *Vergil at 2000: Commemorative Essays on the Poet
and His Influence*, ed. John D. Bernard (New York, 1983), pp.
241–58, argues for a developmental model of Shakespeare's
overall practice of allusion to Virgil, from a 'labored, ostentatious, and self-congratulatory' early phase, to 'subtle and
sharply controlled ... point and irony' around 1600, to
'eristic imitation' at the levels of idea and image (p. 242).
My reading of Queen Margaret's speech will suggest that
early uses may already evince pointedness, irony, and creative reworking of the Virgilian text at the level of idea and
image.

[15] Burrow, *Classical Antiquity*, pp. 25–7.

[16] In this direction, the Martindales note that the Page's attribution of Hecuba's dream of a burning brand to Althaea in *2
Henry IV* (2.2.82–3) may belong to the character and be
meant to be seen to belong to him (*Uses of Antiquity*, p. 7).
Note that York offers a 'correct' allusion to the story of
Althaea in *2 Henry VI* (1.1.231–2). J. W. Binns makes
a parallel point relevant to the argument of this essay about
how 'Latin, and especially its misuse and misunderstanding,

Heather James, who has contributed so much to our understanding of how Shakespeare tells the *Aeneid* but tells it slant, argues that Shakespeare's allusions to Dido as a listening figure have two (cooperative) effects. They evoke a figure whose rapt attention in any given instance points outward to the dynamics of sympathy at work in theatre, and one who, across multiple plays, carries the literary function of directing attention specifically to 'concerns already on Shakespeare's mind when Dido makes her entrance into a given play's field of discourse': 'Dido bristles with the imminence of action ... Dido attends to performance with self-transforming compassion, following another's narrative to its suspenseful plateau but then supplying unforeseeable narrative directions and conclusions.'[17]

Queen Margaret's allusion to Dido, not analyzed by James, enriches her thesis via a text yet earlier than the examples from which it is developed (principally *Titus Andronicus*, *Lucrece*, *Hamlet*, *Othello* and *The Tempest*). At the point in *2 Henry VI* where Margaret paints *herself* as Dido, she bristles with the imminence of action in soliciting a compassionate hearing on her own behalf. Her rhetorical aim is to make of Henry a Dido: one who will hear the story of a near shipwreck who fled a war-torn land and be charmed into an indisseverable fidelity to the spousal bond he has made with the speaker. The threat of abandonment by suicide pregnant in her evocation of Dido's frenzy is a quick-witted defence against an external threat of abandonment. With Suffolk under a sudden louring cloud, her erotic and political power hang in the balance. It is in this context that she makes the Aeneas–Ascanius substitution. The seemingly gratuitous errancy from the *Aeneid* lets her more freely operate the Dido–Aeneas dyad from both sides. It also adds another layer of connotative complexity. In this speculation, I am partly anticipated by Knowles's judicious 'longer note' on lines 116–18:

Shakespeare undoubtedly knew that it is Aeneas, upon Dido's invitation at the opening of Book 2 of Virgil's *Aeneid*, who tells the story of Troy, not his son Ascanius

(see *Titus* 3.2.27–8). In Virgil Venus has Cupid appear as Ascanius bearing gifts from Troy to Dido, to inflame her heart with love (*Aeneid* 1.658–756). Marlowe generally repeats this in *Dido*, but with the sequence reversed, Cupid as Ascanius appearing after Aeneas' harrowing account. [J. Dover] Wilson mistakenly attributes Shakespeare's variant to a misreading of Chaucer's *The Legend of Good Women* (1129–55), which in fact gives the basic Virgilian details. J. A. K. Thomson notes, 'It is thought that this perversion of the *Aeneid* comes from the *Roman d'Énéas* (latter half of the twelfth century), in which it is Ascanius who excites Dido's love' (89). Presumably there must be a more mainstream source which, as yet, remains unidentified. Given the irony of Margaret's speech at this point, perhaps Shakespeare was drawn by the image of Suffolk–Cupid–Ascanius?[18]

Margaret's speech is overtly ironic in that its overwrought piteousness appears to a knowing audience as instrumental (towards maintaining her favourite and her own initiative and freedom of action at court) and hypocritical (it is a break with Suffolk, not Henry, that gives rise to despair). Additional ironies ramify, however, from her evocation and variation of the first books of the *Aeneid*. Suffolk wooed and married Margaret as Henry's proxy in France, although the language of the opening speech of the play, in which Suffolk narrates the surrogate espousal and renounces 'my title in the Queen' (1.1.12), is rhetorically poised between the illocutionary delivery of that title and its subtle reassertion in the present moment by virtue of the re-presentation of circumstance in a way that establishes the complex dependencies and Petrarchism of the Lancastrian ménage.[19] As (courtly) lover, Suffolk is substituted into the

---

contributes to the characterization', although his focus here is on comic characterization, which he distinguishes perhaps too cleanly from the 'appropriate grandeur' evoked by the appearance of Latin in history plays ('Latin Citations', pp. 119–20).

[17] Heather James, 'Dido's Ear: Tragedy and the Politics of Response', *Shakespeare Quarterly*, 52 (2001), 360–82; p. 382.

[18] Knowles, ed., p. 369.

[19] Suffolk's wooing of Margaret is dramatized in *1 Henry VI*, 5.5, although that play probably postdates *2 Henry VI*.

amorous role of Cupid that he first played in France, while King Henry, ever absent yet still 'the substance / Of that great shadow [Suffolk] did represent' (1.1.13–14), is left holding the part of Aeneas at his worst.

Let us return from a textual and interpretative wandering to the Virgilian passage in which Venus concocts the substitution plot that will entrap Dido in passion:

> At Cytherea novas artes, nova pectore versat
> consilia, ut faciem mutatus et ora Cupido
> pro dulci Ascanio veniat, donisque furentem
> incendat reginam atque ossibus implicet ignem:
> quippe domum timet ambiguam Tyriosque bilinguis.
>
> (1.657–61)

But the Cytherean revolves in her breast new wiles, new schemes; how Cupid, changed in face and form, may come in the stead of sweet Ascanius, and by his gifts kindle the queen to madness and send the flame into her very marrow. In truth, she fears the uncertain house and double-tongued Tyrians.[20]

Queen Margaret's 'madding' corresponds grammatically to *furentem*; the idea is reinforced incessantly in book 4, after tales of 'burning Troy' set Dido afire.[21] But it is Venus who fears that the house and hosts receiving Aeneas and Ascanius may be unreliable (*ambiguam*) and double-tongued (*bilinguis*): 'How often have I tempted Suffolk's tongue – / The agent of thy foul inconstancy'. The crux is the substitution *Cupido / pro dulci Ascanio* in Dido's lap, which is scrambled by Margaret into a substitution of Ascanius for Aeneas as the spellbinding narrator. Such a blatant substitution may be a decoy (but also, by the very nature of decoys, a clue, and an anchor) in respect of a delicate series of potential identifications and substitutions, including Knowles's 'Suffolk–Cupid–Ascanius', with several branching terms. I have implied one, namely Margaret–Venus–Dido: she portrays herself as the 'witched' queen, but is the orchestrator of the substitutional logic. Queen Margaret also plays Venus as the inciter of seduction ('How often have I tempted Suffolk's tongue ... to sit and witch me'), but, in a brilliant piece of invention, the admission to having

solicited seduction is transformed into a sign of fidelity: Suffolk's private words are cast as efforts to kindle love for Henry. It is Henry who is excoriated for infidelity and abandonment, associations that place him in the role to which his kingship also answers: Aeneas. Yet this is an Aeneas who has wooed by surrogate, and therefore Margaret places a surrogate in her epic simile.

There remains something unresolved about how the absent Aeneas's role is apportioned among the three principals in Margaret's simile. Suffolk has a claim: riding openly with the queen, as in 1.3, he has provoked rumour and resentment among the people. If King Henry, a boy king, were played by a boy actor (as, of course, was Margaret), there would be special irony in inviting an identification between Suffolk and Ascanius in so apparently awkward a manner: sufficient irony to provoke the name 'Ascanius' as a sort of desperate parapraxis to cover the elder man's obvious amatory role? More securely, the active Margaret appropriates some of Aeneas's endurance – and glamour – in the first part of her speech:

> QUEEN. Was I for this nigh wrecked upon the sea
>   And twice by awkward winds from England's bank
>   Drove back again unto my native clime?
>   What boded this, but well forewarning winds
>   Did seem to say: 'Seek not a scorpion's nest,
>   Nor set no footing on this unkind shore'?
>   What did I then, but cursed the gentle gusts
>   And he that loosed them forth their brazen caves
>   And bid them blow towards England's blessed shore
>   Or turn our stern upon a dreadful rock.
>   Yet Aeolus would not be a murderer,
>   But left that hateful office unto thee.
>
> (*2 Henry VI*, 3.2.82–93)

---

[20] Virgil, *Eclogues, Georgics, Aeneid 1–6*, ed. and trans. H. R. Fairclough, rev. G. P. Goold (Cambridge, MA, 1999), pp. 306–9.

[21] Cf. *ardet amans Dido traxitque per ossa furorem* ('Dido is on fire with love and has drawn the madness through her veins' (line 101)) and, at the moment of her suicide, *subitoque accensa furore* ('in the heat of sudden frenzy' (line 697)).

This passage recalls, in preparing for the Dido allusion, the storm of *Aeneid* 1 ('flavoured', perhaps, by the omens of *Aeneid* 3). Moreover, it illustrates how Margaret makes herself the Aeneas figure in her dramatic context, seeking to evoke compassion and love through a tale of adventure and sacrifice.[22] The tragedy, from Margaret's point of view, is that Suffolk's exile will reprise the separation of Aeneas and Dido. Her words are equally powerless to stop it, although she will be the one to outlive her beloved and wage war for the right to rule.

Thomson and Vincent homed in on the word 'brazen', taking for granted the reference to Aeolus himself. But an adjudicator of sources must take care not to miss the forest for the *silvae*. Aeolus, in this context, clearly evokes the storm of *Aeneid* 1: like Aeneas threatened by the Syrtes and rocks off the coast of Libya, Margaret miraculously escapes shipwreck, paving the way for the allusion to the famous scene of audition that begins later in the same book. The allusion is, in fact, doubly prepared for by the presence of a Virgilian line that at first utterance appears to be an isolated *sententia*:

GLOUCESTER.   What, Cardinal? Is your priesthood
    grown peremptory?
    Tantaene animis coelestibus irae?
    Churchmen so hot? Good uncle, hide such
    malice;
    With some holiness – can you do it?

                        (*2 Henry VI*, 2.1.23–6)

The quotation is too famous to establish on its own that Shakespeare was consulting the text of the *Aeneid* while writing *2 Henry VI*, but, coming in conjunction with the thorough conditioning of Margaret's speech by lines Shakespeare was so often to revisit, it should be read as part of a larger allusive project. Gloucester's handling of *Aeneid* 1.11 also tends to confirm David Riggs's characterization of him as a capable, even an idealized Ciceronian humanist.[23] The rhetorical question is a commonplace, one of the most widely circulating quotations from the *Aeneid* ('Can such wrath belong to heavenly spirits?'), but Gloucester is not merely throwing out a tag. Vexed by his enemies (chiefly Cardinal Beaufort) on a royal hawking

excursion to St Albans, he repurposes Virgil's words to the immediate context. The pointed and sardonic force of the allusion (*coelestibus* denoting not the pagan pantheon but, with heavy irony, politician–ecclesiastics whose thoughts are anything but 'heavenly') is partly elucidated by the technique, frequent in Shakespearian drama, of partial self-gloss: 'Churchmen so hot?' The Cardinal's later retort, playing on Luke 4: 23 ('physician, heal thyself') reverses the technique by omitting the Vulgate's verb, '*cura*': '*Medice teipsum.* – / Protector, see to't well, protect yourself' (52–3).

Use of the *Aeneid* does not end there: a relatively trivial allusion to Troy sets the scene for Bolingbroke's conjuration (1.4.17), and Young Clifford, coming upon his dead father, slain by York, fashions himself into yet another Aeneas-figure, as the outrageous anger of the terrestrial

---

[22] Given the importance of the schoolroom to *2 Henry VI*, Queen Margaret's speech and its affective aims should also be read in light of Leah Whittington's argument for the importance of feminine *ethopoeia* (speeches composed in character) in Elizabethan dramatists' education: 'the schoolboy trained himself to adopt the speech, gestures, and emotions of these grieving women as his own ... The humanist schoolroom, in other words, was a laboratory for compassion'. 'Shakespeare's Virgil: Empathy and *The Tempest*', in *Shakespeare and Renaissance Ethics*, ed. Patrick Gray and John D. Cox (Cambridge, 2014), pp. 98–120; p. 101.

[23] Riggs interprets Gloucester as a 'Ciceronian governor', an unprecedentedly 'balanced portrayal of the ideal ruler through humanistic topics' in *Shakespeare's Heroical Histories: 'Henry VI' and Its Literary Tradition* (Cambridge, MA, 1971), pp. 115, 119. He points a contrast between Humphrey's rhetoric over the articles of peace at 1.1.73–100 and York's 'half-ironic reassertion of the *topoi*' in the soliloquy that closes the scene (pp. 119–21). Chris Fitter suggests that Gloucester may have been deliberately modelled on William Cecil, Lord Burghley, and adduces both Burghley's reverence for Cicero ('carrying *De Officiis* about with him, and ordering Cicero's works from France in portable size volumes') and Bacon's association of Burghley with the phrase *pater patriae*, a singularly rare honorific (at least in the republican period) of which Cicero was the third recipient, for thwarting Catiline's conspiracy. See 'Emergent Shakespeare and the Politics of Protest: *2 Henry VI* in Historical Contexts', *ELH*, 72 (2005), 129–58; p. 147.

spirits shifts the action of this play towards the Senecan ambiance fully evident in *2 Henry VI*:

YOUNG CLIFFORD.   Meet I an infant of the house of
    York,
Into as many gobbets will I cut it
As wild Medea young Absyrtus did.
In cruelty will I seek out my fame.
Come, thou new ruin of old Clifford's house;
            [He takes him up on his back.]
As did Aeneas old Anchises bear,
So bear I thee upon my manly shoulders;
But then Aeneas bare a living load,
Nothing so heavy as these woes of mine. (5.2.57–65)

The last strand in the Virgilian web supplies the other of its most famous iconographical moments, but in an enervated form. Literary subtlety and the effort to self-fashion in the direction of Virgilian heroism are as dead as Old Clifford: the son dedicates himself not to new nation-building but to the special cruelty of civil war. Young Clifford's 'wild Medea' is a nice touch in this respect; the most commonly cited source, Ovid's *Tristia* 4.9, has '*impia . . . Medea*' (line 9), characterizing her wickedness as specially sacrilegious and pointing a contrast with Virgil's *pius Aeneas*.[24] The loss of Virgilian pathos (even more pointed in Q, where Young Clifford is forced immediately to put his father off his back in order to fight with Richard) continues a theme among the Lancastrians established by the death of Margaret's first substitute Aeneas, Suffolk. In that death scene, the change of focus from sovereign passions to civil war is definitively established around an important and underappreciated use of Lucan.

'IMPERIAL TONGUE': SUFFOLK AND LUCAN

SUFFOLK.   Come, soldiers, show what cruelty ye can,
That this my death may never be forgot.
Great men oft die by vile Bezonians.
A Roman sworder and banditto slave
Murdered sweet Tully; Brutus' bastard hand
Stabbed Julius Caesar; savage islanders
Pompey the Great; and Suffolk dies by pirates.
                    (4.1.134–40)

Hadfield comments: 'Any mention of Pompey was likely to have had the effect of triggering a memory of the *Pharsalia*, especially when juxtaposed with the name of Caesar.'[25] Perhaps, but we can go much further. When Suffolk, fleeing to exile, is decapitated aboard a boat at the shore by a man who once served in his livery, this invites a memory of Lucan significantly more precise and vivid than Suffolk's own rather vague recollection of famous Roman deaths. The misalignment between the competence of the scenic allusion and the incompetence of the character's verbal allusion is pointed, part of the design, and Shakespearian: the critical effort strictly to measure the playwright's knowledge by the character's superficial learning again does not do justice to the former.

As Gloucester's quotation of a single line from *Aeneid* 1 sets the scene for the more extended evocation and refraction of *Aeneid* 1–4, so Suffolk utters a snippet of Lucanian text: '*Pene gelidus timor occupat artus*: / It is thee I fear' (118–19).[26] There is

---

[24] Ovid, *Tristia, Ex Ponto*, ed. and trans. A. L. Wheeler, rev. G. P. Goold (Cambridge, MA, 1988).

[25] Hadfield, *Republicanism*, p. 118. Hadfield notes the absence of Pompey from Suffolk's speech in Q, and posits an addition by a Lucan-conscious reviser. The textual difference is consistent with Q's vastly lower utilisation of Roman antiquity, but Hadfield reverses the direction of revision favoured by Knowles, Manley, and others (see n. 2 above), and I will argue the Lucanian presence in F is much deeper and more integrated than adding 'Pompey' to 'Caesar' would effect alone.

[26] Pramit Chaudhuri, 'Classical Quotation in *Titus Andronicus*', *ELH*, 81 (2014), 787–810, has recently mounted a compelling case that the four classical Latin lines and part-lines in *Titus Andronicus* should be interpreted for what they reveal about the characters using them and that the interpretative value of the allusions is enriched by attention to their original contexts. Chaudhuri follows Brian Vickers, *Shakespeare, Co-Author: A Historical Study of Five Collaborative Plays* (Oxford, 2002), and others in attributing *Titus* 4.1 to George Peele, and finds this attribution confirmed by the differences between the techniques of Latin allusion there and in Shakespearian scenes elsewhere in *Titus*. I am attributing to Shakespeare kinds of textual manipulation that Chaudhuri divides between Shakespeare and Peele. For important reasons to reserve judgement over the attribution of *Titus* 4.1, see William W. Weber, 'Shakespeare After All?:

the same partial self-gloss of the more elaborate phrase 'Chill fear almost [i.e. almost wholly?] seizes my limbs'.[27] The quotation is neither as exact nor as recognizable as Gloucester's, although its epic genealogy is clear. Line-terminal *occupat artus* occurs on one occasion in Lucan's *Civil War* (the poem also known under the title *Pharsalia*) and on two occasions in Virgil:

gelidos pauor occupat artus ('fear seizes their chilled limbs') (*Civil War*, 1.246)[28]

subitus tremor occupat artus ('sudden trembling seizes his limbs') (*Aeneid*, 7.446)

cur . . . tremor occupat artus ('why does trembling seize our limbs?') (*Aeneid*, 11.424)

In Lucan the phrase describes the reaction of the citizens of Ariminum, on the Italian side of the Rubicon, to Caesar's crossing. In Virgil, Turnus is the sufferer in book 7 and the speaker in book 11. Suffolk transfers the epithet *gelidus* from *artus* to *timor*, itself a metrically equivalent synonym for *pauor*.[29] The similarity of the sensation described to that in one of Virgil's most famous formulas – *soluuntur frigore membra* ('[his] limbs grew slack with chilling dread' (*Aeneid*, 1.92 and 12.951)) – increases the profile of the '*occupat artus*' locution, but also indicates that Suffolk (and Shakespeare) have reached further into the book of memory, or of commonplaces, and gone beyond the obvious. Perhaps it is going too far to call that avoidance of the obvious 'conspicuous', but to the extent that Suffolk's Latin allusion is part of an effort to fashion a heroic end it is clear that 1.92 (part of the Aeneas–Dido narrative dear to Queen Margaret) and 12.951 (the death of Turnus, perhaps the most famous in epic) offer better value. Moreover, the very inadequacy and incommensurability with epic precedent of Suffolk's death itself forms part of the allusive texture of the scene as a whole, and the likely blending of Lucan and Virgil at the verbal level would be thoroughly consonant with Shakespeare's use of both poets in designing the symbolic and ideological levels of this episode.

Shakespeare's staging of the scene, and the planting of clues to its Latin origins, works on parallels of setting, rhetoric and grisly spectacle. In both cases, the noble prisoner is captured at sea and taken aboard the enemy vessel; delivers a set-piece speech; is beheaded; the body is abandoned, though given more dignified treatment by a sympathetic party; and the head is saved, delivered to the sovereign, and apostrophized. Suffolk is a pale imitation even of Lucan's parodic Pompey, but his fate inaugurates a spate of decapitation that dominates Act 4, figuring the disintegration of the English polity as Pompey's decapitation the disintegration of the Roman.[30] Yet this allusion to Lucan is, so to speak, pregnant with an inevitable allusion to Virgil. One of the emotional high points of Aeneas's narration of the fall of Troy is the death of Priam (the basis of the Player's speech in *Hamlet*). Given the density of allusion to books 1 and 2 of the *Aeneid* established in the previous section (and adding to the circumstantial evidence that 3.2. 116–18 illustrates Margaret's extemporaneous

---

The Authorship of *Titus Andronicus* 4.1 Reconsidered', in *Shakespeare Survey 67* (Cambridge, 2014), pp. 69–84, which also takes allusive practice into account. Janette Dillon, *Language and Stage in Medieval and Renaissance England* (Cambridge, 1998) contains many insights on the cultural semiotics of Latin in post-Reformation theatre, but her reading of the politics of *2 Henry VI* does not systematically address the Latin of this play (pp. 202–19).

[27] *Pene* ('almost') emends F *Pine* (TLN 2285). The word raises mild textual doubts: its value to the sense is unclear, and it disrupts the dactylic hexameter rhythm of the Latin while raising the syllable count of the line from 10 (as in the surrounding blank verse) to 12. See also Binns, 'Latin Citations', p. 122.

[28] Lucan, *The Civil War*, ed. and trans. J. D. Duff (Cambridge, MA, 1928).

[29] Thomson offers a back-handed compliment: 'It needs a certain amount of scholarship to *misquote* in this way' (*Classics*, p. 90).

[30] For a genealogy of the imagery of bodily integrity and the 'head of state' in Roman political thought, and an incisive interpretation Lucan's treatment of the heads of Caesar and Pompey and of Pompey's decapitation in relation to this discourse, see Julie Mebane, 'Pompey's Head and the Body Politic in Lucan's *De Bello Civili*', *TAPA*, 146 (2016), forthcoming.

innovation upon Virgil's text, not Shakespeare's distance from it), it is possible that the germ of the Suffolk scene was the famous passage describing Priam's corpse:

> tot quondam populis terrisque superbum
> regnatorem Asiae. iacet ingens litore truncus,
> avulsumque umeris caput et sine nomine corpus
>
> (*Aeneid*, 2.557–9)

> he who was once lord of so many tribes and lands, the monarch of Asia. He lies, a huge trunk upon the shore, a head severed from the neck, a corpse without a name!

Two passages in Lucan evoke this moment. At the climax of *De Bello Civili* 1, a frenzied Roman matron cries out her visions after the taking of public auguries: *hunc ego fluminea deformis truncus harena / qui iacet, agnosco* ('I recognize that headless corpse lying on the river sands' (1.685–6)). The vision is realized when Pompey's death is narrated at length in book 8: *Litora Pompeium feriunt, truncusque vadosis / Huc illuc iactatur aquis* ('Pompey is battered on the shore, and his headless body is tossed hither and thither in the shallows' (8.698–9)). 'However', as Stephen Hinds teases out, 'what gives this correspondence its real edge is that the trunk of Priam in *Aeneid* 2 seems already itself to be an allusion to the trunk of Pompey, as noted already by Servius' in his ancient commentary.[31] The matron's prophecy constitutes a form of 'allusion troped as recognition', poised between the evocation of Pompey and of Priam, just as Virgil's *sine nomine* gestures at once towards the unstated name of the character and invites the reader to supply the historical name.[32]

In Lucan, an Egyptian takes the embalmed head of Pompey as a trophy to his enemy Caesar, who hypocritically deplores the offering (9.1010–108). In Shakespeare, Caesar's joy and tears are divided: Suffolk's head, saved by a Gentleman (4.1.146–9), is delivered to Queen Margaret, whose lamentations are genuine (4.4.1–6, 14–17), while King Henry's glee at the delivery of Cade's head exhibits a crudity highlighted by comparison with Caesar's artifice:

> KING HENRY.   The head of Cade! Great God, how
>   just art Thou!
> O let me view his visage, being dead,
> That living wrought me such exceeding trouble.
>
> (5.1.68–70)

Yet more macabre is the final distant echo between Queen Margaret's handling of Suffolk's head ('Here may his head lie on my throbbing breast' (4.4.5)) and Dido dandling Cupid disguised as Ascanius at *Aeneid*, 1.718–19: *haec pectore toto / haeret et interdum gremio fovet* ('with all her heart she clings to him and repeatedly fondles him in her lap').

There are other possible instances of variation and reversal. For example, while Pompey seeks to cover his head and face during his decapitation (a dignity denied him by his murderers), Suffolk begins the scene *sine nomine* but asserts his aristocratic dignity by uncovering his Order of the Garter ('Look on my George' (4.1.29)). The most acute irony, however, is a global one governing the entire allusion. The account of Pompey in the text to which Suffolk has alluded verbally is in fact much closer to the circumstances of his imminent execution than the way he puts it: 'savage islanders / Pompey the great'. Suffolk wishes to ennoble his own execution by drawing a parallel to Pompey's; believing his murders to be 'pirates' (the chief note he has sounded throughout the scene is class hostility towards his supposedly 'low' captors), he unconsciously assimilates Roman history to the present and produces 'savage

---

[31] Stephen Hinds, *Allusion and Intertext: Dynamics of Appropriation in Roman Poetry* (Cambridge, 1998), pp. 8–9. Servius: *Pompei tangit historiam, cum 'ingens' dicet, non 'magnus'* ('He alludes to Pompey's fate, though he says '*ingens*' for '*magnus*'). The allusion turns both on the image and Pompey's Latin name, Gnaeus Pompeius Magnus: the cognomen 'Magnus' is the adjective 'great' (in size, as well as other senses); Virgil's description of Priam's body as *ingens* ('huge') lightly veils the pun. See also Andreola Rossi, 'The Aeneid Revisited: The Journey of Pompey in Lucan's *Pharsalia*', *American Journal of Philology*, 121 (2000), 571–91; p. 587; Martha Malamud, 'Pompey's Head and Cato's Snakes', *Classical Philology*, 98 (2003), 31–44; pp. 35–7; and Mebane.

[32] Hinds, *Allusion and Intertext*, p. 9.

islanders'.[33] But Pompey's assailants are agents of King Ptolemy of Egypt, and the fatal sword is wielded by Servitius, a Roman who had once fought in his ranks. Suffolk's failure to respond to the charges articulated by the Lieutenant, who voices grievances articulated by nobles in the chronicle sources,[34] except with class hostility erases the tragic pathos that might have existed given the Virgilian signals in the allusion. A better orator (and politician) could have amplified these and created a connection with Queen Margaret's Virgilian rhetoric. Instead, Suffolk's effort to use Roman antiquity to magnify his death exposes him as an ineffective reader and self-fashioner. While Lucan's Pompey seeks to use his final speech improbably to fashion his death into that of a Stoic hero, Suffolk is instead 'like ambitious Sulla' (84) – a figure guilty of fomenting civil war, but unworthy of sustaining even ironic celebration in Roman epic.[35]

Lucan places great emphasis on Servitius, who effects the actual beheading, as Roman and as a former subordinate of Pompey:

> numquam superum caritura pudore
> Fabula: Romanus regi sic paruit ensis,
> Pellaeusque puer gladio tibi colla recidit,
> Magne, tuo.   (8.605–8)

a tale that will always bring reproach on Heaven – a Roman sword obeyed such a behest of the king, and the head of Magnus [Pompey] was cut off with his own sword by the Macedonian boy.

The assassination has been ordered by a child king, who, as Lentulus reminds Pompey, owes his rule to Pompey's patronage ('*Sceptra puer Ptolemaeus habet tibi debita, Magne*' (8.448)). King Henry, however, is not implicated in Suffolk's murder. It is rather ordered by a Lieutenant for whom Shakespeare devises a biography of service in Suffolk's household:

SUFFOLK.   Obscure and lousy swain, King Henry's
      blood,
   The honourable blood of Lancaster,
   Must not be shed by such a jaded groom.
      . . .
   How often hast thou waited at my cup,
   Fed from my trencher, kneeled down at the board

When I have feasted with Queen Margaret?
Remember it, and let it make thee crestfallen,
Ay, and allay this thy abortive pride.
How in our voiding lobby hast thou stood
And duly waited for my coming forth?
This hand of mine hath writ in thy behalf
And therefore shall it charm thy riotous tongue.
                              (4.1.50–64)

Suffolk is deluded in his expectation that his 'imperial tongue' (123) will govern the supposedly 'riotous tongue' of the 'lousy swain'. The Lieutenant's accusations are better ordered than Suffolk's mere harping on the string of degree. Shakespeare further extends the chronicles by making the Lieutenant of York's party. At this point in the action, Suffolk's fall and obscure death, recalling Pompey's, imply, although the parallel is not pursued in the play's symbolism beyond this level of implication, that the Caesarian initiative now lies with York. Suffolk's light is put out by the claimant to the throne 'whose hopeful colours / Advance our half-faced sun, striving to shine, / Under which is writ "*Invitis nubibus*"' (4.1.97–9). The emblem and its motto ('despite the clouds') figure the imperial self-assertion of the character whose handling of history, politics and Latinity has been the most assured throughout. In the war of words that constitutes one arc across which *2 Henry VI* traces the descent of England into a hideous Lucanian civil war, York is shown more fluent in the imperial tongue.

---

[33] On the social dimensions of the confrontation between Suffolk and his captors, especially the Lieutenant and the gentleman Walter Whitmore, see Thomas Cartelli, 'Suffolk and the Pirates: Disordered Relations in Shakespeare's *2 Henry VI*', in *A Companion to Shakespeare's Works*, vol. 2, ed. Richard Dutton and Jean Howard (Malden, MA, 2003), pp. 325–43.

[34] Cartelli, 'Suffolk and the Pirates', pp. 328–32.

[35] For the classic analysis of Lucan's representation of Pompey's fate as itself a severe burlesque and his final speech as a 'serious parody of the conventional Stoic last moment', see W. R. Johnson, *Momentary Monsters: Lucan and His Heroes* (Ithaca, NY, 1987), p. 81.

'I NEVER READ BUT': YORK, CADE AND THE SCHOOLROOM

Acts and images of reading are ubiquitous in *2 Henry VI*. Gloucester cannot finish reading the articles of peace (1.1.52–3), and figures the infamy that they carry as erasure, 'cancelling your fame, / Blotting your names from books of memory, / Razing the characters of your renown' (96–8). York comments indignantly 'I never read but England's kings have had / Large sums of gold and dowries with their wives' (1.1.125–6). The conjurors' papers, read aloud on stage, convict Eleanor, whose humiliations after her conviction include having verses pinned to her back (2.4.31). Queen Margaret seizes the petitions against Suffolk and tears them up before the petitioners' eyes (1.3. 20–40). York, we note, is himself a reader, whereas the Lancastrians' readings are incomplete, self-destructive, or lead to violent erasure. Yet it is York's scorn for, and assault upon, Henry's 'bookish rule' (1.1.260) that the play represents as threatening to pull down books and rule together in the Cade episode.

York's facility as a reader is illustrated by the conjuration episode. Latin partly sets the scene here, but it is the Latin of witchcraft, superstition and, by implication, of Roman Catholicism.

> *Here do the ceremonies belonging, and make the circle;*
> *Bolingbroke or Southwell reads, 'Coniuro te', etc.*
> *It thunders and lightens terribly, then the* Spirit *riseth.*
> SPIRIT. *Adsum.* (1.4.23)

Asnath gives the answer of a good grammar school pupil (*adsum*, 'present!'), although the F orthography ('*Ad sum*') suggests he may not have earned a place at the very front of the schoolroom. Southwell as the reader of the 'coniuro te' would be consonant with Bolingbroke's prior instructions 'Mother Jourdain, be you prostrate and grovel on the earth; John Southwell, read you; and let us to our work' (11–12). The stage business prescribed and implied in Q is somewhat different: the witch Margery Jourdain calls for a circle in which she will lie to 'talke and whisper with the diuels below, / And conjure them for to

obey my will'; this speech is followed by the directions 'She lies downe vpon her face. / Bullenbrooke makes a Cirkle' (TLN 497–8); Southwell is not mentioned. In a six-line speech 'Bullenbrooke' invokes the spirit ('Askalon' in this text) with the culminating command '*Askalon, Assenda, Assenda*' before the direction 'It thunders and lightens, and then the spirit riseth vp' (TLN 505). In this version, therefore, the audience may not have the benefit of a Latin conjuration, though '*Assenda*' is presumably a stab at Latin *ascende* ('arise!'; cf. the spelling '*Sosetus* [i.e. Cocytus] lake' at TLN 501), and Latin may be the language of the witch's whispers. Jourdain's words may in fact have been made an audible part of the performance, conjurations being theatrical set-pieces that invite elaboration.[36]

Another facet of the conjuration unique to Q is the self-consciousness and explicitness of its sponsor regarding the fact that the participants are constructing a scene of dictation:

> *Elnor.* Here sir *Iohn*, take this scrole of paper here,
> Wherein is writ the questions you shall aske,
> And I will stand vpon this Tower here,
> And here the spirit what it saies to you,
> And to my questions, write the answeres downe.
> (TLN 483–7)

The evocation of the schoolroom in the spirit's '*Adsum*' (F only) answers well to the scenario of question, answer and writing – conducted under the sign of the Latin language – spelled out by the Duchess (Q only).

When the nobles arrive to break up the scene, York dispels this atmosphere with a crisp classical quotation from Cicero's treatise debunking divination:

---

[36] See Alan C. Dessen and Leslie Thomson, *A Dictionary of Stage Directions in English Drama, 1580–1642* (Cambridge, 1999), s. v. 'circle', 'conjure'; Manley, 'Strange's Men to Pembroke's Men', p. 262. Scene 3 of Marlowe's *Doctor Faustus* is a familiar instance of a long Latin conjuration.

YORK. Now pray, my lord, let's see the devil's
   writ.
   What have we here? *(Reads.)*
   The duke yet lives that Henry shall depose,
   But him outlive, and die a violent death.
   Why, this is just
   Aio te, Aeacida, Romanos vincere posse.
   Well, to the rest.   (*2 Henry VI*, 1.4.57–63)

There are some further textual complications
around this passage. Knowles, like most editors
since Rowe, restores the form of the Latin quotation from Ennius's *Annales* given in modern
editions of Cicero's *De Divinatione* ('I declare,
O son of Aeacus, you the Romans can defeat'
(2.116)). F has '*Aio Æacida Romanos vincere posso*'
(TLN 691; 'I declare, O son of Aeacus, the
Romans can defeat'); *posso* is a simple misprint,
but *Æacida* without *te* jeopardizes the clarity, as it
were, of the ambiguity. The Oxford *Complete
Works*, following J. W. Binns, introduces an
alternative emendation that reestablishes the
symmetry, printing accusative *Aeacidam* for vocative *Aeacida*, i.e. '*Aio Aeacidam, Romanos vincere
posse*' (1.4.59; 'I declare the son of Aeacus the
Romans can defeat').[37] That edition omits, however, York's utterance of the text to which he is
reacting (1.4.59–60 in Knowles); we do not hear
the prophecy spoken again until it is handed to
the King at 2.1.180–1. York's speech is not present in Q, and the editors supply at 1.4.57 the
stage direction '*Buckingham gives him the writings*',
duplicating 2.1.178. By not also duplicating the
prophecy itself, a metapoetic irony may be
occluded, of a kind which ties together several
of the uses of classical antiquity analyzed in this
section.[38] F reveals York's cognitive reaction to
'*The duke yet lives that Henry shall depose, / But him
outlive, and die a violent death*': he immediately
associates it with a *locus classicus* for ambiguous
political prophecy from that prime mover of the
humanist classroom, Cicero.

As Cicero removes the line from its context in
Ennius, so the line circulated in antiquity and the
Renaissance free of Cicero's text: St Augustine paraphrases Cicero's example in *De Civitate Dei* 3.17;
and, as William Poole notes, it was used to illustrate

the stylistic vice of *amphibologia* in the *Tabulae* of
Mosellanus, a much reprinted textbook on the
topic in use in English grammar schools.[39]
I would suggest, however, that Shakespeare
might have consulted the quotation in the context
of Cicero's *De Divinatione* 2.116. This treatise is in
two parts: in the first, Cicero's brother Quintus
puts the (Stoic) case for the credibility of divination; in the second, Cicero offers a refutation. It is
thus for the purpose of debunking that he adduces
Ennius's line:

Quis enim est qui credit Apollinis ex oraculo Pyrrho esse
responsum:
   aio te, Aeacida, Romanos vincere posse?
   Primum Latine Apollo numquam locutus est; deinde
ista sors inaudita Graecis est; praeterea Pyrrhi temporibus
iam Apollo versus facere desierat; postremo … hanc
amphiboliam versus intellegere potuisset, 'vincere te
Romanos' nihilo magis in se quam in Romanos valere.

For instance, nobody believes Ennius when he says
that Apollo's oracle gave the following response to
Pyrrhus:
   O son of Aeacus, my prediction is
   That you the Roman army will defeat.

---

[37] As Binns noted, a tilde or stroke over the vowel to indicate
abbreviation of final *–m* was a ubiquitous piece of shorthand
easily overlooked in printing, so the manuscript may have
read *Aeacidā* ('Latin Citations', p. 123).

[38] Manley notes that the F arrangement 'perhaps solidifies
the ironic foundation of the play's prophetic structure,
but at the price of local redundancy', whereas the
Q arrangement appears to be narratively superior and
fulfils the evident aim of the revisions to underscore
Eleanor's guilt ('Strange's Men to Pembroke's Men',
p. 271). I agree, except to argue that the apparent local
redundancy of F emphasizes the prophecies at a moment
when they are marked as 'fake', increasing the dramatic
value of their vindication in the ultimate fates of three
anti-Gloucester conspirators (compare Dillon, *Language
and Stage*, pp. 211–12), and allows for a specific characterization of York in terms of reading practice.

[39] William Poole, 'The Vices of Style', in *Renaissance Figures of
Speech*, ed. Sylvia Adamson, Gavin Alexander and
Katrin Ettenhuber (Cambridge, 2008), pp. 237–51: 'This
was the very example given by Mosellanus for that vice in
his textbook; here Shakespeare may be directly recalling his
time in the classroom' (p. 248).

In the first place Apollo never spoke in Latin; second, that oracle is unknown to the Greeks; third, in the days of Pyrrhus Apollo had already ceased making verses, and, finally ... Pyrrhus would have had sense enough to see that the equivocal line – 'You the Roman army will defeat' – was no more favourable to him than to the Romans.[40]

Latine Apollo numquam locutus est: away with him – he speaks Latin! Cicero's sceptical emphasis on the artificiality of the text as prophecy, in addition to an emphasis on the artifice of its composition that feeds into Renaissance rhetorical textbooks, may have helped the playwright use the character's words to point out his own technique behind them.[41] York first reads the English couplet and pulls from his book of memory a classical analogue ('This is just', i.e. 'This is nothing more than' the Ennian *'Aio te, Aeacida, Romanos vincere posse'*). In terms of composition, however, the playwright begins with a knowledge of the line in *De Divinatione* and devises a contextually apt English version based on the same principle of grammatical ambiguity. York knows how an educated charlatan – or poet – would exercise *inventio* to compose an oracular couplet. (One could also note that a continuous reading, or even a roving eye looking up the page from this section, might have noticed that the previous section concerned a prophecy over the war of Pompey and Caesar (2.114), but not every such textual contingency needs to be conjured.)

In sharp contrast to the epic delusions of the Lancastrians, York's classicism is erudite (e.g. 'Telamonius' (5.1.26), 'Achilles' spear' (5.1.100)) and subordinated to argument and action. Yet part of his activation of the dark side of humanism, the skilled Machiavellian union of force and fraud, is to set on the rebellion of Jack Cade, a rebellion assimilated by Shakespeare to aspects of the stage tradition of peasants' revolts, but with a special emphasis on Cade's hostility to literacy and pedagogy. Richard Helgerson has argued that *2 Henry VI* is both the product and reflection of a class tension between actor-centred and writer-centred models of theatre. Writers with university educations or otherwise aspiring to gentry status composed plays less sympathetic to the commons and to forms of popular culture represented by clowns such as Richard Tarleton. Shakespeare, he argues, mingles kings and clowns in a manner less conducive to popular solidarity than the authors of history plays for Henslowe's companies.[42] Cade's attack on the education system is especially pointed: 'if Cade's war on gentlemen would destroy the social and demographic foundation of the new authors' theatre, his campaign against literacy would destroy its means of production'.[43] This is part of an argument for seeing Act 4 as evidence that the politics of this play are more anti-popular than popular. Helgerson's perspective seems especially persuasive in the context of the present argument, which constructs a more literary *2 Henry VI* than is typically recognized, although the alternative view has several adherents.[44]

The anti-literacy campaign is a Shakespearian innovation. Hall gave a picture at odds with the stage version precisely in this respect:

This capitayn not onely suborned by techers, but also enforced by pryvye scholemasters, assembled together a great company of talle personages: assuring them, that their attempt was both honorable to God and the king, and also profitable to the common wealth, promisyng them, that if either by force or pollicie, they might once take the kyng, the Quene, & other their counsaillers, that neither fiftenes should hereafter be demaunded, nor once any imposicions, or tax should be spoken of.[45]

---

[40] Cicero, *De Senectute, De Amicitia, De Divinatione*, ed. and trans. William Armistead Falconer (Cambridge, MA, 1923), pp. 500–3.

[41] See also *De Divinatione* 2.115: *partim ambiguis, et quae ad dialecticum deferenda sint* ('and some oracles are so equivocal that they must be submitted to a logician to construe them' (translation modified)).

[42] See Richard Helgerson, *Forms of Nationhood: The Elizabethan Writing of England* (Chicago, 1992), pp. 200–3, 237.

[43] Helgerson, *Forms of Nationhood*, p. 213.

[44] See, for example, Annabel Patterson, *Shakespeare and the Popular Voice* (Oxford, 1989); and Fitter, 'Historical Contexts'.

[45] Geoffrey Bullough, *Narrative and Dramatic Sources of Shakespeare*, vol. 3 (London, 1960), p. 114.

Teachers and schoolmasters? Compare the chronicle account with Cade's indictment of Lord Saye:

Thou hast most traitorously corrupted the youth of the realm in erecting a grammar school; and, whereas before our forefathers had no other books but the score and the tally, thou hast caused printing to be used and, contrary to the King his crown and dignity, thou hast built a paper-mill. It will be proved to thy face that thou hast men about thee that usually talk of a noun and a verb, and such abominable words as no Christian ear can endure to hear. (4.7.29–37)

Saye's is the third staged killing in Act 4 that has turned on learning. Preliminary to it is the fate of the Clerk of Chartham:

WEAVER.   The clerk of Chartham: he can write and read and cast account.
CADE.   O, monstrous!
WEAVER.   We took him setting boys' copies.
CADE.   Here's a villain!
WEAVER.   H'as a book in his pocket with red letters in't.
CADE.   Nay, then, he is a conjuror. (4.2.78–84)

Cade anticipates the peremptoriness of Lewis Carroll's Queen of Hearts, and the implicit parallel drawn in the last quoted line to the treason charges levelled against the clerk and the Duchess of Gloucester has some of *Alice in Wonderland*'s zaniness to it, but here the command to 'Hang him with his pen and inkhorn about his neck' is, one assumes, duly executed (100–1). To teach writing becomes a capital crime; the records of the realm are ordered burned, the power of Parliament shall lie wholly in the mouth of this autodidact whose unschooled invention brooks no master (4.7.11–12):

BROTHER.   Jack Cade, the Duke of York hath taught you this.
CADE.   *[aside]* He lies, for I invented it myself.
(4.2.144–5)

This transformation, under Cade's misrule, of the power of writing into the power of speech is illustrated afresh in the macabre scene where a messenger arrives just as Cade declares 'it shall be treason for

any that calls me other than Lord Mortimer' (4.6. 5–6). 'Jack Cade! Jack Cade!' calls the breathless soldier arriving with news of an imminent attack, who is killed on the spot for breaking a statute instantaneously in effect though impossible for the transgressor to have learned. Coolly, the Butcher reads the message of troop movements, taking advantage of the medium of writing.

The confrontation with Saye puts both writing and oratory on the dock: Saye attempts to use humanist eloquence to acquit himself of the charge of humanism:

SAYE.   You men of Kent –
BUTCHER.   What say you of Kent?
SAYE.   Nothing but this: 'tis *bona terra, mala gens*.
CADE.   Away with him, away with him! He speaks Latin.
SAYE.   Hear me but speak, and bear me where you will.
    Kent, in the *Commentaries* Caesar writ,
    Is termed the civil'st place of all this isle.
    Sweet is the country, because full of riches,
    The people liberal, valiant, active, wealthy;
    Which makes me hope you are not void of pity.
(4.7.50–9)

Saye embraces the paradox of his situation by building his defence upon a Latin quip and a classical citation. Here, of all places in *2 Henry VI*, we have evidence of humanist eloquence moving a stage audience in consistency with the ideal of the schoolroom, but the paradox in which Saye is trapped is too watertight: 'I feel remorse in myself with his words', says Cade for the benefit of the theatre audience, 'but I'll bridle it. He shall die, an it be but for pleading so well for his life' (4.7.98–100). As Martin Dzelzainis comments, 'Cade's indictment of Say attacks the very foundations of English humanism', whereas it was 'Shakespeare's grounding in rhetoric' that 'provided both the stimulus and the means to amplify the political content of his plays'.[46] 'Nor is it quite the

---

[46] Martin Dzelzainis, 'Shakespeare and Political Thought', in *A Companion to Shakespeare*, ed. David Scott Kastan (Oxford, 1999), pp. 100–16; pp. 103–4.

case', Dzelzainis goes on to caution, 'that Ciceronian humanism was entirely eclipsed by the new Tacitean version', and the qualification suits the period as a whole.[47] Yet this closely tracks how *2 Henry VI* represents the eclipse of Gloucester and the replacement of his Ciceronian statecraft with competing and internecine imperial ambitions on the part of Suffolk and York.

A final irony. On the rebound, as it were, from his access of pity, Cade returns to the carnivalesque mode in an unwittingly self-undermining fashion: 'The proudest peer in the realm shall not wear a head on his shoulders, unless he pay me tribute; there shall not a maid be married, but she shall pay to me her maidenhead ere they have it; men shall hold of me *in capite*' (4.7.112–16). Editors note how '*in capite*' continues the punning on the legal term for a tenant who holds his lease from the king. It foreshadows the handling of his head after his decapitation. But it also prompts our indignant accusation: *Et tu, Ioannes?* At the apex of Fortune's revolution, the Jack Cade of F stumbles into treasonous facility with the anathematized language. 'He speaks Latin' suddenly recalls Simpcox's suspicious ability correctly to identify colours despite his claim to have been blind from birth (see 2.1.122–6). Perhaps Hall's 'pryvye scholemasters' still lurk in the background.

The Latinity and allusiveness of *2 Henry VI* finally demonstrates not merely that from his very earliest ventures in dramatizing history Shakespeare was often struck with a Roman thought. Shakespeare's quotations and allusions cluster and characterize, interweaving Virgilian pity and Lucanian terror, and, taken together, subtend a critical thematization that placed his culture's whole system of schooling, erudition and habits of thought under scrutiny. In so far as humanist education can generate a Ciceronian governor like Gloucester, or a playwright like Shakespeare, it may be commendable. In so far as it generates the delusive and disintegrative grandeur of *Magni manqués* like Suffolk and York, it may be deplorable. One could frame the latter point in yet sharper and more dialectical fashion: the fragmentary and tendentious humanism practiced by the self-assertive nobility, the severing and instrumentalizing of *capites* (headings) and *corpora* (works) in the rhetorical domain, not only becomes hideously literal, but unleashes a destructiveness that would annihilate the conditions for existence of humanism's better part.

---

[47] Dzelzainis, 'Political Thought', p. 115.

SHAKESPEARE AND THE OTHER VIRGIL: PITY AND *IMPERIUM* IN *TITUS ANDRONICUS*

PATRICK GRAY

The influence of Virgil's *Aeneid* in Shakespeare's *Titus Andronicus* is more extensive than has been recognized to date, largely because Shakespeare studies, surprisingly, still has not entirely acknowledged or addressed the more ambiguous reading of the *Aeneid* put forward in recent decades by the so-called 'Harvard School' of Virgil criticism. This interpretation of the *Aeneid* draws attention to Virgil's sympathy for human suffering, especially his pity for the fallen enemies of Rome. Revisionary critics such as Adam Parry, Wendell Clausen and Michael Putnam argue that the 'melancholy' tone of the poem, resigned, mournful and at times finely ironic, arises from a sense of sorrow at the human cost of establishing the Roman Empire, undermining its ostensible purpose as Augustan propaganda. Virgil's 'private voice' of compassion undercuts his 'public voice' of praise for Augustus's *pax Romana*. Although associated today with criticism that emerged in America in the wake of the Vietnam War, as Craig Kallendorf has shown, this 'pessimistic' reading of the *Aeneid*, what he calls 'the other Virgil', was available in England in the Renaissance, and arguably dates back to antiquity.[1] As apparent from his allusions to Virgil in *Titus Andronicus*, Shakespeare's reading of the *Aeneid* is in keeping with this vision. Virgil's epic is the touchstone and the model for his own critique of *Romanitas*.

Writing in 1978, John Velz complains of 'the neglect of Virgil as an influence on Shakespeare's Rome', and observes that 'there is much untouched ground'.[2] Writing a few years later, in 1986, Robert Miola also sees 'extant criticism on Vergil's presence in Shakespeare's art' as 'surprisingly slight and desultory'.[3] Since then the connection between Shakespeare and Virgil has attracted more attention; critics, however, have tended to focus either on *The Tempest* or on *Antony and Cleopatra*. Miola himself sees Virgil as a 'pervasive presence, a deep source', in Shakespeare's plays, but only 'in Shakespeare's final phase, as in *Hamlet*'. Like Aeneas's ruthless, murderous rampage at the end of the *Aeneid*, Hamlet's 'final revenge' presents a 'paradox' which Miola sees as 'central' to Shakespearian tragedy, as well as Virgil's epic: 'the man of *pietas* and humanity acts in impious *furor*'. In *Titus Andronicus*, a much earlier play, 'allusions to Aeneas and Lavinia' are in contrast 'crudely and baldly inappropriate'. The *Aeneid* is 'stitched onto the play rather than woven into its fabric'.[4] Like Miola, Colin Burrow sees the *Aeneid* in *Titus Andronicus* as a 'counter-plot' to the 'main narratives'. The *Aeneid* 'represents an alternative kind of Roman empire to the one presented on stage': a counterfactual, more optimistic vision of

---

[1] Craig Kallendorf, *The Other Virgil: 'Pessimistic' Readings of the 'Aeneid' in Early Modern Culture* (Oxford, 2007).

[2] John W. Velz, 'The Ancient World in Shakespeare: Authenticity or Anachronism? A Retrospect', in *Shakespeare Survey 31* (Cambridge, 1978), pp. 1–12; p. 12, n. 5.

[3] Robert S. Miola, 'Vergil in Shakespeare: From Allusion to Imitation', in *Vergil at 2000: Commemorative Essays on the Poet and his Influence*, ed. John D. Bernard (New York, 1986), pp. 241–58; p. 241.

[4] Miola, 'Vergil in Shakespeare', pp. 251, 250, 242.

Rome. Virgil is 'a distant, strangled voice'.[5] Heather James argues that Shakespeare in *Titus Andronicus* displaces 'Vergilian authority'; the play 'performs an Ovidian critique of Rome', replacing the 'imperial epic of Vergil' with the 'counter-epic of Ovid'.[6]

Not only in *Titus Andronicus* but in general, critics tend to see Shakespeare as much more Ovidian than Virgilian. In his study of Shakespeare's sources, T. W. Baldwin casts Ovid as 'Shakespeare's master of poetry'.[7] For Burrow, Ovid is 'the Latin poet who had the greatest influence on Shakespeare'.[8] Writing in 1990, Charles and Michelle Martindale conclude, 'Shakespeare has little of the Virgilian sensibility and frequently Ovidianises Virgilian matter'.[9] A decade later, Charles Martindale can see no reason to change his mind: 'Shakespeare is not usefully to be described as a Virgilian poet. By that I mean that his reading of Virgil did not result in a profound modification of his sensibility and imagination'.[10] Burrow, writing a decade later still, feels uneasy about this neat dismissal. 'There is perhaps something slightly nineteenth-century about Martindale's judgment ... Shakespeare was not an imperial and melancholy kind of guy, and so Virgil sat shallow in his mind'. Nevertheless, even Burrow tends to cast Shakespeare's debt to Virgil in terms of 'allusion and stylistic echo' rather than 'sensibility'.[11]

Politically, Heather James is reluctant to align Shakespeare with an author, Virgil, whom she believes he saw as an advocate of Roman imperialism. James acknowledges that 'Vergil himself formulated two distinct approaches to Augustan empire in the *Aeneid*, one panegyrical and the other interrogative': 'Vergil chose to support Augustan ideology in the formal design of the *Aeneid* and test it through "impertinent" questions dispersed throughout the poem'. James is not inclined to grant, however, that Shakespeare himself might have seen the 'interrogative' voice in the *Aeneid* as Virgil's own. 'Literary tradition is not always known for its justice, and so the panegyrical tradition is, in the Renaissance, mostly known as Vergilian while the interrogative is more often

associated with Ovid'.[12] Kallendorf's study of 'the other Virgil' in the Renaissance, published a decade later, gives some reason to doubt this conclusion. James, however, associates Virgil almost exclusively with what she calls the 'panegyrical' voice. Virgil is in practice, for Shakespeare, she suggests, a propagandist, an apologist on behalf of the Roman Empire. He is the 'authority' whom Ovid subverts, rather than himself a voice of subversion.[13]

In terms of temperament, Shakespeare also seems far removed from the world-weary tone of the *Aeneid*: the sadness Aeneas himself describes simply, poignantly, as *lacrimae rerum* ('tears for [the way] things [are]') (1.462). Matthew Arnold observes, 'Over the whole of the great poem of Virgil, over the whole *Aeneid*, there rests an ineffable melancholy ... a sweet, a touching sadness'. He imagines Virgil as 'a man of the most delicate genius ... the most sensitive nature, in a great and overwhelming world'.[14] Shakespeare in contrast seems hearty, exuberant, unrestrained and cheerfully unrefined. As Dr Johnson speculates, citing Thomas Rymer, 'his natural disposition ... led him to comedy'.[15] Looking deeper into Arnold's

---

[5] Colin Burrow, *Shakespeare and Classical Antiquity* (Oxford, 2013), p. 75.

[6] Heather James, *Shakespeare's Troy: Drama, Politics, and the Translation of Empire* (Cambridge, 1997), p. 44.

[7] T. W. Baldwin, *William Shakspere's Small Latine and Lesse Greeke*, vol. 2 (Urbana, 1944), p. 418.

[8] Burrow, *Classical Antiquity*, p. 92.

[9] Charles Martindale and Michelle Martindale, *Shakespeare and the Uses of Antiquity: An Introductory Essay* (London, 1990), p. 43.

[10] Charles Martindale, 'Shakespeare and Virgil', in *Shakespeare and the Classics*, ed. Charles Martindale and A. B. Taylor (Cambridge, 2004), pp. 89–106; pp. 89–90.

[11] Burrow, *Classical Antiquity*, p. 51.

[12] James, *Shakespeare's Troy*, pp. 24, 27, 43.

[13] Martindale and Martindale, *Uses of Antiquity*, p. 43.

[14] Matthew Arnold, 'On the Modern Element in Literature', in Matthew Arnold, *On the Classical Tradition*, ed. R. H. Super (Ann Arbor, MI, 1960), pp. 18–38; p. 35.

[15] Samuel Johnson, 'Preface to Shakespeare', in *Johnson on Shakespeare*, ed. Arthur Sherbo (New Haven, CT, 1968), p. 69; cf. Thomas Rymer, 'A Short View of Tragedy', in

assessment, however, as well as more recent studies of the *Aeneid*, it may be possible to discern some common ground. As Michael Putnam explains, 'the past century has seen a revolution in the interpretation of Virgil'.[16]

The traditional or 'optimistic' interpretation of the *Aeneid* finds in Aeneas an ideal hero, and in the epic as a whole a celebration of the political achievement of Rome, especially, Virgil's patron, Augustus. Rome establishes civilization through self-discipline and the conquest of barbaric opposition. This sense of the *Aeneid* was set forth at the beginning of the twentieth century by two German scholars, Richard Heinze and Viktor Pöschl, and defended in English by T. S. Eliot.[17] After World War II, however, a revisionist, 'pessimistic' school of interpretation began to emerge. 'We hear two distinct voices in the *Aeneid*', Adam Parry argues, 'a public voice of triumph, and a private voice of regret'. Taking up Arnold's sense of Virgil's 'melancholy', Parry presents 'the whole mood of the poem, the sadness, the loss, the frustration', 'the sense of emptiness', as 'produced by the personal accents of sorrow over human and heroic values lost ... Virgil continually insists on the public glory of the Roman achievement, the establishment of peace and order ... But he insists equally terribly on the terrible price one must pay for this glory ... human freedom, love, personal loyalty ... are lost in the service of what is grand, monumental, and impersonal: the Roman state'.[18]

Other critics central to this new school of thought include, in America, Wendell Clausen and Michael Putnam, and in England, Deryck Williams and Oliver Lyne. 'How shall we define the private voice of the poet?', Williams asks. 'We associate it most strongly with Dido and the apparently senseless suffering of her tragedy; and with Turnus who does what he thinks right and loses his life; and with the old king Priam; with Pallas and Euryalus and Lausus and Camilla and the countless warriors who fall in battle ... It is the world of the individual, not the state; a world of *lacrimae*, not *imperium*'.[19] At the heart of this new strain of Virgilian criticism is an emphasis on

Virgil's surprising compassion for the victims of Aeneas's efforts to found to Rome. The human cost of that political accomplishment undermines its putative value. According to Clausen, Aeneas's victory is 'Pyrrhic'. The *Aeneid* 'moves us' because it 'enlists our sympathies on the side of loneliness, suffering, defeat'.[20] Parry finds in the *Aeneid* a 'fine paradox': 'all the wonders of the most powerful institution the world has ever known are not necessarily of greater importance than the emptiness of human suffering'.[21]

Adumbrations of this reading of the *Aeneid* can been seen in earlier criticism, particularly in the tradition arising out of Richard Heinze's account of Virgil's distinctive *Empfindung der handelnden Personen*.[22] *Empfindung* is difficult to translate; essentially, Heinze observes that Virgil identifies with his characters (*der handelnden Personen*); his narration leads the reader to adopt their 'emotional point of view' (*Empfindung*). Brooks Otis, although for the most part opposed to the Harvard School, adopts and refines this concept as what he calls 'empathy', and it looms large, as well, in the work of the influential Italian critics Gian Biagio Conte and Antonio La Penna.[23] As Conte explains, 'the

---

The Critical Works of Thomas Rymer, ed. Curt Zimansky (New Haven, CT, 1956), p. 169.

[16] Michael C. J. Putnam, *Virgil's 'Aeneid': Interpretation and Influence* (Chapel Hill, NC, 1995), p. 22.

[17] Richard Heinze, *Virgils epische Technik* (Leipzig, 1903), translated by Hazel Harvey, David Harvey and Fred Robertson as *Virgil's Epic Technique* (Berkeley, CA, 1993); T. S. Eliot, *What is a Classic?* (London, 1945); Viktor Pöschl, *Die Dichtkunst Vergils: Bild und Symbol in der Aeneis* (Innsbruck, 1950), translated by Gerda Seligson as *The Art of Vergil: Image and Symbol in the 'Aeneid'* (Ann Arbor, MI, 1962).

[18] Adam Parry, 'The Two Voices of Virgil's *Aeneid*', *Arion: A Journal of Humanities and the Classics*, 2 (1963), 66–80; pp. 71, 69, 78.

[19] R. D. Williams, 'The Purpose of the Aeneid', in *Oxford Readings in Vergil's 'Aeneid'*, ed. S. J. Harrison (Oxford, 1990), pp. 1–36; p. 26.

[20] Wendell Clausen, 'An Interpretation of the *Aeneid*', *Harvard Studies in Classical Philology*, 68 (1964), 139–47; pp. 146, 144.

[21] Parry, 'Two Voices', p. 80.

[22] Heinze, *epische Technik*, p. 362.

[23] Brooks Otis, *Virgil: A Study in Civilized Poetry* (Oxford, 1964). For Otis's influence on Virgil studies in Italy, see

poet's narrative voice lets itself be saturated by the subjectivity of the person within the narrative'.[24] These critics' sense of Virgil's emotional engagement with his characters, especially, Rome's enemies, also informs R. O. A. M. Lyne's reimagination of what Parry describes as Virgil's own 'private voice'. Wary of ascribing intention, rather than 'two voices', both Virgil's own, Lyne prefers to speak of an 'epic voice' and 'further voices'. 'Further voices add to, comment upon, question, and occasionally subvert the implications of the epic voice.'[25] Drawing upon narratology, Don Fowler speaks in like vein of what he calls 'deviant focalization'.[26]

In his study of 'the other Virgil' in the Renaissance, Kallendorf sets out 'to show in some detail that there is a continuous tradition of "pessimistic" readings that extends through the early modern period in Europe'. As an opportunity to explore Lyne's concept of 'further voices', and in keeping with the larger tradition of what Otis describes as Virgil's 'subjective style', he turns to Shakespeare's *Tempest*, alongside Ercilla's *La Araucana*, and asks how such a reading of the *Aeneid* might conceivably have influenced Shakespeare's understanding of colonization.[27] Citing Marilyn Desmond, he notes that 'classical studies has just recently begun to develop a postcolonial reading of Virgil', one which emerges out of these critics' sense of Virgil's ambivalence.[28] Desmond writes, 'This strain of Virgil criticism, with its emphasis on the "second voice" or the "doubleness of vision" in the text, complements the focus of a critical attempt to dismantle imperial or colonial discourses of the sort exemplified by the "imperial Virgil".'[29]

Kallendorf draws attention to Caliban, in particular, as an example of a Virgilian 'further voice': 'Caliban occupies a space within the play that Prospero never succeeds in closing off ... Caliban's claims to the island are never refuted; he is overpowered but on this point cannot be silenced.' He has 'an eloquence of his own'; his curses have 'their own kind of power'. 'Thus,' Kallendorf concludes, 'while the main thrust of *The Tempest* is pro-imperial ... the "further voices", especially Caliban's, remind us of the cost of empire, just as in the *Aeneid*.'[30] In a recent essay on empathy and *The Tempest*, Leah Whittington presents a more developed version of this argument, comparing Shakespeare's treatment of Caliban to Virgil's surprisingly sympathetic account of the death of the arch-villain Mezentius. Shakespeare, she argues, imitates 'the poetic strategy of *empatheia* in Virgil's *Aeneid* ... When Virgil allows the narrator's voice to be fragmented and segregated, as different characters emerge to tell the story from their own unique perspectives, to represent the world *in persona* as they see it, the poem reaches out to the reader like an orator – or an actor – trying to engage the faculty of empathy'.[31]

One charge, nevertheless, which continues to be levelled against this kind of 'pessimistic' or 'ambivalent' reading of the *Aeneid* is that of anachronism, more specifically, 'Christian anachronism'.[32] Are our soft hearts nowadays, reading Virgil's epic, merely a projection of our own post-Christian prejudice towards pity? A symptom of what Nietzsche would call *décadence*? As A. D. Nuttall observes, 'Christianity has happened; we are all now either Christian or post-Christian.' Even when secularized, stripped of former Christian theological

---

Don Fowler, 'Deviant Focalisation in Virgil's *Aeneid*', *Proceedings of the Cambridge Philological Society*, 36 (1990), 42–63; pp. 54–8. Antonio La Penna, *L'impossibile giustificazione della storia: un'interpretazione di Virgilio* (Rome, 2005).

[24] Gian Biago Conte, *The Poetry of Pathos: Studies in Virgilian Epic*, ed. S. J. Harrison (Oxford, 2007), p. 30.

[25] R. O. A. M. Lyne, *Further Voices in Vergil's 'Aeneid'* (Oxford, 1987), p. 2.

[26] Fowler, 'Deviant Focalisation'.

[27] For Virgil's 'subjective style', see Otis, *Civilized Poetry*, pp. 41–96.

[28] Kallendorf, *Other Virgil*, pp. viii, 73.

[29] Marilyn Desmond, *Reading Dido: Gender, Textuality, and the Medieval Mind* (Minneapolis, 1994), p. 7.

[30] Kallendorf, *Other Virgil*, p. 124.

[31] Leah Whittington, 'Shakespeare's Virgil: Empathy and *The Tempest*', in *Shakespeare and Renaissance Ethics*, ed. Patrick Gray and John D. Cox (Cambridge, 2014), pp. 99, 105.

[32] Richard F. Thomas, *Virgil and the Augustan Reception* (Cambridge, 2001), p. xii, n. 4.

justification, our assumptions about ethics, as well as politics, have been indelibly shaped historically by 'a transition from an ethical philosophy which essentially sets personal love and devotion to one side to a philosophy which makes personal love the centre of the ethical life'.[33] We are the legacy, in other words, of the latter-day 'transvaluation of values' which Nietzsche condemns as 'the slave revolt in morals'.

One response to this charge is to argue that an 'ambivalent' reading of Virgil's *Aeneid* has been in play since antiquity, independent of Christianity. In a book on what he calls the 'Augustan reception' of Virgil's epic, Richard Thomas looks closely at one of the earliest pagan commentators on Virgil's *Aeneid*, Servius, and reconstructs his opposition: other critics, lost to posterity, whom Servius refuses to name. Addressing them simply as *alii* ('others'), or with various insults, Servius works throughout his commentary to debunk their misgivings in favour of his own more familiar, 'optimistic' take on the poem. In this fashion, Thomas argues, traditional 'Augustan' readers over the centuries have actively suppressed Virgil's intentional subversion of his patron's politics. Thomas casts Virgil himself as a kind of Shostakovich, working against the grain of his imperial commission. Ovid in particular, he maintains, who knew both Virgil and Augustus, understood his fellow poet's predicament; he is not a rival so much as a secret sympathizer.

Another response, however, to the charge of what Thomas calls 'Christian anachronism' is to argue that the *Aeneid* is proleptic. In the third century, Lactantius reimagined Virgil's fourth eclogue as an unwitting prophesy of the coming Messiah, and the sense of Virgil as a pagan forerunner of Christianity has endured ever since. In the twentieth century it was put forward most forcefully by Theodor Haecker in his book, *Virgil, the Father of the West*, and from there picked up and promulgated by T. S. Eliot in his influential essay, 'Vergil and the Christian World'.[34] Haecker appropriates Tertullian's concept of the *anima naturaliter Christiana* and applies it to Virgil, arguing that the poet had an 'adventist' presentiment of the coming of Christ.[35]

Virgil might also be considered 'naturally Christian', however, in another, less mystical sense. In an essay on what he calls 'the Stoic in love', Nuttall reconsiders Haecker's appeal to Tertullian. Virgil, he suggests, anticipates Christianity, not as an inadvertent prophet, but as an ethical avant-garde. His compassion adumbrates the moral revolution, Christianity, which would follow soon thereafter. Christianity, in other words, emerges in response to the same kind of dissatisfaction with the prevailing Roman ethos which Virgil articulates in his epic. It is the public triumph of misgivings about Roman indifference to human suffering which can be discerned in Virgil's *Aeneid*, but remain confined there to what Parry calls a 'private voice', or Lyne, 'further voices'. Hence Virgil's attractiveness, Pöschl argues, as 'a mediator between the antique Roman world and medieval Christianity'. He goes on, in somewhat purple prose: 'In Vergil there is both the granite of ancient Roman grandeur and the delicate bloom of humanity opening upon a new dimension of the soul.'[36]

Seen in this light, J. L. Simmons's argument that Shakespeare's Rome resembles what St Augustine calls 'the City of Man' becomes more plausible.[37] It is not necessary that Shakespeare himself read the *City of God* in order for his vision of Rome to resemble St Augustine's. Both authors are indebted to the same touchstone, Virgil's *Aeneid*, for their sense of Rome's characteristic flaws.[38] This 'earthly city', St Augustine writes, 'was itself ruled by its

---

[33] A. D. Nuttall, 'The Stoic in Love', in *The Stoic in Love: Selected Essays on Literature and Ideas* (London, 1989), pp. 56–67; p. 61.

[34] T. S. Eliot, 'Vergil and the Christian World', *Sewanee Review*, 61 (1953), 1–14; cp. Theodor Haecker, *Virgil, Father of the West*, tr. Arther Wesley Wheen (London, 1934).

[35] For the concept of *anima naturaliter Christiana*, see Tertullian, *Apology*, 17.6 and *Patrologia Latina*, 1:377.

[36] Pöschl, *Art of Vergil*, pp. 54, 58.

[37] J. L. Simmons, *Shakespeare's Pagan World: The Roman Tragedies* (Charlottesville, VA, 1973).

[38] For a more comprehensive account of Virgil's influence on St Augustine, see Sabine MacCormack, *The Shadows of Poetry: Vergil in the Mind of Augustine* (Berkeley, CA, 1998).

desire to rule' (*ipsa ei dominandi libido dominatur*) (1.1). 'Lust for power [*libido dominandi*] existed among the Romans with more unmitigated intensity than among any other people' (1.30). By way of explanation, St Augustine cites Anchises's charge to Aeneas in the Underworld. 'Remember, Roman', he says, 'to rule the nations by your command [*imperio*]', 'to impose the ways of peace, to spare the subjected [*parcere subiectis*], and to battle down the proud' (6.851–3). According to St Augustine, as the Romans fought and conquered other nations, individual pursuit of political dominance was at first kept in check by a desire to be praised for temperance, as well as service to the Roman state. Once the Romans defeated Carthage, however, their most dangerous rival, this 'concern to preserve a reputation' (*cura existimationis*) began to seem old-fashioned and unnecessary, until finally it faded away altogether. Seeking only power, at whatever cost, the Romans began to turn on each other. 'First concord was weakened and destroyed by fierce and bloody seditions; then followed … civil wars … massacres … proscription and plunder' (1.30). As St Augustine sees it, desire for *imperium*, left unchecked, leads eventually, inevitably, to appalling internecine bloodshed. Rome's pitiless civil strife is the polar opposite of the ideal City of God, unified in contrast by Christian *caritas*.

According to Michael Putnam, Aeneas himself undergoes a similar moral degeneration. 'Jupiter early on predicts a time when *Furor impius*, Madness that lacks piety particularly because it is a source of war against internal, not external, enemies, will roar vainly from its prison (1.294–5) … What we are witnessing, then, as the last half of the epic unfolds … is a prototype of civil war, climaxing in Aeneas' killing of Turnus … In scorning his father's command to spare a suppliant [*parcere subiectis*]', Putnam argues, 'Aeneas behaves impiously'. He takes up, in effect, 'the role of savage Juno and of Furor on the loose' (12.946–7). 'From the beginning of the epic,' he explains, '*pietas* is antonymous to a series of negative abstractions including *ira, dolor, saevitia*, and … *furor*.'[39] Yet all of these attributes are applied to Aeneas, in the end. In the

closing lines of the epic, especially, as Aeneas decides to kill Turnus, Virgil describes him as *furiis accensus et ira / terribilis*: 'inflamed with madness and terrible in his wrath' (12.946–7).

Within Virgil's *Aeneid*, one of the clearest and most disturbing indications that Aeneas might not represent an ethical ideal is his decision, towards the end, to offer human sacrifice. He first takes eight captives to be killed offstage, so to speak, as a blood offering on Pallas's funeral pyre (10.517–20, 11.81–2). Then he kills Magus, a suppliant, despite his pleas for mercy, and immediately afterward Haemonides, a suppliant who is also a priest of Apollo. As he describes Aeneas's rampage, Virgil uses an unusual verb, *immolo*, a religious term for sacrifice, to describe not only what will happen to the captives (*immolet*, 10.519), but also Aeneas's killing Haemonides (*immolat*, 10.541), as well as Turnus (*immolat*, 12.949). The choice of diction, Putnam maintains, is meant to be shocking. As Steven Farron explains, human sacrifice was seen within Rome, as well as ancient Greece, as inexcusably alien and abhorrent. Authors as various as Cicero, Ovid and Lucretius all describe it as *impium*.[40] Livy calls it *foeditas* ('foulness, filthiness') (7.15.10). There is a precedent in Homer's *Iliad*: Achilles kills twelve captured Trojans at Patroclus's funeral pyre (18.336–7, 21.27–32, 23.22–3, 23.175–7). Homer's narrator condemns the deed, however, as does Zeus (23.176, 18.357–9). 'Why,' Putnam asks, 'does Virgil choose to end his poem with his precedent-setting hero offering human sacrifice, something no civilized Roman would have done? … The answer must be that Virgil, too, would have us condemn his hero's final deed as

---

[39] Putnam, *Virgil's 'Aeneid'*, p. 202.

[40] Ronald Broude claims, 'Elizabethans do not seem to have been aware' that 'human sacrifice was rarely if ever practiced during the Empire' ('Roman and Goth in Titus Andronicus [*sic*]', *Shakespeare Studies*, 6 (1970), 27–34; p. 30). Given widespread condemnation of the practice, however, by other classical authors such as Cicero, this assumption seems debatable. See S. Farron, 'Aeneas' Human Sacrifice', *Acta Classica*, 28 (1985), 21–33.

the action of someone deranged, driven by fury to violate not only his father's injunction to behave with *clementia* but also a basic tenet of civilized behaviour.'

It is very revealing, then, that *Titus Andronicus* begins with the same kind of human sacrifice that Aeneas offers at the end of the *Aeneid*.[41] As Danielle St Hilaire points out, 'the problem is not, as Bate suggests, that Titus's behaviour is inconsistent with Rome's historical practices, but rather that Titus's sacrifice is entirely consistent with a similarly appalling scene in a Roman text'.[42] Lucius, Titus's eldest son, asks his father Titus for 'the proudest prisoner of the Goths, / That we may hew his limbs, and on a pile /*Ad manes fratrum* sacrifice his flesh' (1.1.96–8). Titus hands over Alarbus, Tamora's son, despite Tamora's pleas, and he is led away forthwith to be hacked apart and burnt. 'With what almost seems to be deliberate perverseness,' Andrew Ettin complains, 'Shakespeare has evoked from Vergil ... moments that display in the Latin poet's works whatever it is that lies on the side of the Roman soul opposite to forbearance and *pietas*.' Shakespeare's allusion to Virgil here is only 'perverse', however, if one sees him, as Ettin does, as 'the celebrator ... of the Augustan virtues', 'one of the writers responsible for our notion of Rome as civilized and virtuous'.[43] Only a few lines earlier, Titus is described as 'surnamed Pius', an epithet that calls to mind Virgil's *pius* Aeneas. Almost immediately, however, the concept itself of *pietas* is put to the question. 'O cruel, irreligious piety!' Tamora cries (1.1.130). Her outburst proves well founded. 'In this early, bloodthirsty play,' Russell Hillier concludes, 'Roman piety precludes and excludes pity.' As a result, Shakespeare's Romans, like Virgil's, are 'locked' into an interminable 'cycle of violent reprisal and counter-reprisal'.[44]

Heather James argues that 'within the first three hundred lines of the play, the Vergilian virtues through which Titus understands himself emerge as bankrupt'.[45] The implicit claim here, however, that Titus's ethos is 'Vergilian' is debatable. In keeping with the Harvard School of Virgil criticism, it may be more accurate to say instead that in the opening scene of *Titus Andronicus*, the author

shows, like Virgil himself, that what Romans such as Titus consider virtuous, the subordination of the individual to the state, is not necessarily a virtue at all, but instead compromised by its indifference to human suffering. As in the *Aeneid*, the moral value of traditional Roman *pietas* is undermined by a harrowing depiction of its human cost. As Miola observes, 'Roman honour, with its subordination of private feeling to public responsibility, transforms the city into barbaric chaos. Titus's vision of Rome and his place in it blinds him to Alarbus, just as it blinds him to his own son and daughter.'[46]

Despite all his plaudits, Titus, especially, the Roman war-hero, comes across as brutally cold and callous, even to his own family. He abruptly kills his own son, Mutius, for daring to try to prevent him from marrying off his daughter, Lavinia, without any thought of her consent, to the new emperor, Saturninus, rather than the man, Bassianus, whom she loves, and to whom she is already betrothed. When his brother, Marcus, accuses him of having 'slain a virtuous son', Titus disavows Mutius, his brothers, and Marcus as well (1.1.339). 'No son of mine, / Nor thou, nor these,

---

41 Some critics assign this and other sections of *Titus Andronicus* to a collaborator, George Peele, rather than Shakespeare himself. See especially Brian Vickers, *Shakespeare, Co-Author: A Historical Study of Five Collaborative Plays* (Oxford, 2002), pp. 148–243. For a recent overview of ongoing debate about the authorship of various sections of *Titus Andronicus*, see William W. Weber, 'Shakespeare after all? The Authorship of *Titus Andronicus* 4.1 Reconsidered', in *Shakespeare Survey 67* (Cambridge, 2014), pp. 69–84.

42 Danielle A. St Hilaire, 'Allusion and Sacrifice in *Titus Andronicus*', *SEL*, 49 (2009), 311–31; p. 314. Cf. Jonathan Bate, *Shakespeare and Ovid* (Oxford, 1993), p. 135, n. 127. St Hilaire goes on to describe in some detail how 'the language of the exchange between Aeneas and his pleading victim closely resembles Titus's dialogue with Tamora'.

43 Andrew Ettin, 'Shakespeare's First Roman Tragedy', *ELH*, 37 (1970), 325–41; pp. 326–8.

44 Russell M. Hillier, '"Valour will weep": The Ethics of Valor, Anger, and Pity in Shakespeare's *Coriolanus*', *Studies in Philology*, 113(2016), 358–96; p. 384.

45 James, *Shakespeare's Troy*, p. 54.

46 Robert S. Miola, *Shakespeare's Rome* (Cambridge, 1983), p. 49.

confederates in the deed / That hath dishonoured all our family' (1.1.340–2). When Lucius asks his father to let his brother, Mutius, be buried in the family tomb, Titus refuses: 'Here none but soldiers and Rome's servitors / Repose in fame' (1.1.349–50). 'My lord, this is impiety in you' (1.1.352), Marcus protests. 'Thou art a Roman; be not barbarous' (1.1.375), Titus reluctantly agrees, but shows no further sign of remorse.

Somewhat surprisingly, given her outrageous cruelty later in play, it is Tamora in contrast who outlines in this opening scene an alternative ethos, more akin to Christianity, and based like Christianity on a different understanding of the divine. 'Wilt thou draw near the nature of the gods?' she asks Titus. 'Draw near them then in being merciful' (1.1.117–18). After the death of her son Alarbus, however, Tamora becomes in contrast a symbol of barbaric ruthlessness. She compares herself to Dido, but she can be understood as a representative of a more general pattern in the *Aeneid*. Women in Virgil's epic, starting with the goddess Juno, are symbols of unrestrained *furor*. When Latinus promises Lavinia to Aeneas, for example, Juno sends a fury, Alecto, to prompt his wife, Amata, to resist this decision. Robert Adger Law points out that the 'barren detested vale' where Shakespeare's Lavinia is raped, as well as what it contains, the 'abhorred pit' where Martius discovers the body of Bassanius, strongly resembles the Vale of Amsanctus in the *Aeneid*, where Alecto temporarily takes refuge.[47] When Martius falls into the pit, he describes it as a 'fell devouring receptacle, / As hateful as Cocytus' misty mouth' (2.3.235–6). Virgil describes Alecto's earthly hiding place in like manner as a 'horrifying cave' (*specus horrendum*) containing the 'breathing-holes of hell' (*spiracula Ditis*). 'An enormous chasm, where Acheron bursts forth, opens wide its pestilent jaws' (*ruptoque ingens Acheronte vorago / pestiferas aperit fauces*) (7.568–70). Alecto aptly personifies the shared character of Aeneas's various female antagonists: her name in Greek means literally 'the unceasing'. Even more so than the other Erinyes, she serves as a symbol of relentless, implacable anger: the *furor* that eventually overtakes Titus,

as well as Aeneas, reducing him to acts of savage barbarism. Seeing his sons' severed heads, Titus's tears abruptly cease: 'Which way', he cries, 'shall I find Revenge's cave?' (3.1.269).

In *Titus Andronicus*, Lavinia finds herself prey to Tamora's sons, Chiron and Demetrius, while Tamora looks on. She pleads for 'pity', but Tamora scoffs: her 'heart' is as impervious to Lavinia's tears as 'unrelenting flint to drops of rain' (2.3.140–1). The language here strongly echoes Virgil's. When Aeneas acknowledges he is planning to leave Carthage, Dido, weeping, accuses him of being born of the rocks of the Caucasus: '*duris genuit te cautibus horrens / Caucasus*' (4.366–7). Afterward, when Aeneas encounters her in the Underworld, the roles are reversed: Aeneas weeps, but Dido is unmoved. '*Nec magis … movetur / quam si dura silex aut stet Marpesia cautes*' ('She was no more moved, than if she had been a hard stone ("flint"), or Parian marble') (6.470–1).[48] As Lavinia pleads with Tamora, Demetrius urges his mother not to spare her, and Lavinia protests, again in language that recalls Virgil's. 'When did the tiger's young ones teach the dam?' she asks Demetrius. 'O, do not learn her wrath! she taught it thee. / The milk thou suckedst from her did turn to marble' (2.3.142–4). When Dido accuses Virgil of being a child of the craggy Caucasus, she also accuses him of having been nursed by Hyrcanian tigers: '*Hyrcanaeque admorunt ubera tigres*' (4.367). 'Marble' here, too, calls to mind *Marpesia cautes*, Virgil's description of Dido, later on, as 'Parian marble'.

Shakespeare seems to have been especially fascinated by Virgil's conceit of the nursing female Hyrcanian tiger as a symbol of paradoxically pitiless femininity. At the end of *Titus Andronicus*, Lucius denounces Aaron as a 'ravenous tiger' (5.3.5) and Tamora, too, as a 'ravenous tiger' (5.3.194). 'Her life was beastly,' he explains, 'and devoid of pity' (5.3.198). The image of the tiger appears in several

---

[47] Robert Adger Law, 'The Roman Background of *Titus Andronicus*', *Studies in Philology*, 40 (1943), 145–53; p. 149.
[48] 'Flint' is the usual sixteenth-century translation of *silex*.

other plays, as well, and always in the same vein, as a symbol of frightening ruthlessness: 'th'Hyrcan tiger' in *Macbeth* (3.4.100); in *Hamlet*, 'rugged Pyrrhus, like th'Hyrcanian beast' (2.2.453). Urging his men 'once more unto the breach', the tiger serves for Henry V as a symbol of 'hard-favoured rage' (3.1.1–8). In *3 Henry VI*, after she has killed his son, York describes Margaret of Anjou as 'more inhuman, more inexorable, / O ten times more than the tigers of Hyrcania' (1.4.155–6). 'O tiger's heart,' he calls her, 'wrapped in a woman's hide!' (1.4.138). Later in the play, the tables are turned: Margaret becomes, as Henry VI says, 'a woman to be pitied much' (3.1.36). 'Her tears will pierce into a marble heart,' he claims; 'the tiger will be mild whiles she doth mourn' (3.1.38–9).

Turning to the other great villain of the piece, Aaron the Moor, it is tempting to surmise that his characterization, as well, may owe something to the influence of Virgil. Specifically, Aaron may be modelled on Virgil's Mezentius. In the *Aeneid*, Virgil describes Mezentius as a tyrant who had once ruled over the Etruscans, '*superbo imperio et saevis ... armis*' ('with arrogant command and savage ... arms'), but whose reign had been overthrown by a popular uprising (8.481–2). Having fled Etruria, Mezentius took refuge with King Turnus, and he appears in the epic fighting at his side against Aeneas. Virgil attributes to this deposed tyrant a memorable form of executing his political enemies: chaining them to corpses, hand to hand and face to face, until the gruesome, bloody fluids of decomposition (*sanie taboque fluentis*) would extend from the dead to the living (8.485–9). Something akin to this peculiar form of torture can be seen in *Titus Andronicus*, when Aaron tricks Titus's sons, Quintus and Martius, into falling into a pit which contains the dead body of Bassianus. Shakespeare lingers over their horror at their proximity to the dead. 'I am surprised with an uncouth fear' (2.3.211), Quintus exclaims, 'A chilling sweat o'erruns my trembling joints' (2.3.212). The pit is an 'unhallowed and blood-stained hole' (2.3.210), 'detested, dark, blood-drinking' (2.3.224): Martius describes the scene as a 'fearful sight of blood and death' (2.3.216).

Other similarities, as well, suggest a connection between Aaron and Mezentius. Both scoff at the gods. 'Thou believest no god' (5.1.71), Lucius says of Aaron. 'Indeed I do not' (5.1.73), Aaron retorts, unrepentant. As Aeneas and Mezentius begin to fight, Aeneas invites Jupiter and Apollo to strike the first blow. Mezentius, however, is undaunted. 'I am not horrified by death,' he boasts, 'nor would I spare any of the gods' (10.880). At another point, Mezentius declares his own right hand and spear his 'god' (*dextra mihi deus et telum*) (10.773). Aaron and Mezentius are also both in some measure redeemed by their heartfelt love for their own progeny. 'This before all the world do I prefer' (4.2.108), Aaron exclaims, holding tight to his newborn son. He vows to feed and raise the child himself and to bring him up 'to be a warrior and command a camp' (4.2.179). Mezentius's love for his son, Lausus, can be seen in contrast in his reaction to his death. After Aeneas kills the young warrior, Mezentius is utterly distraught. He flings dust on his hair and clings to the corpse (*corpore inhaeret*), in an ironic recreation of his own former mode of execution (10.845). Only by killing his son, 'only this way' (*haec via sola*), he tells Aeneas, 'there was, by which you might destroy me' (10.879).

This peculiar weakness of Mezentius, as well as Aaron, is in keeping with another point of resonance between Shakespeare's *Titus Andronicus* and Virgil's *Aeneid*: an emphasis on the relationship between father and son. The word itself, 'son', appears significantly more often in this play than in any other of Shakespeare's plays.[49] More specifically, both works emphasize a father's grief at the death of his son. Much of the action of the second half of the *Aeneid* revolves around the death of two young warriors: Pallas, son of Evander, killed by Turnus, and Lausus, son of Mezentius, killed by Aeneas. Titus's own case is more extreme: he begins the tragedy with most of his sons dead, kills one himself at the beginning, and loses two

---

[49] Along with related words such as 'sons' and 'son's', seventy-three times; the closest points of comparison are *3 Henry VI* (54) and *King John* (36).

more over the course of the play. His chief antagonist, Tamora, loses her sons, as well; one at the beginning and two more at the end. Like Virgil, Shakespeare seems to say that *this*, this tragedy that we see before us, is the cost of *imperium*: the loss of young men's lives. Human sacrifice is a symbol of a more metaphorical sacrifice: the price of *Romanitas*, the blood offering it requires, is casualties in war.

By far the most disturbing aspect of Shakespeare's *Titus Andronicus*, however, is his recasting of Virgil's Lavinia as a kind of Philomela. Like her namesake, Shakespeare's Lavinia is the innocent subject of a bitter quarrel over marriage rights. In the *Aeneid*, Lavinia is initially betrothed to a local suitor, Prince Turnus, but then abruptly handed over to a stranger, Aeneas, prompting a pan-Italian war. In *Titus Andronicus*, Titus agrees to allow the new emperor of Rome, Saturninus, to marry his daughter, even though she is already betrothed to Bassianus. Like Virgil's Turnus, Bassianus refuses to give up his claim. And, as in the *Aeneid*, the result is bloodshed, beginning with the death of Titus's own son. Later in the play, Tamora's sons, Chiron and Demetrius, rape Lavinia and mutilate her, with Tamora's approval, in reprisal for Titus's agreeing to sacrifice their brother, Alarbus. As in the story of Philomela, they cut out her tongue; in addition, however, they cut off her hands. Nonetheless, by indicating pages in Ovid's *Metamorphoses*, Lavinia is able to communicate her plight, prompting Titus to take revenge on Tamora and her sons, much as Philomela's sister, Procne, does to Tereus, by serving her her sons, Chiron and Demetrius, baked in a pie.

Miola argues that Shakespeare's Lavinia 'parodies' Virgil's; her rape is 'in direct contrast' to her namesake's wedding to Aeneas.[50] That sense of contrast, however, reflects his relatively 'optimistic' reading of the *Aeneid*. A more 'pessimistic' reading of the *Aeneid* would suggest that Shakespeare's Lavinia clarifies, by exaggeration, Virgil's own more subtly rendered concerns about the human cost of *Romanitas*, for women as well as men. In *Titus Andronicus*, Tamora is not Lavinia's mother, and she does not carry off Lavinia herself, as Amata does in the *Aeneid*. Yet

some analogy may be in play, nonetheless. In the *Aeneid*, Amata, associated with the Bacchantes, vows that Bacchus alone is worthy of her daughter, and that he alone will have her (7.389–91). What would it mean, however, Shakespeare seems to ask, if Bacchus did indeed take possession of her daughter? Chiron and Demetrius dismember Shakespeare's Lavinia, much as the Bacchantes do Orpheus. When he finds Lavinia afterward, Marcus compares her explicitly to 'the Thracian poet', Orpheus, and recalls her beautiful singing, as well as her 'lily hands ... upon a lute' (2.3.44–51). Voicelessness also signifies Lavinia's lack of agency. In the *Aeneid*, Amata speaks of her own 'maternal right' (*iuris materni*), but never of Lavinia's wishes or concerns (7.402). Shakespeare seems to have found this indifference, like Titus's, horrifying. Lavinia's enforced dumbness, her tongue literally cut out of her mouth, reflects the fact that in the *Aeneid*, she has no say in her own fate. Instead, she is shuffled back and forth as a bargaining chip: a voiceless object of political machination. The name of the son that Titus kills, Mutius, is perhaps, then, not coincidental. He, too, is rendered effectively 'mute'.

Heather James and Jonathan Bate see in *Titus Andronicus* Shakespeare choosing Ovid over Virgil, not just in terms of style, but also in terms of what Martindale calls 'sensibility'. 'Ovid dominates the central acts of the play,' James argues, 'at a direct cost to Vergil as a source of cultural decorum for Titus, Rome, and the play itself.'[51] Citing James, Bate agrees: Ovid is used 'to destabilize a Virgilian, imperial idiom'.[52] Lisa Starks-Estes, too, maintains that Shakespeare uses Ovid 'to revise and, in part, to overturn Virgil, the epic tradition, and its values'.[53] James explains: 'No sooner is Vergilian authority installed through the ritual events and

---

[50] Miola, *Shakespeare's Rome*, pp. 54–5; cf. Miola, 'Vergil in Shakespeare', pp. 242–3. See also James, *Shakespeare's Troy*, p. 55, on Shakespeare's Lavinia as a 'warping' of Virgil's.

[51] James, *Shakespeare's Troy*, p. 43.

[52] Bate, *Shakespeare and Ovid*, p. 103, n. 33.

[53] Lisa S. Starks-Estes, *Violence, Trauma, and 'Virtus' in Shakespeare's Roman Poems and Plays* (London, 2014), p. 11.

ceremonious speeches of the first act than it is deposed by a specifically Ovidian insouciance, marked by the once humourless Titus's laughter upon receiving his severed hand and his sons' heads: "Ha, ha, ha!" (3.1.263).' Shakespeare 'wrenches the play world from Vergilian to Ovidian coordinates' and 'unleashes the floodgates to the outrageous puns, violence, and schematic disjunctions that subsequently pervade the play'.[54]

To what end, however, does Shakespeare evoke Ovid as an alternative to Virgil? James and Bate seem not to notice Virgil's celebrated 'empathy', as well as his subversion of Roman 'authority'. They also overlook Ovid's notorious cruelty: the gleeful, gloating sadism which pervades his representations of violence. Bate observes that '*Titus* reminds the audience of its own Ovidianism' (102): a point hard to dispute, when Ovid's *Metamorphoses* itself makes a cameo on-stage.[55] As A. D. Nuttall asks, however, 'What then of the ethical question-mark which has hung over Ovid for so many centuries? ... There is so much pain and so many rapes in Ovid, and the poet seems in a way not to care.'[56] Shakespeare imitates what James calls 'Ovidian insouciance' not out of affinity, but instead, to subject it to an ethical critique. As Valerie Traub writes, 'any comprehensive account of the impulses and effects of Ovidianism needs to account for its fascination with the erotics of cruelty, including the amplification of such violence in such quintessentially Ovidian texts as *Titus Andronicus*'.[57] What Burrow identifies as the 'Ovidian grotesquerie of *Titus*' is meant to be horrifying, not appealing.[58]

Within classics, a sense of Ovid as witty but cold-hearted, even outright sadistic, is a critical commonplace, dating back to Ovid's own contemporaries. 'One of the oldest and most persistent charges which has been levelled against the Ovid of the *Metamorphoses*,' David Hopkins explains, 'is that the poet trivializes his depictions of pain, anxiety, and suffering by prolixity, by a callous impassivity, and by displays of tastelessly inappropriate wit.'[59] When a poet should 'endeavour to raise Pity', Dryden observes, Ovid instead is 'tickling you to laugh'.[60] If Shakespeare does intend to

question Ovid's amoral aestheticism, it makes sense, moreover, that he would turn to the *locus classicus* for this criticism of Ovid's style, his description of Tereus's rape and mutilation of Philomela (6.550–62). Karl Galinsky cites this scene, in particular, for its 'loving depiction even of the smallest sadistic detail', including especially 'the detail of the cutting out of the tongue and its twitching on the ground'.[61] Shakespeare omits this detail; Marcus's long speech, after he finds Lavinia mutilated, has come in for criticism as over-elaborate, but it is much more sympathetic than Ovid's description of Philomela. As Martindale writes, 'here there is none of the disconcerting precision and coolness of Ovid ... no tone of detachment ... The effect ... is not flippant or disorienting, but rather one of pathos and sorrow'.[62] In other words, Marcus describes Lavinia, not in the style of Ovid, but instead, as Virgil might – with pronounced compassion. His is a eulogy, not a mockery.

Just before he cuts Chiron's and Demetrius's throats, Titus vows to make the 'banquet' he will prepare for their mother, Tamora, 'more stern and bloody than the Centaurs' feast' (5.3.201–2). Although brief, the allusion to Ovid here is again

---

[54] James, *Shakespeare's Troy*, pp. 43–4.

[55] Bate, *Shakespeare and Ovid*, p. 102.

[56] A. D. Nuttall, 'A Kind of Scandal', *London Review of Books* (August 1993), 15–16; p. 16 (review of Bate, *Shakespeare and Ovid*).

[57] Valerie Traub, 'Afterword', in *Ovid and the Renaissance Body*, ed. Goran V. Stanivukovic (Toronto, 2001), pp. 260–9; p. 266.

[58] Burrow, *Classical Antiquity*, p. 106.

[59] David Hopkins, 'Dryden and Ovid's "Wit out of season"', in *Ovid Renewed: Ovidian Influences on Literature and Art from the Middle Ages to the Twentieth Century*, ed. Charles Martindale (Cambridge, 1988), pp. 167–90; p. 167.

[60] John Dryden, 'Preface to Fables Ancient and Modern', in John Dryden, *Major Works*, ed. Keith Walker (Oxford, 1987), pp. 552–71; p. 559.

[61] Karl Galinsky, 'Ovid's Humanity: Death and Suffering in the Metamorphoses', in Karl Galinsky, *Ovid's 'Metamorphoses': An Introduction to the Basic Aspects* (Berkeley, CA, 1975), pp. 110–57; p. 130.

[62] Martindale and Martindale, *Uses of Antiquity*, p. 51. See also Burrow, *Classical Antiquity*, pp. 110–12.

revealing. Galinsky cites the battle of the Lapiths against the centaurs as an especially egregious instance of the poet's tendency toward Grand Guignol: 'Ovid revels in ever new ways of imagining how bodies can be mangled, maimed, or disintegrated.' One centaur is killed, for instance, by having his eyes gouged out by antlers a Lapith finds hanging on a tree; Ovid lingers over the image of his eyeball rolling down his beard (12.265–70). 'Death becomes a ludicrous and sensational event, which the poet views without any empathy for its victims.'[63] Recounting a host of malevolent, murderous pranks, Shakespeare's Aaron boasts:

> I have done a thousand dreadful things
> As willingly as one would kill a fly,
> And nothing grieves me heartily indeed
> But that I cannot do ten thousand more.
>
> (5.1.141–4)

It is Ovid, not Virgil, whom Shakespeare 'parodies' in this play: Shakespeare imitates, even exaggerates, Ovidianism, to the point that it becomes both absurd and revolting. Ovid's style is that of the villains, the barbarians, Tamora, Aaron, Chiron and Demetrius, and it is part of the tragedy that Titus degenerates morally by the end of the play to the point that he takes on this attitude himself. At the beginning of the play, he is callous, indifferent to suffering. By the end, however, Titus is somehow worse: he takes pleasure, like his enemies, in inflicting pain. Ovidianism serves as an index of this moral decline. Like Traub, as well as Starks-Estes, Galinsky sees in Ovid a disturbing 'erotics of cruelty'. Citing Otto Kiefer's study of Roman sexuality, Galinsky argues that this 'cruel and sadistic streak in the Roman character' was 'endemic and never far from the surface'.[64]

Towards the middle of *Titus Andronicus*, in one especially heart-breaking scene, Lucius finds his father wandering the streets of Rome, pleading to the cobblestones for the life of his sons. 'No man is by,' Lucius protests, 'You recount your sorrows to a stone' (3.1.28–9). 'They are better than the Tribunes,' Titus replies, 'When I do weep, they

humbly at my feet / Receive my tears and seem to weep with me' (38, 40–1). Roman authority is in contrast 'more hard than stones' (44). The contrast between 'tears' and 'stones' recalls not only Dido's response to Aeneas's tears, itself a response to his earlier indifference to hers, but also Tamora's rejection of Lavinia's 'as unrelenting flint to drops of rain' (2.3.141), which she casts explicitly as a response to Titus's indifference to her tears for Alarbus. 'Be not obdurate', Lavinia begs (2.3.160). But Tamora professes herself 'pitiless' (162). 'Remember, boys,' she tells her sons, 'I poured forth tears in vain / To save your brother from the sacrifice, / But fierce Andronicus would not relent' (163–5).

'Foolish Lucius,' Titus explains to his son, 'dost thou not perceive / That Rome is but a wilderness of tigers?' (3.1.52–3). Rome seems to be a city, the centre of civilization. But it is little different from the 'wilderness' that surrounds it. In Shakespeare's *Titus Andronicus*, as in Virgil's *Aeneid*, *Romanitas* seems at first to be the opposite of barbarism, but by the end it turns out to be infected with the same savage spirit. 'I am Revenge' (5.2.30), says Tamora, visiting Titus in disguise. But the line could equally well apply to Titus himself. Like Aeneas at the end of the *Aeneid*, the 'Roman' has become 'barbarous'. In a sense, though, he always was. As Shakespeare shows, from a Christian perspective, the common thread connecting Roman subordination of the individual to the glory of the state, as well as of the child to the honour of the *paterfamilias* – Roman *pietas* – and barbaric sadism such as that of Shakespeare's Aaron is a desire for command, control, dominance: the craving for power over others that St Augustine calls *libido dominandi*. And the missing element, the cost of that *imperium*, is pity: a Virgilian sense of compassion for human suffering.

---

[63] Galinsky, 'Ovid's Humanity', pp. 126–7.
[64] Galinsky, 'Ovid's Humanity', p. 138; cf. Otto Kiefer, *Sexual Life in Ancient Rome* (London, 1934).

'THOUGH THIS BE METHOD, YET THERE IS MADNESS IN'T': CUTTING OVID'S TONGUE IN RECENT STAGE AND FILM PERFORMANCES OF *TITUS ANDRONICUS*

CHRISTIAN M. BILLING

I

No subject affecteth us with more delight than history, imprinting a thousand forms upon our imaginations from the circumstances of place, person, time, matter, manner, and the like. And what can be more profitable, saith an ancient historian, than sitting on the stage of human life, to be made wise by their example who have trod the path of error and danger before us . . .[1]

In this article I will consider the relationship between the human body as a material object and visual signifier, and the complex philosophical concepts it is sometimes called upon to articulate in theatrical and cinematic contexts. In particular, I will outline an understanding of the body as a disruptive site that has problematized the creation of theatrical and cinematic meaning, as well as the conveyance of performative intertextual authority, in recent performances of Shakespearian drama. My case study is Lavinia in Shakespeare's *Titus Andronicus*, with a focus on the ways in which Lavinia's body has distracted film and theatre directors (and audiences) as a result of the immediacy of the physical torment it undergoes, and how, ironically, it has turned them away from the potentially feminist performative, literary and historical intertextuality it is intended to provide. My argument centres on the fact that Lavinia is not meant at all times to be a representation of individual human subjectivity; rather, like many Renaissance characters, she is frequently a dramaturgical device incorporated into the play in order to provide a way

into intertextual frames of reference essential to more meaningful understandings of Shakespeare's drama. Unfortunately, approaches to the presentation of dramatic character that incorporate notions of performative intertextuality, abstraction and character-as-metaphor are very much out of fashion in contemporary theatrical and cinematic practice.

Titus is a challenging play, a slippery rhetorical text upon which it is very difficult to get a sustained philosophical grip. Perhaps this is why so many critics and theatre directors have misunderstood it over the years, and have detected in it the kind of cliché of classical allusions that Shakespeare himself ridicules in comic terms in later plays. Some have scorned its supposedly amateurish formal conception.[2] As Bate, Waith, Palmer, James and Rowe have shown in a new critical tradition beginning in the 1950s, however, such responses are just plain wrong-headed. Shakespeare's use of contrasting literary and historical sources is not the mess that unsympathetic critics have claimed it to be. Rather, a playfully eclectic use of classical intertextuality is what gives *Titus* its philosophical cohesiveness: like

---

[1] Henry Peacham, *The Complete Gentleman, The Truth of Our Times, and the Art of Living in London (1622)*, ed. Virgil B. Heltzel (Ithaca, NY, 1962), p. 64. Quoted in Jonathan Bate, 'Introduction', in William Shakespeare, *Titus Andronicus*, ed. Jonathan Bate (London, 1995), pp. 1–122; p. 16.

[2] For a précis of this tradition, see Bate, 'Introduction', pp. 1–36.

a bicycle wheel, the play is held together by the creative tension of significant forces pulling in different directions. In response to T. J. B. Spencer's 1957 accusation that 'the author seems anxious not to get it all right, but to get it all in',[3] Jonathan Bate has famously replied: 'quite so, but this is exactly the point'.[4] Recent philological readings of *Titus* have accordingly outlined the ways in which Shakespeare uses Livy's *Histories* and Ovid's *Fasti* (for Tarquin and Lucretia) to speak about the legitimacy of absolutist monarchy and the move towards republicanism. Equally insightful have been readings that pick up on Shakespeare's choice of the wicked emperor Saturninus from Suetonius and Tacitus – in whose work the tyrant is contrasted with wholesome, pastoral Germans who stand as code in the Renaissance imaginary for Protestant Reformation. Even the fact that Shakespeare chose Virgil's Lavinia, the mother of early Rome, as the mutilated daughter of that empire in decline has been used to demonstrate that 'the founding acts of Empire turn out to contain the seeds of its destruction'.[5]

Of the many horrendous sights in Shakespeare's *Titus Andronicus*, Lavinia's mutilated body stands apart as one of the play's most powerful testaments to the barbarity of both Roman and Gothic cultures. Despite the acts of sensationalist violence that are visited upon it, this body somehow persists; its 'lopped and hewed' trunk remains unremittingly on stage as an awkward and yet perplexingly beautiful signifier of the thorny relationship between human bodies and the concepts they are used to articulate in performance. The text of *Titus Andronicus* asks the Lavinia actor to embrace oxymoron, to use his (or her) body as a 'map of woe, that ... dost talk in signs' (3.2.12), a figurative and emblematic trope pointing to the human cost of the play's central themes: loyalty, revenge, filial duty, the lust for power and dominion. Lavinia's stage and screen body accordingly derives power from the fact that it is a channel through which much of the play's intertextuality is mediated. Much of Lavinia's performative force accordingly comes from the fact that she exists in a symbolic theatre and is presented through a significant distancing device: theatrical transvestism. Transvestite representations of femininity, from the stages of ancient Athens to those of early modern England, derived much of their potency from the fact that audiences did not consider them to be real in all respects, but rather that they could also be understood as rhetorical investigations of the nature of human (both male and female) subjectivity.[6] Lavinia's existence on stage, post-rape and dismemberment, is a biological impossibility that indicates she has more in common with the figurative emblems of Ripa's *Iconologia* than she does any actual human subject. Her dramatic power and performative agency are accordingly rooted in the ways in which she both evokes and resonates against a variety of classical exemplars.

In what follows I consider the fundamental difficulty that seems to exist in attaining a similar theatrical and cinematic reception and interpretation history for *Titus* as that which has been achieved in critical terms. To do this, I shall ask two questions: (1) why does it seem that so few modern directors have been capable of connecting all of the pieces of Shakespeare's complex intertextual theatrical puzzle?; and (2) why do a significant number of directors appear to be more interested in the physical actions undertaken by and upon performers (and particularly female performers) than in the rhetorical language that the same dramatic constructs, or those around them, simultaneously articulate vocally to represent the play's philosophical arguments?

Which brings me to performance.

---

[3] T. J. B. Spencer, 'Shakespeare and the Elizabethan Romans', in *Shakespeare Survey 10* (1957), 27–38; p. 32.

[4] Bate, 'Introduction', p. 17.

[5] See Heather James, 'Cultural Disintegration in *Titus Andronicus*: Mutilating Titus, Vergil and Rome', in *Themes in Drama, vol. 13, Violence in Drama*, ed. James Redmond (Cambridge, 1991), pp. 123–40.

[6] The best discussions of this phenomenon occur in classical philology. See Helene P. Foley, *Female Acts in Greek Tragedy* (Princeton, NJ, 2001); Laura McClure, *Spoken Like a Woman: Speech and Gender in Athenian Drama* (Princeton, NJ, 1999); and Froma I. Zeitlin, *Playing the Other: Gender and Society in Classical Greek Literature* (Chicago, 1996).

II

The first account of *Titus* is a production in the home of Sir John Harrington on 1 January 1596. Jacques Petit, the French tutor to Harrington's household, offers a glimpse of the apparent tension he felt between the performative elements of *Titus* and the play's more sophisticated literary, philosophical and political intentions.[7] Following a performance by an unnamed London company (presumably the Lord Chamberlain's Men), Petit observed, '*on a aussi joué la tragédie de* Titus Andronicus *mais la monster a plus valu que le sujet*'.[8] His opinion is that the play's spectacle (*la monster*) was of greater import than its subject matter (*le sujet*). A second early modern response makes the point even more forcefully. In an account of *Titus* that appeared in a collection of plays translated into German by Frederick Menius in the 1620s, purporting to be a record of plays acted by the English in Germany during the period,[9] we see a version of *Titus* stripped entirely of its intertextual relevance. The cast is cut to twelve speaking parts and two silent extras; all of the play's classical allusions are removed (even to the point of providing just a bucket of sand and a stick for Lavinia – no copy of Ovid's *Metamorphoses* exists here for her to draw the parallels to Philomela that are so important to Shakespeare's text). Jonathan Bate has observed of this written German account of a touring English player version that a '"lower" audience than Shakespeare is implied, one which requires a strong concentration on spectacle and action rather than ornate rhetoric'.[10] The reasons for the absence of any desire to prompt understanding of the play's highly developed intertextuality in this account would appear obvious: profound understanding of Shakespeare's *Titus* can only be achieved by those who: (1) have seen its contemporary theatrical intertexts staged (and thereby derive metatheatrical pleasure in Shakespeare's exploitation of contemporaneous London theatregrams);[11] and (2) also have knowledge of the play's literary and historical intertexts. A popular German audience, separated by language, geographical distance and cultural location,

would have seen few, if any, of the plays that speak to Shakespeare's fashionable staging, nor would they have understood classical allusions made in English. The author of this German-language account of an English touring production, like the French tutor in Harrington's household, accordingly documents an understanding of Shakespeare's text predicated upon only the simplest physical aspects of its performance – the only elements of production they had been able to understand.

Two significant aspects of current film and theatre practice have exactly the same effect as the cultural and linguistic distance that affected the degree and mode of understanding that either Petit or Menius could attain in watching a 'foreign' *Titus*. The first is the prevalence in current British and American film and theatre practice of naturalistic staging techniques, and the dominance of acting processes predicated upon psychological realism, including method acting; the second is the sometimes disorientating presence of female actors in modern performances of early

---

7. Given that Sir John Harrington had connections to the Earl of Essex's faction, it is possible that his commissioning of a performance of Shakespeare's play had more to do with *Titus*'s treatment of the political issue of succession than it did to the play's presentation of acts of physical violence.

8. See Gustav Ungerer, 'An Unrecorded Elizabethan Performance of *Titus Andronicus*', in *Shakespeare Survey 14* (Cambridge, 1961), pp. 102–9. I translate Petit as follows: 'we also had the tragedy of *Titus Andronicus* played to us, but the staging was of more import than the subject matter' (*monster* is the archaic version of the French verb *monter*, which, used in conjunction with an event, can indicate the act of producing it, e.g. *monter un complot* – to hatch a plan; *monter une pièce de theatre* – to stage a play).

9. The play was entitled, with characteristic German brevity, *Eine sehr klägliche Tragaedia von Tito Andronico und der hoffertigen Kaiserin, darinnen denckwürdige actions zubefinden*. See Willy Louis Braekman, 'The Relationship of Shakespeare's *Titus Andronicus* to the German Play of 1620 and to Jan Vos's *Aran en Titus*', *Studia Germanica Gandensia*, 9 (1967), 9–117; and 10 (1968), 9–65.

10. Bate, 'Introduction', p. 45.

11. I refer to the concept of the theatregram as outlined by Louise George Clubb in *Italian Drama in Shakespeare's Time* (New Haven, CT, 1989), pp. 1–26.

1. Vivien Leigh in an abstract forest, with scarlet and white streamers flowing from her mouth and wrists (1955). © RSC Production Archive

modern English drama. Before I turn to the significance of these factors on the performance text that I will consider in most detail (Julie Taymor's filmed *Titus* of 1999) however, I want to consider a number of key theatrical productions from recent years, in order to establish a performative genealogy for this play and the character of Lavinia during the second half of the twentieth century and onwards.

III

According to Milton Shulman, until Peter Brook staged *Titus Andronicus* at the RST in 1955 (Illustration 1), the play had 'only been given two major productions in 100 years'; the same critic added that '[t]he squeamish may well wonder why there have been so many'.[12] Brook's version of *Titus* is considered a landmark production that influenced theatrical approaches to the play for the next thirty years, until Deborah Warner (1987) and

---

[12] Milton Shulman, *London Evening Standard*, 17 August 1955, quoted in Samantha Ellis, 'Peter Brook's *Titus Andronicus*, August 1955', *Guardian*, 25 June 2003, www.theguardian.com/stage/2003/jun/25/theatre.samanthaellis. All further references to contemporary newspaper reviews of Brook's production are from this article.

Bill Alexander (2003) broke decisively from its legacy.[13] Brook omitted unnecessary violence and created horror using elegant and beautiful images. Working within what he considered to be an Artaudian theatrical episteme that made much of Asian symbolism, he emphasized the stylistic nature of Shakespeare's play rather than acquiesce with the excesses of literalized violence that *Titus* has sometimes suggested to less astute practitioners. A key example of Brook's strategy was the vision of Lavinia after her rape and mutilation, in which Vivien Leigh stood in front of an abstract forest, with scarlet and white streamers flowing from her mouth and wrists. The discovery was accompanied by an eerie, slow plucking of harp strings, described as being 'like drops of blood falling into a pool' (Brook composed the music and 'clashed experimentally with pots and warming pans, played with pencils on Venetian glass phials [and] turned wire baskets into harps' in his attempts to write the perfect score).[14]

The lack of gore achieved by Brook's rejection of naturalistic approaches to stage violence ensured that the director 'created an atmosphere in which the [play's] horrors [could] take hold of [the audience]'.[15] Paradoxically, the effect of this tacit elision of violence was an augmentation of the power of the play's viscerality. According to the *Daily Express*, extra St John Ambulance volunteers had to be called in during the run because at least three spectators passed out each night. Other critics drew attention to the evident contradiction, claiming that the production was 'full-blooded and bloodless' whilst observing '[w]hat a gory Gala night Mr Brook could have made of it! And how triumphantly he resisted the temptation!'.[16] The *Manchester Guardian* observed that Brook conjured 'dazzling simplicity out of a terrifying tawny darkness'.[17] Despite no explicit verbal reference or semiotic visual allusion of any kind being made in the production to events of the recent and traumatic past, the *Times* review chillingly concluded that 'There is absolutely nothing in the bleeding barbarity of *Titus Andronicus* which would have astonished anyone at Buchenwald.'[18]

Brook's *Titus* had immense power because it was staged in ways that involved non-literal and non-naturalistic approaches to the play's martial, homicidal and sexual violence. The director claimed that 'the real appeal ... was obviously for everyone in the audience about the most modern of emotions – about violence, hatred, cruelty, pain – in a form that because *unrealistic*, transcended the anecdote and became ... *quite abstract and thus totally real*'.[19] In his attempts to achieve this theatrical 'reality', Brook cut the play by over 850 lines, including the entirety of Marcus's discovery speech in Act 2, scene 3. The discovery of Lavinia was accordingly rendered as silent tableaux within an upstage discovery space, described by the promptbook thus: 'Enter C[entre] Lavinia stands desolate ... Demetrius and Chiron slowly close the column doors meeting C[entre]'.[20]

Faced with the forty-seven lines of sublime poetry that Shakespeare gives Marcus at the discovery of his niece, Brook saw simply an exercise in verbal stylization and replaced words with a powerful stage image – an approach that, according to Jonathan Bate,

Answer[ed] to the first rule of strong theatrical reinvention. The long red ribbons serv[ing] as a translation of the language of the text in that they stand in the same evocative but oblique relation to blood as do such similes as that of the bubbling fountain ... Brook's innovation[s] may ... be said to grow from the original script. And at

---

[13] For a brief account of the production, see Dennis Kennedy, *Looking at Shakespeare: A Visual History of Twentieth-Century Performance* (Cambridge, 2001), pp. 168–71.

[14] Shulman, quoted in Ellis, '*Titus Andronicus*'.

[15] An unnamed critic writing for the *Times*, quoted in Ellis, '*Titus Andronicus*'.

[16] Cecil Wilson, *Daily Mail*, quoted in Ellis, '*Titus Andronicus*'.

[17] Philip Hope-Wallace, quoted in Ellis, '*Titus Andronicus*'.

[18] Harold Hobson, quoted in Ellis, '*Titus Andronicus*'.

[19] Peter Brook, 'Search for a Hunger', *Encore* (July–August 1961), 16–17, quoted in Alan C. Dessen, *Shakespeare in Performance: Titus Andronicus* (Manchester, 1989), p. 15.

[20] Promptbook for Peter Brook's *Titus Andronicus*, Shakespeare Centre, Stratford-upon-Avon; quoted in Bate, 'Introduction', p. 60.

2. Lavinia's dress, designed by Peter Brook. Note the crumpled fabric of the underskirt, resembling tree bark. © RSC Costume Archive

the same time they speak in the new language of the post-Artaudian theatre in which stage events are

ritualized and their correspondence to reality outside theatre is skewed and problematized.[21]

This may well be true; nevertheless, in the early modern period, heightened audience understanding was derived from an appreciation of the emblematic nature of Shakespeare's theatrical spectacle *together with* an acknowledgement of the play's rich vein of literary and historical intertextuality. Without the combination of heavily mediated spectacle (a boy actor representing a totem of femininity, using symbolic representations of bloodshed to articulate the violence that has been enacted upon it) *alongside* the power of literary and historical allusion (communicated through deliberately intertextual Shakespearian verse), the scene's philosophical importance and the power implicit in its reception are both diminished.

In the twentieth century, Brook's production is testament to the fact that *Titus* can achieve significant theatrical power when its violence is rendered metaphorical, when the human bodies onstage are considered not as psychologically complete human entities, but rather as emblematic tools in the communication of raw human emotions (what Brook describes as a quality of performance that enabled his production to '[touch] audiences directly because [it] tapped in it a ritual of bloodshed which was recognised as true').[22] However, to separate the play's spectacle from its literarily and historically specific aural referents is to do much damage to its wider project. Thus Brook, in his very attempt to render symbolic (and therefore universal) the violence of *Titus*, inevitably tied it down to a response appropriate perhaps only to his own historical moment: a European society emerging from the annihilation of the Second World War – acts of genocide that were as yet still unspeakable amongst those who had discovered them.

Many producers of *Titus* in recent years have responded in like manner; such metaphorical abstractions range from Freedman in 1967 to Ninagawa in 2006 – whose Marcus likewise omitted all references to Ovid and instead keened

[21] Bate, 'Introduction', pp. 60–1.

[22] Peter Brook, *The Empty Space* (Harmondsworth, 1990), p. 53.

animalistically as he encountered a kabuki-inspired symbolic representation of the mutilated Lavinia.[23]

IV

So where can we find an alternative to this stripped-down, visually metaphorical but verbally cut tradition? And what alternate valences can a different approach to staging *Titus* in the modern world offer? The answers come from the political landscape of British imperialism towards Ireland during the 1970s. In 1972, Trevor Nunn, Buzz Goodbody and Euan Smith staged a version of *Titus* at the RST that rejected entirely the theatrical symbolism of Brook and its influential legacy. Nunn's production was predicated upon stage realism and, to Colin Blakely, an Irishman who played Titus and saw numerous analogies to Conservative British politics and the occupation of his homeland, the similarities he detected between Rome and Britain (in Ireland) or America (in Vietnam) as empires in decline, led him to observe: 'of all [Shakespeare's] Roman plays it is the most apposite to our present time. It is quite up to date. It takes a look at an empire in decay and a system which has become so hard, so brittle, that it breaks.'[24]

Nunn's production accordingly represented violence in a naturalistic way, with the in-your-face realism of the mass media news camera. This frankness was seen as the only possibility for a team of politicized directors and actors who recognized that 'people can see what violence is really like when they watch the news on television', and confessed: 'whatever we did, it would never be as horrible as that picture of the officer pushing a gun into a man's head in Vietnam'.[25]

The rape of Lavinia was presented as a horrifying physical assault. Subsequent to her violation, Suzman acted a Lavinia who, due to the severity of the assault she had endured, experienced difficulty in standing upright, or in walking; she was hung up by the arms by Chiron and Demetrius during the course of their taunts and, according to Billington, presented 'a pitiable, hunched, grotesque, crawling out of the darkness like a wounded animal' (Illustration 3).[26] As Titus embraced his daughter

upon their first post-rape encounter, Suzman 'presse[d] against her father for comfort like some terrified animal'.[27] In the context of this 'lingering, slow-motion realism ... naturalistic weight and stress', there was no room for Marcus's poetic explications of his niece's state either.[28] The RSC promptbook accordingly shows that twenty-nine of Marcus's forty-seven lines in 2.3 were cut, including all the Ovidian ones.[29]

By contrast, in 1987, Deborah Warner directed an uncut version of *Titus* at the RSC's Swan theatre. Dessen notes that the production

started with no overriding interpretation (or music or design concept), but rather assembled the best actors available, actors who *wanted* to do this script, and then went through, scene by scene, confronting each problem as it emerged, with the designer ... on hand, making sketches so as to adjust design and costume choices to those ongoing decisions. The word repeated constantly among *Titus* personnel was trust: trust in the script, in the audience, in the Swan ... in each other.[30]

The stage of the relatively new and deliberately intimate Swan was practically bare, save for the occasional stage property, sometimes historical, sometimes modern. As a result, Warner displayed a 'stripped simplicity of means [that] enable[d audiences] to feel the terror of a bucket, cheesewire, and a little stage blood'.[31] In Act 2, scene 3,

---

[23] For a detailed account of this production, see Christian M. Billing, 'The Emperor's New Clothes: Review of *Titus Andronicus* (Directed by Yukio Ninagawa) at the Royal Shakespeare Theatre, June 2006', *Shakespeare*, 3 (2007), 203–12.

[24] Colin Blakely, interview by Judith Cook, *Shakespeare's Players* (1983), pp. 88–9, quoted in Dessen, *Shakespeare in Performance*, p. 36.

[25] Blakely, quoted in Dessen, *Shakespeare in Performance*, p. 36.

[26] Michael Billington, *Guardian*, 13 October 1972, quoted in Dessen, *Shakespeare in Performance*, p. 39.

[27] *Leamington Spa Courier*, 20 October 1972, quoted in Dessen, *Shakespeare in Performance*, p. 39.

[28] Billington, quoted in Dessen, *Shakespeare in Performance*, p. 36.

[29] Bate, 'Introduction', p. 60.

[30] Dessen, *Shakespeare in Performance*, p. 57.

[31] Robert Hewison, *Sunday Times*, 4 July 1988, quoted in Dessen, *Shakespeare in Performance*, p. 58.

3. Janet Suzman as Lavinia, hung up on a tree at the beginning of the assault by Chiron and Demetrius. © RSC Production Archive

Lavinia's plight was indicated not by buckets of blood, but by a coating of clay or mud applied to her body, through Ritter's posture, and in the improvised bandages that had been applied to her stumps (Illustration 4). Presented in its entirety in one of the rare examples of textual fidelity since the Second World War, Marcus's monologue became a desperate attempt to rationalize and contextualize a horror that, precisely *because of* her uncle's *oral* explications, was no longer specific to Lavinia (and hence utterly unknown and unexpected), but rather a horror enacted as part of

4. Sonia Ritter and Donald Sumpter in Deborah Warner's discovery scene (1987). © Richard Mildenhall

a long tradition of violence against women. The staging of the scene did not, accordingly, present Lavinia as entirely subdued, the kind of quivering animal who ran to the arms of the nearest patriarch (as in Nunn); rather, 'A two actor scene, wherein [the audience] observe[d] Marcus, step-by-step, use his logic and Lavinia's reactions to work out what has happened, so that the spectators both [saw] Lavinia directly *and* [saw] her through his eyes and images.'[32] The terror was thus mediated through the poetic consciousness of Shakespeare's reworked classical narrative and, halfway through his speech, Marcus moved to hold Lavinia – a position he held up to and including his penultimate line 'do not draw back', which Warner used

---

[32] Dessen, *Shakespeare in Performance*, p. 60.

to highlight the difficulty that Lavinia had, as a rape victim, in moving forwards either emotionally or physically from this utterly devastating moment.

Nevertheless, despite fulfilling all the demands placed upon her by an uncut script, Lavinia did not seem to escape the trauma of this pivotal scene and, as the play progressed, like Suzman before her, she became 'a sub-human ... who in the final two scenes ... has lived so long with the memories of Act II as to become catatonic'.[33] Ritter consequently 'played her part in Titus' plans but left it to the men to take the decisions'.[34] As Dessen observes, 'Ritter responded to the challenges in Lavinia's silences in a powerful and often disturbing fashion that signalled her status as a reflection [of] and, as a result, a victim of the men in this Rome'.[35] Theatre critics likewise saw not an active and assertive woman who became an agent of her own retribution, but a victim of and a servant to the forces of patriarchy – a point that was perhaps made most forcefully by Coveney's description of Lavinia's dead body, following her father's breaking of her neck in Act 5, scene 3, as the falling of 'a discarded dummy on a ventriloquist's knee'.[36] Bate points out the gender-political rationale behind Warner's interpretation:

Warner in her direction of Marcus and Sonia Ritter in her portrayal of Lavinia achieved what they did because rape matters to them as late-twentieth-century women more than it could possibly have done to Shakespeare writing for Marcus and the boy who first played Lavinia ... Watching Ritter and sensing Warner behind Sumpter, one could with Marcus begin to share the rape victim's anguish. The scene was so powerful to so many members of the audience because our culture is more conscious of rape and its peculiar vileness than many previous cultures have been: so it was that the words from the 1590s ... worked a new effect in the context of the 1980s.[37]

Such sentiments have influenced productions from Warner's *Titus* onwards, particularly Alexander's 2003 Royal Shakespeare Company production, for which assistant director Tom Wright and Lavinia actor Eve Myles went to a rape crisis centre for guidance, describing their experience as follows:

It was such a difficult, intense experience – we were in a place where women are daily counselled for exactly the things Lavinia has experienced. We told them the story and they said how remarkably similar it seemed to the stages people go through when they've been raped. The key stage that you reach at the start of recovery is to acknowledge what has happened. Lavinia chooses a very specific moment to write RAPE in the sand. That marks the beginning of her recovery. We also described the very short scene with Chiron and Demetrius after the rape and were told that rapists rationalize very quickly ...[38]

I would like to suggest that a combination of the entirely understandable and ethically proper gender-political imperatives of modern directors in relation to the representation of the act of rape and its consequences, and their less defensible reliance on psychological realism and emotion-recall-based, Stanislavskian systems of actor training and rehearsal to achieve them, has led modern theatre and cinema into a performative cul-de-sac in which more credence is given to prevailing sociological constraints and moral contexts than to either the Shakespearian playtext or its historical and literary intertexts. For a director to guide an actor who is to play Lavinia towards a rape crisis centre rather than

---

[33] Dessen, *Shakespeare in Performance*, p. 65. Nancy Carlin in Oregon in 1986 likewise played Lavinia as Catatonic. See Dessen, *Shakespeare in Performance*, p. 93.

[34] Dessen, *Shakespeare in Performance*, p. 66.

[35] Dessen, *Shakespeare in Performance*, pp. 66–7.

[36] Michael Coveney, *Financial Times*, 14 May 1987, quoted in Dessen, *Shakespeare in Performance*, p. 95.

[37] Bate, 'Introduction', pp. 63–5.

[38] The literality of research was not limited to rape counselling; Tom Wright also tried to find a doctor who specialized in amputations and through the internet found the Limbless Association, an organization that helps people who have lost limbs. They put him in contact with a veteran from the Falklands conflict whose arm had been blown off while defusing a bomb. The research led to work with actors concerning the psychosomatic condition of the phantom limb, which was used in scenes like the fly-killing scene. Wright observes: 'from this we surmised that even after their hands had been chopped off, Titus and Lavinia would imagine their hands were still there and would reach for things' (RSC website for Bill Alexander's 2003 production of *Titus Andronicus*, accessed 23 May 2007 (URL no longer active)).

to offer her copy of Ovid's *Metamorphoses* and a selection of feminist readings that articulate patterns of resistance within those difficult narratives, is to place the performer in a social and psychological context that neither suits the play, nor from which it is easy to escape. Certainly, if psychology, understood through verbal articulation, is to be the exit strategy, then Shakespeare's play-text offers no way out – because Lavinia never tells us how she feels. She cannot. In addition to the manifest inaccuracy of the assumption that they 'were in a place where women are daily counselled *for exactly the things Lavinia has experienced*', in taking recourse in psychology and the trauma of real, lived human experience, Wright and Myles (like most modern directors and actors who approach the role of Lavinia) were closing off many more performative possibilities than they were opening up.

In contrast, by incorporating Ovid at the moments he does, Shakespeare not only locates Lavinia's rape within a narrative tradition in which there is clear classical precedent for the actions that have happened, but also within one that powerfully adumbrates the events of retribution that are to come. The dramatist also significantly offers a route to redemption and release that is predicated not merely upon the vengeful acts of Lavinia's male family members, but upon those of the sufferer *herself* – an intertextual frame of reference that powerfully foreshadows the female vengeance that is to come and highlights not only Lavinia's role in the capture and mutilation of Demetrius and Chiron, but her eventual corporal release from the torment of physical and emotional suffering.[39]

V

Classical scholarship of approximately the past thirty years has demonstrated the ways in which Ovid's poetic output evinces 'recognition of aspects of [the female] condition that are only now becoming common currency'. In particular, *Metamorphoses*, which contains approximately fifty instances of 'forcible rape, attempted rape, or sexual extortion hardly indistinguishable from rape'

provides analyses of the ways in which patriarchal oppression and predatory sexual expectation are endured, avoided and revenged by female characters.[40] In certain instances, Ovidian rape entirely dehumanizes its victims, partly because an overriding generic telos of the *Metamorphoses* is to lead its characters towards final acts of transformation from human into animal or vegetal states. As Curran observes, in Ovid:

> Rape does worse than undermine a woman's identity; it can rob her of her humanity [therefore] transformation into the non-human is uniquely appropriate in the case of rape, for the process of de-humanisation begins long before any subsequent metamorphosis of the woman's body. The transition from human to sex object and then to object pure and simple proceeds by swift and easy stages, its onset being simultaneous with the decision to commit rape. The final physical transformation of so many rape victims is only the outward ratification of an earlier metamorphosis of the woman into a mere thing in the mind of the attacker and in his treatment of her . . .[41]

The Ovidian character who best exemplifies the dynamic of desire, objectification, transformation and inertia is Daphne, the nymph who in her desire to flee the advances of Apollo, is transformed into a tree. In Daphne, Ovid writes version of female experience in which the only line of defence when faced with unconstrained male sexual desire is to become an inanimate material substance incapable of being raped because it does not possess the reproductive biology of human, divine or animal worlds. Daphne avoids ravishment, true, but at the significant price of giving up her human form – and it is important to remember that this was a form that not only led to Apollo's desire of her, but also constituted the corporeal frame in and through which Daphne had been able to perceive of and engage with the world. In phenomenological terms, therefore, Daphne's metamorphosis is not

---

[39] Interestingly, it is to this aspect of Ovid's *Metamorphoses* that female dramatists such as Sarah Kane and Timberlake Wertenbaker have turned in their appropriations.

[40] Leo C. Curran, 'Rape and Rape Victims in the Metamorphoses', *Arethusa*, 11 (1978), 213–41; p. 231.

[41] Curran, 'Rape', p. 229.

merely a loss of agency, it is rather a retreat from all sentient existence as ontological subject. Moreover, such an exit from the world of apprehension and agency seems to be prefigured into Daphne's culturally encoded identity as woman, because '[a]s Daphne runs from Apollo, the effect of the wind on her fluttering clothing and streaming hair corresponds closely to what the wind will do to the branches and leaves of the tree she is to become'.[42]

This physical similarity between the object of Apollo's desire and the objectified tree that is Daphne's teleological destiny is disturbing enough; but what is perhaps more shocking is the willingness of critics to ascribe its non-human, ontologically absent characteristics to the experience of the real women who have been raped throughout history:

After her transformation, Daphne as tree is an exact analogue of a victim so profoundly traumatized by her experience that she has taken refuge in a catatonic withdrawal from all human involvement, passively acted upon by her environment and by other persons, but cut off from any response that could be called human. Ovid's language describing what he and Apollo choose to take as the laurel's 'reactions' (l. 556 and 556–7) has an eerie but psychologically correct ring to it.[43]

The impassive inertia of the rape victim detected here resonates chillingly against the 'catatonia' also perceived by the performance critic, Alan Dessen in relation to Ritter's portrayal of Lavinia. Such a response to the act of rape in textual or performative terms as inertia, absence, the closing in and off of any ability to engage sensorially, corporally and articulately with the world, is also chillingly seen as being 'psychologically correct' by both men.

Fortunately for feminist critics and modern theatre practitioners interpreting the Ovidian influences acting in and through Shakespeare's *Titus Andronicus*, Daphne is not the most prominent intertextual referent pointing towards the modalities of Ovidian rape in the play. Lavinia is much more frequently and systematically compared, by both Shakespeare and his critics, to Ovid's character Philomela, the sister-in-law raped by Tereus and tormented by him in her still living, still

human form through having her tongue cut out and being forced to continue her life in a sequestered, mutilated, silenced form. Unlike the tale of Daphne, however, in Philomela's story the protagonists remain for a long time unremittingly human. As Marder observes: 'While most of the preceding Ovidian tales depict conflicts between human and divine figures, present confusions of animal and inanimate worlds, and involve magical or supernatural operations, the story of Philomela is presented as a human drama among characters who are endowed solely with human powers, proper names, and social positions.'[44]

Because the detailed narrative events of Ovid's tale of Tereus, Procne and Philomela are central to my argument, I will summarise them here: Tereus, a Thracian king, marries a woman called Procne and brings her to his home in Thrace. After a brief period, Procne becomes homesick for her sister, Philomela, and implores her husband to return to her father's home in order to solicit Philomela as a companion for his new wife. Tereus consents and travels to Procne's father's house, where he sees Philomela for the first time. Upon seeing her, he is consumed with a burning passion, and convinces the father to consent to Philomela travelling back to Thrace, ostensibly as companion to her sister. On their arrival in Thrace, however, Tereus drags Philomela into a forest, tells her that he is going to rape her, then rapes her. When Philomela threatens to speak out concerning her ravishment, Tereus cuts out her tongue and rapes her once again. Tereus then locks Philomela in a cottage in the forest. Unable to speak, Philomela uses a loom in the dwelling to weave a communication relating to her rape, using red thread on a white background. She sends the cloth to her sister, Procne. Upon receipt, Procne uses the pretext of a Bacchic festival as an excuse to leave Tereus's palace. She then dances her way to the cottage in which Philomela

[42] Curran, 'Rape', pp. 229 and 230.
[43] Curran, 'Rape', p. 230.
[44] Elissa Marder, 'Disarticulated Voices: Feminism and Philomela', *Hypatia*, 7 (1992), 148–66; pp. 156–7.

is imprisoned. She immediately brings her sister back to the palace and plots appropriate revenge. Although Procne considers castrating Tereus or cutting out his tongue, she is finally moved by the physical similarity between Tereus and their son, Itys. She therefore stabs Itys, decapitates and disembowels him, and puts the remaining cuts of his human flesh into a stew, which she serves to Tereus. As he eats, Tereus asks to see his son; at which point Procne tells Tereus that Itys is now in his stomach. Philomela enters, bearing the decapitated head of Itys, which she throws in the King's lap. When Tereus draws his sword to kill the two sisters, all three protagonists are turned into birds and fly away.

Marder argues that Ovid's tale of Philomela is not simply a powerful exemplar of male aggression and female revenge, but, precisely because its figuration of the male violation of women is framed in relation to access to language, it acts as a metaphor for the modern feminist project.

The text appears to stage two 'rapes': one 'literal' and the other 'symbolic'. While one might assume that the literal rape rapes the body and the figurative rape violates access to speech, the text reverses these two registers. The first actual rape is accompanied and preceded by a speech act that announces the crime. The act of speaking rape is supplemented by the act of 'raping' speech – the cutting off of the tongue – that occurs later. Between these two acts comes the act of sexual domination. The Latin text insists on the convergence between speaking the crime and doing the deed: '*fassusque nefas et virginem et unam vi supererat* . . . [the crime being spoken, he overwhelmed the virgin, by force, all alone]' (l. 524 . . .). One cannot speak 'rape' or speak about rape, merely in terms of a physical body. The sexual violation of the woman's body is itself embedded in discursive and symbolic structures . . .[45]

These 'symbolic structures' relate most profoundly in feminist terms to the ways in which silenced and violated women (all women within a patriarchal world) must, if they are to escape oppression, take ownership of, subvert and refashion male discourses and behaviours in order not only to assert their rejection of such oppression but also their right to exist in a world that exists outside patriarchy and its linguistic and behavioural confines.

But the journey is not a straightforward one, and, despite an ostensibly Maenadic enactment of revenge, Ovid's story does not immediately allow escape from patriarchy, but rather draws attention to the cycles of violence, disenfranchisement and atrocity that inevitably spring from it. To Marder, therefore,

The text invites a feminist reading not only because it recounts the story of a woman's rape, but also because it establishes a relationship between the experience of violation and the access to language. Unable to speak, Philomela weaves the story of her rape. Only after she has been raped and mutilated does Philomela attempt to write. Through weaving, she writes the story because she cannot speak, and the only story she has to tell is that she has lost her voice. She writes out of necessity and in response to violation, but that writing is bound by the terms of violation.[46]

In raping his sister-in-law, Tereus has violated not just the order of familial relations but also the patriarchal order itself. It is for this reason that, in the moment in which Tereus seizes Philomela's tongue and moves to cut it out, Ovid has her tongue call upon patriarchal authority to defend her: 'he seized her tongue with pincers, as it protested against the outrage, calling ever the name of the father [*et nomen patris usque vocantem*] and struggling to speak, and he cut it off with merciless blade' (lines 555–60). At this moment of mutilation, the only language (*lingua*) that Philomela's tongue (also *lingua*) can speak is that of patriarchal authority; and the only response that comes from a male in the light of her invocation of 'the name of father' is one of abuse and violation. Thus Philomela is 'doubly silenced, first by the rapist, and then by the paternal law itself. [Her] tongue speaks only the language of the law: the name of the father. While the horror of the rape violates the paternal order, the effects of the rape disclose the implicit violation *by* the paternal order.'[47]

In Ovid's narrative, once Philomela has experienced this third, metaphorical rape (the first being

---

[45] Marder, 'Disarticulated Voices', p. 158.
[46] Marder, 'Disarticulated Voices', p. 157.
[47] Marder, 'Disarticulated Voices', p. 160.

the announcement by Tereus of his intentions, the second being the physical act of his raping her), she begins of necessity to seek means of articulation through embodied discourses: she weaves, she dances, she cuts, she cooks, she throws, she sings as a bird. It is in the moment of literal and metaphorical rupture that is constituted in/by the rape that Ovid's text begins to provide the possibility of resistance. Interestingly, therefore, there is no definitive indication in the *Metamorphoses* that Philomela uses either script or language as a means of communication subsequent to her violation. Indeed, the most significant things about Ovid's description of the tapestry she produces for Procne (her textile but not necessarily textual message) are its emphasis on the colours of the woven document (red and white) and its use of 'signs' [*notas*] (line 577) – which, in addition to denoting the marks of writing on a page, can be used in Latin to mean 'rupture or puncture', 'branding', 'observation' or 'visual record'. Thus, while Marder is correct to observe

the Latin text implies that the story of Philomela's mutilation and rape is communicated by neither words or pictures. The purple words on a white background figure the bloody writing as tattoo marks on a branded body. Although alienated from her body, this form of writing through weaving represents and writes the mutilated body ... [t]his is a form of writing born from a violation of speech; its clarity and urgency derive from marks of pain. But the language that is derived from pain and mutilation can say nothing outside a discourse of pain and mutilation[48]

the significant *retreat* in the Ovidian text from the world of *language* to a world of *embodiment* is also deeply significant here.

In the feminist discourse of theorists such as Butler and Kristeva, a retreat from language towards embodiment, and particularly embodiment in and through abjection, allows for the creation of a more significant site of resistance than that which is possible through male-authored languages and socialized modes of thought/behaviour.[49] In a corporeal world that rejects the primacy of language, an emphatically embodied evocation of the female other can defy, and eventually replace,

the patriarchal order. This is what the Philomela myth tells us. And it is why the transformation at the end of it is so radically different from that at the end of the myth of Apollo and Daphne. Thus while Tereus's transgression is communicated by the male rapist most emphatically in linguistic terms (before he commits the act of rape he must name it, and subsequent to the act itself he seeks to control knowledge of his crime through control of the access to the means of linguistic production: Philomela's patriarchally instructed *lingua*), Philomela's, and subsequently Procne's, route(s) to the destabilization of Tereus's patriarchal authority are all intensely corporeal. When Philomela's textile expression of history and identity arrives with Procne, the response it provokes in her sister is silence: '*evolvit vestes saevi matroni tyranni fortunaeque suae carmen miserabile legit et (mirum potuisse) silet: dolor ora repressit, verbaque quaerenti satis indignantia linguae defuerunt, nec flere vacat* [opening out the fabric, she reads the wretched state of her sister (a miracle that she is able to) and she is silent. Grief represses her mouth and her questioning tongue fails to find words equal to her rage nor could she weep]' (lines 582–6).

Next, Procne's use of a Bacchic festival as the pretext for her flight to rescue her sister furthers Ovid's exploration of the embodied female other as radical agent. She dances away from the patriarchal world represented by the palace to the forest, the locus of male desire and sexual violence in which Philomela waits; the pair then use Bacchic dance as a means of escaping the confines of the forest. In all their actions, Procne and Philomela embody and enact corporeal sites and behavioural modes of resistance that are mediated *not* through words but *in action*. When 'Procne, rejects a logic of symmetry or exchange [and] refuses to take a tongue for a tongue, or even a penis for a tongue [and when] the weapon that is stronger

---

[48] Marder, 'Disarticulated Voices', p. 161.

[49] See, for example, Judith Butler, *Bodies that Matter: On the Discursive Limits of Sex* (London, 2011), and Julia Kristeva, *Powers of Horror: An Essay on Abjection* (New York, 1982).

than the sword is a language fuelled by excess instead of loss', each articulation of this new 'language' is a corporeal one.[50] Such 'languages' of female agency – motion, action and revenge – are never articulated phonetically or scripturally; rather, they are articulated in performative iterations of movements that are either culturally or generically associated with the female body, or inversions of acculturated female functions such as birthing, sustaining, or nurturing human bodies. Thus Procne

stuffs [Tereus's] mouth and belly with the body of his son, leaving Tereus no room for words. Procne violates her husband by making him gag on the law of the father; she arrests the progression of paternity by feeding him his own child through the mouth. Procne thus uses her own child as a substitute for a tongue. She speaks through her child, forcing the child into her husband's mouth and belly. In the body of the father, the belly becomes the place of the tomb instead of womb. Rather than relying on a logic of exchange and a discourse of loss, Procne transgresses the boundaries of the male body by forcing it to assume the presence of another. Metaphorically, Procne turns Tereus into a pathetic mimicry of a sterile, masculine maternity.[51]

In such a move, all patriarchy is mocked, muted and overcome.

VI

Despite her opinion that *Titus Andronicus* 'speak[s] directly to our times', Julie Taymor's film adaptation gains much of its power from its refusal to render *Titus* as a simile for any event with which a modern audience could easily identify.[52] The film's aesthetic laudably embraces a deliberate eclecticism with regards to historical costume, architectural location and the selection of stage properties.[53] Such plurality militates against audiences interpreting the film's temporal and/or geographical location with any degree of specificity. Taymor accordingly resists the impulse of many directors to render aspects of the violence in *Titus* literal, to speak of the way in which they are 'excited by the play because it seems so contemporary', to render it a story about real people, or to treat it as a simile for mid-twentieth-century European fascism, the ethnic genocide in Rwanda, the religious 'cleansing' of Bosnia, or any

other contemporary conflict.[54] In this respect, her film works well because it echoes what we can presume of the original production's visual style (at least in relation to that notoriously problematic early modern representation of the play, the Peacham manuscript).[55] Taymor's non-naturalistic treatment of the Roman army, her pan-historical depiction of political struggles between Bassianus and Saturninus, her use of puppetry, blue screen graphics and time-slice photography are all excellent translations of the play's original juxtapositional textual and performative modalities into modern media, which contribute to the overall success of the film. Yet there is one significant respect in which I consider Taymor's adaptation to be seriously flawed: her treatment of the rape of Lavinia.

The fifteen minutes of Act 2, scenes 2 and 3 sit uncomfortably with most of the rest of the film because here the director chooses to have the action rendered extremely brutally and naturalistically. From the opening duologue between Tamora and Aaron, the performances are characterized by overt physicality and a hyper-sexualization of the female bodies presented. In the case of Aaron, the lusty performance he is directed to provide runs counter to the sense of nearly all of the speeches he delivers (in which he rejects Venus in favour of Saturn and places his desire for revenge above any sexual desire that

---

[50] Marder, 'Disarticulated Voices', p. 161.

[51] Marder, 'Disarticulated Voices', p. 161.

[52] Taymor's production notes, quoted in George Hannah, 'From Shakespeare's *Titus Andronicus* to Julie Taymor's *Titus*', www.gprc.ab.ca/shakespeare/reviews/titusGeorge Review.html, accessed 29 May 2007.

[53] Indeed, rather than produce several of her props, Taymor raided the properties stores of the Italian film studios *Cinecittà*, making eclectic use of what she found in true Renaissance style.

[54] Bill Alexander, cited on the RSC website, www.rsc.org.uk /titus/current/director.html, accessed 29 May 2007.

[55] The Peacham manuscript is possibly one of the few surviving contemporary illustrations of a Shakespeare play in performance. It shows a scene from *Titus Andronicus* in which Tamora pleads for her sons. It is, however, widely disputed as to whether the scene can reliably be taken as a record of actual stage practice, given its internal inconsistencies.

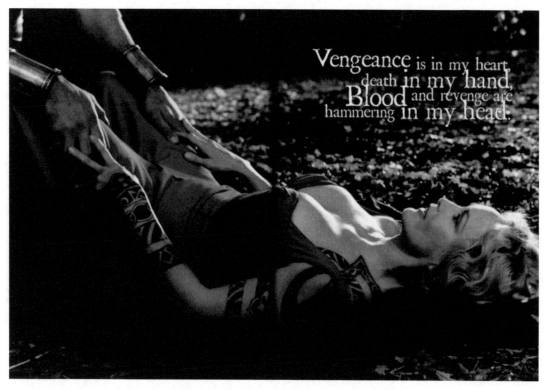

Vengeance is in my heart, death in my hand, Blood and revenge are hammering in my head.

5. Jessica Lange: Tamora as centrefold. © Newmarket Press

Tamora encourages him to have). Significantly, Taymor uses the bodies of the female performers she has cast to provide repeated images of the eroticized and fetishized female form. This is true of her representation of both Lavinia and of Tamora (the latter of whom begins to undress, is caressed on the neck, breasts, buttocks, thighs and belly by Aaron – who also places his fingers in her mouth and kisses her repeatedly, before she dresses once more with almost post-coital luxury). Taymor's spin-off publication, intended to capitalize on the success of her film, *Titus: The Illustrated Screenplay*, makes the point even more graphically as the recumbent body of Jessica Lange spreads across pages 74–5 in the manner of a pornographic centrefold (Illustration 5). From the entrance of Demetrius (04:37)[56] and Chiron (04:55), the voyeuristic realism of Taymor's scene is augmented by an immediacy achieved through the *cinema verité* technique of circling hand-held

camera shots rapidly intercut to provide shifting perspectives every few seconds. The attack of Chiron, and Demetrius, both participated in and overseen by their mother, is sold to the cinema audience as documentary fact. The *Screenplay* provides further evidence of this directorial intention through the use of slightly blurred cinematic frames and grainy black and white photo-journalistic shots (one of the rare occasions the book uses black and white images) (Illustration 6). In the film, Lavinia's gloves are stripped fetishistically (07:44) and Demetrius is made to lick Lavinia's naked hand (07:52) prior to straddling her from behind and cutting the buttons from the back of her dress

---

[56] Numbers in parenthesis indicate timings within the scene, which I take to begin with the cut from Tamora's hunting party to the shot of Aaron placing his dagger in the ground in order to dig a hole in which to hide his gold.

6. Black and white still from *Titus: The Illustrated Screenplay*. Note the grainy nature of the image, evocative of high-speed, low-light news photography, and the limited depth of field. © Newmarket Press

with a knife in close-up (08:18). Chiron subsequently swaps positions with his brother, straddles Lavinia from behind and rips open her dress, once again in close-up, to reveal Lavinia's naked back together with the straps and bodice of a low-cut corset (08:24). A reverse shot is provided next, in which Lavinia clutches her black dress against her stripped torso in an inadvertent revelation of first one shoulder and then both, together with a view of her falling corset straps (08:28). The scene is disturbing; it invites audiences to contemplate both the trauma of rape and the pleasure of highly eroticized, fetishistic sexual intercourse. It is an audacious directorial choice and, like that of other recent stage directors, it is intended to bring home the social reality of rape, together with a notion of the personal desecration it entails.

The problem with such a deliberately scopophilic treatment of the female body, however, is that it goes against the sense of Shakespeare's writing. Lavinia's plea to Tamora to 'tumble me into some loathsome pit / Where never man's eye may behold my body' (2.3.176–7) sits somewhat awkwardly with a scene in which (1) so much visual use is made of both Lavinia's and Tamora's fetishized anatomy and (2) both shot choice and aesthetic approach focus the audience's attention on the immediacy of one particular human subject's graphically real situation.[57] The naturalistic, documentary, almost photo-journalistic style chosen by Taymor to communicate the beginnings of what will culminate in a double rape, not only creates a performance that has more to do with the objectification of the female form in the medium of contemporary pornography than it does Shakespeare's play-text, but also presents what is happening as a series of real and frightening events.[58] In terms of its representation of the social

[57] For a discussion of the scopophilic in relation to the female screen body, see Laura Mulvey, 'Visual Pleasure and Narrative Cinema', *Screen*, 16 (1975), 6–18.

[58] Running the scene by Umberto Eco's acid test is illuminating. See Umberto Eco, 'How to Recognise A Porn Movie', in *Movies*, ed. Gilbert Adair (Harmondsworth, 1999).

reality of rape, this is a commendable set of decisions. But, given that the scene in Shakespeare is a linguistic precursor to the violence that takes place, quite deliberately, *offstage* and in which spectators are accordingly rendered complicit with the act of violence as a result of the fact that they are required to produce in their own mind's eye versions of the rape of Lavinia during the action of the pit scene (albeit guided by Shakespeare's poetic description of the briars that cover it), the fundamental dramatic function of both Shakespearian scenes is lost. Hence, through the strategies of naturalism, cinematic immediacy and the important fact that Taymor provides her spectators with documentary evidence of *other people* committing this act, the essential point is entirely lost that violence that is *not seen* theatrically or cinematically must be *imagined* and therefore renders auditors not only complicit in but also responsible for any and all acts of atrocity that they imagine. Put simply, it is easy for us to condemn Demetrius and Chiron in this film, because we do not mentally commit the act of rape for them.

The full effect of Taymor's decisions to victimize Lavinia absolutely, however, is not seen until the discovery scene of Act 2, scene 3, in which Taymor slowly returns her audience to the symbolic impressionism, expressionism and abstraction that characterize so magnificently the majority of her film. The audio/visual treatment of Marcus's discovery speech intercuts images of the speaker with sustained shots of the raped and mutilated Lavinia, over which the speech continues. By means of this subtle visual intercutting, Taymor is able to exploit a naturalistic version of the cinematic device of the voiceover – a technique that enables Marcus's lines prior to the opening of Lavinia's mouth to be laid over a bravura tracking shot that eventually cranes upwards as blood falls from the mutilated Lavinia's gaping mouth. The affective power of this moment is augmented by a stylized rising 'scream' in Goldenthal's orchestral underscoring (the music is present from the moment it is faded in over an establishing atmosphere of cicadas and birdsong, ten seconds after the

scene's beginning and at Marcus's line 'Who's this? My niece?').

This is undoubtedly powerful cinema. It is an uncomfortable moment of visual spectacle that makes much of the opposition between viewers' appreciation of the aesthetic beauty of Taymor's cinematography and their revulsion at the horror that it depicts. Such representation has a price, however, and the way that this moment has been aesthetically achieved makes its images so shocking that spectators need *time* to contemplate the full terror (and beauty) of what they are witnessing. Accordingly, a thirty-two-second silence follows the falling of blood from the windswept Lavinia's mouth. It is an eternity of screen time, accompanied only by a falling topos of grief in Goldenthal's Debussy-like, impressionistic score.

Unquestionably this is a major moment of Shakespeare cinema history but the cost is great, because it is not just Lavinia who is silenced in the sensory overload of Taymor's representation: Shakespeare's voice is also muted in this treatment, because the thirty-two seconds of verbal silence that Taymor needs for her audience to come to terms with her metaphorically beautiful vision of the ugliness of the results of male brutality replace some thirty lines of text.[59] Significantly, yet unsurprisingly given the genealogy of performance outlined above, these are lines that resonate within the intertextual history of literary considerations of sexual barbarity against women; references that add weight and significance to the rape of Lavinia, rendering it more than the representation of a single woman's plight.

Compounding this focus on Lavinia's pitiful, victimized silence and state of inertia is the fact that Taymor chooses to locate the scene in the

---

[59] The lines are 22–51, in which Marcus relates the violation of Lavinia to the rape of Philomela (Sophocles, *Tereus*; Ovid, *Metamorphoses*). He also connects Lavinia to Orpheus, and thereby to the other significant rape victim of classical literature, Lucretia (Livy, *History of Rome*; Ovid, *Fasti*). On the intertextual relationship of these accounts, and Shakespeare's use of them, see Jonathan Bate, *Shakespeare and Ovid* (Oxford, 1993), pp. 76–7 and 111–13.

7. Lavinia as Doe/Marilyn being attacked by Chiron and Demetrius in the PAN following her revelation of the rape. © 20th Century Fox

muddy, marshy area of a river delta, with shattered sticklike trees protruding from the riverbed's churned-up mud. The vista is evocative of Augustus John's expressionistic scenery for the World War I scenes of *The Silver Tassie* (1928), or photographic stills of devastated Flanders battlefields. In this mutilated landscape of shattered trees, which clearly alludes to iconic images of nature assaulted by men, Taymor has decided to place Lavinia on a shattered stump, with twigs sticking into her own 'stumps' as a visual incarnation of the mockery of hands promised to her by Chiron and Demetrius. The result is perhaps the most powerful image of Lavinia as Daphne to have been created in the performance history of Shakespeare's play.[60]

The tenor of this awkward static victim representation continues in the film's fourth Penny Arcade Nightmare (PAN): which re-presents Lavinia's rape as a psychological haunting. Taymor inserts this mental flashback during the revelation of Lavinia's attackers (prompted by a copy of Ovid) and the inscription of

[STUPRUM] CHIRON DEMETRIUS in the sand. Here, Taymor makes a brave decision to have Lavinia reject Marcus's textual instructions to take the phallically figured stick in her mouth and between her hands in a moment of re-engagement with language through inscription that would simultaneously symbolically refigure her own violation. Yet, despite this, once again, the chosen mode of performance is based on fixation with psychological remembrance of the defilement of the victim, this time through memorial reconstruction in which Taymor presents iconic images of the objectification of Lavinia as an object of male desire/attack. Now taking the form of Marilyn Monroe in *The Seven Year Itch* (Illustration 7), Lavinia in her own memory is 'rooted' on a classical pedestal, attacked by Demetrius and Chiron in the form of tigers and

---

[60] For a discussion of Lavinia as Daphne, see Thomas Cartelli and Katherine Rowe, 'Colliding Space and Time in Taymor's *Titus*', in *New Wave Shakespeare on Film* (Cambridge, 2007), pp. 84–9.

8. Lavinia as Marilyn on a classical column being attacked by Chiron and Demetrius in the form of tigers, from the PAN following her revelation of the rape. © 20th Century Fox

transformed into a fawn, with a doe's head and hooves, which she uses to try to keep her billowing skirts in check (Illustration 8).

Taymor states that she devised the concept of the PAN (used throughout her film) 'to portray the inner landscapes of the mind as affected by the external actions', arguing that '[t]hey depict in abstract collages, fragments of memory, the unfathomable layers of a violent event'.[61] Ironically, of course, by choosing to retreat into Lavinia's psyche and represent her imagined remembrance of rape as a visual essay in victimization, Taymor inadvertently inverts and thereby negates the narrative of Ovid, according to whom, in their revenge, '[Procne] pounced on Itys, *like A tigress pouncing on a suckling fawn ...* And dragged him to a distant lonely part Of the great house... struck him with a knife [as] Philomela slit his throat' (636–42). The original Ovidian imagery is a figuration of Maenadic female revenge, yet this possibility is usurped in favour of the so-called trauma psychology of the objectified rape victim.

VII

The danger in seeing a character like Lavinia in a play like *Titus Andronicus* from the perspective of only our own cultural moment (and its political and gender-political agendas), is that we render the cultural, geographical and historical dialogue upon which Shakespeare's play is based simply a route of transmission – and even there, one in which the line can easily go dead. Conventional understandings of 'source study' see the relationship of Shakespeare and the classics as a one-way street from antiquity to the Renaissance and perhaps not beyond. I want, however, to posit a version of literary, historical and performative intertextuality that is based upon *exchange*: for if antiquity renders up its texts for Shakespeare (and for us), what is required of us during the processes of production and performance is to give back the sense of honour and respect that comes from

---

[61] Taymor, quoted in Cartelli and Rowe, *New Wave*, p. 87.

listening, reading and interpreting them. If we close the borders with antiquity, if we consider Shakespeare's classical allusions to other lands, times and cultures to be unstageable and inappropriate to our own, then we lose not only the possibility of understanding Greek and Roman history, culture and literature *through* Shakespeare, but also the possibility of understanding Shakespeare himself, because for Shakespeare, the classics held deep meanings, not only for his own, but for all historical periods.

In one of the best essays to have been written about Lavinia in recent years, Katherine Rowe criticizes the tendency of certain feminist critics to read her as an emblem of the absolute oppression of the female – a position of subjugation characterized by the violated woman. She suggests that Lavinia should instead be seen as an emblem for the general loss of agency in the play and thus Titus's counterpart, not his opposite.[62] For such an argument to make sense, the character needs to be connected to the Lavinia of Virgil's *Aeneid*, to the Lucretia of Livy's *Histories* and Ovid's *Fasti*, as well as to Shakespeare's explorations of the same

subject in *The Rape of Lucrece*; most importantly, however, she must also be connected to the Philomela of Ovid's *Metamorphoses*. Her plight must be seen from multiple perspectives in a deliberately transhistorical, transcultural and intertextual frame of reference, rather than from the purely personal and psychological ones that characterize our own times. It is difficult for modern directors to do this, for as Dessen has observed,

theatrical professionals ... place great emphasis on 'realism' in the narrative and in the motivation of ... characters, but, especially in this early Shakespeare script, the images (for both the ear and the eye of the spectator) can be especially strong and can exhibit their own logic and consistency. Our sense of theatre or staging, often controlled by unacknowledged assumptions about naturalism, can at times collide with the rationale behind a playscript designed for a pre-realistic stage without any pretence to 'theatrical illusion' at a time when the major literary event was the emergence of Books I–III of *The Faerie Queene*.[63]

---

[62] Katherine Rowe, 'Dismembering and Forgetting in *Titus Andronicus*', *Shakespeare Quarterly*, 45 (1994), 279–303.

[63] Dessen, *Shakespeare in Performance*, p. 86.

THE NOBLE ROMANS: WHEN JULIUS CAESAR AND ANTONY AND CLEOPATRA WERE MADE SEQUELS

MICHAEL P. JENSEN

This article will eventually look at the 1979 radio series *The Noble Romans* presented by the BBC World Service. The series paired *Julius Caesar* and *Antony and Cleopatra*, two plays not usually considered to be a cycle. I first look at previous cycles of these plays starting in the late nineteenth century, and at the unusual moment in the early sixties that had producers of stage, television and radio looking for plays they could turn into cycles, whether the plays were written as sequels or not. This resulted in the Roman cycles on television in 1963 and the Royal Shakespeare Company's stage in 1972. The bulk of my attention will turn to the previously unexplored radio series. I will show that presenting *Julius Caesar* and *Antony and Cleopatra* together tends to treat them as the saga of Antony, and how the series producer designed the programme to achieve this.

There is no evidence that any of the Roman plays were considered sequels in Shakespeare's time. When John Heminges and Henry Condell wanted to emphasize the connectedness of Shakespeare's two tetralogies, they retitled the plays with numerals, such as *1 Henry VI*, and put them in story order in the First Folio. This was not done for his Roman plays. Indeed, the only Roman plays to share characters are *Julius Caesar*, written about 1599, and *Antony and Cleopatra*. While the date of *Antony and Cleopatra* is difficult to determine, it came several years later. In his Arden edition of the play, John Wilders puts it in the range between 1604 and 1608, with the holidays of 1606–7 being the most likely time of composition.[1] This puts the creation of the pair

a minimum of five years apart, whereas the plays in each of Shakespeare's tetralogies were written roughly a year apart. These dates seem to indicate that *Antony and Cleopatra* was not written as a sequel to *Julius Caesar*. Though Mark Antony is an important ensemble character in *Julius Caesar* and the lead male role in *Antony and Cleopatra*, few believe these or any of the Roman plays comprise a cycle.

Indeed, the designation 'Roman Plays' came quite late. The first person to designate seems to be M. W. MacCallum in his 1910 book *Shakespeare's Roman Plays and their Background*. MacCallum believed that subject and Shakespeare's comparative faithfulness to his sources are among the things that distinguish the Roman plays from the chronicle plays and the tragedies.[2] For MacCallum, the Roman plays are *Julius Caesar*, *Antony and Cleopatra* and *Coriolanus*.

Cycles meant performances of linked chronicle plays until 1898, when Sir Frank Benson anticipated MacCallum by presenting *Julius Caesar*, *Antony and Cleopatra* and *Coriolanus* at the annual festival in the Shakespeare Memorial Theatre, Stratford-upon-Avon. These are Shakespeare's

---

[1] John Wilders, 'Introduction', in *Antony and Cleopatra* (London, 1995), p. 74.

[2] M. W. MacCallum, *Shakespeare's Roman Plays and their Background* (New York, 1910), pp. 93–4. I would like to thank Robert S. Miola for bringing MacCallum to my attention. I have been unable to find anything earlier that treats the Roman plays as a unit.

Roman plays[3] excluding *Titus Andronicus*, which was never in the Benson repertory.[4]

Aside from Benson's conscious decision to produce the plays together, these Roman plays were not marketed as a cycle, though Benson may have thought of them that way. *Antony and Cleopatra* was something of a sensation because of the cost of mounting it. The show was the most expensive of all the Benson company productions, and this was the first time the play was produced in Stratford, resulting in this production drawing a disproportionate amount of notice by critics.[5] One wrote that it 'forms to some extent a sequel to *Julius Caesar*, in that the fortunes of Mark Antony are continued', and another observed that Benson, portraying Antony in the two plays, 'never forgot that he was playing the same Antony whose masterly eloquence we have heard over the dead body of Caesar, who shared the soldier's fortunes at Philippi, and fought against famine'.[6] In other words, Benson played the title character in *Antony and Cleopatra* much as he had played the part in *Julius Caesar*. The Benson Company produced the three again in the spring festival of 1912 when Benson took a different approach, playing Antony as 'a masquer and a reveller' in *Julius Caesar* (5.1.62).[7] Critics do not seem to have identified *Coriolanus* as having kinship with the other plays, and the chronologically first story opened last in 1898, then between the others in 1912.

Public perception of cycles was usually reserved for chronicle plays. Benson presented several history cycles starting in 1899. He had previously limited the histories to one or two per year, so this was a change. It is difficult to call the 1899 productions a cycle in part because Benson did not and the stories were not contiguous: *2 Henry VI* opened first, followed by *Richard III*, *Henry V* and *Richard II*. This led to an actual cycle that Benson called a 'week of Kings' in 1901, presenting, in story order, *King John*, *Richard II*, *2 Henry IV*, *Henry V*, *2 Henry VI* and *Richard III*.

Though Margaret Shewring believes this cycle should be understood in context of patriotic feelings stirred by the Boer War[8] and John Dover Wilson writes that 'The epic drama of Agincourt

matched the temper of the moment', these productions seem to have caused some reflection on Shakespeare as the author of cycles.[9] William Butler Yeats testified to the impact of this cycle, 'Partly because of a spirit in the place, and partly because of the way play supports play, the theatre moved me as it has never done before.'[10] Benson produced more history cycles in the festivals of 1905–6, 1910, and 1913–16. Cycles of chronicle plays moved to companies such as the Old Vic and the Birmingham Repertory Theatre from the twenties and through the fifties. History cycles were also broadcast on BBC Radio, such as the eight-part 1945 series adapting the Henry IV plays discussed in this article.[11] The second tetralogy was broadcast on Third Programme in 1947, as was the first tetralogy, with an abridged *1 Henry VI*, in 1952.

Two history cycles in the early sixties had such success that stage, television and radio producers soon immersed Britain in many kinds of cycle. The first was *The Age of Kings*, both of Shakespeare's tetralogies edited for television and broadcast live in fifteen episodes on the BBC in 1960. The series was popular and a critical triumph,

---

[3] I take *Cymbeline* to be essentially an English play with Roman antagonists.

[4] I cannot tell if MacCallum was influenced by Benson's selections. MacCallum was Sydney based, and wrote that he returned 'home only on hurried and infrequent visits' (*Background*, p. ix). Most likely this is coincidence or something was in the culture that emphasized these plays, or, perhaps, deemphasized *Titus Andronicus*.

[5] Lady Benson, *Mainly Players: Bensonian Memories* (London, 1926), pp. 157–8.

[6] Quoted in Sarah Hatchuel, *Shakespeare and the Cleopatra/Caesar Intertext: Sequel, Conflation, Remake* (Lanham, MD, 2011), p. 28.

[7] Hatchuel, *Cleopatra/Caesar*, p. 32.

[8] Margaret Shewring, *Shakespeare in Performance: King Richard II* (Manchester, 1996), p. 91.

[9] Quoted in J. C. Trewin, *Shakespeare on the English Stage 1900–1964* (London, 1964), p. 60.

[10] Quoted in T. C. Kemp and J. C. Trewin, *The Stratford Festival: A History of the Shakespeare Memorial Theatre* (Birmingham, 1953), p. 59.

[11] Michael P. Jensen, 'Lend me your Ears: Sampling BBC Radio Shakespeare', in *Shakespeare Survey 61* (Cambridge, 2008), pp. 170–80; p. 174.

winning the Best Drama award from the Guild of Television Producers. Success was in part due to the 'bold cutting and rearrangement of scenes, with deployment of the full range of [televising] techniques evolved over the past decade ... The serial framework, also, smoothes out the contradictions readable in such different plays as *Richard II, Henry V* and *Richard III*'.[12] Kinescopes were broadcast in the United States and other countries. The US airing generated a mass-market paperback that printed the television dialogue.[13]

The second cycle was *The Wars of the Roses*, presented on stage by the Royal Shakespeare Company in 1963. Appointed to run the Shakespeare Memorial Theatre in 1960, Peter Hall with John Barton abridged and revised the first tetralogy, presenting it as three plays tailored to speak to the politics of the day.[14] Hall had negotiated a contract with the BBC to record selected RSC productions for television.[15] *The Wars of the Roses* aired in 1965, and was also shown in the US, Canada and Australia.[16] The second tetralogy joined the stage repertory in 1964, but was not televised. The success of these large-scale projects inspired many others.

The 1967 series *The Forsyte Saga* is a prime example of this trend in television. John Galsworthy's nine Forsyte novels were adapted in twenty-six sixty-minute episodes, broadcast on BBC 2, and sold around the world. A similar series called *The Pallisers* was adapted from Anthony Trollope's six Palliser novels and broadcast over BBC 2 in 1974. Ambitious projects designed for the theatre include Alan Ayckbourn's 1973 *Norman Conquests*, three plays with the same characters set in three locations at a country-house. The RSC's 1980 *The Life and Adventures of Nicholas Nickleby* was another ambitious project, though not a cycle. The Charles Dickens novel was retooled as a long two-part play. Peter Hall's 1981 National Theatre staging of the *Oresteia* by Aeschylus is another example of many that can be cited, the tip of the proverbial iceberg.

Shakespeare was certainly part of this. The *BBC Television Shakespeare* (1978–85), the televising of the thirty-seven play canon, was itself an ambitious project, but within this series are the two tetralogies. Jon Finch played Bolingbroke/Henry IV in *Richard II* in the first series and in the Henry IV plays in the second series. Actors cast in *1 Henry IV* played their roles through *Henry V*, whenever their characters appeared in multiple plays. These were directed by David Giles. A different group of actors worked through the recurring roles in the first tetralogy, broadcast in the fifth series, and again these plays had the same director, Jane Howell. *Julius Caesar* and *Antony and Cleopatra* were treated separately, broadcast in 1978 and 1980, respectively, without sharing cast or director.

There were also cycles of thematically linked plays. The Prospect Theatre Company toured *Richard II* and Christopher Marlowe's *Edward II* in 1969, with a young Ian McKellen playing both title roles.[17] Of remarkable ambition was *Vivat Rex*, a 1977 twenty-six-part cycle of chronicle plays on BBC Radio 4, presenting edited versions of *Edward II*, the then anonymous (but for some scenes Shakespeare suspected) *Edward III*, the anonymous untitled play commonly called *Thomas of Woodstock*, both of Shakespeare's tetralogies supplemented by the anonymous *Famous Victories of*

---

[12] Susanne Greenhalgh, 'U.K. Television', in *Shakespeares after Shakespeare: An Encyclopedia of the Bard in Mass Media and Popular Culture*, ed. Richard Burt, vol. 2 (Westport, CN, 2007), p. 661.

[13] William Shakespeare, *An Age of Kings: The Historical Plays of William Shakespeare as Presented on the British Broadcasting Corporation Television Series 'An Age of Kings'*, ed. Nathan Keats and Ann Keats (New York, 1961).

[14] Hall renamed the Stratford stage the Royal Shakespeare Theatre, which is how I shall refer to it henceforward.

[15] Richard Pearson, *A Band of Arrogant and United Heroes: The Story of the Royal Shakespeare Company's production of the Wars of the Roses* (London, 1990), p. 70.

[16] David Addenbrooke, *The Royal Shakespeare Company: The Peter Hall Years* (London, 1974), p. 282. The scripts were later published as John Barton and Sir Peter Hall, *The Wars of the Roses: Adapted for the Royal Shakespeare Company from William Shakespeare's Henry VI, Parts 1, 2, 3, and Richard III* (London, 1970). Trevor Nunn revived *The Wars of the Roses* in September 2015 at the Rose Theatre, Kingston.

[17] The plays were televised in 1970.

Henry V, John Ford's *Perkin Warbeck* and *Henry VIII* by Shakespeare and John Fletcher. Neither is a genuine cycle. The Prospect plays are by different authors and do not share characters, but they can be seen as linked by the deposition of unpopular monarchs, and so are interesting to perform together. Some of the plays adapted for *Vivat Rex* are clear sequels, but *Thomas of Woodstock*, *Famous Victories of Henry V*, *Henry VIII* and the plays by Marlowe and Ford are not. Producer Martin Jenkins did some rescripting to give the episodes a flow the original texts lack. This desire to create notable productions, and sometimes force plays not conceived as sequels to speak to each other, was very much in the air when three producers made cycles of Shakespeare's Roman plays.

These cycles differ from one another in content and medium. The BBC Television series *The Spread of the Eagle* was a follow-up to *An Age of Kings*. Its nine episodes were derived from *Coriolanus*, *Julius Caesar* and *Antony and Cleopatra*, the three Roman plays Benson produced in 1898 and 1912, now presented in story order. The two series shared a producer, Peter Dews, a composer, Christopher Whelen, and some of the same actors, notably Robert Hardy as Henry V and Coriolanus, Mary Morris as Margaret and Cleopatra, and Jack May as Richard, Duke of York and Casca. Though handsomely produced, this series was considered a disappointment.

Susanne Greenhalgh summarised the consensus of reviewers, writing that *Coriolanus* failed 'to find a suitably epic style in which to present the battle scenes or an effective mode of acting to capture the formality of ancient Rome'.[18] John Russell Taylor wrote that *Julius Caesar* indulged in 'over-hardy acting', unsuitable sound effects, and complained that dividing the story into three episodes 'broke the back of its dramatic development'.[19] *Antony and Cleopatra* was stagey and Egypt was 'insufficiently sultry'.[20]

There are no continuing characters through these three plays, so serializing them implies continuity where none exists. The *Times* foresaw a 'problem with this series' in a review published the day after the first episode aired, 4 May 1963.

Julius Caesar and *Antony and Cleopatra* have three common characters, and the same actors enacted those parts in both plays, but the reviewer felt that cycling these plays with *Coriolanus* was a stretch.

And stretch they did. Michael Brooks writes: 'Designer Clifford Hatts compensated [for the lack of continuity] to some extent through imaginative visual links – for instance, Rome's great Forum is under construction during *Coriolanus*, but completed by the time the action of *Julius Caesar* gets underway.' Brooks further notes that Keith Michell's Mark Antony occupies the 'lion's share of screen time', which I assume is another attempt to give continuity to the last six episodes.[21] As has been seen, this was not enough to redeem the series for reviewers. Laurence Kitchin summed up the problems of producing this series and Shakespeare generally on television.

The small television screen is notably ill-adapted to Roman mobs ... But audiences in Canada or Bradford are not likely to have such reservations, and so a drastically limited image of Shakespeare gains enormous circulation, infecting audiences in particular with television's allergy to lyricism and rhetoric, in fact to any form of heightened speech ... Compared with the medium's routine output they are excellent; compared with a good stage production they are cramped and perfunctory.[22]

Spread of the Eagle nevertheless outdrew *An Age of Kings* by 4 million viewers to 3.

In 1972 the Royal Shakespeare Company's artistic director Trevor Nunn, with different co-directors, mounted *Coriolanus*, *Julius Caesar*, *Antony and Cleopatra* and *Titus Andronicus* under the umbrella title 'The Romans'. Margaret Lamb speculates that, 'renewed interest in the political settings of Shakespeare's plays, and particularly the

---

18 Greenhalgh, 'U.K. Television', p. 678.
19 Quoted in Greenhalgh, 'U.K. Television', p. 691.
20 Quoted in Greenhalgh, 'U.K. Television', pp. 674–5.
21 Michael Brooks, 'Spread of the Eagle, The (1963)', *Screenonline*, www.screenonline.org.uk/tv/id/466545/index .html, accessed 11 March 2016.
22 Laurence Kitchin, 'Shakespeare on Screen', in *Shakespeare Survey 18* (Cambridge, 1965), pp. 70–4; pp. 71–2.

success of Peter Hall's 1963 *War of the Roses*, prompted the presentation of the four Roman tragedies'.[23] This left Nunn with an even bigger problem than Peter Dews faced with *The Spread of the Eagle*. How do you present not three, but four plays that are not sequels in the age of cycles? Nunn had one plan and the RSC marketing department had another.

Sally Beauman notes that the director allowed 'the programmes and posters produced for the season to suggest that the RSC *was* attempting a classical cycle'.[24] This doubtless cued public expectations, but Nunn had no illusions about story continuity, saying 'there is a superficial relationship between *Julius Caesar* and *Antony and Cleopatra*, because they share some of the same characters, but they're written in different styles'.[25]

Nunn emphasized a different continuity. 'I was interested to begin with that Shakespeare ... returned, on four separate occasions, to the same background, the same society and many of the same concerns for his plays ... Shakespeare seemed to be finding, by using the Roman background, Roman imagery, the opportunity to make free comment about political issues that he just wasn't able to when writing the English history plays.'[26] Peter Thomson characterized this as 'the politics of Rome as Shakespeare pictured them at four different historical crises ... the growth from small tribe to City-state (*Coriolanus*), to Republic (*Julius Caesar*), to Empire (*Antony and Cleopatra*), and to a decadence that is the prelude to Gothic conquest (*Titus Andronicus*)'.[27]

Nunn signalled this with the processions that begin each play. These made 'a quick preliminary directorial statement about the societies that plays examined'.[28] *Coriolanus* opened with a march that included statues of Romulus, Remus and their wolf-nurse, to portray the birth of Rome.[29] *Julius Caesar* began with a dumb-show crowning Caesar with a laurel.[30] *Antony and Cleopatra* began with a billowing canopy and coloured lights, the lovers 'dressed as Egyptian god-monarchs, and revelling in their wealth'. Roman soldiers stood uncomfortably in black, telegraphing the contrast of the Roman and Egyptian worlds in this play.[31] *Titus*

Andronicus featured a life-sized statue of the late Emperor in a decadent posture, a characterization and posture that John Wood's Saturninus embodied when the play began.[32] Nunn's cycling hand is perhaps most clearly expressed in the frames preceding *Coriolanus* and *Julius Caesar*. The feast of Lupercalia commemorates the nursing of Romulus and Remus by the she-wolf. This is the feast celebrated in the opening scene of *Julius Caesar*, not *Coriolanus*. Nunn moves it, creating a new opening for *Julius Caesar* to emphasize his vision for the evolution of the Roman state.

Critics were divided about these dumb-shows and the additional spectacle given to the plays. Irving Wardle did not like it. 'The spectacle was used didactically, wrenching the plays into a simplistic pattern to show the evolution of a society from tribalism to authoritarianism, to colonialism, to decadence – a four play decline and fall.'[33]

It is not entirely artificial since the plays all begin with crowd, or at least group, scenes, but a degree of extratextual continuity was supplied by the stage of the Royal Shakespeare Theatre.[34] New hydraulic lifts allowed 'the floor to rise and change shape in a mechanical extravaganza of technical power. A flick of a switch, it seemed, would slowly transform a flat open space in an off-white box into a set

---

[23] Margaret Lamb, *Antony and Cleopatra on the English Stage* (Rutherford, NJ, 1980), p. 165.

[24] Sally Beauman, *The Royal Shakespeare Company: A History of Ten Decades* (Oxford, 1982), p. 314 (emphasis in the original).

[25] Ralph Berry, *On Directing Shakespeare: Interviews with Contemporary Directors* (London, 1989), p. 69.

[26] Berry, *Directing*, pp. 67 and 69.

[27] Peter Thomson, 'No Rome of Safety: The Royal Shakespeare Season 1972', in *Shakespeare Survey 26* (Cambridge, 1973), pp. 139–50; p. 142.

[28] Beauman, *Royal Shakespeare*, p. 315.

[29] Thomson, 'Rome', p. 142.

[30] Thomson, 'Rome', p. 144.

[31] Beauman, *Royal Shakespeare*, p. 315.

[32] Thomson, 'Rome', p. 148.

[33] Quoted in Beauman, *Royal Shakespeare*, p. 316.

[34] I am hedging a bit since *Antony and Cleopatra* begins with Philo telling Demetrius how the mighty Antony has fallen. The crowd enters during the last four lines (1.1.1–14).

of steps, a pyramid, monument (exterior or interior), a Roman conference room or a galleon, complete with mast.'[35] These configurations could not be used when the plays transferred to the Aldwych Theatre in London, for that stage lacked this equipment. Nunn became 'disillusioned' by the hydraulics and used them sparingly in the last two productions, easing the London transfer.[36] Critics quite liked the season overall, and the plays were popular with audiences.

Some critics still reviewed the perceived character continuity, or its lack, between *Julius Caesar* and *Antony and Cleopatra*. Richard Johnson's black beard as the younger Antony was grizzled in the later play. Breaking with the critics of Benson's generation, those in 1972 praised Johnson for differences in his performances between these plays and dispraised Corin Redgrave for making Octavius the same in both, though Redgrave made a valid choice given the way Octavius is written. Hatchuel noted that critics were habituated to finding continuity between these plays, even though Nunn's productions strived for something else. Certainly, RSC marketing led critics to expect this.[37]

Conversely, the World Service radio series *The Noble Romans* created continuity when it could. This series, produced and directed by Dickon Reed, employed numerous strategies to turn these plays into the story of Mark Antony, just as many critics of Nunn's Roman season expected.

First, let me correct an impression derived from the *BBC Annual Report and Handbook 1981*, covering 1979/80, in a section about the popularity of World Service dramatic programming. Selected listeners were polled to learn their preferences. Those empanelled strongly liked drama broadcasts. The foreign nationals questioned, 88 per cent of the panel, especially appreciated Shakespeare programming. The *Report* connects the polling and the broadcast of *The Noble Romans* on page 53, implying the series was produced as a result of the survey, and indeed the first *Noble Romans* episode was broadcast on 3 November 1977, shortly after the poll results were released in October. Reed

corrects this impression, writing that the series was created independently of the poll and would have been broadcast regardless of the results. There was 'almost a year between my initial decision' to produce the series due to 'the planning meetings and the subsequent writing and physical production, plus delays caused by scheduling of the actual transmission' of the broadcast.[38]

Producing the two plays over six episodes was an undertaking of some ambition, and Reed had recently become well placed to do it. His earliest work as a director was for the School Broadcasting Department (Radio), the education division producing educational dramas and programmes on English history, between 1969 and 1973. These included a twenty-minute version of William Langland's *Piers Plowman* and Ted Hughes's 'Orpheus', which won the Japan Prize for international educational broadcasting.[39] Reed moved briefly to adult educational broadcasting on Radio 3 before transitioning to drama, producing new radio plays, serials and adaptations of novels and plays. In all, he created nearly two hundred dramatic programmes and spent many years as Head of Drama for the World Service, probably starting in 1973.[40]

Reed had limited experience with Shakespeare and other early modern writers when he produced *The Noble Romans*, but he was certainly ready. He began reading Shakespeare in school and acted briefly at the Belgrade Theatre, Coventry, where he played a number of small parts in Warren Jenkins's 1967 production of *Julius Caesar*.[41] Not long after joining the BBC, he produced *War and*

---

[35] Michael Scott, *Text and Performance: Antony and Cleopatra* (London, 1983), p. 44.

[36] Beauman, *Royal Shakespeare*, p. 315.

[37] *Antony and Cleopatra* was recorded for television and broadcast in 1974.

[38] Dickon Reed, email, 21 July 2015.

[39] Reed, email, 21 July 2015.

[40] Dickon Reed, email, 22 July 2015. 'I am reasonably certain that I took on the job of running BBC World Service Drama in 1973'. None of the BBC histories consulted mention Reed, let alone his dates as head of Drama.

[41] Reed, email, 21 July 2015.

Peace in Shakespeare, a twenty-five minute 1969 programme of excerpts from *2 Henry IV* and *Henry V* for Radio 4, and in 1975 Christopher Marlowe's *Edward II* for the World Service. His Shakespeare immersion came in 1977 with *Cry God for Harry*, a cycle derived from the *Henry IV* plays and *Henry V* for the series *Theatre of the Air*. The six-part series recast the RSC's players of Hal and Falstaff from two years before, Alan Howard and Brewster Mason, in their old roles. Narration was supplied by excerpts from Holinshed, 'to help listeners make sense of what was going on'.[42] The series was preceded by a thirty-minute special about the plays and their politics to publicize the show. Curiously, *Cry God for Harry* ran concurrently with the earliest episodes of *VIVAT Rex*, which adapted these plays in different productions. *VIVAT Rex* began with the first *Edward II* episode on 13 February on Radio 4. Reed's series began six days later on the World Service, which creates programming for the rest of the world, though it can be heard in Britain. Reed brought Mason back to portray Falstaff in a ninety-minute version of *The Merry Wives of Windsor* for the World Service in 1978.[43]

The Roman series was a follow-up to *Cry God for Harry*.[44] Both adapted multiple Shakespeare plays over six episodes and both used Shakespeare's main sources to supply narration, but there were differences. *Cry God for Harry*, with six hours to tell the stories of three chronicle plays, two sixty-minute episodes per play, required a fair amount of cutting to fit the stories into their time slots. *The Noble Romans* told the story of just two plays in six hours, and one, *Julius Caesar*, is amongst Shakespeare's shorter dramas. Comparatively little cutting was needed, but the radio scripts would require a lot of other preparation.

The challenge for Reed, as for all Shakespeare audio producers, was to convey to listeners information *seen* on stage and screen. This requires a degree of rescripting, and that is where the producer could best show off the strengths of radio drama.

Reed adds many vocalizations. The majority of these are probably 'Aye', 'Aye, my Lord', and the sound of characters chuckling. These interjections are used mostly as interruptions in longer speeches to indicate that the characters not speaking are listening and reveals their reaction to what is said. This rescripting accomplishes two things. The first is to add aural variety to these scenes, and aural variety adds energy to a performance. It also gives the broadcasts an interactive quality in place of the interaction in a stage performance or film, where audiences see non-speaking characters react to the lines. Reed scripted audio equivalents to these visual reactions.

Another type of rescripting is simple verbal blocking. Listeners cannot see the characters enter at the beginning of *Julius Caesar* 3.1, so Reed added a sound effect of multiple footsteps with a new line spoken by the entering Publius, 'And morning, Great Caesar'. These substitute for the stage direction that names Publius and others entering. There are similar lines to clarify entrances and exits throughout. Such changes are in addition to the accidental changes that occur when an actor unintentionally drops an 'O', or reads a 'ye' as 'you'. These happen many times in *The Noble Romans* and other broadcasts of early modern plays.

The entire series is punctuated by sound patterns that clarify and enrich the action. An example is when the music, alarums, shouts, clangs, blows and other sounds of battle that end *Antony and Cleopatra* 4.6 are heard through 4.7 to indicate that this dialogue occurs during the conflict, then finishes with a cheer by Antony's army preceding his first line in 4.9, 'We have beat him to his camp'. Sound makes the armies seem bigger and the battles longer than battles indicated by four or ten actors running across a stage. Kitchen objected that television was unable to capture the grandeur of such scenes. *The Noble Romans* makes the battle scenes aurally

---

[42] Dickon Reed, email, 19 June 2015.
[43] Reed later produced a two-part *All's Well that Ends Well* for the World Service that was broadcast in two sixty-minute episodes on 21 and 28 November 1981, with repeats on 22 and 29 November. I thank Olwen Terris, whose contact in the British Library found the dates of these broadcasts.
[44] Reed, email, 19 June 2015.

grander than the same scenes on stage and in television productions of that era, such as the BBC Television *Julius Caesar*, also broadcast in 1979.[45]

A quite different effect is achieved in a scene from Episode 5 that corresponds with *Antony and Cleopatra* 4.1. Octavius Caesar enters reading a letter. The letter informs him that Antony has mistreated Caesar's messenger. Reed adds the words 'So, to Antony' between lines three and four to indicate that Caesar is writing the response we hear him speak over the scratching of a quill. This rescripting uses the possibilities of the audio medium to enrich the story-telling, adding details to the pictures listeners create in their mind's eyes.

More rescripting is the narration excerpted from Shakespeare's main source for both plays, Thomas North's translation of Plutarch's *Lives*, 1579, but expanded in 1595 and 1603, dates well timed for Shakespeare's use. The BBC made North a selling point for the series, pointing it out in the press release about the show.[46] This narration was read by Peter Whitman, who would also play Alexas in the *Antony and Cleopatra* episodes.

The readings not only give listeners a dose of Plutarch with their Shakespeare; the quotations seem also to root the drama in fact. The first episode begins with this bit of edited North:

When the empire of Rome was divided into factions, Julies Caesar and Pompey both were in arms the one against the other. The great battle was fought in the fields of Pharsalus where Pompey was overcome. He fled into Africa to Egypt and was slain. After all these things were ended, Caesar went into Spain to make war with the sons of Pompey. This was the last wars that Caesar made, but the triumph he made into Rome for the same did offend as much as anything he had done before because he had destroyed the sons of the noblest man in Rome. But to win himself the love and goodwill of the people, Caesar made common feasts again and general distribution of corn.

Thus spake history? Well, a version of it. These lines are cobbled together from stray sentences from Plutarch's lives of Julius Caesar and Brutus, with some simplification and updating of language to make non-contiguous lines sound contiguous, so this is not pure Plutarch. Rewriting Plutarch

makes sense. He did not write for the radio, so Plutarch's lines could not always be repurposed by Reed without editing. It is interesting, therefore, to see how often Reed could lift sections more or less intact. These lines begin part 2:

On the morning of the ides of March, one Artemidorus, a doctor of rhetoric, who was very familiar with certain of Brutus and Cassius confederates, and therefore knew the most part of all their conspiracy against Caesar, made a little paper written with his own hand of all that he meant to tell him.

Reed adds the words 'on the morning of the ides of March', but the rest is a fairly close paraphrase of Plutarch's life of Julius Caesar, streamlining North's sixty-three words to forty-six that leave out no facts and are easier to absorb when heard. It would have been more accurate, therefore, to say that the narration was 'based on' North, though that would have sounded less impressive. Reed felt that adapting North, as he had Holinshed in the previous series, 'fitted the style of writing far better than any commentary or narration of my own could have done'.[47]

Plutarch creates an illusion of historical accuracy that gives weight to the presentation. This was a sham, of course. Plutarch was a moral philosopher, not an historian. The *Columbia Electronic Encyclopedia* tells us that Plutarch's 'facts are not always accurate. Since his purpose was to portray character and reveal its moral implications, his technique included the use of much anecdotal material'.[48] Most listeners would not be aware of this.

---

[45] Kitchen, 'Screen', pp. 70–4. Kitchen makes *The Spread of the Eagle* emblematic of the problems of producing Shakespeare for television, and then contrasts the limitations of early televised Shakespeare in England with a number of Shakespeare films. He does not discuss the possibilities of audio Shakespeare.

[46] I have not seen the press release, but the *Times* mentions North's Plutarch in the 3 November broadcast listing. This would have been learned from press materials sent by the World Service.

[47] Reed, email, 19 June 2015.

[48] www.infoplease.com/encyclopedia/people/plutarch.html

One might expect that adapting two plays over six episodes would mean that each play would be presented in three parts. *The Noble Romans* could not be structured that way because of the shortness of *Julius Caesar* and the length of *Antony and Cleopatra*, 2,730 and 3,636 lines in the First Folio, respectively. The extra 906 lines resulted in *Antony and Cleopatra* beginning at the midpoint of Episode 3. The structures of both plays caused other division problems.

Taylor's complaint that the episodic treatment of *Julius Caesar* in *The Spread of the Eagle* broke the back of the story very much applies to the episode breaks in *The Noble Romans*. The one-hour length had priority over the structure of the plays. There are no good places to break *Julius Caesar*. Certainly, a bad place to put an interval is at the end of 2.2, the scene in which Decius tempts Caesar to attend the Senate despite Calpurnia's misgivings. Act 2, scene 2 flows to 2.3, Artemidorus's letter of warning to Caesar, followed in 2.4 by the Soothsayer's conversation with Portia, followed by 3.1 when the Soothsayer attempts to warn Caesar. In four consecutive scenes, Shakespeare troubles the path to assassination with warnings, but the clock forced Reed to interrupt after the first. The episode had reached fifty-eight and a half minutes, so it was time to end.[49]

Reed therefore began the second episode with the paraphrased warning from Plutarch's life of Julius Caesar, quoted above. This made 2.3 all but unnecessary, and the Soothsayer was eliminated from 2.4, though his line in 3.1 was retained. One could argue this either way: the impact of the repeated warnings is lost and repetition matters or the quote from Plutarch is a strong beginning to the episode that made Shakespeare's lines unnecessary. Shakespeare's version and Reed's version both have an impact, but they have different impacts.

Not all episode breaks are this problematic. Episode 2 closes at the end of Act 4, Brutus encounters the ghost of Caesar, and Episode 3 begins with 5.1, the meeting between Octavius, Antony, Brutus and Cassius. Breaking the story here has a cost, for the ghost hints at Brutus's

doom, then in the next scene Brutus meets with those who will execute this doom, but the hour was up and this is probably as good a place as any to break the story if the story must be broken.

It is strange, however, when *Julius Caesar* ends with more narration twenty-seven minutes into the third broadcast. This narration from the life of Mark Antony bridges the gap between the two plays. It is quite long, 1,527 words, and the reading takes more than three minutes. Despite the Plutarchian asides, most of the story had so far been told with dialogue and sound patterns. Now a lengthy narrative describes the ending of the battle, 'Antony cast his armour, which was wonderful, rich, and sumptuous, upon Brutus's body and gave commandment to one of his enfranchized slaves to defray the charge of his burial.' It continues with Antony and Octavius parting, the pleasures Antony found in the east, his meeting with Cleopatra and her sensual appeal coupled with Antony's alienation from Octavius, Fulvia's wars with Octavius, and Antony's isolation from all this: 'It seemed all this had nothing touched him, and he yielded himself to go with Cleopatra into Alexandria where he spent and lost in childish sports and idle pastimes the most precious thing a man can spend, and that is time.' Plutarch thus becomes the stitching that joins these plays as a *faux-continuous* narrative, an ancient Chorus recruited to move the action to Alexandra instead of Harfleur.

The episodic structure of *Antony and Cleopatra* better accommodates episode breaks, for the most part. The most problematic break is between Episodes 5 and 6, five ending at 4.5 and six starting with 4.6, parallel scenes in the camps of Antony and Octavius. Reed wrote: 'The break between the 4.5 and 4.6 battle scenes was dictated simply by the time available in each episode. I realized that they should "flow" together but I had little choice in separating them.'[50] There is no quote from

---

[49] Only six lines and a few words were cut in this episode, so time was not much of a problem. The minute and a half to fill the hour would have been used to back announce the programme, announce the broadcast of the next episode, and announce the programme that would follow.

[50] Dickon Reed, email, 26 June 2015.

Plutarch to begin Episode 6, the only time North was omitted at the start of an episode: 'By omitting narration . . . my intention was to 'cut to the chase' and get on with action as quickly as possible.'[51]

Because the plays are not sequels, Reed deploys Plutarch to explain characters and offstage incidents new to this play with the result that there are more Plutarchian interpolations than in *Julius Caesar*. This extra narration may seem curious since Pompey, for example, is not explained to audiences in the theatre when he enters in *Antony and Cleopatra* 2.1. So why did Reed bother? He believes that *Julius Caesar* 'has a much stronger and more easily understood narrative arc than A&C. I felt the listeners needed more guidance in the latter play'.[52]

The quality of the acting is very high. Acting styles have evolved since 1979 and the programme sounds dated to the modern ear, but when compared to Shakespeare audio of the time, these broadcasts come across well. Many performers are noteworthy for their clarity, convincing interpretations, and line readings that seem obviously right. Paul Hardwick as Julius Caesar has excellent condescension when he gives the speech that begins 'I could be well moved if I were as you' (3.1.58–73), in the second episode. The meeting and the striking of a deal between Octavius and Antony in episode four positively sizzles. When Gerard Green as Lepidus suggests that their differences be 'gently heard', he puts an urgent length on 'gently' (*Antony and Cleopatra*, 2.2.20). The discussion between Octavius and Antony builds in hostility step by step until the men realize the consequences of their conflict, then both can be heard moving to positions that will maintain honour while finding common ground, the hostility defusing step by step, just as it had built. It is masterfully handled. There are several moments of such power in every episode.

This is especially impressive when you consider the rehearsal schedule. Martin Jarvis recalls that rehearsals began with a table reading on day one, a break, followed by rehearsal for the rest of the day. Day two was a complete rehearsal that included the radio equivalent of a dress rehearsal:

performing the script as if the show was being recorded, then the actual recording after a break for lunch. That the nuanced and strongly interactive performances were realized with so little rehearsal time speaks to the intelligence and artistry of all involved.[53]

The leads were publicly recognized actors. Edward Hardwicke's many television appearances began in the fifties and included recurring roles in five series and serials prior to *The Noble Romans*. He spent seven years with the National Theatre from 1964 in roles that included Montano in John Dexter's 1965 *Othello*, which famously, and to some notoriously, starred Laurence Olivier. Hardwicke's radio work was limited to just several shows, one of which was playing Rosencrantz in a 1978 Radio 3 version of Tom Stoppard's *Rosencrantz and Guildenstern are Dead*. Hardwicke may have lacked experience playing Shakespeare at the time Reed hired him to portray Brutus, but he was a well regarded actor.

Though appearing in only a half-dozen radio productions prior to 1979, Ian Hogg, Cassius, had a busy television career before *The Noble Romans*. He was a member of the RSC from 1964–8, mixing Shakespeare and roles in modern plays, then returned to the RSC to play the title role in *Coriolanus*, Lucius in *Titus Andronicus* and Menas in *Antony and Cleopatra* in Trevor Nunn's cycle. Hogg had a small role in Peter Brook's 1967 *Marat / Sade* film, but was not in the stage version; played Edmund in Brook's 1971 film version of *King Lear*, but was not in the stage version; and was in both the RSC's 1967 stage and 1968 television productions of *All's Well that Ends Well*, directed by John Barton and Claude Whatham, respectively.

Octavius was portrayed by Martin Jarvis, who had previously played the part while doubling Decius Brutus in a 1972 broadcast of *Julius Caesar* for the series *Play of the Week* on BBC Radio 3. Jarvis had been a presence on both television and

[51] Reed, email, 26 June 2015.   [52] Reed, email, 26 June 2015.
[53] Martin Jarvis, phone interview, 13 May 2015. My thanks to Stacy Keach for putting me in touch with Mr Jarvis.

radio with some very showy parts including Jon in the later episodes of the *Forsyte Saga* (1967), the title role in *Nicholas Nickleby* (1968), and similar literary series for BBC Television. He had an even busier career in radio as an actor and reader, totalling more than eight hundred broadcasts by the time of *The Noble Romans*. Dickon Reed had frequently cast Jarvis in World Service shows and would continue to use him after *The Noble Romans*. Jarvis's Shakespeare broadcasts prior to *The Noble Romans* were Prince Hal/Henry V in *Vivat Rex*, Clarence in *Richard III* (1967), Claudio in *Much Ado About Nothing* (1969), Horatio in *Hamlet* (1971), Cassio in *Othello* (1972), the Dauphin in *Henry V* (1976) and Orlando in *As You Like It* (1978). Reed writes of 'the need to cast actors, like Martin, who had plenty of microphone experience and could deliver a polished performance in a short time'.[54]

Reed cast older for his Antony and his Cleopatra. 'Roy Dotrice [was] best known in RSC Shakespeare terms as portrayer of comic and eccentric old men . . . His slightly elderly and desiccated vocal timbre was distinctive, but in this production I felt he overcame that limitation at least enough to suggest a formerly virile and active general whose powers were definitely now waning. Obviously, this worked best in the second play.'[55] Dotrice worked in Stratford from 1959 to 1965, and returned in 1968, though in modern plays; his featured roles for the RSC included Julius Caesar in 1963 and Bedford and Edward IV in *The Wars of the Roses*. He then settled into a busy television and radio career. His most prestigious television role to precede *The Noble Romans* was probably the title character in *Dickens of London* on Independent Television in 1976. He was also heard in a few radio and other audio Shakespeares, including another old-man part, Justice Shallow, in *Vivat Rex*.

'I cast Maxine Audley, a mature and versatile actress . . . too old to be credible visually as the Egyptian queen, but experienced and confident enough to get the result I was looking for'.[56] Audley began broadcasting in 1941 and eventually acted in plays adapted from Shakespeare's contemporaries. She was Evadne in *The Maid's Tragedy* by

Francis Beaumont and John Fletcher (1954), Aurelia in *The Malcontent* by John Marston (1962), Vittoria in *The White Devil* by John Webster (1969) and Calantha in *The Broken Heart* by John Ford (1970). Her Shakespeare broadcasts include the lead in a forty-five-minute modern version of *Othello*, entitled *Desdemona* (1957), Constance in *King John* (1967), Gertrude in both *Hamlet* (1971) and the 1978 broadcast of *Rosencrantz and Guildenstern are Dead*, and Mistress Page in Reed's *The Merry Wives of Windsor*. Audley had Stratford seasons in 1950, 1955, 1957, 1962, though that latter season was not in Shakespeare, and played Volumnia in *Coriolanus* in the 1977/8 season. She was also a busy television actor from the late forties.

These were the stars, but the success of *The Noble Romans* depended on the entire cast. The rescripted ayes and chuckles gave the series energy and drive by the expert meshing of all the actors, both leads and those in bit parts; the sound effects created by Elizabeth Parker and the sound balance provided by Keith Perrin and Chris Lewis on different episodes made it work.

To finish, let me look at how *The Noble Romans* told the story of Mark Antony. Reed's statement, 'I certainly did see Mark Antony as a through-link, between the two plays', demonstrates his intent, so let us examine the choices that reinforced that intent.[57] Not surprisingly, some aspects of the broadcasts already discussed contributed to this unity.

We have already seen this in the casting. It is unusual to perform these plays with different actors portraying Antony, Octavius and Lepidus.[58]

---

54 Reed, email, 26 June 2015.
55 Dickon Reed, email, 22 June 2015.
56 Dickon Reed in a second email dated 22 June 2015.
57 Reed, second email, 22 June 2015.
58 Unusual, but not unknown. The RSC mostly cross-cast actors in these plays in 2006. Those playing the Triumvir, however, played different roles in each play or did not appear in the other play. Patrick Stewart played Antony in *Antony and Cleopatra*, but did not appear in *Julius Caesar* where Aryion Bakare played Antony. Bakare then switched to Pompey for *Antony and Cleopatra*. My thanks to Philip Lineer for bringing this to my attention.

Casting the same actors in these parts ensured that audiences and critics would find the unities they expected. As for casting in a different sense, Roy Dotrice was very well known at this time and he played the star part in this saga. He has what actors call 'presence', on radio meaning that the ear is drawn to him when he speaks.[59]

Few of Antony's lines were cut compared to other major characters in *Julius Caesar*, just eight. Brutus, Cassius and Portia lose a couple of dozen. Even small- and medium-sized roles such as Lucilius, Messala and the Soothsayer lose more lines than Antony. The result is that Roy Dotrice has a relatively greater percentage of air time. It is wrong to say that Antony dominates the *Julius Caesar* episodes, Reed is too sensible and professional to let the story go off-kilter, but the cuts slightly push the broadcast in Antony's direction.

The cuts in *Antony and Cleopatra* are a bit different. There are no cuts longer than a word to a half-line until part 6. As we have seen, that episode begins at 4.6, which begins the momentum of the next few scenes that alternate between the camps of Octavius and Antony until the defeat of Antony's forces. The only cut in this sequence is the brief 4.12, but with 4.15 the cuts come thick and fast, and many of the lines cut are Antony's or Cleopatra's. This reduces the air time of these characters, but both are so dominant throughout this part of the play that these cuts barely lighten their impact. The play is known for delaying the conclusion with a lot of dialog, anyway, so these cuts get Reed there faster.

It is a shame that some of the play's most beautiful poetry is gone, lines such as,

> Sometimes we see a cloud that's dragonish,
> A vapour sometime like a bear or lion,
> A towered citadel, a pendent rock,
> A forkèd mountain, or blue promontory
> With trees upon't that nod unto the world
> And mock our eyes with air. Thou hast
>   seen these signs;
> They are black vesper's pageants. (4.15.2–8)

and such exchanges as:

> ANTONY.   Not Caesar's valour
> Hath o'erthrown Antony, but Antony's
> Hath triumphed on itself.
> CLEOPATRA.   So it should be,
> That none but Antony should conquer Antony.
> But woe 'tis so! (4.16.14–18)

The more extensive textual cuts in this episode tend to be redundancies and lovely turns of phrase. Narrative dialogue was retained in order to complete the story while obeying the time slot.

Starting with the third episode, Reed exclusively used North's translation of Plutarch's life of Antony for his narration, strengthening Antony's impact on the story despite the cuts in the last episode. Dotrice had a decreased percentage of microphone time, but the narration kept the story Antony-centric.

Audiences attending the Benson and Nunn productions and viewers of *The Spread of the Eagle* saw performances of *Julius Caesar* and *Antony and Cleopatra* a day, a week or more apart. Listeners to *The Noble Romans* heard Act 1, scene 1 of *Antony and Cleopatra* hard upon the last scene of *Julius Caesar*, with which it split the hour. The beginning of the second play, then, was heard in the same sitting, reinforcing the impression that the saga of Antony continued, for in this version it did.

There is also the simple matter of context. The fact that these plays are part of the same series creates its own connection. *Antony and Cleopatra* may not have been written as a sequel to *Julius Caesar* but, as we have seen repeatedly, performing them together creates connections in the minds of audiences, or in this case, radio listeners.

Large and ambitious theatre and media projects still occur today, but there seem to be fewer than in the sixties, seventies and eighties. When Shakespeare is cycled, it again tends to be chronicle plays. Major theatre companies and media producers have not returned to the Roman plays as a cycle. That moment has passed, at least for now.

---

[59] My thanks to actor Jeffrey King for helping me understand the idea of presence.

Presenting the plays separately allows their singular qualities to shine.

Martin Jarvis put this succinctly. He said that while these plays tell 'the story of Rome, they can be *perceived* as the story of Antony. Clearly, Dickon [Reed] wanted to combine them into a cohesive narrative', and Reed did that very well.[60]

APPENDIX I EPISODE BREAKDOWN

Episode 1 'Caesar Must Bleed', *Julius Caesar* 1.1–2.2. Focuses on the conspiracy and the wooing of Brutus, but ends with Caesar's decision to attend the Senate despite warnings to beware on the Ides of March.

Episode 2 'Friends, Romans, Countrymen', *Julius Caesar* 2.3–4.2. Caesar attends the Senate and is assassinated. Antony's funeral oration results in chaos throughout Rome. Cassius and Brutus air their grievances.

Episode 3 'This was a Man', *Julius Caesar* 5.1–5 and *Antony and Cleopatra* 1.1–4. The political power shifts after the battle of Philippi, the conspirators die, and the triumvirate takes control, but their alliance falls apart when Antony is seduced by Cleopatra and the pleasures of Egypt.

Episode 4 'The Serpent of Old Nile', *Antony and Cleopatra* 1.5–2.7. Antony and Caesar attempt to repair their differences. They seem to succeed, which puts a strain on Cleopatra and those around her.

Episode 5 'Sword Against Sword', *Antony and Cleopatra* 3.1–4.5. Antony's return to Cleopatra leads to Rome warring with Egypt. Enobarbus deserts Antony.

Episode 6 'Fire and Air', *Antony and Cleopatra* 4.6–5.2. The Roman and Egyptian forces exchange victories, but Rome prevails. Antony botches his suicide, but eventually dies. The captured Cleopatra kills herself so Octavius may not lead her to Rome in triumph.

---

[60] Martin Jarvis, phone interview, 13 May 2015. The emphasis was in his voice.

SHAKESPEARE'S POEMS IN PIECES: *VENUS AND ADONIS* AND *THE RAPE OF LUCRECE* UNANTHOLOGIZED

KATE RUMBOLD

Shakespeare's narrative poems once defined his reputation. *Venus and Adonis* and *Lucrece* went through multiple editions after their first publication in 1593 and 1594 respectively. They secured Shakespeare's status, gained him a patron, and, in the case of *Venus and Adonis*, set trends for new kinds of verse. They outstripped many of Shakespeare's plays in their print popularity, and in their frequent quotation by contemporaries. By comparison, the sonnets, when they appeared in print in 1609, already seemed rather old-fashioned, and were a 'notorious market failure'.[1] Yet neither the erotic charms of Venus, nor the 'graver' story of Lucrece, were able to secure the narrative poems' popularity much beyond the middle of the seventeenth century. Today, Shakespeare is often described as the greatest ever playwright, and his sequence of sonnets thought to represent 'the fascinating and frustrating centre of Shakespeare's oeuvre and, by extension, the corpus of Renaissance poetry, the canon of English literature, and, by some accounts, the history of modern Western subjectivity'.[2] By contrast, Shakespeare's narrative poems are marginal to his reputation, and little known beyond a scholarly audience. Why did these enormously popular poems disappear, never fully to regain their status?

Some might attribute the vast change in the fortunes of the narrative poems to changing tastes, and a tailing off of interest in the form. After an enthusiastic run of sixteen (between 1593 and 1636) and eight (between 1594 and 1632) separate quarto editions respectively, the once popular *Venus and Adonis* and *Lucrece* ceased to be printed in quarto with anything like such frequency, save for new printings in 1655 (*Lucrece*) and 1675 (*Venus*). Others might attribute the poems' disappearance to the fact that neither *Venus* nor *Lucrece* were included in the First Folio of 1623, nor in any subsequent, oeuvre-defining collection of Shakespeare's works, except as a supplementary text, until the end of the eighteenth century.[3] Their absence from the Folio was, ironically, a result not of their obscurity, but of their popularity: owned by other publishers, they could not be reproduced here.

This article ventures a new explanation for the disappearance of *Venus* and *Lucrece*: a significant but overlooked contributor to this process. The poems' initial popularity indeed contributed to their absence, but not simply because of their exclusion from the Folio. Crucial to their changing status is the intersection between the quartos, the Folio and another form: the anthology or quotation book. I argue that the enthusiastic anthologization of extracts from the poems ironically limited their

---

[1] Lukas Erne and Tamsin Badcoe, 'Shakespeare and the Popularity of Poetry Books in Print, 1583–1622', *Review of English Studies*, 65 (2014), 33–57; p. 52; Catherine Nicholson, 'Commonplace Shakespeare: Value, Vulgarity, and the Poetics of Increase in *Shake-Speares Sonnets* and *Troilus and Cressida*', in *The Oxford Handbook of Shakespeare's Poetry*, ed. Jonathan Post (Oxford, 2013), pp. 185–203; p. 186.
[2] Nicholson, 'Commonplace Shakespeare', p. 185.
[3] Katherine Duncan-Jones and H. R. Woudhuysen, eds., *Shakespeare's Poems* (London, 2007), pp. 514–18.

popularity in the decades and centuries that followed. This is not to lament the dangers of anthologization: selective quotation has, over the centuries, helped to attribute to other parts of Shakespeare's work, notably his plays, qualities of insight and beauty, and promoted the wisdom of Shakespeare himself. Rather, the early seventeenth-century printed anthology established ways of valuing Shakespeare's poems that, because of later restrictions in the form, combined with the increasingly limited circulation of the poems, did not – unlike ways of valuing his plays – subsequently evolve.

Early collections found sententious value in both poems, but also helped to strip them of their dramatic qualities. Lucrece and Venus lost their voices, never fully to regain them. The absence of Shakespeare's poems from the large-scale editions of the seventeenth and eighteenth centuries is thus only part of the story. The eager, sententious anthologization of these initially popular poems at the very beginning of the seventeenth century, swiftly followed by a long hiatus in their inclusion in quotation books, shaped their meaning and availability. To say that *Lucrece* was 'later neglected',[4] as if the poem trailed understandably out of fashion, is to underestimate the effects of both poems' earliest handling on their long-term reception.

This chapter has significant implications for the study of Shakespeare and of literature: it creates new understanding of the current status of poetry in Shakespeare's *oeuvre*, and reveals the role played by the anthology form in constructing, but also limiting, perceived literary value in the seventeenth century and beyond. Building on a growing interest in the fragmentary ways in which literature circulated in the early modern period,[5] it examines the complex intersections of seemingly ephemeral texts with the more substantial material forms of the quarto and folio; confirms the importance of dialogue between the fields of book history and reception history; and, by spanning the sixteenth, seventeenth and eighteenth centuries, traces for the first time the implications of the decisions made by early compilers in not just the decades but also the centuries that followed.

Over one hundred and fifty years separate the first publication of Shakespeare's poem *Lucrece* (1594) and Samuel Richardson's novel *Clarissa* (1748), two literary accounts of a virtuous woman who is raped by an unwanted suitor and dies as a consequence of this fate worse than death. Shakespeare's words are frequently invoked by characters in Richardson's epistolary novel; and, while he is not the most quoted author (he concedes that honour to the rakish Robert Lovelace's 'favourite bard', John Dryden), he is quoted by the widest range of characters, and admired by Clarissa and her attacker alike. Described by Lovelace as 'well read in Shakespeare', Clarissa quotes widely from her 'beloved Shakespeare', both before and after her rape.[6]

Clarissa avoids, however, one of Shakespeare's most obvious analogies for her fate. After the rape, she pours onto paper her outrage at Lovelace's violation. In 'Paper X', her normally articulate prose degenerates into fragments of borrowed verse, ten short quotations scattered crazily across the page. Amidst extracts from recent writers such as Dryden, Otway, Cowley and Garth are two speeches from Shakespeare:

> – Oh! you have done an act
> That blots the face and blush of modesty;
> Takes off the rose
> From the fair forehead of an innocent love,
> And makes a blister there! –

And, rotated through more than ninety degrees at the right-hand edge of the page:

> I could a tale unfold –
> Would harrow up thy soul! –   (p. 893)

---

4 *William Shakespeare: The Complete Works*, ed. Stanley Wells et al. (Oxford, 1986), p. 237.

5 See, for example, Jeffrey Todd Knight, *Bound to Read: Compilations, Collections, and the Making of Renaissance Literature* (Philadelphia, PA, 2013).

6 Samuel Richardson, *Clarissa*, ed. Angus Ross (London, 1985), pp. 761, 1148; Richardson, *Clarissa*, 2nd edn (London, 1749), vol. 3, p. 49. Further references to Ross's edition are given in the main text.

With the 'you' of the first quotation, Clarissa reproaches Lovelace as Hamlet reproaches his mother; with the 'thy' of the second she warns her friend Anna Howe of the dreadful import of her news, as the ghost of Old Hamlet warns his son. In her horror, Clarissa turns not to the words of the raped Lucrece, but to *Hamlet*.

The Lucretia myth is evidently not beyond the knowledge of Richardson nor his characters, since, in a letter to Lovelace signed by 'the miserably abused Clarissa Harlowe', Clarissa rages:

And here my uncle Harlowe, when he knows who I am, will never wish any man to have me: no, not even you, who have been the occasion of it – Barbarous and ungrateful! – A less complicated villainy cost a Tarquin – but I forget what I would say again – (p. 895)

In halting prose, Clarissa alludes glancingly to Tarquin's rape of Lucretia. Lovelace continues the association, wondering 'is death the *natural* consequence of a rape? – and if not the natural consequence, and a lady will destroy herself, whether by a lingering death as of grief; or by the dagger, as Lucretia did' (p. 1439). The servant heroine of Richardson's first novel also invokes the Lucretia story. Pulled on to her master's knee for a kiss, the horrified Pamela, like Clarissa, first summons *Hamlet*:

I said, like as I had read in a Book a Night or two before, Angels, and Saints, and all the Host of Heaven, defend me![7]

Pamela transforms Hamlet's exclamation at the sight of his father's ghost into an earnest plea. When Mr B. 'by Force kissed my Neck and Lips; and said, Who ever blamed *Lucretia*, but the *Ravisher* only?', Pamela rather too grandly replies, 'May I, *Lucretia* like, justify myself with my Death, if I am used barbarously?'

In both assaults, Richardson's heroines first quote from Shakespeare's *Hamlet*, then paraphrase the Lucretia myth. Pamela's self-dramatizing identification with Lucretia invites Mr B's mockery: 'you are well read, I see; and we shall make out between us, before we have done, a pretty Story in Romance, I warrant ye!' Clarissa conveys her greater maturity by her hesitation to declare that, '*Lucretia* like', she might die from this outrageous violation. She begins to invoke Lucretia before stepping back from the reference: 'but I forget what I would say again'. Her hesitation might signal a deliberate rejection of Lucretia's unchristian suicide: 'the moral difference is of course that Lucrece kills herself and Clarissa explicitly rejects this course of action'.[8] But was the Lucretia story for Richardson 'an uncomfortable myth: a myth whose moral implications leave much to be desired',[9] or is there another explanation for its absence?

The lack of verbal borrowings from *Lucrece* in *Clarissa* is illuminating. Richardson was a frequent proponent of the quotation of Shakespeare, and yet there are no references to Shakespeare's poems in any of his works, nor in any other of the eighteenth-century novels I have surveyed; there are, by contrast, hundreds of references to his plays, from Richardson and Henry Fielding to Ann Radcliffe and beyond.[10] If the Lucretia Richardson invokes is cultural shorthand for Livy's story,[11] the novelist acknowledges no debt to Shakespeare's intervening poem; Ian Donaldson's study of the cultural manifestations of the Lucretia story treats Shakespeare and Richardson's respective retellings separately.

Beyond Clarissa's reservations, one explanation for the absence of Shakespeare's *Lucrece* is the limited availability of the narrative poems to eighteenth-century readers, compared to Shakespeare's plays. *Clarissa* was first published in the same

---

[7] Samuel Richardson, *Pamela; or, Virtue Rewarded*, ed. Albert J. Rivero (Cambridge, 2011), p. 29. Further references are given in the main text.

[8] Martin Scofield, 'Shakespeare and Clarissa: "General Nature", Genre and Sexuality', *Shakespeare Survey 51* (Cambridge, 1998), pp. 27–43; p. 40.

[9] Ian Donaldson, *The Rape of Lucretia* (Oxford, 1982), p. 76.

[10] See Kate Rumbold, *Shakespeare and the Eighteenth-Century Novel: Cultures of Quotation from Samuel Richardson to Jane Austen* (Cambridge, 2016).

[11] An ECCO search confirms that Lucretia is frequently invoked as a trope of chastity in the eighteenth century.

decade that a statue of Shakespeare was erected in Poet's Corner, Westminster Abbey. Thanks to the Shakespeare Revival, audiences could see Shakespeare's plays performed on stage and, since Nicholas Rowe's edition of 1709, printed in complete works editions. By contrast, the narrative poems appeared only in supplementary volumes to those editions. They were appended to Rowe's 1709 edition, published by Bernard Lintot, and by Edmund Curll and E. Sanger with an essay by Charles Gildon. They also appeared in a revised volume by Gildon attached to Rowe's second edition in 1714; in a supplementary volume by George Sewell attached to Pope's edition of Shakespeare in 1725; and in a reissue of Gildon's volume attached to Pope's second edition in 1728.[12] Edmond Malone added two volumes, including the narrative poems, to George Steevens's edition in 1780 and then included them in his own: 'Though near a century and a half has elapsed since the death of Shakspeare, it is somewhat extraordinary, that none of his various editors should have attempted to separate his genuine poetical compositions from the spurious performances with which they have been so long intermixed, or taken the trouble to compare them with the earliest editions.'[13] Stressing their authenticity and lamenting their neglect, Malone confirms how marginal the narrative poems are to Shakespeare's growing reputation.

But more importantly, the ways the poems circulated in the eighteenth century did not lend themselves to the kinds of quotation practised by fictional characters such as Clarissa. Shakespeare's poems are not only largely absent from editions, but after 1600, also from most anthologies that excerpted his works. The ways of reading promoted by the early anthologies are not replaced, in the case of the poems, by modes of engagement that will become conventional in the eighteenth century: applying observations to one's own circumstances, borrowing the advice of an admired author, testing and confirming Shakespeare's unusual insight. The circulation of the narrative poems promotes neither identification with a particular character, nor admiration for 'our beloved

Shakespeare'; they will, as a result, remain '*common-placed*' rather than '*quoted*'.[14]

Venus and Adonis and *Lucrece* were extremely well received when they were first published in 1593 and 1594 respectively. As Katherine Duncan-Jones has observed, 'The poems' success was immediate', and both texts were avidly consumed: 'Frequent lending-out and thumbing of copies led to the physical disappearance of virtually the whole print-run.'[15] *Venus and Adonis* was by far Shakespeare's best-selling work, and its dedication to Henry Wriothesley proved lucrative for the Shakespeare family: 'It is virtually certain that the poet immediately used part of his reward for *Venus* to settle his father's many debts, for suits against John Shakespeare cease entirely after the spring of 1593.'[16]

The early publishing history of the narrative poems testifies to their perceived quality. The first editions of both poems were printed (and *Venus and Adonis* published)[17] by Richard Field, a Stratford associate of Shakespeare's, who would 'build on' the achievement of his former master, Thomas Vautrollier, and his widow (later Field's wife), Jacqueline Vautrollier, to make 'a name for himself as one of London's more distinguished printers and publishers'.[18] As Douglas Bruster notes, one of the distinguishing qualities of his

---

[12] *Shakespeare's Poems*, ed. Duncan-Jones and Woudhuysen, p. 519.

[13] *Supplement to the edition of Shakspeare's plays published in 1778 by Samuel Johnson and George Steevens. In two volumes. Containing additional observations by several of the former commentators: to which are subjoined the genuine poems of the same author, and seven plays that have been ascribed to him; with notes by the editor and others.* Advertisement, p. iv.

[14] Jeffrey Paxton Hehmeyer, 'Heralding the Commonplace: Authorship, Voice, and the Commonplace in Shakespeare's *Rape of Lucrece*', *Shakespeare Quarterly*, 64 (2013), 138–64; p. 163.

[15] Katherine Duncan-Jones, *Shakespeare: Upstart Crow to Sweet Swan, 1592–1623* (London, 2011), p. 94.

[16] Duncan-Jones, *Shakespeare*, p. 95.

[17] Lukas Erne, *Shakespeare and the Book Trade* (Cambridge, 2013), p. 147.

[18] Douglas Bruster, 'Shakespeare's Lady 8', *Shakespeare Quarterly*, 66 (2015), 47–88; p. 67.

work, continuing the Vautrolliers' approach, was his remarkable 'carefulness as a printer' and 'attention to detail', which manifests itself in the presentation of Shakespeare's poetry.[19] Adam Hooks valuably cautions scholars, however, against using Field to authorize a certain biographical vision of a Shakespeare personally invested in his print reputation, who collaborated closely with a friend from Stratford, to whom he would remain grateful for the rest of his career, in boosting his status as a poet. Field's 'responsibility for and financial risk in Shakespeare's poetry were limited to two editions within a year, which were sold at the White Greyhound, the shop of his partner, John Harrison'; for him 'the budding poet seems to have been little more than a brief matter of business'. More significant to the popularity of Shakespeare's poems are the 'crucial, if neglected, contributions of two stationers', John Harrison and William Leake.[20] Field transferred the rights to *Venus and Adonis* to Harrison on 25 June 1594, a month after Harrison had entered 'a booke intituled the Ravyshement of Lucrece'. Harrison would promote the two texts as 'companion volumes', publishing a total of seven editions of the narrative poems. Harrison retained the rights to *Lucrece* until 1614, but sold the rights to *Venus and Adonis* in 1596 around the time that he 'ceded his shop at the White Greyhound in St Paul's Churchyard to William Leake'.[21] Leake published two editions of *Venus* before 1600 and three afterwards, and would exploit the popularity of the poem by selling it alongside the rather more dubious poetic collection, *The Passionate Pilgrim*.[22] The poems were evidently valuable commodities.

The immense popularity of Shakespeare's poems is even more apparent when considered in the context of the circulation of poetry books in the early modern book trade. Shakespeare might account for 'no more than 13 of the 284 poetry books published', but when the number of reprints is considered, a different picture emerges: 'With 15 reprints before 1640, *Venus and Adonis* appears to have had unrivalled success among poetry books. With seven reprints, the popularity of *Lucrece* is matched only by a handful of publications, and

exceeds that of 98.6 per cent of the other poetry books published at the time.'[23] This impressive rate of reprinting means that, of the '701 poetry books first published from 1583 to 1622', *Venus and Adonis* is in first place, and *The Rape of Lucrece* in shared fourth place: indeed 'an astounding level of success'.[24] The best-selling *Venus* was formally influential, too: Erne and Badcoe note a 'surge in popularity' of the six-line 'heroic sestet' in the poetry of the 1590s and early 1600s.[25] Shakespeare's *Sonnets*, by contrast, resembled other sonnet collections of this period in failing to achieve even one reprint.

The narrative poems were not only frequently reprinted in the late sixteenth and early seventeenth centuries: their words were much repeated. *The Shakspere Allusion Book*, which traces seventeenth-century references to Shakespeare, placed *Venus* and *Lucrece* fourth and sixth respectively in the list of works most alluded to, with sixty-one documented references to *Venus* and forty-one to *Lucrece*.[26] Going beyond the praise and verbal borrowings recorded in that collection, Sasha Roberts finds documentary evidence to suggest that Shakespeare's poem also offered early modern women a bawdy reading experience, as well as furnishing male readers with rhetorical tools for seduction.[27] By contrast to *Venus*, as Duncan-Jones suggests, contemporary readers might have been disappointed by *Lucrece*, finding this 'graver'

---

[19] Bruster, 'Shakespeare's Lady 8', pp. 67–8.

[20] Adam G. Hooks, 'Shakespeare at the White Greyhound', *Shakespeare Survey 64* (Cambridge, 2011), pp. 260–75; pp. 262, 267, 262.

[21] Erne, *Book Trade*, pp. 147–9.

[22] Erne, *Book Trade*, pp. 149–50.

[23] Erne and Badcoe, 'Popularity of Poetry Books', pp. 47, 49.

[24] Erne and Badcoe, 'Popularity of Poetry Books', pp. 47, 49.

[25] Erne and Badcoe, 'Popularity of Poetry Books', p. 51.

[26] *The Shakspere Allusion-Book: A Collection of Allusions to Shakspere from 1591 to 1700. Vol. II. Originally compiled by C. M. Inglelby, Miss Toulmin Smith, and by Dr F. J. Funivall, with the assistance of the New Shakspere Society: and now re-edited, revised, and re-arranged, with an introduction, by John Munro*, 2 vols. (London, 1909), vol. 2, p. 540.

[27] Sasha Roberts, *Reading Shakespeare's Poems in Early Modern England* (Basingstoke, 2003), pp. 20–59, 62–101.

poem to lack the warmth and titillation they had come to expect.[28] Yet if *Lucrece* was not read to pieces with quite the hunger that its more tantalizing counterpart inspired, it was certainly devoured *in* pieces, with many contemporary allusions.

Significantly, around 1600, a cluster of printed commonplace books drew increasingly heavily on extracts from Shakespeare's poems. Grocer John Bodenham took notes on his wide reading, and publishers and printers in his circle arranged them into collections. The first of these, *Politeuphuia: Wits Commonwealth* (1597), produced for Bodenham by publisher Nicholas Ling, collected 'choice and select admonitions and sentences' from classical and Christian sources. Francis Meres's *Palladis Tamia: Wit's Treasury* (1598) took *Politeuphuia* as a 'model' but used the format to venerate English authors, praising 'honey-tongued' Shakespeare and 'explicitly putting modern vernacular poets on a par with the Greek and Roman classics'.[29] Subsequent collections, however, quoted entirely from English writers, under headings such as 'Feare', 'Lechery', 'Time' and 'Women'; and here, Shakespeare is a significant presence. In *Englands Parnassus: or, the Choysest Flowers of our Moderne Poets*, compiled by Robert Allott and published by Ling, the ninety-seven quotations from 'W. Shakespeare' place the playwright 'sixth out of 60–70 named authors, after Spenser, Drayton, Daniel, Warner, and Lodge'.[30] In *Bel-vedére, or the Garden of the Muses*, compiled from Bodenham's notes by Antony Munday, Shakespeare ranks first, if *Edward III* is included in the count (but less visibly than in Allott, as the compiler runs together numerous brief extracts without attribution).

In both collections, the narrative poems dominate the Shakespearian extracts. *Romeo and Juliet* is Allott's most frequently quoted play (with 12 extracts, compared to 2 from *Love's Labour's Lost*, 2 from *1 Henry IV*, 6 from *Richard II* and 6 from *Richard III*), but it is outweighed by *Venus and Adonis* (25 extracts) and *Lucrece* (38).[31] In *Belvedere*, according to Charles Crawford's count, extracts from *Lucrece* total 91 and *Venus and Adonis* 34, compared to 47 from *Richard II*, 23 from *Edward III*, 13 from *Richard III*, 12 from *Romeo and Juliet*, 10

from *3 Henry VI*, 5 from *Love's Labour's Lost* and 1 from *1 Henry VI*.[32]

Scholars regard the poems' dominance of the commonplace books as a result of the way in which *Lucrece* was first printed. Lesser and Stallybrass trace connections between *Englands Parnassus* and *Bel-vedére* and the nine poetic texts printed between 1594 and 1599 with commonplace markers in their margins. Signalling sententious lines in a poem was an increasingly systematic practice in the 1590s.[33] *Lucrece* was the first text of Shakespeare's to be printed with these markers – and, with *Hamlet*, one of only two marked before 1609 – inviting speculation about authorial intervention.[34]

Approximately twenty-four lines are flagged up in the margins of Q1 *Lucrece*. Commonplace marks called attention to aphoristic lines such as

' The sweets we wish for, turne to lothed sowrs,
' Euen in the moment that we call them ours.[35]

Here, marks reinforce the abstract, proverbial wisdom of a final couplet. Elsewhere, they gesture to single lines, such as the final declarative statement

---

[28] Katherine Duncan-Jones, 'Ravished and Revised: The 1616 *Lucrece*', *Review of English Studies*, 52 (2001), 516–23; p. 517.

[29] Peter Stallybrass and Roger Chartier, 'Reading and Authorship: The Circulation of Shakespeare 1590–1619', in *A Concise Companion to Shakespeare and the Text*, ed. Andrew Murphy (Malden, MA, 2007), pp. 35–56; p. 43.

[30] Neil Rhodes, 'Shakespeare's Popularity and the Origins of the Canon', in *The Elizabethan Top Ten: Defining Print Popularity in Early Modern England*, ed. Andy Kesson and Emma Smith (Farnham, 2013), pp. 101–24; p. 114.

[31] Roberts, *Reading Shakespeare's Poems*, p. 93.

[32] See Charles Crawford, 'J. Bodenham's Belvedere', in *Shakspere Allusion-Book*, vol. 2, appendix D, pp. 489–518.

[33] Zachary Lesser and Peter Stallybrass, 'The First Literary *Hamlet* and the Commonplacing of Professional Plays', *Shakespeare Quarterly*, 59.4 (2008), 371–420; p. 385. See also George K. Hunter, 'The Marking of Sententiae in Elizabethan Printed Plays, Poems, and Romances', *The Library*, 6, (1951): 171–88.

[34] See e.g. H. R. Woudhuysen, 'The Foundations of Shakespeare's Text', *Proceedings of the British Academy*, 125 (2004), 69–100.

[35] William Shakespeare, *Lucrece* (London: Printed for Richard Field, by John Harrison, 1594), G1v.

in a stanza describing Lucrece and Tarquin's 'cat' and 'mouse' negotiations:

His eare her prayers admits, but his heart granteth
No penetrable entrance to her playning,
' Tears harden lust though marble were with rayning.
(E2r)

These marks pick out a truism from the characters' struggle. Flagged-up lines in Q1 are largely narratorial: they tend towards abstraction, rather than the dynamics of characters' thought and speech. After her rape, sententious marks frame not Lucrece's wretched response, but a detached observation on her maid's behaviour:

This plot of death when sadlie shee had layd,
And wip't the brinish pearle from her bright eies,
VVith vntun'd tongue shee hoarslie cals her mayd,
VVhose swift obedience to her mistresse hies.
' For fleet-wing'd duetie with thoghts feathers flies
(I2r)

Instead of the emotional, dramatic image of Lucrece 'sadlie' wiping 'the brinish pearle from her bright eies' and calling 'hoarslie' to her mayd', the marks fix on a passing, alliterated phrase that is more memorably sententious.

Scholars often assume a direct connection between the sententious markings in Q1 *Lucrece* and the heavy quotation of this poem in the printed commonplace books. Lesser and Stallybrass observe that 'nearly half the quotations [in *Bel-vedére*] (91) are from *Lucrece* alone, the only text by Shakespeare prior to Q1 *Hamlet* that was printed with commonplace markers'; and Roberts, noting the number of flagged-up passages in Q1, says that, 'not surprisingly, then', extracts from *Lucrece* dominate the collections.[36] Lesser and Stallybrass note that 'all of the nine commonplaced texts were used either for *Bel-vedére* or *Englands Parnassus* or both', and that Nicholas Ling, his co-publisher John Busby, and printer James Roberts, were involved in the publication of five of the nine: by Robert Garnier, Michael Drayton (two), Edward Guilpin and John Marston. Why, then, 'should we imagine that anyone but the Bodenham/Allott/Ling circle was responsible for the appearance of

commonplace markers in these nine books of vernacular poetry, given how heavily they were using the same texts for their own printed commonplace books?'[37] Yet *Lucrece* is not one of the poems in which Ling and Busby had a hand and, at the time *Bel-vedére* and *Englands Parnassus* were published, the rights to the narrative poems were owned by Harrison (*Lucrece*) and Leake (*Venus and Adonis*) respectively.

Closer inspection of the lines from *Lucrece* excerpted in *Englands Parnassus* and *Bel-vedére* suggests that the sententious markings in Q1 exert relatively little influence on their choices. Allott favours aphorism in his quotations from *Lucrece*, but overlooks most pre-marked lines. Of his thirty-eight quotations from *Lucrece*, the only two also flagged up in Q1 are 'Distresse likes dumpes, when time is kept with teares', and

'Tis double death to drowne in ken of shore,
He ten times pines, that pines beholuding food:
To see the salue doth make the wound ake more
Great griefes greeve most at that would doe it good,
Deere woes rowle forwarde like a gentle flood:
Who being stopt, the bounden bankes ore flowes,
Greefe dallied with, nor law nor limmit knows[38]

These two observations from the same speech of the distraught Lucrece appear in Allott under 'Woe'.

By contrast, Allott extracts numerous aphorisms *not* marked in Q1, including 'All Orators are dumbe where Bewtie pleadeth' (p. 14) and 'True griefe is fond, and testy as a childe' (p. 124). Where the Q1 commonplace markers privileged the narrator, Allott often draws on Lucrece and Tarquin's speeches (including a twenty-one-line monologue from Lucrece beginning 'Times glory is to calme contending kings' (p. 286)). Despite their decontextualization, and the absence of any indication of the speaker beyond 'W. Shakespeare', Allott's less pithy extracts give *some* sense of person and place:

---

[36] Lesser and Stallybrass, 'First Literary *Hamlet*', p. 384; Roberts, *Reading Shakespeare's Poems*, p. 130.

[37] Lesser and Stallybrass, 'First Literary *Hamlet*', pp. 385–7.

[38] Robert Allott, *Englands Parnassus* (London, 1600), p. 306.

Tarquin 'shakes aloft his Romaine blade' before the 'Harmelesse *Lucretia*' (p. 431), and Lucrece's beauty is described, if anonymously, at length (p. 396). Allott's collection, then, is not simply aphoristic: it hints that, as has been increasingly observed, *Lucrece* is 'the work of a dramatist, a poet–playwright who understands the distinct capabilities of each genre, but also permits a trace of each to appear in the other'.[39]

Bel-vedére is only slightly more heavily influenced by the sententious markings in *Lucrece*. Of the 91 extracts from *Lucrece* that Crawford identifies in this collection, only 13, I have found, correspond to the lines marked as sententious in Q1; 7 of those are all fragments of the same two sententious passages, now divided into single lines on the same page under the shared heading 'Of Griefe' (and 'Of Death'). (Twelve of those extracts are also to be found in *Englands Parnassus*.) If the compiler was at all guided by the sententious marks, he, being 'more cavalier with the Shakespearean text',[40] does not reproduce those lines with care: Shakespeare's 'Birds never lim'd no secret bushes feare' (B3r) becomes 'Birds feare no bushes that were never lim'd'; 'Tears harden lust, though marble wear with rayning' (E2r) becomes 'Teares harden lust, though marble weare with drops', and 'But no perfection is so absolute, / That some impurity doth not pollute' (G1r) becomes '*Hardly perfection is so absolute. / But some impuritie doth it pollute*'.[41]

Like *Englands Parnassus*, *Bel-vedére* excerpts numerous aphorisms not flagged as sententious in Q1. It also goes further than Allott to *create* aphorisms where none existed. Where Allott borrowed lengthy passages, *Bel-vedére* works in units of one or two lines. Tarquin and Lucrece are frequently quoted, but their questions and reflections are transformed – sometimes heavy-handedly – into statements. Tarquin's exclamation:

> A martiall man to be soft fancies slaue! (C1v)

becomes in *Bel-vedére*:

> A martiall man ought not be fancies slaue. (p. 85)

With a small rewording, the compiler nudges Tarquin's wry, rhetorical reflection on his infatuation into an unambiguous truth. Likewise, under the heading 'Of Affection, etc.', Tarquin's lines

> Affection is my Captaine, and he leadeth.
> And when his gaudie banner is displaide,
> The coward fights, and will not be dismaide (C3v)

become in *Bel-vedére*

> *Affections gawdie banner once displayed,*
> *The coward fights and will not be dismayed* (p. 162)

The compiler compresses three lines into a resounding couplet; Tarquin's self-dramatizing personification of Affection as 'my captain' is lost.

Lucrece's characterful, rhetorical speeches also become, in *Bel-vedére*, more detached statements. Her already forceful

> Then Kings misdeedes cannot be hid in clay (E3v)

becomes

> Monarchs misdeeds cannot be hid in clay (p. 57)

Without the connective 'Then', the line is detached from the context of rhetorical suit; by replacing 'kings'' with 'Monarchs', it gains the alliterative force of truism. Likewise, Lucrece's address to 'Time':

> O time thou tutor both to good and bad (G4v)

becomes in *Bel-vedére* the more neutral

> Time is a tutour both to good and bad (p. 216)

The personification remains, but the sense of Time's agency (and the speaker's desperation) is diminished without Lucrece's apostrophe. The compiler transforms Tarquin and Lucrece's rhetorical flights and plaints into narratorial observations.

[39] Catherine Belsey, 'The Rape of Lucrece', in *The Cambridge Companion to Shakespeare's Poetry*, ed. Patrick Cheney (Cambridge, 2007), pp. 90–107; p. 92.

[40] Roberts, *Reading Shakespeare's Poems*, p. 132.

[41] John Bodenham, *Bel-vedére, or, the Garden of the Muses* (London, 1600), pp. 145, 121, 42.

Unlike the 'graver' *Lucrece, Venus and Adonis* was never furnished with commonplace marks. As with *Lucrece*, however, the compilers of *Englands Parnassus* and *Bel-vedére* needed no such guide to extract copious moral material. Roberts proposes that, in *Englands Parnassus*, lines 'removed from the context of a seduction narrative, acquire[s] a new tone of grave common sense';[42] placed under headings such as 'Use', they are transformed into proverbial wisdom. It is not quite true to say, though, that Allott's extractions in *Englands Parnassus* transform an erotic poem into an entirely sententious one, for his selections are more diverse than that. Allott takes the majority of his quotations from the narrator, who typically furnishes not proverbs but 'Poeticall Comparisons':

Euen as an emptie Eagle sharpe by fast,
Tires with her beake on feather, flesh and bone,
Shaking her wings, deuouring all in hast,
Till eyther gorge be stuft, or pray be gone,
    Euen so she kist his brow, his cheeke, his chin,
    And where she ends, she doth anew begin.

(p. 423)

This extract is chosen for its violent animalistic imagery rather than for its moral value. It is one of a little-discussed swathe of such 'Comparisons' in Allott, from a variety of authors, that hinge on similitude: 'As that ... Such seemed ... ', 'As when ... Such was ... ', 'Looke how ... Such was ... ', 'Euen as ... So ... ' – or, in this case, 'Euen as ... Euen so ... ' The narrator also provides descriptions (such as of Adonis's horse) and brief observations about love ('Louers hours are long, though seeming short' (p. 192)), but what characterizes these extracts is often their comparative construction:

An Ouen that is stopt, or Riuer staied
Burneth more hotely, swelled with more rage:
So of concealed Griefe it may be said.
Free vent of words, loues fier doth asswage.
But when the hearts atturney once is mute,
The Circuit breakes, as desperate in his sute.

(p. 123)

Shakespeare uses the double image of the 'Ouen ... stopt, or River staied' to articulate the pressure of unexpressed emotion: 'So of concealed Griefe it may be said.' Extracting this passage, Allott models for readers and writers not a moral truth, but a well-deployed double simile.

The characters in *Venus and Adonis* furnish more similes. Allott draws several times upon Adonis's attempt at an indignant distinction between lust and love:

Loue comforteth like sun-shine after raine,
But lusts effect, is tempest after sunne:
Loues gentle spring doth alwaies fresh remaine,
Lusts winter comes ere sommer halfe be donne.
Loue surfets not, but like a glutton dies,
Loue is all truth, lust full of forced lies   (p. 164)

By placing these lines under 'Lechery', Allott seems to extract from Adonis a moral point about the superiority of love to lust. But as in the narrator's observation, this extract in fact furnishes a set of memorable comparisons and contrasts – 'like sun shine after raine', 'is tempest after sunne'; 'Loues gentle spring', 'Lusts winter'; 'like a glutton' – through vividly opposed images of weather, seasons, greed and restraint, and truth and lies.

Allott does not, then, relentlessly turn every part of the poems into moral truism; he also draws attention to compelling poetic images, comparisons and structures. But this is not to say that Shakespeare's characters are unaffected. From Venus' speeches, Allott extracts statements of high emotion on the subjects of 'Love', 'Jealousie' and 'Griefe':

Danger deuiseth shifts; wit waits on feare.   (p. 48)

Grief hath two tongues, and neuer woman yet
Could rule them both, without tenne women's wit.

(p. 123)

Loue can comment vpon every woe.   (p. 182)

O learne to loue, the lesson is but plaine,
And once made perfect, neuer lost againe.   (p. 190)

Miserie is troden on by manie
But being lowe, neuer relieu'd by any.   (p. 204)

Foule cankering rust the hidden treasure frets

---

42 Roberts, *Reading Shakespeare's Poems*, pp. 94.

But gold that's put to vse, more gold begets. (p. 297)

Venus wields proverbial language to seduce Adonis, turning to its reassuringly patterned rhetoric when other, physical forms of persuasion fail: 'Unlike myself thou hear'st me moralize' (line 712). Yet Allott lifts these rhetorical attempts out of Venus's voice to become the proverbial statements and poetic feats of 'W. Shakespeare'; in *Belvedére* they are detached from character and poem.

The effect of such anthologization on both poems is essentially the same: the distinctive voices of Venus and Lucrece (and of Tarquin and Adonis) are lost. Allott's excerpts might mention 'she' and 'Venus' in passing, and her extracts might be emotional, but, in general, her female speech is obscured. The same is true of Lucrece: Allott removes 'quoth she' from her 'Few words shall fit the trespasse best' (p. 307); while in *Bel-vedere*, Lucrece's declaration that 'My woes are tedious though my words are briefe' (I4r), becomes the third-person observation that 'Woe is most tedious when her words are brief' (p. 142). In one sense, as Roberts has observed, this 'excision of character' make Shakespeare's poem more 'widely applicable', even 'universally applicable'. The anthologists turn a poem that deals with rape, publicity, classical Rome and kingship, into advice about behaviour; and Lucrece's self-questioning 'moral dilemmas' into 'staunch truisms'.[43] But in the longer term, however, as this article argues for the first time, the 'excision of character' makes the poem *less* available for application. By transforming Lucrece's debate and Venus' rhetoric into a set of statements and poetical comparisons, anthologization removes their voices from the poem, and limits their capacity to be revoiced by others in future.

Why is this loss of voice so significant in the case of Shakespeare's narrative poems? The choices made by these anthologists will have a long-lasting effect on their reception. In one sense, these collections appear more influential than the quartos themselves. The extracts from *Lucrece* copied into sixteenth-century manuscripts and personal commonplace books and listed in the *Catalogue of*

English Literary Manuscripts 1450–1700 seem to correspond very little, if at all, with the lines flagged up as sententious in Q1, and more closely with the descriptive passages already extracted in print collections. These collections might exert a more powerful influence on the way later readers engage with Shakespeare's poems than the poems themselves.

The anthologies have a lasting influence on perceptions of the poems because the modes of engagement they promote do not evolve. Certainly, all of the lines from Shakespeare's plays extracted in *Englands Parnassus* and *Bel-vedere* are also detached from their original speaker: Friar Laurence and Romeo, for example, provide Allott with the observations that 'Care keepes his watch in euery olde mans eye' (p. 24) and 'Loue is a smoake made with fume of sighes' (p. 173). But while subsequent publications offer new ways of valuing the plays, Venus and Lucrece, unlike Shakespeare's dramatic speakers, do not later regain their voices.

First, the flurry of anthologies that appeared around 1600 was quickly followed by what William St Clair has called a 'clamp-down on the publishing of printed anthologies which drew on previously printed sources' that lasted until 1774.[44] Second, the poems' absence from the First Folio meant that they were not included in the few anthologies that avoided these restrictions. *Venus* and *Lucrece* are absent from John Cotgrave's 1655 *The English Treasury of Wit and Language, collected out of the most, and best, of our English drammatick poems: methodically digested into common places for general use.* Despite the title reference to 'drammatick poems', the collection draws exclusively from plays: 'one hundred percent' of the quotations in Cotgrave's collection 'are dramatic in origin', as opposed to 6–8 per cent of the selections in Allott.[45] Some see this as a sign of the 'rise of the drama in popularity,

---

[43] Roberts, *Reading Shakespeare's Poems*, pp. 132–3.

[44] William St Clair, *The Reading Nation in the Romantic Period* (Cambridge, 2004), p. 66.

[45] Gerald Eades Bentley, 'John Cotgrave's *English Treasury of Wit and Language* and the Elizabethan Drama', *Studies in Philology*, 40 (1943), 186–203; p. 198.

prestige, and dignity in the reigns of James I and Charles I';[46] others as an attempt to rescue plays, 'lately too much slighted',[47] by highlighting 'their literary nature, making them worthy sources for commonplaces'.[48] Most importantly, though, plays were readily available to Cotgrave. Humphrey Moseley, for whom the collection was printed, had recently issued collected editions of Beaumont and Fletcher, Brome, Cartwright, Massinger, Shirley and Suckling, most of whom are well represented. Shakespeare is Cotgrave's most frequently quoted playwright, with 154 extracts to Jonson's 112 and Beaumont and Fletcher's 111. Even though Moseley had no direct connection to the Folio, 'One suspects that part of Shakespeare's appeal for Cotgrave was the fact that an unusually large number of his plays were to be had in a single volume'.[49] If he closely followed the Folio[50], he might naturally overlook the poems.

Third, in a parallel process, the sententious markings in the margins of *Lucrece*, numerous in the 1594 and 1600 quartos, began to vanish in later editions of the poem, until, by 1616, and in all subsequent editions to 1655, only one set remains:

' For thoughts vnstain'd do sildome dreame on *euil*.
' *Birds* neuer limb'd, no secret *bushes* feare:[51]

It is as if the established methods of extracting value from the poems gradually dropped away, without being replaced by new ways of consuming them. By the time restrictions on anthologies and quotation books start to lift, the poems are not readily available for new kinds of engagement.

The ironic exclusion of *Venus and Adonis* and *Lucrece* from a collection of 'drammatick poems' represents the beginning of a process by which Shakespeare's plays come to be venerated as poetry, and his poems marginalized. Edward Bysshe, in *The Art of English Poetry* (1702), apologized for the absence of 'the Good Shakespeare' in the first edition of his collection of 'the most Natural, Agreeable and Noble Thoughts on all Subjects of our modern Poets' because of their unappreciative audience.[52] In his *Complete Art of Poetry* (1718), Charles Gildon compensated for the neglect of Shakespeare and Spenser, 'being satisfy'd that the

charms of these two great Poets are too strong not to touch the Soul of anyone who has a true Genius for Poetry'.[53] Gildon supplied the supplementary volumes of Shakespeare's complete works that included his narrative poems, yet, in his *Shakespeariana, or Select Moral Reflections, Topicks, Similies, and Descriptions from* SHAKESPEAR (1718), drew all of Shakespeare's 'Poetry' from his plays. William Dodd's *Beauties of Shakespear* (1752), the first collection of quotations devoted exclusively to an individual author, gathered the 'finest passages of the finest poet' entirely from Shakespeare's drama.[54]

Because the poems were not included in these later anthologies, their sententious extracts were not recast in a new light. Dodd's *Beauties* has mixed selection criteria, and partly resembles the early printed commonplace books. He includes Romeo's 'Love is a smoke rais'd with the fume of sighs' under the heading '*LOVE*', and Friar Laurence's advice against too hasty marriage under '*Violent Delights, not lasting*'; Juliet is abstracted as '*A Beauty describ'd*' and '*A Lover's Impatience*'. Yet mingled with these commonplaces and descriptions are different ways of viewing the play. Dodd provides long dramatic extracts such as '*The Courtship between* Romeo *and* Juliet, *in the* Garden', '*SCENE VII. Juliet's Chamber, looking to the* Garden', and 'Juliet's *Soliloquy, on drinking the Potion*', with speech prefixes and

---

[46] Bentley, 'Cotgrave's *English Treasury*', p. 198.

[47] Bentley, 'Cotgrave's *English Treasury*', preface.

[48] Laura Estill, *Dramatic Extracts in Seventeenth-Century English Manuscripts: Watching, Reading, Changing Plays* (Lanham, MD, 2015), p. 89.

[49] Bentley, 'Cotgrave's *English Treasury*', p. 203.

[50] Stallybrass and Chartier note that Cotgrave makes 'heavy use' of the Folio but also attributes to Shakespeare drama that does not appear in that collection, p. 54.

[51] *The rape of Lucrece. By Mr. William Shakespeare* (London: Printed by T. S. for Roger Jackson, 1616), B4v.

[52] Edward Bysshe, *The Art of English Poetry* (London, 1702), preface, unpaginated.

[53] Charles Gildon, *The Complete Art of Poetry* (London, 1718), preface, unpaginated.

[54] William Dodd, *The Beauties of Shakespear* (London, 1752), vol. 1, p. xiii.

stage directions.[55] Where no speaker is specified, Dodd's design – play by play with act and scene divisions – means that detached lines are rehoused in a dramatic structure. But because Dodd drew heavily on eighteenth-century editions that included the poems only in supplementary forms, and on earlier anthologies that had excluded them, *Venus and Adonis* and *Lucrece* were not recast, with the plays, as rich sources of dramatic speech, nor of 'sublime' poetic 'beauties'.

Instead, the narrative poems were published in the eighteenth century in ways that might actually have restricted their circulation. Both poems were published in full in a collection of *Poems on Affairs of State, from 1620. to this Present Year 1707. Many of them by the Most Eminent Hands.*

Since the publishing of the last Vol. which was Anno 1704, several Choice Poems have been communicated to me by Ingenious Gentlemen, desiring I would make another Vol. and that such Pieces as Mr. William Shakespear's (the Great Genius of our English Drama) Rape of Lucrece, and Venus and Adonis, which were never printed in his Works, might be preserv'd.[56]

The collection reproduces Shakespeare's narrative poems to recuperate the lesser-known 'Pieces' of the 'Great Genius of our English Drama', previously excluded from 'his Works'. While it arguably increased the poems' visibility, the nationalistic and political company in which it presented them, flanked by 'The Miseries of England, from the Growing Power of her Domestick Enemies' and 'The first Anniversary of the Government under his Highness the Lord Protector: suppos'd to be written by Edmond Waller of Becconsfield Esq; and printed in 1655', might have limited their availability for domestic consumption and quotation.

The Digital Miscellanies Index, a database of eighteenth-century poetic miscellanies, confirms that extracts from *Venus* were not in wide circulation early in the century, beyond *Poems on Affairs of State. Lucrece*, by contrast, is quoted at length in a 1725 letter to *The Plain Dealer*, Aaron Hill and William Bond's short-lived, non-partisan journal of 1724 to 1725 that devoted itself to cultural and social, rather than party political, concerns.[57] The letter's author, 'R. S.', poet Richard Savage, whose work Hill would promote, writes in the wake of the unofficial publication of Shakespeare's narrative poems in a separate volume tacked on to Pope's 1725 edition:

finding the Six Volumes, tho' called *Shakespear's* Works, contained not his VENUS and ADONIS, his TARQUIN and LUCRECE, and numberless other Miscellaneous Pieces, which, for Richness of Fancy, and the many beautiful Descriptions that adorn them, are far from being inferior to some of his more celebrated Labours; I thought myself obliged to become a Purchaser of the Seventh Volume also, which appears to me, to have no Demerit to occasion its Exclusion.[58]

Savage celebrates 'a few of the numberless natural Beauties, which shine every where thro' these charming Pieces', and laments that the poems have not, 'by some of the Wits in *Leading-Strings*, been looked on with equal Favour; because this Edition of it was not midwif'd into the World, by the *great Names* that have condescended, for the *Emolument* of the *Publick*, to shine in the Title Page of the First Six Volumes' (p. 484). Savage wishes to save the poems from the short-sighted judgement of those who disregard them, and to promote to the '*Implicite Witlings*' of the Age, those Beauties which might otherwise escape their Observation' (p. 484). Savage's epigram, '*Pro captu Lectoris habent sua fata Libelli*' ('According to the capacity of the reader, books have their destiny'), suggests that

---

[55] Dodd, *Beauties of Shakespear*, vol. 2, pp. 198, 209, 202, 209, 202–8, 212–15, 215.

[56] *Poems on Affairs of State, from 1620 to this Present Year 1707* (London, 1707), p. iii.

[57] For discussion of the *Plain Dealer*, see Christine Gerrard, *Aaron Hill: The Muses' Projector 1685–1750* (Oxford, 2003), ch. 5, 'The *Plain Dealer* and the Religious Sublime', pp. 105–21.

[58] Aaron Hill, *The Plain Dealer: being select essays on several curious subjects, relating to friendship, love and gallantry, marriage, morality, mercantile affairs, painting, history, poetry, and other branches of polite literature. Publish'd originally in the year 1724, and now first collected into two volumes*, 2 vols. (London, 1730), no. 116, vol. 2, p. 483.

Shakespeare's poems are a victim of their undeserving readership.

By contrast, the DMI reveals that the same speech from *Lucrece* is included in *The Historical and Poetical Medley, or Muses Library* (1738) for negative reasons:

his Genius does not seem so well suited to the Narrative, as the Dramatick Part of Poetry; as I presume, will appear by the many Conceits not only in the Two first Stanzas quoted below; but almost thro' both his Poems of *Venus* and *Lucrece*, tho' his passionate Transition in the last to *Opportunity* is a strong Proof that his Mistakes are more owing to an Excess of Wit, than a Want of it.[59]

The compiler quotes almost exactly the same passage from *Lucrece*, not to admire the beauties but to illustrate the *weakness* of Shakespeare's narrative poetry. The stress is on how unlikely it is that Shakespeare's anaphora-filled rhetorical flights would be spoken by such a character in such circumstances. It is as if the patterned and sententious language – the 'many Conceits' and poetical comparisons – once prized in Allott's collection, are now the sign of Shakespeare's failure.

Thus while *Lucrece* might contain, in Savage's words, 'beautiful Descriptions', the rhetorical flights of Lucrece and Venus do not appear to fit the eighteenth century's sense of the 'propriety' or fittingness of speech and character; they are too much for a character to say.[60] This eighteenth-century collection, like the unofficial volumes that supplemented the major editions, ironically reinforces the boundaries between narrative poetry and drama, resisting the opportunity to regard the poems as extensions of Shakespeare's dramatic art, and delineating them as a lesser form. This compounds the legacy of the early anthologies which initially detached these rhetorical flights from their speakers. Nor does the presentation of the narrative poems mesh with the persona of 'Shakespeare' being constructed, via quotation, in anthologies and fiction. The words of Shakespeare's characters – 'To thine own self be true', or 'Neither a borrower nor a lender be' – become, by selective quotation, the wisdom of 'Shakespeare' himself, but the poems, not present in these anthologies

and novels, escape this treatment, too. They are thus neither available as the dramatic speeches of characters that can be revoiced in new personal situations ('I could a tale unfold'), nor as the insightful observations of 'our beloved Shakespeare'.

In turn, eighteenth-century anthologies would lastingly influence perceptions of the poems. Dodd's *Beauties* was not only reissued into the twentieth century, but silently informed the selections of numerous anthologies of the late eighteenth century and beyond (such as Vicesimus Knox's *Elegant Extracts from Poetry*, a collection designed to support 'the improvement of youth'). After Dodd's death, the dubious publisher George Kearsley borrowed his title but extended his scope: *The Beauties of Shakespeare: selected from his plays and poems* (1783). Under alphabetized headings, extracts from *Venus* and *Lucrece* illustrate 'Fear' and 'Grief', 'Covetousness' and 'Death', 'Happiness' and 'Hare-hunting'. They remain, however, in a separate section, 'The Beauties of Shakespeare's Poems', after an appendix of passages omitted from the plays. But Kearsley's derivative publication would have comparatively little sway over subsequent anthologists, and Dodd's exclusively play-focused choices would persist long after the poems had been rehabilitated by Edmond Malone in *The Plays and Poems of William Shakespeare*.

The marginal status of Shakespeare's narrative poems, then, cannot simply be ascribed to their exclusion from the First Folio of 1623, nor to changing tastes. The sententious quotation of these immensely popular poems in printed commonplace books, followed by their exclusion from

---

59 *The Historical and Poetical Medley, or Muses Library; being a choice and faithful collection of the best antient English poetry, from the times of Edward the Confessor, to the reign of King James the First. With The Lives and Characters of the known Writers taken from the most Authentick Memoirs. Being The most valuable Collection of the Kind now extant, affording Entertainment upon all Subjects whatsoever* (London, 1738), p. 376.

60 See Rumbold, *Shakespeare and the Eighteenth-Century Novel*.

more overtly dramatic anthologies, seems to have limited both *Venus*'s and *Lucrece*'s availability to readers and writers into the eighteenth century: unlike in the case of the plays, the mode of consumption that those collections encouraged was never replaced. Consequently, they are not given voice by new characters like Clarissa, nor celebrated as the wise observations of 'Shakespeare'. While complete works editions would debate the boundaries of Shakespeare's work, later anthologies compound the exclusion of the poems by reproducing the decisions of earlier collections. Printed anthologies thus crucially intertwine with those more familiar subjects of book history, quarto and folio texts, confirming Shakespeare's reputation as the 'finest poet' while continuing – to this day – to position his narrative poems as marginal to his work.

THE OVIDIAN GIRLHOOD
OF SHAKESPEARE'S BOY ACTORS:
Q2 JULIET

HEATHER JAMES

The role of Juliet is the first in Shakespeare's repertory to take shape in relation to Ovid, the Augustan love poet who emphasized and enlarged the roles played by girls in the myth and poetry of his day. It makes intuitive sense to discover the playfully transgressive spirit of imperial Rome's boldest love poet at the heart of Juliet's girlhood. Ovid was Shakespeare's favourite poet: by 1599, Francis Meres could assert that 'the sweete wittie soule' of Ovid had entered into 'mellifluous and honytongued' Shakespeare by metempsychosis.[1] And girlhood mattered intensely to Ovid, who made it a practice to invert Greco-Roman myths, suggesting that they were about girls rather than the gods, demigods and heroes etched into the politics and ideology of Augustan Rome.[2] It seems additionally fitting that Shakespeare would adapt an inventive, iconoclastic and (to at least some of his contemporaries) licentious source from pagan antiquity to reanimate a tale descending from a prior generation of Elizabethans, who translated, reworked and moralized the sensational fiction of early modern Italy. As the 'schoolmaster of love' (*magister amoris*), known for his unrestrained wit (*ingenium*), friskiness (*lasciuia*) and licence (*licentia*) with moral, sexual and rhetorical proprieties, Ovid had what it took to update the moral tale of Arthur Brooks's *Tragicall History of Romeus and Juliet* (1562), based on Matteo Bandello's novella, and turn it inside out. In the playhouses as well as the printing houses of the Elizabethan 1590s, models of classical transmission might well suggest the modern and avant-garde as well as the ancient, especially when it came to Ovid and the genre of erotic elegy.[3]

To say this much and no more, however, is potentially to accept the limitations that a narrow sense of source studies places on the functions of classical adaptation and allusion and thus to miss the force and complexity of Shakespeare's reckoning with Ovid in *Romeo and Juliet*. There is first a question of texts: there simply is no Ovidian girlhood for Juliet in the first quarto of 1597. This edition of the play has important allusions to Ovid, but they have no singular relevance to the part of Juliet. It is not until Q2 of 1599 that Juliet's role takes shape in relation to Ovid and Ovidian models of girlhood; there is consequently a textual component to the metamorphosis of Juliet's part. Second, there is an expressly theatrical dimension to Shakespeare's engagement of Ovid in Q2, focused on the boy actor, whose status is also transformed by the text's Ovidian materials: the boy actor gains every bit as much as the girl he plays.

---

[1] Francis Meres, *Palladis Tamia* (London, 1598), sigs O01v–O02r. In commenting on Shakespeare's revival of Ovid's spirit, Meres is thinking of Shakespeare's poetry rather than his plays.

[2] Deanne Williams has established Shakespeare's investment in girlhood in *Shakespeare and the Performance of Girlhood* (Basingstoke, 2014).

[3] W. R. Johnson described the critical sense of Ovid as 'classically unclassical' in his influential essay, 'The Problem of the Counter-classical Sensibility', *CSCA*, 3 (1970), 123–52. For a study of Ovid's relationship to the innovative literature of the Elizabethan 1590s, see Georgia E. Brown, *Redefining Elizabethan Literature* (Cambridge, 2004).

When modern Shakespearian critics comment on the differences between the 1597 and 1599 quartos of *Romeo and Juliet*, they are not thinking of the allusive programmes at stake in the two texts. They are instead prompted by an idea that emerged over a hundred years ago with the New Bibliography, when A. W. Pollard, in conversation with W. W. Greg, introduced the concept of 'bad quartos', which he pitted against the exemplary citizenship and textuality of the so-called 'good quartos'; the idea first appeared in 1909 and developed further in the twentieth century through the influence of R. B. McKerrow.[4] Pollard decreed that there were five 'bad' quartos (the number would expand along with the persuasiveness of the new bibliography), the first of which was *The Excellent conceited Tragedy of Romeo and Juliet* published by John Danter and Edward Allde in 1597. *Hamlet*, too, had a 'bad quarto', which continues to receive a princely share of critical attention. Yet the 1597 quarto of *Romeo and Juliet*, the first of the bad seeds, has attracted a fair share of interest from scholars concerned with modern editorial practices and early modern performance. In a brilliant essay published in 1982, Random Cloud compares the texts of the 1597 and 1599 quartos in a concerted effort to expose the problems of moralizing the differences between allegedly 'bad' and 'good' quartos.[5] His essay helped to fuel further work by Jonathan Goldberg (1986), Steven Urkowitz (1996) and Wendy Wall (2006), which focused on the practical and ideological implications of the two quartos as scripts for performance.[6] The present chapter draws on critical arguments for viewing the extant texts through the lens of theatre and performance, but seeks out the resources of an untapped ally of early modern theatre studies, namely the changing practice of classical allusion and adaptation in Shakespeare's early tragedy. To be clear at the outset: there is no compelling reason to choose between critical interests in theatrical allusion and classical allusion, as if they represented wholly different agendas to the study of drama in Shakespeare's day. Moreover, Shakespeare's classical allusions,

which concentrate in the 1599 but not the 1597 quarto, do not add to the critical arguments for his supposed intent to cultivate literary authorship, especially if print culture and the more literary qualities of printed texts are imagined to stand at a far remove from (or even the vanishing point of) his sense of the here and now of the theatre.[7] I argue that the opposite is true in the case of *Romeo and Juliet*: the more lavish and bold the allusions to Ovid become, the more they reveal the ways in which Shakespeare, in 1599, had his sights set on the strength, legacy and future of the English theatre.

To begin with some changes between the two quartos: Q2 is longer than Q1 by some 20–25

---

[4] Alfred W. Pollard, *Shakespeare Folios and Quartos: A Study in the Bibliography of Shakespeare's Plays 1904–1685* (London, 1909). Clear and helpful accounts of the rise of the New Bibliography and criticism of it may be found in Laurie E. Maguire, *Shakespearean Suspect Texts: The 'Bad' Quartos and their Contexts* (Cambridge, 1996) and Lukas Erne, *Shakespeare as Literary Dramatist*, 2nd edn (Cambridge, 2013), ch. 8, pp. 216–43.

[5] Random Cloud, 'The Marriage of Good and Bad Quartos', *Shakespeare Quarterly*, 33 (1982), 421–31.

[6] Steven Urkowitz, 'Two Versions of Romeo and Juliet 2.6 and Merry Wives of Windsor 5.5.215–45: an invitation to the pleasure of textual/sexual di(per)versity', in *Elizabethan Theater: Essays in Honor of S. Schoenbaum*, ed. R. B. Parker and S. P. Zitner (Newark, DE, 1996); Jonathan Goldberg, '"What? in a names that which we call a Rose": The Desired Texts of Romeo and Juliet', in *Crisis in Editing: Texts of the English Renaissance*, ed. Randall M. Leod (New York, 1994), pp. 173–202; and Wendy Wall, 'De-generation: Editions, Offspring, and *Romeo and Juliet*', in *From Performance to Print in Shakespeare's England*, ed. Peter Holland and Stephen Orgel (Basingstoke, 2006), pp. 152–70. See also Stephen Orgel, *The Authentic Shakespeare, and Other Problems of the Early Modern Stage* (London, 2002), and Gary Taylor and Michael Warren, *The Division of the Kingdoms: Shakespeare's Two Versions of King Lear* (Oxford, 1983).

[7] Lukas Erne (*Shakespeare as Literary Dramatist*) has influentially asserted the literary imagination and aspiration in Shakespeare's dramatic works, while Patrick Cheney has argued extensively that the ideas of authorship and literary careers are the primary shaping forces in the works of Shakespeare, Spenser and Marlowe. See especially Patrick Cheney, *Shakespeare, National Poet-Playwright* (Cambridge, 2004) and *Shakespeare's Literary Authorship* (Cambridge, 2008).

per cent, and what changes is Juliet's role, which grows by two-thirds.[8] Other characters, such as Benvolio and Friar Laurence, also have more to say in Q2; Benvolio has the additional advantage of surviving the tragic ending of the second quarto, whereas he dies in the first one (as we learn from Montague, who publicly discloses that his wife is dead and then, perhaps thinking forward to the next generation of Montagues, awkwardly adds that young Benvolio has died as well). The Prince is another of the dramatis personae to profit from the change in quartos: he gains a name, Eskales, longer speeches, and, as Wendy Wall has demonstrated, a subtle degree of control over the terms of punishment and pardon to be meted out to the rival families at the play's end. Urkowitz and Wall have both shown that the parts of various characters change in a range of scenes, and argued that these changes reflect a range of performance options affecting the play's handling of character, sexual mores and, for Wall, political ideology.[9] The Prince's speech at the play's end in Q2 shows that final judgement of the play's dramatic action does not rest in the hands of Capulet and Montague as the heads of the feuding households. It might be held in the control of the Prince and state (in the dramatic action) or left to the will of the audience (as a matter of theatre). Juliet, however, has the only role in the play to reap consistent benefits from the extensive change in her part. It is her part that reflects a shift in Shakespeare's idea of the theatre in 1599 and his sense of, or hopes for, its future.

To be frank, less is more for some characters. This is true for Romeo as early as the play's first scene. In Q2, Romeo comes across as a self-involved petrarchan lover, who rejects the deep sympathies of Benvolio, a man of all heart and good will, as his name implies; despite his cousin's unwavering kindness, Romeo prefers his private experience of melancholy to intimacy and only gradually comes around. In Q1, by contrast, Romeo is on edge and with good reason: he is doing everything in his power to shun the advances of Benvolio as an informer, a man in his parents' service, just as Hamlet will shun the overtures of

Rosencrantz and Guildenstern and question Ophelia's loyalties. At the outset of their conference, Romeo pointedly asks, 'Was that my Father that went hence so fast' (B1v), and he never loses sight of the significance of his father's puzzling and speedy exit and Benvolio's likely mission; and he is right, since Benvolio has exhorted both parents to 'stand . . . aside', assuring them that he will 'know [Romeo's] grieuance, or be much denied' (B1r).[10] Q2's Romeo poses the same question but his vague interest in his father's movements rapidly fades to none at all: he has love on the brain and only half minds his cousin's flattering efforts to get him to talk about it. Q1's Romeo, on the other hand, parries Benvolio's efforts to gain his confidences, share his pain and talk of love. Even his references to the Dianlike chastity of his beloved lady, whose name – Rosaline – he refuses to divulge, have a double sense: the object of his devotion is admirably proof against bribes and blandishments but his kinsman is perhaps more susceptible to corruption by 'Saint seducing gold' (B2r). Once he has touched on the seductiveness of bribes, Q1's Romeo is done with his cousin, the 'right good mark-man' (B2r), who aims at Romeo's secrets, whereas Q2's Romeo encourages and extends the conversation, readily falling into step when Benvolio offers to govern his thoughts. 'Be rulde

---

[8] I refer to the difference between the size of the First Quarto and the Second Quarto as growth in the neutral sense of volume. I leave to one side the hypothesis of an earlier edition, which we do not have, that more closely resembles Q2 (i.e., the argument that Q1 is a 'bad quarto' that has little relation to Shakespeare's authorial intentions). If Q1 is imagined to be a reduced and theatre-based version of an original more closely resembling Q2, then we still need to explain why Juliet's part – in relation to Ovid – makes and marks the considerable differences between the two texts.

[9] In emphasizing the patriarchal dimensions of Q2, Wendy Wall usefully refocuses the theoretical arguments laid out by Dympna C. Callaghan in 'The Ideology of Romantic Love: The Case of *Romeo and Juliet*', in her volume, co-edited with Lorraine Helms and Jyotsna Singh, *The Weyward Sisters: Shakespeare and Feminist Politics* (Oxford, 1994), pp. 59–101.

[10] William Shakespeare, *The Most Excellent Tragedy of Romeo and Juliet* (London: John Danter, 1597). All references are to the edition by Charles Praetorius (London, 1886).

by me, forget to thinke of her,' Benvolio says, to which Romeo offers the mild protest, 'O teach me to forget to think' (B2r).[11] While Romeo prolongs the dialogue about love in Q2, he is at pains to shut it down in Q1.

And why shouldn't Q1's Romeo carry a 'grieuance' (B1r) against his parents alongside of his love grief over Rosaline? They are locked in an ancient and violent family feud that may well claim the life of their only son. They are highly motivated to pry into the secrets of his heart and restrict his movements: from the moment Romeo enters the stage, he reads the signs of the first scene's brawl as evidence of the 'loving hate' within his own family as well as the family feud that binds the Capulets and Montagues together in the city of Verona. The second quarto, in short, presents the image of Romeo that is familiar and even clichéd today: he is a young man caught up in petrarchan love-in-idleness and very much at loose ends. But Q1 gives him solid goals: first, evade entrapment by his cousin, the voluntary informant to his parents, and second, go find himself a Capulet to love. Rosaline is nice – she is a niece of the enemy family. But Juliet, as Capulet's sole daughter, is irresistible. Romeo of Q1 knows he is trading up when he meets the entrancing Juliet and learns her identity, while Romeo of Q2 does little more than exchange one infatuation for a fresher and more gratifying one. Romeo of Q2 consequently moves through his version of the play under a cloud of suspicion that prevents him, in the eyes of many Shakespearian scholars, from fully establishing himself as a tragic protagonist on par with Juliet. For Romeo, the choice between the two quartos seems easy: less is more.

The opposite is true for Juliet: more is more. In Q2 she has riveting speeches that give her unquestionable priority in the play. In Q1, by contrast, she has arresting stage directions that bestow moments of concentrated dramatic energy upon her. The best of these tells us how she arrives at the appointed place for her wedding, and the operative word is 'fast': *Enter Iuliet, somewhat fast, and embraceth Romeo.* This stage direction carries the scene or, better, the scene is built around it.

Romeo and the Friar prepare for Juliet's arrival in their opening dialogue, when Romeo anticipates the moment the lovers will 'consummate those never-parting bands, / Witness of our hearts' love, by joining hands' (E4r). Juliet's cue is the Friar's sententious reply, 'Youths loue is quicke, swifter than swiftest speed' (E4r), and she makes good on his maxim. She speeds straight to Romeo's arms and speaks only to him, leaving the Friar to stand back and put words to his sense of wonder: 'See where she comes. / So light of foote nere hurts the troden flower: / Of loue and ioy, see see the soueraigne power' (E4r). In the Friar's account, Juliet is a force of nature, a Lucretian or perhaps a Vergilian Venus, who brings together three distinct senses of the word 'speed' in a visual play on words: swift movement, sovereign power and success or prosperity in the marriage rites Juliet intends to enjoy.[12] Romeo greets her as the daylight that comes to 'waking eyes / (Cloasd in Nights mysts)': he says she is the 'frolicke Day', and she agrees to play the 'Sunne' (E4v) in an erotic game with her beloved, so long as she may draw her radiance and power from his presence. Juliet of Q1 wastes no time on the deferential civilities she pays to the Friar in Q2, where she pauses to address him ('good even to my ghostly confessor') and awaits his signal ('Romeo shall thank thee, daughter, for us both') before

---

[11] William Shakespeare, *The Most Excellent and Lamentable Tragedie, of Romeo and Juliet* (London: Thomas Creede, for Cuthbert Burby, 1599). All references are to the facsimile edition by Charles Praetorius (London, 1886). I generally cite passages from the Q2 edition, except where Q1 is specified.

[12] The *OED* records various relevant meanings for 'speed': sense 2 is 'power, might'; sense 3 is 'success, prosperity, good fortune; profit, advancement, furtherance'; and sense 5 is 'quickness in moving or making progress from one place to another, usually as the result of special exertion; celerity, swiftness; also, power or rate of progress. Lukas Erne, editor of *The First Quarto of Romeo and Juliet* for *The New Cambridge Shakespeare* (Cambridge, 2007), notes the surprise of the Friar's comparison of Juliet to a goddess and cites the encounter of Aeneas with Venus, who 'reveals herself as a true goddess by her gait' (*Aeneid* 1.405), notes to 9.10, lines 11–12.

turning to her Romeo.[13] In Q1, she addresses the Friar only once and that is to let him know he needs to pick up the pace: 'Make hast, make hast,' she chides, 'this lingring does vs wrong' (E4v). The betrothal scene of Q1 has splendid poetry and energy, whose chief function is to comment – like a motto to an emblem – on the visual significance of Juliet when she enters, '*somewhat fast, and embraceth Romeo*'.

The 1597 quarto favours stage directions and dramatic action over the enhanced speech and full-scale monologues of 1599. One of the most celebrated speeches in *Romeo and Juliet*'s modern editions comes when Juliet, who has married her Romeo but not yet consummated their marriage, is alone onstage and gives voice to her passion:

> Gallop apace you fierie footed steedes
> To *Phoebus* mansion, such a Waggoner
> As *Phaethon*, would quickly bring you thether,
> And send in cloudie night immediately.   (F3r)

At this point in Q1, the Nurse puts an elaborate stage direction into action: *Enter Nurse wringing her hands, with the ladder of cordes in her lap*. And here, in this version of the play, Juliet stops her monologue, satisfied with an intense but brief wish that Phaethon, the bold and ill-fated child of the Sun-God, were in charge of his father's sun-chariot on the night of her marriage. Juliet wills the sun to speed towards night with the force and velocity of that mythical day, relayed at length in book 2 of Ovid's *Metamorphoses*, when Phaethon rashly attempted to drive the chariot of the sun, lost control of his horses and put the entire world at risk. Juliet is entirely prepared to seize the day and risk her own world, beginning with the Capulet family and the city of Verona. In Q1, these four vibrant lines say it all. Q2, however, gives Juliet thirty-one lines of fiery-footed meter to deliver a full-scale erotic elegy worthy of the boldest love poets of classical antiquity. When the Nurse enters, it is simply '*with cords*' (G1v) and, it would seem, less hand-wringing than in Q1. The extended version of this speech (to be discussed in more detail below) constitutes Juliet's most overtly Ovidian performance in the play and radically transforms

her part. Even the stakes of her opening allusion to Ovid's Phaethon change and expand. In Q1, Juliet wants the speed and daring of Phaethon and she wants it now. In Q2, she takes more time with her Ovidian allusions and gets more from them, with the result that she launches a stunning reading of the story of Phaethon, stripped of the usual moralizations, as an inspirational figure of youthful ambition: even his fall to earth, shot from the heavens by Jove as king and father of the gods, testifies to his heroic grappling with death, divinity and fathers. In short, Q1 may have action and theatrical energy, but Q2 has volume and energy of speech, and this speech is overwhelmingly allotted to Juliet.

Juliet's part grows most in four scenes, and one scene is pure punishment: in it, Capulet berates his daughter at staggering length as 'mistress minion' (H4v), 'green-sickness carrion', 'tallow-face', 'young baggage' and 'disobedient wretch', 'whining foole', 'puling mammet' and 'hilding' (I1r). In Q1, he also fumes that she is a 'headstrong selfe-wild harlotrie' (H3v). Her verbal evasions make his 'fingers itch' to deliver corporal punishment to the girl who will not agree to his plans for her marriage to Paris, although he once considered her consent indispensable: 'Wooe her gentle *Paris*, get her hart,' Capulet said early in the play, 'My will to her consent, is but a part' (B2r). What vexes him most is that she will neither comply with him nor confide in him, but instead uses 'chopt lodgick' (H4v) to gainsay his paternal role in her life. In both quartos, the non-compliant speech of women puts Capulet in a tyrannical fury. Even his wife says 'You are too hot' (I1r) before taking his side and rejecting her daughter's woeful pleas for intercession: 'Talke not to me, for ile not speake a word, / Do as thou wilt, for I haue done with

---

[13] The Friar of Q2, as Katherine Duncan Jones aptly puts it in her review of the Oxford *Romeo and Juliet* edited by Jill L. Levenson, 'is less poetic and more prudish, resolving that the lovers 'shall not stay alone' until the church has legitimated the union for which they are so pantingly eager' (*RES*, n.s. 52.207 (2001), 446).

thee' (I1v). It falls to the Nurse to say directly what Juliet cannot. 'You are to blame my Lord to rate her so,' she says and is confounded when her master tells her to hold her tongue: 'I speake no treason ... May not one speake?' (I1r). But speech is the very problem: Juliet's gifts of speech – her control over words and silence alike – count as the petty treason of domestic rebellion: 'Graze where you will, you shall not house with me,' Capulet tells her, 'And you be mine, I'le giue you to my friend, / And you be not, hang, beg, starue, dye in the streets, / For by my soule ile nere acknowledge thee' (I1v).[14] In Q2, Juliet is left onstage to reflect on her untenable position as a 'soft ... subject' (I1v) of this world, in need of heavenly aid since she has lost the resources of family. When the Nurse counsels her to submit to her parents, even if it means forgetting Romeo and her marriage vows, Juliet briefly extemporizes with her old confidant and, when finally left alone onstage, spurns the nurse who failed her as the devil's instrument: now cast as 'Ancient damnation' and 'most wicked fiend' (I2r), the Nurse propels Juliet's dramatic exit to find the Friar, who is bound to help her by spiritual law and the risks he has already taken on her behalf.

Capulet's fury seems wildly disproportionate to Juliet's verbal offenses in this scene, as the Nurse's puzzled protests affirm. It is not, after all, as if he knows that his daughter has set aside his name as father, secretly married Romeo, and consummated her marriage in a bedroom within his own house. Yet Capulet intuitively understands that the deepest source of his daughter's rebellion lies in verbal even more than sexual boldness: his own rhetorical abuse, which comes in response to her terse equivocations in the dramatic scene, seems to encompass the far bolder speeches that Juliet delivers in scenes of the play to which he is not privy. These are the very speeches, the bold and fluent monologues that Juliet utters when she is alone onstage or thinks she is alone, that play-goers and readers are most likely to remember and recite. They include her speculative and philosophical monologue on the substance of names in the window or balcony scene; the intense and erotic soliloquy in which she urges on the arrival of her

wedding night; and the fearful and even nightmarish monologue she delivers before swallowing poison, knowing she will wake up, more alone than ever, in the company of the dead buried in the Capulet family tomb. These are also the three scenes that most amplify the volume and energy of Juliet's part between the two quartos, reshape her in relation to Ovid, and fully establish her as Shakespeare's first major heroine in any genre.

Q2 enacts an Ovidian metamorphosis in the role of Juliet as the 'boy heroine', in Phyllis Rackin's felicitous term, through whom Shakespeare rethought the status of the late Elizabethan theatre.[15] This is a lot to claim, and I wish to be clear about the stakes of the Ovidian infusion into an already good play and part. As noted earlier, it has become tempting to think of Shakespeare's classical allusions in terms of a literary programme that Shakespeare may or may not have had in mind for his plays and even to marshal his classical allusions towards the supposed goal of authorship. It is also tempting to interpret these allusions in terms of canon formation, especially if the whole history of classical transmission is attached to the *translatio imperii studiique*, the programme by which cultural authority, gathered at the site of Augustan Rome, is shifted westward in time and space with no mention of the historical forms of resistance or interrogation that attend the passage of empire.[16] In the case of *Romeo and Juliet*, I suggest, Shakespeare was thinking less of his own literary future than of the future directions of his theatre. What did he want the English theatre in London to remember, conserve, animate and forecast in the last years of Elizabeth I's long reign? Ovid had

---

[14] The seminal discussion of the 'subordinate's plot' in acts of domestic rebellion is Francis E. Dolan, *Dangerous Familiars: Representations of Domestic Crime in England* (Ithaca, NY, 1994).

[15] Phyllis Rackin, 'Androgyny, Mimesis, and the Marriage of the Boy Heroine on the English Renaissance Stage', *PMLA*, 102.1 (1987), 29–41.

[16] A clear example of interrogation and resistance may be found in the kernel of *translatio republicae* that is embedded in Vergil's *Aeneid* and extended first in Ovid's *Metamorphoses* and then, no holds barred, in Lucan's *Bellum Ciuile*.

mattered a great deal to the innovative poetry of England in the late 1580s and the 1590s and he mattered also to the English theatre of 1599. The first question to ask is precisely how he mattered in terms of craft and the second is why he mattered, and this is a question that shifts the critical focus from issues of form to aesthetics, theatre, philosophy and politics – in short, to the larger cultural concerns that formal change and innovation engage.

How did Ovid come to shape the role of Juliet in the second quarto of *Romeo and Juliet*? The play's Ovidian materials come chiefly from the counter-epic *Metamorphoses* and the *Amores*, the erotic elegies that launched his career, although the *Art of Love* (a how-to manual about erotic pursuit and fulfilment), the *Heroides* (verse epistles between mythic lovers separated by fortune, accident, or choice) and the *Tristia* and *Epistulae Ex Ponto* (elegies and verse epistles written in Ovid's exile) may also be relevant to this play about erotic instruction, the dialogue of separated lovers and the poetry of exile. Where the *Metamorphoses* are concerned, Juliet's monologue at her window echoes the dramatic monologues delivered by a series of five Ovidian heroines at the outset of their tales of transgressive love in the *Metamorphoses*, while her struggles with fear over the Friar's phial of poison recall the scenes of bodily threat and transformation that conclude four of Ovid's five tales. These early and late scenes, moreover, frame the passionate speech that Juliet delivers on her wedding night. This speech has received some of the most illuminating commentary on the play's rhetoric, genre, image and allusion, and yet it is too bold and combustible to contain by the usual means of scholarly analysis: simply put, it may not be possible to restate, or overstate, its case for seizing the night, setting the opinions of severe old men at a cent (to draw on Catullus 5), and giving in to the mythic and apocalyptic dimensions of passionate love.[17] It is an erotic elegy, designed and destined to renew the astonishing rhetorical, sexual and political energy of the erotic elegies of Ovid's youth, the *Amores*.[18]

Juliet's speeches in Q2 form an extended if implicit argument about the liberties and duties of subjects in the family and the state. In her first soliloquy, Juliet speculates on the substance of a name – puzzling over the relationship of names to the body (there is none) and the law of the father (the connection is made to feel intimate) – while she struggles, in her last soliloquy, with her intense fear of being walled up in the tomb of her forefathers. In argument, theme and word, her speeches recall the dramatic monologues of the famously transgressive heroines of Ovid's *Metamorphoses*, Books 7–10. Medea, Scylla, Byblis, Iphis and Myrrha are adolescent girls in the first rush of love and their love objects are treason to their fathers. Like Juliet, they are young: Iphis, the only one identified by age, may provide the key to Shakespeare's choice to shave two years off the age of the heroine in Arthur Brooks's tale: Ovid's Iphis, too, is just 13 years old. Also like Juliet, each girl enters into a monologue or private counsel on the subject of her duties and choices: each heroine reflects on the unstable nature of passion, the arbitrary force of custom and law, and the tyranny of the name of the father, and each chooses the force that Ovid elsewhere calls a god. In the *Ars Amatoria*, Ovid asserts, *Est deus in nobis, et sunt commercia caeli: / Sedibus aetheriis spiritus ille venit* ('There is a god in us; we are in touch with heaven: from celestial places comes our inspiration'), and he revisits the thought in the *Fasti*, where he says, *Est deus in nobis, agitante calescimos illo: / impetus hic sacrae semina mentis habet* ('There is a god within us. It is when he

---

[17] See especially Catherine Belsey, 'The Name of the Rose in *Romeo and Juliet*', *Yearbook of English Studies*, 23 (1993), 126–41; Gayle Whittier, 'The Sonnet's Body and the Body Sonnetized in *Romeo and Juliet*', *Shakespeare Quarterly*, 40 (1989), 27–41; and Gary McCown, 'Runnawayes Eyes' and Juliet's Epithalamium', *Shakespeare Quarterly*, 27 (1976), 150–70.

[18] The erotic elegies also anticipate the end of the poet's career, when Augustus Caesar relegated the aging poet to Tomis on the Black Sea for a poem written in his youth: the offense (officially) was the licentiousness of the *Ars Amatoria*, a didactic poem on love that extends the project of the erotic elegies in his *Amores*.

stirs us that our bosom warms; it is his impulse that sows the seeds of inspiration').[19] When love moves with divine force, it exposes the social and political investments in casting fathers as gods of their children and princes as gods of their subjects. The Ovidian heroines' arguments *in utramque partem* on the topics of love and filial duties are both passionate and deliberative, even forensic.[20] The heroines come to adulthood and subjectivity over one question: what does the force of love do to a girl?

The first of Ovid's adolescent heroines to find herself torn between dissidence and compliance with the family and state is Medea, the barbarian sorceress of Greek myth and Euripidean tragedy. Ovid radically departs from Euripides' complex version as well as from the more straightforward and misogynistic accounts of her story. As Page DuBois has suggested, Euripides' concern is to present Medea as a deeply ambivalent figure, who embodies 'the problems of difference, animal/ human, Greek/barbarian, male/female'.[21] Every step his Medea takes in the play brings home to the audiences of Euripides' day the social and political contradictions denied in Athenian democracy, in which women, aliens and slaves greatly outnumber male citizens. Ovid's heroine is best seen as a radical updating of the barbarian woman to comment on Augustan ideals. She is moral, introspective, engaging and outrageously smart – in short, everything one would desire in a young citizen of the state. Ovid's young heroine – perhaps like the elegiac poets of Augustan Rome – moves through her narrative by discarding and transcending patriarchal taboos and customs, one bar at a time. She is at first sceptical about her desires for Jason, a 'straunger' and 'husband of another world': 'Love persuades me one, another thing my skill,' she tells herself, 'The best I see and like: the worst I follow headlong still' (T1r). Medea soon gives up her scruples, however, and formally begins her astonishing transformation into a sorceress. She can work wonders and even make old men young, as she proves when she rejuvenates Jason's aged father with a potion composed of 'Charmes' of every 'herbe and weed' and the 'mightie working' of

'Ayres and winds … Elves of Hilles, of Brookes, of Woods alone, / Of standing Lakes, and of the Night' (T3v). Shakespeare famously remembered these words to the end of his own career, when he used her incantatory words to animate Prospero's renunciation of his magic arts in *The Tempest*. For Ovid and Shakespeare alike, Medea's magical power lies in words: even her considerable skill with nature's secrets comes second to her unsurpassed eloquence.

The power of speech is central to Ovid's *Metamorphoses*, and the speeches in which Medea exhibits her powers of persuasion accordingly occupy the majority of Ovid's tale. In Arthur Golding's translation, it takes less than four and a half lines to cover Jason's plan to desert Medea and remarry and her subsequent acts of brideburning and infanticide (the whole of Euripides' play). But her opening monologue runs to 88 lines and her invocation of the powers of moon, stars and earth in her magical incantation takes up 30 lines, while the longer episode devoted to the rejuvenation of Jason's father runs to 137 lines.[22] Medea reveals her full capacity to change the minds of others through words alone when she convinces the daughters of Pelias, Jason's great enemy, to help her slit their father's throat in the false hope that he too will regain youth: Ovid's Medea can talk dutiful daughters into parricide, and this is her greatest heresy in the ideological world of Augustan

---

[19] *Ars Amatoria*, 3.549–50 and *Fasti*, 6.5–6. I quote from the Loeb translations, *The Art of Love and Other Poems*, trans. J. H. Mozley (Cambridge, MA, 1979) and *Ovid's Fasti*, trans. Sir James George Frazer (Cambridge, MA, 1951).

[20] For discussions of classical models for the rhetorical set pieces of schoolboys and the drama of Shakespeare's England, see especially Joel B. Altman, *The Tudor Play of Mind: Rhetorical Inquiry and the Development of Elizabethan Drama* (Berkeley, CA, 1978) and Lynn Enterline, *Shakespeare's Schoolroom: Rhetoric, Discipline, Emotion* (Philadelphia, 2012).

[21] Page DuBois, *Centaurs and Amazons: Women and the Pre-History of the Great Chain of Being* (Ann Arbor, MI, 1991), pp. 118–19.

[22] In Ovid's text, it takes Medea three lines to destroy Jason's new bride and kill her sons, and an additional line to escape the wrath of Jason's sword; her opening monologue is sixty lines, and her magical incantations run to twenty-seven lines.

Rome, where fathers are sacrosanct. By the end of the tale, Ovid's Medea has assumed a new and paradoxical identity as Augustan nightmare and transcendent heroine: her transformation is complete when she sheds her roles as wife and mother, discarding the last claims of patriarchy and the state on her identity. Medea suffers no metamorphosis into bird, beast, fountain or tree, much less a monster, and she receives no punishment. Instead, she talks her way to a triumphant conclusion, which includes an extended world tour in which she surveys the changes and accidents of the metamorphic world she has left behind and below. For Ovid, Medea is the heroine in a *Bildungsroman* about a girl who, against all odds, becomes an incantatory speaker and poet: her fulfilment in her tale is also the fulfilment of his.

Juliet also comes into her own as a dramatic heroine through passionate and incantatory speech. Unlike Medea, she is not granted a comic ending. She owns the story, as the Prince affirms at the play's end, but the story she owns is tragic: 'neuer was a Storie of more wo, / Then this of *Iuliet* and her *Romeo*' (M2r). The reasons for generic doom are not far to seek: her social and gendered position requires her silence. Juliet is beloved by the play's readers and audiences and yet punished within the play for her relationship to speech. As Jonathan Bate notes, she is doubly trapped by the passivity in love typically expected of women and also by her father's will, and she 'alludes to her concomitant linguistic imprisonment' in the first balcony scene through an evocation of Ovid's Echo: 'Bondage is hoarse, and may not speake aloude, / Else would I teare the Caue where Eccho lies, / And make her ayrie tongue more hoarse, then / With repetition of my *Romeo*' (D4r). 'But in the very act of speaking thus,' Bate continues, 'she overcomes her bondage. Unlike the conventionally silent woman, she speaks aloud' until, by the law of the politically charged genre of tragedy, her dramatic speech is silenced.[23] If Juliet transcends the limits imposed on her, it is ultimately through the mediums of performance and print.

The plot about Juliet's woe – rather than her self-authorship – follows the Ovidian model of Scylla, who also finds love among the enemies of her father. The object that initially arrests her thoughts is Minos, the leader of the armed forces gathered for war at the city of her father, Nisus. He is beautiful, and she addresses him in absentia as her 'enemie' and 'Lover' – an antinomy familiar to Juliet – before narrowing in on the main problem: he could ask anything by way of a dowry, 'Save only ... my Fathers realme' (Y1r), which is of course the entirely usual dowry of a sole female child of a rich father. The recognition of limit, however, prompts her to an opposite and optative thought. 'Would God that I were Fatherlesse,' she cries, 'My father only is the man of whome I stand in dreede, / My father only hindreth me of my desired speede' (Y1r). Putting aside her filial pieties and reluctance to seek love through 'traitrous meanes' (Y1r), she takes bold action, moving in the dark of night to her father's bedroom – the ultimate representation of the *arcana imperii* or mysteries of state – to clip the lock of hair containing his virile power and sovereignty, which she then offers (after boldly walking to the enemy camp) to Minos along with herself. Hers is a story of patriarchal closed ranks: she may be heroic and victorious, but she loses her cherished hope when the horrified Minos rejects her and effectively sides with his own great enemy, Nisus. Seeing herself mirrored back not as a lover but as a monster, the anguished Scylla rehearses Minos's condemnation of her and calls on her father to punish her, even as she launches her body at Minos's departing ship and clings to its prow. And it is there that her father, now an osprey, finds her and tears into her flesh – much as old Capulet verbally tears into his only daughter – until she transforms into a bird, the ciris (which Golding suggestively translates as the lark), thus eluding the full rigor of paternal vengeance.

The Ovidian heroines most vulnerable to heavy censure are Byblis and Myrrha, who are tied to their love objects by blood: Byblis loves her

---

[23] Jonathan Bate, *Shakespeare and Ovid* (Oxford, 1993), p. 180.

twin brother Caunus with a fixed determination, while Myrrha reluctantly loves her father Cinyras. These heroines, who are not enviably placed among Ovid's transgressors, bequeath to Juliet their unsentimental analyses of the grammar of blood relations in the volatile context of erotic love. When Byblis falls in love, she initiates a meditation in the poem at large on the 'name of kin', a phrase she repeats and varies as the 'name of kinred' (2Cr). The name of kin enjoys the status of absolute rule to the waking mind but, as Byblis learns in a sexual dream about her brother that makes her blush in her sleep, it has no bearing on the sleeping minds of young girls. The next portion of Byblis's narrative is devoted to her unblushingly reflections on love, names and kinship in her waking hours. The name of kin has no bearing on the gods, Byblis quickly recognizes, who do not hold back (in Christopher Marlowe's phrase) from 'heady riots, incest, rapes'.[24] Inspired with new confidence and purpose, Byblis turns writer, seizing a stylus (or pen, in Golding's translation): 'She doutes, shee wryghtes: shee in the tables findeth lacks. / Shee notes, shee blurres, dislikes, and likes: and chaungeth this for that' (2Cv). Even her final transformation affirms her status as writer, for she metamorphoses into an eternally weeping fountain, an emblem of elegiac lament. Myrrha also thinks of her love as a 'heynous cryme', wishing the gods, godliness and 'holy rites and awe / Of parents' would 'withdrawe' it from her 'vicious mynd' and thus 'dissappoynt [her] wickedness', but she then wavers over the open secret of her society: her love is not deviant since it in fact accords with the practices of the gods and nature and, so, 'infringeth not the bondes of godlynesse a whit' (2D4r). '[E]very other living wyght dame nature dooth permit / Too match without offence of sin' (2D4r), she notes: the heifer, horse, goat and all birds do it and, what is more, so do humans, for there are other 'Realmes (men sayne) / In which the moother with the sonne, and the daughter with the father / Doo match', augmenting the natural bond with 'doubled love' (2D4r). The differences between Ovid's incestuous heroines and Shakespeare's young lovers is obvious, but so are the similarities. Romeo and Juliet, too, want nothing more than to forget 'the name of kin'. They crave the freedom to choose love, as if there were no name of kin, and define it as godly: the aim, as Myrrha puts it, is to be free of the 'spyghtfull lawes' that 'restreyne / The things that nature setteth free' (2D4r). Shakespeare's tragic lovers, like Ovid's transgressive heroines, take on moral absolutes and recast them in the interrogative mood.

Between the tales of the incestuous Byblis and Myrrha, Ovid sets the story of Iphis, whose passion quietly but quite effectively undermines patriarchal rule: she is a girl, raised as a boy and in love with a girl, Ianthe, whom she has every wish to wed and bed. Iphis herself does not grasp the radicalism of her own experience. In her opening monologue, she struggles, as Medea and Scylla did, with a love she fears is 'straunge', 'uncoth' and prodigious' (2C3v), but she does not directly argue with the bars of convention. Iphis is the only one of Ovid's transgressive heroines who does not lay her experience of gender trouble at her father's door, although none has better reason to do so: her father, Ligdus, regretfully informed his pregnant wife, Telethusa, that their poverty required them to abandon the baby if it had the misfortune to be a girl and not, more affordably, a boy. Telethusa, however, followed the promptings of her favoured goddess, Isis, rather than the directions of her husband: when she gave birth to a girl, she dressed and raised her child as a boy. Yet the question of sexual value and viability could be delayed only until Iphis's adolescence. At 13, Iphis has a face 'As eyther a boay or gyrle of beawtie uttered much' (C3v). She is a beauty, betrothed to a beauty, with her father's approval: 'When *Iphys* was of thirteene yeeres, her father did insure / The browne *Iänthee* untoo hir' (C3v). Surrounded by favour and poised to come into her own, Iphis nonetheless experiences love as torment:

---

[24] Quoted from *Hero and Leander* in *The Poems of Christopher Marlowe*, ed. Millar MacLure (London, 1968), p. 144.

How straunge a love? how uncouth? How prodigious
   reynes in me?
If that the Gods did favor mee, they should destroy
   mee quyght.
Or if they would not mee destroy, at leastwyse yit they
   myght
Have given mee such a maladie as myght with nature
   stond,
Or nature were acquainted with. A Cow is never fond
Uppon a Cow, nor a Mare on Mare. The Ram
   delyghts the Eawe,
The Stage the Hynde, the Cocke the Hen. But never
   man could shew
That female yit was tane in love with female kynd.
   O would
Too God I never had beene borne.   (2C3v–2C4r)

Iphis reverses the pattern of Byblis and Myrrha,
who appeal to the law of nature to advance
their case for illegitimate love: she issues
a powerful series of negative examples from
nature that ironically make the case for the
opposing truth. Historical and natural precedent, as well as the bitter genres of epigram
and satire, testify to the fact that women can
indeed be 'tane in love with female kynd'.
Valerie Traub has established that eighteenth-
century adaptation of Ovid's tale of Iphis
responded to the rise of scientific interests in
nature and sexuality, when it becomes increasingly
clear that female same-sex love is a fact of nature;
and I would add that the original tale already made
the case for a sex-positive and gender-troubling
reading of the tale and its heroine through
rhetoric.[25]

   The tale's broadest questions are these: just how
important is the male sex organ to the loving and
erotic union to two girls, already joined by age,
physical beauty, education and mutual love, for
'the hearts of both, the dart of Love did streeke, /
And wounded both of them aleeke' (2C3v)?[26]
And how essential is the father to natural, divine
and civic law? Ovid's heroine inclines to lacerating
self-doubt, defining herself by what she lacks.
But Ovid's text rejects Ligdus's law in favour of
the improvisational and reparative strategies of
Telethusa, who exploited the ambiguity between

the sexes to sustain her daughter's life and prospects: girls can wear boys' clothing, girls and
boys may both go under the name of Iphis, and
her girl can love another girl. Ovid's tale bears out
Telethusa's position twice, first when Iphis dwells
hopelessly on her own love in relation to the
'monstrous' (2C4r) case of Pasiphäe's love for
a bull, improbably asserting that her own 'love is
furiouser than hers, if truthe confessed bee' (2C4r).
Her reason is that Pasiphäe satisfied her desire when
she was 'served by a Bull beguyld by Art in Cow of
tree', created by Daedalus. And yet, Iphis laments,
no such aid exists for her:

If all the conning in the worlde and slyghts of suttle wit
Were heere, or if that *Dædalus* himselfe with uncowth
   wing
Of Wax should hither fly againe, what comfort should
   he bring?
Could he with all his conning crafts now make a boay of
   me?   (2C4r)

Just what could Daedalus, master artisan, do to
bring two girls together in sexual union, if either
of them felt that a phallus was essential? It will be
apparent to Ovid's readers, if not his tortured
young heroine, that Daedalus could invent the
world's best dildo, if required: he constructed
a wooden cow, illustrating his genius for sex toys,·
so why not a phallic counterpart to the far more
difficult proposition of a wooden cow?

---

[25] Valerie Traub, *The Renaissance of Lesbianism* (Cambridge,
2002) identifies the tale of Iphis as 'the Ur-story of *lesbian
desire*' (p. 230) and hones in on two properties of the
narrative and its history: Iphis's romantic fatalism and
the increasingly scientific and open reading of the story
that takes place over the course of the early modern
period.
[26] Laurie Shannon, 'Nature's Bias: Renaissance
Homonormativity and Elizabethan Comic Likeness',
Modern Philology, 98 (2000), 183–210, offers a deft reading
of the theme of likeness and parity in Ovid's tale and its
extensions in Elizabethan comedy. Also illuminating – while
focused on male homoeroticism in marriage plots – is
Mario DiGangi's chapter, 'The Homoerotics of Marriage
in Ovidian Comedy', in *Homoerotics of Early Modern Drama*
(Cambridge, 1997).

Ovid returns to the (in)significance of masculine dominion – the counterpoint to the '(in)significance of lesbian desire' that Valerie Traub has illuminated – at the tale's end, when Telethusa takes her daughter to the temple of Isis for aid.[27] Isis's altar issues a propitious sign, and Iphis leaves the temple with a 'larger pace than ay / Shee was accustomd', a 'face not so whyght', increased strength, and 'her looke more sharper . . . to sight' (2C4v). 'O Iphis,' Ovid's narrator says in apostrophe, 'who ryght now / A moother wert, art now a boay': mother and daughter/son head to the wedding ceremony, where Iphis, 'transformed too a boay / Did take *Iänthe* to his wyfe, and so her love enjoy' (2C4v). The scene of metamorphosis is more impressive for what it ignores (the penis) than for what it describes (secondary sex characteristics): if Iphis undergoes a genital change, it is apparently not worth mentioning. What matters is Iphis's new-found delight in the social dynamics of nerve that come along with her heightened secondary sex characteristics. The law of the phallus requires a different narrative climax, one focused on the advent of the biological nerve, or *nervus* (penis), that Iphis has hitherto lacked. But the text flaunts Lidgus's law: when Iphis and her resilient as well as resisting mother leave Isis's temple, Iphis heads to the wedding altar and marriage bed with 'much more lively spryght', and Juno, Venus and Hymen all attend the marriage in a trifecta of approval for the ambiguous union of Iphis and Ianthe.[28] In Golding's translation, Iphis, 'Did take *Iänthe* to his wyfe, and so her love enjoy' (2C4v), but in Ovid's Latin, there is no need to choose between masculine and feminine pronouns. Iphis may be a boy or she may pass for a boy, and in either case Iphis may still enjoy the love of '*sua . . . Ianthe*'.[29] The feminine possessive adjective, *sua*, attaches to the direct object (Ianthe) regardless of the gender of the subject (Iphis) of the sentence. Only in English are readers required to make a choice between translating the possessive as 'his' or 'her': in Latin, there is active and fully appropriate ambiguity. Iphis is the original of Shakespeare's boy heroines: a boy may play a girl, and a girl may play a boy.

Like Ovid's girls, Juliet struggles with the enormity of patriarchal order more than her natural father. Like Scylla, Medea, Byblis, Iphis and Myrrha, she first sees her love in the aspect of monstrosity and treason. She is stricken when the Nurse tells her, as the Capulet feast disbands, that man exiting the room – the man with whom she danced and spoke and exchanged kisses – is '*Romeo, and Montague, / The onely sonne of your great enemie*' (C4r). Her response bears multiple echoes of Ovid's horror-struck heroines:

> My onely loue sprung from my onely hate,
> Too earlie seene, vnknowne, and knowne too late,
> Prodigious birth of loue is this to mee,
> That I should loue a loathed enemie.   (C4r)

But like Ovid's heroines, she soon overcomes her shock that she loves an 'enemie' and 'stranger' (D1r), and she devotes her mind to chains of thought that are both passionate and philosophical. When Romeo sees her next, she tells him (in absentia, as she thinks), ''Tis but thy name that is my enemie' and, more boldly, 'Denie thy Father,

---

[27] See Valerie Traub, *Renaissance of Lesbianism*, pp. 158–87 and the earlier version of the essay, 'The (In)Significance of "Lesbian" Desire in Early Modern England', in *Queering the Renaissance*, ed. Jonathan Goldberg (Durham, NC, 1994), pp. 62–83.

[28] Gary Ferguson, *Queer (Re)readings in the French Renaissance: Homosexuality, Gender, Culture* (Aldershot, 2008), partly follows Traub's reading of Iphis's tale, but shifts the openness of her discussion towards restrictive absolutes. Traub traces the theme of 'impossible love' in the history of early modern adaptations of the tale, while Ferguson treats it as 'one of the most fundamental and potent statements of the impossibility topos ("What do lesbians do?") and of the equation of sex with phallic penetration' (p. 269). My argument focuses on the philological and rhetorical properties of this Ovidian tale in the context of other stories of boldly transgressive girls in the *Metamorphoses*. Iphis does something far more interesting than make arguments against self-interest: she makes a false counter-argument that completes the case made for her own, quite natural, viable, and appealing, desires.

[29] The very last words of *Metamorphoses* Book 9 home in on the still open question of gender translation: *potiturque sua puer Iphis Ianthe* (line 797). I quote from the Teubner edition, ed. W. S. Anderson (Stuttgart, 1991).

and refuse thy name / And Ile no longer be a *Capulet*' (D2r).

> Thou art thy selfe, though not a *Mountague*,
> What's *Mountague?* it is not hand nor foote.
> Nor arme nor face, ô be some other name
> Belonging to a man.
> Whats in a name [–] that which we call a rose,
> By any other word would smell as sweete,
> So *Romeo* would were he not *Romeo* cald.
> Retaine that tytle, *Romeo* doffe thy name,
> And for thy name which is no part of thee,
> Take all my selfe.   (D2r–v)

Juliet's first experience of love leads her to grapple with the philosophical dilemmas of her situation. She effectively takes up and extends the interrogation of the name of the father begun by Ovid's heroines: she poses these questions, after all, in an enclosed garden that stands as an analogue to the Garden of Eden of Genesis, where Adam names all of the beasts and establishes his dominion over them, and the *hortus conclusus* of the Song of Songs. Shakespeare's Juliet implicitly repeals the right of fathers to determine the will and future for their children by naming them.

Juliet's bold principles are the treason that her father Capulet senses when he says he will disown her, starve her and leave her to wander the streets: it is his wrath that enters into her nightmares. In her monologue before she drinks the poison, she is gripped by 'hideous fears' of patriarchal wrath in the tomb of her forefathers: she fears that her holy father, Friar Laurence, means to poison her to avoid exposure; next, that she will be stifled in the airless vault and 'die strangled' before her Romeo comes; and last, that she will *not* die and no one will come to save her from a life-in-death, packed in with 'the bones / Of all [her] buried [and all male] ancestors', until she runs mad and uses 'some great kinsman's bone, / As with a club' to 'dash out [her] desperate brains' (4.339.53). In Q2, Shakespeare intensifies the plight of the Ovidian heroine, oppressed by the demands of family and painfully isolated from its comforts.[30] Like

Ovid, he pits a girl against the dual imperatives of filial obedience and love to transform her into an iconic and tragic heroine: Ovid's heroines fail, but each one shakes loose some of the mortar holding together the order of patriarchal rule. In Q2, Juliet's thoughts seem to stop time or transcend it, while she enters into an extended engagement with imagined futures. It does not happen this way in Q1, where her thoughts move on clock-time, and each minute rushes towards the end of the two-hours' traffic of the stage.

There is a second way in which *Romeo and Juliet* adapts Ovid. The play draws on the stock types of Roman new comedy, such as the young man (*adulescens*), the girl (*puella*), the angry old father (*durus pater* and *senex iratus*), the braggart soldier (*miles gloriosus*), the nurse (*nutrix*) and the madam (*lena*) who tries to pimp the girl.[31] Romeo, Capulet, Tybalt and the Nurse at times act out these roles. But Juliet does not play the traditional girl of comedy, who is little more than a passive and silent love object for the young man. Shakespeare replaces the *puella* of new comedy with a girl from another genre: the *docta puella* or learned girl of Roman erotic elegy, whose cues are supplied by Ovid, and specifically by the *Amores* and *Art of Love*.

---

30 The First Quarto insists on the role of fathers and patriarchy as early as the prologue, which attributes the tragic deaths of the 'starre-crost Louers' to 'the continuing of their Fathers strife' (A1r), while the Second Quarto refers more generally to the rage and strife of their 'Parents' (A2r). Both quartos focus on problems of patriarchy and fathers, but only the Second Quarto concentrates the plot of adolescent rebellion in the role of Juliet as an Ovidian heroine.

31 In *Shakespeare and the Traditions of Comedy* (Cambridge, 1974), Leo Salingar emphasizes the roles of fortune and the clever servant as they come down from ancient Greece and especially through Rome, while Rosalie L. Colie identifies the roles of *puella*, *adulescens*, *senex iratus* and *nutrix* in *Romeo and Juliet* in her discussion of the technical challenges of creating a tragedy about love, which is typically the subject of comedy, in *Shakespeare's Living Art* (Princeton, NJ, 1974), pp. 135–6.

Sharon L. James has shown that the *docta puella* is an active reader and commentator on the elegiac lover's persuasions.[32] This figure comes down to Shakespeare by way of Petrarch, for whom Laura is sometimes a hauntingly sacred and profane image – a saint bringing erotic sin to the poet-lover – and at other times a fierce critic and commentator on his errors and his verse. Shakespeare assigns this role to Juliet in the play's earliest scenes, where she is gentle but firm with Romeo: there is the push-me-pull-you of the sonnet-like dialogue when they first meet. 'You kisse bith [by the] booke' (C4v) she tells him, raising the delicious question of just which book she has in mind.[33] 'O swear not by the moone th'inconstant moone, / That monethly changes in her circle orbe' (D3r) she tells him later that night, cutting off his letter-perfect poetic protestations, before she passes down her final and absolute instruction, 'Do not sweare at all' (D3v). As Juliet encourages and then checks her exuberant lover ('What satisfaction canst thou haue to night?' (D3v), she inquires, when Romeo suggests that she is leaving him unsatisfied), dismissing him and summoning him back again in the balcony scene, she steps quickly and neatly into the role of the learned girl of Ovidian erotic elegy in the play's early scenes, upsetting the comic order of Roman new comedy.[34]

But Shakespeare goes farther in his updating of Ovid, for his Juliet is not merely the *docta puella* of erotic elegy. She is the play's great erotic elegist, as witness her wedding-night soliloquy in the middle, and at the heart, of the second quarto:

> Gallop apace, you fierie-footed steedes,
> Towards *Phoebus* lodging, such a wagoner
> As *Phaethan* would whip you to the west,
> And bring in cloudie night immediately
> Spread thy close curtain loue-performing night,
> That runnawayes eyes may winke, and *Romeo*
> Leape to these armes, vntalkt of and vnseene,
> Louers can see to do their amorous rights,
> And by their owne bewties, or if loue be blind,
> It best agrees with night.   (G1r–v)

This is the most passionate speech of the play and it draws its fire from Ovidian elegy and myth. In Q2, Juliet moves from her wild image of Phaethon bringing on the night and likely apocalypse – and her celebration of other lawbreaking 'runnaways' – to a stunning recuperation of Night personified and, finally, an even more astonishing fantasy of what will happen when she dies for love, when her family takes revenge, or in the act of love.[35] She calls on Night, a 'sober suted matron all in blacke', to take Romeo

> and cut him out in little starres,
> And he will make the face of heauen so fine,
> That all the world will be in loue with night,
> And pay no worship to the garish Sun.   (G1v)

This is the speech of passion, hope and defiance that anticipates the play's ending in the Capulet tomb, where, as Ramie Targoff has suggested, we see laid out before us the dark side of the philosophical, religious and emotional motivations for seizing the day in love and elegy alike: as Catullus put it in a famous elegy, *Soles occidere et redire possunt: / nobis, cum semel occidit breuis lux, / nox est perpetua una dormienda* ('Suns may set and rise: / for us, when the brief light has set, / one perpetual night must be slept').[36] Juliet imagines Romeo's

---

[32] Sharon L. James, *Learned Girls and Male Persuasion* (Berkeley, CA, 2003), provides a compelling study of the intersection of rhetoric, gender and social history in Roman elegy.

[33] For Diana E. Henderson, *Passion Made Public: Elizabethan Lyric, Gender, and Performance* (Urbana, IL, 1995), the book is emphatically Petrarch's, and Juliet's iconoclasm and agency in the play are marked for the first time by her readiness to participate in the erotic activity of sonnet-making.

[34] For a fuller reading of Juliet's role as educator, see Carolyn E. Brown, 'Juliet's Taming of Romeo', *SEL, 1500–1900*, 36 (1996), 333–55.

[35] Gary Cown argues that Juliet's reference to 'runnawayes' refers to the eternally fugitive Cupid and the epithalamic tradition, but the standard senses of 'runaways' to come up in an EEBO search of the 1590s are the self-evident: they are law-breakers, deserters and escaped apprentices.

[36] Ramie Targoff, 'Mortal Love: Shakespeare's *Romeo and Juliet* and the Practice of Joint Burial', *Representations*, 120 (2012), 17–38. The translation of Catullus 5 is mine.

metamorphosis into little stars, whose beauty will transfix and convert all worldly spectators (Donne's 'Dull sublunary lovers') to reject the wide-ranging decorums associated with the sun.

This is rhapsody. It is Juliet's most dazzling and rule-breaking speech: with creativity and wit, it breaches decorum – rhetorical, sexual and social. It breaks down heteronormative conventions of love, sex and gender, taking seriously its status as an uncensored and full-voltage erotic elegy and not an epithalamion (there is no mention of a marriage bed or rites, and Juliet's speech is no more focused on marriage than Donne's elegy, 'To His Mistress, Going to Bed'). This is true whether the girl Juliet or the boy actor is seen as the desiring speaker. The boy heroine of Q2 is locked in fiery combat with the stars of predestination, social scripts and customs. The iconoclasm of Juliet's speech and imagination achieves an unprecedented intensity for Shakespeare, as if all the radicalism of A Midsummer Night's Dream were channelled into a single speech; or as if all the passion and audacity of Christopher Marlowe were emanating from the slender sides of a girl or a boy.

For it is not just Ovid that is at stake in Juliet's erotic elegy, although all of the characteristics of speech I have enumerated are hallmarks of Ovid's poetry: it's Marlowe's Ovid, beginning with his translation of the Amores in his All Ouids Elegies (1595) and moving into the 'heady riots, incest, and rapes' of the classical gods in the myth of Hero and Leander (1598) and the heart-stopping speeches of desire and yearning in Tamburlaine, Edward II and Doctor Faustus. The power-hungry barons of Edward II address Gaveston as an 'Ignoble vassal, that like Phaethon / Aspirest unto the guidance of the sun (i.e., the English king)' (1.4.16–17); and their allusion to Phaethon's story reveals their own desire to play the role Jove to the bastard son of Phoebus by blasting him to earth from his airy heights.[37] For the humble-born Doctor Faustus, Phaethon speaks powerfully to his dissident passions about God, even at the end of his contract with the devil and Mephistopheles and at the end of his life. 'Lente, lente, currite noctis equi' (5.2.74), Faustus cries out, quoting one of Ovid's erotic

elegies in a painful effort to slow down the momentum of the sun-chariot's horses so that he, even if he cannot seize the day, might not wholly miss it: 'Let me breathe a while' (5.2.121).[38]

Marlowe was dead before Shakespeare wrote any version of Romeo and Juliet. He died in 1593, a year or two before the play's first performance and six years before the publication of Q2, which remembers and revives him through Juliet's arresting speech. The year 1599 was also the most likely for the completion of As You Like It, the pastoral comedy that explicitly recalls Marlowe and ties him to Ovid. The scene in question begins with the entrance of Touchstone, who has attached himself to Audrey in a union that turns him into an ironic version of Ovid: 'I am here with thee and thy goats,' he tells Audrey, 'as the most capricious poet honest Ovid was among the Goths' (3.4.5–6).[39] In the space of a brief allusion, Touchstone invokes the satyr's perspective on erotic elegy and satire: he is at once a comic figure of Ovid among the horny goats of pastoral and a tragic figure of Ovid among the harsh and barbaric Goths of his exile.

I take it that the Goths are crabbed Elizabethan moralists, from Stephen Gosson to the bishops of London and Canterbury, who sought to banish Ovid from print in 1599. The Bishops' Ban suggests one historical point for the recovery of Ovid and Marlowe in the London theatres. The ban included satire and Ovidian elegy: John Davies's satires and Marlowe's translation of All Ouids Elegies were bound together and burned together. But Marlowe's Ovid was revived in the theatre: Ben Jonson devoted his 1601 comical satire, Poetaster, or the Arraignment, to the story of Ovid's emergence as a love poet and his banishment by Augustus; he

---

[37] Quoted from Edward II, ed. Charles R. Forker (Manchester, 1994).

[38] Quoted from Doctor Faustus A- and B-texts (1604, 1616), ed. David Bevington and Eric Rasmussen (Manchester, 1993), A-text.

[39] Quoted from the New Cambridge As You Like It (updated edn), ed. Michael Hattaway (Cambridge, 2009).

focused on the erotic elegies of Ovid's youth and used Marlowe's recently banned translations. Jonson was perfectly capable of translating and adapting Ovid himself, as he abundantly demonstrates in his poetry and plays: he wanted *Marlowe's* Ovid.[40] His point is to reverse the ban on Ovid and Marlowe and restore their playful, wanton and licentious poetry to the stage, and so he presents Ovid, in an early scene, composing and reciting the entire closing elegy of the first book of the *Amores* in Marlowe's translation. This is Shakespeare's point, too, in *As You Like It*, when the shepherdess Phoebe claps eyes on Rosalind disguised as Ganymede and reflects on the power of a verse she remembers from Marlowe's most extended Ovidian poem, *Hero and Leander*: 'Dead shepherd, now I find thy saw of might: / 'Who ever loved that loved not at first sight'?' (3.6.80–2). Touchstone began the round of the allusions to Marlowe's death and his poetic and theatrical afterlife with his reflection – immediately following his allusion to Ovid among the goats and Goths – that 'When a man's verses cannot be understood . . . it strikes a man more dead than a great reckoning in a little room' (3.4.8–10). The worst possible fate for elegies is to wind up in the wrong hands: Orlando pins his elegies to brambles of the forest of Arden, in contrast with the bishops of London and Canterbury, who used brambles to burn *All Ouids Elegies*.

These facts of *As You Like It* are well known to Shakespeare critics and the facts of Jonson's *Poetaster* should be more widely known. Jonson regarded the Bishops' Ban as the chief target of the Ovidian satire, love elegy, and polemics of his own play. Shakespeare's situation is different: he was writing *As You Like It* before the Ban, and Q2 of *Romeo and Juliet* appeared in print in the same year as the Ban. It would appear that Shakespeare was thinking about the theatre's vital need for Marlowe and Ovid at roughly the same time that the bishops were thinking that all of England needed less of them. It is a critical commonplace to emphasize Shakespeare's sense of poetic rivalry with Marlowe as well as Jonson over the status of the classics in poetic authority; and the year 1599 factors heavily in

critical reckonings with the so-called 'poets' wars' and the idea of rivalry more generally.[41] There is room, however, for another hypothesis: Shakespeare had enough time, by 1599, to establish himself as a man of the theatre and a great lover of Ovid and he had enough time left over to sift through the poetic materials and social uses of the theatre and to reflect on what had been lost with Marlowe's death six years earlier.

Joseph Roach has discussed the art of surrogation, in which 'one generation will stand up and stand in for another, and honor the preceding generation by quoting it, but also develop their own ideas and put in their own inventions'.[42] I suspect it was a shock to discover that Marlowe was suddenly part of a prior generation and also that the shock ran deep enough to require time to consider and choose the way to remember him and to innovate beyond him. It is my argument that Shakespeare wanted to recover for the theatre a specific condition of Marlowe's 'mighty line', as Ben Jonson memorably put it: this is its strong ties to the liberty of speech known as *parrhesia* in Greek and *licentia* in Latin, which Michel Foucault characterized as 'fearless speech' and David Colclough as 'bold and open speech'.[43] Like Marlowe,

---

[40] For an account of Jonson's positive engagment of Ovid, see Heather James, 'Ben Jonson's Light Reading', in *A Handbook to the Reception of Ovid*, ed. John Miller and Carole E. Newlands (Hoboken, NJ, 2014), pp. 246–61.

[41] See especially MacDonald P. Jackson, 'Francis Meres and the Cultural Contexts of Shakespeare's Rival Poet Sonnets', *RES* n.s. 56.224 (2005), 224–46; James P. Bednarz, *Shakespeare and the Poets' Wars* (New York, 2001); and Jonathan Bate, *The Genius of Shakespeare* (Oxford, 1998).

[42] I quote from a 2005 interview with Ned Sublette for *Hip Deep*, produced with the support of the NEH, in which Roach places a more optimistic account of the concept of surrogation originally presented in *Cities of the Dead: Circum-Atlantic Performance* (New York, 1996). See www.afropop .org/10424/joseph-roach-talks-to-ned-sublette, accessed 11 March 2016.

[43] Michel Foucault, *Fearless Speech*, ed. Joseph Pearson (Los Angeles, 2001), and David Colclough, in *Freedom of Speech in Early Stuart England* (Cambridge, 2005) and 'Parrhesia: The Rhetoric of Free Speech in Early Modern England', *Rhetorica*, 17 (1999), 177–212.

I suggest, Shakespeare thought of it as 'Ovidian speech', which is both polemical and poetic, and indivisably so. The smallest unit of verse in Ovid's writings is a foot of elegiac meter, which Ovid once described as an arrow or barb linking his erotic elegies to the weapons that his ancestors used to fight for their liberties in the Social Wars with Rome (*Amores* 3.25). Ovid understood erotic elegy as a form of polemic, and Augustus ultimately did, too. The prince's exile of the poet produced the conditions for writers and readers of early modern England to regard Ovid's verse in the same way. Marlowe was bold, iconoclastic and parrhesiastic, an ideal of speech in which a *man* delivers the full contents of *his* mind as if he had no fear of punishment. And Marlowe was gone. His successors in the English theatre were left with a question to reflect on and think through over time: where do you put Marlowe's bold voice, which yearns for liberties and always demands yet more? Shakespeare's presents his solution in *Romeo and Juliet* Q2: not in Marlovian overreaching and transgressive heroes, such as Tamburlaine and Faustus, but in a figure that both overturns and radically extends Marlowe's vision of a theatre invested in parrhesiastic liberties of speech, and that is the part of a girl, played by a boy.[44]

---

[44] My argument for the political desires of the theatre, available to men and women of all social sorts and types, intersects with Stephen Orgel's work on sexuality and gender ambiguity in the early modern theatre in *Impersonations: The Performance of Gender in Shakespeare's England* (Cambridge, 1996). Orgel focuses on the boy actor in the role of a woman as an object of audience desire that cuts across gender lines. I transfer the focus on the productive ambiguity of gender and sexual desires from the body per se to speech, the ability to put the contents of one's mind into words creatively and above all boldly.

'LEND ME YOUR EARS': LISTENING
RHETORIC AND POLITICAL IDEOLOGY
IN *JULIUS CAESAR*

ESTHER B. SCHUPAK

Shakespeare's republican leanings, or lack thereof, as evidenced in *Julius Caesar* have been greatly debated because the drama effectively argues both sides of the case. According to James Shapiro's micro-history, Shakespeare modelled this work on John Hayward's *The First Part of the Life and Reign of King Henry IV*, a popular book that was published a year before the first recorded performance of *Julius Caesar*.[1] Unfortunately, shortly before the first performance of the play, a second printing of the book was consigned to the flames by the Bishop of London. If Shapiro is correct, then Shakespeare's technique of 'juxtaposing competing political arguments, balancing them so neatly that it was impossible to tell in favour of which the scales tipped' was learned from Hayward's book. Indeed, based upon the eventual fate of that book, Shakespeare may have decided not to publish *Julius Caesar* as a text since Elizabeth's censors were more lenient about the spoken word than the printed text.[2]

In any case, because *Julius Caesar* simultaneously enacts both sides of the argument, the balanced nature of the drama makes it difficult to determine Shakespeare's point of view. Thus, Ernest Schanzer's opinion that 'Shakespeare seems to me to be playing on his audience's varied and divided views of Caesar, encouraging and discouraging in turn each man's preconceptions. And since on our view of Caesar depends, very largely, our judgement of the justifiability of the entire conspiracy, the whole drama is thus kept within the area of the problem play.'[3] Schanzer defines the play by this uncertainty.

Perhaps partly because of the uncertainty that prevails in this play, there has been a great deal of scholarly discussion circling the question of whether Shakespeare was in fact a republican, with some viewing a canonical author as necessarily conservative and entangled in prevailing ideologies and others noting his republican connections and the libertarian themes in his work. This article is different in that it represents an attempt to stand outside the traditional argument culture of academia to practise listening rhetoric with regard to the text that Shakespeare has left us, rather than choosing a stance and then picking and choosing evidence, moulding a presentation to suit the argument. Of course, as a twenty-first-century Westerner, I believe in democracy, and I therefore want to believe that Shakespeare held the same views. The text of *Julius Caesar* is open enough to allow me to easily argue this point of view or its diametric opposite or some point in between. But I choose not to.

Rather, I intend to follow Wayne Booth's mode of listening rhetoric (LR), of which, in

---

I would like to thank Bar-Ilan University for the Presidential Fellowship that supported this research.

[1] James S. Shapiro, *A Year in the Life of William Shakespeare, 1599* (New York, 2005), p. 129.

[2] Shapiro, *Year*, p. 129.

[3] Ernest Schanzer, *The Problem Plays of Shakespeare: A Study of Julius Caesar, Measure for Measure, Antony and Cleopatra* (London, 1963), p. 33.

The Rhetoric of Rhetoric, he says: 'When LR is pushed to its fullest possibilities, opponents in any controversy listen to each other not only to persuade better but also to find the common ground behind the conflict.'[4] Too often, but especially when engaged in argument, people listen to each other only for the purpose of formulating an answer; their listening activities are keyed to rebuttal or reply, not to true listening. Similarly, when reading a text, they choose to understand it exclusively through the lenses of their own ideologies and for the purpose of building their own arguments. As such, listening rhetoric represents perhaps more of an idealistic goal than a readily achieved methodology – to listen without an agenda, to truly hear another human being, to respect the integrity of the text, and to search for commonalities rather than differences. Thus, the practice of listening rhetoric is cooperative rather than agonistic.

Furthermore, I intend to use the strategy of 'listening deeply and respectfully' that Gesa E. Kirsch and Jacqueline J. Royster describe in 'Feminist Rhetorical Practices': 'As an inquiry strategy, deep listening is geared toward facilitating a quest for a more richly rendered understanding.'[5] My listening stance will be that of an eavesdropper. In *Rhetorical Listening: Identification, Gender, Whiteness*, Krista Ratcliffe discusses the phenomenon which she calls 'eavesdropping', a rhetorical strategy for listening to the discourse of other groups. According to *Merriam-Webster*, an eavesdropper is one 'standing under the drip from the eaves' in order to 'listen secretly to what is said in private'. For Ratcliffe this strategy entails 'choosing to stand outside ... in an uncomfortable spot ... on the border of knowing and not knowing ... granting others the inside position ... listening to learn'.[6] Eavesdropping, as a subset of listening rhetoric, is the rhetorical mode in which this research will engage. It is also true that eavesdroppers tend to overhear things that they regret listening to, and so I will attempt to listen to those aspects of the texts that I do not wish to hear, that contradict the tenor of my discussion, without moulding and manipulating those aspects so that they conform to my argument. Moreover, listening will

not only be my method of inquiry; it will also be my paradigm for approaching the drama.

Although some reject the notion that the play can be defined in Aristotelian terms, there has been a great deal of critical debate about whether Caesar or Brutus is the tragic hero/protagonist, which is part of the reason why Schanzer defines this as a problem play. On one hand, the title of the play is not *Brutus*, while, on the other hand, it is difficult to pronounce Caesar as the tragic hero, given the fact that his death occurs in Act 3. Of course, this fact is trumped by the reality that Caesar does not remain dead – not literally as his ghost rises, and not thematically as he continues to motivate the action of the play even when no longer alive, or, as Bullough points out, 'the spirit of Caesar lives on in Antony and Octavius, and finally conquers'.[7] Moreover, Brutus comments upon Cassius's and Titinius's suicides: 'O Julius Caesar, thou art mighty yet. / Thy spirit walks abroad, and turns our swords / In our own proper entrails' (5.3.93–5). Since Brutus had spoken with the ghost of Caesar only the night before, this statement can be taken both literally and metaphorically – though dead, Caesar is hardly gone. Therefore, Horst Zander asserts that 'there seems to be an agreement that the protagonist of the play is Caesar and hence that the title of the piece is justified'.[8]

Caesar's arrogance and self-centredness are certainly strong candidates for the position of his tragic flaw, as has been argued in critical literature in the past. However, I will suggest that it is his unwillingness to listen that truly causes his

---

[4] Wayne C. Booth, *The Rhetoric of Rhetoric: The Quest for Effective Communication* (Malden, MA, 2004), p. 10.

[5] Gesa E. Kirsch and Jacqueline J. Royster, 'Feminist Rhetorical Practices: In Search of Excellence', *College Composition and Communication*, 61 (2010), 640–72; p. 649.

[6] Krista Ratcliffe, *Rhetorical Listening: Identification, Gender, Whiteness, Studies in Rhetorics and Feminisms* (Carbondale, IL, 2005), pp. 104–5.

[7] Geoffrey Bullough, *Narrative and Dramatic Sources of Shakespeare*, vol. 5 (London, 1957), p. 55.

[8] Horst Zander, '*Julius Caesar* and the Critical Legacy', in *Julius Caesar: New Critical Essays*, ed. Horst Zander (New York, 2005), pp. 3–56; p. 6.

downfall. Robert Miola observes that even though Caesar is 'shrewd and perceptive', he is still deaf on one side, 'an infirmity perhaps symbolic of a fatal inability to listen'.[9] Moreover, I believe that the significance of this detail is manifest in the fact that it is not found in Plutarch, but was apparently invented by Shakespeare himself. The purposeful insertion of this (mortal) point is indicative of its centrality.

In its most literal sense, we see this fatal tendency illustrated in the succession of forewarnings that Caesar chooses to ignore on his way to the Senate. Calpurnia's prophetic dream, Artemidorus's injunctions to read his written warning, the soothsayer's prophecies all fall – as the saying goes – on deaf ears. But this is only the cherry on top, the dramatic suspense that builds to the assassination; the symbolism goes much deeper into the character of Caesar. The assassination is not an impulse of the moment; it is a long-planned affair involving many conspirators. Moreover, Caesar is sufficiently perceptive to have observed Cassius's 'lean and hungry look', and biologically he hears the petitions for clemency for Publius. However, he is wilfully deaf to the political implications of these facts, just as he is wilfully deaf to the pleadings of Calpurnia, Artemidorus and the soothsayer. This fatal pattern of unwillingness to listen, to truly hear, is depicted in the significant first scene where the audience is introduced to Caesar, when he announces that Calpurnia should be sure to stand in Antonio's path since 'our elders say, / The barren, touchèd in this holy chase, / Shake off their sterile curse' (1.2.9–11). Here Caesar is deaf to his wife's feelings as later he will be deaf to her words and to his political environment.

Caesar's deafness is far more than merely a personal flaw; it is a condition endemic to autocratic forms of government. He does not want to hear because he does not need to hear, a situation that is opposite to that of the elected official whose position is dependent on the mandate of the people. As Susan Bickford writes in *The Dissonance of Democracy*, 'what makes politics possible, and what democratic politics requires, is a kind of listening attention to one another'.[10] She provides two definitions of listening. The first is emotional, listening as empathy:

Listening understood in this way involves neither strategic analysis nor mere toleration of another's utterance. Rather, listening means 'I will put myself in his place, I will try to understand, I will strain to hear what makes us alike, I will listen for a common rhetoric evocative of a common purpose or a common good.' The effort of listening is directed toward figuring out what unites us, and we accomplish this through the exercise of empathy.[11]

This definition is in precise opposition to Caesar's stance in the assassination scene where he claims to be immovable, as 'constant as the Northern Star', distant, cold, 'unshaked of motion' (3.1.60, 70), the antithesis of the warm empathy advocated by Bickford. Another component of listening cited by Bickford is the act of deliberately placing oneself in the background: 'without moving ourselves to the background, we cannot hear another at all'.[12] Shakespeare's Caesar is notably arrogant, incapable of ever consigning himself to a non-central position; he is as immovable as 'Olympus' or the 'Northern Star'.

None of the arrogance that permeates Shakespeare's Caesar is evident in Plutarch. Even Caesar's reply to Artemidorus's plea, 'What touches us ourself shall be last served' (3.1.8), is depicted far more humbly in Plutarch, who merely writes that 'Caesar took it of him, but coulde never read it, though he many times attempted it, for the number of people that did salute him'.[13] While Caesar's arrogance is suggested by the incident in Plutarch where a young Caesar insists that his captors raise his ransom from twenty to fifty talents,[14] as well as by his failure to rise for the Senate,[15] this depiction is ameliorated by his subsequent dashing capture of his former captors and by his immediate repentance for his disrespect to the Senate: 'Thereupon also Caesar

---

[9] Robert S. Miola, *Shakespeare's Rome* (Cambridge, 1983), p. 85.
[10] Susan Bickford, *The Dissonance of Democracy: Listening, Conflict, and Citizenship* (Ithaca, NY, 1996), p. 2.
[11] Bickford, *Dissonance*, p. 13.
[12] Bickford, *Dissonance*, p. 24.
[13] Bullough, *Sources*, vol. 5, p. 85.
[14] Bullough, *Sources*, vol. 5, p. 59.
[15] Bullough, *Sources*, vol. 5, p. 80.

rising, departed home to his house, and tearing open his doblet coller, making his necke bare, he cried alowde to his frendes, that his throte was readie to offer to any man that would come and cut it.'[16] This is hardly the overweening pride of Shakespeare's Caesar. Indeed, according to Christopher Pelling, 'Plutarch gives us a Caesar who is trapped by his past, who sees the dangers, who cannot do anything about it'.[17] Just as is the case with Caesar's deafness, his arrogance is largely a construct of Shakespeare's imagination, as well as a trait subsidiary to Caesar's characteristic deafness.

As a representative of monarchy and autocracy, Caesar's deafness is the antithetical apotheosis of democracy, which in theory represents the voice of the people. And indeed, in contrast to Caesar, Brutus, our quintessential republican, reads and *listens to* the notes from the populace affixed to his ancestor's statue, the praetor's chair, and thrown in to his window. These notes are based upon Plutarch's account in *The Life of Marcus Brutus*.[18] However, Shakespeare transmutes this popular appeal to Brutus into a cheap trick played by his fellow conspirators. Thus, this attempt to listen, while an apt demonstration of Brutus's libertarianism, is doomed because it is based upon deceit – Cassius is the true author of those notes, urging him to 'Speak, strike, redress' (2.1.47). Fraudulent as the letters may be, Brutus's desire to follow the will of the people is clear: 'O Rome, I make thee promise, / If the redress will follow, thou receivest / Thy full petition at the hand of Brutus' (2.1.56–8). If Brutus represents a republican openness to the will of the people, it is a problematic trait as it makes him vulnerable to what Booth refers to as 'rhetrickery', which Booth defines as 'the art of *producing* misunderstanding'.[19] Yet, only two short scenes later, we see Caesar, the antithesis to Brutus's republicanism, failing to listen to most petitions and failing to grant the one petition he does hear, a failure that directly leads to his death.

In the beginning of the play, Brutus is a careful listener: he heeds the (false) letters sent to him; he is persuaded by Cassius; he is persuaded by Portia. However, when Brutus fails to listen, it is this failure that directly leads to his downfall. This occurs most tellingly upon the occasion of the funeral

speeches when, as Garry Wills points out, his speech is 'all about himself',[20] about his honour, what he believes, and '[t]hose who do not believe are not just wrong. They are so *base*, so *rude*, so *vile* as to challenge his virtue and perfection'.[21] His self-centredness results in a kind of deafness to the opinions of the crowd, a deafness that extends to the suggestions of his fellow conspirators. In contrast, Antony is tuned in to his audience, even going so far as to ask their permission. This is illustrated in Joseph Mankiewicz's film *Julius Caesar* (1953) when Marlon Brando's Antony, supposedly overcome by emotion, in reality adopts a listening posture that is visible to the film audience, but not to the Roman crowd. While Brutus demands that they 'hear me', Antony more gently asks: 'lend me your ears'. As Wills explains: 'Brutus gave orders to the crowd. "Believe me! Speak if you dare! Stay here! Listen to Antony!" By contrast, Antony asks the crowd's permission to go on, to read the will, to descend.'[22] This profound failure to attend to the point of view of the populace and to the suggestions of his peers is ultimately fatal to Brutus, to his rhetorical effectiveness, and to the conspiracy.

Wills lists seven decisive instances where Brutus 'overrules' Cassius to the grievous detriment of the enterprise. I would refer to these instances as examples of Brutus's self-centredness and consequent wilful deafness. I will begin with Wills's second example because, in my opinion, his first had no discernible effect on the conspiracy:[23]

---

[16] Bullough, *Sources*, vol. 5, p. 80.

[17] Christopher Pelling, 'Plutarch on Caesar's Fall', in *Plutarch and his Intellectual World: Essays on Plutarch*, ed. Judith Mossman (London, 1997), pp. 215–35; p. 218.

[18] Bullough, *Sources*, vol. 5, p. 95.   [19] Booth, *Rhetoric*, p. x.

[20] Garry Wills, *Rome and Rhetoric: Shakespeare's Julius Caesar*, Anthony Hecht Lectures in the Humanities (New Haven, CT, 2011), p. 54.

[21] Wills, *Rome*, p. 57.   [22] Wills, *Rome*, p. 89.

[23] The first example he gives is: 'When Cassius says that the conspirators must swear to their plot, Brutus forbids it, saying that justice itself will vindicate them without any such bond' (2.1.113–16). In this case, it seems to me that Brutus was quite right as all the conspirators did in fact remain loyal to their project almost to the end.

2. Brutus excludes Cicero from the plot against Caesar, though Cassius urges his inclusion (2.1.140–52). Cicero would have delivered a better defense at Caesar's funeral than Brutus's self-referential one.

3. Brutus rejects Cassius' argument that Antony should be killed along with Caesar . . .

4. Brutus gives Antony permission to speak at the funeral, though Cassius rightly says this is courting disaster . . .

5. Brutus determines that he shall speak first, then leave, telling the crowd to stay with Antony. It is a commonplace bit of advice to public speakers that they should try to speak last, if possible, lest an opponent raise things that cannot be answered in response . . .

6. Brutus decides to go out to battle at Philippi, though Cassius rightly says this is yielding the advantage to their foe (4.3.199–212), a verdict Antony and Octavius endorse (5.1.1).

7. Brutus, though a less experienced soldier than Cassius, takes the foremost military role.[24]

As soon as Brutus begins to mirror Caesar in egoism and inability to listen, his failure as a politician is assured; indeed, from the context of the play, it would seem that had Brutus merely followed Cassius's advice, they most likely would have been successful. As J. L. Simmons observes: 'Brutus, to the consternation of Cassius, becomes a Caesar within the conspiracy', and when he assumes Caesar's deafness, it becomes fatal to him too.[25]

In reaffirming the centrality of listening, I choose not to focus upon the texts of the many republican and anti-republican speeches in this play, as these speeches, and particularly the funeral speeches, have already been subject to three hundred years of exhaustive analysis. Rather, I will employ Krista Ratcliffe's rhetorical tactic of 'purposeful overhearing, or eavesdropping', as a mode for interrogating the libertarian ideologies in this play.[26] Thus, my strategy will emphasize the auditors of these famous speeches, the people of Rome, and their reception of the rhetoric, and rhetrickery, directed at them. Rather than engaging with the upper-class, patrician rhetorical constructs, I will eavesdrop, as it were, upon the people who are subject to the manipulation of the patricians and senators who speak. Ratcliffe uses eavesdropping as a mode for interrogating notions of whiteness and gender, but I will use it to focus upon class as I question Shakespeare's notions of republicanism and his libertarian tendencies. As Simon Barker writes, 'Shakespeare's foregrounding of the role of the populace (however malleable), and its admission of the cry of 'Peace, Freedom, and Liberty' (3.1.111), not only acknowledges a crisis in the absolutism of the Tudor administration, but also anticipates a tendency toward modern democracy. Another point of view, however, suggests that Shakespeare offers a glimpse of a more universal and discouraging vision of the rhetoric-soaked mob.'[27] In choosing to focus upon the common people, Shakespeare highlights their political significance and potential power within the government; however, his negative portrayal of the crowd is hardly conducive to a positive view of democratic institutions. So again, Shakespeare's balanced presentation renders it difficult to discern his point of view: is the role of the crowd to demonstrate the importance of attentiveness to the will of the people or to deride their fickleness?

Bickford observes that in a democracy, speaking and listening are mutually interdependent: 'speaking is . . . inescapably intertwined with listening. The relationship between speaking and listening is characterized by a mutual sensitivity that is not simply interpretive but bodily as well'.[28] This mutual sensitivity implies that the auditor has an effect on the rhetor, who adjusts her language in reaction to the response of the listener. The interaction implies a more active role for the listener than is normally associated with the role,

---

[24] Wills, *Rome*, pp. 125–8.

[25] Joseph Larry Simmons, 'Shakespeare's Brutus: A Man Torn by Conflicting Values', in *Readings on Julius Caesar*, ed. Don Nardo (San Diego, CA, 1999), pp. 61–8; p. 68.

[26] Ratcliffe, *Rhetorical Listening*, p. 104.

[27] Simon Barker, '"It's an actor, boss. Unarmed": The Rhetoric of *Julius Caesar*', in *Julius Caesar*, ed. Zander, pp. 227–39; p. 237.

[28] Bickford, *Dissonance*, p. 143.

and this kind of interplay is visible in many of the scenes of the play that feature a rhetor and a crowd.

The first such scene constitutes the only humorous interlude in the drama. In the opening scene of the play, Flavius and Murellus are the 'straight men' whose humourless rectitude contrasts with the bawdy and clever wit of the commoners. When the cobbler eventually admits that the reason that he and his cohorts are in the street in their holiday garb is because 'we make holiday to see Caesar, and to rejoice in his triumph' (1.1.30–1), Murellus responds with his long-winded 'Wherefore rejoice?' speech, in which he addresses his auditors metaphorically as listeners so stupid as to be rendered inanimate: 'You blocks, you stones, you worse than senseless things!' (1.1.35). Flavius, although less harsh than his fellow tribune, is still clearly contemptuous, referring to them as 'idle creatures' (1.1.1) and 'poor men of your sort' (1.1.57). Moreover, in contrast to the playful wit and good humour of the common people, these tribunes are portrayed as stuffy, self-righteous and completely divorced from any sense of fellowship with the common people for whom it is their task to advocate. As Daniell notes, 'The five tribunes of the people were supposed to maintain the republican tradition, but these two, while detesting tyranny, show no respect for, nor fellow-feeling with the people.'[29]

While initially the common people have a voice in this scene, a voice that is capable of outwitting the hegemonic authority of the tribunes, later on they answer Murellus's rant with silence. It is difficult to know whether this silence indicates that he has succeeded in cowing them, or if they are employing silence as a rhetorical strategy to expedite their exit. In the First Folio, there is a centred stage direction, which, according to Neil Freeman, usually indicates that it was a playhouse direction rather than a marginal direction inserted by the printing house.[30] It reads 'Exeunt all the Commoners' and is followed by Flavius's verbal cue 'See where their basest mettle be not mou'd, / They vanish tongue-tied in their guiltiness'.[31] Flavius's assumption that their audience has been moved is, of course, contestable, or

as Shapiro writes, 'for all we know, the laborers have simply headed off to another part of town, where they won't be bothered by these killjoys'.[32] In fact, this is precisely the way the situation is depicted in Gregory Doran's film *Julius Ceasar* (BBC, 2012), where the revels resume as soon as the tribunes depart. Thus, right at the outset this play asks a question: 'Is the tribunes' sense of the commoners as an easily manipulated rabble correct, or have they underestimated their political savvy?'[33]

While I am not sure that it is possible to arrive at a definitive answer to this sort of question, examining Plutarch's version of this event opens up some interesting possibilities. The primary change that Shakespeare made in his depiction of this initial scene is precisely in his portrayal of the common people; in Shakespeare, they are placed in opposition to Flavius and Murellus, whereas in Plutarch the people are enthusiastic followers of these tribunes.[34]

In choosing this as the beginning point of his narrative, Shakespeare must have been impressed with its significance, and his decision to so completely change the reaction of the common people must also be significant. In Plutarch, the people's opposition to Caesar's monarchic ambitions is apparent, but Shakespeare muddies the waters, making it appear that Flavius and Murellus are working against the will of the people and in contradiction to their mandate as tribunes. Was Shakespeare doing this because he wanted to portray the people as stupid, shallow, easily swayed from their own best interests? Did he want to emphasize the conflict between the patrician and plebeian classes, the fact that the supposedly republican institutions favoured only the aristocracy? Or was he merely trying to achieve a politically safe balance, modelled on Hayward?

---

[29] William Shakespeare, *Julius Caesar*, ed. David Daniell, Arden Shakespeare Third Series (London, 1998), p. 155 n.

[30] *The Tragedie of Julius Caesar*, ed. Neil Freeman, Applause First Folio Editions (New York, 1998), Applause, p. xxvi.

[31] 1.1.61–2.   [32] Shapiro, *Year*, p. 154.

[33] Shapiro, *Year*, p. 161.   [34] Bullough, *Sources*, p. 81.

Another important difference is in Caesar's reaction to the actions of the tribunes: in Plutarch they are prosaically deprived of their positions, but Shakespeare writes the far more ominous 'put to silence' (1.2.286). As Shapiro points out, this is in keeping with the theme of censorship that pervades the text and which severely delimits attempts to draw conclusions with regard to author intentionality.

The next scene to which the common people are central is one that is not directly shown, but rather recounted by Casca as eyewitness. Casca's elitist disdain for the people of Rome comes through clearly, an ironic point of view given his own flat, uninspired diction, a point highlighted by contrast to the rhetorical eloquence of other characters as well as by Brutus referring to him as a 'blunt fellow' (although Cassius chooses to call this flaw 'a sauce to his good wit') (1.2.295, 300). As requested by Brutus and Cassius, Casca recounts the scene at the Lupercal festivities where Antony offers Caesar a crown:

I saw Mark Antony offer him a crown – yet 'twas not a crown neither, 'twas one of these coronets – and, as I told you, he put it by once; but for all that, to my thinking, he would fain have had it. Then he offered it to him again; then he put it by again – but to my thinking, he was very loth to lay his fingers off it. And then he offered it the third time; he put it the third time by. And still as he refused it, the rabblement hooted, and clapped their chapped hands, and threw up their sweaty night-caps, and uttered such a deal of stinking breath because Caesar refused the crown that it had almost choked Caesar; for he swooned and fell down at it. And for mine own part, I durst not laugh, for fear of opening my lips and receiving the bad air.   (1.2.235–50)

Casca oozes contempt for the people, despite the fact that they clearly share his republican values. There is a striking contrast between his jaundiced account and Plutarch's far more objective version:

So when [Antony] came into the market place, the people made a lane for him to runne at libertie, and he came to Caesar, and presented him a Diadeame wreathed about with laurel. Whereupon there rose a certain crie of rejoycing, not very great, done onely by a few, appointed for the purpose. But when Caesar refused the Diadeame, then all the people together made an outcrie of joy. Then Antonius offering it him againe, there was a second shoute of joy, but yet of a few. But when Caesar refused it againe the second time, then all the whole people showted. Caesar having made his proofe, found that the people did not like of it, and thereupon rose out of his chayer, and commanded the crowne to be carried unto Jupiter in the Capitoll.[35]

Another significant contrast between the versions is in the deliberateness of Caesar's actions. Casca's version omits any mention of agency or intentionality on Caesar's part; he merely recounts the events he actually witnessed, whereas Plutarch alleges that this scene was deliberately orchestrated, with agents planted in the crowd to give a 'crie of rejoicing' at the designated moment. In withholding this item, Shakespeare tilts the balance in Caesar's favour, downplaying his monarchic ambitions.

A few lines down, Casca makes an intriguing and important comment: 'If the tag-rag people did not clap him and hiss him, according as he pleased and displeased them, as they use to do the players in the theatre, I am no true man' (1.2.258–61). The analogy between democracy and entertainment, between government and Shakespeare's theatrical enterprise, does not cast a positive light on republicanism, especially when one considers the 'jig' performed at the end of the play, alluded to by Brutus: 'What should the wars do with these jigging fools?' (4.2.189).[36] It also casts light on the function of Shakespeare's theatre itself as an exemplar of and practical experiment in libertarianism:

---

[35] Bullough, *Sources*, p. 81.

[36] Thomas Platter, a Swiss visitor to London, recounts: 'On the 21st of September, after dinner, at about two o'clock, I went with my party across the water, in the straw-thatched house we saw the tragedy of the first Emperor Julius Caesar, very pleasingly performed, with approximately fifteen characters; at the end of the play they danced together admirably and exceedingly gracefully, according to their custom, two in each group dressed in men's and two women's apparel.' (Thomas Platter, *Travels in England: 1599*, ed. Clare Williams (London, 1937), p. 166.)

The Globe experiment has shown that the common play-goers standing in front of the stage are more important in the dramatic process than most theatre historians had acknowledged. Their ability to move around freely, interject and participate in the action, as well as show approval and disapproval, reveals the Elizabethan and Jacobean theatre to have been a relatively democratic public space, certainly when compared to a modern theatre.[37]

Early modern audiences functioned not as passive consumers of theatrical performances, but as active listeners, always ready with a response, whether oral or physical. Performances were interactive and constituted a form of unruly, dynamic listening that embraced the audience as part of the show.

Of course, the relatively low price of admission contributed to the equalizing effect of the theatre. The Accounts of the Master of the Merchant Taylors Company alleges, 'Whereas at our comon playes and such lyke exercises whiche be commonly exposed to be scene for money, everye lewd persone thinketh himself (for his penny) worthye of the chiefe and most commodious place with respecte of any other either for age or estimacion in the comon weale.'[38] Shakespeare's Globe was a microcosm of democracy in action, possibly a release valve in a totalitarian state.

However, it was not only audience participation that rendered the Elizabethan theatre inherently democratic, but also the very act of mimetically enacting a play. As Louis Montrose explains, 'Playing was without a place among traditional callings, and the professional players' assumptions of various roles – their protean shifts of social rank, age and gender – seemed to some to be a willful subversion of the divinely ordained categories of difference that had brought order out of chaos at the foundation of the world.'[39] I would take this observation one step further and suggest that not only did acting *appear* to be a 'willful subversion', but that it actually functioned that way by demonstrating the capriciousness of social rank. That is, if I as a low-born actor can dress as an aristocrat, act like an aristocrat, fight like an aristocrat, then what precisely is the difference between me and a genuine aristocrat? As such, acting smudges hierarchical boundaries.

Casca thus highlights the democratic nature of the Elizabethan stage and its similarity to the political arena. Continuing the comparison, Shakespeare conflates this Lupercal scene with an earlier one in Plutarch, in which Caesar makes the mistake of refraining from standing upon the entrance of the Senate. When he realizes that not only the Senate but also the common people have been angered, he makes the dramatic gesture of laying his throat bare to offer his death to the populace in expiation.[40]

This incident is transmuted into the Lupercal scene when Casca recounts:

Marry, before he fell down, when he perceived the common herd was glad he refused the crown, he plucked me ope his doublet and offered them his throat to cut . . . And so he fell. When he came to himself again, he said, if he had done or said anything amiss, he desired their worships to think it was his infirmity. Three or four wenches where I stood cried 'Alas, good soul!' and forgave him with all their hearts. But there's no heed to be taken of them: if Caesar had stabbed their mothers, they would have done no less. (1.2.263–75)

What Shakespeare invented here was the credulous reaction of the populace, along with Casca's pithy comment about their mothers. Especially when a character is as problematic as Casca, with his vulgar buffoonery and flat prose, it is obviously a mistake to suggest that he is the mouthpiece of the author. On the other hand, the fact that Shakespeare manufactured this seems to point clearly either to anti-republican tendencies or to a desire to portray Caesar as a manipulative demagogue.

The iconic scene of the funeral speeches similarly abounds in instances where Shakespeare has supplemented Plutarch in a manner that depicts the people as far more gullible and susceptible to

---

[37] Andrew Hadfield, *Shakespeare and Republicanism* (Cambridge, 2005), p. 3.

[38] Quoted in Louis Adrian Montrose, *The Purpose of Playing: Shakespeare and the Cultural Politics of the Elizabethan Theatre* (Chicago, 1996), p. 47.

[39] Montrose, *Purpose*, p. 36.   [40] Bullough, *Sources*, p. 80.

manipulation than they are in Plutarch's narrative. Casca's earlier remark about the susceptibility of the people – 'If Caesar had stabbed their mothers' – foreshadows Brutus's ability to explain away his stabbing of their beloved father figure: 'Live Brutus, live, live', 'Bring him with triumph home unto his house', 'Give him a statue with his ancestors' and the staggering 'Let him be Caesar', which ultimately reveals the total lack of political awareness afflicting the common people (3.2.48–51). While their words reveal a breathtaking degree of naiveté, the language in which they speak is so simple as to be almost childlike: ''Twere best he [Antony] speak no harm of Brutus here', 'This Caesar was a tyrant', 'Nay, that's certain. / We are blessed that Rome is rid of him' (3.2.69–71). His portrayal of the simplicity of the populace, while preparing the way for Antony's speech, is so extreme as to suggest irony on Shakespeare part. Moreover, this depiction of the populace stands in stark contrast to Plutarch's account: 'When Brutus began to speake, they gave him quiet audience: howbeit immediatly after, they shewed that they were not all contented with the murther'.[41] Plutarch's populace is neither boisterous nor easily swayed.

Thus, when Antony later brings the populace to a killing rage, in Plutarch he is merely nudging them along a path that they have already begun, whereas Shakespeare causes them to enact a complete reversal of course. Moreover, Plutarch's emphasis is different; it is not so much Antony's demagoguery that wins them over as the facts of the case, namely Caesar's bequest to the Roman populace. Only afterwards does Antony enrage them by the spectacle of Caesar's wounds, whereas in Shakespeare rhetorical power rules the day.[42] Thus, in Shakespeare's drama, the people are clearly more susceptible to manipulation than they are in Plutarch.

Shapiro refers to the Cinna the Poet scene as 'Shakespeare's invention';[43] however, in Plutarch this scene immediately follows Caesar's funeral, just as in Shakespeare. In the scene, which highlights the combustibility of the mob, Shakespeare remained quite faithful to Plutarch's account in almost every detail. The primary alteration is the insertion of Cinna's humorous, quick-witted repartee, his wit earning him no friends among the mob. When they confront him, bombarding him with questions, his response is: 'What is my name? Whither am I going? Where do I dwell? Am I a married man or a bachelor? Then to answer every man, directly and briefly, wisely, and truly: wisely I say, I am a bachelor' (3.3.13–16). In contrast to the first scene where it was the plebeians who were witty, here the answer of the populace is dull and violent: 'That's as much as to say they are fools that marry. You'll bear me a bang for that, I fear' (3.3.17–18). Just as in Plutarch, Cinna the Poet is mistaken for Cinna the conspirator and suffers for it. In fact, Shakespeare exacerbates Plutarch's account of a miserable scene further by turning a tragic error into deliberate injustice: when Cinna declares that he is not Cinna the conspirator, the people are indifferent to the truth: 'Tear him for his bad verses' (3.3.30); 'It is no matter, his name's Cinna' (3.3.33). Shakespeare's only amelioration here is to leave Cinna's fate vague, as nowhere does it explicitly say in the text or in the First Folio stage directions that Cinna is killed; nevertheless, this bit of stage business may have simply been left out of the Folio. As far as the image of the common people is concerned, this scene epitomizes the nadir of their behaviour, the people committing blind, undeserved mayhem on the innocent.

In his performance history of the play, John Ripley points out that until Orson Welles's 1937 fascist interpretation, no known American production enacted the Cinna the Poet episode.[44] As the actor who played Cinna in the Welles staging explained, his character 'symbolised what was happening in the world, if your name was Greenburg – and even if you weren't Jewish'.[45] Indeed, the recent Doran production presents this

---

[41] Bullough, *Sources*, p. 103.

[42] Bullough, *Sources*, pp. 104–5.   [43] Shapiro, *Year*, p. 127.

[44] John Ripley, *Julius Caesar on Stage in England and America, 1599–1973* (Cambridge, 1980), p. 224.

[45] Quoted in Richard France, 'Contemporary Settings Illustrate the Play's Universality', in *Readings on Julius Caesar*, ed. Don Nardo (San Diego, CA, 1999), pp. 55–9; p. 59.

scene as a South African 'necklacing'.[46] However it translates into contemporary contexts, this scene is about the violence of irrational mobs. In their desire to utilize the play as an exponent of republicanism, Americans saw the need to exclude this scene as it illuminates the dangerous aspects of democracy. The very fact that the drama had to be reshaped in this way militates against a view of *Julius Caesar* as unabashedly libertarian.

Certainly, Shakespeare systematically ameliorates the character of Brutus, omitting or changing a number of historical details that negatively characterize him, an action that suggests sympathy with Brutus's republicanism. For example, in the scene where Cassius and Brutus quarrel, Brutus asserts his moral superiority on the basis of financial scrupulousness:

> . . . I can raise no money by vile means.
> By heaven, I had rather coin my heart
> And drop my blood for drachmas than to wring
> From the hard hands of peasants their vile trash
> By any indirection. (4.2.126–30)

Of course, this statement is ironic, because he is perfectly willing to accept this ill-gotten lucre from Cassius's hands. However, the historical Brutus was not averse to usury, lending money to the people of Salamis at the extortionate interest rate of 48 per cent.[47]

Yet, this positive view of Brutus's character is counterbalanced by Shakespeare's negative view of the populace, significantly worse than Plutarch's, who was a self-confessed imperialist.[48] There is no question but that they are portrayed as being extremely susceptible to rhetoric. However, this susceptibility is also found in the other social classes – almost everyone in this play is swayed by rhetorical power. Brutus is persuaded by Cassius to join the conspiracy, as is Casca, but then Brutus's rhetorical power overshadows Cassius's in the strategizing of the conspirators. Moreover, as Anne Barton points out, 'In *Julius Caesar*, the art of persuasion has come to permeate life so completely that people find themselves using it not only to influence others but to deceive themselves. This is true, above all, of Brutus.'[49] We see Brutus

convincing *himself* by the power of his own oratory in the 'It must be by his death' soliloquy as well as in his forum speech. Caesar is first persuaded by Calpurnia to stay home on the day of the assassination, but is then counter-persuaded by Decius Brutus, who leads him to his death. Just as fatally, Antony convinces Brutus to allow him to deliver a funeral oration. Cassius persuades Titinius to help him commit suicide, as Brutus attempts with his own followers with more difficulty, eventually succeeding with Strato. As Velz comments on the pervasiveness of rhetoric in this play, 'The power of oratory to move people, the basest mettle and the most exalted alike, has been shown repeatedly.'[50] In this play, the power of rhetoric to move the auditor cuts across class boundaries.

Moreover, it can perhaps be argued that Shakespeare's portrayal of the people is so negative as to constitute a parody. After all, in the first scene they seem significantly more witty and intelligent than their supposed superiors, only to degenerate into a murderous mob by the Cinna the Poet scene. Shakespeare's compression of the time frame for dramatic purposes further highlights the volatility of the crowd, so much so that it can perhaps be said to cross a line into the absurd. No real crowd could truly swing from one extreme to the next so quickly.

Part of the problem rests with the fact that Shakespeare's definition of republicanism may have substantially differed from our contemporary view, hence Charles Mills Gayley, an early Shakespearian scholar, uses the term

---

[46] Doran, 'Julius Caesar'.

[47] Steve Sohmer, *Shakespeare's Mystery Play: The Opening of the Globe Theatre 1599* (Manchester, 1999), p. 157.

[48] Wills, *Rome*, p. 19.

[49] Anne Barton, 'The Art and Power of Oratory in *Julius Caesar*', in *Readings*, ed. Nardo, p. 127.

[50] John W. Velz, '"Orator" and "Imperator" in *Julius Caesar*: Style and the Process of Roman History', *Shakespeare Studies*, 15 (1982), 55–75; p. 64.

'aristodemocracy'.[51] Daniel Gil explicates this point of view: 'Caesar's absolutist program is counterbalanced by the civic republicanisms of Brutus and the conspirators, for whom the state exists to offer an aristocratic elite opportunities for the exercise of virtue and thus the pursuit of ethical perfection. From the perspective of the conspirators, the state is constituted by patricians seeking to maximize their honor.'[52] In this view, the republicanism of *Julius Caesar* is so different from twenty-first-century political republicanism as to constitute something else entirely. Moreover,

Shakespeare's dance with censorship further complicates any attempt to come to grips with his political point of view.

As such, I have come to recognize that my commitment to listening finally prevented me from drawing any definitive conclusions.

---

[51] Charles Mills Gayley, *Shakespeare and the Founders of Liberty in America* (New York, 1917).

[52] Daniel Juan Gil, '"Bare Life": Political Order and the Specter of Antisocial Being in Shakespeare's Julius Caesar', *Common Knowledge*, 13 (2007), 67–79; p. 72.

PLUTARCH'S PORCIA AND SHAKESPEARE'S PORTIA: TWO OF A KIND?

GEORGE MANDEL

It is well known that the nocturnal conversation between Brutus and his wife, Portia, in Shakespeare's *Julius Caesar* is based on an episode in Plutarch's *Life of Marcus Brutus*,[1] and it is often claimed that Shakespeare followed his source very faithfully here. We read that the conversation was 'taken almost word for word from Plutarch; it is simply North done into verse',[2] or, in a slightly more cautious formulation, that 'In this exchange Shakespeare follows both the ideas and the words of a long passage in Plutarch quite closely'.[3] The role and character of Portia, in particular, are sometimes said to be virtually copies of what Shakespeare found in Plutarch's pages. We are told that '[Shakespeare's] Portia [is] Plutarch's and no more',[4] and that 'the remonstrance of Portia that she is shut out from her husband's counsels, and the proof of courage which she gives', are from Plutarch 'down to the smallest details'.[5] Some commentators point to differences between Porcia (as her name appears in North's text) and Portia while still seeing them as essentially similar. David Daniell, for instance, in the third Arden edition of the play, asserts that Shakespeare put into Portia's mouth language that is 'strikingly different' from Porcia's, and that Portia's speech beginning 'Within the bond of marriage' (*Caesar* 2.1.279ff.) 'is a development [rather than a copy] of that in Plutarch' – but writes nevertheless that 'This episode with Portia, *taken in detail from the prose of North's English* ... is given

I am very grateful to Professor Richard Proudfoot for much help and advice, and especially for his comments on early drafts of this chapter. I would also like to thank Professor Frank Stewart for encouraging me to put my thoughts about *Julius Caesar* down in writing.

[1] On the sources of the play see, e.g., Marvin Spevack, *Julius Caesar* (Cambridge, 2004), pp. 6–13, and the works discussed there, especially the one by Geoffrey Bullough (note 8 below). To these should be added the chapter on *Julius Caesar* by Alessandro Serpieri, 'Giulio Cesare: commento', in *Nel laboratorio di Shakespeare. Dalle fonti ai drammi*, ed. Alessandro Serpieri, Keir Elam, and Claudia Corti, vol. 4, 2nd edn (Parma, 1993), pp. 77–129; William Poole, 'Julius Caesar and Caesars Revenge Again', *Notes & Queries*, 49 (2002), 227–8; and George Mandel, 'Julius Caesar and Caesar's Revenge, yet again', *Notes & Queries*, 59 (2012), 534–6.

[2] Agnes Mure Mackenzie, *The Women in Shakespeare's Plays* (London, 1924) p. 180.

[3] William Shakespeare, *Julius Caesar*, ed. Norman Sanders (London, 2005), p. 144. Broadly similar opinions are expressed by M. W. MacCallum, *Shakespeare's Roman Plays and their Background* (London, 1935), p. 183; Frank Kermode, *The Riverside Shakespeare* (Boston, MA, 1974), p. 1101; David C. Green, *'Julius Caesar' and its Source* (Salzburg, 1979), p. 53; Arthur Humphreys, ed., *Julius Caesar* (Oxford, 1984), p. 13; Mariko Ichikawa, '"Enter Brutus in his orchard": Garden Scenes in Early Modern English Plays', *Shakespearean International Yearbook*, 9 (2009), 214–47; esp. p. 237; Vivian Thomas, *Julius Caesar* (Hemel Hempstead, 1992), pp. 93–5; Serpieri, *Nel laboratorio di Shakespeare*, vol. 4, p. 90.

[4] H. M. Ayres, 'Shakespeare's *Julius Caesar* in Light of Some Other Versions', *PMLA*, 25 (1910), 183–227; p. 188.

[5] Edward Dowden, *The Complete Works of William Shakespeare*, with a general introduction by [A. C.] Swinburne, vol. 8 (London, 1911), p. 88. Dowden is quoting approvingly the opinion of R. C. Trench. Others who see the two characters as essentially the same or very similar include: M. L. Clarke, *The Noblest Roman: Marcus Brutus and his Reputation* (London, 1981), p. 117; G. B. Harrison, *Shakespeare's Tragedies* (London, 1963), p. 74; Paul Stapfer, *Shakespeare and Classical Antiquity* (London, 1880), p. 370.

by Shakespeare new poetic form'.[6] Juliet Dusinberre goes somewhat further than most in distinguishing between the two characters, writing that 'Plutarch's Portia is apologetic in her plea for Brutus' confidence; Shakespeare's demands it as her inalienable right'.[7]

My contention is that to regard Portia as essentially Porcia plus poetry, or as Porcia apart from some minor differences, or as an elaboration or development of Porcia, or as someone who differs from Porcia only in being demanding and unapologetic, is to overlook some significant and far-reaching ways in which Shakespeare altered what he found in his source, and hence to underestimate greatly the differences between the two characters.

Portia from the beginning complains about Brutus's behaviour towards her. He has 'ungently ... stole[n]' from her bed, stared at her with 'ungentle looks', stamped his foot 'too impatiently' and dismissed her with 'an angry wafture' of his hand (2.1.236–7, 241, 243, 245). Porcia makes no such explicit complaints. On the contrary, she says, 'Nowe for thy selfe, I can finde no cause of faulte in thee touchinge our matche'.[8] And, whereas Portia insists that she ought to know Brutus's secret 'by the right and virtue of my place' (268), thus implying that he is failing in his duty to her by refusing to reveal it, Porcia makes no such claim. What she says is

I ... was maried unto thee, not to be thy beddefellowe and companion in bedde and at borde onelie, like a harlot: but to be partaker also with thee, of thy good and evill fortune. Nowe for thy selfe, I can finde no cause of faulte in thee touchinge our matche: but for my parte, howe may I showe my duetie towards thee, and howe muche I woulde doe for thy sake, if I can not constantlie beare a secret mischaunce or griefe with thee, which requireth secrecy and fidelity?[9]

The only duty Porcia refers to is hers to her husband. The only duty Portia mentions, or alludes to, is her husband's to her.[10]

When she sees that neither talking about 'the right and virtue of my place' nor kneeling before

Brutus changes his mind, Portia makes further accusations, this time concerning his behaviour towards her as a whole rather than just during his recent period of agitation. She says, 'Is it excepted I should know no secrets / That appertain to you?' (2.1.280–1), implying that Brutus *never* shares confidences with her, and she further implies that *as a rule* he regards her functions as being only to 'keep with you at meals, comfort your bed / And talk to you sometimes' (283–4). She does not actually say that that is how Brutus habitually behaves towards her, and the accusations sound as though they have been invented for the occasion. Whether or not that is what we are meant to think, the fact that she makes them at all distances her from her original to an even greater extent than do her earlier complaints.

Portia's accusations culminate in the statement that 'If it be no more, / Portia is Brutus' harlot, not his wife' (285–6). As was shown above, Plutarch, too, puts the word 'harlot' into the mouth of Brutus's consort, but there is a considerable difference between the contexts in which the word is used by the two authors, and between the intentions behind its use. Porcia is saying that if she is

---

6 David Daniell, ed., *Julius Caesar* (London, 2006), pp. 66, 215, 212. All quotations from the play will come from this edition. The italics are mine.

7 Juliet Dusinberre, *Shakespeare and the Nature of Women* (London, 1975), p. 113. Dusinberre's comment is accurate but, it seems to me, insufficiently far-reaching.

8 Geoffrey Bullough, *Narrative and Dramatic Sources of Shakespeare*, vol. 5 (London, 1966), p. 98. References in this chapter to Plutarch's version of events are to be understood as being to North's English translation.

9 Bullough, *Sources*, p. 98.

10 Yet some writers state or imply that Portia, in this scene from the play, recognizes duties or obligations to her husband. See Spevack, *Julius Caesar*, p. 11; Joseph Candido, '"Time ... come round": Plot Construction in *Julius Caesar*', in *Julius Caesar: New Critical Essays*, ed. Horst Zander (New York, 2005), pp. 127–38; p. 131; Martin Mueller, 'Plutarch's *Life of Brutus* and the Play of its Repetitions in Shakespearean Drama', *Renaissance Drama*, 22 (1991), 47–93; p. 60 (Mueller, listing supposed points of contrast between Portia and Lady Percy, writes that the latter 'says nothing about wifely duties'); Marc Saint-Marc Girardin, cited by Stapfer, *Shakespeare*, p. 377.

unwilling or unable to share Brutus's evil fortune as well as his good, she is no better than a harlot. Unlike Portia, Porcia is not blaming Brutus; if anything, she is conditionally blaming herself. Admittedly, her words imply that if Brutus does not share his secret with her, he will be preventing her from putting the matter to the test, and denying her the chance to prove to him that she is indeed better than a harlot. To that extent she is implicitly complaining about his behaviour, even though, explicitly, she denies finding any fault with him. Yet even if we are meant to believe that Porcia's words are intended to imply a complaint against her husband, it is not a complaint that Portia ever makes. Porcia regrets Brutus's secrecy for the reason just given; Portia is offended by it. Both are unhappy because Brutus's secrecy limits their role to that of a harlot, and they agree, by and large, on what that role consists of: eating, sleeping and sometimes talking with their husbands. (Porcia does not mention 'talking' but speaks of being Brutus's 'companion in bedde and at borde'.) The difference appears in the reasons why each one feels that this limitation harms her. For Porcia, it means not being able to help Brutus, share his troubles, and show him how much she would do for his sake if only she were allowed to. Portia's reasons for wanting to be told the secret are not stated as clearly but, whatever they are, they are not the same as Porcia's. Nowhere in the scene does Portia say that she wants to help Brutus in his troubles, share his evil fortune as well as his good, or show him how much she would do for his sake if she were allowed to. The nearest she comes to sounding genuinely concerned and sympathetic is when she says 'Dear my lord, / Make me acquainted with your cause of grief' (254–5). That is not a clear statement of a wish to help Brutus, and it falls far short of what Porcia says. Porcia's strong wish to help her husband in his distress is a central element in Plutarch's narrative. It is an element that Shakespeare did not take over.[11]

Another difference between the two presentations lies in the extent to which Brutus's wife feels doubts about her ability to keep a secret. Porcia inflicts the wound on her thigh to prove *to herself*

that she is capable of maintaining confidentiality. Naturally, she then uses the fact of having done so in her attempt to persuade Brutus, but her initial and main motive is to settle her own doubts. That does not seem to be the case with Portia. True, her words 'I have made strong proof of my constancy' (2.1.298) do not tell us whether the proof was directed only at her husband or also at herself. But nowhere else in the scene does she mention self-doubts or show the slightest sign of having had any. Someone reading the play without knowledge of Plutarch's version would probably assume that Portia gives herself the wound simply in order to convince Brutus. Moreover, if Portia had previously been unsure of her ability to keep the secret, she would at least understand, as does Porcia, why Brutus does not want to reveal it to her, and would not make accusations against him that, under the circumstances, would presumably seem unreasonable and exaggerated even in her own eyes.

When Portia is on her knees she enjoins her husband to

> unfold to me, your self, your half,
> Why you are heavy – and what men tonight
> Have had resort to you: for here have been
> Some six or seven who did hide their faces
> Even from darkness.   (2.1.273–7)

There are two distinct demands here, and the second of them – that Brutus tell Portia who his visitors were – is surely one that he will be particularly reluctant to accede to. Portia wants her husband to tell her not only *his* secret, but also the secrets of other people; and that only a few minutes after the audience has heard him hold forth on the subject of the 'several bastardy' that every drop of a Roman's blood is guilty of, 'If he do break the smallest particle / Of any promise that hath passed from him' (2.1.137, 138–9). She is asking Brutus to violate the trust of his companions and do something that may

---

[11] However, the opposite is often stated or implied. See, e.g., T. S. Dorsch, ed., *Julius Caesar* (London, 1965), pp. xliii, lix.

endanger their lives. True, Portia does not actually know that lives may be in danger, but she must sense that something is taking place that involves great peril and that there are weighty reasons for the obvious wish of the visitors to keep their identities hidden. This demand of hers is rarely, if ever, mentioned in discussions of Portia's character, yet it is something not found in Plutarch that Shakespeare put into her mouth, and it presumably gives us some indication of how he saw her. It is hard to believe he would have put it into the mouth of someone whom he meant us to regard as, for instance, a 'perfect wife',[12] nor is it consistent with assertions such as that 'all [Portia] wants at this point is to minister to her husband as she sees him in jeopardy'.[13]

Another feature of the scene that has gone largely unremarked is that Brutus, throughout his conversation with Portia, is aware that Caius Ligarius may arrive at any moment. This awareness could well be the chief determinant of his response to her sudden appearance. His overriding aim now will be to get her to leave before Ligarius appears. How could it be otherwise? And the rest of the scene is entirely consistent with such a notion. Brutus's first response, 'Portia, what mean you? Wherefore rise you now?' (2.1.233), sounds like an expression of alarm and annoyance, as would be natural if he were thinking about the expected arrival of Ligarius. He then tells Portia to go to bed while obviously having no intention of doing the same himself. He cannot, because he is expecting Ligarius. Portia's curiosity about his visitors will alarm Brutus all the more because of the imminent arrival of another potential object of that curiosity. And to add further to Brutus's anxiety, Portia goes down on her knees, in effect making herself immobile.[14] Brutus then tells Portia that she is his 'true and honourable wife, / As dear to me as are the ruddy drops / That visit my sad heart' (287–9). This could well be not, or not primarily, a sincere expression of love, but the utterance of a harassed husband seeking for words that will placate a wife who will not stop questioning and criticizing him even though she knows that he is already under strain. The same holds for his designation of Portia

as 'this noble wife' (302) a few lines later. Brutus is here bestowing on her the most laudatory adjective in his vocabulary, higher in the scale even than 'true' and 'honourable'. The tactic, if it is a tactic, fails – either because Portia is not sufficiently moved by it, or because she has no time to respond. A moment later, knocking is heard and Brutus promises to tell Portia what she wants to know.

When Brutus tells Portia that she is as dear to him 'as are the ruddy drops / That visit my sad heart', his choice of imagery is not the most fortunate. The blood that circulates in one's body is, like the air one breathes, usually taken for granted rather than acknowledged every day with love and gratitude. We become aware of it, and of our dependence on it, only when it surprises us by behaving in an unusual, most often an untoward, way. If we were talking about a real human being rather than a character in a play, we might be tempted to deduce that the simile is more appropriate than the speaker intends: without being aware of it, he is telling us that he speaks words of affection to his wife only when her unexpected behaviour suddenly makes him feel that it would be politic to do so. That Shakespeare intended us to think something like that about his Brutus would be too far-reaching an inference. However, the simile Shakespeare puts into Brutus's mouth does add to the weight of the probability that we do not have to take Brutus's declaration of love entirely at face value.

---

[12] Dowden, *Complete Works*, vol. 8, p. 92. It is fair to call it a demand and not just a request. Admittedly, Portia says 'I charm you' (2.1.270) and goes down on her knees, but before doing so she tells Brutus that she has a right to know, and a moment afterwards she says he is ungentle for making it necessary for her to kneel. Her words have the force of a demand.

[13] Mary Hamer, *William Shakespeare: Julius Caesar* (Plymouth, 1998), p. 49.

[14] Compare her behaviour with that of Constance in *King John*, at the end of her scene with Salisbury and Arthur. When Constance lowers herself to the ground she makes it plain that she is doing so in order to prevent Salisbury from leading her away.

It is often said that what persuades Brutus to change his mind in the play, and promise to tell Portia what she wants to know, is the demonstration of her constancy provided by the revelation of the wound in her thigh.[15] An alternative reading is at least as plausible, however: Brutus promises to tell Portia the secret because that is the only way he can get her to leave before the new arrival is ushered in. Her behaviour throughout the scene, especially her demand for information about his earlier visitors, has made him afraid that, if he does not promise, Portia will stand her ground, see Ligarius and, worse, be seen by him doing so. As it is, she leaves just before Ligarius enters.

This interpretation is well in keeping with Brutus's words at this point. He makes his promise immediately after saying 'Hark, hark, one knocks' (2.1.303). A causal connection is probably implied: he makes the promise *because* someone is knocking.

Considerations of this kind could explain why Shakespeare makes Brutus switch to 'thy' and 'thee' when the knocking is heard, after he and Portia have used 'you' and 'your' to one another throughout the preceding part of their conversation. Brutus is again trying to sound affectionate in the hope that that will make Portia more amenable to his urgings. They could explain, too, why Shakespeare makes Caius Ligarius visit Brutus whereas in Plutarch it is, more naturally, Brutus who goes to the home of the sick Ligarius. And they could explain why Shakespeare reverses the order of events. Plutarch's account gives the clear impression that Brutus talks to Ligarius well before, not after, his conversation with Portia. Apparently Shakespeare wanted the audience to see how alarmed Brutus is by the prospect of Portia and Ligarius catching sight of one another and, as a corollary, by her earlier demand to be given information about his other visitors. Portia's persistence makes her appear much less considerate of her husband than is the case with Porcia.

A different explanation for the alterations to the Ligarius episode has been proposed by Serpieri. He writes that Shakespeare made them in response to 'theatrical needs since, unlike in the narrative form – in which a series of episodes that are connected thematically can occur at various times and locations – thematic unity entails, in the theatre, unity of situation and therefore unity of time and of space'.[16] The two explanations are not mutually exclusive, but it should be noted that Shakespeare's changes go beyond the temporal and spatial rearrangements needed to achieve 'unity of time and of space'. That could have been done simply by having Ligarius arrive just after Portia has left Brutus, with or without an explicit promise that he, Brutus, will tell her everything. (There is no such promise in Plutarch.) Instead, his arrival interrupts a conversation between Brutus and Portia, thus establishing a link between two conversations that, in Plutarch, have no connection with one another. Moreover, the conversation Ligarius is interrupting is one in which we have been shown clearly Portia's wish to know who Brutus's visitors are. It is not surprising, under these circumstances, that Ligarius's arrival alarms Brutus ('Leave me with haste' (2.1.308)). These are substantive, not merely technical, alterations to Plutarch's version of events.

Plutarch tells us of Brutus's great concern that the conspiracy may be detected, and in particular that his own behaviour may arouse suspicion. Characteristically, Shakespeare more or less inverts this part of the story. Plutarch writes that Brutus's anxiety concerning possible discovery led him to have disturbed nights, and it was these that alerted Porcia to her husband's troubled state of mind. In the play there is no indication that Brutus is suffering from that particular anxiety until Portia's behaviour arouses it in him. Before she appears, he deliberates at length over whether killing Caesar is really justified, after which he mentions his sleeplessness but does not link it in any way to a fear of discovery. In Plutarch, that is, Brutus's wife is troubled by her husband's anxiety lest the plot be discovered; in the play, her behaviour is, to a significant degree, the cause of that anxiety, and

[15] E.g., Green, 'Julius Caesar', p. 53.
[16] Serpieri, *Nel laboratorio di Shakespeare*, vol. 4, p. 90.

a little later, in the scene with Lucius, she nearly causes it to be realized. This is another of Shakespeare's additions. In Plutarch's narrative, Porcia faints but does not come close to blurting out the secret.

Shakespeare's additions and alterations to Plutarch lead to a difficulty in the play that is not present in the source. In Shakespeare's version Portia, without at first mentioning the wound to her thigh, tries to persuade Brutus to share his secret with her. Only when it becomes clear that her arguments are not having the desired effect does she do what Porcia does without any preceding attempts at persuasion: allude to the difficulty women allegedly have in keeping secrets and tell Brutus about the wound. But if Portia, unlike her original, thinks it worthwhile first to make an attempt to persuade Brutus by referring to 'the right and virtue of my place', by talking about her 'once commended beauty' (2.1.270) and kneeling before him, and by protesting that he is treating her as a harlot, then she will surely make it *before* giving herself the wound, and will keep that drastic procedure for use only as a last resort. The text of the play does not give the impression that that is what happens. Portia seems to be showing Brutus a wound that she inflicted on herself before their conversation began, rather than cutting herself there and then on the stage, in Brutus's presence. In other words, she apparently inflicted the wound on herself *before* making her attempts to persuade Brutus. It seems that Shakespeare, having made the quite far-reaching changes he wanted to make to Plutarch's version, either did not realize the implausibility they give rise to at this point, or decided to ignore it in the hope that it would not be noticed in performance. In that case he presumably believed its presence was a price worth paying for the ability to show us the things he wanted to show about the interactions between Portia and Brutus. And if we assume that Shakespeare did mean Portia to wound herself on stage, in Brutus's presence – that is, *after* she has tried and failed to persuade him – that would remove the implausibility but would make the contrast between Portia and Porcia even greater. Plutarch

tells us that the latter 'woulde not ask her husbande what he ayled before she had made some proofe by her selfe'.[17] Portia, by contrast, does a great deal of asking, and more than merely asking, before the point at which, we are supposing for the moment, she wounds herself.

In Shakespeare as in Plutarch, the behaviour of Brutus's wife when Brutus has gone to the Senate house shows that she has overestimated her strength. However, in the play this is much more to her discredit than in Plutarch's version of the story. Because Portia, in her conversation with Brutus, displayed not the slightest self-doubt, insisted on her right to know, and demanded information about his visitors, her subsequent weakness is all the more remarkable, and her previous behaviour all the more blameworthy.

One more difference between Plutarch's version and Shakespeare's is relevant to this discussion. Shakespeare makes no use of the story of the painted table at Elea that Plutarch recounts in the *Life of Brutus*.[18] As told there, the story makes us aware how deeply Porcia loves her husband and how great is her distress at the prospect of being separated from him. The story's ending makes us realize, too, that Brutus admires his wife greatly. These things do not sit well with the way in which, I have been arguing, Shakespeare saw his Portia and her relationship with her husband, and it was therefore entirely natural for him to keep the episode out of his play.[19]

This view of the relationship between Portia and Brutus sits reasonably well with the two much discussed announcements of Portia's death later in the play. Brutus's unemotional, almost dismissive, reception of the news when Messala tells him that Portia is dead could simply reflect an actual lack of deep feeling for his wife. And in the earlier

---

[17] Bullough, *Sources*, p. 98.   [18] Bullough, *Sources*, p. 107.

[19] Paul Stapfer regretted 'the absence, in Shakespeare's tragedy, of the beautiful scene in which Brutus and Portia take leave of one another at Elea' (*Shakespeare*, pp. 370–1). But Stupfer had a highly idealized view of the character of Brutus's wife in the play, and thought – wrongly, in my opinion – that Shakespeare shared it.

announcement, which Shakespeare may have intended as a replacement for the later one, Brutus boasts of having shown few outward signs of distress ('No man bears sorrow better' (4.3.145)). Here, as there, the true explanation may be simple: he shows little sorrow because he *feels* little sorrow. But the words he speaks are intended to convey to his hearers that, appearances notwithstanding, the opposite is the case.

The freedom with which Shakespeare treated his source material has often been pointed out.[20] In the specific case of *Julius Caesar*, it is well known that Shakespeare more or less reversed some of the things he found in Plutarch: concerning Caesar's swimming ability, for instance, and Casca's knowledge of Greek. His portrayal of Brutus's wife should be added to the list. He presents her as almost the opposite of the character depicted in his main source. Shakespeare's Portia is not so much an elaboration or development of her Plutarchian original as a radical transformation of her.

---

[20] See e.g. J. Dover Wilson, ed., *Julius Caesar* (Cambridge, 1949), pp. xvi–xviii.

SHAKESPEARE'S UNHOLY MARTYRS: LESSONS IN POLITICS

DOMINIQUE GOY-BLANQUET

In children's books of the 1950s, a martyr was a young girl dressed in white facing a pack of hungry lions. Depending on God's whimsy that day, she was eaten up or she turned the lions into playful puppies. In either case, the circus audience were reduced to tears and instantly converted to her faith. The infamous penalty backlashed, bringing confusion to her oppressors. Her death-day, renamed *dies natalis*, celebrated her birth to eternal life. Martyrdom was the quickest and surest way to Paradise. It seems a long way from Saints Blandine or Ursula to today's self-proclaimed martyrs for their faith – after all, those Christian maids never did much harm to the lions. They have one thing in common, though: the need of an audience who will tell their story to the world. The connection between terrorism and martyrdom has been spelt out unambiguously in the past decades by groups such as the Al-Aqsa Martyrs, who are high on the US State Department's list of Foreign Terrorist Organizations. Despite their claim to be a non-religious group, they took their name from the Al-Aqsa Mosque ('The Farthest Place'), the site where the Prophet Muhammad ascended to heaven, and modelled their action on Shiite Hezbollah.[1] The Arabic name 'shahid' given to suicide bombers has the same meaning, and ambiguity, as the Greek μαρτυρ: a witness.

This hunger for publicity is getting grimmer and more patent with each new spectacular act. Like advertising, terrorism needs constant invention, which dictates new rules and new targets. Earlier generations of terrorists, like Michael Collins's Squad, worked for an end, and sometimes achieved

it. Destroying a railway, crash-landing on a battleship, removing a potential threat or a tyrant, are almost things of the past. The object of attack now matters far less than impact on the media. Aim and target are increasingly disconnected: the killing of Israeli athletes in Munich was not done to win the Olympic Games. The attack against the Twin Towers achieved nothing in practical terms, yet, over a decade later, it remains the unsurpassed reference for media efficiency.

The history of the primitive church proudly records the martyrs executed for their beliefs, even courting death by public gestures of defiance. The glorification of martyrdom, as John Donne would later point out, owed much to the Roman tradition of heroic suicide, which had its own store of edifying tales. In 'high Roman fashion', a slave deserved scorn for the dishonourable choice he had made of giving up his freedom to save his life. Yet if suicide for honour's sake was admired in aristocratic circles, popular opinion was not so favourably inclined. By threatening imperial unity, early Christians became enemies of the state. Pagan Romans were shocked by their recklessness, and suspected them of dementia – a distrust shared by modern historians who denounce their provocative 'extremism', their eagerness to get

---

[1] Recent surveys show that Hezbollah is still regarded as a legitimate resistance movement throughout most of the Arab and Muslim worlds, though their support of President Assad in Syria has partly turned opinion against them.

themselves martyred, which left no choice to otherwise benevolent masters.

Even before the third century, when the Church Fathers tried to restrain the martyrs' alacrity for fear it would deplete the ranks, the Roman emperors had begun to punish suicides by seizing their property.[2] When the empire converted to Christianity, both powers joined forces in condemning them as *felo de se*, felon to oneself, like any other homicide. A popular maxim, quoted twice in Justinian's *Digest*, exposes the motives that will govern the discourse on suicide for centuries: 'he who is capable of killing the one each of us loves best of all is as capable of killing anyone'.[3] Poor Job came to be hailed as a model of forbearance against former heroes like Cato. The once honoured virgins deserved reproof no less than Lucretia for causing their own death. Only Samson escapes St Augustine's strictures, because he destroyed the Philistine Temple in Gaza on a secret order from God: 'the spirit within him, which wrought miracles by him, did prompt him into this act'.[4] But Samson's last prayer in the Bible is a call for revenge, his last words, 'Let me die with the Philistines'. With God's permission, he broke the two pillars that held the temple roof, killing approximately three thousand: 'So the dead which he slew at his death were more than they which he slew in his life.' His motive in Judges sounds closer to private vengeance than Augustine allows: 'I pray thee only this once, O God, that I may be at once avenged of the Philistines for my two eyes.'[5]

From Samson onwards, martyrdom is an impossibly tangled mix of personal, political and religious warfare. Augustine admitted other exceptions to the commandment 'Thou shalt not kill' if it was done in the right spirit. The church made a decisive move from passive to active defence of the faith when it conferred the palm of martyrdom on Crusaders, whether they died fighting for the recovery of Christ's sepulchre in Holy Land or the *reconquista* of Catholic Spain. Soldiers who had killed an enemy in Charlemagne's missionary wars were prescribed long fasting and penance by the Carolingian penitentials. Two centuries later, the Pope would promise them a place in heaven for

the same act – a promise relayed by King Arthur's archbishop Dubricius in the *Historia Regum Britanniae* when he offers absolution to all British men who shall suffer death in the field: to die willingly for their country, 'that in itself is victory and a cleansing of the soul'.[6] There is some basis to the historian Fiori's claim that crusade and jihad are but two faces of a war for sovereignty of one's God over conquered territories.[7]

Looking for Christian martyrs in the Shakespeare canon, one finds only two sanctified by the Roman Catholic Church, both controversial, Joan of Arc and Thomas More, plus a tentative one – Henry VI did not quite make it to sainthood, despite the efforts of his Tudor heirs to have him canonized – and numerous pagans ready to sacrifice themselves for one cause or another. Joan has many features of the martyred maid in French hagiography, but not in Shakespeare's play, where her own supporters call her saint with tongue in cheek. She is caught trading her blood with fiends in exchange for an earthly victory, but fails to win their support. In a symmetrically opposite scene, Henry VI tries to break the pattern of retaliation by offering his life in atonement, a bargain that like hers remains unanswered. In Augustine's *City of God*, selfless oblation is the example of perfect charity, but Shakespeare's plays betray persistent scepticism about the healing virtues of innocent blood and of the gods, Roman or Celtic, who feed upon such sacrifices.

Vengeance and suicide made excellent returns at the Elizabethan box office, yet only a few

---

[2] Paul Veyne, 'Rome antique: le suicide n'est pas obscène', *L'Histoire*, 27 (1980), 38–40.

[3] Justinian, *Digest*, XX, 1.23.3, and XLVIII, 21.3.6. See Paul Veyne, 'Suicide, fisc, esclavage, capital et droit romain', *Latomus*, 40 (1981), 217–68; p. 239.

[4] Augustine, *The City of God*, trans. John Healey, ed. R. G. V. Tasker (London, 1967), I.20, p. 26.

[5] Judges 16: 30, 28 (KJV).

[6] Geoffrey of Monmouth, *The History of the Kings of Britain*, Book 9, trans. Lewis Thorpe (Harmondsworth, 1966), ch. 4, p. 207.

[7] Jean Fiori, *Guerre sainte, jihad, croisade: Violence et religion dans le christianisme et l'islam* (Paris, 2002).

dissenting voices dared dispute Augustine's all round condemnation of self-slaughter. Thomas More's *Utopia* allowed it in specific cases like terminal illness. So did Montaigne, tepidly, who concludes a list of Greek and Roman authors with a small measure of tolerance to suicide: 'Grieving-smart, and a worse death seeme to me the most excusable incitations'.[8] John Donne in *Biathanatos* is probably the first Christian to argue in a scholarly manner that suicide is not a sin, nor a breach of divine or natural law: its prohibition by law-makers has no other legitimate basis than the conservation of states. John Foxe, though he never uses the word 'suicide', obviously had no quarrel with this aspect of martyrdom. His *Actes and Monuments* aims to produce a multitude of 'faythfull witnesses' to a long history of resistance to popes and the doctrine of Rome by so-called heretics. Rather than the lives of bloody warriors, he will record those 'of mylde and constant Martyrs of Christ', who 'declare to the worlde what true Christian fortitude is, and what is the right way to conquere'. The martyrs of his own time deserve no less commendation than those of the primitive church, and bright gory images anticipating *Richard II*: 'They dyd water the truthe with their bloud, that was newly springing up ... They like famous husband-men of the world did sowe the fieldes of the church, that first lay unmanured and wast; these with fatnes of their bloud did cause it to battell and fructifie'.[9] Among the villains who caused their deaths, Thomas More occupies a prominent place as a persecutor of 'heretics'.

One of the most debated features of More's own claim to martyrdom was his 'silence'. His early biographers discuss it at length to refute all suggestions his martyrdom was unheroic. Compared to John Fisher, who had 'hastened to the scaffold',[10] that is, died unequivocally proclaiming his faith and the supremacy of the Pope, More never defied the king nor publicly denounced his policy. More's famous 'silence' was a firm refusal to indict himself. As for Joan of Arc, her trial records reveal a gift for tart rejoinder, allied with a keen desire to live.[11] What Elton says of More is also true of Joan: they fought for their life to the last, reasoning with the

judges and winning legal points until trapped by a low trick.[12] Both would have won their case in court had the verdict been an open one, but both were doomed before the trial began. The plays conspicuously avoid showing them in the courtroom, and never discuss religious issues. In *Henry VI*, Joan tries to save herself by pleading her belly as she does in Holinshed, but is straight away led offstage to be burnt, and deprived of her public martyrdom. The play *Sir Thomas More* makes minimal references to 'those articles' More cannot accept, and shows him going to the Tower 'with all submissive willingness' (4.4). In *Henry VIII* we are not even informed of his death, but then Shakespeare impartially spares us intimations that Cranmer and most protagonists must lengthen the list of victims before we reach the promised happy end, the future accession of Elizabeth. Indeed the entire play, with its alternative title, *All is True*, is a masterpiece of paralipsis.

The case of Thomas More, which raised still sensitive issues, must have dictated caution. Joan's did not need such self-restraint: Shakespeare was better informed about the French Maid than the Tudor chroniclers but no fairer, and probably no more interested in giving her a fair trial.[13] Whether More and Joan are considered victims or enemies of the commonwealth, it is clear in both history and drama that neither 'hastened to the scaffold', even though they were ready for it if

---

[8] Montaigne, *Essays*, trans. John Florio, ed. Ben R. Schneider, Renascence Editions (Eugene, OR, 1999). From *Essais*, ed. Pierre Villey and Verdun-Louis Saulnier, 1595, Book 2, ch. 3.

[9] John Foxe, *Actes and Monuments of Matters most Special and Memorable, happening in the Church* (London, 1576), pp. 4, 9–10.

[10] Thomas Stapleton, *The Life and Illustrious Martyrdom of Sir Thomas More*, trans. Philip E. Hallett, ed. E. E. Reynolds (Fordham, NY, 1966), p. 189.

[11] *Procès de condamnation de Jeanne d'Arc*, ed. Pierre Tisset and Yvonne Lanhers, 3 vols. (Paris, 1960–71).

[12] G. R. Elton, *Policy and Police: The Enforcement of the Reformation in the Age of Thomas Cromwell* (Cambridge, 1972), p. 410.

[13] See D. Goy-Blanquet, 'Shakespeare and Voltaire set Fire to History', in *Joan of Arc: A Saint for All Reasons* (Aldershot, 2003), pp. 1–38.

needs be. Their reluctance to die made them dubious or at best second-rate martyrs by contemporary standards. Nor did they turn their deaths into weapons against their oppressors. More's last letters were written to defend his conscience, not to impeach a tyrant, just as onstage he dies politely begging the king's pardon for his offence.[14] However dangerously subversive their later biographers would make them, neither truly qualifies for terrorism.

The Regent Bedford had written to all the princes of Europe explaining Joan of Arc was a witch who had met the treatment she deserved. Cromwell entrusted to Richard Morison the task of justifying More's death, alerted to the harm it might do in public opinion.[15] The Tudor age made substantial advances in the management of propaganda: both executioners and victims grew expert at handling the tools of media power available, paltry ones, of course, compared with today's. Old-style martyrs could never hope for worldwide broadcast and instant blogging, a serious handicap that left those would-be terrorists, again, relatively harmless. The historical Thomas More may have made a nuisance of himself with memorable puns and famous last words, his death did throw discredit on the regime, but with little immediate benefit to his supporters. Although his and Fisher's executions caused indignant reactions around Europe, they made few adepts, and failed to alter the course of religious change in England.

Shakespeare's suicides do not all aim to testify either, but rather show a large variety of means and motives. Some of his heroines – Juliet, Thisbe – simply cannot face life after their lover's death, and instantly kill themselves without further thought of the world outside. There are strong similarities in the plots of *Romeo and Juliet, Pyramus and Thisbe, Antony and Cleopatra* up to *Cymbeline*, where Imogen breaks the fatal pattern by refusing to give in to despair and rises from the dead to bring her husband's alleged murderer to justice. Some wear their suicide with a difference. Cleopatra may not wish to survive Antony, and will run to death as to a lover's arms, just slowly enough, for she too has an eye on the future, as when she imagines some

squeaking comedian will boy her greatness on the world's stage. Rather than dictated by rash passion, her suicide is modelled on Roman heroism and designed to inflict a defeat to her conqueror. Octavius, who had planned to return to Rome, leading the Egyptian queen captive, is deprived of his petty triumph. The asp is but a dumb witness:

> O, couldst thou speak,
> That I might hear thee call great Caesar ass
> Unpolicied!   (*Antony* 5.2.305–7)[16]

and hers is a small victory that will not affect history. The Republic is living its last moments after centuries of unparalleled glory.

The Rape of Lucrece focuses on the event at the origin of this remarkable Republic, and narrates a wholly different suicide. Before she dies, Lucrece wants revenge and she wants the truth told to posterity. Her death, like Cleopatra's, will be her greatest victory, but it will have a far more meaningful impact on the sequel of events. The sight of her dead body, carried back to Rome by Junius Brutus, will cause the crowds to rebel and depose the Tarquins. Shakespeare does not waste much thought on 'Tarquin's everlasting banishment' or on the end of monarchy. The political consequences of Lucrece's suicide are dispatched in the last two lines, after two long parallel inner debates at the centre of the poem: Tarquin's fight with his conscience, Lucrece's fight with her fear and shame. Yet Shakespeare does take time to recall the fall of Troy, pictured on a painted cloth that invites itself in Lucrece's meditation. No distress can compare with what she sees printed on the face of Hecuba. No worse fate imaginable than the fall of such a magnificent city. No worse

---

[14] 'Our conscience first must parley with our laws' (*Sir Thomas More*, 10.73).

[15] In *Apomaxis Calumniarum Convitiorumque*, Morison claims that all true scholars vindicate the king: More, a poor busy lawyer, could not compete with the learning of Gardiner, Foxe or Tunstall.

[16] *Antony and Cleopatra*, ed. John Wilders, Arden Shakespeare Third Series (London, 1995). All quotations are from the Arden Shakespeare Third Series.

injustice than the death of so many caused by the fault of one individual, made more bitter still by comparison of Helen with herself:

> Show me the strumpet that began this stir,
> That with my nails her beauty I may tear.
> Thy heat of lust, fond Paris, did incur
> This load of wrath that burning Troy doth bear.
>
> (1471–4)

It is this burning sense of injustice that helps her determine how to save her and her husband's honour. The Troy legend already figured significantly in *Titus Andronicus*, where the mutilated Lavinia also wants revenge and manages to tell her story even though deprived of a tongue. At the end of the play, the fatal engine 'That gives our Troy, our Rome, the civil wound' (5.3.86) marks the decline of the Roman Empire, bringing closure to a cycle of violence Shakespeare will deal with in later plays. When asked to explain his sorrow, Titus, like Aeneas, feels unable to 'tell the tale twice o'er / How Troy was burnt and he made miserable' (3.2.27–8), while his daughter Lavinia has for her namesake the bride of Aeneas, Lavinia. The end of Virgil's *Aeneid* offered some consolation for the fall of Troy by sending their descent to found Rome and repeople Europe. In Geoffrey of Monmouth's *Historia*, the surviving Trojans who land in Britain build a capital named Troynovant, ancestor of London.

Where Shakespeare's abrupt ending to *The Rape of Lucrece* excludes any other cause than her suicide to the end of monarchy, Livy shows a more intricate pattern in which the sight of Lucretia's dead body simply brings to culmination a long set of grievances against the despotism and past crimes of the Tarquins. The main features of her sad tale in later versions all draw on Livy:[17] Sextus Tarquin's violent desire for Lucretia; his threat that she will be found dead in a servant's embrace, and made to pass for an adulteress if she resists; the promise she demands of her relatives that they will punish her ravisher; her assertion that only her body was soiled, her heart is pure, as her suicide will prove; the public exposure of her corpse that excites universal horror and eventually causes the

fall of the Tarquins. In Ovid's *Fasti*, Tarquin's blackmail is told in the first person: '"I, the adulterer, will bear false witness to thy adultery [*Falsus adulterii testis aduler ero*]. I'll kill a slave, and rumour will have it that thou wert caught with him"'. And so, 'Overcome by fear of infamy, the dame gave way'.[18] The tale is repeated in Chaucer's *Legend of Good Women* and in Painter's *Palace of Pleasure* but, even though in these four accounts all Lucrece's relatives absolve her of any guilt, she will not forgive herself and chooses to die. There is no sign of the long inner soliloquy that will build up to her resolution in Shakespeare's poem, where Tarquin's threat to defame her if she resists forces her to survive her shame. Even though she did not submit from a wish to live at all costs, her sense of guilt is inspired by the scorn attached to those slaves who chose to live at the price of their honour. Her long deliberation shows her how to clear herself from such blame, her delayed self-slaughter testifies to the truth of her story, making her a credible 'witness' in the eyes of her avengers.

Chaucer writes that the great Augustine 'hath gret compassyoun / Of this Lucresse, that starf in Rome toun'.[19] This is slightly overstating the case: however compassionate, the saint condemns her to the pagans' Hades; on the authority of Virgil, she is among those

> That (guiltless) spoiled themselves through black despite;
> And threw their souls to hell, through hate of light.[20]

Augustine declares her innocent of the rape, and therefore undeserving her death, so it is she who committed the murder of an innocent, unless she experienced pleasure in the intercourse. She must be guilty either of adultery or of murder. So he appeals to the laws and judges of Rome: 'why then

---

[17] Livy, 'The Story of Lucretia', in *The History of Rome*, Book 1, trans. Rev. Canon Roberts (New York, 1912), ch. 57.

[18] Ovid, *Fasti*, ed. J. G. Frazer (London, 1929), II.808–10.

[19] Geoffrey Chaucer, *The Legende of Good Women*, ed. Hiram Corson (London, 1864), lines 1688–9.

[20] *Aeneid*, VI.434–6, quoted in Augustine, *City of God*, I.18, p. 23.

do you so extol the murder of so chaste and guiltless a woman?' Christian women who have been forced 'have the glory of their chastity still within them, it being the testimony of their conscience'.[21] In the next chapter, Augustine develops his argument, linking the prohibition of self-slaughter with that of false testimony: 'Thou shalt not bear false witness against thy neighbour', the Scripture says, but he will be equally guilty 'if he bear false witness against himself: because he that loves his neighbour, begins his love from himself: seeing it is written "Thou shalt love thy neighbour as thyself"'. The commandment 'Thou shalt not kill' 'excludes all exception both of others, and of him to whom the command is given . . . For he that kills himself, kills no other but a man'.[22]

In all these tales, the question of testimony is crucial. What rumour will be spread? How will the story be told to present and future generations? In *Julius Caesar*, this concern is part of a far more complex process, and it is solved at the end by the winner of the war, who now has the power to tell the story his own way, discrediting the conspiracy while appearing magnanimous with his tribute to Brutus:

> This was the noblest Roman of them all.
> All the conspirators save only he
> Did that they did in envy of great Caesar.
>
> (5.5.67–9)

This judgement so perfectly matches Plutarch's that one might believe Antony himself had dictated his facts to the historiographer: 'his very enemies which wish him most hurt, because of his conspiracy against Julius Caesar, if there were any noble attempt done in all this conspiracy, they refer it wholly unto Brutus; and all the cruel and violent acts unto Cassius, who was Brutus' familiar friend, but not so well given and conditioned as he'.[23]

One of More's Latin epigrams, in a sequence discussing monarchy, tyranny and republicanism, is '*sola mors tyrannicida est*', death alone is the remedy for tyranny.[24] But whose death: the tyrant's or the victim's? In Shakespeare's sad stories of the death of kings, no one claims that killing the king is morally acceptable. Even for theorists of

tyrannicide, it was considered a last resort, at best a necessary evil. On stage, neither Richard III, nor King John, nor Henry IV argues long with his conscience before getting rid of a royal rival. Macbeth does, but without shaping it into a political theory. The stuff of terrorism must be sought elsewhere, outside the frame of religious monarchy, among unchristian martyrs, the freedom fighters of *Julius Caesar*. The play was composed shortly after one successful regicide in France, the murder of Henri III by a fanatical monk, and several failed attempts against his successor, the Huguenot Henri IV, generally imputed to the Jesuit influence.[25] Despite Navarre's conversion and due anointment, the attacks continued, with a peak of three in 1599, and his assassination in 1610.

The conspirators of *Julius Caesar* all show a proper martyr's eagerness to die for liberty. Cassius's wily argumentation soon turns their vows into a preference for Caesar's death, when he entreats Brutus to spare his valuable self and kill their oppressor instead. Dante had consigned Brutus to the last circle of hell for his unforgivable treachery. But Shakespeare drew on Plutarch, who was much more favourable to Brutus than was Suetonius, who was the source of most contemporary Caesar plays.[26] Interpreters of Brutus since

---

[21] Augustine, *City of God*, I.18, p. 22–4.

[22] Augustine, *City of God*, I.19, p. 25.

[23] 'Life of Brutus I', in *Shakespeare's Plutarch*, trans. Thomas North, ed. Walter W. Skeat (London, 1875), p. 106.

[24] *Latin Poems*, III.2 (written *c.* 1515 and published in 1518), in *The Complete Works of St Thomas More*, ed. Clarence H. Miller et al. (New Haven, CT, 1984), pp. 144–5.

[25] Henri III was killed on 2 August 1589 by Jacques Clément. Henri IV abjured his Protestant faith on 25 July 1593 and was crowned on 27 February 1594. The Jesuits whose preachings and plottings were held responsible for the attempt of 27 December 1594 were expelled by Parliament. See Voltaire's *Histoire du Parlement de Paris*, in *Œuvres de Monsieur de Voltaire* (1775), vol. 20, p. 169.

[26] Plutarch in 'Life of Brutus' unfavourably compares 'that Junius Brutus', a man so subject to his choler that he had his own sons executed, to 'this Marcus Brutus' who was 'rightly made and framed unto virtue' (*Shakespeare's Plutarch*, pp. 105–6).

then have wavered between alternative readings of his character, virtuous or vain, self-centred, would-be tyrant, hopeless intellectual, naive idealist manipulated by a crafty Cassius, or ethical light of the play. When Cassius complains that like a Colossus, Caesar fills the world, leaving no room for any one else, he echoes the feelings of the First Tribune whose republicanism aims at general levelling, bringing the Colossus down to his petty height. But Brutus means to substitute for this inhuman cosmic order one guided by free men's will, a social ethics based on contract: Shakespeare shows that such an ideal may have appeared within reach, Richard Marienstras observes, and yet straightaway been made impossible by Rome's refusal to subscribe to this contract. In the Forum, the *pro et contra* debate on political assassination denies any legitimacy to Brutus's stillborn righteous order. The play tells the story of his failure, but the fact that ethics was defeated by politics does not erase the value of his attempt.[27]

Coming after the two Henriads, the Roman plays pursue their investigation of power and resistance by other means, in a stage universe where thoughts are freed from the earlier shackles of Christian medieval monarchy, making its political lessons invaluable to various ages and cultures. Brutus's stance against tyranny early awakened sympathetic echoes in America, and enjoyed more performances there than in Britain.[28] Philadelphia's Southwark Theatre saw the first recorded production in 1770, advertised as presenting 'the noble struggles for Liberty by that renowned patriot Marcus Brutus'.[29] Given the proper context, the topicality of the play need hardly be stressed. *Julius Caesar* has often been performed against a background of political assassination, to mourn the death of a charismatic leader, or wishfully execute hated despots. When arrested after his failed attempt against Hitler, Colonel Claus von Stauffenberg had an open copy of the play on his desk, with Brutus's relevant speeches underlined. He had performed it at school with his elder brothers, and clearly cast himself as the liberating hero, but large sections of the German public

did not share his reading of the play.[30] They were fascinated by the figure of the sublime ruler, as were theatre directors. In Jürgen Fehling's 1941 production, Caesar's death was a universal catastrophe, delaying the advent of a new era.[31] In the 'Robben Island Bible', a volume of Shakespeare's plays shared by the prisoners, Nelson Mandela had chosen Caesar's lines, 'Cowards die many times before their deaths; / The valiant never taste of death but once' (2.2.32–3).[32] Death or liberty, the tyrannicides' leitmotiv in the play, takes on a new poignant tone when performed in a high-security prison near Rome in the recent Taviani brothers' *Cesare deve morire*. As the long-term prisoner who plays Cassius confides to the camera at the end of the film, 'now that I have come to know art, this cell has turned into a jail'.

Rather than leaps from passive to active modes of testimony, the name 'martyr' bridges the gap from ancient to modern technology. Terrorism is traditionally defined by the disproportionality between armed forces, which drives powerless individuals to desperate means against mighty oppressors. The world could measure exactly how powerless, when a handful of individuals armed with plastic knives outdid Samson by bringing down the twin pillars of its proudest city on live television. 'Why do they hate us so?' was one of

---

27 Richard Marienstras, 'L'Arbitrage de la cité', in *Shakespeare et le désordre du monde*, ed. D. Goy-Blanquet (Paris, 2012), ch. 17.

28 Charles H. Shattuck, *Shakespeare on the American Stage: From Booth and Barrett to Sothern and Marlowe* (Washington DC, 1987).

29 Horst Zander, 'Julius Caesar and the Critical Legacy', *Julius Caesar: New Critical Essays* (New York, 2005), pp. 3–55; p. 17. Philadelphia alone saw fifteen revivals of the play in twenty years.

30 Michael Baigent and Richard Leigh, *Secret Germany: Stauffenberg and the Mystical Crusade against Hitler* (London, 1994), p. 5.

31 Wilhelm Hortmann, *Shakespeare on the German Stage* (Cambridge, 1998), pp. 143–4.

32 The volume where Mandela signed the passage with the date 'December 16, 1977' was part of the exhibition 'Shakespeare: Staging the World', British Museum, July–November 2012.

many questions raised after the 9/11 attacks – a soul-searching one that came close to an admission of guilt in intellectual quarters, and which made it vital to determine who was the guilty agent, who the initial aggressor. The question implicit behind the searching – in which cases is terrorism justified? – usually admits varying degrees of sympathy for the people driven to violence, whether in tsarist Russia, Ireland, Corsica, Chechnia or Palestine. The development from testimony to publicity makes it ever more crucial to occupy the position of victim in the media. Communications – originally a term used in warfare for transport of ammunition and troops – are more concerned now with public relations.[33] Communications consultants advise politicians on their choice of words, not of weapons. Taking a leaf from the Roman emperors, President Bush requalified suicide bombings into homicide bombings, to focus on the martyrs' victims. Inversely, targeted killing suggests a care to harm none but the intended quarry. Euphemisms like freedom fighter, martyrdom operations, jihad, or crusade all emphasize some virtuous quality in the attempt.

As Donne shrewdly perceived, the laws against suicide are made for the preservation of states. An extremist, as declared enemy of the state, provides governments with the needed excuse for strong reprisals. The more spectacular his success, the more self-defeating, since opinion will accept or even demand extreme preventive measures against further risks. The 7/7 attacks on London's public transport raised more public anger and larger media coverage than the ensuing restrictions on liberties. The drafting of a new law in France to reinforce anti-terrorist legislation after the attack on the Jewish Museum in Brussels raised similar anxieties: the draft included preventive measures against potential terrorists, forbidding them to travel to Syria where they might be trained as jihadists, 'but how does one prove even before they depart that these persons will constitute a threat when they return?' The serpent's egg dilemma. The shootings of the *Charlie Hebdo* cartoonists and at the Bardo Museum in Tunis raised the question again with increased urgency: a parliamentary bill relating to the intelligence services threatens to give excessive power of control to the prime minister at the expense of judges, and to endanger the freedom of the press; the *New York Times* pointed out: 'Parliament has a duty to protect citizens' democratic rights from unduly expansive and intrusive government surveillance'.[34] Yet, since the Paris attacks of November 2015, an overwhelming majority in Parliament have consistently voted to extend the 'state of-emergency' regulations.

Media terrorism has to keep the ball endlessly rolling to occupy media space. The killing irony is that the position of victim can be held only as long as it takes to shoot back. History betrays its limits when it comes to the original responsibility of violence. Even if historians could agree on the identity of the first terrorist, they would be no nearer a resolution of terrorist dialectics: whoever threw the first stone initiated a tie-up in which both parties must endlessly compete for the place and name of victim. Onstage, Titus Andronicus hits first with a human sacrifice in repayment for the death of his sons on the battlefield, but the retaliations are so atrocious that the Andronici are moved up to the victim's place. Incidentally, it was Lucius who first suggested they kill Tamora's eldest son, 'hew his limbs and on a pile / *Ad manes fratrum* sacrifice his flesh', causing her to denounce this 'irreligous piety' (1.1.101–2, 133), and it is Lucius who collects the prize, an emperor's crown, at the end once the cycle of violence is exhausted. Terrorism entertains a perpetual movement of confusion, constant shifts in status between victims and aggressors locked in complicity like a dancing couple. The visionary Henry VI has an intuition of this lethal polarity in his image of war as the fight of sea and wind, 'Both tugging to be victors, breast to breast, / Yet neither conqueror nor conquered' (*3 Henry VI*, 2.5.11–12). To Shakespeare's learned readers, the rape of Lucrece re-enacts the rape of

---

[33] See Carl von Clausewitz, 'Lines of Communication', in *On War*, Book 5, trans. J. J. Graham (London, 1873), ch. 16, p. 274: 'they form the connection between the army and its base, and are to be considered as so many great vital arteries'.

[34] 'The French Surveillance State', Editorial Board, *New York Times*, 31 March 2015.

Priam's sister, Hesione, an 'old aunt' repeatedly evoked in *Troilus and Cressida*, which Troilus considers the original cause of the Trojan War, before Helen was ravished in retaliation (2.2.72–81). If one went still further back, Hercules had abducted Hesione in revenge against her father Laomedon's perjury.[35] 'What frankness with ourselves would be needed to reach the original cause, the futile first cause', once those forces of body and soul are in motion, the philosopher Alain writes: 'How shameful it would be to return to our former quiet after so many promises and pledges to ourselves, without first having shed some of that boiling blood. So much blood and all for nothing?'[36]

Since terrorism is commonly ascribed to dangerous minority groups, it is worth recalling that almost as soon as it started it became an affair of leaders against individuals, not the other way round. In 1584, after the failure of the Throckmorton plot, a Bond of Association to preserve the security of the queen's person had united the whole country under an oath 'to the uttermost of their power, at all times, to withstand, pursue and suppress all manner of persons' that might by any means threaten her safety, confirmed by an Act of Parliament in 1585.[37] In answer to Cardinal Allen's denunciations of the tortures inflicted upon Catholic martyrs by the English government, Cecil and Walsingham's propaganda made Elizabeth a fragile victim exposed to a swarm of dangerous assassins.[38] Her loyal subjects were allowed to execute justice themselves on any suspect, by what amounted to a suspension of the law. The word 'terrorist' itself first occurs in France, applied to the Jacobin faction.[39] They put Terreur on the order of the day against the enemies of the Nation, the foreign coalition threatening their borders, then moved on speedily to execute all 'enemies of the people', anyone considered a threat to the regime, and set up special courts to do the thing properly. Most of the leaders, Robespierre, Saint-Just, and their executioners Fouquier-Tinville, Carrier, Fouché, who were all lawyers, erected terrorism into a mode of government. Setting a momentous precedent, the state was 'legally' fighting dangerous individuals, which included former lawyer friends such as Desmoulins or

Danton, and the more moderate Girondin party. The Girondins, who vainly tried to save the king and resist the institution of a revolutionary tribunal, were mourned as martyrs by European admirers of the young Revolution, for instance, the Lake poets. 'Liberté, que de crimes on commet en ton nom', 'Freedom, how many crimes are committed in thy name', were the last words of their muse Manon Roland as she climbed to the guillotine.[40]

Saint-Just repeatedly argued before the National Assembly that King Louis XVI could and must be tried: 'Hasten to judge the king for there is no citizen who does not have over him the same right that Brutus had over Caesar.' All kings are but rebels and usurpers of authority, made powerful only by slavish subjects: 'Cromwell was no more a usurper than Charles I; for when a people are cowardly enough to be ruled by tyrants, domination is the right of any new comer, neither more sacred or legitimate on one head than the other.'[41] Saint-Just cast himself in the position of heroic conspirator, not the repressive state he did in fact speak for. Only a few months earlier, because still under age, he had been denied access to the Assembly and

---

[35] The story travelled from Apollodorus to Caxton via Ovid's *Metamorphoses* and Lydgate's *Troy Book*.

[36] Alain [Émile-Auguste Chartier], *Mars; or, the Truth about War*, trans. Doris Mudie and Elizabeth Hill (New York, 1930), p. 72; translated from *Mars ou la guerre jugée* (1921).

[37] TNA, State Papers 12/174/1. See Alison Plowden, *Danger to Elizabeth: the Catholics under Elizabeth I* (New York, 1973), p. 204.

[38] William Allen, *A briefe Historie of the Glorious Martyrdom of xii reverend priests*, 1582, ed. Rev. J. H. Pollen (London, 1908).

[39] The Girondins who originally belonged to the club resigned in September 1792, and the Jacobins then took the title of Société des Amis de la Liberté et de l'Egalité.

[40] An avid reader of Plutarch, she was accused of plotting with England, and executed on 8 November 1793. Her husband Jean-Marie Roland who had escaped pursuits after the proscription of Girondins on 31 May 1793, killed himself on 15 November when told of her death. Several Girondins committed suicide.

[41] 'On ne peut régner innocemment', speech to the Convention Nationale, 13 November 1792, in *Œuvres complètes de Saint-Just*, ed. Charles Vellay, vol. 1 (Paris, 1908), pp. 366–70.

vented his frustration with this Shakespearian apostrophe: 'O God, must Brutus languish forgotten, far from Rome! My resolution is made, however. If Brutus does not kill the others he will kill himself.'[42] Shakespeare's *Julius Caesar* had several performances in various French towns immediately after the fall of the Bastille; in Voltaire's adapted translation, *La Mort de César*, whose conclusion was rewritten to suit the contemporary mood, so that, instead of having the last word, Antony is arrested by the Republicans, and Cassius pays homage to a 'statue of Liberty surrounded by a ring of people':

> Républicains, voilà votre divinité;
> C'est le dieu de Brutus, l'auguste Liberté.[43]

Brutus further hits the nail by addressing a prayer to the beloved goddess.[44]

The antique setting of *Julius Caesar* provided an escape from Elizabethan politics and its ruling moral precepts into a world of ambivalence. Shakespeare never says if Brutus was right or wrong, while freely exploring the depths of unholy martyrdom. There is evidence enough of Caesar's ambition, but any proof of his potential tyranny is killed in the egg, the 'serpent's egg'. The signs given by the gods are unreadable, open to opposite interpretations. Only after the deed will the weight of public opinion, carefully manipulated, decide the proper name to give it. Brutus puts it to the mob that their act was a sacrifice, that he himself killed his friend for the good of his country. By labelling the conspirators 'butchers', Antony works up the crowd to a righteous anger, in fact a destructive rage, and himself to the triumvirate. With Octavius he 'pricks' the 'traitors' designed for target killing, wins the war, and the power to impose his version of the murder to be recorded for posterity. Brutus's handicap, like other idealistic terrorists', is that he has no ulterior aim, ambition, or programme: the deed is its own end, since he will not take Caesar's place the crowd spontaneously offers him, with tragic misunderstanding of his motives.

Shakespeare's reading of the conspiracy is impressively lucid, and way ahead of contemporary thought on assassination. Conflicting philosophies, Roman *virtus*, and the age-old prejudice against *felo de se* all combine to expose the coils of heroic martyrdom. *Julius Caesar* captures the exact moment when the oppressed victim feels justified by despair to take up arms against a sea of troubles and by opposing, to end them. Brutus adheres to Pythagoras, while Cassius is a staunch Epicurean. The Pythagoreans condemned suicide as a violent gesture that destroyed the harmony of the body and set the soul wandering in search of appeasement. Epicurus argued that man must not fear death but, like Montaigne, admitted only a few cases in which self-slaughter could be thought legitimate. Yet in the play, Cato's suicide, a gesture of protest against Caesar's rise to despotic power, is the conspirators' model. Cato's son, his daughter Portia, Cassius, Titinius, even the Pythagorean Brutus all take the honourable Roman exit when defeated. So will Antony, in a later play, making room for the empire Brutus had sought to prevent. All these deaths, obviously not decisions of the playwright, are given special prominence in the final scenes.

It is a known fact that the end of the Republic was marked by an unprecedented wave of self-slaughter, which the new authorities encouraged by allowing the suicides' relatives to inherit their property. To Montaigne, who owned himself

---

[42] Letter to Villain-Daubigny, 20 July 1792, in *Œuvres complètes*, vol. 1, p. 349.

[43] Voltaire, *La Mort de César*, III. viii, avec les changements faits par le citoyen Gohier, Ministre de la Justice, à Commune affranchie, Lyon, An II de la République.

[44] See Laurence Marie, 'Art oratoire et Révolution française: jouer Jules César sur les scènes française, anglaise et allemande', Centre de Recherche sur l'Histoire du Théâtre, 2005, www.paris-sorbonne.fr/IMG/pdf/CRHT_Laurence_Marie_Art_oratoire_et_Revolution_francaise__jouer_Jules_Cesar_sur_les_scenes_francaise_anglaise_et_allemande-2.pdf, accessed 11 March 2016; and Marion Monaco, *Shakespeare on the French Stage in the Eighteenth Century* (Paris, 1976), pp. 158–9. Voltaire's denouement was amended by a lawyer, Louis-Jérôme Gohier, Minister of Justice in the Convention from March 1793 to April 1794, who oversaw the arrest of the Girondins.

'besotted' with 'the said ancient, free, just and florishing *Rome* (for I neither love the birth nor like the old age of the same)', their demise amounted to betrayal, for '*Brutus* and *Cassius*, by reason of the down-fall and rashnesse, wherewith before due time and occasion they killed themselves; did utterly lose the reliques of the Roman libertie, whereof they were protectors'.[45] What is not in Plutarch, nor in any other available source, is the subtle rhetoric developed on stage by the conspirators. Their slogan, 'Death or liberty', faithfully records the aristocratic contempt for the slave's condition. The example of Perseus who was offered the choice of a rope or a sword to avoid the humiliation of defeat is their cue: 'So every bondsman in his own hand bears / The power to cancel his captivity' (1.3.100–1). Brutus repeats it to the crowd: 'Had you rather Caesar were living, and die all slaves, than that Caesar were dead, to live all free men?' (3.2.22–4). The crowd can't argue with this reasonable proposition. That Brutus truly is an honourable man makes his intellectual pilgrim's progress all the more chilling.

The conspirators all swear they would rather die than bear Caesar's rule, which is equated with slavery. But on second thoughts, Caesar's death would be a surer way to freedom. The shift is smoothly operated with the rumour that Caesar will be crowned:

> I know where I will wear this dagger then:
> Cassius from bondage will deliver Cassius.
> Therein, ye gods, you make the weak most strong;
> Therein, ye gods, you tyrants do defeat. (1.3.88–91)

It is but a step to the logical conclusion: 'And why should Caesar be a tyrant then?' Tyrants are created by cowards who fear for their lives. Now Cassius reveals he has already moved some noble Romans to undergo 'an enterprise / Of honourable dangerous consequence' (122–3). All that remains to be done is to convince Brutus that Caesar can be better spared than himself. The play consistently dramatizes the closeness between murder and suicide. After hovering in this restricted space, the daggers plunged in Caesar's breast find their ways to the murderers', who stress the proximity of the

deeds with a final sense of recognition: 'Caesar, thou art revenged / Even with the sword that killed thee'. The old maxim, 'he who is able to kill the one each of us loves best' reverberates in Brutus's admission to the crowd, 'as I slew my best lover for the good of Rome, I have the same dagger for myself when it shall please my country to need my death' (3.2.44–7). His last words, 'Caesar, now be still. / I killed not thee with half so good a will' (5.5.50–1) close the circle.

From the Justinian maxim down to Sigmund Freud, the wish to die is treated as intimately tied with the wish to kill. Whether a private act of free will or a public protest, it expresses a need to bear testimony, advertise a grievance, denounce an intolerable oppression.[46] All attempts by commentators or apologists to avoid the ethical stance founder on the violence of the act, which needs to be excused by a legitimate grievance or terrible suffering. Either society or the terrorist is guilty, or sick. In *Julius Caesar* there is no canon against self-slaughter: the dialectics of freedom or slavery moves step by step from *taedium vitae* to self-offering, ritual murder, retaliation and republican suicide, summed up in Brutus's avowal of defeat, 'Slaying is the word: / It is a deed in fashion' (5.5.4–5). The freedom fighters have paved the way for worse oppression than Caesar's. A comprehensive view of terrorist dynamics shows the republican ideal of man's freedom deteriorating from Cato to Brutus into terrorist contempt of human life, beginning with one's own, and locates its impetus in the death urge. Therein, ye Gods ... Shakespeare's plays neither excuse nor reprove martyrdom, till in *Cymbeline* faithful

---

[45] Montaigne, *Essays*, Book 3, ch. 9, 'Of Vanitie'. Book 2, ch. 3, 'A Custome of the Ile of *Cea*', in which he discusses Seneca's stoic formula, 'fortune hath no power at all over him who knoweth how to dye'.

[46] Sigmund Freud, 'Dreams and Occultism' (1933), in *The Standard Edition of the Complete Psychological Works of Sigmund Freud*, ed. James Strachey et. al, vol. 20 (London, 1966), p. 46.

Imogen overcomes the death-wish in order to gain justice. They clearly divide those eager to die for their faith from those with an indestructible zest for life. Cato had refused to beg his life from Caesar, denying him any right over a free man, making his suicide a public gesture to denounce his tyranny. Brutus's failure to win support from the Roman people turned Caesar's sacrificial execution into vain murder, his own suicide a pathetic end to the republican dream.

'A LEAN AND HUNGRY LOOK': SIGHT, EKPHRASIS, IRONY IN *JULIUS CAESAR* AND *HENRY V*

ROS KING

The phrase 'lean and hungry look' (*Julius Caesar*, 1.2.193) is one of those Shakespearian quotations that has become so familiar that we no longer enquire after its implications.[1] Indeed since its meaning seems straightforward – someone who appears lean and hungry, i.e. thin and discontent, and therefore perhaps resentful or jealous – there is no obvious reason to do so. Even so, this description by Caesar of Cassius, presented as observable fact, quickly slides, as has just been demonstrated, into a matter of interpretation. No editors comment on this slippery function, however, preferring simply to note Shakespeare's borrowings: David Daniell in the Arden edition, for example, refers the entire block of twenty-two lines in which the phrase occurs to passages in three of the relevant *Lives* of Plutarch, as translated by Sir Thomas North from the French version by Amyot.

In the *Life of Julius Caesar*, we are told that Caesar 'suspected' Cassius and held him 'in great gelouzie' saying 'I like not his pale lookes'. Then a passage that is more or less repeated in the *Life of Marcus Antonius* adds: '"as for those fatte men and smooth com[b]ed heads," quoth he, "I never reckon of them: but these pale visaged and carian leane people, I fear them most", meaning Brutus and Cassius'.[2] Shakespeare's 'look' preserves North's use of 'looks' as a noun, rather than the intransitive verbal form of customary interpretation (i.e. 'looks lean and hungry'). His version of Caesar's wish – 'Let me have men about me that are fat, / Sleek-headed men' – is intensified with 'and such as sleep a-nights', and subsequently two long scenes that

will show sleepless conspirators in the dark (1.2.191–2; 1.3; 2.1). But he drops the paleness, emphasizing hunger rather than thinness, and adds an extra anxiety about Cassius's powers of looking: 'He reads much, / He is a great observer, and he looks / Quite through the deeds of men' (1.2.200–2). Caesar's disquiet thus becomes a shrewder anxiety about what Cassius *does* rather than a merely superstitious fear about what he looks *like* and what his appearance might presage. The 'lean and hungry look' can now be seen to have a verbal quality about it, conjuring an image of energetic, devouring wolfishness, rather than Plutarch's carrion emaciation. The phrase is sufficiently arresting to have caught on quickly; an EEBO keyword search gives five instances in the century following the play's composition.

In this chapter I argue that the ambiguity of noun-ness and verb-ness in this line exploits contemporary uncertainty concerning the physiology of sight in order to raise a whole set of questions as to the nature of seeing, and also therefore of point of view, and of understanding. Furthermore, active, evocative descriptions, such as this one, that conjure up emotive images of people and

---

[1] Quotations from *Julius Caesar* are from the Arden Shakespeare Third Series, ed. David Daniell (London, 1998); see note to 1.2.191–213. All other Shakespeare quotations are from *William Shakespeare: The Complete Works*, ed. Stanley Wells et al. (Oxford, 1986).

[2] Plutarch, *Lives of the Noble Grecians and Romans*, trans. Sir Thomas North (London, 1579), pp. 792, 975; quoted Daniell, *Julius Caesar*, 325–6.

events (both on and off the stage), are studded through the play to the extent that they become a structural principle of ekphrasis. This contributes to the play's sense of conflict and, through juxtaposition of different points of view, creates a sense of irony that involves readers and spectators in a powerful argument about the disasters of tyranny.

THE ART OF EKPHRASIS

Etymologically, the rhetorical term *ekphrasis* is derived from *ek* (or *ex*) plus *phrasein* – 'out' plus 'to speak' – suggesting a tangible sense of something created in or from words. Over the course of the twentieth century, it came to signify little more than a description of a work of art, but its original meaning is not limited in that way and covers any evocative description of a person, place, thing or event.[3]

The first reference to the word listed in the *Oxford English Dictionary* (where it is spelt 'ecphrasis') dates from 1725. But in Greek lettering it would have been familiar to those with a sixteenth-century education. Numerous versions and adaptations in Latin of Aphthonius's *Progymnasmata*, some explicitly for use in grammar schools, had been published by English printers by the time Shakespeare began to write his plays. This textbook on rhetoric comprises a series of different types of rhetorical construction, each with extensive citation and quotation from the best examples. The section, headed in both Latin and Greek, *Descriptio* and εκφρασις, does not occur until late in the text, but then takes up considerable space, suggesting that it is an advanced skill.[4] It states that ekphrasis can be applied to persons, things, times, places, animals and plants, and is characterized by ἐνάργεια (*enargeia*), vividness: the capacity to lay things, as it were, 'before the eyes'.

Ekphrasis and *enargeia* work together as rhetoric (i.e. as an art of persuasion) by appealing to the memories, values, imagination and experience of those that listen. Together they form 'a conception of language as a quasi-physical force which penetrates into the mind of the listener, stirring up the images that are stored there'.[5] The result is that both speaker and listener feel themselves to be present at the event that is described and emotionally involved with it.

As Quintilian puts it, frequently citing Cicero as his best exemplum, 'The heart of the matter as regards arousing emotions ... lies in being moved by them oneself' (*Institutio Oratoria*, 6.2.26).[6]

The person who will show the greatest power in the expression of emotions [*in adfectibus potentissimus*] will be the person who has properly formed what the Greeks call *phantasiai* (let us call them 'visions'), by which the images of absent things are presented to the mind in such a way that we seem actually to see them with our eyes and have them physically present to us. (6.2.29–30)

He goes on to demonstrate that descriptions that succeed best in placing people and events before the eyes of a listener depend not so much on adjectives as on actions:

Suppose I am complaining that someone has been murdered. Am I not to have before my eyes all the circumstances which one can believe to have *happened* during the event? Will not the assassin *burst out* on a sudden, and the victim *tremble*, *cry for help*, and either

---

[3] For example, while acknowledging that ekphrasis need not be confined to verbal descriptions of works of art or other artefacts, much recent work deliberately restricts itself to that usage; see Catherine Belsey, 'Invocation of the Visual Image: Ekphrasis in *Lucrece* and Beyond', *Shakespeare Quarterly*, 63 (2012), 175–98; and Claire Preston, 'Painting in Words', in *Renaissance Figures of Speech*, ed. Sylvia Adamson, Gavin Alexander and Katrin Ettenhuber (Cambridge, 2007), pp. 115–29. Richard Meek's *Narrating the Visual in Shakespeare* (Farnham, 2009) concentrates on plays that contain a described artwork, apart from a chapter on *King Lear*.

[4] Aphthonius, *Progymnasmata* (London, 1583), sigs. 181v–95; cf. Erasmus *De Copia*, Book 2, *Quinta ratio*.

[5] Ruth Webb, *Ekphrasis, Imagination and Persuasion in Ancient Rhetorical Theory and Practice* (Farnham, 2009), p. 128.

[6] This idea can be found in Aristotle, *Poetics*, 17; Horace, *Ars Poetica*, 101–7; Cicero, *De Oratore*, 2.189. All quotations from Quintilian, *Institutio Oratoria*, are from *The Orator's Education*, trans. and ed. Donald A. Russell (London, 2001). No English printers produced an edition of Quintilian before the late seventeenth century, but the work was widely read and quoted.

plead for mercy or *try to escape*? Shall I not *see* one man *striking* the blow and the other man *falling*? Will not the blood, the pallor, the *groans*, the last *gasp* of the *dying* be imprinted on my mind? (6.2.31; my emphases)

The result will be that the orator seems 'not so much to be talking about something as exhibiting it. Emotions will ensue just as if we were present at the event itself' (6.2.31–2).

The events so described may or may not be true. But, as Hamlet was later to observe, if actors can exhibit emotional identification with their characters 'in a fiction, in a dream of passion', how much more important is emotional identification in those speaking about the trauma of real events (see *Hamlet*, 2.2.551–82):

Let us identify with the persons of whose grievous, undeserved and lamentable misfortunes we complain; let us not plead the case as though it were someone else's but take the pain of it on ourselves for the moment. We shall thus say what we would have said in similar circumstances of our own. I have frequently seen tragic and comic actors, having taken off their masks at the end of some emotional scene, leave the stage still in tears. And if the mere delivery of the written words of another can so kindle them with imagined emotions, what shall *we* [orators] be capable of doing, we who have to imagine the facts in such a way that we can feel vicariously the emotions of our endangered clients?

(6.2.34–5)

The purpose of ekphrasis and *enargeia* in oratory is therefore to generate shared cultural values; listeners get the impression they are 'seeing' the same vision as the speaker, and are thereby encouraged to feel the same emotional response.[7] But Shakespeare's plays bring a variety of characters before our eyes with different values set up in opposition – as befits drama. They recount events which are clearly of varying truth, or which are greeted with varying degrees of emotion and different interpretations by those on the stage. And like real people, these characters exhibit inconsistency.

Thus the same Cassius who strikes fear into Caesar, retells the occasion when he had to rescue Caesar from the Tiber – or perhaps invents it since it is not found in Plutarch. His story is laced with multiple visual elements that lend it verisimilitude, including the following emotive comparison with an image of Aeneas rescuing his father from the ruins of Troy:

I, as Aeneas, our great ancestor,
Did from the flames of Troy upon his shoulder
The old Anchises bear, so from the waves of Tiber
Did I the tired Caesar: (1.2.112–15)

That event lends itself to actual pictorial representation and can be found as a woodcut in Geffrey Whitney's *A Choice of Emblems* (1586) 'moralised' as an exemplum of filial piety.[8] But as a dramatist, Shakespeare is aware that meaning depends on context, and in Cassius's mouth the image is yoked with scorn for Caesar's supposed physical weakness in a rhetorical ploy to persuade Brutus that Caesar is unfit to rule Rome.

Cassius is, nevertheless, also the person whose shocked reaction to the appalling and graphic news of Portia's death by swallowing burning coals allows us to see that Brutus's stoic acceptance of her (excessively) Roman sense of honour is not the only possible Roman reaction.

BRUTUS. ... with this she fell distract,
And, her attendants absent, swallowed fire.
CASSIUS. And died so?
BRUTUS. Even so.
CASSIUS. O ye immortal gods!
Enter Lucius *with wine and tapers.*
BRUTUS. Speak no more of her. (4.3.153–6)

Perhaps it simply cannot be spoken of in front of the servants, but this moment is recapitulated some forty lines later when Brutus and Messala compare what their letters tell them of terrible events in Rome: the proscription and deaths of a hundred (or is it seventy?) senators, including Cicero. Brutus there feigns ignorance of Portia's fate, thus forcing Messala to tell him what he knows. This is something Messala is loath to do, but he admits, 'For

---

[7] Webb, *Ekphrasis*, pp. 131; 152–63. See also Jas Elsner, *Roman Eyes: Visuality and Subjectivity in Art and Text* (Princeton, NJ, 2007), p. 187.

[8] Geffrey Whitney, *A Choice of Emblems* (Leyden, 1586), p. 163.

certain she is dead, and by strange manner'. Brutus's claim that, having once meditated on her death, he has 'the patience to endure it now', is then greeted by Messala apothegmatically (perhaps with relief, perhaps puzzlement, perhaps awe): 'Even so great men great losses should endure'. Cassius, however, observes that although he has as much 'art' as Brutus 'yet my nature could not bear it so' (4.3.179–93).

Such highly charged, contradictory moments, in which what one person sees is at odds with what another understands provide a rhetorical structure that allows space to us as audiences or readers to engage our own imaginations in dialectical reflection on what is spoken. This in turn goes a long way to answer traditional criticism that the construction of the play is problematic, even confused.[9] The play's subject matter – assassination, deposition, civil war – is inherently both emotionally charged and divisive. It is only appropriate that its structure and content should reflect that.

THEORIES OF SIGHT

By transferring the description of Cassius's physical appearance to the nature of his look, Shakespeare has introduced a glancing reference to the extramission theory of sight – the idea expressed by Empedocles and promulgated by Plato and others that the eye sees by throwing out a small beam of light. Despite early contradiction by Aristotle (who argues that rays of light from an object penetrate the watery, translucent medium of the inner eye where they somehow mingle with the translucent soul to produce vision),[10] the theory of extramission has been long-lived, particularly with regard to the sight of beloved objects.

The idea of a lover's 'eye-beam', sometimes tangling with eye-beams emanating from the beloved, features in countless medieval and early modern love poems; but it has recently been reported that as many as 50 per cent of US college students believe extramission to be an accurate account of the process of seeing.[11] Perhaps we should not really be surprised by this (although

I confess I am). The concept supplies an externalizing, physicalized image of the familiar yearning desire of those in love to connect with their beloved, and the irresistible compulsion to gaze on him or her. It is a powerful metaphor for what is felt, and therefore possesses a certain psychological or emotional truth, even though it has been known to be physiologically impossible for almost as long as it has been believed to be actually true. After all, the influence we have on others through 'oversight', or 'looking after' is preserved in the language, and we must all, from time to time, have had the powerful sense that we can actually feel other people looking at us. This is one of the many paradoxes of sight.

The word 'eye' is one of Shakespeare's most frequently used nouns. It runs to nearly six double-column pages in Bartlett's *Concordance*, slightly more than 'hand', and even than 'heart', and nearly three times the incidence of 'ear'. But Shakespeare uses the expression 'eyebeam' only once – suitably enough in *Love's Labours Lost*, in the very bad poem written by the King of Navarre, which is stuffed with over-worn, conventional and slightly nonsensical tropes:

> So sweet a kiss the golden sun gives not
> To those fresh morning drops upon the rose
> As thy eyebeams when their fresh rays have smote
> The night of dew that on my cheeks down flows.
> (4.3.24–7)

Another early play, *Two Gentlemen of Verona*, has a couple of instances of active looking which have their roots in extramission: 'borrows his wit from your ladyship's looks, and spends what he borrows' and 'His mistress / Did hold his eyes lock'd in her crystal looks' (2.4.37–8 and 86–7). Yet in

---

[9] Cf. Rene E. Fortin, 'Julius Caesar: An Experiment in Point of View', *Shakespeare Quarterly*, 19 (1968), 341–7; Ernest Schanzer, 'The Problem of Julius Caesar', *Shakespeare Quarterly*, 6 (1955), 297–308; Ernest Schanzer, *The Problem Plays of Shakespeare* (New York, 1963).

[10] Aristotle, *De Sensu*, parts 2–3.

[11] G. A. Winer et al., 'Fundamentally Misunderstanding Visual Perception: Adults' Beliefs in Visual Emissions', *American Psychologist*, 57 (2002), 417–24.

A Midsummer Night's Dream, we are told 'Love looks not with the eyes but with the mind, / And therefore is winged Cupid painted blind' (1.1. 234–5). That it is not the eye that sees but the brain is another counter-intuitive paradox of sight. This insight dates from classical times but it would only find its demonstration in western science at about the time Shakespeare was writing.[12] In *Julius Caesar*, Shakespeare thus makes metaphorical use of the idea of extramission without necessarily believing in it as a scientific explanation. In this play, ideas about sight bounce around, encompassing myth, superstition, report and hearsay, and influenced by off-stage sounds and internal imaginings. This is perhaps another reason why the play has attracted such long-standing critical disagreement.

French scientist André du Laurens in *A Discourse of the Preseruation of the Sight* translated into English in 1599, the year that *Julius Caesar* was probably first performed, carefully rehearses all of the arguments for the extramission theory of sight before coming down, little by little, firmly on the side of intromission: sight by means of light, reflected from external objects, entering the eye. As part of his extramission theory argument, he states, 'Plinie hath obserued that Tyberius Cesar did make afraid many souldiers with his onely looke, it was so quicke and full of light'.[13] The importance of the military commander's 'look', inspiring and urging his men to victory through a cheerful look, a fierce look, or flashing, energetic eyes is common in classical and sixteenth-century texts on war, both handbooks and literary.[14] Cassius's 'lean and hungry look', however, denotes narrower, personal ambition. It is not so much his physical appearance that, in Shakespeare's version, is disquieting to Caesar, but what the quality of his gaze reveals about his mind and his political aspiration: 'Yon Cassius has a lean and hungry look: / He thinks too much: such men are dangerous' (1.2.193–4).

Cassius later turns out to be a rather unsuccessful general, snatching total defeat from the jaws of possible victory. Firstly, he bows to Brutus's

rhetoric and agrees to press on to meet Octavius's army rather than force Octavius to come to them. This potential error will later surprise the latter, although Mark Antony will claim to have insider knowledge that it is but a ruse to make the conspirators' forces appear stronger than they are (4.3. 197–223; 5.1.1–12). Again, multiple views of the same set of actions. Secondly, Cassius is falling prey to superstitious fears: it is his birthday, 'where I did begin, there shall I end' (5.3.24); and he has seen ominous sights 'ravens, crows and kites / Fly o'er our heads and downward look on us' (5.1.84–5). Most disastrously, and ironically given the previous rhetoric about his gaze and his physical superiority to Caesar (who of course is deaf in one ear), his own eyesight is in fact rather 'thick'. As a result, he asks Titinius to ride off to observe the events of the battle more closely, while asking his bondman, Pindarus, to climb a nearby hill to 'regard Titinius'

---

[12] Renaissance work on optics is dependent on the *Book of Optics* by the physicist Ibn al-Haytham (d. *c.* 1000), and transmitted by Erasmus Vitelo (d. *c.* 1300). The Swiss physician Felix Platter described the retina as an expansion of the optic nerve, with the revolutionary realization that indeed seeing happens in the brain, not in the eye: 'the brightness of the Images which are offered to the Brain by the optick Nerve, where all sensation and distinction is made' (*De Corporis Humani Structura* (1583), translated as *Platerus Golden Practice of Physic* (1664), p. 60). Johannes Kepler's interest in the instruments of astronomy would shortly lead him to refine Platter's observations by arguing that the purpose of the lens in the eye is not itself to see, as Aristotle had thought, but to focus light on the retina (manuscript presented to Rudolph I as a New Year's gift in 1604 and published as his additions to Vitelo's *Ad Vitellionem paralipomena, quibus Astronomiae Pars Optica traditur*, 1604).

[13] André du Laurens, *A Discourse of the Preseruation of the Sight*, trans. Richard Surphlet (1599), pp. 14–46, esp. p. 37.

[14] E.g., 'Like as it auayleth much with wordes and with cherefull looke to gyue courage, and to fill with hope, the army' (*Onosandro Platonico, of the generall captaine, and of his office*, translated out of Greeke into Italyan, by Fabio Cotta, a Romayne: and out of Italian into Englysh, by Peter Whytehorne (1563), p. 68); 'And with a cheerefull looke surueigh'd the Campe. / Exhorting them to charge, and fight like men' (Robert Garnier, *Pompey the Great, his faire Corneliaes tragedie*, trans. Thomas Kyd (1595), sig. I4v).

from a distance.[15] Pindarus catastrophically misinterprets the sight and sound of Titinius meeting a group of fast-riding horsemen as his being pursued and captured by Antony's troops, whereas in fact he is learning news of Brutus's unexpected victory against Caesar. Cassius, in despair, stops Pindarus from observing long enough to understand properly. He has predicted and now sees disaster in his mind, and he commits suicide by compelling Pindarus to stab him (5.3.15–46).

POINTS OF VIEW IN SHAKESPEARE'S HISTORICAL PLAYS

Is *Julius Caesar* a history, a tragedy? And if the latter, whose? Caesar's? Brutus's, even Cassius's? Rome's? And what of the Roman rabble? What construction and opinion of 'the people' do their scenes represent? These are significant ethical questions, which the play lays before its spectators from multiple points of view.

Andrew Hadfield has shown how important the debate about the nature and virtues of republicanism was to Elizabethans, and demonstrates that Shakespeare himself returned to the topic repeatedly from the beginning to the end of his career. *The Rape of Lucrece* records the moment that marks the beginning of Rome's republican period with the banishment of Tarquinius; *Titus Andronicus* deals with the corruption of a Roman emperor; *Antony and Cleopatra* is concerned with the rivalry between the three triumvirs of the post-republican period.[16] Conversely, the struggle for British empery and independence from Caesar's Roman Empire forms the backdrop to *Cymbeline*, while English attempts to resist both tyranny at home and subjection to foreign empire are the subject of history plays from *King John* to *Richard III*. Of course, calls for good government and ethical justifications for resisting tyranny – with arguments justifying tyrannicide if necessary – long predate the Elizabethan period. With slightly different forms of justification depending on broader cultural and religious belief systems, they can be found in works of classical, medieval, early modern and modern political philosophy as well as in the long and honourable tradition of the poet-counsellor.[17]

At the end of the sixteenth century the need for discursive analysis of such issues was pressing. Just four years after *Julius Caesar* was probably first performed, James I's accession medal would show him dressed in Roman clothes, and presented as emperor of the whole Island of Britain as well as king of France and Ireland, while his coronation medal the following year goes a step further with its legend 'James I, Caesar Augustus of Britain, Caesar the heir of the Caesars, presents this medal'. Indeed, James was to cause disquiet amongst some at least of his auditors when he told his assembled parliament that kings sat on the right hand of God and in many respects *were* gods.[18] We can presume therefore that when Elizabethans watched *Julius Caesar*, they were also to an extent watching, and wondering about, themselves.

Dramatic writing is both the very embodiment of ekphrasis and its strange obverse; it is the raw material out of which actors lay living images (stage pictures) before the eyes of spectators, and does not itself need to be descriptive. But in plays on historical subjects, we are aware that the characters depicted in their corporeal stage presences had

---

[15] 'regard Titinius' is the F reading whereas Daniel's edition includes a stray comma, erroneously putting Titinius in the vocative.

[16] Andrew Hadfield, *Shakespeare and Republicanism* (Cambridge, 2005); Robert Miola, '*Julius Caesar* and the Tyrannicide Debate', *Renaissance Quarterly*, 38 (1985), 271–89. Cf. Ronald Knowles, *Shakespeare's Arguments with History* (Basingstoke, 2002), p. 107.

[17] Ernst Kantorowicz, *The King's Two Bodies: A Study in Medieval Political Theology* (Princeton, NJ, 1957); Greg Walker, *Writing under Tyranny: English Literature and the Henrician Reformation* (Oxford, 2005); David Colclough, 'Talking to the Animal: Persuasion, Counsel and their Discontents in Julius Caesar', in *Shakespeare and Early Modern Political Thought*, ed. David Armitage et al. (Cambridge, 2009), pp. 217–33. Cf. Richard Edwards's play, *Damon and Pythias* (1564), where the tyrant Dionisius is advised by Eubulus (Good Counsel), and where the Prologue invites comparison with Elizabeth's court by claiming not to do so: 'Wee talke of Dionisius court, wee meane no court but that'.

[18] Ros King, *Cymbeline: Constructions of Britain* (Aldershot, 2005), pp. 80–2.

a previous actual existence, and may have ongoing contemporary significance. The words and their embodiment by actors can therefore conjure up images that are subtly different from those already present in individual memories or imaginations.

Conversely, while the need to telescope long tracts of historical time and great events into the purview of a play, can encourage description of things happening offstage, it is often more dramatically effective to encapsulate huge historical processes in a single scene, even a single gesture or stage image. The scene in which the representatives of the houses of York and Lancaster confront each other in a garden, and respectively pluck white and red roses to represent their cause (*1 Henry VI*, 2.4), probably never happened, but it sums up thirty years of turbulent history in one ekphrastic image. It has influenced the way in which that history has been told ever since.

The power of ekphrastic imagination is overtly exploited in another play written at about the same time as *Julius Caesar*, and which has likewise acquired critical notoriety as 'ambivalent': *Henry V*.[19] The Chorus opens that play half humorously denying the capacity of mere actors, their words, and assorted odd props to present the actuality of a great military campaign, and famously uses that lack as a prompt to audiences to engage. The audience is instructed to imagine the historic scene by visualizing detailed actions: '*Think*, when we talk of horses, that you *see* them, / *Printing* their proud hoofs i'th'*receiving* earth' (*Henry V*, 1.0.26–7; my emphasis). Shakespeare intends us to collude in seeing the churning and compaction of the soil by invading cavalry as something that the very land of France is eager to embrace.

The play is also indebted to borrowings from classical *ekphraseis*. The Duke of Burgundy's lament for the terrible effects of the war on the agriculture and economy of the French countryside is a textbook ekphrastic exercise, the origin of which seems to be Demosthenes's much cited description of the sack of Phocis, in which 'a few details ... stand for the whole event and bring to mind a vivid scene of devastation'.[20] Burgundy's

lament is rather more drawn out, lasting more than twenty lines. France lies in ruins:

> Her vine, the merry cheerer of the heart,
> Unprunèd dies; her hedges even-plashed
> Like prisoners wildly overgrown with hair,
> Put forth disordered twigs.   (5.2.41–4)

It is an elegiac, emotive picture, but if the rhetorical purpose of ekphrasis is to make the listener share the speaker's perspective, it can only miss its mark. The principal listener, Henry, has his own rather different memories of the war, its purposes and its hardships. This, added to the length, may account for Henry's impatient response. If, he says, the Duke really wants the peace 'Whose want gives growth to th'imperfections / Which you have cited', then Burgundy and the French

> must buy that peace
> With full accord to all our just demands,
> Whose tenors and particular effects
> You have enscheduled briefly in your hands.
>   (5.2.68–73)

An ekphrastic literary trope thus gives way to a concrete stage picture with a rather different agenda. We now realize that Burgundy is holding, but not looking at, a written copy of Henry's demands; he is not simply lamenting, but stalling because the King of France wants further talks (5.2. 68–82).

The Chorus's description of Henry's embarkation for France is similarly more complex than it at first appears. Holinshed simply states that the King and his army embarked for France in a thousand ships, but the Chorus instructs us to 'suppose' that we have 'seen' Henry embark at Southampton, but in such a way that we 'play with' our 'fancies'. The scene has an antique and epic quality in its choice of language. The ships' ropes are 'hempen tackle' and their sails are 'threaden'. Rather than merely waving in the wind, their flags are 'silken

---

[19] See Norman Rabkin, 'Rabbits, Ducks, and *Henry V*', *Shakespeare Quarterly*, 28 (1977), 279–96.

[20] Webb, *Ekphrasis*, p. 153. Cf. Quintilian, *Orator's Education*, 8.3.67–9, also quoted in *Progymnasmata* (1583), p. 185.

streamers', 'fanning' Henry's face in the persona of the sun-god 'Phoebus' himself. The ships' bottoms are 'huge', the 'surge' is 'lofty'. There is scarcely a noun that is not graced with an adjective, but more important is the lively sense of movement in which we too, in imagination, are invited to be physically involved: we are to 'grapple' our minds 'to sternage of this navy', so vast that as we simultaneously stand watching from the 'rivage' (seashore), we see an entire 'city on th'inconstant billows dancing' (3.0. 1–18). This use of the odd and poetic term 'rivage', which occurs nowhere else in Shakespeare's plays or poems, and the particular combination of curiously antique words and images in this passage indicate that something more is going on than a simple recounting of an event in medieval history. Indeed, many of its individual words can be found (in almost the same order) in the famous ekphrastic description in North's Plutarch of Cleopatra's barge on the river Cydnus when she first beguiles Mark Antony:

on either hand of her, pretie faire boyes ... fanned wind upon her. Her ladies ... tending the tackle and ropes of the barge, out of which there came a wonderfull passing sweete savor of perfumes, that perfumed the wharfes side, pestered with innumerable multitudes of people. Some of them followed the barge all alongest the rivers side: others also ranne out of the citie to see her comming in.[21]

Shakespeare's 'rivage' echoes North's 'rivers side', but is also a curiously redolent term for the topography of the scene, since the Solent, where it takes place, is not only sea but a confluence of rivers. Yet it may seem strange that a description of a military expedition should be inspired by one of the most extravagant seduction events in recorded history. Shakespeare's hallmark as a dramatist, however, is the way in which he introduces images near the beginning of a work that he can transform or undercut towards the end. This invasion will be ratified, excused (call it what you will) by a love affair: 'for I love France so well that I will not part with a village of it, I will have it all mine; and Kate, when France is mine, and I am yours, then yours is France and you are mine' (5.2.173–6). He is only partly joking.

The *Henry V* Chorus is notoriously unreliable: the things he describes or tells us to expect never happen in quite the way he says they will. This is an almost inevitable pitfall of ekphrastic description because of the speaker's presumption of a shared cultural outlook with his listener, which may not in fact be shared, and his desire to persuade that listener to a particular point of view. Peter Wagner describes it thus: 'Ekphrasis, then, has a Janus face: as a form of mimesis, it stages a paradoxical performance, promising to give voice to the allegedly silent image even while attempting to overcome the power of the image by transforming and inscribing it.'[22] In a play where successive characters with different outlooks make such assumptions, it becomes a powerful device for evoking turmoil.

EKPHRASIS AND INTERMEDIALITY

By its very nature, ekphrasis is intermedial (from event or image into words, via memory of similar events or images, to a reconstructed image of the event or image in the mind of the listener); it is also often intertextual, and can thus, intentionally or not, come to signify more than is overtly set down.[23] In *A Choice of Emblemes*, Geffrey Whitney had used the death of Brutus as illustration for the motto *Fortuna virtutem superans* – Fortune conquers the valiant. Whitney's moral hope for the collection as a whole is expressed on its title page: that through 'the office of the eie, and the eare, the minde maye reape dooble delighte throughe holsome preceptes, shadowed with pleasant deuises: both fit for the vertuous, to their incoraging: and for the wicked, for their admonishing and amendment'. In this case, the woodcut shows a figure in Roman armour, bent over, his bared

---

[21] Plutarch, *Lives*, p. 981.

[22] Peter Wagner, *Icons-Texts-Iconotexts: Essays on Ekphrasis and Intermediality* (New York, 1996), p. 13. Cf. Elsner, *Roman Eyes*, pp. 192 and 199 for discussion of duplicity and irony in mimetic art.

[23] Cf. Wagner, *Icons-Texts-Iconotexts*, p. 28; Webb, *Ekphrasis*, p. 95.

breast resting on the tip of an upright, naked sword. The verse tells how Brutus 'sawe his friendes, lie bleeding on the grounde', and how his remaining friends have urged him 'to flee', but he refuses 'with courage great', stating 'my flight with hands shalbe'. He concludes:

Oh Prowes vaine, I longe did loue thee beste,
But nowe, I see, thou doest on fortune waite.
　Wherefore with paine, I nowe doe prooue it true,
　That fortunes force, maie valiant hartes subdue.[24]

The message seems straightforward: Brutus's suicide is the action of an honourable and valiant man in the face of overwhelming fortune. But Brutus is an ambivalent figure: on the one hand stoic defender of liberty and the Republic; on the other, conspirator and murderer. In an attempt, presumably, to clinch the heroic aspects, a lengthy marginal note refers us, in Latin, to the dispute between Ajax and Ulysses over which of them should inherit the armour of Achilles. It first directs us to an emblem earlier in the book in which a 'doleful dame', Prowess herself, is shown sitting on Ajax's tomb. She is tearing her hair because Agamemnon's judgement in favour of the 'filed tongue' of Ulysses, caused Ajax, the 'onelie man of warre', to fall insane and kill himself.[25] It then selectively quotes from the story as retold by Ovid in *Metamorphoses* 13, concluding '*Ne quisquam Aiacem possit superare, nisi Aiax*'; no one but Ajax can conquer Ajax. Those familiar with Ovid's story, however, will also remember that Ajax had attempted to take revenge for Agamemnon's judgement, but the gods rendered him insane so that he merely slaughtered a flock of sheep, stabbing himself when he came to his senses. Ovid also tells how Ajax's blood caused a hyacinth to spring from the ground – the same flower that had sprung up after the accidental death of the boy Hyacinth during a game of discus with Apollo. The flower, Ovid says, bears on its petals the letters AI, denoting both the boy's pain, and the first two letters of Ajax's name. The marginal annotation thus gives intertextual references (both within the *Emblemes* and external to it) that supply both visual and aural stimuli – the doleful dame, the anguished cry of

a boy, the ranting of Ajax, the springing to life of a flower – that are emotive but also potentially ambiguous, even incompatible with the proposed meaning of the emblem.

Whitney was a client of the Earl of Leicester and was in his retinue during his military expedition to Holland; the *Emblemes* had started as a manuscript gift to the earl and had been published at the behest of various leading Dutch humanist scholars. The tenor of the Brutus poem suggests that any Christian anxiety Whitney may have had about the sinfulness of suicide has disappeared in the attempt to reinforce Leicester's heroic credentials. But the marginal gloss to other images and their verbal descriptions only serve to muddy this message – something that would be intensified for later readers familiar with Ajax the 'beef-witted lord' of Shakespeare's *Troilus and Cressida*, or Harington's *Anatomy ... of Ajax* (1596), a satire on the Elizabethan court, including a specific reference to Leicester. In explicating and contextualizing, Whitney has rather undermined himself, despite his attempts to control and limit his references.

COMPLEXITY

The complexity of vision in *Julius Caesar*, however, usefully takes doubt not just about the morality of the conspirators' actions but about their political efficacy to a new level of ethical debate. It presents us with a situation in which one bad government, which is afraid of its own shadow, impotent and subject to superstition, is replaced not by the revolutionaries (who in fact have no political manifesto other than the removal of the tyrant) but by more of the same. Old-fashioned augury is replaced by newfangled spin – and continuing civil war. Tellingly, for a work of poetic literature, this all too familiar nightmare process has no space for poets or public intellectuals. The various poets who make brief appearances are each noted for their 'bad verses'. And Cicero, the most commonly read legal thinker in sixteenth-century English

---

[24] Whitney, *Emblemes*, p. 70.　　[25] Whitney, *Emblemes*, p. 30.

schoolrooms, who in *The Laws* defends tyrannicide according to the principle of natural law, and who wrote an entire oration in favour of the poet Archias, stressing the public and private value of the arts, is curiously peripheral. This must be deliberate. Shakespeare cannot have been ignorant of Cicero's political and legal importance – whether from his school studies, his reading of Plutarch's *Lives*, which includes a Life of Cicero, or through the good offices of his Stratford contemporary, the printer Richard Field, who through marriage to Vautrollier's widow had acquired the rights to print not only the *Lives*, but also Cicero's works in England. Quentin Skinner has exhaustively catalogued Shakespeare's familiarity with Cicero, and the technical accuracy of the rhetorical speeches in *Julius Caesar* and other plays from the same period of Shakespeare's career. He also notes the emotional uses of *enargeia*. But while recounting the disposition of elements within single speeches, he largely ignores Shakespeare's juxtaposition of characters, speeches and events through an entire play, and therefore the dialectic that is set up by this selection and arrangement in the mind of the reader/spectator.[26]

When Shakespeare makes Brutus describe Cicero's entrance in Caesar's train after the failed crowning at the Lupercal games, it is with a glancing and uncomplimentary reference to extramission, which balances Caesar's earlier description of Cassius:

> and Cicero
> Looks with such ferret and such fiery eyes
> As we have seen him in the Capitol
> Being crossed in conference by some senators.
>
> (1.2.184–7)

The ferret's 'look' may be fierce, but it is a tiny animal, and Caesar is no rabbit. This Cicero has already lost all influence, and Caska will shortly joke about his ineffective intervention at the games: 'Ay, he spoke Greek ... those that understood him smiled at one another, and shook their heads; but for mine own part, it was Greek to me' (1.2.278–83).[27]

We see Cicero just once more in the following scene, in talk with Caska in a thunderstorm, clearly not believing Caska's ekphrastic tales of strange sights within sights: the man he 'saw' with the hand that flamed 'Like twenty torches joined; and yet ... remained unscorched'; the lion that 'glazed' upon him, yet forbore to attack him; and the 'hundred ghastly women ... who swore they saw / Men, all in fire, walk up and down the streets' (1.3.14–25). But he sees no point in disagreeing:

> Indeed it is a strange-disposed time.
> But men may construe things after their fashion
> Clean from the purpose of the things themselves.
>
> (1.3.33–5)

It is the kind of sardonic put-down for which, Plutarch says, he was famous. He cannot bother himself to engage with the misconceived rumour-mill that is public discourse. Or perhaps more fairly, he realizes that the wild rumour, which has resulted in people seeing what they have been conditioned by the times to see, is not susceptible to reasoned argument.

Later, Brutus will veto the other conspirators' suggestion that Cicero should be invited to join them, on the grounds that 'he will never follow anything / That other men begin' (2.1.150–1). But like Cicero, Cassius and Brutus have also bowed out of the social, political process. They decided not to accompany Caesar's train to the games, but they, and we, hear the roars from the crowd and the flourish of trumpets, punctuating Cassius's attempts to encourage Brutus to thoughts of tyrannicide. These sounds enabled them (and us) to imagine the scene in which the crown is offered to Caesar. Their own relationship is not easy. Brutus, Cassius says, has appeared unfriendly of late. The language used mixes sight expressed as a metaphor of extramission with words connoting troubled, interrupted or false sight to create an image of disrupted friendship:

---

[26] Quentin Skinner, *Forensic Shakespeare* (Oxford, 2014).

[27] In life, Cicero's career was marked by alternating periods of banishment and supreme power. He was murdered the year after Brutus's and Cassius's rebellion by Mark Antony in retaliation for the *Philippics*, a set of orations he wrote against Antony. See Plutarch, *Life of Cicero*.

CASSIUS.　Brutus, I do observe you now of late.
　　　I have not from your eyes that gentleness
　　　And show of love as I was wont to have.
　　　You bear too stubborn and too strange a hand
　　　Over your friend, that loves you.

Brutus acknowledges the truth of this:

　　　　　　If I have veiled my look,
　　　I turn the trouble of my countenance
　　　Merely upon myself . . .

He asks that Cassius should not

　　　　　　construe any further my neglect
　　　Than that poor Brutus, with himself at war,
　　　Forgets the shows of love to other men.

And in response to Cassius's desire that he look at his own face, he notes a further paradox of sight, that 'the eye sees not itself / But by reflection, by some other things' (1.2.32–53).

Having imagined the scene in the capitol through sound effects and as something to 'fear' (and after both the return of Caesar and his train in some disarray, and then their exit), we are invited to see it again in more graphic detail, but this time as something to laugh at.

CASKA.　I saw Mark Antony offer him a crown – yet 'twas not a crown neither, 'twas one of these coronets – and, as I told you, he put it by once; but for all that, to my thinking, he would fain have had it. Then he offered it to him again; then he put it by again; but to my thinking, he was very loth to lay his fingers off it. And then he offered it the third time; he put it the third time by; and still as he refused it the rabblement hooted, and clapped their chopped hands, and threw up their sweaty nightcaps, and uttered such a deal of stinking breath because Caesar refused the crown that it had almost choked Caesar; for he swooned and fell down at it. And for mine own part, I durst not laugh, for fear of opening my lips and receiving the bad air.　(1.2.236–49)

This speech supplies us with multiple points of view and emotional responses – from Mark Antony, from Caesar, from the crowd – all mediated through Caska's irony. The informality and colloquialism of ''twas not a crown neither, 'twas one of those coronets' betrays the tawdriness

of the occasion and the failure to stage-manage it properly. It is also ironic that Caesar's desire for the crown cannot be satisfied because the crowd greets his show of refusal with such rapture. He wants to be a tyrant by the consent of the people! Conversely and even more ironically, by killing him, the conspirators will actually hasten the end of the republic they claim to be defending.

In Shakespeare's play, community, allegiance, friendship and marriage are all stretched to breaking point. The people are at odds with their tribunes; Cassius deceives Brutus into taking the action that *he* wants him to take by throwing counterfeit messages in at windows; Brutus and Cassius argue before Phillipi; and there is no companionateness between husbands and wives. Brutus cannot bring himself to communicate with Portia, while Caesar publicly announces that Calphurnia is barren and orders Antony to touch her during the race on the Lupercal.[28] Expressed as a series of commands to both Calphurnia and Antony as to what each should do, it becomes a highly visual verbal image, which at least to modern and presumably to Elizabethan eyes is humiliating. Mark Antony even draws attention to Caesar's autocracy, and to the strangeness of the ritual, abrogating his own responsibility: 'When Caesar says "Do this", it is performed' (1.2.10). As Colin Burrow observes, 'when Shakespeare represents a religious ritual, he, like Plutarch before him, will tend to emphasise the alienness of Roman custom'.[29]

With such dislocation of social relations, it is inevitable that the revolution only serves to breed violence; the rabble on the streets tears an innocent person to pieces because it cannot distinguish between people with identical names – 'I am Cinna *the poet*' (3.3.29, my emphasis) – while Caesar's successors sit down and coldly trade close

---

[28] Cf. Cicero's wife Terentia, who 'had gotten more knowledge from her husband of the affayres of the state, than otherwise she had acquainted him with her housewifery in the house, as Cicero himself reported'. Cicero later divorced her (Plutarch, *Lives*, pp. 922, 933).

[29] Colin Burrow, *Shakespeare and Classical Antiquity* (Oxford, 2013), p. 215.

relatives to death, reducing individuals to no more than a 'prick' or mark, 'Look, with a spot, I damn him' (4.1.6).

Cassius has asserted the classical defence against a charge of tyrannicide: that is, self-defence against the enslaving behaviour of the tyrant, and which, in the aim to reassert natural justice, thereby enacts God's will:

> Cassius from bondage will deliver Cassius.
> Therein, ye gods, ye make the weak most strong;
> Therein, ye gods, you tyrants do defeat. (1.3.90–2)

He acknowledges that in doing so, he too is acting the part of tyrant but claims to be able to shake this off:

> If I know this, know all the world besides,
> That part of tyranny that I do bear
> I can shake off at pleasure.   *Thunder still.*
> (1.3.98–100)

But the thunder sound-effect is ominous, even blackly satirical. Cassius's readiness to 'make a mighty fire', and his denigration of Rome itself as 'trash', 'rubbish', 'offal' (1.3.107–9), that can now, logically, be burned on that fire is chilling, especially so, perhaps, to us who have heard similar sentiments from countless twentieth- and twenty-first-century demagogues, dictators and terrorist fanatics.

Cassius is not alone. Mark Antony, the man who is about to woo the people with promise of bequests made in Caesar's will, not only has no intention of delivering those bequests but privately vows to revenge Caesar in the bloodiest of civil wars:

> Blood and destruction shall be so in use,
> And dreadful objects so familiar,
> That mothers shall but smile when they behold
> Their infants quartered with the hands of war:
> (3.1.265–8)

Criticism has tended to ignore this horror. Like the plebs in the play, it has been beguiled by Antony's subsequent rhetoric and also perhaps by Shakespeare's later manifestation of him as the great but flawed lover – or perhaps just by the

Richard Burtons and other gorgeous actors who have played the role. This Antony is rather the cruel tyrant attacked by Cicero in the *Philippics*. Examples of Cicero's copious, graphic, *ad-hominem* rhetoric are ubiquitous in Plutarch and Erasmus. But Shakespeare gathers these hints to dramatize the dangers and the failure of oratory; his characters condemn themselves.

JUXTAPOSITION AND IRONY

Colin Burrow states that *Julius Caesar* lacks 'obtrusive imagery'; he observes the 'relative absence from it of puns or lexical innovations, its tendency to rely heavily on monosyllables', which gives it a sense of an alien culture far removed from Elizabethan England, and suggests that it was this alienness that kept Shakespeare safe from accusations of sedition. He notes the conspirators' rhetorical identification of themselves with the 'thews and sinews' of early Romans, and reiterates an oft-noted feature: that Shakespeare rephrases Plutarch in terse, often monosyllabic language that speaks 'marmoreal' Romanness.[30] All this is true, and in first drafting this article I rather surprised myself by the number of times I began to reach for the word 'irony' to describe the play and its techniques. Burrow himself makes the briefest passing reference to irony, while Garry Wills, commenting on Brutus's funeral oration, remarks: 'Brutus layers his figures, interlaces them, piles them up, runs one through another, violating the teaching of Quintilian, reducing the crowd to cowed silence. Its rhetoric is so overdone that it approaches what is comic elsewhere in Shakespeare.'[31] Yet as Quintilian himself remarks, 'Irony too: is not this even in its severest form almost a kind of joke?' (*Institutio Oratoria*, 6.3.68).

In the mouths of individual characters, the play demonstrates the truth of Plato's *Gorgias* that most

---

[30] Burrow, *Classical Antiquity*, pp. 216–19.
[31] Burrow, *Classical Antiquity*, p. 220; Garry Wills, *Rome and Rhetoric: Shakespeare's Julius Caesar* (New Haven, CT, 2011), p. 54.

oratory is mere sophistry. Whether Antony's ironic 'For Brutus is an honourable man' or Brutus's 'Believe me for mine honour and have respect to mine honour, that you may believe', they are all variously deluding themselves, each other, and the people, but always for their own individual self-interest. The power and value of the *play*, however, lie in its juxtapositions, which prevent the rhetoric of language and image from exerting the meanings that the character-speakers intend.

We are not the audience for Antony's and Brutus's funeral orations (despite the attempts of so many modern productions to turn us into a crowd of Roman citizens), because we are also watching, and marvelling, at the way the crowd gets turned:

> Look, in this place ran Cassius' dagger through:
> See what a rent the envious Caska made:
> Through this, the well-beloved Brutus stabbed,
> And as he plucked his cursed steel away
> Mark how the blood of Caesar followed it,
> As rushing out of doors, to be resolved
> If Brutus so unkindly knocked or no. (3.2.172–8)

Who knows which of the holes in that bloody cloak were actually made by Cassius, Caska or Brutus? We can see how the rhetoric achieves its effects – with verbs and actions – and we can make our own meanings.

In other words, though Roman approaches to honour and militarism have often been valorized in Western European culture, this play does not force us to accept them without question. In it, Shakespeare sets up a pervasive pattern of different ways of seeing and understanding. This structure expresses the ethical complexity of the political situation, which strangely, in its very alienness, makes it a play for our time, as well as for his own; Nigerian-born Theo Ogundipe, soothsayer in the 2012 RSC production which was set in modern Africa, describes the play as 'Perfect for Africa, because of the way Africa is run'.[32]

We are still nonplussed in the face of tyranny; our legal structures and international organizations are incapable of acting to alleviate the acknowledged suffering of innocent people under tyrannous regimes.

Instances of politically motivated murder seem not to have diminished since the conspiratorial designs of Brutus or the revolutionary speeches of Robespierre that proclaimed 'death to tyrants' (Robespierre 1794). In the recent Iraq war the question of tyrannicide was raised once again; should Saddam Hussein be killed to free the Iraqi people . . .? It was a contemporary manifestation of an ancient quandary which demonstrates that international societal norms governing tyrannicide warrant serious investigation.[33]

We should therefore not expect the play to be straightforward in its expression of a problem that has not, after all, gone away; its strangeness is useful to us, since it offers space for reflection. It is not that Shakespeare is sitting on the fence, playing safe with political ambiguity, rather that he is painting a picture of a bleak world that has gone beyond the operation of normal politics. Shakespeare's use of ekphrasis, *enargeia* and irony is not simply an ornamental way of speaking. The dramaturgy of competing emotional images creates an argument about the ethical and practical problems associated with both resistance to tyranny and internecine war, which are as relevant today as they have ever been. If we find the play's language 'marmoreal', alien and ungiving, it is perhaps a prompt that its characters' solutions to the problems in which they find themselves should not be ours.

---

[32] Royal Shaksepeare Theatre, www.rsc.org.uk/explore/shake speare/plays/julius-caesar/julius-caesar-gregory-doran-2012-videos.aspx, accessed 17 February 2015. The production had found its inspiration in Nelson Mandela's underlining of a passage from the play in the so-called Robben Island 'Bible', the disguised copy of Shakespeare's complete works that circulated amongst the political prisoners.

[33] Shannon K. Brincat, '"Death to tyrants": The Political Philosophy of Tyrannicide – Part 1', *Journal of International Political Theory*, 4 (2008), 212–40.

'HER STRONG TOIL OF GRACE': CHARISMATIC PERFORMANCE FROM QUEENS TO QUAKERS

INEKE MURAKAMI

Recounting the meeting on the river Cydnus where Cleopatra first 'pursed up' (2.2.194) his commander's heart, Enobarbus says:

> The barge she sat in, like a burnished throne
> Burned on the water. The poop was beaten gold;
> Purple the sails, and so perfumèd that
> The winds were love-sick with them. The oars were
>   silver,
> Which to the tune of flutes kept stroke, and made
> The water which they beat to follow faster,
> As amorous of their strokes.   (2.2.198–204)

As many have recognized, this extravagant imagery cleaves closely to Shakespeare's source. Yet, where North's Plutarch reads like the inventory of a royal treasury, 'the poope wherof was gold, the sailes of purple, the owers of silver', Enobarbus's speech is a fever dream of enchanted objects vying for erotic union with their numinous mistress.[1] The queen exerts such centripetal force that

> The city cast
> Her people out upon her, and Antony,
> Enthroned i' th' market-place, did sit alone,
> Whistling to th' air, which but for vacancy
> Had gone to gaze on Cleopatra too,
> And made a gap in nature.   (2.2.20–5)

What is this power that induces the otherwise plain-spoken Roman soldier to describe air yearning to rush forth and drink in the sights? What force drives the people to abandon the already enthroned Antony to a dangerous vacuum, to swarm the barge, which only *resembles* a burnished throne, and throng the wild banks of the river in a manner that makes the market a dull alternative?

The spectre of mass enchantment suggests that this force is charisma: the not entirely legitimate gift of grace associated, since Max Weber, with political authority. Like other Shakespearian accounts of charismatic performance, from the 'new-made King' Bolingbroke's entry to London in *Richard II* (5.2.45), to Coriolanus's triumphal return to Rome, the power Enobarbus describes is both focused and barely contained.[2] Unlike other such accounts, however, the character at its centre is female. Some of the most virtuosic charismatic performances in the canon are adduced to Cleopatra, yet she tends to be overlooked in this respect.[3] This is due, perhaps, to the frustrating opacity for which even her most admiring commentators feel compelled to apologize.[4] We do not

---

[1] 'The Life of Marcus Antonius', in *Plutarch's Lives of the Noble Grecians and Romans Englished by Sir Thomas North, Anno* (1579), vol. 6 (New York, 1967), p. 25.

[2] *Richard II*, 5.2.7–21; *Coriolanus*, 2.1.202–18. Studies of charisma in Shakespeare tend to focus on the tragedies and histories. One exception is Richard Burt's 'Charisma, Coercion, and Comic Form in *The Taming of the Shrew*', *Criticism*, 26 (1984), 295–311.

[3] Raphael Falco's chapter in *Charismatic Authority in Early Modern English Tragedy* (Baltimore, MD, 2000) is one exception, although it extends a familiar assumption that Cleopatra's charisma is significantly more erotic and therefore less political than the male variety (pp. 172, 178).

[4] For example, Barbara Bono concedes to critical complaints that 'her motives are never completely clear' (*Literary Transvaluation: From Virgilian Epic to Shakespearean Tragicomedy* (Berkeley, CA, 1984), p. 184), while Sara Munson Deats notes that even Cleopatra's admirers tend to treat her 'as an archetype and emblem, rather than a complex,

know Cleopatra's motives, or whether to attribute her performances to impulse or design, because she lacks the soliloquies charismatic characters usually employ to interpret their own actions.

This absence is usually attributed to Shakespeare's ambivalence toward his sources, from Plutarch to the late Elizabeth Tudor, but what if Shakespeare maintains our distance strategically, in order to foreground the technique and effects of charismatic political theatre?[5] If *Antony and Cleopatra* extends a meditation on charisma, seen as early as *1 Henry VI*, perhaps our distance from the queen is a kind of proto-Brechtian countermeasure to the fog of identification. Similarly, the focus on a female character tends to foreground charisma's *function* as an extraordinary politics that operates *beside* normative (patriarchal) politics, for being queen in this period does not automatically confer the degree of authority Cleopatra wields. It is charisma, as much as the Roman order she adapts, that baits her political angling.

This chapter posits *Antony and Cleopatra* as, in part, Shakespeare's exploration of how charisma works. Focusing on a scenario,[6] or set-piece, of regal femininity which links Cleopatra to Elizabeth I, Shakespeare reveals a dialectic of play that renders the imaginative space of charismatic performance transformative for queens and commoners alike. I explore the latter potential especially in the second half of this study, where I demonstrate how the charismatic performances of even non-elite Quaker women foster a collective expansion of the possible. Quaker women's success, like Elizabeth's, confirms what *Antony and Cleopatra* suggests: that charisma permits the disruption of norms because it is based on the collaborative exchanges of performance.[7] Charisma enchants not as a by-product of delusional mass submission but, on the contrary, because it articulates and materializes communal aspirations.

To prepare for the above analyses, the section that follows suggests where extant theories of charisma remain useful, and where they might be revised to account more satisfactorily for the seemingly intractable contradictions apparent in the

critical literature. By approaching charisma as a type of deep play, I naturalize what is popularly pathologized, and recover the communal, creative potential Shakespeare seems to intuit.

ENCHANTED STAGES

Charisma, like performance, has a long history of exercising its best students' capacity for definition. We find works that discuss something like charisma as early as Plato's *Republic*, and premodern meditations from Longinus to Bacon raise versions of the questions that continue to vex modern commentary:[8] is charisma a psychological or a social phenomenon? Is it the personal quality of

---

interiorized character' (*Antony and Cleopatra: New Critical Essays* (New York, 2005), p. 17).

[5] Arguing that the death of Elizabeth I is the 'precondition' for the play, Katherine Eggert revisits key studies of the resemblance between the two queens in *Showing Like a Queen: Female Authority and Literary Experiment in Shakespeare, Spenser and Milton* (Philadelphia, 1999), pp. 132–4. For a list of historical incidents on which comparisons are typically drawn, see Helen Morris, 'Queen Elizabeth I "Shadowed" in Cleopatra', *Huntington Library Quarterly*, 32 (1969), 271–8; pp. 271–2.

[6] I borrow 'scenario' from performance theorist Diana Taylor to denote the 'formulaic structures' of repeatable behaviour that inform social roles (*The Archive and the Repertoire: Performing Cultural Memory in the Americas* (Durham, NC, 2003), pp. 19–28). Scenarios make up the larger 'repertoire' by which we transfer cultural knowledge in ways that exceed the 'archive' of written, built or filmed records. The repertoire includes 'gestures, orality, movement, dance, [and] singing' (p. 37).

[7] I argue that charisma draws on the dynamic of performance, or 'theatricality', discussed shortly. For an overview of debates around these terms, see Tracy C. Davis and Thomas Postlewait, 'Theatricality: An Introduction', in *Theatricality*, ed. Tracy C. Davis and Thomas Postlewait (Cambridge, 2003), pp. 1–39. Both a cognitive operation and a social relation, what I term 'performance' is closest to Josette Féral's 'theatricality' ('Foreword', *SubStance*, 31, special issue 'Theatricality' (2002), 3–13).

[8] Dionysius Longinus, *On the Sublime*, trans. Stephen Halliwell, Loeb Classical Library 199 (Cambridge, MA, 1995), p. 162; *Francis Bacon: The Major Works including New Atlantis and the Essays*, ed. Brian Vickers (Oxford, 1996), p. 445. Early modern theorists include Castiglione, Machiavelli and Bacon.

an exceptional individual or mass delusion? Is its nature primarily religious or political? Does it thwart or stimulate critical thought?[9] To begin to think through these apparent contradictions, I start by noting that some of the most nuanced insights still belong to Weber, charisma's first and best-known modern investigator.

Weber's initial theory of charisma is instructive, not only for its resistance to the above dichotomies, but also for the political implications of its history of revision. Weber's emphasis in his final years seems to have influenced most readers to overlook the importance of reception in the early version of charisma in *Economy and Society*, where it is not so clearly a personal power.[10] The charismatic leader appears to be 'endowed with supernatural [or] superhuman' qualities. Yet, as Weber insists, these attributes are merely '*thought of*' as the basis for power. In fact, charisma resides in the 'recognition' its name designates as *charis* – a 'gift of grace', which extends *not* from the Christian deity but from the many '*subject to* charismatic authority'. Thus, while charisma describes an authority that operates 'outside the realm of everyday routine and the profane sphere', its power comes, importantly, from below, making charisma communitarian.[11]

This complex, yet underdeveloped version of Weberian charisma has not gone entirely unrecognized.[12] Most relevant to present purposes is political theorist Andreas Kalyvas's inclusion of Weber's early thinking in a 'politics of the extraordinary', in which Weberian charisma, refined by Schmitt's 'constituent power' and Arendt's 'new beginnings', is identified as the force that allows radical, democratic mobilizations to redefine the content and aims of community.[13] For Kalyvas, Weber's abandonment of charisma's collective power after 1913 in all but his writing on religion speaks to his growing distrust of the multitude. His work with the Weimar Republic and the precipitous rise of National Socialism convinced Weber of charisma's danger. In its ability to move people to overturn not just the legal and bureaucratic machinery of state but also the perception of reality itself, charisma could empower demagogues to act on a people's darkest fantasies. Weber's

response was to focus his political writing on normative bureaucratic and juridical politics, against which charismatic movements could be delegitimized as a threat to political stability, a tool for Caesarian domination.[14] From this vantage point, the shift in Weber's thought appears not as the revision of a fundamentally flawed analysis but as a (perhaps) paternalistic response to the perceived threat of abuse.

It is precisely charisma's collective capacity to shape the world, socially and materially, that draws Kalyvas, like Bourdieu before him, to revisit

---

[9] The best-known example of the first question is Clifford Geertz's complaint about reducing Weber to either psychological or sociological terms; see 'Centers, Kings and Charisma: Reflections on the Symbolics of Power', in *Culture and its Creators: Essays in Honor of Edward Shils*, ed. Joseph Ben-David and Terry Nichols Clark (Chicago, 1977), 150–71; pp. 50–1. C. Stephen Jaeger adopts an admirably mixed approach in *Enchantment: On Charisma and the Sublime* (Philadelphia, 2012), but with interests that are more aesthetic and modernist than mine. The second question concerns what Falco calls the 'central paradox' of early modern tragedy: the clash between group ideal and charismatic leader's individuality (*Charismatic Authority*, p. 1). The question of charisma's religious or political basis seems unnecessarily exclusive to Andreas Kalyvas, *Democracy and the Politics of the Extraordinary: Max Weber, Carl Schmitt, and Hannah Arendt* (Cambridge, 2008). On the final question of charisma and critical thinking is where I depart from all here but Kalyvas.

[10] Among those who read charisma as a personality trait that inspires primitive, religious frenzy, are Wolfgang J. Mommsen, *The Age of Bureaucracy: Perspectives on the Political Sociology of Max Weber* (New York, 1974), pp. 72–94, and Luciano Cavalli, 'Charisma and Twentieth-Century Politics', in *Max Weber: Rationality and Modernity*, ed. Sam Whimster and Scott Lash (London, 1987), pp. 317–33; p. 318.

[11] Max Weber, *Economy and Society* (1921), in *The Theory of Social and Economic Organization*, trans. A. M. Henderson and Talcott Parsons (New York, 1947), pp. 359–61. The italics in the quotation are mine.

[12] See, for example, Pierre Bourdieu's sparse but trenchant comments in *Language and Symbolic Power*, trans. Gino Raymond and Matthew Adamson (Cambridge, 1991) and *In other Words: Essays Towards a Reflexive Sociology*, trans. Matthew Adamson (Stanford, CA, 1990).

[13] Kalyvas, *Democracy*, p. 10.

[14] Weber, *Economy and Society*, pp. 1119, 154.

Weber's early work.[15] My interest in the mechanics of performance makes my approach somewhat different. Specifically, I want to press Weber's insight that the way charisma shapes communities 'from within', transforming their symbolic and ethical foundations, begins with 'a subjective or internal reorientation' of the regulatory fictions that frame the world.[16]

First, we need to take seriously Weber's description of the 'magical' sensation of the 'gift of grace', and consider it in terms of the exchanges that connect individuals, creating groups. Second, we need to recognize that the analytical method of focusing on either a charismatic leader *or* a follower imposes a narrow fixity that is at odds with what is a dynamic, dialectical process. What is required, I suggest, is an approach specifically attuned to interpersonal dynamics and the effect of repeated events; a method that posits continuity between the mundane interactions which are its usual study, and heightened religious or aesthetic experience.

On the basis of his clinical observations of children, D. W. Winnicott noted that the 'play' that first occurs between a child and its primary caregiver lays the groundwork for 'what will always be important' in adult life, namely, the imaginative work at the heart of cultural experiences, from art to religion.[17] The 'transitional space' created during play is neither 'inner psychic reality' nor 'external world', so actions that transpire there are invested with dream meaning and feeling. This sensation intensifies when an other, perceived as sharing transitional space, interacts through an object as solid as a security blanket or as fleeting as a smile, in a way that seems to anticipate or mirror the child's desires.[18] Play becomes truly social when the (m)other begins to introduce ideas of her own into the game, rupturing narcissistic omnipotence with the 'to and fro' of reciprocal work, the unpredictable excitement of being *with*. Coaxed to accommodate new objects and ideas, the child learns to tolerate the frustration of compromise. Through the repetition of such play, s/he discovers that objects in transitional space, including the other, are trustworthily responsive

but also 'the not-me' that establishes a sense of reality.[19] Play satisfies most profoundly when tension is maintained between the enchanted internal world and the hardy external one, bridging the real and the phantasmal. This accounts for Weber's magic, a sensation subsequent social scientists have associated with both religious and political enthusiasm.

Weber also underscores the importance of a dialectic between the mirroring and rupture of convention when he notes: 'every charismatic authority subscribe[s] to the proposition, "It is written ... but I say unto you ..."'[20] Once we affirm a shared tradition, our concession to the other's novel idea ('I say unto you') may create affective bonds that put us 'beside ourselves'.[21] As part of a collective, we may then forge, as in Artaud's theatre, 'the chain between what is and what is not, between the virtuality of the possible and what already exists in materialised nature'.[22] Play, then, is the blueprint for theatrical performance and collaborative politics, actions initiated, like good theatre, by our initial recognition – the gift of attention with which we grace an other.

Charisma's to and fro motility reveals the limitation of approaches that fixate on a single element: actor or participant, mirror or rupture. Our play

---

[15] Kalyvas, *Democracy*, pp. 24–5; Bourdieu, like Kalyvas, reads charisma as dialogic, between individual and group (*Language and Symbolic Power*, p. 129).

[16] Weber, *Economy and Society*, pp. 1116, 363.

[17] D. W. Winnicott, *Playing and Reality* (London, 1971), pp. 12, 51. Féral also adapts Winnicott's transitional space as the cognitive 'framing' of quotidian space that initiates theatrical experience ('Theatricality', p. 98).

[18] Winnicott, *Playing*, pp. 111–17. This magic also occurs in solo play with a 'transitional object', like the famed security blanket (p. 233).

[19] Winnicott, *Playing*, pp. 47–8.

[20] Weber, *Economy and Society*, pp. 361, 755.

[21] Judith Butler's communitarian politics urge a decentring of the self through emotions that 'bind us to others, transport us, undo us, implicate us in lives that are not our own' (*Precarious Life: The Powers of Mourning and Violence* (New York, 2004), p. 25).

[22] Antonin Artaud, *The Theater and its Double*, trans. Mary Caroline Richards (New York, 1958), p. 27.

model resists narrowing charisma to a characteristic like charm by locating its suprarational effects in the exchange of conventional symbols and allusions: a repertoire of cultural knowledge. As the primal scene for communal experience, play locates rupture within a healthy range of social activity. This seems important given the tendency to pathologize charisma as mass enthralment. It is, ostensibly, this peril that motivates the last of the dichotomous questions with which I opened this section: whether charisma fosters or suppresses critical thinking. This question, like those before it, seeks to freeze a process whose contours unfold only over time. Is there a *moment* in the oscillation of this dialectic that 'uncouples the critical sense, [and] overrides judgment . . . lessen[ing] individual will', as many contend?[23] Certainly. This is Longinus's lightning bolt of sublimity, the psychic blow that shatters our composure. But while charisma may temporarily arrest our critical faculties, it ultimately stimulates them.

Rather than make this case through more abstract exposition, I want to return to Enobarbus's Act 2 attempt to convey to Maecenas and Agrippa how the sight of Cleopatra 'beggared all description' (2.2.205). The trope of ineffability is familiar period shorthand for the shock of encounter, yet Enobarbus's description of her 'O'er-picturing that Venus where we see / The fancy outwork nature' (207–8) forecloses the possibility of mere platitude. The painting alluded to is Apelles's *Venus Anadyomene*, which Shakespeare knew through Pliny – an image Enobarbus has internalized by the time he claims the queen exceeds its charms by as much as Apelles's work was said to have surpassed its model. Notably, to relay the queen's extraordinary effect, Enobarbus turns to the critical method of comparison and contrast.

A rupture Enobarbus does not relay, but one which some in Shakespeare's audience can be expected to have known, is Cleopatra's refusal to appear where she has been summoned. As Linda Woodbridge reminds us, social situatedness is often literalized in this period, rendering where a person stands, walks or reclines something of an index of

their political power.[24] It is significant, therefore, that Cleopatra appears not in the Tarsian square where Antony expects to upbraid her for aiding Cassius and Brutus against Caesar, but on the river. Nor does she sit contritely, but lolls amidst symbols that move Enobarbus and others to recognize her Cytherean qualities. In return for bracketing off the Cydnus as enchanted space, Enobarbus seems to see gold burn on the water, masochistic waves trail after oars that beat them, lovesick winds flock to the sails, and tackle tumesce in 'flower-soft hands' (2.2.217). This is no unmediated utterance of astonishment but an experience reconstructed in tranquility. The account contains as many similes, leaving room for doubt – her gentlewomen are '*like* the Nereides' (213) – as transformative metaphors, revealing the vicissitudes of Enobarbus's judgement.

The anecdote moves Agrippa to recall how Cleopatra charmed the previous Caesar to forgo war for love, a memory which, in turn, elicits this peculiar recollection:

ENOBARBUS.   I saw her once
  Hop forty paces through the public street,
  And having lost her breath, she spoke and panted,
  That she did make defect perfection,
  And breathless, pour breath forth.   (2.2.235–9)

Those familiar with Venus's gait in *The Aeneid*, or with the many early modern echoes wherein aristocratic women are mistaken for goddesses, recognize how Cleopatra ruptures convention. Significantly, she impresses not by walking like a goddess but by bringing off a gait which Enobarbus's tone suggests ill suits most ladies. The queen who can out-Venus Venus turns out to be the one who can make the 'vilest things / Become themselves in her' (244–5). To understand

---

[23] Jaeger, *Enchantment*, p. 22.

[24] Linda Woodbridge discusses place and mobility in 'Imposters, Monsters, and Spies: What Rogue Literature can Tell us about Early Modern Subjectivity', *Early Modern Literary Studies*, 9, special issue 'Interactive Early Modern Literary Studies Dialogues' (2002), http://purl.oclc.org/emls/iemls/dialogues/01/woodbridge.html, accessed 11 March 2016.

how Cleopatra's breathless exertions redeem human imperfection, we need to recognize that this street performance, accrued to performances past, relies on juridical work done by one who grants Cleopatra the gift of grace to alter the repertoire of regal femininity. Enobarbus's critical recreation and affirmation of Cleopatra's hop makes hopping a queenly possibility ever after.

SCENARIO I: THE ROYAL HAND

From here, I would like to turn quickly to the kind of account Shakespeare may have used to refresh his memory of Elizabeth Tudor after her death. Bernard Garter's festival book, *The ioyful receiving of the Queenes most excellent Maiestie* (1578), is not the most famous of such accounts, but offers a strong version of the type of political performance Shakespeare seems to work through in *Antony and Cleopatra* nearly thirty years later. Elizabeth was 45 years old when she first visited Norwich, by size and prosperity the 'second city' of the realm.[25] She had had twenty years to master the craft of political performance but, as some have noted, an East Anglian progress was by no means an assured success. The region was a hotbed for puritans and recusants. The patriarch of the most powerful local family, the Earl of Norfolk, had been executed only six years earlier for his part in the Ridolfi Plot, and several locals remained under suspicion. Complicating matters were the crown's marriage negotiations with the Catholic Duke of Anjou, the last to be entertained with the like level of seriousness. The French delegation was invited to accompany the queen and it was an open secret that Alençon himself was to meet the party and woo her in person.[26]

The political intricacies of this progress have raised speculation that the queen and her council hoped to play the expected staunch Protestantism of Norwich residents against Anjou's expressed demand to remain Catholic in marriage. Others have suggested that consideration of Anjou's proposal was itself a tactic designed to keep this younger brother of France out of the conflict between Lowland rebels and their Spanish

Catholic overlords.[27] I mention these difficulties to emphasize the highly charged nature of such events, and the conflicting interests of those involved. Elizabeth's ultimately successful use of political performance is not, to my mind, diminished by acknowledging with critics like William Leahy that even 'propagandistic' accounts like Garter's show traces of disunity.[28] Charisma is unlikely ever to have been universally overwhelming.

In the tradition of festival books, Garter captures the splendour of the progress's entry. We are treated to the cheers of the citizens and the richly appointed procession of city fathers before the 'terrestriall paradise' of streets beautified with the queen's colours and insignia.[29] The mutual displays of affection between Elizabeth and her people are quasi-conventional since Mulcaster's pre-coronation book, but given that moments of apparent monarchical improvisation appear in stories by ambassadors disinclined to flatter England, this feature seems more than conventional. At the first pageant, in which adult and child performers showcased the city's manufacture of woollen fabrics, from taffeta to 'Tuft Mockado', Elizabeth stepped close and 'particularlye viewed' the spinning and weaving. She heard the boy

---

25 B[ernard] G[arter], *The ioyfull receyuing of the Queenes most excellent Maiestie into hir Highnesse citie of Norvvich* (London, 1578), STC (2nd edn), 11627, title page. For historical context, see Zillah Dovey's *An Elizabethan Progress: The Queen's Journey into East Anglia, 1578* (Madison, WI, 1996).

26 Dovey, *Progress*, p. 62.

27 *Elizabeth I and her Age*, ed. Susan M. Felch and Donald V. Stump (New York, 2009), p. 238; and Dovey, *Progress*, p. 16.

28 William Leahy, *Elizabethan Triumphal Processions* (Aldershot, 2005), is the most provocative of a number of studies, like *Dissing Elizabeth: Negative Representations of Gloriana*, ed. Julia Walker (Durham, NC, 1998), that problematize the cult of Elizabeth. Leahy's admonition against taking encomiastic work at face value is salubrious, but his claim that certain spectators' failure to be 'interpellated by [Elizabeth's] spectacular presence' signifies a 'failure' of performance is less convincing, not least because it misreads Althusser, for whom there are always some individuals who do *not* respond to the hail (pp. 86, 90).

29 Garter, *ioyfull*, sig. A2v.

representing the Commonwealth of Norwich, and gave 'great thanks' to the people.[30] While this set the tone for her responsiveness, a speech later that week moved her to call the French and 'divers English Lords' to her side, where she 'willed them to harken, and she hirselfe was very attentive, even untill the end therof'.[31]

This oration, by Master Stephen Limbert of the grammar school, was probably delivered off schedule, as he seemed flustered at greeting her, after her party was rained out of an excursion to Mount Surrey. '[H]ir Maiestie drewe neare unto him and, thinking him fearfull, saide graciously unto him: "Bee not afeared". He aunswered hir againe in English: "I thanke your Maiestie, for your good encouragement", and then with good courage entred into [his] oration.'[32] The main conceit of Limbert's speech compared Elizabeth to the life-giving Nile, source of the enriching rivers of 'godlynesse, justice, [and] humilitie'. He praised her for keeping England out of the wars, and extolled her addition of land to the city's hospital for the poor, insisting that if she could see the 'hidden' 'creckes' of the citizens' minds, she would find infinite good will in those 'narrow straightes'.[33] Thanking the schoolmaster, the queen replied, 'It is the best that ever I heard, you shal haue my hande', and she 'pulled off hir gloue, and gaue him hir hand to kisse'. She then returned immediately to her lodgings, appearing no more that evening, save to inquire after Limbert's name. She left the city on Friday with the 'water standing in her eies'.[34]

Garter's account illustrates both the specular and disruptive moments of charismatic performance. The decorations and pageants reflect the inherited world, reproducing royal iconography: Elizabeth as justice-dealing biblical heroine, font of all virtue, blended Tudor rose. The queen, in her performance of royal but attentive affect, mirrors, in turn, the people's hopes. For Jonathan Goldberg, accounts like Norwich demonstrate how Elizabeth made ordinary people her 'co-partners' in a 'mutual exchange of affective gifts'.[35] What he implies, and what accounts like Garter's suggest, is that a not inconsiderable part of her charisma derived from her performance of ideal reception. She offers gestic and verbal feedback, and forces auditor roles upon those accustomed to being the centre of attention.

Playing to the city's expectations, Elizabeth embodies the role of Norwich's high sovereign, mirroring through approval their production of her charismatic authority. She also confirms Norwich's ego ideal: industrious Protestant masters of manufacturing and commerce. Limbert, who represents Everycitizen in his oration, is seen loving and being loved by the monarch, thanking and being thanked by one whose charismatic presence, 'creates the illusion of full participation in a higher kind of life'.[36] Both psychoanalytic and political theorists tell us that this relational recognition of self in the other transforms from the inside out, linking individuals to community. In Norwich and as Norwich, Limbert appears as the object that satisfies the queen's desire because for the luminous moment of the kiss, he is that object.

Yet, in offering her hand to a commoner, a favour not granted to either the mayor or other Norwich dignitaries, Elizabeth alters the frame of convention, opening the scene to new possibilities for action and identification. The hand-kiss ruptures the reflection of her entry in a moment that blurs boundaries between participant and player, between working port city and its distant, dazzling other, the royal court, as the two converge at the city gate. Peter Stallybrass and Ann Rosalind Jones remind us that extension of the naked hand in early modern courtly etiquette was a mark of great favour, especially when emphasized by the erotic gesture of pulling off the glove.[37] Indeed,

---

[30] Garter, *ioyfull*, sig. B7.   [31] Garter, *ioyfull*, sig. Ev.
[32] Garter, *ioyfull*, sig. D2v.   [33] Garter, *ioyfull*, sig. E1r.
[34] Garter, *ioyfull*, sigs. E1v and F1v.
[35] Jonathan Goldberg, *James I and the Politics of Literature* (Baltimore, MD, 1983), p. 29. Unlike James I, Elizabeth 'provided a mirror of the people's hopes and wishes in her attentiveness to the pageants' (p. 30).
[36] Jaeger, *Enchantment*, p. 18.
[37] Peter Stallybrass and Ann Rosalind Jones, 'Fetishizing the Glove in Renaissance Europe', *Critical Inquiry*, 28 (2001), 114–32; p. 124.

this is how Shakespeare's Antony understands it in Act 3, when he orders Caesar's messenger whipped for his presumption to kiss that 'kingly seal' which a servant 'that will take rewards' should 'shake' to look upon (3.13.126, 124, 141). Given Elizabeth's expertise in 'the silent language of the hand', it seems not unreasonable to suppose that for Limbert's oration, which reflects Elizabeth *Regina*'s best self, she marks him with a public gesture with which he will likely be identified for the rest of his life.[38] Her charisma rubs off on those she touches, in much the same way the royal touch was believed to have healing powers that could pass even to coins.[39] At the same time, the gesture's reiteration of her 'stately stouping to the meanest sort' renews the charismatic bond through which Elizabeth, in part, receives her power.[40]

Moving from Garter's account to Shakespeare's more self-consciously fictionalized one reveals how the latter exposes the inner workings of the former. Focusing on two closely related scenes in the play, we find that, to produce the charismatic effect, the enchanting mirror image must be offered and accepted, but what Shakespeare suggests hundreds of years before Weber, is that charismatic political performance also requires a felicitous rupture that puts us beside ourselves, where new perspectives may be considered.

Like Limbert's oration, Act 2, Scene 5 revolves around a disruptive use of the royal hand. The scene opens in Cleopatra's court, where an eagerly awaited messenger has arrived from Rome. The queen greets him with the following statement of conditions: if he bears the good news that Antony is 'free and healthful', he will have gold and '[m]y bluest veins to kiss – a hand that kings / Have lipped, and trembled kissing' (2.5.38, 29–30). She also warns that for bad news, 'The gold I give thee will I melt and pour / Down thy ill-uttering throat' (33–4). Unfortunately for the honest messenger, the news he carries is of Antony's marriage to Octavia. Cleopatra strikes him, curses him and ignoring his pleas for 'patience' responds with more blows and increasingly hyperbolic threats (62). When she brandishes a knife, the messenger flees. Five scenes later, coaxed back into the royal

presence, the messenger has changed his tune. Pumped for information about Octavia, he asserts that the new bride 'creeps' rather than strides in 'majesty', that her face is 'round, even to faultiness', and that she possesses a forehead 'as low as she would wish it' (3.3.18, 30, 33). For this depiction, he is rewarded with praise, gold and the promise of future employment.

As Katherine Eggert and others have shown, scene 2.5 emphatically eroticizes the courtly gesture.[41] In this, it recalls the Petrarchan politics and mercurial caprice of the recently deceased monarch. By replacing the hand-kiss with a blow, and dilating the moment to imagine the after-effects of this rupture, Shakespeare reveals the potentiality at the core of the performance. This enables us to make sense, retrospectively, of the political force of Elizabeth's theatrics at Norwich. I suggest that Cleopatra's blows violently, but no less literally, collapse the space between servant and queen, disrupting the hierarchy of ordinary politics to momentarily close social distance. We are made privy, through the intimacy of this problematic variety of touch, to how rupture can liberate the commoner in the serious play of the charismatic relationship. Cleopatra's blows induce him to see a new possibility in the messenger function: invention rather than reportage. In the space deterritorialized by the slap, the creative servant may enchant with fictions about the rival Octavia's homeliness. And if he becomes, in this respect, no more than the 'common liar' (1.1.62) denounced

---

[38] Mary Hazard, *Elizabethan Silent Language* (Lincoln, NE, 2000), p. 7. Hazard cites more examples of the queen's expert deployment of this gesture, including her refusal to honour the anti-Protestant Bishop Bonner during her pre-coronation entry (pp. 7–8, 204).

[39] For Elizabeth's ambivalence toward the superstition of the curative royal touch, see Stephen Deng, *Coinage and State Formation in Early Modern English Literature* (New York, 2011), pp. 137–44.

[40] Sir John Hayward, *Annals of the First Four Years of the Reign of Queen Elizabeth*, ed. John Bruce, Camden Society First Series, 7 (London, 1840), pp. 6–7.

[41] Eggert, *Showing Like a Queen*, pp. 133, 136.

by the Roman Demetrius at the play's beginning, it is not a role the play itself condemns.[42]

While the messenger revises his role, the enchanted space also frees the queen to become something other than royal Egypt – in this case an ordinary, jealous lover, competing with her rival. Shakespeare reveals that the queen's desire to rupture the messenger's reflection of impervious, regal femininity may be no less urgent than her servant's desire for her favour. On the contrary, Cleopatra's desire, as perceived by the messenger post-slap, becomes the *condition* of his transformation, from deliverer of news to a more valued gossip whose inventions are precisely what the queen deems 'fit for [the] business' (3.3.36) of keeping long-distance love alive.

AMBIGUOUS VISIBLES

I turn now to performers who substantiate the more radical implications of Shakespeare's meditation: that because transcendence of social norms derives from the serious play of a performance dialectic, charisma is ultimately communitarian and transformative even for the non-elite. Like queens, pre-Restoration Quaker women warrant their performance of charismatic authority through the reflection and revision of theological conventions already powerful in the cultural imaginary. Yet, lacking royal resources, Quakers patently reject status-based exceptionalism and embrace a scenario that allows for what social anthropologist Athena Athanasiou calls 'plural performativity', socially transformative performance inextricable from the collective.[43] To understand how this choice instrumentalizes performance which, in turn, allows Quaker women to rearticulate their political identities, we must know something about the doctrine which justifies this.

Weber observed that charismatic social movements target the emancipatory aspirations of their audience.[44] This was certainly true of Quakerism. Fundamental to what drew women in particular – Quakers' public activism, eschewal of social stratification and deeply affective spirituality – was the doctrine of Inner Light. Extending earlier Protestant iterations of the 'light of conscience',

Quakers believed themselves recipients of 'the light of Christ', a divine power that induced the 'quaking' of their group's moniker, and offered the chance for a prelapsarian 'perfection' unimaginable from the vantage point of the Calvinist doctrine of depravity.[45] This internal Christ called women as readily as men to demonstrate obedience, whether it meant travelling to distant corners of the world, organizing petitions or donning sackcloth and ashes as a sign of the Lord's immanent wrath.

Consequently, women were at the forefront of the movement from its inception in the unusually tolerant atmosphere following the abolition of the English prelacy in 1642. The Inner Light provided a basis for Quakers' radical assertion of a universal spiritual equality that rendered all social difference 'outward' form, and all co-religionists Friends.[46] Consequently, they eschewed all '*fashion[s] of the world*' that sought to place man above man: all forms of 'honour which is from below'.[47] Hailing

---

[42] See Janet Adelman's influential argument that characters' presentation of competing accounts blurs the hard distinctions audiences expect between truth and fiction (*The Common Liar: An Essay on 'Antony and Cleopatra'* (New Haven, CT, 1973), p. 30).

[43] Athena Athanasiou defines plural performativity as occurring when 'the collective demand [that] emerges from . . . singular histories, becomes something plural' without effacing the 'personal and the singular' (*Dispossession: The Performative in the Political, Judith Butler, Conversations with Athena Athanasiou* (Cambridge, 2013), p. 157).

[44] Max Weber, *Sociology of Religion*, trans. Ephraim Fischoff (Boston, MA, 1993), p. 102.

[45] Rosemary Moore, *The Light in their Consciences* (University Park, PN, 2011), stresses the cross-pollination and inter-group movement between Familists, Anabaptists, Quakers, etc., in the revolutionary era more than pioneering studies like William Braithwaite, *The Beginnings of Quakerism*, 2nd edn (Cambridge, 1961). The name Quaker, like Puritan, began as a slur. Self-identifying as Children of Light, or Friends, Quakers eventually adopted the pejorative term as a badge of honour.

[46] Phyllis Mack, *Visionary Women: Ecstatic Prophecy in Seventeenth-Century England* (Berkeley, CA, 1992; repr. 1995), p. 157; Moore, *Light*, pp. 80–1.

[47] George Fox, *Some Principles of the Elect people of God who in scorn are called Quakers, for all people throughout all Christendome to read over, and thereby their own states to consider*, Library of the

mostly from middling or serving-class backgrounds, and therefore amongst those most burdened by displays of deference, Quakers must have found adherence to inward truth almost immediately liberating. Their refusal to bow, use honorary titles, or replace 'thou' with the honorific 'you' when addressing superiors, contributed to their pre-Restoration reputation as troublemakers and disturbers of the peace.[48] 'Hat honour' became a trial of faith when hauled before authorities for vagrancy or disruption of church services, as often occurred. Mary Tompkins, ordered by a magistrate to remove her hat, swept it from her head and cast it to the ground. Stamping on it, she declared, 'See I have your honour under my feet'.[49] In one swift action, Tompkins seizes the common signifier of deference to literalize her contempt for it, then glosses her gesture to avoid misconstrual. The way outward things, or 'visibles', could mask inward truth was, for Quakers, an embodied conundrum from the start.

The notion, then, that the Quaker concern with inward things rendered the outward insignificant is an oversimplification.[50] Early Quakerism was not a *contemptus mundi* religion but sought, as Hugh Barbour writes, 'to transform the world, not to shut it out'.[51] Their apprehension of difference between spiritual and carnal forms allowed for something like a critical distance from discursive constructions of cultural institutions and the bodies these sought to control. The performance of 'signs and wonders' to legitimize their calling depended not on the 'transcendence' of materiality, but on its reinscription.[52] Detractors famously attacked the group's condemnation of conventional structures, from steeples to aristocratic fashions, but, if iconoclastic negation was all Quakers performed, the movement would have played itself out quickly. Instead, their ability to positively resignify the mundane in a way desirable to those outside the group lent them charisma and staying power.

SCENARIO II: THE PROPHETIC SIGN

Like the female monarchs who interested Shakespeare, Quaker women cannily established a protective conventional frame for their performances. Acts of 'prophecy', denoting not so much prognostication as 'biblical exegesis' and the calls to repentance issued by those summoned by God, fed cultural assumptions about feminine receptivity, self-sacrifice and unlettered wisdom.[53] It granted adepts authority as a form of spiritual exceptionalism. In this, Quaker women tapped a larger English tradition whose more spectacular examples include Margery Kemp, Anne Askew, the Holy Maid of Kent and Anna Trapnel.[54] The doctrine of the Inner Light, however, allowed Quaker women to position their exceptionalism more firmly within contemporary social conventions. Therefore, while Patricia Crawford is right to caution us not to conflate 'secular' with spiritual equality, the fact

---

Society of Friends, London (hereafter LSF) (London, 1661), pp. 4–6.

[48] Thomas Underhill lists typical Quaker disturbances in *Hell Broke Loose: or An history of the Quakers both old and new*, LSF (London, 1660), pp. 30–2.

[49] George Bishope relays the incident in *New England judged, not by man's, but the spirit of the Lord: and the summe sealed up of New-England's persecutions*, LSF (London, 1661), p. 2.

[50] The contrast Kate Peters makes between spirit and flesh, for example, somewhat undermines her argument for print's central importance to the movement in *Print Culture and the Early Modern Quakers* (Cambridge, 2005), pp. 2, 135. Similarly, Mack writes that Quaker women alienated themselves from their gender (*Visionary*, pp. 172–8).

[51] Hugh Barbour, *The Quakers in Puritan England* (New Haven, CT, 1964), p. 15. Most Quaker histories describe a shift from radical, quasi-democratic beginnings in Nottinghamshire, 1647, to a more sober, routinized organization after 1660. Ann Hughes reminds us, however, that the Quaker desire for respectability was always mediated by the 'living, more radical tradition' of their inception. 'Early Quakerism: A Historian's Afterword', in *The Emergence of Quaker Writing: Dissenting Literature in Seventeenth-Century England*, ed. Thomas N. Corns and David Loewenstein (London, 1995), pp. 142–8; p. 147.

[52] Elaine Hobby, 'Prophecy, Enthusiasm, and Female Pamphleteers', in *The Cambridge Companion to Writing of the English Revolution*, ed. N. H. Keeble (Cambridge, 2001), pp. 162–78; p. 167.

[53] Kenneth Carroll, 'Early Quakers and "Going naked as a sign"', *Quaker History*, 67 (1978), 69–87; p. 70.

[54] See Diane Watt, *Secretaries of God: Women Prophets in Late Medieval and Early Modern England* (Suffolk, 1997).

is that 'prophecy' enlarged women's access to public roles, allowing ordinary women to occupy positions of leadership as travelling ministers, writers, agitators and administrators of funding and international events.[55]

For prophets who relied on the mystical Christ disseminated through his many-membered church, it was 'collective identity that mattered most'. They prized the intermittent dissolution of boundaries that isolated individuals from this unified body.[56] Prominent among these were the normative matrices of gender. The unusual 'fluidity of gender' in early Quakers has occasioned a significant amount of discussion, but evidence suggests that the Quaker understanding was more complex than the critical conclusion sometimes espoused that Quakers disavowed gender as a 'negative abstraction' without 'descriptive value for individual, sanctified women'.[57] It seems implausible, for example, to suppose seventeenth-century women believed they could 'circumvent traditional ideas about female inferiority' by simply performing masculinity.[58] On the contrary, Quaker women seem to have mirrored some gendered conventions in order to rupture others. Most did this not to elevate individual personality but to present their embodied activities, like those of their male counterparts, as the 'signs and wonders' Scripture extolled as the mark of true prophecy.[59]

It was widely known, for example, that Paul forbade women from speaking in church.[60] Yet, as one Quaker pamphlet defending female prophets explained, Quaker women, 'taught of God himself', 'who dwelleth in them, and walketh in them, and is their Teacher', demonstrated their obedience by proselytizing *wheresoever* moved to speak. Here, the wonder of the Inner Light suspends the Pauline proscription.[61] It is a rupture seen in practice nearly twenty years earlier, when Priscilla Cotton and Mary Cole addressed 'the Priests and People of England' from their jail cell in Exeter. Exploiting the cultural convention equating women with weakness, Cotton and Cole claim the Pauline ban is 'not spoke only of a Female', but rather, 'it's *weakness* that is the Woman by the scriptures forbidden' to speak in

church.[62] Weakness, for early Quakers, was an overdependence on book learning: the type gained at university and typically used to silence women. 'Indeed', Cotton and Cole assure the priests responsible for their incarceration, 'you *yourselves* are the women that are forbidden to speak in the church'. Stripped of their usual tactics by the resignification of 'Woman' as academic vanity, the priests 'railed on us with filthy speeches', 'becom[ing] women'.[63] In contrast, Cotton and Cole, authorized by the Inner Light, could wield 'the aggressive language of [male] Old Testament prophets' in church or other public spaces.[64]

This is clearly different from 'blending' 'sexual categories'.[65] Indeed, the 'wonder[ous]' point of

---

[55] Patricia Crawford, *Women and Religion in England, 1500–1720* (New York, 1993), p. 161.

[56] Mack, *Visionary*, p. 20; Moore, *Light*, p. 155. For an argument that Quaker gendering was a harbinger for modern 'queer' identities, see A. G. Myles, 'Border Crossings: The Queer Erotics of Quakerism in Seventeenth-Century New England', in *Long Before Stonewall: Histories of Same-sex Sexuality in Early America*, ed. Thomas A. Foster (New York, 2007), pp. 114–43.

[57] Crawford, *Women and Religion*, p. 180; Mack, *Visionary*, pp. 173, 177.

[58] Hobby, 'Prophecy', p. 166.

[59] For example, 2 Corinthians 12: 12, in which Paul invokes the 'signes, and wonders' that legitimize his mission. Also John 4: 48, and Daniel 3: 32, in which Daniel 'declare[s] the signes and wonders, that the hie God hathe wrought towarde me'. All biblical citations are from *The Geneva Bible: A facsimile of the 1560 edition* (Madison, WI, 1969).

[60] 'Let your women keep silence in the Churches: for it is not permitted unto them to speak' (1 Corinthians 14: 34–5).

[61] George Keith, *The Woman-Preacher of Samaria, a better preacher, and more sufficiently qualified to preach than any of the men-preachers of the man-made-ministry in these three nations*, LSF (London, 1674), p. 5. Margaret Fell's *Women's Speaking Justified* (1666) also defends female prophets, but I concur with those who find Fell 'more careful and conservative' than the prophets (Peters, *Print Culture*, p. 131).

[62] Priscilla Cotton and Mary Cole, *To the Priests and People we discharge our consciences, and give them warning*, LSF (London, 1655), pp. 6–7; italics mine.

[63] Cotton and Cole, *To the Priests*, pp. 7–8.

[64] Mack, *Visionary*, p. 187.

[65] Rachel Trubowitz, 'Female Preachers and Male Wives: Gender and Authority in Civil War England', in *Pamphlet*

a 'sign' is often the way it reiterates a beholder's internalized norm, in order to revise it. The very difference between the spectacular signifier, say, Cleopatra's slap, and its apparent signified, the proffered queenly hand, encourages participants to develop, through the interpretive work we saw modelled by Shakespeare's spectators, a new, more personally relevant meaning. Quakers invoked certain attitudes about corporeal femininity to justify the extraordinary work they accomplished in the world. When the prophet Dewance Morey describes her preaching as the miraculous communication of 'a poor, despised Earthen Vessel' through whom the Lord has seen fit to speak, she brings gender and status to the fore to reveal herself a sign of the Lord's power to use even 'the weak things of the world to confound the things which are mighty'.[66] Echoing Jonah,[67] Morey exhorts the king to 'come down from his Throne, and sit in the Dust' with her and repent:

O, *England*! Thy warning has been doubled . . . for I have also been made to go [through] thy Streets of *London* in sackcloth with dust upon my head, and a rod in my hand for a Sign unto thee; proclaiming that dreadful and terrible Famine that is swiftly coming on upon thee from the God of Life.[68]

Female prophets in cities from Bristol to Bridgetown testified in the streets, fasted publicly and appeared in churches and before Parliament with the dishevelled hair, bare limbs and symbolically overdetermined props that bespoke the immanence of divine judgement.[69] Prophets like Morey, who stressed their aversion to becoming such 'wondering stock[s]',[70] gained the additional licence of reluctant obedience.

The scenario that put this protection most sorely to the test was the practice of going 'naked' 'as a sign'.[71] That 'naked' was ever full nudity has been contested; it may, rather, have meant to strip to one's shift, or go about in sackcloth, without other covering.[72] The scenario was modelled, again, on Old Testament prophets like Isaiah of 20: 3, who battles his aversion to going 'naked, & barefote thre yeres, *as* a signe & wondre vpon Egypt, & Ethiopia'.[73] To go 'naked at the word

of the Lord' was to divest oneself of all 'garments through which class and gender were made visible', to decry the bareness of professions and worldly prestige while delivering a clarion call to repent.[74] It was, in other words, a highly confrontational act in which the flouting of social conventions, especially for women, fed opponents' assertions that Quakers were 'the most immodest, obscene, people in the world'.[75] As such, going naked was a high-risk performance undertaken more frequently by men than women. For the latter, who appear not to have committed their thoughts about the experience to paper, we rely on accounts by supportive male co-religionists and scandalized enemies. What all make abundantly clear, is the knife's edge of convention upon which these performances turned.

Prophets explained that the impulse to go naked arose in the conscience, where it gnawed until one 'durst not withstand' it.[76] Once the prophet complied, accounts typically describe the great dread

---

Wars: Prose in the English Revolution, ed. James Holstun (London, 1992), pp. 112–33; p. 119.

[66] Dewance Morey paraphrases 1 Corinthians 1: 27–8 in *A true and faithful WARNING from the Lord God, sounded through me, a poor despised Earthen Vessel, unto all the Inhabitants of England*, LSF (1665), p. 1.

[67] Jonah 3: 6–9.   [68] Morey, *True and faithful*, pp. 1, 5.

[69] For more on Quaker millenarianism and the use of props, from carrying lit torches at midday to smashing a pitcher at the door of Parliament to signify its immanent destruction, see Kenneth Carroll, 'Sackcloth and Ashes and Other Signs and Wonders', *Journal of the Friends Historical Society*, 53 (1975), 314–25.

[70] William Simpson, *From one who was moved of the Lord God to go a sign among the priests & professors of the Prophets, Apostles, and Christs WORDs*, LSF (London, 1659), p. 8.

[71] Simpson, *From one who was moved*, p. 8.

[72] Patricia Crawford and Laura Gowing, *Women's Worlds in Seventeenth-Century England* (New York, 1999), p. 256.

[73] Isaiah 20: 3.

[74] Francis Howgill, *A Woe against the Magistrates, priests, and people of Kendall in the county of Westmorland* (London, 1654), LSF, p. 4. Stallybrass and Jones, *Renaissance Clothing*, p. 207.

[75] Underhill, *Hell Broke Loose*, p. 30.

[76] Simon Eccles, *Signes are from the Lord, to a People or Nation to forewarn them of some eminent Judgment near at hand* (London, 1663), LSF, p. 1.

that came over viewers. Reaction to this feeling could be aggressive, but Quakers turned this to their advantage by publishing narratives of patient 'sufferings' that generated public sympathy. These quasi-hagiographical stories contributed not inconsiderably, if Kate Peters is correct, to solidifying Quaker identity and encouraging the 'growth of a successful, national movement'.[77] One well-known account by Quaker leader Richard Hubberthorne concerns 'little Elizabeth Fletcher' and her companion, Elizabeth Leavens, who were the first to evangelize Oxford between 1653 and 1655. The young women walked together in the apostolic manner, through 'the streets, in the market-place, in the synagogues, and in the colledges'. And despite the fact that

Elizabeth Fletcher was a very modest, grave young woman, yet Contrary to her owne will or inclination, in obedience to the Lord, [she] went naked through the Streets of that City, as a sign against the Hippocritical profession they then made there, being then Presbyterians & Independents, which profession she told them the Lord would strip them of, so that their Nakedness should Appear, which shortly after ye return of King Charles the 2nd, was fulfilled upon them, they being turned out or made Hippocritically to Conforme.[78]

The reaction of some Oxford students and residents was remarkably brutal, perhaps because in the notoriously homosocial university milieu, two young women wandering 'freely' to 'declare against sin and ungodliness' were unable to make the conventions they tapped legible.[79] Slight and 'naked' in her shift, with her hair down, feet and legs bare, the scenario 19-year-old Fletcher evoked for university boys was probably not the Old Testament prophet. She may, rather, have embodied the sartorial shorthand of theatre wherein a woman in her smock was 'simultaneously sexualized and made vulnerable'.[80] Accompanied by the lower-born Leavens, who held Fletcher's clothing, the two may have brought to mind a young gentlewoman and her maid at bedtime. The difference was that Fletcher vigorously castigated observers to leave off their 'pride, covetousness, lust, and all uncleanness'.[81] The powerfully

erotic symbolism of a young woman in her smock combined with a shaming message toward those either accustomed to occupying, or being trained to occupy, authoritative roles, may have impaired the intended mirroring, without which rupture proves intolerable.

Had Fletcher gone naked through a more urban area, like the east end of London, which saw a significant amount of prophetic activity in those years, she might have fared better.[82] A cursory glance at Ephraim Pagitt's anatomy of 'Sects' in his 1654 pamphlet, *Heresiography or a Description of the Heretickes and Sectaries Spring up in these Latter times*, gives a sense of the apparent ubiquity of female prophets in the ferment of London's relative religious freedom.[83] In this context, the repetition of prophetic acts stabilized allusive links to the biblical scenario. Going naked in London may have incurred arrest, followed by whipping or imprisonment, but it seldom met with the level of rough justice Fletcher and Leavens experienced in Oxford.

The women were 'mocked, buffeted and shamefully used, being tied together at *Johns* Colledge and pumped [held under a water pump with their mouths forced open until they nearly drowned], and kicked and buffeted, and thrust into a pool called "Giles" pool'. Hauled before the city magistrates and vice chancellor of the university, the girls were condemned to be 'soundly whipped' out of town as vagabonds.[84] Elizabeth Fletcher never recovered from the 'cruel usage' that included

---

77 Peters, *Print Culture*, pp. 9–10.
78 Hubberthorne, *True Testimony*, p. 2.
79 Hubberthorne, *True Testimony*, p. 2.
80 Stallybrass and Jones, *Renaissance Clothing*, p. 213.
81 Hubberthorne, *True Testimony*, p. 2.
82 The intense activity around one of the first Quaker meeting houses (1656) is memorialized today in the name Quaker Street, in the Spitalfields neighbourhood.
83 Ephraim Pagitt, *Heresiography or A description of the hereticks and sectaries of these latter times . . .*, Early English Books 946 (London, 1547), p. 17. See Mack's chart of female prophets around London's east end in *Visionary*, pp. 416–24.
84 Hubberthorne, *True Testimony*, pp. 2–3, 10.

being dashed down onto a gravestone. She died of her injuries soon afterwards.[85]

The standards by which I cite the Fletcher and Leavens episode as an example of successful charismatic performance probably require clarification. If we are to believe Hubberthorne, 'there was many in the City that have so much of the Light of Christ made manifest in them, as to acknowledge them [Fletcher and Leavens] to be servants of the Living God, and to own them in their sufferings, and to confess the appearance of Christ in them before men, and in love did accompany them out of the City, and did own them in their persecution'.[86] In other words, some people at one of the key training centres of orthodox English clergy were converted, or 'convinced' in Quaker parlance, by Fletcher and Leavens's performance. Where it failed as Old Testament prophecy, it succeeded as martyrdom. Warning Oxford 'thy desolation is coming', Hubberthorne exhorts the community to submit to the Inner Light, mend their ways and stop persecuting 'the saints'.[87] Fletcher and Leavens also opened the way for other prophets, like Jane Whitehead who, during her far less violent mission to Oxford was also 'confirm[ed] of many in the truth'.[88] On a smaller scale, Elizabeth Leavens, despite very humble origins, went on to become a religious leader in her own right. Sent to head a border mission in Wales, she met and married Thomas Holme, another Quaker prophet who had gone naked as a sign earlier in his career. The two were made pastoral overseers of Wales.[89]

If the success of charisma is measured by the performer's convincement of others, and impact on 'the body politic and society at large', Quakers were, on the whole, highly successful.[90] Evidence of female prophets' efficacy in initiating conversions and instantiating new communities abounds. Elaine Huber confirms an earlier historian's estimate that by 1690 there were some 60,000 English Friends, 'or one out of every 130 persons then living in England' was a Quaker.[91] It is also worth noting that, of the unprecedented abundance of female-authored texts in the period, a 'disproportionate share' were written by Quakers. An estimated 20 per cent of all seventeenth-century women's publications were Quaker-authored.[92] Peter's speculation that print may have been used to normalize the 'actual presence of preaching women' becomes more intriguing in light of the fact that there were even more female prophets than writers (220 prophets between 1640 and 1660), most of whom did *not* publish.[93] Or did they?

In his journal, the Quaker leader, George Fox, declared that there were three legitimate ways to 'publish the truth': 'by word, by writing and by signs'.[94] Here is Fox, decades after Quakers had distanced themselves from their more ecstatic beginnings, putting two *performed* modes of publishing on a par with printing. His words confirm my sense that to focus *only* on the archive of written texts, without considering the repertoire they attempt to capture and elucidate, is to exclude from analysis not only a crucial technique of Quaker publishing, but also a possible key to how ordinary women, and by extension, other marginalized people, used charismatic performance to carve out leadership roles for themselves, reconfiguring political relations.

Admittedly, those who endeavour to read the Quaker repertoire face not only the infamous ephemerality of performance, but the fragmentary, second- or even third-hand nature of accounts

---

85 Huber, 'A Woman Must Not Speak', p. 164; Hubberthorne, *True Testimony*, p. 4.

86 Hubberthorne, *True Testimony*, p. 4.

87 Hubberthorne, *True Testimony*, pp. 2, 10.

88 Theophila Townsend, *A Testimony concerning the life and death of Jane Whitehead, that Faithful Servant and Hand-maid of the Lord . . .*, LSF (London, 1576), p. 6.

89 Barbour, *Quakers in Puritan England*, p. 133; Moore, *Light*, pp. 32, 136.

90 Peters, *Print Culture*, pp. 1, 10; Jaeger, *Enchantment*, p. 5.

91 Huber, 'A Woman Must Not Speak', pp. 164, 154.

92 Patricia Crawford, 'Women's Published Writings, 1600–1700', in *Women in English Society: 1500–1800*, ed. Mary Prior (London, 1985), p. 213. That so much writing survives is partly attributable to the seventeenth-century Quaker practice of preserving two copies of every Quaker-related document since the movement's beginning.

93 Peters, *Print Culture*, p. 150; Mack, 'Women as Prophets', p. 24.

94 *The Journal of George Fox*, ed. John L. Nickalls (Cambridge, 1952), p. 407.

imbued with passionate pro- or anti-Quaker sentiment. These issues cause some historians to balk at
the Friends' archive, citing the way propaganda
muddies events.[95] But in thinking about charisma,
historical accuracy seems, finally, less important
than *reception* – 'the emotional response of the reader
or viewer'.[96] What Quaker performances affirm,
with Shakespeare, is that charisma beguiles not
because it forces a mass surrender of plebeian will
but, on the contrary, because its emancipatory
promise speaks to participants across the social spectrum, embodying wishes and reshaping norms to the
community's will.

This is why Egyptian improvisation ultimately
co-opts Roman triumph, with the latter's staid
reproduction of triumphs past.[97] This is why, even
if Shakespeare can no more conceive of a stable
charisma than Weber, he nevertheless celebrates
Cleopatran charisma at the play's end. In real time,
Caesar dominates the scene, reacting to news that
the queen's suicide has thwarted his plan to display
her in his spectacular reentry to Rome. Yet, his final
command reduces him to a choric function:

> High events as these
> Strike those that make them, and their story is
> No less in pity than his glory which
> Brought them to be lamented. Our army shall
> In solemn show attend this funeral,
> And then to Rome. Come, Dolabella, see
> High order in this great solemnity. (5.2.354–60)

Caesar becomes, here, the gazed-upon participant
in Cleopatra's procession, and not, as he intended,
the other way around. Nor is it entirely clear
what moves the troops more: Caesar's orders or
the dead queen's 'strong toil of grace' (342). Her
visage, which now 'looks like sleep, / As she
would catch another Antony' (340–1), disrupts
space-time, blurring the line between past and
present as Caesar echoes Enobarbus's account of
her arrival on Cydnus where, by being precisely
where she was not supposed to be, Cleopatra
recursively justified the sovereignty her performance asserted. In the end, Caesar adds to
Cleopatra's extraordinary politics by projecting
her into the anagogical space of 'glory', where she
continues to feed the social imaginary from
whence she drew.

---

[95] Peters discusses historians' misgivings about the reliability of
these sources in *Print Culture*, pp. 8–9.

[96] Jaeger, *Enchantment*, p. 4.

[97] I follow here the many who read Cleopatra's finale as
a victory. Heather James, for example, sees an Isis-like
apotheosis in 'The Politics of Display and the Anamorphic
Subjects of *Antony and Cleopatra*', in *Shakespeare's Late
Tragedies*, ed. Susanne Wofford (Upper Saddle River, NJ,
1996), pp. 208–34, while Linda Woodbridge describes how
Cleopatra outgames Caesar in '"He beats thee 'gainst the
odds": Gambling, Risk Management and *Antony and
Cleopatra*', in *Antony and Cleopatra: New Critical Essays*, ed.
Sara Munson Deats (London, 2005), pp. 193–212.

CORIOLANUS AND THE 'COMMON PART'

ROBERT N. WATSON

This article seeks to briefly explore some roots of *The Tragedy of Coriolanus*: historical, philosophical, psychological, sociological, theological, even etymological roots. The play grows, I believe, from a synergistic set of underlying tragic questions. How can a person who aspires to embody a cultural ideal – in this case, the ancient Roman criteria for manly virtue – survive his entanglement in the life within and around him that compromises or contradicts that ideal? How, in other words, does a devotion to nobility, integrity and a centred self that is always like itself (*sui similis*: a Senecan tag Shakespeare echoes repeatedly) endure reminders of all it has in common with supposedly lower forms of life, its dependency on give-and-take with a community, and the casting and shattering of that self into parts? How would that revered legacy have withstood the Christian and especially Calvinist doctrines of Shakespeare's world – doctrines that deemed no person self-sufficient, and insisting that all must instead depend on a communion of bread and blood for eternal life, and that God alone is 'resolute, and immutable, always one, and like himself, not wavering or varying in those things which once he willed' (Lipsius, *De Constantia*, 1.17; 1584: p. 53)? How, finally, does this tragic topic reflect the transhistorical reality of the human mind and spirit delimited by the mortal body?

In Caius Martius Coriolanus's war against 'the beast / With many heads' (4.1.1–2), the boundaries defining the human species and the human individual stand or fall together. Human exceptionalism is coded as Roman exceptionalism in Coriolanus's animal epithets for those who fall short of his ideal.

Taken together, his hatred of the undifferentiated plebian masses, his embarrassment about his wounds, his determination to 'stand / As if a man were author of himself / And knew no other kin' (5.3.35–7), and his threats to purge with fire anyone who threatens to compromise or complicate his martial definition of himself and the Roman body politic offer a fascinating limit case to the classical project of selfhood. Historical contexts, close reading and data mining all reveal this play's ambivalence about the Senecan insularity of its title character.[1]

Just a few years before Shakespeare wrote *Coriolanus*, Sir William Cornwallis's *Discourses upon Seneca the tragedian* warned that 'No extreme continueth' because nature 'hath given limits to all things, and to all things courses fitting their natures'; otherwise 'there would be nothing, for combating against one another, & setting their forces one against another; the Victor would convert all things to his owne nature, and that would destroy nature, whose glory is the multiplicitie of her instruments, and the working of them with one another'. That conversion is practically the mission statement of the disincorporation called Caius Martius Coriolanus, who threatens his fellow Roman soldiers that he will 'leave the foe / And make my wars on you' (1.4.40–1) and who 'would

---

[1] Gordon Braden's influential *Renaissance Tragedy and the Senecan Tradition: Anger's Privilege* (New Haven, CT, 1985), p. 57, demonstrates how Senecan tragic personae 'strain to take a fantasy of individual autonomy beyond almost any kind of limit'.

depopulate the city and / Be every man himself'
(3.1.266–7).

This protagonist's disdain for both the creatureliness and the interchangeability of Rome's plebeians, and thereby for their appetite for
individual and collective survival, seems valid
even as it proves fatal. The tragic dilemma is therefore Hegelian. Its fulcrum is the transition from the
waning classical values of the play's setting to the
waxing Christian-communitarian values of its original audience. The particular historical moment of
the play's action, when Rome was moving from
monarchy to republic – 'between the heroic age of
personal achievement and the age of the city-state
in which an organic society will be the moral
standard'[2] – is homologous to the protagonist's
struggle to maintain a self-dominion that subju-
gates his own potential commonness. That the
play was written at a political moment when King
James was testing the limits of his sovereignty over
the House of Commons, referring to his opponents
there disdainfully as 'Tribunes of the people' and
'plebeian tribunes',[3] is probably no mere coincidence. Scholars connecting the composition of
Coriolanus to the Midlands uprisings of 1607 generally focus on food shortages.[4] But Shakespeare
may have associated Coriolanus's destructive self-
enclosure, which excludes food and community as
the loci of mingled life, more specifically with the
social tragedy then called enclosure. Class arrogance in agronomics resembled a broader human
presumptuousness that Coriolanus epitomizes, and
in eight other plays Shakespeare uses the word
'common' – which haunts this play – to refer to
land open to shared grazing.

Coriolanus's mistrust of connection manifests itself
even in his peculiar verbal style. As Russ McDonald
has demonstrated so compellingly, this protagonist's
speeches 'eschew connectives, both within and
between sentences, and such withholding creates
a disjunctivity that sets every utterance apart from
every other', creating 'a language in which the inter-
dependence of sentences is suppressed, clauses do not
touch'.[5] His key rhetorical quirk is asyndeton – the
omission of a conjunction that would normally hold
parts of a sentence together.[6] So the protagonist's

rhetorical style is as Senecan as his tragic character;
structurally as well as explicitly, he uses language to
break rather than build connections. Sean Benson
observes that 'the driving imagery and language of
the play concern themselves with fragments, which
are often represented as synecdochic parts of some
larger whole ... Similarly, Coriolanus's life is fragmented by the many relational roles he must
assume'.[7] Lawrence Danson convincingly highlights
the prevalence of synecdoche and metonymy in the
play[8] – a language of parts with ambiguous relation
to the whole. The question of whether the tragic
hero can separate himself from common life without
shattering the identity he seeks to consolidate –
a theme prominent also in Macbeth – informs the
plot of Coriolanus from beginning to end, this article
will argue, and pervades the play's peculiar diction as
well as its peculiar syntax.

The opening scene evokes the same passage
from First Corinthians evoked by Bottom's synes-
thetic rhapsody toward the end of Midsummer
Night's Dream:

God hath tempered the body together, and hath given
the more honor to that part which lacked, Lest there
should be any division in the body, but that the members
should have the same care one for another. Therefore if
one member suffer, all suffer with it; if one member be
had in honor, all the members rejoice with it.

(12: 24–6, Geneva Bible)

[2] John Velz, 'Cracking Strong Curbs Asunder', English Literary Renaissance, 13 (1983), 58–69; p. 62.
[3] Quoted by Peter Holland in the introduction to his Arden edition of Coriolanus (London, 2013), p. 105. Citations of Coriolanus are taken from this edition. Except for King Lear, as cited below, all other Shakespeare references are taken from William Shakespeare: The Complete Works, ed. Stanley Wells et al. (Oxford, 1986).
[4] For an important early example, see E. C. Pettet, 'Coriolanus and the Midlands Insurrection of 1607', in Shakespeare Survey 3 (Cambridge, 1950), pp. 34–41.
[5] Russ McDonald, Shakespeare's Late Style (Cambridge, 2006), p. 56.
[6] McDonald, Late Style, p. 57. On the Senecan as opposed to the Circeronian style of this speaker, see p. 61.
[7] Sean Benson '"Even to the gates of Rome"', Comitatus, 30 (1999), 96.
[8] Lawrence Danson, Tragic Alphabet (New Haven, CT, 1974).

But Coriolanus's dream city hath no Bottom. What happens in *Coriolanus*, from the opening scene onward, is this failing to happen. Through the belly-fable, Menenius preaches the Pauline sermon to the plebeian mob, but just as they seem ready to convert, in swaggers Caius Martius – a stony-hearted, honour-hoarding heretic in this religion of collectivity. The fable about 'incorporate friends' proposes, and the rest of the play uneasily explores, a continuity between communities of bread and communities of blood.

The idea of shared bread – established by the opening debate about the sharing of grain – turns up with remarkable persistence in the mouths of the play's compromisers and conciliators: 'company' (in each of the first four acts), 'accompany', 'accompanied', 'companion', 'companions' and 'companionship'. Food provides everyone with what Menenius calls 'that natural competency / Whereby they live' (1.1.134–5). If '*trans-*' is the Latin prefix that haunts *Midsummer Night's Dream*, in *Coriolanus* it is surely '*cum-*' (abetted by 'part', in tension with 'sole', 'lone' and – five times each – 'whole' and 'wholesome'). The word 'common' appears more often here than in any of Shakespeare's other works; it is the unnamed antagonist of the plot, and a cause of all the debates. It also seems worth noting that the very next play Shakespeare wrote exploits the same root to characterize its protagonist's aversion to adulterate mixtures: Leontes rants that affection

> **Com**municat'st with dreams – how can this be? –
> With what's unreal thou **co**active art,
> And fellow'st nothing. Then 'tis very credent
> Thou mayst **co-**join with something, and thou dost –
> And that beyond **com**mission . . .
> (*The Winter's Tale*, 1.2.142–6)

If Leontes's breakdown is a symptom of his hubristic denial of the shared appetites and mortality of the human body – a denial (I argued long ago) he shares with Coriolanus[9] – then this verbal correlation is all the more significant.

My sense that anxiety about mixture and (especially) human interaction manifests itself in the frequent deployment of the Latin *cum-* and *part-*

prefixes in *Coriolanus* is supported by statistical study. Both quantity and frequency might contribute to an audience's sense of this topic's importance, and as Illustrations 9 and 10 show, *Coriolanus* contains far more of these co-/com-/col-/cor-words than any other Shakespeare play, with only *Richard II* having a higher percentage of such words (by a minuscule difference of 70 vs. 69 per 10,000; the next closest is *Henry V* at 62).[10] When the sample is reduced to only those words that actually refer to mixtures or human interactions, *Coriolanus* stands out starkly atop the list (Illustrations 11 and 12), with 71 instances where the other plays average only 30, and the highest percentage as well.[11] Furthermore, the cumulative subliminal effect of these instances would have been strongly augmented by the 34 namings of Coriolanus,[12] 17 of Corioles and 18 of Cominius, as well as 10 of

---

9 Robert N. Watson, *Shakespeare and the Hazards of Ambition* (Cambridge, MA, 1984), pp. 222–79.

10 This statistical work was conducted with the excellent assistance of Craig Messner, a doctoral student at UCLA. We derived a list of words beginning 'co' and 'part' from Shakespeare concordances and trimmed it to include only those whose prefixes were plausibly derived from the Latin '*cum-*' or '*part-*' roots. We used the texts at www.ibiblio.org /xml/examples/shakespeare/, which are already marked up in XML and thus make it easy to omit stage directions, character lists, speech headings, and other meta-features. We then ran the text of plays believed to be entirely or almost entirely by Shakespeare through a Python algorithm Craig Messner developed for this purpose, and finally converted the results to bar graphs using the Python plotting library called matplotlib.

11 This category was narrowed by eliminating 113 words beginning with *co-* that derived from a different root or drifted away from any implication of combinatory work, leaving the 184 that pointed toward mixture and/or interaction. All these lists will be available on https://github.com /messner1/

12 Peter Holland, '*Coriolanus*: The Rhythms and Remains of Excess', in *The Forms of Renaissance Thought*, ed. Leonard Barkan, Bradin Cormack and Sean Keilan (London, 2009), p. 151, observes that those who focus (probably anachronistically) on the *-anus* at the end of the protagonist's name somehow 'never explore the Latin heart of his name in the "Cor" that opens it'. But where Holland takes this syllable to signal 'heart', I am interested in its contribution to the pervasive theme of combination.

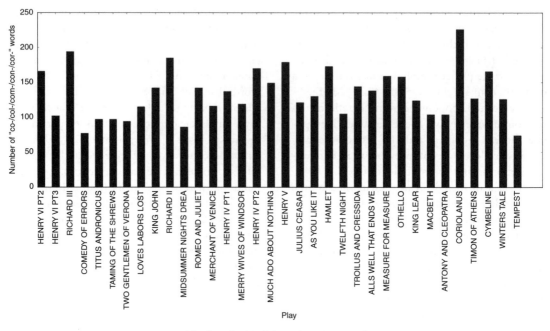

9. Number of co-/col-/com-/con-/cor- words.

Shakespeare's 35 uses of 'corn', the sharing of which is the initial main topic of the plot. These are not included in my charts because they do not share the *cum-* etymology, but they might still have contributed to an audience's sense of relentless pressure toward mingling (much as the interplay of Duncan's name with 'dun' and the many echoes of 'done' haunts *Macbeth*). That verbal pressure ironically becomes all the more intense through Caius Martius's attainment of a *cognomen ex virtute* supposed to honour what he did alone, as that same achievement ironically drives him into the interactive role of candidate for the consultative position of consul.

My other hunch – that anxiety about parts (body parts, theatrical parts and participation) would be reflected, at the same micro-level, in a notably high number and rate of *part-* prefixes – proved to be similarly verifiable: *Coriolanus* again surpasses all the others in both number and rate (Illustrations 13 and 14).[13]

The last thing this protagonist wants is to 'mutually participate' in 'the appetite and affection

common / Of the whole body' (1.1.98–100). Attention to these word-roots seems especially well justified in a play where Menenius plays off the suffixes of the tribunes' names – Sicinius Velutus and Junius Brutus – with a jeering homophone: 'I find the ass in compound with the major part of your syllables' (2.1.56–7). And attention to prefixes may be apt in a play where Shakespeare – although this derives from Plutarch – shows his hero finally caught between forces beginning with the same consonant: the Volscians, Volumnia, Virgilia, and Valeria.

In contrast to Volumnia, Coriolanus's wife Virgilia is horrified by the idea of him exchanging blood, and she 'will not out of doors ... not over the threshold ... I will not forth ... I must not', despite Valeria's admonishment that 'you confine yourself most unreasonably' (1.3.73–112). Virgilia's

---

[13] Here I omitted 'Parthian' and 'partridge' as etymologically unrelated.

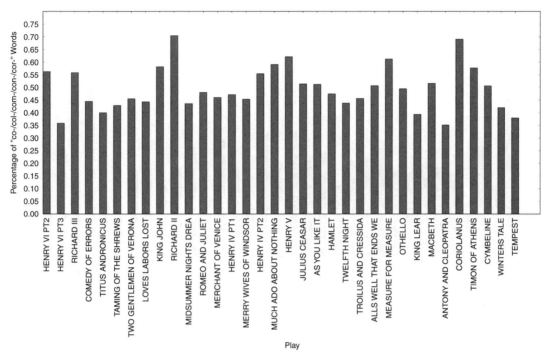

10. Co-/col-/com-/con-/cor- words as percentage of play words.

determination to sustain herself in an intact domestic sphere seems to be a gendered counterpart to her husband's imperviousness in battle, and designed superstitiously to ensure that such insularity extends to his body: marital chastity evoking martial impenetrability. But her domesticity also signals a more positive view of collective life. Twice here we are superfluously reminded that Virgilia is sewing (1.3.54, 84–8) – the same kind of function Shakespeare gives Bottom the weaver, who must lace together all the living worlds of *Midsummer Night's Dream*. Anthropologists have observed that 'The ritual and discourse that surround its manufacture establish cloth as a convincing analog for the regenerative and degenerative processes of life, and as a great connector, binding humans not only to each other but to the ancestors of their past and progeny who constitute their future.'[14] Sewing thus extends Virgilia's role as a counterpart to Coriolanus, who

has, according to the tribune Sicinius 'unknit himself / The noble knot he made' by alienating his fellow Romans (4.2.31–2), tearing up what the First Citizen, in the first scene, describes as 'this our fabric' in which the various social roles work together as various parts of the human body do. As flesh of his flesh and mother of his son, Virgilia weaves Coriolanus back into that fabric.

To be fully human – or, at least, fully Roman, which from Coriolanus's perspective is much the same thing – is to be integral and impenetrable. Caius Martius's first words depict the people as itchy 'scabs' (1.1.161): the maddeningly incomplete boundary of the skin-bound self. They represent the same unpleasantly liminal case that King Lear invokes with his alienated flesh and blood:

---

[14] Annette B. Weiner and Jane Schneider, eds., *Cloth and Human Experience* (Washington DC, 1989), p. 3.

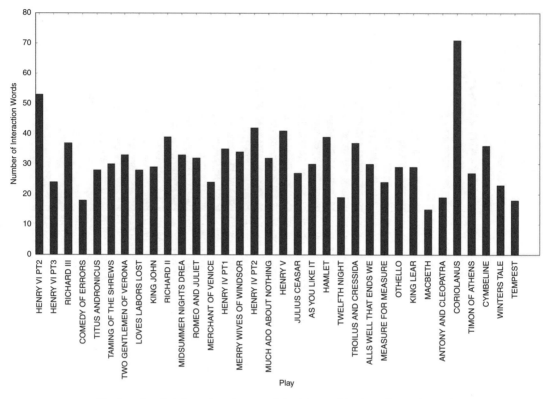

11. Number of co-/col-/com-/con-/cor- words implying combination or human interaction.

But yet thou art my flesh, my blood, my daughter,
Or rather a disease that's in my flesh,
Which I must needs call mine. Thou art a boil,
A plague sore, or embossed carbuncle,
In my corrupted blood.[15]

When Rome's soldiers fail to show 'hearts more proof than shields' (1.4.26), he curses them as dermatological diseases of the body politic and as non-human (because non-heroic) bodies:

All the contagion of the south light on you,
You shames of Rome! You herd of – boils and plagues
Plaster you o'er, that you may be abhorred
Farther than seen, and one infect another
Against the wind a mile! You souls of geese
That bear the shapes of men ...   (1.4.31–6)

Failing to defend the boundary of the Roman body politic makes these commoners failures of the moral boundary of humanity and failures of the skin boundary of the individual.

Their collective cowardice allows Coriolanus the solo conquest that wins him his new name and also converts the carbuncle from a symptom of mortally permeable flesh to its other meaning: a fiery jewel, hard and sharp as a sword fresh from the forge. When a Roman soldier reports that the Volsces 'Clapped to their gates', leaving Coriolanus 'himself alone / To answer all the city', Titus Lartius exclaims

O, noble fellow,
Who sensibly out-dares his senseless sword
And, when it bows, stand'st up! Thou art left, Martius.

---

15 *King Lear*, 2.2.410–15; Arden Shakespeare Third Series, ed. R. A. Foakes (London, 1997).

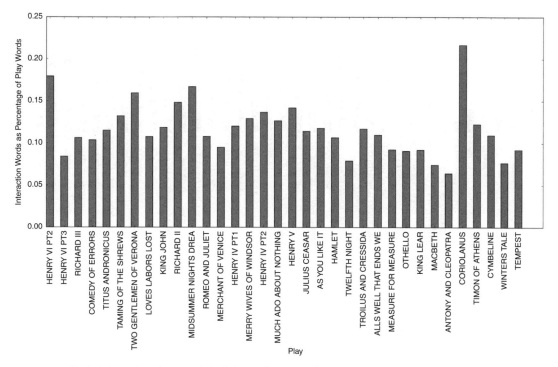

12. Co-/col-/com-/con-/cor- words implying combination or human interaction as percentage of play words.

A carbuncle entire, as big as thou art,
Were not so rich a jewel.   (1.4.55–60)

Yet, in order to win the plebeians' votes for consul, Coriolanus will be obliged to display the wounds that resemble the more fleshly kind of carbuncle, the swollen red markers of a body whose integrity is under threat. A similar ambiguity haunts the word 'tent' in this play, which three times refers to a soldier's habitation, but twice refers to the medical practice of propping open an infected wound: again the idea of a valiant enclosure sits in tension with the idea of mortal openness.

Cominius wonders what human form he sees returning from Corioles 'That does appear as he were flayed? O gods / He has the stamp of Martius' (1.6.22–3). If a person's outline is the envelope of skin, then what are the borders and markers of Coriolanus's self? Cominius – whose name echoes 'common', but with an ennobling *différance* – worries that perhaps Coriolanus 'come[s] not in

the blood of others, / But mantled in your own' (1.6.28–9); another uneasy question suiting a scene of birth, again on the contested borderlines of self and other. This hero, however, insists that his enemies have been porous while he remained enclosed:

CORIOLANUS.   Alone I fought in your Corioles' walls
And made what work I pleased. 'Tis not my blood
Wherein thou seest me masked.   (1.8.9–11)

Is that alien blood merely a mask – a *persona* – or instead an expression of this person's truest self?

Thanks, paradoxically, to his many wounds, this mortal creature can now be replaced by a *cognomen* signalling his solitary enclosure, his epitomizing achievement:

HERALD.   Know, Rome, that all alone Martius did fight
Within Corioles' gates: where he hath won,

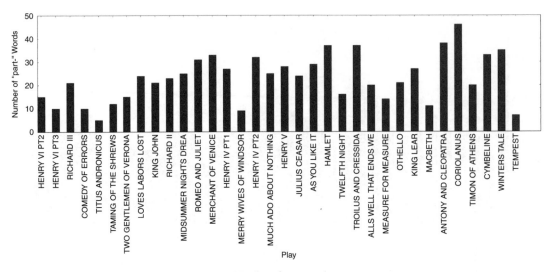

13. Number of part- words.

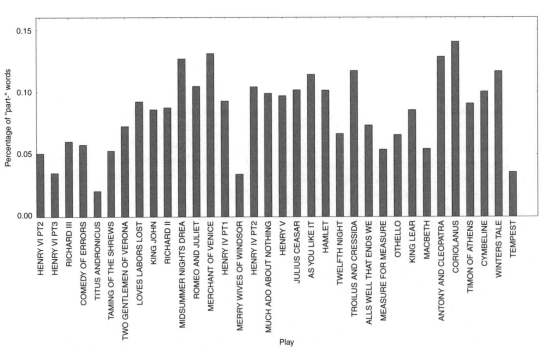

14. Part- words as percentage of play words.

With fame, a name to 'Martius Caius'; these
In honour follows 'Coriolanus'.   (2.1.157–60)

The tension between 'all' and 'alone' in 'himself alone
to answer all the city' (1.4.55–6) is further compressed
here. In both cases, it precipitates out the 'one'.

In the distribution of the spoils from this victory,
Coriolanus requests no more than 'my common
part with those / That have beheld the doing'
(1.9.39–40), but there is a sarcastic sting in the end
of his egalitarian and communitarian gesture. He
considers such spoils a spoilage: he will go no further
into 'the common muck of the world' (2.2.124).
Then, in an incident so irrelevant to the plot that it
begs for thematic interpretation, Coriolanus forgets
the name of the poor man who sheltered him and
now needs his rescue (1.9.81–91) – plausibly, another
instance of his pre-conscious refusal of the mutual
dependency of life.

Cominius proceeds to depict Coriolanus as
a warrior who 'cannot in the world / Be singly
counterpoised', and who is repeatedly bound in
encircling garlands, reserving for him the role of
the phallic aggressor rather than the one penetrated:

> When he might act the woman in the scene
> He proved best man i'th' field, and for his meed
> Was brow-bound with the oak. His pupil age
> Man-entered thus, he waxed like a sea,
> And in the brunt of seventeen battles since
> He lurched all swords of the garland.
>   (2.2.94–9)

And thus engaged, thus engorged, he enforced the
birth of his new, renamed, swordlike, martial self:

>   from face to foot
> He was a thing of blood, whose every motion
> Was timed with dying cries. Alone he entered
> The mortal gate of th' city . . .   (2.2.106–9)

Again Coriolanus is isolated; he makes his way into
the world, not vice versa. When Menenius urges the
people to 'think / Upon the wounds his body bears,
which show / Like graves i' the holy churchyard',
Coriolanus has to insist the wounds are not really
penetrations of his body or spirit, let alone signals of
mortality: 'Scratches with briars, / Scars to move
laughter only' (3.3.48–51). But the jokes are on him.

This self-betrayal of showing those wounds makes
Coriolanus aware that the 'part' called 'half' – both
words to which I will return – comes between 'the
one' and 'the other': 'I am half through: the one part
suffered, the other will I do.' But he won't. For
Coriolanus, 'to make his requests by particulars,
wherein every one of us has a single honour' (as
a plebeian describes the process at 2.3.42–4) would
be to share the honourable 'singularity' the tribunes
complain he demands (1.1.273). It would grant particularity to the commoners while he is trapped
playing 'a part / That I shall blush in acting'
(2.2.143–4):

> . . . such a part which never
>   I shall discharge to th' life.
> COMINIUS.   Come, come, we'll
>   prompt you.
> VOLUMNIA.   I prithee now, sweet son, as thou hast
>   said
>   My praises made thee first a soldier, so,
>   To have my praise for this, perform a part
>   Thou hast not done before.   (3.2.106–11)

The reassurance that his common touch will be
merely a dramatic part comes with the unwelcome
implication that his supposedly spontaneous and
characteristic posture as a martial hero was also
merely a scripted performance.

Before the scene is over, exasperated by the
mixed character of a government whose parties
(the term Menenius uses for these political opposites at 3.1.316) are simultaneously even and at odds
in a common cause, Coriolanus swears by an
immortal and pre-eminent selfhood:

>   By Jove himself,
>   It makes the consuls base; and my soul aches
>   To know, when two authorities are up,
>   Neither supreme, how soon confusion
>   May enter 'twixt the gap of both and take
>   The one by th'other.   (3.1.108–13)

'Other' (like 'many', and as in 'one infect another'
at 1.4.34) is again inherently the foe of the one;
and later Aufidius will comment that it is
Coriolanus's 'nature, / Not to be other than one
thing' (4.7.41–2). In fact, the word 'one' appears
more often in *Coriolanus* than in any of

Shakespeare's earlier plays. Coriolanus's fear of 'confusion' here is validated when the tribunes orchestrate a 'din confused' from the plebeians to enforce his execution (3.1.111, 3.3.20), and he disdains 'congregations' and any 'consent' that derives from his fellow citizens rather than from Jove (3.2.12, 5.3.71).

The Senate can reasonably hope that the tribunes will offer 'your kindest ears and, after, / Your loving motion toward the common body' (2.2.50–1). That, however, is exactly the kind of openness and intimacy that Coriolanus cannot tolerate. Menenius tells the tribunes, 'He loves your people, / But tie him not to be their bedfellow', because he wants no connection to 'Your multiplying spawn' (2.2.62–3, 76); later he will insist that 'I have not been common in my love' (2.3.93). The tribunes, as the representatives of the common people within the body politic, represent the common burdens of mortal creatureliness within Coriolanus. What Menenius urges against their excessive pride – 'an interior survey of your good selves' (2.1.38) – would be no less corrosive to the pride of Coriolanus. Menenius then flees the interview in order to protect himself from very much the same contagions – multiplicity, animality, commonness: the census of the senses – that repel Coriolanus: 'More of your conversation would infect my brain, being the herdsmen of the beastly plebeians' (2.1.91–2).

The etymology of 'ambition' links it to the practice of canvassing for votes, and Coriolanus seems uneasily aware that the election will compromise rather than institutionalize his sovereignty, driving him toward the identity of consul which (as the Latin root again indicates, and the play's use of various forms of 'counsel' reflects) is founded in an interactive rather than an autonomous function. It is a relationship of mutual dependency, rather than the imperial role that, ironically, young Caius Martius helped eliminate when he fought against the tyrant Tarquin (2.2.85–93), thus establishing the republic that now repels him.

When the citizens describe their role in the making of Coriolanus as consul, it becomes clear (largely through a swarm of alliterative m-words: 'multitude' and 'monster' thrice each, 'many' and 'members' twice each) why that political role threatens his bodily integrity:

THIRD CITIZEN.   ... we are to put our tongues into those wounds and speak for them. So, if he tell us his noble deeds, we must also tell him our noble acceptance of them. Ingratitude is monstrous, and for the multitude to be ingrateful were to make a monster of the multitude, of the which we, being members, should bring ourselves to be monstrous members.
FIRST CITIZEN.   And to make us no better thought of, a little help will serve; for once we stood up about the corn, he himself stuck not to call us the many-headed multitude.
THIRD CITIZEN.   We have been called so of many ...
(2.3.6–17)

Later in the scene, Coriolanus hurries to change back into more dignified clothes and, 'knowing myself again, / Repair to th' Senate-house' (2.3.145–6) – the discriminating locale that cures the disease of a marketplace where exchange erases transcendent values. He is practically a hypochondriac in his hyper-vigilance for symptoms of that disease, seemingly anticipating Karl Marx's insight that a wage-labourer 'sells his very self, and that by fractions'.[16] When a citizen argues that no special respect is owed to Caius Martius for his military service to Rome, because 'he pays himself with being proud', that too seems to be an insight about commodification and alienation; what Coriolanus feels are inherent expressions of his noble valour are reconceived as a social economy of payment and exchange, even within his supposedly integral self. His own mother says he fights 'Like to a harvest-man that's tasked to mow / Or all or lose his hire', which might have reminded Shakespeare's original audiences of the role of enclosure in the explosion of wage-labour. Coriolanus is indignant about showing the people his wounds, 'As if I had received them for the hire / Of their breath only', and hates to seem to 'Crave the hire'. He sardonically asks those citizens 'Your price o' the consulship?', only to be reminded that

---

[16] Karl Marx, *Wage-Labour and Capital* (New York, 1933), ch. 2, p. 20.

they do not see this as quite the alienated and quantified transaction he implies: 'The price of it is to ask it kindly.' Later he says he 'would not buy / Their mercy at the price of one fair word' (3.3.89–90). Perhaps the word 'money' shares more than the obvious auditory association with 'many' and 'meinie' (a Volscian solider says, 'The wars for my money', because men in peace-time 'less need one another' (4.5.233–4)).

As in *A Midsummer Night's Dream*, the boundary of the human individual and the boundary of the human species collapse simultaneously. Coriolanus asks 'the tribunes of the people, / The tongues o' the common mouth',

> Are these your herd?
> Must these have voices, that can yield them now
> And straight disclaim their tongues? What are your
>   offices?
> You being their mouths, why rule you not their teeth?
>   (3.1.24, 34–7)

Menenius's belly-fable is clearly lurking in the plebeians' minds when they pursue this metaphor: 'The noble tribunes are the people's mouths / And we their hands' (3.1.273–4). When Sicinius asks a rhetorical question still often audible from the left wings in the twenty-first century – 'What is the city but the people?' – the citizens respond, 'True, / The people are the city' (3.1.199–200). The shifting number of the verb is revealing. Coriolanus complains that the 'meinie' compromise 'the honoured number' (3.1.68–74) – an echo of his complaints about the 'many' who threaten his unique selfhood and Aufidius's complaint that his 'seconds' have 'shamed' him by intervening in his single combat with Coriolanus (1.8.15–16). For Aufidius, as for Coriolanus, the only honourable number (because the loneliest) is one: the Roman 'I'. 'I would I were a Roman; for I cannot, / Being a Volsce, be that I am'.

Coriolanus warns the Senate that these 'min-nows' or 'fragments' threaten the distinction of identity, which even his oppositional syntax strives to defend:

> If you are learned,
> Be not as common fools; if you are not,

Let them have cushions by you. You are plebeians,
If they be senators, and they are no less
When, both your voices blended, the great'st taste
Most palates theirs.   (3.1.100–5)

Again the intimacy of a shared mouth disgusts him. In response, the tribune Brutus sees no reason for the plebeians to join mouths with someone who disdains their love: 'Why shall the people give / One that speaks thus their voice?' (3.1.119–20).

Coriolanus's answer, in its evocation of failed birth and feeding, again suggests anxiety about the core of shared life: 'Even when the navel of the state was touched, / They would not thread the gates. This kind of service / Did not deserve corn gratis'; furthermore, their complaints, 'All cause unborn, could never be native / Of our so frank donation. Well, what then? / How shall this bosom multiplied digest / The Senate's courtesy?' (3.1.124–33). He therefore urges the Senate to

> pluck out
> The multitudinous tongue; let them not lick
> The sweet which is their poison. Your dishonour
> Mangles true judgment, and bereaves the state
> Of that integrity which should become't.
>
>   (3.1.156–60)

What defends 'integrity' – wholeness – against the 'multitudinous' alternative is Coriolanus's favourite integer: the single self, standing up like a lone sword against the mindlessly appetitive mass of living flesh. But playing 'a part which never / I shall discharge to the life' has shattered even Coriolanus's body into discordant parts (3.2.106–24); his attack on the unifying belly-fable dismembers him when it reverts to micro-cosm. The tribunes, speaking 'Upon the part o'th' people' (3.1.211), condemn him to death.

Ignoring Cominius's advice that he either 'make strong **part**y or defend yourself / By **calm**ness' (3.2.95–6). Coriolanus provokes the exile that suits his deeper purpose. His fare-ill speech renews his complaints about the stinking mob of decaying animals (disguised as Romans) trying to corrupt his unity and uniqueness: 'You common cry of curs whose breath I hate / As reek o'th'rotten fens' whose 'carcasses ... do corrupt my air' (3.3.119–22). Thus begins a flurry of alliteration in Coriolanus's speech that continues through his arrival in Antium, and could signal subliminally, at the micro-level, an insistent sameness always threatening to collapse into otherness, always on the brink between doubleness and difference. He tells his mother that 'the beast / With many heads butts me away', and while 'common chances common men could bear', he must 'go alone, / Like to a lonely dragon' (4.1.1–2, 5, 29–30); the way 'calm' echoes the doubled 'common' in the preceding line may reinforce Coriolanus's determination to be furious instead, and no other Shakespeare play has more uses of 'calm-', or of 'many'.

Coriolanus's earlier compulsion to flee the shared domestic space of Rome manifested itself in his nostalgia for confrontations with Tullus Aufidius, mirror of his martial self – confrontations that establish his identity by offering to liberate him from it: 'were I anything but what I am, I would wish me only he' (1.1.226–7). The subjunctive hides what is, for Coriolanus, an inconvenient truth: we are each (as microbiology, racial genetics, depth psychology, sociology and many other disciplines have shown) many things other than what we are. Having strenuously separated from the body politic of Rome, Coriolanus arrives in Antium – another name that hints at an apt prefix – weirdly eager to enter another co-mingling: comparing his former identity with Rome to friends 'whose double bosoms seems to wear one heart . . . who twin, as 'twere, in love / Unseparable', Coriolanus now seeks to join his flesh and blood with the Volscians, like friends who 'interjoin their issues' (4.4.13–22).

The very first mention of Tullus Aufidius makes clear that Coriolanus finds him so alluring because Aufidius allows Coriolanus to inhabit his favoured role of heroic warrior, especially in difficult single combat: 'Were half to half the world by th'ears and he / Upon my party, I'd revolt to make / Only my wars with him' (1.1.228–30). The word 'half' appears more often in *Coriolanus* than in any other Shakespeare play, including four more instances seemingly imposed in this first Act for no particular reason: 'half an hour' (twice, about two different

events), 'half a hundred years', and 'Within this mile and half'. As the story progresses, however, instead of making Coriolanus whole, Aufidius intensifies the divisions between the halves already constituting Coriolanus's identity in order to destroy him.

Aufidius knows how to flatter his guest, calling him 'all-noble Martius' and 'thou Mars', and seeming to accept that he could never penetrate his foe's body, only encircle it: 'Let me twine / Mine arms about that body, where against / My grained ash an hundred times hath broke / And scarred the moon with splinters' (4.5.108–11). But Aufidius's homoerotic rhapsody culminates ominously with these two mirrored men waking 'half dead with nothing' (4.5.127); it may actually impose a divided self, again signalled by the word 'half'. Within a dozen lines, that poison pill in the humbly offered feast resurfaces: 'Therefore, most absolute sir, if thou wilt have / The leading of thine own revenges, take / Th'one half of my commission' (4.5.138–40).

So much for 'absolute' ('Free from dependency, autonomous; not relative' (*OED* A1)); to halve is to have not. The tension between the implications of the 'com-' root and the 'sol[e]' root are probably not accidental, since the same pairing (with the addendum of 'part-') recurs two scenes later when Aufidius's lieutenant wishes 'for your **part**icular, – you had not / Join'd in **com**mission with him; but either / Had borne the action of yourself, or else / To him had left it **sol**ely'. In uniting with the enemy that he assumes verifies his martial self, Coriolanus immediately joins the kind of commensal event by which human otherness had always threatened to get inside the gates of the self. He repeatedly accepts food, drink and popularity with the multitude. Departing Rome, he had vowed to 'exceed the common or be caught / With cautelous baits and practice' (4.1.32–3); he is now unwittingly trending toward the latter.

The meal might seem to be Coriolanus feeding at last on his greatest foe: a first servingman recalls that Coriolanus 'was too hard for [Aufidius] directly, to say the truth on't: before Corioles he scotched him and notched him like a carbonado', and a second servingman adds, 'An he had been cannibally given, he might have broiled and eaten him too'. This is hardly good news for Aufidius, who has his own bifurcation problems: 'the bottom of the news is, our general is cut i'th' middle and but one half of what he was yesterday; for the other has half, by the entreaty and grant of the whole table' (4.5.188–202).

But Aufidius has already decided to sacrifice his integrity, to avenge his wounded vanity; it is Coriolanus's integrity that is now at risk. However disguised as a martial project, this is still the common experience of feeding that kept threatening to invade Coriolanus's fantasy of the self as sword. His mother (as Janet Adelman has discussed)[17] wanted feeding to be subsumed by battle: 'the breasts of Hecuba / When she did suckle Hector looked not lovelier / Than Hector's forehead when it spit forth blood / At Grecian sword contemning' (1.3.42–5). Cominius describes Coriolanus's return to battle as a man coming 'to a morsel of this feast / Having fully dined before', which Coriolanus complains makes it seem 'as if I loved my little should be dieted / In praises sauced with lies' (1.9. 10–11, 51–2). So, in Antium, he is being served, but ill-served. The supper table is the altar where the soldier is redomesticated, and the god of unity is sacrificed into his mortal parts. The final surrender of his violent mission to tender sentiments of fleshly kinship is actually only the culmination of a process that had been insidiously underway since that first embrace and feast in Antium.

Back in Rome, the tribunes, celebrating a 'more comely time', a time of calm for the commons, recognize that Coriolanus's self-regard depended on self-containment, on the absence of others except as opponents:

BRUTUS. Caius Martius was
A worthy officer i'th' war, but insolent,
O'ercome with pride, ambitious past all thinking,
Self-loving.
SICINIUS.   And affecting one sole throne
Without assistance.   (4.6.27–33)

That addendum is revealing in its redundancy. At the core of 'insolent' lurks another 'sole'; at the heart of the haughtiness is the isolation. The etymology – from *absolutus*, meaning 'made separate' or 'set free' – may be different from that of 'sole', but both similarly evoke Coriolanus's project. Perhaps the most striking of the play's four versions of 'insolent' is Sicinius wondering how Coriolanus's 'insolence can brook to be commanded / Under Cominius', where the repetition of the 'com-' prefix emphasizes the tension between working alone and working with others, and aurally links Cominius to the latter. Nor can Coriolanus's old supporters imagine this solitary figure at one with another: 'He and Aufidius can no more atone / Than violent'st contrariety' (4.6.73–4). But, in Antium, *contra-* has become an alternative *com-*: Cominius confirms that Coriolanus has 'join'd wi'th' Volscians', and the many evolve toward an army of one, at some level superior to the massed 'clusters' of ordinary Roman life (4.6.90, 125, 131). Coriolanus's Volscian followers may resemble that 'multiplying spawn', but they are generated by martial charisma rather than biological functions.

The great son of Rome brings a high fever to cleanse the body politic of all life forms that do not epitomize this supposed Roman self, and the umbilical cord of his Roman origins will be not only cut but cauterized. Cominius reports that Coriolanus now acknowledges neither shared blood, even with a noble Roman warrior, nor the title Rome gave him for his noblest battle:

I urged our old acquaintance and the drops
That we have bled together. 'Coriolanus'
He would not answer to, forbade all names.
He was a kind of nothing, titleless,
Till he had forged himself a name o'th' fire
Of burning Rome.   (5.1.10–15)

---

[17] Janet Adelman, '"Anger's my meat": Feeding, Dependency, and Aggression in *Coriolanus*', in *Shakespeare: Pattern of Excelling Nature*, ed. David Bevington and Jay Halio (Newark, NJ, 1978), pp. 108–24.

Might this name (in parallel with 'Coriolanus') be Romulus, and this his chance to give new birth to his decadent imperial city, as well as to his compromised martial identity? Menenius had earlier analogized Coriolanus to a creature loved to death by a wolf (2.1.8–10), and certainly being a suckled canine would hardly suit Coriolanus's determination to transcend nursing on milk amid 'the common cry of curs'. But as he returns in vengeance, the Romans are the wolf he is hunting (4.6.112). Sloughing off human father figures such as the anonymous old Volscian and Menenius, Coriolanus will allow his identity to be permeated or penetrated only by the god Mars (lurking in his *nomen* and linked to him by multiple attributes of Mars, including fatherlessness, in classical texts and Renaissance mythographies)[18] and the demi-god Hercules (twice explicitly associated with him, and twice more via a fiery battle against a many-headed Hydra). These were the two warriors most often proposed as Romulus's father; and a servingman reports that Coriolanus was welcomed in Antium 'as if he were son and heir to Mars' (4.5.194–5).

Menenius is reluctant to make a claim on Coriolanus's filial loyalty, given the rebuff of similar claims by Cominius, who 'was sometime his general, who loved him / In a most dear particular. He called me father – / But what o' that?' (5.1.2–4). Yet the seeds of Coriolanus's destruction are already showing some shoots. His own diction inadvertently evokes the breast and the family:

> my remission lies
> In Volscian breasts. That we have been familiar,
> Ingrate forgetfulness shall poison rather
> Than pity note how much. Therefore, be gone.
> Mine ears against your suits are stronger than
> Your gates against my force.   (5.2.83–8)

His determination to make his body a fortress of isolation – and his inability to see that subservient communing with the Volsces defeats that project – could hardly be clearer.

Even his exalted title of 'general' implies the compromises of shared humanity. The word 'general' appears more often than in any other Shakespeare play, including ones such as *Othello* and *Troilus and Cressida* where the term for the top military commander is similarly relevant. Although it is mostly used in that sense here, Menenius speaks of 'the general food' in the opening belly-fable, Coriolanus complains about the plebeians' 'general ignorance', and his mother condemns them as 'general louts'. Political exaltation again carries a thinly veiled threat to render the transcendent person merely a generic one.

The Volscian soldiers do not yet recognize that paradox: 'The worthy fellow is our general: he's the rock, the oak not to be wind-shaken' (5.2.107–8). Menenius's claim to have been 'on the party of your general' proved, not surprisingly, unavailing (5.2.30–1). Then, however, the rhetorical winds, and with them the emotional temperature, start to rise. The next scene begins with Aufidius endorsing Coriolanus's self-praise for having 'stopped your ears against / The general suit of Rome', in obedience to the Volsces (5.3.5–6). But only fourteen lines later, the 'general' Coriolanus finds that stopping his ears may not stop his eyes, widely supposed in Shakespeare's culture to be the main channel to the heart. The fabric of his proudly asserted self-containment begins to fray at the fringes: 'Shall I be tempted to infringe my vow / In the same time 'tis made? I will not' (5.3.20–1). 'Shall I be tempted' is a question that answers itself, and does so by reminding us that the psychological self is always divided, despite the disciplinary functions of the will.

If Caius Martius's symbolic death and rebirth at the gates of Corioles lifted him free from his hereditary identity by granting a new name reflecting his martial deeds, then the confrontation at the gates of Rome calls him back to his first birth, his dependencies and dependants, and the meaning of common blood:

> My wife comes foremost, then the honoured mould
> Wherein this trunk was framed, and in her hand
> The grandchild to her blood. But out, affection!
> All bond and privilege of nature break!

---

18 Peggy Muñoz Simonds, 'Coriolanus and the Myth of Juno and Mars', Mosaic, 18.2 (1985), 33–50.

Within three lines, what dissolves instead is his metallic, statuary self: 'I melt, and am not / Of stronger earth than others'. His son 'Hath an aspect of intercession which / Great Nature cries "Deny not"' (5.3.22–33).

For a moment he rallies, determined to let Rome be the penetrable field, while himself remaining uncreaturely and purely autonomous:

> Let the Volsces
> Plough Rome and harrow Italy, I'll never
> Be such a gosling to obey instinct, but stand,
> As if a man were author of himself
> And knew no other kin.   (5.3.33–7)

But this resolution, too, fails within a few lines, rendering Coriolanus again a creature of theatrical and fleshly 'parts':

> Like a dull actor now,
> I have forgot my part and I am out,
> Even to a full disgrace. Best of my flesh,
> Forgive my tyranny.   (5.3.40–3)

This resembles the Mad Hatter defending to Alice his decision to butter his watch on the grounds that it was 'the very best butter', and Coriolanus continues to try to frame his concessions to his biological identity with superlatives:

> You gods, I prate
> And the most noble mother of the world
> Leave unsaluted. Sink, my knee, i'th' earth;
> Of thy deep duty more impression show
> Than that of common sons.   (5.3.48–52)

That adjective again: in trying to remain more than common flesh, he yields to common flesh. As he sinks back into the earth, and back into the allure and mutual obligation of family life, the whole project of radical autonomy is systematically retracted. Nor is identity unique or even possessory: in a line that richly anticipates *The Winter's Tale*, Volumnia presents Coriolanus's son as 'a poor epitome of yours, / Which by th'interpretation of full time / May show like all yourself'. Time makes the self (back) into the all – a fact at once tragic and comic – and his Senecan determination to be 'like himself' (2.2.46) and 'like me formerly' (4.1.53) must be deferred hopefully into a next generation.

When Coriolanus returns to the enclosure of Rome, his mother stands blocking the gates – gates which partly represent the passageway through which he first emerged into the world as a separate being.[19] If he thinks he is a self-made man, and thinks being a wholly self-contained being is the ideal, she will remind him that she surrendered her own bodily integrity to bring him into being, when she could instead have prevented his birth. Pushing through those gates to erase his compromising Roman identity will in fact only confirm disgracefully the messy truth of his biological derivation.

Wavering, he begs not to be told to 'capitulate / Again with Rome's mechanics. Tell me not / Wherein I seem unnatural' (5.3.82–4). But, as in *A Midsummer Night's Dream*, what those mechanics or mechanicals largely represent is the natural aspect – the functional body, as opposed to abstract ideal – of the human animal. Even the term 'capitulate', although familiar enough as a term for negotiating terms under headings, suggests that both Coriolanus and the Roman state will be obliged to mingle their higher faculties – the *caput* and the Capitol – with the mere vessel (yet mostly master) of human life that Hamlet (2.2.124) calls 'this machine'.

Volumnia warns him against 'Making the mother, wife and child to see / The son, the husband and the father tearing / His country's bowels out' (5.3.101–3). His identity is multiple because it is relative and derivative, made of 'parts' that will only become more deeply engaged as he tries to free himself:

> If I cannot persuade thee
> Rather to show a noble grace to both parts
> Than seek the end of one, thou shalt no sooner
> March to assault thy country than to tread –
> Trust to't, thou shalt not – on thy mother's womb
> That brought thee to this world.   (5.3.120–5)

'Tread' persists as Coriolanus's mode of domination (even over himself, at 1.1.254–6), set against

---

[19] Watson, *Hazards of Ambition*, pp. 174–5.

'trade', which derives from it and links the class disdain of both the protagonist and his mother to a disdain for exchange (an emergent meaning of 'trade') as a means of survival. The bawdy sense of 'tread' proposes an oedipal crisis, but one centred (like most post-Freudian views of early childhood psychology) less on sexuality than on differentiation. His mother's intervention is 'most mortal to him' – mortal, as in fatal, but also fatal because mortal, because his claim to self-authorship and transcendence has been exposed as unsustainably 'unnatural'. Asking Coriolanus to 'reconcile' the warring sides is demanding a surrender of the anti-'con-' project that matters more deeply to him than any battle between city-states; it would be a compromise, but – as events prove – a compromise is, for him, an ultimate defeat.

Uneasily awaiting the outcome of this final plea for mercy, the people's politician Sicinius (as he does so often) raises the relevant question about Coriolanus's apparent escape from the con- condition of a fellow Roman: 'Is't possible that so short a time can alter the condition of a man?' Menenius answers in terms that seem to endorse Coriolanus's transcendence, but keep remanding him to the zoo and its feeding troughs:

MENENIUS.   There is differency between a grub and
    a butterfly; yet your butterfly was a grub. This
    Martius is grown from man to dragon. He has
    wings; he's more than a creeping thing.
SINCINIUS.   He loved his mother dearly.
MENENIUS.   So did he me and he no more remembers
    his mother now than an eight-year-old horse.
    The tartness of his face sours ripe grapes ... there
    is no more mercy in him than there is milk in a male
    tiger.   (5.4.11–28)

These admirations of Coriolanus's transcendence (including his disdain for feeding) contain within them subversions of it: he has no stable self, and no immunity to the identification with non-human creatures that was his primary rhetorical weapon against his domestic enemies.

Coriolanus thus implicitly becomes the butterfly his son and his metaphoric sons in the Volscian army will dismember[20] – the disastrous end of his

effort to rise above his vermicular condition – and Eric Brown argues that Aristotle's definition of insects as creatures that are simultaneously whole beings and separable parts guides many of the play's key insect references.[21] Furthermore, the son's 'confirmed countenance' in chasing the butterfly is a double-barrel shot of the 'con-' prefix, with the latter word derived from the idea of containment: a holding together that, in this case, leads to a tearing apart.

George Bernard Shaw called *Coriolanus* 'the greatest of Shakespeare's comedies'. Shaw enjoyed turning conventional views upside-down, not least regarding Shakespeare, but one can easily imagine a comedy celebrating the survival of ordinary Romans achieved by eliminating a fanatically militarist and disciplinarian leader. *Coriolanus* is not, however, that play. Caius Martius is not just the 'puritan' Malvolio (*Twelfth Night*, 2.3.135) on steroids, although he does seem at moments to represent a revision of monasticism and martyrdom, redirected from Christian to classical aims of glory with some of the old emphasis on works and purgation intact.

Still, from one exalted perspective, this is a comedy after all: 'The gods look down and this unnatural scene / They laugh at' (5.3.184–5). Like the performers of the Twelve Worthies in *Love's Labour's Lost* (5.2.579), Coriolanus feels 'o'er-parted': ridiculed out of his role as an immortal Roman hero. Not only is the battle against the complexity of a human self (including its Roman macrocosm) difficult; victory would be Pyrrhic. Explicitly and subliminally, Shakespeare calls his audience's attention to the way human beings are, from a tragic perspective, unitary, and from a comic view, parts shared in common.

Aufidius understands that Coriolanus's failure to complete his cleansing of Rome constitutes the triumph of his mortal aspect. An 'empoisoned'

[20] Watson, *Hazards of Ambition*, pp. 215–16.
[21] Eric C. Brown, 'Performing Insects in Shakespeare's *Coriolanus*', in *Insect Poetics*, ed. Eric C. Brown (Minneapolis, 2006), pp. 29–30, 48.

Coriolanus cannot 'purge himself with words', despite claiming to be 'returned your soldier, / No more infected with my country's love / Than when I parted hence' (5.6.8, 71–3). But parted he has been; made back into a part of the human and Roman collectives that seek survival above all, because parts of himself turned him against the parts of himself that cast him into a more heroic role. He could defeat a whole city of Volscians alone, but he cannot overcome his own disabling multiplicity. He had vowed to 'fight against my cankered country' (4.5.92–3), but the *contra-* root of 'country' – a word that, in its various forms, occurs forty times in *Coriolanus*: twice as many as in any other Shakespeare play – has become an insurmountable paradox.

Aufidius refuses to use 'thy stolen name, / "Coriolanus", in Corioles (5.6.91–2). A few scenes earlier, one Volscian watchmen taunted the retreating Menenius by asking, 'Now, sir, is your name Menenius?' and the other added, ''Tis a spell, you see, of much power. You know the way home again' (5.2.94–6) – a devastatingly apt anticipation of the taunt that is about to send the 'boy' Coriolanus back home to his mother earth without the name he had achieved. Aufidius twice calls Coriolanus 'traitor', echoing not only the charge of the tribunes but also – aurally, via the Latin *trāditor* – the project of treading on the trades (as Aufidius and perhaps his confederates apparently 'Tread' on Coriolanus's corpse at 5.6.130–5). Coriolanus responds with predictable boasts, but his integrity is forfeit. Rather than admit to the unmanly leaking of tears, he claims to 'sweat compassion' (5.3.196), but the *cum-* prefix word undermines the already shaky claim. Now he is the one seeking 'conditions' (5.3.205) – the *cum-* prefix word that humiliated Aufidius earlier (1.10.3–7).[22] His foes are now the sword, and he merely the stain: 'Cut me to pieces, Volsces men and lads; / Stain all your edges on me' (5.6.112–13). In his final line he reprises his favourite boast – 'Alone' – but the mob will then 'Tear him to pieces' to avenge their relatives he killed, including a 'Marcus' who recalls Coriolanus's own patronymic (5.6.117–23). I think Shakespeare may have recognized, in the classical tradition of the *sparagmos*, in which the protagonist is literally torn to pieces, something toward which he could build the story of a man torn apart by the very nature of community. Thus concludes the tragedy of the uncommon, the tragedy of the insular man. Kinship – the life of us all – is inevitably the death of him.

A stage direction specifies that *'Two conspirators'* kill Coriolanus: a violation of singularity tied to another con- word, framed by five consecutive cries of 'kill' and four of 'hold'. Then a penitent Aufidius surrenders himself to the 'censure' of his community and says, 'Take him up. / Help three o'th' chiefest soldiers; I'll be one . . . Though in this city he / Hath widowed and unchilded many a one' (5.6.143, 149–53). Why, in just the last twenty-five lines of the play, does Shakespeare impose a two, a three, a four, and a five, along with 'many a one', if not to remind us again of the singularity that has been destroyed?

A Volscian lord offers a command that momentarily grants Coriolanus, posthumously, an honourable identity separate from the body that has taken him the way of all flesh, but that separation promptly collapses in the second sentence:

> Bear from hence his body
> And mourn you for him. Let him be regarded
> As the most noble corpse that ever herald
> Did follow to his urn. (5.6.143–6)

Another of the lords then absolves Aufidius of 'a great part of blame'. The very last word is 'Assist': Caius Martius Coriolanus disappears in the midst of a collective exit.

---

22 McDonald, *Late Style*, p. 55 notes that 'condition' is '*con* and *dicere*, or "speaking with"'.

CORIOLANUS AND THE POETICS OF DISGUST

BRADLEY J. IRISH

In the final days of 1811 a London newspaper reviewed a recent production of *Coriolanus*, starring the renowned John Philip Kemble. To conclude his report, the anonymous critic summarized Caius Martius and his tragedy:

He affects to bow down, in spirit, and succumb before the Gods; yet, when his hot nature bursts forth into a summary and fatal resolution, he vomits blasphemy, and challenges the wrath of Jove, by denying his homage to the will of Heaven! He affects to be a patriot of the sternest order, yet he places the pretensions of his own swelling vanity above the institutes and ancient ceremonies of the land.[1]

Though much could be said about this reading of the play, I want to focus on a single image: that of Coriolanus vomiting, his curses encompassing not just a verbal violence, but a visceral one as well. The notion was hardly original; it is easy enough to imagine the mouth of Martius as a site of varied expulsion, and Shakespeare himself would have encountered a similarly eruptive Roman in his reading of Plutarch:

So *Martius* being a stoute man of nature, that neuer yeelded in any respect, as one thinking that to ouercome alwaies, and to haue the vpper hand in all matters, was a token of magnanimitie, and of no base and faint courage, which spitteth but anger from the most weake and passioned part of the heart, much like the matter of an impostume.[2]

In his rage, Coriolanus again ejects a diseased substance from his body. Here, 'the matter' is the pus and filth of an infected abscess, perhaps from an impacted tooth or an inflamed bowel – his disgust

for the Roman plebs is somatized, a sympathetic response to the moral revulsion equally occasioned by their presence. Coriolanus is a man often disgusted, in both body and soul.

Nowhere does Shakespeare use the term *disgust*, a word that began its career in the English language just as he was settling into his as a playwright. Yet there's little doubt that the sentiment is present in Shakespeare's plays; we have no trouble speaking of Hotspur, disgusted by the mincing of a foppish courtier, or of Hamlet, repulsed by the mysteries of feminine sexuality. In *Coriolanus*, disgust is a key component of the relationship between Rome's citizens and Rome's protector, and it is surprising that more has not been made of this affective node in scholarly treatments. Stanley Cavell comes closest, noting that 'the value of attending to this particular play' involves mapping 'the pervasive images of food and hunger, of cannibalism and disgust' that dominate it.[3] But his assertion may be pushed further: *Coriolanus*, I argue in this

Portions of this chapter were presented in the 'Disgusting Shakespeare' seminar at the 2015 meeting of the Shakespeare Association of America; I thank Natalie Eschenbaum, Paul Budra and Emily King for their feedback. I am also grateful for the invaluable advice of Frank Whigham, Eric Mallin, James Loehlin, Ayanna Thompson, Cora Fox, Bradley Ryner, Ian Moulton and Peter Holland.
[1] David George, *Coriolanus* (New York, 2004), p. 92.
[2] Plutarch, *The Lives of the Noble Grecians and Romanes* (London, 1595), p. 243.
[3] Stanley Cavell, *Disowning Knowledge in Six Plays of Shakespeare* (Cambridge, 1987), p. 146.

article, is a play fundamentally about the experience of being disgusted.

Long recognized by affect theorists as a core emotion of human experience, disgust is a concept of enormous conceptual richness. It is underpinned by an array of behavioural and affective mechanisms that are inflected by culture even as they transcend it. These dynamics of disgust, I suggest, correlate with the stylistic, thematic and dramaturgical investments of *Coriolanus*, and equally inform the strands of critical concern apparent in recent studies of the play. Disgust is an emotion about boundaries, about entries and expulsions, about the regulation of bodies, both literal and symbolic; it is an emotion about blood and guts, about disease and illness, about the incorporation and elimination of food. These are, it should be immediately clear, concepts essential to Caius Martius and his tragedy – and, as such, disgust functions as a master trope in *Coriolanus*, variously guiding the action and manner of the play.

This article contributes to the growing body of recent scholarship on emotion in the Renaissance.[4] Yet rather than emphasizing historical phenomenology (the dominant critical approach), I instead anchor my main theoretical claims elsewhere, drawing upon the robust body of empirical and theoretical research on disgust that has emerged in the past two decades.[5] By placing these contemporary theories alongside an historicist treatment of disgust, I hope to demonstrate how revulsion is anchored at the heart of *Coriolanus* – and hope to suggest a new approach for scholars working on emotion in the early modern period. Accordingly, this article has three objectives, which are of increasingly expansive interpretive significance. The first, most obviously, is to demonstrate how tending to the dynamics of disgust can elucidate *Coriolanus*; disgust underwrites not only the play's imagery, but also its narrative structure, a framework dominated by cycles of incorporation and expulsion. The second is to provide a model of disgust that might prove valuable in other treatments of the period – be it in service of Shakespeare or Jonson, Sidney or Spenser, Marston or Nashe. But most importantly, my ultimate aim is to provide an example of how literary studies of emotion might benefit from a more direct engagement with current work in the sciences. Though the experience of disgust in the early modern period was undoubtedly governed by a unique set of particular circumstances, there is much to gain by exploring the more universalist affective logic that helped shape the emotion's historically and culturally contingent forms. Historicism only tells half the story of early modern emotionality; recent approaches to Renaissance emotion, which have so crucially contextualized our understanding of the topic, can only be enriched by expanding their theoretical purview, and bringing the insights of modern scientific research to bear upon their findings.

A BRIEF HISTORY OF DISGUST

For over a century, disgust has been deemed a core emotion of human experience – disgust elicitors in a cross-cultural context reliably predict a stereotypical set of responses, including facial behaviour, physiological changes and neuroanatomical activation. Yet it has also traditionally been the least understood of the so-called 'basic' emotions, and it has only been in the past two decades that disgust has become subject to extended investigation.[6] To begin most obviously: disgust

---

4 See, for example, Gail Kern Paster, *Humoring the Body: Emotions and the Shakespearean Stage* (Chicago, 2004); *Reading the Early Modern Passions: Essays in the Cultural History of Emotion*, ed. Gail Kern Paster, Katherine Rowe and Mary Floyd-Wilson (Philadelphia, 2004); *The Renaissance of Emotion: Understanding Affect in Shakespeare and his Contemporaries*, ed. Richard Meek and Erin Sullivan (Manchester, 2015); *Shakespeare and Emotions: Inheritances, Enactments, Legacies*, ed. R. S. White, Mark Houlahan and Katrina O'Loughlin (New York, 2015).

5 For a similar methodology, see Bradley J. Irish, 'The Rivalrous Emotions in Surrey's "So Crewell Prison"', *SEL: Studies in English Literature, 1500–1900*, 54 (2014), 1–24. See also Patrick Colm Hogan, *What Literature Teaches us about Emotion* (Cambridge, 2011).

6 For an overview of research, see Bunmi O. Olatunji and Craig N. Sawchuk, 'Disgust: Characteristic Features, Social Manifestations, and Clinical Implications', *Journal of Social and Clinical Psychology*, 24 (2005), 932–62.

is an emotion about food – or, more precisely, about spoiled food. It is an emotion about vomit, about nausea, about noxious, putrid smells; it is about how we know what we can eat, and how we know what we cannot. Since Darwin's investigation in *The Expression of the Emotions in Man and Animals*, food (and its rejection) has been recognized as central to the operation of disgust; in the early twentieth century, A. Angyal confirmed that fear of 'oral incorporation' was disgust's fundamental motivation, and in the following decades researchers have largely agreed that the primary domain of disgust is the mouth, the site of both ingestion and vomit.[7] In a foundational article of modern research, Paul Rosin and April E. Fallon similarly define disgust 'as a food-related emotion', and subsequent research has identified food aversion behaviour as the fundamental component of disgust's physiological response – which includes, most centrally, the induction of nausea.[8] Disgust is what Jonathan Haidt and his colleagues call the 'guardian of the mouth', the sentiment that crucially prevents us from incorporating infectious or dangerous substances.[9]

Yet disgust is also about much more than food – it is an emotion about blood, about pus, about shit, about wounds, about death, about corpses. It is clear that oral incorporation alone cannot fully account for the phenomenology of disgust, as we obviously experience revulsion in many circumstances that have little to do with food. Accordingly, investigators have identified a variety of different domains in which disgust triggers can be identified, radiating outward from the emotion's origins as oral defence. Many of these domains continue to constellate around the issue of contamination – though, as we will see, the source of this contamination becomes increasingly abstract as we travel further from disgust's original purview. In an influential essay, Jonathan Haidt and colleagues introduced the 'Disgust Scale', an articulation of the emotion's various forms across a series of discrete domains.[10] Their research suggests that disgust elicitors can be broadly categorized into two tiers. The first set, elicitors of *core disgust*, attends to the emotion's origins in orality:

when we are disgusted by *food, bodily products* or *animals* (particular organisms associated with food or excrement, such as maggots, cockroaches or rats), we are experiencing a visceral, somatic warning against oral incorporation. These core elicitors originate as 'an evolutionary adaption for an omnivorous species living with the constant threat of microbial contamination'.[11]

The second set of disgust elicitors expand beyond orality. In a process of cultural evolution, core disgust seems to have enlarged its purview, as a regulator of *sex, hygiene*, the *body envelope* (the physical integrity of the human body) and *death*. These domains, research suggests, have in common their ability to remind human beings of their fundamentally animal origins – and as such, this category of *animal-reminder disgust* serves an important cultural function, as a 'defensive emotion that guards us against the recognition of our animality, and perhaps ultimately, of our own mortality': 'Humans cannot escape the evidence of their animal nature. In every society people must eat, excrete, and have sex. They bleed when cut, and ultimately they die and decompose. We propose that most cultures have found ways to "humanise" these activities, through rituals, customs, and taboos that serve to differentiate humans from animals.'[12] Because of the need to efface our animality – to insist that our lives have a higher meaning, and extend beyond death – we have developed an emotion that discourages us from

---

7 Charles Darwin, *The Expression of the Emotions in Man and Animals* (New York, 1873), pp. 257–61; A. Angyal, 'Disgust and Related Aversions', *Journal of Abnormal and Social Psychology*, 36 (1941), 393–412; p. 394.

8 Paul Rozin and April E. Fallon, 'A Perspective on Disgust', *Psychological Review*, 94 (1987), 23–41; p. 23.

9 Jonathan Haidt et al., 'Body, Psyche, and Culture: The Relationship between Disgust and Morality', *Psychology and Developing Society*, 9 (1997), 107–31; p. 111.

10 Jonathan Haidt, Clark McCauley, and Paul Rozin, 'Individual Differences in Sensitivity to Disgust: A Scale Sampling Seven Domains of Disgust Elicitors', *Personality and Individual Differences*, 16 (1994), 701–13.

11 Haidt et al., 'Individual Differences', p. 712.

12 Haidt et al., 'Individual Differences', p. 712.

engaging that which suggests the opposite: disgust is an emotion of avoidance, by which we attempt to evade both the physical threat of illness and the existential threat of confronting our own material nature. These behaviours entail the response of 'pure disgust', the emotional form 'devoid of moral connotations'.[13]

But perhaps more suggestive to our study of literature and culture is the myriad of instances in which the emotion of disgust seems occasioned by violations of the *moral order* —at least, according to ordinary language. Some researchers have claimed that the lay sense of 'moral' disgust is, strictly speaking, a linguistic slippage – that is, when we claim to be *disgusted* by an act of racism, for example, we are really just mislabelling the experience of anger.[14] Yet there is an overwhelming body of evidence to suggest a deep connection between the visceral, embodied experience of pure disgust and the so-called 'disgust' that is elicited by socio-moral transgressions. And while the elicitors of this socio-moral disgust are certainly shaped by culturally specific variation,[15] the semantic congruence of disgust's visceral and socio-moral forms occurs across a wide linguistic spectrum: in countless language families, a single word signifies both eruptions of the stomach and eruptions of the social order.[16] Elaborations of disgust, it seems, exist on a spectrum – and as a guardian of social boundaries, socio-moral disgust is a culturally inflected elaboration of pure disgust's biological purview.

That socio-moral infractions elicit a genuine disgust response – sometimes called the 'moral dyspepsia' thesis – has received ample substantiation in the laboratory setting. The recent work of Gary D. Sherman and colleagues reveals that viewing morally offensive images – such as, for their college student test subjects, depictions of racism – predicts the same somato-visceral responses typically associated with food-based, core disgust. That morally objectionable content should elicit the tightening of the throat and a queasiness in the chest and stomach – involuntary behaviours poised to block the ingestion of offensive food and, if necessary, reject it – suggests the continuity between the biological origins of disgust and its

culturally conditioned adaptations.[17] Research similarly finds that the appraisal of consensual sibling incest induces a state of 'oral inhibition' ('nausea, gagging and diminished appetite') in test subjects – even though the morally repulsive act in question has no connection to food consumption.[18] That the orality of the disgust response adheres in such moral examples suggests that these emotional elaborations are mapped across a spectrum. And unsurprisingly, neurological research suggests that both pure and moralized disgust responses are underpinned by a similar anatomical architecture: functional MRI reveals that both domains 'recruited remarkably overlapping neural substrates' in the medial and lateral orbitofrontal cortex.[19]

It seems clear that humans evolved a *primary* disgust system as a biological safeguard, which then became elaborated broadly in a variety of culturally (and, of course, historically) determined, *complex* forms.[20] In its complex form, moral disgust

---

[13] Jorge Moll et al., 'The Moral Affiliations of Disgust: A Functional MRI Study', *Cognitive and Behavioral Neurology*, 18 (2005), 68–78; p. 68.

[14] See Edward B. Royzman and John Sabini, 'Something it takes to be an Emotion: The Interesting Case of Disgust', *Journal for the Theory of Social Behaviour*, 31 (2001), 29–59.

[15] See Jonathan Haidt, Silvia Helena Koller and Maria G. Dias, 'Affect, Culture, and Morality, or Is it Wrong to Eat Your Dog?', *Journal of Personality and Social Psychology*, 65 (1993), 613–28.

[16] Haidt et al., 'Body, Psyche, and Culture', p. 117.

[17] See, for example, Gary D. Sherman, Jonathan Haidt and James A. Coan, 'The Psychophysiology of Moral Disgust: Throat Tightness and Heart Rate Deceleration', unpublished manuscript. I am thankful to Dr Sherman for sharing his study with me.

[18] Edward B. Royzman, Robert F. Leeman and John Sabini, '"You make me sick": Moral Dyspepsia as a Reaction to Third-Party Sibling Incest', *Motivation and Emotion*, 32 (2008), 100–8; p. 100.

[19] Moll et al., 'Moral Affiliations', p. 75. See also Bruno Wicker et al., 'Both of us Disgusted in *my* Insula: The Common Neural Basis of Seeing and Feeling Disgust', *Neuron*, 40 (2003), 655–64; and P. Wright et al., 'Disgust and the Insula: fMRI Responses to Pictures of Mutilation and Contamination', *NeuroReport*, 15 (2004), 2347–51.

[20] Sarah L. Marzillier and Graham C. L. Davey, 'The Emotional Profiling of Disgust-Eliciting Stimuli:

(or *indignation*, as it is called by some researchers) guards not the body, but the soul – it is that which involves 'the protection of the self as a spiritual entity from degrading and polluting influences', as articulated within a particular cultural context.[21] Charged with 'the protection of the soul or the world from degradation and spiritual defilement', moral disgust keeps vigil over 'regulative concepts such as sacred order, natural order, tradition, sanctity, sin, and pollution' – just as disgust in its pure form stands watch over the literal violation of our material self.[22] The connection is elegantly characterized by Haidt and colleagues: disgust, having 'evolved to help our omnivorous species figure out what to *eat* in the physical world, now helps our social species figure out what to *do* in the cultural world'.[23]

But what of the word itself? From the Latin *gustare* (to taste), *disgust* entered the English language at the close of the sixteenth century; the earliest printed appearance that I have located occurs in John Florio's Italian dictionary *A Worlde of Words* (1598).[24] In Florio's translation, we can immediately detect the semantic congruence of disgust's visceral and generalized, socio-moral forms: *sgusto* is rendered with the English cluster 'disgust, distast, vnkindnes, dislike'.[25] This usage is confirmed in Randle Cotgrave's *A Dictionarie of the French and English Tongues* (1611), which translates *Desappetit* as 'a queasinesse, or disgust of stomacke' and *Desaimer* as to 'fall into dislike, or disgust'.[26] When the Catholic loyalist Anthony Copley denounces both Jesuit and Protestant prophecy, his expression equally suggests the proximity between moral disgust and distaste: 'So likewise of her Maiesties end how disasterously they haue prophecied, and do expect, I am sure you haue heard and do disgust as much as I. But what talke I of Protestants, seeing that also vpon very religious Catholikes they haue augured no lesse fatally, for being their known or but suspected distasters?'[27] That both *disgust* and *distaste* are deployed in this context suggests the immediate connection between the concept's gastric origins and its moral elaboration. Though some researchers, as I have shown, assert that the socio-moral usage of *disgust* is merely a figurative extension of disgust's true visceral form (the form suggested by its etymological origins in distaste), both applications seem to enter the English language simultaneously in the early modern period.

This linkage is crucial to *Coriolanus*, a play indebted stylistically to images of visceral disgust and, thematically, to sentiments of moral disgust. In his introduction to the play, R. B. Parker details the variety of 'image-clusters' that dominate the text; these include, he suggests, 'images related to *food eating* (and *cannibalism*), *animals, perversions . . . of sex, bodily fragmentation* and *the body as diseased*.[28] This catalogue correlates almost exactly with the list of conceptual objects that (as seen above) researchers have identified as the core elicitors of human disgust: *food, bodily products, animals, sex, hygiene, body envelope* and *death*. Though such categories are variously prominent in Shakespeare's plays, their concentration here is telling: *Coriolanus* is overwrought with images associated with disgust, from the 'stinking breaths' (2.1.229) of the 'beastly plebeians' (92) to the 'large cicatrices' (144) and 'unaching scars' (2.2.147) that

---

Evidence for Primary and Complex Disgusts', *Cognition & Emotion*, 18 (2004), 313–36.

[21] Moll et al., 'Moral Affiliations', p. 69.

[22] Paul Rozin et al., 'The CAD Triad Hypothesis: A Mapping Between Three Moral Emotions (Contempt, Anger, Disgust) and Three Moral Codes (Community, Autonomy, Divinity)', *Journal of Personality and Social Psychology*, 76 (1999), 574–86; p. 576; Richard A. Shweder et al., 'The "Big Three" of Morality (Autonomy, Community, Divinity) and the "Big Three" Explanations of Suffering', in *Morality and Health*, ed. Allan M. Brandt and Paul Rozin (New York, 1997), p. 138.

[23] Haidt et al., 'Body, Psyche, and Culture', p. 108.

[24] John Florio, *A Worlde of Wordes, or Most Copious, and Exact Dictionarie in Italian and English* (London, 1598), p. 370.

[25] Florio, *Worlde of Wordes*, p. 370. Florio confirms the generalized form in the definition of *Disparére*, rendered 'a disopinion, a diuersitie in conceit . . . Also a disgust or vnkindnes' (p. 108).

[26] Randle Cotgrave, *A Dictionarie of the French and English Tongues* (London, 1611), sig. Bb; Aa6v.

[27] Anthony Copley, *Another Letter of Mr. A.C. to His Dis-Iesuited Kinseman* (London, 1602), p. 25.

[28] *Coriolanus*, ed. R. B. Parker (Oxford, 1994), pp. 77–81.

mark the bloody body of Rome's hero.[29] In constructing *Coriolanus*, Shakespeare seems to have taken his cue from the lexicon of disgust, missing little opportunity to deploy language associated with that which makes us sick.[30] The cumulative effect of such images underscores a central facet of the play: the world of *Coriolanus* is inhabited by ill, compromised bodies, unsettled by the pangs of hunger, the soldier's blade or the moral disgust experienced so viscerally by its title character.

When discussing the play's interest in fragmented, anatomized bodies, scholars of *Coriolanus* have regularly deployed Bakhtin's familiar paradigm of bodily construction; Michael D. Bristol, for example, grids the play's corporeal politics within the battle of Carnival and Lent, the 'central event of popular festive life' in early modern Europe.[31] Yet, despite the obvious value of Bakhtinian approaches, we must be careful to avoid formulaic notions of the classical and carnivalesque body: *Coriolanus* is not, as Zvi Jagendorf notes, a play of 'Rabelaisian abundance', but is instead populated by starving plebs, rotund senators and an abundance of porous bodies, confounding any easy class distinction.[32] The concept of disgust, I suggest, is one such way to advance a more nuanced account of the body in *Coriolanus*. Given the intimate connection of visceral and socio-moral disgust, the concept of revulsion provides a useful way of integrating a discussion of the physical body (and its various tortured forms) with the play's larger conceptual issues, such as matters of political incorporation, self-sufficiency and popular participation. To consider the *disgusted* body is to think of a body that is capable of being violated both physically and ethically – often from the same root cause. *Coriolanus* depicts this association throughout, taking a wide cue from the spectrum of disgust.

IT'S HARD TO STOMACH: FOOD AND DISGUST IN CORIOLANUS

If *Coriolanus* is a play about disgust, then it follows closely that it is a play about food; the emotion, as seen above, originated as a governor of oral incorporation, and its visceral sensation is located primarily in the digestive tract. Kenneth Burke famously emphasized 'the last two syllables of the hero's name', and there is indeed a way that the play is preoccupied with all things alimentary, from food entering the mouth to exiting the anus.[33] The action of *Coriolanus* is framed by issues related to food: it begins with the starving plebeians of Rome rioting for corn, and ends with the plebs of Antium devouring Coriolanus in a symbolic feast.[34] Other key moments of the plot concern food and its consumption. When the banished Coriolanus arrives at the house of Aufidius, he finds his rival 'feast[ing] the nobles of the state' (4.4.8); conversely, Coriolanus's ill-reception of Cominius is attributed to the fact that 'he had not dined' and that 'veins unfilled ... are unapt / To give or to forgive' (5.1.50–3). Stylistically, the rhetoric of food, digestion and cannibalism overwhelms the play: there is no dearth of references to gnawing teeth and growling stomachs, and it's telling that its governing metaphor, the trope of the body politic, is introduced by Menenius's celebrated 'fable of the belly'. Furthermore, for a contemporary audience, the play likely spoke to a set of relevant issues from their own gustatory experience: *Coriolanus* has been linked topically to several food-related social phenomena, such as the Midlands enclosure riots of 1607, or the Great Dearth of 1593–7.[35] And if there is any remaining

---

[29] *Coriolanus*, ed. Peter Holland (London, 2013). All parenthetical citations from the play refer to this edition.

[30] For a discussion of the play's relevant imagery, see Gail Kern Paster, 'To Starve with Feeding: The City in *Coriolanus*', *Shakespeare Studies*, 11 (1978), 123–44.

[31] Michael D. Bristol, 'Lenten Butchery: Legitimation Crisis in *Coriolanus*', in *Shakespeare Reproduced*, ed. Jean E. Howard and Marion F. O'Connor (New York, 1987), p. 215.

[32] Zvi Jagendorf, '*Coriolanus*: Body Politic and Private Parts', *Shakespeare Quarterly*, 41 (1990), 455–69; p. 458.

[33] Kenneth Burke, *Language as Symbolic Action: Essays on Life, Literature, and Method* (Berkeley, CA, 1966), p. 96.

[34] See Paster, 'To Starve with Feeding', p. 123.

[35] See Arthur Riss, 'The Belly Politic: Coriolanus and the Revolt of Language', *ELH*, 59 (1992), 53–75; and Nate Eastman, 'The Rumbling Belly Politic: Metaphorical Location and Metaphorical Government in *Coriolanus*', *Early*

doubt that Shakespeare emphasized food, we need only look to the alterations of his source: in Plutarch's account, the plebeians rise primarily to end 'the sore oppression of usurers', while in *Coriolanus* they instead resolve 'rather to die than to famish' (1.1.3–4).[36]

Die, famish, or perhaps something else: to kill Caius Martius, suggests the First Citizen in the play's opening lines, is to 'have corn at our own price' (1.1.9–10). Immediately denounced as the embodiment of the patricians – whose ruthless agrarian policy is to hoard the harvest – the hero of Rome is precariously cast as the cause of its citizens' empty stomachs, an irony made all the more cutting by his own 'surplus' (41) of faults and vices, which cannot help but mock the 'leanness' (18) of the plebs. Although the eruption against Martius and the patricians is clearly symptomatic of a deeper fault-line within Rome's social organization, the plebeians are careful here to couch their action not in the language of political opposition, but rather in that of naked sustenance; 'I speak this in hunger for bread', claims the First Citizen, the primary agitator of the riot, 'not in thirst for revenge' (22–3). With this pat distinction (*hunger* for *bread* / *thirst* for *revenge*), Shakespeare introduces a central preoccupation of *Coriolanus*: the Roman body as a site of both visceral sensation and metaphoric possibility, a semantic range that accounts for the play's pervasive interest in how bodily matters function as both literal and figurative signifiers. In these opening moments, when the plebeians control the linguistic terrain, the focus remains overwhelmingly visceral: though Martius may be cursed as 'a very dog to the commonalty' (26), it is the multitude, more accurately, who in their hunger are reduced to the barest form of animal life.[37]

But despite this early focus on Caius Martius, it is Menenius who first takes up the patrician case. He does so, quite crucially, by transforming the body into a different kind of rhetorical object; one that conveys information not in the sensual experience of its pangs and aches, but in the potency of its symbolic application. This entails, of course, his famed 'fable of the belly',

the long-standing trope of political theory that forms one of the most memorable moments in *Coriolanus*. The familiar allegory details 'a time, when all the body's members / Rebelled against the belly' (91–2), spiteful of the latter's apparent leisure; the situation is defused when the belly reminds that it is he who receives and distributes 'that natural competency / Whereby they live' (134–5). For Menenius, the fable has clear enough bearing on the Republic's current troubles: 'The senators of Rome are this good belly', he suggests helpfully to the plebs, 'And you the mutinous members' (143–4). With good reason, the fable of the belly has inspired considerable commentary from scholars of the play, who routinely deem it a rhetorical failure; James Holstun, for example, calls it an 'almost contemptuously inappropriate' response to the plebeian rising, while Arthur Riss observes that Menenius 'does not merely fail to restrain the revolt, he actually legitimizes it'.[38] While I am in full agreement with this assessment, I think that the contemptuousness of Menenius has even been understated: though perhaps a reflection of his rhetorical naiveté, the form of the allegory equally reveals the deep disgust he harbours towards the plebeians.

The fable of the belly is, of course, a story about digestion, and as such, it has a natural affinity with the domains of disgust. As Frank Whigham has revealed, images of the alimentary tract were inscribed with a rich 'social coding' in an early modern period fraught with anxieties concerning 'class ingestion, retention, and evacuation'; surely this machinery is also active in the famous fable, which is, fundamentally, an attempt to justify

---

Modern Literary Studies, 13 (2007), http://purl.oclc.org/emls/13–1/eastcori.htm, accessed 11 March 2016.

[36] Plutarch, *Lives*, p. 237.

[37] On the play's biopolitics, see James Kuzner, 'Unbuilding the City: *Coriolanus* and the Birth of Republican Rome', *Shakespeare Quarterly*, 58 (2007), 174–99.

[38] James Holstun, 'Tragic Superfluity in *Coriolanus*', *ELH*, 50 (1983), 485–507; p. 487; Riss, 'Belly Politics', p. 62.

Rome's rigid social hierarchy.[39] As the bodily system devoted to incorporation and elimination – and thus to food, faeces and vomit – digestion thus offers a material cognate to the social disgust that implicitly defines Menenius's response to the plebeians – and that will find explicit expression in Caius Martius. But the stuff of literal disgust is equally active here: though the fable, Anny Crunelle notes, 'does not explicitly mention elimination', there is still a series of scatological puns on *tale/tail, pretty/prat* and *but/buttock*.[40]

Indeed, in the stunted digestion of this allegorical body, the stomach is said to deliver the 'flour' to its members, who in return 'leave [him] but the bran' (140–1) – that is, the inedible waste of the distribution process, which receives no further mention in the fable. As Jonathan Goldberg suggests, this crucial incompleteness codes the belly as 'undeniably anal': the stately stomach, he argues, 'assumes the position of the anus, receiving what is normally expelled; a closed economy is imagined in which waste is consumed'.[41] For Peter Holland, the belly is thus a 'vision of a hyper-efficient system', in which 'there is no waste to be disposed of, no excess to the consumption, no outside to which the waste is turned' – an assertion to which, I imagine, Menenius would assent, insofar as it substantiates the rhetorical fiction of his fable.[42] But there is also, I think, a way in which this image undoes itself, much to the detriment of Menenius and his senatorial interests. Though the fable's stomach indeed receives the body's waste, there is nothing in the passage to indicate that it is further consumed: perhaps instead it remains unprocessed, a heap of slowly spoiling refuse, much like the musty grain in the patrician's silos. Rather than a finely tuned fantasy of Roman engineering, the patrician's stomach may well be an overburdened midden, housing waste but doing little to dispose it further. This is the reading of the Second Citizen, who deems the belly 'the sink o'th' body' (117) – and there is certainly a way that Menenius may be seen as a partly constipated figure, swollen with the bloat of his own rhetoric.

Shakespeare intensifies this excremental association, by portraying Menenius as an explicitly *digesting* body. In the midst of his fable, the senator is famously interrupted by a flare-up of his own belly, providing a convenient opportunity for some metacommentary:

SECOND CITIZEN.   Well, sir, what answer made the belly?
MENENIUS.   Sir, I shall tell you. With a kind of smile,
Which ne'er came from the lungs, but even thus –
For, look you, I may make the belly smile
As well as speak –   (101–5)

Though slightly obscure, Menenius breaks some kind of wind here – either *upward* or *downward*, as the early moderns put it.[43] There are two things to be emphasized about this moment. First, Menenius's attempt to co-opt his body's (potentially embarrassing) intrusion, and incorporate it into his fable, is perhaps the most naked example of his rhetorical obtuseness in this sequence: quite remarkably, he thinks it wise to stress that his body is literally processing food directly in front of the starving plebs. But given the gravity of the moment, it is also worth considering that the 'belly smile' might be rather disgusting – as a reminder both of his grotesque corporality *and* his grotesque contempt for the plebs. Menenius here unites two modes of the signifying body. By drawing attention to his own senatorial belly, he provides the visual correlative to the Senate's role in the famous fable: he exemplifies the stomach, through and through, offering it to the plebs – quite perversely, in these circumstances – as an object of both literal and figurative contemplation.

---

[39] Frank Whigham, 'Reading Social Conflict in the Alimentary Tract: More on the Body in Renaissance Drama', *English Literary History*, 55 (1988), 333–50; p. 333. See also Bruce Thomas Boehrer, *The Fury of Men's Gullets: Ben Jonson and the Digestive Canal* (Philadelphia, 1997).

[40] Anny Crunelle, '*Coriolanus*: The Smiling Belly and the Parliament Fart', *ANQ*, 22 (2009), 11–16; p. 11.

[41] Jonathan Goldberg, *Shakespeare's Hand* (Minneapolis, 2003), p. 177.

[42] Peter Holland, '"Musty Superfluity": *Coriolanus* and the Remains of Excess', in *Shakespeare et l'excès*, ed. Pierre Kapitaniak and Jean-Michel Déprats (Paris, 2007), p. 94.

[43] See note 47 below.

But what, more specifically, does it mean to associate Menenius with the stomach, or to say generally that 'the senators of Rome are this good belly' (143)? Besides activating this network of digestion and disgust, the patricians' linkage with the stomach equally invokes a variety of other associations within the humoural discourse of the early modern period. As has been widely demonstrated, early modern concepts of the embodied self were not governed by a Cartesian binary of body and mind; in the early seventeenth century, physiology and psychology were endlessly entangled, just as the body itself was thought to experience a more porous engagement with its environmental context than is customary in a post-Enlightenment framework.[44] Accordingly, to speak of the belly, as Menenius does, is to unlock (in this case, perhaps, unwillingly) a set of dispositional associations as well. In early modern usage, the word *stomach* entailed not only 'the pipe wherby meate goeth dowen', but also sentiments like 'indignation, anger, vehement wrath, hatred, displeasure, abhorring of anie thing that liketh not'.[45] These are, of course, all emotions with a clear linkage to disgust – and indeed, as has been seen, some current researchers have argued that *indignation* is simply verbal shorthand for the feeling of moral disgust.

The stomach, then, was a festering pool for a host of angry, hostile eruptions. Within the humoural framework of the early modern period, this emotional set forms a taxonomy of choler, and it is probably not surprising that nowhere in Shakespeare does the word *choler* appear more than in *Coriolanus*. Yet while the usage of the term indeed invokes the now familiar physiological theory of the early modern period – with the elaborate sociocultural and dispositional implications it entails – there is also a more direct way in which *choler* circles back to matters of the stomach and disgust. In contemporary usage, *choler* also denoted what is now usually referred to as *cholera* – that is, the affliction of the bowels that 'purgeth vncessantly both vpward and downeward'.[46] Though distinct, both senses of the word are nonetheless entangled by their shared roots in the Latin

cholera, tellingly defined by one sixteenth-century lexicon as 'The humour called Choler. Also a sicknesse of the stomacke, with a troblous flixe and vomite ioyned wyth great daunger'.[47] To complicate matters further, this network of meaning must also include the etymologically distinct, but phonetically proximate *colic* – the 'wynde of the great Guttes' that is, we will see, later invoked by Menenius.[48]

Choler, the humour, induces a figurative stomach that erupts with temperamental anger; *choler*, the infirmity, induces a literal stomach that erupts with vomit and faeces. Both expressions are intimately related, and both correlate to the spectrum of disgust: rage and indignation form the basic expression of moral disgust, while the bodily wastes function as indicators and elicitors of visceral disgust. The opening scene of *Coriolanus*, I suggest, enacts this range of meaning by staging both senses of *stomach* in progression. That is to say, by casting the Senate as the *stomach* of his fable, Menenius equally assigns it a dispositional orientation toward his plebeian audience – one that finds imminent expression in the tongue of Martius, whose venomous rhetoric amplifies the implicit force of his comrade's allegory.

The indignation of Caius Martius, it follows, makes good on the rhetorical groundwork installed by Menenius, by excavating the latent disgust of the belly fable. Despite the inappropriateness of his attempt, Menenius at least tries to partly hide his contempt for the plebeians; he enters the scene with a reputation of 'one that hath always loved the people' (46–7), and he doesn't denounce Rome's 'rats' (157) until after the obvious failure of his fable. Coriolanus, however, has little time for

---

44 See note 4 above, especially the work of Paster.

45 Thomas Thomas, *Dictionarium Linguae Latinae et Anglicanae* (London, 1587), sigs. Kkk4v–5.

46 Pliny, *The Historie of the World*, vol. 2 (London, 1634), p. 46.

47 Thomas Cooper, *Thesaurus Linguae Romanae & Britannicae* (London, 1578), sig. T1r.

48 William Bullein, *Bulleins Bulwarke of Defence Against All Sicknesse, Soarenesse, and Woundes That Doe Dayly Assaulte Mankinde* (London, 1579), fo. 2v.

such niceties: his choler, his disgust and his *stomach* are evident from the moment he takes the stage. Though his opening invective draws widely on the lexicon of disgust – with images of illness, animals and bodily fragmentation – it is most ripe with images of food and digestion: a thematic cluster apt for those plebs who would 'feed on one another' (183) and with whom he would gladly 'make a quarry' (193).[49]

In fact, Martius seems to be disgusted by the very fact that Rome's citizens are hungry at all:

They said they were an-hungry, sighed forth proverbs –
That hunger broke stone walls, that dogs must eat,
That meat was made for mouths, that the gods sent not
Corn for rich men only. With these shreds
They vented their complainings.   (200–4)

Contempt drips from this passage, as do the images of visceral disgust, which cast the plebs as *dogs* and their plaints as *shreds*. But most telling is the remark that the rioters *vented* their complaints to the senators (to *vent*, as Holland notes, 'can mean to fart, to shit or to piss').[50] Martius, quite perversely, attaches a scatological weight to their hunger pangs; unable to excrete food from their empty bellies, they instead excrete words from their mouths, the site of the dirty teeth and rotten breath that so repulse him.[51] Indeed, for Coriolanus, the commoners are the refuse of the Republic, an association confirmed by his reaction to the pending Volscian assault: 'I am glad on't', he exclaims, 'Then we shall ha' means to vent / Our musty superfluity' (220–1). Coriolanus sees the pending war as a fine way to process Rome's overflowing waste heap: it is not just the Senate, but Rome itself which is constipated, overburdened with the festering waste of the common mobs.[52]

HEAL THYSELF: ROMAN DISEASE AND THE STRUGGLE FOR DISGUST

It is a remarkable image: plebeians as the waste of the Roman body politic, an impacted mass which must be expelled for the good of the Republic. In crafting this, perhaps the pre-eminent social fantasy of Caius Martius, Shakespeare takes a cue from his source in Plutarch. In the comparable passage, the patricians respond similarly to news of the Volscian assault:

So the wise men of ROME began to thinke … how by this occasion it was very meete in so great a scarsitie of victuals, to disburden ROME of a great number of citizens: and by this means aswell to take away this new sedition, and vtterlie to ride it out of the citie, as also to cleare the same of many mutinous and seditious persons, being the superfluous ill humours that greeuouslie feede this disease.[53]

As has been seen, Shakespeare's use of the word *vent* enables a specifically scatological reading of this moment; this is, I have argued, consistent with the larger thematic agenda of the play's opening movement, which explores Rome's social conflict via the class-inflected rhetoric of digestion and disgust. But while the excretory context is not explicit in the source-text, North's rendition is nonetheless suggestive for the related discourse that it activates: by comparing the common mob to a humour that must be purged, the passage is indebted to early modern medical practices, casting the plebeians as a kind of social pathology. Unsurprisingly, the rhetoric of disease is closely associated with the bodily matters we have thus far explored, and illness and contamination are key domains under the umbrella of disgust. If the healthy body is disgusting in its natural functions of excretion, the pathologized body is even more disgusting in its disintegration and decay – and as such, images of disease and illness form the second crucial component of how *Coriolanus* establishes its affective mode.

---

49 See *OED*, 'quarry, n.': 'A collection or heap of all the deer or other game killed during a hunt'.
50 Holland, 'Musty Superfluity', p. 93.
51 Goldberg notes that Coriolanus experiences the words of plebeians 'as shit hurled at him' (*Shakespeare's Hand*, p. 178).
52 In *Pierce Penniless* (1592), Thomas Nashe similarly recommends military service for the 'certain waste of the people for whome there is no use'; see Jo Anne Shea, 'Rhetorical Economies in Thomas Middleton's City Comedies' (Ph.D. dissertation, University of Texas at Austin, 1998), p. 36.
53 Plutarch, *Lives*, p. 241.

In his opening speech, Martius deploys the rhetoric of disease to express his contempt for the multitude:

What's the matter, you dissentious rogues,
That, rubbing the poor itch of your opinion,
Make yourselves scabs?   (1.1.159–61)

With this introduction, Shakespeare activates a variety of thematic concerns associated with disease and disgust. Yoking an image of physical degradation with one of sedition, Coriolanus presents a multitude that is both materially and politically compromised – and he is disgusted in both terms – visceral and socio-moral. The notion of scabbiness itself bridges the literal and metaphoric senses of disease: in this ambiguous phrasing, Coriolanus presents the multitude as physically covered in scabs and as the scabs of the body politic. For him, popular political action is self-defeating, and even rather indulgent: unable to restrain themselves, the plebeians scratch their bodies bloody, inviting further discomfort in the act of seeking relief. This implicit image of self-consumption – participating in the play's larger motif of cannibalism – is made more explicit in Martius's next salvo: 'your affections are / A sick man's appetite, who desires most that / Which would increase his evil' (172–4). The multitude is again cast as diseased – and, more importantly, as driven mad by their illness. Coriolanus continues to deflate the political seriousness of the uprising, by dismissing it as something like a fever-dream – not to be heeded, and more harmful than helping. And given the context, this medical advice is all the more perverse: while Martius speaks metaphorically of a 'sick man's appetite', the plebeians before him really are hungry, and their appetites really are being ignored by the patricians.

News of the Volscian assault pre-empts further discussion. In battle, however, Martius finds renewed cause to lament Rome's ailing body politic, denouncing his comrades as a social plague:

All the contagion of the south light on you,
You shames of Rome! You herd of – boils and plagues
Plaster you o'er, that you may be abhorred
Farther than seen, and one infect another
Against the wind a mile!   (1.4.31–5)

These are the 'common file' (1.6.43) of the Roman army, those who fled to the trenches while Martius penetrated the gates of Corioles alone. Coriolanus here deploys the rhetoric of disease with an unprecedented concentration – one that is only matched, as will be seen, in reaction to his own banishment. Again, visceral and socio-moral forms of repulsion intermingle, as Martius conjures a vision of physical repulsion to match the disgust occasioned by the soldiers' shameful retreat. In the context of combat, his metaphors are particularly apt; the waves of panic that overtake a breaking rank mirror the trajectory of a plague-wind, and there is an obvious justice in casting an incurable blight on those who fled their appointed death by an enemy's blade. Though Coriolanus was disgusted enough by the plebeian uprising, he is, given his own martial investments, supremely repulsed by the plebs' execrable conduct in the field.

But it is not simply the plebeians who elicit the rhetoric of disease from Coriolanus and the aristocratic party: as proxies for the multitude, Sicinius and Brutus are equally painted as a source of contamination and infection. A notable example inaugurates the second act, in which Menenius and the tribunes, waiting for news of the Volscian assault, turn their discussion to matters of state. In the midst of their banter, Menenius attacks the tribunes with a particularly strange elaboration: 'When you are hearing a matter between party and party, if you chance to be pinched with the colic, you make faces like mummers, set up the bloody flag against all patience and, in roaring for a chamber-pot, dismiss the controversy bleeding, the more entangled by your hearing' (2.1.70–5). While editors routinely note that the passage conflates a variety of the play's stylistic investments (images of disease, warfare, legality, etc.), I think a simple question must be asked: why, when mocking the tribunes for their parochial scope, would Menenius jump to a vision of their violent, bloody evacuation? Menenius makes a clear thematic linkage: in his fantasy, proximity to the plebeians – here specifically, entanglement in the daily rhythms of their life – correlates with the onset of a painful illness, the force of which loosens the boundaries of continence and turns the body inside-out. Though a Bakhtinian account may explain the image of the boundless plebeian body, I think the larger issue here is one of contagion: the tribunes are compromised by their dealings with the plebs, whose social repulsiveness finds a correlative in their bodily ailments. And quite appropriately, the illness is coded as specifically excretory – the disease of the plebeians is one that manifests the raw material of disgust, a fetid reminder of its origin in the common mob. Given the perennial fullness of his own belly, it is unsurprising that Menenius distances himself from the tribunes, now a source of contagion themselves: 'More of your conversation', he dismisses, 'would infect my brain, being the herdsmen of the beastly plebeians' (91–2).

It is no surprise that Coriolanus and his colleagues thus cast the plebs and their representatives as 'measles' (3.1.80) on the body politic. Rome is 'sure of death', Coriolanus rails, lest this popular influence be purged 'with a dangerous physic' (155–6). Yet, despite the obvious ferocity of this rhetoric, it is equally important to recognize that Caius Martius has no monopoly on being disgusted: the tribunes also rely on disgust-based imagery in their attempts to agitate the populous against the military hero. In fact, it is Coriolanus's very disgust for the plebs that enables this rhetorical strategy: guided by the tribunes, the citizens are incited by the very disgust-response that they themselves elicit in their protector.

We have already seen how disgust for the rabble manifests in Coriolanus – this visceral response, I have argued, underpins his characteristic indignation, a term synonymous with moral disgust. The tribunes identify this 'soaring insolence' as the key to toppling Coriolanus, and it is indeed the posture of *insolence* – associated by one contemporary dictionary with 'pride, hautinesse, stomacke' (2.1.248) – that is invoked to enflame the moral anger of his opponents.[54] In their first moments on stage, Sicinius and Brutus lay the groundwork for this strategy: contempt for the plebeians, they note, is virtually encoded in Coriolanus's bodily expression, seated in his 'lips',

'eyes' and 'taunts' (1.1.250). It is this famous pride, swollen with class-based contempt, that enables the tribunes to orchestrate his undoing:

> BRUTUS.   I heard him swear,
> Were he to stand for consul, never would he
> Appear i'th' market-place nor on him put
> The napless vesture of humility,
> Nor, showing, as the manner is, his wounds
> To th' people, beg their stinking breaths.
>
> (2.1.225–30)

The concentration of imagery in this passage suggests the proximity of visceral and socio-moral disgust elicitors. Coriolanus is sickened both by the populace and by the notion of submitting himself to them: the implications of humility, it follows, are as stomach-turning as the smell of the unwashed masses. The central charge of insolence encompasses both registers: when Sicinius implores the masses to 'forget not / With what contempt . . . he scorned you', he asks them to acknowledge their status as both materially and politically repulsive (2.3.217–19).

But once the tribunes establish Caius Martius's indignation, they are able to wrench free the rhetoric of disgust and fashion it to their own purposes. Coriolanus is cast as a disease of the state, a figuration *enabled* by his own constant professions of disgust: by announcing himself as sickened by the commoners, he unwittingly enables the tribunes to construe his insolence as a dangerous infection, which itself must be purged for the sake of the state's social harmony. In Shakespeare's elegant construction, Coriolanus and the plebs are thus locked in what might (quite inelegantly) be called an affective feedback loop. Martius, to start, is doubly disgusted by the plebeians: viscerally, by the grotesqueness of their bodies, and morally, by their cowardice, ingratitude and presumption. He consequently casts them as a pox on Rome's body – crafting a metaphor that, by emphasizing illness and decay, perversely reflects the material

---

[54] Richard Perceval, *A Dictionarie in Spanish and English* (London, 1599), p. 125.

circumstances of their lived experience. But here's the rub: Coriolanus's social arrogance inflames its own populist resentment in the plebeians, who, with the help of the tribunes, themselves diagnose this very snobbery as its own disease of state. What is evident here, above all else, is the fluid relationship between forms of disgust; matters of pride and indignation effortlessly inspire images of illness and disease, while being associated with such elicitors is enough to arouse contempt in even the most powerless subjects. In this manner, disgust (and indignation) become trapped in a mutually reinforcing emotional circuit: the plebs are disgusted by Martius's flagrant dismissal of their political voice, while Coriolanus is himself disgusted that they are bold enough to want one at all.

For their part, the tribunes insistently cast Coriolanus as a sickness of the state, aping the rhetoric with which he condemned the populace. In this construction, he is a one-man social plague, threatening to 'depopulate the city, and / Be every man himself' (3.1.266–7). As self-appointed physicians of the state, Sicinius and Brutus work to ensure that Coriolanus's damning influence 'shall remain a poison / Where it is, not poison any further' (88–9). When Menenius urges a temperate approach to Coriolanus, Brutus assures him that the case is far too severe: 'Sir, those cold ways / That seem like prudent helps are very poisonous / Where the disease is violent' (221–3). This rhetorical motif culminates in the conclusion to scene 3.1, in the final moments before Coriolanus and his allies retreat from the mob. Here, Sicinius most nakedly denounces Coriolanus as an infection of the state: 'He's a disease that must be cut away' (296). Despite the attempts of Menenius to disarm the metaphor – 'O, he's a limb that has but a disease: / Mortal to cut it off, to cure it easy' (297–8) – the tribunes stand by their diagnosis:

SICINIUS.   The service of the foot,
    Being once gangrened, is not then respected
    For what before it was.

BRUTUS.   We'll hear no more.

(to the Citizens) Pursue him to his house and pluck him
    thence,
Lest his infection, being of a catching nature,
Spread further.   (307–12)

Are the citizens, then, pathogens or antibodies? It depends on who you ask. It is hard not to associate this violent, angry mob with the spreading infection that Brutus describes, and Coriolanus and his party surely perceive their assault as requiring a healing 'physic' (3.2.34). But, co-opted by the tribunes, the pathologizing discourse has equally been turned against Coriolanus, and he too is transformed into a diseased subject.

In the showdown between plebs and patricians, the central political question may thus be framed in strikingly material terms: who, the play asks, has the greater right to be disgusted? As both parties stake claim to the politics of disgust, they paint their opposition as a blight on the body politic, to be healed only by their own purging physic. Shakespeare makes much, I think, of this fundamental similarity, which is revealed especially in the moments following Coriolanus's banishment. Here, Martius unloads a barrage of disgust-based rhetoric:

You common cry of curs whose breath I hate
As reek o'th' rotten fens, whose loves I prize
As the dead carcasses of unburied men,
That do corrupt my air, I banish you.
                                (3.3.119–22)

Though anchored in the familiar metaphor of contamination, the explosive imagery of this passage correlates remarkably with the disgust elicitors I reviewed in the first section of this chapter: Coriolanus runs the gamut of disgust, framing his repulsion in terms of hygiene, animalism, dead bodies and, of course, illness. But even more telling, I think, is his famed declaration of reciprocal banishment. Having lost the current battle – and by extension, being condemned as the source of Rome's illness, at least in the court of plebeian opinion – Coriolanus makes a final effort to invert the sentence of the tribunes, just as they inverted his own pathologizing discourse. Though intended as a distancing move, confirming his own fantasies of self-sufficiency, the manoeuvre ironically confirms his proximity to the tribunes, with whom he shares a central rhetorical premise.

In *Coriolanus*, the clash between plebeians and patricians manifests largely in the struggle to affirm one's repulsion. Yet, while both parties attempt to pathologize their adversaries – in order to distinguish Rome's healthy body from its diseased counterpart – the effect of this rhetorical mirroring, I suggest, ultimately works to undermine the class difference in which the play's characters are so invested. Accordingly, when the banished Coriolanus famously takes his leave like 'a lonely dragon [to] his fen' (4.1.30), a simple question lingers: does he set off to the same rotten fen in which he earlier located the plebs?

CORIOLANUS: THE ALLEGORY OF DISGUST

Disgust is known by many theorists as the 'gate-keeper emotion'; it oversees the boundaries of the self and social order, guarding the integrity of both from internal disruption and foreign contamination. It is thus unsurprising that it is of central importance to *Coriolanus*, a play that is, if nothing else, about the opening and closing of gates. We have already seen Shakespeare's vast deployment of disgust-related imagery – most notably (but by no means exclusively) images of digestion and disease – and I have suggested that disgust functions as an affective touchstone in the rhetorical conflict between the plebeians and the patricians – each party struggling to assert just how much it is repulsed by its counterpart. I want in closing to expand my focus, by exploring how some of the conceptual issues associated with disgust – matters of incorporation and purgation, integrity and violation – manifest in the larger structural features of the play. *Coriolanus* is preoccupied with thresholds, and its dramatic architecture is dominated by a series of ritualized entries and expulsions. For much of his time on the stage, Coriolanus is entering or exiting a city gate – sometimes forcing, sometimes forced, but always with profound consequence for those within and those without. To consider these concerns in an

affective framework provides means for aligning the play's stylistic and structural features: the abundances of images associated with disgust elicitors find dramatic expression in the shape of the narrative, which ultimately enacts an allegory of disgust.

As noted above, readers of *Coriolanus* have long viewed Caius Martius as a character enchanted by the fantasy of his own completeness; in this sense, he perhaps exemplifies the Bakhtinian notion of the classical body, that 'strictly completed, finished product . . . isolated, alone, fenced off from other bodies'.[55] For Coriolanus, it is the plebeian body that is marked by its fundamental incompleteness: he spends a great deal of the play railing in this manner against 'the mutable, rank-scented meinie' (3.1.68), whom he tellingly denounces as 'fragments' (1.1.217) during the climax of the food riots. Yet this dichotomy is also routinely challenged by the play, which cannot simply be read within Bakhtin's paradigm. The body of Coriolanus is far from pristine: it is one that wounds, and scars, and bleeds, sometimes to a shocking extent. Coriolanus's commitment to notions of the bounded self is further compromised by his own role as guardian of Rome's social order: as the Republic's war-machine, he is fundamentally tasked with puncturing and penetrating the wholeness of once firm boundaries, whether cleaving apart an enemy soldier or breaching the gates of an enemy compound. In structural terms, Coriolanus spends a great deal of the play as an invading force, trying to encroach upon a place where he's not wanted – be it Corioles, Antium, or in the final sequence, Rome itself.[56] Accordingly, he regularly assumes the status of a foreign body – a term that, with its saliency in multiple discourses, helps account for him both as a political and a symbolic subject.

It is, of course, in the assault on Corioles that Martius wins his greatest renown, and it is in this

---

[55] Mikhail Bakhtin, *Rabelais and his World* (Bloomington, IN, 1984), p. 29.
[56] On concepts of the foreign body, see Jonathan Gil Harris, *Foreign Bodies and the Body Politic: Discourses of Social Pathology in Early Modern England* (Cambridge, 1998).

initial action that Shakespeare establishes the narrative pattern of invasion and entry that dominates the play. Many readers, especially those with psychoanalytic interests, have associated the gates of Corioles with female genitalia, variously reading immersion in the symbolic vagina/womb in terms of rape and rebirth – a sequence thought, with good reason, to reflect Coriolanus's ambivalent bond to the overbearing Volumnia.[57] While this approach is certainly suggestive, I do think that it might be usefully expanded, by associating the assault on Corioles with the play's larger interest in the violation of bodily integrity. My basic suggestion here is that, in breaching the Volscian walls, Martius mirrors the trajectory of a contaminant that corrupts a body – that is, the same mechanism through which one is disgusted by a noxious substance, be it spoiled food, a dangerous pathogen, or a morally offensive sentiment. With the declaration that 'the gates are ope' (1.4.44), Rome's premier soldier clears the lane for his entry into foreign ground; in the moments that follow, he is incorporated into the body of Corioles, 'himself alone / To answer all the city' (55–6). Despite his comrades' cowardice, Caius Martius undoes the Volscians from the inside-out, gutting the defenders within their walls before welcoming his fellow Romans. In this moment, he is the infection – the spoiled blood and rotten humours that Corioles would expel, if only it possessed a suitable purgative.

And it is crucial, I think, that Martius is injured in the siege. Despite the victory, his own body is not preserved intact, and Lartius insists that the conquering hero retire from subsequent engagement: 'Worthy sir, thou bleed'st. / Thy exercise hath been too violent / For a second course of fight' (1.5.14–16). Despite his fantasy, Martius's is no classical body; it is subject to the same intrusion and violations that it inflicts upon its unfortunate opponents. But this is hardly an impediment: the quick-thinking Martius is able to appropriate the injury – to own his wounds, so to speak – by exploiting the features of early modern medical discourse, and casting the blood as restorative: 'The blood I drop', he assures Lartius, 'is rather

physical / than dangerous to me' (1.6.18–19). Unlike those of the unfortunate Volscians, these wounds merely enliven him for the next round of combat. Yet at the same time, blood is blood, and there is equally a sense in which the source of spillage is ultimately indistinguishable, commingled as it is on Caius Martius's body. This is the effect of his subsequent entry in the camp of Cominius, where he arrives as a bloody spectacle: 'Who's yonder', the general asks, 'That does appear as he were flayed?' (21–2). Not only a source of amazement, Martius appears here as an object of disgust: soaked in gore, it is he who is now turned inside-out, in the manner of a skinned deer. Though much of the blood is Volscian, its effect is to make him the anatomy; Martius is again the defiler and the defiled, consistent with the struggle for disgust displayed elsewhere in the play.

In fact, the success of Coriolanus in the field is explicitly measured by the degree of injury to his own body; Volumnia and Menenius eagerly anticipate cataloguing his new wounds, 'every gash ... an enemy's grave' (2.1.151–2). In the action of war, Martius is distinctly not disgusted by the blood and gore of violated flesh; his fantasies of integrity are temporarily suspended, replaced by a moral standard that rewards the shedding of blood and tearing of bodies, both his enemies' and his own. Yet after the din of war has faded, and Coriolanus has donned civilian garb anew, he reassumes a classical orientation of the body – incessantly defending his own corporal boundaries, and thoroughly repulsed by the common mob. Coriolanus, it seems, embraces injury as a visceral sensation – one suspended in the time-bending action of combat – but cannot assess its meaning in the aftermath; his injuries only smart when they 'hear themselves remembered' (1.9.29), and he'd rather suffer his 'wounds to heal again / Than hear say how [he] got them' (2.2.67–8). Coriolanus is

---

57 See, for example, Coppélia Kahn, *Man's Estate: Masculine Identity in Shakespeare* (Berkeley, CA, 1981), and Sean Benson, '"Even to the gates of Rome": Grotesque Bodies and Fragmented Stories in *Coriolanus*', *Comitatus*, 30 (1999), 95–113.

thus particularly unnerved by the electoral procedure of the consulship – a populist gauntlet that demands he peddle his punctured body, placing it in nauseating proximity with the garlic-eaters. In Plutarch, the returning hero embraces Roman custom, displaying his 'many woundes and cuts' without the protest of his dramatic counterpart.[58] Shakespeare's rendition insists upon Coriolanus's inability to tolerate this contact: not only a reflection of social antagonism, it reveals a deep anxiety about the proximity of the plebeian body to his own.

Why is Coriolanus repulsed by the idea of exposing his body to the rabble? Disgust is primarily a guardian of boundaries, and we know that Coriolanus fiercely asserts the social distinction that separates him from the multitude. Yet in its current state, his war-ravaged body might actually be thought to resemble that of the plebs: it is compromised by sores and cuts and a fundamental state of rupture. Coriolanus, as has been seen, casts the rabble as *scabs* during his initial moments on the stage – but he, we must assume, is literally scabby, the open and half-healed wounds of Corioles set in relief by the faded scars of battles passed.[59] To expose himself, it follows, is to reveal physical affinity with the plebeians – a material congruence that equally implies social cohesion. For obvious reasons, Coriolanus works to disavow any notion that he and the citizens enjoy a transactional parity:

> To brag unto them 'Thus I did, and thus',
> Show them th'unaching scars which I should hide,
> As if I had received them for the hire
> Of their breath only.   (2.2.146–9)

Yet there is another sense of exposure, entailing not display, but communicability – that is, not exposure *of*, but exposure *to*. If his current state makes Coriolanus resemble the plebeians, it also makes him more susceptible to them: here, the openness of his wounded body threatens both physical and social contamination. Perhaps the most naked testament to the frailty of corporal boundaries, a scab is the threshold between injury and integrity; it is an extension of the body proper, under continual threat of rupture or infection. Fearful of plebeian contagion on his best days, Coriolanus is particularly reluctant to subject his compromised body to the trauma of interaction with the rabble. Assaulted by enemy steel, the gates of his body have been unfastened; to offer it to the plebeians as such is to grant them access unopposed. '[W]e are', tellingly remarks one citizen, 'to put our tongues into those wounds' (2.3.6–7) – a statement that, I think, captures a disgusting fear of Martius. Popular political action, Coriolanus later exclaims, 'bereaves the state / Of that integrity which should become't' (3.1.159–60); these common tongues, with their rotten teeth and stinking breath, equally undermine the integrity of his own self.

Yet such attempts to inoculate himself against the plebs are unsuccessful; after his failure in the political arena, Coriolanus is himself diagnosed as a pathogen to Rome, an invading body that must be purged for the good of the state. Though ostensibly antithetical, his return to Rome – the play's second crucial entry – thus proves to be analogous to the capture of Corioles: he is ultimately cast as a foreign agent in both cities. A basic problem of *Coriolanus* is one of (military) incorporation; the play explores the fate of the war-machine in times of peace. But unlike Cincinnatus – the other pre-eminent solider-statesman of early republican Rome, who was successfully reintegrated into civilian life – Coriolanus ultimately proves to be indigestible by the Roman body politic: chaff of the senatorial belly, he is a necessary ingredient of peacetime living, but one that ultimately must be disposed of and expelled after serving its purpose. In her perceptive reading of the play, Paster suggests that, 'in banishing Coriolanus', Rome effectively 'devours' its

---

[58] Plutarch, *Lives*, p. 242.

[59] Gail Kern Paster observers that, in this scene, the play allows no distinction 'between new and old wounds, between flowing blood and healed-over scars' (*The Body Embarrassed: Drama and the Disciplines of Shame in Early Modern England* (Ithaca, NY, 1993), p. 97).

hero.[60] But this, I think, is only half the story, and the analogy must be pressed further. Rome does not simply devour Coriolanus, it also shits him out – expelling that which, now exhausted, resists any further incorporation into the healthy state. That his banishment is a popular action only amplifies the scatological implications: progression through the alimentary tract is inherently demo-cratic, as that which is differentiated at the time of oral incorporation finds itself homogenized by the anus.[61] In this manner, Coriolanus is declared utterly abject by the plebeians, an object of repul-sion even to them. This is the ultimate humiliation for Martius, who has strived endlessly to guard against such social contamination.

In banishing Coriolanus, the Roman citizens are said to 'have pushed out [the] gates the very defender of them' – and much is made of this irony as the narrative continues (5.2.40–1). Indeed, *Coriolanus* is a play thoroughly devoted to the collapsing of apparent opposites – be it attacker/defender, patrician/pleb, Roman/Volscian, and of course, disgusting/disgusted. Ultimately, I think that such an opposition defines the role of Coriolanus in Rome's political body, as an agent ultimately undone by the nature of his own utility. To extend the bodily metaphors, Coriolanus func-tions like pus – matter that, in being expelled, bears witness to the body's own defence – or like the curing purgative – a remedy that, in the violence it induces, is ejected alongside the offending matter it relieves. Yet whether he is shat, popped or vomited out, he must finally be cast away – an object that, by virtue of being purged, is no longer distinguish-able from the very threats he once himself repelled.

This trajectory is immediately literalized when Coriolanus enters the gates of Antium, his third such symbolic entry thus far in the play. After humbling himself before his rival, Coriolanus is readily incorporated into the Volscian political body, thus confirming his new identity as Rome's enemy. Unsurprisingly, he deploys the rhetoric of disease and disgust when denouncing his former home, vowing to 'fight / Against [his] cankered country with the spleen / Of all the under-fiends' (4.5.92–4). This is quite appropriate, I think,

because the manner of his revenge serves as another metaphor of infection. Having been cast away as refuse, Coriolanus is transformed into a pure con-taminant: literally now a foreign body to Rome, he acquires the ability to tear down his former home from without, through the same means of violent incorporation that undid Corioles. Rome is, in effect, contaminated by its own filth; it shat where it eats, so to speak. The folly of its ways is confirmed by the symbolic reversal that follows, in which Coriolanus now assumes the role of gatekeeper – first ejecting Cominius, then Menenius from the presence of his war camp. By initiating this assault on Rome, Coriolanus is (as Volumnia notes) effectively 'tearing / His coun-try's bowels out' – he aims to destroy the symbolic organ that expelled him, as well as a conceptual metaphor of the play (5.3.103–4). By concurrently activating associations of food, disease and bodily violations, this image exemplifies the play's structural debt to the dynamics of disgust in a way unlike any other.

Coriolanus, we know, never orchestrates this infection of Rome; his plans for violent invasion are pre-empted by the offer of congenial incor-poration, through which he is to be reintegrated into both his familial and civic roles. A Roman messenger celebrates the news, tellingly cast in the language of purgation:

> The Volscians are dislodged and Martius gone.
> A merrier day did never yet greet Rome,
> No, not th'expulsion of the Tarquins.
>
> (5.4.41–3)

Yet things aren't so happy in Antium. Aufidius and his conspirators prepare for the return of Coriolanus – the final of the play's long progression of entries, and the one that will bring ruin to the Roman hero. As Aufidius reveals his plot, Shakespeare tellingly balances images of incorpora-tion and expulsion:

---

60 Paster, 'Starve with Feeding', p. 137.
61 See William Ian Miller, *The Anatomy of Disgust* (Cambridge, MA, 1998), p. 99.

> Him I accuse
> The city ports by this hath entered and
> Intends t'appear before the people, hoping
> To purge himself with words.   (5.6.5–8)

In the final moments of the play, the status quo is restored: Coriolanus is once against cast as an invading pathogen. This time, however, he threatens to undermine the city with the spirit of reconciliation – a danger that Aufidius must neutralize, before he contaminates the Volscian plebs with his pacifying rhetoric. Indeed, the returning Coriolanus begins his address to the Antiates by declaring himself innocuous:

> Hail, lords! I am returned your solider,
> No more infected with my country's love
> Than when I parted hence.   (71–3)

For his immediate audience, it is difficult to square this claim with his subsequent celebration of peace. And while mercy may have bought Coriolanus re-entry into his native land, it does little to endear him to the Volscians, who took him for a strand of ill far less susceptible to remedy. As the articles of treason are revealed, Coriolanus is indicted for failing to exhibit (what is thought to be) the characteristic brutality that fuelled his assault on Corioles, and that occasioned his banishment from Rome: the Volscians were sold a bill of goods, and the man before them – who 'at his nurse's tears ... whined and roared away' the conquest of Rome – does not live up to the 'stolen name' of Coriolanus (99–100; 91). It is clear that Aufidius is disgusted by the accommodating behaviour of Coriolanus, whom he famously denounces as a 'boy of tears' (103). This, the final blow, triggers the Roman's familiar indignation – a violent outburst that, in a crippling irony, only provides the final pretext for the Volscian coup. In witnessing the rage of Coriolanus, the plebeians are at last reminded of the violence to which it was once directed: 'He killed my son! My daughter! He killed my cousin Marcus! He killed my father!' (121–3). In this bloody spectacle – which is also clearly a symbolic feast – the Volscian citizens 'tear him to pieces' (121), sentencing Coriolanus to the same fate as his many unfortunate victims in the field. Blood, wounds, stomachs, indignity – this is the stuff of raw disgust, and it is present as ever in the play's final moment.

THE HOUSEHOLD OF HEROISM: METAPHOR, ECONOMY AND *CORIOLANUS*

VERENA OLEJNICZAK LOBSIEN

THE HOUSEHOLD AS EXTENDED METAPHOR

To look at Shakespeare's last tragedy, *Coriolanus*, with an interest in its economic structures may not seem an obvious choice of task. True, in the first act there are allusions to the situation in contemporary England, the recent famine, the problems of communal supply and in particular the bread riots that had taken place in the Midlands only a year or so before the first performance of the play, in 1608. But its eponymous hero does not seem to owe his memorable stature to his economic skill (or lack of it). He is admired in the first place for his martial feats. Still, as I shall try to show, economics and heroism need to be considered together, at least, in this instance. They do not converge in any overt thematic sense, but they are linked in an interesting manner on the play's metaphorical and allegorical plane. I shall argue for a close correspondence between the guiding, large-scale metaphors in *Coriolanus* and the structures that demand an explanation in economical terms.

In doing so, I shall, more than once, refer to classical antiquity. This is not only because metaphor and allegory belong to the repertory of classical rhetoric; even more important is the classical resonance of the concept of 'economy' – literally, the household. It will be seen that the household metaphor in *Coriolanus* can only be understood if we take into account the nuanced significance *oikonomía* had acquired in the writings of the classical authors. At the same time, the transformation it receives within its new, Shakespearian context will be found to hold up to critical inspection aspects of the ancient concept that had hitherto not only gone unquestioned but were cultivated, even celebrated, as important dimensions of contemporary English Renaissance culture. Shakespeare's literary revision of the household metaphor thus throws light on the metaphor's ideological validity as part of Elizabethan *romanitas* as well as on the dubious nature of the notions of heroism founded upon it.

THE ECONOMIES OF *CORIOLANUS*

The drama's story bears retelling. It harks back to historical events that took place in the late fifth century BC, during the early Roman Republic. In a situation of famine, the victorious warrior Caius Martius Coriolanus, having single-handedly, in an almost superhuman military performance conquered the Volscian stronghold Corioles, is urged by his friends and family to stand for consul. He does so truculently and with great reluctance. In particular, he is unwilling to comply with the ancient custom of soliciting the people's votes by presenting his wounds in public. In the end he conforms with a bad grace, barely able to keep his temper. As the plebeians soon after revoke the trust they have hesitantly and with misgivings placed in him, he chooses exile. Enraged and moved by an implacable anger against Rome, he then joins forces with his former enemies. Only his mother Volumnia manages to dissuade him from devastating the city at the head of a Volscian army. However, by thus averting the destruction of Rome, she also seals her son's death at the hands of the Volscians: they kill him as a traitor.

Readings of the play have tended to focus above all on the protagonist's exceptional prowess, his psychology and the nature of his heroism; on Shakespeare's 'classicism' with respect to his major source, Plutarch, and on the politics he seems to advocate;[1] on the psychodynamics of the hero's relationship to his mother; or on gender aspects.[2] Several studies have drawn attention to the characters' rhetoric, in particular the way in which Coriolanus himself responds to names and naming.[3] So far, however, the mainstream of critical debate appears to have passed by the peculiar metaphorical structure of *Coriolanus* – with the obvious exception of discussions of Rome as body politic provoked by Menenius's retelling of the familiar 'fable of the belly' early in the play.[4]

The fable of the belly is, however, not the only motif that goes back to Shakespeare's principal source, Plutarch's *Lives of the Most Noble Grecians and Romanes*.[5] In many ways, *Coriolanus* is perhaps the most 'Roman' of the so-called Roman plays in the canon. Still, it is, at first glance, not an allegorical play. Although Plutarch presents the hero as a potential embodiment of male virtue, of valour as the mainstay of *romanitas*, it is difficult to conceive of him as a version of Everyman or to discern his didactic potential. In fact, the hero's very uniqueness, his singularity as a warrior, his defiant individualism and his repeated insistence on his autonomy and solitariness ('Alone I did it', 5.6.117)[6] appear to render him particularly unsuitable to the kind of general representativity expected of a personification of mankind.[7] The other characters do not invite allegorical readings either, and the plot as a whole, firmly anchored in Plutarch, seems to offer no moral edification except the most trivial ('Pride comes before a fall', etc.). Yet, as I would claim, the play as a whole is nonetheless structured by a type of extended metaphor.[8]

In brief, I am claiming that, in *Coriolanus*, a classical economic model of the commonwealth gives way to a concept of the heroic soul as an inner household conceived along Stoical lines, while this in turn is presented in the process of tragically losing its equilibrium. This ideal *oikonomía*, threatened by being corrupted through economic as

---

[1] For a reading of the play that draws out the parallels between Plutarch's and Shakespeare's presentations of the early Republic and early modern England as situations of political as well as ethical change, see Colin Burrow, *Shakespeare and Classical Antiquity* (Oxford, 2013).

[2] E.g. Janet Adelman, '"Anger's my meat": Feeding, Dependency, and Aggression in *Coriolanus*', in *Representing Shakespeare: New Psychoanalytic Essays* (Baltimore, MD, 1980), pp. 129–49; Janet Adelman, *Suffocating Mothers: Fantasies of Maternal Origin in Shakespeare's Plays, 'Hamlet' to 'The Tempest'* (London and New York, 1992); see also Coppélia Kahn, *Roman Shakespeare: Warriors, Wounds, and Women* (London, 1997).

[3] See, e.g., Carol M. Sicherman, '*Coriolanus*: The Failure of Words', *ELH*, 39 (1972), 189–207, or Michael West and Myron Silberstein, 'The Controversial Eloquence of Shakespeare's Coriolanus – an Anti-Ciceronian Orator?', *Modern Philology*, 102 (2005), 307–31; also Verena Olejniczak Lobsien, 'Passion und Imagination. "Signs and Tokens" der Leidenschaft in *Coriolanus*, *Titus Andronicus* und *Cymbeline*', *Shakespeare Jahrbuch*, 140 (2004), 45–65.

[4] E.g. David G. Hale, 'The Death of a Political Metaphor', *Shakespeare Quarterly*, 22 (1971), 197–202; or, with observations regarding the economic implications of the metaphor that concur with mine, Zvi Jagendorf, '*Coriolanus*: Body Politic and Private Parts', *Shakespeare Quarterly*, 41 (1990), 30–45.

[5] Translated 1595 by Thomas North; see Geoffrey Bullough, *Narrative and Dramatic Sources of Shakespeare*, vol. 5 (London, 1966), pp. 505–49.

[6] *William Shakespeare : The Complete Works*, ed. Stanley Wells et al., 2nd edn (Oxford, 2005).

[7] Ronald Horton offers one of the few attempts at reading *Coriolanus* allegorically ('The Seven Deadly Sins and Shakespeare's Jacobean Tragedies', in *Shakespeare and Spenser: Attractive Opposites*, ed. Julian B. Lethbridge (Manchester, 2008), pp. 242–58; pp. 250–2). Focusing on the hero, he concludes: 'The play features wrath' (p. 252). However, as I shall argue, wrath is not at the root of Coriolanus's failure. (He does get very angry, but he is untouched by the self-conscious egotism that would permit an equation of his anger with the mortal sin of wrath, just as he is free from personal vanity.) Still, there may indeed be a 'responsiveness' in Shakespeare to medieval allegory (p. 258), perhaps to Spenser, but, as Horton notes, the 'sticking point' in determining the allegorical quality of Shakespeare's plays is 'the function of allegory as moral-didactic vehicle' (p. 257). Here, the transfer does not work. Both Coriolanus's anger and its renunciation are symptoms rather than causes.

[8] For concept, history and various realizations of allegory as *metaphora continua* see, among many others, C. S. Lewis, *The Allegory of Love: A Study in Medieval Tradition* (Oxford, 1936; repr. 1973); Rosemond Tuve, *Allegorical Imagery: Some Medieval Books and their Posterity* (Princeton, NJ, 1966);

well as political transactions, brings about its own collapse. The hero's downfall thus uncovers a fatal ambivalence within the household metaphor together with systematic tensions in the doctrines on which it relies.

Parallel to the tragedy's bipartite structure before and after Coriolanus's banishment from Rome, two metaphorical models of economy are evoked. One is concerned above all with political processes; the other primarily with interactions of the human (masculine) body and soul. One occurs fairly early, in relative isolation; the other can be seen to structure the play indirectly, coming to the fore in its latter part. One receives an exegesis; the other achieves its effects by combining its 'system[s] of implications' so that they result in an impasse for the hero.[9] In Shakespeare's play they are arranged so that they begin to question each other. With the hero's failure, the perfect human 'economy' he had seemed to represent is also shown to fail. As he appears more and more 'economical', metaphorical structures begin to proliferate on all levels of the play. As they multiply, they become increasingly questionable.

'A PRETTY TALE'

The first part of *Coriolanus* is dominated by the fable of the belly (1.1.87–156). This is the only passage that explicitly presents and explicates an allegory.[10] Placed in the mouth of Menenius, a patrician, this 'pretty tale' (1.1.88) leaves no doubt as to its strategic and manipulative purpose. Hence, its rhetoric falls rather flat. Everybody seems to know what Menenius is going to say, and his plebeian listeners repeatedly anticipate his arguments. Both the familiarity of the allegory and the transparency of its ulterior aim contribute to a distancing effect. As he is finally provoked to address one of the hecklers as 'the great toe of this assembly' (1.1.153), the organological magic has already collapsed and the grand oratory is about to degenerate into a slanging match.[11] Menenius's speech appears framed, as if in quotation marks. Together with its topical nature, this awakens some curiosity as to the possible variations the

speaker has to offer on his well-known theme. And in fact, his 'tale' appears to be pointed not only towards the functionality of all the body parts and in particular the seemingly 'idle and unactive' stomach for the whole – 'Still cupboarding the viand' (1.1.97, 98) – but also towards their economic relationship.

This is, in other words, not merely an outworn commonplace in the shape of an organological allegory. Menenius puts a psycho-physiological slant upon his narrative that serves to dynamize the belly's function as 'the storehouse and the shop / Of the whole body' (131–2). He describes it as a distributive agency, processing and fairly spreading the resources by conveying them to all its 'incorporate friends' (128) so that, as it claims in its prosopopoeia, even 'The strongest nerves and small inferior veins / From me receive that natural competency / Whereby they live' (136–8). By the belly's 'audit', all body parts 'do back receive the flour of all' (142–3). Thus, in the speaker's allegoresis, its economic, distributive justice is placed beyond doubt and so is the Roman senators' legitimate power: 'For examine / Their counsels and their cares, digest things rightly / Touching the weal o'th' common, you shall find /

Gay Clifford, *The Transformations of Allegory* (London, 1974); Angus Fletcher, *Allegory: The Theory of a Symbolic Mode* (Ithaca, NY, 1964); Gerhard Kurz, *Metapher, Allegorie, Symbol* (Göttingen, 1982); for an early modern understanding of allegory, see also George Puttenham, *The Arte of English Poesie*, ed. Gladys Doidge Willcock and Alice Walker (Cambridge, 1936); for its philosophical and theological implications, see Henri de Lubac, *Typologie Allegorie Geistiger Sinn: Studien zur Geschichte der christlichen Schriftauslegung*, trans. Rudolf Voderholzer (Freiburg, 2007).

[9] Max Black, 'Metaphor', in *Models and Metaphors: Studies in Language and Philosophy* (Ithaca, NY, 1962), pp. 25–47; p. 41.

[10] With probable sources in the English texts of Livy, *Romane Historie* (1600), trans. Philemon Holland; and William Camden, *Remaines of a greater worke concerning Britaine* (1605). See Bullough, *Narrative and Dramatic Sources*, vol. 5, pp. 496–505 and 551–2.

[11] As Zvi Jagendorf has pointed out, the 'organic metaphor of body, reduced to the small change of this grotesque and demeaning synecdoche, cannot retain its cohesive force ... Too many signifiers are chasing too few signifieds, and that is a sure sign of economic trouble' ('*Coriolanus*', p. 460).

No public benefit which you receive / But it proceeds or comes from them to you' (147–51).

All this harks back to the older meanings of *oikonomía*. In its ancient, Hesiodic and Aristotelian sense, economy did not in the first place refer to the market, to the exchange of commodities, to mercantile processes of commerce or trade. What it primarily referred to was the house, the people living in it, and the relations they held towards each other, together with the particular justice connected with the distribution both of goods and power within the *oikos*. The function of this kind of speech is clear. If the economy of a city is conceived as a household along these lines, the power relations that determine and regulate it will appear quasi-natural and literally close to home: familiar, domestic, beyond questioning and dispute, nothing to be feared or distrusted.

But there are additional aspects. The metaphor of the larger social community, indeed the world, as a body also refers to the Stoical tradition. In Seneca's outline of the idea, the whole cosmos can be compared to a living being. It is created by Nature and held together by divine *pneuma*, a body of which we are the members: 'all that you behold, that which comprises both god and man, is one – we are the parts of one great body. Nature produced us related to one another, since she created us from the same source and to the same end. She engendered in us mutual affection, and made us prone to friendships. She established fairness and justice.'[12] For Seneca, this is a model of universal connectedness and mutuality, equally the wellspring of fairness. As we shall see, it is not least this ancient notion of organic coherence as matrix and paradigm of politic order at the origin of distributive justice that Shakespeare's tragedy calls into doubt.[13]

True, Menenius does allude to an organological model of the state as body politic, with every organ and member contributing to the wellbeing of the commonwealth. As part of medieval and early modern political theories, this might have carried considerable ideological appeal in addition to its legitimatory impact.[14] As part of the doctrine of the 'king's two bodies', allegorical organology

assisted in conceptualizing royalty by mapping the way a monarch's mortal body was seen to be related to the office and institution of kingship. However, not only does its immediate effect on the plebeian listeners remain questionable; it also fails to work on a larger scale. The perfect functionality of the body politic as presented in the abstract will find no correspondence in the actual corporate reality of Rome. Nor will it be represented by any of the available bodies natural. In accordance with one of the classical 'master tropes' of political rhetoric,[15] Menenius models the polis of Rome as an organism that macrologically reflects the human body and its internal economy; an organism that in order to retain its unity and to remain whole needs to avoid division and rebellion. But the dismemberment it conjures up as something to be feared has, in the play, already taken place. It is about to intensify as plebeians and patricians find themselves increasingly in opposition, their interests irreconcilable. And this becomes clear not so much in spite of the affirmative gesture the allegory is meant to make, but to some extent because of it. In addition to this falling apart into inimical factions, one of the major limbs of the body politic is about to be severed, for the hero Coriolanus will, only a little later, opt for exile and join the ranks of the enemy.

---

[12] '[O]mne hoc, quod vides, quo divina atque humana conclusa sunt, unum est; membra sumus corporis magni. Natura nos cognatus edidit, cum ex isdem et in eadem gigneret. Haec nobis amorem indidit mutuum et sociabiles fecit. Illa aequum iustumque composuit'(Seneca, 'Epistle 95.52', in *Ad Lucilium Epistulae Morales*, trans. Richard M. Gummere, vol. 3 (Cambridge, MA, 1925), pp. 90–1).

[13] This is in fact a metaphoric outline of social or biological *oikeiosis* (see below); cf. also Robert Bees, *Die Oikeiosislehre der Stoa: I. Rekonstruktion ihres Inhalts* (Würzburg, 2004); and Robert Bees, 'Das stoische Gesetz der Natur und seine Rezeption bei Cicero', in *The European Image of God and Man: A Contribution to the Debate on Human Rights*, ed. Hans-Christian Günther and Andrea Aldo Robiglio (Leiden, 2010), pp. 125–77.

[14] Ernst H. Kantorowicz, *The King's Two Bodies: A Study in Medieval Political Theology* (Princeton, NJ, 1957).

[15] Jagendorf, '*Coriolanus*', p. 455.

Menenius's euphemistic version of political government, then, loses its apologetic force because of the already apparent idiosyncrasies, corruption and lust for power of individual members of the ruling elite as well as the inconstancy – and the shrewdness – of the people. It also fails to find a counterpart in the person of the hero. He certainly has the aristocratic format and the makings of becoming a kingly leader. His 'valour' might have resulted in the political 'virtue' anticipated by his general Cominius (2.2.84). But the expectable and intensely Roman link between the two qualities[16] is never forged. Coriolanus turns out to be incapable of realizing his promise, and the senatorial 'belly' never grows into a part of the king's two bodies. Despite its initial suggestiveness,[17] the play does not pursue or affirm either the monarchist or the republican implications of the ancient metaphor to the full. They never acquire the striking political significance unfolded in other Shakespearian contexts.[18]

HOUSEHOLD MATTERS: ECONOMIES OF BODY AND SOUL

As the explicit politico-economical allegory fades, so attention is drawn to a second, implicit household metaphor. Now, Coriolanus's predicament, his state of mind and body, and his attempts to cope with the dilemma in which he appears caught move to the foreground. Here, however, the metaphorical substratum is never articulated in so many words. Unlike the organological economy, the psychophysiological model of the soul as an internal household in interaction with corporeality remains implicit. It is perceptible only as an underlying pattern that is realized in its dramatic effects. It has to be recognized by way of its consequences. The descriptive and analytic challenge it presents is, in other words, one of literary hermeneutics – of interpretation against the foil of Elizabethan transformations of antiquity.

To some extent, this is prescribed by the traditionality and the topical currency of the metaphor. That the cooperation of body and soul as well as the soul's internal dynamics can be regarded in terms of

an *oikonomía*, with the soul ruling the body, and reason in the position of the *despotes* or *paterfamilias* governing the other faculties, is a commonplace that may be found in Plato (*Phaedo*, 79–84e)[19] as well as in Aristotle (*Politics*, I, 1254b).[20] It appears to possess even greater, seemingly self-evident relevance for Stoic thinkers. Here, however, the dominant notion is that of *oikeiosis*,[21] of an accord, an

---

[16] Stressed, as frequently pointed out, in Plutarch; cf. also Burrow, *Shakespeare and Classical Antiquity*, pp. 229–31.

[17] And probably also for historical reasons: Rome, after all, had only just embarked on the way of republican government in Coriolanus's lifetime.

[18] For instance, in *Richard II*.

[19] *The Collected Dialogues of Plato*, ed. Edith Hamilton and Huntington Cairns (Princeton, NJ, 1973).

[20] *The Complete Works of Aristotle*, ed. Jonathan Barnes, vol. 2 (Princeton, NJ, 1984).

[21] The idea is systematically present from Zeno and Chrysippus to Cicero, Seneca, Epictetus, Marcus Aurelius; see e.g. excerpts A–H in ch. 57, 'Impulse and Appropriateness', in *The Hellenistic Philosophers*, ed. A. A. Long and D. N. Sedley, vol. 1 (Cambridge, 1987), with the translations and commentary, pp. 346–54. Cf. also the discussions in Pierre Hadot, *The Inner Citadel: The Meditations of Marcus Aurelius*, trans. Michael Chase (Cambridge, MA, 1998); Maximilian Forschner, *Die stoische Ethik: Über den Zusammenhang von Natur-, Sprach- und Moralphilosophie im altstoischen System* (Darmstadt, 1995); Bees, *Die Oikeiosislehre der Stoa*; Michel Foucault, *Die Sorge um sich: Sexualität und Wahrheit 3* (Frankfurt-on-Main, 2000); A. A. Long, *From Epicurus to Epictetus: Studies in Hellenistic and Roman Philosophy* (Oxford, 2006); and Martha Nussbaum, *The Therapy of Desire: Theory and Practice of Hellenistic Ethics* (Princeton, NJ, 1994). In his explanation of the concept, Bees stresses that human assumption of self-ownership is in fact a response to, indeed an organic correlative of, a prior 'having been given' by Nature. It is Nature who is the first giver of self, body, family, offspring, species, etc. to the individual, not so much and certainly not only the individual who then actively takes possession of all that. Bees, 'Das Stoische Gesetz der Natur'; cf. also *Die Oikeiosislehre der Stoa*, p. 171. There is, in other words, a close connection, even a reciprocity, between individual and social or natural *oikeiosis* so that 'to live in accordance with nature' always implies 'with one's own nature' as well as 'with nature as a whole' – at least for the older Stoa. The emphasis on individual *oikeiosis* and the difficulties associated with an ethics of self-care appear, if not Hellenistic, as early modern reduction of a complex that originally sought to include large-scale, macro-cosmic relationships as well.

instinctive attunement with oneself that every human being senses from the moment of birth and later grows capable of reflecting and affirming. It is an assumption and appropriation of oneself, a self-awareness (*sensus sui*) that leads to care of and responsibility for oneself (*cura sui*). It also creates in us the wish to live in continuity with our nature (*homologoumenos zen*), and thus to be constant and true to ourselves.

In the context of early modern Aristotelian-Galenic theories of the faculties, the concept of the inner household acquires even stronger topological connotations, as the internal senses are, with their individual powers and competences, located in ventricles or 'chambers' of the mind.[22] This strengthening of the literal sense of the household metaphor also appears connected with the attempt to ascribe the various tasks and functions in an increasingly normative fashion to specific agencies. In particular, it is linked with an emphasis on the dominance of reason over other parts of the sensitive soul, above all those close to the sensual and affective realm. The household of the soul is to be ruled rationally, and it is mandatory to be master of one's passions. Only a well-governed individual will be fit for public service, his inner household micrologically corresponding to, and thus able to build and stabilize, the greater order of the commonwealth. It is, however, precisely along the lines of rational inner *oikonomía* that Coriolanus fails. While he is shown to excel in terms of constancy, his failure to keep order in his internal household begins to undermine his heroism.

It should be added that in Renaissance England these notions had become commonplace to an extent that tended to obscure their different origins. Elizabethan stoicism drew its ethical ideas mainly from Hellenistic, above all Latin authors, such as Cicero and Seneca. Their texts were comparatively accessible as well as widely available, and their writings lent themselves to teaching purposes. Many of the basics had thus curdled to precepts and maxims, thereby assuming the brief and memorable literary format also favoured by some Stoic thinkers (such as Epictetus, Marcus Aurelius, or, for that matter, Seneca). It is in this

shape that not only Elizabethan students and grammar school boys, but also Shakespeare's hero would have imbibed the kind of everyday Stoicism that provided the mainstay of early modern English *romanitas*.[23]

Geoffrey Miles has argued that the dilemma of Coriolanus arises from an irreconcilable contradiction between two versions of Roman Stoicism – a clash within the mindset he has been led to cultivate between 'a Senecan Stoic heroism aspiring to divinity' and 'the decorous Ciceronian playing of a social role'.[24] True, although Seneca and Cicero both discuss the relationship between the eminent individual and his social context, they appear to differ with respect to the stress they place on exemplary constancy and the obligations of public life respectively. But neither considers it altogether impossible to balance the competing demands of the individual and the civic. On the contrary, the wise man finds himself under an obligation to place his talents at the service of the community.[25] Looked at in the overarching terms of an economy of the self within its natural and

---

[22] Cf. Dominik Perler, ed., *The Faculties: A History* (Oxford, 2015).

[23] For Coriolanus's ruinous dependence on the 'precepts that would make invincible / The heart that conned them' (4.1.10–11) and that he was raised on by Volumnia, see Sicherman, 'Coriolanus', pp. 196–7; for the pervasive presence of stoical commonplaces in Shakespeare and some of the problems he associates with uncritical adherence to them, cf. also Verena O. Lobsien, '"Stewed Phrase" and the Impassioned Imagination in Shakespeare's *Troilus and Cressida*', in *Love, History and Emotion in Chaucer and Shakespeare*, ed. Andrew J. Johnston, Elisabeth Kempf and Russell West-Pavlov (Manchester, 2016), 125–40.

[24] Geoffrey Miles, *Shakespeare and the Constant Romans* (Oxford, 1996), p. 157.

[25] While the principle (that theoretical insight ought to lead to active engagement in public affairs) seems never in doubt, the realization appears to be a more delicate matter, as becomes obvious for instance in Seneca's citation of Zeno's dictum about the Stoic sage in *De otio*, 3, 2: 'Zeno says: "He will engage in public affairs unless something prevents him"' – 'Zenon ait: "Accedet ad rem publicam, nisi si quid impedierit"' (Seneca, *Moral Essays*, vol. 2, trans. John W. Basore (Cambridge, MA, 1932), pp. 184–5); see also Bees, 'Das Stoische Gesetz der Natur', p. 170.

communal contexts – and both Seneca and Cicero[26] repeatedly suggest this larger perspective – this does not seem to be an insoluble task. Still, Coriolanus indubitably fails. Measured against Stoical norms, he appears flawed on several counts: he neither commands perfect *apathia* nor adequate sociability, let alone the ability to combine both in strategic affability.

It is this deficiency and its gradual emergence in the course of the play that the household metaphor renders visible. It directs our attention towards the way Senecan and Ciceronian emphases are made to interact and, in the person of the hero, begin to conflict. By Roman standards, constancy and magnanimity ought to be sides of one and the same coin – in fact, to constitute a perfect metaphorical whole: the valiant soldier perfectly equipped to be a virtuous statesman; the warrior qualified to 'stand for' consul in a literal as well as figurative sense. In *Coriolanus*, however, this does not seem to work. While the hero's temper, his excessive anger, makes him successful in the battlefield, it disqualifies him for political rule. He cannot, for the life of him, perceive an analogy between military indifference towards pain, terror and hardship and political self-control.

Shakespeare's tragedy thematizes the Stoicist ideology of self-government in a manner that both emphasizes and challenges it. Coriolanus's mentality is offered as an example of the difficulties created by its central metaphor. At first, the hero is presented as a paradigmatic realization of Stoical *romanitas* conceived along the lines of fortitude, constancy and imperviousness to pain. It is his eminent constancy, his invincible determination to be true to his 'nature' (e.g., 3.2.14, 4.7.35), that renders him incapable of acting any other part but that of the man he is. Yet his superiority with respect to individual *oikeiosis* finally breaks his neck. The play thus uncovers a problem at the heart of the Stoical economy of the soul and unfolds its tragic potential. By the time the hero's glorious autonomy culminates in a fantasy of male self-creation ('As if a man were author of himself', 5.3.36), it has become obvious that (and how) he will fail in exactly those respects in which he had appeared exemplary. The extraordinary mastery over his body and his subjugation of part of his passions to his will lead to an increasing reification, verging on the monstrous, as he exults: 'O' me alone, make you a sword of me?' (1.7.76; cf. 2.2.109: 'a thing of blood'; also 4.6.94). And yet the hero's management of anger appears clearly deficient. He is not only incapable of suppressing his disgust and fury, but transparently unwilling to dissimulate them when political reason and expediency demand that he perform in public the person he is (cf. 2.3 and 3.2). In Coriolanus, individual excellence and the exigencies of civility clash. He cannot bring himself to fulfil the conflicting demands addressed to the 'great soul' to be at the same time true to itself and to act its magnanimity, in Volumnia's words: 'perform a part' (3.2.109). In her son's view, this amounts to being 'False to my nature' (3.2.14) – to play-acting, hypocrisy, self-demeaning inauthenticity.

We might argue, then, that Coriolanus is constitutionally incapable of metaphor. In a way, his attitude seems to anticipate an ethics of discourse articulated much later, in 1667, by another protagonist of linguistic purity, this time in the service of empiricism and scientific rationalism – by Thomas Sprat, historian of the Royal Society, in his invective against the abuses of eloquence and

---

[26] E.g. in *De finibus*, III, 64 (the speaker is 'Cato', defending Stoic doctrine): 'Again, they hold that the universe is governed by divine will; it is a city or state of which both men and gods are members, and each one of us is a part of this universe; from which it is a natural consequence that we should prefer the common advantage to our own' – 'Mundum autem censent regi numine deorum eumque esse quasi communem urbem et civitatem hominum et deorum, et unumquemque nostrum eius mundi esse partem; ex quo illud natura consequi ut communem utilitatem nostrae anteponamus' (Cicero, *De finibus bonorum et malorum*, trans. H. Rackham (Cambridge, MA, 1914), pp. 284–5). If the whole world is indeed a 'Cosmopolis' (editor's marginal note), it is only natural for the wise man to act accordingly, i.e. take responsibility for the commonwealth in standing for public office.

the indirections of metaphorical speech.[27] Coriolanus seems to share Sprat's enmity towards 'the easie vanity of *fine speaking*'[28] because it threatens the plainness that has hitherto seemed to align him with his own inner truth in an apparently unmediated manner.

SHAKESPEARE'S CRITIQUE OF HEROIC ECONOMY: THE FAILURE OF METAPHOR

What is it that ultimately causes the hero's temper to break? Why can he not remain indifferent and perform politically, serve his country and work for the greater good? Why can he not play the man he is,[29] act the person others see in him and try to harness to communal purposes? In the end, it is not only constancy taken to an extreme, or a hidden systematic friction between Senecan and Ciceronian varieties of Stoicism that prevents the heroic individual from conforming to social demands; it is a clash of metaphors and of metaphorical implications, together with an ingrained resistance to a certain kind of metaphorical exchange, that create a complex aporia Coriolanus is incapable of solving. Within this multilayered complex, several ideas are conflated and a number of different strands intertwined that I shall, in closing, try to disentangle.

Shakespeare's drama creates a constellation in which the good household of the individual soul is put under pressure to become another kind of economy. Individual *oikeiosis*, the perfect, constant self-appropriation and self-coherence as Coriolanus seemed to have achieved them are to become subservient to an all-embracing political 'household' – an economy that, unlike the older type of *oikonomía*, is based on mercantile processes and aims at gain. The politics of the Roman senatorial elite are presented as founded on a symbolic exchange that will yield profit in terms of power, ideological and material dominance. Their behaviour conforms to an impulse to make something out of nothing, more and yet more of a little. In accordance with this monetarian logic, Coriolanus would have to buy his office at the price of his self. He would have to exchange

truth to his nature for functionality within a larger social nexus that, as indicated by the fable of the belly, also pretends to possess a quasi-natural, organic existence. To be true to one, here, implies to be false to the other. Even worse, the transition between them is imagined as the assumption of a *persona*, the playing of a role that is fundamentally alien to the warrior self the hero identified with.

Now there is, as T. S. Eliot and others have observed, a systematic link between Stoicism and performativity, a tendency, as Eliot put it, towards 'self-dramatization'.[30] As the Stoic sage acts his solo part in the eyes of the gods and the world, so this histrionic dimension becomes evident.[31]

---

[27] While formerly metaphors were employed 'to represent *Truth*, cloth'd with Bodies; and to bring *Knowledg* back again to our very sense, from whence it was at first deriv'd to our understandings', now, Sprat foams in his *History of the Royal-Society of London*, 'they are in open defiance against *Reason*, professing not to hold much correspondence with that, but with its Slaves, *the Passions* ... Who can behold without indignation how many mists and uncertainties these specious *Tropes* and *Figures* have brought on our knowledg?' (*Critical Essays of the Seventeenth Century*, ed. J. E. Spingarn, vol. 2 (Oxford, 1908), pp. 116–17). Nothing, from this perspective, is more pernicious than 'this vicious abundance of *Phrase*, this trick of *Metaphors*, this volubility of *Tongue*, which makes so great a noise in the World' (p. 117).

[28] Spingarn, ed., *Critical Essays*, vol. 2, p. 117.

[29] Thus Coriolanus to his mother: 'Would you have me / False to my nature? Rather say I play / The man I am' (3.2.13–15).

[30] T. S. Eliot, 'Shakespeare and the Stoicism of Seneca', in *Selected Essays* (London, 1932; repr. 1966), pp. 126–40.

[31] Cf. Thomas G. Rosenmeyer, *Senecan Drama and Stoic Cosmology* (Berkeley, CA, 1989), with reference to passages such as the following from Seneca's *Naturales quaestiones* (II.59.11–12): 'So, rise up all the more bravely against the threats of heaven, and when the universe burns on all sides think that you have nothing to lose in so glorious a death. But if you believe that disturbance in heaven, that discord of tempests, is being prepared against *you*; if clouds pile up, collide, and roar on *your* account; if such a great fiery force is being scattered around for *your* destruction, then reckon it a comfort that your death is valued at so much' (Seneca, *Naturales Quaestiones I*, trans. Thomas H. Corcoran (Cambridge, MA, 1971), p. 197). For this kind of histrionic self-awareness, compare Epistles 101 and 82, 25.5, 11.8, 80.7 and 120.22 in Seneca, *Ad Lucilium Epistulae Morales*, trans.

Increasing habituation will render the cosmic perspective dispensable, the attitude self-sufficient, in accordance with Seneca's conviction: 'it is a great rôle – to play the rôle of one man. But nobody can be one person except the wise man; the rest of us often shift our masks'.[32] This paradoxical 'acting' of identity, resulting in resistance against multiformity and a perfect self-mastery that does not require any support outside itself, marks one of the extremes of Stoic self-fashioning. It is perhaps the most spectacular effect of its systematic emphasis on self-monitoring. Both its outlines and its cost become perceptible in Shakespeare's *Coriolanus*.

They are laid open to inspection by the explicit demand addressed to the hero to play his part in a drama directed not by himself. It is precisely because this doubles the inherently histrionic structure of the Stoic 'truth to oneself' that it succeeds in exposing it – as metaphor. For this metaphoricity is the fundamental condition of theatre: as the actor impersonates another character, concealing his own, he acts out a metaphorical structure. In a sense, he becomes a metaphor. Following the same logic, George Puttenham in his poetics refers to '*Allegoria*' as the 'the Courtly figure', or even as 'the Courtier or figure of faire semblant',[33] for allegory, too, requires the dissimulation of another, co-present meaning. It is this kind of artful, courtly as well as theatrical figuring that Coriolanus tries to resist: 'You have put me now to such a part which never / I shall discharge to th' life' (3.2.105–6). In fact, this is not only against his nature; it is the opposite of nature – a poetics of the self that Coriolanus cannot but fail to perform.

To this, however, Shakespeare's drama adds yet another complication. To the dissimulation required of the ideally constant Stoic in standing for consul a further metaphorical layer is added as his predicament is presented in economical terms. This is not merely a stage play with heightened duplicity – the drama of the Stoic self duplicated and exposed in political performance – but a public bargain. The action required of Coriolanus can be seen as ritual initiation into a form of political government that demands a self-governance of its candidates which forces them to exaggerate aristocratic *sprezzatura* until it becomes hypocrisy, and then to sell it. In doing so, it brings the Stoic hero under unbearable pressure, with him the household model of the soul.[34] Fittingly, all this is staged in the forum, that is, literally in the 'market-place' (3.2.131), with Coriolanus's friends and family urging him to put his heroic self on offer while entering a process of mercantile, pseudo-commercial exchange. He is expected to conform to a world of 'policy' (3.2.49) in which he will gain the people's votes by offering in return to public inspection the wounds he received in conquering Corioles. He will win favour if he is ready to turn his body into a commodity and his words to merchandize; to pay lip-service to notions he does not believe in and pander to the interests of those he considers worthless. Indeed, to him they are no more than commodities themselves, 'woollen vassals, things created / To buy and sell with groats' (3.2.8–9). This, then, marks the breaking point. Coriolanus cannot bring himself to embark on this type of economy: 'I would not buy / Their mercy at the price of one fair word' (3.3.94–5). Instead, unwilling by his body's action to 'teach [his] mind / A most inherent baseness' (3.2.123–4), he choses 'a world elsewhere' (3.3.139) – with disastrous consequence.

Richard M. Gummere, vols. 1–3 (Cambridge, MA, 1917–25); see also the discussion in Gordon Braden, *Renaissance Tragedy and the Senecan Tradition: Anger's Privilege* (New York, 1985).

[32] Ep. 120. 22: 'Magnam rem puta unum hominem agere. Praeter sapientem autem nemo unum agit, ceteri multiformes sumus.' (Seneca, *Epistulae Morales*, vol. 3, pp. 394–5).

[33] Puttenham, *Arte of English Poesie*, pp. 186 and 299 (in the marginal gloss, it is '*Allegoria*, or the Figure of false semblant', p. 186, with Puttenham's vacillation between 'faire' and 'false' indicating the duplicity and moral ambiguity inherent in dissimulation).

[34] At the same time, it pushes the honorific dimension also present in ancient economic theory to an extreme: Xenophon's *Oeconomicus* also recommends strategies to the 'gentleman farmer' that are to a great extent symbolical investments and which lead to social recognition and honour; cf. Xenophon, *Memorabilia. Oeconomicus. Symposium. Apology*, trans. E. C. Marchant and O. J. Todd (Cambridge, MA, 1923; repr. 1997).

Shakespeare's play of heroic valour, pride and choler, of magnificent arrogance and aristocratic anger at the 'baseness' of political exchange; his analysis of unmanageable passion at the democratic imposition of selling one's own merit at prices set by one's inferiors, modulates into tragedy as its mercantile mechanism proves inescapable. Unfortunately but consistently, 'elsewhere' this logic persists, too, in inverted form. The model of unequal exchange – the logic of the marketplace – also underlies the patterns of retaliation and revenge that Coriolanus now finds himself caught in as he becomes the leader of a Volscian army ready to attack Rome. Ultimately, things turn into catastrophe, as not only the logic of political exchange but also the model of the perfect household returns – with a vengeance, one is tempted to say. It rebounds on the hero no longer metaphorically, but literally, as Coriolanus's family now arrive to seek out their *despotes*. As his mother's appeal to familial values and bonds prevails, the hero's fantasy of male autonomy collapses. In combination, both types of economic logic together work his death.

Due to the complex metaphoricity of the play, this fatal dynamic works equally on the literal level and the figurative level. As individual 'honour' is turned into an object of exchange for political 'voices' (e.g. 3.1.123), the affective household of the heroic individual is thrown off balance. As the virtue it had regarded as its own reward and its core value is to become subject to supply and demand, to calculation (how many wounds in how many wars?), to appraisal and negotiation between tribunes and senators, impassability is lost. Coriolanus is shown to teeter on the edge of corruption, as his noble 'sovereignty' (4.7.35) as well as the ideal inner economy it was founded on can no longer be sustained. Under conditions of political pressure and in the economical theatre of the market, *oikeiosis* appears as unfeasible as equanimity.

Coriolanus's failure can thus be considered as an emblem of the deficiencies of certain classical ideas both of individual and public governance. For a moment, both stand revealed as strategies of commodification. For Shakespeare's contemporaries,

they were growing into normative ideas and absolute metaphors. Yet, the author's final tragedy presents, through the refusal of its tongue-tied hero[35] to engage in dissimulation, an eloquent criticism of a central dimension of Elizabethan classicist ideology. It does so in a metaphorical mode. As the underlying economic structures both of the masculinist, Stoicist ideal of Roman virtue and of Roman politics are uncovered, *Coriolanus* clears the space for a radical interrogation of an ancient homology between the self and society that Renaissance culture had learned to take for granted.

As regards the viability of the philosophical concepts brought into play, the result is ruinous. Organological, cosmic *oikeiosis* is presented as mere propaganda. Its naturalness appears as euphemism for the self-interest of those in power, and the corporeality conjured up in the fable of the belly merely serves to mask political disintegration. The Roman belly is no provider but an insatiable consumer about to devour its own substance. Correspondingly, individual *oikeiosis*, instead of microcosmically mirroring the larger processes of give and take, fruitful exchange or mutual nourishment in its own, smaller household of human faculties, brings forth a self-limiting and ultimately self-incapacitating one-sidedness in the hero's monomanic insistence on constancy and truth to himself. Although in theory both individual and social *oikeiosis* should be in harmony,[36] mutually reflecting each other, their interaction redounding to the benefit of all, in *Coriolanus* they dramatically fall apart. Instead of concurring, in both, the natural and metaphysical aspects recede and the ethical and political predominate – with disastrous consequences. In Shakespeare's construal, both *oikeioseis* appear contradictory and in contradiction to each other. The cosmopolis can neither be perceived as

---

[35] For a discussion of his 'controversial eloquence', see also West and Silberstein, 'Controversial Eloquence'.

[36] That there are great internal tensions and potential problems here was already obvious to thinkers in classical antiquity; even to those in evident sympathy with Stoicism such as Cicero, whose *De finibus* bears eloquent witness to these in its dialogic structure.

functional organism nor as well-furnished household or distributive agency, dispensing to each their due; the heroic self will not function as actor. Micro- and macrocosm are not in harmonious sympathy but linked in a mutually desctructive manner. As both become increasingly 'economified', they no longer enhance but begin to militate against each other. Thus the play not only discredits Stoicist mentalities, but also pulls into its devaluative vortex the metaphoric mechanisms on which they are based.

The metaphoricity of Shakespeare's tragedy works simultaneously on several planes – ideological as well as poetological. Like its hero's anger, the play's criticism is directed not only (as, for instance, in *Timon of Athens*) against the logic of political economy superseding older modes of *oikonomía* with their emphasis on small-household subsistence and tight social networks.[37] Shakespeare's critique is more radical and, literally, closer to home. It touches the tools of his own trade by turning equally against the processes of metaphorical exchange and transfer. Not only are the mechanisms of micro-macrological reference challenged but also the metaphorical principles of the stage, which demand that one person act another, dissimulating his own identity. Apart from that, *Coriolanus* needs to be read as a problematization of Stoic heroism and, by way of that, of early modern economy. The nexus of ideas spread out in the metaphorical texture of Shakespeare's play embraces not only household matters but also issues of individual psychology combined with ancient as well as modern 'techniques of the self'.[38] In addition, it addresses the political logic of the marketplace together with modes of governing a commonwealth that imply a blatantly unequal distribution of ressources.

It does so by indirection. In a recent article in the *Shakespeare Jahrbuch*, Jean Howard has pointed out that Shakespeare's

approach to the capitalist transformations of his society is . . . not just about economic practice. That is, he does not directly portray financial institutions like The Royal Exchange . . . Rather, he attends primarily to social relations and to mentalities – that is, to the way in which the ideologies that sutured a feudal way of life were profoundly disrupted by economic forces that remain at best shadowy presences in his plays, but inexorably were altering relations between people.[39]

In *Coriolanus*, these 'forces' work through metaphor and by thematizing metaphorical ways of mapping relationships between the self and the world. They do so by exposing failure, in particular the failure of the household concept. In fact, my own article might have been subtitled 'The Functions of Failure', for, as we could see, Shakespeare's play foregrounds the tragic destruction of the exemplary individual by itself. His hero conforms, perfectly and all too successfully, to a prevailing ideology. But at the same time, *Coriolanus* demonstrates the failure of the metaphor that provides the matrix of *oikeiosis* and the mainstay for the ideology surrounding it: the extended metaphor that seeks to elevate the performative principle of 'acting one man only' (*unum hominem agere*) to the fulcrum on which not only individual but also communal as well as economic action turns.

On the poetological plane, this failure is wholly functional. In its collective, allegorical version (the fable of the belly), thereby also in its material, indeed corporeal accentuation, the economic metaphor is exposed as a political lie. Rome appears as anything but a unified bodily whole with all its parts contributing to its alimentation and prosperity. Instead, there are division, injustice and famine, with a suspicion that the hero himself may be implicated in practices of hoarding grain for profit. In an even more spectacular manner, the household metaphor is invalidated in its application to the psychophysiological condition of the individual subject. As attention is directed towards the mind and character of the hero – and despite his

---

[37] As celebrated, for instance, in Hesiod's *Erga*, see *Hesiod: Works and Days*, ed. Martin L. West (Oxford, 1978). For economic criticism with respect to Shakespeare, see also Peter F. Grav, 'Taking Stock of Shakespeare and the New Economic Criticism', *Shakespeare*, 8 (2012), 111–36.

[38] As outlined in Foucault, *Dic Sorge um sich*.

[39] Jean Howard, 'Shakespeare and the Consequences of Early Capitalism', *Shakespeare Jahrbuch*, 150 (2014), 30–45; p. 35.

own attempts to reduce himself and his vulnerable body to a fighting 'thing' – we have seen that it is precisely the perfect realization of the metaphor that turns out most detrimental. Here, it is the dramatic action that works towards allegorization and its simultaneous subversion. Through the way the Stoic concept of the inner household is unfolded in the play, we are placed in a position to observe how its conventional didactic applicability crumbles. However, even as the economic metaphor is shown to disintegrate, the process turns it into an instrument for thinking. As the knowledge it had seemed to carry is emptied of value, as its performance leaves its hero vulnerable to friends and foes, finally and literally, both mortified and mortally wounded, the household of the soul and its Stoic management, with it the ideological charge it carried for an Elizabethan public, stand to lose their cultural and educational glamour. Looked at through the optic provided by Shakespeare's play, this is no longer a viable model for (male) self-fashioning, nor for the (communal) fashioning of others.

Shakespeare challenges Elizabethan *romanitas*, in other words, by means of his textual economy. He gradually unhinges it through the way his text employs one of its central metaphors: unfolding it allegorically, in topical narrative as well as by means of a dramatic questioning of its transfer potential. Taken seriously, both in the state and in the individual, the household metaphor is seen to fail on all accounts – and with it, its economic unfoldings. Its deficiencies become apparent through the textual transformations engineered by Shakespeare's drama. This kind of critique is the prerogative of literature.

'THOSE ORGANNONS BY WHICH IT MOOVES': SHAKESPEARIAN THEATRE AND THE ROMISH CULT OF THE DEAD

THOMAS RIST

I am thy father's spirit,
Doomed for a certain term to walk the night,
And for the day confined to fast in fires
Till the foul crimes done in my days of nature
Are burnt and purged away. But that I am forbid
To tell the secrets of my prison-house
I could a tale unfold whose lightest word
Would harrow up thy soul, freeze thy young blood,
Make thy two eyes like stars start from their spheres,
Thy knotty and combinèd locks to part,
And each particular hair to stand on end
Like quills upon the fretful porcupine.

(*Hamlet*, 1.5.9–20)[1]

. . . a man feels that he has a soul, and consequently a force, because he is a social being.

(Emile Durkheim)[2]

How seriously would Shakespeare have taken the notion of his theatre as a cult of the dead? Concluding Stephen Greenblatt's *Hamlet in Purgatory*, this question has in different times received different answers.[3] Suggesting the playwright took the cult of the dead very seriously, in 1745 Colley Cibber spoke of eighteenth-century critics inferring Shakespeare's Catholicism 'from the solemn Description of Purgatory given us by his Ghost in *Hamlet*'.[4] When scholars addressed the matter in the twentieth century, the question moved from the solemnity of the Ghost to its reliability: 'What if it tempt you toward the flood . . . draw you into madness?' (*Hamlet*, 1.4.50–5).[5] When in the new millennium Peter

Marshall made the problem of 'Hamlet's Ghost Critics' the very problem of the Reformation, it was clear that Shakespeare and pretty much everyone else took seriously the cult of the dead.[6] The principal remaining question was only how directly the cult bore on the theatre. Coming to understand Hamlet's Ghost as just one manifestation of the religious practices of commemoration that are everywhere in Shakespeare, to commentators the underpinning of much early modern theatre by the Catholic, and to contemporaries Romish, cult of the dead is ever more clear.[7] The other outstanding question is how

---

[1] All Shakespeare quotations are from *William Shakespeare: The Complete Works*, ed. Stanley Wells et al. (Oxford, 1986).

[2] Emile Durkheim, *The Elementary Forms of the Religious Life* (London, 1915; repr. 1964), p. 366.

[3] See Stephen Greenblatt, *Hamlet in Purgatory* (Princeton, NJ, 2001), p. 258.

[4] David Chandler, 'Catholic Shakespeare: The Making of the Argument', *English Language Notes*, 44 (2006), 29–41, p. 30.

[5] See, notably, Eleanor Prosser, *Hamlet and Revenge* (London, 1967).

[6] For Marshall's acknowledgement of Hamlet's Ghost criticism prefiguring his view of the Reformation, see *Beliefs and the Dead in Reformation England* (Oxford, 2002), p. 232. The phrase 'Hamlet's Ghost Critics' is Greenblatt's.

[7] As the *OED* observes, 'Romish' compounds 'Roman' with 'Roman Catholic'. The term came into frequent use in the sixteenth century (the first cited example is from Tyndale, 1538), and evocatively highlights the link between 'Rome'

fully Shakespeare and contemporary dramatists endorsed the cult. Starting with a localized answer, this article addresses both of these far-reaching questions. As well as evoking Purgatory, the Ghost's address to Hamlet is already a paradigm of theatre. Commanding attention, the Ghost speaks and performs. Being his audience, Hamlet listens and responds.[8] According to contemporary associations of Purgatory with purgation, the passage even foregrounds explanation of how performed tales cathartically 'harrow' an audience.[9] *Hamlet*'s prime example of purgatorial cult is also a paradigm for performed action in the round. Why?

The short answer is that performance is a religious as much as theatrical activity and that early modern England did not clearly distinguish between the theatrical forms. 'Drama did not simply move, as scholars once argued, from inside to outside the church. Drama we might consider secular was sometimes performed inside churches, at least from the sixteenth century, if not before, just as drama that we would consider religious might be performed outside churches'.[10] New theatres such as the Globe shared audiences, actors and playwrights with theatres recalling former religious use such as the Blackfriars, and until the late sixteenth century competed and collaborated with theatres still actively involved in religious performance such as at St Paul's.[11] From 1603, the last performed Corpus Christi play in England is contemporary with *Hamlet*.[12] Each theatre competed for audiences with the popular sermons performed, for example, at Paul's Cross. Set speeches and responses, singing including Latin dramatizations of biblical material, ritual acts including from liturgy and the mass, characterize theatrical as well as church performances.[13] Early modern performance was simultaneously religion and entertainment. The longer answer to why the cult of the dead becomes a paradigm of theatrical action in *Hamlet* is that rituals of funeral inextricable from that cult characterized the drama long before Shakespeare's play. Beginning with a play in which English religious unease is the backdrop, the following section recounts the developing linkage.[14]

THEATRICAL HISTORY: THE DEAD IN THEATRE BEFORE *HAMLET*

When in *The Defense of Poesie* Sir Philip Sidney denounced England's pre-Shakespearian theatre, the one play 'of these that I have seen' that he admired was Sackville and Norton's *Gorboduc*.[15] Though he does not say so, the play's performance at court at Elizabeth I's request, and its topical treatment of an England without heirs to the throne, partly explains this.[16] Yet Sidney's

---

and 'Roman Catholicism' in early modern England. Like 'catholic' (meaning 'universal'), the term also encompassed some of the stranger theories at the end of this piece. Further etymological significance emerges in my comments on *Titus Andronicus* below.

[8] For the scene as a 'theatrical microcosm' in this respect, see Thomas Rist, 'Transgression Embodied: Medicine, Religion and Shakespeare's Dramatized Persons', in *Staged Transgression in Shakespeare's England*, ed. Rory Loughnane and Edel Semple (Basingstoke, 2013), pp. 120–35; p. 129.

[9] See Thomas Rist, 'Catharsis as "Purgation" in Shakespearean Drama', in *Shakespearean Sensations: Experiencing Literature in Early Modern England*, ed. Katharine A. Craik and Tanya Pollard (Cambridge, 2013), pp. 138–53.

[10] Janette Dillon, *The Cambridge Introduction to Early English Theatre* (Cambridge, 2006), p. 2.

[11] See Thomas Rist, 'Shakespeare Now and Then: Communities, Religion, Reception', in *Writing and Religion in England, 1558–1689: Studies in Community-making and Cultural Memory*, ed. Roger D. Sell and Anthony W. Johnson (Farnham, 2009), pp. 114–15. For discussion of theatricality at St Paul's in special relation to commemorating the dead, see Thomas Rist, *Revenge Tragedy and the Drama of Commemoration in Reforming England* (Farnham, 2008), pp. 75–95.

[12] For discussion of this Corpus Christi performance, see Dillon, *Early English Theatre*, p. 83.

[13] Dillon, *Early English Theatre*, p. 1.

[14] My method follows that proposed by Wilson-Okamura. Its aim is the 'scholar's task' of grasping its subject 'as a whole', which will entail leaving some 'gaps'. See David Scott Wilson-Okamura, *Virgil in the Renaissance* (Cambridge, 2010), pp. 8–11. For discussion of the religious backdrop as 'unease', see Henry James and Greg Walker, 'The Politics of Gorboduc', *English Historical Review*, 110 (1995), 109–21; pp. 109–10, 116–17.

[15] See 'The Defense of Poesie', in *Sir Philip Sidney: The Major Works*, ed. Katherine Duncan-Jones (Oxford, 2008), p. 243.

[16] For details of this stage history, see the introduction in *Gorboduc or Ferrex and Porrex*, ed. Irby Cauthen (London,

emphasis on 'funerals' as an essence of tragedy provides further explanation.[17] Although this aspect of the document is hitherto unnoticed, the eyewitness account of *Gorboduc* found in the Yelverton Collection of the British Library also notes the play was a 'tragedie' whose sequence of events included an entrance of 'mourners'.[18] Interpreting the play, the eyewitness reiterates this funereal emphasis: 'The shadowes were declared by the *chore*. First to signyfie unytie. The 2. howe that men refused the certen and tooke the uncerten, whereby was ment that yt was better for the Quene to mary with the L.R. knowne than with the K. of Sweden. The thryde to declare yt cyvill discention bredeth mourning'.[19] According to the eyewitness, in fact, mourning is central in the three identified ways that the play 'signifie[s]'. It alone, notably, receives no more than a single, explicit mention.

Since there are just six eyewitness accounts of London plays from 1567 to 1642, the conjunction of mournful action with tragedy in Sidney and the anonymous *Gorboduc* witness is exceptional evidence that mourning and tragedy were fundamentally interlinked in contemporary understandings of the genre.[20] That Sackville and Norton placed mournful action in a dumbshow also merits comment: 'in a play full of static action and long sententious speeches, these sequences of elaborate visual spectacle and movement were the most engaging and therefore most memorable parts of the play' – the more so since here was 'the first known use of dumbshows on the English stage'.[21] Projecting mourning through a dumbshow, Sackville and Norton gave it a striking prominence: one answering to Sidney and the eyewitness accounts of its tragedy. As shall now be seen, the eyewitness's 'moral commentary' on the dramatic meanings of the dumbshow particularly show that besides being a 'well-educated minor courtier' in Norman Jones and Paul Whitfield White's words, he was a reliable and astute observer of *Gorboduc*.[22]

Gorboduc not only shows the mourning of the dead common in Elizabethan drama thereafter, but in various ways it too comments on its centrality in

tragedy. It does so through the figure of the Chorus and the dumbshow separating each dramatic act. These especially make the play not just 'full of stately speeches and well-sounding phrases, climbing to the height of Seneca's style', in Sidney's phrase, but also one 'as full of notable morality'.[23] The dramatic moralizing of the action of *Gorboduc* cannot be overstated. Giving unusually full descriptions of the dumbshows that schematically precede each act, the text names each description as 'The Order and Signification of the Dumb Show'. Repeatedly bringing out this signification ensures an action always imbued with moral meaning. Basing itself in moral axioms, the Chorus ending each act presents the morality in words.

The Chorus ending Act 3 therefore works in tandem with the dumbshow preceding Act 4. Quoting the Chorus in full brings out its extensive intervention in the dramatic meaning, as well as its means of arguing from moral maxims:

> The lust of kingdom knows no sacred faith,
> No rule of reason, no regard of right,
> No kindly love, no fear of heaven's wrath;
> But with contempt of gods and man's despite,

1970), pp. xi–xxx; pp. xii–xiii. All quotations from *Gorboduc* are from this edition.

[17] Illustrating distinctions between comedy and tragedy, Sidney's contrast is of 'hornpipes with funerals'. He considers these features in classical and English dramatic precedents. See 'Defense of Poesie', p. 244.

[18] Quoted in Norman Jones and Paul Whitfield White, 'Gorboduc and Royal Marriage Politics: An Elizabethan Playgoer's Report of the Premiere Performance', *English Literary Renaissance*, 16 (1996), 3–17; pp. 3–4.

[19] Quoted in Jones and White, 'Gorboduc', p. 4.

[20] Jones and White observe five eyewitness accounts of London drama of the period including that of the Yelverton collection ('Gorboduc', p. 3). Sidney's insistence that he has seen *Gorboduc*, and other plays, makes a sixth.

[21] Jones and White, 'Gorboduc', pp. 5, 16.

[22] Quoted in Jones and White, 'Gorboduc', pp. 4–5. In emphasizing the critical perceptiveness of the eyewitness's moral commentary, though, my following reading differs from Jones and White. They consider the moral commentary of the eyewitness 'typical', citing Simon Foreman – a haphazard commentator – as a parallel example (p. 5).

[23] 'Defense of Poesie', p. 243.

Through bloody slaughter doth prepare the ways
    To fatal sceptre and accursed reign.
The son so loathes the father's lingering days,
    Nor dreads his hand in brother's blood to stain.

O wretched prince, nor dost thou yet record
    The yet fresh murders done within the land
Of thy forefathers, when the cruel sword
    Bereft Morgan his life with cousin's hand?
Thus fatal plagues pursue the guilty race,
    Whose murderous hand, imbrued with guiltless blood,
Asks vengeance still before the heaven's face
    With endless mischiefs on thy cursed brood.

The wicked child thus brings to woeful sire
    The mournful plaints to waste his very life.
Thus do the cruel flames of civil fire
    Destroy the parted reign with hateful strife.
And hence doth spring the well from which doth flow
    The dead black streams of mourning, plaints, and woe.
                    (*Gorboduc*, 3.1.170–91)

Dramatic moralizing here begins with the chaos falling on kingdoms where individuals lust for power and ends with a kingdom in mourning, making political theory and funerary performance inextricable dramatic highlights. In 'The Order and Signification of the Dumb Show Before the Fourth Act' that follows immediately afterwards, this order reverses. Instead of moving from the political to the funerary, the dumbshow moves from the funerary to the political:

> *The Order and Signification of the Dumb Show*
> *Before the Fourth Act*
> First, the music of hautboys began to play, during which there came forth from under the stage, as though out of hell, three Furies, Alecto, Megaera, and Tisiphone, clad in black garments sprinkled with blood and flames, their bodies girt with snakes, their heads spread with serpents instead of hair, the one bearing in her hand a snake, the other a whip, and the third a burning fire-brand, each driving before them a king and a queen which, moved by Furies, unnaturally had slain their own children. The names of the kings and queens were these: Tantalus, Medea, Athamus, Ino, Cambises, Althea. After that the Furies and these had passed about the stage thrice, they departed, and then the music ceased. Hereby was signified the unnatural murders to follow; that is to say, Porrex slain by his own mother, and of King Gorboduc and Queen Videna, killed by their subjects.[24]

Clad in black garments, the three furies bring to life the funeral imagery of 'dead black streams of mourning, plaints and woe' concluding the Chorus. Yet by the dumbshow's end, this imagery has become explicitly political in the 'signified ... unnatural' murders of Gorboduc, Videna and Porrex. From the beginning of the Chorus to the end of the dumbshow, the metatheatrical commentary has swirled from political theory to funerals and from funerals back again to political theory. Besides illustrating their immediate dramatic centrality, *Gorboduc* here begins the process of making English political theory and funerals inseparable on the English stage. The focus on 'vengeance' and 'Fury' points towards English revenge tragedy. The presentation of funerary remembrance as an agent in historical development points to the history play. These forms receive significant development by the playwrights and friends Christopher Marlowe and Thomas Kyd.[25]

Marlowe's history *Tamburlaine Part II* (hereafter *Tamburlaine II*) has been influentially treated as the weak follow-up to *Tamburlaine I*, where the hero has lost his all-conquering vim.[26] Comparing the dramatic Prologues of the two plays shows this is misleading. While both plays address brutal conquest, the Prologue to *Tamburlaine* promises a 'stately tent of War' backed by the 'high astounding terms' of its hero. The Prologue to Part II is quite different:

> *The generall welcomes Tamberlaine receiv'd*
> *When he arrived last upon our stage,*
> *Hath made our Poet pen his second part,*
> *Wher death cuts off his progres in his pomp,*
> *And murderous Fates throwes all his triumphs down.*

---

[24] *Gorboduc*, p. 44.

[25] For discussion of Marlowe's friends, including Kyd, see Lisa Hopkins, *Christopher Marlowe: A Literary Life* (Basingstoke, 2000), p. 47.

[26] See Harry Levin, *The Overreacher: A Study of Christopher Marlowe* (London, 1954). The influence is present, for example, in David Fuller's 'Introduction', in *The Complete Works of Christopher Marlowe*, vol. 5, ed. David Fuller and Edward J. Esche (Oxford, 1998), p. xxxix. All quotations from *Tamburlaine* (Part I or Part II) are from this volume.

But what became of fair Zenocrate
And with how manie cities sacrifice
He celebrated her sad funerall,
Himself in presence shall at large unfold. (2.0.1–9)

The first sentence addressing the audience presents Tamburlaine supplanted by death. Retaining death's emphasis, the second sentence initially moves away from Tamburlaine entirely, making sacrifice and the 'sad funeral' of Zenocrate the emphasis, and only readmitting Tamburlaine to the drama as its narrator. Conjuring a very different audience response from the prologue of *Tamburlaine I*, death, funeral and sacrifice are the dramatic focus of *Tamburlaine II*. The subtitle to *Tamburlaine II* reinforces this focus. Indeed, 'With his impassionate fury, for the death of his *Lady and Love, faire Zenocrate*: his *fourme* of exhortation and discipline to his three sons, and the maner of his own death' not only makes the death scenes of Zenocrate and Tamburlaine the centre of the drama; in 'exhortation', it presents the other listed features (fury, the drama of the sons) as products of Zenocrate's death.[27]

According to the promise of the prologue and also the subtitle, funeral becomes the dramatic theme overtly with the death of Zenocrate in Act 2, scene 4. The scene ends with Tamburlaine mourning her:

For she is dead? Thy words doo pierce my soule.
Ah sweet *Theridamas*, say so no more:
Though she be dead, yet let me think she lives,
And feed my mind that dies for want of her.
Where'er her soule be, thou shalt stay with me,
Embalmed with Cassia, Amber Greece, and Myrre,
Not lapt in lead but in a sheet of gold,
And till I die thou shalt not be interred.
Then in as rich a tombe as *Mausolus*,
We both will rest and have one Epitaph
Writ in as many severall languages,
As I have conquered kingdomes with my sword.
This cursed town will I consume with fire,
Because this place bereft me of my love:
The houses, burnt, wil look as if they mourn'd,
And here will I set up her statua,
And march about it with my mourning campe,
Drooping and pining for *Zenocrate*.
(*Tamburlaine II*, 2.4.125–42)

Various points need emphasis from this speech developing the prologue and subtitle. Rather than a 'thirst of raigne' (2.7.12), as in *Tamburlaine I*, conquest and violence here become expressions of mourning.[28] This is immediate in the images of the burnt houses 'as if they mourned' and of Tamburlaine's 'mourning camp' on the march. According to the speech and later evidence, this second image will be a lasting one. Extending mourning for the term of the play, and so delivering on the subtitle's claim that death 'exhorts', Tamburlaine here states that rather than burying her, Zenocrate will accompany his march across the world. How often her hearse reappears on stage as a reminder is unclear. With the images of the burning town and mourning army, it is certainly there in the stage direction of Act 3, scene 2: '[Enter] TAMBURLAINE *with* USUMCASANE, and . . . four [souldiers] bearing the hearse of* ZENOCRATE, *and the drums sounding a dolefull martch, the Towne burning*'. It is also there in Tamburlaine's final request, at the climax of the play, to 'fetch the hearse of fair *Zenocrate*. / Let it be plac'd by this my fatall chair, / And serve as parcell of my funerall' (5.3.211–13), as he looks on the hearse, in Tamburlaine's last speech celebrating 'eies [that] injoy your latest benefite' (5.3.225). Following its initiation in Act 2, scene 4, the metaphor of conquest as funeral also receives considerable elaboration:

TAMBURLAINE.   So burne the turrets of this cursed town,
  Flame to the highest region of the air:
  And kindle heaps of exhalations,
  That, being fiery meteors, may presage
  Death and destruction to th' inhabitants.
  Over my Zenith hang a blazing star,
  That may endure till heaven be dissolv'd,
  Fed with the fresh supply of earthly dregs,

---

[27] 'Exhortation' comes from the Latin 'ex' (out of) and 'hortari' (to urge). Thus, the urge to fury and the drama of the sons is out of the death of Zenocrate.

[28] For the 'thirst of reign' speech as exhibiting 'many' of the play's 'characteristic qualities', see Fuller, 'Introduction', p. xxxix.

Threatening a dearth and famine to this land,
Flieng dragons, lightning, fearful thunderclaps,
Sindge these fair plains, and make them seem as black
As is the island where the Furies maske,
Compassed with Lethe, Styx, and Phlegethon,
Because my dear *Zenocrate* is dead.

CALYPHAS.   This Piller, placed in memorie of her,
Where in Arabian, Hebrew, Greek, is writ
This towne being burnt by Tamburlaine *the great*,
Forbids the world to build it up again.

AMYRAS.   And here this mournful streamer shall be
    plac'd,
Wrought with the Persian and Egyptian armes,
To signify she was a princesse borne
And wife unto the Monarke of the East.

CELEBINUS.   And here this table as a Register
Of all her virtues and perfections.

TAMBURLAINE.   And here the picture of *Zenocrate*,
To shew her beautie, which the world admired.
Sweet picture of divine *Zenocrate*,
That, hanging here, will draw the Gods from
    heaven:
And cause the stars fixt in the Southern arke,
Whose lovely faces never any viewed
That have not passed the centre's latitude,
As pilgrims travel to our Hemi-sphere,
Only to gaze upon *Zenocrate* . . .

(*Tamburlaine II*, 3.2.1–42)

Reiterating the funereal image of the burnt-black landscape, in this dialogue Tamburlaine initially also repeats both his and the subtitle's logic of conquest: 'Because my dear Zenocrate is dead'.[29] Implying the use of material memorials onstage, Calyphas then alludes to 'this pillar, placed in memory of her' commemorating Zenocrate and the rationale of conquest, and there are further commemorative materials in the mournful streamer, 'table' registering her virtues and a 'picture of Zenocrate / To show her beauty'. As part of the wider treatment of conquest as funeral, this unusually developed and also focused use of stage properties transforms the procession of victories originating in *Tamburlaine I* into one vast funeral procession. While *Tamburlaine I* in broad terms proposes a human triumph over death, *Tamburlaine II* returns drama to its ritual origin in funeral.

A parallel process is visible in Kyd's revenge tragedy *The Spanish Tragedy*, where Hieronimo also keeps a beloved family member unburied to the end. Though they are even more sustained, his laments emphasizing personal suffering recall *Gorboduc* more than *Tamburlaine II*, although the dramatic motif of the corpse preserved from burial until the denouement shows a collaboration of ideas between Marlowe and Kyd. In *The Spanish Tragedy*, the unburied family member is a son, Horatio, rather than a wife, and remaining a corpse to the end, the son does not receive even the partial ritual of a hearse accorded to Zenocrate. Yet the conjunction of withheld funeral ritual with bloodthirstiness, in which violent language and action expresses a memorial process simultaneously with the dramatic procession of events, corresponds in each play. As Tamburlaine produces Zenocrate's hearse before dying, therefore, Hieronimo produces his son's corpse:

> I see your looks urge instance of these words.
> Behold the reason urging me to this!
> *Shows his dead son.*
> See here my show; look on this spectacle!
> (*The Spanish Tragedy*, 4.4.86–8)[30]

Since *The Spanish Tragedy* begins with Andrea's 'rights of burial not performed' (1.1.21–2), the action of both plays is framed by the funerary. Tamburlaine's arrangement of hearse and throne indicates the art involved. As a 'parcell' (5.3.213) of his funeral, the arrangement is as wrapped up as a body in a cloth and as closed as a corpse in a coffin. In *Tamburlaine II*, this is the arrangement of the dramatic end, the close of events. Yet it is even more suggestive for *The Spanish Tragedy*, where the show of the corpse exists in a wider show that is itself the show of Andrea and Revenge, and where

---

29 As noted, the play's subtitle said fury arose 'for the death of his Lady'.

30 All quotations from *The Spanish Tragedy* are from *The Spanish Tragedy by Thomas Kyd*, ed. Clara Calvo and Jesus Tronch, Arden Early Modern Drama (London, 2013).

the action begins and ends in narratives of life underground. Parcelling, here, is a claustrophobic principle of organization, where the 'endless tragedy' (4.5.48) is being continually wrapped up for a funeral.

I have argued for a collaboration of ideas of funerary theatre in *Tamburlaine II* and *The Spanish Tragedy*, but setting the stage for debate, the plays diverge over funerary religion. Tamburlaine's allusion to 'as rich a tombe as Mausolus'', where he and Zenocrate 'will rest and have one Epitaph / Writ in as many severall languages / As I have conquered kingdomes with my sword' (*Tamburlaine II*, 2.4.134–6), has three important functions for the ensuing action. First, it associates the epitaph over the tomb with the babble of Roman Catholicism in its Protestant guise as Babylon, making Catholic memorial, particularly associated with prayer for the purgatorial dead, an incoherence.[31] Second, it transforms the ensuing conquests leading to Babylon into his and Zenocrate's material epitaph, where the many voices of the conquered cultures evidence the memorial incoherence. Third, it anticipates Tamburlaine's death, where Zenocrate's corpse is a reminder of the ordained funeral and 'here ... all things end' (*Tamburlaine II*, 5.3.250). Funeral babble leading to Babylon brings us to the Apocalypse, in a coherent sweep of dramatized Protestant propaganda.[32] This is not to say that Tamburlaine's empire is straightforwardly a Catholic one, or that the play is straightforwardly anti-Catholic. Though its mixed religious signals extend incoherence beyond the funerary, they do not do so coherently.[33] Making the dramatic bête noire the Catholic ritual for the dead, what is coherent is the association of dramatic action with funeral and this association with Babylon's end of days.

This is in sharp contrast with *The Spanish Tragedy*, where Babylon receives no mention and is certainly not a geographical locus. It has been suggested that Hieronimo stating his play 'Soliman and Perseda' will be performed in sundry languages means it was so performed, signalling Babylon. Yet, at best, the signal is indirect and, as Mulryne notes, the reading only has purchase 'if the play was

indeed performed in "sundry languages"'.[34] What Johnson identified as an 'unusual' editorial interpolation claiming various languages for 'Soliman and Perseda's' original performance makes this suspect, especially since the playlet is integral in the larger drama and understanding it is important.[35] Since the interpolation itself presents understanding the playlet as necessary, it is safest to assume the playlet was performed in English, as the text presents it.[36] It has recently been argued that the play only became anti-Catholic in its later rather than original performances, and that Elizabethan Hispanophilia presents as relevant a context for the play as Elizabethan Hispanophobia.[37]

The funerary contrast is also sharp in the plays' presentations of obligations to the dead, which, as has been seen, divided Protestants from Catholics. From its first induction, funerary obligation to the dead is central to *The Spanish Tragedy*, when, delineating supernatural laws for the play, the Ghost of Andrea says 'my rites of burial not performed, / I might not sit amongst his [Charon's] passengers' (1.1.21–2). The phrase delineates as a supernatural law that funerals benefit the dead, and that to lessen

---

[31] For discussion of contemporary associations of prayer for the dead and purgatory, see especially Marshall, *Beliefs*.

[32] Marlowe probably knew Foxe's *Acts and Monuments* from its second edition. See Fuller, 'Introduction', p. xxiii.

[33] For Protestant and Catholic influences on Marlowe in the Tamburlaine plays, see Fuller, 'Introduction', p. xxiii. Jeff Dailey observes 'several ... religious messages' in *Tamburlaine II* in 'Christian Underscoring in *Tamburlaine the Great, Part II'*, *Journal of Religion and Theatre*, 4 (2005), 146–59; p. 147.

[34] J. R Mulryne, 'Nationality and Language in Kyd's *The Spanish Tragedy*', in *Travel and Drama in Shakespeare's Time*, ed. Jean-Pierre Maquerlot and Michèle Willems (Cambridge, 1996), pp. 87–105; p. 93.

[35] See S. F. Johnson, 'The Spanish Tragedy, or Babylon Revisited', in *Essays in Shakespeare and Elizabethan Drama in Honour of Harding Craig*, ed. Richard Hosley (London, 1963), pp. 23–36; p. 23.

[36] Rist, *Revenge Tragedy*, p. 39.

[37] Eric Griffin, 'Ethos, Empire, and the Valiant Acts of Thomas Kyd's Tragedy of "the Spains"', *English Literary Renaissance*, 31 (2001), 192–229; and Griffin, 'Nationalism, the Black Legend, and the Revised *Spanish Tragedy*', *English Literary Renaissance*, 39 (2009), 336–70.

their suffering, the living must complete the funerals of the dead. Drawing this supernatural line in a Virgilian context in which English contemporaries recognized Purgatory, the idea of a complete funeral implies a Catholic one, in view both of Spain and of the brevity of the funerary rite of the Book of Common Prayer by traditional standards.[38] Implicit in the benefits the living bestow on the dead are the ties of friendship that defined medieval ideas of community.[39] These ties become explicit in Horatio's claim to have recovered Andrea's corpse in battle, sighing and sorrowing 'as became a friend' (1.4.37). They are writ larger in Isabella's speeches of mourning for her son, and still larger in those of Hieronimo, kith and kin equally emphasizing the bonds of community as those of affect:

HIERONIMO.   Here, Isabella, help me to lament,
  For sighs are stopped, and all my tears are spent.
  . . .
ISABELLA.   O gush out, tears, fountains and floods of
      tears!
  Blow, sighs, and raise an everlasting storm,
  For outrage fits our cursed wretchedness!
                                (*The Spanish Tragedy*, 2.4.36–46)

Just as it earlier 'became' the friend, mourning the dead here 'fits' the parents. Just as mourning from the induction must be complete, so it here opposes truncation. The result is the picture of a society whose shared belief is in the unadulterated performances of funeral rituals. Extending from the audience of Andrea's ghost to the theatrical audience in its ambit, the affirmed social value extends to us.

The strength of this affirmation is clear in its contrast with *Tamburlaine II*. Instead of a communal value affirmed by a succession of characters, in Marlowe's play mourning the dead is Tamburlaine's idiosyncratic preoccupation. The idiosyncrasy emerges in various ways. While both plays affirm the 'everlasting' possibilities of outrage, Tamburlaine's rage in mourning, spilling across borders to annihilate cities and armies, reveals how strictly limited Hieronimo's aggression is. In *Tamburlaine II*, the whole world can burn for one person. By contrast, *The Spanish Tragedy*'s

presentation of mourning is proportionate. Horatio mourns for Andrea. Bel-Imperia mourns for Andrea. Hieronimo and Isabella mourn for Horatio, their son. Each act of mourning denotes a symmetrical relationship alien to Tamburlaine's burning grief, and for all the hyperbole, Hieronimo's final destruction is relatively small in scale.[40]

That is a comparative analysis, but *Tamburlaine II* bears out the claim in particulars. From the prologue onwards, the play expresses a lack of conviction in its funerary presentation. Introducing the topic after Tamburlaine's 'pomp' (Prologue, 4) with a conjunction ('But') is weak and the whole introduction of the theme by the Prologue is bathetic. When it invites Tamburlaine to reveal the sacrifices of Zenocrate's funeral 'Himself . . . at large', it abnegates responsibility for the funeral while introducing it, in an act of carelessness the play compounds by making Orcanes, not Tamburlaine, come forward. As seen, the funerary theme itself, then, only comes to the fore in Act 2, scene 4. The result is a funerary theme simultaneously central and underwhelming that is found consistently wanting before it has begun.

When in Act 2, scene 4 the theme arrives, the idiosyncrasy of *Tamburlaine II* is at its height. After the thirty-seven lines hymning 'divine Zenocrate' with which Tamburlaine opens the scene, his bathetic question 'how fares my fair Zenocrate?' (2.4.41) receives the most bathetic of responses:

---

[38] For discussion of early modern readings (following Augustine) of Virgil's underworld as Purgatory, see Wilson-Okamura, *Virgil in the Renaissance*, pp. 173–8. Critics who have read Kyd's underworld in these terms include Lucas Erne, *Beyond 'The Spanish Tragedy': A Study of the Works of Thomas Kyd* (Manchester, 2002), p. 53; Lorna Hutson, *The Invention of Suspicion: Law and Mimesis in Shakespeare and Renaissance Drama* (Oxford, 2007), p. 280; Rist, *Revenge Tragedy*, pp. 31–3.

[39] For detailed discussion of this point first raised by Eamon Duffy, see Lucy Wooding, 'Remembrance in the Eucharist', in *The Arts of Remembrance in Early Modern England: Memorial Cultures of the Post Reformation*, ed. Andrew Gordon and Thomas Rist (Farnham, 2013), pp. 19–36.

[40] Hieronimo's methodical search for evidence amid his grief is relevant here. See G. K. Hunter, 'Ironies of Justice in The Spanish Tragedy', *Renaissance Drama*, 8 (1965), 89–104.

I fare, my Lord, as other Empresses,
That when this fraile and transitory flesh
Hath suckt the measure of that vitall aire
That feeds the body with his dated health,
Wanes with enforced and necessary change.
(*Tamburlaine II*, 2.2.42–6)

This is a polite way of saying 'wake up, and smell the coffee', but immediately and until the end of the scene Tamburlaine refuses its analysis of reality with ever grander and more deluded gestures. Theridamas makes the point: 'Ah, good my Lord, be patient, she is dead, / And all this raging cannot make her live' (*Tamburlaine II*, 2.4. 119–20). Since it follows immediately after, Tamburlaine's determination to turn the world funerary black in memory of Zenocrate is at odds with Zenocrate's and Theridamas's assertions of the real, making him idiosyncratic even as their bathetic interventions undercut his pathos. Commemorating Zenocrate through world annihilation is in equal measure mad in two of the senses in which contemporary drama plays with the term: angry and insane.[41] In stark contrast with *The Spanish Tragedy*, where the two senses are in play, but where a relatively circumscribed outrage allegedly 'fits' a loved one's mourning and also more or less fits it in upshot, *Tamburlaine II* goes out of its way to ensure funerary affect is beyond the pale.[42] Perhaps the action following Act 2, scene 4 somewhat redeems the affect by making it a 'new normal', as psychologists say; or rather, by asserting an old normal, since violence is a celebrated norm of *Tamburlaine Part 1*.[43] Relevantly, too, the extremity of Tamburlaine's mourning for Zenocrate, being idiosyncratic by the standards of the play until Act 2, scene 4, as well as by the religiously varying norms of the period, moderates the satire of Babylonian funerary ritual in Catholicism. His final words are replete with paradox:

Farewel my boies, my dearest friends farewell,
My body feeles, my soul doth weepe to see,
Your sweet desires depriv'd my company,
For *Tamburlaine*, the Scourge of God must die.
(*Tamburlaine II*, 5.3.245–8)

By contrast with *The Spanish Tragedy*, where true to the promise of storms that are 'everlasting', Hieronimo's destruction in Spain provokes more, overt mourning, the grief here is curtailed and evasive.[44] Though the body feels grief, it contrasts with the soul, where grief is visible, suggesting that these words apart, the body – all we can see of Tamburlaine – expresses no grief. Yet the elegiac farewells accompanying the weeping of the soul acknowledge grief, leaving this culmination of the funeral performance begun in Act 2, scene 4 uncertain. Is this the incoherence of Babylon finally affirmed according to the play's satirical strand, or a grandeur before death affirming the hero's tragedy that overturns satire? There is no direct answer. Yet closing with a death of Tamburlaine set against the friends and children he leaves behind emphasizes the division of the living from the dead that is at the heart of Reformation differences of commemoration. Allowing the Apocalypse to register either Protestant propaganda or a hyperbole of grief suggesting Catholic, commemorative largesse, the play closes in religious dilemma. Since despite commemorative differences Protestants and Catholics both felt the loss of loved ones, one effect of the uncertainty may be diminishing religious oppositions.

The Spanish Tragedy and *Tamburlaine II* were hugely successful in their era. Taken with the

---

41 The *OED* dates the definition 4 of 'mad' as 'insane, crazy, mentally unbalanced' back to 1330, citing *The Comedy of Errors* as a contemporary, dramatic example. It dates definition 6.b ('angry, irate') back to 1400, with many early modern examples, including from the Great Bible (1539) and the King James Bible (1611). Though no dramatic example is cited in this category, the Shakespearian instance of definition 1 ('Of an animal: abnormally aggressive') applies the sense to a human: 'The venome clamours of a iealous woman, / Poisons more deadly then a madd dogges tooth' (*The Comedy of Errors*, 5.1).

42 For discussion of this 'upshot', see Rist, *Revenge Tragedy*, pp. 41–3.

43 See for example, Eric Maisel, 'The New Normal: Mental Health in the Context of Inevitable Struggle', *Psychology Today*, 1 February 2013.

44 For discussion of how mourning in Kyd 'survives the play', see Rist, *Revenge Tragedy*, p. 40.

court-endorsed *Gorboduc* acclaimed, among others, by Sidney, they set the stage for an Elizabethan and later drama that is widely concerned with commemorating the disputed dead of the Reformation. To these three can be added another hugely popular play, *Titus Andronicus*. The relevant major innovations of this play are aligning funeral controversy with 'popish tricks and ceremonies' (5.1.76) explicitly; accentuating the ancient Rome and Roman Catholic connotations in 'Romish' through their simultaneous performance; making Rome personify mourning (1.1.70); very substantially enlarging the justification of immoderate grief found in *The Spanish Tragedy*; underlining the arguments for grief with negative images of restricted funerary ritual, where the ritual is either a punishment or insult; and aligning the blood and paste through which Titus redeems Rome with a 'coffin' (5.2.187), creating a link precisely sacramental, since altars (unlike Protestant communion tables) traditionally contain the bodies of saints.[45] Yet *Gorboduc* and *Tamburlaine II* also point in the direction of the history play. This significant dramatic development requires attention.

THEATRICAL HISTORY 2: HISTORIES

With its simultaneous connotations of 'story' and 'history' in the period, the term *histories*, devised by John Heminges and Henry Condell in the First Folio, testifies to the interaction of what we today call the history play with other contemporary dramatic genres. Yet Heminges and Condell clearly understood the past as having special prominence in the plays. Their implicit recognition that the genre concerned the dead is explicit in Thomas Nashe's recollection of *1 Henry VI*, in the context of plays 'for the most part borrowed out of our English Chronicles, wherein our forefathers' valiant acts, that have lain long buried in rusty brass and worm-eaten books, are revived':

How would it have joyed brave Talbot, the terror of the French, to think that after he had lain two hundred years in his tomb, he should triumph again on the Stage, and have his bones new embalmed with the tears of ten thousand spectators at least (at several times), who, in the tragedian that represents his person, imagine they behold him fresh bleeding![46]

According to the funerary metaphors and the rich understanding of impersonation, in which both Talbot and his actor triumph on the stage, *1 Henry VI* was a lively encounter with the dead. If that gets lost in abstract phrases like 'history play' or 'the past', Nashe reminds us that the dead are history's content.[47] The description also makes the actor the commemorator of history, meaning both performer and narrative in the history play is commemorative. While the plays treated hitherto make remembering the dead a development of narrative, the implication is that commemoration of the dead (both presentation of the dead and its re-presentation by commemorative performers) defines the genre.

This is also the implication of the history plays themselves, which move forward by looking backward, making the actor a commemorator and making audiences his commemorative observers. Every history play except *Henry V* begins with a backward glance, which normally takes the form of a commemorated death. *The First Part of the Contention of the Two Famous Houses of York and Lancaster* begins with the 'grief, / Your grief, the common grief of all the land' at the passing away of Henry V with his French legacies, Anjou and Maine (*2 Henry VI*, 1.1.73–4). *The True Tragedy of Richard Duke of York and the Good King Henry the Sixth* initially follows with battle, blood and the lofted head of the Duke of Somerset. In an image of the dead giving birth to the future, Richard throws the head down saying 'Thus do I hope to shake King Henry's head' (*3 Henry VI*, 1.1.20).

---

[45] For detailed discussion of these points, see Rist, *Revenge Tragedy*, pp. 44-60. The observation of sacramentality, though, is new. For these connotations in 'Romish', see *OED* definitions 1 and 2.

[46] See 'The Defense of Plays' in 'Pierce Penniless', in Thomas Nashe, *The Unfortunate Traveller and Other Works*, ed. J. B. Steane (London, 1972; repr. 1985), pp. 112-14.

[47] See especially Robert Harrison, *The Dominion of the Dead* (Chicago, 2003).

Foregrounding the funerary theme, *The First Part of Henry the Sixth* – probably written after the two other plays – opens with Henry V's funeral, which makes funeral the premise of the sequence. Especially since his image of the risen Talbot recalls one of 'Henry's corpse ... burst[ing] his lead and rise[n] from death' (*1 Henry VI*, 1.1.62–4), Nashe's analysis of Shakespeare's history as a dramatic resurrection was precise.[48]

With greater or lesser funerary emphasis, other history plays give the past similarly commemorative forms. *Richard II* opens with 'Old John of Gaunt, time-honoured Lancaster' (1.1.1). *Richard III* opens with a 'buried' past, where 'arms are hung up for monuments' (1.1.4; 6). *1 Henry IV* opens with King Henry on England's 'blood' (1.1.6) spilt in the 'intestine shock' (1.1.12) of civil war. *2 Henry IV* brings Rumour with true and false commemorations of Shrewsbury Field. In this context, the innovation of the Chorus of *Henry V*, focusing on imagining the living king, stands out. Harry, who in the Chorus does not emerge from a past but is instead 'like himself' (1.1.5), is a fresh start. Nevertheless, Act 1, scene 2 delves deep into his heredity, over which the ensuing drama is a battle. Its conclusion is Shakespearian commemoration at its most formal:

> Do we all holy rites:
> Let there be sung *Non nobis* and *Te Deum*,
> The dead with charity enclosed in clay.
>
> (*Henry V*, 4.8.122–4)

In the same way nation and religion earlier merged in Henry's commemoration of the day of St Crispin, so history and heredity here merge with the grand funerals of Roman Catholicism. At England's high watermark in the cycle and the play's soberest moment of triumph, *Henry V* claims the commemorative unity of its historical and temporal, funerary and religious modes.[49] Returning to lineage in the marriage to Catherine in Act 5 and then looking beyond Henry's death, temporal history seems one long funeral in preparation. Next to the emergence of plays of violent commemoration including *Tamburlaine II* and the revenge tragedies, the emerging history play, as written by Shakespeare and interpreted by Nashe,

Heminges and Condell, contributes pointedly to the early modern association of theatre and Rome's cult of the dead. By the time of *Hamlet*, Act 1, scene 5, that connection was thoroughly established. The remaining question for the scene is the presence of the Ghost. Since in the scene's presentation of actor and audience the Ghost provides narratives preoccupying Hamlet, the question is important. Why does Shakespeare equate his religious ghost with narrative in *Hamlet*? What precedents for this exist? In providing an answer, I shall move between the plays already considered, treating them each as 'history' according to the term's early modern connotations of narrative and narrative especially concerned with temporal events.[50]

SPIRITS OF HISTORY

Hamlet, Act 1, scene 5 is not the play's first association of narrative and ghost. In Act 1, scene 1, Horatio proposes he, Francisco and the sentinels sit to hear Barnardo's 'story' (1.1.30) of the Ghost's appearance, so that it is into a story-telling tableau that the Ghost enters, linking him with narrative twice. Since in Act 1, scene 1 and Act 1, scene 5 the Ghost also evokes the past (indirectly or directly), we may speak with Derrida-inspired critics of Shakespeare's hauntology.[51] Yet early modern examples of the haunting past are both more

---

[48] Nashe, it seems, substituted Shakespeare's image of Henry rising from his tomb for an image of Talbot doing so.

[49] My reading of *Henry V* here develops that of Philip Schwyzer in *Literature, Nationalism and Memory in Early Modern England and Wales* (Cambridge, 2010), pp. 126–51.

[50] The treatment is also in line with the inclusivity of early modern dramatic presentations of genre. For discussion, see Dillon, *Early English Theatre*, pp. 141–71.

[51] Derrida's prime example of history haunting the present is Hamlet's Ghost. See *Specters of Marx: The State of the Debt, the Work of Mourning and the New International*, trans. Peggy Kamuf (New York, 1994), p. 1. Derrida and Hamlet's Ghost are acknowledged as inspirations in Marvin Carlson's wide-ranging study of theatre's spectral functioning in *The Haunted Stage: The Theatre as Memory Machine* (Ann Arbor, MI, 2003).

personal and more overtly literary than *Spectres of Marx* or *The Haunted Stage* allow. 'As the soul of Euphorbus was thought to live in Pythagoras, so the sweet witty soul of Ovid lives in mellifluous and honey-tongued Shakespeare.'[52] Like the two scenes from *Hamlet*, Francis Meres's consideration of *Venus and Adonis* twice presents a dead soul as the source of later human agency, making animation (from the Latin *anima* or soul, but having the sense of 'living') a matter in which the dead are the soul of liveliness, in narrative as more generally.[53]

Evoking the dead as what lives, and being key in good theatre, 'animation' bears emphasis. The Ghost's claim that his story could 'freeze thy young blood' (1.5.16) educes early modern Galenic physiology, in which spirits, described by Gail Paster as the 'energetic faculties ... that make the body move and feel', animate bodies.[54] The ghostly play on 'spirits' – both personal and medical – underlines the importance of animation in the scene, especially in its causes. What animates Hamlet, causing him to act? Is it a spirit from the dead or of his physiology? Recent readings of *Hamlet* as also of the epoch suggest one cannot affirm either cause without affirming the other, since medicine and religion in the pre-Cartesian, 'Galenic moment' were interdependent.[55] At root, the cause is theological, since, as Paster observes, discussions of physiological spirits even among more materially minded medical theorists were implicitly a 'celebration of *pneuma*'s breakaway force'.[56] Yet as important as the First Cause are the causal links between it and Hamlet. According to the scenes, those links take two forms: the Ghost and the narratives of the past. The implication is not only that ghost and historical narrative are the same, and that these are bound up with Purgatory and purging, but also that these ghosts animate history. That is a claim very close to Nashe's indication, in his analysis of *1 Henry VI*, that in the histories the dead 'triumphe againe on the Stage'. What other dramatic precedents for the claim that narrative is a mysterious ghost exist?

An answer is already in *Gorboduc*, where the 'Order and Signification of the Dumb Show

Before the Fourth Act' explains introducing the Furies and the dead: 'Hereby was signified the unnatural murders to follow' (4.0.13). Spirits stand for narrative in this authorized explanation, particularly a fictional narrative of historical events to come, showing the ghost-as-narrative motif was flexible long before Shakespeare. *The Spanish Tragedy* places the motif front and centre: the opening narrative is spoken by the Ghost of Andrea and recounts his history, making the Ghost the voice of history while also making history the content of the ghost. Since understanding *The Spanish Tragedy*'s plot depends on the speech, the ensuing drama, overseen and eventually ended by the Ghost, equates dramatic narrative, in this case a fictional presentation of history, with the dead.

Tamburlaine II presents physiological spirits instead of ghosts. Physicians surround Zenocrate and also Tamburlaine's deathbeds, and 'spirits' are the centre of their practice:

---

[52] Francis Meres's famous comment on *Venus and Adonis* (1598).

[53] For 'anima' as 'soul', see the *OED* etymology for 'anima'. Interestingly, 'anima' contrasts with 'animus', these being the irrational and rational parts of the soul respectively. The *OED* also traces the etymology of 'animation' from Classical Latin, meaning 'form of life', through various early modern examples. Definition 4 specifically pertains to 'Senses relating to life, quickening, bringing into action'.

[54] See Gail Kern Paster, 'Nervous Tension: Networks of Blood and Spirit in the Early Modern Body', in *The Body in Parts: Fantasies of Corporality in Early Modern Europe*, ed. David Hillman and Carla Mazzio (London, 1997), pp. 107–28 ; p. 111. For discussion of Hamlet's 'young blood' in terms of physiology, see Rist, 'Catharsis as "Purgation"', p. 149.

[55] For detailed discussion of the 'Galenic moment' in these terms, see Charles Parker, 'Diseased Bodies, Defiled Souls: Corporality and Religious Difference in the Reformation', *Renaissance Quarterly*, 67 (2014), 1265–97; esp. p. 1269. For analysis of Hamlet in these terms, see Rist, 'Catharis as "Purgation"' and 'Transgression Embodied'.

[56] Paster, 'Nervous Tension', p. 115. Explicitly for the author of the *Novum Organum* (*sic*), Francis Bacon, all the universe besides the 'passive' earth consists of 'pneumatic matter'. See '3.3. Matter Theory and Cosmology' under 'Francis Bacon', in *Stanford Encyclopaedia of Philosophy*, http://plato.stanford.edu/entries/francis-bacon/, accessed 18 June 2015.

PHYSICIAN.   I view'd your urine, and the Hipostasis
  Thick and obscure doth make your danger great.
  Your vains are full of accidentall heat,
  Whereby the moisture of your blood is dried.
  The *Humidum* and *Calor*, which some holde
  Is not a parcell of the Elements,
  But of a substance more divine and pure,
  Is almost cleane extinguished and spent,
  Which, being the cause of life, imports your death.
  Besides my lord, this day is Criticall,
  Dangerous to those whose *Chrisis* is as yours:
  Your Arteries, which alongst the vains convey
  The lively spirits which the heart ingenders,
  Are parcht and void of spirit, that the soule,
  Wanting those Organnons by which it mooves,
  Cannot indure by argument of art.
  Yet if your majesty may escape this day,
  No doubt, but you shal soon recover all.

                   (5.3.82–99)

The detailed and final medical analysis goes to the heart of the liveliness of Tamburlaine, who is animated or dead according to a rationale in which spirits move the soul. The analysis defines the play's idea of humanity, making the life of the soul the definition of living, and explaining action and so theatre as the soul's visible manifestation. Although there are no ghosts in *Tamburlaine II*, the souls traditionally emerging as ghosts at death are essential.

Those inner spirits are also in *The Spanish Tragedy*, most obviously in the Ghost of Andrea's introduction of his 'soul' as the 'eternal substance' that 'Did live imprison'd in my wanton flesh / Each in their function serving the other's need' (1.1.1–3). Yet the inner spirits equated with action are almost as evident in Revenge, who is both a personified feeling ('vengefulness') and a personified action. The opening of *The Spanish Tragedy* turns the explanation of action of *Tamburlaine II* inside out, showing through an external association of spirit, feeling and action the physiologized religion Marlowe diagnosed within Tamburlaine's body. *The Spanish Tragedy* complements this heightened visibility with a third form of spiritual intercession:

  And all the saints do sit soliciting
  For vengeance . . .   (4.1.33–4)

The third form of spiritual impetus is the saints of Roman Catholic Spain. Their association with Revenge, and so with Purgatory, brings out the religion underpinning personal action.[57]

A single example sufficiently illustrates for the present how the three forms of spirituality explain action in Shakespeare's histories. Four short scenes after Buckingham has identified the day of his death as 'All-Souls' day' (5.1.10; 12), in a passage identifying 'Dream' (5.5.100) as part of a spirit's arsenal, in *Richard III* the Ghost of Prince Edward, of Clarence and of Rivers tell Richard they will 'sit heavy on thy soul tomorrow' (5.5.71, 85, 93). The message is also the tenor of the Ghost of Henry, Gray, Vaughan, the Princess and Lady Anne to Richard, and the broken spirit of Richard is visible in his waking soliloquy of doubt and broken phrases (5.5.131–60). Also visited by the ghosts, but with encouragement, Richmond awakes in high spirits, the two characters evidencing the causal relation of spirits to feeling to action. Stressing this, Richmond comments: 'Methought their souls whose bodies Richard murdered / Came to my tent and cried on victory. / I promise you, my soul is very jocund' (5.6.184–6). Moving from 'their souls' to 'my soul' in the context of feeling underlines the causal connection. The following success and failure of Richmond and Richard stresses it all the more.

Notable here is the interchangeability of terms: 'ghost', 'soul', 'spirit'. The first two remain subspecies of the third in general discourse. The third, while the focus of more strictly physiological discourse in the period, was connected to the soul (and so the soul in death: the ghost), as seen. Each term, of course, can denote religion, which the play brings out not only in 'All-Souls'', but also in its presentations of prayer. Following the claim that 'saints pray' (4.4.75) for Richard's demise, the Ghost of Lady Anne says to Richmond that she 'pray[s] for thee' (5.5.120). The implication is that

---

[57] For Purgatory relating to justice and revenge, see Hutson, *Invention of Suspicion*, pp. 275–7 and Rist, *Revenge Tragedy*, pp. 27–74.

the Ghost of Anne is a saint, which must be true if, as the play repeatedly asserts, the Tudors come to the English throne through the providence of 'God and good angels' (5.5.129); but which strikingly implicates the medieval cult of the saints not only in the picture of spirituality *qua* human agency and theatrical action but also in the majesty of Elizabeth I and the operations of providence.[58]

CONCLUSION

By the time Shakespeare wrote *Hamlet*, there was considerable precedent in English theatre for thinking of the institution and much else as an expression of the cult of the dead of Rome.[59] With differing emphases as a remarkably high number of contemporaries had observed, Sackville and Norton, Kyd, Marlowe and Shakespeare himself had done so before. Hamlet's response to the Ghost's narrative in Act 1, scene 5 reproduces an established paradigm of theatre. The 'perturbèd spirit' (1.5.183) having disturbed the persons of Act 1, scene 1, the explanation of theatrical action is part of a wider analysis of action in which spirits move persons. Drawing on the semantics of religion and medicine simultaneously, Act 1, scene 5 brings out the 'purge' (1.5.13) of this action; and Hamlet's pained inactivity following the scene conforms to the Ghost's claim that his tale might harrowingly freeze him, according to the spiritual logic.[60]

Yet according to these plays, the cult of the dead might be redescribed as a cult of the living. It is their repeated claim that as agents producing movement, spirits keep bodies from immobility, itself unsurprisingly associated with death: when the spirit traditionally leaves the body or, as Marlowe has it, when the spirit and soul want 'those organnons by which it mooves'.

Emphasizing the logic of movement, Marlowe's description raises one last question. What value might this explanation of theatre and action have today beyond the historical? In view of the rise of the New Historicism, Cultural Materialism, the 'turn to religion' and the critical practices these have influenced, the answer is a lot, since these share what Greenblatt identified as a 'desire to speak with the dead', 'the familiar if unvoiced motive of literary studies'.[61] Acknowledging the embarrassment that buries this motive 'beneath thick layers of bureaucratic decorum', Greenblatt described a conundrum: 'If I never believed that the dead could hear me, and if I knew that the dead could not speak, I was nevertheless certain that I could re-create a conversation with them.'[62] Explanation follows: 'for the dead had contrived to leave traces of themselves, and those traces make themselves heard in the voices of the living'.[63] Yet this explanation requires another: a society 'that posits an occult network linking all human, natural, and cosmic powers and that claims on behalf of its ruling elite a privileged access to the linked powers ... generates vivid dreams of access to the linked powers'. That too requiring explanation, Greenblatt avoided further regress by writing about something else.[64]

---

[58] For parallel reading, see Jean-Christophe Mayer, *Shakespeare's Hybrid Faith: History, Religion and the Stage* (Basingstoke, 2006), p. 56; also Katherine Goodland, *Female Mourning and Tragedy in Medieval and English Renaissance English Drama: From the Raising of Lazarus to King Lear* (Aldershot, 2005), p. 149.

[59] The genre omitted from specific consideration in this article is comedy, but its narratives too evoke remembrance of the dead. For perspectives, see Rist, 'Merry, Marry, Mary: Shakespearean Wordplay and *Twelfth Night*', in *Shakespeare Survey 62* (Cambridge, 2009), pp. 81–91, especially 88–90; Suzanne Penuel, 'Missing Fathers: *Twelfth Night* and the Reformation of Mourning', in *Studies in Philology*, 107 (2010), 74–96; and Andrew Gordon, 'The Ghost of Pasquill: The Comic Afterlife and the Afterlife of Comedy on the Elizabethan Stage', in *The Arts of Remembrance in Early Modern England: Memorial Cultures of the Post Reformation*, ed. Andrew Gordon and Thomas Rist (Farnham, 2013), pp. 229–46.

[60] For discussion, see Rist, 'Transgression Embodied', pp. 129–30; also 'Catharsis as Purgation', p. 151.

[61] Stephen Greenblatt, *Shakespearean Negotiations: The Circulation of Social Energy in Renaissance England* (Oxford, 1988), p. 1.

[62] Greenblatt, *Shakespearean Negotiations*, p. 1.

[63] Greenblatt, *Shakespearean Negotiations*, p. 1.

[64] Thus, only 'something' survived of 'this initial conception'. Greenblatt, *Shakespearean Negotiations*, p. 2.

Yet illustrating the problem of causation, the regress is important. How do the dead 'contrive' to leave traces? How do societies 'generate' dreams? What, in short, energizes 'social energy'? The answer 'people' (or in literature, 'readers') is inadequate. What energizes them?

As suggested at the outset, the 'father of sociology' Emile Durkheim considered this regress-inducing question of energetic 'force' (in his phrase) a normal reason for human belief in the soul.[65] In the 'hodgepodge of Galenic theory and Vesalian anatomy' mingling with the 'corporal hermeneutic' of sanctity and corruption, certainly, the Renaissance had spiritual and soulful answers, especially from Rome's church.[66] Today, biology, theoretical physics and philosophical theology – containing continuities with the premodern – dispute answers of other kinds, but the underlying question, the logic of causation, occupies each.[67] Whether speaking of evolution, string theory, energy, or God, causation retains in popular and academic discourse the fascination it held on the Renaissance stage. Though we may not subscribe to the agency of the dead, the phrase can serve as a metonym for 'organnons', energy or indeed (with its attention to motive) character, until such

time as the disputes resolve. Nothing comes of nothing, as Lear observes, while, in its emphasis on analogy, the spiritualism of the Renaissance had the quality of drama.[68]

---

[65] For specific discussion of the belief in terms of causality and the philosophical regress, see Durkheim, *Elementary Forms*, p. 366.

[66] Parker, 'Diseased Bodies', p. 1268. As Parker notes, some early modern Protestants also accepted this hermeneutic 'embraced by Catholics for centuries' (p. 1266).

[67] Since Darwin and Stephen Hawking are well known, only 'philosophical theology' may need introduction here, so see Alasdair MacIntyre's recent explication of Thomist philosophy: 'this presupposes some source of existence, some being whose being is not to be understood either as a composite of form and matter or as one in whom essence and existence are distinct, but as a being whose essential is his esse, God' (*God, Philosophy, Universities: A History of the Catholic Philosophical Tradition* (London, 2009), p. 74).

[68] See Wayne Shumaker, *The Occult Sciences in the Renaissance: A Study of Intellectual Patterns* (Berkeley, 1972), pp. 193–7; esp. p. 197. Much like Greenblatt, Shumaker was embarrassed by and disavowed the 'occult', while recognizing its importance 'for the literary period in which I specialise' (p. xvi). Pertaining to the causes of action, Shumaker's observation that in the Renaissance occult 'the whole world is alive' (p. 225) also merits mention. I am grateful to Stanley Wells for his comments on an earlier draft of this chapter.

'ANOTHER PART OF THE FOREST': EDITORS AND LOCATIONS IN SHAKESPEARE

PETER WOMACK

I

Until recently, most editions of Shakespeare headed each scene with a note of its location: 'A ship at sea'; 'Troy. A room in Priam's palace'; 'Another part of the forest'. As is well known, these headings have no textual authority: in the Folio and the Quartos, a scene typically starts by specifying which characters are to enter, but with nothing to indicate where they are supposed to be. With very few exceptions, the locations are the work of eighteenth-century editors, reproduced or emended by their nineteenth- and twentieth-century successors.

Over the past half-century the scholarly consensus has moved against this practice. As G. E. Bentley put it in 1964: 'Why should such a careful distortion of Shakespeare's plays have been carried out and copied for centuries? The answer is ignorance. Ignorance of the theatre for which Shakespeare wrote and of his careful planning of his plays for it.'[1] In regarding location as an invariable and necessary piece of information, he argued, the editors showed their failure to understand the 'placeless' early modern stage and its dramaturgy.[2] They read Shakespearian drama as if the theatre of their own time, with its proscenium arch and representational scenery, were the only possible kind. Not only that; by integrating this unthinking assumption with the standard text of the plays, they misdirected the imaginations of generations of readers. Twenty years later, Alan Dessen enthusiastically endorsed Bentley's account, and added: 'Thanks to generations of editing and typography, modern readers have thereby been conditioned to *expect* placement of a given scene ("where does it occur?"), regardless

of the fluidity or placelessness of the original context or the potential distortion in the question "where?"'[3]

Dessen clearly feels that his explicit project – to recover Shakespeare's lost 'theatrical vocabulary'[4] – is made both necessary and difficult by this accretion of irrelevant expectations: he and his followers have the air of scraping away the deposits left by alien interpretations in order to expose the true Shakespearian drama underneath.[5] In similar vein, in 1994, Barbara Mowat argues that Nicholas Rowe's influential editorial locations 'encourage readers of the plays to read them novelistically, or to imagine them within a proscenium arch on a stage filled with backdrops and furniture'.[6] Lear rages on

---

[1] G. E. Bentley, *Shakespeare and his Theatre* (Lincoln, NE, 1964), pp. 55–6.

[2] This argument was not new in 1964: for a lively earlier statement, see Harley Granville-Barker, 'A Note upon Chapters XX. and XXI. of *The Elizabethan Stage*', *Review of English Studies*, 1 (1925), 60–71. It was from the 1960s on, though, that the theatrical and critical *consensus* shifted.

[3] Alan C. Dessen, *Elizabethan Stage Conventions and Modern Interpreters* (Cambridge, 1984), p. 84.

[4] The phrase is from a later book of Dessen's: *Recovering Shakespeare's Theatrical Vocabulary* (Cambridge, 1995).

[5] For example, this is a dominant trope in the work associated with the replica Globe, such as Pauline Kiernan, *Staging Shakespeare at the New Globe* (London, 1999), and Christie Carson and Farah Karim-Cooper, *Shakespeare's Globe: A Theatrical Experiment* (Cambridge, 2008).

[6] Barbara Mowat, 'Nicholas Rowe and the Twentieth-Century Shakespeare Text', in *Shakespeare and Cultural Traditions*, ed. Tetsuo Kishi, Roger Pringle and Stanley Wells (London, 1994), pp. 314–22.

the heath, and Hamlet encounters his father's ghost on the platform of the castle, merely because an editorial whim has posed them against these backdrops. By the end of the twentieth century, then, it was a truth universally acknowledged, at least in academic circles, that locative headings had been an unwarranted interference in Shakespearian reception, now happily detected and removed.[7]

In standing back from this new orthodoxy, I do not mean to argue that it is simply mistaken. Bentley's argument was founded in part on Bernard Beckerman's *Shakespeare at the Globe*, which had appeared a little earlier, in 1962. This resolutely empirical study inspected all the scenes in all the Shakespeare plays that can be shown to have been staged at the first Globe, and asked what kind of placing each one implied. To classify his findings, Beckerman decided that he needed four categories.[8] Some scenes were located in much the way that later editors expected: that is, the audience was told exactly where the action was supposed to be taking place. In others, there was no indication whatsoever; the scene was simply unlocated. In a third and quite large category the action had, as he termed it, a 'general' location, which meant that it was unambiguously located, but in an extensive place such as 'London' or 'Egypt', with nothing to fix its position within those boundaries. And finally there were some examples, not numerous but evidently not anomalous, in which the implied setting changed in the course of a scene. In sum, Shakespearian locations could be specific, general, unstated or fluid, according to the requirements of the narrative.

Beckerman's categorization of particular scenes is questionable and, in any case, opaque. But no one has seriously contested his demonstration that the Shakespearian mode of dramatic location is variable: the representation of place is done in different ways for different scenes. It follows that when subsequent editors insisted on heading every scene with a specified and consistent location, they were imposing a misleading uniformity on the flexible dramaturgy of the early modern stage. But if we are right about this, then it seems to me that we should be more surprised. It is surprising

that the entire tradition of Shakespearian editing, from Rowe in 1709 to Arden 2 in 1951–82, should have fallen prey to such a basic misconception.[9] It is surprising that scholars who laboured with bardolatrous passion to restore the authentic Shakespearian text should nevertheless have been content to add an inauthentic supplement to every single scene. And it is surprising that an editorial convention, unquestioned for well over two centuries, should then have been so abruptly discredited. Simply to take it that the scales fell from our eyes, so that we can now see the truth about Shakespeare that was hidden from all our predecessors, would be to demonstrate just the transhistorical complacency of which we accuse them. We are fairly sure they were not right, but it is still worth asking what it is that made them think they were.

II

As Dessen points out, the most systematic exponent of editorial location was Edmond Malone, whose immense Variorum Shakespeare appeared in 1790.[10] Introducing the edition, Malone promises that the reader will 'find the place in which every scene is supposed to pass, precisely ascertained: a species of information, for which, though it often throws light on the dialogue, we look in

---

[7] The most prominent collected editions of the period were the Oxford Shakespeare, edited by Stanley Wells and Gary Taylor (1986), the Norton Shakespeare, edited by Stephen Greenblatt (1997), and the Complete Works, edited by Jonathan Bate and Eric Rasmussen for Macmillan as part of the RSC Shakespeare series (2007). The Oxford abandoned locative headings; the other two relegated them to somewhat shame-faced footnotes.

[8] Bernard Beckerman, *Shakespeare at the Globe* (New York, 1962), pp. 63–9.

[9] The successive editions are magnificently surveyed in Andrew Murphy, *Shakespeare in Print: A History and Chronology of Shakespeare Publishing* (Cambridge, 2003).

[10] *The Plays and Poems of William Shakspeare*, in ten volumes, edited by Edmond Malone (London, 1790). This edition is intensely studied in Margreta de Grazia, *Shakespeare Verbatim: The Reproduction of Authenticity and the 1790 Apparatus* (Oxford, 1991).

vain in the ancient copies'.[11] The terminology here – 'ascertain', 'information' – implies that Malone's locations are factual discoveries, systematically based on evidence. Dessen rejects this claim to validity:

many of the texts widely used by actors, directors and critics give prominent typographical position to such locales as 'a wood' or 'a room in the castle', designations that have no authority other than the theatrical or literary tastes of an early editor ... [W]hat exactly does 'another part of the forest' (to cite a notorious example) mean when linked to a production designed for a large open platform where the 'forest' is largely if not totally the product of the 'imaginary forces' of the spectator? I know of no evidence that the audience at the Globe or Blackfriars shared this obsession with place. Rather, as Gerald Eades Bentley reminds us, Shakespeare 'wrote with the Globe, not the Drury Lane, in mind, and he wrote a drama of persons, not a drama of places' in which, normally, 'the audience is expected to concentrate wholly on words and actions and to ignore the place where the action may have taken place'.[12]

'Another part of the forest' is the heading Malone provides for several scenes in *As You Like It*. What makes it a 'notorious example'? Dessen does not explain, but I think he means that the phrase is a sort of *reductio ad absurdum* of Malone's toponymic labours. The insistence on treating Shakespearian locations as if they were geographical data is comically undermined by the undifferentiated and explicitly imaginary Forest of Arden that is conjured up on a bare stage by the words of the playwright and the imaginations of the spectators. The play affords Malone so little 'information' of the kind he seeks that he is reduced to offering the empty distinction between one part of the forest and another part of the forest as if it meant something. Palpably, he is asking the wrong kind of question; he is like someone trying to fix the latitude and longitude of a place in a dream.

However, if in a contrarian spirit we attempt a defence of the notorious phrase, it is not impossible to think of reasonable arguments. Take one example of Malone's use of it: *As You Like It*, Act 3, scene 5.[13] At the end of Act 3, scene 4, Corin has come to Rosalind and Celia to say that Silvius is courting Phoebe at this very moment:

> Go hence a little, and I shall conduct you,
> If you will mark it.   (3.4.50–1)

Rosalind replies, 'Bring us to this sight', and all three leave the stage. Then Silvius and Phoebe come on, and Silvius has seven lines before Rosalind, Celia and Corin re-enter. The narrative continuity is obvious. When the trio left the stage, it meant that Corin was 'conducting' Rosalind and Celia to the place where they would find Silvius and Phoebe; and now, when they join Silvius and Phoebe on the stage in the new scene, we understand that they have arrived and found them. Both scenes are clearly set in the Forest of Arden. But a reader or spectator who thought that 3.5 begins with Silvius and Phoebe arriving at the very spot that Rosalind and Celia have just vacated, and so almost meeting them by chance, would be misinterpreting the sequence of exits and entrances. In order to follow the story, in the most elementary sense, we must suppose that the action of 3.5 happens a short distance away from the place where the action of 3.4 happens. The most economical way to spell out this necessary supposition is precisely to say that 3.5 is located in 'another part of the forest'. Thus Malone's ascription is not gratuitous, and it is not an expression of his 'theatrical or literary tastes': it is a logical deduction from the Folio text.

Moreover, the deduction is unaffected by the presence or absence of scenery. The need to suppose a change of place is a function of the narrative: it applies in exactly the same way whether *As You Like It* is being presented on an illusionistic set, or acted on a bare stage, or read as a poem with no stage at all. Malone himself did not assume pictorial scenery: he knew that Shakespeare's stage had none, and argued the point at length against rival scholars who believed otherwise.[14] The two

---

[11] Malone, *Shakspeare*, vol. 1, pp. lviii–lix.

[12] Dessen, *Elizabethan Stage Conventions*, pp. 84–5. The quotation from Bentley is from *Shakespeare and his Theatre*, p. 57.

[13] All Shakespeare quotations and scene and line numbers are from *William Shakespeare: The Complete Works*, ed. Stanley Wells et al., 2nd edn (Oxford, 2005), unless otherwise noted.

[14] Malone, *Shakspeare*, vol. 1, part 2, pp. 66–89.

issues – location and scenery – are certainly connected, as will be seen. But they are not the same, and the relationship between them is more complicated than Dessen implies.

What is Malone assuming, then, if it is not a scenic stage? The crucial concept is 'supposing': the datum he is concerned to ascertain is 'the place in which every scene is supposed to pass'. A play says to its audience: we know that these things are not really happening, but let us suppose that they are. This sophisticated pretence, this supposition, means treating the actions and utterances and emotions of the characters as if they were real. But any real event must necessarily happen at a particular time and place. So if we are to suppose an event, we must know when and where to suppose that it is occurring. If we cannot do that – if a dramatic event is left floating nowhere in particular – then it is to that extent *not* like a real event, and so loses some of its intelligibility and power. Quite how this suppositious place is communicated to the audience – whether by naturalistic scenery or by words spoken on a bare stage – is a secondary question. What matters primarily is just that the audience should know *somehow or other* where the characters they are watching are supposed to be. That is why Malone thinks it helpful to provide locations for his readers. In coming to that conclusion he is making any number of dubious philosophical assumptions, but he is not simply 'obsessed' with place, he is not regarding dramatic location as 'an end in itself',[15] and he is not mentally putting Shakespeare's plays on the stage of Sheridan's Drury Lane. Rather, like Dessen or Bentley, he is considering the conditions of effectiveness of the spectators' 'imaginary forces'.

Nor is this project personal or eccentric. More often than not, Malone's ascriptions merely confirm or refine those of earlier editors: in this respect, as in others, the Variorum is a consolidation of the eighteenth-century editorial tradition. The work of location had been going on, in similar terms, ever since Nicholas Rowe's edition of 1709. Take one of Barbara Mowat's examples from Rowe: his decision that Hamlet meets his father's ghost on 'the Platform before the Palace'.[16] Mowat represents this platform

as an arbitrary invention, which then survived through dozens of subsequent editions out of habit. But that does less than justice to Rowe's close reading.

When Horatio and Marcellus tell Hamlet about the appearance of the ghost, his first reaction is to ask 'But where was this?' (1.2.212). The naturalness of the question is itself part of the context of Rowe's specification. Like anybody confronted with an ontologically dubious event, Hamlet tries to get a handle on it by pinning it down to a particular place. In effect, he shares the assumption we have attributed to Malone: if his informants cannot say where the ghost was, he is less likely to regard it as real. So their categorical answer – 'My lord, upon the platform where we watch.' – has the force of an insistence that they genuinely did see something. Hamlet's next move is correspondingly definite:

> So fare ye well.
> Upon the platform 'twixt eleven and twelve
> I'll visit you.   (1.2.250–2)

Then the same characters appear at the opening of 1.4, and almost at once have this exchange:

HAMLET.   What hour now?
HORATIO.   I think it lacks of twelve.
MARCELLUS.   No, it is struck.   (1.4.3–5)

Here, almost pedantically, we are given to understand that Hamlet has joined the others at the time he told them he would; so we naturally see the stage, whatever it looks like, as the place where they said they would be. Once again, so far from being a gratuitous supplement to the Shakespearian text, the editorially supplied location is a deduction from it that is both inescapable and dramatically relevant.

This particular case gets more complicated, however. The ghost appears and gestures to Hamlet to accompany it 'to a more removèd ground' (1.4.42).

---

[15] Dessen, *Elizabethan Stage Conventions*, p. 85.
[16] *The works of Mr William Shakespeare; in six volumes*, ed. Nicholas Rowe (London, 1709), vol. 5, p. 2382. The scene is 1.4 in modern editions.

This makes the question 'where?' still more urgent, Hamlet insisting on following the ghost to another place, and Horatio and Marcellus desperately trying to compel him to stay where he is. Hamlet prevails and exits with the ghost; after a brief discussion, his friends follow him off. The stage is empty for a moment, then the ghost re-enters with Hamlet, who immediately says: 'Whither wilt thou lead me? Speak. I'll go no further' (1.5.1). At this point, then, we are in a situation closely analogous to 'another part of the forest': the narrative requires us to imagine that the fresh action is happening somewhere close to the location of the previous scene, but not on exactly the same spot. Rowe, like the Folio, simply heads 1.5 with the re-entrance of Hamlet and the ghost: throughout his edition his concern with location is rather casual and inconsistent. But Lewis Theobald in 1733 observes the additional difficulty and adds: 'SCENE changes to a more remote Part of the Platform'.[17] This uneasy solution proved resilient: Malone accepted it, and it passed from him into the collected editions of the nineteenth and twentieth centuries.

This enduring historical stability is significant because it is in fact typical: editors agreed on the great majority of the locations assigned to individual Shakespearian scenes, even though they were cantankerously hostile to one another on many other issues. The reason for the uncharacteristic harmony is the one we have already seen: that once the question of place is raised at all, it can usually be answered unambiguously on the basis of the text. The editors came to the same conclusions because they were looking at the same evidence. This suggests that place on the Shakespearian stage may be a good deal less fluid than its more excitable modern exponents propose. A sort of dramaturgic libertarianism can make early modern theatre appear phantasmagoric, as if the audience were prepared to be transported to multiple imaginary places at the actors' lightest word.[18] The solidity of the eighteenth-century editors' deductions alerts us, on the contrary, to the extent of the drama's representational *fixity*. As long as readers and editors continued to ask where *Hamlet*, Act 1, scene 5 is supposed to take place, the answer continued to be 'A more remote Part of the Platform'. The reason the formulation lasted so well, despite its inherent feebleness, was just that it was not a whimsical imposition upon the Shakespearian text but a demonstrable fact about it.

III

If that is so – if Shakespeare does routinely provide materials by which the location of his scenes can be 'ascertained' – then arguably his theatre cannot have been indifferent to the question of place after all. Perhaps it *did* matter that the spectators should understand where they were supposed to be. This suspicion is rather surprisingly confirmed by the Chorus in *Henry V*. In a way, these speeches form a *locus classicus* of the 'placeless' Elizabethan stage, because of their flamboyant insistence on the transformative power of the audience's imagination. 'Our swift scene flies / In motion of no less celerity / Than that of thought' (3.0.1–3), soaring effortlessly above the pedestrian calculations of editors and scene painters. But there is also an interesting moment when the speaker's confidence falters, and he seems to get in something of a tangle:

> The sum is paid, the traitors are agreed,
> The King is set from London, and the scene
> Is now transported, gentles, to Southampton.
> There is the playhouse now, there must you sit,
> And thence to France shall we convey you safe,
> And bring you back, charming the narrow seas
> To give you gentle pass – for if we may
> We'll not offend one stomach with our play.
> But till the King come forth, and not till then,
> Unto Southampton do we shift our scene.
>
> (2.0.33–42)

---

[17] *The works of Shakespeare: in seven volumes*, ed. Lewis Theobald (London, 1733), vol. 7, p. 250.

[18] See for example Doug Eskew, '*Coriolanus* and the Paradox of Place', *Early Modern Literary Studies*, 15 (2009–10), https://extra.shu.ac.uk/emls/15-1/eskecori.html, accessed 11 March 2016; and Lloyd Edward Kermode, 'Experiencing the Space and Place of Early Modern Theater', *Journal of Medieval and Early Modern Studies*, 43 (2013), 1–24.

In this passage there is both an assumed confusion and, I think, a real one. The assumed confusion has to do with the business of conveying the audience from London to Southampton, and then across the sea and back. The Chorus highlights these movements with a mock-sheepish consciousness of their absurdity. Look for example at the line, 'There is the playhouse now, there must you sit'. It is not needed – the speech flows more easily if you simply cut it – and its conceit makes the transaction sound sillier than it needs to be. After all, he has already said that the geographical scope of the story is to be encompassed by the spectators' imaginations: that is, to the extent that they manage to 'be' in Southampton, they cease to be in the playhouse. Either way, there is no question either in reality or in imagination of relocating the *building*. The logical levels involved are being deliberately and playfully muddled up. A similar game with locative convention informs the promise that the Channel crossing will not offend anyone's stomach: teasingly, theatre offers a voyage that is guaranteed not to make you seasick. Whatever may be the point of these jokes for the play as a whole, they turn on an ironically felt doubleness: the audience are of course sitting in the theatre on the Bankside, but for the purposes of the play they must also be in Southampton, at sea, and in France. The company is not after all taking the contradiction casually in its stride; it is aware of it, sublimely or comically or something in between, as an anomaly.

As for the real confusion, it comes in the last two lines:

> But till the King come forth, and not till then,
> Unto Southampton do we shift our scene.

The main thrust of the speech has been that we are going to Southampton and then to France, but these concluding lines belatedly acknowledge that, in fact, the next scene is going to be in London, and we will not get to Southampton until after that. There are several possible ways of understanding this hiccup: it has the interesting effect, for instance, of placing the death of Falstaff as a sort of unofficial interruption to the planned progress of the play. But however that may be, it produces in the Chorus itself an unaccustomed moment of uncertainty: to Southampton! – oh, wait a minute, not just yet. The clause 'till the King come forth, and not till then' is self-contradictory as it stands: surely the Chorus intends to say that *when* the King comes forth, we will be in Southampton, but that *until* he does we are not. The King's 'coming forth' is an event in the theatre, not in the story – it is the entrance we should look out for to get our bearings; but then the clarification is itself unclear. The Chorus has been playing in the ambiguous space between the stage and the world it signifies, and just for a second he loses his way. The eighteenth-century editors are not the only ones who need to know where they are supposed to be.

The passage is interesting not only for its awareness of the difficult poetics of dramatic location, but also for what it is doing with the word *scene*. This has multiple senses in early modern English,[19] but in both its occurrences here it could be glossed as 'the place where the action is set'. Other Shakespearian choric speakers use it in the same way: the scene 'lies' in Troy, or the actors 'lay' the scene in Verona. For us, talk of shifting the scene naturally suggests changing the physical appearance of the stage: this sense was not unimaginable – in 1605 Ben Jonson uses the word to refer to a painted landscape seen in a masque[20] – but of course it is not what is literally meant here. Rather, to 'shift our scene' to Southampton means to change our message about *what place the stage is to stand for*. That such an announcement is even possible is another indication that the gap between Shakespeare and his eighteenth-century editors is not so wide as has been supposed. Their theatre had painted flats, and his did not, but both had a concept of 'the scene' as

---

19 See Bruce R. Smith, 'Scene', in *Early Modern Theatricality*, ed. Henry S. Turner (Oxford, 2013), pp. 93–112.

20 'First, for the scene, was drawn a landscape consisting of small woods', Ben Jonson, *The Masque of Blackness*, line 6, in *The Cambridge Edition of the Works of Ben Jonson*, ed. David Bevington, Martin Butler and Ian Donaldson, 7 vols. (Cambridge, 2012), vol. 2.

something that can be specified and that remains the same until it is changed. The idea that a scene is *set* somewhere does not necessarily presuppose scenery.

IV

It is nonetheless true that a theatrical revolution separated Rowe and Theobald and Malone from the conventions of the Shakespearian stage. When professional playing resumed in London in 1660, both the founding managers, Thomas Killigrew and William Davenant, equipped their theatres with wings and shutters so as to be able to present pictorial scenes. For dramatists, the significance of this innovation was not so much the scenery itself, which had existed, in some forms and some contexts, long before 1642; rather, it was the fact that scenery was now compulsory. Once the scenic machinery was installed, it could not simply be left blank. It was necessary to paint *something* on the carefully arranged surfaces, and so the question 'where is this scene set?', which a pre-1642 performance could in principle choose to ignore, was posed inescapably by the design of the building.[21]

This is a far-reaching change, but it does not transport us all at once into a world where every scene of every play has its own specific place. Apart from anything else, the commercial conditions of Restoration theatre, with its large repertoires and rapid turnover, made it impracticable to provide every play with its own custom-made sets. A class of spectacular productions, often billed as 'operas', did indeed feature specially painted perspective scenes; and it was in order to present shows of this kind that the scenic apparatus was most of all needed. But there was no reason to invest so lavishly in the performance of ordinary plays. Shakespearian revivals, like newly written tragedies and comedies, normally used generic designs: as one well-known account expresses it, ten painted scenes would be

sufficient to answer the Purposes of all the Plays in the Stock, in which there is no great Variety, being easily reduced to the following Classes, 1st, Temples. 2dly, Tombs. 3rdly, City Walls and Gates. 4thly, Outsides of

Palaces. 5thly, Insides of Palaces. 6thly, Streets. 7thly, Chambers. 8thly, Prisons. 9thly, Gardens. And 10thly, Rural Prospects of Groves, Forests, Deserts, &c.[22]

There is an early glimpse of this system, for example, in the text of Nahum Tate's adaptation of *King Lear*, performed in 1681. Typically for its time, the first edition is inconsistent in its notation of place. Some scenes, like the original Shakespearian text, have no locative headings at all; some have fairly specific ones ('Gloster's House', 'Goneril's Palace'); and three are headed 'The Field Scene'.[23] This last phrase is clearly a playhouse direction rather than a narrative one: it indicates not where the action is to be supposed to occur, but which back shutters the theatre is to use. Any stage manager would understand an instruction to set up 'the field scene'.

So the relationship between scenery and place is ambiguous: what looks at first sight like a mechanism for specifying location is deflected by an equal tendency to generalize. The actors perform in front of landscape paintings and domestic interiors which represent more or less stereotypical 'classes' of place, selected from a finite repertoire of possibilities. It is not after all quite true that the scene is happening somewhere in particular. To explore the ambiguity, we can take advantage of the fact that two of the early editors themselves produced scripts which mediate between Shakespeare and the theatre of the early eighteenth century. Nicholas Rowe's *The Tragedy of Jane Shore*, first performed at Drury Lane in 1714, was explicitly 'written in imitation of Shakespeare's

---

[21] See Edward A. Langhans, 'The Theatres', in *The London Theatre World, 1660–1800*, ed. Robert D. Hume (Carbondale, IL, 1980), pp. 35–40; and David Thomas, ed., *Theatre in Europe: A Documentary History. Restoration and Georgian England, 1660–1788* (Cambridge, 1989), pp. 83–100.

[22] *The Case of the Stage in Ireland* (Dublin, 1758), pp. 36–7, quoted in Sybil Rosenfeld, *Georgian Scene Painters and Scene Painting* (Cambridge, 1981), p. 24. A more generous inventory of over forty stock scenes owned by the Covent Garden theatre in 1744 is printed in Thomas, ed., *Theatre in Europe*, pp. 317–18.

[23] Nahum Tate, *The History of King Lear* (London, 1681), pp. 28, 41, 45.

style', and Lewis Theobald adapted *Richard II* for performance at the Lincoln's Inn Fields Theatre in 1720.[24] How in practice did they rewrite Shakespeare for their pictorial stage?

The surprising answer is that both plays are much *less* interested in place than their respective originals. Jane Shore was the mistress of Edward IV; Rowe's play is a five-act tragedy about her repentance and death, which borrows lines and characters freely from Shakespeare's *Richard III*. It has four locations: 'The Tower', 'An Apartment in Jane Shore's house', 'The Court' and 'The Street'. The first three of these are almost indistinguishable in practice: the effective setting for all of them is an anonymous semi-public room where the principal characters are free to come and go. In other words, this is the generalized but socially exclusive space of Racinian tragedy: what might indicatively be called 'Insides of Palaces'. The final setting is prompted by Gloucester's cruel persecution of Jane: she is thrown out on the street, and the stage becomes the street in question. This location is therefore more dramatically significant than the others, but no less generalized: it represents not any particular street but 'the street' as a social and moral idea.

In Theobald's *Richard II* the dissolution of place is even more extreme. The play tells the story of Richard from his return from Ireland through to his death – that is, it corresponds to the last three acts of Shakespeare's play. But it rearranges the events so that everything takes place in the Tower of London: the Tower replaces Flint as the castle where Richard confronts the returned Bolingbroke, Westminster as the venue for the ceremony of abdication, and Pomfret as the prison where Richard meets his death. In short, Theobald takes a chronicle play and imposes on it a neoclassical unity of place. Not only that; he supplements the story with a love affair between Aumerle and a daughter of the Earl of Northumberland. This leads to the tightly plotted deaths of both lovers and Aumerle's father, and so matches the spatial closure of the Tower with the formal closure of tragedy.

In their different ways, then, both these early editor-adaptors move their respective history plays

into the neutral or at least weakly differentiated space of feeling. Broadly speaking, the motives of action are those of French classical tragedy: love, jealousy, honour, paternal authority, female distress. Since these emotions are understood to be universal, the specific context of their utterance is relatively unimportant. Location loses its urgency: the conversations are intense, but most of them take place in interchangeable rooms of state. The generic scene – the apartment, the field – is not merely what happens to be dictated by the economics of the theatre; it is appropriate in any case to the dramatic logic of what happens in front of it. The scene painter is employing the *same* generalizing rhetoric as the dramatist. Ironically, it is here in the eighteenth century, rather than in Shakespeare's own theatre, that we really encounter Bentley's form: 'a drama of persons, not a drama of places'. In these adaptations, written to be played in front of painted backdrops, the persons are general instances of human nature, and so the places are literally negligible.

What this shows by contrast is that Shakespeare, denizen of the allegedly placeless stage, is vividly interested in place. Theobald's spatial unification of *Richard II* abstracts the play from an insistent geographical diversity: Shakespeare required his stage to stand for the Welsh coast, the queen's garden, Flint Castle, Westminster Hall, Pomfret and the distances involved in the York family's desperate race to get to the King. Like other plays in the tetralogies, *Richard II* declares its national ambition by going out of its way to attach events to particular parts of England and Wales. *Richard III* does not do that, but it is not indifferent to place either. Take, for example, its handling of the Tower of London. In Theobald's *Richard II* the Tower has no differentiating force because nothing happens anywhere else. Shakespeare's *Richard III*, on the other hand, stages three journeys towards it: Clarence under guard, Hastings in a tragicomic state of false security, and

---

24 Nicholas Rowe, *The Tragedy of Jane Shore* (London, 1714); Lewis Theobald, *The Tragedy of King Richard the II* (London, 1720).

the Princes coaxed, bullied and reluctant. All are travelling to their deaths: the question of where we are has become a savagely significant one, dismissed as trivial only by the foolish and the doomed. When Malone observed in passing that the location of a scene in Shakespeare 'often throws light on the dialogue', he was understating his case.

V

All the same, my defence of the locative heading is not leading up to a call for its reinstatement. There undeniably is something about the categorical specification of place that resists and represses the energies of the Shakespearian scene. But it is not so much that the editors are concerned with place and the drama is not; rather, it is that their respective concerns are not of the same kind. We can explore the difference by returning to the platform at Elsinore.

The reason that 'a more remote Part of the Platform' sounds comically maladroit is that it fails to rise to the sophistication of the way the stage is being used. When Horatio and Marcellus go off at the end of Act 1, scene 4, they are evidently unsure about disobeying the Prince, but urge one another on to follow him in case he is running into danger. It is therefore a hurried exit: the impression is that they are only a few seconds behind Hamlet. When Hamlet re-enters, though, the ponderous rhythms of the ghost's speech immediately impose themselves, and the arrival of Horatio and Marcellus is delayed until the ghost has told its tale, scented the morning air and departed. How does it take them so long to catch up with someone they were pursuing so closely? It is as if the place where Hamlet speaks with his dead father is not just 'a more remote part of the platform', but is remote in a more radical sense too, sealed into a spectral time and space beyond the reach of ordinary human searching. The ghost's subsequent cries from under the stage confirm this impression that it confounds the normal rules of location: Hamlet exclaims '*hic et ubique*', and wanders around the stage trying to divine the right spot for the oath.

This is exactly the kind of effect that Dessen's work really has highlighted: Theobald's

common-sense suggestion is mocked by a spatial ambiguity which is made possible by the indeterminacy of the open stage. But that does not exemplify a general fluidity. On the contrary, it is explicitly a disturbance produced by the unnatural apparition. 'O day and night, but this is wondrous strange!' (1.5.166); these are not normal stage conditions. Place, as well as time, is out of joint, and as was seen, Shakespeare first establishes time and place rather literal-mindedly, in order to prepare the uncanny effect of their breaking down. In other words, the place of the action *is* specified, with urgent insistence, but at the same time the specification is subverted by a dramatic action that outruns its categories. So location, it could be said, acquires a *dialogical* character, as different actors define it in contesting ways. Hence the incongruous effect of the editorial attempt to turn it into a monological datum. It is not that place is less germane than Malone supposes; it is that it is more complicated.

A different example, not overtly 'supernatural', will help to generalize this point. What is the location for *Macbeth*, Act 1, scene 7? Malone makes it 'A Room in the Castle', and once again, his logic is hard to resist. The Folio's own scene heading reads:

> *Ho-boyes. Torches.*
> *Enter a Sewer, and diuers Seruants with Dishes and*
>   *Seruice ouer the Stage. Then enter Macbeth*

That is to say, a feast is in progress and we are to suppose the stage to be a room near the hall where the food is being served. When Macbeth enters, it is presumably by the door through which the servants have just exited. In *there*, just out of sight, the king and the courtiers are having supper; *here* is therefore a kind of ante-room, where the waiters line up with the dishes and the host takes temporary refuge from the strain of the occasion. It is obvious where the action is meant to be taking place, and, as before, the obviousness is unaffected by the presence or absence of scenery.

But when Macbeth embarks on his soliloquy, the fact of an open stage – the configuration of the Globe or the Blackfriars – is suddenly crucial.[25] Almost inevitably, the actor moves downstage, and as he does so, he leaves the locating bustle of the tiring-house doors behind him and enters a space where there is nothing but him. The 'information' that this is 'A Room in the Castle' is not cancelled, but it is weakened, and what grows correspondingly stronger is the connection between the actor and the audience, who are, to an increasing extent as he approaches the edge of the platform, above, below and around him. It is to that ring of faces that he says:

> And pity, like a naked new-born babe,
> Striding the blast, or heaven's cherubin, horsed
> Upon the sightless couriers of the air,
> Shall blow the horrid deed in every eye
> That tears shall drown the wind. (1.7.21–5)

In the 'Room in the Castle', Macbeth is alone: no one can see or hear the preparation of the deed. But in his imagination it is witnessed by a horrified and pitiful crowd – and so of course it is, in the theatre. Not that, in a crudely metatheatrical sense, Macbeth knows he is in a play. Rather, the actor's situation at the centre of the theatre substantiates Macbeth's mental life.

What does that do to the workings of location? When an actor speaks on an empty stage, we have to take his word for where he is: 'this castle', 'here in the forest'. And in a way, this soliloquy of Macbeth's does include that deictic gesture: 'But *here* upon *this* bank and shoal of time', 'we still have judgment *here*' (1.7.6, 8). However, this is a universalizing 'here' rather than a specifying one. 'Here' is the world; Macbeth appears in a cosmic and emblematic field; he places himself not in an identifiable spot ('a room', 'Inverness') but on a bank or shoal in the gulf between heaven and hell. His speech makes the stage into a different *kind* of place.

But then what happens is that Lady Macbeth comes through the door at the back and says, 'He has almost supped. Why have you left the chamber?' (1.7.29). That is to say, in effect, 'what are you doing *here*? you need to be *there*', and so she grabs the stage back from the universal attribution that Macbeth gave it when he had it to himself, and insists that it goes back to being the room

immediately outside the banqueting chamber where the king is finishing his supper. Macbeth is in an open space, conscious of 'every eye' upon him; Lady Macbeth is sure that they are alone in a room of their own house. The same thing happens later with the knocking at the gate: Macbeth, alone onstage, hears an unlocated summons – 'whence is that knocking?' (2.2.55) – full of the irony of its inability to wake Duncan; Lady Macbeth re-enters briskly and says 'I hear a knocking at the south entry: retire we to our chamber' (2.2,63–4). The scene is 'located' for her *as it is not for him*.

Here is dialogic location at its most intense. The stage is capable of two radically different codings at the same moment. One conforms to the positivistic assumptions of the eighteenth-century editors, whereas the other accords the stage the metaphoric fluidity proposed by their twentieth-century critics. Not only that; the opposing conventions are given the voices of the scene's great antagonists: the incompatibility is not of the order of naivety (as if 'the Elizabethans' were simply *insouciant* about place on the stage), but is consciously and fiercely dramatized. Macbeth and Lady Macbeth contend with each other for the power to say where they are. Certainly the contest loses its urgency if a limitedly literal-minded definition of the space is simply ratified by editorial fiat. But it is no less diminished if, on the other hand, the impulse to locate the action in a consistent imagined world is simply dismissed as irrelevant. The theatrical energy is conflictual through and through: neither Macbeth nor Lady Macbeth can be allowed, as it were, to win the argument. The unfashionable value of Malone's principle, then, is just that it takes the question of location seriously. In the end, Shakespeare's 'swift scene' cannot be pinned down to a positive place – but it is only when you try that the impossibility gets interesting.

---

[25] The account of the scene that follows is based on watching it in performance at the reconstruction of the Globe on Bankside, in the production by Eve Best, summer 2013.

UNMANNING JULIET

DENISE A. WALEN

INTRODUCTION

In Act 3, scene 2 of *Romeo and Juliet*, sometimes called the 'cords scene', the actress playing Juliet is faced with an appreciable challenge. In a compact scene, she waxes sexually rhapsodic imagining the consummation of her marriage, plunges into despair believing her recently and secretly married husband dead, is torn with bitter hate when she hears he has killed her cousin, steels herself with the knowledge that her husband lives, is stricken with grief at the report of his banishment, then manages to compose herself preparing to meet him one last time. The emotional range originates from and combines with an exceptional rhetorical virtuosity fashioned of lyrical metaphors, puns, oxymora, antithesis and rhyme. The technical and emotional requirements of the scene reflect its importance. In the middle of the dramatic action overall, 3.2 presents a turning point for Juliet. Beginning the scene as an eager and passionate young girl, the character as she has been in the first two acts of the play, the brief but intense emotional and oratorical journey transforms Juliet into a sober, serious and wary young woman, the character as she will remain through the end of the action.

Despite the importance of 3.2, with all of its textual resonance in the development of Juliet's character, productions rarely present it without some reduction of the lines. Far more surprising (because, of course, Shakespeare is often reduced for performance), nearly all professional productions eliminated the entire scene for some fifty years, from the late nineteenth century through

to the early twentieth. While it may seem easy to blame the supposed corrupting influence of the theatre – the desire to purify the script or simplify the hermeneutics and wrangle the text into a momentary directorial concept – critical theory has in the twentieth century questioned the theatrical viability of this scene, implying the validity of its reduction if not its elimination. Of course, the origin texts of *Romeo and Juliet* 3.2 are problematic, issuing from the differing First (Q1) and Second (Q2) Quarto editions, the former offering a concise version of 3.2. These separate but related elements constitute a range of interpretive options in the 'recursive temporality' of the play.[1] That is, Shakespeare's multiple texts, production scripts and attendant performance enactments that issue from those texts, and textual criticism of the texts contribute not only to our momentary understanding of the play, but to our comprehension of past and the potential for future perceptions of it as well.

The Lucy Maynard Salmon Research Fund of Vassar College generously supported the writing of this article. The librarians at the New York Public Library for the Performing Arts, the Beinecke Rare Book and Manuscript Library at Yale University, the Booth-Hampden Collection at the Player's Club, and the Shakespeare Centre Library all provided substantial help in locating material. Collections at the Folger Shakespeare Library and their staff proved invaluable to this chapter.

[1] Gina Bloom, Anston Bosman and William N. West, 'Ophelia's Intertheatricality, or, How Performance is History', *Theatre Journal*, 65 (2013), 165–82; p. 170.

It is helpful to expand on the theory of intertheatricality in understanding this approach. According to Gina Bloom, Anston Bosman and William West, 'intertheatricality foregrounds how theatrical performances relate to one another'.[2] According to the theory, any one theatrical performance may relate to and connect with a variety of other theatrical performances (of various plays) and performance practices, including 'dances, spectacles, plays and songs'.[3] Within this multiplicity, any performance may 'contribute to and draw from a nonsequential field of performance possibilities' that share a 'repertoire of gestures, actions, and styles'.[4] On a simplistic level, the red nose of a circus clown may appear on the nose of the Fool in *King Lear*. Intertheatricality does not rely on a linear temporality; rather, it is interested in recurrence. In broadening the theory on one hand to include texts and criticism as well as performative gestures, and collapsing it on the other to focus on one play, this article explores not only how theatrical performances of *Romeo and Juliet*, with all their attendant cultural and historical layers, relate to one another, but also how they are imbued with and contribute to knowledge and understanding of the original printed play-scripts that preceded them and the textual criticism that followed. The article follows Barbara Hodgdon's idea of 'performance work', which 'invites a redirected critical praxis – one which embraces Shakespeare's play-texts, their variant critical re-formations, and performance texts'.[5] The approach is predicated on W. B. Worthen's argument that the literary and theatrical dichotomy in the study of Shakespeare is not 'mutually exclusive', that a 'variable consubstantiality' exists, and that 'despite the polemical distinction between a 'literary' and a 'theatrical' Shakespeare, there is considerable common ground between them'.[6]

I will examine the unstable text of 3.2 *Romeo and Juliet*, the production history of its fifty-year disappearance, and the textual criticism surrounding it in the twentieth and twenty-first centuries. I argue that the reduction and elimination of 3.2 in performance is not the effect of simple theatrical expedience, but a complex recurrence that emerges from diverse and somewhat disparate sources, found within the early textual variants, arising among various performances for multiple reasons, and reconstituted in textual criticism. Consequently, the reduction and elimination of 3.2 diminishes the characterization of Juliet by removing the text that presents the character's marked psychological struggle and process of maturity.

TEXTUAL INSTABILITY OF 3.2

Romeo and Juliet exists in two early substantive versions, Q1, published in 1597, and Q2, published in 1599. The Folio version derives primarily from Q2 by way of other later quartos. The two earliest versions are strikingly different – Q2 is nearly eight hundred lines longer than Q1 and the texts have hundreds of variants in words and phrases. Character, of course, emerges from the available text a dramatic author creates and that text is interpreted and reiterated – if not revised and remade – by individual performers, readers and spectators. Jill Levenson argues that in early plays like *Romeo and Juliet* Shakespeare portrayed character through variations in the poetry and that in his later work he reduced his reliance on rhetorical devices and found 'less contrived means for portraying character'.[7] Therefore, in a play such as *Romeo and Juliet* the text conveys character in a heightened form and differences in the text

---

[2] Bloom et al., 'Intertheatricality', p. 169.
[3] Jacky Bratton, *New Readings in Theatre History* (Cambridge, 2003), pp. 37–8.
[4] Bloom et al., 'Intertheatricality', p. 169.
[5] Barbara Hodgdon, 'Absent Bodies, Present Voices: Performance Work and the Close of *Romeo and Juliet's* Golden Story', *Theatre Journal*, 41 (1989), 341–59; p. 359.
[6] W. B. Worthen, 'Intoxicating Rhythms: Or, Shakespeare, Literary Drama, and Performance (Studies)', *Shakespeare Quarterly*, 62 (2011), 309–39; pp. 310–13.
[7] Jill Levenson, 'Changing Images of Romeo and Juliet, Renaissance to Modern', in *Images of Shakespeare: Proceedings of the Third Congress of the International Shakespeare Association*, ed. Werner Habicht, D. J. Palmer and Roger Pringle (Newark, DE, 1988), pp 151–62; p. 152.

impact the conception, signification and citationality of the character.

The role of Juliet is one of the most substantial female roles in Shakespeare. Textually, she is Romeo's equal in Q2, as the two characters share a similar number and length of long speeches.[8] Lynette Hunter and Peter Lichtenfels have commented that the exceptional balance in the roles is best displayed in the arrangement of 3.2 and 3.3.[9] Structurally, the couple develops in a somewhat oppositional pattern. While Romeo is more prominent in the early half of the play, Juliet becomes more active in the later half and is the driving force and focus of the action all through Act 4.[10] In fact, the character grows more independent and vocal as the play progresses; a transformation noted with grave disapproval by her parents who experience the change as a movement from the reverential child deferring to their 'consent' in 1.3 (Q2, C1r, line 18), to the 'disobedient wretch' they encounter in 3.5 (I1r, 6).[11] Juliet's role is not only sizeable; a number of critics have also remarked on the significance and centrality of her part.[12] In her Oxford edition of the play, Levenson notes Juliet's 'resolve', comfortable 'sexuality', 'autonomy' and responsibility for the 'course of events' in the play, her 'risk-taking' and strategizing in the face of danger, all of which make her a compelling and substantive character.[13] Juliet not only shares lines and speeches with Romeo; she is jointly responsible for the action of the play. Juliet is a heroine with a strong interior life surprising for a female character in tragedy.[14]

However, Q1 presents a very different image of Juliet from Q2's. Juliet's role in Q1 is nearly 40 per cent shorter than in Q2, with half as many long speeches and only a third of the lines from those speeches.[15] For example, her sixteen-line soliloquy – 'The clocke strooke nine when I did send the Nurse' (Q2, E4v, 25) – that opens 2.4 is a mere six lines in Q1. Juliet's affecting potion soliloquy of Act 4 is only half as long: of a vigorous forty-four lines in Q2 only eighteen appear in Q1. The active engagement of the character in Q2 is also significantly different from what it is in Q1. According to Steven Urkowitz, in Q1

a relatively innocent Juliet enjoys a supportive female community and is a passive victim of the male codes embedded in Veronese society, while in Q2 the character is isolated and wary but 'capable of sophisticated self-protective strategies'.[16]

The most drastic textual difference in the play affecting Juliet's character may be found in 3.2. There, twenty-nine lines are absent from the opening Q1 soliloquy. All that exists in Q1 of that intense adjuration is

> Gallop apace you fierie footed steedes
> To *Phœbus* mansion, such a Waggoner
> As *Phaeton*, would quickly bring you thether,
> And send in cloudie night immediately.[17]
>
> (F3r, 15–18)

---

[8] Irene Dash, *Wooing, Wedding, and Power: Women in Shakespeare's Plays* (New York, 1981), p. 94.

[9] Lynette Hunter and Peter Lichtenfels, *Negotiating Shakespeare's Language in Romeo and Juliet* (Farnham, 2009), pp. 151–2.

[10] Evelyn Gajowski, *The Art of Loving: Female Subjectivity and Male Discursive Traditions in Shakespeare's Tragedies* (Newark, DE, 1992), p. 44.

[11] William Shakespeare, *The Most Excellent and Lamentable Tragedie, of Romeo and Juliet*, Q2, STC 22323 (London, 1599). All subsequent references to Q2 will be cited in the text.

[12] See, for example, William Shakespeare, *Romeo and Juliet*, ed. René Weis (London, 2012), p. 7; and Marjorie Garber, *Shakespeare After All* (New York, 2004), pp. 205–8.

[13] William Shakespeare, *Romeo and Juliet*, ed. Jill L. Levenson (Oxford, 2000), pp. 27, 30, 39, 41.

[14] Hunter and Lichtenfels, *Shakespeare's Language*, p. 152.

[15] See Kathleen O. Irace, *Reforming the 'Bad' Quartos: Performance and Provenance of Six Shakespearean First Editions* (Newark, DE, 1994), p. 185.

[16] Steven Urkowitz, '"A Cleane Smocke": Shakespeare's Aesthetics of Revision in Romeo and Juliet', paper presented at the fifth Blackfriars Conference, Staunton, Virginia, 21–25 October 2009; and Steven Urkowitz, 'Two Versions of Romeo and Juliet 2.6 and Merry Wives of Windsor 5.5.215–45: An Invitation to the Pleasures of Textual/Sexual Di(per)versity', in *Elizabethan Theater: Essays in Honor of S. Schoenbaum*, ed. R. B. Parker and S. P. Zitner (Newark, DE, 1996), pp. 222–38.

[17] William Shakespeare, *An Excellent conceited Tragedie of Romeo and Juliet*, Q1, STC 22322 (London, 1597). All subsequent references to Q1 will be cited in the text.

Juliet's command for the sun to set, clouded in classical allusion, suggests her anticipation for the night but lacks the blunt articulation of sexual desire and wanton abandon found in the longer Q2 version of the speech. These four brief formal lines that rely for understanding on knowledge of Greek mythology also provide the actor with little opportunity to intimate all the carnal yearning of the longer soliloquy. Even if the actor knew what was expected from the Q2 passage, assuming it was available to Shakespeare's boy actor, these lines hardly lend themselves to mimetic expressions of sexual excitement. Phaeton no longer alliteratively 'whip[s]' his horses 'to the west' with the erotic appeal of prurient fetish (Q2, Grv, 2), he simply brings them, albeit quickly. The reckless and threatening action, the lack of control imagined by the allusion is muted in the lost gesture of the adolescent Phaeton whipping the horses and careening, wildly, toward the west. The Q1 Phaeton is simply quick and functional; the Q2 Phaeton is impulsive, exciting and dangerous.

The remainder of Juliet's soliloquy in Q2, an epithalamium celebrating her wedding, considers the sexual pleasures she expects to enjoy when she and Romeo consummate their marriage that night. Gary McCown argues that the irony surrounding Juliet's self-presentation of the speech, when others should perform it for her as the bride, evokes pity and pathos.[18] While that is so, it is true primarily because the audience knows of Romeo's banishment while Juliet does not. In the epithalamium, the text expresses Juliet's interior vitality and the earnest longing of her character, suggesting neither disappointment nor despair:

> come civill night,
> Thou sober suted matron all in blacke,
> And learne me how to loose a winning match,
> Plaide for a paire of stainlesse maydenhoods.
> Hood my unmand bloud bayting in my cheekes,
> With thy blacke mantle, till strange love grow bold,
> Thinke true love acted simple modestie:
>
> (Q2, GIV, 9–15)

The text makes Juliet sexually eager, sensually expectant, and the night is her ally for the 'amorous

rights' (GIV, 7) she plans to perform with Romeo. Her blood is bating in her cheeks; that is, fluttering or pulsing as a physical sign of her sexual excitement as well as a sign of embarrassment. She would have her blushes covered by the 'blacke mantle' of the night so that no one will see her agitation and excitement. The night will also bring Romeo; it will bring the cover of darkness that will allow him to enter the Capulet house and Juliet's chamber. It will shroud their lovemaking from prying eyes and help assuage or cover any sense of internal embarrassment. The night is metaphorically a matron that will help her 'learne' an empirical lesson she craves to experience; that will provide the opportunity for a physical education she has no practice in even if she has received certain information. She is at the moment of the speech 'unmand'; that is, untrained or not tamed, therefore wild as well as uneducated in lovemaking. She is also 'unmand' because she is sexually unfamiliar with men, uncoupled, without a sexual male partner or the relief a man such as Romeo will provide her. Juliet calls on the night to 'Hood', in the sense of both concealing and taming her desire by bringing Romeo to her so she may quench and satisfy her passion. For all its erotic impulsiveness, the speech also contains a note of innocence. Juliet and Romeo are 'a paire of stainlesse maydenhoods', but once they come together their 'strange love' will 'grow bold' allowing them to commit such lascivious, carnal acts that they will put the 'simple modestie' of 'true love' to shame. The intricate rhetoric and metaphors of the speech, the paradox of losing virginity to win love, convey excitement, caution, fear, anticipation, embarrassment, sex and violence, and present a complex character; a Juliet eager to experience what the night has to offer.

Once the night comes, Romeo will 'Leape' (GIV, 6) into Juliet's active and apparently capable 'armes' (6) where he will 'lie upon the winges of night' (17), perhaps assuming a passive position in

---

[18] Gary M. McCown, '"Runawayes Eyes" and Juliet's Epithalamium', *Shakespeare Quarterly*, 27 (1976), 150–70; p. 170.

their lovemaking. After all, she considers herself as much an active agent that has 'bought' (25) this love and plans to possess it, even as she has been 'sold' (26) and hopes to be 'enjoyd' (27). The character expresses herself as both a passive object or commodity and a consumer. The speech has its own sexual impulse growing in a spiral tension as Juliet repeatedly invokes the night to 'come' (9, 16, 19) and her rhetoric intensifies until her paroxysm when she imagines Romeo cut out in little stars once she 'die[s]' (20) which was, of course, a common euphemism for an orgasm. She appears neither naive about nor ignorant of what this, her wedding night, holds, and is rather aware of and eager, in fact, 'impatient' (29) to experience the 'amorous rights' of a lover. Mary Bly argues that Juliet shows an unexpected sexual knowledge for a chaste young Elizabethan woman and is surprisingly immodest, although not bawdy, for a virginal, Petrarchan heroine.[19] To be sure, Juliet's imagination, fed by the fecund ribaldry and vicarious desire of her nurse, seems to run wild with sexual possibilities. The speech represents Juliet's agency or the character's willingness to actively participate in the action through which she and Romeo will consummate their marriage by achieving a sexual union that satisfies both partners. The Q2 speech presents a fully developed three-dimensional image of the character and affords the audience a psychological perspective lacking in Q1, which presents only briefly Juliet's mild impatience.

The dialogue between Juliet and the Nurse that follows the opening speech is also significantly different. What is a robust scene of 152 lines in Q2 appear as a meagre 60 in Q1. Levenson has discussed the rhetorical and specifically Petrarchan devices Shakespeare uses in the Q2 version of the scene in some detail, noting how 'changes in the verse from moment to moment convey the shifting contours of [Juliet's] personality'.[20] As the scene progresses, Juliet's exuberant expression of erotic nuptial longing and desire is disrupted by the arrival of the Nurse. This interruption quickly enough dislocates the amatory verse and throws Juliet into confusion marked by 'laboured wordplay'

distinguished, argues Levenson, by a series of monotonous puns. 'Hath *Romeo* slaine himselfe? say thou but I [aye], / And that bare vowell I shall poyson more / Then the death [d]arting eye of Cockatrice' (G2r, 12–14). According to M. M. Mahood, these 'quibbles' not only express the extent of Juliet's troubled psyche, but also reverberate with multiple meanings that intensify the character by extending the eye imagery of the opening soliloquy and producing the sound effect of shrill lamentation.[21] These lines do not appear in Q1 and are often cut in performance.

The grief Juliet expresses when she believes Romeo dead, 'O break my hart, poore banckrout break at once' (G2r, 24), is in sharp contrast to the enthusiastic erotic imagining of the opening soliloquy she just concluded. Without Romeo, she plans to 'end motion' and 'resigne' herself to 'Vile earth', where she and Romeo will share one grave (G2r, 26). The lines reflect Juliet's utter anguish and foreshadow the play's final scene where she and Romeo lie together dead in the Capulet tomb. In Q1, the character never expresses this grief, but instead questions why she has been 'severd' from Romeo and why fate would 'envie' their 'happie Marriage' (F3v, 2, 4). The question has as much a ring of peevish indignation as it does tormented suffering. Then, with Juliet believing that Romeo is dead, she receives the news that Tybalt has been slain and becomes equally distraught in both texts.

The realization that Romeo is alive and has in fact killed Tybalt sends Juliet into an angry tirade in which she complains that Romeo's beauty conceals a villainous soul. The oxymora that Juliet uses to describe Romeo – he is a 'Bewtifull tirant, fiend angelicall' (Q2, G2v, 7) – signals how furious she is when she thinks that she has been deceived by Romeo's appearance. The wild variations of the comparisons Juliet makes indicate that the

---

[19] Mary Bly, 'Bawdy Puns and Lustful Virgins: The Legacy of Juliet's Desire in Comedies of the Early 1600s', in *Shakespeare Survey 49* (Cambridge, 1996), pp. 97–109; pp. 98–101.

[20] Levenson, ed., *Romeo and Juliet*, pp. 58–9.

[21] M. M. Mahood, *Shakespeare's Wordplay* (London, 1957), pp. 56, 70.

character is unsettled, torn between her love for Romeo and her anger at his violent behaviour. In his analysis in *The Osier Cage*, Robert O. Evans reveals Juliet to be a 'masterful rhetorician' who possesses a sophisticated intellectual acuity.[22] According to Evans, under severe mental duress Juliet must choose whether she will condemn or excuse the actions of the man she recently married and whom she has known only briefly. The oxymora demonstrate the depth of her conflict, Romeo is 'A dimme [damned] saint, an honourable villaine' (G2v, 11). In Q2, the character swings back and forth over thirteen lines warring internally between her love and anger, lamenting at the end 'that deceit should dwell / In such a gorgious Pallace' (G2v, 16–17). In Q1, the text offers only four lines of contradictory doubt, which is a weak expression of inner tension, and the concluding question sounds a note of petulance rather than regret: 'O serpents hate, hid with a flowring face: / O painted sepulcher, including filth. / Was never booke containing so foule matter, / So fairly bound. Ah, what meant Romeo?' (F3v, 17–20). This shows adolescent irritation rather than the deep struggle presented in Q2.

Juliet's emotions shift again when she defends Romeo from criticism by the Nurse, 'Blisterd be thy tongue / For such a wish, he was not borne to shame' (Q2, G2v, 23–4). In a second long and carefully wrought speech at the end of the Q2 scene, Juliet criticizes herself for not supporting Romeo: 'Ah poor my lord, what tongue shal smooth thy name, / When I thy three houres wife have mangled it?' (G2v, 31–2). She reasons that Romeo killed Tybalt only in self-defence and concludes that she should comfort herself with the knowledge that he is still alive. 'My husband lives that *Tybalt* would have slaine, / And *Tybalts* dead that would have slain my husband: / All this is comfort' (G3r, 2–4). This rhetorical process and intellectual perception ennoble Juliet. As the Q2 speech continues, Juliet remembers that Romeo has been 'banished' (G3r, 9). At the thought, her comfort turns to 'woe' (G3r, 12) and her true grief emerges. The prospect of losing Romeo is terribly sobering. This second long speech, developed over

thirty-one lines, includes Juliet's anger at the Nurse, her defence of Romeo, self-criticism, a rationalization of Tybalt's death and sustained grief at Romeo's banishment. In Q1, the process happens so quickly it serves to make Juliet appear erratic verging on the hysterical.

After the shifting tensions of such an emotionally fraught scene, 3.2 ends with what Harley Granville-Barker appreciatively called 'fine simplicity, set in formality'.[23] Juliet determines with a quiet, almost stoic resignation to 'die maiden widowed' (G3r, 32) and reluctantly accepts her profound grief by saying 'ile to my wedding bed, / And death not *Romeo*, take my maiden head' (G3r, 33–4). The line alternately suggests a long and solitary life, or death from heartbreak or suicide. The Nurse has difficulty breaking into Juliet's solemn contemplation, but her promise to find Romeo gives Juliet hope that her 'true Knight' will come to 'take his last farewell' (G3v, 3–4). The character's thoughtful reasoning, ability to master her emotions and quiet resolve show Juliet at her best in the Q2 version of this scene and demonstrate how integral the text of 3.2 is in establishing the character's maturation.

If sexual explicitness and excess mark Juliet's opening speech and expose a healthy sexual appetite, sound judgement, pragmatism and endurance distinguish the second speech and reveal a decidedly mature intellect. Juliet also makes the critical decision here to abandon family for her husband, a decision that isolates her in the play but may elevate the character in the eyes of the audience. The scene asserts a sixteenth-century poetic discourse that emphasizes passion, emotion and sexual desire over societal and familial directives.[24] Juliet begins the scene in a blissful erotic reverie, quickly becomes anxious and confused, then grief-stricken, then wildly angry, then rational, and concludes it in

[22] Robert O. Evans, *The Osier Cage: Rhetorical Devices in Romeo and Juliet* (Lexington, KY, 1966), pp. 34–41.

[23] Harley Granville-Barker, *Prefaces to Shakespeare* (London, 1930), p. 20.

[24] Dympna Callaghan, *Romeo and Juliet: Texts and Contexts* (Boston, MA, 2003), p. 248.

somber but determined resignation and resolve, moving toward a tragic stature. The combination of rhetorical devices that play out across 3.2 in the Q2 version not only clarify the action of the play; they expand our knowledge of the character by showing her emotional response and intellectual reasoning. This complex textual construction of the character is absent in the much shorter version of Q1, which presents an erratic character. The Q1 Juliet is emasculated, unmanned in another sense, and appears an anxious, innocent, wilful girl – reactionary, petulant, frenetic – in comparison to the young woman achieving a new level of maturity and sophistication found in Q2.

THEATRICAL (IN)STABILITY OF 3.2

The text of *Romeo and Juliet* in performance has proven equally unstable. In the Restoration, James Howard turned it into a tragicomedy with Romeo and Juliet alive at the end.[25] Thomas Otway's heavy adaptation in *The History and Fall of Caius Marius* remained popular from 1679 through to the early decades of the eighteenth century. He eliminated 3.2 but moved the 'Gallop apace' speech to the comic scene between Juliet/Lavinia and the Nurse, replacing 'the clocke strooke nine' speech.[26] Theophilus Cibber presented his own version of *Romeo and Juliet* in 1744.[27] Then David Garrick's adaptation of 1750, with an abridged 3.2, remained the standard acting version of the play from the mid eighteenth century through to the mid nineteenth century. Garrick's 3.2 is not as short as the Q1 version of the scene, but still reduces the sexual energy of the epithalamium, excises the puns and nearly eliminates the oxymora.[28]

While many production scripts continue to edit 3.2 for performance, especially the scene's opening soliloquy, puns and oxymora,[29] a number of famous productions and their popular female stars eliminated the scene altogether in the late nineteenth century. The first actress to delete 3.2 was the accomplished Adelaide Neilson, whose Juliet lasted in critical memory long after her early death. She was the quintessential Juliet – her youth and beauty never altered by advancing age – and other actresses

aspired to emulate her success.[30] Exactly when or why Neilson cut the scene after playing the role to ecstatic praise for years is unclear. The *New York Times* reviewer of 1874 commended her 'force' in this scene, and the promptbook for her performance at Augustin Daly's Fifth Avenue Theatre in 1877 shows it intact, although with reductions on an already edited acting version (Illustration 15).[31] However, sometime during her final US tour in 1879–80, after announcing her retirement when she was only in her thirties and at the height of her career, Neilson dropped the scene to the objections of the New York and Boston critics. The *Times* advised, 'Her Juliet . . . would be still more fascinating if she could be induced to restore the second scene of the third act'.[32] She died within three months of this, her final New York performance.

Her contemporary, and some thought successor, Mary Anderson, who mounted a lavish production at the London Lyceum in 1884, received mixed reviews in the role and collected some especially harsh criticism for this scene. The London *Times* found her 'one of the noisiest and most hysterical Juliets' to receive the news of Tybalt's death.[33] The great critic William Archer believed that in

[25] John Downes, *Roscius Anglicanus* (London, 1709), p. 22.

[26] Thomas Otway, *The History and Fall of Caius Marius* (London, 1680), pp. 31–2.

[27] Theophilus Cibber, *Romeo and Juliet* (London, 1748), pp. 33–6.

[28] David Garrick, *Romeo and Juliet* (London, 1750), pp. 38–40.

[29] William Shakespeare, *Romeo and Juliet*, ed. James N. Loehlin (Cambridge, 2002), pp. 176–82; Russell Jackson, *Shakespeare at Stratford: Romeo and Juliet* (London, 2003), pp. 72–3.

[30] George. C. D. Odell, *Shakespeare from Betterton to Irving*, vol. 2 (New York, 1920), pp. 258–9.

[31] See 'Dramatic: Miss Neilson at Booth's', *New York Times*, 21 April 1874, p. 5; and William Shakespeare, [*Romeo and Juliet*] ([London, n.d.]), Folger Shakespeare Library PROMPT Rom. 22, p. 40.

[32] See G. E. M., 'The Juliets of the Stage: Miss Neilson's Performance in the Poet's Drama of Love', *New York Times*, 9 May 1880, p. 2; 'Music and the Drama: Miss Neilson as Juliet', *Boston Daily Advertiser*, 17 February 1880, p. 1, col. B.

[33] 'The Theatres: "Romeo and Juliet" at the Lyceum', *The Times*, 3 November 1884, p. 8, col. A.

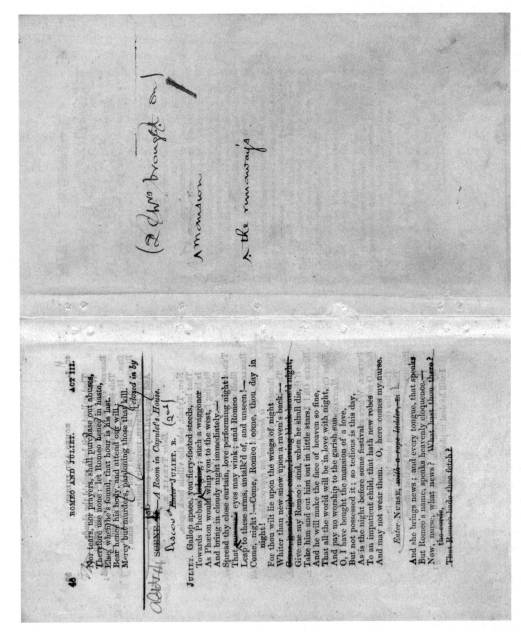

15. Adelaide Neilson's promptbook, pp. 40 and facing. Reproduced by permission of the Folger Shakespeare Library.

this role she had 'never quite thrown off the shallow conceptions and bad habits adopted while she was yet a girl in her teens'.[34] Even her friend and staunch ally Owen Meredith, who was otherwise rhapsodic about her performance, found this scene 'disappointing' and Anderson lacking 'evidence of genuine emotion'.[35] Henry Baker, remarking that this scene is a 'crucial test upon which so many actresses break down', thought that Anderson relied on 'exaggerated, maudlin sentiment' and judged the scene 'crude and formless, half-conceived' and 'lacking the power of expression'.[36] Anderson had compelling reasons to drop the scene.

In her autobiography, Anderson mentions her 'disappointment' with the role, being 'humiliated', and therefore 'resolved . . . to restudy and remodel the part'.[37] She prepared a new acting version for her return to America in 1885.[38] Her script, in fact, cut the end of 3.1 as well as all of 3.2 and picked up at 3.3, which is Romeo's scene with Friar Laurence (Illustration 16). The influential American critic William Winter notes in his *Tribune* review of the New York production, that 'Juliet's 'banished' scene Miss Anderson now omits – just as Miss Neilson did, and wisely; for it conflicts with Romeo's kindred scene, and it anticipates a dramatic effect which should not arrive so soon'.[39] While Winter suggests that Anderson eliminated the scene to correct Shakespeare's faulty dramatic structure, another reason for dropping the scene was given by the Boston critic of the *Daily Advertiser*. He found it 'rather odd that she should have omitted the entire scene' and considered 'perhaps there was forethought in the omission, inasmuch as the neglected passage requires exceptional passionate force in the actress'.[40] Apparently Anderson cut the scene because she could not or would not present the passion it required, and it had proved a critical embarrassment during her London run.

A succession of other productions followed suit, including those of Robert B. Mantell, who clearly eliminated the scene from the promptbook of his touring production in 1887 (Illustration 17), even though he had prepared it to be the first scene of his

fourth act; Maggie Morton, who left the scene out of her printed acting edition of the play in 1888; and Margaret Mather.[41] Mather's production played opposite and rivalled Anderson's in the fall of 1885. The fiery Mather, a regional success who had never appeared in New York, debuted there in October with *Romeo and Juliet*, just before Anderson's return. Mather proved a mediocre actress; however, her manager, John M. Hill, so brilliantly produced and marketed the production to the New York audience that Mather's Juliet ran more than ten consecutive weeks, which was an unprecedented triumph for a Shakespeare production. Her promptbook presumably for the Union Square theatre, using the Samuel French acting edition, shows all of 3.2 carefully cut from the script, which places a scene break after Romeo's line 'O, I am fortune's fool' (Illustration 18).[42] The initial *New York Times* review mentioned her acting in this scene and one wonders if Hill, who

---

[34] William Archer, 'Miss Mary Anderson', *The Theatre: A Monthly Review of The Drama, Music, and the Fine Arts*, new series, 6 (London, 1885), 175–82; pp. 179–80.

[35] Owen Meredith, 'Miss Anderson's Juliet', in *Shakespeariana 2* (Philadelphia, 1885), pp. 1–22; p. 14.

[36] Henry Barton Baker, 'Some Famous Juliets', *Frank Leslie's Popular Monthly* (July–December 1885), 295–303; p. 303.

[37] Mary Anderson, *A Few Memories* (New York, 1896), pp. 182–3.

[38] See the US edition, William Shakespeare, *Romeo and Juliet . . . Performed By Miss Mary Anderson And Company, In London, England, Under the Direction of Mr. Henry E. Abbey, November 1884* ([New York, 1885]), p. 31.

[39] Quoted in William Winter, *The Stage Life of Mary Anderson* (New York, 1886), p. 144.

[40] 'Music and the Drama: Miss Anderson as Juliet', *Boston Daily Advertiser*, 1 December 1885, p. 4, col. D.

[41] William Shakespeare, *Romeo and Juliet* (New York, n.d.), Folger Shakespeare Library PROMPT Rom. 17, pp. 39–42; and William Shakespeare, *Romeo And Juliet As Produced In Five Acts, By Miss Maggie Morton* (Hereford, 1888), pp. 28–9.

[42] William Shakespeare, *Romeo and Juliet*, French's Standard Drama (New York, n.d.), Margaret Mather Promptbook, Billy Rose Theatre Division, New York Public Library for the Performing Arts, p. 40.

Romeo and Juliet.   31

Stand not amazed :—the prince will doom thee death,
If thou art taken,—hence !—be gone !—away !
   Rom.   O ! I am fortune's fool !

Scene 2.   *Friar Laurence' cell.*

Enter Friar Laurence *and* Romeo.

   Fri.   Romeo, come forth ; come forth, thou fearful man ;
Affliction is enamor'd of thy parts,
And thou art wedded to calamity.
   Rom.   Father, what news ? what is the prince's doom ?
What sorrow craves acquaintance at my hand,
That I yet know not ?
   Fri.   Too familiar
Is my dear son with such sour company :
I bring thee tidings of the prince's doom.
   Rom. What less than dooms-day is the prince's doom ?
   Fri. A gentler judgment vanish'd from his lips,
Not body's death, but body's banishment.
   Rom. Ha ! banishment ? be merciful, say—death :
For exile hath more terror in his look
Much more than death : do not say—banishment.
   Fri. Here from Verona art thou banished ;
Be patient, for the world is wide.
   Rom. There is no world without Verona's walls :
But purgatory, torture, hell itself, hence banished is
Banished from the world, and world's exile is death ;
Then, banished is death mistermed, calling death banished.
Thou cut'st my head off with a golden axe,
And smilest upon the stroke that murders me.
   Fri. O deadly sin ! O rude unthankfulness !
Thy fault our law calls death ; but the kind prince,
Taking thy part, hath brush'd aside the law,
And turn'd that black word death to banishment :
This is dear mercy, and thou seest it not.
   Rom. 'Tis torture, and not mercy : heaven is here
Where Juliet lives, there is
More felicity in carrion flies : they may seize
On the white wonder of dear Juliet's hand,
And steal immortal blessing from her lips,
But Romeo may not—he is banished.
Hadst thou no poison mixed ;
No sharp ground knife, no sudden means of death,
Though ne'er so mean, but banished to kill ?

16. William Shakespeare, *Romeo and Juliet* . . . *Performed By Miss Mary Anderson* ([New York, 1885]), p. 31. Reproduced by permission of the Folger Shakespeare Library.

And to't they go like lightning; for ere I
Could draw to part them, was stout Tybalt slain;
And as he fell, did Romeo turn to fly.
This is the truth, or let Benvolio suffer.

Cap. He is a kinsman to the Montague:
Affection makes him false; he speaks not true.
I beg for justice; justice, gracious Prince;
Romeo slew Tybalt, Romeo must not live.

Prince. Romeo slew him, he slew Mercutio;
Who now the price of his dear blood hath paid.

Mon. Romeo but took the forfeit life of Tybalt.

Prince. And we, for that offence, do banish him.
I have an int'rest in your heady brawls;
My blood doth flow from brave Mercutio's wounds;
But I'll amerce you with so strong a fine,
That you shall all repent my loss in him.
I will be deaf to pleading and excuses,
Nor tears nor prayers shall purchase our repeal;
Therefore use none; let Romeo be gone,
Else, when he is found, that hour is his last.
Bear hence this body, and attend our will:
Mercy but murders, pardoning those that kill.

[*Exeunt, Capulet,* R., *he rest,* L.

SCENE II.—*Juliet's Chamber.*

Enter JULIET, L.

Jul. Gallop apace, you fiery-footed steeds,
Tow'rds Phœbus mansion: such a waggoner
As Phaeton, would whip you to the west,
And bring in cloudy night immediately.—
Spread thy close curtain, love-performing night,
That the runaway's eyes may wink; and Romeo
Leap to these arms, untalked of, and unseen:—
Come, night!—Come, Romeo! come, thou day in night!
For thou wilt lie upon the wings of right,
Whiter than new snow on a raven's back.—
Give me my Romeo, night!—and, when he dies,
Take him and cut him out in little stars;
And he will make the face of heaven so fine,
That all the world will be in love with night,
And pay no worship to the garish sun.—

ACT - IV -
SCENE - 1 -
LIGHT FANCY

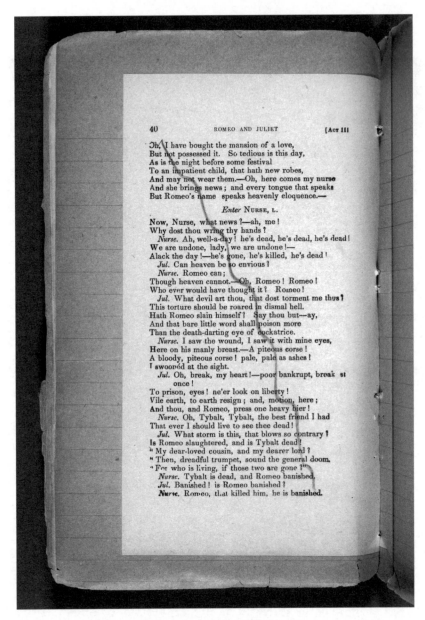

18. Margaret Mather's promptbook, p. 40.

clearly knew Mather's limitations, had her delete it after he saw Anderson's revised version.[43]

The next important production to drop the scene was an English version mounted by Johnston Forbes-Robertson at the London Lyceum in 1895.

[43] 'Miss Margaret Mather', *New York Times*, 14 October 1885, p. 5. See also Charles H. Shattuck, *Shakespeare on the American Stage: From Booth and Barrett to Sothern and Marlowe*, vol. 2 (Washington DC, 1987), p. 113.

Forbes-Robertson played Romeo to the Juliet of the great Mrs Patrick Campbell. She, like Anderson, was considered inadequate in the role, not because her acting failed to meet the challenge, but because her approach was thought decidedly too modern for the character. She could play Pinero's second Mrs Tanqueray brilliantly, but audiences had difficulty accepting the youthful innocence and grand passion of Juliet encompassed in the new realistic acting style. The London *Times* reviewer found her Juliet 'to be a forward young person, of an apathetic manner and somewhat lax morals, engaged in a somewhat questionable intrigue'.[44] William Archer thought she 'glaringly misrepresented' Juliet and acted with 'temperament' but 'no skill'.[45] Still, he was disappointed to miss her delivery of the 'Gallop apace' speech, which she dropped from performance early in the run.[46] Forbes-Robertson's printed acting edition notes the 'scene is sometimes omitted' (Illustration 19).[47] I. Zangwill, in the *Pall Mall Magazine*, seemed less surprised but no less disturbed that Campbell had cut the speech, and argued that the lines were too lyrically poetic for the naturalistic delivery favoured by Campbell and her New Woman approach.[48] George Bernard Shaw, who thought Mrs Campbell beautiful but her performance 'immature', ostensibly softened his criticism by laying some of the blame for her failure on Shakespeare's script. He wrote, 'It should never by forgotten in judging an attempt to play Romeo and Juliet that the parts are made almost impossible, except to actors of positive genius, skilled to the last degree in metrical declamation, by the way in which the poetry, magnificent as it is, is interlarded by the miserable rhetoric and silly logical conceits which were the foible of the Elizabethans.'[49] Mrs Patrick Campbell failed to be an effective Shakespearian actress and instead cut the text, just as Mary Anderson had done, because it exposed her limitation in the role.

The following US season included several productions of *Romeo and Juliet* that omitted 3.2. Otis Skinner presented a production with his wife, Maud Durbin, in Chicago in the fall of 1896.[50] Durbin's promptbook shows the scene cut with

no markings to suggest it was ever rehearsed (Illustration 20).[51] Earlier that same spring, New York witnessed the duelling productions of Julia Marlowe and Robert Taber at Palmer's Theater in competition with Augustin Daly's production starring Mrs Cora Brown Potter and Kyrle Bellew. Daly mounted his production of *Romeo and Juliet* to rival Marlowe's and to ruin her return to New York, where she had not performed for nearly a decade.[52] Both productions cut all of 3.2 from their scripts. In fact, Winter thought it foolish that Marlowe had attempted the scene in her earlier performance of the play in 1887, noting that 'In the prodigality of her youthful, undeveloped powers she made use of the difficult, exacting colloquy between Juliet and the Nurse about the banishment of Romeo, which more judicious performers discreetly omit, and to which she proved unequal.'[53] In the spring of 1896, without 3.2, Marlowe became a successful Juliet and this remained one of the signature roles of her career.[54] Unfortunately, the critics were not as kind to

---

44 'Lyceum Theatre', *The Times*, 23 September 1895, p. 5, col. D.

45 William Archer, *The Theatrical World of 1895* (London, 1896), p. 286.

46 Archer, *Theatrical World*, p. 290.

47 William Shakespeare, *Romeo & Juliet ... arranged for the stage by Forbes Robertson and presented at The Lyceum Theatre on Saturday, September 21st, 1895 With Illustrations by Hawes Craven* (London, 1895), p. 47.

48 I. Zangwill, 'Without Prejudice', *Pall Mall Magazine*, September to December 1895, 648–56; pp. 649–50.

49 Bernard Shaw, *Shaw on Shakespeare*, ed. Edwin Wilson (New York, 1961), p. 181.

50 'Amusements: Grand Opera-House', *Daily Inter Ocean*, 25 September 1896, p. 7, col. C.

51 William Shakespeare, *Romeo and Juliet* (New York, 1894) promptbook signed by Maud Durbin, Harvard Theatre Collection 355, pp. 89–93.

52 Charles Edward Russell, *Julia Marlowe: Her Life and Art* (New York, 1926), pp. 271–85.

53 William Winter, *Shakespeare on the Stage* (New York, 1915), p. 191.

54 'Juliet in Another Guise', *New York Times*, 10 March 1896, p. 5; Edward Dithmar, 'The Theatres', *New York Times*, 15 March 1896, p. 10; and 'Romeo and Juliet at Palmer's – Mr. and Mrs. Taber', *New-York Tribune*, 10 March 1896, p. 7, col. A.

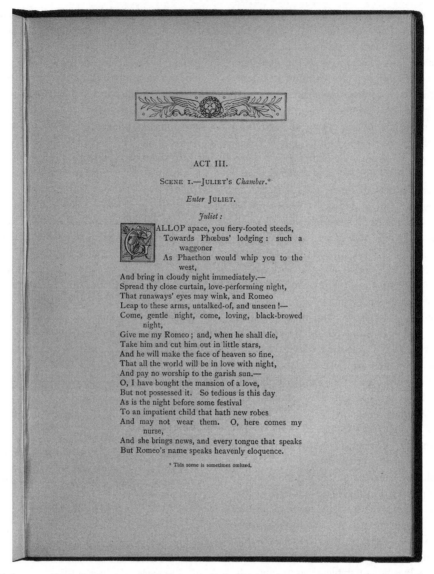

ACT III.

SCENE I.—JULIET'S *Chamber.**

Enter JULIET.

Juliet :

GALLOP apace, you fiery-footed steeds,
 Towards Phœbus' lodging : such a
     waggoner
 As Phaethon would whip you to the
     west,
And bring in cloudy night immediately.—
Spread thy close curtain, love-performing night,
That runaways' eyes may wink, and Romeo
Leap to these arms, untalked-of, and unseen !—
Come, gentle night, come, loving, black-browed
     night,
Give me my Romeo; and, when he shall die,
Take him and cut him out in little stars,
And he will make the face of heaven so fine,
That all the world will be in love with night,
And pay no worship to the garish sun.—
O, I have bought the mansion of a love,
But not possessed it.   So tedious is this day
As is the night before some festival
To an impatient child that hath new robes
And may not wear them.   O, here comes my
     nurse,
And she brings news, and every tongue that speaks
But Romeo's name speaks heavenly eloquence.

* This scene is sometimes omitted.

19. William Shakespeare, *Romeo & Juliet . . . arranged for the stage by Forbes Robertson* (London, 1895), p. 47. Reproduced by permission of the Folger Shakespeare Library.

Mrs Potter. In a scathing review, the *New York Times* complained that 'the play has been "cut" to suit her weakness to a preposterous extent'.[55] Daly arranged the script for this production, using Henry Irving's version, and the rehearsal copies show the scene was eliminated without being rehearsed (Illustration 21).[56] During the late

[55] 'Mrs. Potter as Juliet: Some Portions of the Great Love Tragedy Performed Last Night at Daly's Theatre', *New York Times*, 4 March 1896, p. 4.

[56] William Shakespeare, *Romeo and Juliet* (New York, *c.* 1883), Rehearsal copies, Folger Shakespeare Library PROMPT Rom. 7, pp. 30–1 [rehearsal copy no. 6 checked for the Nurse].

ROMEO AND JULIET.

And she brings news; and every tongue that speaks
But Romeo's name speaks heavenly eloquence.—

Enter Nurse, with cords.

Now, nurse, what news? What hast thou there? the cords
That Romeo bid thee fetch?

Nurse. Ay, ay, the cords.
                           [*Throws them down.*

Juliet. Ay me! what news? why dost thou wring thy
    hands?

Nurse. Ah, well-a-day! he's dead, he's dead, he's dead!
We are undone, lady, we are undone!
Alack the day! he's gone, he's kill'd, he's dead!

Juliet. Can heaven be so envious?

Nurse.   Romeo can,
Though heaven cannot.—O Romeo, Romeo!—
Who ever would have thought it?—Romeo!   40

Juliet. What devil art thou, that dost torment me thus?
This torture should be roar'd in dismal hell.
Hath Romeo slain himself? say thou but ay,
And that bare vowel I shall poison more
Than the death-darting eye of cockatrice:
I am not I, if there be such an I;
Or those eyes shut, that make thee answer ay.
If he be slain, say ay; or if not, no.
Brief sounds determine of my weal or woe.

Nurse. I saw the wound, I saw it with mine eyes—   50
God save the mark!—here on his manly breast:
A piteous corse, a bloody piteous corse;
Pale, pale as ashes, all bedaub'd in blood,
All in gore-blood; I swoonded at the sight.

Juliet. O, break, my heart! poor bankrupt, break at once!
To prison, eyes, ne'er look on liberty!
Vile earth, to earth resign; end motion here,
And thou and Romeo press one heavy bier!   60

Nurse. O Tybalt, Tybalt, the best friend I had!
O courteous Tybalt! honest gentleman!
That ever I should live to see thee dead!

Juliet. What storm is this that blows so contrary?
Is Romeo slaughter'd, and is Tybalt dead?
My dear-lov'd cousin, and my dearer lord?
Then, dreadful trumpet, sound the general doom!
For who is living, if those two are gone?

Nurse. Tybalt is gone, and Romeo banished;
Romeo that kill'd him, he is banished.

Juliet. O God! did Romeo's hand shed Tybalt's blood?   70

Nurse. It did, it did; alas the day, it did!

Juliet. O serpent heart, hid with a flowering face!
Did ever dragon keep so fair a cave?
Beautiful tyrant! fiend angelical!
Dove-feather'd raven! wolvish-ravening lamb!
Despised substance of divinest show!
Just opposite to what thou justly seem'st,
A damned saint, an honourable villain!
O nature, what hadst thou to do in hell,   80
When thou didst bower the spirit of a fiend
In mortal paradise of such sweet flesh?
Was ever book containing such vile matter
So fairly bound? O, that deceit should dwell
In such a gorgeous palace!

Nurse.   There's no trust,
No faith, no honesty in men; all perjur'd,
All forsworn, all naught, all dissemblers.—
Ah, where's my man? give me some aqua vitæ.—
These griefs, these woes, these sorrows, make me old.
Shame come to Romeo!

Juliet.   Blister'd be thy tongue   90
For such a wish! he was not born to shame:
Upon his brow shame is asham'd to sit;
For 't is a throne where honour may be crown'd

20. Maud Durbin's promptbook, pp. 90–1. Source: Houghton Library, Harvard University.

SCENE II. *Verona.—The Loggia.*

Enter JULIET.

JUL. Gallop apace, you fiery-footed steeds,
Towards Phœbus' lodging; such a waggoner
As Phaeton would whip you to the west,
And bring in cloudy night immediately.—
Spread thy close curtain, love-performing night!
That runaway's eyes may wink; and Romeo
Leap to these arms, untalk'd of, and unseen!—
Come, night!—Come, Romeo! come, thou day in night!
For thou wilt lie upon the wings of night
Whiter than new snow on a raven's back.
Come, gentle night; come, loving, black brow'd night,
Give me my Romeo: and, when he shall die,
Take him and cut him out in little stars,
And he will make the face of heaven so fine,
That all the world will be in love with night,
And pay no worship to the garish sun.—
O! I have bought the mansion of a love,
But not possess'd it.   So tedious is this day,
As is the night before some festival
To an impatient child, that hath new robes,
And may not wear them.   O! here comes my nurse,
And she brings news; and every tongue that speaks
But Romeo's name, speaks heavenly eloquence.—

Enter NURSE, *with Cords.*

Now, nurse, what news?   What hast thou there? the cords
That Romeo bade thee fetch?
   NURSE. Ay, ay, the cords.
   JUL. Ay, me! what news?   Why dost thou wring thy hands?
   NURSE. Ah well-a-day! he's dead, he's dead, he's dead!
We are undone, lady, we are undone!—
Alack the day!—he's gone, he's kill'd, he's dead!
   JUL. Can heaven be so envious?
   NURSE.   Romeo can,
Though heaven cannot.—O Romeo! Romeo!—
Who ever would have thought it?—Romeo!
   JUL. What devil art thou, that dost torment me thus?
   NURSE. I saw the wound, I saw it with mine eyes,—
Here on his manly breast: a piteous corse,
Pale, pale as ashes,—I swooned at the sight.
   JUL. O break, my heart!—poor bankrupt, break at once!
To prison, eyes! ne'er look on liberty!
Vile earth, to earth resign; end motion here;
And thou, and Romeo, press one heavy bier!
   NURSE. O Tybalt, Tybalt, the best friend I had!
That ever I should live to see thee dead!
   JUL. What storm is this, that blows so contrary?
Is Romeo slaughter'd: and is Tybalt dead?
   NURSE. Tybalt is gone, and Romeo banished;
Romeo, that killed him, he is banished.
   JUL. O God!—did Romeo's hand shed Tybalt's blood?

   NURSE. It did, it did; alas the day! it did.
   JUL. O nature! what hadst thou to do in hell,
When thou didst bower the spirit of a fiend
In mortal paradise of such sweet flesh?
O, that deceit should dwell
In such a gorgeous palace!
   NURSE.   There's no trust,
No faith, no honesty in men; all perjur'd,
All forsworn, all naught, all dissemblers.—
Shame come to Romeo!
   JUL.   Blister'd be thy tongue,
For such a wish! he was not born to shame:
Upon his brow shame is asham'd to sit;
For 'tis a throne where honor may be crowned
Sole monarch of the universal earth.
O, what a beast was I to chide at him!
   NURSE. Will you speak well of him that kill'd your cousin?
   JUL. Shall I speak ill of him that is my husband?
Ah, poor my lord, what tongue shall smooth thy name,
When I, thy three-hours wife, have mangled it?
Back, foolish tears, back to your native spring;
Your tributary drops belong to woe,
Which you, mistaking, offer up to joy.
My husband lives, that Tybalt would have slain;
And Tybalt's dead, that would have slain my husband:
All this is comfort.   Wherefore weep I then?
Some word there was, worse than Tybalt's death,
That murder'd me: I would forget it fain;
But, O! it presses to my memory,
Like damned guilty deeds to sinners' minds:
Tybalt is dead, and Romeo—banished!
Romeo is banished!   To speak that word
Is father, mother, Tybalt, Romeo, Juliet,
All slain, all dead.—*Romeo is banished!*—
There is no father, and my mother, nurse?
   NURSE. Weeping and wailing over Tybalt's corse.
   JUL. Wash they his wounds with tears: mine shall be spent,
When theirs are dry, for Romeo's banishment.
Take up those cords:—Poor ropes, you are beguil'd,
Both you and I; for Romeo is exil'd:
   NURSE. Hie to your chamber: I'll find Romeo
To comfort you: I wot well where he is.
Hark ye, your Romeo will be here at night;
I'll to him; he is hid at Laurence' cell.
   JUL. O find him! give this ring to my true knight,
And bid him come to take his last farewell.

[*Exeunt.*

A. W. Verm

SCENE III.—*Verona.   A Secret Place in the Monastery.*

Enter FRIAR LAURENCE.

FRIAR. Romeo, come forth; come forth, thou fearful man:
Affliction is enamour'd of thy parts,
And thou art wedded to calamity.

nineteenth century, actresses who attempted Juliet often failed in 3.2 and critics such as Winter and Shaw argued that the play was structurally more sound without it or that the poetry was beyond the skills of most actresses, but many of those who did eliminate it were accused of transforming the role to suit the defects of their acting. An actress approaching the character of Juliet was presented a nearly impossible task given the contradictory and arbitrary nature of the criticism surrounding the part.

On her way to popular fame and fortune at the turn of the century, Maude Adams tried her hand at classical acting and appeared as Juliet at the Empire theatre in New York on 8 May 1899. However, Adams was not a classically trained actress and the critics took note. Edward Dithmar of the *New York Times* championed her, arguing that what she lacked in 'classical tragedy' she more than made up for in 'natural eloquence and seeming spontaneity of expression'; but he conceded that she went untested in 'the great scene in which Juliet learns of Tybalt's death and Romeo's banishment'.[57] The acting edition Adams published reveals that her script omits all of 3.2, skipping from the latter half of 3.1 to the opening of 3.3 (Illustration 22).[58] Another reviewer of the *New York Times* remained neutral regarding Adams script, stating that she was merely following 'recent custom' by omitting the scene.[59] However, one Boston reviewer found her omissions inexcusable and attributed their absence to her desire to fit the play to her own 'moderate powers'.[60] William Winter was her most severe critic, both at the time in his *Tribune* review and years later, reminiscing that her performance 'ceased to be frivolous only when it became mildly hysterical'.[61] According to biographer Acton Davies, Adams knew her limitations with the role and cut the script so that her production created 'a simple girlish creature of infinite charm' rather than the assertive, independent young woman that emerges in Q2.[62]

By the early twentieth century, only twenty years after Neilson first eliminated the scene in performance, it became common – customary according to the *Times* reviewer – to cut 3.2 from

productions. Frank Benson's touring company eliminated the scene. The promptbook that he used at the Shakespeare Memorial Theater roughly from 1898 to 1911 does not include it.[63] When Marlowe joined with E. H. Sothern in 1904, she continued to leave this scene out of *Romeo and Juliet*, a play they successfully included in their repertoire through 1924. None of the many promptbooks Marlowe and Sothern left behind include the scene.[64] Productions by Margaret Anglin, John Doud, Windsor P. Daggett, Priestly Morrison and the commercial productions of Walter Hampden and Winthrop Ames all eliminate the scene.[65] The evidence from the

57 Edward A. Dithmar, 'The Week at the Theatres', *New York Times*, 14 May 1899, p. 17.
58 William Shakespeare, *Maude Adams Acting Edition of Romeo and Juliet* (New York, 1899), pp. 71–2.
59 'Maude Adams as Juliet', *New York Times*, 9 May 1899, p. 7.
60 'Maude Adams, Her Boston Appearance as Juliet at the Hollis', *Boston Daily Advertiser*, 23 May 1899, p. 8, col. A.
61 William Winter, 'A Sad Affair at the Empire: "Romeo and Juliet"', *New York Tribune*, 9 May 1899, p. 8, col. F; Winter, *Shakespeare on the Stage*, p. 189.
62 Acton Davies, *Maude Adams* (New York, 1901), p. 85.
63 William Shakespeare, *Romeo and Juliet* [(n.p., n.d.)], F. R. Benson Promptbook, Shakespeare Centre Library, Shakespeare Birthplace Trust, n.p.
64 See, for example, [William Shakespeare,] *Romeo and Juliet*, typescript prompt copy, Folger Shakespeare Library PROMPT Rom. Fo. 5, pp. 31–2.
65 William Shakespeare, *Romeo and Juliet* (n.p., n.d.), Margaret Anglin Promptbook, Billy Rose Theatre Division, New York Public Library for the Performing Arts, n.p.; William Shakespeare, [*Romeo and Juliet,*] promptbook of John Doud [(New York, n.d.)], Folger Shakespeare Library PROMPT Rom. 41, pp. 55–6; William Shakespeare, *Shakespeare's Tragedy of Romeo and Juliet* (New York, 1901) Promptbook of Windsor P. Dagget, Billy Rose Theatre Division, New York Public Library for the Performing Arts, pp. 55–8; William Shakespeare, *Romeo and Juliet* (New York, [1882]) Promptbook of Priestley Morrison, Billy Rose Theatre Division, New York Public Library for the Performing Arts, n.p.; William Shakespeare, *Romeo and Juliet*, (n.p., n.d.), Walter Hampden Promptbook, Hampden-Booth Library, Player's Club, p. 141; William Shakespeare, *Romeo and Juliet* [Boston, 1906] Typewritten sides for nineteen characters for Winthrop Ames production, Billy Rose Theatre Division, New York Public Library for the Performing Arts, n.p.

ROMEO and JULIET

BENVOLIO.
O Romeo, Romeo, brave Mercutio's dead!
Here comes the furious Tybalt back again.
[Looking off R. C.
[Re-enter TYBALT.

ROMEO.
Alive, in triumph! and Mercutio slain!
[Picks up MERCUTIO's sword.
Now, Tybalt, take the 'villain' back again
That late thou gavest me, for Mercutio's soul
Is but a little way above our heads,
Saying for thine to keep him company;
Either thou, or I, or both, must go with him.

TYBALT.
Thou, wretched boy, that didst consort him here,
Shalt with him hence.

ROMEO.
This shall determine that.
[They fight. TYBALT falls. Bell. Murmurs within.

BENVOLIO.
Romeo, away, be gone!
The citizens are up, and Tybalt slain;
Stand not amaz'd; the prince will doom thee death,
If thou art taken. Hence, be gone, away!

ROMEO.
[Up C.] O, I am fortune's fool!
[Exit ROMEO and BENVOLIO, L. U. E. Enter officer, guards and servants of Prince, citizens, etc.

71

ROMEO and JULIET

SCENE III.—FRIAR LAURENCE's Cell. Monday afternoon. ROMEO discovered. Enter FRIAR LAURENCE, who locks iron gates.

Romeo!   FRIAR LAURENCE.

ROMEO.
[In chair, R. C.] Father, what news? What is the prince's doom?
What sorrow craves acquaintance at my hand,
That I yet know not?

FRIAR LAURENCE.
Too familiar
Is my dear son with such sour company;
I bring thee tidings of the prince's doom.

ROMEO.
What less than doomsday is the prince's doom?

FRIAR LAURENCE.
A gentler judgment vanished from his lips,
Not body's death, but body's banishment.

ROMEO.
[Rises.] Ha, banishment! be merciful, say death;
For exile hath more terror in his look,
Much more than death; do not say banishment.

FRIAR LAURENCE.
Hence from Verona art thou banished.
Be patient, for the world is broad and wide.

72

22. William Shakespeare, Maude Adams' Acting Edition of Romeo and Juliet (New York, 1899), pp. 71–2. Reproduced by permission of the Folger Shakespeare Library.

promptbooks of these productions indicates that all cut the script shortly after Romeo kills Tybalt, removing the Prince's pronouncement, along with all of 3.2, and picking up again with the scene between Romeo and Friar Laurence, so that the audience learns at the same time as the character of Romeo's banishment. This effect was what William Winter praised when Mary Anderson first dropped the scene.

As the twentieth century progressed so important productions continued to discard 3.2. Their promptbooks show Jane Cowl, Eva Le Gallienne and Katharine Cornell all eliminated the extraordinary 'Gallop apace' soliloquy and the emotionally vibrant exchange with the Nurse that follows.[66] Cowl made history by portraying the role in 174 consecutive performances, and received praise from the *New York Times* for presenting the character as a 'charming, simple girl'.[67] While Cowl played to sold-out houses, not all reviewers were appreciative. Joseph Brewer, writing in *The Spectator*, resented the 'expurgated production' in which he thought, 'Miss Cowl was largely relieved of doing any acting'.[68] Le Gallienne, who also directed the production for her Civic Repertory Theater in 1930, cut her script lightly.[69] In fact, critics credit Le Gallienne with restoring scenes usually cut from performance and fashioning a swiftly paced, dynamic script of passion and violence. However, Le Gallienne eliminated both 1.3 and 3.2, noting in the programme that she cut the latter 'simply because it retards the action'.[70] Critics such as Burns Mantle praised her choice, commenting that the lines about cutting Romeo out in little stars make Juliet appear psychotic and the character benefits from their absence.[71] Cornell brings the trend among actresses full circle, having begun her productions of *Romeo and Juliet* without 3.2, but eventually reinstating the scene, reversing the process that Adelaide Neilson began. Cornell and husband/director Guthrie McClintic felt compelled by tradition to follow a conventionally cut script. While some encouraged him to include the 'Gallop apace' scene, he saw 'no reason' to do so. But, when the production struggled on the company's historic tour of 1933,

McClintic reapproached the staging and restored the text for the Broadway run that played to critical acclaim in 1934/5.[72]

The above production history presents no single cause for omitting 3.2 in performance, but demonstrates the close relation among a group of performances. Clearly certain actresses, or their manager/directors, cut this challenging scene from their productions rather than risk critical ridicule. The role may, in fact, suffer from the debilitating paradox expressed by Helena Faucit, that an actress young enough to look the part lacks the emotional maturity to perform the role well, although that seems simplistic.[73] The scene also suffered in this

---

[66] William Shakespeare, *Romeo and Juliet* [London, 1902], souvenir copy of Jane Cowl production, Harvard Theatre Collection 359, pp. 71–3; William Shakespeare, *Romeo and Juliet* [n.p., 1909], Eva Le Gallienne Promptbook, Beinecke Rare Book and Manuscript Library, Yale University, n.p.; and William Shakespeare, *Romeo and Juliet*, typescript for Katharine Cornell's 1933 tour, Billy Rose Theatre Division, New York Public Library for the Performing Arts, n.p.

[67] 'Jane Cowl, Juliet, Ends Record Run', *New York Times*, 10 June 1923, p. S5.

[68] Joseph Brewer, 'The Theatre: The New York Stage of To-Day', *Spectator*, 31 March 1923, p. 552, Col. B.

[69] William P. Halstead, *Shakespeare as Spoken: Statistical History of Acting Editions of Shakespeare* (Washington DC, 1983), vol. 14, p. 794.

[70] Civic Repertory Theatre Records, C.R.T. Programs 4th, 5th, and 6th Seasons, 21 April 1930, New Haven, Yale University, Beinecke Rare Book and Manuscript Library.

[71] See Burns Mantle, 'Le Gallienne's Version puts New Life into Tragedy', *Springfield Republican*, 4 May 1930; and Burns Mantle, 'Fourteenth St Shakespeare: Eva Le Gallienne Revives 'Romeo and Juliet' in Her Own Way', *New York Daily News*, 4 May 1930, in Civic Repertory Theatre Records, Press Books of the Civic Repertory Theatre, New Haven, Yale University, Beinecke Rare Book and Manuscript Library.

[72] Tad Mosel, *Leading Lady: The World and Theatre of Katharine Cornell* (Boston, MA, 1978), pp. 318, 324, 345–56.

[73] Helena Faucit Martin, 'Juliet', in *On Some Of Shakespeare's Women by One Who Has Impersonated Them* (private circulation, 1885), pp. 28–88; pp. 28–9. None of these Juliets was particularly young. Mary Anderson was 26 when she played the part in 1885 and Cowl and Cornell were 40 when they first took on the part. See also Jackson, *Shakespeare at Stratford*, pp. 125–8.

historical moment, suiting neither waning Victorian interests nor waxing modern sensibilities. On the one hand, Victorian critics ignored Juliet's anguish and heroic resolve in 3.2, favouring the Gothic quality of Juliet's terrorized imaginings in the potion scene and the frightening visual effects of the tomb scene.[74] On the other, the rhetorical style of the scene clashed with the modern, naturalistic performance approach favoured by actresses such as Mrs Patrick Campbell. Critics also argued that dramaturgical necessity required any production to eliminate 3.2 because it detracts from Romeo's scene with Friar Laurence. Further, while never articulated in the production criticism, staging practices of Victorian realism played a part in textual cuts. The many scenes of a Shakespeare play, presented with any pictorial authenticity, required large amounts of time to shift scenery and props on and off the stage. Even with severe cuts, many of these productions ran for well over three hours.[75] By the turn of the twentieth century, some productions merely followed theatrical precedent and cut the scene simply because other productions cut it.

Early productions influenced later ones either directly or indirectly. William Winter applauded Mary Anderson's decision to omit 3.2 'just as Adelaide Neilson did'. Johnston Forbes-Robertson, who played Romeo to Anderson's cut version of Juliet in 1885, may very well have encouraged Mrs Patrick Campbell to drop the scene early in the run of his Lyceum production in 1895. Performing Romeo and Juliet in New York at the same time that Anderson mounted her newly cut version, Margaret Mather eliminated the scene during her own run of the play. Otis Skinner, who served for a brief period as an actor/manager for Mather in 1890,[76] eliminated the scene when he mounted his production with wife Maud Durbin. By the time Maude Adams presented her version of the play in 1899, theatre critics accepted the omission of 3.2 as an established theatrical convention. When Guthrie McClintic directed Romeo and Juliet with wife Katharine Cornell in 1933, he was given access to the Sothern/Marlowe promptbooks and had no intention of staging 3.2 until his production failed and he took a closer look at the full text.

The connections between theatre professionals, both as friends and rivals, must certainly have influenced the recurring production choice to eliminate 3.2 in performance.

Before dismissing these stage cuts as the vagaries and vestiges of the Victorian era, it is important to realize that significant movie versions seen by millions of spectators have reduced or nearly eliminated the scene. Franco Zeffirelli, who defined the play for generations, eliminated both the 3.2 soliloquy and the potion speech of Act 4 because he felt the young Olivia Hussey was not up to the demands of the text.[77] Levenson explains that Zeffirelli's movie uses gesture instead of language in 3.2 and that by decreasing the text he reduces Juliet's emotional reaction to that of 'an adolescent sorely disappointed and oddly formal in her expression of grief'.[78] More recently, Baz Luhrmann allowed Claire Danes only eleven of the 'Gallop apace' lines.[79] Danes speaks less than twenty lines from the entire scene sitting alone in her room in separate shots interspersed between Tybalt's death, the proclamation of Romeo's banishment and Romeo's scene with Friar Laurence. So much of Juliet's later dialogue is sacrificed to visual narration that Danes is reduced to tearful, forlorn looks and despondent sobbing raves. These filmic Juliets, the contemporary equivalent of earlier popular theatre versions, are passive young female victims of patriarchal societies entrenched in violence. Like Hussey, Danes is rendered a frustrated adolescent, infantilized by the loss of a much broader

---

[74] Carol J. Carlisle, 'Passion Framed by Art: Helen Faucit's Juliet', Theatre Survey, 25 (1984), 177–91; pp. 177–9.

[75] Anderson's printed acting version notes, 'As the setting of the scenery is very elaborate, the Management beg the indulgence of the audience for any delays that may occur this evening'.

[76] Otis Skinner, Footlights and Spotlights: Recollections of My Life on the Stage (Indianapolis, 1924), pp. 192–8.

[77] Loehlin, ed., Romeo and Juliet, pp. 78, 176; Romeo & Juliet, directed by Franco Zeffirelli, Paramount Pictures, 1968.

[78] See Levenson, 'Changing Images', pp. 159–60.

[79] Loehlin, ed., Romeo and Juliet, p. 176; William Shakespeare's Romeo + Juliet, directed by Baz Luhrmann, Twentieth Century Fox, 1996.

emotional range. With the loss of text, these Juliets become, like the Juliet of Maude Adams or Jane Cowl before them, 'simple' and 'girlish'. These film Juliets, like their earlier stage sisters, lack the psychological depth available to the character that exists in the rich dramatic language of the Q2 text. They have more in common with the Q1 Juliet, who is a simpler, more innocent, adolescent version of the character.

TEXTUAL CRITICISM OF 3.2

One of the theories surrounding the textual variants of Q1 and Q2 *Romeo and Juliet* exhibits an intriguing correlation to the production history of the play and the reasons 3.2 was eliminated in the late nineteenth century. Scholars have offered several theories that attempt to explain the relationship between the Q1 and Q2 texts. Each of these theories provides a thoughtful hypothesis about the relationship between the two versions; however, the theories have not satisfactorily ended conjectures because no conclusive evidence exists regarding the origin of the texts and their relation to each other. The most prominent and most vigorously challenged is memorial reconstruction, which argues that Q1 represents the Q2 text as poorly remembered by actors or spectators.[80] Other scholars argue that Shakespeare expanded Q1 to create Q2.[81] More recently, a number of scholars have rejected the impulse to identify one specific relationship between the two texts and suggest that their multiplicity is more intriguing and enlightening than attempting to identify their provenance.[82] However, the theory that most directly impacts the production history of 3.2 is that Q2 is the original script, which was abridged for performance, and Q1 represents that condensed performance script.[83] In this case, textual theory seems to be informed by performance as it follows and reflects stage practice and popular performance criticism, and also informs performance as it imagines and explains the textual variants that provide the material substance of the 3.2 play-script.

Lukas Erne is the most prominent adherent of the theory that the shorter Q1 represents a performance text, and he argues that the longer Q2 represents a literary one. In *Shakespeare as Literary Dramatist*, he writes that Shakespeare conceived the longer versions of his plays, including the second quarto of *Romeo and Juliet*, as literary texts with complex characters appropriate for a literary medium but that Shakespeare thoroughly expected the plays to be abridged and altered for stage performance.[84] Erne further argues that Q1 *Romeo and Juliet* displays an orality and theatricality that reflect the play as performed on the early modern London stage. A number of other scholars present similar theories. George Winchester Stone, Jr argues that Shakespeare 'overwrote his plays to indicate character development for his actors'.[85] He asserts that as a man of the theatre, Shakespeare anticipated his company would alter the Q2 script of *Romeo and Juliet* to fit the circumstances of performance and expected the actors to do their best to create a character based on their knowledge of the Q2 text even if they did not speak all the lines of the Q2 script. Jay L. Halio argues that Shakespeare shortened the play himself to meet performance requirements.[86] Robert

---

[80] See, for example, Harry R. Hoppe, *The Bad Quarto of Romeo and Juliet: A Bibliographical and Textual Study* (Ithaca, NY, 1948), p. 57; Irace, *'Bad' Quartos*, pp. 56, 115–31, 141–2.

[81] See, for example, Donald Foster, 'The Webbing of *Romeo and Juliet*', in *Critical Essays on Shakespeare's Romeo and Juliet*, ed. Joseph A. Porter (New York, 1997), pp. 131–49.

[82] See, for example, Paul Werstine, 'Narratives about Printed Shakespeare Texts: "Foul Papers" and "Bad" Quartos', *Shakespeare Quarterly*, 41 (1990), 65–86, p. 86.

[83] A number of scholars have argued that Shakespeare and/or his company cut his plays for production. See, for example, Andrew Gurr, 'Maximal and Minimal Texts: Shakespeare v. The Globe', in *Shakespeare Survey 52* (Cambridge, 1999), pp. 68–87; p. 70.

[84] Lukas Erne, *Shakespeare as Literary Dramatist* (London, 2003), pp. 220, 243–4; Lukas Erne, *The First Quarto of Romeo and Juliet* (London, 2007), pp. 32–3.

[85] George Winchester Stone, Jr, '*Romeo and Juliet*: The Source of its Modern Stage Career', in *Shakespeare 400: Essays by American Scholars on the Anniversary of the Poet's Birth*, ed. James G. McManaway (New York, 1964), p. 198.

[86] Jay L. Halio, 'Handy-Dandy: Q1/Q2 Romeo and Juliet', in *Shakespeare's Romeo and Juliet: Texts, Contexts, and Interpretation*, ed. Jay L. Halio (Newark, DE, 1995), p. 137.

Burkhart agrees that the company cut the script for production, but argues that the text is a touring version carefully made only when necessity forced the company to travel during the summer of 1596.[87] David Farley-Hills essentially supports Burkhart's argument, believing that the Q1 *Romeo and Juliet* represents 'a version intended for the stage', 'for performance by a touring troupe in the provinces', which was prepared by a redactor from Shakespeare's foul papers.[88] The earliest version of this argument, however, was presented in 1934, the same year Cornell and McClintic were grappling with 3.2 in performance. In his *Shakespeare and the Homilies*, Alfred Hart argued that Q1 is clearly an acting version prepared by an 'Elizabethan play-adapter' for production in the London theatres.[89] When Hart published his theory he would have been familiar with the highly reduced versions of *Romeo and Juliet* common in the theatre, and one wonders how much contemporary theatre practice affected his argument about the sixteenth-century theatre texts, an argument that clearly influenced later generations of textual critics.

Hart and Erne believe that the differences in Juliet's Q1 and Q2 speeches are part of the abridgement made for the acting version of the play, and both argue that excision of long poetic passages like those in 3.2 is necessary in performance. Erne argues that while Juliet's speeches might appeal to a reader, they add nothing to the plot and lack theatrical interest.[90] Hart believes that the company wanted to rid the script of tedious and non-dramatic rhetoric, concluding that 'brisk dialogue' is the 'quintessence and life of drama'.[91] Similarly, Brian Gibbons thinks the opening soliloquy of 3.2 was reduced for a 'provincial audience ... impatient with lyric utterance'.[92] According to Farley-Hills and Halio, the company was apparently willing to sacrifice character to the expedient of plot and worked toward an increased rate of action to enhance the dramatic effect.[93] Halio maintains that the company skilfully cut 3.2 in order to protect the 'essential features' of the scene while quickening the pace. In his discussion of stage business in the 1940s, Arthur Sprague found that 3.2 had

little 'interest' because it lacked physical activity, which seems to support what Erne, Hart, Halio and Farley-Hills argue about its lack of dramatic appeal.[94] The recurring theory argues that the Q2 version of 3.2 is not theatrically viable and was reduced for performance to enhance the scene's dramatic appeal resulting in the Q1 text.

The textual arguments regarding the non-dramatic nature of 3.2, which emerged in the 1930s with Alfred Hart, focus on its challenging rhetorical qualities, and therefore follow and reiterate performance critiques that plagued a number of actresses in the role. Remember that in the 1880s Henry Baker thought the scene broke 'many actresses', and that in 1896 William Winter thought any 'judicious' actress should eliminate 'the difficult, exacting colloquy'. Shaw suggested in his review of Mrs Patrick Campbell, although not very persuasively given his droll tone, that the stylistic excess of Shakespeare's language in 3.2 – his 'miserable rhetoric' – is almost impossible for a performer to master. In his 1930 prefaces, Granville-Barker sympathizes with any actress who 'shirks' 3.2, saying that the verbal conventions in the scene are both Shakespeare's 'success' and 'failure', calling for an operatic virtuosity from the performer incompatible with modern stage practice.[95] He explains that the scene was perfect for the boy actor of Shakespeare's theatre, trained

---

[87] Robert E. Burkhart, *Shakespeare's Bad Quartos: Deliberate Abridgments Designed for Performance by a Reduced Cast* (The Hague, 1975), p. 65.

[88] David Farley-Hills, 'The "Bad" Quarto of *Romeo and Juliet*', in *Shakespeare Survey 49* (Cambridge, 1996), pp. 27–44; p. 28.

[89] Alfred Hart, *Shakespeare and the Homilies* (Melbourne, 1934), pp. 125–30. Hart believes Q1 is a mutilated memorial reconstruction of this shortened acting version.

[90] Erne, *Literary Dramatist*, pp. 225–7.

[91] Alfred Hart, *Stolne and Surreptitious Copies: A Comparative Study of Shakespeare's Bad Quartos* (Melbourne, 1942), p. 163.

[92] William Shakespeare, *Romeo and Juliet*, ed. Brian Gibbons (London, 2008), p. 8.

[93] Farley-Hills, '"Bad" Quarto', p. 28; and Halio, 'Handy-Dandy', pp. 131–3.

[94] Arthur Colby Sprague, *Shakespeare and the Actors: The Stage Business in his Plays (1660–1905)* (Cambridge, 1945), p. 307.

[95] Granville-Barker, *Prefaces to Shakespeare*, pp. 18–19, 63–4.

in rhetoric and declamation – although he notes that much of the rhetoric is missing from Q1 – and argues that 3.2 is not suited to the modern actress or audience. As an actor, manager, playwright, critic and scholar, Granville-Barker is heavily influenced in his textual criticism of 3.2 by performance – early twentieth-century theatre conventions – and his knowledge of popular stage criticism. His notation that the most stylized language of 3.2 is absent from the Q1 text suggests that, despite the declamatory perfection of early modern boy actors, performance considerations may also explain the provenance of the early quartos. Stanley Wells has commented more recently on the challenge the language of the play provides actors and identifies the wordplay of 3.2 as especially problematic, although not untheatrical.[96] Understanding the texts as scripts for performance inspired a performance-based analysis of the play and the relation between Q1 and Q2.

Performance critics had another objection to the scene: its structural weakness. Eva Le Gallienne cut 3.2 from her Civic Repertory production, to the delight of critics, because she said the scene retarded the action. According to Winter, Mary Anderson did well to exclude 3.2 from performances in the 1880s because it weakened the effect of Romeo's scene with Friar Laurence immediately following. George Odell surmised that the scene was cut so often because it seemingly 'detracted from the dramatic effect of Romeo's 'banished' scene'.[97] Granville-Barker saw the structural arrangement as an indication of Shakespeare's youthful inexperience as a playwright.[98] The scene, according to Winter, Odell and Granville-Barker, was dramaturgically deficient, weakening the stronger scene that followed by making it repetitive and taking away the surprise for the audience of learning along with Romeo of his banishment. Of course, the Q2 text of 3.2 presents the psychological development of Juliet's character and offers a balance with Romeo in 3.3. After all, with 3.2 missing, the script focuses less on the way the quarrel affects the domestic feminine space that Juliet inhabits and instead concentrates on the violence that erupts within competing patriarchal systems of authority. By eliminating

Juliet's scene of tragic consequence, her decision to choose her new husband over familial affiliation, and following 3.1 immediately with 3.3, these performance scripts emphasize Romeo's dilemma and heighten his tragic status over Juliet's equally wrought ethical impasse. The growing autonomy of Juliet's character, her reasoning-out of the emotional dilemma into which she has been plunged, is treated as an intrusion into the play's essential action.

The textual criticism regarding the provenance of the early quartos, at least as it affects 3.2, historically follows and theoretically echoes the stage practice of theatre professionals and the performance criticism that analyzed, explained and evaluated their choices. In the case of 3.2 *Romeo and Juliet*, it is possible to see how theatrical performance in the late nineteenth and early twentieth centuries could have influenced the textual criticism of the original quartos. At the turn of the twentieth century, theatre professionals and performance critics assessed 3.2 to be rhetorically difficult and structurally weak, both because the stylized language slows the action and because the scene was believed to detract from the effect of 3.3. Similar concerns quickly found their way into textual arguments regarding the provenance of the quartos. Textual critics began to argue that Q1 represents an edited script used for performance by Shakespeare's company because the heightened language in the original Q2 text slows the pace and action of the play. This textual criticism supports the persistent reduction of 3.2 in performance by arguing that the longer Q2 version of the scene is a literary version never meant and inappropriate for performance while the shorter Q1 text – with its naive, anxious Juliet – is the script meant for performance. When textual critics privilege the Q1 text as the more theatrically viable, they also privilege the simple, innocent characterization of Juliet as the more stageworthy.

---

[96] Stanley Wells, 'The Challenges of *Romeo and Juliet*', in *Shakespeare Survey 49* (Cambridge, 1996), pp. 1–14; pp. 7–9.

[97] Odell, *Shakespeare from Betterton to Irving*, vol. 2, p. 402.

[98] Granville-Barker, *Prefaces to Shakespeare*, pp. 20–1.

CONCLUSION

The earliest published quartos of *Romeo and Juliet*, subsequent performances and attendant production scripts and reviews of those performances, and the textual criticism that analyzes and explains the early texts, have conspired together in an unconscious collaboration to present a Juliet on stage that is often less than the Juliet in Q2. The quarto texts, performance and criticism all contribute to an immediate, temporary conception each time the play is read or seen or read about. Any one of these three elements informs and influences an understanding of the other elements, and as each element layers new meaning and redirects knowledge about *Romeo and Juliet*, so it affects both the comprehension of the play's past and the potential of future perceptions. The 1597 quarto provided a textual example of a brief 3.2, a scene that presents the character of Juliet as an anxious, naive girl rather than the sophisticated woman that emerges in the longer quarto version of 1599. Productions tend to reduce the scene in performance, and for over fifty years at the turn of the twentieth century the scene disappeared entirely from productions, because, performers and stage critics argued, the language is rhetorically difficult, it slows the dramatic action, and it weakens the structure of the plot. Some textual critics echo these production arguments as they look back past the performance history of the texts and attempt to understand the relationship between the two different early quartos. Textual, performative and critical continuities intermingle over a long theatrical tradition to present a broad unanimity – a characterization of Juliet that remains an adolescent figure. The Q2 text propels Juliet as an active agent into the tragic structure of the play and without it she is a passive victim of consequences: childish, reactive and submissive. The condensing or loss of 3.2 in performance does more than speed the action and quicken pacing; it produces Juliet's operative decline. The interior life of the character, her psychological composition, suffers from the loss of the text. In the case of 3.2 *Romeo and Juliet*, the earliest text, performance practices and textual criticism seem to conspire against a scene critical to character formation.

THE SECOND TETRALOGY'S MOVE FROM ACHIEVEMENTS TO BADGES

CERI SULLIVAN

In a passionate response to the King's insistence that the crown should get any prisoners of war, Hotspur famously reaches for the moon:

> By heaven, methinks it were an easy leap
> To pluck bright honour from the pale-faced moon,
> Or dive into the bottom of the deep...
> And pluck up drowned honour by the locks,
> So he that doth redeem her thence might wear,
> Without corrival, all her dignities.
> But out upon this half-faced fellowship!
>
> *(1 Henry IV* 1.3.200–6)[1]

Most comment follows Northumberland and Worcester in thinking Hotspur is spouting 'a world of figures/ ... But not the form of what he should attend' (1.3.208–9). It gets called empty huffing, suitable for an apprentice's audition piece, as in the Induction to *The Knight of the Burning Pestle* (c. 1607). The lines do not seem to require much more: 'bright honour' is a conventional collocation in the sixteenth century (here, shining like the disc of the moon) and 'drowned honour' is a hairy personification, perhaps a bit muddy from lying around on the bottom. In either state, the honour (a concrete dignity) should be captured and worn by one man alone. The only historical gloss editors offer is a suggestion that 'half-faced' may refer to the paired profiles of Philip and Mary on the Marian shilling.

Leslie Hotson noted a reference to the Percy badge: the crescent moon.[2] However, he did not point out that the Percy silver crescent moon usually encloses a fetterlock (a double manacle, which locks two fists together). Together, crescent and lock appear to be a full-faced moon with big

eyes; looked at another way, this becomes two faces in profile, opposing each other. There is, for instance, a man in each of the five crescents-with-fetterlocks on the margin of the first folio of British Library MS Arundel 130 (dated 1446–61), an ordinal and annotated breviary owned by Henry Percy, 3rd Earl of Northumberland.[3] Though the crescent moon had been borne by the Percys since 1386, Hotspur was the first of his family to combine a crescent and lock, initially on his seal. Henry Percy, the 9th Earl of Northumberland, revived the collocation of the two, which appeared on his seals from 1588.[4] So the passage from *1 Henry IV* (probably first performed early in 1597) may show a Percy yearning to retrieve a badge of honour – the moon and its locks – from the alternative possibility that the family's moon has embraced a double-faced man like Henry.

This article will argue that the wearers of 'dignities' in the second tetralogy make repeated attempts

---

[1] William Shakespeare, *King Henry IV Part 1*, ed. D. S. Kastan, Arden Shakespeare Third Series (London, 2002).

[2] Leslie Hotson, *Shakespeare by Hilliard* (London, 1977), pp. 156–8. The battle cry of 'Esperance! Percy!' is accurately reported by Shakespeare (2.3.70, 5.2.96).

[3] London, British Library, MS Arundel 130, fo. 1r, www.bl .uk/catalogues/illuminatedmanuscripts/ILLUMIN.ASP? Size=mid&IllID=3014, accessed 6 November 2014.

[4] W. H. D. Longstaffe, 'The Old Heraldry of the Percies', *Archæologia Æliana*, n.s. 4 (1860), 157–228; pp. 178–80, 183, 213, 217–18, 223; *Northumbrian Monuments, or the Shields of Arms, Effigies, and Inscriptions in the Churches, Castles, and Halls of Northumberland*, ed. C. H. H. Blair, Newcastle upon Tyne Records Committee 4 (Newcastle upon Tyne, 1924), pp. 133, 152.

to separate their heraldic signs from such 'half-faced fellowship'. Accordingly, heritable heraldic achievements (based on descent and marriage) give way to badges (personal signs of loyalty to one man), which are recast as national badges. The argument starts with the revolutionary connotations of the Percy badge in the 1560s to 1590s. It then turns to Henry IV's anxiety over the permanent abatement of his family coat of arms. Neither coat nor badge will do for his son, who – first separating the gage from the badge – looks to an emblem of place of birth (not dynasty), which was worn in the 1590s by that unofficial 'Prince of Wales', the 2nd Earl of Essex.

Many critics have weighed the claims of the abstract quality of honour in *1 Henry IV*, balancing between what David Scott Kastan calls 'the fat knight's deflating nominalism' and Hotspur's 'committed essentialism'.[5] Here, though, I want to keep to the heraldic honour as a concrete noun. Gerard Cox traces it as a recurrent image in *1 Henry IV*.[6] Hal promises to call to account the 'child of honour and renown, / This gallant Hotspur', wishing that 'every honour sitting on his helm, / ... were multitudes' to be plucked off (3.2.139–40, 142–3). Blount, one of 'many marching in [the king's] coats' (5.3.25), in an inglorious tactic to spread any risk offered to the King, is the second such 'coat' to be taken by the Douglas, who jokes that he will kill the king's 'wardrobe, piece by piece' (5.3.27). Falstaff concludes that honour is a 'mere scutcheon' (5.1.139–40), referring to the escutcheon, a shield with armorial bearings (in this period, the use of the word was not confined to funeral hatchments), so the dead Blount seems to him a coat worn by 'grinning honour' (5.3.33, 60). Though Hal threatens Hotspur that 'the budding honours on thy crest / I'll crop to make a garland for my head' (5.4.71–2), in the event he covers the dead man's face with his own 'favours' (5.4.95). In doing so, Cox argues, Hal shows himself to be a truly magnanimous prince, not a counterfeit heir to the throne.[7]

A complete achievement of arms comprises shield, supporters, crest, mantle, helm and motto (though only the shield is essential). Arms and crests are personal to their bearers (and with due difference, their families). Coats of arms cannot be sold or alienated as long as there are kindred of the family still alive. There is only one way they can be lost: by attainder, which works corruption in the blood, extinguishing all civil rights and capacities, among them the right to bear arms (both weapons and coats of arms). By contrast, badges are heraldic insignia which are not associated with the shield or helm, though they may be displayed in conjunction with a coat of arms. Badges may be worn as marks or cognisances by retainers or adherents.[8] They are thus simple communal signs, more instantly recognizable than the armorial shield, and worn by the common man as well as the leader. Rapid recognition was important in battle (rival badges gave their names to the Wars of the Roses). But in peacetime, too, badges were widely and habitually displayed on pennons, seals, costume, military equipment, horse trappings, household furniture and plate. Heraldry experts claimed that they were natural signs in civil society (as with the tattoos of the New World inhabitants).[9] Thus a working knowledge of heraldry was not confined to the armigerous ranks, a fact also suggested by the popularity of published guides such as Gerard Legh's *The Accedens of Armorie* (1562, 1568, 1576, 1591, 1597, 1612), abridged by John Bossewell as *Workes of Armorie* (1572, 1597), John Ferne's *The Blazon of Gentrie* (two editions in 1586), Edmund Bolton's *The Elements of Armories* (1610) and John Guillim's *A Display of*

---

[5] *King Henry IV Part 1*, ed. Kastan, pp. 70 and 77.

[6] Gerard H. Cox, 'Like a Prince Indeed: Hal's Triumph of Honor in *1 Henry IV*', in *Pageantry in the Shakespearean Theater*, ed. David M. Bergeron (Athens, GA, 1985), pp. 130–52.

[7] Cox, 'Like a Prince'.

[8] *Boutell's Heraldry*, rev. John P. Brooke-Little (London, 1973), pp. 163–4. Guy Cadogan Rothery lists references to badges across a range of Shakespeare's plays in *The Heraldry of Shakespeare: A Commentary with Annotations* (London, 1930), ch. 5.

[9] Edmund Bolton, *The Elements of Armories* (London, 1610), pp. 20–2.

Heraldrie (1610, 1611, and onwards into the eighteenth century).

The legend told about the Percy family badge was that the Crusader William de Percy, who died in sight of Jerusalem in 1096, adopted the crescent.[10] A verse chronicle from the early sixteenth century, probably by William Peeris, a clerk to the 5th Earl of Northumberland, traces the genealogy of the Percys from the Norman Conquest onwards. Peeris claims that William de Percy, fighting at the 'Ponnte Terrible', was granted a portent, a moon 'i[n]verysyng her light' as it shined on his shield, so encouraging his side to victory. 'And therfor the Perses the cressant doth renew', Peeris says the chronicles conclude.[11] Six copies of Peeris's work exist, including one at the Percy seat of Alnwick Castle and another at the British Library, where it is part of a manuscript which contains an illustration of the Percy moon receiving its light from the Tudor sun of Henry VIII.[12]

During Shakespeare's lifetime, the Percy badge was kept in public view by the family's Catholic faith. One of the leaders of the Northern Rising of 1569 was Thomas Percy, 7th Earl of Northumberland. Quixotic and brief as it was, the Rising had the character of a crusade, recovering holy places from Protestant desecration. Wearing red crosses, men at arms marched under the banners of the five wounds of Christ; masses and anthems were sung in Durham Cathedral and surrounding parish churches; altar stones and holy water stones were brought out of hiding and reinstalled, and Protestant books and communion tables were burned.[13] Trying Percy in 1571, after the failure of the Rising, the state flourished a prophecy said to have been found among the earl's papers. At the rising of the moon one lion would be overthrown and two other lions united (referring to Northumberland, Elizabeth, and a projected marriage between the country's two most eminent Catholics, Mary Stuart and the Duke of Norfolk) – a document Percy dismissed as 'foolish Prophecy'.[14]

Patriotic ballads dating from the aftermath of the Northern Rising saw the potential of the Percy badge to symbolize changeable loyalties and folly. John Barker's 'The Plagues of Northomberland' (1570) tells how 'the Moon, in Northomberland, / After the change, in age well conne / Did rise in force, then to with stande / The light and bright beams of the Sonne', opposing 'the false beames of the glystringe Moon'. William Elderton's 'A Ballat Intituled Northomerland Newes' (1570) asks 'What meane ye to follow the man in the Moone', and reminds hearers of how an earlier 'Percie provoked King Harry to frowne'. William Kirkham's 'Joyfull Newes for True Subjects' (1570) rejoices that 'the Man in the Moone' has been brought down.[15]

The execution of Thomas Percy was not the end to questions about the family's loyalty to the crown, which continued over the succeeding decades.[16] He was named as a Catholic martyr (with other northern rebels) by Father Richard

---

[10] Edward Barrington de Fonblanque, *Annals of the House of Percy*, 2 vols. (London, 1887), vol. 1, p. 20.

[11] A. S. G. Edwards, 'A Verse Chronicle of the House of Percy', *Studies in Philology*, 105 (2008), 226–44; pp. 231–2, dealing with Alnwick Castle MS 79.

[12] A. G. Dickens, 'The Tudor Percy Emblem in Royal MS 18 Dii', *The Archaeological Journal*, 112 (1955), 95–9; plate xiv, p. 97, referring to earlier Galfridian prophecies about an eclipsed Percy moon reviving in conjunction with a kingly Edwardian sun.

[13] Diana Newton, *North-East England, 1569–1625: Governance, Culture and Identity* (Woodbridge, 2006), pp. 118–25. The specifically Catholic impetus behind the Rising in the North of 1569, challenged by revisionist historians, has recently been reasserted, K. J. Kesselring, '"A cold pye for the Papistes": Constructing and Containing the Northern Rising of 1569', *Journal of British Studies*, 43 (2004), 417–43. On the 7th Earl's actions during the Rising, see Fonblanque, *Annals*, vol. 2, pp. 22–3, 35–41, 46, 57.

[14] William Cobbett, *Cobbett's Complete Collection of State Trials and Proceedings for High Treason, and Other Crimes and Misdemeanors*, 33 vols. (London, 1809–26), vol. 1, p. 997. Hotspur threatens a key military alliance by impatience over Glendower's belief in such prophecies (3.1.12ff.).

[15] Claire Lamont, 'Shakespeare's *Henry IV* and "the old song of Percy and Douglas"', in *Shakespearean Continuities: Essays in Honour of E. A. J. Honigman*, ed. John Batchelor, Tom Cain, and Claire Lamont (Basingstoke, 1997), ch. 4; pp. 65–8.

[16] Thomas Percy may have come to mind again when his widow died in October 1596 and was buried at Westminster Abbey. William Camden, *Reges, reginae, nobiles,*

Bristow in 1574. In 1584 Cardinal William Allen repeated that Percy was 'a Saint and holie Martir' for refusing the state's offer of mercy if he altered his religion.[17] The attainder of the 7th Earl specifically reserved the rights of his brother Sir Henry Percy – who had stayed loyal to Elizabeth during the Rising – to inherit the title. Nonetheless this 8th Earl was also suspected of involvement in Catholic plots against the queen, and was imprisoned. When in 1585 he was found shot through the heart in the Tower of London, all sides doubted the government's claim of suicide.[18]

The death of the 8th Earl marked a brief recrudescence in the way the family was perceived. Able to convince Elizabeth throughout the 1580s and 1590s of his personal loyalty, the 9th Earl of Northumberland, Henry Percy, was installed as a Knight of the Garter in 1593, and was selected to carry the Garter to a newly elected Stranger Knight, Henri IV of France, on 8 July 1596.[19] The Percy crescent and fetterlock would have been highly visible during the notably opulent ceremonies of installation.[20] George Peele wrote a congratulatory dream poem on the occasion, in which a number of the most prominent contemporary authors (including Edmund Spenser, Samuel Daniel and Edmund Campion, but not Shakespeare) are unwilling to follow Philip Sidney and Christopher Marlowe into the grave while there is still a possibility that they can honour the 9th Earl. Peele's Edward III, the founder of the Garter, urges Percy to 'Become thy badge, as it becommeth thee'.[21] Until 1605 this was the standard line: George Chapman, praising the arts and sciences in a commendatory poem on *Sejanus* (1605), celebrates how 'Northumber ... with them, his crescent fills'.[22] In the same year, William Camden cites an anonymous anagram about the Percy name, 'with a relation to the Crescent or silver Moone his Cognisance': '*Percius HIC PURE SINCERUS, Percia Luna / Candida tota micat, pallet at illa polo*' ('Percy, he is truly sincere; the Percy crescent shines completely brightly though it is pale in the sky').[23]

But after the 9th Earl supported a limited measure of toleration for Catholics, and his cousin,

Thomas Percy, was cited a ring-leader in the Gunpowder Plot, Henry Percy fell under royal suspicion and was imprisoned in the Tower for fifteen years from 1606.[24] In 1609, John Davis, writing master to the Percy daughters, prudently focuses on the future (10th) earl, urging him to learn to read as 'A perfect Pierc-ey that in darknesse cleeres ... / So, Percies fame shall pierce the Eie of Daies / Then, by those Raies my Pen (inflam'd)

& *alij in ecclesia collegiata B. Petri Westmonasterij sepulti* (1600), sig. H1v.

[17] Richard Bristow, *A Briefe Treatise of Diuers Plaine and Sure Waies to Finde Out the Truth in this Doubtfull and Dangerous Time of Heresie* (1574; repr. 1599), fo. 73r; William Allen, *A True, Sincere and Modest Defence, of English Catholiques* (London, 1584), pp. 48–9; Julian Lock, 'Percy, Thomas, Seventh Earl of Northumberland (1528–1572)', *Oxford Dictionary of National Biography* (Oxford, 2004–15), www.oxforddnb.com/view/article/21956?docPos=5, accessed 6 November 2014.

[18] Carol Levin, 'Percy, Henry, Eighth Earl of Northumberland (*c.* 1532–1585)', *ODNB*, www.oxforddnb.com/view/article/21938?docPos=9, accessed 6 November 2014.

[19] Fonblanque, *Annals*, vol. 2, p. 201. The task eventually went elsewhere, Peter J. Begent and Hubert Chesshyre, *The Most Noble Order of the Garter: 650 Years* (London, 1999), pp. 234–5.

[20] The Garter processions from London to Windsor had become so flamboyant that the knights for installation in 1597 were ordered to limit their trains to fifty attendants. Stephanie Trigg, *Shame and Honor: A Vulgar History of the Order of the Garter* (Philadelphia, 2012), p. 153. On the Garter entertainments that year, see Giorgio Melchiori, *Shakespeare's Garter Plays: Edward III to The Merry Wives of Windsor* (Newark, DE, 1994), ch. 5.

[21] George Peele, *The Honour of the Garter* (London, 1593), sigs. C4r, D1r.

[22] George Chapman, in Ben Jonson, *Sejanus His Fall* (1605), ed. P. J. Ayres (Manchester, 1990), p. 60; Hotson, *Shakespeare*, pp. 156–8.

[23] William Camden, *Remains Concerning Britain* (London, 1605), ed. R. D. Dunn (Toronto, 1984), pp. 149, 490. When the 9th Earl died in 1632 the inventory for Petworth showed that many family rooms had green hangings marked with white crescents (even the brewhouse kept a half-moon branding iron). G. R. Batho, ed., *The Household Papers of Henry Percy, Ninth Earl of Northumberland (1564–1632)*, Camden Third Series 93 (London, 1962), pp. 114, 117, 118.

[24] Mark Nicholls, 'Percy, Henry, Ninth Earl of Northumberland (1564–1632)', *ODNB*, www.oxforddnb.com/view/article/21939?docPos=10, accessed 6 November 2014.

shall runn, / Beyond the Moone, to make thy Moone a Sunne!'²⁵ The rebellious inflections of the crescent continue in a conflated version of the two parts of *Henry IV*, put together for an amateur performance at some point after 1613. The most substantial change to the original substituted, for three lines by Henry on the Holy Land ('over whose acres walked those blessed feet, / Which fourteen hundred years ago were nailed / For our advantage on the bitter cross' (*1 Henry IV*, 1.1. 25–7)), nine lines on the king's longing to assume the honours of the opposition:

> And force proude Mahomett from Palestine.
> The high aspiring Cresant of the turke,
> Wee'll plucke into a lower orbe, and then
> Humbling her borrowed Pride to th' English lyon,
> With labour and with honour wee'le fetch there
> A sweating laurell from the glorius East
> And plant new jemms on royall Englands crowne.
> We'll pitch our honores att the sonnes uprise
> and sell our selves or winn a glorious prize
>
> (1 Henry IV, appendix 3, p. 350)

The vocabulary used picks up the fight between the physical badges in the rest of *1 Henry IV*: a crescent will be reduced to an orb lower than the sun, its honours plucked off to make a new crest for the crown.

1 Henry IV's planetary references are usually read from the point of view of the victor. The regular use of imagery associated with the heraldic royal badges of Richard II and Henry IV – sunbursts, suns in splendour, and clouded suns – has long been noted.²⁶ As Hal reflects on himself as a sun which permits clouds to smother it before it breaks forth (1.2.187–93), he pre-empts his father's memory about how Richard failed to shadow his 'sun-like majesty' (3.2.79), so merely tiring the eyes of onlookers, rather than dazzling them with brief glimpses of royalty. When Falstaff plays the King he teases Hal about whether the Prince can be a true 'son of England', for could a 'blessed sun of heaven prove a micher'? (2.4.399, 397–8). Vernon's account of Hal and his men before the Battle of Shrewsbury carries on the theme: 'Glittering in golden coats like images . . . / gorgeous as the sun

at midsummer' (4.1.99,101), an enthusiasm hushed by Hotspur as 'worse than the sun in March' (4.1.110). The King's advice to Hal to act 'like a comet', to steal 'all courtesy from heaven', so as to 'pluck allegiance from men's hearts, /. . . Even in the presence of the crowned King' (3.2.47, 50, 52–4), sees allegiance as a disputed physical favour, to be snatched by the Lancasters. As in the Dering manuscript, the King unwittingly echoes Hotspur's determination to 'pluck' honour from the face of the moon and 'out of this nettle, danger, [to] pluck this flower, safety' (2.3.8–9). The passage is approvingly cited by an anonymous common-placer, picking out bits from *1 Henry IV* sometime before 1603 (now BL Additional MS 64078): 'As he may pluck allegiance from mens harts even in the presence of ye Queene' is noted (daringly resexing the monarch to fit the circumstances).²⁷

Some commentators find that the Prince's emblem of the sun naturally evokes Falstaff's counter-emblem of the moon. Falstaff's self-description (perhaps sketched in the tavern's 'Half-moon' chamber, 2.4.26) is as one who goes 'by the moon and the seven stars, and not by Phoebus' (1.2.13–14), one of 'Diana's foresters . . . minions of the moon' (1.2.24–5), amongst whom Hal ironically places himself in lamenting how 'the fortune of us that are the moon's men doth ebb and flow like the sea, being governed, as the sea is, by the moon' (1.2.30–2). But the rebels in the ranks above Falstaff also ebb and flow with the moon, plucking honour from it, seizing crescents of land in its shape, and so, in the King's view, waxing ripe to be forced to 'move in that obedient orb again / Where you did give a fair and natural light,/ And be no more an exhaled meteor' (5.1.17–19). The 9th Earl of Northumberland knew one of

---

²⁵ John Davis, *Humours Heav'n on Earth* (1609), sig. A2v.

²⁶ For instance, James Hoyle, 'Some Emblems in Shakespeare's Henry IV Plays', *ELH*, 38 (1971), 512–27; Saxon Walker, 'Mime and Heraldry in *Henry IV Part 1*', *English*, 11 (1956), 91–6; pp. 95–6.

²⁷ Hilton Kelliher, 'Contemporary Manuscript Extracts from Shakespeare's *Henry IV Part I*', *English Manuscript Studies 1100–1700*, 1 (1989), 144–81; pp. 157, 173.

these sections of *1 Henry IV* well enough to refer to it fleetingly in a letter to the Earl of Salisbury in 1628: they should deal 'in a straight line, without turnings and windings, as Henry Hottspurre would have it when Mortimer and he devided England in a mappe' (referring to the passage in which Hotspur claims that 'A huge half-moon' has been cut from his proposed share of the land, by the curve of the river Trent, 3.1.98).[28] The climax of the battle between the two badges comes when Hal and Hotspur fight, for 'Two stars keep not their motion in one sphere' (5.4.64). With the disappearance of Hotspur go both the references to concrete badges of honour and to the moon. They do not reappear in the second part of the play (performed in 1597–8), bar in a 'particular ballad' which Falstaff threatens if his deed of honour is overlooked, where 'I in the clear sky of fame o'ershine you as much as the full moon doth the cinders of the element' (4.3.50–2).[29]

In fact, Falstaff's coat of arms would not bear much scrutiny. A standard heraldic topos is to list the dishonourable acts which 'abate' (or 'rebate') an achievement of arms. Guillim, Bossewell and Legh give nine causes of abatement: boasting of some valiant act which was never performed, killing a prisoner after he asks for quarter, lying to the sovereign or commander-in-chief, cowardice, adultery, drunkenness, revoking a challenge given or accepted, mistreating a woman, and treason.[30] In *1 Henry IV*, Falstaff energetically and comprehensively works his way down the first eight of the nine reasons for abatement, in the three fields of 'action' which he sees: Boar's Head, Gad's Hill and Shrewsbury. Take, for instance, the first cause of abatement ('too much boasting of himself in martiall actes'), which Legh exemplifies in the behaviour of 'Sir William Pounder, muche bragging of his knighthood, who semed to bee a Lyon, by countenaunce, but in his heart, was no lesse than a fearefull Hare'.[31] Falstaff boasts to the Prince about Gad's Hill (seven of the eleven assailants taken on by Falstaff himself, but 'the lion will not touch the true prince' (2.4.263)). The other reasons follow on: stabbing the already-dead Hotspur, lying to the king about who had killed him (Hal

comments that 'if a lie may do thee grace / I'll gild it' (5.4.157–8)), a 'coward on instinct' (2.4.264) at both Gad's Hill and Shrewsbury, pretending to be dead when Douglas challenges him, whoring, drunk on the battlefield and at the tavern (2.4. 515–28, 5.3.56), and filching from the Hostess (3.3. 65–74). These 'vices' of sluggishness or half-heartedness in chivalry are punished, in heraldry, by the removal or addition of charges on the coat of arms.

But Falstaff never ventures on the last and greatest cause of abatement of an achievement: treason. The legal consequence of this offence is attainder; the heraldic consequence is that 'the dignitie [of the escutcheon] is not blemished only in some points ... but is essentially annihilated in the whole', says Guillim.[32] Ferne describes how 'the Armes of Traytors and Rebels may be defaced and removed from all places wheresoever they were fixt or set: neither be their children or sequell suffered to beare the same againe, except there happen a restauracion, or new repaire of the bloud, to be made up by the free grace of the Soveraigne'. He gets warmer: 'so jealous is a soveraigne prince of the safety of his country, his person & state, that as God threatneth to inflict punishment unto a 3. and 4. generation of those, which by Idolatarie, and false worship, have sought to diminish the glorie of his Godhead: so earthly Princes do with justice punish the offsprings, and generations of Traytors'.[33] As Guillim gravely states, eight of the abatements can be reversed, by true descendants of a false knight, but the issue of

---

[28] Helen H. Sandison, 'The Ninth Earl of Northumberland Quotes his Ancestor Hotspur', *Review of English Studies*, 12 (1936), 71–5; p. 75.

[29] William Shakespeare, *The Second Part of King Henry IV*, ed. A. R. Humphreys, Arden Shakespeare Second Series (London, 1966).

[30] Gerard Legh, *Accedens of Armorie* (London, 1597), 70v–74r; John Guillim, *A Display of Heraldrie* (1610), pp. 31–6. John Bossewell terms these vices unfitting gentlemen, rather than abatements, in *Workes of Armorie* (London, 1597), p. 9r.

[31] Legh, *Armorie*, p. 71v.   [32] Guillim, *Heraldrie*, p. 35.

[33] John Ferne, *The Blazon of Gentrie* (London, 1586), pp. 267, 275–6.

those convicted of high treason can never regain the family's achievements. An attack on the sovereign state is 'not so much offensive against the person of the Prince, as it is against the Majestie of the Eternall God, whose Image he beareth. And the welfare of the Subjects depending on the safety of the Soveraigne, the danger intended to the one, hath in it a guilt of endammaging the lives of millions'. It can never be forgotten. Guillim prescribes that the offender's coat armour be razed, his shield reversed, his spear trunked, his spurs hewn from his heels, his sword broken over his helm, his crest divided, his horse's tail and mane docked, any statues of him pulled down, the issue of his blood attainted, his body destroyed, his family name ended, and his possessions given to another, 'so that by such his degredation, he receiveth farre greater shame ... then' ever hee received honour by his advancement'. [34] Nor is this a bygone punishment, Guillim says, remembering how the family of the man who murdered Henri IV had recently been deprived of their surname.

The ceremony of degradation from the Order of the Garter provided an exciting instance of abatement for the heraldry texts. [35] Henry VIII's statutes for the order codified three absolute 'points of reproach': heresy, flight from battle, and treason. If a knight was deemed to have committed one of these, then Companions were summoned to the Chapel of St George at Windsor Castle. The Garter King of Arms read out the Instrument for the Publication of Degradation, which required that the offender's 'Arms, and Ensignes, and Achievements' be 'expelled', so that 'all other Noble men, thereby may take Example'. [36] As he did so, one of the heralds climbed a ladder to the top of the knight's stall, and tossed down into the quire the offender's banner (which displayed his coat of arms), crest, mantling and sword. Then the Officers of Arms kicked the achievements out of the quire through the chapel, out of the door, across the lower ward, and into the castle ditch. This final humiliation was sometimes curtailed as a mark of the monarch's clemency (Lord Cobham's achievements, for instance, did not get as far as the ditch, on 12 February 1604). After the achievement

had been thrown down, the stall plate was removed. Only the Register of the Garter remained to show that the offender was ever a Companion, and this was marked in the margin of his name with 'Vah proditur' ('Fie on you traitor'). The ceremony was infrequent, since execution tended to come before the next meeting of the order. Just three knights were degraded in Elizabeth's reign, one of whom was Thomas Percy, the 7th Earl of Northumberland, on 27 November 1569, and the other, the 2nd Earl of Essex, on 25 January 1601. [37]

Stephanie Trigg argues that the legend about the inception of the order, and the rituals surrounding the election or degradation of knights, are less concerned with any feelings of shame in the courtiers and more with the social and political power of the king, which has to induce the effect of shame. 'In contrast to shaming in a spiritual or religious context, chivalric shaming is primarily the activity of the shamer, not the shamed', and is an instrument of power. [38] In Richard II (first performed in about 1595), Bolingbroke complains that the King has reduced him in this way: 'From my own windows torn my household coat, / Rased out my imprese, leaving me no sign / Save men's opinions and my living blood / To show the world I am a gentleman' (3.1.24–7). [39] By contrast to Richard – and despite repeatedly invoking the register of heraldic achievement – the Lancasters are never

---

[34] Guillim, Heraldrie, pp. 35, 36. See also Edmund Spenser, The Faerie Queene, ed. A. C. Hamilton (London, 1977), 5.3.37, 6.7.26–7.

[35] William Segar and John Selden lovingly detail the medieval and current ceremonies. See William Segar, Honor Military, and Civill (London, 1602), pp. 54–5, 75; and John Selden, Titles of Honor (London, 1614), pp. 338–9. Ferne refers to the ritual without specifying it as a Garter ceremony (Gentrie, p. 276).

[36] Begent and Chesshyre, Garter, p. 270, and on the absolute points of reproach in the statutes, pp. 63–4, 71–2. Henry also required that Companions be gentlemen of blood, for three generations back.

[37] Fonblanque, Annals, vol. 2, pp. 49–51.

[38] Trigg, Shame, p. 133.

[39] William Shakespeare, King Richard II, ed. C. R. Forker, Arden Shakespeare Third Series (London, 2002).

able to produce this shame effect in their retainers, be they noble (the Percys) or parodic (Falstaff). Indeed, the family are vulnerable to charges that they themselves cannot honourably bear the royal coat of arms. The punishment of abatement for treason is reserved not for Falstaff, not for Hotspur, but for King Henry. By deposing Richard II, Henry has made his issue 'disabled to succeede in bloud', as Ferne puts it.[40] The dominant imagery in the second part of *Henry IV* is that of illness specifically caused by corruption of the blood breaking through the skin (rather than the weakness consequent on wounds, bruises, and broken limbs, which are the normal effects of civil war, referred to in the opening lines of *1 Henry IV*). *2 Henry IV* laments over 'the body of our kingdom / How foul it is', what rank diseases grow, / ... near the heart of it' (3.1. 38–40), how 'distemper'd' (3.1.41), that it 'breaks into corruption' (3.1.77) and is full of a 'burning fever, / And must bleed for it; of which disease / Our late King Richard being infected died' (4.1. 56–8), how 'The blood weeps from my heart / When I do shape ... / [The] rotten times' (4.4. 58–60), and how even the crown might 'infect my blood with joy' (4.5.169).[41] On his deathbed, the King refers simultaneously to his act of usurpation and to the stain on his coat: 'all the soil of the achievement goes / With me into the earth. It seem'd in me / But as an honour snatch'd with boist'rous hand'. Yet he hopes that Hal will have an unblemished coat, since as son he 'the garland wear'st successively' (*2 Henry IV*, 4.5.189–91, 201). Shakespeare transfers the latter phrase from the Prince's terse statement, in Holinshed, that since the father got the crown, the son can keep it without challenge (4.5.201n). Reassigning the comment emphasizes how Henry still looks to a primary technique to create the effect of legitimacy (where chivalric honours are a shorthand of history), even though the Lancaster coat has been permanently abated for treason.

There may be a further contrast between the Percys and the Lancasters, in their frequent references to the Crusades. At first Shakespeare follows Holinshed in crediting the truth of Henry's determination to recover Jerusalem from the Infidel (as does the Dering version). Henry starts by hoping warring sides will unite in marching 'As far as to the sepulchre of Christ / (Whose solider now, under whose blessed cross / We are impressed and engaged to fight)' (*1 Henry IV*, 1.1. 19–21), and refers to 'our business for the Holy Land' (1.1.48), and again, 'Our holy purpose to Jerusalem' (1.1.101). The issue returns in *2 Henry IV*, where Henry at first still speaks of the English Civil War as a distraction from his true and holy purpose 'unto the Holy Land' (3.1.108). Holinshed speaks of the king's 'roiall iournie as he pretended to take into the holie land' (*2 Henry IV*, appendix 1, p. 200), 'pretended' here meaning 'intended'. But Shakespeare suddenly picks up the other meaning of pretence, departing from Holinshed. When the dying king speaks to his son, he abruptly reframes the Crusade, now seen as a way to extinguish the effects of his own treason,

> To lead out many to the Holy Land,
> Lest rest and lying still might make them look
> Too near unto my state   (4.5.210–12)

But even this pragmatic reason is undercut by a banal mistake over the title of a room:

> It hath been prophesied to me, many years,
> I should not die but in Jerusalem,
> Which vainly I suppos'd the Holy Land.
> But bear me to that chamber; there I'll lie;
> In that Jerusalem shall Harry die
>   (4.5.236–40)

Admittedly, the practical problem of getting a corpse offstage means that the dying often ask to be moved, but the passage goes out of its way to emphasize the anti-climax. It contrasts with the honourable action of the Crusader William de Percy, buried near Jerusalem and recalled in his

---

[40] Ferne, *Gentrie*, p. 267.

[41] Holinshed carefully reports that though the king's weakness was rumoured to be leprosy it was in fact an apoplexy (Shakespeare, *2 Henry IV*, ed. Humphreys, pp. 200–1), to be treated by blood-letting. Phillip Barrough, *The Methode of Phisicke* (1583), pp. 25–6.

family badge, and perhaps by the actions of a more recent 'Crusader', the 7th Earl, Thomas Percy.

If the coat of arms will not do for the child of a traitor, what of the badge? Although commentary on *Henry V* (performed in 1599) tends to discuss the play's exchanges of gloves and leeks in the same breath, the gage and the badge have different functions in heraldry. A gage is an improvized synecdoche of a man's honour, a part of his clothing or equipment caught up at a moment, to offer as a visible reminder that action will follow his stated intention.[42] This temporary expedient marks a private exchange of promises, usually that the wearers will fight each other when a suitable time comes (though sometimes, John Kerrigan points out, subsequent circumstances will make it more honourable not to redeem the pledge).[43] By contrast, a badge is an enduring sign of commitment to a public cause, which may be worn by the family and all grades of retainer. Henry's aim (giving up the coat of arms as lost) is to persuade each noble to exchange his gage, not for another man's gage but for Henry's badge (and preferably not the one that the Dauphin offers, the tennis ball).

As prince, Hal had been agile in evading signs thrust upon him. *Richard II* starts with Bolingbroke and Mowbray ritually casting down their gages before each other, a scene repeated with ironic hyperbole before Henry, when Aumerle's faction hurl gages at Henry's supporters. Holinshed specified these tokens as hoods. Shakespeare generalizes this: they are 'gages' (1.1.69, 146, 161, 174, 176, 186; 4.1.26, 35, 47, 84) or 'the manual seal of death', 'my honour's pawn' and 'my bond of faith' (4.1.26 and note, 56, 71, 77). In both scenes, the action peters out after the monarch declares that the 'differences shall all rest under gage' (4.1.87, 106). Private signs interrupting public affairs will never be ransomed. The Prince treats such signs bathetically. Hotspur tells the King how Hal has refused to attend a noble tournament; he would rather 'unto the stews, / And from the common'st creature pluck a glove / And wear it as a favour' (5.3.16–18).

Gloves provided the income with which John Shakespeare, a glover and whittawer since at least

1556, attempted to acquire a coat of arms, in around 1576. Biographers assume that William (not John) renewed the application in 1596 and extended it in 1599 (the years in which the second tetralogy was performed). Applications were expensive, particularly if the claim was as fragile as that of the Shakespeares. Although the family received a grant of arms on 20 October 1596, theirs was one of the instances later used to cite Garter for awarding coats to base and ignoble persons, and in 1599 they were refused permission to incorporate the Arden connection into the coat.[44] C. W. Scott-Giles pointed out that Shakespeare's king makes the unusual offer (4.3. 62–3) that the real Henry V did to his soldiers. By a writ of 1417, in the first attempt to forbid the assumption of arms unless acquired by descent or assigned by due authority, the king specifically exempted those who fought with him at Agincourt.[45] Even in the 1590s a herald might make a standard enquiry about such Agincourt service, if other parts of an application for a coat seemed to lack substance.

In *Henry V*, the King first has to deflate any emblem that could be preferred before the sovereign's. The night before Agincourt, the King first engages his glove to Williams, after the battle retrieves it again by command, and then gives it back to Williams, filled with crowns. Williams's glove is engaged to the King before the battle, and after it handed by Henry to Fluellen, with a back story that Henry had 'plucked' the favour from the helm of the Duke of Alençon, in a noble hand-to-hand duel (a detail about the gage altered from

---

[42] Ferne, *Gentrie*, pp. 312–17; William Segar, *The Booke of Honor and Armes* (1590), pp. 75–85.

[43] Kerrigan, 'Oaths', p. 562.

[44] S. Schoenbaum, *William Shakespeare: a Documentary Life* (Oxford, 1975), pp. 166–73; Katherine Duncan-Jones, *Ungentle Shakespeare: Scenes from his Life* (London, 2001), pp. 85–6.

[45] A. R. Myers, ed., *English Historical Documents, 1327–1485* (London, 1969), p. 1117; C. W. Scott-Giles, *Shakespeare's Heraldry* (London, 1950), p. 121; William Shakespeare, *Henry V*, ed. T. W. Craik, Arden Shakespeare Third Series (London, 1995).

Holinshed, 4.7.152–3n.). Fluellen pronounces this to be 'great honours' (4.7.157), and Henry is sure a fight will follow, for Williams 'By his blunt bearing ... will keep his word' (4.7.173). So far so legitimate, under the rules of heraldry. Ferne explains that using a proxy in challenges across ranks is as honourable as it is necessary, since great men must be open to challenge (or they might become tyrannical) but, at the same time, discipline must be maintained.[46] Henry specifically checks this point (and in doing so nearly lets out the secret that 'the answer of his degree' to Williams, made as though he is a soldier in the ranks, is not that which his real rank would require or permit as a 'gentleman of great sort' (4.7.133–4)). Then, assembling as many people as possible to view the scene, Henry publicly dishonours the gage by not following through on the fight, but instead paying off the challenger handsomely and tossing the gage itself back to Williams with a casual 'wear it for an honour in thy cap / Till I do challenge it' (4.8. 60–1), which is as good as saying never, since he does not allow the challenge when there is plenty of opportunity.

Marilyn Williamson and John Kerrigan argue that Henry, belatedly realizing that his status debars him from fighting in person, ransoms his word by shuffling the fight onto Fluellen, and tipping Williams.[47] But this does not account for the very public way in which Henry makes sure that every-one gathers together to witness that the gage is a sign of merely personal honour. The King wants it replaced by a national badge, one that he and any other 'common man' (4.8.52) can wear and be accountable for. In John Selden's words, Henry wants to exchange the sign of a relationship between 'Peers' of the 'Greater Nobilitie' for a sign of 'Paritie' between the 'Lesse Nobilitie' of knights, squires, gentlemen and yeomen.[48] So he reaches for the leek with its minimum sign-up qualification: the place where its bearer's 'limbs were made' (3.1.26).

On three occasions in *Henry V* leeks are worn in caps. Pistol, talking to the Welshman 'Harry Le Roy' the night before Agincourt, threatens to knock Fluellen's 'leek about his pate / Upon Saint Davy's day', earning the stern warning 'Do not you wear your dagger in your cap that day, lest he knock that about yours' (4.1. 55–8). After the battle, Fluellen reminds Henry that under his grandfather 'the Welshmen did good service in a garden where leeks did grow, wearing leeks in their Monmouth caps, which your majesty know to this hour is an honourable badge of the service; and I do believe your majesty takes no scorn to wear the leek upon Saint Tavy's day'. He gets a warm response to this auda-cious reminder that the King is a brother Welshman, fighting in a common cause: 'I wear it for a memorable honour, / For I am Welsh' (4.7. 97–104). Back in London after victory, when Pistol mocks the leek in Fluellen's cap, Fluellen beats him with it, forces him to eat it, and offers a leek-skin plaster. Serves Pistol right for disrespecting 'a memorable trophy of predeceased valour', Gower observes (5.1.72–3).[49] The scenes, Allison Outland notes, are generally dismissed as knockabout, mates teasing each other after a tense mission, but could be read as a patronizing game to put the lower ranks back in their place (where Pistol acts as Williams did, and Fluellen as Henry).[50] Megan Lloyd attri-butes the scene to irritation with Welsh 'shoving' in 1590s London.[51]

When the French are not chatting about their equipment (guidons, banners, horses and armour – and 'are those suns or stars on it ...' (3.7.

---

[46] Ferne, *Gentrie*, pp. 320–1; see also *Richard II*, 4.1.22–30.

[47] Marilyn L. Williamson, 'The Episode with Williams in *Henry V*', *Studies in English Literature, 1500–1900*, 9 (1969), 275–82; John Kerrigan, 'Oaths, Threats, and *Henry V*', *Review of English Studies*, 63 (2012), 551–71; pp. 562–4.

[48] Selden, *Titles of Honor*, p. 344.

[49] On the violent assertion of Welsh nationalism in London in the 1590s, see W. P. Griffith, 'Tudor Prelude', in *The Welsh in London, 1500–2000*, ed. Emrys Jones (Cardiff, 2001), p. 26.

[50] Allison M. Outland, '"Eat a leek": Welsh Corrections, English Conditions, and British Cultural Communion', in *This England, that Shakespeare: New Angles on Englishness and the Bard*, ed. Willy Maley and Margaret Tudeau-Clayton (Farnham, 2010), ch. 4.

[51] Megan S. Lloyd, *Speak it in Welsh: Wales and the Welsh Language in Shakespeare* (Lanham, 2007), ch. 4.

70–2)), they are gloating about how a captured Henry will 'for achievement offer us his ransom' (3.5.60), a phrase echoed by Henry with 'achieve me, and then sell my bones' (4.3.91). Ransoms or ramsoms (both forms are common) is a species of wild garlic (*Alium ursinsum*), which with the other members of the onion family was long valued as a good 'poore man's treacle' (healing balm).[52] Fluellen follows conventional medical advice when he claims that raw leek skins mashed with salt will cure Pistol's head wound. As food too, this plant family was popular (and thought even healthy, if cooked).[53] Biblical commentaries expounded on how, in Numbers 11: 5, the 'murmuring Israelites' longed after leeks, onions, and garlic, desired not only 'by people of low degree and base calling, but of noblemen and wealthy personages also' (unusual in a period when one marker of rank was whether meat was eaten as a dietary staple or an occasional flavouring).[54] Everyone could afford garlic, onions and leeks ('not worth a leek' was a common saying). So Henry reaches for leeks as well known to heal wounds, and cheap enough for all ranks to eat, to plaster on themselves, and even to wear as a sign (unlike the expensive coat of arms).

Where on the clothing the leek is worn is also relevant. Henry is not Welsh by descent but by place of birth, Monmouth. Fluellen's mention of the Monmouth cap brings back the seven mocking references to 'Harry Monmouth' by his enemies, who cannot bring themselves to call him Prince of Wales (*1 Henry IV*, 5.2.49, 5.4.58; *2 Henry IV*, 0.29, 1.1.19, 1.1.109, 1.3.83, 2.3.45). These seven allusions are countered by seven repetitions of 'Monmouth' by Fluellen, in comparing Henry to Alexander (4.7.11–51). Monmouth was excluded by the 1536 and 1543 Acts of Union from participating in the Welsh Courts of Great Sessions, and included in the Oxford assize circuit, making it necessary to refer in many subsequent statutes to 'Wales and Monmouthshire'.[55] Monmouth men effectively had dual nationality. In taking a leek for his Monmouth cap, Henry is taking an inclusive, cheap and healing ransom for his achievement.

The Tudor rose (if not the shamrock and the thistle) could make a similar claim, but it is not mentioned by the play. So is the audience being invited to recognize who, in the late 1590s, was conspicuously wearing the green and white Percy colours, in the leek? A. E. Hughes finds little evidence that the leek was seen as a national emblem before the 1590s. He notes that Mary Tudor's privy purse accounts show payment for a leek presented to her by the royal bodyguard (the yeoman of the King's Guard) on St David's Day in 1537, 1538 and 1544, that is, over precisely the period in which the Acts of Union were passed. The same amount was paid to the Guard each time, suggesting to Hughes that it was a custom that the leek be worn on that day.[56] However – even after admitting that negative evidence is always incomplete – it is surprising that no later evidence of wearing the leek appears in sources where such an emblem would be noted. There is no record in the ordinary of Welsh arms that a leek was borne as a badge, or on a coat, or as a crest.[57] There is evidence that St George's Day was kept solemnly at court, where the red cross and the red and white rose were much in evidence, but none that St David's Day ever was.[58] The same is true outside court, in the

---

[52] Rembert Dodoens, *A Niewe Herball*, trans. Henry Lyte (London, 1578), pp. 636–9, 641–2; Anglicus Bartholomeus, *Batman Uppon Bartholome*, trans. John Trevisa (London, 1582), pp. 313v–314r; Barrough, *Phisicke*, p. 33; A. E. Hughes, 'The Welsh National Emblem: Leek or Daffodil?', *Y Cymmrodor*, 26 (1916), p. 152.

[53] Joan Fitzpatrick, *Food in Shakespeare: Early Modern Dietaries and the Plays* (Aldershot, 2007), pp. 38–44.

[54] Levinus Lemnius, *An Herbal for the Bible*, trans. Thomas Newton (London, 1587), p. 162. Hotspur reaches for 'cheese and garlic' as the food of the poor (*1 Henry IV*, 3.1.158).

[55] George Owen, *The Dialogue of the Government of Wales (1594)*, ed. J. Gwynfor Jones (Cardiff, 2010), pp. 83, 160 n. 115; Geraint H. Jenkins, *A Concise History of Wales* (Cambridge, 2007), pp. 146–8.

[56] Hughes, 'Leek or Daffodil?', 147–90; pp. 156–9.

[57] M. P. Siddons, *The Development of Welsh Heraldry*, 4 vols. (Aberystwyth, 1991–93), vol. 3, pp. xi–xxiii.

[58] John Nichols, *John Nichols's The Progresses and Public Processions of Queen Elizabeth I: A New Edition of the Early*

Welsh volumes of the Records of Early English Drama.[59] Although Robert Dudley, the Earl of Leicester, had extensive holdings in north Wales, his household accounts show no sign of such celebrations.[60] Henry VIII used a red dragon, not a leek, when acknowledging his Welsh ancestry, a practice followed by his daughters.[61] Elizabeth's personal badges were displayed during her travels (for instance, at her reception into Norwich in 1578), and marked on gifts to her (for instance, embroidered on the prayer book Sir William Cecil gave her as a New Year's gift), but there are no representations of leeks, even on gifts from Welshmen (though many other vegetables and fruits appear, from fennel to figs).[62] Major histories, like Holinshed's *Chronicles*, do not note that the Tudor Welsh wear the leek. Looking at printed fiction, J. O. Bartley cites the Welsh language, pride of birth, musicality and love of mountains (and the sheep and goats on them, and hence the cheese and wool from them) as the usual signifiers of a Welshman up to the mid 1590s.[63] In *1 Henry IV* and *The Merry Wives of Windsor* (performed at some point between 1597 and 1602), for instance, Glendower and Evans are notable for their Anglo-Welsh locutions, their love of music and their interest in genealogy, but cheese and garlic, not leeks, are the foodstuffs mentioned.[64] Then suddenly, from 1597, this rather outmoded symbol becomes widely visible as an emblem of Wales (to the English, at least).[65] This is so even when it would be more decorous not to put a smelly vegetable next to dainty flowers, as for instance in Michael Drayton's *England's Heroicall Epistles* (1597), where Owen Tudor woos Katherine, the widow of Henry V, by offering to unite the leek with the lily of France and the rose of England.[66]

What changed in the late 1590s to make the leek such a prominent badge? Editors dismiss Fluellen's anecdote that wearing the leek commemorates previous military service by the Welsh under the English.[67] However, they credit Francis Osborne's claim that the leek was customarily worn on St David's Day by the 2nd Earl of Essex. The anecdote first appears in the life of Essex given in Francis Osborne's *Miscellany of Sundry Essayes*

(1659). One must be cautious here. Essex had been executed when Osborne was 8 years of age (over half a century before), and Osborne was not at court until an adult, so presumably he was going by report.[68] Nonetheless, that report seems credible. Osborne was in the service of the Pembroke family, becoming Master of Horse to William Herbert, the 3rd Earl of Pembroke. The family had vast estates in Wales, and the 2nd Earl headed the Council of Wales and the Marches until his death in 1601. Osborne specifies that his information comes from discussing Essex's situation with those present at the

---

Modern Sources, ed. Elizabeth Goldring et al., 5 vols. (Oxford, 2014), vol. 1, p. 180; vol. 3, pp. 251–5.

[59] *Records of Early English Drama: Cheshire, including Chester*, ed. Elizabeth Baldwin, Lawrence M. Clopper and David Mills, 2 vols. (London, 2007); *Chester*, ed. Lawrence M. Clopper (Manchester, 1979); *Wales*, ed. D. N. Klausner (London, 2005). Even in Wales, celebrations for St George's Day are recorded, but none for St David's Day. See *Wales*, ed. Klausner, pp. 306–7.

[60] Simon Adams, ed., *Household Accounts and Disbursement Books of Robert Dudley, Earl of Leicester, 1558–1561, 1584–1586* (Cambridge, 1995).

[61] Hughes, 'Emblem', p. 163.

[62] Nichols, *Progresses*, vol. 2, p. 792; Jane A. Lawson, ed., *The Elizabethan New Year's Gift Exchanges: 1559–1603* (Oxford, 2013), 63.100.

[63] J. O. Bartley, *Teague, Shenkin, and Sawney: Being an Historical Study of the Earliest Irish, Welsh, and Scottish Characters in English Plays* (Cork, 1954), ch. 3.

[64] *1 Henry IV*, 3.1; William Shakespeare, *The Merry Wives of Windsor*, ed. Giorgio Melchiori, Arden Shakespeare Third Series (London, 2000), 1.2.12, 3.1.11–29, 5.5.136–42.

[65] All Bartley's examples are taken from after 1597. Possibly St David's Day, too, became more noticeable: Rowland White, the steward of Sir Robert Sidney, dates his 1 March letter in 1596 as just that, but his letters on that day in 1597 and 1599 are dated 'our St Davies Day'. Henry Sydney, ed., *Letters and Memorials of State, in the Reigns of Queen Mary . . . [to] Oliver's Usurpation*, 2 vols. (London, 1746), vol. 2, pp. 23–7, 93, 173.

[66] Michael Drayton, *Englands Heroicall Epistles* (1597), p. 40r.

[67] Though Iolo Morganwg cites an undated legend that wearing a leek commemorates the battle of Crécy, Hughes says dryly that it is 'somewhat remarkable' that no earlier references to the legend can be found ('Emblem', pp. 164–8).

[68] 'Osborne, Francis (1593–1659)', *ODNB*, www.oxforddnb.com/view/article/20875?docPos=1, accessed 6 January 2014.

time. Essex – who in his first year at Cambridge had studied Legh's *Armorie* – was a master of using *imprese* to make political points, and his 'publications' of this sort remained in their viewers' memories for many years afterwards.[69] In an essay dealing with 'Politicall deductions from Essex's death', Osborne (a commonwealth man himself) considers that Essex was so popular in Wales that many Welshmen would have risen with him in 1601, or at least sent him safely to Ireland, to join other rebels. Osborne then adds to this counter-factual history that the Earl's

security might have been more, and losse lesse, had he gone into Wales, when he passed through London, where he had great love both by Inheritance from his Father (a good Landlord) and his own purchase, always of a liberall Nature. Nor did he fail to wear a Leek on St David's Day, but besides, would upon all occasions vindicate the Welch Inhabitants, and own them for his Countrymen, as Queen Elizabeth usually was wont, upon the first of March.[70]

As far as the queen goes, the last phrase might allow one to infer that Elizabeth too wore the leek on 1 March, or that on that day she acknowledged the Welsh as kin, or, alternatively, that she did both on that day (but only on that day). Osborne's anecdote is not necessarily an uncomplicated statement of royal support for a Welsh folk custom. By contrast, Osborne's interlocutors remember Essex as aggressively pro-Welsh ('vindicate'), and someone who made a point of wearing the leek ('nor did he fail').

Wearing the leek regains some of its political connotations if it is seen as specifically associated with Essex, at a time when the regime was nervous of his military power and his popularity. When Shakespeare's Henry attaches the leek to himself, he brings it under sovereign control, making a personal badge into a national emblem.

Studies of the representations of Essex generally discuss him in terms of Ireland, partly because Shakespeare gives a rare direct reference to contemporary events, in the allusion by the Act 5 Chorus to Essex's command of the invasion forces in 1599. Essex's father, too, had led a previous invasion of

Ireland. But contemporaries were equally as aware of the family's connections to Wales. The family fortunes had arisen with the appointment of Sir Walter Devereux, the great-grandfather of the 2nd Earl, to the Council of Wales and the Marches in 1513. By 1525 Devereux was seneschal chancellor and chamberlain to the household of Mary Tudor. The family continued to flourish in west Wales over the century. From boyhood, the 2nd Earl of Essex was attentive to the goodwill of his family's Welsh connections.[71] His stepfather, Leicester, took him on a tour of his north Wales estates in 1578. In 1584, at the family home of Lamphey, Pembrokeshire, Essex kept open house for his neighbours over the winter, and also fondly recalled the moments of 'contemplative retirednesse in Wales' (in his *Apologie* of 1600).[72] At Lamphey he established strong ties to his family's followers and servants, taking some of the household with him as servants when he arrived at court for his first prolonged and independent visit in late 1585. Throughout his political life, Essex stood up for his Welsh servants and put forward Welshmen for promotion. Essex's influence in Wales grew still further over the 1590s when the Lord President of the Council of Wales and the Marches, Sir Henry Herbert, 2nd Earl of Pembroke, fell into prolonged ill health.[73] In 1594

---

[69] P. Hammer, *The Polarization of Elizabethan Politics: the Political Career of Robert Devereux, Second Earl of Essex, 1585–1597* (Cambridge, 1999), pp. 29, 202–3, 214.

[70] Francis Osborne, *A Miscellany of Sundry Essayes ... Together with Politicall Deductions from the History of the Earl of Essex* (London, 1659), pp. 216–19. Welsh support for Essex, but not the anecdote about the leek, appears in Osborne's *Historical Memoires on the Reigns of Queen Elizabeth, and King James* (London, 1658), pp. 88–9.

[71] Hammer, *Essex*, pp. 23, 158, 272–9.

[72] Robert Devereux, Earl of Essex, *An Apologie of the Earle of Essex* (c. 1600), sig. A1v.

[73] 'Devereux of Lamphey, Pembs., Ystrad Ffin, Carms., Vaynor and Nantariba, Mont., Pencoyd, Brecknock', *Dictionary of Welsh Biography*, http://wbo.llgc.org.uk/en/s-DEVE-REU-1100.html?query=devereux&field=content, accessed 6 November 2014; 'Devereux, Robert, Second Earl of Essex (1565–1601)', *ODNB*, www.oxforddnb.com/view/article/7565?docPos=9, accessed 6 November 2014; Hammer, *Essex*, pp. 21, 35–66, 122,

Essex sealed the Pembrokeshire bond of association for the defence of the queen, and was appointed *custos rotulorum* for Pembrokeshire.[74] After this, although he did not visit Wales personally again, his colleagues on the Privy Council continued to hear a great deal about his Welsh estates, since Essex cited them as a pretext for withdrawing from court whenever he wanted to mark his displeasure at decisions made against his advice.[75]

Essex's two principal aides in military affairs were Welshmen. Roger Williams, born in Penrhos, Monmouthshire, was Essex's second-in-command of the cavalry at Tilbury in 1588. He allowed Essex to stow away on the 1589 mission to Lisbon (against the express orders of the queen), and was the supporter (then successor) to Essex, as commander of the English Army in France in 1592. Williams, personally courageous, and delighting in charges, rallies and single combat, was also an expert in the professional arts of war. His *Briefe Discourse of Warre* (1590) influentially argued that English forces should be reorganized along continental lines.[76] He died in 1595 with Essex at his side (leaving all his property to the earl). Essex gave instructions for his funeral (co-organized by Williams's cousin, Sir Gelly Meyrick), paid for it, and attended it in person. Son of the Bishop of Bangor, Meyrick had been brought up on his mother's estate near Lamphey, and attached himself to Essex from his university days onwards.[77] For all Essex's military ventures Meyrick organized supplies, sourced troops (mostly from south Wales, Radnorshire and Carmarthenshire), and administered their pay and the disposal of prizes. In return, Essex made him steward of his household in 1587, knighted him on the Cadiz expedition, and prompted Elizabeth to grant him extensive lands. Although Londoners disregarded Meyrick as Essex's factotum, and insulted him about his birth and upbringing, he was deemed powerful in Wales.[78] He twice sat as a member for Welsh constituencies, became deputy lieutenant for Radnorshire (against strong protest by the Earl of Pembroke), and was *custos rotulorum* for the county by 1599.[79]

Williams and Meyrick were key to how Essex worked his Welsh connections in raising troops.[80]

The usual method was for the queen and the Privy Council to order the county lieutenants to provide a certain number of men, equipped and armed. The temptation for the county lieutenants (and their pressmen) was to put local interests above national ones, and provide substandard troops and equipment (a possibility which Falstaff exploits (*1 Henry IV*, 4.2.10–47; *2 Henry IV*, 3.2.236–72)). For the 1599 Irish expedition, Essex was permitted to follow continental practice, and raise the troops himself. County lieutenants were asked to provide arms and equipment. Two of the four captains Essex used for this task were ordered to concentrate on Wales and the Marches, to find two-fifths of the total force.[81] Thus, over the four years in which the

---

297–8, 379–80; Alexandra Gajda, *The Earl of Essex and Late Elizabethan Political Culture* (Oxford, 2012), ch. 5.

[74] His sister Dorothy married the 9th Earl of Northumberland around 1595, though the initial good relations between the brothers-in-law were sour by 1597. See Fonblanque, *Annals*, 2.205; Hammer, *Essex*, p. 281.

[75] Sydney, *Memorials of State*, vol. 2, pp. 23–7.

[76] 'Williams, Sir Roger (1539/40–95)', *ODNB*, www.oxforddnb.com/view/article/29543?docPos=1, accessed 6 November 2014. The editor of Williams's work disputes the suggestion that Williams is a source study for Fluellen, given the latter is a conservative in military affairs, and the former a noted innovator in the new model tactics. Roger Williams, *The Works of Sir Roger Williams*, ed. John X. Evans (Oxford, 1972), pp. lxxvi, 158, 162.

[77] Hammer, *Essex*, pp. 26, 31; 'Meyrick, Sir Gelly (c. 1556–1601)', *ODNB*, www.oxforddnb.com/view/article/18639, accessed 11 March 2016.

[78] Michael McGarvie, *The Meyricks of Bush: The Story of a Pembrokeshire Family* (Glastonbury, 1988), ch. 2; David Mathew, *The Celtic Peoples and Renaissance Europe: A Study of the Celtic and Spanish Influences on Elizabethan History* (London, 1933), ch. 18.

[79] Neither man's coat bore a leek. The Meyricks of Bodorgan bore 'Gules, two porcupines passant Argent, armed Or'. Williams bore 'Argent, a dragon's head erased Vert, holding in his mouth a dexter human hand couped at the wrist, proper and bloody', Siddons, *Welsh Heraldry*, 2.381, 2.598–9.

[80] Mathew, *Celtic Peoples and Renaissance Europe*, pp. 336–59, 368–70.

[81] Neil Younger, 'The Practice and Politics of Troop-Raising: Robert Devereux, Second Earl of Essex, and the Elizabethan Regime', *English Historical Review*, 526 (2012), 566–91; Hammer, *Essex*, p. 127.

tetralogy was first performed, the Essex faction stood out as a distinctively Welsh group, expert in war, and able to supply and lead the large-scale military expeditions which the state felt it required to keep its borders intact. It was political sense to sport the Welsh badge.

More speculatively, one of the ways in which Essex built up this group might also be discerned as a motif of honour which is discussed in the plays. A major accusation against Essex, Paul Hammer argues, was that he courted from the public the sort of attention and warmth that was generally reserved for the monarch.[82] Hammer distinguishes between Essex's power base (drawing on structural relationships like that of landlord and tenant), which was relatively small for his rank, and his following, which was large, and needed to be nursed along by patronage, courtesy and explanation about the political positions he was taking.[83] Any play about deposition watched by the Essex group might well, Hammer thinks, echo warnings to Essex about not courting popularity over the head of the queen.[84] Shakespeare's Richard II acidly complains about Bolingbroke's manipulative courtesy to all ranks, but when the latter becomes king he recommends it as a tested political technique for amassing a following when one does not have a power base. Back from banishment, he had aimed to 'pluck allegiance from men's hearts / . . . Even in the presence of the crowned King' (1 Henry IV, 3.2.52–4), as the pre-1603 commonplacer of the play had noted.[85] Public notice here is a disputed favour or badge, which is to be plucked off the opposition. One wonders how many of the cheering Londoners lining four miles of streets to send Essex on his way to Ireland – three weeks after St David's Day in 1599 – wore the leek.[86]

To sum up: in *Henry V*, the tetralogy's search for a national badge, in preference to a dynastic achievement of arms or a personal gage of honour, concludes when the monarch translates the badge of a powerful faction into a national badge. But perhaps some thought should also have been given to the Percy moon as well as the Welsh leek. Two years later, on the afternoon before the Essex uprising, Sir Charles Percy, younger brother of the ninth Earl of Northumberland, commissioned Shakespeare's company to revive an old play about the deposition of Richard II.[87]

---

[82] Paul E. J. Hammer, '"The smiling crocodile": The Earl of Essex and Late Elizabethan "Popularity"', in *The Politics of the Public Sphere in Early Modern England*, ed. Peter Lake and Steven Pincus (Manchester, 2007), ch. 4; Hammer, *Essex*, pp. 270ff., 292ff.

[83] Shakespeare's Henry V, like Essex, justifies why he consorts with soldiers, 'a name that in my thoughts becomes me best', says the king (3.4.6); Essex, *Apologie*, sig. B3r.

[84] Paul E. J. Hammer, 'Shakespeare's *Richard II*, the Play of 7 February 1601, and the Essex Uprising', *Shakespeare Quarterly*, 59 (2008), 1–35.

[85] For instance, the letters that Essex sent to the lieutenants to equip these expeditions differ markedly from those usually sent. The latter stressed the facts and gave the rationale for the war. Essex's letters focused on the personal affection that any help given would show both the queen and him.

[86] Nichols, *Progresses*, ed. Goldring, vol. 4, pp. 70–1.

[87] E. A. Barnard, *New Links with Shakespeare* (Cambridge, 1930), pp. 65–6. Charles Percy had been knighted by Essex in 1591, and served under him in Ireland in 1599. That Percy family habitually referred to Shakespeare's drama is suggested by the 9th Earl's reference to 1 Henry IV in writing to Salisbury, and Charles Percy's reference to 2 Henry IV in a note asking for London news (dated 27th December [?] 1600). *The Shakspere Allusion-Book: a Collection of Allusions to Shakspere from 1591 to 1700*, ed. C. M. Ingleby, L. Toulmin and F. J. Furnivall, 2 vols. (Londo, 1909), vol. 1, pp. 86–7n.

'LET ME NOT TO THE MARRIAGE OF TRUE MINDS': SHAKESPEARE'S SONNET FOR LADY MARY WROTH

JANE KINGSLEY-SMITH

Let me not to the marriage of true minds
Admit impediments; love is not love
Which alters when it alteration finds,
Or bends with the remover to remove.
O no, it is an ever-fixèd mark,
That looks on tempests and is never shaken;
It is the star to every wand'ring bark,
Whose worth's unknown, although his height be taken.
Love's not Time's fool, though rosy lips and cheeks
Within his bending sickle's compass come;
Love alters not with his brief hours and weeks,
But bears it out even to the edge of doom.
              If this be error and upon me proved,
              I never writ, nor no man ever loved.[1]

Perhaps one of Shakespeare's most familiar and best-loved poems, Sonnet 116 has often struck readers as curiously detached from the rest of the collection, sharing 'no obvious thematic connections' with the other poems.[2] Carol Thomas Neely perceives 'an "I", drained of particular personality, [which] speaks to no clearly defined audience. Although a dramatic situation is implied, none is realised: neither speaker, audience nor occasion is particularised'.[3] But particularity may be in the eye of the beholder. Although the sonnet's transcendent definition of ideal love is the reason for its success, I will argue that it was written for a unique historical situation – namely the marriages of William Herbert, 3rd Earl of Pembroke, and of his cousin (who was also his mistress), Lady Mary Sidney, in September–November 1604. This new reading is consistent with recent lexical analysis, which places sonnets 104–26 in the early seventeenth century.[4] It also addresses some of the

structural difficulties posed by Sonnet 116, while undermining further the assumption of a simple binary division between two addressees – the so-called Fair Youth and Dark Lady – within the Sonnets as a whole.[5] But perhaps most importantly, Lady Mary Wroth emerges as an original reader of Sonnet 116, and one who responded creatively to that poem throughout her literary career. Acknowledging that Wroth's influence may extend to other Sonnets, we may wish to describe her influence as patronage and to rethink the ways in which Shakespeare was inspired to write the Sonnets, as well as for whom.

The crux upon which this argument turns is lines 7–8, 'It is the star to every wand'ring bark, / Whose worth's unknown, although his height be taken'.

---

[1] All quotations from the Sonnets are taken from *Shakespeare's Sonnets*, ed. Katherine Duncan-Jones (London, 1997). I am grateful to Ilona Bell, Penny McCarthy and Mary Ellen Lamb for generously sharing their work with me before its publication. Stanley Wells, Ilona Bell, Clare McManus and Andy Kesson also offered valuable suggestions on a draft version. The italics in the sonnet are mine.

[2] Paul Edmondson and Stanley Wells, *Shakespeare's Sonnets* (Oxford, 2004), p. 32.

[3] 'Detachment and Engagement in Shakespeare's Sonnets: 94, 116, 129', *PMLA*, 92 (1977), 83–95; p. 88.

[4] See MacDonald P. Jackson, 'Vocabulary and Chronology: The Case of Shakespeare's Sonnets', *Review of English Studies*, 52 (2001), 59–75; p. 75.

[5] See Heather Dubrow's important refutation of this binary in '"Incertainties now crown themselves assur'd": The Politics of Plotting Shakespeare's Sonnets', *Shakespeare Quarterly*, 47 (1996), 291–305.

The notion of calculating the 'worth' of a star has always seemed strangely inappropriate, not least because 'star' is such a fixed sign of value within the Petrarchan system. Moreover, the assumed permanence of the star as the epitome of constant love seems oddly undermined by its worth's being 'unknown'. Critics have wrestled with the phrase, conscious that how they interpret it will divide them into the ranks of the mawkish or the cynical. Katherine Duncan-Jones glosses 'worth's unknown' as 'the value of which is beyond human measurement'.[6] But for John Kerrigan, line 7 is part of the couplet's insistence that no man could love like this: 'the lover can take Love's altitude, but not reach up and grasp the star, experience its "worth"'.[7] Stephen Booth's parenthetical observation – '"Worth" is imprecisely used in this line' – is appealing.[8] But what if 'worth' were not only a term for 'high value' but also a means of praising someone called 'Wroth'?

Lady Mary Wroth (1587–1653), née Sidney, herself a famous sonneteer and romance writer, would invite the pun on wroth/worth on numerous occasions. It was used of her by Nathaniel Baxter in one of the poems in *Ourania* (1606), which praises Mary and her sister as 'Ladies of worth' (B3v); by William Browne in his description of Wroth as a shepherdess 'full of Worth' in *Britannia's Pastorals* (1613); and by Josuah Sylvester in his elegy for her brother, *Lachrimae Lachrimarum* (1613), which includes the marginal observation:

Although I know None, but a *Sidney's* Muse
Worthy to sing a *Sidney's* Worthyness:
None but Your Owne *AL-WORTH* Sideides
In whom, her *Uncle's* noble Veine renewes.   (H2)

Wroth also used it extensively about herself: her sonnet sequence *Pamphilia to Amphilanthus*, prose romance *Urania* and the pastoral comedy *Love's Victory* all include puns on 'worth/worthy' as well as the ubiquitous 'Will'.[9]

Shakespeare was clearly not averse to punning on names in the *Sonnets*, with multiple references to 'Will', and an allusion to 'hate away' (Hathaway) in Sonnet 145. In Sonnet 116, the reference to 'worth's unknown' seems to draw attention to its

own secrecy. That its covert referent is Wroth is strengthened by the fact that it relates back to 'star' and also forwards to 'height'. As suggested above, the worth of Wroth was often seen to depend upon her shared lineage with Sir Philip Sidney, who had invested the Petrarchan cliché of beloved-as-star with a deeper meaning by naming his sonnet sequence *Astrophil and Stella* (published 1591). That the historical figures of Sidney and Lady Penelope Devereux, later Rich, existed behind these masks was acknowledged by Elizabethan readers including Sir John Harington and Thomas Campion.[10] Moreover, Wroth was considered unusually tall for her sex, as glanced at perhaps in Browne's reference to her being apt to 'fit /The height of praise unto the height of wit' (M1v).[11] For this reason, the addressee of William Herbert's poem, 'One with admiration told me . . .', has also been identified as Wroth:

Then he blames the work of Nature,
'Cause she framed thy body tall,
Alleging that so high a stature
Was most subject to a fall,
Still detracting from *thy worth*
That which most doth set thee forth.   (44)[12]

---

[6] Duncan-Jones, *Shakespeare's Sonnets*, p. 342.

[7] John Kerrigan, *The Sonnets and A Lover's Complaint* (Harmondsworth, 1986; repr. 1999), p. 54.

[8] Stephen Booth, *Shakespeare's Sonnets* (New Haven, CT, 1977), p. 385.

[9] For further discussion of Wroth's puns, see Marion Wynne-Davies, '"For *worth*, not weakness, makes in use but one": Literary Dialogues in an English Renaissance Family', in *"This Double Voice": Gendered Writing in Early Modern England*, ed. Danielle Clark and Elizabeth Clarke (Houndmills, 2000), pp. 164–84.

[10] See Alison Wall's entry on 'Rich [née Devereux], Penelope', in the *Oxford Dictionary of National Biography*.

[11] Margaret P. Hannay, *Mary Sidney, Lady Wroth* (Farnham, 2010), p. 90.

[12] All quotations from Herbert's poetry are taken from Robert Krueger's 'The Poems of William Herbert, Third Earl of Pembroke', B.Litt. thesis (Oxford, 1961). The italics in the passage are mine. The identification with Wroth is made by Gary Waller in *The Sidney Family Romance: Mary Wroth, William Herbert, and the Early Modern Construction of Gender*

But perhaps the most important effect of coupling 'worth' and 'height' in Sonnet 116 depends on another interpretation of this term (spelled 'higth' in the 1609 Quarto). I cannot avoid hearing a pun on 'hight' as in 'named',[13] which directs us to that moment when Lady Mary became a 'Wroth' through her marriage in 1604 – a marriage that would prove famously unhappy, and 'unworthy' of her.[14] Thus, the paradox of 'worth's unknown, although his height be taken' does more than stress the impossibility of valuing a star. Rather, it makes the point that at the very moment when she became a 'Wroth', Lady Mary remained unappreciated by her new husband, who might have accurately gauged her wealth and social position, but was ignorant of her true worth, including perhaps her capacity for deep romantic attachment. This reading would also justify the awkward use of the masculine pronoun, '*his* height be taken'.

Shakespeare's interest in the plight of Lady Mary was probably driven initially by the fact that she was the cousin of William Herbert, 3rd Earl of Pembroke, not only the dedicatee of the First Folio but most likely to be the 'only begetter' of the Sonnets.[15] She was also Pembroke's mistress, producing two illegitimate children by him some time after the death of her husband, including a son called William.[16] At exactly what point the relationship between the two cousins became romantic and/or sexual remains unknown, but it may well have predated the weddings of 1604. Josephine A. Roberts notes the way in which the relationship between Pamphilia and Amphilanthus in Part 2 of Wroth's *The Countess of Montgomery's Urania* is sealed by a *de praesenti* marriage, described as 'the knott never to bee untide', although they both subsequently marry other people.[17] Furthermore, a letter by Lady Mary's father dated 10 October 1604 alludes to the new husband's dissatisfaction with the marriage: 'I finde by him that there was some what that doth discontent him: but the particulars I could not get out of him'.[18] Critics have conjectured that either he had discovered the degree of affection between Lady Mary and her cousin, or that she was no longer a virgin.[19] There are also strong indications that Pembroke's

marriage was affected by his relationship with Wroth. Having delayed his union with the considerable fortune of Lady Mary Talbot for so long that at least one commentator assumed it would never happen, Pembroke finally married just two months after Mary. Like his cousin's union, this also became the subject of gossip, with Rowland Whyte having to reassure the bride's parents that Pembroke was a loving husband and that she was well treated.[20] Moreover, although he had facilitated the marriage by making a substantial contribution to Lady Mary's dowry, Pembroke seems to have acknowledged the suffering it caused him in

---

(Detroit, 1993), pp. 182–3, though he does not acknowledge the pun on 'worth'.

13 Shakespeare uses this term to mean 'named' four times: twice in *Love's Labour's Lost* (1.1.168, 249), and once in *A Midsummer Night's Dream* (5.1.138) and *Pericles* (15.18). I have found no evidence that he transformed it into a noun but it would be a very simple conversion. All quotations from Shakespeare's plays are taken from *William Shakespeare: The Complete Works*, ed. Stanley Wells et al., 2nd edn (Oxford, 2005).

14 Ben Jonson confided to Drummond that 'My Lord Lisle's daughter, my Lady Wroth, is unworthily married on a jealous husband', in *Informations to William Drummond* in *The Cambridge Edition of the Works of Ben Jonson*, ed. David Bevington, Martin Butler and Ian Donaldson, 6 vols. (Cambridge, 2012), vol. 5, p. 377.

15 The case for Herbert has been made extensively and persuasively by Duncan-Jones in *Shakespeare's Sonnets*, pp. 55–69.

16 Hannay argues for 1624 as the year Wroth gave birth to twins, citing John Chamberlain's letter: 'Here is a whispering of a Lady that hath been a widow above seven years, though she had lately two children at a birth. I must not name her though she be said to be learned and in print' (*Mary Sidney*, p. 251).

17 See Josephine A. Roberts, 'Introduction', in *The First Part of The Countess of Montgomery's Urania*, ed. Josephine A. Roberts (Tempe, AZ, 1995; repr. 2005), p. lxxiv, and also her '"The knott never to bee untide": The Controversy Regarding Marriage in Mary Wroth's *Urania*', in *Reading Mary Wroth*, ed. Naomi J. Miller and Gary Waller (Knoxville, KY, 1991), pp. 109–32.

18 As quoted by Josephine A. Roberts, *The Poems of Lady Mary Wroth* (Baton Rouge, LA, 1983), pp. 11–12. All quotations from Wroth's poetry are taken from this edition.

19 See Roberts, *First Part*, p. xc, and Hannay, *Mary Sidney*, pp. 107–8.

20 Hannay, *Mary Sidney*, p. 96.

his own poetry. In the lyric 'Muse get thee to a Cell', the speaker complains:

Who says that I for things ne'er mine am sad?
That was all mine which others never had.
No sighs, no tears, no blood but mine was shed
For her that now must bless another's bed.

There is evidence, then, not only that Wroth and Herbert registered private feelings about one another in their literary work, but also that they responded to one another's poetry within the context of a relationship.[21] A poet on familiar terms with either of them might have ventured his own (more circumspect) contribution to the theme.

Recently, critics have tied themselves in knots trying to deny that Sonnet 116 has anything literal to say about 'marriage',[22] a response in part, I would suggest, to the overwhelming confidence that popular culture has demonstrated in its matrimonial content.[23] However, the sonnet begins and ends with allusions to the Book of Common Prayer; not only 'if either of you know any lawful impediment why ye may not be lawfully joined in matrimony', but also 'to love and cherish, till death do us part' – these allusions gain greater resonance if we read them in the context of the Wroth and Herbert weddings of 1604.[24] The measured, ceremonial tone of Shakespeare's opening lines now confers legitimacy on a love that is outside the bounds of marriage – an epithalamium for an extra-marital love. The possibility of impediments is acknowledged, anticipating the emotional infidelity of the lovers to one another when they have so recently given themselves to other people, but the sonnet confronts this objection only to dispel it. Hereafter, the union of mere bodies and the 'marriage of true minds' is implicitly juxtaposed, offering reassurance that true love will not be altered by the couple's nuptial circumstances. The sonnet's inherently anti-materialist perspective – that love transcends pleasure in physical beauty ('rosy lips and cheeks') and that it endures to 'the edge of doom' – flatteringly directs attention away from the fact that both addressees were making financially astute marriages.

At the same time, we cannot ignore the poem's structural and tonal ambivalence, created not only

by the final couplet, but also by the repressed 'me' of the opening line. The impression that these parts are detachable might explain why the sonnet has often been appropriated without them, but to contextualize it historically is to bring these parts into greater artistic unity. One way of reading 'Let me not', meaning 'may I never', would be as the continuation of an imagined discussion or argument between Shakespeare, Herbert and Wroth on the subject of their marriages. The poem could even be understood as an act of atonement, with Shakespeare rejecting an earlier cynical stance, not difficult to imagine from the author of *Troilus*

---

21 On Wroth and Herbert's dialogue through their poetry, see Garth Bond, 'Amphilanthus to Pamphilia: William Herbert, Mary Wroth, and Penshurst Mount', *Sidney Journal*, 31 (2013), 51–80; and Mary Ellen Lamb, '"Can you suspect a change in me?": Poems by Mary Wroth and William Herbert, Third Earl of Pembroke', in *Re-Reading Mary Wroth*, ed. Katherine R. Larson and Naomi J. Miller with Andrew Strycharski (New York, 2015), pp. 53–68; 58–60. See also Ilona Bell's groundbreaking study of how Wroth censored the more explicit material before publication in 'The Autograph Manuscript of Mary Wroth's *Pamphilia to Amphilanthus*', in *Re-Reading Mary Wroth*, pp. 171–82.

22 Richard Strier argues that 'The poem is about how persons who are "true minds" love (that is, with constancy to their object, regardless of how the object behaves); it is not, despite how the famous opening line and a half sounds, about how "true minds" love each other'. 'The Refusal to be Judged in Petrarch and Shakespeare', in *A Companion to Shakespeare's Sonnets*, ed. Michael Schoenfeldt (Oxford, 2010), pp. 73–89; p. 82.

23 In the BBC's updating of *Much Ado About Nothing*, directed by Brian Perceval for the ShakespeaRe-Told season (2005), Benedict plans to read the poem as part of his best man duties at the wedding of Hero and Claudio, only to receive Beatrice's withering response: 'How original!'

24 Penny McCarthy also focuses on the events of 1604, arguing that the scandalous secret being covered up by Wroth's marriage was her pregnancy by Shakespeare with a child that she later miscarried. 'Autumn 1604: Documentation and Literary Coincidence', in *Mary Wroth and Shakespeare*, ed. Paul Salzman and Marion Wynne-Davies (London, 2015), pp. 37–46. I tend to see the Wroth–Shakespeare relationship as platonic, but am intrigued by the connections McCarthy pursues between Wroth's and Shakespeare's writing, and by her acknowledgement of a possible 'worth/wroth' pun in Sonnet 150, p. 42.

and Cressida (c. 1602–3). Similarly, the couplet – 'If this be error and upon me proved / I never writ, nor no man ever loved' – becomes less 'a Pistol-like piece of swaggering' than an affectionate over-compensation.[25] Rather than 'the poet protesting too much, losing confidence in his protestations . . . anticipating rebuttal', one might see the poem as a piece of self-conscious romantic hyperbole intended to soothe ruffled feelings.[26]

This is not, however, to overlook the deep strain of melancholy and forced self-abnegation that runs through it – and we might find something here of Shakespeare's own difficulty if we join up the present biographical speculations with the more famous narrative of his passion for a young aristocrat, identified as Pembroke. If Shakespeare earned his place of intimacy with the couple through his ability to idealize their love, to do so was to acknowledge how far he was excluded from it. This inevitably complicates his relationship with the poem, and might explain the shifts between detachment and engagement which characterize the speaker's role: from 'Let *me* not', to the impersonal asseveration 'Love is not love', to the passionate, even breathless 'O no . . .' The sonnet performs the requisite flattery of its readers while also giving voice to an idealized, unreciprocated love that flatters the poet.

It remains to be asked, what evidence is there for Shakespeare circulating the manuscript of this poem 'among his private friends', defined as Wroth and Herbert? The answer is, of course, very little. And yet, this would seem to be a critically propitious moment to envisage the scenario, given the exciting work that has been done recently on Wroth and Herbert, and Wroth and Shakespeare.[27] As Mary Ellen Lamb puts it, 'The long-term physical proximity underlying the familial and later sexual relationship [of Wroth and Herbert] . . . created the reading of each other's poetry as all but inevitable'.[28] Following their marriages, in the winter of 1604, they could both be found at Baynard's Castle in London, a place where Wroth kept some of her writing, and from whence they might partake of the festivities at court, including performances of *Othello* and *Measure for*

Measure.[29] Furthermore, if we look ahead to Wroth's literary relationship with Ben Jonson, we find a similar kind of writing circle to the one I am imagining for Shakespeare. William Drummond recalled the genesis of Jonson's 'Song. That Women Are But Men's Shadows': 'Pembrok and his lady discoursing the Earl said that Woemen were mens shadowes, and she maintained *them*, both appealing to Johnson, he affirmed it true, for which my Lady gave a pennance to prove it in Verse: hence his Epigrame.'[30] Michael G. Brennan has argued that this lady is far more likely to have been Wroth than Herbert's wife, and offers it as an example of her 'enjoying poetic banter with Pembroke and Jonson'.[31] If this were something both relished in 1612, then there is no reason why it should not also have been a feature of their discourse in 1604.

But perhaps most importantly, there is evidence that both William Herbert and Mary Wroth had read Sonnet 116, for they both reuse the phrase 'Love is not love' in their own original verse: Herbert in a lyric beginning 'If her disdain least change in you can move' (2), and Wroth in the

[25] Duncan-Jones, *Shakespeare's Sonnets*, p. 343.

[26] Kerrigan, *Sonnets and A Lover's Complaint*, p. 53.

[27] See, for example, Gayle Gaskill's discussion of Shakespeare's and Wroth's sonnets alongside one another, though she 'neatly sidestep[s] the unanswerable question of whether Wroth was familiar with Shakespeare's sonnets'. 'Mary Wroth and Shakespeare: A Conversation in Sonnets', in *Mary Wroth and Shakespeare,* ed. Salzman and Wynne-Davies, pp. 47–60; p. 47. See also Naomi J. Miller's compelling fictional representation of Shakespeare and Wroth in her novel, *The Story-maker,* currently under submission. An extract appears as 'Reimagining Mary Wroth Through Fiction', *Sidney Journal*, 32 (2014), 39–64.

[28] Mary Ellen Lamb, '"Can you suspect"', pp. 53, 54.

[29] Roberts, *Poems*, pp. 244–5.

[30] *Works of Jonson*, vol. 1, p. 142.

[31] Michael G. Brennan, 'Creating Female Authorship in the Early Seventeenth Century: Ben Jonson and Lady Mary Wroth', in *Women's Writing and the Circulation of Ideas: Manuscript Publication in England, 1550–1800,* ed. George L. Justice and Nathan Tinker (Cambridge, 2002), pp. 73–93; p. 85.

poem 'As these drops fall' (U29).[32] We might assume this to be a memorable phrase for any reader of the 1609 Sonnets – one that would inspire frequent repetition and imitation – but this is surprisingly not the case. A search of the Chadwyck-Healy database to include all phrases beginning 'love/loue is not' between 1590 and 1640 produces only three examples of 'love is not love' in poetry and these are Shakespeare, Herbert and Wroth. If we expand the search to drama, we find only a further two: Shakespeare's *King Lear* (c. 1605, Q 1608) and Barksted and Machin's *The Insatiate Countess* (c. 1608, pub. 1613).[33] The fact that Wroth and Herbert published the only extant poems including this phrase might suggest that they were not dependent on the Quarto but had read Shakespeare's lyric in a manuscript, and hence that they were creatively engaged with Shakespeare on a more direct and personal level. What they do with the phrase may offer us a deeper insight into the kind of readers they were for him.

William Herbert appropriates the phrase in his lyric 'If her disdain least change in you can move', part of a 'poem-and-answer set'[34] created with his friend, Sir Benjamin Rudyerd, which was printed in 1660 but circulated in manuscript much earlier, and probably written in the early years of the seventeenth century when Herbert and Rudyerd were at the Inns of Court together.[35] The Shakespeare allusion appears in the first stanza:

> If her disdain least change in you can move
> > You do not love,
> For while your hopes give fuel to your fire
> > You sell desire.
> Love is not love, but given free,
> And so is mine, so should yours be.　　　　(2)

The phrase serves as a touchstone to prove the truth of professed affection, and in this way it remains true to its purpose in Sonnet 116. However, its context is more overtly homosocial, operating within Petrarchan conventions according to which reciprocal affection by the woman is not expected or even desirable for the purposes of poetry. Furthermore, the impact of the Shakespearian phrase is partly lost by its being a restatement of what has already been

said: 'If her disdain least change in you can move / You do not love'. The argument was apparently clear in the speaker's mind, and he made it in his own words first, but when it needed reiteration he turned to Shakespeare (whose *King Lear* had placed it in a similar context of male rivalry). In this respect, the lyric is consistent with much of Pembroke's verse, described by Gary Waller as '"coterie social transactions", written for or within a group of friends, perhaps on particular, though relatively common, social or erotic occasions'. Its casual appropriation of another writer's words is of a piece with its relaxed attitude towards lyric convention:

> [Pembroke] is content to let the dominant aesthetic ideology of the male-dominated court and its acceptance of the decorativeness of lyric poetry speak through his verse without the anguish of having to call into question the system that brought them into being. He finds a pattern of discourse already existing and a role waiting for him to fill.[36]

The case was obviously vastly different for his cousin, Lady Mary Wroth, and it is no surprise to

---

[32] I am indebted to Duncan-Jones for the connection between Sonnet 116 and Pembroke's lyric, 68. The connection with Wroth's writing is my own.

[33] In *King Lear*, Shakespeare reuses his own phrase in the mouth of the King of France as he proleptically chides Burgundy for abandoning Cordelia once her price has fallen: 'What say you to the lady? Love's not love / When it is mingled with regards that stands / Aloof from th'entire point' (1.1.238–40). It is notable that although the phrase is now elided, 'Love's not', Shakespeare retains it in the same position, after the caesura. In *The Insatiate Countess*, the phrase is used by Gniaca to upbraid Isabella for her abrupt transfer of her affections: 'Wrong not yourself, me, and your dearest friend: / Your love is violent, and soon will end. / Love is not love, unless love doth persèver: / That love is perfect love that loves forever', *Four Jacobean Sex Tragedies*, ed. Martin Wiggins (Oxford, 2009), 3.2.79–82.

[34] See Arthur Marotti, 'Manuscript, Print and the Social History of the Lyric', in *The Cambridge Companion to English Poetry, Donne to Marvell*, ed. Thomas N. Corns (Cambridge, 1993), pp. 52–79; p. 55.

[35] Krueger lists the poem as appearing in six additional manuscripts, from the 1620s, in *Poems of Herbert*, p. 2. On the possibility of its being written as early as 1603, see Waller, *Sidney Family Romance*, p. 165.

[36] Waller, *Sidney Family Romance*, pp. 166, 167.

find her poem (and indeed her poetic canon) demonstrating a deeper and more ambivalent engagement with Shakespeare's Sonnets.[37]

Most obviously, Sonnet 116's fantasy of an enduring and unalterable love speaks to one of the overarching themes of Wroth's literary work, namely the desire for constancy.[38] Its recurrence in *Pamphilia to Amphilanthus* and in both parts of the *Urania* seems likely to have been prompted by Wroth's relationship with the errant Pembroke, whose sexual transgressions were well known and who might easily qualify as a 'remover [who] removes'. A further point of contact is the desire in Wroth's poetry to identify true love, as opposed to the false and meretricious. Notable examples include, in *Pamphilia to Amphilanthus*, Song 5: 'Unworthy love doth seeke for ends / A worthy love butt worth pretends / Nor other thoughts itt proveth' (P35), and the lyric beginning 'It is nott love which you poore fooles do deeme / That doth apeare by fond, and outward showes' (P46). What is particularly fascinating about Wroth's engagement with Sonnet 116 is the fact that it seems to have endured over the course of more than fifteen years, and that her response to the poem shifted considerably – from resentment of its persuasiveness, to identification with its image of unrequited love, to optimism that it might affect some alteration in her life.

In Book 1 of *The First Part of . . . Urania*, which was published in 1621 but perhaps written between 1618 and 1620, the character of Bellamira (whose name means 'beautiful Mary') meets Amphilanthus (an obvious analogue for Pembroke).[39] She laments her abandonment by a king who at first pursued her so ardently that her father married her off to someone else in order to preserve her virtue. But after her husband's death, the king's affections waned:

When I was a Widdow, and suffered so many crosses, my poore beauty decayd, so did his love, which though he oft protested to bee fixed on my worth, and love to him, yet my face's alteration gave his eyes distaste, or liberty from former bands, to looke else where, and so he looked, as tooke his heart at last from me, making that a poore servant to his false eyes, to follow still their change. I grieved for it, yet never lessned my affection . . .
(390)

Bellamira uses the terms 'fixed', 'worth', 'love' and 'alteration' in close proximity to one another, suggesting a link with Sonnet 116. Her claim that once her beauty was lost, her lover's affections strayed, resonates ironically with the sonnet's observation that 'Love's not Time's fool, though rosy lips and cheeks / Within his bending sickle's compass come'. We might speculate that Wroth was here recalling her own private experience. The years 1614–16 had been particularly traumatic, with the deaths of her husband and then her son (at this point her only child), as well as considerable financial pressures, and she might well have considered her beauty to have faded, with a resultant slackening of Pembroke's affections. From such a vantage point, she might remember with bitterness and resentment the use Pembroke had once made of Sonnet 116 in Bellamira's allusion to his 'protest[ing] to bee fixed on my worth'. At the same time, Shakespeare's sonnet underpins her own heroic, unrequited passion, with its celebratory imagery of a love that 'bears it out, even to the edge of doom'.

When Amphilanthus asks Bellamira to share some of her verses, she expresses a deep sense of alienation from her own poetry and, by implication, from her own past:

---

[37] Dubrow argues for the 'extraordinary affinities between Wroth and Shakespeare' as sonneteers, including 'doubts about their own poetic achievements', their 'complex relationship to narrativity', the isolation and alienation which characterize both speakers, and their shared obsession with betrayal. See *Echoes of Desire: English Petrarchism and its Counter-Discourses* (Ithaca, NY, 1995), pp. 145–6. See also Ilona Bell's discussion of the ways in which 'Shakespeare's strategies of evasion and concealment resemble Wroth's' in 'Sugared Sonnets among their Private Friends: Mary Wroth and William Shakespeare', *Mary Wroth and Shakespeare*, ed. Salzman and Wyne-Davies, pp. 9–24; p. 16.

[38] See, for example, Elaine V. Beilin, '"The onely perfect vertue": Constancy in Mary Wroth's *Pamphilia to Amphilanthus*', *Spenser Studies*, 2 (1981), 229–45.

[39] Hannay, *Mary Sidney*, p. 37. Roberts also argues that Bellamira is one of the key fictional self-portraits Wroth created in her work, specifically 'highlight[ing] her private relationship with Pembroke' (*First Part*, p. lxxi).

'Truely Sir,' said she, 'so long it is since I made any, and the subject growne so strange, as I can hardly cal them to memory which I made, having desired to forget all things but my love, fearing that the sight, or thought of them, would bring on the joyes then felt, the sorrowes soone succeeding.'   (390)

There may be a trace here of Wroth's own perceived distance from Sonnet 116, whose romantic idealism is a relic of her youth, and which may be similarly painful to re-examine. Nevertheless, Bellamira offers up to Amphilanthus the lyric 'As these drops fall', which she describes herself as having written after the king's neglect had begun but before she despaired of ever recapturing his affection: 'one time after he had begun to change, hee yet did visite mee, and use mee somtimes well, and once so kindly, as I grew to hope a little, whereupon I writ these lines' (391). The poem expresses relief that her lover is softening towards her, but also fears that the change may not be lasting. The final two stanzas read:

But if like heate drops you do wast away
Glad, as disburden'd of a hot desire;
Let me be rather lost, perish in fire,
Then by those hopefull signes brought to decay.

Sweete be a louer puer, and permanent,
Cast off gay cloathes of change, and such false slights:
Love is not love, but where truth hath her rights,
Else like boughs from the perfect body rent.
                                                    (U29, 17–24)

This allusion to Sonnet 116 works in contrasting ways on the levels of fiction (Bellamira) and autobiography (Wroth). For Bellamira at the time of writing, 'Love is not love' becomes itself an 'ever-fixèd mark' within the oceanic instability of their relationship (6, 9) – an ideal to aspire to. There might also be an echo of Sonnet 80 in the desire that she be 'not by those hopefull signes brought to decay' (20) through the same excess of love and hope.[40] But as she recites the lyric now before Amphilanthus, there is no chance of the quoted sonnet being able to move the absent lover. The same cannot be said of Wroth, for whom the key feature of the lyric is that it is performed before

Amphilanthus, i.e. Pembroke, as reader of the romance. In this context, the phrase 'Love is not love' potentially forces Pembroke to confront his falling-off from the romantic sentiments that inspired Sonnet 116. It also upbraids him with his own poetry, wherein he appropriated 'Love is not love' as an avowal of his unalterable passion. For all that the poem has lost any possible influence over Bellamira's romantic affairs, it retains a certain power over those of Wroth. Furthermore, by reading the line 'Love is not love, but where truth hath her rights' against the backdrop of Sonnet 116, which is so explicit in its allusion to the marriage ceremony, 'rights' potentially becomes 'rites'. Neither Bellamira nor Wroth may be asking for these to be performed literally – although Bellamira (like Wroth) is free in her widowhood to marry, her beloved (like Pembroke) is still married. Yet there might be an allusion to the other kind of rite owed to love, namely sexual consummation, and if 1624 is the correct date of Wroth's delivery of twins, then this appeal was not made in vain. In this sense, Wroth appropriates a sonnet which celebrates unreciprocated passion, in terms that belie any possibility of physical intimacy, and transforms it into a powerfully erotic poem, which draws attention to the physical desires of the female speaker, as well as lingering suggestively over her 'perfect body'.[41]

Of the two intended recipients of Sonnet 116, then, Lady Mary Wroth seems to have experienced the deepest affinity with the poem, to the extent that she could still recall its imagery (and its

---

[40] 'Then if he thrive, and I be cast away / The worst was this: my love was my decay'. Sonnet 80, which includes puns on 'worth', is discussed further below.

[41] There is an additional use of 'Love is not love' by Wroth in Rodomandro's masque which celebrates the triumph of Honour over Cupid in the second part of the *Urania*. The third stanza of the song reads: 'Love's nott Love, that vainely flings / Like a harmfull waspe that stings / Therin I did miss / Desire should nott bee stil'd love / Butt with honors wings to move / Bright love tells us this' (N5, p. 198). On the love-god's importance in Wroth's work, see Jane Kingsley-Smith, *Cupid in Early Modern Literature and Culture* (Cambridge, 2010), pp. 121–32.

emotional context) more than fifteen years after it was written. It remains to ask whether this affinity had developed into a more lasting relationship between herself and the poet. As Duncan-Jones observes, Shakespeare's idea of patronage initially looks to have been overwhelmingly male:

Other ambitious writers in this period cultivated and sought to please, not only the Queen, but also courtly patronesses, the wives, widows, and daughters of noblemen. Such ladies often had considerable wealth and influence, as well as leisure in which to read and respond to literary works which would perhaps be given little more than a cursory glance by their menfolk ... Yet there is not one single instance of Shakespeare addressing a work to a well-known woman, whether royal, noble or gentle. From the Earl of Southampton to Sir John Salisbury to Mr W. H. to Francis Manners, Earl of Rutland, Shakespeare's visible patrons were all male.[42]

There remains the possibility of an 'invisible' patron. John Dover Wilson speculated that the Countess of Pembroke commissioned the first seventeen sonnets as a coercive gift for her son on his seventeenth birthday.[43] There may be a graceful compliment in Sonnet 3's avowal: 'Thou art thy mother's glass, and she in thee / Calls back the lovely April of her prime' (9–10), April also being the month of Herbert's birth. This would suggest a more flexible idea of patronage as something not necessarily rendered explicit through a dedication or title, but registered within the poem through covert allusion: the function of the verse is not to celebrate the patron's virtues but to perform a persuasive act on their behalf.

The evidence for Wroth acting as a patron whilst being influenced in her own poetry brings us back to Jonson. In 1612 he dedicated *The Alchemist* to Wroth, one year after he had dedicated *Catiline* to Pembroke, and what Brennan describes as 'the implicit pairing in patronage of William Herbert and Lady Mary Wroth' was notably replicated in the 1616 Folio, where *The Alchemist* was immediately followed by *Catiline*, and where an Epigram to Herbert was succeeded by one to Wroth.[44] We referred earlier to the possibility that Wroth had inspired Jonson's 'Song. That Women Are But Men's Shadows', and it would certainly be possible

to read this kind of playful but also private patronage back into the first decade of the seventeenth century, and her acquaintance with Shakespeare. As Brennan states, 'By the end of 1604 Lady Mary ... was already firmly ensconced in the personal circles of both the new king and queen', and this 'early prominence at the new Stuart royal court' might well have translated into early efforts of dedication and solicitations for patronage.[45]

If we reconsider all of Shakespeare's sonnets which contain the word 'worth', we can glimpse the possibility of Wroth functioning not as a Dark Lady but as a 'Begetter'. The word 'worth' appears in eighteen poems, and, as we might expect in a collection so often concerned with questions of value, many of these appear unremarkable. However, there are at least two which might give us pause, both dealing with poetic inspiration and/ or patronage. Sonnet 38 reads:

How can my Muse want subject to invent
While thou dost breathe, that pour'st into my verse
Thine own sweet argument, too excellent
For every vulgar paper to rehearse?
O give thyself the thanks, if aught in me
Worthy perusal stand against thy sight:
For who's so dumb, that cannot write to thee,
When thou thyself dost give invention light?
Be thou the tenth Muse, ten times more in worth
Than those old nine which rhymers invocate;
And he that calls on thee, let him bring forth
Eternal numbers to outlive long date.
    If my slight Muse do please these curious days,
    The pain be mine, but thine shall be the praise.[46]

Like 116, this sonnet stands out from the surrounding poems, and Helen Vendler suggests that it might once have belonged to a different group:

38, though it has some matter (and the words 'worth' and 'praise') in common with 39, bears no thematic trace of

---

[42] Katherine Duncan-Jones, *Ungentle Shakespeare: Scenes from his Life* (London, 2001), p. 150.
[43] John Dover Wilson, *The Sonnets* (Cambridge, 1966), p. c.
[44] Brennan, 'Creating Female Authorship', pp. 76, 84.
[45] Brennan, 'Creating Female Authorship', p. 74.
[46] The italics in the sonnet are mine.

the separation of lovers which is the common content of 36 and 39. It seems to me that a 'break' such as this one lends credence to the argument . . . that in arranging the sequence Shakespeare (or another editor) made room for some earlier and less practiced sonnets among the ones more clearly written in close temporal sequence.[47]

'Earlier and less practiced sonnets', or perhaps later ones, are addressed to a different, female patron. This would certainly explain the awkwardness of the speaker's demand 'Be thou the tenth Muse' to a man, given that Muses are conventionally female. The addressee's identification as Wroth might be suggested not only by allusions to 'worth' and 'Worthy', but by the fact that this is one of Shakespeare's most Sidneian sonnets.[48]

The other patronage poem which resonates in this context is Sonnet 80:

O how I faint when I of you do write,
Knowing a better spirit doth use your name,
And in the praise thereof spends all his might,
To make me tongue-tied speaking of your fame.
But since your worth, wide as the ocean is,
The humble as the proudest sail doth bear,
My saucy bark, inferior far to his,
On your broad main doth wilfully appear.
Your shallowest help will hold me up afloat,
Whilst he upon your soundless deep doth ride;
Or, being wracked, I am a worthless boat,
He of tall building, and of goodly pride.
    Then if he thrive, and I be cast away,
    The worst was this: my love was my decay.

Possible evidence of Wroth's familiarity with this sonnet was produced above, and the sonnet's use of the terms 'worth', 'worthless' and 'worst' starts to look like deliberate wordplay. The inclusion of a pun on 'wilfully'[49] suggests that Shakespeare might be coupling his patrons, Herbert and Wroth, together, just as Jonson would do in the Folio years later. Furthermore, the poem bears some interesting thematic similarities with 116. Where, in that sonnet, the worthy star offered guidance to the 'wandering bark', here the worthy ocean supports the poet's 'saucy bark' – a connection which did not go unnoticed by John Benson, who placed 116 immediately after a conflation of 80 and 81 in his *Poems* (1640).[50]

To conclude, if we accept the Pembroke/Wroth marriages of 1604 as a context for Sonnet 116, the implications for our understanding of the rest of Shakespeare's *Sonnets* are profound. For a start, we have a precedent for there being occasional sonnets within the collection – the fact that we have not been able to explain an occasion does not mean it did not exist. We are also encouraged to be more receptive to Q's fragmentation into small clusters and sub-groups, so that there can be more than one patron, just as there seems to be more than one 'Fair Youth' and 'Dark Lady'. Indeed, the major impediment for me in identifying the 'worth' pun more extensively is the centripetal force by which it will draw Wroth back towards the role of Dark Lady.[51] To return to women's function in the *Sonnets* as confined to the subject of misogynist invective is not the intention of this chapter. Rather, its most important discovery seems to me to be the emergence of Lady Mary as a sympathetic and highly engaged reader for Shakespeare, one whose concerns and experiences influenced his writing, which then offered creative stimulus to her own. The ways in which she interprets 'Let me not' suggest a profound understanding of the conflicts which structure it – 'a marriage of true minds' indeed.

---

[47] Helen Vendler, *The Art of Shakespeare's Sonnets* (Cambridge, MA, 1997), p. 191.

[48] Duncan-Jones observes the echoes of *Astrophil and Stella* 3 (*Shakespeare's Sonnets*, p. 186), while Vendler comments on the rarity of Muses in Shakespeare's collection: 'The fact that the Muse appears chiefly in the context of poetic rivalry suggests that it is the use of this figure by other poets which occasions its appearance in Shakespeare' (*Art*, p. 198).

[49] This is also noted in Vendler, *Art*, p. 358.

[50] Benson's editing of the *Sonnets* has only recently received serious attention from scholars who have shown him to be in many ways a sensitive reader. See, for example, Margreta De Grazia, *Shakespeare Verbatim: The Reproduction of Authenticity and the 1790 Apparatus* (Oxford, 1991), pp. 163–73; and Cathy Shrank, 'Reading Shakespeare's *Sonnets*: John Benson and the 1640 *Poems*', *Shakespeare*, 5 (2009), 271–91.

[51] See Gaskill's argument that Wroth puts on the role of Dark Lady only to redefine its terms: 'Wroth's lady is "as dark as night" because the love object, her "chief light", who once shone on her like the sun, has withdrawn' ('Wroth and Shakespeare', p. 51).

VOLUPTUOUS LANGUAGE AND AMBIVALENCE IN SHAKESPEARE'S SONNETS

MATS MALM

PHYSICAL AND LINGUISTIC DESIRE

Although it is uncontroversial to propose that Shakespeare's sonnets take a peculiar place in literary history, this place is still in need of clarifying. Their aspects of desire and sexuality, and the ways they have been understood, both when they were first published in 1609 and in later times, are an inexhaustible issue, as not least the studies of Margreta de Grazia, Peter Stallybrass and Robert Matz have demonstrated.[1] On the other hand, the issue of desire is firmly connected to the strong metalinguistic character apparent already in the introductory sonnets, which promise reproduction and memory not through family and offspring but by the 'eternal lines' of the very sonnets. These two aspects obviously are central for understanding the specificity of Shakespeare's sonnets, and much attention has been directed toward them, but the complex manner in which desire and metalinguistic discourse overlay each other calls for further analysis. This article aims to clarify how the sonnets relate to a traditional notion of what is best termed 'voluptuous language', and how this notion on the one hand gives an historical explanation of the ambivalent desire expressed in the sonnets, while on the other hand is recast by Shakespeare into a novel kind of imagery. The examination will also shed light on that dramatized desire which Stephen Greenblatt once spoke of in terms of 'fiction and friction'.

The close connection between the two desired characters of the sonnets and the desire for language itself was efficiently pointed out by Joel Fineman, who emphasized that 'the poet's various characterisations of desire very much correspond to the way he characterizes language, either as something visual or as something verbal'. In representing vision, language, according to Fineman, also perverts vision in a way that connects to the relative purity and perversion of the desire for the young man and the dark lady: Fineman here opposes a 'homogeneous visuality' to a 'linguistic heterogeneity'.[2]

Nuancing Fineman's argument and stressing the importance of writing itself, Douglas Trevor has pointed at how the sonnets attempt 'first to recreate the initial fairness of the first love object – the male friend – as it is compromised through his inconstant, unbecoming behaviour, and then, much more quickly, redressing the duplicity of the dark lady, fixing her infidelity within the poem's constant art'.[3] Shakespeare does effectuate decisive changes in the love objects of the sonnet tradition. Love is sexualized, but especially important, while

---

[1] Margreta de Grazia, 'The Scandal of Shakespeare's Sonnets', in *Shakespeare's Sonnets: Critical Essays*, ed. James Schiffer (New York, 2000), pp. 89–112; Peter Stallybrass, 'Editing as Cultural Formation: The Sexing of Shakespeare's Sonnets', *MLQ*, 54 (1993), 91–103; Robert Matz, 'The Scandals of Shakespeare's Sonnets', *ELH*, 77 (2010), 477–508.

[2] Joel Fineman, *Shakespeare's Perjured Eye: The Invention of Poetic Subjectivity in the Sonnets* (Berkeley, CA, 1986), pp. 17–18.

[3] Douglas Trevor, 'Shakespeare's Love Objects', in *A Companion to Shakespeare's Sonnets*, ed. Michael Schoenfeldt (Malden, MA, 2007), pp. 225–41; p. 234.

previous sonnets in the tradition, keeping their desire chaste and unearthly, had as their objects the beloved and God, God in Shakespeare's sonnets has no place as an ultimate desired object. Trevor concludes that Shakespeare not only changes the traditional triad lover–beloved–God and creates a triangle of desire when addressing two loved ones; he also, in the end, 'replaces a single love object – the Laura or Stella figure of the Petrarchan sonnet tradition with a literary object, the poems themselves'.[4]

Joyce Sutphen, in accordance with previously expressed notions of a (relative) stability in the first part and anarchy and variability in the second part, instead demonstrated that memory and writing enable the poet to conquer loss and oblivion in the sonnets up to 126, while this project is shattered in the latter part, and turned toward the dark lady.[5]

While these considerations are highly pertinent to an understanding of the specificity of Shakespeare's sonnets, in order to better understand their place in literary history (and thus better understand their specificity), they have to be more firmly founded in their historical tradition. Fineman's contraposition of 'linguistic heterogeneity' and 'homogeneous visuality' can be deduced from a traditional anxiety concerning language itself, which does not oppose the verbal to the visual in an actual sense; rather, it concerns rhetorical lucidity in a very special sense. Trevor's focus on the constancy of the poems themselves, as opposed to the inconstancies of love, effectively develops the old notion of poetry's ability to immortalize as formulated by Horace. However, this tradition is paralleled by another tradition of antiquity, where it is not the constancy of poems that is the burning topic, but the inconstancy of language itself. In view of this, Trevor's observation, that the sonnets leave the traditional sonnet triad lover–beloved–God and instead introduce the poems themselves as love objects, may be nuanced: it appears rather that God is replaced not by the poems but by language itself.

Similarly, Sutphen's observations on how the force of memory and writing vanishes toward the end of the collection can be contextualized: in effect, desire and language in Shakespeare's sonnets to a great extent connect to a pre-existing set of notions, which however are implemented in an entirely new manner: Shakespeare, as Fineman pointed out, sets linguistic desire in poetic motion in a new way that enables a new kind of subjectivity and thematization of lust in the sonnet genre.[6] However, this linguistic desire has its roots in the notion of voluptuous language, a notion of antiquity which during the Renaissance came to be implemented in poetry in more ways than the one displayed by Shakespeare.

In order to clarify the effects of this, I will first give a brief account of the background, and then discuss particular points of contact with this tradition in Shakespeare, in order to propose a deeper understanding of the structure of desire in the sonnets and the structure of the sonnets in the collection.

THE NOTION OF VOLUPTUOUS LANGUAGE

There is reason to believe that in order to more fully comprehend the critique launched at poetry in early modern England, we must appreciate the notion of voluptuous language inherent in the rhetorical tradition and the iconographic arguments surrounding it. Whereas the obvious points of critique concerned poetry's content – corrupting people by presenting bad examples and immoral ways of life – rhetoric naturally divided discussion into content and form,

---

[4] Trevor, 'Shakespeare's Love Objects', pp. 229, 239.

[5] Joyce Sutphen, '"A dateless lively heat": Storing Loss in the Sonnets', in *Shakespeare's Sonnets*, ed. Schiffer, pp. 199–217. See also de Grazia, 'Scandal'.

[6] Fineman, *Perjured Eye*, p. 18. Fineman uses the description 'linguistic desire' for the latter, new kind: 'For Shakespearean "Will" . . ., is the name of a linguistic desire, the name of a desire *of* language, which is at once more personal and more painful than it is structurally possible for any visionary poetics of ideal (and therefore desireless) desire even to imagine' (p. 26). Trevor develops the argument of corrupted vision and the power of writing into a discussion of the sonnets as such as objects of desire.

and it was the deceptive attractions of form, *elocutio*, that were the critical point, rather than issues of content. This debate was visually represented through iconographical characters: the lusting, deceitful and uncontrollably sexual harlot of Asianism was visualized most forcefully by Dionysius of Halicarnassus (born *c.* 60 BC),[7] but more importantly and influentially, Quintilian (*c.* 35–*c.* 100) in his *Institutio oratoria* offered two separate female images to define the virtues and vices of rhetoric:

Healthy bodies, with sound blood and strengthened by exercise, acquire good looks by the same means as they acquire strength; they are tanned, slim, and muscular. On the other hand, if one feminises them by plucking the hair and using cosmetics, the very striving for beauty makes them disgusting. Again, decent and impressive apparel lends men authority, as the Greek verse bears witness, but a womanish and luxurious dress, instead of adorning the body, exposes the mind within. In the same way, the translucent and many-coloured style [*elocutio*] of some speakers emasculates subjects which are clothed in this kind of verbal dress ... Eloquence should be approached in a higher spirit; if her whole body is healthy, she will not think that polishing her nails or styling her hair has anything to do with her well-being.[8]

The deceitful and consciously attractive, painted and adorned verbal ornamentation *Elocutio* emasculates and effeminizes (*effeminat*) men, and is thus in the end a threat to society. Beside her stands *Eloquentia*, rhetoric as a whole, being not painted or deceitful but healthy and virtuous. Implied, by their side, is the orator, attracted to both but virtuously to pure *Eloquentia*, voluptuously to sordid *Elocutio*. The cosmetics, adornments and garments of *Elocutio* are here the exaggerated use of *colores rhetorici*: rhetoric's different means of making discourse pleasurable. This includes imagery and visualizations, but not least language's more physical means: rhymes, alliterations, rhythms and metre, which create a sensual body, as it were, of sound.

This iconography of language thus embodies the attraction of language: obviously, man's linguistic desire is the starting point; but it is also represented as a fear of being overwhelmed, seduced, violated,

contaminated, effeminized by this seductive language.[9] Linguistic pleasure is so closely associated with physical pleasure and its moral system of condemnation, that the images receive great force and at times result in a vibrating ambivalence toward what we would today call aesthetic pleasure. Attraction to language and poetry in its pure, clean and honourable form was uncomplicated – but succumbing to its sensually seductive, lustful and deceptive form was condemnable. Where the line was to be drawn was a constant matter of negotiation. Any critic of rhetoric or poetry could easily choose to focus on the harlot-like image of *Elocutio*, while any defender could focus on pure *Eloquentia* or use both images to clarify rhetoric's and poetry's virtues as well as their vices. This is what happened in the English seventeenth- and eighteenth-century debate, where especially Stephen Gosson (1554–1624) in his critique of poetry actualized Plato's suspicion of rhetoric and poetry, and Philip Sidney (1554–86) in his *Defence of Poesie* (first published in 1595) endeavoured to rebuild the image of virtuous *Eloquentia* as *Poesie*, while defining the seductive female image of *Elocutio* as not at all belonging to poetry:

Now for the outside of it [Poesie], which is words, or (as I may tearme it) *Diction*, it is euen well worse: so is it that hony-flowing Matrone *Eloquence*, apparrelled, or rather disguised, in a Courtisanlike painted affectation. One time with so farre fet words, that many seeme monsters, but must seem straungers to anie poore Englishman: an other time, with coursing of a letter, as if they were bound to follow the method of a Dictionary: an other

---

7 Dionysius of Halicarnassus, Περι Των Αρχαιων Ρητορων, *Dionysius of Halicarnassus: The Critical Essays in Two Volumes*, trans. and ed. Stephen Usher, vol. 1 (Cambridge, MA, 1947), pp. 4–7.

8 Quintilian, *The Orator's Education*, vols. I–V, trans. and ed. Donald A. Russell (Cambridge, MA, 2001), vol. 3, Book 8, Pr. 19–22.

9 See Jacqueline Lichtenstein, *The Eloquence of Color: Rhetoric and Painting in the French Classical Age*, trans. Emily McVarish (Berkeley, CA, 1993), esp. pp. 37–54, aiming at Renaissance art theory; and Mats Malm, *Voluptuous Language and Poetic Ambivalence: The Example of Swedish Baroque* (Frankfurt-on-Main, 2011), for a study aiming at literary analysis.

time with figures and flowers, extremely winter-starued.[10]

Related images are to be found in John Rainolds (1549–1607), Fulke Greville (1554–1628), and others.[11]

In early modern society and its notions of morals, passion and sensuality, this could produce a particular dynamic which connects to new medial possibilities to represent mankind and the world, and to the urge to test the limits of art, society and morals. This ambivalence, it appears, in many respects concerns issues of the baroque.[12]

Since Plato, whom Quintilian quotes in order to clarify his own critical stance to voluptuous language, the problem of rhetoric, art and representation as such has been that they flatter and entice with beautifying but false colours, complexions, adornments and ever-shifting variability.[13] The notion of voluptuous language can be found in explicit theoretical arguments, but also in poetry itself. Poetry, of course, often comprises more or less explicit statements of its own conditions, but in some contexts the notion of voluptuous language has also affected poetic discourse as such. It can be taken for granted that the notion as theoretically outlined was known to Shakespeare, and in the section that follows some fundamental traces will be exemplified. However, since Shakespeare indulges in linguistic pleasures more often than any other poet of his time, the ambivalence of linguistic desire becomes substantial.

LANGUAGE'S UNRELIABILITY AND ATTRACTION

Shakespeare's mistrust of descriptions and metaphors is obvious in several of the sonnets, but it is less obvious how this unreliability of language is connected to the attraction of language. I will now examine the thematics and their connection with tradition, in order to analyze how they are actually implemented.

Shakespeare does not resort to the simple allegorical images of rhetoric in his sonnets, although he reveals his acquaintance with the basic image of decorative and deceptive Rhetoric

in the guise of *Elocutio* in *Love's Labour's Lost* (1590s), as Berowne exclaims: 'Fie, painted rhetoric!' (4.3.237).[14] The connection between content and form is underscored in Sonnet 82, when purity in essence, *res*, is juxtaposed with appearance, *verba*: 'Thou art as fair in knowledge as in hue'. The opposition between virtuous content and style, and rhetorical cosmetics and abuse, is then further explicated:

... when they have devised
What strainèd touches rhetoric can lend,
Thou, truly fair, wert truly sympathized
In true plain words by thy true-telling friend;
    And their gross painting might be better used
    Where cheeks need blood: in thee it is abused.[15]

---

[10] Philip Sidney, *The Defence of Poesie* (London, 1595), I3r. See Heinrich Plett, *Rhetorik der Affekte: Englische Wirkungsästhetik im Zeitalter der Renaissance* (Tübingen, 1975), p. 144; Wayne Rebhorn, *The Emperor of Men's Minds. Literature and the Renaissance Discourse of Rhetoric* (Ithaca, NY, 1995), p. 142; and Mats Malm, 'Linguistic Desire and the Moral Iconography of Language in Early Modern England', in *Pangs of Love and Longing: Configurations of Desire in Premodern Literature*, ed. Anders Cullhed et al. (Newcastle upon Tyne, 2013), pp. 144–56.

[11] See the overview in Rebhorn, *Emperor*, pp. 64–79; 133–9, and Heinrich F. Plett, *Rhetoric and Renaissance Culture* (Berlin, 2004), pp. 501–52. Much evidence points at Shakespeare being intimately acquainted with Quintilian through basic education. On the use of Quintilian, see T. W. Baldwin, *William Shakspere's Small Latine & Lesse Greeke*, 2 vols. (Urbana, IL, 1944), vol. 2, pp. 197–239, but the notion of voluptuous language was well established elsewhere as well (cf. Malm, *Voluptuous Language*).

[12] See Malm, *Voluptuous Language*, where the argument is developed from a limited material.

[13] In several respects it concerns iconoclasm, expressions of which in poetry have been treated in previous research. See e.g. John N. King, *English Reformation Literature: The Tudor Origins of the Protestant Tradition* (Princeton, NJ, 1982) and *Spenser's Poetry and the Reformation Tradition* (Princeton, NJ, 1990); Ernest B. Gilman, *Iconoclasm and Poetry in the English Reformation* (Chicago, 1986); and Peter C. Herman, *Squitterwits and Muse-haters: Sidney, Spenser, Milton and Renaissance Antipoetic Sentiment* (Detroit, 1996).

[14] See *William Shakespeare: The Sonnets and a Lover's Complaint*, ed. John Kerrigan (Harmondsworth, 1986), p. 202.

[15] Quotations are from *William Shakespeare: The Complete Works*, ed. Stanley Wells et al. (Oxford, 1986).

The abundant metapoetic traits in Shakespeare's sonnets make it immediately clear – not surprisingly – that he, as would any author within the rhetorically dominated system, instinctively divides between content and form, rhetoric's *res* and *verba, inventio* and *elocutio*. He repeatedly speaks of his invention in the sonnets, in 76 (one of the most consistently metapoetic sonnets) in direct connection to the dressing in words ('in a noted weed') – the metaphor of verbal dress obviously deriving from the idea that *res*–invention–body may be draped in various *verba*–elocution–raiment and corresponding to the metaphor of verbal cosmetics. Shakespeare thematizes the conflict of beautifying and deceptive language as contrasted to 'true' content most obviously in Sonnet 101:

> O truant muse, what shall be thy amends
> For thy neglect of truth in beauty dyed?
> Both truth and beauty on my love depends;
> So dost thou too, and therein dignified.
> Make answer, muse. Wilt thou not haply say
> 'Truth needs no colour with his colour fixed,
> Beauty no pencil beauty's truth to lay,
> But best is best if never intermixed'?
> Because he needs no praise wilt thou be dumb?
> Excuse not silence so, for't lies in thee
> To make him much outlive a gilded tomb,
> And to be praised of ages yet to be.
> > Then do thy office, muse; I teach thee how
> > To make him seem long hence as he shows
> > now.

The traditional notion that truth and virtue need no adornment, as they are beautiful enough in themselves, presupposes the idea that beautifying is also feigning: adornment thus belongs to vice and lie. This idea, an inherent part of the notion of voluptuous language as established by Plato, is here destabilized first by the juxtaposition of *truth* to *beauty*, which appears to motivate the use of more linguistic colour/adornment than would be strictly necessary. In the end, the very old notion that poetry immortalizes is adduced as the final argument for representing. It may noted, though, that the objection that 'Truth needs no colour' is

not directly answered, since this critique concerns the adding of adornment but the answer only defends representing the beloved 'as he shows'. The battle of content and form is thus actualized, and handled by twisting the argument in another direction.

The opposition between content and form, based in the issue of voluptuous language, is an important part of that mistrust toward metaphor which is apparent in the Sonnets but which cannot be properly understood on its own. In one of the most well-known sonnets, number 130, the opposition between content and deceptive words is so commonplace and at the same time so elegantly fashioned that it nearly escapes attention:

> My mistress' eyes are nothing like the sun;
> Coral is far more red than her lips' red.
> If snow be white, why then her breasts are dun;
> If hairs be wires, black wires grow on her head.
> I have seen roses damasked, red and white,
> But no such roses see I in her cheeks;
> And in some perfumes is there more delight
> Than in the breath that from my mistress reeks.
> I love to hear her speak, yet well I know
> That music hath a far more pleasing sound.
> I grant I never saw a goddess go:
> My mistress when she walks treads on the ground.
> > And yet, by heaven, I think my love as rare
> > As any she belied with false compare.

While the surprising effect of the sonnet lies in negating love poetry's extolling clichés, it actually thematizes the problem not only of 'false compare' but also of false representation.[16] This false representation is directly connected to erotic desire – physical in the sense that it is meant to lead to a particular result – but it is also connected to linguistic desire in the sense that it is rhetoric's colours that are thematized and visualized as sensual (vision, hearing, smell, inviting to touch and taste)

---

[16] Kerrigan, *Shakespeare*, pp. 18–33, poignantly treats these and other sonnets' problematization of metaphor and comparison, but not the issue of representation as such.

enhancement and lie, making the woman described a more sensually attractive object than she is in reality.

While this critique of representation is fairly obvious, the effect of it only shows when it is connected to the thematics of the preceding poem. Sonnet 129 has received much attention for its spectacularly elaborate form, and the form has been connected to the moral content.[17]

Th'expense of spirit in a waste of shame
Is lust in action; and till action, lust
Is perjured, murd'rous, bloody, full of blame,
Savage, extreme, rude, cruel, not to trust,
Enjoyed no sooner but despisèd straight,
Past reason hunted, and no sooner had,
Past reason hated as a swallowed bait
On purpose laid to make the taker mad,
Mad in pursuit and in possession so,
Had, having, and in quest to have, extreme;
A bliss in proof and proved, a very woe,
Before, a joy proposed; behind, a dream.
   All this the world well knows, yet none knows well
   To shun the heaven that leads men to this hell.

In commentaries, it is usually pointed out how the sexual act as well as its fore- and aftermath are elegantly described without many sexual or physical words being used, and that even the concluding lines, which sound definitely moralizing, are destabilized by the contemporary use of 'hell' for the vagina. Moreover, commentaries usually dwell on the many stylistic features of the poem, ranging from anaphors and alliteration to parallelisms and antitheses. That is, the poem offers an exceedingly attractive stylistic body, adorned in every adornment possible to squeeze into fourteen lines. From one point of view, what the poem actually says corresponds to the form; it all concerns pleasure, delight, attraction, lust. However, the poem's proposition is entirely moral, renouncing the pleasures and ending in the conclusion that these lusts should be shunned. While the poem's content, invention, idea recognizes the attraction of pleasure but actually denounces it, its form, elocution, style paradoxically engage unreservedly in the attractions and delights – not of the physical body, but of language.

Among Shakespeare's Sonnets, this one is unusual in so strongly thematizing the problem of voluptuousness and lust – not one-sidedly moralizing, but putting forth a problem vibrating with complications. The intensity of the language clearly demonstrates that it is not only physical desire that is at stake, but also linguistic desire. This is entirely in accordance with the traditional notion of voluptuous language, which is based on the presumption that language is endowed with a body: physical morals (or immorality) are tantamount to linguistic morals (or immorality). However, the nerve of the poem appears to consist in the ambivalence toward desire on different levels, since the poem does not reject voluptuous language in the same way as it does voluptuous carnality. In a sense, the sonnet calls for being understood as a proposition of the kind that would later be elaborated with the rise of aesthetics and disinterested pleasure as Immanuel Kant would define it: the morals of language and art are *not* easily equatable with the morals of the actual body.[18] At the same time, by staging linguistic desire in form, overlaying corporeal desire in content, the sonnet partakes in the old debate about voluptuous language. Thus, Sonnets 129 and 130 in different ways thematize the same opposition between content and form, *res* and *verba* – by way of desire.

Since Plato, the uncontrollable nature of representation and elocution is in itself the problem of a culture in which stability and adherence to universal virtues are the norm. There thus arises a peculiar duplicity concerning constancy and writing, which is especially apparent in Shakespeare's Sonnet 105:

---

[17] See particularly Roman Jakobson and Lawrence G. Jones, *Shakespeare's Verbal Art in Th'Expense of Spirit* (The Hague, 1970); and Helen Vendler, 'Jakobson, Richards, and Shakespeare's Sonnet CXXIX', in *I. A. Richards. Essays in his Honor*, ed. Reuben Brower et al. (New York, 1973), pp. 179–98.

[18] On the negotiations of the norms connected to the notion of voluptuous language in the aesthetics of the eighteenth century, see Malm, *Voluptuous Language*, pp. 255–65.

Let not my love be called idolatry,
Nor my belovèd as an idol show,
Since all alike my songs and praises be
To one, of one, still such, and ever so.
Kind is my love today, tomorrow kind,
Still constant in a wondrous excellence.
Therefore my verse, to constancy confined,
One thing expressing, leaves out difference.
'Fair, kind, and true' is all my argument,
'Fair, kind, and true' varying to other words,
And in this change is my invention spent,
Three themes in one, which wondrous scope affords.
    Fair, kind, and true have often lived alone,
    Which three till now never kept seat in one.

As Kerrigan puts it, 'Almost bare of metaphor, with a chaste rhetorical "colour" scheme, it exemplifies in verbal terms the flatness of *constancy*.'[19] The question is why. Whilst the pun of this poem is obviously that the speaker is not guilty of worshipping more than one god – as what he worships is the Trinity, here transformed into the 'Fair, kind, and true', one essential aspect of idolatry that structures the poem is that of adoration of surface, attractive representation. Superabundant decoration in churches was thrown out in England and elsewhere not only because it was considered wrong to adore saints and others, but also, and not least, because it was considered wrong to adore representations as such, especially when the representations were colourfully adorned. Decoration and ornament directed worship from the referents to the signs, hence the tangible resistance toward decoration in Protestant and Reform theory (also in Catholic theory, but as a rule, the resistance to ornament was used as an argument against Catholicism).[20] When the speaker's love must not *show* the beloved in this way, it means that the love-poem must not ornament its subject, the beloved. Ornament is many-coloured and varying: here, constancy and simplicity both of love and representation (verse) is repeatedly underlined. The poet, here as elsewhere, must find words for it, but they must not be enticing, misleading or deceptive: they must on the contrary be 'Fair, kind, and true'. Virtuous love, as well as language, is constant; desirous love, as well as language, is inconstant. This simple dichotomy may

not have been Shakespeare's unreserved confession, but it certainly was the dominating paradigm of his time. Sonnet 105 thus exemplifies the exact opposite to the explorations of voluptuous desire of Sonnet 129, yet draws upon the same notions of the virtues and vices of language. In 105, chaste *Eloquentia* rules; in 129, voluptuous *Elocutio*. The idea of language's attractions and the dichotomy of true essence versus false linguistic cosmetics and garb are thus pervasive in Shakespeare's sonnets, thematically connecting to traditional notions of voluptuous language. Still the question remains, how these notions and particularly the female apparitions are actually transformed in Shakespeare's sonnets.

OBJECTS OF DESIRE

As was pointed out by Trevor, the Sonnets themselves offer constancy as a counterbalance to the inconstancy of love. Whilst this is consistent with notions of writing's power in love-sonnets elsewhere, as well as with the old notion of poetry's ability to immortalize, it should be pointed out that the constancy of writing and poetry, both in the sense of literary stabilizing and of durability of the written word, are balanced – or, rather, unbalanced – by a pervasive notion of the inconstancy of language; that language which is associated with exaggerated elocution, cosmetics, adornment, pleasure and effeminacy. The effect of this is that language and love overlay each other in a way which covers constancy as well as inconstancy.

It is true, and seminal, that Shakespeare removes God from the traditional tripartite sonnet structure lover–beloved–God, and that the poems which the speaker creates certainly provide a kind of solution. To Trevor, the young man and the dark lady are important because they are 'loved in expressly literary terms – as literary creations, not real people',

---

[19] Kerrigan, *Shakespeare*, p. 310. As Trevor, together with Fineman, comments, 'my love' in verse 5 should not be understood as the beloved but as the speaker's 'love put into being by poetry itself' (Trevor, 'Love Objects', p. 232).

[20] I refer to the argument and references adduced in Malm, *Voluptuous Language*, pp. 47–57.

which leads 'back to the verse itself'.[21] This would substantiate the idea that the Sonnets themselves are introduced as a love object, but the matter appears rather to be that the desire for the loved characters is overlaid with desire for and of language. That is, it is not the literary creations that are loved, but literary language itself. This means that the traditional Petrarchan triad lover–beloved–God has turned into a triad lover–beloved(s)–language. The Horatian trust in poetry's constancy is thus problematized by another notion of antiquity.

There are reasons to consider the beloved(s) as substantially different from the traditional beloved, through the merging of the young man and the dark lady – adding the illicit to the licit so as to catch all aspects of desire and reflect it further. And as they simultaneously represent the desire of language, it is language that takes the place of God in the traditional triad. It is then not the actual poems that are the objects of desire, but language itself – the chaste desire for pure language, corresponding to *Eloquentia*, and simultaneously, ambivalently and tremblingly, the linguistic desire for voluptuous language, corresponding to *Elocutio*: the uncontrolled and uncontrollable, effeminizing and immoral harlot of the rhetorical tradition. The Sonnets obviously give no conclusive or homogeneous proposition, but in a complex way portray the objects of physical desire as well as linguistic desire.

These double objects of desire – the beloved and language instead of God – consequently form the negated conclusion of Sonnet 116:

> Love's not time's fool, though rosy lips and cheeks
> Within his bending sickle's compass come;
> Love alters not with his brief hours and weeks,
> But bears it out even to the edge of doom.
>   If this be error and upon me proved,
>   I never writ, nor no man ever loved.

The last verse is usually interpreted 'I never wrote and no man loved' or 'I never wrote or loved a man'.[22] In this case, loving and writing are strictly paralleled, but their parallelism is stronger than so. As Stephen Booth points out, the 'error' in the preceding verse gains effect by actualizing legal process and legal language: the juridical formula 'writ of error' (a kind of fault in proceedings) ties 'error' to the verb 'writ'.[23] However, this connection also suggests the *noun* 'writ': writing. The verses may thus be read as a statement of Shakespeare's renegotiated Petrarchan triad lover–beloved–language 'I never loved writing, nor any man/human'.

It appears obvious that besides the erotic and sexual desire of Shakespeare's Sonnets, part of their nerve resides in a linguistic desire handed down in tradition. Desire here is not negotiable in categories of hetero- or homosexuality, nor in terms of actual corporeality. Departing from the voice produced by the body, it takes place in verboreality and is linguistic, although it, as a rule, needs corporeal metaphors and graphic visualizations to be explicated. In Shakespeare's Sonnets, desire for the young man is overlaid by desire for pure language, while desire for the dark lady is overlaid by desire for voluptuous language.

Analogous to physical desire, linguistic desire trembles between the virtuous, constant and true on the one hand, and the voluptuous, inconstant and deceptive on the other. So close are these desires, that even though Shakespeare does not exploit the iconography of voluptuous language in the same allegorical way as do Greville, Sidney and others, his desired objects to a very great extent are subjected to the same rules and appear in very much the same way. So, while the curious 'master-mistress' of Sonnet 20 cannot be reduced to an image of language or rhetoric, the correspondence between its juxtaposition of images and rhetoric's juxtaposition of images is overwhelming.

> A woman's face with nature's own hand painted
> Hast thou, the master-mistress of my passion;
> A woman's gentle heart, but not acquainted
> With shifting change as is false women's fashion;
> An eye more bright than theirs, less false in rolling,

---

[21] Trevor, 'Love Objects', p. 234.

[22] See for example Trevor, 'Love Objects', p. 238.

[23] *Shakespeare's Sonnets*, ed. Stephen Booth (New Haven, CT, 1977), pp. 386–7.

Gilding the object whereupon it gazeth;
A man in hue, all hues in his controlling,
Which steals men's eyes and women's souls amazeth.

The androgynous male beloved is opposed to the feminine false in just the same way as *Eloquentia* with her masculine, that is, non-feminine traits is traditionally opposed to *Elocutio* with her feminine and effeminating traits: a natural beauty, true and unadorned, with a complexion/hue that stirs amazement but is controlled, versus the shifting falseness and deceptive mien that is designed to entice lascivity. In this sense, the androgyneity of the beloved young man is consistent with the image of good rhetoric: this female icon, according to its misogynous origin, differs from bad rhetoric precisely through the lack of excessive 'feminine' apparel: through being more masculine – a linguistic 'master-mistress'. The two desires of the poet as formulated in Sonnet 144 thus correspond to an ancient debate on language:

> Two loves I have, of comfort and despair,
> Which like two spirits do suggest me still.
> The better angel is a man right fair,
> The worser spirit a woman coloured ill.

It remains uncertain whether it is the eye of the master-mistress or of the others which gilds the object it sees in Sonnet 20, but in either case, it is obviously the act of adorning representation that is the issue. This sonnet is particularly tightly connected to the next one, number 21, which expresses an easily recognizable attitude, but in this case obviously concerning poetry:

> So is it not with me as with that muse
> Stirred by a painted beauty to his verse,
> Who heaven itself for ornament doth use,
> And every fair with his fair doth rehearse,
> Making a couplement of proud compare
> With sun and moon, with earth, and sea's rich gems,
> With April's first-born flowers, and all things rare
> That heaven's air in this huge rondure hems.
> O let me, true in love, but truly write,
> And then believe me my love is as fair
> As any mother's child, though not so bright
> As those gold candles fixed in heaven's air.

The 'muse' will here be a synonym for the rival poet who does differently than the 'I', and the 'painted beauty' could simply be a painting or a person beautified with cosmetics,[24] but the negative associations are evident in the following verses and as the 'I' contrasts with the will to be true and write truly. The 'painted beauty' thus establishes dame *Elocutio* as we know her from Quintilian and iconographical descriptions in Shakespeare's vicinity. In this way, Sonnet 20 sets up the negative example of the poet who, unlike the 'I', writes under the influence of feigned and beautified representation, while the 'I' in Sonnet 21 writes under the influence of the unadorned, natural beauty which we recognize as the personification of good rhetoric.

As Kerrigan points out, this sonnet connects to the critique of simile and metaphor in Sonnet 130, and the two sonnets (or sonnet pairs) have the same introductory role within the first and second group of sonnets respectively.[25] The critique, as we have seen, concerns not only simile and metaphor, but also language and artistic representation on the whole. We may also note that the poet's desire for language is doubled by the young man's: the rival poet attracts the young man through his voluptuous language, which implies that the speaker's relation to the young man is based on attraction – to his language. The young man's linguistic desire is also effectuated by a version of rhetoric's iconology in Sonnet 82, where the muse instead of rhetoric corporealizes poetry and language in order for the young man to be able to be 'married to my muse'.

THE SONNET SEQUENCE

The division of the Sonnets into one part where, after the introductory sonnets, the object of desire is the fair young man, and one part where the object of desire is the 'dark lady', has been

---

[24] *Shakespeare's Sonnets*, p. 166.
[25] Kerrigan, *Shakespeare*, pp. 23–4.

frequently discussed. The main critique, as formulated by Heather Dubrow, concerns the 'plotting' of the Sonnets: not only reading biographical information into them, but also construing a consistent development in them.[26] However, the critique concerns various attempts to construe the addressees and the plot, and does not dismiss the idea as such of a divide between Sonnets 126 and 127. Such a break is apparent in a number of ways, not least through the relative initial stability and the concluding instability and through Sutphen's demonstrating of how the poet's use of memory and writing to control oblivion and loss fails toward the end. The shift between Sonnets 126 and 127 thus concerns not only the objects of desire, but also the way they are represented. In essence, this means that the two parts not only develop different objects of desire, but also different kinds of desire. Sonnet 127 reads:

> In the old age black was not counted fair,
> Or if it were, it bore not beauty's name;
> But now is black beauty's successive heir,
> And beauty slandered with a bastard shame:
> For since each hand hath put on nature's power,
> Fairing the foul with art's false borrowed face,
> Sweet beauty hath no name, no holy bower,
> But is profaned, if not lives in disgrace.
> Therefore my mistress' eyes are raven-black,
> Her brow so suited, and they mourners seem
> At such who, not born fair, no beauty lack,
> Sland'ring creation with a false esteem.
> > Yet so they mourn, becoming of their woe,
> > That every tongue says beauty should look so.

The dark lady, the new object of desire, is here introduced in a way that makes her the vehicle of an elaborate thematization of representation. The word 'beauty' appears five times only in this sonnet.[27] Whilst this demonstrates the importance of the phenomenon, it is not as a general concept that beauty appears, but as a personification. Beauty has a name, an heir, is slandered, is sweet, then has no longer a name (in the sense of good reputation), no longer dwells in a bower, is profaned and even lives in disgrace.[28] Shakespeare meets the problem of desire by introducing not the pure and virtuous

female character, but instead presenting the deeply problematic dark lady, exaggerating the problems rather than dodging them. As Stephen Booth has pointed out, 'Fairing the foul with art's false borrowed face' with its 'ostentatious alliteration, consonance and assonance makes the line sound "beautified", artificially tricked out'.[29] Thus, curiously, 'my mistress' has black eyes, which is further elaborated with the same conventional idea of natural beauty versus painted beauty. The personification of Beauty thus results in two personifications, and this embodies the thematics and imagery of the sonnets: the natural, constant and virtuous image on the one side, and on the other, the faked, enticing, ever-changing woman who is beautiful only insofar as nature has been painted and lent a new, artificially created face. The issue at stake is thus representation, and the imagery again corresponds to the traditional imagery of good rhetoric, *Eloquentia*, versus bad rhetoric, exaggerated *Elocutio*.

The notions of voluptuous language and the twofold iconography of rhetoric were a general heritage, discretely but broadly transmitted and handled. As I have shown, it is also on the linguistic and metalinguistic levels that constancy and fairness are connected with the young man of the first part, while infirmity and feigning are connected with the woman. So, even though the first part is also filled with deliberations of the problem of representation and authenticity, it relates to that past age when natural beauty prevailed, while the falseness, incertitude and inconstancy of the latter part is announced by the words on false beautification. The young man part connects to the image of

---

[26] Heather Dubrow, '"Incertainties now crown themselves assur'd": The Politics of Plotting Shakespeare's Sonnets', in *Shakespeare's Sonnets: Critical Essays*, ed. James Schiffer (New York, 2000), pp. 113–33.

[27] Sutphen, 'Dateless lively heat', p. 211.

[28] In the 1609 edition, 'Beautie' begins with a capital only once, but whether that orthography was intended from the beginning is impossible to know.

[29] *Shakespeare's Sonnets*, p. 435.

good rhetoric, while the dark lady part connects to the image of bad rhetoric – and the growing focus on the unreliability of language and representation as such is entirely consistent with the fact that, as Sutphen has pointed out, it is only in the former part that memory and writing can provide consolation of loss. From this perspective, the opposition between vision and language which Fineman distinguished can fundamentally be understood as the ancient opposition between pure, unadorned language and misleading, cosmetically coloured language.

Thus, the desire for the young man is overlaid primarily by desire for good, true, virtuous language, and the desire for the dark lady is overlaid by desire for detrimental, false, voluptuous language. While Trevor is correct in pointing out how the sonnet triad of desire lover–beloved–God was abandoned here, it appears that God is not substituted by the poems themselves, but by language. It is not only the traditional notion of poetry's ability to consolidate that is implemented in the Sonnets; the traditional, highly iconographical, notion of language's inconstancy is too. This means that although writing and the poems themselves function as a consolation for the Shakespearian 'I', as for other sonneteers, Shakespeare fills this function with a vibrant complexity.

All of this relates to the speaker's own use of voluptuous language, as he explicitly tries to choose true language but in the end is left with excessive, voluptuous language. The underlying assumption from antiquity onwards is that whoever submits himself (for the subject will always be 'he') to linguistic desire will be effeminated, made useless by it, and whoever delivers voluptuous language thereby reveals his effeminacy. Consequently, in Sonnet 147, the speaker's love is explained through the will to deliver pleasure:

> My love is as a fever, longing still
> For that which longer nurseth the disease,
> Feeding on that which doth preserve the ill,
> Th' uncertain sickly appetite to please.

This can be understood as the reason for the whole deliberation on linguistic desire: *Elocutio*'s appetite and will to please to speak with Quintilian, the same qualities in the poet and rhetorician to speak with Plato. The novelty of Shakespeare's Sonnets thus to a considerable part rests on very old notions, staged in a new, elusively artistic way.

When Stephen Greenblatt explicated the sexual chafing of Shakespearian comedy as a kind of representative, verbal foreplay, he focused much on the issue of sexual identity. As he concluded that 'for Shakespeare friction is specifically associated with verbal wit; indeed at moments the plays seem to imply that erotic friction *originates* in the wantonness of language and thus that the body itself is a tissue of metaphors or, conversely, that language is perfectly embodied', so we may conclude that an underlying premise was the notion of linguistic desire and the direct relation between voluptuous language and the physical body that conveys or receives it.[30] Friction is here not the result of fiction. Friction arises as the sounds and syllables lustfully rub against each other, creating a garb of voluptuous language for the poet, for the listener, and for the reader who re-enacts the poem's ingratiating voice.

---

[30] Stephen Greenblatt, *Shakespearean Negotiations: The Circulation of Social Energy in Renaissance England* (Oxford, 1988), p. 89.

SYMPATHETIC SONNETS

KATHARINE A. CRAIK

I

This story begins with one famously unreasonable reader. Delia Bacon was born in Ohio in 1811, the youngest daughter of a Congregationalist minister. She had no formal education after 14, but her teachers described her formidable eloquence and 'fervid imagination'.[1] Bacon is remembered now, when she is remembered at all, as the first person seriously to question the authorship of Shakespeare's plays. Bacon spent four years in England in the 1850s, pursuing her theory that Shakespeare's works were written not by a single person but rather by a group of courtiers exiled from the centre of power who were working in a determinedly proto-republican spirit. Chief among these, significantly, was Bacon's namesake: Francis Bacon. Delia Bacon's method was to find a 'system of philosophy' in Shakespeare's lines which, she came to believe, registered with a comparable system in the writings of Francis Bacon. She had not set out to find it; but, as Nathaniel Hawthorne explained, she gradually 'began to see, under the surface, the gleam of this hidden treasure'.[2] Truly understanding Shakespeare was all about the experience of reading, for Bacon, rather than seeing the plays performed in the theatre. They became too rushed and crowded, she argued, when they were staged; only by absorbing oneself in their pages could the 'repose, the thought, and sentiment of actual life' be properly realized.[3] According to one of her students, Bacon's method was to 'saturate herself with the play, as it were; to live in it, to call into imaginative consciousness the loves, hopes, fears, ambition,

disappointment, and despair of the characters, and under this intense realization to divine, as it were, the meaning of the play'. It was precisely this absorption in the plays which broke Bacon, according to Hawthorne:

Unquestionably, she was a monomaniac; these overmastering ideas about the authorship of Shakespeare's plays, and the deep political philosophy concealed beneath the surface of them, had completely thrown her off her balance . . . From her own account, it appears she did at one time lose her reason; it was on finding that the philosophy, which she found under the surface of the plays, was running counter to the religious doctrines in which she had been educated.[4]

Delia Bacon's methodology, together with Hawthorne's remarks, suggest something of what is at stake for selfhood and subjectivity when we read. A series of intensely experiential encounters with Shakespeare involved Bacon in a recalibration

---

[1] This description is attributed to Catherine and Mary Beecher who ran the Female Seminary where Bacon was educated for a year. See James Shapiro, *Contested Will: Who Wrote Shakespeare?* (London, 2010), p. 93.

[2] Nathaniel Hawthorne's preface to Delia Bacon's *The Philosophy of the Plays of Shakespeare Unfolded* (London, 1856), pp. ix and x.

[3] The quotation is taken from Bacon's preface to her play *The Bride of Fort Edward, Founded on an Incident of the Revolution* (New York, 1839) available via Project Gutenberg www.gutenberg.org/files/7235/7235-h/7235-h.htm.

[4] Nathaniel Hawthorne, *Our Old Home: A Series of English Sketches* (Columbus, OH, 1970), p. 106. See also Shapiro, *Contested Will*, pp. 99 and 110.

of all that she thought she was, as the faultlines between fiction and lived experience started to erode. Her education and upbringing had been rooted in the myth of the founding fathers in accordance with the great Puritan, evangelical tradition. But her theory that the plays were written collaboratively, in a republican spirit, sat uneasily with the myth of America she had grown up with. Few critics have remarked upon the coincidence of names between Delia Bacon and the man she believed lay at the heart of Shakespeare's works, Francis Bacon, and she never sought to prove a genealogical link. But searching for the origins of Shakespeare's works, Delia Bacon was also uncovering a new version of her own origins – and a new version of herself.[5]

There are many different ways to read Bacon's story. The more fantastic elements of her methodology, together with her unshakeable conviction that her scholarly mission involved unravelling an 'endlessly deferred Gnostic secret', share something with the later, wilder excesses of the anti-Stratfordians.[6] Her insistence that Shakespeare could not have written the plays because he was a commoner is now particularly difficult to countenance, although more sympathetic readers might find in her writings the beginnings of the debate about collaborative dramatic production which is now such an important strand of Shakespeare studies.[7] For the purposes of this article, Bacon's life opens up questions about reading as an embodied practice with profound implications for personal integrity and wholeness. Bacon published her theories as *The Philosophy of Shakespeare Unfolded* (1857), an extraordinary volume which vividly captures the strangeness of literary experience, bearing witness as it does to an intensely collaborative exchange between author, text and reader. For Hawthorne, this exchange is evidence of Bacon's 'monomania' – an *idée fixe* in which the mind loses its reason in one particular respect but remains sound in others. I suggest instead that Bacon's relinquishment of herself in the act of reading, together with her sense (never fully articulated) that she was somehow involved in the texts' production as well as their reception, sheds interesting

light on reading practices that we have long since forgotten. Bacon's story may be famously wild and improbable, but can we take seriously the unfashionable possibility that reading involves processes of identification, reidentification and unidentification which oblige us to reconsider who we think we are? Scholars have recently tended to figure the early modern reading experience as medicinal, therapeutic or self-regulatory, often drawing on the templates of usefulness or sweetness (*utile et dulce*). But reading literature, especially Shakespeare, also involves enthusiasm, recognition and sympathy – none of which are easy to square with these familiar templates.

Shakespeare's Sonnets make an interesting test case as they theorize their readers' experience in sometimes painful detail. The first 126 sonnets in particular, addressed to the friend, offer a series of meditations on the act of reading – many of which are animated by reflections on the sonnets' own greatness (and smallness). The Sonnets have remained remarkably resistant to our usual strategies for discussing early modern habits of reading, perhaps because at the heart of the experience they describe lies a kind of possession, or enthusiasm, which looks neither useful nor delightful. In order to think afresh about how it feels to encounter the Sonnets, this article considers them alongside the Greek rhetorical treatise *Peri hypsous* (or *On the*

---

[5] For a recent discussion of Delia Bacon's early contributions to the authorship debate, see Graham Holderness, 'The Unreadable Delia Bacon', and Alan Stewart, 'The Case for Bacon', in *Shakespeare Beyond Doubt: Evidence, Argument, Controversy*, ed. Paul Edmondson and Stanley Wells (Cambridge, 2013), pp. 5–15 and 16–28. Nicholas Royle revisits Delia Bacon's interest in Francis Bacon through Freud's 'engagement with the power of the proper name'. See 'The Distraction of 'Freud': Literature, Psychoanalysis and the Bacon-Shakespeare Controversy', in *Shakespeare and his Authors: Critical Perspectives on the Authorship Question*, ed. William Leahy (London, 2010), pp. 58–90; p. 62.

[6] Holderness, 'Unreadable Delia', p. 15.

[7] Bacon's first published essay, in *Putnam's Monthly* (January 1856), scorns those who 'refer the origin of these works to the illiterate man who kept the theatre'. See Martin Pares, *A Pioneer: In Memory of Delia Bacon* (London, 1958), p. 7.

Sublime) probably written in the 1st century AD by the author known as 'Longinus'. Longinus's theories overlap in many respects with earlier Greek and Roman writers, but his treatise is different in its sustained attention to the overwhelming effect of encountering excellence in speech and writing. Using examples drawn from epic, tragedy and, significantly, love poetry, Longinus describes how audiences become profoundly involved – enthralled, inflamed, astonished – by particular passages of literature or rhetoric.

Longinus's theories are usually regarded as peripheral to early modern literary culture, partly because *Peri hypsous* tends to be considered in isolation from other traditions of classical thought. Its English readership is generally believed to have been confined to a small scholarly audience England before Nicolas Boileau's *Traité du sublime* (1674) proved foundational to the modern conception of Shakespeare as an original genius, and inspired John Dryden, John Dennis, Joseph Addison and Sir Joshua Reynolds.[8] The textual history of *Peri hypsous*, however, begins much earlier than this. Its first printed appearance was in the Basle edition of 1554, which included the Greek text together with marginal notes in Latin, followed by the Venetian edition of 1555. The first translation into Latin was Domenico Pizzimenti's in 1566, followed by Franciscus Portus's Greek text in 1569–70, Portus's further (undated) Latin commentary and Petrus Paganus's Latin 1572 translation. *Peri hypsous* began influencing the period's literary theory as early as 1575 when a translation into Italian by the Florentine scholar Giovanni da Falgano appeared in manuscript.[9] The availability of the text in Latin and vernacular translations and commentaries, as well as several editions in the original Greek, justifies the serious scholarly attention it has already enjoyed among historians of early modern literature and culture. Scholars including Patrick Cheney, Arthur Kinney and Brian Vickers have all noted the likely importance of *Peri hypsous* to Renaissance thinkers increasingly interested in rhetoric's appeal to volition as well as cognition.[10] More recently, Caroline van Eck and others have shown how widely print and

manuscript editions of the work were circulating in Latin and vernacular languages, arguing that Longinus was figuratively (as well as literally) translated across Europe through theories of architecture and the visual arts. We now know that Longinus's ideas were reaching early modern audiences through more complex and diffuse channels than previously believed.[11] Yet despite this, the complex textual history of *Peri hypsous*, together with the critical tendency to consider the treatise in isolation, mean that its importance to early modern culture, and to the sonnet tradition in particular, remains largely uncharted. The assumptions arising from the long-held critical consensus that Longinus was virtually unknown in England until Gerard Langbaine's 1636 Oxford edition are ripe for revision, however. Longinus's theories of reception were trickling into English literary and theatrical culture as early as the 1590s, partly through continental writings on the writing and reading of sonnets, and this sheds new contextual light on Shakespeare's own consideration, in his Sonnets, of the astonishments and self-reversals which attend committed acts of reading.

---

[8] Jonathan Lamb has surveyed Longinus's importance to eighteenth-century aesthetics and politics. See 'The Sublime', in *The Cambridge History of Literary Criticism*, vol. 4, *The Eighteenth Century*, ed. H. B. Nisbet and C. Rawson (Cambridge, 1997), pp. 394–416. On the importance of Boileau for the 'developing appreciation of Shakespeare's distinctive artistic stature', see David Hopkins, *Conversing with Antiquity* (Oxford, 2010), pp. 37–54; 38.

[9] The early textual history is outlined by Bernard Weinberg, 'Translations and Commentaries of Longinus, On the Sublime, to 1600: A Bibliography', *Modern Philology*, 47 (1950), 145–51.

[10] Patrick Cheney, *Marlowe's Republican Authorship: Lucan, Liberty, and the Sublime* (Basingstoke, 2009), pp. 12–21; Arthur F. Kinney, *Humanist Poetics: Thought, Rhetoric and Fiction in Sixteenth-Century England* (Amherst, MA, 1986), pp. 199–201; and Brian Vickers, *In Defence of Rhetoric* (Oxford, 1988), pp. 297–9 and 307–10. See also David Sedley, *Sublimity and Skepticism in Montaigne and Milton* (Ann Arbor, MI, 2005), p. 10.

[11] See *The Early Modern Reception and Dissemination of Longinus' 'Peri Hupsous' in Rhetoric, the Visual Arts, Architecture and the Theatre*, ed. Caroline Van Eck et al. (Leiden, 2012).

II

As explorations of reading and reception, the Sonnets and *Peri hypsous* have some interesting impulses in common. Longinus wrote *Peri hypsous* as a response to the impoverished state of contemporary writing, bemoaning 'that passion for novelty of thought which is the particular craze of the present day' and criticizing those with an 'insatiable passion for starting strange conceits'.[12] The date and authorship of *Peri hypsous* are both uncertain, and the text exists only in mutilated form. Around two-thirds is thought to survive: there are six lacunae in the only authoritative textual source, which dates from the tenth century, and the ending is missing altogether. Longinus was writing in response to a contemporary problem, namely the excesses of style prevalent among first-century writers and orators. By way of remedy, he offered a clear and definitive account of the five origins of 'excellence and distinction in language': namely, great thoughts, strong emotion, figures of speech, noble diction and dignified arrangement of words.[13] Whilst the best examples of speech and the written word have 'beauty, clearnesse, weight, [and] strength', truly excellent rhetoric and literature also have emotional intensity, or 'height' (*hypsos*). It is this elusive aspect of writing that Longinus strives to describe. Ornament may sooth or bring pleasure, and persuasive words may change minds – but in truly great writing,

the effect of genius is not to persuade the audience but rather to transport them out of themselves. Invariably what inspires wonder, with its power of amazing us, always prevails over what is merely convincing and pleasing. For our persuasions are usually under our own control, while these things exercise an irresistible power and mastery, and get the better of every listener.[14]

Great writing does not persuade people of something useful, or delight them with something beautiful. Instead, it involves a kind of enthusiasm, and necessitates a relinquishment of will. *Hypsos* can therefore be translated not only as sublimity or height, but also as rapture. Its effects are variously described as a 'flash of lightning', 'a whirlwind',

a 'thunderbolt', or a sense of 'Gigantick and transcendent' scale to which one cannot help but abandon oneself. In the words of Longinus's first English translator, John Hall, 'many are so rapt and transported with the conceptions of another, that they are possessed'.[15] The overwhelming effects of sublime rhetoric on audiences, and the loss of reason such effects inevitably involve, do not however represent a source of anxiety and shame. Instead they signal the writer's superlative achievement – and the matching commitment of the reader.

It follows, then, that attentive readers tend to focus upon the most profoundly affecting passages, rather than on those which challenge their point of view through careful reasoning: 'our attention is drawn from the reasoning to the enthralling (*ekplektikon*) effect of the imagination'.[16] A productive exchange takes place between those who speak and write passionately, and audiences who find themselves entranced by them so that 'the true sublime naturally elevates us: uplifted with a sense of proud exaltation, we are filled with joy and pride, as if we had ourselves produced the very thing we heard' (pp. 178–9).

The best aesthetic experiences come when we encounter words or thoughts which look particular to us, so that to experience great writing is, finally, to be persuaded not just that the text is *about* us, but rather that it comes *from* us, 'as if we had ourselves produced the very thing we heard'. Our powerful sense as readers that the text was made not just for (but also *by*) ourselves accompanies the fiercest, richest and most generous experiences of reading. The sublime therefore involves embracing 'the true sublime'

[12] *Peri hypsous (On the Sublime)*, trans. W. H. Fyfe and rev. Donald Russell (Cambridge, MA, 1995; rev. edn 1999), pp. 177, 171. All quotations refer to this edition.

[13] *On the Sublime*, p. 163. For a lucid summary of the treatise's engagement with the literary and rhetorical culture of the time, see J. W. H. Atkins, *Literary Criticism in Antiquity: A Sketch of its Development* (London, 1934), pp. 210–53; 219.

[14] *On the Sublime*, pp. 162–3.

[15] *Of the Height of Eloquence* (1652), sigs. F8v, E6r, D6r, C8v and D7r.

[16] *On the Sublime*, pp. 224–5.

until we experience it as our own; elevated by grandeur, we enter into a sympathetic state of greatness. This process of identification, which breaks down barriers between writers and audiences, is central to Longinus's theory of excellence.[17]

To readers steeped in sixteenth-century humanist pedagogy, certain aspects of Longinus's theory must have seemed, as John Logan has written, 'highly idiosyncratic and unorthodox at best, subversive and incomprehensible at worst'.[18] *Peri hypsous* must have offended many conservative Renaissance scholars at a time when good habits of reading were founded on very different classical theories of audience reception. These theories lay behind the Renaissance conviction that reading and listening resembled forms of self-discipline against which men (in particular) could learn to calibrate the unruly movements of their affections.[19] Renaissance readers would nevertheless have encountered theories of inspired authorship, and the intense involvement of audiences, in the work of other classical theorists besides Longinus. The ancient treatise on poetics most frequently consulted, Horace's *Art of Poetry*, suggests that orators' keenly felt emotions become their auditors' ('si vis me flere, dolendum est / primum ipsi tibi', 'If you would have me weep, you must first feel grief yourself').[20] Longinus's text also shares much in common with Plato's theory in *Ion* of the rhapsode's ecstasy which draws listeners inexorably, like a magnet, until they too experience a form of possession; with Cicero's discussion in *De Inventione* of rhetorical vividness, capable of placing scenes before each listener until he experiences them 'as if he were present, and not by words alone'; and Quintilian's theory in *Institutio Oratoria* of the ability of *phantasia* to penetrate the listeners' emotions and, in so doing, to produce *enargeia*.[21] But none of these sources puts forward a theory of reception adequate to account for the extraordinary sympathies described and enacted through Shakespeare's Sonnets.

For the Sonnets have often possessed and overwhelmed their readers. Oscar Wilde's obsessive scholar Cyril Graham, who shoots himself with a revolver in *The Portrait of Mr W. H.* in order to demonstrate his 'firm and flawless' belief that the dedicatee of the 1609 volume, Mr W. H., was the beautiful young Elizabethan actor Willie Hughes, reminds us of the Sonnets' extraordinary ability to entrance and beguile – or, as Longinus would have it, to 'get the better of every listener'.[22] The first 126 sonnets are indeed partly about the overwhelming effect they are designed to have on readers, not only their immediate addressee, the young man, but also later readers in posterity. Part of the way this happens, of course, is through the vigorous mental power of the speaker. As Longinus reminds us, 'Sublimity is the echo of a noble mind' – and nobility is construed not as careful perfection, but rather as a more capacious form of excellence which in turn develops the readers' own minds 'to some degree of grandeur'. It is the author's own 'high spirit' which makes great writing endure, 'for what is truly great bears

---

[17] For an account of the history of 'identification' in classical rhetoric and literature, and its links to an ethics of reading in twentieth-century literary theory, see Christy Desmet, *Reading Shakespeare's Characters: Rhetoric, Ethics, and Identity* (Amherst, MA, 1992), pp. 10–34.

[18] John Logan, 'Longinus and the Sublime', in *The Cambridge History of Literary Criticism*, vol. 3, *The Renaissance*, ed. Glyn P. Norton (Cambridge, 1999), pp. 529–39; 529.

[19] See my earlier discussion in *Reading Sensations in Early Modern England* (Basingstoke, 2007), pp. 11–34.

[20] *Satires, Epistles, Ars Poetica*, trans. H. R. Fairclough (Cambridge, MA, 1991), pp. 458–9.

[21] Plato, *The Statesman, Philebus and Ion*, trans. W. R. M. Lamb (Cambridge, MA, 1975), pp. 420–21; Cicero, *De Inventione*, trans. H. M. Hubbekk (Cambridge, MA, 1976), pp. 158–9; Quintilian, *Institutio Oratoria*, trans. Donald A. Russell (Cambridge, MA, 2001), pp. 60–1, 374–5. See Ruth Webb, 'Imagination and the Arousal of the Emotions in Greco-Roman Rhetoric', in *The Passions in Roman Thought and Literature*, ed. Susanna Morton Braund and Christopher Gill (Cambridge, 1997), pp. 112–27. For a recent account of inspired authorship in the Renaissance, see Margaret Healy, 'Poetic 'Making' and Moving the Soul', in *Shakespearean Sensations: Experiencing Literature in Early Modern England*, ed. Katharine A. Craik and Tanya Pollard (Cambridge, 2013), pp. 173–90.

[22] 'The Portrait of Mr W. H.' in *Complete Works of Oscar Wilde* (London, 1994), pp. 302–50; p. 311; *On the Sublime*, pp. 162–3.

repeated consideration ... the memory of it is stubborn and indelible'.[23] Many of Shakespeare's sonnets indeed focus on their own ability (or inability) to endure, a problem usually tied up with the speaker's nature. In Sonnet 32, for example, the speaker imagines his readers – both the beloved and those encountering the sonnet many years later – resurveying his poetry not for its style but for the love which inspired it:

If thou survive my well-contented day
When that churl death my bones with dust shall cover,
And shalt by fortune once more resurvey
These poor, rude lines of thy deceasèd lover,
Compare them with the bett'ring of the time,
And though they be outstripped by every pen,
Reserve them for my love, not for their rhyme
Exceeded by the height of happier men.
O then vouchsafe me but this loving thought:
'Had my friend's Muse grown with this growing age,
A dearer birth than this his love had brought,
To march in ranks of better equipage;
    But since he died, and poets better prove,
    Theirs for their style I'll read, his for his love.'[24]

The speaker protests that he cannot write in a high register – unlike 'happier men' in the future whose verse will exceed and outstrip his own. But their height looks meretricious, evidence only (as the next quatrain indicates) that they 'march in ranks of better equipage'. Their writings may suggest 'the bett'ring of the time', but they are not unique, and their lustre is only temporary. If the beloved resurveys (rereads) these present lines, however, he will 'Reserve them for my love, not for their rhyme'. The speaker's voice then switches to the beloved's voice from line 10 onwards; and in the sonnet's closing couplet, the beloved speaks decisively as both reader and writer.

Importantly, then, the speaker's love emerges in and through the beloved's act of rereading. It is through reading about love that his own thoughts become 'loving' (line 9). If this sonnet has its own kind of height that trumps the height of others, this emerges through the beloved's loving act of reading. And when the reader of the sonnet becomes the speaker of the sonnet, as he does in its second half, the sonnet is not only about him reading, but

also – more surprisingly – by him reading. The sonnet's complaint about its poverty of style is radically unconvincing; this is a case study in height, even as it claims not to be. As such, it is a confident statement of how the intense emotional engagement involved in writing can be accessed – and shared – by dedicated acts of reading, rereading, resurveying. In imagining how the struggle for poetic authority belongs to readers as well as writers, this sonnet captures something important about the emotional risks involved in hazarding oneself into the lines of another.

This is not the only place in the sequence when the reader becomes the writer, the beloved becomes the lover, and the speaker's sonnet becomes that of the friend. Many of the sonnets explore these various kinds of inseparability, taking their cue from the proverb 'A friend is one's second self' so that sympathetic acts of reading become an extension of the sympathies involved in friendship.[25] The procreation sonnets indeed formulate an elaborate theory of identification through their insistent vocabulary of printing, issuing and the creation of new forms (both literary and material): 'if thou issueless shalt hap to die'; 'thou no form of thee hast left behind'; 'Thou shouldest print more, not let that copy die'; 'When your sweet issue your sweet form should bear'.[26] Now the continuation of the beloved's memory (and his blood line) depends on his successful mobilization of the energies involved in acts of literary making. The speaker inscribes the beloved as a book which

---

[23] *On the Sublime*, pp. 185, 161 and 179–81. G. M. A. Grube describes how radically Longinus departs in this way from his predecessors. See *The Greek and Roman Critics* (Indianapolis and Cambridge, 1995), p. 344.

[24] *William Shakespeare: The Complete Works*, ed. Stanley Wells et al., 2nd edn (Oxford, 2005), p. 783, emphasis mine. All quotations follow this edition.

[25] See for example Sonnet 39, line 2: 'thou art all the better part of me'; Sonnet 42, line 13: 'my friend and I are one'; and Sonnet 62, line 13: ''Tis thee, my self, that for myself I praise'. See also Colin Burrow's notes to Sonnet 39 in his edition of *Complete Sonnets and Poems* (Oxford, 2002), p. 458.

[26] See Sonnet 9, lines 3 and 6; Sonnet 11, line 14; and Sonnet 13, line 8 (Wells et al., ed., *Complete Works*, p. 780).

deserves to be read more widely, and the speaker himself looks to be intimately involved in these acts of reissuing – for he is the one who deals in forms, prints and copies. These sonnets imagine a collaborative enthusiasm based on the energies of reading and writing, and the generative properties of the imagination, much akin to Longinus's theory that the most intense and rewarding experiences of reading are those in which we feel 'as if we had ourselves produced the very thing we heard'.

Shakespeare's sonnets have long been understood as a powerful revelation of first-person experience. As Raphael Lyne has recently argued, they put forward an 'epoch-making assertion of the primacy of inner experience as a means of constructing a view of reality'.[27] I argue that the sequence offers, rather, an epoch-making assertion of the primacy of *reading* as a means of constructing reality as the beloved emerges through his encounters with the sonnets, and through his imagined identification with the speaker and the poems themselves. These are sonnets of extraordinary technical virtuosity, but the sonneteer does not propose that their excellence resides in stylistic flourish. Instead, their power emerges through the sympathies – consensual and coercive – they posit between speaker and reader. As Nicholas Cronk has suggested, 'The rhetorical complexion of literary criticism in the sixteenth and seventeenth centuries [tends to] focus attention on the poet as "maker" of the text rather than on the reader (listener) as "maker of sense" of the text.'[28] In the Sonnets, however, textual meaning is created through the sympathetic energies involved in reading. More than that, text and reader emerge as mutually constitutive: the reader only really exists – and may only continue to exist – through a sustaining sympathy with the writer and the text. For this reason, the acts of reading inscribed into the Sonnets look neither careful nor reasonable. Reprimanding, reproaching, cajoling and remoulding the reader, they appeal instead to what we might call the rhetoric of the sublime, which transforms the beloved by separating him from himself.

III

Shakespeare's Sonnets are everywhere novel and strange in the decisive break they make with the European tradition of sonneteering. Despite this, the speaker directs some of his most pointed criticisms towards poets who attempt novelty and strangeness for their own sake.[29] Longinus's insistence that greatness is not found in mere correctness, or over-niceness, also resonates powerfully in the Sonnets. 'The greatest natures are least immaculate', Longinus had argued, and the Sonnets' extraordinary force does lie partly in the speaker's imperfections.[30] It is true, too, that they are full of examples of rhetorical figures identifiable as bona fide features of the sublime – asyndeton, hyperbaton, rhetorical questions, and so on. But more interestingly, and central to both *Peri hypsous* and the Sonnets, is the question of how great writing transforms those who immerse themselves in it.

This same question lies at the heart of late sixteenth- and early seventeenth-century debates about poetry's forcibleness. We know that Aristotelian ideas about the transformative effects of tragedy were already reaching England through continental intermediaries, shaping sixteenth- and seventeenth-century literary theory.[31] We have, however, tended to neglect the later Greek criticism, even though readers have long detected Longinus's influence in both Sir Philip Sidney's *An Apology for Poetrie* (published in 1595) and

---

[27] Raphael Lyne, *Shakespeare, Rhetoric, Cognition* (Cambridge, 2011), p. 213.

[28] Nicholas Cronk, 'Aristotle, Horace, and Longinus', in *Cambridge History of Literary Criticism*, vol. 3, pp. 199–204.

[29] See for example Sonnet 76 where the speaker defends his decision to eschew 'new-found methods and . . . compounds strange' (line 4).

[30] For Longinus, 'grandeur flawed in some respects' is preferable to 'moderate achievement accompanied by perfect soundness and impeccability' (*On the Sublime*, pp. 266–7).

[31] See Tanya Pollard, 'Audience Reception', in *The Oxford Handbook to Shakespeare*, ed. Arthur Kinney (Oxford, 2012), pp. 452–67; Sarah Dewar-Watson, 'Shakespeare and Aristotle', *Literature Compass*, 1 (2004), 1–9; and Stephen Orgel, 'Shakespeare and the Kinds of Drama', *Critical Inquiry*, 6.1 (1979), 107–23.

George Puttenham's *The Arte of English Poesie* (1589).[32] Ben Jonson's discussion of literary imitation in *Timber* (published 1640) shows similarities with a passage in *On the Sublime* dealing with the 'diligent and strict imitation of such famous Poets and Writers as have gone before us'.[33] And Longinus's theories had filtered through to the universities long before Milton's brief allusion to *On the Sublime* in *Of Education* (1644), often cited as the treatise's first mention in print in England.[34] In a lecture delivered at Oxford in 1574, for example, the popular and influential John Rainolds, reader in Greek at Corpus Christi, had explored Longinus's discussion of the place of figures in sublime style. Invoking the authority of *Peri hypsous*, Rainolds had decried those who deployed small elaborate devices of expression (*verborum exornatiunculis*) to lure inexperienced listeners away from the more appropriately bracing effects of sublime rhetoric.[35] As the author of voluminous letters written against the theatre, published in 1599 as *The Overthrow of Stage Plays*, Rainolds had a more pressing reason than most to acquaint himself with Longinus's theories about how words might impact forcefully upon bodies and selves. His contemporary, Henry Dethick, referred to poetry's 'excellent sublimity' in his treatise on poetry, *Oratio in Laudem Poëseos* (1575), and employed a vocabulary familiar from Longinus when he celebrated poets who experienced 'a burning ardour of mind, as if in a kind of violent impulse' which could arouse similarly ardent emotions among listeners.[36]

Rainolds and Sidney almost certainly knew one another and it seems likely that Sidney, like Rainolds, was familiar with one or other of the Latin translations of Longinus which were available before Langbaine's. Deeply read in continental literary theory as well as in the Latin and Greek classics, Sidney was fascinated by the aesthetic freedoms offered by what he called in the *Defence* poetry's 'heart-ravishing' intensity, which was able to 'strike, pierce, [and] possess ... the soul'.[37] Sidney's account of how poetry impresses itself forcibly upon the imagination resembles Longinus's account of the searing quality of

rhetorical excellence. As Genevieve Guenther has shown, Sidney puts forward a theory of poetry working like a charm which carries hearers away immediately and irresistibly, thus combining ideas of poetry's rhetorical force with metaphysical ideas of perfection.[38] Sidney's own reworking of the sonnet tradition was influenced by Italian literary theorists, including Minturno and Scaliger. From them, he drew the idea that poetry can mould the disposition of even the most resistant reader, and that imaginative language has a powerful generative agency. Italian theorists were themselves increasingly recognizing in the sixteenth century that fiction (including poems) was *sub specie rhetoricae*, and were turning to Demetrius, Hermogenes and Longinus to augment their readings of Cicero, Quintilian and Aristotle's *Rhetoric*. Petrus Paganus described Petrarch's grave style in his undated commentary on the Sonnets, and also himself translated *Peri hypsous* into Latin. These same connections are developed in *Commentarius in Longinum* (c. 1570), attributed to Franciscus

---

[32] Cronk provides fuller discussion of Longinus's place in sixteenth- and seventeenth-century literary criticism in 'Aristotle, Horace, and Longinus', pp. 199–204.

[33] See Elizabeth Nitchie, 'Longinus and the Theory of Poetic Imitation in Seventeenth- and Eighteenth-century England', *Studies in Philology*, 32.4 (1935), 580–97; pp. 589–90.

[34] See T. J. B. Spencer, 'Longinus in English Criticism: Influences Before Milton', *Review of English Studies*, n.s. 8.30 (1957), 137–43; p. 137; and Colin Burrow, 'Combative Criticism: Jonson, Milton, and Classical Literary Criticism in England', in *Cambridge History of Literary Criticism*, vol. 3, pp. 487–99; pp. 496–7.

[35] John Rainolds, 'Oratio 3. Post Festum Natalis Christi, 1573', in *Orationes Duodecim* (1619), pp. 327–8. See William Ringler, 'An Early Reference to Longinus', *MLN*, 53 (1938), 23–4.

[36] *Latin Treatises on Poetry from Renaissance England*, trans. J. W. Binns (Signal Mountain, TN, 1999), pp. 26–55; pp. 26–7 and 32–3.

[37] *An Apology for Poetry, Or, the Defence of Poesy*, ed. Geoffrey Shepherd, rev. R. W. Maslen (Manchester, 2002), pp. 83 and 90.

[38] Genevieve Guenther, *Magical Imaginations: Instrumental Aesthetics in the English Renaissance* (Toronto, 2012), pp. 19–22.

Portus, which deals with 'sublime, magnificent, and grave forms of expression', discussing how poets first experience a certain state of the soul before producing a similar effect among readers.[39] Cesare Crispolti's *Lettione del sonnetto* describes the sublimity of the sonnet form more specifically, drawing from Minturno to argue that the sonnet, despite its modest size, 'moves, arouses and ravishes the reader as if with a secret miracle'. And Patrizi cites Longinus in his treatises on poetry, including *Della poetica*, arguing that 'a supremely great subject will reduce to wonderment the properly attuned reader'.[40] All of these theorists showed Longinus's particular usefulness for conceptualizing the demands placed upon readers by the compressed sonnet form. Taken together with the evidence of *Peri hypsous*' visibility in English literary culture, we can begin to refine our understanding of the rhetorical sources that lie behind English practices of sonnet writing and reading, including both Sidney's and Shakespeare's. Longinus's theories about the heightened emotion involved in reading, and the particular forms of identification such emotion demanded, were already trickling into literary culture in the 1590s – and Shakespeare and Sidney were both writing in a cultural milieu increasingly receptive to their rediscovery.

We have long acknowledged the importance of the passions in the vast Latin literature on oratorical persuasion to early modern ideas about literary inspiration. We have not yet, however, fully recognized the influence of the different strands of rhetorical theory which emerged in the empire. These strands seem better equipped to accommodate the intensely experiential readings inscribed into this sequence, especially what T. G. Bishop, in his study of rhetoric and wonder in Shakespeare's theatre, has called their 'powerful dynamic of imaginative coercion and consent'.[41] If it is frustratingly difficult to pin down Shakespeare's familiarity with the Greek tradition at the level of verbal echo, it nevertheless seems certain, as A. D. Nuttall has argued, that Shakespeare was drawn to 'Greek effects' – especially plot structures, habits of expression and other shapes of thought.[42] Among the most important

of these, I argue, was a theory of audience reception based on the will rather than cognitive understanding. As Shakespeare knew, words could work in thrillingly unpredictable ways. This was and remains one of the fundamental animating principles of the theatre; and Shakespeare's Sonnets, too, explore these same ideas of reception and unreasoned self-transformation.

Determining the sources of the Sonnets is fraught with difficulty, however, for the sequence bears no transparent relationship to its origin. Some sonnets are indeed best approached as 'anti-source' poems thanks to their radical re-writing of Petrarchan and Ovidian convention. If Shakespeare was influenced by Longinus, he did not reproduce his theories in any straightforward way. Sonnet 55 allows us to see this more clearly:

> Not marble nor the gilded monuments
> Of princes shall outlive this powerful rhyme,
> But you shall shine more bright in these contents
> Than unswept stone besmeared with sluttish time.
> When wasteful war shall statues overturn,
> And broils root out the work of masonry,
> Nor Mars his sword nor war's quick fire shall burn
> The living record of your memory.
> 'Gainst death and all oblivious enmity
> Shall you pace forth; your praise shall still find room
> Even in the eyes of all posterity
> That wear this world out to the ending doom.
> > So, till the judgement that yourself arise,
> > You live in this, and dwell in lovers' eyes.

Like many of the sonnets, this one offers both a promise and a threat. It describes itself as a 'powerful rhyme', and part of its power lies in the fact that it will be read in the future. The sonnet

---

[39] Bernard Weinberg, *A History of Literary Criticism in the Italian Renaissance*, vol. 1 (Chicago, 1961), pp. 188–9.

[40] Weinberg, *History of Literary Criticism*, vol. 1, pp. 236–7 and 785.

[41] T. G. Bishop, *Shakespeare and the Theatre of Wonder* (Cambridge, 1996), p. 29.

[42] A. D. Nuttall, 'Shakespeare and the Greeks', in *Shakespeare and the Classics*, ed. Charles Martindale and A. B. Taylor (Cambridge, 2004), pp. 209–22; p. 215.

will be a 'living record' of the beloved because (and here's the threat) 'You live in this'. It is true that 'these contents' will shine more brightly than 'unswept stone besmeared with sluttish time'; line 10, which describes how the beloved will 'pace forth' and 'find room', suggests a sense of expansiveness. But this is curtailed by the idea that the lover will find room only 'in the eyes of all posterity' and that he will 'dwell in lovers' eyes'. His pacing forth is restricted to the tiny movements of the reader's eyes as they scan the page, for the sonnet seems to work to reduce the beloved down to its own modest scale. The same thing happens in Sonnet 81:

> The earth can yield me but a common grave
> When you entombèd in men's eyes shall lie.
> Your monument shall be my gentle verse,
> Which eyes not yet created shall o'er-read . . .

The procreation sonnets, with their determined 'reissuing' of the beloved, had sketched a sympathy between the reader and the author which looked productive thanks to the generative energies it had imagined – both textual and sexual. But here the sonnet's littleness seems to impose itself upon the beloved, and the act of reading suspends the beloved in space and time 'till the judgement that yourself arise'.[43] If reading involves a kind of sympathy, it also serves to shrink the beloved, now, into what the sequence elsewhere mocks as its own paltry achievement:

> For I am shamed by that which I bring forth,
> And so should you, to love things nothing worth.[44]

We recall that Longinus's theory of reception had employed the language of physical violence and cruelty to describe the risks involved in abandoning oneself to the imagination. The most powerful words are those which overcome us entirely. Longinus had emphasized that such assaults can be recuperated for the reader, empowering us in turn. But as Bishop points out, this violent confrontation must also involve a darker sense of threat or loss: 'for blessing or for maim, poem reaches out for reader, spectacle for spectator. And in the process, it attacks the ordinary

boundaries that keep cognitive and social worlds stable'.[45]

It is precisely these boundaries which Shakespeare's Sonnets attack when they describe the sympathies which emerge between readers and writers, and between readers and poems. In so doing, they bear witness to the difficulty of reconciling identification, and overwhelming passion, with the impulse towards order and quantification which had long been a mainstay of rhetorical and literary theory. After all, Longinus effectively severs the close connection between *ratio* and *oratio*, which had formed the cornerstone of Roman rhetorical efficacy and which became central to Renaissance humanist scholarship. It is not surprising, then, that Sonnet 55 and others like it suggest that the transformative sympathies associated with 'powerful rhyme' are disorienting as well as elevating. The passionate exchanges which take place in these poems between readers and writers suggest the risk as well as the exaltation implicit in the rich spatial vocabulary of *hypsos*. In this, they anticipate later interpretations of the sublime in the later seventeenth and eighteenth centuries which would fully explore its association with struggle and violence.

Scholars of the early modern theatre have previously described, from different perspectives, the ways in which words and spectacle could threaten bodily and emotional integrity. One model is the hapless Elizabethan play-goer, familiar from antitheatrical polemic, for whom the processes of identification involved in theatre-going brought about a catastrophic scattering of the self. The unlettered groundlings were thought especially vulnerable to these kinds of theatrical experiences. Thomas Heywood described in *An Apology for Actors* (1612) how plays could prick the consciences of murderesses and adulteresses, for example, who identified so keenly with the events depicted

---

[43] Sonnet 55, line 13.   [44] Sonnet 72, lines 13–14.

[45] See Bishop's exploration, through Longinus, of 'the psychology of wonder' in early modern English drama in *Shakespeare and the Theatre of Wonder*, p. 30.

onstage that they were compelled to confess their crimes.[46] We are familiar, too, with the compulsive – usually female – reader of early modern romance, helplessly swept along by narrative pleasure. These examples leave us with the sense that Renaissance readers who were taken by force, and who submitted to the identification involved in intense textual encounters, were either insolent, childish or mobbish. But extra-rational, enthusiastic literary encounters in this period were not necessarily forbidden or pathologized. Shakespeare's Sonnets test the values and risks of impassioned practices of reading, even as they explore love's constancy and equipoise. The emotional involvement, heightened experience of self and potential for change that they describe resound more closely with early modern descriptions of spiritual ecstasy, where the experience of being ravished, transported and exhilarated by the holy spirit among a community of fellow believers was to involve oneself in an experience much like *hypsos*.[47] The rich conceptual vocabulary of 'height' allows us to take seriously the possibility that literary encounters, as much as spiritual ones, could be charged with the powerful dynamic of astonishment and self-transformation.

---

[46] Pollard, 'Audience Reception', p. 466.

[47] For an exploration of how Longinus's vocabulary of height and sublimity translates into Christian spiritual ardency, see Debora K. Shuger, *Sacred Rhetoric: The Christian Grand Style in the English Renaissance* (New Jersey, 1958), pp. 28–30.

AUTHENTICATING THE INAUTHENTIC: EDMOND MALONE AS EDITOR OF THE APOCRYPHAL SHAKESPEARE

REIKO OYA

ORIGINAL CORRUPTION

In the radical lexical shift of the late eighteenth century, 'authenticity' became a quality to be secured not by a vague consensus among authoritative figures but by a rigorous examination of palpable, external evidence. According to Margreta De Grazia, this new concept of authenticity, which epitomized the spirit of the Enlightenment, and its concomitant supposition of the presence of the original, defined the editorial practice of Edmond Malone (1741–1812).[1] His monumental edition, *Plays and Poems of William Shakspeare* (1790),[2] characterized as it was by the editor's pursuit for objectivity and quest for unmediated original documents, marked a significant departure from the editorial conventions that had been developed continuously over time by the eighteenth-century Shakespearians contracted by publisher and bookseller Jacob Tonson and his successors. Rejoicing that 'the era of conjectural criticism and capricious innovation' was finally over, Malone tried to present the reader with 'what Shakspeare wrote, supported at once by the authority of the authentick copies', by which he meant 'the first quarto copy' or 'if the play appeared originally in folio ... the first folio' (*Plays and Poems*, vol. 1, pt 1, pp. lii–liii, lv–lvi). What will happen, then, if the piece to be edited was not included in the authoritative First Folio, and the earliest quarto, or octavo for that matter, was inaccurate textually, piratical in its origin, and 'inauthentic' overall? This was precisely the problem Malone had faced as he embarked on his first

major Shakespearian project ten years before the landmark 1790 publication.

Collecting materials excluded from the Johnson-Steevens *Plays of William Shakespeare* (1778), Malone's *Supplement* (1780) published the narrative and lyric poems attributed to Shakespeare with various degrees of credibility, and the apocryphal plays that had appeared in the second impression of the Third Folio in 1664.[3] Alongside *Venus and Adonis* and *The Rape of Lucrece*, whose publication Shakespeare himself endorsed by attaching dedicatory letters, poems of very obscure origin (*The Passionate Pilgrim*, the Sonnets and 'A Lover's Complaint') and seven apocryphal plays (*Pericles*, *Locrine*, *Sir John Oldcastle*, *Lord Cromwell*, *The London Prodigal*, *The Puritan* and *A Yorkshire Tragedy*) were published with full editorial apparatus for the first time.

In an effort to settle the authorship of the apocryphal plays, Malone relied heavily on

---

This chapter benefited greatly from the pertinent and productive comments I received from Donatella Pallotti, Yuji Kaneko, Ann Thompson and Matthew Hanley. I also wish to thank the reviewers for their extremely helpful suggestions.

[1] Margreta De Grazia, *Shakespeare Verbatim: The Reproduction of Authenticity and the 1790 Apparatus* (Oxford, 1991), pp. 49–93.
[2] Edmond Malone, ed., *The Plays and Poems of William Shakespeare, in ten volumes* (London, 1790). Hereafter cited parenthetically in the main text.
[3] Edmond Malone, ed., *Supplement to the Edition of Shakspeare's Plays Published in 1778 by Samuel Johnson and George Steevens*, 2 vols. (London, 1780). Hereafter cited parenthetically as *Supplement*.

internal and stylistic evidence. Of the seven plays, he believed only *Pericles* to be genuinely Shakespearian, commenting that

the piece itself furnishes internal and irresistible evidence of its authenticity. The congenial sentiments, the numerous expressions bearing a striking similitude to passages in his undisputed plays, the incidents, the situations of the persons, the colour of the style, at least through the greater part of the play, all, in my apprehension, conspire to set the seal of Shakspeare on this performance.

(*Supplement*, vol. 2, pp. 158–9)[4]

Although 'why this drama was omitted in the first edition of Shakspeare's works, it is now impossible to ascertain' (*Supplement*, vol. 2, p. 184), such intrinsic qualities as 'sentiments', 'expressions', 'incidents', 'situations' and 'colour' were enough for Malone to settle the authorship of *Pericles*. His dismissal of the remaining six plays was also based, to a great extent, on aesthetic grounds. Whilst distrusting the title-page statement '*newly set foorth, overseene, and corrected by W. S.*' of *Locrine* (1595), he emphasized that 'the piece itself affords abundant internal evidence that not a single line of it was written by Shakspeare' (*Supplement*, vol. 2, p. 189). The editor similarly set out to 'vindicate Shakspeare from having written a single line' of *Lord Cromwell* (1602), by pointing to 'The poverty of the language, the barenness of incident, and the inartificial conduct of every part of the performance' (*Supplement*, vol. 2, p. 446).[5] The editor's heavy reliance on internal evidence was inevitable. After all, the plays constituting the Shakespeare Apocrypha almost by definition lacked authentic documentary sources. They were not included in the First Folio and their early quarto texts were often seriously corrupt. Even worse, 'external evidence' such as attributions on printed title pages quite recklessly pointed to Shakespeare's authorship.[6]

Introducing the 1790 *Plays and Poems*, Malone claimed to 'have endeavoured, with unceasing solicitude, to give a faithful and correct edition of the plays and poems of Shakspeare' (*Supplement*, vol. 1, p. i). As if to underline the new edition's authenticity, Malone dropped both the six apocryphal plays and the discussion of the internal

evidence that had justified their omission.[7] In the meanwhile, he did include *Pericles* in the 1790 edition, even though, by then, he had disavowed Shakespeare's sole authorship and accepted George Steevens's suggestion that 'it was originally the production of some elder playwright, and afterwards improved by our poet, whose hand was acknowledged to be visible in many scenes throughout the play'. Malone's new conclusion was once again deduced from internal evidence. While *Pericles* 'was printed with Shakspeare's name in the title-page, in his life-time' and that 'at a subsequent period it was ascribed to him by several dramatick writers', Malone wished 'not to rely on any circumstance of that kind; because in all questions of this nature, internal evidence is the best that can be produced' (*Plays and Poems*, vol. 3, p. 636). Malone unfortunately did not clarify exactly what he meant by 'questions of this nature', or why internal evidence should be more important than external evidence in authorship attribution. With regards to the plays excluded from the First Folio, such as *Pericles*, there probably were no documents authentic enough for Malone to rely on, no matter whether he was to support or repudiate Shakespeare's authorship. However, in the

---

[4] MacDonald P. Jackson surveys the markers of Shakespeare's authorship with reference to *Pericles*, in *Defining Shakespeare: 'Pericles' as Test Case* (Oxford, 2003). For the authorship of *Pericles*, see also *William Shakespeare: A Textual Companion*, ed. Stanley Wells et al. (Oxford, 1987), pp, 130–1.

[5] For Malone's discussion of the authorship of *Sir John Oldcastle*, *The London Prodigal*, *The Puritan* and *A Yorkshire Tragedy*, see *Supplement*, vol. 2, pp. 269–70, 449, 533–4, 675.

[6] See C. F. Tucker Brooke, 'Introduction', in *The Shakespeare Apocrypha* (Oxford, 1908), pp. vi–lvi; Gary Taylor, 'Works Excluded from this Edition', in *Textual Companion*, pp. 134–41.

[7] After the printing of the main body of the 1790 edition, Elizabethan theatre impresario Philip Henslowe's *Diary* was discovered and lent to Malone, who immediately incorporated excerpts from it in 'Emendations and Additions' (*Plays and Poems*, vol. 1, pt 2, pp. 288–329). Malone believed that the *Diary* definitively established the apocryphal status of the six plays, and of *1 Henry VI* and *Titus Andronicus*. Except for the case of *Sir John Oldcastle*, Malone's interpretation of the document is not supported by modern scholarship.

1790 edition, he would question even the First Folio editors John Heminge and Henry Condell's attribution and would argue that two of the plays in the 1623 collection, *1 Henry VI* and *Titus Andronicus*, were not by Shakespeare. Malone's defiance of the authority of the First Folio prompts us to scrutinize his editorial principle and practice further.

DECANONIZING FIRST FOLIO PLAYS

Editing the three *Henry VI* plays for the 1790 edition, Malone noticed a stylistic quality that pertained only to Part 1. He had been 'long struck with the many evident *Shakspearianisms*' in the trilogy so that he had never examined 'with attention any of the arguments that have been urged against his being the author of them':

I am now surprised ... that I should never have adverted to a very striking circumstance which distinguishes this *first* part from the other parts of *King Henry VI*. This circumstance is, that none of these Shakspearian passages are to be found here [i.e., in Part 1], though several are scattered through the two other parts. I am therefore decisively of opinion that *this* play was not written by Shakspeare.   (*Plays and Poems*, vol. 6, pp. 3–4)[8]

The term 'Shakspearianisms' refers to the characteristic words and phrases (and versification patterns, as Malone would argue later in the same passage) that repeatedly appear in the playwright's canonical works. Eighteenth-century editors liked to use these parallel passages to illustrate Shakespeare or, as Samuel Johnson put it, 'The meaning assigned to doubtful words will be supported by the authorities of other writers, or by parallel passages of Shakespeare himself'.[9] Editing the Sonnets for the 1780 *Supplement*, Malone had used them not only to elucidate difficult passages but also to establish Shakespeare's authorship, arguing that the 'general style of these poems, and the numerous passages in them which remind us of our author's plays, leave not the smallest doubt of their authenticity' (*Supplement*, vol. 1, p. 581). As De Grazia observes, Malone's cross-referencing tied the Sonnets and the plays

together and canonized the sonnet sequence.[10] Whilst the force of parallel passages in the authorship issue is, in fact, highly debatable in itself,[11] the testimony of their *absence* in *1 Henry VI* is even more ambivalent. Malone registered parallel passages and verbal echoes according to his subjective standard of what should count as significantly similar, and the number of collected samples depended heavily on his industry and enthusiasm. Indeed, recent scholarly editions reveal the fallaciousness of Malone's reasoning by routinely cross-referencing *1 Henry VI* to other Shakespearian plays and poems.

Still more problematic was Malone's treatment of *Titus Andronicus* in the 1790 edition. He branded the Senecan tragedy as 'A Tragedy Erroneously Ascribed to Shakspeare', and placed it after 'A Lover's Complaint' in the final volume, using the poetical works 'as a barrier between this spurious piece, and his undoubted dramas' (*Plays and Poems*, vol. 10, pp. 373, 377). Questioning the legitimacy of Heminge and Condell's attribution, Malone speculated that the play was included in the First Folio simply because Shakespeare 'wrote a few lines in it, or gave some assistance to the authour, in revising it, or in some other way aided him in bringing it forward on the stage' (p. 375). Malone's misgivings over Shakespeare's authorship of the 'tragedy of blood' are in themselves nothing out of the ordinary: eighteenth-century editors and

---

[8] In 'Dissertation on the Three Parts of *King Henry VI*', Malone discusses both the external and internal evidence relating to the *Henry VI* trilogy at length (*Plays and Poems*, vol. 6, pp. 378–429). For recent discussion on the authorship of Part 1, see Edward Burns, 'Introduction', in *Henry VI, Part 1*, The Arden Shakespeare (London, 2000), pp. 73–90; *Textual Companion*, pp. 112–13.

[9] Johnson, 'Proposals for Printing, by Subscription, the Dramatick Works of William Shakespeare' (1756), in *The Yale Edition of the Works of Samuel Johnson*, vol. 7, *Johnson on Shakespeare*, ed. Arthur Sherbo (New Haven, CN, 1968), p. 57.

[10] De Grazia, *Verbatim*, p. 153.

[11] See Brian Vickers's survey of the use of verbal parallels, *Shakespeare, Co-author: A Historical Study of Five Collaborative Plays* (Oxford, 2002), pp. 57–75.

critics repeatedly challenged the canonicity of this 'so very shocking' play on aesthetic grounds, and recent computer-based attribution scholarship also seriously questions Shakespeare's sole authorship.[12] What is singularly unconvincing is Malone's ratiocination, which was based on a theatrical anecdote recorded by Edward Ravenscroft, an adapter of the tragedy for the Restoration stage:

The tradition mentioned by Ravenscroft in the time of King Charles II. warrants us in making one or other of these suppositions. 'I have been told' (says he in his preface to an alteration of this play published in 1687), 'by some anciently conversant with the stage, that it was not originally his, but brought by a private author to be acted, and he only gave some master touches to one or two of the principal parts or characters.'

(*Plays and Poems*, vol. 10, p. 375)

Malone should have known better. Gerard Langbaine, to whom Malone would directly refer later in the same passage, had already suspected that the disreputable Ravenscroft ('the *Leech*, that lives upon the Blood of Men') might have invented the story of Shakespeare's improvement of *Titus Andronicus* to justify his own practice as an adapter.[13]

Malone was in fact aware of Francis Meres's listing of *Titus Andronicus* among Shakespeare's plays in *Palladis Tamia* (1598), but dismissed the ascription by arguing that 'Meres might have been misinformed, or inconsiderately have given credit to the rumour of the day', and that 'The internal evidence furnished by the piece itself, and proving it not to have been the production of Shakspeare, greatly outweighs any single testimony on the other side' (*Plays and Poems*, vol. 10, p. 376). Malone's handling of *Titus Andronicus* shows that he was quite capable of making misguided use of, and drawing unreasonable conclusions from, the documentary sources he meticulously collected, and of defying the authorship attribution of even the First Folio on aesthetic grounds.

In the second edition of *Plays and Poems*, which was posthumously published in 1821, Malone promoted his theory about *Titus Andronicus* even further by marking 'those passages in which he

[i.e., Malone] supposed the hand of Shakspeare may be traced … with inverted commas'.[14] Malone had actually used similar symbols in the 1790 edition of *2* and *3 Henry VI*. In it, he carefully collated the First Folio texts of the two plays with what he regarded as their source materials (*The First Part of the Contention* and *Richarde Duke of York*), and marked the lines 'retouched, and greatly improved by him [i.e., Shakespeare]' with inverted commas and 'his own original production' with asterisks (*Plays and Poems*, vol. 6, p. 115). To the regret of Malone's literary executor, James Boswell, Jr, who supervised the second edition, the markings in the 1821 text of *Titus and Andronicus* were based 'upon no other ground than this, has it any claim to a place among our poet's dramas?' Malone seized 'upon every line possessed of merit as belonging of right to our great dramatist' (*Plays and Poems 1821*, vol. 21, p. 261). Indeed, Malone's 1821 text of *Titus and Andronicus* bore a sinister resemblance to Alexander Pope's notorious Shakespeare edition (1723–5), in which 'some of the most shining passages are distinguish'd by comma's in the margin' according to the editor's aesthetic judgement.[15] The concurrence of the two editors' marginal signs was particularly ironical, as Malone's greatest achievement was supposedly his departure from the editorial aestheticism and egotism that Pope's imperious commas epitomized.

As far as textual editing was concerned, Malone was no doubt a meticulous collector

---

[12] *Textual Companion*, pp. 113–15. See also Vickers's discussion that *Titus* was begun by George Peele, in *Shakespeare Co-author*, pp. 148–219, and William W. Weber's response to it, 'Shakespeare After All?: The Authorship of *Titus Andronicus*, 4.1 Reconsidered', in *Shakespeare Survey 67* (Cambridge, 2014), pp. 69–84.

[13] Gerard Langbaine, *An Account of the English Dramatic Poets* (Oxford, 1691), pp. 417–18, 464–7.

[14] Edmond Malone and James Boswell, eds., *The Plays and Poems of William Shakspeare*, 21 vols. (London, 1821), vol. 21, p. 261. Hereafter cited parenthetically as *Plays and Poems 1821*.

[15] Pope, 'The Preface of the Editor', in *The Works of Mr William Shakespear*, 6 vols. (London, 1723–5), vol. 1, p. xxiii.

and collator of early quartos and folios, even though his break from the editorial conventions of the eighteenth century was not as clear-cut as De Grazia suggests.[16] He rigorously collated even those plays which he believed to be inauthentic, and refrained from tampering with the texts of *1 Henry VI* and (excepting the problematic inverted commas) *Titus Andronicus*. Regrettably, the same level of textual integrity was not preserved in his editions of the apocryphal poetic miscellany, *The Passionate Pilgrim*.

JAGGARD, BENSON AND MALONE

The Passionate Pilgrim is a collection of twenty poems published in two editions in 1598(?)–9 by William Jaggard. Although the poems are ascribed to 'W. Shakespeare' on the title page, only five of them are demonstrably Shakespearian: Poems 1 and 2, which are either early or corrupt versions of Sonnets 138 and 144 in the 1609 collection, and Poems 3, 5 and 16, which are extracted, with some variations, from the 1598 quarto edition of *Love's Labour's Lost*.[17] Despite these (largely) Shakespearian pieces, the anthology is obviously spurious as it includes poems by other authors without due credit: Poems 8 and 20 very probably belong to Richard Barnfield; Poem 11 to Bartholomew Griffin; and Poem 19 to Christopher Marlowe and Walter Raleigh.[18] The remaining eleven are of unknown authorship. In the third edition (1612), Jaggard knowingly included Thomas Heywood's Ovidian translations from *Troia Britannica* (1609). The translator was understandably mortified and lodged a protest against the publisher in *An Apology for Actors* (1612).[19]

Jaggard's fraudulent publication of *The Passionate Pilgrim* kept annoying Shakespearian scholars and editors, prompting Algernon Charles Swinburne to famously denounce him as an 'infamous pirate, liar, and thief', and *The Passionate Pilgrim* as a 'worthless little volume of stolen and mutilated poetry, patched up and padded out with dirty and dreary doggerel'.[20] Recent researchers, however, have shown how cleverly Jaggard cashed in on Shakespeare's reputation as a popular poet and

dramatist.[21] Technically not a pirate, Jaggard assembled a hybrid collection to capitalize on the success of Shakespeare's *Venus and Adonis* and its companion piece *The Rape of Lucrece*, of his *Love's Labour's Lost* and *Romeo and Juliet*, and of his 'sugred Sonnets'. Indeed, Jaggard's 'counterfeiting of Shakespeare's authorial persona'[22] was ingenious and problematic enough to compel Shakespearian editors from the nineteenth century onwards to routinely reproduce at least part of the 1599 collection (but somehow not the 1612 additions) in their respective Complete Works, the uncertain origin of the poems notwithstanding.

Malone's treatment of *The Passionate Pilgrim* was as tortuous and inconsistent as that of any other editor. Whilst editing the *Supplement*, Malone believed that a majority of the poems were Shakespearian ('Most of these little pieces bear the strongest marks of the hand of Shakspeare' (*Supplement*, vol. 1, p. 709)). At this stage, he apparently had no trouble in seeing 'the strongest marks' of Shakespeare in Barnfield's Poems 8 and 20 and Griffin's Poem 11. The normally judicious editor's misattribution alerts us to the peril of reliance on internal evidence in the authorship question, when

---

16. For Malone's dependence on the received text, see Simon Jarvis, *Scholars and Gentlemen: Shakespearian Textual Criticism and Representations of Scholarly Labour, 1725–1765* (Oxford, 1995), pp. 185–8.

17. For ease of reference, I follow Colin Burrow's numbering of the poems in William Shakespeare, *The Complete Sonnets and Poems* (Oxford, 2002). Poetical texts are from Malone's editions.

18. For the authorship of *The Passionate Pilgrim*, see Hyder E. Rollins, 'Date and Authenticity', in *A New Variorum Edition of Shakespeare: The Poems* (Philadelphia, 1938), pp. 538–58.

19. Rollins, 'William Jaggard, Heywood', in *Variorum Poems*, pp. 533–8.

20. Cited in Rollins, *Variorum Poems*, p. 535.

21. See, among others, Colin Burrow, 'Introduction', in *Complete Sonnets and Poems*, pp. 74–82; Patrick Cheney, *Shakespeare, National Poet-Playwright* (Cambridge, 2004), pp. 151–72; Francis X. Connor, 'Shakespeare, Poetic Collaboration and *The Passionate Pilgrim*', in *Shakespeare Survey 67* (Cambridge, 2014), pp. 119–30.

22. Cheney, *Poet-Playwright*, p. 160.

good documentary evidence either does not exist or is out of reach.

Malone treated *The Passionate Pilgrim* not as a poetic anthology in its own right, but rather as a miscellany of Shakespeare's uncollected short poems. He not only 'rejected' Poem 19 ('Live with me' and 'Love's Answer') as 'Marlowe's',[23] but also removed the Shakespearian Poems 1 and 2, as 'having been already laid before the reader' as Sonnets 138 and 144 of the 1609 sequence (*Supplement*, vol. 1, p. 709).[24] Somewhat inconsistently, the editor kept the three *Love's Labour's Lost* poems. The comedy was certainly not printed in the *Supplement*, but it was in the Johnson-Steevens edition to which Malone's publication was a companion.[25] To replace the omissions, Malone problematically inserted two new poems at the end of the sequence. One was a short lyric from *Measure for Measure* (4.1.1–6):

> Take, oh, take those lips away,
> > That so sweetly were forsworn;
> And those eyes, the break of day,
> > Lights that do mislead the morn:
> But my kisses bring again,
> Seals of love, but seal'd in vain.
>
> Hide, oh, hide those hills of snow
> > Which thy frozen bosom bears,
> On whose tops the pinks that grow,
> > Are of those that April wears.
> But first set my poor heart free,
> Bound in those icy chains by thee.
> > (*Supplement*, vol. 1, pp. 731–2)

Malone discussed the poem's authorship and defended its inclusion in *The Passionate Pilgrim* as follows:

This little poem is not printed in *The Passionate Pilgrim*, probably because it was not written so early as 1599. The first stanza of it is introduced in *Measure for Measure*. In Fletcher's *Bloody Brother* it is found entire. Whether the second stanza was also written by Shakspeare, cannot now be ascertained. All the songs, however, introduced in our author's plays, appear to have been his own composition; and the present contains an expression of which he seems to have been peculiarly fond.

(*Supplement*, vol. 1, p. 731)

The editor's muddled explanation fails to clarify why this particular song had to be added to *The Passionate Pilgrim*, and his sweeping proposition 'All the songs ... introduced in our author's plays, appear to have been his own composition' is demonstrably wrong.[26] Malone's other addition was 'The Phoenix and the Turtle', an allegorical poem first published in a poetic miscellany that supplemented Robert Chester's *Love's Martyr* (1601). According to Malone, the title-page description of the 1601 publication 'leaves us, I think, no room to doubt of the genuineness of this little poem' (*Supplement*, vol. 1, p. 732). Even if we accept Shakespeare's authorship, Malone's inclusion of these two poems in *The Passionate Pilgrim* seems quite haphazard and 'inauthentic', in the sense that his editorial decision was not supported by any authentic documentary sources.

As a matter of fact, Malone's addition to *The Passionate Pilgrim* was anticipated, and indeed very probably inspired, by John Benson's 1640 publication, *Poems: Written by Wil. Shake-speare, Gent.*, in which the two pieces were similarly printed at the end the collection. Most tellingly, 'Take, oh, take those lips away' was one of the only two songs Benson selected for inclusion in the *Poems* out of the numerous lyrics found in Shakespeare's dramatic canon. Malone's reliance on the 1640 anthology is very ironical, as Benson has long

---

[23] Malone followed the authorship attribution of *England's Helicon* (1600) as regards 'Come live with me'. 'Love's answer' has traditionally been assigned to Walter Raleigh.

[24] Malone meanwhile referred to the 1599 texts of the two poems in the footnotes of their 1609 counterparts (*Supplement*, vol. 1, pp. 694, 698).

[25] Malone's other modifications include: division of Poem 14 into two pieces after line 12; removal of the title for the second part of the collection ('Sonnets to Sundry Notes of Music').

[26] For the sources of the songs in Shakespeare's plays, see Peter J. Seng, *Vocal Songs in the Plays of Shakespeare: A Critical History* (Cambridge, MA, 1967); Ross W. Duffin, *Shakespeare's Songbook* (New York, 2004). Fletcher's authorship of the second stanza is studied in Gary Taylor and John Jowett, '"With new additions": Theatrical Interpolation in *Measure for Measure*' and Appendix IV ('The Text of "Take oh take those lips away"'), in *Shakespeare Reshaped, 1606–1623* (Oxford, 1993), pp. 107–236, 272–95.

been the villain of the publication history of Shakespeare's Sonnets. According to the Variorum editor Hyder Edward Rollins, Benson 'pirated Thorpe's text [i.e., the 1609 quarto edition of the Sonnets], but took such great pains to conceal his piracy that he has deceived many modern scholars, just as apparently he hoodwinked the wardens of the Stationers' Company'.[27] And it was Malone who single-handedly rectified the wrong for the rest of us:

Malone gave the first really important critical text of the sonnets, as of the other poems, and (with the aid of Steevens and others) the first commentary. His effect on the text was immense: for the majority of editors before 1864 he left little to do except to insert (or omit) an occasional hyphen, to change a period or comma here or there, to modernize some archaic spelling . . . Truly, one knows not whether to marvel more that he in that misty time could see so clearly, or that we in this supposedly clear age walk so stumblingly after him. He will be praised of ages yet to come.[28]

From the end of the twentieth century onwards, researchers have gradually discarded Rollins's denunciatory view and placed Benson's publication in its historical and cultural contexts.[29] However, Benson's 'cavalier' publication is still a perfect foil for Malone's 'enlightened' approach. In the words of De Grazia, Malone's 'edition of the 1609 Sonnets conclusively supplanted John Benson's 1640 *Poems: Written by Will. Shake-speare. Gent.*, the hybrid edition in which Shakespeare's Sonnets had been read in the late seventeenth and eighteenth centuries, and permanently secured the sequence a position within the corpus of Shakespeare's works'.[30] Malone's *Supplement* and his two subsequent editions of *Plays and Poems* certainly superseded the Bensonian concoction as far as the 1609 Sonnets was concerned. However, the eighteenth-century editor perpetuated the legacy of the 1640 publication when he handled Shakespeare's *other* sonnet sequence, *The Passionate Pilgrim*.

REORDERING THE SEQUENCE

In the *Supplement*, Malone followed Thomas Percy's suggestion[31] and argued that the four poems on the theme of Venus and Adonis (Poems 4, 6, 9 and 11) in *The Passionate Pilgrim* were 'essays of the author [i.e., Shakespeare] when he first conceived the idea of writing a poem on the subject of Venus and Adonis, and before the scheme of his poem was adjusted' (*Supplement*, vol. 1, p. 710). Although the relation between the Venus and Adonis pieces in *The Passionate Pilgrim* and Shakespeare's narrative poem *Venus and Adonis* is certainly 'tantalizing', recent researchers largely disagree with Malone and believe that the four poems are '[a]lmost certainly not' by Shakespeare but rather 'reflections at one remove on the Venus and Adonis story as told by Shakespeare' and 'attempts at Shakespearian pastiche'.[32]

Malone identified two more poems in *The Passionate Pilgrim* as belonging to the Venus and Adonis group, even though the two mythological characters are not mentioned in them. He believed that Poem 10 ('Sweet rose, fair flower') was 'intended for a dirge to be sung by Venus on the death of Adonis', and, by following Thomas Percy, that Poem 12 ('Crabbed age and youth') was 'intended for the mouth of Venus, weighing the

---

[27] H. E. Rollins, *The Sonnets, A Variorum Edition*, 2 vols. (Philadelphia, 1944), vol. 2, p. 18.

[28] Rollins, *Variorum Sonnets*, vol. 2, p. 39. Ann Thompson pointed out to me that, in the final passage of the quotation, Rollins is echoing Philip Sidney's eulogy on Chaucer in *The Defense of Poesy*.

[29] See among others Arthur F. Marotti, 'Shakespeare's Sonnets as Literary Property', in *Soliciting Interpretation: Literary Theory and Seventeenth-Century English Poetry*, ed. Elizabeth D. Harvey and Katharine Eisaman Maus (Chicago, 1990), pp. 143–73; Sasha Roberts, *Reading Shakespeare's Poems in Early Modern England* (Basingstoke, 2003), pp. 158–72; Cheney, *National Poet-Playwright*, pp. 1–12.

[30] De Grazia, *Verbatim*, p. 134.

[31] See Percy's commentary on 'Youth and Age', in *Reliques of Ancient English Poetry*, 3 vols. (London, [1765]), vol. 1, pp. 219–20.

[32] Burrow, 'Introduction', in *Complete Sonnets and Poems*, pp. 79–80. See also C. H. Hobday's case for Shakespeare's possible authorship of the four Venus and Adonis poems, in 'Shakespeare's Venus and Adonis Sonnets', in *Shakespeare Survey 26* (Cambridge, 1973), pp. 103–10.

comparative merits of *youthful* Adonis and *aged* Vulcan' (*Supplement*, vol. 1, pp. 715, 717). Not everyone was convinced. George Steevens, for one, did 'not ... perceive how this little poem [i.e., Poem 12] could have been put, with any singular propriety, into the mouth of the queen of Love, if due regard were paid to the classical situation of her and her husband' (*Supplement*, vol. 1, p. 717). In the 1790 edition, Malone would let his hypothesis about the Venus and Adonis poems disrupt the original sequence of *The Passionate Pilgrim*.

During the ten intervening years between the *Supplement* and *Plays and Poems*, Malone kept accumulating hard facts about *The Passionate Pilgrim*, but his newly acquired knowledge did not necessarily add to the authenticity and credibility of his editorial practice. He purchased a collection of Richard Barnfield's poems published by one John Jaggard in 1598,[33] and found in it Poems 8 ('If music and sweet poetry agree') and 20 ('As it fell upon a day') of *The Passionate Pilgrim*. Malone concluded that William Jaggard, who was John's brother, knew the true author to be Barnfield and deliberately 'inserted these two pieces in the *Passionate Pilgrim* as the productions of Shakspeare' (*Plays and Poems*, vol. 10, p. 321). He dropped Poems 8 and 20 from the 1790 edition. Malone also obtained a copy of the 1612 edition of *The Passionate Pilgrim* and, thanks to his friend Richard Farmer's *An Essays on the Learning of Shakespeare* (2nd edn, 1767), learned about Heywood's attack on Jaggard in *An Apology for Actors* (*Plays and Poems*, vol. 10, p. 322).[34] These two cases of blatant authorship misattribution should have alerted Malone to Jaggard's questionable business ethics. However, he took the title-page statement of the 1612 edition ('The Passionate Pilgrime, or Certaine Amorous Sonnets, between Venus and Adonis') at face value and advanced his grouping of the Venus and Adonis poems:

The title-page above given fully supports an observation I made some years ago, that several of the sonnets in this collection seem to have been essays of the authour when he first conceived the notion of writing a poem on the subject of Venus and Adonis, and before the scheme of his work was completely adjusted.

(*Plays and Poems*, vol. 10, p. 322)

Malone went on to rearrange *The Passionate Pilgrim* in accordance with this hypothesis ('I have not adhered to the order in which they stand in the old copy, having classed all those which relate to Adonis together'), placing Poems 4, 6, 9, 11, 12, 10 and 7 (in this order) at the beginning of the collection. Once again, Malone's reordering echoed the notorious reshuffling of the 1609 sequence of the Sonnets and other materials in Benson's 1640 anthology.

James Boswell, Jr had grave reservations about Malone's grouping of the Venus and Adonis poems. To him, Malone's ascription of Poem 10 ('Sweet rose, fair flower') to the Venus and Adonis group 'shows how the clearest head may be led away by a favourite hypothesis' (*Plays and Poems 1821*, vol. 20, p. 404). Whilst Malone trusted the title-page statement of the 1612 edition, Boswell thought that 'So many instances have been given of Jaggard's want of fidelity in this publication, that I am afraid all confidence must be withdrawn from the whole' (*Plays and Poems 1821*, vol. 20, p. 396).

Boswell was aware that one of the Venus and Adonis poems (Poem 11) had first appeared in Bartholomew Griffin's *Fidessa* (1596), and very probably belonged to this minor sonneteer rather than to Shakespeare. As he observed, Griffin's authorship 'will throw some additional doubt upon Mr Malone's conjecture' concerning the possible connection between the mythological lyrics in *The Passionate Pilgrim* and *Venus and Adonis* (*Plays and Poems 1821*, vol. 20, p. 396). In

---

[33] *The complaint of poetrie, for the death of liberalitie. [With] The combat, betweene conscience and couetousnesse in the minde of man [and] Poems: in diuers humours* (Lond. G.S. for I. Iaggard, 1598). Malone's copy is now in the possession of the Bodleian Library (Mal. 282 (2)).

[34] Malone's copy of the 1612 edition had two title pages, one with Shakespeare's name printed on it and the other without it probably as a result of Heywood's protest. See *Plays and Poems*, vol. 10, p. 321.

fact, there is strong reason to believe that Malone knew, and deliberately neglected, Griffin's publication to defend his grouping of the Venus and Adonis pieces.

OVERLOOKING THE EVIDENCE

The emergence of scholarly editing of English secular literature was one of the key cultural phenomena of the eighteenth century. As Marcus Walsh's detailed study shows,[35] the works of Shakespeare and Milton, which were acquiring the status of national scripture, were edited by such eminent intellectuals as Alexander Pope, Richard Bentley and Samuel Johnson. These Shakespearian and Miltonian scholars improved their editorial technique and knowledge by learning from (and sometimes reacting against) each other. Whilst editing Milton's shorter poems (*Poems upon Several Occasions: English, Italian, and Latin* (1785)), renowned Oxford scholar and poet Thomas Warton certainly consulted Malone's 1780 *Supplement* as a way to establish Shakespeare's influence on the younger prodigy. Malone, in his turn, studied Warton's Milton edition as soon as it was published and noticed in its footnotes references to a very rare edition of *Venus and Adonis*. He sent an enquiry to the senior scholar (17 March 1785):

In the notes you some times mention an edition of Venus and Adonis, in 1596, so particularly, that I imagine it is in your possession. If that should be the case, I shall be extremely obliged to you, if you lend it to me for a few days. – When I was preparing my edition of Shakspeare's Poems, I advertised repeatedly that I would pay a considerable price for the first edition of the Venus & Adonis in 4to 1594, and also for the small 8vo in 1596, but I never could meet with either of them; and was forced to print this poem from an edition in 1600, which was given to me by Dr Farmer.[36]

Warton immediately agreed to lend him the precious edition, which was 'bound up with many coeval small poets, the whole making a Dutch-built but dwarfish volume'.[37] The poems bound together with the 1596 *Venus and Adonis* were as follows:

H[enry] C[onstable], *Diana, or, The excellent conceitful sonnets, '1584'* [1594].

[Samuel Daniel], *The complaynt of Rosamond. Augmented; The complaint of Rosamond; The tragedie of Cleopatra*, 1594.

Richard Barnfield, *Cynthia, with certaine sonnets and The legend of Cassandra*, 1595.

Bartholomew Griffin, *Fidessa, more chaste then kinde*, 1596.

R[ichard] L[ynche], *Diella, certaine sonnets, adioyned to the amorous poeme of dom Diego and Gineura*, 1596.

Gervase Markham, *The poem of poems, or Sions muse, contayning the divine Song of king Solomon, devided into eight eclogues*, [1596].

Gervase Markham, *The most honourable tragedie of sir Richard Grinuile, knight*, 1595.[38]

Of these seven pieces, Malone already had the volume of Daniel's works, but other materials, including Griffin's *Fidessa*, were apparently new to him.[39]

Malone spent a considerable amount of time studying the unique collection of Elizabethan poems ('treasures for a poetical antiquary'): he had promised to return the volume to Warton 'in a few days', but ended by borrowing it for more than a month, sending it back to its owner on 25 April 1785 with a letter of apology ('I am quite ashamed that I have not returned you the little volume which you were so obliging as to send me, before this time').[40] He not only collated the 1596 *Venus and Adonis* for the 1790 *Plays and Poems*, but apparently studied other pieces in the volume, as he cited a parallel passage from '*Diella, Certaine Sonnets adioyned to the amorous poeme of Dom Diego and Ginevra, by R. L., 1596*' in a footnote to *The Merchant of Venice* (*Plays and Poems*, vol. 3, p. 100). There is another telltale sign: in the 1780

---

[35] M. Walsh, *Shakespeare, Milton, and Eighteenth-Century Literary Editing* (Cambridge, 1997).

[36] *The Correspondence of Thomas Warton*, ed. David Fairer (Athens, GA, 1995), p. 510.

[37] Warton to Malone, 19 March 1785, in *Correspondence*, p. 512.

[38] The collection of the seven poems and the 1596 *Venus and Adonis* are now in the possession of the Bodleian Library, Oxford (Mal. 436; Arch. G d.44 (1)).

[39] Malone to Warton, 28 March 1785, in *Correspondence*, p. 512.

[40] James Prior, *Life of Edmond Malone* (London, 1860), p. 178; Malone to Warton, 25 April 1785, in *Correspondence*, p. 528.

Supplement, Malone had mistakenly cited Markham's work ('*The Tragedie of Richard Grinvyle, Knight*') in the list of 'unpublished plays' (*Supplement*, vol. 1, p. 78), without realizing that it was actually an heroic poem in octave stanzas.[41] From the 1790 edition, Malone silently rectified the error by removing Markham's poem from the list (*Plays and Poems*, vol. 1, pt 1, p. 365). Still, Malone did not notice that Poem 11 of *The Passionate Pilgrim* was printed prominently as Poem 3 of Griffin's *Fidessa* in the same volume.

In July 1787, Malone tried to borrow the volume again, but Warton was unfortunately away from his home in Oxford and was 'hindered from accommodating you immediately with the *Venus and Adonis*'.[42] In fact, Malone's interest might not have been primarily in the 1596 *Venus and Adonis* in the collection at this stage: when he applied for a loan of the volume yet again on 6 November 1787, he would state explicitly that he had already finished editing *Venus and Adonis* ('I ... have no urgent occasion for it, *Venus and Adonis* being printed').[43] Malone's 1790 publication still failed to assign Poem 11 of *The Passionate Pilgrim* to Griffin even in 'Emendations and Additions' and 'Appendix', which printed the editor's last minute corrections.

Following the death of Thomas Warton in 1790, his brother Joseph Warton sent Malone the invaluable collection of poems as a keepsake. Malone 'took out that piece [i.e., the 1596 *Venus and Adonis*] in order to place it with my other early editions of Shakspeare's pieces', and rebound it and the other poems separately.[44] Malone kept revising *Plays and Poems* after the publication of the 1790 edition, but with spectacular obstinacy did not register Griffin's *Fidessa*, and remained resolutely *un*enlightened. He left countless memoranda and instructions at his demise in 1812 to Boswell but, as is clear from the junior editor's complaint, information about *Fidessa* was not among them.

Strictly speaking, Griffin's verse-book does not definitively settle the authorship of Poem 11 of *The Passionate Pilgrim*. The title-page ascription of *Fidessa* might be just as untrustworthy as that of *The Passionate Pilgrim*, even though Griffin's dedication of the former to William Essex of Lamborn and his address to the 'Gentlemen of the Innes of Court' certainly make it look like a very legitimate publication. All the same, Malone's neglect of *Fidessa* is profoundly regrettable, as it shows that the great Shakespearian editor did not always make good use of external evidence even when it was (literally) in his own hands. Either through inattention or deliberate ignorance, Malone failed to register the important testimony Griffin's *Fidessa* bore about the authorship of the Venus and Adonis poems, and missed the good chance to reflect on, and if necessary abandon, his problematic reordering of *The Passionate Pilgrim*.

---

[41] John Payne Collier was the first to point out Malone's slip in the *Supplement. The History of Dramatic Poetry*, 3 vols. (London, 1831), vol. 2, p. 237.

[42] Warton to Malone, 29 July 1787, in *Correspondence*, p. 577.

[43] Malone to Warton, 6 November 1787, in *Correspondence*, p. 587.

[44] Prior, *Life of Malone*, p. 179.

PAPER WORLDS: A STORY
OF THINGS LEFT BEHIND

BARBARA HODGDON

ABSOLUTE BEGINNERS

While exploring the RSC collection, I came across a curiously wrought lantern resembling a toy – a typical 'bullseye' lantern with a green lens, topped by 'opera glasses' that vent smoke from the candle inside, giving light to the lens (Illustration 23).[1] In a cartoon by Alfred Bryant titled 'Horrible London', George R. Sims, costumed as a policeman, shines such a lantern on the London underworld.[2] This lantern, the property of Eugene Aram, an eighteenth-century English philologist and infamous murderer, celebrated in Edward Bulwer-Lytton's novel as a Romantic figure torn between violence and visionary ideals, once belonged to Henry Irving. Did Irving see himself as a similar figure? Perhaps. On the night of Aram's offence, Irving performed the story of his murder as a dramatic poem: moreover, not only did he take the central role in W. G. Wills's play *Eugene Aram* but he also kept the lantern on his dressing-room table and, so the story goes, carried it onstage when he played Hamlet – one of those intensely convenient anecdotes through which an object has an enclosed contextual resonance, turns back on itself, gains meaning through user and use.[3]

To write about objects that echo down the mind's corridors is to write a memoir, touch a past history. Just as this tiny lantern supposedly illuminates London's underworld, I adopt it to guide me through the rooms within rooms, layer upon layer of subterranean levels nested like Russian dolls, of another underworld, an archive of my own.[4] Beginning with a single object, my enquiry might be called an installation, in the sense that Peter Greenaway's *Prospero's Books* brings together images with marginalia, commentary and drawings, held in tension though not necessarily brought into synthesis. Put another way, I conjure a paper theatre in print, make of the page a theatrical scene – a place reminiscent of a memory theatre like Robert Fludd's *Ars memoriae*, built on his image of the Globe – that houses a selection of properties, costumes and set models, archived as digital photographs. By including the historical gossip that burrs on to these remains, I fashion an anecdotal ethnography centred on the body, beginning with 'hands, eyes, voice, ears and so mobilizing both time and space',[5] but with special emphasis on capturing theatre as a temporal experience, transforming acting into looking and the shape and movement of the text into the conditions of the photograph.[6] What kind of virtual stage

---

[1] All the illustrations used in this chapter are photographs taken by Richard Abel as part of research at the RSC Collections.

[2] David Mayer supplied this information (email, 15 July 2015); the lantern, measuring 10 x 7.5 x 7.5 cm, is listed in the catalogue of Irving's effects.

[3] My thanks to David Howells for information about Irving's connection to Eugene Aram.

[4] For the idea of layered passageways, see Tom Gunning, 'The Exterior as *Interieur*: Benjamin's Optical Detective', *boundary* 2.30 (2003), 114. See also Gaston Leroux, *The Phantom of the Opera* (London, 1985), esp. pp. 225, 259–60.

[5] See Jacques Derrida, *Paper Machine*, trans. Rachel Bowlby (Palo Alto, CA, 2005), p. 44.

[6] See Barbara Hodgdon, 'Photography, Theater, Mnemonics; or, Thirteen Ways of Looking at a Still', in *Theorizing Practice:*

23. The lantern owned by Henry Irving. Image taken by Richard Abel as part of informal research at the RSC Collections.

might use and *reuse* costumes, properties and set designs borrowed from archival 'stuff'?[7] As with Sophie Calle's *Ghosts*,[8] which places empty frames and written memories of the paintings stolen from the Isabella Stewart Gardner Museum in their place, writing evokes presence from loss, the past becomes the present inside my head,[9] demonstrating the performative quality of all seeing.

Imagining such a virtual stage, then, is not simply a notation system but an alternative starting point located outside the body, so that I occupy a double position, both inside *and* outside the work, intent on mapping points upon a graph, material details for a sketch of theatrical thinking and display, resembling a Mobius strip. Reaching toward each image, I search for what Benjamin calls the 'tiny spark of contingency' signalling the here and now, that half-hidden place where the future nests and where a flashed look might rediscover it. I watch echoes of theatrical stuff reverberate across differing fields, leading the gaze through several lenses – and tenses – part and parcel of the 'deep time' that lends such echo objects[10] the gliding,

---

Redefining Theatre History, ed. W. B. Worthen with Peter Holland (London, 2003), pp. 88–119; esp. pp. 102, 105.

[7] See Gabriella Giannachi, *Virtual Theatres: An Introduction* (London, 2004), pp. 1, 10, 12, 125–6. See also T. Schiphorst, 'Merce Cunningham: Making Dance with the Computer', *Choreography and Dance* 4.3 (1997), 94.

[8] Sophie Calle, *Ghosts – Last Seen* (New York, 2013).

[9] I borrow from Margarethe Bohr's line, speaking of memory, in Michael Frayn's *Copenhagen* (London, 1998), p. 6.

[10] See Walter Benjamin, 'A Little History of Photography', in *The Work of Art in the Age of its Technological Reproducibility and*

floating character of a jazz riff: swooping, rising, stretching and extending one moment into a solo, then segueing to slow motion, enlarging or reducing particular fragments – enabling a long-past minute to greet a possible future through eloquent paper-dreaming in the present.

TOY THEATRE THINKING

Presiding over this collection of stuff is Shakespeare's hand – represented by his delicately embroidered gloves, preserved as in a reliquary, laid against red velvet, bearing the phrase, 'Presented to David Garrick in the belief that they were Shakespeare's Gloves', and framed, sealed within its own permanent time,[11] directing the gaze, first, to set models. Singling out these particular photographs for re-viewing works somewhat like the classical mnemonic of placing a thought or image within a fictive theatrical architecture.[12] Braiding production technologies with modes of performance, the digital photograph thematizes a hyperframe, a master code for thinking performance in print.[13] Clearly, these belong backstage, in what Antony Sher calls 'a shadowy, blue-lit area which is locked in permanent night-time',[14] where actors are waiting to come on through stage doors or aisles – in transit. Some models are more finished than others: take, for instance, Motley's unit set for Glen Byam Shaw's *Antony and Cleopatra* (1953) at the Shakespeare Memorial Theatre. As displayed in the archive, it shows the tiny figures of Cleopatra and her court at the top of four upright stairs; a broad empty space, squared off by two columns (a distant memory of Globe-space?), separates her from Antony and his soldiers, clustered together at a down-left open door, just outside a false proscenium, barely within frame. A caption glosses the set design, which 'allowed for instantaneous shifts from Egypt to Rome and back again, making the play's sprawling forty-seven scenes run smoothly together'.[15] The moment shown, however, is an invention, for it is not dramatized in the play. Writes Peggy Ashcroft, who played Cleopatra: 'The two worlds were set

in the heat of the lighting and the coldness of the lighting, and the banners or whatever extraneous objects were brought in.'[16]

In a slightly different category, a model of Farrah's design for Terry Hands's 1978 *Coriolanus* also appears on display: set on a table next to shelves filled with classical busts, it resembles a mock-up that might be shown to actors at an early rehearsal. It shows a signature scene – Coriolanus (Alan Howard) borne aloft by five soldiers, his face and parts of his costume bloodied, his figure nearly

---

Other Writings on Media, ed. Michael W. Jennings et al., trans. Edmund Jephcott et al. (Cambridge, MA, 2008), p. 276. I borrow 'deep time' from Siegfried Zielinski, *Deep Time of Media: Toward an Archaeology of Hearing and Seeing by Technical Means*, trans. Gloria Custance (Cambridge, MA, 2006); similarly, I borrow Barbara Maria Stafford's title but not her contextual apparatus from *Echo Objects: The Cognitive Work of Images* (Chicago, 2007).

[11] Shakespeare's gloves are included in the RSC Collection, Shakespeare Birthplace Trust.
[12] See Frances A. Yates, *The Art of Memory* (Chicago, 1966).
[13] See Barbara Hodgdon, 'Shopping in the Archives: Material Memories', in *Shakespeare, Memory and Performance*, ed. Peter Holland (Cambridge, 2006), p. 139.
[14] Antony Sher, *Year of the Fat Knight*, p. 176.
[15] Glen Byam Shaw's pre-performance notes reveal that he considered deleting some scenes. 2.3: Its only purpose is to introduce audiences to Octavia; otherwise it could be cut. 2.4: 'Cabinet ministers' prepare for war. 3.4 and 3.5, Both scenes are very short, could be combined. 3.8: Caesar making battle plan. 3.9: Antony making battle plan. 4.2: Shows state of Antony's mind, but could be cut. 4.3: Soldiers hear music under the earth ('It could be cut but first I should like to know what Shakespeare meant by it'). 4.7 (Antony wins battle) and 4.8 (Having won the battle, Antony returns to Cleopatra rather than keeping his attention fixed on beating Caesar): one or the other might be cut but not both. 4.10: Antony makes battle plan. 4.11: Caesar makes battle plan. Byam Shaw's preparation notes are in the Shakespeare Centre Library, Shakespeare Birthplace Trust. See also Michael Mullin's interview with Peggy Ashcroft (2 September 1977) in the Shakespeare Centre Library, Shakespeare Birthplace Trust. Act and scene numbers in this selection are taken from *Antony and Cleopatra*, ed. John Wilders, The Arden Shakespeare, 3rd edn (London, 1995).
[16] Peggy Ashcroft, interview with Michael Mullin, 3 June 1977, RSC Collection, courtesy of the Shakespeare Birthplace Trust.

overwhelmed by Corioli's golden-topped walls. This model has the aura of a second-order performance, a performance-about-performance that works not just as a mnemonic of my presence but also as a means of integrating surviving fragments.[17] The model's detailed miniature world, among the most fragile remains, resembles a Joseph Cornell box: surprisingly, this hint of experience that precedes performance becomes its means of survival. Both written texts and visual images of objects – costumes, props, embodied practices – take on the traits that properly belong to documents, including their permeability, their 'open-ness'.

Writes Carlo Ginzburg: 'By digging into texts ... uncontrolled voices can be made to emerge ... Fiction, fed by history, becomes material for historical reflection or else for fiction.'[18] Were these models situated in display cases at some point (as with costume memorabilia such as Desdemona's handkerchief, embroidered with strawberries, which became further contextualized by placing casts of Ellen Terry's hands and face and a monogrammed handkerchief beside the embroidered one)? If so, the display case not only fashions a convenient (ahistorical) theatrical lie, but also incorporates a particular way of thinking, touching lightly on an optical unconscious that becomes more fully revealed in photography, which makes visible the invisible, if only in print.[19]

Two images of *Troilus and Cressida* sets offer an even more complex instance (Illustration 24). One is a mock-up bearing a label giving title, date (1985) and location (Stratford-upon-Avon Theatre) and naming the director, Howard Davies, the designer, Ralph Koltai, and the actors, Anton Lesser and Juliet Stevenson. Koltai has confined the play in a unit set, crafted a domesticated story-telling space dominated by a sweeping staircase that bisects that space. The partially black and white tiled floor (brown- or blood-stained) reveals a bare space (filled, in performance, with a grand piano), a paned door angled against a bar for supporting the staircase, and frazzled-up carpeting. Soiled draperies hang from sections of crenellated moulding. It's a set poised for *re*telling an old story: what

comes to mind is the acerbic grin and wry tones of Laurence Olivier's Archie Rice, 'Don't clap too hard – it's a very old building'.[20]

This image reveals an (almost) habitable space, making it easy to imagine populating it with actors, choosing costumes, boots and props from the collection and constructing stick figures to play out a scenario. The production's poster does just that, showing Clive Merrison at the piano and Troilus (Anton Lesser) at the bottom of the staircase looking up at Cressida (Juliet Stevenson) – a near echo of *Romeo and Juliet*'s balcony scene celebrating Koltai's stage design. Another photo, taken from on high, looks down at bits and pieces of the set – an arch, an upright bar, a ladder, a slatted blind, two paned doors, joined – half arranged, half not, where the strength of the arch holds these fragments together. Playing with this jumble entails constructing a virtual paper model that prepares for a *material* space where a play might take place. Viewed together, these two images sync up, make a tense-ful story, riffing remains to remember: like Benjamin's 'angel of history', the detritus of the past invites a spectator to see the flow of events, so that, as in Brecht's 'Portrayal of Past and Present in One', she may experience the 'progression of one-thing-after-another'.[21]

---

[17] Speaking about how such fragments bridge exterior and interior, shattering dichotomies, Benjamin compares 'the splitting of the atom, liberating the energies of history from the narcotic of the "once upon a time"'. *Arcades Project* (463), N3, 1; N3, 4 (see n. 25); see also Gunning, 'Exterior as *Interieur*'.

[18] Carlo Ginzburg, 'Introduction', *Threads and Traces / True False Fictive*, trans. Anne C. Tedeschi and John Tedeschi (Berkeley, CA, 2012), p. 3.

[19] See Rosalind E. Krauss, *The Optical Unconscious* (Cambridge, MA, 1993), p. 179.

[20] John Osborne, *The Entertainer* (London, 1959), p. 60.

[21] See Gabriella Giannachi, *Virtual Theatres: An Introduction* (London, 2004), p. 12. Benjamin is meditating on Klee's *Angelus Novus*, 1920, now in the Israel Museum in Jerusalem. See also Walter Benjamin, 'Theses of Philosophy', IX, 'On the Concept of History', in *Selected Writings*, vol. 4 (1938–40), ed. Howard Eiland and Michael W. Jennings, trans. Edmund Jephcott et al. (Cambridge, MA, 2003), p. 392; and Bertolt Brecht, 'Portrayal of Past

24. Ralph Koltai's *Troilus and Cressida* set, 1985. Dir. Howard Davies. Image taken by Richard Abel as part of informal research at the RSC Collections.

Material details of sets – such as the golden fleur-de-lys-patterned slats for *The Plantagenets* (London, 1989), complete with a paper layout of structural supports – are among the most fragile remains. Compellingly mysterious, they are a teaser for 'the real thing'.[22] Several are tiny golden doll's-house figures – stunning leftovers from *Plantagenets*, seemingly purpose-built to inhabit imaginary castles (Illustration 25). One is a carefully articulated knight on horseback, complete down to reins and tail, holding a drawn sword in one hand, a lance in the second; the other, a tree – and not just any tree but *the* eponymous tree, the one bearing plucked red and white roses, Lancaster and York, emblematic badges marking points of origin for the Wars of the Roses. A third, a faceless figure in a

red-covered bed, stands in for all the losses from battle after battle, from single combats working out revenge.[23] Together, the three set model images encapsulate a small-scale history – a microhistory, comparable to a close-up.[24]

and Present in One', trans. John Willett (1938), in *The Methuen Book of Theatre Verse*, ed. Jonathan and Moira Field (London, 1991), pp. 116–17.

[22] Pollock's Toy Theatres in London are the time-honoured example. On toy theatres, see A. E. Wilson, *Penny Plain and Twopence Coloured: A History of the Juvenile Drama* (London, 1932).

[23] See 2.4.25–120, *King Henry VI, Part I*, ed. Edward Burns; The Arden Shakespeare 3rd edn (London, 2000).

[24] Miriam Bratu Hansen, 'Benjamin, Cinema and Experience', *New German Critique* 40 (1987), 179–84.

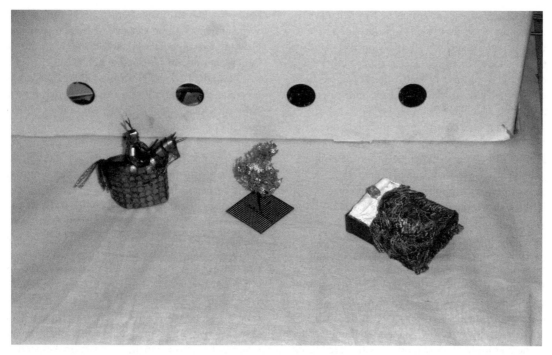

25. Fragments from *The Plantagenets*, Stratford, 1988. Dir. Adrian Noble. Image taken by Richard Abel as part of informal research at the RSC Collections.

WEARING

So many things in an overcoat! – when circumstances and men make it speak.

(Walter Benjamin, *The Arcades Project*)[25]

So many things, too, in a photograph, even when, as with a fragment of Peggy Ashcroft's dress for Cordelia, deep description here stands in for the image. A tag, basted on to the costume's lining, identifies pertinent details: designed by Leslie Hurry for a production of *King Lear* directed by John Gielgud and Anthony Quayle in 1950 and marked Number 050 in the Royal Shakespeare Company Collection. The fragment is deep blue; a pink facing with hooks and eyes attached is turned back to reveal the lining, which bears a red smudge. Scrollwork crafted from stitched-together feathers and golden beads frames the blue fabric – Mary's colour, the colour of truth. What sense of the body

does such a fragment carry? In histories of theatrical stuff, costumes subscribe to what Michel de Certeau calls a 'scriptural economy'[26] to mark the disjunction between orality and writing and to play out how that disjunction becomes inscribed on the body – a body that, as De Certeau remarks, 'is itself

---

[25] Walter Benjamin, *The Arcades Project*, trans. Howard Eiland and Kevin McLaughlin; prepared on the basis of the German volume, ed. Rolf Tiedmann (Cambridge, MA, 1999), I5a2. Gunning mentions this citation in 'Exterior as *Interieur*', p. 110.

[26] Michel de Certeau, *The Practice of Everyday Life* (Berkeley, CA, 1984), esp. pp. 131–2. See also Bruno Latour's notion of a 'culture of inscription' in *Pandora's Hope: Essays on the Reality of Science Studies* (Cambridge, MA, 1999); and Lisa Gitelman, *Paper Knowledge: Toward a Media History of Documents* (Durham, NC, 2014).

defined, delimited, and articulated by what writes it'. Costume, writes Paola Dionisotti, 'is a frame to hang a performance on'.[27] It becomes a stand-in for the body, engaging all that burrs onto it in a continuing theatrical archaeology, an endless tapestry of writing that works as both discipline and myth: discipline because writing is a form of socialization and control, and myth because writings accumulate with the weight of history itself in which showing – either by means of a photographic image or a thick description of an image[28] – is wrapped with knowing. Writes Benjamin, 'It is through the camera that we first discover the optical unconscious just as we discover the instinctual unconscious through psychoanalysis.'[29] As soon as writing is framed, that frame becomes a 'provocative matrix with which to see images, as Polonius saw the camel in the clouds or Leonardo the figures in the fire'.[30] And in more than one case, such showing involves recycled materials, reanimating folds of fabric, giving them another life. Some costumes, like my mother's satin-lined black velvet cloak, heavy with Chanel No. 5, echo still with the touch and smell of previous wearers.[31] The navy blue anorak worn by David Tennant's Hamlet (2008), for example, is heavily sweat-stained, and his deep red T-shirt, stamped with prominent black outlines of pectoral and deltoid muscles, looks as though it has been either laundered or lightly worn whereas a lighter red version seems unworn, as if made only to be archived.

Antony Sher writes of a corridor on the ground floor of the backstage area near the stage door, where a constant low noise is heard. It probably comes from heating, air conditioning or plumbing, but Sher reads it as distant applause, echoes trapped during theatre renovations and now housing a selection of costumes.[32] What body memories do these costumes carry? Do they serve a talismanic function? Clothes are material presences, theatrical properties that oftentimes transgress social boundaries. Peggy Ashcroft's dress for Cleopatra, for instance (Illustration 26), sculpts her body with Greekish drapes into a figure dressed out of the Parthenon frieze – a modern knock-off of an ancient silhouette in soft yellow fabric, sashed in

blue, that evoked gasps from post Second World War audiences, long deprived of such colourful illusions. Press reports of Ashcroft's body measurements, panopticon-like (and of her fake eyelashes, à la Elizabeth Taylor), confirmed that Cleopatra's greatest asset is her body, seemingly denying how Ashcroft's idea of the role as based on her political power countered that notion. Theatre's Egyptian dish, Cleopatra also is its fashion plate, tempting onlookers to desire the costume (or clothes) of 'the other' – the figure on the stage, on the runway, at the corner table.

Costumes that also belong centre-stage in my memory space include others worn by Ashcroft in a series of roles, from Cordelia in John Gielgud and Anthony Quayle's King Lear (1950) to Cleopatra in Glen Byam Shaw's Antony and Cleopatra (1953) to Queen Margaret in John Barton and Peter Hall's Wars of the Roses (1963–4), dresses that trace her progress from young girl to warrior queen and aging virago, mourning her dead husband, her lover and her son. Finally, her last Shakespearian role was the Countess of Rossillion in All's Well That Ends Well (1982). I recall seeing her sit, take her glasses from her cardigan's pocket, carefully put them on, pause, slowly open the envelope, another pause, read Bertram's letter, pause, put letter and envelope in her lap. Making the past present, I watch her repeat those precisely timed

---

[27] Dionisotti cited in Carol Rutter, *Clamorous Voices: Shakespeare's Women Today*, ed. Faith Evans (London, 1988), p. xxii.

[28] See Derrida, *Paper Machine*, p. 44.

[29] Walter Benjamin, *Work of Art*, p. 37.

[30] Krauss, *Optical Unconscious*, p. 284; 'Vision', writes Krauss, 'is a form of cognition' (p. 15). See also Walter Benjamin, *Arcades Project*.

[31] The Museum of London holds the bald wig, moustache and beard worn by George Robey, who played Falstaff in Olivier's film of *Henry V* – the front of the wig still caked with a pinkish, plastic-like film from his make-up. See M. R. Holmes, *Stage Costume and Accessories in the London Museum* (London, 1968), p. 21; Sher, *Falstaff Diaries*, p. 106.

[32] Antony Sher, *Year of the Fat Knight*, p. 176.

26. One of Peggy Ashcroft's gowns for Cleopatra, 1953, dir. Glen Byam Shaw. Image taken by Richard Abel as part of informal research at the RSC Collections.

movements over and over – gestures of a practical woman, alive with the hope that Bertram still might agree to woo Helena.

The Countess's costume – a simple every-day blouse and skirt topped by a grey-coloured sweater-jacket, embroidered with details tracing the body – has a deep performative history in which the aura of performance transferred from that jacket, now known as 'The Peggy', when Ashcroft wore it at Petruchio's house, in the scene with Grumio and also with the Tailor (4.1.106ff.; 4.3.65ff.), to its wearing in another performance – Estelle Kohler's Paulina in Gregory Doran's *Winter's Tale* (1999) – and then, circling back, passed to Alexandra Gilbreath's Katherina in Gregory Doran's *Taming of the Shrew*

(2003). Do this in remembrance of me, this story of borrowed robes: as costumes travel, they engender narrative; anecdotes 'make' identities. Curiously, given the central 'essence' of this costume, what remains curious is its absence in the archive; even in photographs, it is more often than not invisible or passed over, a visible invisible, blurred by distance, out of shot, half forgotten, half remembered.

A long back-story lies behind such borrowings, recyclings, deeds of gift and stories of loss. Given the economies of the theatrical trade, Lady Macbeth's first dress, a gift from Irving to Stratford's Benson Company, had been originally intended for a court train of the First Empire, presumably for the Napoleonic reception in Sardou's *Madame Sans-Gene*.[33] Like the famous 'baldric of Porthos',[34] it kept its beauties for the front only; the back, made of plainer, cheaper stuff, was covered with a mantle or shawl. Ellen Terry writes of a red cloak for Lady Macbeth cut from the same fabric used for Mephistopheles's doublet three years earlier – making an uncanny connection between the Lady and the Tempter – that she was not permitted to wear for fear that her gown would catch spectators' eyes, distracting their attention from Macbeth, fresh from the slaughter of the grooms, supposedly the 'appropriate' object of the gaze. A richer example of recycling comes from the Lady's dress for the banquet scene: a mantle of vermillion velvet, rich with embroidery and jewels, over a gown made by combining a bodice made of strips of rich-looking oriental brocade and three bands of green silk and gold braid with sleeves edged with gold fringe and a skirt of deep red silk – its cobbling together of parts revealed only through detailed scrutiny of the mantle's embroidery.[35] If one removed the train from this, or from many a late nineteenth- or early twentieth-century theatrical costume, the dress itself, its design and fabric, would echo contemporary fashions.

THE ARMOURY

For other stand-out items, I go backstage once more. Scanning the prop tables, I find an array of swords. Richard Burton's sword for Henry V, only its hilt visible from a swirl of tissue paper, gives little sense of its heft, which is left to the imagination. Not so with the sword Irving carried as Hamlet, its provenance spelled out on the blade, heavy with names – 'Sword by Wilkinson for Henry Irving "Hamlet"'. It is the ancestor of a more talismanic weapon, the sword reputedly worn by Edmund Kean as Richard III and later by Irving when he played the role. On Irving's death, that sword came, perhaps via Ellen Terry, to Kate Terry Gielgud, who gave it to her son John when he played Hamlet at the Lyceum. Gielgud then gave the sword to Laurence Olivier (like Irving, a permanent ghost in the archive), engraved with these words: 'This sword, given to him by his mother Kate Terry Gielgud 1938, is given to Laurence Olivier by his friend John Gielgud in appreciation of his performance of Richard III at the New Theatre, 1944.' This, of course, is an old story – one that bears retelling not just as an instance of gift exchange but also because it is a story that keeps growing, gathering commentary that enriches and expands its parameters. One story recounts that at Olivier's memorial service in Westminster Abbey, Frank Finlay, his Iago, carried this sword in a procession of objects placed on the high altar; another story says it was Derek Jacobi; yet another claims that the sword was buried with Olivier, who thought no one worthy to receive it from him. Reacting to the sound of Olivier's voice speaking Henry V's St Crispin's Day speech – 'From this day to the ending of the world / But we in it shall be remembered, / We few, we happy few, we band of brothers' – Ian McKellen mouths the words, as though attempting to catch his cadence.[36] Henry V's tomb, I recall, is located

---

[33] Holmes, *Stage Costume*, p. 21.
[34] The phrase derives from Alexandre Dumas, *The Three Musketeers*, ch. 4, 'The Shoulder of Athos, the Baldric of Porthos and the Handkerchief of Aramis' (London, 1846), esp. p. 51. A theatre historian's joke – 'only on this side' – lurks here.
[35] Holmes, *Stage Costume*, pp. 21, 57.
[36] *King Henry V*, 4. 3.58–60. Arden Shakespeare Third Series, ed. T. W. Craik (London, 1995).

below the abbey's Edward the Confessor Chapel: when the original carved figure's head and hands were stolen, their replacement was modeled on Olivier's hands.[37]

Or take the double-quilloned, cross-bladed boar sword fashioned by Brian McKnight, a freelance engineer and expert at making armour and weaponry for medieval reconstructions.[38] Like many but not all theatrical remains in the RSC Collection, this sword bears a tag naming its provenance: 'Richard III 1984, Sword for killing boars – used by Richmond to kill Richard'. Hefting it, I was surprised by its weight and now wonder whether the Richmond-actor rehearsed with a lighter model. Perhaps not, for this particular weapon is used only once, and the dramatic effect of raising it with difficulty enhances its importance. Is there, perhaps, a rift – or riff – here between historical and theatrical figures, between real and virtual actors, making the page a trace of the object, its stand-in?

SPARENESS

Just as the boar sword might be called *Richard III's* iconic object – the essential property that completes the narrative, so too with the iconicity of clothing in Peter Brook's *A Midsummer Night's Dream* (1970 and world tour) which begins with their origins in the costumes borrowed from Chinese acrobats and is displayed in the vibrant purple, daffodil yellow, verdant green and the sting of scarlet in the robes that punctuate the brilliantly white surround. In addition to a photographic record (catalogued in my *Shakespeare, Performance and the Archive*),[39] the archives also offer an array of materials that tell a different story, among them the shirts, trousers and gowns adorned with haphazardly placed dots of blue, covered, near the end, with satin-lined cloaks with soft furlike collars and then casually though deliberately dropped to reveal the brilliant cream-satin underdresses and suits (Illustration 27). I remember searching in vain for Titania's feather, wondering how many there were during *Dream*'s long world tour, nor do I find Oberon's and Puck's

trapezes or those of the 'fairies', here called 'AVs' (for audio-visuals) or the giant 'slinkies' that fell from above. But I did find other significant properties – the discs and wands that stand in for 'the little western flower' and get passed from Oberon to Puck as they swing aloft as well as a selection of the coloured freekahs (Illustration 28). Their archive tag reads 'sound makers': like balloons, they are capable of being twisted into shapes, making a mirror for Bottom or turning into a musical instrument: when tossed in a circle, they produce a haunting melody, a back-up soundtrack for actors' voices. For me, however, the star object is Snug the Joiner's lion mask.

When sorting through leftovers, I might easily have bypassed Snug's mask (Illustration 29), resigned it to jumble sale or flea-market status. But something about this curious object made me stop. Initially, I was struck by my sheer pleasure in discovering and handling it, an evocative mnemonic tied to an awareness that it had been so obviously and lovingly used (by Barry Stanton, who played Snug at one point in the production's history) and so well kept – ragged with marks of decay that rendered its life history and afterlife in material terms, giving it an extraordinary 'thingness'. If nothing else, it expresses a child's idea of a lion – a lion that could fit only in a gigantic doll's-house zoo.

Leaving this toy theatre, I return to my study and, from my desk, pick up a heavy mallet weighing a pound and a half, painted red with splashes of black, showing signs of heavy use (Illustration 30). Made by the RSC's Props Workshop for Snug the Joiner, it was dropped during previews, relegated to the 'hell' for unused props, its future uncertain. Such discarded props may travel to rehearsal rooms down the years – the horses made for John Barton's *Richard II* wait, like sleeping perennials, to be

---

[37] See Sher, *Falstaff Diaries*, p. 107.

[38] My thanks to Roger Howells, the Official Historian of the Shakespeare Centre Library, for this information. McKnight also made a shaft for Sher's Richard III crutch.

[39] See Barbara Hodgdon, *Shakespeare, Performance and the Archive* (London and New York, 2015).

27. The satin cloak from *A Midsummer Night's Dream*, 1970. Dir. Peter Brook. Image taken by Richard Abel as part of informal research at the RSC Collections.

ridden again and hats, belts, gloves and daggers become items of actors' souvenir culture. David Tennant (probably) took the hat he wore as Hamlet; David Brierly (once head of the RSC Collection) appropriated a dagger used by Anthony Quayle and gave it to his son; Anthony Sher displays Desdemona's handkerchief on his wall, a mnemonic of his Iago. Snug's mallet has a

different history. Laurence Burns, the deputy stage manager who made the promptbook for the performance, ferreted it out from the under-backstage dock cellar where previously used or rejected props gather (including wooden and papier mâché goblets, cups, bowls, weaponry and small furniture) and took it home, where it stayed for forty-five years, brought back into the world when

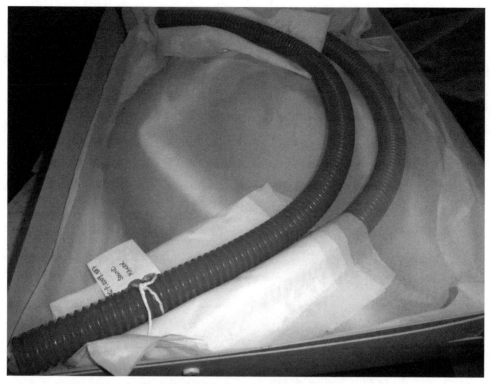

28. Freekahs from Peter Brook's *A Midsummer Night's Dream*, 1970. Image taken by Richard Abel as part of informal research at the RSC Collections.

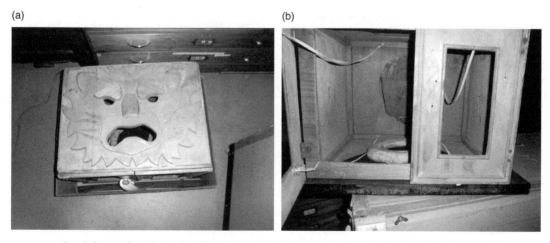

29. Snug's lion mask made by the RSC's Properties Workshop under William Lockwood for Peter Brook's *A Midsummer Night's Dream*, 1970. Image taken by Richard Abel as part of informal research at the RSC Collections.

30. Mallet made by the RSC's Properties Workshop under William Lockwood for Snug the Joiner (Barry Stanton) in Peter Brook's *A Midsummer Night's Dream*, 1970. Image taken by Richard Abel as part of informal research at the RSC Collections.

"'No, I am no such thing; I am a man as other men are": and there, indeed, let him name his name; and tell them plainly, he is Snug, the joiner'[40] with an anecdote that occurred at a spectacle presented to Queen Elizabeth wherein

Harry Goldingham was to represent *Arion* upon the dolphin's backe; but finding his voice to be verye hoarse and unpleasant, when he came to perform it, he tears off his disguise, and *swears he was none of Arion, not he, but even honest Harry Goldingham*; which blunt discoverie pleased the queene better than if it had through in the right way – yet he could order his voice to an instrument exceeding well.[41]

A century and a half later, the mallet appears as a paper trace in Sally Jacobs's post-performance costume design for the *Dream*'s so-called mechanicals (now held at the Victoria & Albert Theatre and Performance Archive), where it is pictured among several tools – a hacksaw, a hammer – and a carpenter's tool bag and lunch pail. All such theatrical leftovers, such remains, ultimately return to paper – that is, return to their origins, to their initial form as 'first version', 'manuscript', 'rough draft', whether writing with pencil, pen or computer as an idea inscribed on fleshly paper,[42] returning the echoes of the voice or song that it carries – to be reperformed, as here, in an imagined paper theatre.

Burns sent me a photograph of it and, later, the mallet itself. Although it occasionally gets repurposed in the kitchen for a variety of tasks (often to pound recalcitrant chicken breasts), its more appropriate place is in my study, where its major role is to cue lost-past stages and spaces to reappear, evoking paper traces that play out a partial history. One such trace comes from Charles Kean's historical and explanatory notes (1856), glossing Snug's

---

[40] See *A Midsummer Night's Dream*, ed. Harold F. Brooks, The Arden Shakespeare 2nd edn (London, 1979), 3.1.42–4.

[41] *Shakespeare's Play of A Midsummer Night's Dream: Arranged for Representation at the Princess's Theatre: with historical and explanatory notes by Charles Kean. As first performed on Wednesday, October 15th, 1856* (London: J. K. Chapman, 1856), p. 35.

[42] See Derrida, *Paper Machine*, p. 47.

AN INTIMATE AND INTERMEDIAL FORM: EARLY TELEVISION SHAKESPEARE FROM THE BBC, 1937–1939

JOHN WYVER

In the twenty-seven months between February 1937 and April 1939 the fledgling BBC Television service from Alexandra Palace broadcast more than twenty Shakespeare adaptations. The majority of these productions were short programmes featuring 'scenes from' the plays, although there were also substantial adaptations of *Othello* (1937), *Julius Caesar* (1938), *Twelfth Night* and *The Tempest* (both 1939) as well as a presentation of David Garrick's 1754 version of *The Taming of the Shrew*, *Katharine and Petruchio* (1939). There were other Shakespeare-related programmes as well, and the playwright himself appeared in three distinct historical dramas. In large part because no recordings exist of these transmissions (or of any British television Shakespeare before 1955), these 'lost' adaptations have received little scholarly attention. In this article I explore the traces that remain of these pre-war broadcasts, paying particular attention to *Scenes from Cymbeline*, *Macbeth* and *Othello* (all 1937) as well as *Katharine and Petruchio*. The surviving records include scripts and production notes preserved in the BBC Written Archives Centre (WAC) at Caversham, listings and articles in *Radio Times*, and reviews and recollections. I also outline the the production environment and cultural context for interwar television Shakespeare, and detail some of the intermedial connections of these productions with the theatre, radio and the cinema of the 1930s.

Pre-war television Shakespeare in Britain features only minimally in the extensive literature focused on small-screen adaptations of the plays.

In his foundational *A History of Shakespeare on Screen: A Century of Film and Television*, Kenneth Rothwell gave brief details of certain pre-war productions and quoted from a small number of contemporary reviews. Critical analysis of these broadcasts, however, has been limited because all television drama until the mid 1950s was played live before electronic cameras, and in the medium's first decade recording technology had not been invented. The first BBC Television Shakespeare production of which even a partial archival copy is preserved is the 1955 studio production of *Romeo and Juliet* with Tony Britton and Virginia McKenna as the lovers.[1] This was captured using the recently introduced technique of tele-recording, which involved filming the screen of an electronic monitor on which the live broadcast was being shown. Tele-recordings exist of a number of BBC productions from the 1950s, including *Othello* (1955), directed by Tony Richardson, and *The Life of Henry V* (1957), with John Neville as the King. By the mid 1960s videotape recording was also being utilized widely, although some later broadcasts have also been lost, including the second half of the Royal Shakespeare Company's 1968

Research for this chapter was undertaken as part of AHRC-funded Screen Plays: Theatre Plays on British Television research project at the University of Westminster.

[1] The Shakespeare database of the British Universities Film and Video Council (BUFVC) is an exceptional resource for information about all BBC Television adaptations, including whether or not an archival copy is known to exist; http://bufvc.ac.uk/shakespeare/

staging by John Barton of *All's Well That Ends Well* and *The Tempest* (1968, BBC) with Michael Redgrave as Prospero.

Writing about the first years of television drama, John Caughie has suggested that the lack of recordings 'makes the recovery of the early history of television form and style an archaeological, rather than a strictly historical procedure'.[2] In his book *The Intimate Screen: Early British Television Drama*, Jason Jacobs developed just such an archaeological study, acknowledging that the WAC resources were central to his work. 'This *written* archive,' Jacob detailed, 'provided programme and policy information – studio plans, camera scripts, memos, etc. – which was invaluable in the process of reconstructing the visual sense of early television drama.'[3] Jacobs noted that other published sources were also important, including reviews and criticism published in the *Radio Times*, *Listener* and *BBC Quarterly*. He was more sceptical about the use of stills, because 'the vast majority of them are production stills, presumably taken during camera rehearsals',[4] but such images can nonetheless offer useful information as well as a resonant visual sense of the moment. Technical manuals, anecdotal and biographical sources and oral history interviews can also be valuable for the interrogation of this period of television drama.

These traces from the period reveal key concerns about the new medium, including the importance of 'liveness' and a sense of 'intimacy'. 'The live immediacy of television is its defining characteristic', Jacobs wrote of the ways in which the medium was discussed in these years. Moreover, 'television is a medium of "intimacy"; it is the delivery of images to the private domestic sphere ... and the visual "closeness" described by the television close-up, that are the characteristic features of television'.[5] One aspect of this 'intimacy' is demonstrated by the way in which two or three actors in early television broadcasts are invariably bunched together in publicity photographs, grouped in such a way as to be visible most effectively to the studio cameras with their narrow fields of vision and minimal depth of focus. John Caughie has argued that 'the absence of expressive *mise en scène* and editing – the absence, in other words, of "style"' in this period, 'was the logical aesthetic of a technology whose essence was conceived in terms of immediacy, relay and the "live".'[6] Pre-war television was also a profoundly *intermedial* form that was shaped in significant ways by radio, by the theatre and to an extent by the cinema of the time. The only models available to television producers were those of pre-existing forms of performance and, throughout the writings of both practitioners and commentators, early television is constantly compared with radio, theatre and cinema. Recalling his earliest BBC Television broadcasts from Alexandra Palace, the service's programme planner, Cecil Madden, who had been a theatre playwright, wrote,

The only technique I knew was of the stage, so I divided up the studio into three stages behind one another, separated by curtains. The three cameras were placed roughly in line but at different heights ... We played an act on stage one, then the curtains parted and cameras moved on to stage two, and then again to stage three. It worked quite well, saved time, was continuous, since cameras could not cut as in films and as television can cut today. Only fades could take one camera to another.[7]

At the same time, like most television producers, Madden was dissatisfied by the reliance on stage techniques. 'I wanted to create something that would be pure television, owing nothing to stage or films', he wrote in his memoirs.[8]

Radio was the other determining medium of early television, and the new form's presentation of Shakespeare extended, as it did in many other contexts, BBC Radio's dramatizations of the plays. The first radio transmission of a Shakespeare scene

---

[2] John Caughie, 'Before the Golden Age: Early Television Drama', in *Popular Television in Britain*, ed. John Corner (London, 1991), pp. 24–5.

[3] Jason Jacobs, *The Intimate Screen: Early British Television Drama* (Oxford, 2000), p. 4, emphasis in original.

[4] Jacobs, *Intimate Screen*, p. 5. [5] Jacobs, *Intimate Screen*, p. 28.

[6] Caughie, 'Golden Age', p. 32.

[7] Cecil Madden, *Starlight Days: The Memoirs of Cecil Madden*, ed. Jennifer Lewis (London, 2007), p. 15.

[8] Madden, *Starlight Days*, p. 89.

appears to have been almost exactly fourteen years before the first extract from the plays on television. Although the account is disputed, the invariably accurate BBC Programme Record details that a broadcast on 16 February 1923 from Marconi House in London's Strand via the 2LO transmitter included the 'tent scene' (*Julius Caesar*, 4.3) with Shayle Gardner and Hubert Carter.[9] By the end of 1923, in addition to further transmissions of excerpts, some accompanied by critical commentary from Professor Cyril Brett, producer Cathleen Nesbit had adapted and broadcast full-length productions of *Twelfth Night* (in which she took the role of Viola), *The Merchant of Venice*, *Romeo and Juliet* and *A Midsummer Night's Dream*. In 1936, the year the television service started, BBC Radio broadcast six full-length Shakespeare plays, including a version of B. Iden Payne's Shakespeare Memorial Theatre production of *Much Ado About Nothing*. Various excerpts were also broadcast, with a programme on 9 July featuring scenes from Robert Atkins's Open Air Theatre presentation of *As You Like It* with Margaretta Scott, a production that, the following year, would also feature in television's first such broadcast.

Central to the production of early Shakespeare on radio, as was also to be the case for the first television broadcasts of the plays, were relationships with the London theatre of the day. Several of the earliest television broadcasts were derived from contemporary stagings, as will be explored, and actors invariably had extensive theatre experience. In 1964, J. C. Trewin offered this summary of the state of Shakespeare in the capital during television's pre-war years: 'From 1933 until the war an addict could usually get a London performance somewhere: at the Old Vic for eight months of the year . . . at the Open Air Theatre in Regent's Park during the summer; and frequently, at any season, in the West End, which had in seven years a mixed score of revivals.'[10] Trewin despaired at the lack of accomplished Shakespeare in the provinces throughout the 1930s, and felt that the achievement of the Festival company in Stratford-upon-Avon was mixed at best. Describing the 1937 season there, he wrote of 'the Sargasso weed of

Memorial Theatre conservatism'.[11] For Trewin, the most consistent centre of Shakespeare performance was the Old Vic, where producer Tyrone Guthrie and others could regularly call on actors of the calibre of Laurence Olivier and Ralph Richardson, both of whom appeared in early television broadcasts.

Although John Logie Baird had organized experimental television broadcasts in Britain from May 1932 to September 1935, regular transmissions began on 2 November 1936 from two small BBC studios at Alexandra Palace. Just prior to this, broadcasts had been made from Alexandra Palace to the annual 'Radio Show' exhibition at Olympia. In what the *Times* described as 'the first organised television programmes in this country', a mixed programme of variety, comedy, newsreels and film excerpts was broadcast solely for the exhibition twice daily between 26 August and 5 September.[12] Among the half-hour compilation of excerpts from feature films was a scene with Elisabeth Bergner and Laurence Olivier from director Paul Czinner's movie *As You Like It*, which was released on 3 September. *As You Like It* was also the play chosen for the first known British television broadcast of Shakespeare. Three months after the start of the regular television service, in the afternoon of 5 February 1937, Act 3, scene 2 of the play was given an 11-minute transmission with Margaretta Scott as Rosalind and Ion Swinley as Orlando. When the service began, it could be received by just a few hundred viewers who lived close to the transmitter at Alexandra Palace, and the range had hardly been extended by the time the service closed down at the start of the Second World War. By this point, however, the number of predominantly middle-class viewers (for the sets were expensive) had

---

[9] See BUFVC, 'Scenes from Shakespeare [16/02/1923]', Shakespeare database, http://bufvc.ac.uk/shakespeare/index.php/title/av37818, accessed 5 October 2014.

[10] J. C. Trewin, *Shakespeare on the English Stage 1900–1964* (London, 1964), p. 144.

[11] Trewin, *English Stage*, p. 172.

[12] 'First television broadcast', *The Times*, 26 August 1936.

31. Margaretta Scott (Rosalind) and Ion Swinley (Orlando) in Robert Atkins's production of *As You Like It* for *Scenes from Shakespeare* (BBC, 1937). Reproduced by permission of the BBC Photo Library.

risen to perhaps thirty thousand. Initially, there was an hour of programmes in the afternoon from 3.00 to 4.00 p.m. and an hour from 9.00 p.m. in the evening (which was soon extended to two hours). Sunday broadcasts were prohibited until 3 April 1938, when a seven-days-a-week service was inaugurated with a performance of Clemence Dane's drama *Will Shakespeare*. But television remained very much the poor relation of radio, with constant internal arguments about funding. Only after the Treasury provided extra finance was the BBC able to approach its target of twenty hours of broadcasts each week.[13]

The television service's programme planner, Cecil Madden, wrote later that '"a play a day" was the target we set ourselves at the outset, and so it turned out'.[14] The pre-war service broadcast more than 400 excerpts and adaptations of plays, all but a handful of which had been written for the theatre. Whilst this total fell some way short of Madden's aspiration, television nonetheless presented a remarkable range of work. In the three

---

[13] Asa Briggs, *The History of Broadcasting in the United Kingdom*, vol. 2, *The Golden Age of Wireless* (Oxford, 1965), p. 616.
[14] Madden, *Starlight Days*, p. 104.

months before the *As You Like It* excerpt, the service had offered scenes from fourteen plays including the Scottish comedy *Marigold*, T. S. Eliot's *Murder in the Cathedral*, and Lady Gregory's one-act comedy *The Workhouse Ward*. All but three of these presentations were drawn directly from current theatre productions and involved the stage cast going into one of two small studios and acting out a scene conceived for the stage in front of two or three electronic cameras. The two studios were of the same size, with a narrow production space of roughly 20 x 10 metres. The sets initially were exceptionally spare and generic, in part because the studios were on the first floor and there was no goods lift and in part because the same studios were needed almost immediately before and after each transmission for variety shows or discussion programmes.[15]

The connections between Shakespeare in the British theatre and television's first productions began with Margaretta Scott reprising her Rosalind from the 1936 Regent's Park Open Air Theatre production. Robert Atkins, who was running the Regent's Park theatre with its founder Sydney Carroll and who was to become a key figure in television Shakespeare across the next decade, is credited as the producer of the 5 February broadcast. Stephen Thomas, who was a staff producer for the BBC, 'presented' the broadcast for television, which indicated that the performances and staging had been imported and Thomas's responsibility was the disposition of the cameras. There was a similar relationship between theatre and television for Margaretta Scott's next television appearance in Shakespeare, just six days after the scene from *As You Like It*. In January, the actress had played Beatrice in a limited number of performances of *Much Ado About Nothing* for the Bankside Players.[16] This company, also run by Robert Atkins, had conjured up a temporary theatre known as the Ring in a boxing arena at Blackfriars. On the semblance of an Elizabethan platform stage, Ms Scott performed here with Jack Hawkins as Benedick, but when she returned to the BBC Television studio for a ten-minute excerpt from the play on 11 February 1937 her foil was Henry Oscar.

Between February and April there were eleven brief Shakespeare broadcasts, including scenes from *A Midsummer Night's Dream* (18 February), *Twelfth Night* (distinct excerpts on 20 February and 12 March) and *Richard III* (9 April). Henry Oscar was the actor who appeared most frequently in these, playing Henry V to Yvonne Arnaud's Katherine in the evening of 5 February, giving Mark Antony's funeral oration from *Julius Caesar* in the afternoon of 11 February, and on 25 March playing Macbeth (3.4) opposite Margaret Rawlings. With its running time of thirty-four minutes, this broadcast by producer George More O'Ferrall was a step towards more ambitious productions later in the year, as was his compilation of scenes from *Twelfth Night*, which also ran for thirty-four minutes on 7 May. The close relationship between television's first 'scenes' and contemporary theatrical productions is also demonstrated by the presentation from Alexandra Palace on 12 March of the 'letter scene' from *The Merry Wives of Windsor* (2.1). The *Radio Times* billed this as being performed by Robert Atkins's Bankside Players, with Violet Vanbrugh as Mistress Ford and Irene Vanbrugh as Mistress Page. Atkins was presenting *The Merry Wives of Windsor* with the Vanbrugh sisters at the Ring on Sunday evenings, and just three days after the broadcast, the reviewer for the *Times* was complimentary about the stage production, writing: 'The wives ... conduct their mischief with a graciousness which puts even its victim in a pleasant light. Not that their performances, though free from malice, miss any facet of the fun ... It is an extremely lively production, and Mr Robert Atkins, using the Elizabethan stage as to the manner born, has gained pace and a rare measure of intimacy.'[17]

---

[15] See Martin Kempton's online resource, 'The BBC's TV studios in London', www.tvstudiohistory.co.uk/old%20bbc%20studios.htm#alexandra, accessed 10 October 2014.

[16] 'G. W. B.' (George W. Bishop), review of *Much Ado About Nothing*, *Sunday Times*, 24 January 1937.

[17] 'Blackfriars Ring: *The Merry Wives of Windsor*', *The Times*, 15 March 1937.

Broadcasting well-known scenes from Shakespeare's plays during television's first year paralleled not only the practice at the beginning of BBC Radio but also that of early cinema. As Judith Buchanan has written, 'The pioneering years of cinema (1895–c. 1906) saw the release of a handful of films offering brief, cinematically animated, visual quotations from Shakespeare plays. This approach was in tune with the era's film-making impulses in relation to adaptation more generally, which typically privileged brief cameo references to literary works over a consistent narrative drive.'[18] Even before silent Shakespeare films began in Britain in 1899 with W. K. L. Dickson's scenes from Herbert Beerbohm Tree's staging of *King John*, there was an earlier tradition of such 'scenes' in other cultural forms, including magic lantern slides and pantomime. For all its novelty as a technology, television extended an approach to Shakespeare that would have been familiar to audiences and accepted by them in other contexts. The new medium was also soon to follow the older one, the progress of which has been further described by Buchanan: 'In the transitional era (c. 1907–13) ... this cherry-picking approach to a literary or theatrical source ceded to more sustained engagements with story-telling and to a desire to tell autonomous narratives cinematically. A parallel, related, development in the film industry during this period was the increase in the lengths of films.'[19]

Television Shakespeare demonstrated its intermedial relationship with radio when extracts from *Julius Caesar* were shown on 1 April 1937 with Malcolm Keen as Brutus, Robert Holmes as Cassius and Mary Hinton as Portia. This broadcast was presented for television by Stephen Thomas 'in conjunction with Peter Creswell's sound programme production'.[20] On the previous Sunday, Creswell had produced for the BBC's National Programme a live two-hour adaptation of Shakespeare's play. In the published cast-list for this, however, Malcolm Keen is credited as Mark Antony and Brutus was Ion Swinley. Cast members of the radio production had gone to Alexandra Palace four days after the radio broadcast to reprise

scenes before the cameras. The success of early television transmissions such as this was recognized in July 1937, when the television critic of the *Observer*, who was reviewing *Pyramus and Thisbe*, adapted by producer Jan Bussell as a stand-alone excerpt of *A Midsummer Night's Dream*, suggested that, 'The television studios have been very successful in giving us bits and pieces of Shakespeare'.[21] A less laudatory response is recorded in a *Radio Times* article headed 'View of a Viewer' in June 1937. Jean Bartlett outlined her impressions after watching television for six months, and she compared the Shakespeare adaptations unfavourably with broadcasts of excerpts from West End plays:

Shakespeare ... invariably falls flat, even when distinguished artists are playing the selected arts [sic]. Non-Shakespeareans are frankly bored – they cannot get the hang of the thing before it is over; and lovers of Shakespeare are irritated by brief episodes suspended in mid-air and inevitably devoid of the play's original stagecraft, and viewed from two cameras alternately at rather uninteresting angles.[22]

By the autumn the service was planning more ambitious broadcasts, although the relationship with the theatre remained central. The first production regarded as being 'full-length' was the sixty-seven-minute adaptation of *Othello*, produced by George More O'Ferrall on 14 December, but before this the television studios were visited by two more productions from the theatre. On 25 October 1937, in a half-hour afternoon broadcast, scenes were given from *Measure for Measure* by the cast of Tyrone Guthrie's Old Vic production. Just a month later, in both the afternoon and the evening of 29 November *Scenes from Cymbeline* were restaged by nine cast members from Andre

[18] Judith Buchanan, *Shakespeare on Silent Film: An Excellent Dumb Discourse* (Cambridge, 2009), p. 74.
[19] Buchanan, *Silent Film*, p. 75.
[20] *BBC Television Programme Records, vol. 1, 1937–38* (London, 1939), p. 25.
[21] 'Television', *Observer*, 11 July 1937.
[22] Jean Bartlett, 'View of a Viewer', *Radio Times Television Supplement*, 4 June 1937.

van Gyseghem's production of the play at the Embassy Theatre. This stage production had opened on 16 November 1937, thirteen days before the television broadcast. The staging is notable for being the first to use George Bernard Shaw's variation for Act 5, although the broadcast scenes were selected only from Acts 1 and 2. The broadcast is the first Shakespeare broadcast for which a WAC production file exists, and included within it is a detailed camera script that offers a strong sense of the 'look' of early television drama.[23] The presentation began with a music cue played from a 78 rpm disc of the London Symphony Orchestra performing Rimsky-Korsakov's *Cortege des Nobles*. The announcer spoke over the onscreen caption, 'Cymbeline': 'Now we are to see scenes from Andre van Gyseghem's production of *Cymbeline* from the Embassy Theatre, by permission of Ronald Adam.' With the caption still in place, the minor actors were introduced by name before a mix to a shot of one actor accompanied by an explanatory voiceover, 'Iachimo is played by George Hayes', and then another mix to a shot of three characters: 'The Queen by Olga Lindo, Posthumus by Geoffrey Toon and Imogen by Joyce Bland.' The next mix revealed a further caption – 'The Palace Garden' – and then the television image returned to the previous three-shot. On a cue from the cameraman, the Queen began to speak. Each of these mixes at this time would have taken four to six seconds to complete; cutting live between studio cameras was impossible until 1946.

The first scene was drawn from Act 1, scene 1 and ran from the entry of the Queen, Posthumus and Imogen. After the repeat of the caption 'The Palace Garden' and a brief music cue, 1.3 was played in full with Imogen, Pisanio and, for the final lines out of the total of forty-eight, a Lady. Both of these 'Palace Garden' scenes were acted in No.1 studio at Alexandra Palace in front of a minimal setting that included three trees in tubs. Both garden scenes were also covered by just two fixed-lens cameras, which were mounted on dollies allowing forward and backward movement. In the first of these scenes, which might have lasted

perhaps six minutes, there were just four shot-changes by mixing from one camera to the other; the second, which would probably have run for between two and three minutes, was played in a single shot. The scene then shifted to (another caption) 'Philario's House in Rome' for 1.4, and then to 'Imogen's Bedroom' for, first, the 'wooing scene' (1.6), and then the 'trunk scene' (2.2). The final element of the selection returned to 'Philario's House in Rome' for 2.4, the first 192 lines of which were played – which might have lasted a further six minutes or more. The whole of this scene appears to have been shot by camera no. 4. The timings, of course, are approximate, but if the presentation did indeed play its total of 790 lines in thirty minutes – an average of twenty-six lines per minute, not allowing for breaks or music – the verse-speaking would have had to be very fast. It is quite possible, however, that the broadcast overran its allocated slot, as many did, sometimes by as much again as the scheduled time. In contrast, and judged by later standards, the visual rhythm would have seemed funereally slow. There were perhaps just twenty-five shot changes during the broadcast, and half of these were accounted for by captions.

In retrospect, perhaps the most notable pre-war 'scenes from' Shakespeare broadcast, and the one of which most historians would covet a recording, was the half-hour presentation of *Scenes from Macbeth* with Laurence Olivier. Olivier opened in Michel St Denis's production of the Scottish play at the Old Vic on 26 November 1937, the first night having been postponed for three days because of the complexity of the production. Earlier that year Olivier had played Hamlet and Henry V for the company, as well as Sir Toby Belch in *Twelfth Night*, and he was still to take on the role of Iago to Ralph Richardson's Othello. *Macbeth* had settings and costumes by the design team Motley and incidental music composed by Darius Milhaud. The presence of the queen at a matinee on 29 November

---

[23] BBC WAC T5/121 Drama: Cymbeline 1937–1956.

indicated how significant an event this was in the theatre season. But her presence may also have been because Lilian Baylis, the indefatigible founder of the Old Vic, died on the eve of the opening night at the age of sixty-three. The *Times* celebrated the staging as 'lucid' while recognizing that its 'outstanding merit' was Olivier's performance, of which the critic wrote:

Sometimes still he misses the full music of Shakesperian verse, but his speaking has gained in rhythm and strength, and his attack upon the part itself, his nervous intensity, his dignity of movement and swiftness of thought, above all his tracing of the process of deterioration in a man not naturally evil give to his performance a rare consistency and power.[24]

The production and responses to it are documented in reviews, biographies and in photographs that preserve its bizarre costumes, headdresses and decor. Trewin noted also that it was played in 'excessive gloom'.[25] Two weeks after the opening, on Friday 10 December, members of the company made the journey up the hill to Alexandra Palace to play scenes from their staging before the cameras. (The *Radio Times* had announced the broadcast for the previous week, but Baylis's death presumably delayed this.) The live transmission that afternoon was witnessed by a correspondent for the *Times*, and the brief review reveals that it included at least one of the scenes with the witches, Lady Macbeth reading her husband's letter in 1.5, the exchange with his wife before Macbeth goes off to murder Duncan, and the appearance of Banquo's ghost at the banquet. The anonymous reviewer pointed out advantages that television had over the theatre: 'The weird sisters . . . were able to use the resources of the television camera in order to vanish in a most convincing way. Banquo's ghost, too, was more effective than in the stage production, for, instead of a masked effigy, the real Banquo was there, and then he faded away, leaving Macbeth staring at the spot where he had been.'[26] At the same time, the article acknowledged the technical limitations of the television image at this point in the medium's development. 'Few of the characters [around the table],' the review observed,

'were shown on the screen at the same time, and there was no complete picture of the banquet.' The limitations of early cameras ensured that it was the intimacy of the exchanges between the murderous couple that were most successful.

The main problem for the reviewer of this stage-to-screen translation was one that has remained a concern through to the present day in discussions of multi-camera presentations of staged plays:

Mr Laurence Olivier and Miss Judith Anderson [as Lady Macbeth] were also extremely effective, though they made no attempt to moderate their voices to television scale, and still spoke to the utmost recesses of an imaginary theatre, whereas their smallest whispers would have been heard by the unseen audience. *The conventions of the theatre must be got rid of if television is to stand on its own.*

As in Cecil Madden's writing, this review reveals the desire and the prescription that for the medium 'to stand on its own' it must be liberated from its fundamental theatricality. The reviewer continues the intermedial comparisons by praising the 'cinematic' qualities of another recent television broadcast, also of a stage play although not of a specific theatre presentation. (Eric Crozier had mounted on the afternoon of 6 December a studio production of Moss Hart and George Kaufman's comedy about Hollywood, *Once in a Lifetime*.) 'The technique of the cinema . . . was freely drawn on for *Once in a Lifetime*, which was excellent entertainment from the first moment to the last, and the ingenuity by which the scenes were made to succeed one another without loss of time was remarkable. *If television can be as good as this, it will be real rival to the films.*'

Othello followed *Scenes from Macbeth* just four days later, and was announced in its *Radio Times* listing on 14 December 1937 with simply the title of the play. In the published *BBC Programme Records*, however, the broadcast is listed as *Scenes from Othello*. The *Radio Times* schedule featured

---

[24] 'Old Vic', *The Times*, 27 November 1937.
[25] Trewin, *English Stage*, p. 174.
[26] 'Broadcasting: Televised Drama', *The Times*, 13 December 1937, emphasis added here and elsewhere.

George More O'Ferrall's broadcast lasting thirty-five minutes from 3.25 until 4.00 p.m., much as had his thirty-four-minute adaptation of scenes from *Twelfth Night* back in May. A repeat presentation was listed for 9.00 p.m. on Saturday 18 December. Also promised was a cast headed by Diana Wynyard as Desdemona and Ralph Richardson as Othello, along with the television regular Henry Oscar as Iago, Olga Lindo as Bianca and Dorothy Black as Emilia. Production documents in the BBC Written Archive, however, as well as *BBC Programme Records*, confirm that while Dorothy Black and Olga Lindo appeared, the casting for the three principals was entirely different. As it does with *Scenes from Cymbeline*, a production file for this *Othello* transmission exists, and this reveals that just fifteen days before transmission, the expected casting of the principals was Richardson, Oscar and, as Desdemona, Jessica Tandy. Producer George O'Ferrall was also looking after the broadcast of the Old Vic's *Macbeth*, and he was clearly concerned about the lack of time. 'I will be rehearsing *Macbeth* and *Othello* simultaneously,' he noted. 'I will have very little ordinary rehearsal before coming to the studio, and *Othello* is going to be a bigger production than anything I have so far contemplated.'[27] Director of Television Gerald Cock had his own concerns about the broadcast, and on 3 December issued a memo with the following caution to be read out before the programme: 'This great tragedy of Shakespeare contains passages which may be considered unsuitable for children. We are sure viewers will use their discretion on this occasion.' By 8 December the cast featured Celia Johnson as Desdemona, Baliol Holloway as Othello and D. A. Clarke-Smith as Iago. Anthony Quayle was also on board as Cassio. This is confirmed by another memo from O'Ferrall, this time to the wardrobe department, which specified that the costumes should be '"Venetian" period', and that Celia Johnson would 'need to wear her night robe for the bedroom scene beneath her day gown'.

The production file includes an opening page to the script as well as a page for the conclusion, but between the introduction of the cast (single shots of the principals speaking a fragment of text) and the final credits there is only the frustrating typed instruction 'Play as rehearsed'. No detailed reconstruction is possible as can be done with *Scenes from Cymbeline*, although a simple floor plan on a sheet of foolscap paper is preserved. This indicates the relative positions of basic rostra, steps and balustrades, an Italian chest and a bed, as well as the three studio cameras. And there is a further trace of the production in another *Times* review. 'The watching of televised drama,' the critic wrote, 'especially of Shakespearian drama, is an astonishing experience to the spectator who is completely new to the medium.' And after expressing reservation that the distance of figures on a screen must be 'from the stage and the tradition of Shakespeare', the reviewer was grudgingly admiring:

There are times, especially when Iago is alone on the screen – although it is by no means Mr D. A. Clarke-Smith's fault – when the memories of the primitive cinema are irresistibly conjured up, but there are other times when the tiny screen seems magnified to the proportions of the theatre and Othello is the great man, spiritually and physically, that he was ... at the end of this constricted but fluid adaptation of *Othello*, the impression is that a great play, and not merely a conjuring trick, has been performed.[28]

Once again, there are the intermedial references to both film and the stage. A second, and similarly positive, review of this production amounts to only two sentences. '*Othello* ... was an unqualified success', a writer identified as 'E. H. R.' recorded. 'It had been rehearsed for television, which is essential if the best is to be got out of a play.'[29]

After the war, George More O'Ferrall reflected on his experience producing early plays for the medium, asserting that 'From the beginning of television I felt that it was a good medium for Shakespeare.' In an article for the *Radio Times* alongside his 1947 presentation of *Hamlet*, the

---

[27] BBC WAC T5/379 TV Drama: Othello 1937–1950.
[28] 'Televised Drama', *The Times*, 15 December 1937.
[29] 'E. H. R.', 'Television', *Observer*, 19 December 1937.

producer reflected on the quality of intimacy in two forms divided by nearly four hundred years:

in its method of presentation [television] comes nearer to the Elizabethan theatre, for which the plays were written, than the modern theatre can do ... The Elizabethan theatre was often only about 80 feet square, so that an actor playing, say, the part of Hamlet, was able to come right out on to the apron stage to speak the lines 'To be or not to be ...' with the audience all round him, and some of them only a few feet away. Shakespeare wrote the speech with such conditions in mind, and I feel that in television we get as near these conditions as possible, with the actor playing Hamlet in close-up and the whole of his audience now numbered in many thousands, sitting only eight to ten feet away from him.[30]

In addition to the excerpts from his plays, Shakespeare was a prominent presence in other early programming. On 5 March 1937, Irene Vanbrugh and the scholar and critic G. B. Harrison introduced a fifteen-minute programme in which were shown 'models and costumes from the Shakespeare Exhibition to be held the following week in aid of the Shoreditch Housing Association'.[31] The following month, on Shakespeare's birthday, the television service offered a masque to Mendelssohn's music based on the fairy scenes of *A Midsummer Night's Dream*, with choreography by Andrée Howard. Another significant dance-work drawn from Shakespeare was *Cross-Garter'd*, a twenty-minute piece choreographed by Wendy Toye to music by Frescobaldi for Marie Rambert's dance company and based on the letter scene from *Twelfth Night*. Back in 1931, Anthony Tudor had choreographed an earlier ballet on the theme for the company, while Toye's version was presented at the tiny Mercury Theatre on 14 November 1937. On 3 December, Toye danced the role of Olivia for the cameras, although as Janet Rowson David has written, 'The ballet misfired on television because the changes in Malvolio's dress were not apparent. On his first entrance he was seen only from the waist up, so on his next entrance there was nothing with which to compare the cross-garter'd hose.'[32] One final Shakespeare trace during 1937 was a version on 16 December by producer Eric Crozier of Ferenc

Molnár's playlet comedy *Prologue to King Lear*. An actor, played onscreen by William Devlin, is so taken over by the role of Lear that he begins to speak in Shakespearian verse.

Three different actors also played William Shakespeare in historical dramas during 1937 and 1938, although it appears that we can only be certain of two of them. Henry Oscar portrayed the playwright in Clemence Dane's biographical drama *Will Shakespeare* on 3 April 1938, and then on November 27 Clement McCallin was the suitor in *The Wooing of Anne Hathaway* by Grace Carlton. Before these two full-length plays, in the summer of 1937 producer Royston Morley presented Maurice Baring's one-act comedy *The Rehearsal*, published in 1919. During preparations for *Macbeth* at the Globe in 1595 (which was the date of the first performance according to early twentieth-century scholarship), Mr Shakespeare has to respond to Richard Burbage's truculence by quickly composing 'Tomorrow and tomorrow and tomorrow'. Although *BBC Programme Records*, unlike the *Radio Times*, lists the cast, it is not possible to match these names with roles. Clemence Dane's popular fantasy, first produced on the stage in 1921 and broadcast several times on the radio in the 1930s, speculates about connections between the playwright, the 'Dark Lady' who is identified as Mary Fitton, and Christopher Marlowe. Writing for the *Observer*, 'E. H. R.' hailed this as 'the best dramatic production we have had from Alexandra Palace ... the whole play was a thrill for viewers and a triumph for television.'[33] Grace Carlton's play is set in the Hathaways' cottage between 1581 and 1597 and had been staged by the Birmingham Repertory Company from 5 to 18 November before it was given in the Alexandra Palace studio five days after its final theatre performance.

---

[30] George More O'Ferrall, 'Televising *Hamlet*', *Radio Times*, 5 December 1947.

[31] *Radio Times*, 26 February 1937.

[32] Janet Rowson Davies, 'Ballet on British Television, 1933–1939', *Dance Chronicle*, 5.3 (1982), 245–304; p. 265.

[33] 'E. H. R.', 'Television', *Observer*, 10 April 1938.

After *Othello* had demonstrated that Shakespeare's own plays could be presented at longer than an hour, BBC Television mounted in 1938 and 1939 three 'full-length' productions of Shakespeare's plays together with David Garrick's version of *The Taming of the Shrew* before the war shut down transmissions, on 1 September 1939. Producer Dallas Bower was involved in each of these ambitious productions,[34] beginning with a two-hour presentation in late July 1938 of *Julius Caesar* set in a contemporary fascist state. The critic for the *Times* approved of Bower's approach: 'the play, stripped of its classical trappings, becomes a present-day drama of power politics, and the atmosphere of intrigue and unrest is unfortunately but too real in certain countries today.'[35] The review was written just six weeks before the Munich Crisis. Bower was the first of two senior producers appointed to the BBC Television service in 1936, having previously worked in the film industry as a sound technician, editor and director. He was assistant director on the 1936 feature film of *As You Like It* and Olivier later acknowledged that it was Bower who gave him the idea to make his wartime film of *Henry V*, on which he receives an associate producer credit. In his personnel file at Caversham there is a note from 1939 by director of television Gerald Cock describing Bower as 'incorrigibly "highbrow" – and as such valuable'.

After *Julius Caesar*, Bower oversaw the first outside broadcast of a Shakespeare play from the theatre, when *Twelfth Night* was transmitted live from the Phoenix Theatre on 2 January 1939, with Peggy Ashcroft as Viola in Michel St Denis's staging. A production photograph (Illustration 32) shows the central camera of three that were mounted in the circle. This was only the second outside broadcast of a play from the theatre, and critics were among those getting used to the visual language. Reflecting that the production's 'lyric beauty defies the vigilance of mechanical eyes which alter their range minute by minute', the reviewer for the *Times* recorded that 'the impression given was one of extreme restlessness. Viola was now a tiny figure scarcely distinguishable from half-a-dozen others equally diminutive and now

rather more than life-size, taking up half the screen.'[36] Grace Wyndham Goldie, writing for the *Listener*, was considerably more enthusiastic: 'I sat in my own sitting room the other night and watched *Twelfth Night* being performed on the stage of the Phoenix Theatre. And the miracle of television came home to me afresh. There was the actual feeling of being in a theatre.'[37]

A month after *Twelfth Night*, Bower was back in the studio with an adaptation of *The Tempest* with incidental music written by Sibelius and Peggy Ashcroft as Miranda. The ambitious production was plagued by technical problems, and Bower wrote a memo to Cock summarizing the reasons for 'the disastrous results'.[38] Despite this, the aspirations and achievement of the broadcast were recognized by at least one critic: 'picture after picture of Prospero and Miranda were memorable as being beautifully placed on the screen and giving us an intimate picture of the two, more intimate than any theatre performance can be.'[39] The traces that remain of Bower's productions in these months, which also included a bold version of Pirandello's *Henry IV*, indicate that this is a moment of confident experimentation, even if not always of creative success, in television drama.

Dallas Bower was also the producer of television's last pre-war Shakespeare adaptation. On 12 April 1939 he presented *Katharine and Petruchio* (often spelt as *Catharine*) from Garrick's 1754 'acting edition' of *The Taming of the Shrew*. The one-hour broadcast was live, and the matinee repeat ten days later meant that the company had to return to the studio to play it once again. Garrick conceived *Catharine and Petruchio*,

---

[34] See John Wyver, 'Dallas Bower: A Producer for Television's Early Years', *Journal of British Cinema and Television*, 9.1 (2012), 26–39.

[35] 'Televised Drama: Julius Caesar in Modern Dress', *The Times*, 1 August 1938.

[36] 'Television from a Theatre', *The Times*, 3 January 1938.

[37] Grace Wyndham Goldie, 'Television: From the Stalls', *Listener*, 19 January 1939.

[38] BBC WAC T5/508, TV Drama: Tempest, The 1938–51.

[39] 'Televised Performance of *The Tempest*', *The Times*, 7 February 1939.

32. Production still of the BBC Television outside broadcast of *Twelfth Night* from Phoenix Theatre, London, 2 January 1939. On stage are Peggy Ashcroft (Viola), Esmond Knight (Orsino), William Devlin (Antonio) and others. Reproduced by permission of the BBC Photo Library.

'altered from Shakespeare's *The Taming of the Shrew*, with alterations and additions' as an hour-long entertainment to follow a full-length play. The Christopher Sly frame of Shakespeare's original is dropped and the play begins after Bianca is married. Much of the comic business is also excised and the romance between Catharine and Petruchio is emphasized. As with the other productions considered here, the *Radio Times* listing is one of the key traces of this 'lost' broadcast. The magazine in these early years of television is often infuriatingly inconsistent in the credits it provides, but in this case there is what appears to be a full cast-list and, at three names, a rather fuller list of creatives than is often the case.

From the cast members, Austin Trevor, who took the lead as Petruchio, was known in the 1930s for playing Hercule Poirot in the first three feature film adaptations of Agatha Christie's novels.

Margaretta Scott, who played Katharine, has already featured prominently in this discussion of pre-war Shakespeare. Like Ms Scott, Vera Lindsay (Bianca) was a regular at the Old Vic in the 1930s: she was Olivia in Michel Saint-Denis's 1939 production of *Twelfth Night* with Peggy Ashcroft, and Iris in Bower's studio production of *The Tempest*. Also in that *Tempest*, and taking roles in *Katharine and Petruchio*, were Alan Wheatley (Hortensio), Stuart Latham (Biondello) and Erik Chitty (Tailor). After only just over two years there is a strong sense of a repertory company, albeit loosely defined, at Alexandra Palace. These actors, with their newly developed expertise of playing before the electronic cameras, could be called on by a production like Bower's, which was one of four new drama presentations that week alone. And that group had extensive links with the classical and the experimental theatre of the day, as well as with the feature film industry. As for the creatives, the incidental music credit to James Hartley acknowledges a BBC staff composer who had also created music for Dallas Bower's *Julius Caesar*. More notable, perhaps, is the 'Costumes by Elizabeth Haffenden' credit, because a 'Costumes' credit is exceptionally rare on any pre-war television drama. In 1939 Elizabeth Haffenden was right at the start of an illustrious career which would embrace costumes for many of the Gainsborough melodramas of the 1940s as well as Oscars for best costume design on *Ben Hur* in 1959 and *A Man for all Seasons* in 1966. Her involvement in *Katharine and Petruchio*, and her credit in the *Radio Times*, suggests that visual excess was perhaps more important to this production than it was to many others made within tight budget constraints in a tiny Alexandra Palace studio for a fuzzy monochrome screen image. But there is no credit for Alexandra Palace in-house designer Malcolm Baker-Smith, who, we learn from a review in the *Times*, created 'a charming Italian setting', which complemented the 'beautiful' costumes.[40]

Other traces of *Katharine and Petruchio* include *Playback*, an unpublished autobiographical fragment by producer Dallas Bower in which he misremembers *Katharine and Petruchio* as 'the first Shakespeare play to be seen on television'. Bower also suggests that Garrick's shortening of Shakespeare 'greatly improv[ed] the overall shape of the play', and he celebrates the fact that he secured 'a whole fourteen days' rehearsal'.[41] The recovery of *Katharine and Petruchio* is also assisted by two contemporary reviews: a short note from 'E. H. R.' for the *Observer*, and a rather more extensive – and more approving – anonymous review from the *Times*. Asserting that Garrick's text features only the most uproarious elements of a play that is 'undoubtedly a farce', 'E. H. R.' lamented that the words were spoken so quickly that fully 'fifty per cent of the words were unintelligible'.[42] Yet the speed of the verse seemed not to have concerned the writer for the *Times*. 'Much care had been taken,' the reviewer reflected, 'by Mr Dallas Bower in preparing the production, which, unlike some television plays,

was planned down to the last detail ... The first sight of Katharine (Miss Margaretta Scott) and Bianca (Miss Vera Lindsay) in their loggia was a lovely picture and the changes from long shots to close-ups were particularly successful.'[43] As in other early reviews, a critical vocabulary is beginning to emerge for this new form of television drama, which is developed further when the reviewer observes that all of this achieved 'a unity which at once brought home how different a planned production is on the screen from one that is adapted from the theatre'. A concern is again apparent to establish the medium's specificity, and the desire for it not to be beholden to radio, to the cinema or to the theatre, despite the centrality of each of these to television's formation.

This production of *Katharine and Petruchio* can also be understood as an element of the Georgian revival of the 1930s, when, as Alexandra Harris has outlined, many aspects of the literary and visual styles of the eighteenth century were being recovered and celebrated by writers and artists of the moment.[44] Harris has detailed how this revival, related perhaps paradoxically to the concerns of modernism, can be recognized in the writings of Lytton Strachey and Virginia Woolf, in the picturesque art of John Piper and the poems of Geoffrey Grigson, and in the renewed enthusiasm for Georgian design demonstrated by figures including the visual artists Eric Ravilious and Edward Bawden. Bower's production appears to have shared their concerns.

In early April 1939, around a fortnight before *Katharine and Petruchio*, new productions of *The Taming of the Shrew* opened both in London and at the Memorial Theatre in Stratford-upon-Avon. At the Old Vic, Tyrone Guthrie produced a pantomimic *Shrew* in which, for Ivor Brown for

---

[40] 'Televised Plays', *The Times*, 17 April 1939.
[41] *Playback*, unpaginated ms in the author's possession.
[42] 'E.H.R.', 'Television', *Observer*, 16 April 1939.
[43] 'Televised Plays', *he Times*, 17 April 1939.
[44] See Alexandra Harris, *Romantic Moderns: English Writers, Artists and the Imagination from Virginia Woolf to John Piper* (London, 2010), pp. 59–85.

the *Manchester Guardian*, 'Old Padua is but New Palladium writ small. Mr Guthrie, evidently feeling for moderns that "the *Shrew*" won't do, leads Shakespeare up the Crazy pavement ... Shakespearean slap-stick never slapped harder.'[45] In Stratford on 3 April 1939, the director Komisarjevsky opened a spectacular production with Alec Clunes and Vivienne Bennett. Of this, Ivor Brown wrote that it had been conceived 'half as a Restoration *raree*-show, half as Italy's old comedy of pantaloons and clown'.[46] And as he also observed: 'The people who grumble at the Stratford theatre as being timid and parochial overlook the licence annually granted to our Russian genius to make antic hay with the less important comedies.'

Dallas Bower's choice of *Katharine and Petruchio* may have been a competitive response to these two high-profile exuberant productions. And how better to do that than to turn 'a riotous comedy' into what the *Times* reviewer described as 'a polite entertainment' – Shakespeare, courtesy of David Garrick, 'pruned and tidied up'? Such speculation takes the argument here beyond the knowledge that can be achieved of the 'lost' pre-war Shakespeare productions. Despite the absence of recordings of these broadcasts, aspects of their achievement *can* be recovered, as research into *Scenes from Cymbeline*, *Macbeth* and *Othello* as well as *Katharine and Petruchio* has shown. Despite, or perhaps because of, its tiny audience, pre-war television and its rich range of Shakespeare adaptations saw a good deal of bold experiment in an intimate and fundamentally intermedial form; a form which was searching for, and starting to forge, its own specificity while being entwined with the radio, with the theatre and with the cinema of the time.

---

45 Ivor Brown, 'Old Vic: *The Taming of the Shrew*', *Observer*, 2 April 1939.

46 Ivor Brown, 'The Stratford Festival', *Observer*, 9 April 1939.

TAGGING THE BARD: SHAKESPEARE GRAFFITI ON AND OFF THE STAGE

MARIACRISTINA CAVECCHI

GRAFFITI EVERYWHERE

'The original Globe theatre was built on this site in 1576'. This assertion is painted in black letters on a sprayed wall in New Inn Broadway, in Shoreditch (Illustration 33), an area of London that has become something of an open-air gallery. The writing on the wall probably appeared in August 2008 after the discovery of the remains of 'the Theatre'. It abbreviates a long story since, according to the legend, it was 'the Theatre' built on the site that was later dismantled and rebuilt piece by piece on the South Bank with the new name of 'the Globe'. As always with street art, it is difficult to ascertain precisely when and why it came into existence, and yet despite (or thanks to) its inaccuracy, this graffiti, and the entire wall in New Inn Broadway (also featuring a quotation from Shakespeare's *Macbeth*), invite us to embark on an exciting journey to track down new and different versions of Shakespeare's stories scattered on the walls not only of London but across the world.

These references to the Globe and to *Macbeth* may mean Shakespearian scholars, who are perhaps over-eager to find Shakespeare everywhere and, at the same time, are not fully aware of the grammar and secrets of street art, might be tempted to interpret the wall as a sort of 'Shakespearian anthology'. Thus, the grand aerosol painting representing a showy and monstrous Ariel, possessed of demonic powers over both fire and water, who seems to be fighting with the elements to arouse a fire tempest at sea, might be read as conjuring up the image of 'the fire and cracks / Of sulphurous roaring'

(*The Tempest*, 1.2.204–5). Prospero's/Shakespeare's magic wand has been replaced by a spray can, which, significantly, visual artist Jake Bresanello describes in almost Renaissance terms as being 'like a miracle of alchemy': 'it's a gas, it's a solid, it's a liquid'.[1] Even the moustachioed king riding his scrawny horse might evoke Shakespearian kings (or fools) – perhaps he is even Richard III finally riding the very horse for which he gives up his reign! We are obviously moving in the realm of suppositions and hypotheses, for it is impossible to know the motives that inspired these graffiti and their relation to Shakespeare. However, this is not always so, and in some cases the source of inspiration is explicit. The 'Double double toil & trouble' painted in precise blue-on-black letters on the same New Inn Broadway wall by Tom Bingle (a graffiti artist from Bristol known as INKIE, whose tag appears in blue on the lower part of the wall) unequivocally reveals its Shakespearian roots (*Macbeth*, 4.1.10).

The graffiti wall in New Inn Broadway visually epitomizes the unique connection between Shakespeare and street art. Many traces of Shakespeare have been disseminated in the graffiti world and, conversely, the grammar of graffiti has often been used and indeed still is appropriated by theatre directors who wish to bring Shakespeare and his work up to date for today's audiences.

---

[1] Jake Bresanello, quoted in Peter Drew, 'Who Owns the Street', YouTube video, 12:33, posted by 'PrecedePictures', 2 December 2013, www.youtube.com/watch?v=SBDStTM iRhk, accessed 11 March 2016.

33. A graffiti-sprayed wall in New Inn Broadway, Shoreditch, London. Photograph by Maria Christina Cavecchi.

Since its explosion in mid to late sixties Philadelphia and New York, the global spread of graffiti writing has 'moved at the speed of MTV and pop culture',[2] and even the quotation of Shakespeare's lines has proliferated very quickly and continues to do so on the walls of buildings, houses and handrails, in capital cities, small towns or rural villages. Graffiti quoting Shakespeare's verses spring up everywhere, but so far the incidence of Shakespeare in graffiti has never been documented, even though street art is today the object of considerable academic interest, to the point of being defined as 'the quintessential art movement of the twenty-first century'.[3] And while even a major museum such as Tate Modern held an exhibition of street art in London in 2008, it remains a field of study that has been largely neglected by Shakespearians, even though it can offer meaningful contributions to Shakespeare studies.[4]

Following in the footsteps of Iain Sinclair in his 'Skating on Thin Eyes', we might walk through the streets of London (and indeed the whole world) armed with a camera and a notebook, 'recording and retrieving the messages on walls, lampposts, doorjambs'.[5] One might also surf the internet to spot the many and various occurrences of Shakespeare in graffiti disseminated in its meanders, and might perhaps even venture to 'tag' them,

[2] Cedar Lewisohn, *Street Art: The Graffiti Revolution* (London, 2008), p. 39.

[3] Anna Wacławek, *Graffiti and Street Art* (New York, 2008), p. 8.

[4] See Mariacristina Cavecchi, 'Taggare il Bardo. Shakespeare e i graffiti', in 'Shakespeare in the Maze of Contemporary Culture', ed. Carlo Pagetti and Mariacristina Cavecchi, special issue, *Stratagemmi Στpaththmata. Prospettive teatrali*, 24–5 (2012/13), 227–53.

[5] 'Skating on Thin Eyes' is Iain Sinclair's first walk in his *Lights out for the Territory: 9 Excursions in the Secret History of London* (London, 1997), p. 1.

following the increasingly popular web practice of adding personal categorizations to artefacts of information. After this preliminary reconnaissance, it might finally be possible to set up a first corpus of Shakespeare-related graffiti, 'an unpredictable anthology', where the Elizabethan playwright would figure among the catalysts of what Sinclair calls the 'spites and spasms' of our contemporary life.[6]

An analysis of this corpus of Shakespeare-related graffiti would allow us to tackle the work of Shakespeare from a very different vantage point, thus helping us to gain a better understanding of the way the Elizabethan playwright's work and language are perceived and appropriated in contemporary subcultures. The practice of graffiti, which is the result of an unsanctioned, extemporary, individual and anonymous action (generally, therefore, illegal) appropriates the most canonical and institutional author of all and frees his work from the stranglehold of institutions both academic and theatrical. Indeed, street art has undeniably 'reinvented' and reinvigorated the work of the Elizabethan playwright: on the one hand, it has offered and is still offering a fuller and less predetermined Shakespearian experience; on the other hand, it has restored to Shakespeare's plays their subversive, destabilizing nature and their ability to articulate a variety of complementary/conflicting meanings, some of which are anti-establishment – as Juliet Fleming reminds us, 'undisciplined' drawing and writing on domestic and public walls was also a common practice in Elizabethan England.[7]

Uncontrolled by any political or cultural institution, unsanctioned Shakespearian lines or imagery on the walls participate in the destiny and nature of all other unsanctioned art projects: they contribute to the unauthorized visual alteration of city spaces and to graffiti writers' questioning of the boundaries between public and private uses of space, by 'infus[ing] the public sphere with moments of fracture, spaces of disruption and subjective uses of territory'.[8] In a short documentary *Who Owns the Street* (2013), Australian graffiti artist Peter Drew, the author of a series of Shakespearian graffiti that I will discuss later, explores the theme of ownership of streets and public spaces and highlights the complex relationships between graffiti

writing and 'post-graffiti art'.[9] Graffiti writing, or more colloquially 'graff', is the movement 'most closely associated with hip hop culture (though it pre-dates it)' whose central concern is the 'tag' or signature of the author;[10] what is generally known as 'post-graffiti art' (or simply 'street art') is characterized by 'wide-ranging stylistic, technical and material innovations, which place less emphasis on lettering with markers and spray-paint and more weight on fashioning varied artistic interventions into the cultural landscape of a city'.[11] Whereas graff is 'functionally inaccessible to outsiders', who have no 'direct path to entry into its meaning and purpose', and is therefore generally misunderstood and even despised by city councils and the general public, post-graffiti art produces less visually cryptic art and considers the question of communication and community as being of value.[12] Even though still illegal, this latter form is often tolerated and can sometimes actually be the result of commissioned public art projects. Drew's docu-film underlines the contradictory position of city councils such as Adelaide city council (and I would add London's and Glasgow's as well), which on the one hand commission public artwork projects that have to be street-art-inspired, but on the other hand prosecute street art and street artists who go out at night to paint, because, ultimately, they cannot control their creative outputs.

Street Shakespeare lives in a constant tension between the grammars of graffiti and post-graffiti; Shakespeare's works are appropriated both by writers who spray-paint verses and by artists who explore more formal art techniques such as stencilling, printmaking and painting to create largely

---

[6] Sinclair, 'Skating', p. 1.

[7] Juliet Fleming, 'Wounded Walls: Graffiti, Grammatology, and the Age of Shakespeare', *Criticism*, 39 (1997), 1–30.

[8] Wacławek, *Graffiti*, pp. 73–4.

[9] Drew, 'Who Owns the Street'.

[10] Lewisohn, *Street Art*, p. 15.

[11] For a description of the differences and the relationships between graffiti and post-graffiti, see Wacławek, *Graffiti*, p. 30.

[12] Wacławek, *Graffiti*, p. 55.

figurative works inspired by the plays. Furthermore, the proliferation of images of Shakespeare's face on city walls, from New York[13] to Ekaterinburg, Russia[14] or Hirai, Japan,[15] seems to work and to affect the urban environment in the same way tags do. Indeed, it would be legitimate to ask whether the dissemination of these recognizable variations of the Droeshout portrait of the First Folio, where Shakespeare's portrait is often 'the subject of carnivalesque inversion',[16] with a moustache or aviator sunglasses, might itself be considered tagging, a mark of 'tribal' and transgressive practice, such as is described by Jean Baudrillard in his important essay on graffiti, 'KOOL KILLER, or The Insurrection of Signs': 'a scream, an interjection, an anti-discourse, as the waste of all syntactic, poetic and political development, as the smallest radical element that cannot be caught by any organized discourse'.[17] Eventually, we might discover that Shakespeare's face, rather than being simply a commercially valuable marketing brand, might actually be something of far greater value, an image capable of investing streets, neighbourhoods and even nations with new life and meaning.

It should moreover be underlined that not only does this dissemination of spray-painted or stencilled versions of Shakespeare's faces share the unique dynamic between authorship and anonymity which characterizes the practice of graffiti but also that the many anonymous graffiti versions of his plays end up proving Roland Barthes's assumption concerning 'the death of the author'. On the one hand, a tag allows the writer to be recognized throughout a city while maintaining anonymity and at the same time gaining notoriety within the subculture. On the other hand, by their very nature, graffiti and street art seem to resist the idea of the individual author who, as Barthes argues, is responsible for 'releasing a single theological meaning (the "message" of the Author-God)' and is allied with other oppressive principles of authority in the dominant culture. Graffiti and street artists are rather more keen to consider as their interlocutors a community of readers and viewers who engage with the full semantic potential of works

which are to be considered as 'multi-dimensional space[s]' in which a variety of languages, 'none of them original, blend and clash'.[18] Thus, even if in an indirect and unintentional way, street Shakespeare ends up questioning the concept of individual authorship, on which most Shakespeare criticism is based, and offering a uniquely modern vision both of the Elizabethan playwright's notorious 'unconcern to preserve in stable forms the texts of most of his plays' and of the Elizabethan collaborative enterprise of dramatic production in which Shakespeare was involved.[19] In street art it often happens that various artists, at different times, add their logos or other images to an original work, sometimes actually changing its original meaning, as might well be the case with the New Inn Broadway wall in Shoreditch.

Moreover, whilst it is site-specific and therefore underwrites traditional, local values, street art seems to respond to the need for a more transnational gaze, so that this area of investigation may contribute to explore the way Shakespeare negotiates between global and local politics and aesthetics. Most artists are concerned with the

[13] See the photo published in 'Literary Graffiti Tells a Story', 'A Picture of Politics' (blog), 26 April 2012, https://apictureofpolitics.wordpress.com/2012/04/26/literary-graffiti-tells-a-story/, accessed 11 March 2016.

[14] Flickr, 8 May 2008, www.flickr.com/photos/30741072@N00/2601054907/, accessed 3 November 2014.

[15] 'Shakespeare Graffiti in Japan', Deviant Art http://reaperc.deviantart.com/art/Shakespeare-Graffiti-in-Japan-303699419, accessed 11 March 2016. Two more Shakespeare faces are published by 'meandmysarcasm', 'Saturday Brings You ... Shakespeare Graffiti', 'Coffee and Missing Stars' (blog), 20 July 2013, https://coffeeandmissingstars.wordpress.com/2013/07/20/saturday-brings-you-shakespeare-graffiti/.

[16] Douglas Lanier, Shakespeare and Modern Popular Culture (Oxford, 2002), p. 112.

[17] Jean Baudrillard, 'KOOL KILLER, or The Insurrection of Signs', in Symbolic Exchange and Death, trans. Iain Hamilton Grant (London, 1993), p. 79.

[18] Roland Barthes, 'The Death of the Author', Aspen, 5–6 (1967), www.ubu.com/aspen/aspen5and6/threeEssays.html#barthes, accessed 11 March 2016.

[19] Terence Hawkes, That Shakespeherian Rag: Essays on a Critical Process (London, 1986), pp. 75–6.

physical, aesthetic and sociopolitical nature of their locations, often choosing their sites for the relationship they themselves enjoy with particular places; at the same time, however, the language they use is accessible and universal. It is perhaps not accidental that the plays by Shakespeare most quoted from or referred to by graffiti writers are the plays that people know best, or those that are most frequently staged: *Hamlet*, *Romeo and Juliet*, *Macbeth*, *The Tempest*. These are also the plays that fascinate young artists because their main characters are generally the same age as the artists. Their lines and images, inevitably frozen by centuries of rereadings and by a myopic preoccupation with the canon, are reappropriated on the walls either to express individual feelings or to tell stories of collective interest, and share with street art the paradox of being at once criminalized yet acclaimed, accessible yet cryptic, anonymous yet identifiable, site-specific and at the same time global.

An ongoing interchange and reciprocal contamination are detectable between onstage and offstage graffiti, and this continues to produce original results, even though the comings and goings between the spaces of the street and the theatre inevitably pose problems and even questions, since both imply a continuous shifting from the uncodified and unsanctioned language of the streets to a language that has been 'domesticated' and that has lost its spontaneity, freedom and illegality. As the celebrated godfather of the street stencil Blek le Rat says, graffiti in galleries, museums and – I would add – in theatres are only 'the shadow of the real thing'.[20]

ACTING SHAKESPEARE ON THE STREET (AND ON THE WEB)

'All the world's a stage', and on many walls of its streets abridged versions of Shakespearian plays or simply individual Shakespearian scenes or characters crop up unannounced, transforming chipped walls and unattended corners of the city into a public stage.

Peter Drew's 'Emoticon Hamlet' is a site-specific project. Between April and September 2013, the Australian artist created a series of sixteen illegal wheat-paste figures accompanied by speech bubbles that depict Hamlet's second act soliloquy (2.2. 297–311) and imagine the Prince as a modern character whose head had been replaced by a pixelated emoticon. The emoticon faces, spouting Shakespearian verses, popped up all over Glasgow, even though, not being part of a commissioned, legal project, some were quickly removed by the city council (Illustration 34).

According to Drew, the pieces were intended to surprise passers-by who accidentally encountered them, and were 'a way of questioning whether subtle and complex emotions, which once characterized great art, can have a place in the age of digital communication'.[21] Although his message may not have been instantly interpreted by Glaswegian pedestrians, the artist hoped that the pictures would at least prompt questions: 'I don't expect the passer-by to see the whole purpose of the project from one glance, but I hope they might enjoy the sight of it and feel curious to find out more.'[22] Moreover, by highlighting and examining the problem of the ordinary passer-by's reception and responses to graffiti and to *Hamlet*, the 'Emoticon Hamlet' project questions the traditional reception of Shakespeare and the process of negotiation between the Elizabethan playwright and the city and its marginal subcultures. The very fact that in the streets these pieces appear suddenly and unexpectedly from nowhere and are often viewed quickly and distractedly while passing by implies a new and different way of encountering Shakespeare that goes against the common viewing experience we are used to when we see a play in a theatre. Because it is scattered throughout the city, 'Emoticon Hamlet' dismantles the linear and logical sequence of the Shakespearian soliloquy in

---

[20] Lewisohn, *Street Art*, pp. 70, 127.
[21] Peter Drew, interview with Rachael Fulton, 'Much Ado about graffiti as street artist tackles Shakespeare project', *STV News*, 19 May 2013, http://news.stv.tv/west-central/225789-shakespeares-hamlet-is-the-subject-of-peter-drews-glasgow-street-art/
[22] Drew, quoted in Fulton, 'Much Ado'.

34. Peter Drew, *Emoticon Hamlet*, published 1 October 2013 on the artist's website. Courtesy of the artist.

favour of a series of fragments; the possibility for the viewer to see all of the pieces is left either to chance or to the viewer's decision to go and seek out the others. The pieces were installed around the city centre, including brick walls in Dundas Lane and Ashton Lane, a cobbled backstreet in the west end of Glasgow, crowded with students from the nearby university. A couple were also placed in industrial areas, but the majority were placed in built-up commercial and residential areas. With their accessible imagery, the pieces aimed to communicate with everyone, though obviously at different levels, according to people's different cultural, political, social or ethnic backgrounds. Reactions were varied: some people stopped in admiration or puzzlement; others just gave a quick or distracted look, too busy with their errands or everyday routine. Some viewers probably recognized the emoticon boy as the Prince of Denmark and his lines as part of his soliloquy in

the second act of the tragedy, others didn't. Some passers-by may even have encountered more than one of these Hamlets and may have started asking themselves questions about the possible meanings of this seriality. In any case, although someone might see them without really looking at them, Drew's emoticon Hamlets, as with most street art, function as 'reminders' of free thought, free expression, individuality. Indeed, Drew's art is an unsanctioned interventionist practice that rebels against established art forms and challenges Shakespeare's status both as a canon and as a potential global commodity. By exploiting Shakespeare, the Australian artist aimed to reclaim public spaces for the community rather than leave them to the will of the council; as happened with his documentary *Who owns the Streets*, 'Emoticon Hamlet' heated up debate about the legacy and legality of street art and its forms of negotiation with the urban space. Moreover, because his 'Emoticon Hamlet' project was not part of Glasgow City Council's 'Clean Glasgow Campaign' – the initiative which uses publicly funded street art to regenerate rundown areas – and therefore went against the council's anti-graffiti policy, it was considered illegal and therefore a potential cause for expulsion from the Glasgow School of Art, where he was completing his master's degree.

It is precisely by virtue of its own illegality that Drew's work, as with most forms of street art, is relegated to and interacts with those marginal spaces that are 'unrestricted, unobstructed, exposed, empty, isolated, forgotten, unmanaged and bleak', 'not necessarily liminal by way of geography, but rather by way of use'.[23] Interestingly, such interstitial spaces or non-spaces, which 'are part of the infrastructure that creates a city but does not define it (at least not from a consumption-driven capitalist standpoint)', might be considered as the modern equivalent of the 'liberties' of Elizabethan London: those areas that were part of the city yet fell outside the jurisdiction of the Lord Mayor, places of anarchy that were similarly transformed into spaces of free expression and beauty by the creative outburst of theatre productions.[24]

It is interesting to note that street Shakespeare lives also in that other domain of contemporary 'liberties', the internet, where he appears in photographs that are often published both on websites specifically dedicated to the preservation of graffiti history and on image-hosting websites such as Flickr or Panoramio. As often happens with street art, before it was removed or modified either by the passing of time or by city councils' anti-graffiti campaigns, Drew's Emoticon Hamlets were photographed and then published and described on the artist's website.[25] Thus, Shakespeare exists in the domains of the street and the net and negotiates between the physicality and materiality of street art and the immateriality of its virtual replica, between the contingency of a precise location and the globality of the web dis-location.

Online, the works can be accessed by a greater number of people by virtue of the medium, but, in turn, the medium itself distances the viewer from them. One need only consider the case of the huge,

vibrant street painting on a red-sprayed brickwall photographed by Keith Palmer and published on Flickr.[26] Dedicated to the famous star-crossed lovers, it comprises five different scenes illustrated in overlapping black frames: as such, it is an abridged version of *Romeo and Juliet*'s plot complemented by the two last lines of the tragedy ('For never was a story of more woe / Than this of Juliet and her Romeo') and by some lines by Friar Laurence ('These violent delights have violent ends / And in their triumph die like fire and powder, / Which as they kiss consume' (2.5.9–11)). Populated by rough and vividly expressive characters, the scenes (or frames) are distinctive in terms of style, technique, colour and narrative, even though we do not have access to the impact they may have on the specific urban context for which they were created. As often happens with the graffiti that are photographed and published on the web, it is impossible to know the name of the artist or to determine exactly where or when the paintings were made, and obviously all these uncertainties make it hard to correctly understand the actual reasons which inspired them. Most plausibly, the artist's idea was simply to recreate his or her own street version of the tragedy. From the photograph we can assume that the mural is located in a suburban area, with sheds and also barbed wire in the background, and that it adopts a visual language reminiscent of a coarse rural context rather than one showing the magnificent palaces of the two Veronese households. This might be an attempt to offer a 'low' version of the tragedy that might be more suitable to this abandoned suburban contest. However, in the absence of any clear relationship to its site of diffusion, this particular narration exists in a sort of void, so that a complete reading is impossible. Unless we actually

---

23 Wacławek, *Graffiti*, p. 114.   24 Wacławek, *Graffiti*, p. 114.

25 Peter Drew, 'Hamlet Emoticons', 'Peter Drew Arts' (blog), 1 October 2013, http://peterdrewarts.blogspot.com.au /2013/10/hamlet-emoticons.html.

26 Keith Palmer's photo of the graffiti is published on 'Graffiti – Romeo and Juliet', Flickr, 14 June 2012, www.flickr.com /photos/keifeh/7187732421/, accessed 11 March 2016.

experience the work live, we cannot access its impact in a particular urban context. As Anna Wacławek suggests, by mediating a personal engagement with the work, the internet 'dilutes' the viewing experience, since the physical encounter with the work itself is missing (or mediated).[27]

If Shakespearian characters and plots find new life on the walls of houses, buildings and shop shutters, so conversely, the ephemeral art of graffiti and street art find a new home on stage, where they gain fresh recognition, even though this ends up betraying the very premises of graffiti as an anarchic form of expression.

SKETCHING SHAKESPEARE GRAFFITI ONSTAGE

Directors of Shakespeare have often been seduced by the practice of graffiti and have used it to update the Elizabethan playwright and sometimes to make him 'cooler'. Various productions have appealed to graffiti and post-graffiti in different ways and forms, depending on where and when they were staged, but no attempt has yet been made to build a corpus of such plays. It is not my intention to do so here, but merely to suggest how important a study of the reciprocal influences between Shakespearian theatre and street art might be, and to offer a few preliminary considerations concerning this reconstruction.

First of all, it should be pointed out that graffiti and post-graffiti displayed on stage are no longer graffiti either literally or symbolically, since they lose the immediacy and energy that they held in the streets. Furthermore, many writers consider graffiti as a rebellion against a system of consumption, and the illegal and free nature of their art is essential to their involvement in subcultures.[28] No longer 'a transformation of the urban environment', nor 'a subversive addition to the cultural landscape of signage',[29] they do not carry the same sociocultural, personal or political weight, even though they are often used onstage as signs of transgression, subversion or illegality, often evoking a marginal, bleak and unrestricted urban environment.

The act of scrawling graffiti and graffiti visuals have thus become the scenic gesture or

background of quite a few *Hamlets*, the Prince of Denmark being the Shakespearian character who more than any other is capable of mirroring young people's preoccupations and of speaking the language of youth. Interestingly, as early as the *Hamlet* directed by Robert Falls at the Wisdom Bridge Theatre, Chicago in 1985, graffiti was an expression of the individual self but also an expression of public and political issues. On the one hand, it contributed to characterizing the Prince, played by Aidan Quinn, who danced to New Wave music and recited the famous soliloquy 'To be or not to be' after scrawling the first line on a stage wall with white spray paint; on the other hand, according to the director, graffiti set the tone of the play, as it was to be interpreted as 'the first signs of frustration in any modern society'.[30] In fact, the grammar of graffiti has also unexpectedly made its way into the opera-house: in director and scenic designer Thaddeus Strassberger's production of Ambroise Thomas's rarely performed opera of *Hamlet* (Washington National Opera/Minnesota Opera/Lyric Opera of Kansas City, 2008–13), graffiti lined the walls of the dead King Hamlet's palace in a mid-twentieth-century Denmark ruled by a fascist dictatorship which clearly evoked the cold war.[31]

Over the past two decades there has been, moreover, a definite rise in interchanges and forms of collaboration between theatre and street art. Often theatre designers try their hand at actually painting graffiti, on other occasions they work together with graffiti artists or students from art schools to design their sets. Czech designer Miloň Kališ created an enormous sheet of white paper that hangs

---

[27] Wacławek, *Graffiti*, p. 179.

[28] Lewisohn, *Street Art*, pp. 134–5.

[29] Wacławek, *Graffiti*, p. 60.

[30] Sharon Cohen, 'The '80s Hamlet: New Wave Music, Graffiti and a Slinky', *AP News Archive*, 5 March 1985, www .apnewsarchive.com/1985/The-80s-Hamlet-New-Wave-Music-Graffiti-and-a-Slinky/id-d88879f493771161 95aaf23f cedda3e5, accessed 11 March 2016.

[31] See images of the show at www.tstrassberger.com/hamlet, accessed 11 March 2016.

across the stage for Lit Moon's internationally acclaimed production of *Hamlet* directed by John Blondell, Santa Barbara's adventurous director, whose *3 Henry VI* played at 2012 Globe to Globe Festival.[32] According to Blondell, Miloň's set reflected the play's movement toward death, destruction and chaos: 'the paper start[ed] out clean, pristine, unaltered, and unadorned. It end[ed] as a tattered mess – much like the action of the play'.[33] Indeed, it was the set designer's intention that events unfolded on and around this sheet of paper, recalling both the blank page of a book and the practice of graffiti writing itself. The ghost of Hamlet's father scrawled 'Remember' across the surface, while other characters scribbled bits of dialogue until these outbursts of graffiti writing inscribed the entire backdrop with the many intrigues of Elsinore.

Even one of the greatest abstract theatre designers, Ralph Koltai, who has worked as associate designer for the Royal Shakespeare Company, used evident gang-symbol graffiti when he depicted 'an urban wasteland – a materialistic society's littered junkyard ankle-deep in refuse' for Michael Bogdanov's modernized version of *Timon of Athens* at Chicago's Ruth Page Theatre in 1997.[34] Outstanding evidence of the official theatre's interest in street art is the fact that the Royal Shakespeare Company, which has used its own artists to design its sets over a period of a hundred years, asked Graffiti Kings, the only street art company with official British government approval, for a graffiti project which related to 'the current generation and the up and coming generation that are intrigued by street art'.[35] Thus, award-winning set designer Soutra Gilmour collaborated with Graffiti Kings for Jamie Lloyd's production of Tarrell Alvin McCraney's *American Trade* (Hampstead Theatre, London, 2011) to create a set 'that is on the border between graffiti and pop art'.[36] Even though it was limited to a single production and not, in fact, a Shakespeare play, this joint venture is nonetheless significant and shows the company's genuine interest in the forms and languages of the street.

Sometimes there have been surprising coventures between playwrights and street artists

and attempts have been made at 'importing' on to the stage some of street art's freshness and spontaneity. It is worth mentioning urban artist Will Powell's amazing graffiti for the set of the 2014 production of *The Bomb-itty of Errors*, a 'hip-hoppin', high-energy, hilarious ad-rap-tation' of Shakespeare's *The Comedy of Errors*.[37] Written by Jordan Allen-Dutton, Jason Catalano, GQ, and Erik Weiner, it was presented by Queensland Shakespeare Ensemble (QSE) by arrangement with Origin™ Theatrical, in association with the University of Queensland's O-Week. This adaptation declares its close link to the world of graffiti starting with the title, which refers to the practice of 'bombing' (graffitist slang for applying graffiti intensively to a location).[38] Remarkably, QSE, a community-based, not-for-profit organization based in Brisbane (Queensland, Australia), whose scope is 'to engage Southeast Queensland communities with Shakespeare in order to strengthen the connections and relationships between community members' and to create 'evocative, engaging theatre that awakes the senses and impassions the lives

---

[32] Lit Moon's production of *Hamlet* began in Santa Barbara, CA, in 2000 and was last seen locally in March 2014. Images of the set were published in the company's website, www.litmoon.com/hamlet.html (no longer accessible).

[33] Blondell, quoted in Margot Buff, 'Hamlet, Man of Action', *Prague Post. The Czech Republic's English-language newspaper*, 22 July 2004, www.praguepost.cz/archivescontent/39613-hamlet-man-of-action.html, accessed 11 March 2016.

[34] Justin Shaltz, '*Timon of Athens* Performed by Shakespeare Repertory at the Ruth Page Theatre, Chicago, Illinois, on May 22nd, 1997', *Shaltz Shakespeare Reviews*, http://shaltz shakespearereviews.com/reviews/timon_of_athens_1997_shakespeare_rep.php, accessed 11 March 2016.

[35] Darren Cullen, 'Royal Shakespeare Company Graffiti Project', *Graffiti Kings*, http://graffitikings.co.uk/royal-shakespeare-company-graffiti-project/, accessed 11 March 2016.

[36] Phillip Fisher, 'American Trade', *British Theatre Guide*, www.britishtheatreguide.info/reviews/RSCamericantrade-rev, accessed 11 March 2016.

[37] See 'The Bomb-itty of Errors', *Queensland Shakespeare Ensemble*, www.qldshakespeare.org/bombitty.html, accessed 11 March 2016.

[38] M. J. Whitford, *Getting Rid of Graffiti: A Practical Guide to Graffiti Removal* (London, 1992), p. 1.

of its audiences and artists', decided to ask for the help of a street artist, an artist, that is, who by his very nature is interested in contending and negotiating with the territory and its community.[39] Moreover, the QSE production offered an opportunity for theatre to come into contact not only with street art but also with video art. A video showing the artistic process through which Powell developed the graffiti was used to promote the play and was posted on YouTube, thus creating a dynamic link between the streets, the stage, the screen, and the internet community.[40]

Street artists are often sought by university productions, and understandably so, since graffiti has entered the world consciousness through the language of teenagers and youth culture. This was the case with the gritty, hip-hop *Romeo and Juliet* at the Cornell University Schwartz Center for the Performing Arts in 2009, with a cast comprising Cornell students and professional actors.[41] According to director Melanie Dreyer-Lude, Shakespearian tragedy 'speaks especially to teenagers, with its universal themes and issues for young people'.[42] In her production the action took place in a contemporary, urban environment undergoing gentrification, where the opposition between the Capulets and Montagues pointed to 'current environmental tensions such as economic stability, unemployment, class struggle and youth violence'.[43] The set, designed by Kent Goetz, professor of theatre, film, dance and a scenic designer, was a towering urban conglomeration complete with graffiti walls done by students from Ithaca High School led by local graffiti writer Jay Stooks of the Greater Ithaca Activities Center. Intriguingly, the graffiti were the result of spontaneous contributions: Goetz first met with Stooks to devise a graffiti mural for a plywood construction wall on the set; later, in order to give the wall an 'authentic layered look with many generations of marks',[44] Goetz and Dreyer involved members of the Ithaca High School Graffiti Club by inviting them to add their designs to the wall under the direction of art teacher Jocelyn Lutter Carver; then, Cornell students took part in an Open Tagging Party on the stage during which the entire set was made into an available surface;

finally, the cast also added their drawings. According to Goetz, 'by the time the set is fully decorated, so many hands, from so many different constituencies, will have played a part in realizing this design', offering a clear example of theatre's effort at importing on to the stage some of the spontaneous and uncontrollable aspects of street art.[45]

As a last consideration, I would argue that what makes the difference in the use of graffiti or post-graffiti work in a Shakespearian production is precisely the degree of engagement or the relationship the works are able to create within the community of spectators and within the group of actors. At times they are just part of the decor, at others, they play a major role. *38*, the remarkable theatrical happening organized by Claude Poissant in Montreal in September 1996 in collaboration with Théâtre Urbi et Orbi and Théâtre d'Aujourd'hui, is a clear example of the former. Over five days, thirty-eight authors under the age of 38 staged their ten-minute pieces that liberally adapted Shakespeare's thirty-eight plays against a huge backdrop covered with graffiti of the titles of the thirty-eight plays. The huge Shakespeare graffiti worked as a fixed set that constantly reminded the audience of the original texts behind the adaptations, thus revealing the process of negotiation carried out on the stage. According to theatre critic Diane Godin:

---

[39] http://archive.is/B30x4, accessed 23 October 2015.

[40] The video is online at 'The Bomb-itty of Errors 2014', YouTube Video, 1:30, posted by 'Queensland Shakespeare Ensemble', 21 February 2014, www.youtube.com/watch?v=cNzTGx2A82g, accessed 11 March 2016.

[41] A trailer of the show is available at 'Romeo and Juliet at the Schwartz Center', *Cornell Cast*, 20 November 2009, www.cornell.edu/video/?videoID=538, accessed 11 March 2016.

[42] M. Dreyer-Lude at http://pma.cornell.edu/schwartz-center/detail.cfm?customel_dataPageID_27136=29978Kent (no longer accessible).

[43] 'Romeo and Juliet at the Schwartz Center', www.cornell.edu/video/?videoID=538, accessed 11 March 2016.

[44] Susan S. Lang, 'Real Graffiti will Splatter the Set for Upcoming "Romeo and Juliet" performances', *Cornell Chronicle*, 3 November 2009, www.news.cornell.edu/stories/2009/11/high-school-students-contribute-graffiti-set-design, accessed 11 March 2016.

[45] Kent Goetz, interview with Susan S. Lang, 'Real Graffiti'.

Le décor de *38* ... en disait long sur l'esprit qui animait l'événement: une immense toile installée au fond de la scène était couverte de graffiti derrière lesquels on pouvait lire les titres qui composent l'oeuvre du grand Will. Or, si le graffiti sont le plus souvent associés à une volonté subversive, ils constituent, en fait, une tribune tout ce qu'il y a de plus démocratique, où les messages à caractère sociopolitique côtoient ceux d'un genre plus personnel.[46]

Albeit in a very different way, twenty years after this Montreal Shakespearian marathon, David Leveaux staged *Romeo and Juliet* at the New York Richard Rodgers Theatre (2013) against a backdrop entirely overwritten with graffiti that, however, on closer analysis, function as simple decor. Conversely, that same year, on the other side of the Atlantic, for her production of *Coriolanus* at the Donmar Warehouse in London, Josie Rourke managed an extremely engaging and challenging use of graffiti.

Two different but equally successful Shakespearian productions, Leveaux's and Rourke's, are particularly interesting as they illustrate two opposing ways in which contemporary practitioners use graffiti to articulate meaning and mirror the contradictory impulses that characterize street art.

ROMEO AND JULIET GOES BUSINESS: MARKETING SHAKESPEARE GRAFFITI

With his Broadway *Romeo and Juliet*, David Leveaux seemed to have set himself the task of amending what did not work in his previous production of the same play at the Royal Shakespeare Theatre of Stratford-Upon-Avon in 1991. He started by lowering the age of the two leading actors; Michael Maloney and Clare Holman were perhaps too mature for their roles, to the point that 'they looked as though they should be worrying about their children's school fees rather than their own teenage romantic obsessions',[47] and as many reviewers remarked, the play's passions lacked the impetuousness of youth.[48] Hence the decision to focus his new production on 'the miracle of love between two young people' and to address the play with 'as much heat and directness as possible for a modern audience'[49] by setting the action in our contemporary time and casting 26-year-old,

two-time Tony nominee Condola Rashad as Juliet and movie star Orlando Bloom as Romeo, who arrives onstage on a motorbike, his jeans fashionably torn at the knees – not really a teenager but nonetheless a teenage idol thanks to his roles in the film series *The Pirates of the Caribbean* and Tolkien's trilogy *The Lord of the Rings*. In spite of Leveaux's good intentions, once again the cast did not work as he had hoped, and the two lovers seemed 'more ill-matched than star-crossed'.[50] One of the most prized and interesting features of the play was the set designed by Jesse Poleshuck, who revisited and updated Alison Chitty's design for the 1991 production. In Chitty's design a huge screen just upstage of the proscenium arch could be 'flown out altogether or, to provide doors, windows, vistas, or glimpses of other rooms, many combinations small and large of its fifty-two panels could be separately removed';[51] the panels, 'framed in antique gilt, derived from and alluded to Italian Renaissance frescoes, and their rich, mellow colors ... provided a very satisfying background to the deep crimsons and dark blues of the silks and satins of the sumptuous Renaissance costumes' and suggested the mood of solemnity and

---

46 Diane Godin, '*38*: Shakespeare graffiti', *Jeu: revue de théâtre*, 82 (1997), 165–9. 'The set design of *38* said a lot about the spirit animating the event: a huge backdrop was covered with graffiti, featuring the titles of the plays by our great Will. Or, when the graffiti are very often associated with a subversive intention, they actually amount to an absolutely democratic tribune, where sociopolitical messages jostle with more personal ones.'

47 Sheridan Morley, '*Romeo and Juliet*', *Spectator Archive*, 3 July 1992, p. 38, http://archive.spectator.co.uk/article/4th-july -1992/38/theatre, accessed 11 March 2016.

48 Peter Holland, *English Shakespeares: Shakespeares on the English Stage in the 1990s* (Cambridge, 1997), p. 78.

49 Leveaux, quoted in 'Romeo and Juliet Study Guide', Yale Repertory Theatre, www.broadwayhd.com/pdf/Romeo .YaleStudyGuide.pdf (no longer available).

50 Jeremy Gerald, 'Orlando Bloom's Biker Romeo Stunts Juliet', *Bloomberg*, 21 September 2013, www.bloomberg .com/news/2013-09-20/orland-bloom-goes-hog-wild-in- tame-romeo-jeremy-gerard.html, accessed 11 March 2016.

51 Robert Smallwood, 'Shakespeare Performed: Shakespeare at Stratford-upon-Avon, 1991', *Shakespeare Quarterly*, 43 (1992), 341–56; p. 347.

35. David Leveaux's *Romeo and Juliet* (2014). Photo by Carol Rosegg.

foreboding'.[52] Conversely, in the Broadway *Romeo and Juliet* the set evokes a contemporary Italian city whose past Renaissance splendour is evoked just by a wall whose upper half shows a fresco with 'Botticelli-esque figures'.[53] This moveable wall dominating the stage is overwritten with graffiti and is primarily made to slide in and out of view to indicate various locations (Illustration 35). With sections that split, descend and rise, it also becomes a powerful visual metaphor of the tragedy's many divisions and oppositions as well as epitomizing Leveaux's attempt at merging past and present and making Shakespeare once again our contemporary. The decision to use graffiti stems precisely from this effort to update the story and from the director's reflections on the centrality of language in Shakespearian tragedy:

It's the thrill of watching two people, who, in part, fall in love because they both find in each other an equal excitement in their ability to conjure images and to reinvent a world that is different from the way their parents and elders see it. I think part of the pleasure and the fun of the play is that joy of experiencing what the English language can do. Young people are always pushing at the borders of language, particularly now with new techniques of social communication.[54]

The grammar of graffiti writing is therefore appropriated by Leveaux and Poleshuck precisely because it is a practice begun and sustained primarily by youth and because it is one of the many expressions of youth's experimenting with

[52] Smallwood, 'Shakespeare Performed', p. 347.
[53] Ben Brantley, 'Such Sweet Sorrow. Orlando Bloom and Condola Rashad in *Romeo and Juliet*', *New York Times*, 19 September 2013, http://rashad-in-romeo-and-juliet.html?pagewanted=all, accessed 11 March 2016.
[54] Leveaux, quoted in 'Romeo and Juliet Study Guide'.

language and 'pushing [it] at the borders'. As Ben Brantley points out, Leveaux 'hopes to capture some of the youth appeal' of Franco Zeffirelli's screen version of 1968,[55] while other reviewers have remarked that this production 'may also prompt thoughts of the musical *West Side Story*'.[56] Indeed, Leveaux's colour-specific casting for the two feuding families (the Capulets are black and the Montagues white) and the central image of the graffiti wall might recall the atmosphere of Robert Wise and Jerome Robbins's 1961 film, which can be considered one of the earliest examples of the way Shakespeare was very quickly appropriated by the emerging form of graffiti writing.[57] Interestingly, the film, which is set in a gang-ridden West Side in New York in the mid 1950s and which translated social conflicts into ethnic struggle, depicted the racial confrontation and clash between two youth bands by means of the newly born practice of 'tagging'. Invented in the 1960s as an attempt to claim public space by getting the writers' names out on the streets as a visual demonstration of existence, tagging was largely associated with gangs whose members wrote on walls in order to demarcate their territory. Philadelphia gangs such as Dogtown and The Moon as well as New York gangs such as the Black Spades and Tomahawks 'had a tradition of writing their gang name in their neighbourhoods so as to represent their presence and control over a particular turf'.[58] In the wake of such gang practices, in the film, too, the crucial oppositions between the 'Jets' (a heterogeneous group of young white European immigrants who call themselves 'Americans' and are the self-appointed owners of the streets and the basketball court) and the newly arrived Puerto Rican 'Sharks', who want to settle in their territory, are visualized in the tags of the two gangs' names written on the walls and on the road surfaces to physically mark out the space they inhabit. Thus, in the scene where the Sharks are chasing after the Jets, the camera zooms in on the wall drawing of a shark with its mouth wide open, exposing its sharp teeth, which are supposed to show how dangerous all Puerto Ricans can be ('The Sharks bite hard'). Soon afterwards, the

Puerto Ricans provoke the Americans and, in return, the Jets, unwilling to give up ('We fought hard for this turf and we ain't just going to give it up ... These PR's are different. They keep on coming like cockroaches'), declare their intention to expel the Puerto Ricans from their territory through a graffiti that reads 'Sharks stink'. Throughout the prologue the camera pans rapidly over the tags of the two 'writing crews'[59] but so insistently that tagging here emerges as something like the mark of a 'pirate'. This is the term used by Lady Pink, who has been extremely active in terms of shaping and popularizing the New York subway writing scene and was 'the first woman to have made a significant impact on the movement',[60] to define graffiti writers and herself: 'Maybe we're a little bit more like pirates ... We defend our territory, whatever space we steal to paint on, we defend it fiercely'.[61] Both the characters in *West Side Story* and the real-life graffiti writers are pirates, rule defiers, for whom tagging provides a life-affirming element of risk. Such a risk is hinted at right from the start of the film in a highly dynamic and kinetic sequence which foretells the tragic denouement of the story; as Lewisohn, the curator

---

55 Brantley, 'Such Sweet Sorrow'.
56 Simon Saltzman, 'A CurtainUp Review: *Romeo and Juliet*', *CurtainU: The Internet Theater Magazine*, www.curtainup .com/romeoandjulietbway13.html, accessed 11 March 2016.
57 Cinema can be seen as playing a fundamental role in fixing forever this ephemeral art generally doomed to be removed or modified either by the passing of time or city councils' anti-graffiti campaigns. Functioning as 'a time machine', cinema also proves an important source for understanding and documenting not only the evolution of graffiti writing, but also the metamorphosis of the relationship between street art and the Elizabethan playwright.
58 Wacławek, *Graffiti*, p. 43.
59 Writing crews 'typically consist of writers with equivalent levels of skill and make writing a fun, communal practice ... Crews are loosely organised and function as a peer group of friends who paint together in order to share ideas and innovations, and to aid each other in the field' (Wacławek, *Graffiti*, p. 26).
60 Lewisohn, *Street Art*, p. 46.
61 Lady Pink, quoted in Jeff Chang, *Can't Stop Won't Stop: A History of the Hip-Hop Generation* (London, 2007), p. 124.

36. The graffiti wall at Juliet's house in Verona. Photograph by Alice Equestri.

of Tate Modern's 'Street Art in London' exhibition writes, tagging is 'an often dangerous and potentially deadly pastime, but it is on this perilous illegality that the activity thrives'.[62] However, as Baudrillard suggests, it is precisely through tagging that 'a particular street, wall or district comes to life through them [i.e. tags], becoming a collective territory again'.[63]

Leveaux reinterprets the feudal fight in terms of rival ethnical gangs in the wake of *West Side Story*, and yet risk and death do not seem to be part of the practice of his graffiti. Indeed, the wall is already decorated when the performance starts and the characters are never actually seen spray painting it. This graffiti wall is just a backdrop which is intended to vaguely convey a sense of modernity and perhaps a whiff of urban guerrilla warfare. Far from displaying those marks of aggression that characterize gang graffiti, it recalls, rather, the wall of Juliet's famous house in Via Capello in Verona. Instead of being

gritty, harsh or coarse, Poleshuck's wall is crammed with hearts and names (or their abbreviations) of lovers from all over the world and it is therefore somehow reminiscent of the multi-coloured graffiti messages left by thousands of couples who have pledged eternal love under the famous balcony from which Shakespeare's Juliet is supposed to have talked to her Romeo (Illustration 36).

Poleshuck's appropriation of the graffiti of Juliet's house is a far cry from the spectacular guerrilla actions of the legendary graffiti artist that Arturo Pérez-Reverte imagined in his novel *El francotirador paciente* (*The Patient Sniper*, 2013); his hearts drawn on the wall have nothing to do with the red hearts through which Sniper and his tribe

---

[62] Lewisohn, *Street Art*, p. 45.
[63] Baudrillard, 'KOOL KILLER', p. 81.

turn not only Juliet's house but the entire city of Verona into the object of a systematic vandalistic bombing, into a true battlefield. On the other hand, Poleshuck's reproduction on his wall of the graffiti of Juliet's house is not very different from the inoffensive and highly aesthetic appropriations of Marc Quinn in his *Love Paintings*. One of the most original exponents of Young British Art, Quinn chose Juliet's house, a place of fantasy and imagination, where the 'myth' of Shakespeare's tragedy mingles with common people's dreams of love, as the locus of his installations in Verona for a side event of the Venice Biennale (May–September 2009). Here he developed his *Love Paintings*, 'ready-made paintings of pure emotion':[64] large graffiti-saturated pictures created out of the marks left by tourists who, while believing they were drawing or writing on the courtyard wall, were actually inscribing white canvases mounted in the entrance of the house. Far from being scatological and transgressive, Poleshuck's graffiti are, like Quinn's *Love Paintings*, 'graffiti of dreams and aspiration':[65] a conversion, as it were, of graffiti, from illegal urban iconography to legal art on canvass, they ultimately fail to convey the urge, passion and violence of an impeded love and resemble instead that type of contemporary art which has gained great popularity among a certain New York elite, who, from the late 1990s, made street art into a mainstream phenomenon and big business.[66]

It is worthwhile noting that on the official site of 'Broadway's *Romeo and Juliet*' spectators are invited to visit the merchandise stand in the main lobby of the Richard Rodgers Theatre to get a free 'love-lock' to hang on the Love Lock Fence outside the theatre: 'Just like the famous Love Locks walls in Paris and London, you can share the love at *Romeo and Juliet* on Broadway with our Love Locks Fence!' Intriguingly, by inviting the audience to take part in the event and forget the adverse destiny of the two Shakespearian lovers, this merchandising strategy closes the circle by recalling, once again, the love pilgrimage to Juliet's house in Verona, and contributes to defuse the outrageous and rebellious potential of the graffiti.

THE WALL OF CORIOLANUS

Where Poleshuck's graffiti might be seen as mere harmless decor, in Josie Rourke's chilling adaptation of *Coriolanus* for the Donmar Warehouse (2013), set and costume designer Lucy Osborne makes the onstage use of graffitiing walls into a pivotal Brechtian *Gestus*, which produces 'a sociopolitical landscape, evoking recognition of historical and contemporary references'.[67] The Rome of *Coriolanus* isn't Imperial Rome, or even the Republic in its prime. Rather, it is a 'dark, uncertain place, rife with upheaval and built on blood'.[68] As the leaflet handed round during the performance stresses, this is 'a gloomy, shadowy place; a harsh urban environment defaced by graffiti'. The setting is bare and functional; the spectators sit on three sides of the stage and a painted brick wall rises up at the back. Osborne drew inspiration for her set by looking at both the Roman walls and Roman graffiti but also by looking at the more contemporary ways in which walls have been used to register protest and anger. For this reason the lower half of the wall, up to a height of about three metres, is coloured blood-red following the Roman tradition, while the rest of the wall above, which rises to the full height of the auditorium, is dirty white. Right from the beginning, 'this story of class-warfare in an emergent democracy and of the psychologically crippling effects of the aristocratic martial code'[69] is told with a strenuous clarity: while Coriolanus's little

[64] Danilo Eccher, *Marc Quinn: Myth* (Milan, 2009), p. 70.

[65] Eccher, *Quinn*, p. 70. [66] Lewisohn, *Street Art*, p. 81.

[67] 'Resident Assistant Director Oonagh Murphy's Rehearsal Diary', in *Donmar Behind the Scenes: Coriolanus*, p. 17, www.donmarwarehouse.com/~/media/Files/Coriolanus %20Behind%20the%20Scenes%20Guide.ashx, accessed 11 March 2016.

[68] Hannah Price in *Donmar Behind the Scenes*, p. 6.

[69] Paul Taylor, *Coriolanus*, theatre review, 'Tom Hiddleston has Blazing Stellar Power', *Independent*, 18 December 2013, www.independent.co.uk/arts-entertainment/theatre-dance/ reviews/coriolanus-theatre-review-tom-hiddleston-has-blaz ing-stellar-power-9012848.html, accessed 11 March 2016.

37. A scene from Josie Rourke's *Coriolanus* at London's Donmar Warehouse (2013). Photograph by Johan Persson.

son Martius traces a red rectangle painted on the stage, a couple of discontented plebeians, in modern hoodies, spray in white paint 'Annona Plebis' on the graffiti-strewn back wall (Illustration 37). These words remain in place throughout the performance, perhaps as a reminder to the audience of the right the plebeians had been awarded in 494 BC to protest against corn shortages and inflated grain prices with the help of their appointed council and its tribunes. Unlike Poleshuck's wall, this scenic structure is well and truly alive, gradually growing as more and more graffiti saying 'Grain at our own prices' scrawl themselves on the back wall digitally, while pulsating snatches of electronic music accompany the offstage voices of plebeians shouting for grain. Other slogans such as 'Meat was made for mouths', 'Hunger breaks stone walls', and 'Even dogs must eat!' appear and disappear throughout the action, mirroring graffiti's ephemeral nature. Slogans shouted out loud by the plebeians and occasionally by the patricians, condemnations, and even offences also appear on the wall. When, after the battle of Corioli, Martius (Tom Hiddleston) selflessly refuses any share of the spoils and is hailed as a hero (1.10) the wall is crammed with the name 'Martius' repeated innumerable times; the wall is later strewn with the word 'traitor' when he is accused by the tribunes of being a tyrant and a traitor of the people (3.3). Osborne's graffiti, whether they are written on the wall by the actual gesture of actors onstage, or added graphically using projections and cinematically lit by Mark Henderson, essentially convey the idea of people reclaiming the public sphere and their right to publicly express their discontent. At the same time, this graffiti-daubed wall is precisely the symbol of what undoes Coriolanus: the opinions of precisely those common people whom he despises without being able to disguise his contempt. Before the confrontation between Caius

Martius and Tullus Aufidius, on the street in front of Aufidius's house in Antium we see one of the actors cleaning the words 'Annona Plebis' from the wall. It is a gesture of censorship which perhaps contributes to characterizing the nature of the Volsces, but which also reminds one of the way graffiti are removed today not just by city councils' anti-graffiti campaigns but also by the many regimes that are always extremely wary and controlling of all forms of public expression.

In her rehearsal diary, assistant director Oonagh Murphy explains how truly innovative the use of the wall was. It acted as a space for messages throughout the production: 'Giving us a sense of the Berlin Wall, or walls in Londonderry or the Gaza strip, this wall becomes, from the very start of the play, a place for democratic speech, the speech of the people. The wall is used to ask for fairer grain prices, to condemn Coriolanus and to stage protest.'[70] During rehearsals, the company discussed the political implications of Shakespeare's Roman play and its analogies with contemporary view of politics with Stewart Wood, political advisor to two successive Labour governments. Wood likened the Senate of *Coriolanus*, as a governing structure, to the House of Lords, and also invited the company to think of the 'Madisonian principle, which champions a sort of qualified democracy, by keeping full power away from the mob'[71] and of those critical moments in political history when, without a collective spoken decision or consensus, it is generally accepted that a leader will come into power, as happened, for example, with Nelson Mandela after he left Robben Island.[72] According to Murphy, conversations with Wood prompted the company to articulate their newfound understanding of how 'close we are now in our society to the revolutionary zeal that the play opens with':

Talk turns to the London Riots, rising electricity prices, Russell Brand inciting the collapse of existing governing structures, and a city where the cost of living is pushing people further and further to its margins. 'What is the city but its people' – a key notion through the play (the word city is mentioned more in *Coriolanus* than in any other Shakespearian play) – could be used as a slogan for the reclamation of London, or any other globalized

contemporary metropolis. The exclamation that the play begins with, a rally cry for redistribution of power, would not be out of place in our newspapers, streets and Twitter feeds, post-2008. And so, *Coriolanus* feels as cynical, misanthropic, and complicated as necessary to speak to audiences today.[73]

Indeed, it is through the image of the wall that Josie Rourke invites the audience to reread Coriolanus's tragedy in the light of modern times and tensions; the wall should encourage the audience to find other walls at other points in time used to highlight and expose political machinations; it should lead them to think of other periods when the poorer sections of society have rioted or acted in protest against those that have the greater share of riches; it should ultimately contribute to make spectators understand 'that humans have consistently struggled with questions of fairness and democracy through their history'.[74]

Arguably, Osborne's wall, where public grievances are spelled out in the form of scrawled graffiti and which is devised to simultaneously reference the writing on the walls in Pompeii and Berlin, seems particularly to evoke all those graffiti that flourished in the wake of the revolutionary wave of demonstrations, riots and civil wars of the so-called Arab Spring. In Tunisia, Egypt and even in Syria, in the months during and following the revolution, street art played a major role by reclaiming public spaces that used to be controlled by the government. For the first time in years, artists and ordinary citizens were allowed to express themselves freely.[75] In a remote geographical and political setting and for very different reasons, once

---

[70] 'Murphy's Rehearsal Diary', p. 21.
[71] 'Murphy's Rehearsal Diary', p. 15.
[72] 'Murphy's Rehearsal Diary', p. 15.
[73] 'Murphy's Rehearsal Diary', p. 15.
[74] Rourke, in *Donmar Behind the Scenes*, p. 7.
[75] Tunisia Graffiti Project, http://tunisiagraffitiproject .wordpress.com/, accessed 27 November 2015; Mia Gröndahl, *Revolution Graffiti: Street art of the New Egypt* (Cairo, 2013); Rima Marrouch, 'Graffiti war in Syria', 'The Arab World in Revolution(s)' (blog), *ARTE*, 12 March 2012, http://monde-arabe.arte.tv/en/rima-marrouch-graffiti-war-in-syria/, accessed 11 March 2016.

38. Photo of graffiti by Margaret Litvin posted on the website Shakespeare in the Arab World on 9 September 2011.

again we find the walls of the streets reciting Shakespearian lines and contributing to further strengthen the cultural bond between Shakespeare and graffiti. Thus, that most famous of all Shakespearian lines, 'to be or not to be', is quoted in connection with the demand for political and social change ('together for a better Egypt') on a wall in Tahrir Square in downtown Cairo;[76] this square is claimed to be 'the epicenter of Egypt's revolution'[77] and, like nearby Mohamed Mahmoud Street, has since the '25 January Revolution' effectively become an open-air gallery showcasing street art on political and social issues (Illustration 38).

This graffiti is very different from the huge post-graffiti murals which can be seen on Cairo's walls and is most probably not the product of a single artist

but rather the work of various and extemporaneous participants. It should be read as a battle cry summoning the imminent 2011 Arab Spring ('with our rivloution [sic] be or not to be'), confirming that Shakespeare has been 'transplanted into Arab soil'[78] and proving his vocation for playing a central role in

---

[76] The photo of the graffiti was posted by Margaret Litvin, 'Tahrir Graffiti', 'Shakespeare in the Arab World' (blog), 9 September 2011, http://arabshakespeare.blogspot.it /2011/09/tahrir-graffiti.html, accessed 11 March 2016.

[77] Ahmad Shokr, 'The Eighteen Days of Tahrir', in *The Journey to Tahrir: Revolution, Protest, and Social Change in Egypt*, ed. Jeannie Sowers and Chris Toensing (London, 2012), p. 40.

[78] Nadia Al-Bahar, quoted in Graham Holderness, 'Arab Shakespeare', *MIT Global Shakespeare*, 25 July 2013, http:// globalshakespeares.mit.edu/blog/2013/07/25/arab-shakespeare/, accessed 11 March 2016.

the forging and articulating of many different national identities besides that of Britain. As Margaret Litvin argues, in the context of the Arab political debate, 'Hamlet's main contribution has been a slogan – "Shall we be or not be?" – an urgent, collective calls to arms',[79] and Arab writers read the line 'to be or not to be' 'not as a meditation on the individual's place in the world but as an argument about collective political identity'.[80] Significantly, the pidgin English in which this street-art call for independence from the regime of President Hosni Mubarak was declared, on the one hand, reminds us of the history of a country that was under British military and political control for a long time and, on the other, tells a story that can be understood internationally and which offers a very different version of the revolutionary events from that given by the state media. According to Mohamed Fahmy, who goes by the pseudonym Ganzeer, the graffiti artist mostly famous for the *Tank vs Bike* mural on Mohamed Mahmoud Street and for starting the series of *Martyr Murals*, 'uncensored street art is the only way we can tell our story'.[81] As Ganzeer explains in an interview, he chose graffiti over other types of artistic expression 'because there was a need for alternative media . . . We can't rely on unbiased news by watching TV shows and state media anymore, with all the prejudiced propaganda'.[82]

In the wake of the anonymous graffiti in Tahrir and of the many others produced by the Arab Spring revolution, the graffiti in Rourke's *Coriolanus* is meant to be anti-authoritarian and irreverent, a voice for the powerless and the have-nots, advocating social and political consciousness and, unlike Poleshuck's graffiti, free from the dictates of the marketplace.

Poetic, everyday, or coarse, subversive or commodified, but always engaging, graffiti and post-graffiti art have appropriated Shakespeare and his work by dismembering and also disfiguring his lines and images on walls, and have started to dialogue with theatrical spaces that, conversely, turn to the grammar of street art to restage Shakespearian plays. The Shakespeare–graffiti bond has therefore become a strong and illuminating metaphor for questioning the Elizabethan playwright's iconic status in this new millennium.

---

[79] Margaret Litvin, *Hamlet's Arab Journey: Shakespeare's Prince and Nasser's Ghost* (Princeton, NJ, 2011), p. 8.

[80] Litvin, *Hamlet's Arab Journey*, p. 9.

[81] Jack Stuart, 'Tahrir Graffiti: History through Art', *Independent*, 2 April 2012, http://academic.aucegypt.edu/independent/?p=3936, accessed 11 March 2016.

[82] Ganzeer, interviewed by Stuart, 'Tahrir Graffiti'.

WILLIAM DUGDALE'S MONUMENTAL INACCURACIES AND SHAKESPEARE'S STRATFORD MONUMENT

TOM REEDY

The funerary monument to William Shakespeare in Holy Trinity Church, Stratford-upon-Avon, is a typical 'scholar monument' of the type that developed in the late sixteenth century and was popular for memorializing academics and clerics well into the seventeenth century (see Illustration 39).[1] Erected probably not later than 1618,[2] it depicts a half effigy of the poet attired in a *subfusc*, an academic gown with the sleeves ribboned and pinned back like a short cape as worn by Oxford University undergraduates, and engaged in his earthly profession, writing. The first published depiction of the monument appeared in William Dugdale's 1656 *Antiquities of Warwickshire*.[3] The engraving, thought to be by Wenceslaus Hollar or one of his workmen, was based on a sketch made by Dugdale probably in 1649,[4] and both depictions differ markedly in some respects from the monument as it appears today.

An article published in 2006 in the *Times Literary Supplement* by Sir Brian Vickers asserted that the monument had been installed originally for Shakespeare's father, John, and later remodelled to suit his poet son.[5] Based on this and subsequent discussion in the letters column, Lois Potter wrote in her 2012 Shakespeare biography that 'it is not certain whether the [monument] image ever showed the poet'.[6] A year later, a team of scholars from Aberystwyth University presented a lecture flatly declaring that 'The original funerary bust remembers a businessman who is clutching a sack of corn, approximately a bushel's worth, holding it safe and ready to sell to the highest bidder.'[7]

Vickers's inspiration was a web page authored by Richard Kennedy, an Oxfordian,[8] 'The Woolpack

My grateful thanks to Sir William Dugdale for his kind permission to use the Merevale Hall archives and to Tilly May for her invaluable assistance. For their permission to publish their photographs, thanks to John Cheal, Jack Heller, Mike Leadbetter, Fr Lawrence Lew, OP, Kenneth R. Mays, Aiden McRae Thomson, walwyn, and the Warwickshire County Record Office.

[1] Peter Sherlock, *Monuments and Memory in Early Modern England* (Aldershot, 2008), p. 150.

[2] Katherine Duncan-Jones and H. R. Woudhuysen, eds., *Shakespeare's Poems* (London, 2007), p. 438. John Weever copied the monument inscription while visiting churches in parts of Staffordshire, Warwickshire and Shropshire, probably not later than 1617–18, based on the dates in his unpublished manuscript.

[3] William Dugdale, *The Antiquities of Warwickshire Illustrated* (London, 1656), p. 520.

[4] Tom Reedy, 'William Dugdale on Shakespeare and his Monument', *Shakespeare Quarterly*, 66.2 (2015), 187–95; p. 195.

[5] Brian Vickers, 'The Face of the Bard?', *TLS*, 18 and 25 August 2006, pp. 16–17. Vickers makes several errors: Gheerart and Garret are variants of the same name; the monument plaque does not mistake Shakespeare's age at death, and writing cushions are common in such monuments of the period.

[6] Lois Potter, *The Life of William Shakespeare: A Critical Biography* (Chichester, 2012), 436.

[7] Jayne Archer, Richard Turley and Howard Thomas, 'Reading with the Grain: Sustainability and the Literary Imagination', 2013 INSPIRE Lecture on Literature and Sustainability, p. 9, www.sidthomas.net/pdf/paperpdfs/144 .pdf. See also www.youtube.com/watch?v=dfnUeZd7tQQ, 12:15–12:32. Both accessed 19 August 2015.

[8] A person who believes that Edward de Vere, the 17th Earl of Oxford, wrote the works of Shakespeare.

39. From left: Shakespeare's monument as it appears today; Dugdale's sketch of 1649; and Hollar's engraving as it appears in Dugdale's *Antiquities of Warwickshire* (1656), p. 520. Photographs by Mike Leadbetter and Tom Reedy.

Man: John Shakspeare's Monument in Holy Trinity Church, Stratford-upon-Avon'.[9] Kennedy assumes that Dugdale's drawing was accurate at the time of execution and argues that the monument originally honoured Shakespeare's father, John, a glover, farmer and illegal wool-trader and money-lender, for his civic service as alderman and High Bailiff, the equivalent of modern-day mayor. He identifies the large pillow the figure clutches in the drawing as a wool pack, 'an emblematic token of his mortal accomplishment'.

Kennedy is not the first to claim that Dugdale's engraving was accurate and that the original monument was substantially altered. The monument was repaired and 'beautified' in 1749 under the supervision of the Rev. Joseph Greene, the first of several restorations over the centuries.[10] Ten years later Greene reported that dissimilarities between the 1740 Shakespeare memorial in Westminster Abbey and the Stratford bust had raised questions in the public mind over whether the renovation had changed the effigy.[11] In 1844,

Peter Cunningham, one of the charter members of what would become the Shakespeare Birthplace Trust, declared his faith in the accuracy of Hollar and Dugdale.[12] And in 1904, Charlotte Stopes proposed that the current effigy was modelled upon a 1744 engraving and had replaced the

---

9 Vickers, 'Face', p. 16, http://webpages.charter.net/stairway/WOOLPACKMAN.htm, accessed 19 August 2015.

10 The latest in 2013.

11 [Joseph Greene,] Letter, *Gentleman's Magazine*, 29.6 (June 1759), 257, repr. in *The Correspondence of the Reverend Joseph Greene (1712–1790)*, ed. Levi Fox (London, 1965), pp. 172–3. Robert Bell Wheler also documents the reasons for the doubt in his *History and Antiquities of Stratford-upon-Avon* (Stratford-upon-Avon, 1806), pp. 72–3.

12 [Peter Cunningham,] 'A Fine Day at Stratford-upon-Avon', *Fraser's Magazine for Town & Country* (November 1844), 505–17; esp. p. 515. Cunningham was rebutted by 'A Letter from Richard Greene, Esq. to Oliver Yorke, 'Touching' Shakspeare's Monument at Stratford-upon-Avon', *Fraser's Magazine for Town & Country* (December 1844), 731–4.

original that depicted Shakespeare shortly before his death with his hands laid 'on a large cushion, suspiciously resembling a woolsack', a conjecture that to her chagrin was adopted by Sir George Greenwood and became a cornerstone of anti-Stratfordian argument.[13] Both Stopes and Greenwood were rebutted by Andrew Lang in 1912 and M. H. Spielmann in 1923.[14]

Lang pointed out the blatant discrepancies between the monument of George Carew, Earl of Totnes, and his wife Joyce, née Clopton, also in the Stratford church, and the corresponding engraving in Dugdale's book. Stopes replied that 'The drawing of the Carew Clopton monument does not appear in [Dugdale's] Diary, which means that *the Clopton family, and not Dugdale, was responsible for its drawing and its inaccuracies.*'[15] Spielmann added that the monument to William Clopton (father of Joyce) in the same chapel is also portrayed inaccurately by Dugdale, but Greenwood only repeats Stopes's previous answer to Lang.[16] Both Stopes and Greenwood had seen Dugdale's sketchbook,[17] which contains a drawing of the Clopton monument, but neither mentioned that drawing or addressed the question of why the family would have supplied a drawing of one monument but not the other.

Dugdale's artistic accuracy is the crucial heart of the argument. In addition to the Shakespeare, Carew and Clopton monument sketches, many of his other original monument sketches are preserved in the ancestral library at Merevale Hall in north Warwickshire.[18] A careful and methodical comparison of the surviving monuments, Dugdale's sketches and the corresponding engravings in his *Antiquities* reveals that the major discrepancies between the Shakespeare monument, Dugdale's drawing and Hollar's engraving – the incorrect facial features, the disproportionate head and limbs, the cushion/sack, the inaccurate architectural features, and the strangely-constructed putti – are also found in other monument representations by Dugdale and Hollar, and therefore they are much more likely the result of Dugdale's unfaithful artistic portrayals than any later alterations of the monument.

Not all the images in Dugdale's *Antiquities* are inaccurate. On page 154 the engraving of the wall

memorial to Ellen Campion (d. 1632) in the church of St John the Baptist, Baginton is astonishingly detailed and accurate. The signature 'W. Hollar fecit' suggests that Hollar probably used his own drawing for the engraving, and indeed it compares well with his signed engraving of William Aubrey's monument published by Dugdale in his *History of St Paul's Cathedral* (1658).[19] But on the same page as the Campion engraving, the depiction of the brass memorial to William Bagot (d. 1407) and his wife Margaret in the same church (Illustration 40) follows the inaccuracies in Dugdale's sketch (B27v): the sloped shoulders, the changed visages, the disproportionately smaller heads, and the inaccurately drawn costumes, all of which are present in Dugdale's drawing of the Shakespeare monument.

No drawings survive of the monument of William Peyto (d. 1639) at St Giles Church, Chesterton (Illustration 41), or of the tomb of Sir

---

[13] Charlotte C. Stopes, 'The True Story of the Stratford Bust', *Monthly Review* (April 1904), 150–9; esp. pp. 154, 156. An expanded version was reprinted in *Shakespeare's Environment* (London, 1914), pp. 104–23; and G. G. Greenwood, *The Shakespeare Problem Restated* (London, 1908), pp. 245–9.

[14] Andrew Lang, *Shakespeare, Bacon, and the Great Unknown* (London, 1912), pp. 177–91; M. H. Spielmann, *The Title-Page of the First Folio of Shakespeare's Plays* (London, 1924), pp. 14–25.

[15] Lang, *Unknown*, pp. 179–80; Stopes, *Environment*, p. 123, emphasis original.

[16] Spielmann, *Title-Page*, p. 19; G. G. Greenwood, *The Stratford Bust and the Droeshout Engraving* (London, 1925), pp. 13–14.

[17] Stopes, *Environment*, p. 122; Greenwood, *Stratford Bust*, p. 9.

[18] The volume, stamped 'DUGDALE/WARWICK/7/ORIGINAL/MANUSCR' in gold on the spine, is comprised of two separate booklets bound together. The first booklet (which I designate 'A') consists of eighteen leaves, most depicting coats of arms displayed in church windows, the majority copied by Dugdale from other sources dating from the first three decades of the seventeenth century, but some taken by Dugdale himself. A few epitaph transcriptions are scattered among the sketches. The second section (designated 'B' in my references) consists of thirty-four folio leaves, most containing sketches and inscriptions in pencil and ink.

[19] William Dugdale, *The History of St Pauls Cathedral in London, From its Foundation until these Times* (London, 1658), p. 96.

40. From left: William and Margaret Bagot brass memorial, St John the Baptist, Baginton © walwyn-professor-moriarty.com; Dugdale's undated drawing, photo by Tom Reedy, reproduced courtesy of Sir William Dugdale; Hollar's engraving from Dugdale's *Antiquities*, p. 154.

41. From left: bust of William Peyto, St Giles Church, Chesterton. Photograph by Aidan McRae Thomson; engraving of bust from Dugdale's *Antiquities*, p. 383.

42. From left: detail from the tomb of Sir Thomas Lucy, St Leonard's Church, Charlecote Park. Photograph by Tom Reedy; detail of engraving from Dugdale's *Antiquities*, p. 402.

Thomas Lucy (d. 1640) in St Leonard's at Charlecote Park, but their engravings are obviously inaccurate. Lucy's monument bust (Illustration 42) sports a shaped moustache and conical goatee remarkably similar to that on Shakespeare's bust, but the sketcher or engraver or both rendered them in the same manner as the Shakespeare depictions: turning down the lines of the moustache, blunting the goatee and spreading it upward along the jaw-line to meet the tips of the moustache.

Dugdale's undated sketch of the monument of Sir Fulke Greville (d. 1559) and his wife Anne in St Nicholas Church in Alcester survives (B33r) (Illustration 43). The engraver improves the drawing but renders it even more inaccurately, mistaking the positions of the praying hands, tightening Greville's collar and transforming the woman's hairpiece.

CUSHION

The cushion upon which Shakespeare rests his hands is probably the most blatant difference between the existing monument and the early depictions. Stopes writes that 'the hands are laid

stiffly, palms downward, on a large cushion, suspiciously resembling *a woolsack*'.[20] Vickers says the effigy is 'resting his hands on a woolsack' the eighteenth-century renovators 'transformed ... into some kind of cushion, a wholly unsuitable writing surface',[21] and Archer, Turley and Thomas describe it as 'a sack of corn'.[22] However, comparisons to other sketches by Dugdale reveal that the Shakespeare depiction is consistent with those: though the cushions are almost uniformly lozenge-shaped with tassels, Dugdale drew them out of perspective as if they were set up on edge with all four corners and tassels revealed. It appears that the hatching that delineates the cushion edge in the sketch was mistaken by the engraver to depict the cushion as a puffy, oval shape.

In the church of St Theobald and St Chad in Caldecote, three members of the Purefoy family are portrayed: Francis (d. 1613) and William (d. 1615) are on one wall monument and Michael

---

[20] Stopes, *Environment*, p. 109.
[21] Vickers, 'Face', pp. 16–17.   [22] Archer et al., 'Grain', p. 9.

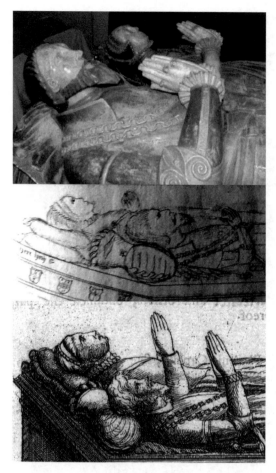

43. From top: detail from tomb of Sir Fulke and Lady Anne Greville, St Nicholas Church, Alcester; detail of Dugdale's sketch; detail of engraving from Dugdale's *Antiquities*, p. 573. Photographs by Tom Reedy. Sketch reproduced courtesy of Sir William Dugdale.

'suspiciously resembling a woolsack'. Yet no question exists that these monuments placed on the walls of a private chapel are the same as those depicted in Dugdale's *Antiquities*.

Dugdale's and Hollar's depictions of the Edward (d. 1592) and Dorothy Holt wall memorial in the parish church of St Peter and St Paul, Ashton, Birmingham (Illustration 45) present dissimilarities that parallel the Shakespeare monument depictions. The figures' eyes are cast downward; in the sketch and engraving, they gaze upward. Her headdress has changed from a Tudor hood to a veil or a scarf. Both Dugdale and Hollar have changed the shell in the background into vague petal-like rays. The beard of the male figure, the angle of the couple's arms, the depiction of the cushions, the height of the altar, and the relative distance of the figures from the arch all deviate from those of the monument.

In the drawing of the wall monument of Robert (d. 1603) and Mary Burdette in All Saints Church, Seckington (Illustration 46), Dugdale transgenders one of the daughters and moves the figure to the left to balance the number of sons and daughters. His continuing problem with perspective is apparent: again, he depicts the cushions as pillows, which are in turn transformed into carpets by the engraver, who apparently is not Hollar. The books on each side of the lectern are tipped upward at an impossible angle in the same manner as the cushions; the engraver leaves them out. The relative distance of the figures from the arch, the position of the arms, and the changed countenances of the figures are all congruent with the disparities in the Shakespeare monument sketch. The details of the coats of arms, however, are pictured accurately.

PUTTI

Vickers also lists the features of the putti placed on either side of the coat of arms as evidence that the monument was changed. He notes that in the drawing their legs dangle off the cornice, that the right putto holds an hourglass instead of an inverted torch, and that the present-day figures, with their curled locks and pompadours, are more

(d. 1627) is singly on another, with all figures kneeling on cushions (Illustration 44). Dugdale's original sketches are lost, but the engravings exhibit many of the characteristics that Vickers takes for evidence that the Shakespeare monument has been altered: the subjects' appearances are changed, especially the facial hair; their costumes differ markedly, especially in the number of armour plates; the overhead arches are wider, and the relative distance between the arches and the heads of the subjects differ. The tasselled cushions are very similar to those of the Shakespeare monument, but they are engraved

44. Details of the monuments of (top, from left) Francis, William and Michael Purefoy; Hollar's engravings in Dugdale's *Antiquities*, pp. 790–1. Photographs by Tom Reedy.

45. From top: detail of the Holt memorial in the parish church of St Peter and St Paul, Ashton, Birmingham, photograph by Aidan McRae Thomson; detail of Dugdale's undated sketch, photograph by Tom Reedy, reproduced courtesy of Sir William Dugdale; Hollar's engraving from *Antiquities*, p. 642.

46. From top: detail of the Burdette monument at All Saints Church, Seckington, photograph by Aidan McRae Thomson; Dugdale's drawing dated 1 August 1639, photograph by Tom Reedy, reproduced courtesy of Sir William Dugdale; engraving from Dugdale's *Antiquities* p. 814.

suitable to the Georgian than the Jacobean period (Illustration 47).[23]

Dugdale's drawing follows the basic poses of the putti on the monument, with the exception of the figure on the right, whose left leg is crossed over its

right, possibly a misconstrual of the inverted torch being held by the figure's left hand. Both putti are also precariously perched with their legs hanging

---

[23] Vickers, 'Face', p. 17.

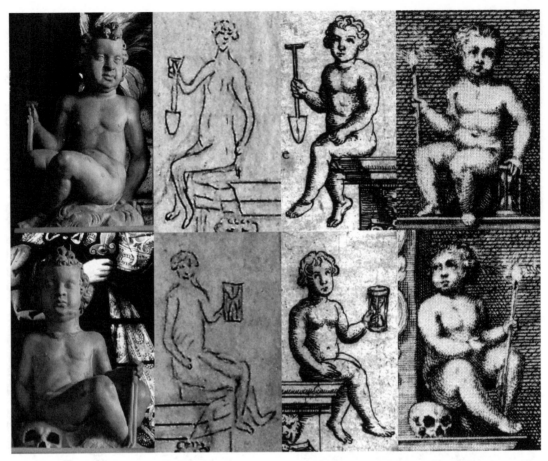

47. The putti from the Shakespeare monument representing labour and rest, from left, as they appear today © John Cheal; Dugdale's sketch, photograph by Tom Reedy, reproduced courtesy of Sir William Dugdale; Hollar's engraving; and Vertue's engraving from Alexander Pope's 1725 edition of Shakespeare's plays.

off the ledge of the cornice, a position not seen in any such tableau that I have been able to find. Enough examples of Dugdale's draftsmanship have been presented to show that he often changed the positions of appendages, and these are well within his range of error. While it may seem an error unlikely to have been made had Dugdale been sketching on site, he took similar liberties with the putti in his drawing of the heraldic shield of Basil Feilding taken from his tomb in the church of St Edith in Monks Kirby, Warwickshire (Illustration 48), which Dugdale notes was taken by himself in May 1637.[24] More likely he worked from separate sketches of the putti, having

forgotten their exact placement on the monument, hence the erasures and redrawings.[25]

George Vertue's engraving of the monument for Alexander Pope's 1725 edition is clearly based

---

[24] 9v.

[25] It is not clear which pages of the booklet were sketched on site and which were copied and redrawn later. While the majority are laid out symmetrically with a rule and straight edge and appear to be fair copies of rough sketches taken on site, the design of the page with Shakespeare's monument is awkward. Unlike all other pages in the booklet, the Carew tombstone epitaph is interrupted and continues on the verso, and Shakespeare's epitaph and those of his family are found twenty-two pages earlier. See Reedy, 'Dugdale', pp. 194–5.

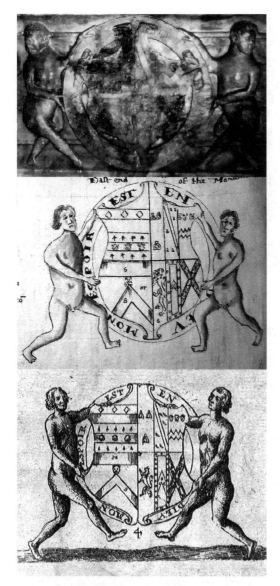

48. Detail from end of the tomb of Basil Feilding and Goodith (Judith), his wife, in the church of St Edith, Monks Kirby; Dugdale's drawing dated May 1637; engraving from *Antiquities*, p. 54. Photographs by Tom Reedy, reproduced courtesy of Sir William Dugdale.

in the hand of the left putto and the torch handle in the hand of the putto on the right are visible to an observer standing on the floor, which was approximately eighteen inches lower before the renovation in the late nineteenth century. The artist could have taken those to be representations of candles or torches. Finally, a comparison of the Shakespeare monument putti with one from the tomb of Sir William Pope, later Earl of Downe (d. 1631) (Illustration 49), confirms that the hairstyles of the allegorical figures are consistent with others of the same general era.[27] Almost identical putti are present on the tomb of Roger Manners, 5th Earl of Rutland, built 1618–19 by Nicholas Jansen, brother and business partner of Garret Jansen, the builder of Shakespeare's tomb.

One change noted by Vickers indeed might have occurred when the monument's architrave was replaced in 1748 or earlier.[28] Leopard heads could have been present on the frieze above the acanthus ornaments when Dugdale sketched the monument. Decorative rosettes or heraldic shields survive on several similar monuments at Oxford University all made about the same time as Shakespeare's, as the three examples of Illustration 50 show. As this study establishes, he routinely omitted many details and distorted others in his sketches, but my limited survey of monuments uncovered no examples of Dugdale adding features that were not present, though some poorly-sketched details obviously confused the engravers.

Seven rosettes attach to the ceiling of the arch above the Shakespeare effigy (Illustration 51), and two could have been attached to the frieze as in Ralph Hutchison's monument. However, given

upon a detailed eyewitness drawing.[26] Vertue placed what appear to be candles or torches in the hands of the putti and perched them on an hourglass and skull respectively. Only the spade handle

[26] Except for basing the face upon the Chandos portrait and the variations of the putti, Vertue's depiction is architecturally identical to the present-day monument. See Sidney Lee, *A Life of William Shakespeare*, rev. edn (New York, 1916), pp. 523–4.

[27] Pope's monument was executed by Nicholas Stone, who from 1615 is recorded working with the tomb-maker Bernard Janssen (Johnson) of Southwark, possibly a brother of Gerard Janssen (Johnson), the sculptor of Shakespeare's monument.

[28] Levi Fox, ed., *The Correspondence of the Reverend Joseph Greene (1712–1790)* (London, 1965), p. 171.

49. Left and right, the two putti from the Shakespeare monument © John Cheal, compared with, middle, a putto on the William Pope monument in All Saints Church, Wroxton. Fr Lawrence Lew, OP.

50. From left: wall funerary monuments of Ralph Hutchinson (d. 1606), St John's College Chapel, Oxford, photograph by Kenneth R. Mays; Robert Hovenden (d. 1614), All Souls College Chapel, Oxford; John Spenser (d. 1614), photograph by Jack Heller. Corpus Christi College Chapel, Oxford, photograph by Kenneth R. Mays.

Dugdale's inventive depictions of other monuments, another plausible explanation is that he exaggerated the front volutes of the decorative capitals and placed them higher, and the engraver, being more familiar with architectural elements, took them for decorative devices and added the front volute to the capital. If they were present, the rosettes or leopard heads could have been lost

51. From left: rosettes inside the arch of Shakespeare's monument, detail of capital; details of Dugdale's sketch; Hollar's engraving from *Antiquities*. Photographs by Tom Reedy, reproduced courtesy of Sir William Dugdale.

sometime between 1649, when Dugdale sketched the monument, and 1725, when Vertue's engraving appeared in Pope's edition of Shakespeare.

Critics of the monument have avoided discussing the similarities between the effigy and Dugdale's drawing, focusing instead in the differences. But the similarities vastly outnumber the differences, especially in the effigy's dress. Vickers himself calls attention to the description by John Aubrey, who saw the monument sometime between 1640 and 1670 and described it perfectly:

Mr William Shakespeare [Poet] in his monument in the Church at Stratford upon Avon, his figure is thus, viz. a Tawny satten doublet I thinke pinked and over that a black gowne like an Under-graduates at Oxford, scilicet the sleeves of the gowne doe not cover the armes, but hang loose behind. When I learnt to read 1632 of John Brome the parish Clarke of Kington St Michael, his old father [above 80] who had been Clarke there before, dayly wore such a Gowne, with the sleeves pinned behind. I doe beleeve that about the later end of Queen Elizabeths time 'twas the fashion for grave people, to weare such Gownes.[29]

Though Vickers calls attention to the 'pinked', or slashed, doublet in the present-day monument, despite the identical depiction of it in the Dugdale drawing, he confuses a jerkin, a sleeveless jacket

with a closed front, with the *subfusc* gown the effigy is wearing, which is always open in the front.

Vickers also gives credence to Barbara Whittington-Jones's theory that the monument is now situated in a different place on the wall than the hypothetical original monument. In 1964 Whittington-Jones claimed that 'all photographs of John Hall's monument[30] reveal four nails or knobs in the chancel wall exactly where one would expect the broader Dugdale to have been secured to the wall – there is one nail on either side and near the top of each square pillar, and one on either side of the central section immediately below the window-sill',[31] which Vickers says 'must have held the solid backing frame of the original monument'. The four holes are clearly visible in Illustration 39. However, no such holes or knobs are present in photographs taken in the

---

[29] Bodleian Library, Oxford, MS Top. Gen. c 25, fo. 203v; Kate Bennett, 'Shakespeare's Monument at Stratford: A New Seventeenth-Century Account', *Notes & Queries*, 47 (2000), 464.

[30] Presumably Whittington-Jones means the Shakespeare monument; no monument to John Hall exists in the church.

[31] Barbara Whittington-Jones, 'The Dugdale "Shakspere"', *Quarterly Review*, 302 (1964), 267–70; p. 270.

52. Shakespeare's monument *c.* 1890. Reproduced courtesy of Warwickshire County Record Office Collections.

nineteenth century or early twentieth century (see, for example, Illustration 52). The original purpose of the holes was to hold a detachable steel cage that was installed around the monument in response to a threat to deface the monument during the suffragette period.[32] Nor does the monument hang; it is set into the stone of the wall, which is clearly visible in Vertue's 1725 engraving.

Finally, other evidence discredits the idea that the monument honours Shakespeare's father. In 1577 and 1591, John Shakespeare was listed

as a person who refused to attend Church of England services in violation of the law; the reason given was that he was in fear of being arrested for debt. In 1570 he was accused of usury, and in 1572 he was fined for two counts of unlicensed

---

[32] Val Horsler, Martin Gorick and Paul Edmondson, *Shakespeare's Church: A Parish for the World* (London, 2010), p. 83.

dealing in wool.[33] It is extremely unlikely that the church would have welcomed a monument in its chancel depicting John Shakespeare's illegal profession, no matter what position he had held on the town council; the appropriate garb would have been the fur-trimmed bailiff's gown with a ceremonial mace. William Shakespeare bought the remaining thirty-one years of a lease of church tithes in 1605, almost four years after his father's death, which obligated him as a lay rector to help maintain the chancel.[34] As a tithe-holder, he was entitled by custom to burial in the chancel, and his wealth provided his family the means to pay for it.[35]

The logical implications of the visual and historical evidence presented are clear: unless one is prepared to argue that all these monuments have been substantially altered since Dugdale first depicted them — an argument without credibility — then Shakespeare's Stratford monument appears today substantially the same as when Dugdale sketched it in 1649, and the discrepancies between it and his depiction are due to the limitations of his artistic ability. A few years after Shakespeare's burial, a monument was erected near his grave to honour his memory, a monument in all essential features identical to that which stands today.

---

[33] Potter, *Life*, pp. 42–3.

[34] B. Roland Lewis, *The Shakespeare Documents*, vol. 2 (Stanford, CA, 1940), p. 373.

[35] J. O. Halliwell-Phillipps, *Outlines of the Life of Shakespeare*, 11th edn, vol. 1 (London, 1907), p. 268; Lewis, *Documents*, vol. 2, p. 525.

SHAKESPEARE PERFORMANCES IN ENGLAND (AND WALES), 2015

STEPHEN PURCELL

When I started to plan my first year as *Shakespeare Survey*'s new theatre reviewer, I became suddenly aware of the responsibility of the position. What should I see, and what should I leave out? One cannot undertake a task like this without a certain amount of hubris: the title 'Shakespeare Performances in England' (I've retained the parenthetical 'and Wales' that was added by Carol Rutter) makes an implicit claim to represent the annual theatrical output of an entire country (and a little of a second). Such a thing of course is impossible, and regular readers will know that the review tends to confine itself largely to the Shakespearian work of the major subsidized theatre companies and to high-profile commercial productions. This article will not stray far from this remit, although I have attempted to cover the work of a number of smaller-scale fringe and touring companies in order to give an impression of the range of Shakespearian performances undertaken in England in 2015. That impression can only be partial, and it is based just as much on when and where I happened to be able to travel as it is on anything else.

COMEDIES

I began my reviewing year with a performance that was underground in both senses of the word. Performed in the basement of Hackney's Arcola Theatre, the Arcola Queer Collective's radical version of *A Midsummer Night's Dream* brought Shakespeare's play into provocative dialogue with modern LGBT politics. Nick Connaughton's adaptation transported both the audience and the action of the play to a cabaret bar called La Forêt – a refuge, in the words of Puck's introduction, for 'misfits and outcasts, the queer and the fabulous' – that we were told faces the prospect of imminent closure and being turned into a soulless Caffè Nero (a nod, perhaps, to the recent fate of Madame Jojo's nightclub in Soho). The bar was owned by Oberon, a drug-dealing 'tran-tastic leather-clad drag king', and his drag-queen partner Titania (played respectively by cabaret performers Rubyyy Jones and Miss Cairo). Over the course of the night, this pair oversaw a transgressive celebration of sexual difference as Hermia (Krishna Istha) escaped to the club with her girlfriend Lysander (Bex Large), pursued by a bisexual Demetrius (Phil Rhys Thomas) and his male ex-lover Helena (Damien Kileen).

An abridged edit of Shakespeare's play was interspersed with modern monologues that had been sourced verbatim from members of London's LGBT community. Thus, for example, Demetrius shared with the audience his struggles with HIV, Hermia her arguments with a bigoted religious mother, Helena his difficulties coming-out as a young gay man. The most radical moment, though, came towards the end of the show, when Bottom (Camilla Harding) woke from her 'dream', apparently broke down, and called the assistant director from the auditorium; she would, she asserted, no longer be oppressed by binary categories of gender, and indeed refused all gender-specific language and pronouns for the rest of the show. In its frame-breaking and simultaneously playful and combative questioning of the under-lying gender politics of Shakespeare's own art, the moment was reminiscent for me of Mistress Quickly's outburst in the recent all-female *Henry IV* at the Donmar Warehouse.

In fact, gender binaries were inverted and deconstructed throughout the show. Theseus doubled with Titania, and Hippolyta with Oberon, so that the mortal royals were played by actors of the 'correct' biological sex and the fairies technically cross-gender. But as a transvestite male-to-female performer, Miss Cairo – Theseus and Titania – was troubling any fixed sense of gender identity from the moment she stepped onstage as Theseus. Wearing glasses over a black lace mask and a long gender-ambiguous cardigan, it was impossible to tell whether this stage figure was male or female (one could argue it was a kind of double-drag, male-to-female-to-male). As Titania, she appeared in a pastiche of conventional femin-ity, with massive fake eyelashes, a blonde Pamela Anderson wig, vertiginous heels and a scarlet corset and thong – the latter so miniscule it made a deliberate and frequent display of her male geni-talia, to whoops of appreciation from many in the audience around me.

The production clearly achieved its stated aim of 'providing a voice' for the LGBT community, and this voice could be heard not only from the stage but, on the night I saw it, among the loud and enthusiastic audience. There were times, however, when I wondered whether Shakespeare's text could have been integrated into this project more skilfully. In their false eyelashes and lacy masks, Theseus and Hippolyta already belonged to a transgressive underground, meaning that the oppressively 'straight' world from which the lovers longed to escape never really made an appearance. Pronouns were generally changed to cover the reassigned genders of many of the characters, but not without some scars: 'We should be wooed, and were not made to woo' did not make much sense when spoken by a male Helena to a male Demetrius, for example, and Oberon's 'Effect it with some care, that they may prove / More fond on them than them upon their love' – rendered,

unlike any other lines in the play before this point, gender neutral so as to make it possible for Puck to mistake the instruction – was simply indecipher-able. But perhaps the fissures between the text and the performance subtly made their own transgres-sive point.

I found myself viewing my second *Dream* – Nick Bagnall's production for the Liverpool Everyman (Illustration 53) – through the lens of the Arcola production, as a similar exploration of gender, sex and power. This one, designed by Ashley Martin-Davis, opened with a plain black set, scrawled all over with chalk drawings of a magical forest. Cynthia Erivo's batlike Puck descended from the ceiling on wires, spinning vertically, her black tail-coat hanging down like wings and, with a flourish, she summoned the play into being. Sharon Duncan-Brewster's Hippolyta burst into the space, pacing furiously as if she were caged and, after a short silence, Garry Cooper's Theseus came in carrying her high-heeled shoes, withholding them from her with a combination of playfulness and menace. In the scene that followed, Hippolyta took a keen interest in Demetrius from the first mention of his affair with Helena. She inspected him angrily, stand-ing much too close for his comfort, until Theseus's 'What cheer, my love?' called her back to herself.

As the action moved to the forest, the black rear wall ascended to reveal a huge mirror stretched across the back of the stage, before which was strewn a jungle of large pieces of crumpled white paper. Titania's all-male fairies were dressed from head to toe in black, their movements deliberately graceless, their voices rough, and their faces obscured with stockings as if they were armed robbers. Duncan-Brewster doubled as Titania, and her speech begin-ning 'Be kind and courteous to this gentleman' was converted into a sensual cabaret number with the fairies as her backing group. This Titania reminded me of Caryl Churchill's Skriker: a powerful but damaged supernatural creature inhabiting a dark world of wild unconscious urges. Resplendent in a glittering silver dress, she nonetheless spent all her scenes hobbling around on a single high-heeled shoe while carrying the other. She was both in control and out of control, and the imbalance and physical

53. *A Midsummer Night's Dream*, 5.2, Liverpool Everyman, directed by Nick Bagnall. Cynthia Erivo as Puck, with company. © Gary Calto.

ungainliness lent to her performance by her footwear recalled Theseus's use of Hippolyta's shoes as a token of power in the first scene. By the end, her 'How I dote on thee' was delivered sobbing, almost despairing, with a sense that despite the effects of the flower, she was aware that her agency was being delimited by an outside force.

Garry Cooper's Oberon was clearly malevolent, a fuller manifestation of the nastiness and hunger for power hinted at in his Theseus. He was a strangely Beckettian figure: barefoot, grizzled and bare-chested in a black suit. Hunched forwards, stilted in his movement, lurching and jumping around the stage, his posture, like Titania's, suggested a wounded supernatural force. His voice rasped, and he looked simultaneously decrepit and like a wolf preparing to pounce. But this was not an entirely malicious figure: when Demetrius made it clear to Helena that he was

threatening to rape her, the invisible Oberon took a threatening step towards the young man.

Matt Whitchurch's interpretation of Demetrius was central to the production. Like all of the lovers, he was played as a teenager and costumed (initially, at least) in the tie, grey V-neck jumper and blazer typical of a conservative independent school – these were repressed adolescents discovering sexuality for the first time. For Demetrius, this carried a sense of menace (he seemed on the verge of undressing as he asked Hermia 'what should I get therefore?'), but it was when he professed his supposed love for Helena at the end that the production really did something unusual. Whitchurch delivered the speech entirely to Theseus, gesturing vaguely at Helena as he described her as 'food' and emphasizing the fact that he was referring to her repeatedly as 'it'. Hippolyta patted him uncertainly on the shoulder as she exited, as if approving of this ostensibly honourable turnaround but also worrying that it was not an entirely desirable outcome.

Emma Curtis's Helena was far from oblivious to the implications of Demetrius's objectification of her, and her lines 'I have found Demetrius like a jewel, / Mine own, and not mine own' were delivered with a steely resentfulness. Her worst fears were confirmed when Demetrius followed up his order 'Let's follow him' by beckoning and whistling to her as if she were indeed his spaniel. The discomfort of this moment was augmented by the final scene, in which several lines were reassigned to produce a greater contrast between Demetrius and Lysander. While Hermia and Lysander were happily entangled on one side of the stage, Lysander interrupting the mechanicals' play only to make positive interventions, Demetrius became increasingly boorish and unpleasant. Helena sat beside him looking tense and shrinking away from him. The destructive interruptions to Moonshine's speech were given entirely to Demetrius, who got up on to the stage to physically bully Starveling. When Thisbe dropped her mantle, Demetrius forced a resisting Helena to get up, trying to encourage her to sabotage the play by stealing it. As the iron tongue of midnight tolled twelve and the lovers filed offstage to bed, Helena was clearly not facing the happy ending she had anticipated. Over his closing speech, Theseus seemed momentarily, in voice and posture, to become the sinister Oberon again.

Bagnall's *Dream* was not the first Shakespearian production this year to make the image of a woman staggering around on a single high-heeled shoe one of its central metaphors. Indeed, I was reminded, as I watched it, of Rupert Goold's *The Merchant of Venice* at the Almeida Theatre, itself a remounting and partial re-envisioning of Goold's 2011 production for the RSC. As in 2011, this production culminated in Susannah Fielding's Portia tottering on her one high-heeled shoe, a blonde wig half on, crying through a showbiz smile as she listened to a recording of Elvis Presley's 'Are You Lonesome Tonight?'

As this suggests, it was Portia, not Shylock, who was the central tragic figure in Goold's production.

Portia was reinvented here as the star of *Destiny!*, an American reality TV gameshow documenting the marriage lottery devised for her by her late father. Both she and Nerissa (Emily Plumtree), the show's host, spoke with Southern accents while off-air, but switched to Californian valley girl accents whenever the 'ON AIR' sign illuminated (Portia's routine about her undesirable suitors, for example, thus became a highly camp and self-conscious turn for the television). Each of the casket scenes was relayed live on stageside television screens, accompanied by the tropes of gameshows: suspenseful drones, piped applause, even a cheesy catchphrase ('The ancient saying is no heresy: / Hanging and wiving goes by destiny!'). Portia was in 'off-air' mode at the start of her first scene with Bassanio (Tom Weston-Jones), flirting with him in her Southern accent; she readopted her television persona on 'Go, Hercules!', and he (inexplicably) entered the TV show dressed as a Roman soldier. By the time he chose the leaden casket, the stageside monitors had stopped relaying the events. Neither he nor Portia was immediately sure that he had chosen correctly – the casket contained not a picture of Portia, but a dictaphone, which he played to reveal the voice of Portia as a child reading the rhyme (her father's plan had evidently been in place a long time). As Portia pledged herself to him, she took off her wig and dropped her TV accent, and by the time Nerissa and Gratiano interrupted, they were clearly no longer on air.

Once again, the Arcola *Dream* gave me a helpful way of thinking about this production – namely the notion of drag as a metaphor for the performance of gender and identity. Portia was triply in drag in this production. First, as the reality television star, complete with blonde wig, frilly socks and killer heels; she was coy, camp and theatrical, playing the sought-after celebrity trophy wife and loyal daddy's girl (she promised to 'die as chaste as Diana, unless I be obtained by the manner of my daddy's will'). But the 'real' Portia, the Portia who fell back into her Southern accent when off-air, was also a drag act of sorts – she seemed happiest playing the dutiful wife and the gracious hostess, but her gestures in this guise, clasping her heart as she affected being moved by Jessica's thanks to her, or welcoming Antonio to her house, were equally hollow and uncomfortably reminiscent of the more obviously fake gestures of her television persona. Thirdly, of course, there was the cross-gender drag she adopted for the trial; but it was in this drag that she came closest to an unillusioned conception of her various identities, allowing the racist streak signposted in her interactions with Morocco full expression as she mocked and impersonated Shylock, and looking on in dawning realization that her husband and Antonio were lovers.

In the final scene, these three identities came into collision. Portia broke down in tears as she revealed her identity as the doctor, watching despondently as Scott Handy's Antonio reached over her lap to make Bassanio promise to keep the ring (she realized that Antonio could extract a promise from Bassanio that she could not). On 'You are all amazed!', she rushed over to her bag, threw on her wig, put on one of her high heels, and readopted her valley girl accent as she narrated the unlikely story of Antonio's three argosies having 'richly come to harbour suddenly'. The characters onstage took stock of the terrible choices they had made: Antonio had seen Bassanio's darker side; Nerissa realized that Gratiano was abusive (he had violently twisted her arm as he protested his innocence about the ring); Jessica understood that Lorenzo saw her as a means of getting rich; all three husbands realized they had exposed their baser motives. Over the closing moments, Elvis's monologue reminded us 'You know, someone said that the world's a stage, and each must play a part'.

Perhaps Shylock was in drag in this production, too. Ian McDiarmid's Shylock also wore a wig for most of the first half – he took it off forcefully at the end of his scene with Tubal, and replaced it with a yarmulke for the trial scene. But whereas in the 2011 production Patrick Stewart had played Shylock as a smart, quiet investment banker, a clear victim of the anti-Semitic society around him, McDiarmid opted for a more theatrical interpretation: a flamboyant spiv with a heavy German accent, more a payday lender than Stewart's serious

businessman. Like Portia, he seemed to be almost parodying the cultural identities that others had forced upon him.

McDiarmid's Shylock was oddly unknowable, and very much the second fiddle to Fielding's Portia. In contrast, in Jonathan Munby's *Merchant* at Shakespeare's Globe, Jonathan Pryce's dignified and vulnerable Shylock was the most human figure on stage. 'I hate him for he is a Christian' was, in this performance, a simple statement of fact, and Pryce responded to the audience laugh it provoked as though it simply confirmed that we were on his side. When he objected that Antonio's practice of lending money gratis 'brings down / The rate of usance here with *us* in Venice', he made an inclusive gesture to the auditorium. Similar gestures resurfaced on the words 'He hates *our* sacred nation', and, cleverly, on 'Your worship was the last man in *our* mouths' – the first-person plural co-opting the audience into complicity with Shylock, since indeed, in a sense, we *had* just been discussing Antonio.

Munby's Venice was one in which worth was measured by wealth and not by virtue. Mike Britton's set covered the entire front of the Globe's tiring-house with a facade that resembled a grubby iron casket or money chest. Jessica's eagerness to 'gild [her]self / With some more ducats' made perfect sense in this world, as did Antonio's reputation as an upright citizen despite his outrageous public treatment of Shylock. Indeed, while Shylock remained polite throughout his first scene with Antonio (Dominic Mafham), the latter threw Shylock's holy book to the floor and grabbed him by the beard (Shylock's 'Why, look you, how you storm!' seemed a desperate attempt to restore a civil tone). There was an audible murmur of shock and disapproval when Solanio spat in Shylock's face after the line 'I am a Jew', and Pryce's depiction of paternal grief made it impossible for the few spectators who seemed to want to laugh at lines like 'fourscore ducats at a sitting!' to continue much beyond his sobbing delivery of 'I had it of Leah when I was a bachelor'.

The trial scene introduced a discordant note of Christian iconography into this dynamic, as a horizontal bar was suspended from the roof, and Antonio's arms were attached to it. Antonio thus became an embodiment of the crucifix, even though little else about the production had asked us to see him as an especially self-sacrificing or otherwise Christ-like figure (in fact he was more than usually vicious). But as Rachel Pickup's Portia played her trump card, the scene once again allowed space for sympathy with Shylock. When Antonio demanded that he become a Christian, Shylock cried 'No, please, no!'; one of the Christians knocked his yarmulke from his head, causing him instinctively to cover his head with his hand. He left the stage sobbing, exposed, clearly considering his forced conversion a traumatic and identity-shattering prospect.

After this deeply unsettling moment, the final sequence of the play was jarring. Whereas Goold's production had wrung every drop of awkwardness from the conclusion to the rings plot, Munby's reasserted a tone of romantic comedy. It seemed to be riding over the potential discomfort of the play's conclusion: Bassanio and Gratiano were simply momentarily flummoxed, Portia and Nerissa triumphant, Antonio joyful in hearing the news about his ships, all the couples happily reconciled. But then, in the final moments, Jessica sunk to her knees and wailed out a lament, and as the stage suddenly filled with clergy and a crucifix, we saw the scene of Shylock's baptism. A hollow-eyed Shylock was led by a priest to the front of the stage, where a font opened up, and the rite played out slowly and painfully. It was a shocking undercutting of the mood of the previous sequence and a reassertion of the ambivalence of the play's ending.

By June, then, I had seen two productions of this play – the first with Portia as its protagonist, the second with Shylock. In Polly Findlay's version for the RSC (Illustration 54), I saw a third, in which – unusually – *The Merchant of Venice* was focused on its title character. As the audience entered, Jamie Ballard's Antonio stood alone onstage, quietly weeping. His first speech became a soliloquy, and he gestured towards the audience on 'you say it wearies you'; we had said no such

thing, of course, so the line seemed to indicate a character with an inferiority complex bordering on paranoia. This reading would become clearer as the evening progressed. Bassanio (Jacob Fortune-Lloyd) and Antonio had not been alone together for more than a few lines before they passionately kissed each other. Antonio broke off to ask about Portia, and Bassanio answered with a frankness that bordered on emotional abuse; that he could be so oblivious to Antonio's evident sexual jealousy indicated the dysfunctionality of their relationship. Antonio waved off Bassanio's line 'To you, Antonio, / I owe the most, in money and in love' as if he were deeply embarrassed by it. The second half opened like the first, with Antonio weeping alone onstage; Shylock brought the Jailer on to arrest him, and Antonio responded as if he had been anticipating, or even in some way looking forward to it. Antonio and Bassanio shared another intense kiss towards the climax of the trial scene, as a horrified Portia (Patsy Ferran) looked on; this did perhaps explain Portia's sudden interest in testing Bassanio's fidelity by begging his ring of him, but it was odd that Bassanio did not appear to remember this kiss upon Portia's revelation in the final scene. Over the last few lines of the play, the characters left two by two, leaving Antonio conspicuously alone again. He did not leave the stage at all, but sat down, as if exhausted, on a stageside bench.

Like Jonathan Pryce, Makram J. Khoury played Shylock as much more of a victim than a villain, though he seemed less interested than Pryce in establishing a direct relationship with the audience. Khoury's Shylock was a man of straightforward principles, expecting honest dealing from others as he dealt frankly and honestly with them. The production cut the words 'for he is a Christian', making Shylock's hatred of Antonio a business principle rather than deep-seated religious intolerance. If Shylock was not guilty of religious hatred, though, some of the Christian characters certainly were. In an echo of the Globe production, both Antonio and Salerio (Owen Findlay) spat squarely in Shylock's face, and he responded at first with hurt bewilderment ('Why, look you how you storm!') and then with an

54. *The Merchant of Venice*, 4.1, RSC, Royal Shakespeare Theatre, directed by Polly Findlay. Jacob Fortune-Lloyd as Bassanio, Jamie Ballard as Antonio and Patsy Ferran as Portia, with company. Photograph by Hugo Glendinning.

understandable determination to fight back. Indeed, it seemed very short-sighted of Antonio and his friends in both productions to vent their hatred for Shylock in such a way at precisely the moments when their opponent held all the cards; Salerio's shock on the line 'thou wilt not take his flesh' seemed especially naive when he had just treated his addressee with such public and violent contempt.

The production's attempts to divide the characters into victims and perpetrators of social prejudice extended to both Portia and Jessica. Portia's line 'may all of his complexion choose me so' was cut, so that the play's heroine was not tainted by the racist attitudes the production was determined to emphasize in many of its other characters. Scarlett Brookes's Jessica, meanwhile, was an unambiguous victim of patriarchy, trapped for the duration of her first two scenes at the top of a huge golden tower,

before throwing down a heavy casket of cash that Lorenzo and his friends wasted no time in delightedly opening up. By the end of the play, she was limp and worn down, her new husband overbearing and controlling.

The weakness of the production was in the ambiguity of its setting. It wanted to condemn the society it depicted as racist and patriarchal, yet never made clear which society it was depicting: the costumes were largely twenty-first-century, but Johannes Schütz's set was entirely symbolic (a gigantic pendulum swinging before a huge golden wall). Rina Mahoney's Duke was a female character, rendering it puzzling that Portia and Nerissa felt the need to dress as men in order to pass themselves off as lawyers. The imaginary Venice of Findlay's production was relatively liberal, in that everyone appeared to be accepting of Antonio and Bassanio's homosexual relationship,

55. *Measure for Measure*, 3.1, Cheek by Jowl, Barbican Theatre, directed by Declan Donnellan. Anna Khalilulina as Isabella and Peter Rykov as Claudio. Photograph by Johan Persson.

but it was also viciously anti-Semitic. It was unfortunate that a production so concerned with social attitudes could not be more specific about the target of its criticism.

The tendency to filter a play through the perspective of a single central character was also present in Declan Donnellan's *Measure for Measure* for Cheek by Jowl's Russian company (Illustration 55), which visited the Barbican in April. Nick Ormerod's set was a mostly bare stage, flanked by five large red boxes. The opening sequence featured the entire ensemble moving around the space in unison, flocklike, led by a company member in grubby and torn prison overalls (it would later become clear that this figure was Igor Teplov's Barnadine). Some moments in, a suited figure – whom we later learned to be the Duke (Alexander Arsentyev) – detached himself

from this group by standing still when it moved on. The group then seemed to stalk this solitary figure, crawling towards him at one point as he backed away in fear. The ensemble remained onstage for almost all of the two-hour production that followed, their presence seeming to haunt the Duke whenever he became aware of it. When he was not in a scene, the Duke tended to stand at the front of this flock, flanked by Barnadine, who often gently touched him to encourage him to watch and notice what was going on.

The Duke almost never looked directly at Barnadine, staring at him only once in a moment of horror as he first entered the prison. Later, during his first 'real' meeting with Barnadine, he cradled this unruly and unruled figure while the mimetic world of the play fell away in a stunning *coup de théâtre*. Dreamlike music blared out, and the three red boxes across the back of the stage spun around to reveal what was inside each of them: a blindfolded Claudio (Petr Rykov) strapped to an electric chair, a petrified Isabella (Anna Khalilulina) pointing upwards in religious rapture, and Pompey (Alexey Rakhmanov) having sex, mechanically and animalistically, with a prostitute. The production seemed to be staging a confrontation between the Duke and his sublimated thoughts about death, desire and sexuality.

The suggestion was very much that we were viewing a psychodrama from the Duke's perspective. At moments of emotional trauma, the whole ensemble would start to pound their heads, skip wildly, or disperse. When Isabella accused her brother of 'a kind of incest', the thus-far naturalistic scene suddenly erupted into a nightmarish frenzy, as Claudio, held by members of the ensemble, attempted to rape his sister before being presented with a double bass, which he proceeded to caress as though it were a woman's body, and then to straddle in a sexualized manner, plucking out a bass line to the accompanying waltz. The Duke intervened to lead Isabella and the rest of the company skipping hand-in-hand in a long human chain as he explained, and they enacted, the Mariana plot. The play was edited so that scenes bled into one other, keeping the story-telling fluid and the psychology of the Duke at the forefront. Act 4 especially was reduced to mere fragments, losing much of Mariana and most of the comic subplot. Scene changes were generally achieved by having the ensemble rush into the acting space en masse, picking up a player and subsuming them back into the ensemble, before depositing another and moving away. This achieved not only a breathless pace but also a dreamlike blurring of one scene into another.

The Duke's psychodrama reached its climax in the final scene, as he returned to his public role and once again repressed his destructive thoughts and desires – now visible only in slight twitches of his hands and face. When he proposed marriage to Isabella, she was caught up entirely in her own grief, staring at her brother, who had moments earlier rejected her attempt at reconciliation. All three couples ended the play in a simultaneous waltz, Claudio and Juliet cradling their newborn baby, Angelo limp and carried around the space by Mariana, and the Duke gazing fixedly at Isabella while she avoided eye contact.

Though the framing of the production positioned the Duke as its protagonist, it did not short-change Isabella, whose scenes with Angelo (Andrei Kuzichev) were a high point. Confronting each other either side of a wooden table, both played out the clash between violence, desire and repression that was central to the production's reading of the text. In their first scene, Isabella grew in confidence, planting herself in the chair opposite Angelo and leaning back in it as she spoke. A police guard hovered on the periphery of the space, repeatedly making as if to intervene and physically remove her, but each time, Angelo would wave his hand to delay physical intervention. Their next meeting, of course, had no third party observers, and this allowed Angelo to make his move. Over the speech beginning 'Who will believe thee, Isabel?', he sat her on his table, reckoned her up, and then approached her slowly, she tense with anger and fear, he parting her legs, lifting her dress, slowly removing one shoe and one sock. As his lips made contact with her leg, she pulled away, and he pressed her against the desk in an aborted attempt at rape (the Duke, watching, had to be restrained from intervening by Barnadine). Her 'To whom should I complain?' was subsequently delivered to the audience with one shoe on and one shoe off – surely by this point, given the similar images in Bagnall's *Dream* and Goold's *Merchant*, one of the defining images of the troubled sexual politics of Shakespearian comedy in 2015.

Dominic Dromgoole's *Measure* at the Globe was a much more light-hearted (though no less interesting) rendering of the play. In a pre-show reminiscent of Brueghel's *Fight Between Carnival and Lent*, jaunty folk music played while two Wendy-houses of ill repute were wheeled into the yard and colourful low-lifes emerged from them. Dean

Nolan's zealous Constable Elbow prowled the galleries, entering the yard to remonstrate with the transgressors and ending up in a comic physical tussle. All this while Dominic Rowan's Duke sat on the stage, his back to the audience.

The comic characters – many of them played by cast members returning from the Wanamaker Theatre's anarchic *Knight of the Burning Pestle* – dominated the production. The first two scenes of Act 2 were intercut, lending the production a faster, more farcical rhythm and allowing the first part of 2.1 to end on a punchline ('Once, sir? There was nothing done to her once!'). Overdone, Elbow and Froth spent much of this scene getting tangled in a cartoon of illicit sexuality and inept attempts to police it, to boisterous laughter from the audience. The early scenes were interspersed with transitional vignettes in which Elbow literally 'pulled down' the 'houses of resort' in the yard with a comic bullishness; later, these vignettes became more disturbing scenes of control and oppression as a struggling prostitute was branded on her face with a red-hot iron, and another was dragged screaming to prison. The audience was thus positioned very much on the side of 'carnival' and unrestrained sexuality in the face of increasingly disturbing oppression. If this ran the risk of constructing prostitution as a victimless crime, however, this suggestion was rather undercut by a moment when Trevor Fox's Pompey wheeled the unconscious Mistress Overdone (Petra Massey) onstage in a cart, and observing a potential customer, offered the body of his drunken charge for 'Four shillings. Two if she wakes up'. It got a laugh, but not an entirely comfortable one.

Kurt Egyiawan's Angelo was young and nervous, spiralling across the stage when Isabella touched his chest on the words 'Go to your bosom'. The intercutting of 2.1 and 2.2 meant that his speech beginning 'What's this?' was a stand-alone soliloquy, which he delivered with huge physical and vocal energy; his next appearance (at the start of 2.4) was also a lively soliloquy, which had the cumulative effect of suggesting a hurtling momentum to the awakening of his sensuality. Mariah Gale's Isabella was convinced

until a relatively late moment in this second scene that her conversation with Angelo was merely hypothetical, an exciting thought experiment rather than a real dilemma. It was not until 'Plainly conceive, I love you' that she realized the truth of her situation, and responded with a sudden and ferocious anger, hurling Angelo across the stage. For a moment, he looked visibly sickened by his own loss of control.

Dominic Rowan's Duke was, like Mark Rylance's at the Globe in 2004, a largely good-natured bumbler rather than a controlling Machiavellian: he was improvising his plan as he went along, and making up moral justifications on the hoof. There were audience chuckles as he ducked having to explain the bed-trick plan to Mariana, Isabella glaring at him as she realized the buck had been passed her way ('Take then this your companion by the hand, / Who hath a story ready for your ear'). This interpretation helped to give the play the structure and momentum of a farce: Rowan's Duke was almost like Basil Fawlty as the plot reached fever pitch, frantically reconfiguring his plan as Barnadine refused to be executed and reacting with mania to every twist ('O, 'tis an accident that heaven provides!'). In his conversation with Lucio, this Duke was not so much deliberately goading his subject into slandering him as naively testing his own reputation: he was, as Escalus puts it shortly afterwards, 'One that, above all other strifes, contended especially to know himself'.

This interpretation gave the final scene a strange ambiguity. The Duke was so coolly in control in his deliberate and sustained manipulation of Isabella's grief that this suddenly seemed like a very different character. The fact that we had been primed to find this *Measure* funny went some way to alleviate this difficulty – when the Duke first proposed to Isabella, she threw her hands to her head and turned toward the audience, inviting us to laugh at the ill-timed inappropriateness of his offer. But this turned into something more thoughtful over the lines that followed. As the Duke attempted to wrap events up to everyone's satisfaction, Isabella picked up and caressed his discarded friar's habit; she loved him, but she loved him (as, judging by reactions, did much of the audience) in his incarnation as a genial friar, not as a suddenly inscrutable figure of power. When he repeated his proposal over the play's final lines, she looked out to the audience as if she were asking for guidance, before moving over to the Duke and taking his hand.

Like Cheek by Jowl's production, Joe Hill-Gibbins's *Measure* at the Young Vic seemed especially interested in the gaze of the Duke. This production opened with a teeming mass of inflatable sex dolls writhing around behind a gauze curtain; the curtain drew back and Zubin Varla's Duke emerged from amongst them, his shirt unbuttoned and his fly unzipped. He spoke his dialogue in 1.1 with a kind of twitchy detachment, as if shellshocked by the depths of his own depravity. At the end of the scene, he left the stage by an upstage door and immediately entered a hidden space behind the back wall, which became visible to the audience as live camera footage from it was projected on to the wall in front (audience members of Hill-Gibbons's 2013 *Edward II* at the National will remember a similar device). The Duke himself took the camera as he assumed the mantle of Friar Lodowick.

From this moment on, the camera became both a metaphor and a means for the violence of the gaze. The Duke pointed his camera at all the scapegoats he could find, from the resigned Claudio (Ivanno Jeremiah) to the resistant Pompey (Tom Edden), displacing his own self-loathing on to them: Claudio and Julietta's private sex tape was displayed 'to th' world'; Angelo shrunk from it as he began to examine Pompey and Froth, leaving the task to Escalus. In 2.3, as the Duke approached Julietta with his camera, both the projected image and the live body of actor Natalie Simpson showed Julietta flinching up against the wall as the camera invaded her pain; the Duke pointed it, and thus our gaze, intrusively at her belly as he referred to 'the sin you carry'. The production was making no attempt here to make us complicit with this act of symbolic violence – rather, it became uncomfortably clear that who gets to look at what and how is irrevocably tied up with acts of coercion from those in power.

The text was heavily cut, playing at 1 hour 50 minutes without an interval; several scenes ended with mid-conversation blackouts rather than exits, lending it a cinematic rhythm, and most secondary characters were either cut entirely or, as in the case of the Provost and Elbow, conflated (presenting actor Hammed Animashaun with the unenviable task of attempting to play in one character both an empathetic man of 'honesty and constancy' and an angry figure of fun). Extensive cuts to the last two acts, and a near constant score of incidental music, added to the sense that this production was primarily a filmic examination of the psychologies of a small ensemble of central characters as they buckled under pressure.

Romola Garai's Isabella was slow and guarded, anxious not to put a foot wrong as she entered what she plainly perceived was dangerous territory; Paul Ready's Angelo likewise picked his words very carefully, hesitating and backtracking whenever he said something that might undermine the moral equivocation he was attempting to make ('Nay, I'll not warrant that; for I can speak / Against the thing I say'). As in Cheek by Jowl's production, their second scene culminated in an explosion of violence, but as he pinned her to the floor, both bodies were tense, stiff, almost frozen. By the end of Isabella's conversation with Claudio, the production was starting to feel like Shakespeare-as-Strindberg: trapped, unhappy characters lashing out at one another with everything they have.

At this point, though, it started to veer into self-parody. Cath Whitefield's Mariana wore a fraying wedding dress beneath a tatty overcoat, a kind of twenty-first-century Miss Havisham, and her mascara was smudged in what read to me as a pop-culture pastiche (rather than a nuanced psychological portrait) of the spurned woman. This was augmented by the fact that the moment she was named by the Duke, she was shown screaming along to Alanis Morissette's 'You Oughta Know': 'And I'm here / To remind you / Of the mess you left when you went away!' The moment raised a cynical laugh as the scene cut quickly to a truncated version of 4.2 and Mariana said apologetically, 'I cry you mercy, sir, and well could wish / You had not found me here so musical.'

As Act 4 progressed, Hill-Gibbons seemed to be doing all he could to detach his audience from the characters whom he had previously built up with such naturalistic detail. As Isabella was told the news of Claudio's (apparent) death, she flung herself against a bank of sex dolls in grief, while in the final scene, Mariana clung madly to Angelo as he was promised in marriage to her; when I saw the production, both moments were met with the laughter they appeared to be inviting. Isabella's unhidden horror at the Duke's proposal, and his manic attempt to organize the resisting bodies of the ensemble into a happy-ending tableau, made for a funny but supremely uncomfortable ending.

In the production's most interesting reinvention, John Mackay played Lucio as fully aware of the Duke's disguise from their very first encounter. 'What news, friar, of the Duke?' was the start of a playful attempt to goad the Duke into giving himself away; 'A little more lenity to lechery would do no harm in him' was an attempt to speak truth to power in the manner of Lear's Fool. There was no doubt, here, of the veracity of Lucio's claim that the Duke 'had some feeling of the sport', given the production's opening scene and the rising panic in the Duke's voice over this exchange. In the final scene, the Duke's insistence that Lucio should hold his tongue was delivered with the vehemence of a tyrant, while Lucio's dismissive description of the Friar was a coded accusation of the Duke's hypocrisy. Lucio paid a high price for his honesty: the Duke's sentence of whipping and hanging was clearly meant in earnest, and as the Duke assembled the whole ensemble into a line facing the audience at the end, the only figure missing was Lucio, weeping on the ground before them. Thus, surprisingly, Lucio emerged as the most heroic figure of the production.

The other two comedies I saw this year were both at Shakespeare's Globe: the first was Blanche McIntyre's in-house *As You Like It* (Illustration 56), and the second was Max Webster's touring *Much Ado* (Illustration 57). Both productions made me think further about the relationship between celebration and restraint in Shakespearian comedy. McIntyre's *As You Like It* reminded me just how deeply the play reflects upon time; its uneven structure is an ingenious device which, in a production like McIntyre's, puts the audience through the very phenomenon that Rosalind observes when she notes that 'Time travels in divers paces with divers persons'. After the quick pace of the court scenes, the play slows down when the characters enter the forest. At the Globe, this was a holiday space outside time: though the production was in Elizabethan costume, modern props began to intrude. Rosalind entered the forest with a huge Ordnance Survey map, Celia with a gigantic pack of belongings that included an espresso maker. Later, Touchstone would don a pair of sunglasses. The production lingered on the pleasant agonies of Rosalind's wait for Orlando, and quite sensibly rushed through the plot elements that happen largely offstage (Oliver's conversion, and the development of his love for Celia). Its score, by 'nu-folk' musician Johnny Flynn, echoed this fusion of the traditional and the anachronistic.

Michelle Terry's Rosalind was masterful at manipulating time herself. Her thoughts seemed at moments to be galloping ahead of her speech so much that she gabbled; at other times, she asserted a calm control over the chaos around her. This was a Rosalind who had been taken by surprise by the violence of physical attraction: she intermittently contorted herself with displays of pleasure and checked herself with nervous self-consciousness. At moments, it was as though Rosalind were stepping in and out of the play, switching between the roles of actor and spectator ('I'll prove a busy actor in their play', she exclaimed as she scampered into the yard in anticipation of the next scene).

For all its timelessness, the production was also underpinned by an awareness that our time on earth is limited, and reminders of death appeared

56. *As You Like It*, Shakespeare's Globe, directed by Blanche McIntyre. Simon Harrison as Orlando and Michelle Terry as Rosalind. Photograph by Simon Kane.

throughout the play. Indeed, the opening sequence was the funeral service of Sir Rowland de Boys, and James Garnon's Jacques became strikingly introspective over the lines 'And so from hour to hour, we ripe and ripe, / And then from hour to hour, we rot and rot'. Even Phebe's letter, finishing on 'Or else by him my love deny, / And then I'll study how to die', prompted a moment of reflection for its onstage listeners, punctuated beautifully by the tolling of the bell of St Paul's as ten o'clock struck.

Webster's *Much Ado*, a revival of 2014's touring production, featured a lead performance by Emma Pallant as Beatrice that in some ways recalled Terry's Rosalind. Pallant's Beatrice spoke so quickly that she came across as both a brilliantly quick wit and, at times, someone whose words

were spiralling out of her own control. Her response to Don Pedro's marriage proposal, here intended more seriously than she at first realized, was charmingly graceless and increasingly awkward; her 'believe me not, and yet I lie not; I confess nothing, nor I deny nothing' was a masterclass in comic timing. But it was in its use of the audience that this production interested me most. It was played in a robust, populist style that evidently responded to its origins in open-air touring: lines were delivered direct to the audience as frequently as possible, with several dialogues played 'out front' in the style of music hall, two characters standing side by side (though of course this was rather complicated by the fact that 'out front' is not really possible in the Globe). Christopher Harper's Benedick was particularly skilled at manipulating

57. *Much Ado About Nothing*, 2.1, Shakespeare's Globe, touring, directed by Max Webster. Emma Pallant as Beatrice, with company. Photograph by Bronwen Sharp.

audience response, soliciting no fewer than four rounds of applause in a single speech, and at one point getting three laughs in as many words:

> *(Loud exclamation)* Love!
> *(Quietly incredulous)* Me!
> *(Suddenly baffled)* Why?

This constant flirtation with the audience, though, had the knock-on effect of encouraging spectators to laugh, cheer and boo at every opportunity and, by the wedding scene, I had the impression that the company was trying hard to keep a lid on the wild responses that the comedy of the first half had unleashed, playing the scene at a furious pace lest the audience invade any unfilled silence. Benedick's asides functioned here as a lightning rod for the laughter that the audience evidently wanted to contribute – but, as the pause following Pallant's

moving delivery of 'I love you with so much of my heart that none is left to protest' was filled with an insincere audience 'aah', I found myself wondering whether some spectators had become afraid of allowing real emotion into what had started as a hilarious romp. Where McIntyre's *As You Like It* managed to tiptoe delicately between carnival and lent, Webster's *Much Ado* seemed trapped in the former.

TRAGEDIES

My first tragedy of the year was another experimental piece, and once again it took me underground: this time to the Waterloo Vaults, to see Filter Theatre's touring production of *Macbeth*. Like two of the three *Measures* I would see later in the year (discussed above), this production used heavy symbolism and inventive staging to explore the psychology of its characters. Its interest was almost exclusively in the central two characters, and the text was edited accordingly: Duncan's first scene, for example, featured only as snippets overheard on the radio. The cast of seven, costumed in rehearsal clothes, doubled as onstage musicians and creators of sound effects. The soundtrack, reminiscent of 1970s progressive rock, relied almost entirely on synthesized and sampled noises, and seemed only to play when either Ferdy Roberts's Macbeth or Poppy Miller's Lady Macbeth were onstage.

Filter have used onstage electronic sound effects in their previous Shakespearian work (2008's *Twelfth Night* and 2012's *A Midsummer Night's Dream*), but where in those earlier productions the 'rock gig' aesthetic added a sense of carnivalesque playfulness, here it created intensity. There were moments of the company's characteristic cheekiness – Lady Macbeth threw jelly babies at Macbeth as she accused him of cowardice, each shot accompanied by a percussive knock, and Paul Woodson's Porter entered through the audience reading from a copy of *Brodie's Notes* on the play. But both of these playful moments had serious undertones. The former was grounded in the staccato rhythms of the dialogue, emphasizing Lady Macbeth's verbal and psychological tactics, while the latter descended into a nightmarish sequence of paranoia: Macbeth had just smeared himself with stage blood, and the Porter covered him with white feathers and, following this, Macbeth took over the reading of *Brodie's Notes*, intercutting it with the lines of Shakespeare's Porter and Macbeth himself while circus-like music and layered sound samples gained in volume underneath his voice.

The soundtrack, then, seemed largely to represent Macbeth's unconscious mind: every noise appalled him. Banquo's ghost knocked on Macbeth's forehead, and a heavy, hollow echo sounded. Macbeth pressed his ear to the wall, and we heard a booming, resonating bass. Macbeth 'killed' Macduff's children by turning off the baby monitor that was playing recorded sounds of a crying baby, and the sample of the crying child returned to haunt him at the end. We heard the birds of Birnam Wood closing in on him in a cacophonous crescendo. This emphasis on soundscapes was matched by a kinaesthetic use of the body: Roberts walked and then ran in a circle around Miller as she delivered Lady Macbeth's 'Come, you spirits' speech, climaxing in a literally breathless verbal exchange with her. In the claustrophobic space of the Waterloo Vaults, as the noise of trains rumbled overhead and then melted into the deep, pulsating electronic score, Filter's production was almost Artaudian in its attempt not merely to represent but actually to embody the 'heat oppressed brain' of its protagonist.

My next *Macbeth* – Jatinder Verma's touring production for Tara Arts (Illustration 58) – was set, according to its programme, in a 'British-Asian extended family'. This was sometimes rather literal, and at other times more metaphorical. The script had been only lightly edited, so the production's intermittent attempts to make the play work naturalistically in a specific modern British-Asian context seemed rather jarring – this was at once both a modern family in twenty-first-century clothes, living in a domestic space with a modern electric standard lamp, and a group of noblemen fighting for the crown of Scotland (the costume design wittily addressed this duality, clothing the Macbeths in tartan sashes for the banquet scene). But when the production adopted a more overtly symbolic register, the setting was less perplexing and more rewarding.

The British-Asian setting allowed British and Indian cultures to play different roles in the world of the play. Claudia Mayer's set was dominated by the garlanded portrait of the most recently deceased king (or family patriarch): thus, immediately after Duncan's murder, his portrait replaced that of his predecessor, and smiled benevolently over the action for the rest of the play, until the final moments, when it was replaced by a glowering image of Macbeth. The male politicians and warriors of the opening act wore Western suits and trenchcoats, speaking with a variety of English

58. *Macbeth*, 3.1, Tara Arts, touring, directed by Jatinder Verma. Shalini Peiris as Servant, Robert Mountford as Macbeth, Shaheen Khan as Lady Macbeth, John Afzal as Ross. Photograph by Talula Sheppard.

accents. The working-class northern accent of Ralph Birtwell's Duncan suggested a self-made businessman rather than a king; the received pronunciation of Robert Mountford's Macbeth, a privately educated nephew or cousin, perhaps. Shaheen Khan's Lady Macbeth was a modern British-Asian woman in leather trousers and an asymmetric jersey top. The witches, in contrast, were *hijras*, transgender figures apparently associated in India with liminality, prophecy and sometimes spiritual leadership. Played by male actors, they spoke with Mumbai accents, and sang and danced. According to Verma's programme notes, these figures represented the world 'of memory, of superstition, of faith' and, for him, the pull exerted by the homeland on Asian emigrants.

Like Filter's otherwise very different production, Verma's was accompanied from start to finish by an onstage musician. Rax Timyr used both

acoustic and electronic percussion instruments to punctuate sequences of dialogue and to accompany fight scenes, striking aural crashes not only for physical blows but also for moments of realization and discovery. For me, the production was at its strongest in Act 5, when it largely abandoned the semi-naturalistic family drama it had attempted to construct in the early acts. The English army was represented by five male actors, who stood in a line across the back of the playing space throughout the act, marching in slow motion. Green banners rolled down the back wall for Birnam Wood, and Macbeth 'strutted and fretted' frantically in front of this. He brought his wife's corpse on to the stage for the final scene, dressing her in his royal robes and addressing some of his questions to her. When confronted by Macduff, he fought ferociously; then three of the actors standing anonymously at the back of the stage grouped together to form

59. *Macbeth*, Tang Shu-wing Theatre Studio, Shakespeare's Globe, directed by Tang Shu-wing. Ng Wai Shek as Macbeth and Rosa Maria Velasco as Lady Macbeth. Photograph by Helena Miscioscia.

a final tableau of the witches, the percussion rallied to create a moment of hiatus and anagnorisis, and Macbeth gave up the battle, offering himself up for execution with the lines: 'Before my body / I throw my warlike shield. Lay on, Macduff, / And damn'd be him that first cries, "Hold"'. Then, to the audience – recognizing that he had met his prophesied end, and the play could conclude – 'Enough'. Red banners dropped from the top of the back wall as Macduff struck the fatal blow.

Tang Shu-wing's Cantonese-language production of the play, which visited Shakespeare's Globe in August (Illustration 59), was also interested in exploring the pull of the past. Chan Chi Kuen Ricky's backdrop of misty blue mountains was spread across the front of the tiring-house, while a large white sheet covered most of the floor.

As the performance started, two performers in neutrally coloured modern dress moved jerkily towards the front of the stage; the stageside surtitles informed us that this was a modern couple dreaming of the world buried beneath modern China. The woman (Rosa Maria Velasco) backed out quickly while her husband (Ng Wai Shek) stayed on the floor. Three male witches, dressed in dirty white ragged robes, entered humming eerily; these figures would be recalled throughout the play, not only in the reappearances of the witches themselves, but also in the trio of murderers in white veils who would do Macbeth's bidding.

Numerous edits served to focus this production, like Filter's, on its protagonists. Duncan's first scene was cut, so that his first appearance was his arrival at Dunsinane with a full retinue in spectacular historical Chinese costume. The Porter was missing, in keeping with the production's detached and ceremonial style, and the witches had no dialogue beyond their exchanges with Macbeth, rendering them more ethereal than usual. The murder of the Macduffs was moved to the middle of the scene in which Ross relates the news of it to Macduff: his wife and son appeared from the discovery space, while the three murderers entered silently behind them, killing them with a single symbolic gesture. The figures of both murderers and victims remained onstage for the rest of the scene.

In fact, the production was full of ghosts of this sort. Duncan's ghost, his face newly decorated in white and red and his mouth streaming with two red ribbons, entered the stage following his murder; Banquo returned in a similar manner after (but interestingly not during) the banquet scene in which Macbeth hallucinated his appearance. Lady Macbeth entered the space in slow motion, wearing a simple black dress, following her death, at the moment when Macbeth realized the imminence of his own. She watched his death at Macduff's hands, which was again done symbolically, without physical contact.

The Globe's discovery space was used as a kind of 'space of oblivion'. Unseen stagehands would part the backcloth from behind to reveal a dark cavernous nothingness, into which various characters would depart: Lady Macbeth to plant the daggers, Macbeth to kill Duncan, Banquo to his death. At the start of her descent into madness, Lady Macbeth stared silently into the emptiness of the space. When the witches showed Macbeth the line of kings, a reflective surface at the back of the tiring-house was lit up by a single spotlight and Macbeth ran frenziedly towards it (the Globe was empty enough on the day I saw the production that this was not lost on two-thirds of the audience, as it would have been in a full theatre).

Acting styles veered from the highly symbolic to the almost naturalistic. Characters frequently entered the stage in extreme slow motion, with a codified gesture indicating their dominant emotion (fear, guilt, grief and so forth). Though the Macbeths played their early scenes in a largely realistic register, their performances became more heightened as the tragedy progressed: during his 'To be thus is nothing' soliloquy, for example, Macbeth's body became physically deformed, in line with the moral contortions of his speech.

The opening was reincorporated upon the central characters' demises. Lady Macbeth's final exit before her death saw her slowly backing into the darkness of the discovery space, rubbing her hands. Macbeth died lying down on the stage, as he had been at the start. Then Lady Macbeth woke her husband from his dream, and the two looked contemplatively out at the yard. A groundling presented Macbeth with a black umbrella (the only moment of real direct contact between the stage and yard in the whole piece); Macbeth raised the umbrella while his wife sang a lament, and the two of them very slowly entered the space of oblivion that had opened up behind them. It was a powerful, unsettling, dreamlike experience.

The two *King Lear*s I saw this year were linked by a shared desire to read the play as some sort of Christian allegory. In the case of the first, Caroline Devlin's production for the Guildford Shakespeare Company, this was probably dictated by the location of the performance: it was the fifth in a series of productions designed for performance in Guildford's magnificent eighteenth-century Holy Trinity Church, following *Hamlet*, *Richard III*, *Macbeth* and *Othello*. But whereas those plays refer frequently to Christian theology, *King Lear* does so rarely if at all. Indeed, the numerous references to and invocations of 'the gods' hit the ear rather awkwardly in this inescapably Christian space.

The production did not attempt to play down the theology its space seemed to be imposing on the play. The rood screen, ornately decorated and topped with a huge golden crucifix, dominated the set throughout, while behind it, a golden painting in the dome of the apse was intermittently illuminated to reveal the figure of Jesus gazing down. Christ himself thus made a flickering appearance during the desolation of Lear's scene in the storm, for example, and later, as Matt Pinches's Edgar spoke the play's final lines gingerly holding the crown, the mural lit up in an ambiguous image of redemption and judgement. (Edgar had snatched at his brother's face during their final duel, attempting to gouge out his eyes in revenge for their father's mutilation, before pulling away and staring at his hand in shocked recognition of the barbarism of his own act.)

The production, like its venue, was strongly iconographic, opening with a series of tableaux of Lear and his daughters, while the Fool's prophecy played over the speakers. The second half started with the image of Emily Tucker's heroic Cordelia returning to England, frozen like the figurehead of a boat as huge expanses of fabric billowed behind her like waves parting beneath the prow of a ship. Any figure framed in the centre of the stage was, of course, also standing beneath a very conspicuous symbol of salvation: a fact that lent some irony to the numerous scenes of cruelty or despair.

The production did seem to be at odds with the space at times. The chancel was curtained off, but the curtains in front of it were made from a thin, gauzelike fabric and often backlit. For reasons that elude me, this holiest part of the building was used as the locus for much of the play's 'sinful' behaviour: Goneril and Oswald (Rosalind Blessed and Timothy Allsop) could be seen in silhouette in a steamy embrace before their entrance in 1.3, while Cornwall and Regan (Richard Neale and Sarah Gobran) could likewise be seen drinking cocktails before their appearance at Gloucester's castle in 2.1. Goneril emerged from her tryst with Oswald in scarlet lingerie, the stereotypical temptress: not only was this a frustratingly reductive reading of the character, but it also seemed a wrong-headed use of the space itself.

Lear (Terence Wilton stepping in for Brian Blessed due to ill health) was a confused innocent, almost like a 5-year-old encountering betrayal and death for the first time. His attempts to reckon up his daughters' love mathematically ('thou art twice her love'), his mad obsession with their ingratitude ('Hast thou given all to thy two daughters?'), and his hopelessly impotent threats ('What they are, yet I know not') were sweetly funny; there was something endearingly childlike about the simplistic moral categories through which he had previously understood the world, and of which he was unwilling to let go. Of course, it helped that Goneril and Regan were uncompromisingly evil in this production.

Northern Broadsides' touring production of *Lear*, directed by Jonathan Miller, pushed the Christian allegory further. Isabella Bywater's set placed most of the action on a simple dais framed by two wooden poles and a top bar over which a small curtain was draped. In this and many other respects, the production recalled the form of medieval pageant theatre: the text was heavily cut, and the company's customary use of Yorkshire accents for most of the characters evoked the York Corpus Christi plays. The most striking parallel, though, was Miller's reading of the play as a straightforwardly moralistic folk-tale. This was a battle between good and evil – the demurely dressed Cordelia (Catherine Kinsella) contrasting with her spiteful, scheming sisters (Helen Sheals and Nicola Sanderson), and the aggressive, charmless and thoroughly bad Edmund (Sean Cernow) playing off against the Christ-like Edgar (Jack Wilkinson), whose Poor Tom was dressed in a loincloth and a crown of thorns, his bare chest marked with gashes. The production missed a trick, I think, in not allowing Cernow's Edmund to adopt the manner of the medieval Vice, seducing the audience into sinful complicity. As it was, it was hard to see the character as much more than – in the words of Mike Poulton's programme notes – an 'absolute bastard'.

Miller also seemed to concur with Poulton's notes in his presentation of Goneril and Regan. Modern attempts to 'find excuses for Goneril's extraordinary behaviour', says Poulton, are 'politically correct ... nonsense'; Regan has likewise 'come in for a lot of misplaced sympathy', and the sisters are nothing more than 'a pair of vicious schemers'. Thus, in Miller's production, Lear's elder daughters were clearly conniving from the start, whispering and glancing to one another throughout the first scene, while Jos Vantyler's Oswald was a smirking, sneering, cowardly fop. When Cornwall ordered Kent to be put in the stocks, the assorted characters on the stage could barely contain their glee – Regan even applauded.

Barrie Rutter's Lear was thus very clearly 'a man / More sinned against than sinning'; this production was not interested in questioning his right to autocratic rule. Since we never saw any of the hundred knights, I was much more inclined to believe Lear's own account of them as 'men of choice and rarest parts, / That all particulars of duty know', than that of the obviously untrustworthy Goneril. For most of the evening, I found myself frustrated by this flattening of the play into a morality drama, but as it neared its conclusion and the text itself began to resist this reading more emphatically, I found myself warming to the concept. In 5.3, Lear was happy to be bundled off to prison not because he had resigned himself to a tragic fate, but because he was still unshakeable in his confidence that he was good, and good would prevail. Watching this version of the final scene, I could glimpse for the first time how upsetting and bewildering Shakespeare's cruel conclusion might have been to an audience familiar with the happy ending of the chronicle history.

I realize, looking back over these reviews, that I saw many productions this year that confined themselves, more or less, to 'two hours' traffic': Northern Broadsides' *Lear*, Filter's *Macbeth*, and the *Measure for Measures* by Cheek by Jowl and the Young Vic all stuck to this running time by making heavy abridgments. Terry Hands's *Hamlet* – the director's swansong for Clwyd Theatr Cymru – clocked in at just under three hours, but managed this with only minor edits. The revelation of this production, for me, was just how much this play makes sense when it is played *fast*: the cast spoke their lines at a machine-gun pace throughout, and this reaped rewards.

Hamlet is often played, in Olivier's words, as 'the tragedy of a man who could not make up his mind' – of a pained introvert who spends too much time thinking and not enough doing. I have never been comfortable with this reading of the character. Lee Haven-Jones's Hamlet was clearly a great intellect – indeed, he was frequently reminiscent of Benedict Cumberbatch's fast-talking Sherlock Holmes, who was surely being referenced in Hamlet's trenchcoat and chunky-knit scarf (anticipating August's sold-out Barbican production starring Cumberbatch, perhaps). But far more satisfying in Haven-Jones's performance was the sense that, like a darker version of Terry's Rosalind or Pallant's Beatrice, this was a character whose thoughts were running away so fast that they were derailing, leading him into dangerous territory before he had had a chance to slam on the brakes.

This speed had numerous advantages. Firstly, it demonstrated that this is a play about thinking. Beckett is said to have advised that his play *Not I* should be spoken 'at the speed of thought', and Hands's *Hamlet* seemed to be attempting this: I found a delight in being constantly surprised by the sudden eruption of the play's familiar lines, as if they were being invented for the first time. Moments at which characters' thought processes became interrupted – Polonius's 'What was I about to say?', for example, or Hamlet forgetting the Priam speech – were like intellectual stumbles, obstacles jutting out from the rapid flow of the dialogue. It helped to explain why the characters do the things they do: they react before they have finished reflecting. Mark Bailey's set, a wall and floor of shiny black mirrors, was full of reflective surfaces but, though it was almost constantly visible to us, Hamlet never saw his own reflection in this play and, by implication, never arrived at a proper understanding of himself. As he told the players how important it was for them to 'hold, as 'twere, the mirror up to nature', he failed to notice Ophelia (Caryl Morgan) sobbing uncontrollably at the back of the stage, where she had remained since the 'Get thee to a nunnery' scene. His misogynistic outbursts in both of these scenes (physically as well as verbally violent) were palpably those of a man who thought not too *much* but too *quickly*.

Secondly, the speed of the dialogue emphasized the extent to which the characters, Hamlet especially, are caught in a machine-like social and political system that will thunder mercilessly onwards with or without them. (I was reminded of the television work of Aaron Sorkin here, not least *The West Wing*.) This was highlighted in the early court scenes, when the members of Claudius's court would quickly and silently arrange their bodies according to the King's movements around the stage, following wherever he led. A silent Reynaldo shadowed Polonius, using a clipboard to transcribe everything anyone said. This production allowed the lines spoken by several characters at once to be unashamedly in unison – it was not pretending to be naturalism, but exploiting the energy and rhythms of the verse.

Finally, the speed enabled a pace that the play is not normally able to achieve in performance: it allowed the interval to be placed just after 'How all occasions . . .', lending both halves a much neater arc than is usually the case. This placing of the interval meant that the first half charted Hamlet's fretful process of decision-making, finishing with his final soliloquy and resolution to revenge: the black mirrors were pulled away for this scene to reveal a bright white cyclorama, against which the trenchcoated prince was briefly silhouetted (I read this as a reference to Friedrich's *Wanderer above the Sea of Fog*, an icon of introspection evoked in the publicity images not only for this production, but also for Gregory Doran's of 2008). But this also meant that the thoughtful, questioning Hamlet was entirely absent from the second half – the character did not return to the stage until the grave-digger scene, from which point onwards he was mysterious, aloof and impenetrable. In a sense, we had lost Hamlet before the interval.

The staging of the final scene made the most of this. Hamlet really was 'incensed', fighting wildly with Laertes in the background, blind to the fact that his mother was dying downstage centre. In Carol Royle's performance, Gertrude's decision to drink was an advised one: she wanted to see if her suspicions of Claudius (Simon Dutton) were true, and if they were, she did not want to live. 'I pray you, pardon me' was spoken direct to Hamlet, but he did not register its import. She turned downstage as the poison took hold, sorrowful and resigned. Claudius stood sadly at her shoulder, while Hamlet fought obliviously behind them: the thinking man had finally given way to the man of action, and there was the tragedy.

Yukio Ninagawa's Japanese-language *Hamlet*, which visited the Barbican in May, treated the play more symbolically. Tsukasa Nakagoshi's set was a ramshackle nineteenth-century Japanese street encircled by higgledy-piggledy wooden balconies, in a vague approximation of an Elizabethan playhouse. In a nod to the production's own position at an intersection between European and Japanese cultures, it was set during the Meiji period, an era of increasing Westernization in Japan: Ayako Maeda's costumes thus mixed traditional Japanese robes with Western-style waistcoats and lapels. These costumes and Motoi Hattori's lighting rendered this, for the most part, a production in three colours: red, white and black. The red belonged to Claudius's court, who not only wore a rich crimson, but were also bathed in a deep red light during most of their scenes. Hikari Mitsushima's Ophelia was clothed entirely in white, and her early scenes were brightly lit, associating the character with purity. Black, of course, was Hamlet's colour, and Tatsuya Fujiwara's Prince wore it for the duration of the show. He spent most of the first court scene leaning against a post at the side of the stage on the periphery of the red light, physically broken with grief; he likewise lurked around the edges of the red wash during his conversation with Polonius in 2.2, confining himself to the darkened balconies at the back and sides.

At first, every scene featuring these characters seemed to be dominated by their associated colours in the lighting, but as the play progressed, this began to be complicated. Ophelia's white rather than Claudius's red lit 3.1, leaving Mikijiro Hira's Claudius looking blanched and exposed as his guilty conscience made itself felt ('How smart a lash that speech doth give my conscience!'). At the beginning of the second half, he appeared for his soliloquy of 3.3 ('O my offence is rank') dressed entirely in white, in a bright wash, and proceeded, in a ritual of self-purification, to undress, pour water over his head, and self-flagellate. Just as Claudius had been temporarily overwhelmed by the white state, so was Ophelia overcome by the red: the unrelenting red lighting of her mad scenes made her costume look crimson, just as the cruelties of the world it represented had overrun her mind.

It was in the figure of Hamlet that these colours achieved their greatest symbolic complexity. Hamlet gained a bright red scarf for 2.2, and stepped wholeheartedly into the red light for the first time as he met Rosencrantz and Guildenstern: the suggestion seemed to be that he was starting to embrace the Machiavellian side to his nature that he had hitherto suppressed. As he delivered the first half of his 'Now I am alone' soliloquy, sixteen narrow white spotlights cut through the red wash to converge at the spot where he was standing, neatly emblematizing his struggle between introspection and fury, lucidity and paranoia. On 'About, my brains!', the red faded to black, and Hamlet shifted from angry, feral movements to stillness and weeping. This symbolism resurfaced in surprising ways as the play progressed: I had been expecting the red light to return, for example, on "Tis now the very witching time of night', but I was mistaken – the white light in fact suggested a triumph of rational thought ('Let me be cruel, not unnatural') over the desire to 'drink hot blood'. This suggestion was not followed through in the closet scene, however, when Hamlet began to sexually assault his mother – stopped only by the intervention of the ghost.

The production's limited colour palette meant that when other colours appeared, they made for a visual shock. Fortinbras (Kenshi Uchida) appeared briefly in 4.4 in electric blue, accompanied by a blue flag, and at the end, as the royal family lay dead and dying, numerous blue flags crashed through the windows before a bare-chested Fortinbras emerged, still dressed from the waist down in bright blue, to claim the throne. In contrast to the stooping elderly courtiers of Denmark, Fortinbras's soldiers were young and athletic: their leader seemed to be attired as he was in order to display his youthful physique. An old era had died, and a new one was being ushered in.

I returned to the Barbican for a second *Hamlet* in August. Lyndsey Turner's highly anticipated production was a rich jumble of different takes on the play: personal, political, psychological and symbolic (Illustration 60). Its opening seemed to pitch

the production as one that would be focused primarily on the mind of its central character: rather than the guards on the battlements, we got Benedict Cumberbatch's Hamlet sitting in a private room, playing Nat King Cole's *Nature Boy* – a song about a 'strange enchanted boy' who is shy, sad and wise – on a portable record player. 'Who's there?' asked Hamlet, usurping not only the play's first line but also its second: 'Stand and unfold yourself'. In came Horatio (Leo Bill), and the scene cut to their dialogue from the end of 1.2. Thus both Hamlet and the existence of the Ghost were presented to the audience in a more sure-footed and perhaps conventional way than the text usually allows, while the political context and sense of general paranoia conveyed in Shakespeare's first scene was elided. (Apparently early previews opened with Hamlet's 'To be or not to be' soliloquy, but this was transposed in the version I saw to the end of Polonius and Hamlet's exchange in 2.2.)

The second scene revealed Es Devlin's lavishly realistic set: a palatial reception room under a sweeping staircase and a huge chandelier, decorated all over with candles and garlands for Claudius and Gertrude's wedding. The large cast filled the stage as a combination of high-society wedding guests and servants. The scene proceeded in a largely naturalistic register until Hamlet's first soliloquy, which established a convention for most of his soliloquies to come: the text was edited so that the action would break, mid-scene, while the stage was still crowded with people; the lights would snap to a ghostly twilight in which the walls were illuminated with X-ray-like projections (perhaps exposing the rottenness of Denmark as existing within the very fabric of its buildings); and the cast would jerk in unison like a faulty video recording before proceeding in slow motion as Hamlet stepped forward to deliver his speech. When Hamlet wished that his 'too too solid flesh would melt', the wedding guests sitting at the long banquet table twitched, zombie-like, and the numerous servants at the outskirts of the room slowly advanced upon them. As Hamlet leapt on to the table amidst the oblivious aristocrats and

60. *Hamlet*, 3.3, Barbican Theatre, directed by Lyndsey Turner. Benedict Cumberbatch as Hamlet. Photograph by Johan Persson.

advancing servants, I thought I was watching a fantasy tableau of impending revolution.

This moment introduced the production's political angle. The large cast meant that the stage was often full of supernumeraries, generally servants and soldiers. The central aristocratic characters tended to talk as if oblivious to, or at least unconcerned by, the presence of these subordinates; Laertes (Kobna Holdbrook-Smith) even gestured towards them as he referred to 'unvalued persons' in his conversation with Ophelia (Siân Brooke). Ophelia herself appeared to become such a person at one point, Claudius (Ciarán Hinds) and Polonius (Jim Norton) talking across her following her scene with Hamlet. Act 1, scene 3 was edited so that a long procession of soldiers crossed the stage beneath Marcellus and Barnardo (Dwane Walcott and Dan Parr) as they kept watch on the balcony; Horatio's speech explaining Norway's military

action from 1.1 was transferred to this moment, and given to their captain.

It gradually became clear that the production was set during a period of social upheaval and political protest in or around the 1960s. Horatio was established early on as a proto-republican, expressing his contempt for the sycophants who had bought tacky commemorative dinner plates emblazoned with Claudius's picture; Matthew Steer's Rosencrantz was costumed in such a way that he evoked the young Bob Dylan. That this was a production about 'the wind of change' became materially evident in the closing moments of the first half, when Claudius was left alone having ordered Hamlet and his companions to England: the doors to the palace suddenly blew open, and a gale of debris blasted in (an echo of the similar climactic pre-interval *coup de théâtre* in the Almeida Theatre's recent *Oresteia*, where it had made a lot more narrative sense). For the entirety of the second half, the palace was covered in a mountain of earth, and as the play's aristocratic characters stumbled in and around it, we seemed to be witnessing a visual metaphor for the remains of a dying social order. In 4.5, Laertes broke into the palace flanked by a large group of armed followers in the proletarian outfits of a popular revolution.

Oddly, the final scene excluded the crowd and once again obscured the story's sociopolitical aspect. Where at the start of the second half we had seen Sergo Vares's Fortinbras alongside numerous members of his army, at the end, he appeared onstage alone, ordering Horatio (of all people) to 'bid the soldiers shoot'; Horatio obediently slunk off upstage, all his progressive zeal sapped. It was a puzzling moment in a production full of such oddities: why had Hamlet been so full of praise for a troupe of players who were presented as old-fashioned hams? Why had Gertrude's closet scene been played in the same semi-public setting as the play-within-the-play, and why were all the guards and servants suddenly nowhere to be found? But while this *Hamlet* was occasionally baffling and often self-contradictory, it was consistently thought-provoking and surprising.

The year saw a slew of *Romeo and Juliet*s across the UK; I managed to get to only two of them. Polina Kalinina's production for Shakespeare at the Tobacco Factory, like Turner's *Hamlet*, took the generational struggles of the 1960s as its keynote, both in costume and characterization. Its most striking quality was its overriding feeling of youth: Daisy Whalley's Juliet, with her childlike costumes, guardedly self-conscious movement and upward vocal inflections, was a plausible 13-year-old, while both Sally Oliver's Nurse and Fiona Sheehan's Lady Capulet were women in their late twenties or early thirties who had evidently had their children when they were teenagers themselves. Indeed, Oliver's performance was one of the revelations of the production: a far cry from the usual comic turn, Oliver rarely tried for laughs, playing the Nurse as a glamorous and intelligent young woman, and invested the character with emotional realism. She sadly fingered the crucifix on her necklace upon the line 'Susan is with God',

and made the same gesture at moments of crisis throughout the play; in this production, Juliet was clearly a surrogate for the Nurse's own deceased daughter. This Nurse cared deeply for Juliet and clearly thought her too young to be married, joking about her forthcoming sexual encounters with uncertainty rather than the usual lustiness, and defended her fiercely from her angry father.

Kalinina's in-the-round staging gave the play a great deal of dynamism, as characters paced in large circles or chased each other around the periphery, while a raised platform in the middle provided a calm centre that was somehow outside of time. During the Capulets' ball, steampunk-costumed revellers danced energetically to a throbbing soundtrack, but fell suddenly into a frozen silence whenever characters occupied the central circle in order to converse: thus, for example, Romeo and Juliet's first meeting literally froze time. Later, Juliet stood serenely on her central balcony, while Paapa Essiedu's Romeo rotated quickly, almost hungrily, around her. The dynamic was not entirely without sinister undertones.

Like Hands's *Hamlet*, this production was remarkable for its speed. Its use of language, however, was very different. Where Hands had exploited the relentless pulse of the metre, this production largely ignored it, often altering lines (presumably in the interests either of running time or of avoiding anachronism) so that they no longer scanned as verse. Indeed, the cast largely played the dialogue with naturalistic cadences, repeating words and phrases or muttering ('Tybalt is ... Tybalt is dead'). As in Baz Luhrmann's film, Juliet woke up as Romeo was dying, her arms and legs starting to stir before he had even taken the poison. The Friar's intervention was thus cut in its entirety, reducing Juliet's moment of recognition to the slightly clunky 'Romeo! Romeo? Romeo ... What's here, closed in my true love's hand?', and she killed herself by cutting her own throat, truncating her dying lines to 'O happy dagger, let me die'. For me, this realist tendency pulled against both the heightened drama of Shakespeare's plot and the performance's own inventive staging, and threatened to veer into the melodrama of soap opera.

61. *Romeo and Juliet*, Shakespeare's Globe, touring, directed by Dominic Dromgoole and Tim Hoare. Whole company. Photograph by Helena Miscioscia.

There were no such risks in Dominic Dromgoole and Tim Hoare's touring production for Shakespeare's Globe (Illustration 61). Like Kalinina's, this production took its cue from Juliet's concern that the lovers' actions are 'too rash, too unadvised, too sudden', playing at a frenetic pace with much fast-talking and charging around, but where Kalinina's relied heavily on emotional realism, the Globe's was unstoppably playful. This was also a radical edit of the text in which scenes were intercut throughout, emphasizing the breakneck speed with which the events of the play transpire. The exchange between Lady Capulet, Juliet and the Nurse in 1.3 began well before Romeo and Benvolio's dialogue of 1.2 had finished, and Romeo's scene with Mercutio and Benvolio in turn started while 1.3 was ongoing, so that Mercutio and Romeo's conversation about love was intercut

with Lady Capulet and Juliet's. Morning broke on both Juliet and the Friar at once in 2.2 and 2.3, and the Nurse was still onstage with Romeo in 2.3 as Juliet complained, in her 2.4 soliloquy, that the Nurse was taking too long in her errand. Act 3, scene 1 started *before* 2.5, so that the scene in which Mercutio and Benvolio anticipate fighting with the Capulets was already underway as Romeo and Juliet were married. Naturally, Juliet's lament over Romeo's banishment (3.2) was intercut with Romeo's own (3.3); when the Nurse entered the latter scene, it became evident that she had only *just* 'come from Lady Juliet'. Such intercutting became less feasible following Romeo's departure to Mantua, of course, and the pace of the performance slowed considerably from this point on as a result.

Not only the young were guilty of over-haste in this production. Matt Doherty's Paris had taken his leave and was virtually offstage when Steven Elder's Capulet called him back with 'Sir Paris, I will make a desperate tender / Of my child's love'; so comic was the older man's evident impatience that 'Wednesday is too soon, / O' Thursday let it be' got a big laugh. This impulsiveness soon became terrifying: in his rage, just before his exit in 3.5, Capulet picked up a wooden stool as if to hit the cowering Juliet with it, to be stopped only by an intervention from the Nurse.

What made this production especially effective, though, was its theatrical playfulness. The actors were already onstage and in the yard as the audience entered, playing musical instruments and chatting (often flirtatiously) with the groundlings. This was not so much a 'pre-show' as it was a simple display of the actors as performers – an approach also evident in the fact that all eight cast members wore plain modern trousers and shirts throughout, donning semi-Elizabethan jerkins, doublets, gowns and dresses as the play demanded (all the actors aside from the two leads played multiple roles). Some costume changes took place in full view of the audience, Tom Kanji's Benvolio, for example, switching mid scene into Friar Laurence as Romeo threw a habit over his shoulders. Music was used liberally throughout, as were comic sequences of tightly choreographed movement.

In many respects, the production was more reminiscent of the riotous, celebratory performances of 2012's Globe to Globe festival than it was of the Globe's usual in-house fare. Like Grupo Galpão's *Romeu e Julieta*, for example, or the National Theatre of Greece's *Pericles*, the fact that this production had *not* been directed specifically for the Globe space paradoxically meant that it suited it all the better – the actors conspicuously inhabited the here and now of performance, being consistently interactive, responsive, inventive. Samuel Valentine's Romeo forged an easy confidentiality with the audience as he, and we, gazed up at Cassie Layton's Juliet on her balcony. The distance between the lovers over this scene included the audience physically in every enactment of emotional intimacy; Romeo descended into the yard, unkissed, as he observed to the surrounding spectators that 'Love goes toward love, as schoolboys from their books, / But love from love, toward school with heavy looks', before Juliet returned to the stage, and he rushed through the groundlings with schoolboyish urgency to finally claim his kiss. Like McIntyre's *As You Like It*, this production worked not as a realistic depiction of the heady thrills of love, but – almost – as a shared experience of them.

This year's tragedies were rounded off by Iqbal Khan's *Othello* for the RSC (Illustration 62). Khan's production reinvented Shakespeare's Venice as a modern, superficially equal-opportunities meritocracy, casting disabled actress Nadia Albina as its ruthlessly efficient Duke and making use of race-conscious casting in the roles not only of Othello (of course) but also of Iago, Emilia and Montano. The casting of black actor Lucian Msamati as Iago was deeply illuminating: his Zimbabwean-accented Iago was much more of an outsider in Venetian society than Hugh Quarshie's received-pronunciation Othello, and whereas Othello was clearly valued by Venice's military establishment, Iago had been overlooked for promotion and was frequently treated by others as though he were invisible. This Iago was happy to humour the racism of Roderigo and Brabantio in order to ingratiate himself, referring to Othello as 'the Moor' in an attempt to reverse the system of social exclusion and inclusion that had so far favoured his rival over him.

The presence of other black and ethnic minority cast members made it clear that this was set in a multicultural society, and as a result the racial tensions of the play became more nuanced, more interesting, and more topical than is usually the case. Iago's manipulation of Cassio in 2.3 began not with a rowdy drinking song, but with a quiet and dignified solo chant drawn from the character's African heritage: Jacob Fortune-Lloyd's white Cassio responded by mocking it, and then attempted to steal Iago's thunder by performing a rap. This clumsy appropriation of black culture led Cassio into a rap battle with the black soldier Montano (David Ajao), a contest won by the latter

62. *Othello*, 3.3, RSC, Royal Shakespeare Theatre, directed by Iqbal Khan. Hugh Quarshie as Othello and Lucian Msamati as Iago. Photograph by Keith Pattison.

when he mocked Cassio for 'taking orders from the Moor'. Cassio's violent response was clearly a result of his having lost status in this complicated, racially charged exchange.

Quarshie's Othello was a hardened military man, coolly issuing orders while his soldiers tortured a hooded prisoner. The soldiers left behind the drill with which they had threatened their prisoner, allowing Joanna Vanderham's Desdemona to pick it up and idly toy with it in the scene that followed: a metaphor, I think, for the way in which she plays with Othello's love for her, little realizing that the favour she is asking is awakening an aspect of his personality that she has not yet encountered. This hinted-at violence later erupted with terrifying force as Othello demanded 'the ocular proof' from Iago, pulling a plastic bag over his subordinate's head and threatening to suffocate him in what was presumably a well-practised tactic of 'aggressive interrogation' from his military

career. Iago's account of sleeping next to Cassio, so often awkwardly funny in performance, here had the ring of a story invented in the heat of the moment by a desperate man in fear for his life.

Msamati's Iago was alternately engaging and disturbing. At the end of 2.3, having begun his manipulation of Cassio, he turned to the audience with a charming shrug and said, 'What? What ...?' before beginning 'What's he then that says I play the villain?' The rapport with the audience established over the first half of this speech made his subsequent shift into an inexplicable hatred for Desdemona all the more alienating. It soon became clear that this Iago was deeply neurotic about sex, reacting with palpable discomfort whenever he made physical contact with Desdemona or with Ayesha Dharker's Emilia. The fact that the latter was played by an actor of Asian heritage lent another layer to the production's exploration of internalized racism: Iago consistently devalued and underestimated his wife, his blind spot for her reflecting Venetian society's similar treatment of him. This Iago was not an arch-manipulator in control of every detail, but an increasingly frantic improviser struggling to rein in the destructive forces he had unleashed, surprised and panicked by their intensity. When Othello fell into his trance, Iago's 'Work on, / My medicine, work!' was delivered by Msamati more as 'Work on … My medicine *works*!', changing it from an expression of masterful control to an exclamation of surprise.

The production's sustained exploration of the submerged – both social and psychological – was made manifest in its central visual symbol, a small rectangular pool in the centre of the stage. Iago and Roderigo's gondola floated unsteadily in it over the first scene; Othello's soldiers ducked the head of their prisoner into it; Othello himself hid in it, beneath a temporary platform, in order to overhear Cassio, Bianca and Iago. It seemed significant that Vanderham's calmly defiant Desdemona allowed her composure to falter only briefly during Act Four, as she dangled her feet in the water and heard an ominous knocking.

HISTORIES

Twenty fifteen gave me the opportunity to see nearly all of Shakespeare's history plays, albeit, in many cases, in heavily adapted form. First up was James Dacre's *King John*, which I saw at Shakespeare's Globe in June. The production had opened in London's Temple Church, and would subsequently tour to Salisbury Cathedral and the Church of the Holy Sepulchre, Northampton. These ecclesiastical settings were clearly invoked in Jonathan Fensom's design: virtually all the action took place on one of the four stretches of a large cruciform red carpet, one part of which stretched across the front of the Globe stage and the other part of which extended from the front of the tiring-house out into the yard, on a narrow stage extension. This left the Globe's upstage corners used only by a group of musicians in monastic habits.

The strict geometry of the acting space lent itself to highly schematized staging. The stage picture was frequently a perfectly balanced image of characters in contention or alliance with one another, echoing the play's sequences of symmetrical verbal sparring between paired opposites: John and King Philip, Eleanor and Constance, the Bastard and Austria, the Dauphin and Blanche. This also served to clarify the ever-shifting allegiances and enmities of the play: characters would literally cross the space to stand behind the figures with whom they were aligning. Choral music and sequences of ensemble movement throughout the play augmented a sense of the performance as a kind of ritual in itself.

Dacre's production seemed especially concerned with religious rituals and their sociopolitical effects, staging a succession of church ceremonies: John's coronation, the marriage between the Dauphin and Blanche, Pandulph's excommunication of John, and John's subsequent re-coronation. In the half-holy, half-profane setting of the Globe, however, it was clear that these were empty rituals, devoid of any moral absolutes, the means merely of legitimating or contesting power. Dacre's staging encouraged us to share the cynical perspective of Alex Waldmann's Bastard, who shouted many of his quips from the yard (the only character to stand amongst the spectators in this way), picked out groundlings to illustrate his examples ('now can I make any Joan a lady'), and stood, both onstage and off, enjoying the play's verbal and physical skirmishes as pure theatre. His frank admission of his materialistic motives ('Gain, be my lord, for I will worship thee') seemed somehow refreshingly honest in contrast with the other central characters' equivocatory attempts to invoke divine legitimation for their actions. Indeed, the audience was so acutely aware of this that John's double-dealing provoked a number of hearty laughs. 'O, this will make my mother die with grief!' lamented Arthur (Laurence Belcher) at the start of 3.3; 'So shall it be', replied Jo Stone-Fewings's John, in a punchline transposed from the scene's first line.

This cynicism took on a metatheatrical dimension as the two kings attempted to persuade the people of Angiers to back their claims, addressing a citizen who stood in a central gallery of the auditorium; it was as if they were attempting to convince the audience themselves. When the Bastard attempted to turn the kings against Angiers by pointing out that the audience were indeed behaving like an audience ('these scroyles of Angiers flout you, kings, / And stand securely on their battlements / As in a theatre, whence they gape and point / At your industrious scenes and acts of death'), he shifted the relationship between stage and audience into something more confrontational: having been cast as neutral observers of the play's political struggles, we were now temporarily antagonized by both sides.

The RSC's *The Famous Victories of Henry V* – a conflation of *Henry IV Parts 1* and *2* and *Henry V* aimed at 'younger audiences' – maintained a highly interactive metatheatrical frame, but found few opportunities for audience interaction within the Shakespearian text itself. Directed and adapted by Owen Horsley, *The Famous Victories* used episodes from all three plays to tell the coming-of-age story of the young Henry V (Martin Bassindale): *Part 1*'s early Falstaff scenes were quickly followed by Hal's meeting with the King and then the Battle of Shrewsbury, skittering from the last of the Boar's Head scenes to the thick of *Part 1*'s climactic battle in under five minutes. We were whisked straight from Shrewsbury to Henry IV's deathbed, and then to Hal's coronation and his rejection of Falstaff. The last section of the play gave us the edited highlights of *Henry V*, suffering something of a narrative drop: these scenes clearly belonged to a completely different story (there had been no mention of France until the dying Henry IV had instructed his son to 'busy giddy minds with French quarrels'), and the absence not only of Falstaff but also of Bardolph, Pistol and the rest of the Eastcheap gang obscured any sense of continuity with the previous scenes. Chorus passages from *Henry V* were adapted in order to apply to the earlier plays ('Now all the youth of England is on fire', for example, became a prologue to Shrewsbury), and Horsley made inventive use of a new pair of proletarian characters

called John and Derek, who resurfaced throughout the performance to report the latest news to each other using lines adapted from Shakespeare. These characters returned in the second half as the common soldiers with whom Henry V speaks on the eve of the Battle of Agincourt.

The show began with a long interactive sequence in which the cast of seven co-opted their young spectators into the game of putting on the show. Bassindale asked everyone to pose as a knight, and then as a 'lazy old knight who just drinks and eats all the time'; we were then cast as Falstaff's 'mad wags' and primed to answer 'How now, Sir John!' whenever actor Simon Yadoo addressed us as such. Another cast member gave us a lesson in miming archery, and then we were taught a drinking song: all of these set-ups, of course, got pay-offs later on in the performance. Some school groups had evidently been asked in advance to make particular props for the performance – a treasure chest, masks, maps and a crown – and these were collected by the actors during the pre-show sequence. The paper crown was passed along the line of actors as they gazed at it in awe, and then they launched into the Shakespearian text with the prologue from *Henry V*.

It was striking that the audience interaction then largely dried up as the cast played out the Falstaff scenes from the beginning of *Part 1*. Horsley was evidently comfortable with the rephrasing of lines for clarity – 'buckram', for example, being replaced with 'disguises' – but Yadoo's Falstaff was given little opportunity to interact with the audience outside the Shakespearian text, rendering the character oddly distant in comparison with the lively back-and-forth of the pre-show. The production really came to life whenever the cast played out some sort of gamelike action – hiding Falstaff, for example, or miming the swords and providing live sound effects during fight sequences (at one point, the children were encouraged to 'throw' Hal his mimed sword after he 'dropped' it). Concluding with another refrain of the drinking song that had opened the show, the performance illustrated that it was adept at inviting its young spectators to get involved, but that it had not, perhaps, responded as clearly as it might have done to the possibilities for audience interaction in the texts themselves. And what, I wondered, was the reformed Hal doing singing a drinking song?

The National Theatre of China's *Richard III*, which returned to Shakespeare's Globe in July following its visit to the 2012 Globe to Globe festival, formed an intriguing companion piece to Tang Shu-wing's *Macbeth* (discussed above). Where the latter gave us a Richard-like Macbeth whose contorted physique embodied his black and deep desires, Wang Xiaodong's Mandarin-language *Richard III* borrowed heavily from *Macbeth* (Illustration 63). As Zhang Hao's Richard turned round to deliver his first soliloquy (here repositioned so that it interrupted an opening speech by King Edward), he struck a pose reminiscent of Macbeth seeing the dagger; before long, three witches had entered the stage and made the prophecy 'that "G" / Of Edward's heirs the murderer shall be', each at once a chappy finger laying upon her skinny lips.

Richard's deformity was visible only during his soliloquies. During these speeches, he mimed a withered arm and a hunched back, limping on tiptoe; at all other times he was straight-backed, athletic and sinuous. This conceit seemed to suggest that his deformity was a hidden identity, psychological rather than physical. With no knowledge of Mandarin, I was unable to tell from the Globe's stageside scene descriptions whether or not the other characters' references to his disability had been cut, but the surtitles did make it clear that he considered himself 'deformed', and his disability certainly started to become visible to other characters towards the end.

Inventive use of a wide variety of performance disciplines lifted the narrative into a heightened register. As in all three of this year's *Macbeth*s, an onstage musician (Wang Jianan) used percussion to pinpoint each moment of reversal or recognition. Zhang Xin's scenes of lamentation as Lady Anne were sung in the style of Chinese opera, breaking down into speech as Richard wore her down. The production made extensive use of Cai

Jingchao and Zhang Zhiyong, a pair of acrobatic clowns who played nearly all of the anonymous murderers, guards and messengers, and even combined to play a two-headed Tyrell, one crouching down in front of the other. The murderers were tumblers, somersaulting on to the stage for their first appearance; they entered the scene in which they murder Clarence in comic 'darkness', groping around and stumbling over each other, both equally fearful and reluctant to commit the murder. After killing the princes, each wore a single red glove, which they took off and gave to Richard, who then wore both (in a visual echo of Macbeth's bloodstained hands) for the rest of the play.

Prophecy was central to the production, casting Richard more as a tragic puppet of fate than as the author of his own destiny. Queen Margaret, so often excised completely, had her role expanded here: she returned to the central balcony upon each major death (Clarence, Edward, Hastings, Anne, the princes and Buckingham) to repeat the part of her curse that had just been fulfilled, while a bloodstain spilled down one of the six white vertical banners beneath her. She Nannan's Margaret was blind, angry and ancient, sweeping her staff dangerously around the space in order to disperse the other figures onstage: part Tiresias, part Fury, she was a figure from Greek tragedy. Margaret was joined by Lady Anne and Queen Elizabeth in donning the cloaks and masks of the witches at the end of 4.4, and all three remained onstage while the clowns' reports of various betrayals and invasions heralded the start of Richard's downfall. The production added a scene in which Richard met the witches again on the eve of battle, and they predicted his demise. Margaret, of course, returned to repeat her curse on Richard as his defeat became inevitable, and black ink spilled down all six banners; another glut of red was added as he was finally killed (not just by Richmond but by the entire company). Richard seemed to be reaching up for something as he died, in an echo of his opening pose. As Richmond was crowned, Margaret's ghostly voice could be heard once again, predicting another usurpation; the narrative thus became

63. *Richard III*, National Theatre of China, Shakespeare's Globe, directed by Wang Xiaodong. Zhang Hao as Richard III.

a classically tragic vision of autocratic power as an endless cycle of ambition, bloodshed and defeat, rather than the redemptive Tudor propaganda of Shakespeare's play.

If the two Chinese productions hosted by the Globe invited comparison, so did the Globe's own *King John* and *Richard II* (Illustration 64). Indeed, the two were advertised on the same flyer, similarly framed photographs of Jo Stone-Fewings' John and Charles Edwards' Richard sharing equal space. Both productions started with a non-Shakespearian coronation scene, and

424

64. *Richard II*, 4.1, Shakespeare's Globe, directed by Simon Godwin. Charles Edwards as Richard II and David Sturzaker as Bolingbroke. Photograph by Johan Persson.

both incorporated the same mortality-defying benediction from the *First Book of Kings*: 'God save the King! Long live the King! May the King live for ever!' The scene that opened Simon Godwin's production showed a child-Richard carrying a toy horse to his coronation; he promised (using the words of Edward II's real-life coronation oath) to uphold peace and justice and, as soon as he was crowned, audience members in the upper gallery let loose handfuls of golden confetti. These golden flakes continued to flutter around in the air for much of the scene that followed, like snow in a snow globe: a neat image of the gilded fragility of Richard's subsequent reign.

Like the aristocracy of Dacre's *King John*, Richard and his supporters were initially characterized as decadent and selfish. As in the 2013 RSC production by Gregory Doran, Richard spent most of the play in full-length white gowns. His self-satisfied favourites wore rich colours, taking unashamed pleasure in Bolingbroke's humiliation and laughing sycophantically at Richard's jokes. When news of Gaunt's death was delivered, Richard's opportunism was so unfeeling as to be comic: 'So much for that,' he said offhandedly, swilling a cup of wine. No sooner had he issued instructions for Gaunt's valuables to be seized than Bushy, Green and others began to collect the golden goblets that the assembled party were drinking from; one even started to pick up a small table. When York (William Chubb) objected, Richard petulantly grabbed the cup from his uncle's hand himself.

Bolingbroke's followers were men's men, macho, angry and resentful (there was a hint of homophobia in Northumberland's description of the King as 'degenerate'). In David Sturzaker's performance, however, Bolingbroke himself was upright and charismatic, full of righteous anger. There was no menace in his meeting with York, meaning that his uncle's capitulation to him was a result of his impassioned persuasion rather than realpolitik. Even Bolingbroke's invective against the bound and beaten Bushy and Green seemed founded upon an unshakeable belief that he was in the right. There was little sense, as he took the King captive, that this Bolingbroke knew his performance of loyalty to Richard's crown was a sham: he had managed to convince himself he was acting honourably. I found it hard to tell whether the production was attempting a problematic whitewashing of Bolingbroke here (Richard's conduct at John of Gaunt's death had, after all, been inexcusable), or whether it was a chilling demonstration of the dangerously unstoppable energies that self-righteousness can unleash. Both Richard and Bolingbroke are equally prone to self-deception in the interests of legitimizing their self-interest, but this production encouraged us to laugh at it only in Richard. It was not until the deposition scene that the parallels between the two men started to emerge: Bolingbroke seemed reluctant as Richard stage-managed him into participating in an image of their equivalence ('On this side my hand, and on that side thine'), and later, as Richard pondered his reflection, he turned the glass towards Bolingbroke, illogically suggesting that Bolingbroke too would see Richard's reflection there. Whether this was indicative of Richard's all-consuming self-centredness or a subversive hint that Bolingbroke was not so very unlike the man he was deposing was unclear: perhaps it worked as both.

Paul Wills's set gave the Globe stage an additional thrust that extended into the yard; the small gap between the extension and the main stage was just wide enough for a line of groundlings to stand in, and the production made frequent and inventive use of the heads of these spectators.

Bolingbroke seemed to be bidding farewell to the audience as he bade farewell to 'England's ground' in the first act, and Richard likewise cupped and patted the heads of groundlings upon his return in the third ('So weeping, smiling, greet I thee, my earth, / And do thee favours with my royal hands'); where Bolingbroke had treated these spectators with 'humble and familiar courtesy', Richard seemed patronizing and comically out of touch. A little later, though, Richard's 'For God's sake let us sit upon the ground' became a moment of humility and connection to his surroundings. On his admission 'I live with bread like you, feel want, / Taste grief, need friends', he tenderly reached out to the nearest groundling. To my ear, the audience laughter here sounded sympathetic for the first time, rather than scornful as it had been earlier in the scene.

This subtle shift in the production's subject positioning had its payoff at the end, when the dirty and mistreated Richard was visited in prison by his former groom (Angus Imrie, the same young actor who had played Bagot). Flashes of Richard's arrogance returned as he railed against his horse's pride before the groom suddenly held up the toy horse that the child Richard had carried to his coronation. 'Forgiveness, horse!' thus became Richard's reaction to a reminder of his coronation oaths – and a recognition of his failure to fulfil them. Like Doran's 2013 version and the BBC's 2012 adaptation for *The Hollow Crown*, this production rewrote the final act as a Judas narrative in which Richard met his death at the hands of his closest friend Aumerle (Graham Butler), here aiding rather than completely replacing Exton (Richard Katz). Exton instructed Aumerle to take Richard's body to King Henry, making rather a puzzle of his own involvement – why had he organized Richard's murder if he has no desire to take the credit? The only answer I could come up with was that he was following secret orders and manipulating Aumerle – an ambivalence that was borne out in the final scene as Sturzaker's inscrutable Henry made a display of his guilty feelings in a way that did not quite have the ring of truth about it. I left the theatre energized and ambivalent

65. *Henry V*, RSC, Royal Shakespeare Theatre, directed by Gregory Doran. Alex Hassell as Henry V, with company. Photograph by Keith Pattison.

myself, unsure of the steer the production had been attempting to give me, and excited about the ambiguity.

In what was rapidly becoming the keynote of 2015's history plays, Gregory Doran's *Henry V* in Stratford (Illustration 65) also made the audience one of its central images. Spectators in the centre stalls were lit throughout the play, once again allowing a small section of the audience to stand in as a synecdoche for the whole. This gave Alex Hassell's Henry a visible crowd to address during his scenes of oration. He rushed alone on to the stage at the start of Act 3 and delivered 'Once more unto the breach' unambiguously to us, seemingly frustrated that we would not (indeed *could* not) follow him on to the stage. He physically demonstrated how he expected us to 'Stiffen the sinews' and to 'set the teeth and stretch the nostril wide', and assured us that he saw 'noble lustre' in our eyes. Was he sincere, or was he working us? Fortunately,

perhaps, we lost our temporary roles as members of his army at the end of the speech, when a group of actors charged from the back of the auditorium to cry 'God for Harry, England, and Saint George!' and resume the attack on Harfleur.

As in Dacre's *King John*, the audience was also put at the receiving end of violent rhetoric. In 3.3, we became the citizens of Harfleur, allowing for one of the production's most interesting effects: now we were given a Henry who was addressing *us* as his enemies, threatening *us* with rape and murder and, if we had been seduced by his rhetoric in 3.1, we were now asked to imagine ourselves as the victims of that same persuasive act of speech. By the next time we were cast as Henry's soldiers, our role was more complex: 'We would have all such offenders so cut off,' he announced in 3.6 in response to Bardolph's execution, glaring round at us as if not only issuing an order but daring us to judge him. Hassell's St Crispin's Day speech,

427

addressed directly to us from the top of a cart, was spine-tinglingly rousing, and it illustrated once again the dangerously self-forgetful power of beautiful speech: minutes later, he would shout 'Then every soldier kill his prisoners' in rage, the terror of the hooded onstage figures bringing home the horrible reality of this order. Interestingly, Hassell eschewed direct address in the one speech that might typically demand it, Henry's soliloquy in 4.1, which he played much more inwardly than his earlier addresses to the audience might have suggested. Spectators were cast in actual fictional roles in this production rather than as extradiegetic confidantes.

Like most productions of *Henry V*, this was a performance that was self-conscious about its own theatricality. Before the start, the bare back wall of the stage was on display, behind an exposed lighting rig and some artfully arranged props and set dressing: this was 'backstage'. In front of all this was the throne, familiar from the previous three instalments in Doran's tetralogy (and all four publicity images), upon which rested the crown. Oliver Ford Davies wandered on in a blue cardigan and red scarf, casually fingering the crown while the house lights were still up; Hassell strode on, snatched the crown from him, and shared a glance of annoyance with the audience before exiting. Davies's Chorus then addressed us as if he were already impatient with our collective inability to imagine the historical world he wished to invoke. He veered between absent-minded enthusiasm and a slightly patronizing air of tolerant explanation throughout the play. Act 2's prologue was repositioned to introduce an adaptation of 2.2, in which the conspirators entered behind the Chorus when they were named, ready to start the scene. As their attempts to begin their dialogue were repeatedly blocked by the increasingly tetchy Davies, still in full flow, it became impossible to read these stage figures as anything other than frustrated actors – the implication being that these were not fully motivated human beings but rhetorical constructions, crafted by the shifting iterations of history into mere signifiers in a story of valiant kingliness. Almost the whole cast told Davies to

'shog off' when he repeatedly insisted on apologizing for their presentation of Agincourt during Act 4: history here was not the monologic narrative that Davies's lecturer-like Chorus wanted to impart to us, but rather a process of collaborative storytelling that was multivocal, contested and ambiguous.

London audiences will be able to see this production alongside Doran's *Richard II* and *Henry IV* plays over the winter of 2015/16, and all four have been filmed for DVD. Certain moments were clearly designed with sequential viewing in mind. In the final scene, Burgundy's long speech advocating peace was reassigned to Jane Lapotaire's Queen Isobel, an as yet unseen character, which allowed this actor to bookend the tetralogy: from her impassioned speech as the Duchess of Gloucester urging revenge at the start of *Richard II*, to its opposite now. The *Henry IV* plays, meanwhile, were evoked not only in the further development of Hassell's youthful and impulsive Henry, but also in the twilight melancholy of the scenes featuring the Eastcheap characters – notably 2.3, when Sarah Parks's Mistress Quickly seemed suddenly full of doubt and fear as she listened to the echoing song of the menfolk marching off to war. I have to admit to losing patience with 3.2, however: as so often, Jamy was a one-joke character with a hilariously incomprehensible Scottish accent, while the Irish MacMorris was a mad pyromaniac with cartoonish bombs strapped to his torso. For me, these lazy stereotypes worked against an otherwise brilliantly nuanced production.

My reviewing year concluded with Trevor Nunn's revival of *The Wars of the Roses* at Kingston's Rose Theatre. John Barton and Peter Hall's 1963 adaptations turn *Henry VI Parts 1, 2* and *3* and *Richard III* into three plays, titled *Henry VI*, *Edward IV* and *Richard III* respectively. It was exciting to have the chance to see these adaptations in the theatre, and the experience of watching them over a single day was oddly reminiscent (I'm outing myself here) of binge-watching *Game of Thrones*, the popular historical fantasy television series liberally name-checked in the publicity and programme (even John Napier and Mark Friend's set seemed to be inviting the comparison, its centrepiece throne topped with the hilts of three swords). The Barton/Hall productions were of course adapted for television in 1965, so perhaps it should be no surprise that each half of each play functions as a self-contained episode in a longer saga.

The first play, *Henry VI*, worked well. Its dominant characteristic was its series of one-off soliloquies at the ends of scenes in which successive characters (Winchester, Suffolk, York, Hume and many others) confided their Machiavellian plans to the audience – a device that Shakespeare spreads throughout the first two parts of *Henry VI*, but that was confined mostly to the first play here. The cumulative effect of these gave the impression of a kingdom in which almost everyone is a self-serving equivocator, and lent a kind of ironic detachment to the interleaving scenes of political manoeuvring. Whilst its first half covered the majority of Shakespeare's *Part 1* (we heard Joan of Arc burning to death as the interval began), its second half told the story of the self-destruction of the king's council from *Part 2* and climaxed in Gloucester, Suffolk and Winchester's deaths.

Edward IV was less focused in its dramatic structure. It opened with a tableau of Henry, Margaret and their young son (played in the first half by a child actor), the existence of the latter indicating clearly that several years had passed since the events of the previous play. The Jack Cade plot was dispatched within about half an hour in order to focus on York's rebellion. In a second neat illustration of the passing of time, York's eldest three sons appeared on a balcony as playing children before they descended the stairs as adults; the fact that the young men were still playing with each other set up both Kåre Conradi's Edward and Michael Xavier's George as boyish and impulsive (an impression borne out by their respective marriage choices), and provided a nice introduction to Robert Sheehan's disarmingly likeable Richard. Rutland, York and the Cliffords were all dead by the interval, and the second half focused on the after-effects of Edward's marriage with Lady Grey.

The focus narrowed to Richard over the course of the day. By the conclusion of the second play, the adaptation had caught up with the end of *Henry VI Part 3*, and the last instalment was a relatively uncomplicated *Richard III*. There were great narrative advantages to be had in presenting it at the end of a full day of the *Henry VI* plays: firstly, we already had a relationship with Richard, and Sheehan easily made the audience laugh during the opening soliloquy and subsequent scenes. Spectators who had seen the previous plays would have understood the complicated tensions between the King, the Queen and Clarence; Clarence's guilty conscience thus made more sense, as did Edward's reputation as a libertine (*Edward IV* had shown him being surprised in his tent with a lover). Richard's recollection of Henry's conversation with the young Richmond became a recollection for the audience too, because we had witnessed it. At the climax, the ghosts of Henry and Prince Edward linked the sequence to the earlier plays. Most importantly, Joely Richardson's Margaret was not just a mad figure from *Richard III*'s murky back story, but a woman with whom we had spent the day: her name, when invoked by characters as they met their dooms, actually meant something beyond her ability to prophesy. Even the usually impenetrable 'I had an Edward, till a Richard killed him' exchange stood a chance of making sense in this context.

The three plays contained numerous foreshadowings and echoes of each other. When Margaret snatched a letter meant for Henry during the second play, she was re-enacting a moment in which Andrew Woodall's Gloucester had done the same during the first. The final play's opening tableau of King Edward and Queen Elizabeth put them on the same balcony that Henry and Margaret had occupied at the start of the second; when Alexander Hanson's Buckingham held Richard's hand as the latter mounted the throne, it recalled a similar moment earlier in the day when the same actor's York had been helped to the throne by Timothy Walker's Warwick. For all of these moments of patterning, though, the production missed a trick in failing to use doubling more symmetrically: with the actors of two of York's sons doubling as the Dauphin and Alençon, for example, it might have been sensible to cast the third as Reignier; doubling Young Talbot with the Son Who has Killed his Father also seems to cry out for a Talbot who doubles with the Father Who has Killed his Son (admittedly these were both done a few years ago in Michael Boyd's RSC productions).

Alex Waldmann's performance as Henry continued the metatheatrical trend in Shakespeare's histories this year (including Waldmann's own performance in the Globe's *King John*, discussed above). His Henry was very much an apprentice king, nervously adjusting his crown and making constant glances at Gloucester as if seeking affirmation from his mentor. His performance of kingship was unpractised: he sat cross-legged in his throne and, at one point, walked off without his sceptre before returning sheepishly to collect it. He seemed aware that 'King' was a theatrical role he was not quite pulling off yet, stepping in and out of it as though he were an enthusiastic novice actor alternately pleased and frustrated by his progress in the part. This aspect of the production was foregrounded in a Barton-scripted exchange between the King and Gloucester:

KING. *(to Gloucester)*
    Young though I am, my lord, the time is come
    That I must choose and act for mine own self.
    If I am King, then I must act the King.

GLOUCESTER. *(aside, to audience laughter)*   I would thou couldst . . .

Henry's 'bookish rule' was symbolized by the Bible that he carried around for most of the first two plays. He pretended to be reading it in order to avoid having to deal with the squabble between Vernon and Basset in the first play; Margaret threw it to the ground in anger at the start of the second, following which he picked it up carefully and kissed it. He had it with him at his death, when he wore a white tunic and Richard a black one; after Richard stabbed him, he clutched the crucifix that hung around his neck and kissed his murderer on the forehead. Richard was clutching the Bible

as he delivered his line 'I am myself alone', making the heresy of the character's individualism clear.

Sheehan's Richard was also self-consciously theatrical. He had a tendency to deliver his lines ironically, as if he were quoting something vaguely silly: *he* did not see himself as 'Deformed, unfinished, sent before my time / Into this breathing world', but he knew that *others* did. He had an infectious enjoyment of words, pausing on 'leave the world for me to . . . *bustle* in' as if carefully selecting the right verb. If this Richard had learned anything from the first two plays, it was that power is theatrical – and Sheehan's Richard loved performing. He shared the prospect of 'inductions dangerous' with us as if it were the most exciting thing in the world and, after having wept real tears during his seduction of Lady Anne, puffed with mock exertion. As the character's soliloquies petered out, however, Sheehan's connection with the audience waned and, towards the end, where some actors start to hint at the King's buried conscience, he gave us little more than a snarling, rasping tyrant. The arrival of Laurence Spellman's softly-spoken Richmond came as something of a relief after Sheehan's abrasive shouting; in an echo of Henry (and, more cynically, of Richard at Baynard's Castle), Richmond carried a Bible during the play's concluding moments.

It is tempting to conclude this article by attempting to pick out the key themes of Shakespearian performance in England (and Wales) in 2015, though of course it is likely that such a list will say more about my own viewing habits than anything else. Nonetheless, I found myself struck by the number of productions that staged some kind of battle between the forces of desire and restraint, or that employed metatheatrical game-playing in order to reflect on the performance of gender, power or identity. Fast-paced productions seemed especially dominant: 2015 was a year for protagonists who thought and acted too quickly. I saw a number of radical edits, and nearly all the productions discussed here interpolated non-Shakespearian lines or speeches – sometimes these were self-advertising, as in the Arcola's *Dream*, while others, like Barton's pastiche Shakespeare in *The Wars of the*

Roses, were virtually imperceptible. Christian iconography was used frequently (in Munby's *Merchant*, both *Lears*, Dacre's *King John*, and the cathedral-like sets of Khan and Doran's RSC productions), and often confusingly. Most of the productions I saw this year were interested in the psychologies of their central characters, but these were just as often represented non-naturalistically (Cheek by Jowl's ensemble movement, Ninagawa's colour-coded lighting, Filter's soundscapes, Khan's hidden pool) as they were by actors performing in a realist idiom. Several productions featured successful examples of both: Sally Oliver's Nurse, John Mackay's Lucio and Lucian Msamati's Iago, for example, reinvented Shakespeare's characters in nuanced psychological portraits within productions with strongly symbolic dimensions.

It became clear this year that – for now, at least – Shakespeare's Globe has eclipsed the RSC as the most prolific producer of Shakespeare in England. The influence of the Globe was clear artistically, too: the tendency not only to address the audience directly but also to cast them in some sort of dramatic role was evident not just in all of the Globe's own shows, but also in Findlay's *Merchant* and Doran's *Henry V* at the RSC. Others were more interested in *representing* their audiences, and several companies (notably the Arcola Queer Collective and Tara Arts) made particular efforts to stage the experiences of minority groups. Most productions made use of race-blind casting, though the casting of Khan's *Othello* was productively race-aware. Trevor Nunn's *Wars of the Roses*, however, gained media attention for all the wrong reasons when the director misguidedly attempted to defend its all-white cast on the grounds of 'historical verisimilitude'. Perhaps he should have kept quiet: the all-white casts of several other productions passed without comment. Whilst numerous productions adapted the Shakespearian texts to turn male characters into women, meanwhile, gender-blind casting remains unusual and confined largely to small supporting roles.

A majority of the productions I saw employed either in-the-round or thrust staging – those by the RSC and the Globe exclusively so (though not, in the case of the latter, without occasional sightline problems). There was a fairly even split between productions in modern dress (a term I use here to mean twentieth- or twenty-first century costume) and those in costumes from earlier historical periods – although the distinction is fairly arbitrary, since numerous productions (McIntyre's *As You Like It*, Tang Shu-wing's *Macbeth*, Dromgoole and Hoare's *Romeo and Juliet*, Doran's *Henry V*) featured a deliberately anachronistic mix. In a period in which the mainstream of British theatrical production is increasingly defined by its re-mediation (all the main-house Globe and RSC productions, Donnellan's *Measure for Measure* and Turner's *Hamlet* were filmed for broadcast to remote audiences), numerous unbroadcast productions brought media technologies into the performances themselves (Goold's stageside screens, Hill-Gibbins's roving camera, Filter's live sound effects). It was ironic that Turner's *Hamlet*, a production that hit the headlines when its star made a plea for his fans to put away their camera-phones, made use of such emphatically filmic devices as the freeze-frame and slow-motion – and, with its opulent and detailed aesthetic, was clearly designed with its international broadcast in mind. It will be interesting to see whether these trends continue in 2016.

PROFESSIONAL SHAKESPEARE PRODUCTIONS IN THE BRITISH ISLES, JANUARY–DECEMBER 2014

JAMES SHAW

Most of the productions listed are by professional companies, but some amateur productions are included. The information is taken from *Touchstone* (www.touchstone.bham.ac.uk), a Shakespeare resource maintained by the Shakespeare Institute Library. Touchstone includes a monthly list of current and forthcoming UK Shakespeare productions from listings information. The websites provided for theatre companies were accurate at the time of going to press.

ALL'S WELL THAT ENDS WELL

Arpana Company. Shakespeare's Globe, London, 5–10 May.
www.shakespearesglobe.com
Director: Sunil Shanbag
Performed in Gujarati – part of Globe to Globe.

York Shakespeare Project. The Frigate Theatre, York, 27–30 November.
www.yorkshakespeareproject.org
Director: Maurice Crichton

ANTONY AND CLEOPATRA

Shakespeare's Globe Theatre. Globe Theatre, London, 29 May–24 August.
www.shakespearesglobe.com
Director: Jonathan Munby
Cleopatra: Eve Best
Antony: Clive Wood
Enobarbus: Phil Daniels

Adaptation

Eric and Cleopatra
David Graham Productions. New Vic Theatre, 18–23 August.
Loose parody of historical plot with a sixties soundtrack.

AS YOU LIKE IT

Shakespeare at the Tobacco Factory. The Tobacco Factory, Bristol, 13 February–2 May and tour to 21 June.
www.sattf.org.uk
Director: Andrew Hilton

Maddermarket Theatre Company. Maddermarket Theatre, Norwich, 27 March–5 April.
www.maddermarket.co.uk
Director: Chris Bealey
Rosalind: Laura Landamore

Stamford Shakespeare Festival. Rutland Open Air Theatre, Tolethorpe Hall, Little Casterton, 10 June–16 August.
www.stamfordshakespeare.co.uk

Taking Flight Theatre Company. Cyfartha Castle Grounds, Merthyr Tydfill, 12–21 June and tour to 19 July.
www.takingflighttheatre.co.uk
Director: Elise Davison
Production involving disabled actors.

Stafford Gatehouse Theatre. Ludlow Shakespeare Festival, Ludlow Castle, Shropshire, 14–22 June.
www.staffordgatehousetheatre.co.uk
Director: Peter Rowe

Oxford Shakespeare Company. Wadham College
Gardens, Oxford, 30 June–15 August.
www.oxfordshakespearecompany.co.uk
Director: Michael Oakley

Peter Huntley Productions. Southwark Playhouse
London, 22 September–18 October.
http://southwarkplayhouse.co.uk
Director: Derek Bond

THE COMEDY OF ERRORS

Propeller Theatre. Lyceum Theatre, Sheffield,
1 January–21 June.
http://propeller.org.uk
Director: Edward Hall
All-male company.

Rumpus Theatre Company. Greenwich Theatre,
London, 21–25 January.
www.rumpustheatrecompany.co.uk
Director: John Goodrum

The Merely Players. Cockpit Theatre, London,
15 March and 20 April.
www.thecockpit.org.uk/shakespeare
Director: Scott Ellis

Bard in the Botanics. Botanic Gardens, Glasgow,
27 June–12 July.
http://bardinthebotanics.co.uk
Director: Gordon Barr

Festival Players Theatre Company. Whittington Castle,
Whittington, 31 May and tour to 31 August.
www.thefestivalplayers.co.uk
Director: Michael Dyer

The Handlebards. Glastonbury Abbey, Glastonbury,
2 June and tour to 10 August.
www.peculius.com
Four actors cycling UK tour.

GB Theatre Company. Reading School, Berkshire,
6 July and UK tour to 23 August.
www.gbtheatrecompany.com
Director: Ed Viney

Groundlings Theatre Company. Groundlings Theatre,
Portsea, Hampshire, 10–12 July; Rose Playhouse,
London, 16–27 July.
Director: Richard Stride

Theatre by the Lake. Theatre by the Lake, Keswick,
26 July–8 November.

www.theatrebythelake.com
Director: Ian Forrest

Shakespeare's Globe Theatre. Globe Theatre, London,
30 August–12 October.
www.shakespearesglobe.com
Director: Blanche McIntyre

St James Theatre. St James Theatre, London, 15–19
September.
www.stjamestheatre.co.uk/events/comedy-of-errors

CORIOLANUS

Donmar Warehouse, London, 6 December–8
February 2014. Broadcast live in cinemas around the
world as part of National Theatre Live, beginning
30 January.
www.donmarwarehouse.com
Director: Josie Rourke
Coriolanus: Tom Hiddleston
Volumnia: Deborah Findlay
Menenius: Mark Gatiss

Lazarus Theatre Company. Tristan Bates Theatre,
London, 18 August–6 September.
http://lazarustheatrecompany.webs.com
Director: Ricky Dukes

HAMLET

The Faction. New Diorama Theatre, London,
4 January–22 February; Greenwich Theatre, London,
26–28 February.
www.thefaction.org.uk
Director: Mark Leipacher
Voice of Ghost: Simon Russell Beale

Hamlet Globe to Globe
Shakespeare's Globe. Middle Temple Hall, London,
18–20 April; Globe Theatre, Bankside, London,
23–26 April and international tour to 2016.
www.shakespearesglobe.com
Directors: Dominic Dromgoole and Bill Buckhurst

Hamlet: Ladi Emeruwa and Nadeem Hayat
Small-scale production claiming to visit all 205 nations
on Earth.

Hiraeth Artistic Productions. Riverside Studios,
London, 28 May–22 June.
Director: Zoe Ford
Hamlet: Adam Lawrence

Wilderness of Tigers. Bard in the Botanics. Botanic Gardens, Glasgow, 3–12 July.
www.wildernessoftigers.com
Director: Alasdair Hunter

Butterfly Theatre. Redcliffe Caves, Bristol, 21–26 July.
http://wearebutterfly.com
Part of Bristol Shakespeare Festival.

Cog & Sprocket Productions. SpaceCabaret @54 (Venue 54), Edinburgh, 11–16 August.
Adaptor and Director: Jo Marsh

Royal Exchange Theatre Company. Royal Exchange Theatre, Manchester, 16 September–25 October.
www.royalexchange.co.uk
Director: Sarah Frankcorn
Hamlet: Maxine Peake

Citizens Theatre Company. Citizens Theatre, Glasgow, 24 September–11 October.
www.citz.co.uk
Director: Dominic Hill
Hamlet: Brian Ferguson

Watermill Theatre. Watermill Theatre, Newbury, 13–17 October.
www.watermill.org.uk
Adaptor: Beth Flintoff
Director: Justin Audibert
75-minute version for three actors.

ACS Random. Park Theatre, London, 2–14 December.
www.acsrandom.co.uk
Director: Andrew Shepherd

Adaptation

Bard Heads
Finding the Will. Artrix Studio, Bromsgrove, Birmingham, 10 February.
www.findingthewill.com
Solo piece featuring interviews with Osric.

The Middle
Sick! Festival, BSMS Teaching Building, Brighton and Sussex Medical School, Brighton, East Sussex, 18 March 2013; and on tour through 2014.
http://michaelpinchbeck.co.uk
Director: Michael Pinchbeck

Courtyard Productions. Courtyard Theatre, London, 30 April–24 May.
www.thecourtyard.org.uk

Director: Rupert Holloway
First Quarto.

Ophelia
A Play, a Pie, and a Pint. Òran Mór, Glasgow, 30 June–5 July.
Director: Stewart Laing
Three-hander focusing on Ophelia, Polonius, Laertes and Hamlet plotlines.

Baron's Court Theatre, London, 28 January–2 February.
Adaptor: Nick Pelas

Blind Hamlet
Actors Touring Company. Assembly Roxy, Edinburgh, 31 July–25 August and tour to 9 October.
www.atctheatre.com
Playwright: Nassim Soleimanpour
Director: Ramin Gray
A writer's experience of going blind with only passing reference to Hamlet.

Actors
Underscore Theatre Company. Paradise in the Vault (Venue 29), Edinburgh, 12–17 August; 19–25 August.
Backstage, 30 minutes before the curtain rises on an amateur production of Hamlet.

Tragic (When My Mother Married My Uncle)
Subway Theatre Company. Cumbernauld Theatre, Cumbernauld, Glasgow, 25–27 September; and Scottish tour.
Director and Playwright: Iain Heggie
Comic retelling updating the action and language to the present day.

HENRY IV, PART I

Royal Shakespeare Company. The Royal Shakespeare Theatre, Stratford-upon-Avon, 15 April–6 September. Broadcast to cinemas worldwide as part of the RSC's Live from Stratford-upon-Avon, beginning 14 May; and on tour to January 2015.
www.rsc.org.uk
Director: Gregory Doran
Falstaff: Antony Sher
Henry IV: Jasper Britton
Prince Hal: Alex Hassell

Thrice Ninth Productions. The Rose Playhouse, Bankside, London, 29 July–9 August; St James Theatre, London, 29 September–3 October.
http://thriceninth.com

Director: Michael Yale
Performed by five actors in under 70 minutes.

Adaptation

Henry IV
Bard in the Botanics. Botanic Gardens, Glasgow,
19 July–2 August.
http://bardinthebotanics.co.uk
Director: Gordon Barr
Adaptation of *1* and *2 Henry IV*.

Henry IV
Donmar Warehouse, London, 3 October–29 November.
www.donmarwarehouse.com
Director: Phyllida Lloyd
King Henry: Harriet Walter
All-female production. Adaptation of *1* and *2 Henry IV*
with same female prison framing device as used in
Lloyd's 2012 all-female production of *Julius Caesar*.

HENRY IV, PART 2

Royal Shakespeare Company. Royal Shakespeare
Theatre, Stratford-upon-Avon, 15 April–6
September. Broadcast to cinemas worldwide as part of
the RSC's Live from Stratford-upon-Avon,
beginning 14 May; and on tour to January 2015.
www.rsc.org.uk
Director: Gregory Doran
Falstaff: Antony Sher
Henry IV: Jasper Britton
Mistress Quickly: Paola Dionisotti
Prince Hal: Alex Hassell

Adaptation

Henry IV
Bard in the Botanics. Botanic Gardens, Glasgow,
19 July–2 August.
http://bardinthebotanics.co.uk
Director: Gordon Barr
Adaptation of *1* and *2 Henry IV*.

Henry IV
Donmar Warehouse, London, 3 October–29
November.
www.donmarwarehouse.com
Director: Phyllida Lloyd
King Henry: Harriet Walter

All-female production. Adaptation of *1* and *2 Henry
IV* with same female prison-framing device as used
in Lloyd's 2012 all-female production of *Julius
Caesar*.

HENRY V

Michael Grandage Company. Noël Coward Theatre,
London, 3 December–15 February 2014.
www.michaelgrandagecompany.com
Henry V: Jude Law
Director: Michael Grandage

Guildford Shakespeare Company. Guildford Cathedral,
11–26 July.
www.guildford-shakespeare-company.co.uk
Director: Caroline Devlin

Groundlings Theatre Company. Groundlings Theatre,
Portsea, Hampshire, 13 July; The Rose Playhouse,
Bankside, London, 15–26 July; and on tour.
www.groundlings.co.uk
Director: Helen Oakleigh

Bard in the Botanics. Botanic Gardens, Glasgow,
18 July–2 August.
http://bardinthebotanics.co.uk
Director: Jennifer Dick

Adaptation

Pocket Henry V
Propeller Theatre Company. Bonnington Theatre,
Nottingham, 22 February and UK tour to April.
Director: Edward Hall
A 60-minute adaptation for young audiences. Played
with *Pocket Dream*.
Harry the King
Mingled Yarn. Zoo Southside (Venue 32), Edinburgh,
10–25 August.
60-minute adaptation performed by two female actors

JULIUS CAESAR

Shakespeare's Globe Theatre. Globe Theatre, Bankside,
London, 20 June–11 October.
www.shakespearesglobe.com
Director: Dominic Dromgoole
Brutus: Tom McKay
Julius Caesar: George Irving

11:11 Productions. CLF Arts Cafe, Bussey Building,
London, 7–25 October.
www.clfartcafe.org

Fluellen Theatre Company. Grand Theatre Arts Wing,
Swansea, 15–17 October.
www.fluellentheatre.co.uk

Proud Haddock Theatre. Chelsea Theatre, Inner
London, 3–15 November.
http://proudhaddock.com

KING JOHN

Hammerpuzzle. The Egg, Theatre Royal, Bath,
9 March.
www.hammerpuzzle.co.uk
60-minute version.

KING LEAR

National Theatre. Olivier Theatre, London,
23 January–28 May. Broadcast to cinemas around the
world by National Theatre Live, 1 May.
www.nationaltheatre.org.uk
Director: Sam Mendes
King Lear: Simon Russell Beale

Darker Purpose Theatre Company. The Cockpit,
London, 11–29 March.
Director: Lewis Reynolds
King Lear: David Ryall

Shakespeare's Globe Theatre. New Theatre Royal,
Portsmouth, 3–5 July; Globe Theatre, Bankside,
London, 6–23 August; and on tour.
www.shakespearesglobe.com
Director: Bill Buckurst
King Lear: Joseph Marcell

Adaptation

Lear
The Steam Industry. Union, London, 6–28 June.
www.philwillmott.org
Director: Phil Willmott
Queen Lear: Ursula Mohan

King Lear with Sheep
Sussex Ox at the Hay Barn, Jevington Place, East Sussex,
15–16 August; and on tour.

Director: Missouri Williams
King Lear: Suffolk Cross Sheep #1
Cordelia: Suffolk Cross Sheep #2
An adaptation with sheep.

Lear's Daughters
Footfall Theatre. Hope Theatre, Islington, 9–20
December.
www.thehopetheatre.com
Director: Isabelle Kettle
All-female company.

LOVE'S LABOUR'S LOST

Royal Shakespeare Company. Royal Shakespeare
Theatre, Stratford-upon-Avon, 23 September–14
March 2015. Broadcast live in cinemas throughout the
United States beginning 2 April 2015.
www.rsc.org.uk
Director: Christopher Luscombe
Rosaline: Michelle Terry
Berowne: Edward Bennett
Paired with *Much Ado About Nothing*, which was billed as
Love's Labour's Won.

Adaptation

Love's Labour's Lost . . . and Won
Progress Theatre Company. Caversham Court Gardens,
Caversham, 16–26 July.
www.progresstheatre.co.uk
The Nine Worthies replaced with a 20-minute play-
within-a-play, alternating between *The Taming of the
Shrew* or *Much Ado About Nothing*.

MACBETH

Bradford Playhouse, Bradford, 4–8 February.
www.thenewbradfordplayhouse.co.uk
Audience encouraged to keep mobile phones on to
receive social networking messages from the cast.

Blue Orange Theatre. Norden Farm, Maidenhead,
25 February and tour to 3 April.
www.blueorangetheatre.co.uk

Further Stages Theatre Company. Studio, New
Wimbledon Theatre, London, 1 March.
www.furtherstages.com
Director: Craig Ritchie

SHAKESPEARE PRODUCTIONS IN THE BRITISH ISLES 2014

Daniel Krupnick Productions. Bridge House Theatre, Penge, 26 March–19 April.
www.BHTheatre.co.uk
Director: Guy Retallack

Courtyard Productions. Courtyard Theatre, London, 6–23 May.
www.thecourtyard.org.uk
Director: June Abbott

Festival Players Theatre Company. Kington and Dormston Village Hall, 15 May; and UK tour summer 2014.
www.thefestivalplayers.co.uk
Director: Michael Dyer

The Handlebards. Larmer Tree Gardens, Salisbury, 1 June and tour to 9 August.
www.peculius.com
Four actors on a cycling UK tour.

Illyria Theatre Company. Hawth Amphitheatre, Crawley, 13 June and tour to 24 August.
www.illyria.uk.com

RIFT. Balfron Tower, Poplar, London, 4 July–16 August.
Director: Felix Mortimer
http://macbeth.in/collections/macbeth
Performed overnight from 8 p.m. until 8 a.m., including overnight accommodation.

Chester Performs. Grosvenor Park Open Theatre, Chester, 4 July–23 August.
Director: Alex Chifton

GB Theatre Company. Reading School, Reading, Berkshire, 7 July; Bristol Shakespeare Festival, Brandon Hill Park Playground, Bristol, 12–13 July; and UK tour to 22 August.
Director: Ed Viney

Creation Theatre. The Gardens at Lady Margaret Hall, Oxford, 1 August–13 September.
www.creationtheatre.co.uk

Heartbreak Productions. Wimpole Estate, 1 August and tour to 6 September.
www.heartbreakproductions.co.uk

Filter and Tobacco Factory Theatre Companies. Tobacco Factory, Bristol, 3–20 September.
www.tobaccofactorytheatres.com

Mercury Theatre Company. Mercury Theatre, Colchester, 2–18 October.

www.mercurytheatre.co.uk
Director: Daniel Buckroyd

Macbeth – in pitch black.
London Contemporary Theatre (in association with South Hill Park Arts Centre). St George's Theatre, Great Yarmouth, 1 November.
Performed in the dark.

Omnibus Theatre. Clapham Common, London, 11–29 November.
www.omnibus-clapham.org
Director: Gemma Kerr
Lady Macbeth: Jennifer Jackson
Macbeth: Gregory Finnegan
Promenade performance.

Ballet

Mac/Beth
De Oscuro. Clywd Theatre Cymru, Mold, 3–4 December.
Composer: Conor Linehan

Opera

Opera North. Leeds Grand Theatre, Leeds, 7–22 February and tour to 20 March.
www.operanorth.co.uk
Composer: Giuseppe Verdi

Northern Ireland Opera. Grand Opera House, Belfast, 21–3 February.
www.niopera.com
Director: Oliver Mears
Composer: Giuseppe Verdi

Scottish Opera. Citizen's Theatre, Glasgow, 22–29 March and tour 25 September–1 November.
www.scottishopera.org.uk
Director: Dominic Hill
Composer: Giuseppe Verdi

Adaptation

Macbeth – Blood Will Have Blood
China Plate and Contender Charlie and Warwick Arts. The Albany, London, 4–8 March and tour.
www.chinaplatetheatre.com
Adaptor: Nick Walker
Adaptation for young audiences narrated by the Porter.

Macbethalone!
Stroud Theatre Company. Playhouse, Salisbury, 14 April
and UK tour.
www.stroudtheatrecompany.co.uk
Director: Chris Garner and Polly Teale

Lady M.
Het Vijfde Bedjrif. Olympus Theatre, Gloucester,
20 July.
Solo piece from the perspective of Lady Macbeth's
servant.

Read Not Dead
Sam Wanamaker Playhouse, Globe Theatre, London,
20 July.
Co-ordinators: Ben and David Crystal
An original pronunciation staged reading
using cue scripts.

Hecate's Poison: Enter the Three Witches
Players Tokyo. Quaker Meeting House (Venue 40),
Edinburgh, 1–23 August.
Adaptor: S. T. Sato
Adaptation narrated by Hecate.

Macbheatha
White Stag Theatre Company and David Walker.
Summerhall (Venue 26), Edinburgh, 11–24
August.
www.white-stag.co.uk
60-minute adaptation performed in Gaelic.

Macbeth – Son of Light
Quids-in Theatre Company. theSpace@Surgeon's Hall,
Edinburgh, 11–23 August.
www.quidsintheatrecompany.com
Exploring the relationship between the historic Macbeth
and Shakespeare's character.

Macbeth – After Verdi
Third World Bun Fight. Barbican, London, 16–20
September.
http://thirdworldbunfight.co.za
Director: Brett Bailey
Composer: Giuseppe Verdi
The plot involves a group of refugee performers who use
Verdi's *Macbeth* to tell their story.

Macbeth the Remix
Findhorn Bay Arts and Arts in Motion. Brodie Castle,
Brodie, 26–28 September.
www.findhornbayartsfestival.com
Multimedia reworking with community
involvement.

MEASURE FOR MEASURE

King's Shakespeare Company. The Bierkeller, Bristol,
21–25 July.
Student-led company based at King's College, London.
Part of the Bristol Shakespeare Festival.

THE MERCHANT OF VENICE

Playing Shakespeare for Globe Education at the Globe
Theatre, Bankside, London, 6–28 March.
www.shakespearesglobe.com
Director: Bill Buckhurst
Shylock: Ognen Drangovski

Rain or Shine Theatre Company. The Old Barn, Purley
on Thames, 6 June and tour to 31 August.
www.rainorshine.co.uk

Ashrow Theatre Company. Guildhall Theatre, Derby,
7–11 October.
www.ashrowtheatre.com

Almeida Theatre, London, 15 December–14
February 2015.
www.almeida.co.uk
Director: Rupert Goold
Shylock: Ian McDiarmid
Portia: Susannah Fielding

Adaptation

The 21st-Century Merchant of Venice
The Drayton Arms Theatre, London, 10–14 June.
Director: Carol Allen
21st-century adaptation with female Shylock.

THE MERRY WIVES OF WINDSOR

Principal Theatre Company. Bloomsbury, London,
17 July–2 August and tour.
www.principaltheatrecompany.com
Director: Christopher Geelan

A MIDSUMMER NIGHT'S DREAM

Propeller Theatre Company. 23 January–1 February and
tour to 21 June.
http://propeller.org.uk
Director: Edward Hall

All-male company.

Immersion Theatre. Brockley Jack Theatre, London,
4–8 February and tour to 20 March.
www.immersiontheatre.co.uk
Director: James Tobias and Amy Gunn

Highland Shakespeare Company. Cambo House, St
Andrews, Fife, 11–17 February; and at Fingask Castle,
Perthshire, 22–23 February.
Director: Sunny Moodle
A winter outdoor production.

Bristol Old Vic and Handspring Puppet Company.
Barbican, London, 6–15 February, Old Vic, Bristol,
7 March–4 May; Barbican, London, 10–15 February
and tour.
www.bristololdvic.org.uk
Director: Tom Morris
Featuring puppets from the company that designed the
puppets for *War Horse*.

Deafinitely Theatre. The Globe Theatre, Bankside,
London, 2–7 June.
www.shakespearesglobe.com
Director: Paula Garfield
Performed in British Sign Language.

Oddsocks. Forum Theatre, Billingham, 13 June and tour
to 18 August.
www.oddsocks.co.uk

Chapterhouse Theatre Company. Harewood House,
Harewood, Leeds, 19 June and tour to 30 August.
www.chapterhouse.org

Permanently Bard. The Boater, Bath 2–3 August, and
tour to September.
Director: Sean Turner
Show commissioned by, and played in, Fuller Breweries
pubs.

The Malachites. Rockwell House, Shoreditch, London,
4–13 August.
www.themalachites.co.uk
London Contemporary Theatre, 7–8 August,
South Hill Park Arts Centre, Bracknell, and tour to
25 August.
www.londoncontemporarytheatre.com
Director: Lotte Wakeham

Rose Bridge Theatre Company. The Courtyard,
Hoxton, 20 August–7 September.
www.rosebridgetheatre.com
Director: Adam Morris

Ballet

Northern Ballet. Theatre Royal, Norwich, 13–17 May
and tour to 14 September.
www.northernballet.com
Composer: Felix Mendelssohn

The Royal Ballet. The Royal Opera House, London,
31 May–13 June.
www.roh.org.uk
Composer: Felix Mendelssohn

*The Genius of Balanchine: Apollo/A Midsummer Night's
Dream*
The Mariinsky (Kirov) Ballet. Royal Opera House, 8–9
August.
www.roh.org.uk
Choreography: George Balachine
Composer: Felix Mendelssohn

Opera

Oberon
New Sussex Opera Chorus. Lewes Town Hall;
Devonshire Park Theatre, Eastbourne; Cardogan
Hall, London, November.
www.newsussexopera.org
Composer: Carl Maria von Weber

Adaptation

I, Peaseblossom
Company of Angels. The Junction, Cambridge, 23–24
February and tour to 16 May.
www.companyofangels.co.uk
Playwright and performer: Tim Crouch
Director: John Retallack
Solo piece from Peaseblossom's perspective.

Pocket Dream
Propeller Theatre. E. M. Forster Theatre, Tonbridge,
8 September and UK tour to 7 November.
Director: Edward Hall
60-minute adaptation for young audiences. Played with
Pocket Henry V.

Shaking up Shakespeare – A Midsummer Night's Dream
Queen's Theatre, Hornchurch, London, 20 September.
www.queens-theatre.co.uk
One-man show.

A Midsummer Night's Dream (As You Like It)

Barbican (in association with the RSC). Barbican
Centre, 12–15 November.
www.barbican.org.uk/theatre
Director: Dmitri Krymov
Performed in Russian with English surtitles. Focuses on
the staging of Pyramus and Thisbe.

MUCH ADO ABOUT NOTHING

Royal Exchange Theatre, Manchester, 27 March–3
May.
www.royalexchange.co.uk
Director: Maria Aberg
Beatrice: Ellie Piercy
Benedick: Paul Ready

Shakespeare's Globe Theatre. Theatre Royal, Margate,
11–13 April and tour to 31 August.
www.shakespearesglobe.com
Director: Max Webster

Chapterhouse Theatre Company. Neeld Hall,
Chippenham, 25 June and tour to 31 August.
www.chapterhouse.org

Burnt Out Theatre. Clandon Wood National Burial
Reserve, Guildford, 5–6 July and tour to 20 July.
www.burntouttheatre.co.uk

Lion and Unicorn Theatre, London, 29 July–23 August.
http://giantolive.com

Royal Shakespeare Company. Royal Shakespeare Theatre,
Stratford-upon-Avon, 3 October–14 March 2015.
www.rsc.org.uk
Director: Christopher Luscombe
Beatrice: Michelle Terry
Benedick: Edward Bennett
Billed as *Love's Labour's Won* to pair with *Love's Labour's
Lost*.

Adaptation

Much Ado About Som'at'
RumDoxy Theatre. Crescent Theatre, Birmingham,
7–8 February; Barn Theatre, Cirencester, 21 February
and tour.
www.rumdoxytheatre.co.uk
Adaptor and Director: Jo Hopkins
All-female cast of four.

Much Ado About Zombies
Thread Theatre Company. Space on the Mile (Venue
39), Edinburgh, 11–16 August.
www.threadtheatre.co.uk
A theatre company performs at Edinburgh during
a zombie apocalypse.

What's All the Fuss About?
Regent Theatre, Stoke, 14–18 October.
Playwright: Catherine O'Reilly and Tim Churchill
Upbeat musical loosely based on *Much Ado About
Nothing*.

OTHELLO

Orangutan Productions. Riverside Studios, London,
16 January–8 February.
www.orangutanproductions.co.uk
Director: Rebekah Fortune

Guildford Shakespeare Company. Holy Trinity Church,
Guildford, 5–22 February.
www.guildford-shakespeare-company.co.uk
Director: Caroline Devlin

Clatterhouse Theatre. Drayton Arms, Old Brompton
Road, London, 2–27 September.

Icarus Theatre Collective and Original Theatre
Company. King's Theatre, Southsea, 12–13
September and tour to 7 April 2014.
www.icarustheatre.org
Director: Max Lewendel

Frantic Assembly and Theatre Royal Plymouth. Theatre
Royal, Plymouth, 4–11 October; Oxford Playhouse,
Oxford, 21–5 October; Lyric Hammersmith,
London, 14 January–7 February 2015; and on tour.
www.franticassembly.co.uk
Director: Scott Graham
Revival of the 2008 Frantic Assembly production.

Opera

Otello
English National Opera. Coliseum, London,
13 September–17 October.
www.eno.org
Composer: Giuseppe Verdi

Adaptation

Desdemona: A Play About A Handkerchief
Park Theatre, London, 13 May–8 June.
www.parktheatre.co.uk
Playwright: Paula Vogel

Unity Theatre with Brazuka. Unity Theatre, Liverpool,
    30 May.
www.unitytheatreliverpool.co.uk
Choreography: Elisio Pitta
Part of PhysicalFest 2014. Combining elements of Afro-
    dance, capoeira and classical ballet.

RICHARD II

Adaptation

Richard II Live!
Hip-Hop Shakespeare, Purcell Rooms, South Bank
    Centre, London, 25–27 March.
Director: Akala
Hip-hop version.

RICHARD III

Hiraeth Artistic Productions. Upstairs at the Gatehouse,
    London, 7 February–1 March.
www.upstairsatthegatehouse.com

Lazarus Theatre Company. Blue Elephant Theatre,
    London, 4–29 March.
www.lazarustheatrecompany.com
Director: Gavin Harrington-Odedra

Scrawny Cat Theatre Company. The Rose Playhouse,
    Bankside, London, 1–26 April.
http://scrawnycat.co.uk
Director: Charlotte Ive
All-female cast of four.

Custom/Practice. The Cockpit, London, 30 April–18
    May; Greenwich Theatre, London, 20–22 June.
www.custompractice.co.uk
Director: Rae McKen

Iris Theatre. St Paul's Church, Covent Garden, London,
    25 June–25 July.
www.iristheatre.com

Director: Daniel Winder

Jamie Lloyd Productions. Trafalgar Studios, London,
    1 July–27 September.
http://thejamielloydcompany.com
Director: Jamie Lloyd
Richard III: Martin Freeman

Theatre Collection, Upstairs at the Lord Stanley,
    London. 10 October–2 November.
www.theatrecollection.net
Theatre Royal, Norwich, 11–13 December.
www.theatreroyalnorwich.co.uk

Adaptation

Drag King Richard III
Stance Theatre Company. Riverside Studios, London,
    29 July–3 August.
http://stancetheatre.co.uk
Director: Roz Hopkinson

ROMEO AND JULIET

The Merely Players. Cockpit Theatre, London,
    16 March.
Director: Scott Ellis

Venture Wolf Productions. London Theatre, New
    Cross, London, 1–6 April.
www.venturewolf.com

Jack in a Box Productions. Trinity Buoy Wharf,
    London, 27–31 May.
http://jackinaboxproductions.com
Director: John Askew

Lord Chamberlain's Men. Kings Ely, Cambridge,
    10 June; Bristol Shakespeare Festival and UK tour
    to September.
Director: Andrew Normington

Antic Disposition. Temple Church, 30 August–7
    September.
www.anticdisposition.co.uk
Director: John Risebero and Ben Horslen

HOME. Victoria Baths, Manchester, 17 September–4
    October.
Director: Walter Meierjohann

Sherman Cymru. Main House, Cardiff, 7–18
    October.
www.shermancymru.co.uk
Director: Rachel O'Riordan
O'Riordan's inaugural production as Sherman Cymru's
    artistic director.

Kaleidoscope Youth Theatre. Pavilion Arts Centre
    Studio, Buxton, 14 October.
www.buxtonoperahouse.org.uk

London Theatre Workshop. Eel Brook Public House,
    London, 4–22 November.
http://londontheatreworkshop.co.uk
Director: Brandon Force

Pepper's Ghost Theatre Company and The Play's the
    Thing Theatre Company. Stantonbury Theatre,
    Milton Keynes, 10–13 December.

Ballet

Moscow City Ballet. St George's Hall, Bradford,
    12 January and tour to 11 March.
Composer: Prokofiev

Scottish Ballet. King's Theatre, Glasgow, 19–26 April
    and tour to 24 May.
www.scottishballet.co.uk
Composer: Prokofiev
Director: Krzysztof Pastor

English National Ballet. Royal Albert Hall, London,
    11–22 June.
www.ballet.org.uk
Composer: Prokofiev

Mariinsky Ballet Company. Royal Opera House,
    London, 28–31 July.
Composer: Prokofiev

Ballet Cymru. Royal Albert Hall, London, 11–22 June
    and tour.
www.welshballet.co.uk

Juliet and Romeo
Royal Swedish Ballet. Sadler's Wells
    Theatre, 24–7 September.
Choreography: Mats Ek
Composer: Tchaikovsky

Adaptation

Before Juliet
Manchester Shakespeare Company. Three-Minute
    Theatre, Manchester, 17–22 March.
www.manchestershakespearecompany.com
Playwright: Hannah Ellis and John Topliff
Director: Gina Frost and Matt Cawson
Modern adaptation with Juliet played with a personality
    disorder.

National Theatre. NT's Temporary Theatre, London,
    29 October–14 November.
www.nationaltheatre.org.uk
Director: Bijan Sheibani
Adaptation for children.

Romeo and Juliet: A Plunderphonica
Stagepunk Theatre. Bread and Roses Theatre, Clapham,
    London, 4–9 November.
www.breadandrosestheatre.co.uk
Composer: Matthew Reynolds
Director: Simon Jay
Dance version for two performers.

West Side Story
Palace Theatre, Manchester, 10 December–4
    January 2014 and tour to 13 September.
http://westsidestorytheshow.co.uk.
Composer: Leonard Bernstein
Director and Choreography: Joey McKneely

THE TAMING OF THE SHREW

Stamford Shakespeare Festival. Rutland Open Air Theatre,
    Tolethorpe Hall, Little Casterton, 1 July–23 August.
www.stamfordshakespeare.co.uk

Folksy Theatre. Threave Estate, Castle Douglas,
    Dumfries and Galloway, 17 July; Bristol Shakespeare
    Festival, 25–6 July and UK tour to 24 August.
www.folksytheatre.co.uk

Immersion Theatre. Brockley Jack Theatre, London,
    30 September–18 October; and UK tour to
    12 November.
www.immersiontheatre.co.uk
Directors: Amy Gunn and James Tobias

XWire Entertainment. London Theatre, New Cross, London, 14–19 October.
www.thelondontheatre.com

Adaptation

First Encounter: The Taming of the Shrew
RSC Ensemble. Courtyard Theatre, Stratford-upon-Avon, 4–8 February and tour to 22 March.
www.rsc.org.uk
Director: Michael Fentiman
Petruchio: Katy Stephens
Katherine: Forbes Masson
75-minute version with cross-gender casting.

Shrew
C cubed. (Venue 16) Riddle's Court, 322 Lawnmarket, Royal Mile, Edinburgh. 31 July–25 August.
Director and Performer: Ami Jones
Sequel from Kate's perspective.

Kiss Me, Kate
John Wilson Orchestra. Royal Albert Hall, London, 2 August.
Part of the BBC Prom 21.

Taming Who?
Intermission Youth Theatre. St Saviours Church, Walton Place, London, 29 October–22 November.
www.iyt.org.uk
Playwright: Darren Raymond
Adaptation set during university induction week.

THE TEMPEST

Oxford Chamber Theatre. London Theatre, New Cross, London, 4–16 March.
www.thelondontheatre.com

Miracle Theatre. Sterts Theatre, Liskeard, 13 June and UK tour to 30 August.
www.miracletheatre.co.uk

Royal Shakespeare Company and Ohio State University. The Other Place, at the Courtyard Theatre, 24 June–4 July.
www.rsc.org.uk
Director: Kelly Hunter

Six actors perform with an audience of children with autism.

Moving Stories Theatre Company. Minack Theatre, Penzance, 30 June–4 July.
www.movingstories.org.uk
Director: Emma Gersch

The Pantaloons. Stansted Park, Rowland's Castle, Hampshire, 11 July and UK tour to 30 August.
www.thepantaloons.co.uk

Tree Folk Theatre Company. Cockpit Theatre, London, 15 July–3 August.
www.thecockpit.org.uk

Breakfast Cat Theatre in association with Steampunk Shakespeare Company. Charles Cryer Studio Theatre, Secombe Theatre, Carshalton, 1–4 October.
www.suttontheatres.co.uk

Waterloo East Theatre, London, 8–26 October.
www.waterlooeast.co.uk

Adaptation

Bard Heads
Finding the Will. Artrix Studio, Bromsgrove, 10 February.
www.findingthewill.com
Solo piece composed of interviews with Miranda 25 years after the shipwreck.

I, Caliban
Company of Angels. The Junction, Cambridge, 23–24 February and tour to 31 May.
www.companyofangels.co.uk
Director: John Retallack
Plawright: Tim Crouch
Solo performance from Caliban's perspective.

This Last Tempest
Uninvited Guests and Fuel. Brewery Arts, Kendal, 9 October and tour to 29 November.
A sequel – Caliban and Ariel remain on the island and use magic learned from Prospero.

Return to the Forbidden Planet
Cut to the Chase Theatre Company. Queen's Theatre, Hornchurch. 6–15 November and tour to May 2015.
www.queens-theatre.co.uk
Director: Bob Carlton

TITUS ANDRONICUS

Shakespeare's Globe Theatre. Globe Theatre, Bankside, London, 24 April–13 July
www.shakespearesglobe.com
Director: Lucy Bailey
Titus: William Houston
Tamora: Indira Varma
Subtitled *Brutality of the Highest Order*. Reported in national newspapers for causing audience members to faint.

Theory of Everything and Resltess Buddha for Bold Tendencies. Multistorey car park on Rye Lane, Peckham, London, 30 August–21 September.
www.thetheoryofeverything.co.uk
Director: Pia Furtado
Inaugural production at Peckham's multistorey car park.

TROILUS AND CRESSIDA

Lazarus Theatre Company. Tristan Bates Theatre, London, 18 August–6 September.
www.lazarustheatrecompany.com
Director: Ricky Dukes

TWELFTH NIGHT

Filter (in association with the RSC). Tobacco Factory, Bristol, 9–14 September and tour to 1 February 2014. First performed at the RSC Complete Works Festival 2006.
www.filtertheatre.com
Director: Sean Holmes
Loose adaptation concentrating on knock-about comedy.

Octagon Theatre. Howell Croft South, Bolton, 27 February–22 March.
www.octagonbolton.co.uk
Director: David Thacker

Liverpool Everyman Theatre, Liverpool, 12 March–5 April.
www.everymanplayhouse.com
Director: Gemma Bodinetz
Malvolio: Nicholas Woodeson
Sir Toby Belch: Matthew Kelly
Viola: Jodie McNee
First production in the rebuilt theatre which was closed 2011–14.

Chrysalis Collective. Bearpit Theatre, Stratford-upon-Avon, 13–17 May.
Director: Christa Harris
Cygnet Theatre. Friars Gate, Exeter, 11 June–19 July.
http://cygnettheatre.co.uk
Director: Jacquie Crago

Oddsocks. Forum Theatre, Billingham, 12 June and tour to 26 August.
www.oddsocks.co.uk

Guildford Shakespeare Company. Guildford Castle Gardens, Guildford, 12–18 June.
www.guildford-shakespeare-company.co.uk
Director: Tom Littler

Madcap Theatre Productions. Mary Arden's Farm, Wilmcote, Stratford-upon-Avon, 4–5 July and tour to 9 August.
www.madcaptheatreproductions.co.uk

Merely Players. Cockpit Theatre, London, 10 August.
www.themerelyplayers.com
Director: Scott Ellis

PurpleCoat Productions, Arts Depot, London, 7 September.
www.artsdepot.co.uk

English Touring Theatre and Sheffield Theatres. Crucible Theatre, Sheffield, 23 September–18 October and on tour.
www.ett.org.uk
Director: Jonathan Munby

Adaptation

I, Malvolio
Octagon Theatre, Bolton, 10–11 March; Curve Theatre, Leicester, 23–24 May.
www.timcrouchtheatre.co.uk
Playwright: Tim Crouch
Directors: Karl James and Andy Smith
The story retold from Malvolio's perspective.

Twelfth Night Re-imagined
Young Shakespeare Company. Regent's Park Open Air Theatre, London, 21 June–12 July.
https://openairtheatre.com
Director: Max Webster
For younger audiences. Publicized with the subtitle 'reimagined for everyone aged six and over'.

THE TWO GENTLEMEN OF VERONA

Royal Shakespeare Company. Royal Shakespeare
    Theatre, Stratford-upon-Avon, 22 July–4 September;
    Newcastle Theatre Royal, 7–11 October. Broadcast
    to cinemas worldwide as part of the RSC's Live from
    Stratford-upon-Avon, 3 September.
www.rsc.org.uk
Director: Simon Godwin
Proteus: Mark Arends
Valentine: Michael Marcus

THE WINTER'S TALE

Richard Burton Company. Royal Welsh College of
    Music and Drama. Bute Theatre, Raymond Edwards
    Building, Cardiff, 3–13 December.
www.rwcmd.ac.uk
Director: Joe Murphy
Lion and Unicorn Theatre, London, 9 December–3
    January 2015.
www.giantolive.com

Ballet

Royal Ballet. Lindbury Studio Theatre, Royal Opera
    House, London, 10 April–8 May; broadcast live in
    cinemas, 28 April, and on tour.
www.roh.org.uk
Choreographer: Christopher Wheeldon
Composer: Jody Talbot
World premiere.

POEMS AND APOCRYPHA

Arden of Faversham
Royal Shakespeare Company. Royal Shakespeare
    Theatre, Stratford-upon-Avon, 6 May–2 October.
www.rsc.org.uk
Director: Polly Findlay

The Rape of Lucrece
Royal Shakespeare Company. Opera House, Cork, 5–7
    June; Swan Theatre, Stratford-upon-Avon,
    23 June–4 July; Queen Elizabeth Hall, South Bank
    Centre, London, 9–12 July.
www.rsc.org.uk
Director: Elizabeth Freestone
Performer: Camille O'Sullivan

Shakespeare's Sonnets
Royal Festival Hall, Southbank Centre, London, 1 June.
www.southbankcentre.co.uk
A complete reading of 154 sonnets featuring Simon
    Russell Beale and Harriet Walter.

Sonnet Walks
York Shakespeare Project. Performed in York,
    25 June–6 July.
Director: Helen Wilson and Tom Straszewski
A series of sonnets performed during York walking tours
    narrated by either Henry V or Katherine.

The Sonneteer
Sebastian Michael and Tom Medcalf with Optimist
    Creations. Greenside @ Nicolson Square (Venue
    209), Edinburgh. 1–23 August.
www.thesonneteer.info
A biographical play about Shakespeare's composition of
    the sonnets.

MISCELLANEOUS

The Complete Works of Shakespeare (Abridged)
Reduced Shakespeare Company. City Varieties Music
    Hall, Leeds, 19 September and tour to 20 November.
www.reducedshakespeare.com

Ellen Terry with Eileen Atkins
Shakespeare's Globe Theatre. Globe Theatre, Bankside,
    London, 12 January–23 February.
Director and Adaptor: Eileen Atkins
Devised from Ellen Terry's lectures on Shakespeare.

Muse of Fire
Shakespeare's Globe, Bankside, London, through 2014.
Exhibition and interactive theatre for children aged 6–11
    that takes audiences through unseen areas of the Globe.

The Other Shakespeare
Pitchfork Production. St Mary's Church, Guildford,
    19 April and tour.
www.pitchforkproduction.com
Playwright: Roy Chatfield
Director: Ian Flintoff
One-woman show from the perspective of Anne
    Hathaway.

The Players Advice to Shakespeare
New Theatre of Ottawa. C Nova, India Buildings,
    Victoria Street (Venue 145), Edinburgh, July 3 –
    25 August.

90-minute monologue. An actor from Shakespeare's
company recounts how he inspired the playwright.

See What I See
Eyestrings. Burton Taylor Theatre, Oxford, 27–28 June.
Exploration of sanity through Shakespeare's work.

Shakespeare in Hell
Brite Theater and So Potent Arts at the Northcott
Theatre, Exeter, 4–7 June and UK tour.
Ariel conducts a tour through Dante's hell and discovers
various Shakespeare characters.

Shakespeare in Love
Disney Theatrical Productions and Sonia Friedman
Productions. Noël Coward Theatre, London,
23 July–10 January 2015.
Director: Declan Donnellan
Adapted by Lee Hall from the *Shakespeare in Love*
screenplay by Tom Stoppard and Marc Norman.

Shakespeare's Deadly Sins
Conor McKee Productions. Mill at the Pier, Wigan,
9 October and tour to 19 October.
Exploration of the deadly sins through Shakespeare's
work.

Shakespeare's Greatest Hits

In Voice and Verse. Leicester Square Theatre, London,
23 April; New Cavendish Club, London, 29 May; and
tour.
www.invoiceandverse.co.uk
Selection of speeches and sonnets performed by
a musical/theatrical trio.

Shakespeare's Lovers
Faction Theatre Company. Bridewell Theatre, London,
25 March–11 April.
www.thefaction.org.uk
Director: Sean Turner
Selection of love scenes.

Where Late the Sweet Birds Sang
Rose Theatre. Rose Playhouse, London, 4–29 November.
www.rosetheatre.org.uk
Director: Martin Parr
A selection of sonnets with musical accompaniment.

Winter's Rages: Shakespeare in Speech and Song
Rose Theatre. Rose Playhouse, London, 2–14
December.
www.rosetheatre.org.uk
Director: Sophie Kochanowska
Shakespeare and song performed by actor, soprano and
piano.

1. CRITICAL STUDIES
reviewed by CHARLOTTE SCOTT

SHAKESPEARE ON TRIAL

One of the things that struck me this year is the increasing diversity of literary criticism. This is not necessarily a good thing. While on the one hand the scattered and variable angles on Shakespeare reveal capacious and wide-ranging interests, there is little to suggest, this year at least, that the field is moving its agendas forward and developing schools of interests and methodologies that will come to shape and redefine our study of Shakespeare. There are many fine books this year, but they remain somewhat atomized – each scholar carving out a single isolated territory that has little or no connection to a wider commitment to our collective understanding of the subject. This, of course, may well be the legacy of a highly pressured output culture where scholars are valued for productivity rather than the longer perspective.

No one can accuse Quentin Skinner of a failure in quality or productivity but, as erudite as *Forensic Shakespeare* is, it situates itself as a lone voice in the pursuit of Shakespeare's relationship to humanist and, more specifically, judicial rhetoric. The study sets out to examine 'the two phases of his literary career in which he became deeply absorbed by the dramatic possibilities of forensic eloquence'. Central to Skinner's project is a concern with the classical precepts of rhetoric, especially 'invention' and 'disposition', through which he attempts to shift the emphasis away from Shakespeare's legal competence towards a more thoroughly articulated focus on rhetorical precepts. Skinner claims: 'I am repeatedly able to point to passages where he follows complex rhetorical arguments to the letter, and can sometimes be shown to be quoting from specific classical manuals in the course of doing so.' As the tone here suggests, Skinner's book is committed to revealing Shakespeare's interest in, even dependence on, classical rhetoric and the effects this reading had 'on his practice as a dramatist'. This is not especially surprising to Shakespearians and if Skinner has a fault it is the overemphasis of this point. But the book is at its best on rhetoric and there is nobody better informed or more articulate on the subject of classical rhetoric than Skinner. His discussions of Cicero and the *Ad Herennium*, for example, are deeply nuanced and thoughtful: he is an immensely sensitive reader of the minor variations and discrepancies between Quintilian, Cicero and the *Ad Herennium* and points to subtle points of interpretation and emphasis (not least of all the long-debated question of *Ad Herennium*'s authorship, which in Skinner's reading is neither the work of Quintilian nor Cicero). Equally attentive to vernacular texts, Skinner returns repeatedly to the thesis that Shakespeare is not drawing on legal texts but judicial rhetoric, and the distinction is vital. Most fascinatingly in this respect is the question of the trial, dominant in what Skinner refers to as Shakespeare's 'forensic plays': 'and thus with the question of how to develop an argument in accusation or defence before a judge'. Focusing on the argument rather than the outcome shifts our attention to the art of persuasion rather than justice. The vocabulary tends to centre on three connected terms, each of which can be specifically traced to classical texts as well as their vernacular adaptations. These terms are principally concerned with range, matter and 'controversy', or debate; in other words, argument and eloquence. Although conceptually no scholar has ever been in any doubt as to Shakespeare's dependence on the terms of classical rhetoric, Skinner's project is to uncover the precise ways that Shakespeare imports judicial terminology and borrows from and paraphrases rhetorical texts to specific ends. He therefore traces a very specific and linear development in Shakespeare's writing that begins with *Romeo and Juliet* and engages 'the technicalities of judicial rhetoric at a new level of detail and complexity'. Working towards an apotheosis in *Hamlet*, Skinner observes the development of this fascination with forensic rhetoric in *The Merchant of Venice* and *Julius Caesar*. In *Hamlet*, however, it reaches new levels of intricacy through the use of the '*constitutio coniecturalis*, where the speaker's aim is to employ conjecture to uncover some hidden truth'. Understood in this way, conjecture becomes central to the development of drama precisely because of the ways it forms a central point of both conflict and resolution. Through the filter of rhetorical texts the terms and understanding of these figures become more mobile. In *Hamlet*, for example, Skinner shows how Shakespeare establishes the dynamic between ghost father and son by directly invoking judicial causes (although the characters of course do not technically stand trial). Here the interpretative possibilities become much more rewarding as Skinner releases these terms from their legal constraints and develops deft readings as he observes that few of

Shakespeare's characters are judges in the legal sense but many, including Hamlet, 'have a judicial role to play in hearing, assessing and delivering a verdict on the truth of what they are told'. We, too, as audience members are often put in this position and so being attentive to the terms through which Shakespeare directs our attentions emphasizes the formative links between performance and persuasion. Sometimes Skinner's readings render the speeches slightly formulaic in their dependence on judicial rhetoric and the emotional and intellectual control they purport to exercise over the audience's response: 'If we find ourselves engaged by it, it is not because Shakespeare has produced a successful representation of real life; it is rather because he has constructed a satisfying rhetorical and dramatic effect.' There's a transparency here that is both fascinating and disappointing, as though we are being invited to see that the magician's illusions are all tricks: something we all know, perhaps, but don't necessarily want to witness. Taking us through the various parts of rhetoric and the studied way in which both matter and locution are choreographed to affect the listener we begin to see how the highly stylized tropes of judicial rhetoric develop in Shakespeare's work into something much more subtle and conversational. The second cluster of plays Skinner analyzes includes *Measure for Measure*, *Othello* and *All's Well*. But he returns again and again to *Hamlet* where Shakespeare seems at his most ambitious and his most eclectic, drawing on Quintilian, Cicero, *Ad Herennium* as well as Leonard Cox and Thomas Wilson. At the centre of many of Skinner's readings, however, is a renewed claim for the formative relationship between narrative and emotion, between empathy and persuasion: 'To Elizabethan writers on stage performance, it came to seem that the basic concern of the theatre was with *repraesentatio*, the attempt to re-enact and re-present past events with so much vividness that we feel we are witnessing them.'

Perhaps one of the most compelling elements of Skinner's argument is how particular speeches reflect an almost textbook response to certain situations.

Observing the ghost of his murdered father, for example, Hamlet seems to follow Cox and Wilson's precepts on determining the veracity of his claims:

First, we must look to see if the suspected party 'blushed or waxed pale'. Next we must attend to whether he 'stutted & coulde nat well speke.' Lastly, it will obviously be incriminating if 'after the dede as done he fled.' Thomas Wilson adds that we should also consider more generally 'how he kept his countenance.'

Skinner presents very engaging and detailed accounts of how judicial rhetoric develops through vernacular translations into a comprehensive language of performance and persuasion. There is no doubt that one of the greatest gifts of this book is the attention to the rhetorical texts themselves and their vigorous and learned analysis. The book's larger claim for Shakespeare's dependence on rhetorical manuals rather than legal processes seems less significant within the context of a humanist education in which oratory is a wide-ranging art. The emphasis here on imitation rather than innovation puts Shakespeare in a different working context and arguably dismantles some of the power of language. Skinner's insistence that we see behind the curtain, as it were, is revealing but not always rewarding. Nevertheless what emerges from this book is a renewed concern with the pleasures and performance of language; the glorious fight for objectivity and the debt that art owes to life.

Maintaining the relationship between art and life is central to Robert Ellrodt's *Montaigne and Shakespeare*, which returns our attention to one of the most recalcitrant themes of this period, indeed the book's subtitle: 'The Emergence of Modern Self-consciousness'. Ellrodt's work has consistently focused on forms of self-consciousness in Montaigne and how we can identify individual structures of thought through experience, imagination and forms of sensibility. Here he returns to the question of selfhood and how we identify the development of subjectivity as well as the relationships between self-knowledge and self-assertion. The first half of the book examines Montaigne

and the cultural-historical contexts in which he was writing. From this perspective, Ellrodt writes: 'Montaigne's mode of self-scrutiny is unprecedented'. Establishing the various modes through which the self can emerge in literature – allegory, elegy, satire, sentiment or spirituality, for example – Ellrodt defines a trajectory through which Montaigne establishes his own unique representation of self-consciousness. Attending to the Sonnets and three formative tragedies (*Hamlet*, *Macbeth* and *Lear*), the book demonstrates a progressive self-awareness in Shakespeare's work that supports the evolution of well-defined characters as well as a coherent representation of individual subjectivities. Central to many of the debates raised here is the question of an essential self versus a culturally contrived self. Ellrodt maintains his commitment to a belief in essence and 'the originality of their aesthetic intuitions of transcendence is highlighted'. One of the highlights of this book is its careful treatment of self-analysis and the sensitive ways Ellrodt observes the subtle differences between emotion and introspection. The section on the Sonnets is especially engaging, as Ellrodt hears a persistent voice hammering through the strains of various subjectivities. Referring to Sonnet 129, for example, he writes: 'Yet, through this apparent impersonality, the paradoxes of desire, through the clash of consonants and contraries, convey to the reader the fits and starts of strained subjectivity.' Recognizing the quality of subjectivity as 'strained' reinforces the complexities of both truth and revelation.

In this way, the illusion of the self is no less valid or unconvincing than the thing itself, and rather than negate a sense of continuous identity it raises the questions of memory, imagination, projection and emotion. What emerges from the readings of the Sonnets is that the appearance of objectivity is created by 'the poet's ability to keep different emotions, different judgments, in balance' and 'thus maintaining the mind of the reader in a state of perplexity up to the final statement'. What is especially rewarding about this book is that Ellrodt reads through the various manifestations of sentiment and self that can appear across a range of words, tones and contexts. He is not especially concerned with the individual behaviours of words but with the ways they relate or resonate across the speech, sonnet or scene. In the midst of this, Ellrodt discerns a complex play of priorities that are less focused on the representation or pre-servation of the self and more on the individuation of the self:

Yet the poet, I think, cares little for the immortality of the young man he never names, nor even for his own immortality (he has not the pride of Ronsard); he seeks to convince himself of the immortality of love, a love able to create its own certainty (or consented illusion) of an unalterable constancy in the sonnet on 'the marriage of true minds'.

Although Ellrodt analyzes some of the most important narratives within the development of Western conceptions of selfhood and addresses Montaigne's reception and development of forms of subjectivity, this book speaks to a much wider remit than the relative dynamic between the two titular authors. It is a wonderful book that ranges across a vast array of forms of identification that seek to express or define themselves in relation to essence, others, God, memory or the physical world. Ellrodt's ability to move fluently between the ancient and early modern worlds as well as linguistics, psychoanalysis and philosophy is inten-sely rewarding. He writes beautifully and the book is a celebration of the multiple, complex and myr-iad worlds of Shakespeare in which we find a radical coherence that renders the self continu-ous, if not always aware.

'THE CENTRE CANNOT HOLD'

In *The Circulation of Knowledge in Early Modern English Literature*, edited by Sophie Chiari, the con-tributors set out to examine the various meanings and effects of 'circulation', from the transmissions of texts, ideas and objects to the implications that such movements may imply. Here the central con-cern is forms of transgression, disruption and abstraction as 'things' move around and between

the outputs of early modern literature. The central concept, however, is transgression, since many of the chapters proceed from the basis that through transmission 'what was deemed transgressive for one individual or social category was considered as simple transmission by another'. Paradoxically, however, there seems no such thing as 'simple transmission' in this collection; all movements are also initiations. The book is divided into four main sections loosely organized around the themes of transmission, initiation, knowledge and gender/ genre. The first three sections are exclusively devoted to our period and cover a range of plays by Shakespeare as well as Marlowe, Jonson, Marston and Middleton. Beyond the plays, how-ever, there are numerous other avenues for exploration, including classical humanism and art. Anne-Valerie Dulac's chapter traces the movement of the word 'miniature' from Hilliard's paintings to Sidney's *Arcadia*. Observing Sidney's unique use of the word in the wonderful description of Philoclea 'playing in the water,' she writes, 'not only is Sidney transmitting an Italian word to the English language but he is here also transgressing lexical usage as he is giving the word the meaning of a small-scale representation.' Almost all the contri-butions here are deeply thoughtful in the dynamics they explore both in subject matter and literary texts. A chapter on transmission and transgression in *Measure for Measure* and *Doctor Faustus* begins from the standpoint of medieval morality and diverges into a detailed interrogation of the seman-tics of power and misrule. In contrast, Joseph Sterrett examines the term 'sanctuary' in Shakespeare's plays and how it moves from a space for the 'organis[ation] of collective values' to a metaphor 'for the interior person or as a boundary that defines revenge'. The terms of transmission and transgression in this volume necessarily give way to ideas of violation, imposi-tion and failure that are explored over a very wide range of material and perspectives. Given the emphasis on forms of transgression, it is not surpris-ing that we encounter Foucault early on, through Richard Wilson's thoughtful exploration of the translated phrase 'Ship of Fools' where 'Foucault's lunatic hulk would inspire scores of post modern fictions and psychedelic artworks'. If Richard Howard's translation enabled this hulk to take passage, then numerous critics jumped onboard. Greenblatt is equally important to Wilson's analysis as he considers how New Historicism took up the central questions of power and subversion in Foucault's work. 'The limit and transgression depend on each other', Foucault had written in his 'preface to Transgression'; but in Shakespeare, where the Ship of Fools became the ship of state, it seems he found at last a form of symbolic transgression that was itself 'as mad as the vexed sea singing aloud (*King Lear*, 4.3.2)'. Wilson's often lyrical contribution provides an excellent point of entry into this varied and engaging collection where nothing is fixed and the far-away is always near at hand, in images of elsewhere.

In *The Renaissance Extended Mind*, Miranda Anderson moves from the circulation of transgression to the distribution of cognition. Keeping the attention on knowledge but shifting our theoretical approach to the cognitive and psychoanalytical, Anderson outlines the 'extended mind' as the 'dynamism (and constraints) involved in mind- and subject-world interactions'. By this she seems to suggest that we broaden our understanding of the mind beyond the representation of thought to body, action, environment, impulse and effect. Moving through phenomenology, embodiment, technology, biology and philosophy, Anderson establishes her methodological range as consistent with a period in which 'the Renaissance displays an especially marked consciousness, concern and celebration about human cognitive extendedness'. The majority of the book is dedicated to analyzing the various approaches to cognition, both in contemporary theory and in Renaissance attitudes to the relationships between subject and object. Formulating the theories of the extended mind to a paradigm (which she then refers to as EM), Anderson states that the Renaissance is especially fascinating because 'unlike the current EM, the soul and mind are also portrayed as capable of intellectual flights, a God-like extendedness that the mortal body constructs. This suggests that

current EM could itself extend what it considers under the rubric of the extendedness.' Despite Anderson's range and ambition, such statements are difficult to read, as is reducing the subject of your book to an acronym. The latter sections of the book, however, deal specifically with Shakespeare and are perhaps more grounded because of their focus on the textual relations between subjects and objects. The sections on *Measure for Measure* analyze mirror motifs and provide some rewarding readings of the mobility of metaphors of reflection. Extending our awareness of reflection through bodies, objects, relationships, fantasies, ceremonies and gestures, Anderson shows how Angelo's failure is one of both projection and limitation. By way of the mirror, Anderson discusses a number of other plays including *King Lear*, *Hamlet*, *Richard II* and *Macbeth* from which she observes 'the blurring of supposed boundaries between the objective and subjective, outside and inside, past and present, human and animal, mind and world by making evident their dynamically entwined natures'. Moving through the mobility of the mirror metaphor, Anderson explores various forms of reflection specifically associated with female vanity and 'Shakespeare's depiction of women's attempts to refashion the frames constraining their subjectivity'. Her pursuit of the extended mind allows her to examine the multiple and intricate ways that characters – and indeed humans – are in a constant process of individuation through conscious and unconscious forms of interaction. In this process she demonstrates that there is no reliable reflection since all the factors that determine and contribute to character are 'variably divisible or dynamically in play'.

'WHO IS IT THAT CAN TELL ME WHO I AM?'

In *Shakespeare and the Power of the Face*, however, the body becomes a text through which we 'read strange matter'. This collection, which has been edited by James Knapp, ranges over the multiple ways the face can reflect character (in its broadest sense) through both physiognomic (fixed features) and pathognomonic (expressions, etc.) interpretations. While all the chapters here understand the face as expressive, they are divided according to their various methodologies. The first section examines early modern texts on physiognomy and how 'the success of face-reading depends on a deep awareness of both the eloquence of the human countenance and its manipulative quality'. In Shakespeare's plays this dynamic is fully exploited and the face becomes a fascinating and contested site of both power and weakness. Sibylle Baumach's chapter, which opens the collection, examines how the face, as 'a document of power', can exert itself as well as function as 'a versatile metaphor' and a 'theatrical paradox'. She links the early modern texts on physiognomy with discourses of fascination and how the face is a provocative index of character as well as desire. Many of the contributions here touch on *Othello* and the play's tragic exploration of visual fascination. Baumach's chapter explores a number of plays where she discerns that 'Shakespeare's experimental physiognomic theatre emerges as both a mediator of and remedy against fascination'. Moving from the contexts to cosmetics, the next section examines complexions, expressions and eruptions. Here the chapters by Farah Karim-Cooper, Loreen L. Gise and Sean Lawrence and David Goldstein record how the face can behave and how this imposes affective fields of interpretation. Gise's attention to the frown or furrowed brow is fascinating as she looks at a small number of court proceedings where the husband's (or wife's) facial expressions are cited as examples of emotional cruelty. Maintaining the subtle links between expression and emotion, Goldstein examines the relationships between faces and hospitality in *Lear* and *Macbeth*. The final section of the book deals more specifically with performance and how the plays assume a wide-ranging and varied repertoire of facial expressions, gesture and deportment. Catherine Loomis's chapter demonstrates a 'cultural practice in which a person's looks and gestures were read at least as carefully as George Whitney's emblems'. Her comparison is pertinent,

as the collection demonstrates, since the face – however we imagine or perceive it in these plays – becomes a contested and powerful site for the understanding of character in action.

In Katherine Duncan-Jones's *Portraits of Shakespeare*, the focus moves from the dramatic face to the playwright's face, although many of the points made in Knapp's collection remain pertinent. As Duncan-Jones points out, the ongoing fascination with Shakespeare's appearance reveals a deeply embedded belief in the correlation between faces and character. In this way, the three earliest-surviving images of Shakespeare have been nothing short of disappointing: bald, receding, and slightly fleshy, the images we have of Shakespeare relentlessly fail to record most cultural fantasies as to what such a unique writer *should* look like. This elegantly written book looks to the wider culture of portraiture in the period to examine form, convention and style in the ways it may have impacted on the earliest images of Shakespeare. Examining monuments, engravings and frontispieces, Duncan-Jones explores the contexts through which the images are being produced as well as how we interpret them. Attentive to the changing expectations of images as well as the multiple ways Shakespeare has been marketed and visualized, this book scrutinizes the authenticity of many of the now iconic renditions of the playwright, not least of all the various ways they have been altered or touched up in the centuries after his death. Ultimately dismissive of the verisimilitude of both the Cobbe and Droeshout images, Duncan-Jones rests her case with the Chandos portrait:

It shows a subject in a relaxed mood, wearing the casual clothes traditionally donned by players offstage. His lips are very slightly parted, as if he is just about to speak. While the great body of Shakespeare's writings bear witness to his versatility in articulating the passions and aspirations of a huge array of characters, this painting, uniquely, hints at Shakespeare's own voice and presence.

It seems that *Macbeth*'s Duncan was wrong: there *is* an art to find the mind's construction in the face.

Moving back from the man to his works, there are two general introductions on Shakespeare this year that sit very nicely together. Stanley Well's contribution to the Oxford series of Very Short Introductions is especially welcome since it provides a characteristically lucid, witty and insightful survey of the life and works in a remarkably concise form. Wells divides the book thematically and chronologically so as to provide a very accessible and comprehensive overview of the shape of Shakespeare's career as well as its context. Beginning with a brief biographical survey, he defines the salient links to Stratford through both education and family. Moving through the development of the early modern theatre and the explosion of drama in the 1590s, Wells devotes the latter sections to genre and the development of Shakespeare's comic and tragic form. The final sections concentrate on the Roman plays and tragi-comedy, including romance and collaboration. Wells manages to touch on almost every play, provide a section on the Sonnets and the narrative poems as well as keeping an unerring eye on performance and reception. His knowledge, as well as love for, the drama is everywhere evidenced by the witty reflections, piercing observations and lucid judgements – Lady Macbeth 'sins', for example, 'through a denial of imagination, seeking to rationalize the inexplicable'. Most rewarding, perhaps, is the deeply ingrained belief in Shakespeare's work as a critical resource as well as the product of a highly professional and attentive writer. Closing with the words of George Bernard Shaw, one thing resonates throughout this perfect little book: 'I pity the man who cannot enjoy Shakespeare.' But Wells, unlike Shaw, is neither high-minded nor conflicted in his admiration for the playwright – as he says, affected by him or not, 'He is in the water supply; he is here to stay.'

Paul Edmondson's *Shakespeare* also offers an introduction to the subject and writer, but strikes a different note to the VSI. This book embarks on the journey through Shakespeare's life and work as a quest to discover the rich pleasures and complexities of the Elizabethan and Jacobean theatres.

The interrogative tone is upheld by an almost effervescent energy, which supplies each section with a narrative through which Edmondson engages with both historical context and textual detail. The look and feel of the book suggests a youthful audience. Each section begins with a pithy subtitle and many of the chapters are accompanied by jaunty images and captions reminiscent of graphic novels. Edmondson's tone is profoundly inclusive and he writes very clearly and transparently on the contexts of Shakespeare's art. Humanism and the practicalities of playing companies are dealt with fluently, as are the many other concerns that shape the drama from revision, collaboration, biography, textual production, props, actors and gossip. The latter sections of the book directly engage the reader in ways of approaching Shakespeare from attending performances to reading aloud. The final chapter confronts the question of Shakespeare's place within the English canon: here Edmondson demonstrates very lucidly the legacy of Shakespeare for generations of writers, recalling Maya Angelou's remark: 'Of course, he was a black woman. I understood that. Nobody else understood it, but I know Shakespeare was a black woman. That is the role of art in life.' There's no better testimony to the field of Shakespeare studies and this book captures the rich pleasures of understanding the work both in context and now.

STAGE, SPACE, TIME AND THE SEA,
THE SEA . . .

I now focus on a more sporadic collection of books which variously engage with specific elements or representations in the plays. Two books deal with the sea, or more specifically, the storm. In Gwilym Jones's *Shakespeare's Storms* we encounter the weather and the water through theatrical and linguistics effects as well as synaesthesia; in Christopher Pye's *The Storm at Sea: Political Aesthetics in the time of Shakespeare* the weather is an altogether different beast. For Pye, the storm at sea is a metaphor for the 'interval between theo-centric institutions and the appearance of the for-mal state'. This 'interval' is especially compelling in this book because it foregrounds aesthetic auton-omy as a 'privileged space in which the problem of foundations as such is engaged'. The Renaissance is unique, Pye suggests, because it defines an era when 'The appearance of the aesthetic as a self-conscious formation is indissociable from that pro-blem of autogenesis of the social domain as such; the aesthetic work is where the intractably political because structurally irresolvable question of society's own capacity to 'incarnate' itself is most directly enjoined.' In this way the aesthetic, in its broadest terms, slips through various categories of power and the individual from 'the Machiavellian polis to the 'rationalised' state'. Pye's analysis is driven by his understanding of art (as a comprehensive rather than limiting term) as cap-able of creating its definitions as well as autonomies and this in turn 'engages the problem of founda-tions, including the abyss of its own grounds'. The pertinence of Shakespeare, as well as da Vinci and Hobbes, who are also discussed here, is that their work engages in different ways with the aesthetic as an escape from, as well as a reflection of, socially structuring categories. The sections on Shakespeare address *Hamlet, Othello* and *The Tempest* as well as *The Winter's Tale*. As this selection suggests (although I kept expecting *Macbeth* to crop up), the subject under discussion is law, sovereignty and the autonomous subject. One of the most resonant points here, especially in rela-tion to *Hamlet* and the later plays, is the way these plays present themselves as 'works whose inclusive aesthetic form incorporates the audience in its unstable, performative effects'. The chapter on *Hamlet* situates the tragedy alongside Kyd's *Spanish Tragedy* and examines the political resonance of art and revenge where the aesthetic becomes not only 'the inescapable limit point of dramatic mimesis, but at the core of the drama as a scene of political and historical foundations'. Despite its theoretical den-sity, this is a very astute book that reinvigorates some of the key debates surrounding ontology and auton-omy. Pye ranges over a number of fascinating texts

and situates the dynamic between the visual and the textual at the centre of his complex but rewarding treatments of socio-political foundations and the citizen-subject. Moving from Hobbes's *Leviathan* to *The Tempest* he writes:

On the one hand, the humanist play, by virtue of the aestheticization that should secure sovereignty, encounters at the deepest reaches of conscience an inhuman dimension that in some sense already antici-pates the automaton of state: it is not hard to get from the dispersed and agentless voice of Prospero's island to the impersonal apparatus of state, a phantasm in its own right.

Such phantasms in *The Tempest* are less spectral and more special in Jones's book, which attends to the representations of weather on Shakespeare's stage. As Jones states, 'Shakespeare was remarkably fond of storms, not only in the stage effects . . . but in the metaphors and similes he gives to his char-acters.' Attending to the various ways that the weather divides and rules in Shakespeare's plays, Jones observes a pattern that he perceives as pro-gressive or linear in its development as Shakespeare becomes increasingly concerned with fiercer and more destructive storms. Jones's particular interest is in how weather can be produced on stage as well as the 'environmental irony' of open-air theatres. Central to this discussion is the extent to which early modern theatre-goers were required to associate weather with augury or the paranormal. Similarly, to what extent did thunder and lightning begin its theatrical career through associations with satanic forces or development from them? Despite the specific associations between sound and weather created through thunderous effects, Jones observes how such sounds are mobilized across a range of instances, including conjuration, spiri-tual manifestations and the supernatural. The extent to which we can discern the moral or emotional effects of thunder is continually modu-lated by the context, so that it is never exclusively allied to evil, for example, but more flexibly asso-ciated with moments of revelation or high drama. As Jones's book demonstrates, the more remark-able the stage effects, the more resonant the metaphor. Central to the book's larger interest in recreating the potentials of early modern stage effects is a keen historical interest in how early modern audiences experienced their plays as well as their weather. In this way, the book explores the multiple ways the weather was coded as symbolic (reflecting divine intervention), portentous (supernatural) and instrumental (producing very real effects on the productivity of a fundamentally agrarian society). Focusing on these different concerns, Jones reads the weather in a number of different plays, including *Julius Caesar*, *King Lear*, *Macbeth*, *The Tempest* and *Pericles*. The chapters are for the most part organized around meteorological emissions – thunder, wind and lightening, for example – but the argument converges through a central interest in the relationship between physical experience and cognitive response – what C. S. Lewis might call the 'emotional weather'.

Keeping with the stage is Darlene Farabee's *Shakespeare's Staged Spaces and Playgoers' Perceptions*. Farabee is concerned with the trafficking of space and how the drama transports its audience. Through the term 'stage craft', she explores the various and often complex ways that the specific use of spaces directs our interpretations of the play. Highlighting how entrances and exits can determine our knowledge of both place and time, the book examines how allegiances are set through the order in which we, as audience, or character, as participant, arrive at the scene. Farabee's terms of analysis are wide-ranging, and here she uses 'stage craft' to encompass almost every strategic element of drama from the soliloquy to the cellar. The attention of the book, however, is largely on location, illusion and what we might call stage grammar, in other words, the effects produced by the spatial awareness of both character and object. The book acknowledges the extent to which many of these effects are defined by directorial decisions and that attending or watching a performance necessarily defines our response to questions of stagecraft. Farabee's interest lies in a combination of the historicist and the performative, but she does not address spatial theory or the epistemologies of space. Combining her particular interests, however, she presents readers with contexts through which to understand the idea of perception as a governing function of place in both *A Midsummer Night's Dream* and *The Tempest*. In the former, she is less concerned with the place of the wood and more with sleeping and dreaming; in *The Tempest*, the discussion centres not on the chorography of the 'bare isle' but on the experience of travelling. The middle chapters deal with the spatial effects produced through close readings of the texts, and here Farabee turns to *Macbeth*, *Hamlet* and *Richard II*. Central to her discussion of these plays is an acute attention to the strategic ways characters inhabit their dramatic space for the development of both character and action.

In Patricia Lennox and Bella Mirabella's edited collection, *Shakespeare and Costume*, the focus turns to the cultural aesthetics of the stage space through the use of costume. The contributors present a range of interests and expertise as the chapters move through documentary reconstruction, strategic symbolism and the production of meaning through fashion and self-fashioning. Although the narrative emphasis of the book is on performance and how costume both reflected and shaped the development of drama, there is a sustained commitment to the mobility of clothes and how we understand them. To that end, although the first section of the book lends itself to reconstructing Elizabethan attitudes to the performance of clothing, the period is not privileged as unique. Rather, the collection demonstrates the ongoing importance of the effects of costume in performance and how they contribute to our understanding of the plays. Although the first three chapters are necessarily speculative in their reproduction of Elizabethan stage costume, they explore the revealing apparatuses of socially constructive clothing including livery, and the visual effects of both splendour and modesty. Charting the relationships between social status and clothing, we move from Maria Hayward's piece on the performance of power in the deportment of monarchs both on stage and in royal progresses, to Erika Lin's thoughtful contribution on livery, which explores the formative relationships between private performance and public playhouse and the networks of debt, loyalty and affiliation produced through clothing. Catherine Richardson moves us down the social scale to the minor gentry as she examines the role of clothing in *The Merry Wives*, especially as a signifier of reputation. In an emotive chapter on shoes, Natasha Korda hones in on the foot, not only as marker of movement, distance and presence but also as a strangely intimate image of life. Here Korda examines early modern play-texts as records of those who performed them as both character and actor. Within this, Korda observes some very entertaining insights, not least of all that 'playtexts reveal that the social aspirations of female characters onstage could sometimes indeed be measured by the altitude of the chopines'. Looking at the practicalities, visual effects, costings and gender definitions of shoes, Korda produces a fascinating chapter on the ways 'shoes mediate the human actor's contact with its changing environment, and the ways in which the actor's body continually shapes and is reshaped by that contact'. The second section of the book attends to the use of costume from the Restoration to the present day, and uses a range of evidence to examine the dramatic effects of costume on the stage. Thinking about the late nineteenth and early twentieth centuries, Russell Jackson explores clothing in *As You Like It* and the challenges of cross-dressing for Rosalind/ Ganymede. Here he traces the changing conventions of female decorum and the complex codes of sexually appropriate behaviour in the theatre. Central to the success of these codes, however, was their subtle erosion and the provocative ways directors had to produce a sexually ambivalent character through dress, while retaining a necessary degree of moral anxiety. Jackson adds a further dimension to his contribution by highlighting the often incongruous dynamic between late nineteenth-century theatrical realism alongside 'the femininity of the figure adopting a swaggering outside but revealing her gender-specific charms in the respectable and licensed context of a classic play'. This and many of the chapters in this collection produce very compelling readings of the relationships between social convention and theatrical production. The latter sections are geared more specifically to looking at productions of the twentieth century and Patricia Lennox provides a compelling reading of the Nurse in *Romeo and Juliet*, demonstrating how representations moved from the genteel to the bawdy through the use of both costume and language. The collection concludes through the perspectives of two renowned costume designers who discuss the experiences and challenges of dressing Shakespeare's characters over the last fifty years. This thoughtful and intelligent collection produces a variety of interests and attitudes to clothing in the period. Each chapter is driven by a different focus and reveals a fascinating reciprocity between the bodies, words and clothes that dress the stage.

THIS GOODLY BOOK

Shifting our gaze to the female body, we turn to Kay Stanton's *Shakespeare's 'Whores'*. The book rather arrestingly begins with an assertion from the author that she 'is NOT a whore'. Her point, of course, is that like many women, she has been referred to as such by a certain type of man who uses the term as a baggy form of abuse. Using this insight as a bridge to Shakespeare's women Stanton observes: 'Of the 59 instances of forms of the word "whore" in Shakespeare's works, 51 come from 21 male characters, leaving only 8 instances from a total of 5 female characters, and only 1 of these, professional sex worker Doll Tearsheet of *2 Henry IV*, "owns" the term by choosing to describe herself by it.' Understanding the word as a form of abuse, why it operates as such within the plays and the male mouth, as well as the social and sexual anxieties it reveals is only part of Stanton's project here. The more polemical ambition of the book is to reclaim the term as an expression of uninhibited sexuality, which, for Stanton, is better expressed under the name Venus. To that end the book explores the various types and archetypes through which women are both limited and characterized within the drama. Almost all these types are defined according to their relationship to sexuality – virgin, whore, goddess, wife, etc. Some of the most compelling characters here are what Stanton calls 'woman-in-between' (borrowing the term from Jean Bolen), like Helena in *All's Well*, as 'she moves between archetypes and within a society quick to stereotype her'. Shifting between the two perspectives of feminism and psychology, Stanton builds on the understanding that women are shaped by the goddess concept as well as patriarchal forces. In this way the symbolic economy of social formation determines certain paradigms through which women can seek to express themselves. Exploring the various ways that Shakespeare's female characters inhabit or express their sexuality, Stanton analyzes the relationships between erotics, politics and poetics in the plays. Here she mainly concentrates on the comedies and the late plays, understanding that genre, too, plays a large part in the preconditioning of female sexuality. On tragedy, for example, Stanton notes: 'The high concentration of appearances of the word "whore" demonstrate that Shakespeare considered men's failure to accommodate themselves to the idea of female sexual choice and integrity to be particularly instrumental in war, violence and, ultimately societal suicide.' The book begins by identifying the power of the name 'whore' and the characters who try to rewrite their destinies. The most devastating here is, of course, Desdemona. Central to this focus is the interpretative resonance of the sex worker and the theoretical relationship between prostitution and marriage, for example. Stanton brings recent feminist critiques to bear on the question of whether the word can be reclaimed as a form of expression rather than an insult. In Shakespeare she discerns a progressive liberalism that allows multiple 'whores' to take the stage by granting themselves 'sexual freedom equal to that which men grant to themselves, regarding the concept of "whore" not as an accurate description of such freedom, but only as a stance of male-constructed female representation that travesties the majesty of our sexual power.' The question is both rhetorical and personal, and Stanton's book examines the various dynamics between shame and power, liberation and oppression written into Shakespeare's 'whores'. Many of the book's central questions come together in the chapter on Cleopatra, the book's apparent hero. Here Stanton provides a sophisticated analysis of the formative effects of myth and tragedy on the production of the symbolic apparatus of sexuality. The latter half of the book explores the pursuit of female desire through a range of instances, including the Sonnets and *A Lover's Complaint*, before culminating in a discussion of cross-dressing and the possibility of 'full androgynous potential'. The book's final section is on Venus and Shakespeare's interest in the creation of desire, as well as its satisfaction and exploitation. Central to Stanton's book is a renewed emphasis on how women are interpreted as well as represented, and part of the pleasure of this book is her vigorous claim for self-awareness – in how we read and think about sexuality as well as celebrate it: 'If Venus is "porno" (*porne*) and Shakespeare is graphic (written), when they embrace, we have 'pornography' through Venus and Shakespeare that male *and* female should be able to enjoy equally, not in debased slavery, but in jouissance.'

Paul Cefalu, in *Tragic Cognition in Shakespeare's Othello*, begins with the instruction to imagine 'what it would be like to be Iago'. Cefalu's point is that Iago is unique amongst Shakespeare's villains because he demonstrates an ability 'to fixate on those aspects of cognition that ordinarily lie between conscious and nonconscious experience'. In other words, he is powerfully, hyper-aware of the experience even as he renders it manifest. The book's interest in cognition follows on from an understanding of the value of psychoanalysis in allowing us to 'evaluate Iago's inimitable mentalizing, the very manner in which those cognitive abilities are pathologized in the play'. To this end, Cefalu uses cognitive and psychoanalytic theories to explore the limits of both knowledge and tragedy within the play: 'But it is Schopenhauer who is Iago's philosopher, for Iago's turning of his will away from life, his contraction of the world as (cognitive) representation into absolute ego, his resigned approach toward death, his heroic escape from the neural sublime, all provide him with the tragic catharsis that . . . is unachievable for us.' It is unachievable for us, Cefalu states, because Iago can close 'the explanatory gap between cognition and consciousness that for us will no doubt remain inexplicably open'. The book is largely concerned with analyzing this gap and what it means for Iago. Iago's success largely depends on his ability to identify and manipulate the weaknesses of others, but even this, as Cefalu observes, reduces him to something of a caricature. Instead, Cefalu concentrates on Iago's ability to mind-read, as it were, and the book develops its narrative through various explorations of Iago's cogitations. What develops from this are various theories about how the mind works and the seemingly irrational or counter-productive moves that Iago can make which create fulfilment precisely because they engage the mind in a fictive pattern of fulfilment. Working towards the central question of catharsis or fulfil-ment, Cefalu traces the multiple mental moves that Iago makes, how he makes them and, to some extent, why he makes them. The final section turns to Othello as a comparative case, and here Cefalu explores the possibility of extended cogni-tion whereby 'Othello's memory, not simply his ability to infer, deduce, gather evidence, now *includes* Iago.' The great irony here, however, is that, according to Cefalu, all our memories include Iago: 'in such re-imaginings of Iago, we likewise project on to him the catharsis that, as obsessive interpreters of his motives, we do not enjoy ourselves'.

Keeping within the tragic vein, Dympna Callaghan's contribution to the Arden Language and Writing series addresses *Hamlet* and provides a comprehensive and thoughtful account of various ways of approaching the play. This series is expli-citly aimed at students of Shakespeare and, although the overarching commitment is to the exploration of the language, the series also aims to approach each play from specific angles through which we can gain a deeper understanding of the

text. In many ways, the series attempts to produce the perfect lesson plan whereby the instructor assumes a basic knowledge of the play but invites students into the rich experiences of deeper under-standing. In this way each section uses a specific focus to open up various discussions on variant texts, etymology and explication, rhetoric, revenge, politics and gender. This list, however, is much more reductive than the book's, which cleverly nuances and explores many of the major aspects of the play through lateral approaches. Callaghan produces an excellent habit of interro-gating language through both the surprising and the mundane: there is a section on 'fat Hamlet', which looks at the play's frequent uses of the word and whether our hero is wide in the girth. Similarly, a section on 'naked' Hamlet reveals the ways words can work differently both at an allego-rical and literal level as well as the deep compres-sion of meaning in this play and the power of suggestion. Callaghan has brief sections on philo-sophy and tragedy, gender and power (whores, widows and vulnerable young women) and the book is a remarkable example of compression and precision. There is a lot of material here, and Callaghan lucidly navigates between versification, textual problems, theatrical contexts and a central focus on some of the major speeches of the play. There is also an astute attention to dramaturgy and performance – the aside, for example, through which Callaghan explores when words are no longer our own, that is, they are sententious phrases borrowed from a culture of moral reflexes, or they are said not in earnest but in affect. Here, and throughout the book, Callaghan writes with the intention of opening up discussions, providing possible ways in and allowing for the coexistence of different interpretations. There is little on critical history or reception (beyond brief mentions of possible interpretations, be they feminist, materi-alist or psychoanalytical); that is not the remit of the book, however, which is instead to provide a comprehensive and thoughtful attention to lan-guage as a way of understanding and relishing the drama as well as inviting students of the play to think about their own approaches and interests and harness them accordingly. This Arden series is a great asset to anyone studying or teaching Shakespeare, and Callaghan's book on *Hamlet* is a shrewd, intelligent and perspicacious representation of the series' aims.

FAITH, HOPE AND CHARITY

Turning from the scholar prince to questions of faith, two books this year deal with religion: David Loewenstein and Michael Witmore's collection *Shakespeare and Early Modern Religion*, which offers a fresh and varied collection of chapters on the subject, and R. Chris Hassel, Jr's *Shakespeare's Religious Language: A Dictionary*. Although both books use the term 'religion' they are much more centred on Western religion and in particular, Christianity. Hassel Jr's dictionary provides a thoughtful companion to anyone interested in the religious language of Shakespeare's plays. It is comprehensive, if by no means exhaustive, and offers a range of entries – some purely definitional, some more discursive. Most entries provide a reference to the line or lines in Shakespeare where the word is mentioned, so it is very useful to anyone wanting to cross-reference the plays. Hassel's interpretation of what constitutes 'religious language' is astute and includes many broader references to things like fasting, hags or luxury, for example. Some of the entries on nouns are the most intriguing, especially for the ways in which they work across the plays. In *Measure for Measure*, for example, we can see the word 'evil' used in reference to sex but to murder in *Hamlet*. It is specifically geared to Shakespeare so tends only to include those words that resonate in his plays but this, of course, is revealing in itself. Hassel is very even-handed and never gets drawn into ethical discourses in his definitions: the section on conscience, for example, enumerates its appearances within the plays and the dizzying complexities of how and where he uses it. Hassel demonstrates rather than discusses these complexities, but this is also the book's virtue, since it is remarkably concise, intelligent and accessible. In *Shakespeare and Early Modern Religion*, the fourteen chapters consider the idea, role, context and expression of

religion in a range of plays. The first section deals largely with contexts and the legacies of the Reformation, examining residual Catholicism and what Felicity Heal calls 'Shakespeare's metropolis'. In her excellent chapter, Heal examines how London offered a 'multifaceted official Protestantism, with its ideological roots in Calvinist theology; a culture of the godly for whom intense preaching had become the focus of experimental faith; formal liturgical ritual maintained in cathedral and court; and the beginning of a new form of religious identity that was to become English Arminianism by the 1630s'. Heal's contribution, and the collection more generally, emphasizes the effects that religious intensity had on the structures and patterns of the city, the culture of preaching and the well-rehearsed public hostility to Catholicism. Attending to the frenetic world of worship, Heal reveals a pullulating and mobile community of Christians fed on the powerful rhetorical structures of faith. Shakespeare, however, 'refused to stage those forms of Protestant propaganda to which his fellow Londoners were routinely exposed'. As a whole, however, the collection is less interested in rehearsing Shakespeare's elusive inclinations and more invested in exploring the plurality of religious interests and how the drama stages debates as to the expression and identities of early modern religious thought. Although the interest here is religion, many of the chapters recognize the interactions between politics and nationhood, and the ethical problems they produce. Beatrice Groves's chapter tackles the interrelationships between political and religious rhetoric in *King John*; Peter Lake addresses the interaction of secular and religious sensibilities in *Julius Caesar*; and Adrian Streete traces the complex conflicts between Lucretian and Protestant responsiveness to natural law in *Measure for Measure*. Through an analysis of *King Lear*, Loewenstein argues that Shakespeare exploited the potential of tragic theatre to represent competing and provocative religious views. Loewenstein proposes that 'King Lear deeply challenges a providential view of the world and universe in a culture that widely believed that God actively intervenes in human affairs to punish, chastise, test and reward.' Following the explosive potential of theatre to represent divisive sensibilities, Ewan Fernie looks at the demonic in *Macbeth*. In Michael Witmore's chapter, proverbial wisdom becomes the focus in a range of plays where he considers 'Shakespeare's adaptations of wisdom practices' and the 'depth of their theatrical power when staged as communal ritual'. Most interesting here is his consideration of *The Merchant of Venice* and the casket scene. Moving the question of 'faith' beyond an exclusively Christian identity, Richard McCoy examines the role of belief in the secular context of theatrical illusion. The latter section moves the discussion in a number of different directions, including a 'post-secular perspective', which seems to mean a renewed interest in the dynamic between the religious and non-religious elements of the dramas. The final chapter is important in moving away from an overarching Western narrative to an examination of non-Christian theologies, including Islam and Judaism. Here Matthew Dimmock suggests that Shakespeare, unlike many of his contemporaries, did not write a 'Turk', nor did he conflate Islam and Judaism as a collective threat to Christianity. Dimmock's reading of *The Merchant* is sensitive to the ways in which 'in drawing on dramatic precedent and the Bible, but offering a shared scriptural language whose valid interpretation is always a Christian prerogative, Shakespeare creates a Judaism that is neither a viable alternative to Christianity nor (in the Marlovian sense) satirical'. Ultimately, for Dimmock, Shakespeare's representations of the two Abrahamic non-Christian religions are essentially theatrical rather than theological; in other words, Shakespeare's non-Christians are 'already encoded in the playhouse' but that it is 'Shakespeare's decision to render non-Christian religion as background rather than foreground that sets him apart from the bombast of the 1580s and early 1590s'. *Shakespeare and Early Modern Religion* is a thoughtful and wide ranging collection that in various ways aims to nuance the debates that surround both spirituality and religious practice. The desire to move away from absolutist or essentialist readings of religious expression makes this a strong book that seeks to explore how religion seeped into secular as well as doctrinal ceremonies.

As evidenced in Cummings's book (reviewed here in 2015), the interest in the Reformation is changing: scholars are no longer in search of boundaries and allegiances but the porous, mercurial relationships between belief and behaviour, dogma and doctrine. One of this year's finest books attends to this shifting focus and re-examines how the Reformation not only sought to redefine religious behaviour but the emotions that attended it. Steven Mullaney's *The Reformation of Emotions in the Age of Shakespeare* begins with the premise that the changing of state religion in this period made huge demands on the ways people felt and expressed or understood those feelings: 'there was indeed a reformation of emotions in the early modern period, it took place most significantly in the domain of what we might call the social emotions, in the social and hence lived world of feeling, as opposed to the theoretical or polemical discourses of medical treatises'. Mullaney's attention to the 'lived world of feeling' drives him to ask 'What did it feel like to be an Elizabethan?', but such a question is less nebulous than it first appears, because the point of Mullaney's thesis is how the Elizabethans asked this of themselves. Observing the proliferation of 'cultural performances' (in its widest sense), Mullaney identifies Elizabethan social media as 'affective technologies'. Central to this thesis is the impact of crisis (religious, political, economic) in redefining the imperatives of performance (both narrative and theatrical). Despite the emphasis on variety and fracture, feeling here is largely collective rather than individual where the theatre 'keep[s] members of an affective and cognitive community up to date with themselves'. Despite the allure of such a statement, Mullaney is not claiming that the Elizabethans were deeply self-aware people, nor that the stage is reflective or even necessarily discursive; rather, the book is committed to the complex and multivalent ways that emotions and world interact. The theatre is a powerful site for the exploration of this thesis because it presents rather than codifies its emotional landscapes. The book begins with an exploration of the 'social logic' of emotions; in other words, the various ways that Elizabethan drama engaged with emotional constructs and sought to delimit the experience of them on the Elizabethan stage. Here revenge tragedy becomes a case in point where Mullaney argues less for drama as didactic or even representative but as 'antimimetic', ironic and 'catalysed' by alienation rather than identification. In this context, *The Merchant of Venice* is identified as 'inextricably implicated in the prejudice and hypocrisy with which it works and on which it depends'. Chapter 2 explores the first tetralogy and how history is constituted as both memory and forgetting. Here, trauma plays an unequivocal part in the cultural organization of those processes (linked specifically to the loss of the Eucharist), but the idea of history emerges as an 'experience rather than an idea or an argument' and is therefore constructed as much by what it fails to record as what it represents. The final chapter turns to Habermas and 'the social life of theatre' where Mullaney examines the idea of publication as performance, whether in print or on stage. Thinking about 'publication', he defines the stage as a place in which 'thoughts and feelings and beliefs could be made public in sixteenth century England'. The overarching attention to how social emotion is identified, exploited and deployed is fascinating and Mullaney writes beautifully: his attention to the theatre presents the drama of this period as somewhat radical in its ability to disclose – in sympathy and revulsion – the affective lives of the audience:

Early modern amphitheatre drama provided a kind of inhabited or at least regularly occupied affective technology, a place where players, playwrights, and their audiences could explore the social imaginary they shared, in all is faultlines and gaps and dissociations – could probe and feel and even touch some of the critical integuments and sinews of the social body that had become disarticulated in the upheavals of 'embodied thought' that constituted the reformations of early modern England.

Such reformations are taking place all the time and many of the finest books this year remind us of the small revolutions that take place every day in the study, classroom or mind.

BOOKS REVIEWED

Anderson, Miranda, *The Renaissance Extended Mind* (Basingstoke, 2015)

Callaghan, Dympna, *Hamlet, Language and Writing* (London, 2015)

Cefalu, Paul, *Tragic Cognition in Shakespeare's Othello: Beyond the Neural Sublime* (London, 2015)

Chiari, Sophie, ed., *The Circulation of Knowledge in Early Modern English Literature* (Ashgate, 2015)

Duncan-Jones, Katherine, *Portraits of Shakespeare* (Oxford, 2015)

Edmondson, Paul, *Shakespeare* (London, 2015)

Ellrodt, Robert, *Montaigne and Shakespeare: The Emergence of Modern Self-consciousness* (Manchester, 2015)

Farabee, Darlene, *Shakespeare's Staged Spaces and Playgoers' Perceptions* (Basingstoke, 2014)

Hassel, R. Chris Jr, *Shakespeare's Religious Language: A Dictionary* (London, 2015)

Jones, Gwylim, *Shakespeare's Storms* (Manchester, 2015)

Knapp, James A., ed., *Shakespeare and the Power of the Face* (Ashgate, 2015)

Lennox, Patricia, and Bella Mirabella, eds., *Shakespeare and Costume* (London, 2015)

Loewenstein, David and Michael Witmore, eds., *Shakespeare and Early Modern Religion* (Cambridge, 2015)

Mullaney, Steven, *The Reformation of Emotions in the Age of Shakespeare* (Chicago, 2015)

Pye, Christopher, *The Storm at Sea: Political Aesthetics in the Time of Shakespeare* (New York, 2015)

Skinner, Quentin, *Forensic Shakespeare* (Oxford, 2014)

Stanton, Kay, *Shakespeare's 'Whores': Erotics, Politics and Poetics* (Basingstoke, 2014)

Wells, Stanley, *Shakespeare: A Very Short Introduction* (Oxford, 2015)

The works reviewed this year range widely, from studies of the 'global' scope of twenty-first century Shakespearian performance, to the public/private intimacy of the Jacobean indoor theatre and even to the enforced intimacy of prison Shakespeare. In one way or another, they converge on the theme of 'interpretive communities': the points at which the various contributions of performers, audiences and scripts coincide, and in which the interpretive opportunities and pressures of playing spaces and the wider society can be identified. I begin with the figure onstage at the centre of the theatrical audience's attention, move to the theatres and issues of spectatorship connected with them, and end with that 'global' reach afforded by international festivals and the film, television and digital media.

The psychology of acting, its essential and unavoidable doubleness, and the relation of these factors to the performance and reception of Shakespeare's plays in 'the long Stanislavskian century' are the themes of Cary Mazer's *Double Shakespeares: Emotional-Realist Acting and Contemporary Performance*. Mazer's applause for Declan Donellan's approach, 'throwing out the Strasbergian bathwater without throwing out the Stanislavskian baby', encapsulates the book's project, an exploration of ways 'of allowing the theatre to be fully representational without succumbing to twentieth-century psychoanalytical fallacies; and of giving free play to the dramatic subject without denying actors their bodies, their emotions and their selves' (66). Mazer pursues this and related ideas through an impressive and stimulating range of examples. These include the animation *Bolt* (2008), which can assume a general understanding in its audience of what is meant by The Method; 'the-play-must-go-on' narratives, such as the Canadian television series *Slings and Arrows*, heavily invested in 'the paradigm of histrionic emotional identification' (105); the metatheatrical boarding-

school drama of Joe Calarco's *Shakespeare's R&J*; Phyllida Lloyd's doubly doubled 2012/13 production of *Julius Caesar*, performed as if by inmates of a women's prison; and his own experiences as a dramaturg. 'Rehearsal narratives', both fictional and factual, sharing tropes of exploration, discovery and self-realization, suggest a dimension of the relationship between the audience and the dramatic event: 'Spectatorship is irresistibly transformative because the actors have transformed themselves' (110). This is effectively an account of the stories we tell ourselves and are told about the way the stage tells us stories, and it yields insights on a number of levels, not least when disguise within the fiction reflects or refracts our own preoccupations. An example is Mazer's comment on contemporary cross-dressing, which aims 'to heighten the theatricality, the phenomenological doubleness, of the theatre event, in order to destabilize assumptions about the coherence and subjectivity of the dramatic character, while at the same time allowing the actors to represent them via Stanislavskian emotionalist acting techniques' (85–6). This may suggest a distinction between early modern and 'contemporary' performance, with the former not sharing the aim Mazer identifies as 'problematiz[ing] binaries of gender without inadvertently reinforcing and essentializing these binaries' (86). Like its other case studies, the book's account of Declan Donnellan's all-male *As You Like It* (first seen in 1991) measures the distance between Shakespearian texts in their own time and in an era that is 'post' Stanislavski himself as well as a good many variations on and oppositions to his ideas. The complex interrelationships of audiences, performers and texts exist in the 'not me … not not me' identified by Richard Schechner (cited by Mazer, 83), but the cumulative effect of *Double Shakespeares* is to establish this as a source of pleasures rather than anxieties: play-acting, as described by Mazer, is serious but, even when the events enacted are in themselves disturbing or tragic, in the last analysis performance is *fun*.

Stimulating approaches to Shakespearian acting are offered by two books addressed to that valuable and much sought-after person, the intelligent general reader. *Performing King Lear: Gielgud to Russell Beale* by Jonathan Croall is an 'oral history of *King Lear* over the last half-century or so' (2) bringing together comment by actors, directors and critics on notable performances, not all of them as well known as those announced by its title. The physical and emotional demands of the role, and the variety of approaches to the nature of Lear's madness are vividly described, and the combination of 'insider' views from performers and directors, with those of 'outsiders' – critics, other actors – makes for a multifaceted and fascinating book.

The revelations about the ways and means of the different actors are especially valuable. At one level of physical and emotional technique is the slight, five-foot-tall Kathryn Hunter (Leicester Haymarket, Young Vic and Japan, 1997), who reflects on her approach to the great male tragic role, played by her as a fragile 80-year old: 'I had to keep checking that I wasn't thinking like a woman, and was attending to a male mentality. But although there has to be a certain amount of transformation, it mustn't be to the point where you lose the feminine element.' Her guiding principle was that 'as an actor you try to enter the appropriate frame of mind, and then the physical action looks after itself' (69). One day Hunter found herself following an old man into a supermarket: 'He was quite small and frail, but he had a real sense of authority. I thought, "If he were wearing a crown and was surrounded by dignitaries, why couldn't he be King Lear?"' Nicol Williamson's work towards his performance in Terry Hands's 2001 Clwyd Theatr Cymru production in Mold was rather different. 'Academic analysis didn't interest him,' Hands recalls of the week spent 'exploring the text in detail; on the island of Rhodes'. 'Instead he simply was Lear throughout the day. Whether in

bars, shops, during interminable lunches, or on walks, he blustered, confronted, dominated, insulted, ate, drank and showed extraordinary, if wayward generosity' (145). Once in the rehearsal room, though, 'Nicol contributed to all aspects of the work', including the weekly session on Shakespeare's Sonnets (147). Croall cites contrasting critical judgements by Charles Spencer, who found Williamson 'vocally underpowered' and 'depressingly superficial', and Michael Coveney, who admitted the actor was ' all over the place' but insisted that 'you knew you were in the presence of true greatness' in a performance 'fretted with moments of gold dust and heartbreak' (148).

Stanley Wells's *Great Shakespeare Actors: Burbage to Branagh*, consists of chapters on the careers of thirty-nine notable performers, all but one (Tommaso Salvini) in the English-speaking theatre, and ten of them women. The difficulties presented by making the choice and the limitations unavoidably incurred are acknowledged, and the emphasis is – as the author explains – 'on individuals rather than on the productions in which they appear or the directors who contribute often to a great but (to audiences) unidentifiable extent, to their performances' (1). This being said, the value of the book is perhaps enhanced by the nature of the restrictions, and the paradoxical freedom they confer. The broader frame of theatrical and cultural history is outlined in the introduction and in two intercalated discussions: 'Who was the first great Shakespeare actress?' and 'Who was the first great American Shakespeare actor?'

The accounts of actors necessarily outside the author's own experience give a convincing impression not only of the effect of their performances but also – whenever possible – the means by which they were achieved and the prevailing theatrical conditions. As well as drawing effectively on significant written accounts by actors and critics, Wells is particularly persuasive in analyses of visual and aural evidence, such as Ellen Terry's recordings of speeches: 'the range of the voice is exceptionally wide, and she sings Ophelia's snatches of song with true beauty of tone, achieving a true inwardness in grief'. In the comment that follows, Wells points to an important distinction that holds true not only for the study of acting styles from the past, but also for the negotiations of modern actors with Shakespearian texts: 'This is not naturalistic speaking, but in its imaginative identification of actor with character it creates a profound impression of emotional reality' (123). Similarly, the description of Gielgud's speaking – much better represented by the recording techniques of later decades than that of his great aunt – draws attention to its dominant characteristics, and the actor's ability to 'create the sense of a mind at work, the words newly minted from within the man who speaks them' (173). Reporting Audrey Williamson's account of Ralph Richardson's Falstaff in 2 Henry IV he reflects: 'I kick myself for not having paid my half-crown and climbed the steps to the gallery to experience this performance' (169). Wells's incisive and sympathetic descriptions of performances he himself has witnessed in a long theatre-going career are vivid and sympathetic. Telling moments are recalled with an eye for their significance in the play as well as their local effect, such as the 'real love and tenderness' with which Ian Richardson, as Ford in The Merry Wives of Windsor, knelt to ask his wife's forgiveness 'in a manner which in retrospect humanized the entire role' (223). Wells does not hesitate to discern the actor's personality as it is reflected in the characters they inhabit. For him, this is a legitimate and important element of the experience of theatre-going. Of Judi Dench he writes that, 'the generosity of her art reflects and is enabled by the generosity of a great spirit' (230). Great Shakespearean Actors is itself generous in identifying and responding to the appeal and – where appropriate – limitations of actors in past and present.

Wells is grateful that Sir Donald Wolfit was his 'first experience of Shakespeare on the stage when, as a schoolboy, [he] saw his Othello in Hull during the 1940s'. He admits, though, that his 'main memory' of the performance was 'of him opening his eyes while lying on stage while having a fit and gazing around the theatre, clearly anxious to see how full the house was' (164). There was, as Wells observes, 'more than a touch of the magniloquent Vincent Crummles' about this powerful, dedicated and often sublimely egotistical actor. Wolfit's career and personality have been represented even-handedly by Ronald Harwood's 1971 biography, and inform his play The Dresser (1980) and Peter Yates's film version released in 1983. But the play's character 'Sir', while sharing some of Wolfit's idiosyncrasies and his power as an actor, is a dramatic construct rather than a portrait.[1] Far from being a physical and mental wreck, dying in his dressing room during a wartime tour, Wolfit was a vigorous and effective performer whose career continued into the 1960s. Laurence Raw's Theater of the People: Donald Wolfit's Shakespearean Productions 1937–1953 draws on the actor's personal papers, held since 1990 in the Harry Ransom Center, University of Texas. Documenting in hitherto unavailable detail Wolfit's relationships with managements, funding bodies and – above all – his audiences, Raw conveys the effectiveness of what was a social as well as artistic mission. Especially in his wartime work, Wolfit 'proved beyond question that theatre had something to say in the past, present, and future, and that it could be readily appreciated by everyone'. This 'theatre for the people' was 'in its own way as political as People's Theatre', but unlike that movement's explicitly socialist agenda, Wolfit's worked 'through an intense, perhaps subliminal communication between actors and audience' (xii–xiii). Having 'positioned himself as an opponent of the establishment as represented by the Old Vic, the Entertainments National Service Association, or the Arts and British Councils' (xiii), Wolfit pursued a career that was at once self-consciously heroic and idealistic, aiming 'to create a theatre for the people without any form of external interference that would fulfill the public service duty of uplifting

---

[1] Harwood makes the distinction clear in the foreword to the play: 'Sir is not Donald Wolfit. My biography ... must serve to reflect my understanding of him as a man and as a theatrical creature' (The Dresser (Oxford, 1980), p. 7).

playgoers, educating them *and* bringing them together' (50, emphasis in original). The relationship between wartime Shakespearian performances and the official and unofficial enhancement of morale was not a simple matter of propaganda, even in such apparently straightforward examples as Olivier's 1944 film of *Henry V*. On the one hand, Wolfit's presentation of Richard III as 'a contemporary tyrant', speaking in hectoring tones, utterly lacking in empathy and even sporting a wig with a Hitlerian cowlick, prompted the London *Evening Standard* to promise 'if you wish to see what Hitler would have done in 1495 then this is your meat' (46). On a less direct and melodramatic level of relevance, his Shylock was a complex character in a production that suggested (Raw argues) that there was little difference between the Jew-hating Christians on stage and the commonplace xenophobia of audiences watching them (72). Wolfit had a firm and well thought-through conviction of the importance of his work and its potential social influence that balanced the extravagances often induced by his bruised ego and resentment of the theatrical establishment.

Wolfit's grandiloquent curtain speeches, often accompanied in the case of King Lear by exhibitions of his physical exhaustion, were not unwelcome as performances of his emotional engagement with the audience as well as the role he had played. He was both the humble servant of the spectators and the playwright, and the man who had commanded their utter attention for the duration of the play. This was a conspicuous act of sharing, and audiences for the most part rose to the occasion, especially in wartime. The dynamic in the plays' own time between actor, spectator, stage and script dominates *Moving Shakespeare Indoors: Performance and Repertoire in the Jacobean Playho*use, edited by Andrew Gurr and Farah Karim-Cooper. If a consensus emerges among the varied and expert chapters, it is that (as John Astington observes in 'Why the Theatres Changed'), 'the statue scene in *The Winter's Tale* or the storm in *The Tempest* would have looked and sounded different at the [King's] company's two theatres, but variability of

venue for given plays had long been a condition to which actors adjusted themselves' (28). Andrew Gurr, in 'The New Fashion for Indoor Plays', suggests that 'The major problems in transferring plays between the Globe and the Blackfriars arose far less for the players than they did for their audiences' (203). Differences in the prices of entrance and in the structure of the Globe and the Blackfriars meant that, as Astington points out, although 'the forms of the early stage and theatre space were multiple, the change effected at the indoor theatre was to select one of those older forms and apply it to a new social and commercial setting' (31).

How did the experiences of seeing and hearing plays differ between the two venues? A number of contributions consider the question in sociological as well as what might be called stage-management terms, and some address dramaturgical issues. In 'The Audience of the Indoor Theatre' Penelope Woods argues for an increased erotic dimension to the play-going experience, in which 'the circulation of looks and longing and fumbling informed what has been described as itself a noticeably sexualized dramatic turn' (163). Woods suggests that the 'vulnerability of Desdemona's gradually undressed body in the scene preceding her murder' was 'instrumental in the production of the keen voyeuristic pity' with which Henry Jackson responded to an Oxford performance of *Othello* in 1610 (154–5). Would this have been more intense indoors than in the outdoor playhouse? This is arguable, but somehow the boy player (admittedly referred to throughout in Jackson's Latin with the feminine pronoun *illa*) tells us more about the emotional and verisimilar conviction produced by spectacle (as distinct from oratory) than the specific erotic effect of the 'male gaze'. Woods's argument concerning the Blackfriars itself, though, is supported by Farah Karim-Cooper's account of the effect of dress and makeup in the audience, 'To Glisten in a Playhouse: Cosmetic Beauty Indoors', and Martin White's '"When torchlight made an artificial noon": Light and Darkness in the Indoor Jacobean Theatre'. As for dramaturgy, Bart von

Es proposes that the 'merging of traditions' meant that 'Shakespeare gradually incorporated aspects of Blackfriars convention at the same time that indoor poets, notably Fletcher, expanded their focus to incorporate the capacities of adult players' (249).

Tiffffany Stern, considering the Second Blackfriars 'as a place of nostalgia', looks back to the site's previous incarnations to support a claim that the 'ex-monastery, ex-parliament, ex-boy theatre and would-be court theatre' was 'always defined by being not something or somewhere else' (114). Stern suggests that the space's history 'will have been creatively appealing to Shakespeare' and 'will have provided a space in which he and other Londoners could explore their conflicted feelings about past and present, Catholicism and Protestantism' (103). Is caution in order here? The 'perhaps' is significant and 'will have' is one of those verbal devices that can plunge downwards as well as soar upwards on the snakes-and-ladders board of critical-historical argument. Firmer if less suggestive ground is provided in the volume's first section, 'The Context of Hard Evidence', in particular by Jon Greenfield's account of the 'practical evidence' and its application to the construction of the Sam Wanamaker Playhouse. In one vivid analogy, we are informed – and perhaps comforted in our experiences of flatpack furniture – by the suggestion that 'the problems encountered by the purchaser of Ikea self-assembly furniture are in some ways the same as those encountered when building a historic timber frame'. Assembly must follow the prescribed order and the structure 'must be strong enough in its half-constructed state to avoid self inflicted damage' (49). Oliver Jones, in 'Documentary Evidence for an Indoor Jacobean Theatre', and Mariko Ichikawa, in 'Continuities and Innovations in Staging', provide between them an effective guide to the 'hard evidence'. The section headed 'Materiality Indoors', as well as Stern's proposal for the Blackfriars experience as in part a 'wistful' (her word) search for time past, includes discussion of acoustics, lighting and – inevitably – audiences. The book's final group of

chapters, 'The New Fashion for Indoors', with its focus on the play-texts, may serve as reminder that 'hard' and 'soft' are relative terms. So, for that matter, were the definitions in the period of the public/private distinction. A useful addendum to *Moving Shakespeare Indoors* is provided by Eoin Price's short but informative monograph *'Public' and 'Private' Playhouses in Renaissance England*, in which a careful survey of paratexts and other evidence 'assesses how [the theatres] were conceived of by the people who built them, worked in them, attended them and wanted them shut down' (5). It emerges that, like many other labels, these could be used by contemporaries without strict regard for stability and (more important) for different purposes.

Bettina Boecker's *Imagining Shakespeare's Original Audience, 1660–2000* has the subtitle *Groundlings, Gallants, Grocers*, suggesting the stratification by class that has characterized influential accounts of that elusive assembly – or rather, assemblies. As several of the chapters in *Moving Shakespeare Indoors* also testify, assessing the interplay between the drama and its patrons is an engrossing but ultimately frustrating business, almost as chancy as show business itself. Boecker's study demonstrates the ways in which since the Restoration, accounts of those 'original' audiences have been freighted with ideological assumptions and turned to critical account. Most important is the manner in which, as she points out, 'A whole class of Elizabethan spectators seems to have come into existence on the basis of a host of diffuse eighteenth-century references to a couple of questionable early modern references' (51). 'Groundlings' have been invented and reinvented, usually with appeal to Hamlet's animadversions on their predilection for inexplicable dumb-shows and noise. Sometimes they have been offered as evidence for the democratic virtues and energy of Shakespeare's theatres, at others as an excuse for reprehensibly indecorous elements of the plays. Appeals to them as social and political exemplars have been tricky: 'Given that nationalism depends on a fundamentally positive concept of the people, singling out the groundlings as responsible for

Shakespeare's moral and artistic lapses presents a considerable argumentative difficulty' (79). On the level of aesthetics, and as an explanation for such 'artistic lapses', it is intriguing to find how persistent the notion has been of an audience childishly willing to suspend disbelief or who, in the words of Muriel St Clare Byrne, writing in 1927, possessed 'the childish faculty of overlooking without effort any discrepancies which shatter the illusion of reality', balanced by 'an imaginative capacity distinctly superior to that possessed by the modern audience' (83). Like so many of the examples cited by Boecker, this is significant in both historical and historiographical terms: what, exactly, does it tell us about the 'modern audience' of the late 1920s, at least as seen by Byrne? For William Poel, the important members of Shakespeare's audience would seem to be the 'gallants' with whom he peopled the edges of his reconstructed platform stages, a living reminder of the performance's authenticity and representatives of the 'highly educated intellectual elite' that formed the principal audience for the Elizabethan Stage Society (89).

Boecker reminds the reader that Alfred Harbage's accounts – *Shakespeare's Audience* (1941) and *Shakespeare and the Rival Traditions* (1952) – are redolent respectively of New Deal idealism and the defence of democracy in the Cold War context: these are 'the people' as we see them in the films of Frank Capra, or in Preston Sturges' *Sullivan's Travels* (1941), in which a jaded Hollywood director of escapist movies goes on the road as a hobo in search of the 'real' people and learns a few truths about what the public wants and needs. In contrast to the lax attitudes of the more 'refined' audiences of the 'private' playhouse, the preference of those at the Globe (Harbage writes) is for 'the charm of courtship, the dignity of wedded love, and the power of familial affection'. As Boecker observes, 'Established notions about which part of the population had the most beneficial influence on Shakespeare's drama are thus turned on their head' (143). The replica of the first Globe on London's South Bank has fostered what might be described as groundling pride, with

T-shirts identifying the wearer as one of an 'authentic' and honoured band: 'Groundling – proudly standing since 1599'. In the theatre's marketing strategy, Boecker writes, 'the standees impersonate the empowerment and sense of participation that the institution routinely promises it patrons' (146).

The nature and influence of audiences, in relation to acting and criticism, are addressed in *Women and Shakespeare in the Eighteenth Century*. Fiona Ritchie explores the ways in which 'the advent of the professional actress contributed significantly to the nature and popularity of stage productions of Shakespeare in the long eighteenth century and to the reception of his works in this period' (13). The criticism and scholarship of Charlotte Lennox, Elizabeth Montagu, Elizabeth Griffith and Elizabeth Inchbald exemplify the relationship between theatrical and literary spheres – both Griffith and Inchbald had experience as performers and playwrights. The women's specific contributions ranged from the editorial work and identification of the plays' sources to such crucial insights as those of Griffith, whose approach to the Shakespearian character, 'informed by her theatrical experience, acknowledges its moral complexity, which vexed many commentators' (97).

Among women whose careers were predominantly theatrical, Ritchie discusses Hannah Pritchard, Susannah Cibber, Catherine ('Kitty') Clive in the 'age of Garrick', and Dorothy Jordan and Sarah Siddons towards the end of the century. The designation of an 'age' by the name of David Garrick points to an important element of Ritchie's argument: the male actor's achievements have tended to predominate over those of the women who took leading roles opposite him. The actresses were notable for their cultural significance and economic power as well as their influential stage interpretations of major roles. In Pritchard's case we move into the realm of the lifestyles of the rich and famous. She was appointed dresser to the wedding of the future Queen Charlotte and for the coronation, and a 'generous dress allowance' for the clothes she wore on stage allowed her to showcase fashions that might be purchased at 'Pritchard's Warehouse', the business she and her husband owned in Covent Garden (46). Ritchie's study also encompasses the responses of female play-goers, from Elizabeth Pepys, who knew when it was not worth staying out a poor performance, to those who, towards the end of the period, set a standard for emotional, 'sentimental' response: 'In the case of sentimental drama, women's ability to feel and to inspire virtues worked together: by making their intensely emotional responses to drama visible in the theatre, women were displaying the "proper" reaction to these plays and demonstrating that they had internalized the moral lesson shown on stage' (159–60). Because the auditorium remained lit, 'audience members could see each other as easily as they could see the actors'. This supported what Ritchie characterizes as an 'interpretive community' in which 'as the actors performed for the audience, playgoers frequently performed for each other' (160). Although 'going to the theater to see and be seen' is usually inflected (and satirized) pejoratively, the audience's sense of itself is constructed as benign and positive. The liberating admission of feeling into the critical responses of female spectators, together with 'the sentimentalizing of Shakespeare through dramatists' adaptations and actor's performances' are valuable elements of the century's 'developing sense of sociability' (174). Alongside its perceptive account of the achievements of the women whose on- and offstage activities it discusses, this invitation to revisit and reassess sentimentality and the influence of some remarkable eighteenth-century women is one of the most effective contributions of Ritchie's engaging and persuasive study.

In *Lincoln and Shakespeare* by Michael Anderegg, attention is focused on the influence of Shakespeare on one remarkable nineteenth-century man. Abraham Lincoln enjoyed Shakespeare, regaling his companions on the campaign trail with recitations from memory of whole scenes, making discriminating observations on professional performances, and taking particular pleasure in the Falstaff of James Hackett. By all accounts, Lincoln was an effective reciter, and in his own oratory he showed a fair degree of histrionic talent, appropriately subdued to the seriousness of the task in hand. Anderegg surveys the evidence for the president's theatre-going in a chapter that is especially informative about theatre in the cities of Illinois during the 1850s and 1860s, if only by its demonstration of the times when 'he more often than not … missed opportunities to see Shakespeare' (63). When he did get to the theatre, his tastes were catholic, and Leonard Grover, manager of the National Theatre in Washington DC recalled that he was 'not exacting'. As well as the National's 'classical representations', he enjoyed lighter fare: 'On one occasion he said to me, "Do you know, Mr. Grover, I really enjoy a minstrel show"' (69). The president's relationship with Hackett, whose pre-eminence as Falstaff was widely attested, was founded on mutual respect and a shared admiration for Shakespeare's work. It seems to have foundered, or at least fizzled out, when the actor was too persistent in requesting appointment as consul in London, and it had been threatened at an early stage by the appearance in the newspapers of a letter from Lincoln that Hackett had had printed for 'private' use. There was a degree of Falstaffian guile in the tirelessly self-promoting Hackett, and Anderegg suggests a parallel between the cooling of Lincoln towards him and Hal's rejection of his Eastcheap friend. In one of their discussions of *1 Henry IV*, John Hay noted, the president asked why the acting version omitted 'one of the best scenes', when the Prince and Falstaff alternate roles as the King and his son in 2.5. Hackett replied that it was 'admirable to read but ineffective on stage', because 'there is generally nothing sufficiently distinctive about the actor who plays [King] Henry to make an imitation striking' (95). The light this sheds on actor-managerial thinking is one of the many insights into the general Shakespearian culture of nineteenth-century America afforded by Anderegg's carefully researched, and elegantly written book.

Yet another set of interpretative communities is documented in the sixteen chapters in *Shakespeare on the University Stage*, edited by

Andrew James Hartley. These encompass a rich variety of emphases and purposes in engagement with the texts, from George Rylands's influential but heavily prescriptive work on language at Cambridge to the diverse cultural and ideological contexts of students and faculty in China and India. In his afterword W. B. Worthen reflects on the tensions between different constituencies within institutions – the 'turf wars' of English and theatre departments or of rival teachers in both – and in his introduction Hartley points out ruefully that 'among the student community, as opposed to the community of importance to faculty and administration, it may well be that ... student-generated productions are the most significant, the highest profile, the ones they most care about' (21). The common experience of colleagues in my own and other universities supports this, and it is also likely that performance opportunities beyond the departmental programme are made all the more enticing by their inhabiting an assessment-free zone. In the case of Rylands, a strong motive was what Michael Cordner identifies as ' a comprehensible ambition to develop an alternative to what was perceived as the professional stage's maltreatment of Shakespeare' (58). If there had been a drama department (under whatever aegis or title) at Cambridge, Rylands would surely have found himself at odds with any faculty member whose approach corresponded to almost all the post-Stanislavskian techniques appropriate to actor training in the twentieth century, as his relationship with Michael Redgrave suggests. As Cordner notes, in Redgrave's notion of performance 'textual fidelity and individual creativity coexist ... to mutually beneficial effect' (57).

In their discussions of the less rarified, but at times more issue-driven world of North American university drama, the separate studies attend to the agenda defined by Andrea Stevens in 'Shakespeare without Resources: Staging Shakespeare in the Midwest': 'how each institution conceives of its own mission; defines artistic "success" and "failure"; imagines its audiences and negotiates – and in many cases, capitalizes upon – those constraints of time,

money, space, personnel, and perception of audience expectations' (111). Paul Menzer's 'The Laws of Athens: Shakespeare and the Campus Economy' tracks 'the disparities of surplus and scarcity that prevail in a performance of Shakespeare on American college and university campuses'. Proposing that these productions enact 'the way in which the Shakespeare industrial complex prepares both the producers and the consumers' by orienting them towards 'what constitutes "appropriate" Shakespeare today', Menzer suggests that they share the 'symbiotic pulse of action and reaction between lavish and austere Shakespeare' that characterizes 'the twentieth-century history of Shakespeare in performance' (203). Perhaps within the educational world the truly significant division is that noted above between the 'departmental' and 'extra-departmental' projects, though there is also bound to be some tension between institutional favouring of high-definition quasi-professional execution in 'prestige' shows of one kind or another, pedagogic imperatives, and the artistic and intellectual appetites of the students themselves. Menzer's analysis of the 'labour relations' in campus productions staged by 'para-professionals' characterizes them as 'an expression of youthful naivety within the framework of adult law' (202). This may seem unduly pessimistic, and other chapters point to fresh, radical interventions by means of Shakespeare, including Chad Allen Thomas's 'Queering Shakespeare in the American South', which shows how 'campus Shakespeare can be a tool for repurposing cultural norms, in addition to reaffirming or disrupting social values' (216). In 'Women who will make a Difference: Shakespeare at Wellesley College', Yu Jin Ko draws attention to the importance of the college's Shakespeare Society, founded in 1877, as an adjunct to the institution's broader agenda: 'cross-gender casting ... serves as an emblem for a more general form of female striving, especially within and educational context' (60).

An even wider range of interpretive communities is documented in *Shakespeare on the Global Stage*, edited by Paul Prescott and Erin Sullivan, with its examination of (as its subtitle indicates) 'performance and festivity in the Olympic year'. This topic has already been given a thorough airing in two earlier publications: *A Year of Shakespeare: Re-living the World Shakespeare Festival*, edited by Paul Edmondson, Paul Prescott and Erin Sullivan, and *Shakespeare Beyond English: A Global Experiment*, edited by Susan Bennett and Christie Carson.[2] Nevertheless, the new collection has fresh insights arising from the Olympiad as (at the time of writing) the great globe itself is readied for the year of Shakespearian commemoration, 2016. The imagery of the Olympic opening ceremony still haunts the imagination and puzzles the will, and Paul Prescott's 'Shakespeare and the Dream of Olympism' brings interpretation of the 'Isles of Wonder' into contact with the ambitions of the founder of the modern Olympic movement, the 'incurable anglomaniac' Pierre de Coubertin, who was 'heavily inspired by key developments in mid-nineteenth century British culture' – not least the educational obsession with sport that, via *Tom Brown's Schooldays*, inspired him to visit Rugby School (7). As Prescott points out, the Victorian origins of this enthusiasm for the beneficial moral effect of manly sports coalesced with the legacy of the Great Exhibition in generating 'the World's Fair logic of concentrated display of exotic wares and bodies' inherent in 'the structure if not the spirit of the 2012 Globe to Globe Festival' (9). The presence of the dark satanic mills in that opening ceremony begins to make more sense. An interview with its writer, Frank Cottrell Boyce, sheds further light on the process by which this brilliant, enjoyable but faintly disturbing pageant was arrived at: 'Without thinking about it, I called it 'Isles of Wonder' and after that, loads of wonderful island imagery just sort of seeped in' (45). Boyce and the director Danny Boyle 'had a couple of meetings and presentations with politicians, but we were completely protected from issues about budget or ideology or anything like that' (48). (Surely ideology, as always, had a tendency to 'seep in'?)

Back on the (Southwark) Globe stage companies from three Balkan countries were invited to perform their independently devised productions of the three parts of *Henry VI*, producing a constellation of historical resonances that Stuart Hampton-Reeves analyzes in 'States of the Nations: *Henry VI*, the London Olympics and the Spectacular City'. These performances of plays that 'call attention to the faultlines in any articulation of national identity' were 'an uncanny reminder that the ideals of the nation, even of the Olympic nation, also have their nightmares' (95). Collette Gordon, in '"Mind the Gap": Globalism, Postcolonialism and Making up Africa in the Cultural Olympiad', identifies the faultlines of another kind that fissure the misleading definition of a continent's 'national' identity embodied in several productions 'populated by a network of Europe-based theatre-makers with access to and a stake in African theatre or its brand as it operates in London and the international circuit' (202). Somehow, we can infer from her contribution, the liberalizing impulse of cultural exchange has become tainted by neo-imperialist globalization and that World's Fair inclination towards the 'display of exotic wares and bodies'. Erin Sullivan's discussion of 'Olympic Shakespeare and the Idea of Legacy' frames the sporting/cultural jamboree 'within the temporally and economically oriented concepts of inheritance, investment, consolidation, speculation and pay-offs', striving not to suggest that everything was 'reducible to a bottom line', but at the same time taking her cue from Theodor Adorno's insistence that 'Whoever speaks of culture speaks of administration as well, whether this is his intention or not' (289). The cumulative effect of these and the other essays and interviews in *Shakespeare on the Global Stage* is sceptical and bracing but not reductive, although the best approach may be to read them alongside the reviews in *A Year of Shakespeare: Re-living the World Shakespeare Festival*, to be reminded of the pleasures as well as contradictions of what was by any measure an extraordinary and rewarding undertaking.

---

[2] See 'Shakespeare in Performance', in *Shakespeare Survey 67* (Cambridge, 2014), pp. 474–9.

From a wide and universal theatre to one that is cabin'd, cribbed and confined: the 'Shakespeare Behind Bars' (SBB) programme at Luther Luckett Correctional complex in Kentucky. This has been documented in a film of the same name, as well as in articles by its founder Curt Tofteland and the actor/inmate Hal Cobb, and in Amy Scott-Douglass's *Shakespeare Inside: The Bard behind Bars*.[3] The aim, as Tofteland describes it, is not so much *re*habilitation as habilitation, enabling the performer to escape from 'the shadow of his past criminal actions' and to achieve 'the possibility of transforming himself into the human being he wants to be'.[4] The discovery and exercise of their own agency on the part of the inmates is paramount in the long period of study and rehearsal. In *Prison Shakespeare and the Purpose of Performance*, Niels Herold discusses SBB in the light of the plays' engagement with confession and penance in a post-Reformation regime that had desacralized this aspect of spiritual life. In the prison environment it is hardly surprising that scenes and speeches of repentance should acquire a specific resonance, but arguably this is a renewal rather than an innovation pure and simple. Citing *King Lear*, Herold points out that 'Shakespeare's characters seem to discover themselves and become vivid as stage fictions precisely by being cast aside or exiled, driven to root around in an interior space that cuts them off from action prescribed by masculine codes of honour, those for example that prevail behind bars for inmates trying to survive in a dangerous homosocial world' (63).

Identification with characters and situations, especially those of passionate anger, might include (for example) Leonato in *Much Ado About Nothing* as well as the more egregious instances of criminality, but it is the latter that are the most striking and complex: 'Since all of Macbeth's serial crimes can be viewed as ineffective attempts to beat back prophetic fate at its own game, for an inmate actor trying to acknowledge his own past and redeem it through this particular Shakespearian play-world, the role is going to present formidable challenges' (78). In the case of *The Tempest* – in which Hal Cobb played Prospero – the issues of anger and forgiveness on the part of the leading character acquire an additional layer of metatheatrical force when, in the Epilogue, the 'inmate actor' must appeal to the non-inmate audience to 'set [him] free' by their 'indulgence'. He must remain on his island/prison, while they will return to the outside world. Herold's study offers an intriguing insight into aspects of the plays that may pass unnoticed in many contemporary, secular readings or performances. The work undertaken by the inmates involves a degree of introspection cognate with Stanislavski-oriented rehearsal techniques, extending even to casting, which is decided by the performers themselves. SBB takes place in a world within the regime of mass incarceration that constitutes a formidable social problem in the United States, and its relationship with the 'inside' world as well as that of the 'outside' facilitators and audiences superimposes the introspection of the dramatic characters with that of actors seeking to 'build a role' and prisoners who are or have become introspective by force of circumstance and through their own past actions.

Issues of surveillance, punishment and repentance figure in *Shakespeare, Dissent and the Cold War*, in which Alfred Thomas compares the twentieth century's confrontation between Communist bloc and the Western allies, with the religious and political conflicts of the playwright's time, and the regime of surveillance and summary punishment to which recusants were subjected. In some respects this cross-referencing of one era's preoccupations with those of another is rewarding, but in others it veers towards speculation regarding authorial intention and audience reception. Accounts of the context of the plays are coupled with discussion of such twentieth-century interpretations as Grigori Kozintsev's two Shakespeare films, and Tom Stoppard's *Cahoot's Macbeth*. To what

---

[3] Curt L. Tofteland and Hal Cobb, 'Prospero behind Bars', in *Shakespeare Survey 65* (Cambridge, 2013), pp. 429–44; Amy Scott-Douglass, *Shakespeare Inside: The Bard behind Bars* (London, 2007).

[4] Tofteland and Cobb, 'Prospero behind Bars', p. 431.

degree did Shakespeare and a fair proportion of his audience, having weathered the religious and political upheavals of their lifetime, remain Roman Catholic – at least in long-held and shared assumptions that could be accommodated more or less to the prevailing regime under Elizabeth and James? Even at the level of persisting beliefs, it is surely a major step to go from lingering traits of Catholicism to active subversion. It seems perfectly plausible that the surveillance state of Hamlet's Denmark would resonate 'with Catholics whose houses were routinely ransacked for concealed priests and signs of the forbidden Mass' (38). On the other hand, Thomas is on less firm ground when he asserts that the various examples of exile in the plays are used by Shakespeare 'to comment obliquely on the fate of many of his exiled Catholic countrymen'. Shakespeare's subversive activism is not necessarily proved by the analogy Thomas draws with the 'many leading intellectuals and reformers, such as the playwright Vaclav Havel', who 'resisted going into exile in order to write and make known their beliefs in spite of police harassment and frequent imprisonment' (44). In this reading of the playwright's purposes, the King's 'seemingly omniscient knowledge of plots against his life' turns *Henry V* into 'a veiled critique of the encroachments of the Tudor monarchy into the lives of ordinary people carefully displaced onto the medieval past' (45). The play is remarkable in its balancing of scepticism and admiration in its presentation of the leading character and his motives, but in 2.2 it is difficult to identify even implicit disapproval of the King's knowledge of the treachery of Scrope, Cambridge and Grey being acquired 'by interception which they dream not of' (2.2.7). Rather than have them confess 'upon examination' before being brought before the king, as Holinshed relates, Shakespeare dramatizes the situation by having them read the documents that they expect will be their 'commissions' but which contain the facts of their transgression.[5]

The 'equivocator' in the Porter's monologue in *Macbeth* has undoubted significance as a reference to the strategy advocated for recusants or insurgent priests under interrogation, but does this support effectively the contention that Shakespeare is 'intent on commenting critically on the murky and murderous politics of Jacobean England, a world that foreshadowed the double dealings of the twentieth century Cold War' (143)? The key words here are 'intent on'. The artist's intentions are well documented in the case of the 'Aesopian' mode of Kozintsev's films or the plays of Vaclav Havel, but in arguing from these cases back to the less knowable intention of the early modern playwright Thomas is moving from direct evidence in the twentieth century to a mixture of circumstantial evidence and supposition in the earlier period. Despite this, the book's analyses of Shakespearian production in the twentieth-century Cold War are often insightful and persuasive, and his account of the context of the German poet Ingeborg Bachmann's 'Bohemia lies on the sea' is especially rewarding.

Shakespearean Echoes, edited by Adam Hansen and Kevin J. Wetmore, Jr, ranges across the spectrum of Shakespearian adaptation and influence in contemporary culture, from *Game of Thrones* to *Romeo y Julieta*, the Argentinian *telenovela* the key to whose 150 episodes is (Alfredo Michel Modenessi observes in his lively and comprehensively informative essay) 'good old-fashioned abuse and violence in all its forms' (94). Among the other contributions, Sharon O'Dair's 'Cursing the Queer Family: Shakespeare, Psychoanalysis and *My Own Private Idaho*' is persuasive in examining the fixations of both the director and the film's critics on Freud and his inheritors. O'Dair observes that 'the homeless and homosexual Mike Waters ... wants to create new forms of family and kinship but fails, and fails because director Gus Van Sant cannot silence the echoes

---

[5] Holinshed in Geoffrey Bullough, *Narrative and Dramatic Sources of Shakespeare, IV: Later English History Plays* (London, 1962), pp. 384–5.

of Shakespeare and Freud percolating in his mind' (131). He 'simply begs the question posed by his film about family and home, about kinship, and about the queer subject –"why Mike's on the street"' (135). The wider implications of O'Dair's argument amount to a warning for the academy: 'polite tip-toeing around the inadequacies of psychoanalysis' has characterized even sophisticated critical discourse, and 'humanists' inability in 20 or 30 years to shed psychoanalysis from their professional interpretive repertoires bodes poorly for our ability to help effect progressive social change regarding kinship or the family' (140). The contributors to *Shakespeare on Screen: Othello*, edited by Sarah Hatchuel and Nathalie Vienne-Guerin, discuss details within films; reassess versions that are famous; and bring little known films into the critical arena. Aimara da Cunha Resende's account of two adaptations from Latin America and Jennifer Drouin's 'Othello in Québec: André Forcier's *Une Histoire inventée*' are adroit in their presentation of remarkable productions that have not yet 'travelled'. Incrementally, such studies contribute to the change in critical praxis advocated by Mark Thornton Burnett in *Shakespeare and World Cinema*, shifting attention away from an Anglophone canon while also 'bear[ing] in mind the complex interplay between expectation and the material realities of filmic practice'.[6]

'World Cinema' in another sense was a constituency that Orson Welles was ambitious to inhabit. Of the making of books about Orson Welles there seems to be no end, just as during his lifetime there seemed to be no limits to his self-refashioning. Habitually making and remaking films and stage performances during and after both production and post-production, Welles also cut, recut and (in interviews) redubbed accounts of his own life. Sebastian Lefait's contribution 'Othello Retold: Orson's Welles's *Filming Othello*' in *Shakespeare on Screen: Othello*, describes the ways in which Welles reshaped the film itself in the excerpts included in the 1978 documentary, adding new complications to the tangled textual history of the 1952 film. Simon Callow's retelling of the oft-told tale of the film of *Othello* in *One Man Band*, the third volume of his magisterial biography of Welles, benefits from such new material as the diary of Fay Compton (Emilia) and a detailed account of the theatrical production he subsequently directed and starred in for (of all managements) Laurence Olivier Productions. This resembled many other projects in which the actor-director struggled and bullied his way to a success that was then squandered through a combination of hubris, self-absorption and heroic fecklessness in his dealings with actual and potential backers and collaborators.

The puzzling quality of Welles's acting in *Othello* is summarized perceptively: 'an inert, almost cataleptic performance ... which deeply undermines the audacity, originality and swagger of his film' (119). In similar fashion, his Lear in the 1953 American television production directed by Peter Brook has remarkable clarity in speech, but 'what [Welles] lacks is a sense of the lived life contained in the line, or of poetic feeling'. Admirable in the rhetorical mode, he 'again seems not to bring anything of himself to the role; it is hard to know why he is playing the part, other than that, as Edmund Hillary so memorably remarked of Everest, it is there' (139–40). A stage production in 1956 at New York's cavernous City Center theatre proved to be yet another case of Welles snatching opening-night success from the jaws of defeat and then failing to follow through. The book ends with what Callow regards as Welles's real Shakespearian triumph on film, and 'one of [his] very best, richest, most detailed, most human performances; whether it is strictly Shakespeare's Falstaff is neither here nor there' (397). Moreover, '*Chimes at Midnight* is not filmed theatre: it is the sort of film Shakespeare might have made, had he had the medium at his disposal' (405).

---

[6] Mark Thornton Burnett, *Shakespeare and World Cinema* (Cambridge, 2013), p. 12.

An impressive range of primary sources, published and unpublished, enriches Callow's account, which moves deftly from the works to the man and back, just – one feels – as Welles intended. The new volume begins with his departure from America in 1947 and ends with the completion of *Chimes at Midnight* (aka *Falstaff*) in 1965. Callow convincingly suggests that Falstaff was the inevitable expression of the complex of father-and-son relationships in both Welles's life and the Shakespearian material. The acknowledged nostalgia for the lost garden of 'Merrie England' in *Chimes at Midnight* was of a piece with Welles's feelings about the time when he was still a boy wonder in years as well as in his carefully cultivated aura. The radio years of the thirties and forties were an artistic age of innocence for Welles, but the delight in making it up as he went along strained the loyalty of many of his co-workers, sometimes (as in the case of John Houseman) to breaking point, especially in the less accommodating world of theatre and film production. Callow adds to the already rich store of anecdote accumulated around Welles's enterprises, but never loses touch with the excitement and artistic achievement of even the fragmentary results. Time and again, though, actors and other associates are alternately warmed by the generosity of the actor-director-author and shocked by his sudden tantrums. During rehearsals for the 1956 *King Lear* 'there was a lot of hatred of Orson in the room', reported Alvin Epstein, who played Lear's Fool. Callow notes that when '[At] the end of three weeks the disgruntled company moved into the theatre for technical rehearsals ... Welles disappeared into the blackness of the auditorium and addressed the actors through a megaphone' (221–2). Rarely available – or inclined – to 'make personal contact' with the actors, here as on other occasions he seems to have treated them as so much raw material for the making of his personal vision. The one-man band was a high maintenance machine, but the combination of gaiety and ruthlessness cast its spell widely – globally, so to speak.

WORKS REVIEWED

Anderegg, Michael, *Lincoln and Shakespeare* (Lawrence, KA, 2015)

Boecker, Bettina, *Imagining Shakespeare's Original Audiences, 1660–2000: Groundlings, Gallants, Grocers* (Basingstoke, 2015)

Callow, Simon, *Orson Welles: One Man Band* (London, 2015)

Croall, Jonathan, *Performing King Lear. Gielgud to Russell Beale* (London, 2015)

Gurr, Andrew, and Farah Karim-Cooper, eds., *Moving Shakespeare Indoors: Performance and Repertoire in the Jacobean Playhouse* (Cambridge, 2015)

Hansen, Adam, and Kevin J. Wetmore, Jr, eds., *Shakespearean Echoes* (Basingstoke, 2015)

Hartley, Andrew James, ed., *Shakespeare on the University Stage* (Cambridge, 2015)

Hatchuel, Sarah, and Nathalie Vienne-Guerin, eds., *Shakespeare on Screen: Othello* (Cambridge, 2015)

Herold, Niels, *Prison Shakespeare and the Purpose of Performance: Repentance Rituals and the Early Modern* (Basingstoke, 2015)

Mazer, Cary M., *Double Shakespeare: Emotional-Realist Acting and Contemporary Performance* (Madison, WI, and Teaneck, NJ, 2015)

Prescott, Paul, and Erin Sullivan, eds., *Shakespeare on the Global Stage: Performance and Festivity in the Olympic Year* (London, 2015)

Price, Eoin, *'Public' and 'Private' Playhouses in Renaissance England: The Politics of Publication* (Basingstoke, 2015)

Raw, Laurence, *Theatre of the People Donald Wolfit's Shakespearean Productions 1937–1953* (Lanham, CO, New York and London, 2016)

Ritchie, Fiona, *Women and Shakespeare in the Eighteenth Century* (Cambridge, 2014)

Thomas, Alfred, *Shakespeare, Dissent and the Cold War* (Basingstoke, 2014)

Wells, Stanley, *Great Shakespeare Actors: Burbage to Branagh* (Oxford, 2015)

3. EDITIONS AND TEXTUAL STUDIES
reviewed by PETER KIRWAN

CONVERGENCES

Early in *The Shakespearean Archive*, Alan Galey sets out his ambitious project to explore 'the convergence of texts, technologies, documents, data sets, and new media experiments that have come to constitute the Shakespearian archive in the digital age' (2). This 'convergence' of technologies and methodologies underpins much of the work in Shakespearian textual studies that has emerged in the last year, culminating in the appearance – as this chapter was submitted – of the first major reinvention of an existing Complete Works edition in a 'born digital' form: the third Norton Shakespeare, itself harbinger to the forthcoming multi-platform New Oxford Shakespeare. Yet, as the works reviewed this year demonstrate, the negotiation between text and technology needs to look backwards as well as forwards, contextualizing the extent and nature of innovations.

I begin with monographs by Galey and J. Gavin Paul that seek some historical understanding of the interfaces via which readers encounter texts, and which understand the printed edition as just one manifestation of a much more complex set of relationships and engagements, arguments also raised by chapters in Brett Hirsch and Hugh Craig's recent collection on *Digital Shakespeares*. I then look to two new projects aimed at reaching the Generation Y/Z classroom: the new *Bedford Shakespeare* which, despite its modest remit in comparison to other anthology editions, intervenes fascinatingly in the question of interfaces for classrooms; and the new Shakespeare: Made in Canada series, which edits the plays with a particular eye on Canadian readers. I then turn my attention to the 1603 quarto of *Hamlet*, which is the focus of new monographs by Zachary Lesser and Terri Bourus, who respectively seek to expose the layers of thinking that have created particular myths around this text and make a new case for its origins. Whilst the implications of these studies are

yet to be felt in editorial practice, these books point to the possibility of serious rethinking of variant texts. Finally, I turn to recent additions to the third series of the Arden Shakespeare: Lois Potter's revision of her 1997 *The Two Noble Kinsmen* and a brand new *Macbeth* that finally replaces Kenneth Muir's 1953 edition. The contrast between Arden's established template and the new digital platforms advanced by the critical works reviewed here illustrates the range of approaches available for attempting to mediate the ever-expanding Shakespearian archive.

SHAKESPEARIAN INTERFACES

Galey's engagement in *The Shakespearean Archive* is with the idea of cultural memory, for which the 'archive' functions as both metaphor and physical embodiment; the archive is the 'technologizing of memory' (64). He is interested in the technologies via which we remember, and Shakespeare's role as both authorizer and subject of new 'information architectures' (80), a term which evokes the vaults and warehouses of physical storage (the book contains more than one reference to the closing image of *Raiders of the Lost Ark*) but which comes to stand for a spatial understanding of any information interface. 'All books materialize parts of networks of information that can never be represented in their totality, only imagined' (81). In his third chapter he discusses the Catalogue that visualizes the 1623 Folio's information architecture and the prefatory material which sets out the material book's relationship to Heminge and Condell's archive of materials, and relates these to the implicit invitation to the 1870s reader of Howard Furness's New Variorum Shakespeare 'to own, if not necessarily to read, their very own Shakespeare archive' (99). Each book is a project of epistemic management, whether predicated on selection (the critical edition) or comprehensiveness (the Variorum).

Lezlie Cross's chapter 'Acting in the Paratext', the other major study of Furness's Variorum published this year, takes discussion of his choices further by surveying his integration of performance texts, actorly interpretations and performative options into critical discussion of the texts, building up a database of creative decisions alongside textual variants within the pages of his editions.

The material book, however, is only one small part of Galey's interdisciplinary project, which also points out the lazy and slippery usages of 'archive' by literary scholars with no investment in how archives actually function. Galey's more ambitious argument is that current debates around digital innovations in Shakespeare are a continuation of long-standing negotiations between Shakespeare and new technology. One case study is Teena Rochfort Smith's 1883 prototype of a four-text *Hamlet*, which uses complex typography to mark the relations between four columns of text in an oblong book. Galey reads this as an early version of XML (27) and argues that Smith was the pioneer of interface design. From this, Shakespeare continually reappears as the test case for new technologies, often simply as a quotation for advertising (the stereoscope in 1856) or legitimization (Alexander Graham Bell's use of 'To be or not to be' in early demonstrations of the telephone to demonstrate the technology's gravitas (175)), but also as a fetishized object, as in Collier's 1858 photographic facsimile of *Hamlet* (1603) and the Royal Ordnance Survey's facsimile of the First Folio alongside other archivable heritage documents of perceived national importance. By the time Galey reaches the use of the First Folio as a substrate for weapons-level encryption during the Second World War, a shiver was running down my spine at the ease with which this contingent and unstable book/text/archive was being built upon.

The real value of Galey's book is in demonstrating and theorizing the rich back history of digital Shakespeare, prioritizing methodology and purpose. If Howard Furness's instigation of the New Variorum was designed effectively to synthesize his vast research library into easily navigable volumes, then digital editors might see experiments with new media in the same light. Galey also provides warnings for those undertaking new digital experiments on corpus analysis, arguing for appropriate historicization of data. Pointing to the difficulties posed by those projects that use the Moby Shakespeare as a kind of essentialized Shakespeare, he argues that 'Shakespeare is not a data set to be massaged into a tolerable margin of error, like the linguistic corpora for which text-analysis methods were developed. Shakespeare's texts are always human artifacts travelling through time, and they carry their histories with them' (265). More pointedly, any reference to 'archives' or 'the text' that elides the *specific* histories of *specific* archives and texts risks participating in the same kinds of essentialism that forget how current states of knowledge have come into being; a problem addressed further by Zachary Lesser in the book discussed below.

Douglas Bruster's important investigation ('Shakespeare's Lady 8') into the history of the printers' ornament that adorns the title pages of *Venus and Adonis* and *The Rape of Lucrece* offers a timely reminder of what is still to be gleaned from paying attention to historical details of the interface that might be passed over as 'merely' illustrative or mechanical. Whilst appropriately cautious, Bruster notes that this ornament is often used 'to decorate, even brand, works associated with France, Protestantism, and aristocracy' (88). His article traces the networks of texts similarly marked, implying that the performance of the page carried ideological loadings that have been hitherto overlooked. J. Gavin Paul's *Shakespeare and the Imprints of Performance* is also concerned with historical interfaces, more specifically with how the critical edition negotiates with performance. He begins by arguing that *The Tempest* is unique among Shakespeare's plays in having a title that also doubles as an opening stage direction, the title immediately evoking performance elements that defy textual codification (xxiii). Paul is concerned to represent the printed text as an interface that allows the reader to experiment imaginatively with ideas of performance, rejecting 'the inability of texts to adequately represent the realities of performance' (5), and he takes a broad historical view of the history of the critical edition to achieve his end. Where Galey approaches his materials with a historian's eye, Paul comes in as a reader, drawing attention to the subjectivity of the reading experience which may be detached from linear progression and time (unlike the linearity of theatre spectatorship). He notes that the more an edition tries to replicate the diversity of performance through paratextual materials, the more unlike a linear performance it becomes.

In surveying the traces of performance in printed early modern drama, Paul suggests that 'all printed drama reminds readers of what has been taken away from them' (78), a remark aligned with Galey's observations about the driving forces behind archival practices. Paul resists binaries posed by Lukas Erne and others between the literary and the theatrical, suggesting that the two are instead synergistic. His perspective moves in and out of physical proximity to the text, even down to the level of white space. Paul then traces the development of performance paratexts through the eighteenth-century editorial tradition, from Rowe's act/scene divisions and engravings to Capell's introduction of shorthand notations for indicating changes of address, asides and irony. Taking into account twentieth-century performance commentary and twenty-first-century electronic archives that embed performance, Paul's scope is commendable and his focus on the agency of editors necessary, particularly in his observation that it is the selectivity, not the exhaustion, of editorial choices that makes an interface useful (169).

This leads into Paul's most provocative argument against 'unediting' and the contemporary tendency to enhance the 'openness' of a text by introducing as few stage directions as possible. In the debate between openness and foreclosure, he suggests that the relegation of staging possibilities and alternatives to the margins 'can coexist with the foreclosure of ambiguity in the edited playtext' (134), and that 'the flexing of a reader's perceptual muscles can occur under either scenario – the issue is whether these muscles are used to rein in potentialities in the playtext that have been left exposed by an editor, or to wrest control from an editorially imposed reading that has smoothed over ambiguities in advance' (135). I agree with Paul that openness may in fact be read as emptiness; an 'unedited' text that marginalizes performance to the commentary may absent itself from performance possibility. However, the very terms Paul uses to suggest the 'flexing of muscles' and 'wresting of control' required to envision alternatives against the editor's foreclosure of meaning suggests that Paul is working with an idealized, particularly confident and aggressive reader; I am not persuaded that all readers are so prepared to work against their texts.

The book's message is somewhat frustrated by Paul's desire to coin a new critical term, *performancescape*, definitions and redefinitions of which permeate the book. He defines it as 'a property of dramatic texts that is activated as a reader negotiates between the text proper and various forms of textual mediation' but also 'a conceptual tool for articulating and thinking through the interpretive demands – and opportunities – that printed plays pose to readers' and 'a flexible model for discussing the interactions between editors, dramatic texts, and readers' (all 21). In resisting other useful models such as *mise-en-page* or M. J. Kidnie's 'virtual performance' and trying to create a term that covers, effectively, the entire network of potential imaginative and implied performances encoded into a printed text, the term becomes redundant through the need for constant rearticulation. Yet even if the value of this book cannot be reduced to a new term, that should not detract from its significant contribution to the ways in which the interface between page and stage is articulated, and to its interrogation of the purpose and value of performance commentary. If nothing else, editors reading Paul's book might come away more confident in their right to pursue a particular set of performance options for a text in the spirit of energizing and enabling the reader to engage, and more importantly disagree, with their vision of the stage.

Paul's historical exploration of new media, from Rowe's engravings to embedded videos, is continued in Brett Hirsch and Hugh Craig's special issue of *The Shakespearean International Yearbook* on *Digital Shakespeares: Innovations, Interventions, Mediations*, which showcases several projects that integrate performance and textual scholarship as well as surveying the fates of major digital Shakespeare projects over the last decade. From Hirsch and Craig's introduction to a cluster of reviews of recent digital projects, the main value of this yearbook is as a state-of-the-field comment on current innovations. Between the warnings of Sarah Neville and Eric Rasmussen about electronic editions that squander their potential and fail to navigate between advertised materials effectively, and the graveyard of abandoned projects enumerated by Hirsch and Craig, the prospective instigator of any digital Shakespeare project will do well to heed the lessons here. Interestingly, and in line with Galey and Paul, the recurring sticking point is the value of editorial selection and subjectivity. Rosemary Gaby's discussion of her own experience editing *1* and *2 Henry IV* for the Internet Shakespeare Editions praises the online edition for being able to make the meaningful connections to other English history plays and associated materials that stand-alone print editions can only partially represent, but also emphasizes the role of the editor in making these connections available, Gaby's hyperlinks defining and limiting the reader's journey.

The most innovative of the projects described here to my eye is that detailed in a multi-authored article 'SET Free: Breaking the Rules in a Processual, User-Generated, Digital Performance Edition of *Richard the Third*' by Jennifer Roberts-Smith and eight colleagues (69–99): a *Simulated Environment for Theatre* 'edition' of *Richard III*. This virtual edition stages the play with avatars in a reconstruction of a small theatre. The strategy here involves destabilizing the core text to situate the play as part of a network, and the text itself is fragmented into speech bubbles above avatars, contextualizing individual speeches temporally and spatially. Further, the user/reader can change the staging choices by moving the avatars, as well as editing the text themselves. With pop-up windows allowing links to video of live performance and

textual apparatus, this model (conveniently illustrated here with screenshots) appears to trump previous virtual world experiments such as the Second Life Globe through its reconceptualization of the two-dimensional space of the critical edition as a four-dimensional performance edition, combining the subjectivity and linearity of performance noted by Paul with the flexible interactivity that enables readerly engagement.

The time for rhetoric about the infinite possibilities of digital media is, these books and articles seem to suggest, over. Between Galey's insistence on the contingencies of archives, Paul's call for editorial intervention, and the contributors to Hirsch and Craig's volume pointing repeatedly to the necessity of the digital editor/curator limiting and guiding readers' choices, the arguments here suggest that curators of digital archives need to be attending to the mediating interface rather than to what lies beneath.

NEW INTERFACES FOR THE CLASSROOM

Given the above discussions, it is fitting that this year marks the launch of a major new 'born digital' Complete Works, the third edition of *The Norton Shakespeare*. While the print edition has arrived, the digital version is at the time of going to press only available in partial form, and as such I defer full discussion until the next issue as much of the edition's new work, including full alternative texts for several plays and in-text editorial and performance notes, is only available in the digital version. For initial purchasers of the physical book, the interface will look little different to the second edition, preserving the single-column text and many of the prefatory materials that contribute to a book so bulky it still relies on tissue-thin paper to fit into a single volume; innovations of design are deferred to the digital volume. By contrast, the other bulky anthology of Shakespeare aimed at classrooms to be published this year, Russ McDonald and Lena Cowen Orlin's *The Bedford Shakespeare*, offers something surprisingly new. The text is that of the New Cambridge Shakespeare, as are the glosses (trimmed down significantly). The edition itself is, rarely, not a 'Complete Works', focusing instead on the 'twenty-five most frequently taught plays' (ix). Given that it offers no new textual scholarship, and that its focus on the American classroom puts it into direct competition with the more expansive and modern Norton, it runs the risk of being over-looked. And yet, McDonald and Orlin have put together a beautifully presented and consistently fascinating edition that has the potential to inspire the instructor as well as the student.

The limitations of the volume are obvious, omitting the poems as well as a substantial number of the plays and thus reinforcing the 'core' canon of Shakespeare. The volume is pitched squarely at the Shakespeare 'beginner', as McDonald's opening chapter 'Approaching Shakespeare' (1–5) indicates in its recommendations to avoid notes, take breaks, concentrate and so on. This is one of three 'practical' chapters (the other two are 'Screening Shakespeare' and 'Staging Shakespeare'), that offer entry-level introductions to modes of reading and interpreting Shakespeare. Quite why these contributions are highlighted in the prefatory materials for particular attention is unclear, especially as the other twenty-two thematic chapters interleaved in alphabetical order with the plays are more focused. What sets the Bedford Shakespeare apart is the extent and quality of its illustration; a five-page section on 'Texts' (1625–9) introduces the basics of printing and some of the key debates, but comparative images of differences in compositorial spelling within the First Folio make absolutely explicit what mere description fails to do. The elisions necessary to briefly introduce, for instance, theories of 'foul papers' and 'fair copy' are understandable given the target audience. Similar sections cover everything from 'Renaissance' to 'Genealogy', 'Society' to 'Language' with efficiency and variety.

Much more valuable is the presentation of the texts themselves, demonstrating the value of the interventionist editor staging their own 'performance' of a text. Each play is prefaced by a short 'Preview' of 'need-to-know' information, along with a synopsis, and followed by an extended analysis ('View') and a timeline of highlights in the play's afterlife. The decision of what a reader should know before or after their 'encounter' with the text opens provocative questions about the linearity of the readerly experience. Yet the text itself is interspersed with what the book calls 'pop-up materials' (vii), a phrase which inevitably conjures up the electronic interface and disrupts the linearity of the codex. The text is illustrated lavishly with photographs, drawings and critical commentary. To take one example, *The Comedy of Errors* is accompanied by a 1560 map of the Mediterranean, extended discussions of the aural texture of lines, quotations from Ephesians on the submission of servants and wives, illustrative photographs of stage productions from three continents, contrasting opinions by Nicholas Rowe and Eamon Grennan of the play's wordplay, critical passages on metamorphosis and farce, a nineteenth-century etching of Dromio and 'Dowsabel', a 1586 image from an emblem book of a siren, and examinations of different theatrical treatments of Dr Pinch and the Dromios. The materials are designed to provoke different kinds of understanding and instigate critical debate, filling the function of seminar handouts. Whilst many teachers may prefer to create their own materials, the sheer volume of synthesized images and commentary here make this a tremendous resource.

The other classroom-facing texts published this year are the first volumes in Oxford University Press's Shakespeare: Made in Canada series, under the general editorship of Daniel Fischlin. The series has launched with *Romeo and Juliet* and *The Tempest*, with four more editions and an edited collection on Canadian adaptations announced to follow. The series is immediately distinctive for its cover art featuring the peculiarly ugly Sanders Portrait, owned by the Canadian Lloyd Sullivan, who introduces the case for its authenticity on the inside back cover of each book. Irrespective of its claims to authenticity, it still reminds me of nothing so much as Cecilia Gimenez's 'restoration' of *Ecce Homo* but, more importantly, its presence is part of the series' reclamation of Shakespeare's particular and specific resonance in a Canadian context. Both volumes are prefaced by a Canadian artist bringing their own concerns to bear: Sky Gilbert proclaims Romeo the 'first metrosexual' (*Romeo*, ix); Daniel David Moses professes ambivalence about *The Tempest*'s colonial English aspirations (*Tempest*, x). The introductions by Fischlin (*Tempest*) and Jill Levenson (*Romeo*) prioritize Canadian productions and scholarship; figures such as Northrop Frye, Susan Bennett and Margaret Atwood dominate the contributions, alongside productions from the Stratford Shakespeare Festival in Ontario and other Canadian adaptations. Fischlin discusses *The Tempest* in relation to its encounter narratives (8) and maps the early 'garrison mentality' of Canada onto *The Tempest*, while also pulling out the poignant quality of Trinculo's 'dead Indian' in the Canadian context. Levenson focuses on sources and adaptation, looking at the development of the *Romeo and Juliet* myth and the specificity of the patriarchal structures of Shakespeare's play before going on to discuss a range of Canadian productions.

The difficulty with student-facing editions is tone. As with the *Bedford Shakespeare*, there is no textual commentary in the Made in Canada series, glossing over any textual cruces. This edition seems to assume a lower-level audience than the *Bedford*, with its 'Ten Tips for Reading Shakespeare', its reductive character descriptions and, most intrusively, a lengthy synopsis before every single scene that disrupts the readerly experience. Here, the difference in format is important; the *Bedford* takes advantage of different typefaces, box colours and page layouts to stage its in-text interventions around the text of the play, whereas the much more basic Made in Canada has a start–stop feel, especially when very short scenes come surrounded by prose summary. Yet while Made in Canada seems to assume an audience that needs its hand holding, the specificity and interpretive complexity of the introductions speaks to a higher level. Where the interface of the *Bedford Shakespeare* implies a reader who is enthusiastically discovering the plays and their multiple contexts, Shakespeare: Made in Canada assumes a reader who is diffident

towards Shakespeare but enthusiastic about Canada. The editors know their audiences, of course, and it is gratifying to see the expansive but potentially intimidating *Norton* complemented by editions that seek to address specific rather than comprehensive audiences.

RE-EVALUATING *HAMLET* (1603)

It is fortunate, both for the authors and for their readers, that the year's two new monographs on the history and origins of the 1603 quarto of *Hamlet* were published too close together for either to take account of the other's arguments as part of their demolition of previous work on the subject. Lesser's *Hamlet after Q1* is a systematic dismantling of flawed narratives that have crept up around Q1 since its belated rediscovery in the nineteenth century; Bourus's *Young Shakespeare's Young Hamlet* enacts a forceful, occasionally aggressive dismissal of much recent work on *Hamlet* in its pursuit of Q1's origins in Shakespeare's youth. Whilst both Bourus and Lesser respond briefly to each other's earlier work, their two monographs stand as coincidental and often complementary reinvestigations of a fascinating text. Cumulatively, they demand that scholars rethink established narratives about the origins and status of this text, and Bourus's more revolutionary conclusion – that Q1 is in fact an early version of *Hamlet* written by Shakespeare in the late 1580s – can, in its essentials, be accommodated within Lesser's broader framework of caveats and warnings about this play's history. Whilst the books disagree in several respects, the contribution of each is vital.

Lesser's book turns on the uncanny belatedness of Q1, rediscovered in 1823 and thus entering anachronistically into a tradition of textual scholarship that struggled to accommodate it. His project here is a systematic querying of received facts which originated in this moment of uncanny accommodation. As a study of the development of patterns of thought at a particular moment in history, it shares much with Galey, especially in chapter 1 where he shows that a long-standing acceptance of Shakespeare as an author who revised his early versions was giving way to a Romantic concern with originality and spontaneity, as well as authorial biography, at precisely the moment Q1 was unearthed (34). Lesser shows how the debates over this play, exemplified by John Payne Collier (arguing in accordance with the priority of discovery that Q1 was a stenographic corruption of the 'real' *Hamlet*) and Charles Knight (insisting that the texts proceeded in chronological order demonstrating Shakespeare's development) polarized the debate according to Romantic notions of biography and authorial genius. Both narratives invested in Shakespeare's authorial priority, and both were synthesized by the next generation, who created the conjectural 'ur-*Hamlet*' to account for all peculiarities of the text. The 'ur' play becomes something of a catch-all solution to problems of *Hamlet*.

Nineteenth-century attitudes pervade the rest of the history of Q1. Lesser argues, persuasively, that the 'bawdy pun' of 'country matters' was in fact not perceived to be sexual by editors *until* the discovery of Q1, whose variant 'contrary' allowed an alternative reading; his argument here is that insistence on the pun has disguised many other alternative readings of the passage, and that treatment of Q1 as a later, bowdlerized version (again, on the uncanny assumption that Q1 is later than Q2/F) misses the fact that Q1 is arguably more explicit in its sexual punning and implicit staging of Hamlet's head in Ophelia's lap (110). More controversially, but again persuasively, Lesser argues that Q1's version of 'To be or not to be', rather than being a simplified version of the more familiar versions, is in fact the most structurally coherent, syntactically unified and astute in its command of the irony of the commonplace tradition surrounding 'conscience makes cowards of us all' (198–9). Audaciously, he suggests that it is the Q2 version of the speech, with its fragmented rhetoric, that exhibits the traces of being 'cobbled together' as a reconstruction of Q1.

The implications that begin emerging in these observations mesh with Bourus's argument that Q1 does in fact represent the earlier version of *Hamlet*, a version which she dates to the late 1580s.

The first three chapters of her book take a similar tack to Lesser's in dismantling previous theories about Q1 – especially those of piratical printers, memorial reconstruction and shorthand reports. Bourus leans heavily on sleight of hand to make her points; at one point she introduces Kathleen Irace's identification of actorly 'interpolations' in Q1 and provides a list. She then reveals that this list is not Irace's but in fact Bourus's own application of Irace's methodology to Q2, proving that the methodology is flawed. Bourus only then reveals and deconstructs Irace's *actual* list. Such gambits prioritize style over substance, as also in her unnecessarily personal attack on Tiffany Stern's credentials and conference presentation style as a way into critiquing her arguments about shorthand reportage. My frustration here is that Bourus's arguments are perfectly legitimate, but that the occasional aggression (filled with rhetorical questions and punchy connections) undermines rather than enhances her authority. She is candid about the fact that, in her lengthy chapter dismissing Stern's work on shorthand, she defers key evidence explicitly supporting the use of shorthand in the period until she has already undermined the reader's belief in the theory (89, some twenty pages into her dismissal of Stern's argument), but one surely unintended consequence of this is to discourage the reader from trusting the author.

The tone is unnecessary as Bourus's caveats, cautions and hypotheses make a great deal of sense. Bourus is a sensitive reader of the three texts who finds plenty of evidence to support her claims that Q1 systematically portrays a younger prince and, consequently, a younger Ophelia, Queen and Laertes. She uses her own experience of directing a version of Q1 starring a young actor as *Hamlet* to support these claims, arguing persuasively that Q1 works as a fast-moving text about young people, though more emphasis on the alternatives explored in rehearsal, rejected choices and comparative practical experiments would have offered a more methodologically sustained application of practice-as-research. Bourus's argument that Shakespeare wrote the play for a young

Burbage and revised it for the same actor (104–10) is entirely persuasive, but her assertion that an audience would perceive a younger queen as a more political agent than an older queen who could no longer bear children does not take account of the semiotics of boy actors for whom age-blindness is necessarily part of the drama. Yet the literary reading makes sense, and is supported by Lesser's account of the effect of the Q1 text on Victorian performance with its allusion to the Ghost's 'nightgown'. Long before Freud and Olivier turned the bedchamber into Hamlet's own sexual fantasies, the 'nightgown' turned the scene into Hamlet's redemption of his mother from her 'incest' with Claudius and prioritized a sexual attachment between the Ghost and Queen (134–42). Bourus's argument that Q1 dramatizes Hamlet's concern that the Queen produce no new heirs again fits well with this, making the 'bedchamber' scene about the political implications of the Queen's sexuality rather than Hamlet's own repressed longings.

One of the main points of disagreement between Lesser and Bourus concerns the reasons why Nicholas Ling was involved in the publishing of two very different quartos of *Hamlet* in consecutive years. Lesser outlines the range of theories, from Ling gazumping James Roberts (who had entered the play in the Stationers' Register in 1602) by putting out the 1603 quarto and establishing a right to the property, to the possibility of collaboration between the two (which would not explain why Ling would go into competition with himself), to the possibility that Q1 had sold out remarkably quickly and that the commercial rationale for a reprint coincided with the new availability of the text underlying Q2. The latter is the possibility pursued by Bourus, who suggests that the 'enlarged' claim of Q2 may be designed to alert readers to a higher price and re-market the book to those who had already bought it. Lesser's more complex theory argues that the *similarities* of presentation between Q1 and Q2 are more important than the differences, and that the new text was designed to be sold alongside the first, perhaps offering versions 'as originally staged' and 'as

newly expanded'. Lesser's theory (which might recall the 2006 release of double DVD sets of the original *Star Wars* trilogy featuring both George Lucas's newly remastered versions and reproductions of the original 1977 release to appease purists) is attractive for its explanation of the similarities between Q1 and Q2 and its non-reliance on the coincidence of a new copy becoming available as the original edition sold out. The theory also aligns with Bourus's sense of two authoritative versions; both Lesser and Bourus agree that there is nothing illegitimate about the publication of Q1, and that the two texts offer two different snapshots of the play's history.

Taken as a pair, these two monographs both destabilize and rewrite the history of Q1 *Hamlet*. Both volumes are more effective in what they dismantle than in what they construct to fill its place, and I suspect that the questions raised by both will endure longer than any one of the new theories. What Bourus does offer, however, is the most cohesive, reinforced and persuasive account to date of how Q1 *Hamlet* functions as an early Shakespearian drama, revised in 1602 at a point of artistic transition following the death of Shakespeare's own father. Her narrative takes into account theatrical, literary, biographical, textual and historical factors; and, further, it supports Lesser's metacritical arguments about the interpretive blind spots caused by the assumption that Q1 must come later.

Also advancing the significance of an early quarto is Lukas Erne's brief note on *Romeo and Juliet* ('"I have forgot why I did call thee back"'). Here, Erne notes that a stray italicized '*Romeo*' in the text of Q1 before Juliet's line 'I have forgot why I did call thee back' is not a hanging speech prefix but the very calling out of his name that she then responds to. Erne proposes a new set of stage directions for the extract that make clear the pattern of near departures and returns. Whilst editors may not wish to adopt so specific a set of suggestions, he makes a strong case for the inclusion of the earlier quarto's extra calling of Romeo's name.

NEW CRITICAL EDITIONS

In March 2015, Bloomsbury announced the fourth series of the Arden Shakespeare under the general editorship of Peter Holland, Zachary Lesser and Tiffany Stern, an announcement which suggests the conclusion of Arden 3 is finally imminent, and which presumably puts no small pressure on the editors of the remaining eight outstanding editions. Yet with several of the previously published Arden 3s now approaching their twentieth birthdays, Bloomsbury is stepping up the publication of updated reprints of selected editions, along the same lines as Cambridge University Press's revised editions discussed in last year's review. Following the reissued *Sonnets* and *The Tempest*, readers can expect updated editions of *Othello*, *Troilus and Cressida*, *Hamlet*, *Much Ado About Nothing* and others by the end of the quatercentenary year, creating a substantial corpus of what presumably must now be called 'Arden 3.5'. Unlike the Cambridge editions, where David Lindley's revision of his own *The Tempest* was a rare exception, the vast majority of the new Ardens will be reconsidered by their original editors, and it will be instructive to see what opportunities this affords for revision.

Lois Potter's second edition of her 1997 *The Two Noble Kinsmen* is largely a reprint. The introduction and appendices remain substantively unchanged, with the exception of a brief new section concluding the introduction, 'Additions and Reconsiderations' (147–70). This section concentrates on new scholarship on collaboration since the 1997 edition, and is an important reminder of how significant the shift in favour of collaborative authorship has been in the last eighteen years, although Potter notes that the play's unique status as an *avowed* collaboration means it has paradoxically received much less attention than the more controversial claims for other plays (148). Whilst collaborative authorship is now widely accepted, Potter further notes that the play's interpretive issues 'are now more likely to be interpreted as sites of contention between Shakespeare and Fletcher' (150), a potentially troubling statement if it implies a return to nineteenth-century disintegrationist logic. Potter continues to see both plots intricately connected in theme and content, making the case for the play's coherence, and she wisely notes that it is easier to point out 'faultlines' of difference than the more seamless meshes of thought and imagery (155). Brief sections on performance and translation acknowledge that the play is getting more outings, and she tantalisingly mentions a Spanish translation conducted by two translators in an attempt to capture the play's dual voices, but this section is disappointingly brief. She confuses two of my own reviews of the play in recent performance; it was not the 2011 production in Stratford that provided a token single performance of the play during a year featuring stagings of all of Shakespeare's works, but the 2006 (not 2005) production she discusses earlier (166).

Whilst the introduction is printed in a larger font that allows it to sprawl much more luxuriously over more pages (one hopes for purposes of the reader's comfort, not to make the volume look more extended than it actually is), the presentational layout of the text and notes adheres rigidly to the 1997 edition, allowing for only minor changes. Most of these correct small errors flagged up in reviews of the first edition, including the significant correction to 'Kinsman' in 3.1.69 where the 1997 edition reads 'Cousin'. The main substantive textual change is to 2.5.13 and is outlined in more detail in the 'Additions and Reconsiderations' (156) where Potter takes up MacDonald Jackson's suggestion that it is Arcite's *seat* in horsemanship (following the 1679 Folio reading), rather than *feat*, that better anticipates his eventual fate. There are some more substantive changes in the stage directions, such as the clarification that horns sound '[offstage]' at 3.1.96 and 107.

A potentially more questionable emendation concerns the opening stage direction to 3.5, which Potter updates from '*Enter* Schoolmaster [GERALD] *and five* Countrymen' to '*Enter* SCHOOLMASTER [Gerald] *and six* Countrymen (*one costumed as a* Bavian)', which takes the text even further from the quarto's call for the schoolmaster, four countrymen, the Bavian, two or three wenches, and a taborer. Practically, this corrects the alignment of stage direction with speech prefix for the Schoolmaster, and provides an entrance for the Bavian; while Potter retains her note suggesting that the query as to the whereabouts of the Bavian, countrywomen and taborer may suggest they enter later in the scene, she now mandates that the Bavian enters from the start. This much is sensible, though I wonder why the countrywomen may not also enter at the start; while the Taborer's initial exchange with 3 Countryman at 3.5.25 does imply his entrance at this point, the countrymen's introductions of the women at 26–8 read to me more as the men introducing/presenting their partners to Gerald rather than greeting new arrivals. The number of men is a difficulty; Potter's increase to six assumes that there must be five in addition to the Bavian in order to 'couple' (3.5.33) with the women, of whom five are named. Yet the quarto calls for four men and two to three women, which is also the number needed for the dance itself (three couples plus the clown and the fool/Bavian). The five women's names cause a problem, but not one that seems to warrant swelling numbers. Potter's silent omission of the comma after 'legs' in 3.5.27, 'And little Luce with the white legs and bouncing Barbary', inadvertently risks offering a solution by treating 'bouncing Barbary' as a further attribute of Luce, though I cannot see any textual justification for this.

Sandra Clark and Pamela Mason's new *Macbeth* begins by noting, among other of the play's 'superlatives', that this is 'the fastest moving, the most economical of the tragedies' (1), and the same is true of their brisk and efficient edition. This *Macbeth* breaks no new ground in text, interpretation or presentation, concentrating instead on marshalling existing scholarship. This is most obvious in the avoidance of the authorship question; Middleton is excluded quietly from the introduction and commentary (apart from in passing references to contemporaneous plays) and the ongoing debate about his contribution is placed into an appendix. Instead, the introduction (credited primarily to Clark) concentrates on the most tried and tested aspects of the play: genre, historical context, language, the theme of time, sources and stage

history. The narrowness of the focus leads to some disappointing omissions. There is no engagement with contemporary theoretical or political approaches to the play: Freud gets half a sentence, the play's interest for feminist criticism is unexplored and, given the edition appears a year after the Scottish referendum on independence, there is only a single brief reference to the rise of Scottish nationalism. Clark unapologetically mentions screen treatments only in passing, a decision which is unfathomable to me given that this is one of Shakespeare's most frequently and most richly filmed plays, and that students are far more likely to encounter a film than the stage productions noted here. More problematically, the list of stage productions discussed includes only a single one not produced in England, and they overwhelmingly focus on London and the RSC. The play's rich tradition of non-anglophone, multicultural, fringe, North American, Scottish and avant-garde production is absent here; and the stage history rarely impacts on discussion elsewhere in the volume. *Macbeth* is, for this edition, a historical rather than a living text.

The edition's conservatism is not, of course, solely a disadvantage. On the subjects that the introduction *does* explore, Clark is authoritative and passionate. The 'Language' section incorporates a lengthy discussion of the play's concern with 'doing', linking Macbeth linguistically to the Sisters and pursuing that link through, for instance, Macbeth falling into rhyming couplets after meeting with them in 4.1 (48). Clark's concern is to demonstrate that the play realizes 'dramatic language as its most expressive' (62), which she sees as key to the play's economic compression of meaning and complexity into a brisk narrative, and this feeds into the main interpretive essay on the play's engagement with time. Clark demonstrates the carefully delineated temporal structure but finds the play straining constantly forward to its own success/ion, while at the same time threatening to come full circle. The kinds of close textual analysis here, combined with the edition's sensible exploration of source material and the historical context, will make it a fine edition for teaching purposes. Clark is particularly interested in the multiple aspects of the Jacobean context, from other plays treating the material to James's interest in his own ancestry, that bear on the play, and in discussions of primogeniture and tanistry she elucidates a complex set of shifting practices (35–8). The performance history, despite the limitations in scope I noted above, is particularly insightful in discussing the problems of the play's ending (116–21) and the implications of dying offstage for the character of Macbeth. Where stage history emerges elsewhere, as in the evidence of *The Knight of the Burning Pestle* for the influence wielded by Banquo's ghost (14), the introduction integrates its interests most effectively.

Mason's text adheres closely to the Folio, often preserving ambiguity in stage directions where other editors mandate action, such as at 2.3.119 where the editors do not mandate a faint for Lady Macbeth on 'Help me hence, ho', a decision justified at length in Mason's textual essay (313–17) where she suggests that the insistence of a male editorial tradition on a faint (genuine or feigned) speaks to 'a wider sense of female duplicity and the exploitation of feminine traits for more sinister motives' (314). Later in the same passage the edition exhibits a curious conflict of identity where Mason adds an exit for Lady Macbeth after Banquo's 'Look to the lady' (2.3.126) in accordance with the editorial tradition, while also including a note referring to Mason's own argument elsewhere that the Folio's openness should be retained. Notwithstanding, the treatment of stage action is light and sensible. Act 5 is split into nine scenes (making the standard extra divisions to the Folio's 5.7) and Clark's commentary notes include a wealth of perceptive commentary on staging options and ambiguities, from whether 'Bellona's bridegroom' refers to Macbeth or Macduff (1.2.55) to how hautboys and torches operated on the early modern stage (1.6.0.1) and notes on different modern productions' approach to the size of Macduff's family (4.2.6). More extended discussion offers staging alternatives; Clark and Mason justify their retention of the Folio's comma after 'Seyton' in 5.3.19 (rather than a question or exclamation mark) to indicate that 'Macbeth may believe Seyton is there, or perhaps he assumes he is close' (280), offering a different angle on Macbeth's isolation and lack of authority at this point. Glossing throughout is generous but efficient, clarifying ambiguous passages with brief analogies; pleasingly, there are no unnecessary 'Longer notes'.

Mason treats the text diligently, and I found only one error in dialogue, 'in the pit' for the Folio's 'at the pit' at 3.5.15. The editors punctuate carefully to clarify sense, adhering to the Folio as far as possible and generally only deviating in cases where there is consensus among modern editors. Another error creeps in at 2.2.11–12, where the silent removal of the comma after 'deed' in 'The attempt, and not the deed, / Confounds us' makes nonsense of the line; other modern editions either preserve both of the Folio's commas or remove both. The most significant problem, however, is the erratic expansion of contractions, particularly 'th''. At times this is done sensitively, as at 2.3.111 where the unusual expansion of 'Th'expedition' creates a stronger pentameter line to my ear; but at 3.3.13 ('the palace' for 'th'palace'), 3.4.99 ('the Hyrcan' for 'th'Hircan') and 3.5.24 ('vaporous' for 'vap'rous') the editors render the lines unmetrical. In other places contractions are left untouched, making it difficult to find a rationale.

Mason's appendix on the text concentrates primarily on the Folio text's lineation and sparing use of exclamation marks, both of which are followed to a greater extent than is usual by this edition, although the editors do work to create consistent blank verse where possible. Sandra Clark, in another appendix essay revealingly titled 'The Folio Text and its Integrity' takes up the question of the play's authorship. In surveying the history of arguments for the play's status as a revision and the identity of the reviser, Clark summarizes 'The Folio text of *Macbeth* is probably not the original version that Shakespeare wrote in 1606; but the extent to which it differs may well be very slight, and confined to 3.5 and two passages in 4.1' (336). She agrees on balance that the songs from *The Witch* fit better in the context of that play and that the revisions therefore most likely took place after Shakespeare's death, but does not agree that this implies Middleton's influence on the remainder of the play. As with the text, then, the edition takes a conservative position on authorship, offering explanations for the explicit presence of non-Shakespearian material but nothing further. Middleton is accordingly given no privileged role in the textual notes, although the editors do note that the entrance direction 'meeting' (1.2.0.2 and 3.5.0.1) is associated more with Middleton and Heywood than with Shakespeare.

Advancing the case for Middleton's presence in the play, Gary Taylor's latest contribution to the debate ('Empirical Middleton') attempts to set out a methodology for 'microauthorship' that allows empirical attribution of short sections of text (approx. 60 words) to one author of another. The value of Taylor's article is more in highlighting the caveats and cautions of such an approach, whose local and very specific focus must necessarily work at the level of relative probabilities rather than certainties. Whilst not all readers will be persuaded that strings of two, three or four words are the best means of establishing shared authorship of two different texts, which is Taylor's premise here, the extensive data he gathers will be a useful contribution to the ongoing methodological questions over whether and how authorship can be determined at such a local level. With the new Norton and new Oxford Shakespeares both imminent and both promising new approaches to canon, chronology, copy text, revision and collaboration, these questions will no doubt be at the forefront of developments over the coming year.

WORKS REVIEWED

Bourus, Terri, *Young Shakespeare's Young Hamlet: Print, Piracy, and Performance* (New York, 2014)

Bruster, Douglas, 'Shakespeare's Lady 8', *Shakespeare Quarterly*, 66 (2015), 47–88.

Clark, Sandra, and Pamela Mason, eds., *Macbeth* (London, 2015)

Cross, Lezlie C. 'Acting in the Paratext: Theatrical Material in Horace Howard Furness's New Variorum Shakespeare', *Shakespeare Bulletin*, 33.2 (2015), 191–213

Erne, Lukas, '"I have forgot why I did call thee back": Editing Romeo and Juliet's Leave-Taking in the Balcony Scene', *Notes & Queries*, 62 (2015), 93–5

Fischlin, Daniel, ed., *The Tempest: Shakespeare Made in Canada* (Ontario, 2013)

Fischlin, Daniel, ed., *Romeo and Juliet: Shakespeare Made in Canada* (Ontario, 2013)

Galey, Alan, *The Shakespearean Archive: Experiments in New Media from the Renaissance to Postmodernity* (Cambridge, 2015)

Greenblatt, Stephen, et al., eds., *The Norton Shakespeare*, 3rd edn (New York, 2015)

Hirsch, Brett D., and Hugh Craig, eds., *The Shakespearean International Yearbook 14: Special Section, Digital Shakespeares* (Farnham, 2014)

Lesser, Zachary, *Hamlet after Q1: An Uncanny History of the Shakespearean Text* (Philadelphia, 2015)

McDonald, Russ, and Lena Cowen Orlin, eds., *The Bedford Shakespeare* (Boston, MA, 2015)

Paul, J. Gavin, *Shakespeare and the Imprints of Performance* (New York, 2014)

Potter, Lois, ed., *The Two Noble Kinsmen*, rev. edn (London, 2015)

Taylor, Gary, 'Empirical Middleton: *Macbeth*, Adaptation, and Microauthorship', *Shakespeare Quarterly*, 65.3 (2014): 239–72

ABSTRACTS OF ARTICLES
IN *SHAKESPEARE SURVEY 69*

ROBERT MIOLA

Past the Size of Dreaming? Shakespeare's Rome
This chapter reviews criticism of Shakespeare's Roman works, assesses the current
state of play, and indicates future directions. The principal works are *The Rape of
Lucrece, Titus Andronicus, Julius Caesar, Antony and Cleopatra, Coriolanus* and *Cymbeline*.
Topics include politics, religion, Shakespeare's sources and new approaches to gender,
sexuality, printing and publication.

MICHAEL SILK

Puns and Prose: Reflections on Shakespeare's Usage
Not all roads lead to Rome. Contrary to received opinion, the punning in
Shakespeare's (and his English contemporaries') serious drama challenges classicizing
norms; so too the prose. The discussion foregrounds *Hamlet*, rhetorical theory, conceits, etymologizing, English language-consciousness and hybridity in language and
literature, and the logic of the two practices.

DAVID CURRELL

**'Away with him! He speaks Latin': *2 Henry VI* and the uses of Roman
Antiquity**
Classical allusions resonate significantly across *2 Henry VI*. York handles his Roman
thoughts deftly, while the Lancastrians' terminate in Suffolk's unwitting parody of
Lucan's Pompey. Yet one Yorkist stratagem – Cade's rebellion – engenders an anti-
literacy so radical it would destroy the very humanism that brought Roman antiquity
to Shakespeare's stage.

PATRICK GRAY

Shakespeare and the other Virgil: Pity and *Imperium* in *Titus Andronicus*
Shakespeare's reading of the *Aeneid* is in keeping with the 'Harvard School' of
criticism, which emphasizes Virgil's sadness at the human cost of Roman *imperium*.
In Shakespeare's own critique of *Romanitas, Titus Andronicus*, Virgil's empathy serves
as a counterpoint to Ovid, whom Shakespeare associates in contrast with gleeful,
barbaric cruelty.

CHRISTIAN M. BILLING

**'Though this be method, yet there is madness in't': Cutting Ovid's Tongue
in Recent Stage and Film Performances of Shakespeare's *Titus Andronicus***
This chapter considers performances of Lavinia from the perspectives of acting and
directing techniques and literary intertextuality. Using performance analysis and
classical philology, Billing demonstrates how psychologically motivated approaches to
the character of Lavinia lead to the suppression of intertextuality and a diminishment
of potentially feminist interpretations by modern artists.

MICHAEL P. JENSEN

The Noble Romans: When *Julius Caesar* and *Antony and Cleopatra* were made Sequel
Producers in the 1960s–80s sometimes paired plays that were not sequels as if they were. Different combinations of Shakespeare's Roman plays were produced by BBC Television (1963), the RSC (1973) and the BBC World Service (1979). This chapter studies the strategies that turned these cycles into the saga of Mark Antony.

KATE RUMBOLD

Shakespeare's Poems in Pieces: *Venus and Adonis* and *The Rape of Lucrece* Unanthologized
Shakespeare's *Venus and Adonis* and *Lucrece* once defined his reputation; today, they seem marginal to his *oeuvre*. Scholars attribute this to changing tastes, or to the poems' exclusion from the Folio. This chapter, however, reveals how, ironically, the anthologization of the poems around 1600 limited their availability to future readers.

HEATHER JAMES

Shakespeare's Juliet and Ovid's Myths of Girlhood
The part of Juliet in *Romeo and Juliet* grows and takes shape in relation to Ovid and the Ovidian models of girlhood in the Second Quarto: why? This chapter argues that Shakespeare adapts Ovid and, more particularly, Christopher Marlowe's Ovid to reimagine the future of the English theatre in 1599.

ESTHER B. SCHUPAK

'Lend me your ears': Listening Rhetoric and Political Ideology in *Julius Caesar*
Shakespeare's republican leanings – or lack thereof – as evidenced in *Julius Caesar* have been debated because the drama effectively argues both sides of the case. Using listening rhetoric as its method, this chapter examines the question of whether this play is truly republican and analyzes the political ideology the drama enacts.

GEORGE MANDEL

Plutarch's Porcia and Shakespeare's Portia: Two of a Kind?
The chapter argues that, contrary to what is usually said or implied, Shakespeare made very far-reaching changes to the character of Brutus's wife as portrayed in Plutarch's 'Life of Brutus'. The conclusion is that 'Shakespeare's Portia is not so much an elaboration or development of her Plutarchian original as a radical transformation of her'.

DOMINIQUE GOY-BLANQUET

Shakespeare's Unholy Martyrs: Lessons in Politics

For all its recent spectacular developments, terrorism has its roots in ancient heroic martyrdom, driven by a similar need to bear testimony. Coming after the two Henriads, Shakespeare's Roman plays pursue their investigation of power and resistance in a stage universe where thoughts, freed from the shackles of Christian medieval monarchy, expose his unholy martyrs' tangled mix of political and personal motives.

ROS KING

'A lean and hungry look': Sight, Ekphrasis, Irony in *Julius Caesar* and *Henry V*
Shakespeare's version of the description of Cassius's 'look' in North's Plutarch exploits classical and early modern uncertainty concerning the physiology of sight. In both *Julius Caesar* and *Henry V*, Shakespeare creates ambiguity and irony through his uses of North, and through techniques of *ekphrasis* ('vivid description') and *enargeia* ('laying before the eyes'). The results valuably involve readers and spectators in imaginative debate.

INEKE MURAKAMI

'Her strong toil of grace': Charismatic Performance from Queens to Quakers
This chapter posits *Antony and Cleopatra* as a meditation in which Shakespeare reveals a dialectic of play that renders charisma transformative for queens and commoners alike. Accounts of Quaker performances confirm this, and suggest that charisma enchants not as a delusion of mass submission but as the articulation of communal aspirations.

ROBERT N. WATSON

Coriolanus and the 'Common Part'
In *Coriolanus*, Latin *cum-* and *part-* prefixes relentlessly emphasize the tension between insular and divided identities. Classical ideals of proud autonomy collide with Christian ideals of humility centred on companionship – literally, shared bread. The protagonist refuses to 'mutually participate' in 'the appetite and affection common / Of the whole body'.

BRADLEY IRISH

***Coriolanus* and the Poetics of Disgust**
This chapter argues that *Coriolanus* is about the experience of being disgusted. The dynamics of disgust, as understood by modern researchers, underwrite the stylistic, thematic and dramaturgical investments of *Coriolanus*, uniting the play's imagery (dominated by motifs of digestion, disease and decay) with its narrative structure (dominated by waves of incorporation and expulsion).

VERENA OLEJNICZAK LOBSIEN

The Household of Heroism: Metaphor, Economy and *Coriolanus*

Coriolanus is analyzed with a focus on the classical metaphor of the household, shown to structure the play on the level of political *oikonomia* and on that of the hero's *oikeiosis*. While Coriolanus's self-government fails tragically, the figurative power of the household metaphor and the economic paradigm are also called into question.

THOMAS RIST

'Those organnons by which it mooves': Shakespearian Theatre and the Romish Cult of the Dead
The idea of the Romish arising in the sixteenth century combined connotations of ancient Rome with Roman Catholic religion, where rituals remembering the dead brought pasts to life. This chapter demonstrates the ritual remembrance defining early modern theatre in action, narrative and recent apprehension.

PETER WOMACK

'Another part of the forest': Editors and Locations in Shakespeare
A 300-year-old editorial practice of heading every scene in Shakespeare with a note of its location has been abandoned in the last few decades. Recovering the assumptions underlying this discredited convention enables us to think more precisely about the working of imaginary location in early modern drama.

DENISE A. WALEN

Unmanning Juliet
This chapter argues that the reduction and fifty-year elimination of 3.2 from performances of *Romeo and Juliet* is the effect of a complex recurrence found in the original quarto editions, rehearsed in the play's performance history, and reconstituted in textual criticism, which results in the diminishment of Juliet's character.

CERI SULLIVAN

The Second Tetralogy's move from Achievements to Badges
Wearers of 'dignities' in the second tetralogy allow heritable heraldic achievements (based on descent and marriage) to give way to badges (personal signs of loyalty to one man), recast as national badges (including the leek, worn in the 1590s by the unofficial 'prince of Wales', the 2nd Earl of Essex).

JANE KINGSLEY-SMITH

'Let me not to the marriage of true minds': Shakespeare's Sonnet for Lady Mary Wroth
This chapter argues that Sonnet 116 was written for the marriages of Lady Mary Wroth and William Herbert, 3rd Earl of Pembroke, in autumn 1604. Both addressees incorporate the phrase 'Love is not love' into their own lyric verse, with Wroth returning to this sonnet repeatedly throughout her literary career.

MATS MALM

Voluptuous Language and Ambivalence in Shakespeare's Sonnets
The strong – and ambivalent – sensuousness in Shakespeare's sonnets is clearly connected to their metalinguistic character, but the question is how this interaction should be understood. In this chapter a notion of voluptuous language, deriving from antiquity, is made the point of departure for clarifying the complex problem.

KATHARINE A. CRAIK

Sympathetic Sonnets
Readers have often found themselves astonished by Shakespeare's Sonnets. This chapter considers the Sonnets alongside Longinus's *Peri hypsous* (*On the Sublime*), and argues that the rich vocabulary of *hypsos*, or height, reveals a powerful dynamic of sympathy and identification at the heart of the reader's experience.

REIKO OYA

Authenticating the Inauthentic: Edmond Malone as Editor of the Apocryphal Shakespeare
Although widely regarded as the epitome of Enlightenment reason, Edmond Malone (1741–1812) revealed his unexpectedly illogical sides when he edited the apocryphal Shakespeare. This chapter reassesses Malone's editorial philosophy and practice by scrutinizing his handling of the plays and poems of inauthentic origin, with special attention to *The Passionate Pilgrim*.

BARBARA HODGDON

Paper Worlds: A Story of Things left Behind
This chapter explores materials left behind once actors have left the stage. Constituting a layered installation that brings together images, marginalia, commentary and drawings, these materials turn the page into a theatrical scene, a place reminiscent of a memory theatre, housing a selection of properties, costumes and set models, archived as digital photographs.

JOHN WYVER

An Intimate and Intermedial Form: Early Television Shakespeare from the BBC, 1937–9
Between February 1937 and April 1939 a fledgling BBC Television service from Alexandra Palace broadcast more than twenty Shakespeare adaptations. Although no recordings exist of these transmissions, this chapter explores their surviving written traces. It also outlines the production environment, cultural context and intermedial connections of inter-war television Shakespeare.

MARIACRISTINA CAVECCHI

Tagging the Bard: Shakespeare Graffiti on and off the Stage

Graffiti and post-graffiti art have appropriated Shakespeare by dismembering his lines and images on walls and have started to dialogue with theatrical spaces that, conversely, turn to the grammar of street art to restage Shakespearian plays. The Shakespeare–graffiti bond has become an illuminating metaphor for questioning the Elizabethan/Jacobean playwright's iconic status in the new millennium.

TOM REEDY WILLIAM

Dugdale's Monumental Inaccuracies and Shakespeare's Stratford Monument

A comparison of surviving monuments with their engravings in William Dugdale's *Antiquities of Warwickshire* (1656) and corresponding working sketches reveals that suspicions that William Shakespeare's Stratford monument has been altered are unfounded.

INDEX

INDEX

INDEX

INDEX